THE DEMOCRATIC–
REPUBLICAN
SOCIETIES, 1790-1800

THE DEMOCRATIC-REPUBLICAN SOCIETIES, 1790-1800

A Documentary Sourcebook of Constitutions, Declarations, Addresses, Resolutions, and Toasts

EDITED, WITH AN INTRODUCTION, BY

PHILIP S. FONER

Foreword by RICHARD B. MORRIS

GREENWOOD PRESS
WESTPORT, CONNECTICUT · LONDON, ENGLAND

Library of Congress Cataloging in Publication Data

Main entry under title:

The Democratic-Republican societies, 1790-1800.

Bibliography: p.
Includes index.
1. United States—Politics and government—
Constitutional period, 1789-1809—Sources.
I. Foner, Philip Sheldon, 1910-
E310.D4   320.9'73'04   76-5260
ISBN 0-8371-8907-1

Library of Congress Catalog Card Number: 76-5260
ISBN 0-8371-8907-1

Greenwood Press, Inc., 51 Riverside Avenue,
Westport, Connecticut 06880

320.9
D383

Printed in the United States of America

The collision of opposite opinions produces the spark which lights the torch of truth.

> Patriotic Society of
> Newcastle, Delaware, 1793

It is an agitation to establish *Constitutional Societies* in every part of the United States, for the purpose of watching over the rights of the people, and giving an early alarm in case of government encroachments thereupon.

> *Norwich (Connecticut) Packet,*
> August 9, 1792

It must be the mechanics and farmers, or the poorer class of people (as they are generally called) that must support the freedom of America; the freedom which they and their fathers purchased with their blood—the nobility will never do it—they will be always striving to get the reins of government in their own hands, and then they can ride the people at pleasure.

> *Woods's Newark Gazette,*
> March 19, 1794

Contents

Foreword

The era of the American Revolution not only witnessed the achievement of independence and the forging of federal union by the new American nation, but it also fostered the beginnings of a re-formation of American society along republican principles. As the men of '76 saw it, republicanism involved more than the substitution of an elected chief executive for a hereditary monarch. It meant basing a political system on broad moral principles and recognizing the people as constituent power.

There is, then, more than a chronological nexus between the years culminating with the adoption of the federal constitution and the decade of the 1790s, in which the main tasks of organizing and operating the new government were entrusted to men of Federalist principles. The Revolutionary War had demonstrated the potentialities of popular action. It was the culmination of a movement which combined mass organization and elitist direction. In this respect, as well as in its desire to bring about a "renovation" of society, the 1790s, as this illuminating collection of documents bears out, had a special affinity with the Revolutionary years. Dr. Foner, in his introduction and notes to the rich collection of documents bearing on the organization and avowed purposes of the Democratic-Republican societies, shows how heavily these societies drew upon the example of the old Patriot infrastructure. The revival of the Sons of Liberty and other similar organizations with patriotic titles makes this parallel striking indeed.

Many people in the 1790s, just as in the 1770s, came to regard the government as conspiring to encroach upon their individual liberties. What distinguished the later period was the popular concern that a first step toward ending civil liberties would be the threatened entente with England, the old foe, against France, the venerated ally. As these documents make abundantly clear, it was not disagreement over domestic policy or over the details of the Hamiltonian fiscal program which precipitated the founding and proliferation of the Democratic-Republican societies, but rather the growing tension between the Washington administration and the successive French revolutionary governments about the course, conduct, and character of the French Revolution, and America's responsibilities to France resulting from the wartime alliance.

The opposition party that emerged was not genetically connected with the old anti-Federalist party or faction, although it recruited numerous members from that camp. The masses, especially the workers in cities and towns, had supported the federal constitution with enthusiasm. The answer to why they now turned against the party in power is found in Dr. Foner's scholarly introduction. Therein he spells out the kind of program they now articulated, and his examples are abundantly buttressed in the rich documentation that follows. Even though foreign policy may have sparked their rise, the Democratic-Republican societies, as he makes clear, were home-grown products not a foreign importation. The documentation also bears out the contention that, aside from opposing a British connection, the societies turned to the domestic scene and had what they deemed social inequities as their targets. They sought the elimination of imprisonment for debt, a more humane penal system, the ending of excessive court costs, and public education. Above all, they vigorously repelled any alleged threats to the sovereignty of the people.

Henceforth, no one should feel comfortable in studying the emergence of the Jeffersonians as a full-scale national party, in seeking to comprehend the political and social crises of the 1790s, or in relating American foreign policy in these years to internal dissent without recourse to this admirably full collection covering the activities of the Democratic-Republican societies from Maine to Georgia.

Richard B. Morris

Preface

For a long time a major controversy among historians of the postrevolutionary era revolved about the origin of Thomas Jefferson's Democratic-Republican party. One of the questions debated was whether the members of the Democratic-Republican party, which carried Jefferson to the presidency in 1800, were also members of the group that had opposed the adoption of the federal Constitution in 1787 and 1788. Another was how it was possible for Jefferson and his associates to fashion, in so brief a period, a party that soon became dominant.

During the last two decades, various monographs that have appeared have substantially altered the traditional answers to these questions. These studies have demonstrated that in the formation and development of the first political parties, local rather than national, foreign rather than domestic, issues were often paramount and that a large majority of those who were usually considered Republicans throughout our early national period were initially Federalists. The Republicans became the majority party by developing techniques to organize the electorate and get out the vote.

In recent years, too, a growing interest has emerged in the central importance of a republican ideology in the early Republic. It is becoming increasingly clear as a result of new studies that republicanism meant something more to the post-revolutionary generation than the absence of monarchy, more even than the way of structuring political power. It implied a view of human society, a statement about man's nature.

As historians have developed an increasing interest in the organization, techniques, and policies of the state and local parties of our first party system and in the implications of the republican ideology in the postrevolutionary period, a new sensitivity has developed to the Democratic-Republican societies that arose in the United States in 1793 during the widespread enthusiasm for the French Revolution. The story of the societies, their demonstrations in support of the French minister Genêt, their opposition to the pro-British and anti-French Federalist policy after the Proclamation of Neutrality of 1793, their activity in securing the free and uninterrupted navigation of the Mississippi River, their contributions to the wide variety of reforms, their supposed connection with the Whiskey Rebellion, the fear and hatred they stirred among Federalists, climaxed by Washington's unjust denunciaton of them as "self-created" (extragovernmental and therefore subversive) is a familiar one. The studies of Charles D. Hazen, Bernard Fäy, William Miller, and especially Eugene P. Link have provided us with a general picture of these societies. In addition, particularistic studies of our early parties, especially Alfred F. Young's massive one on the origins of the Democratic-Republicans in New York State, have shown the societies in action on the local level. Finally, studies of the newspapers of the era, particularly Donald H. Stewart's detailed monograph on the Republican press, have thrown considerable light on the role of the societies in skillfully presenting Republican views on key issues, thereby helping fashion the political party of Thomas Jefferson that soon became dominant.

There has, however, been a need for a compilation of the basic documents of the Democratic-Republican societies—their constitutions, minutes of their meetings, accounts of their celebrations, and the manifold resolutions, addresses, and toasts presenting their views on the conduct of government and issues of the day and by means of which they contributed to the development of the Republican ideology and to forging the party of Jefferson into a potent political force. What is presented here is the first such compilation. Included are the basic documents of every Democratic-Republican society from Maine to Georgia whose source material has been preserved either in manuscript or printed form. By "basic," I mean documents that reflect the views of the societies on national and international issues rather than those that deal only with internal organizational matters or more parochial issues.

Space limitations prevented the inclusion of the orations before the societies, usually given on the Fourth of July. Nevertheless, I have discussed and partly summarized the major ones in the introduction and notes; all are included in the bibliography and can be consulted easily in microfiche reproduction. It was impossible for the same reason to include all the letters in the contemporary press defending and denouncing the popular societies, but a sufficient number are presented to give the reader a picture of this significant debate in our early history. In the appendix the reader will find a list of other letters in the press on the societies. Also included in the appendix is a list of the occupations of those members of the Democratic Society of Pennsylvania, the leading such society in the nation, whose trades and professions are listed in Philadelphia's contemporary trade directories. Finally, the appendix includes the documents of the most important of the countersocieties the Federalists organized to offset the influence of the Democratic-Republican Societies—the Constitutional Association of the Borough of Elizabeth, New Jersey.

The introduction and notes that accompany these documents are intended to provide what is essential for an understanding of the background of the documents; however, the identification of persons cited in the documents does not pretend to be complete. Biographical information on a number of officials and members of the societies does not exist even in local societies and local histories. For the student who wishes to pursue further the history of the Democratic-Republican societies, a comprehensive bibliography is included.

Acknowledgments

The compilation of this volume would have been impossible without the kind cooperation of the staffs of many historical societies, state libraries, college and university libraries, and public and private libraries. I wish to take this opportunity to express my gratitude to the staffs of the Historical Society of Pennsylvania, New-York Historical Society, American Antiquarian Society, Massachusetts Historical Society, Vermont Historical Society, Maine Historical Society, Connecticut Historical Society, New Jersey Historical Society, Western Pennsylvania Historical Society, Maryland Historical Society, Kentucky Historical Society, Historical Society of Delaware, Minnesota Historical Society, Charleston (South Carolina) Library Society, Library of Congress, New York State Historical Association, New York Public Library, Boston Public Library, Peabody Institute Library (Baltimore), State Law Library (Kentucky), Virginia State Library, Kentucky State Archives and Records Center, State Education Department of the University of the State of New York, Columbia University Library, Harvard University Library, University of North Carolina Library, University of Pittsburgh Library, University of Pennsylvania Library, New York University Library, and University of Delaware Library. I owe a special debt to the interlibrary loan department of Lincoln University Library for assistance in obtaining materials from libraries and historical societies.

I wish to thank Professor Alfred F. Young of the Department of History of Northern Illinois University for a number of valuable suggestions as to the scope of the project.

Lincoln University, Pennsylvania   PHILIP S. FONER

THE DEMOCRATIC–
REPUBLICAN
SOCIETIES, 1790-1800

1 | The Democratic-Republican Societies: An Introduction

Returning from a visit to the South Carolina backcountry, Federalist William Smith wrote to Alexander Hamilton on April 24, 1793, that groups of "banditti-like" people were reading Philip Freneau's *National Gazette* and discussing its advice to organize into societies and voice their opposition to Federalist policies.[1] Freneau, the "poet of the American Revolution," had published the first issue of the *National Gazette* in Philadelphia on October 31, 1791. Until October 1793, when his paper was discontinued for financial reasons, Freneau, with his sharp wit and acid pen, attacked the idea that the administration in power with George Washington as President was always in the right. Such a doctrine, which he called more suited to a monarchy than to a republic, was the prelude to tyranny; it was a totally evil practice that stifled inquiry and rendered impossible the task of distinguishing between good and bad rulers and good and bad measures. Instead, public opinion must be freely expressed to keep officials to their duty. Indeed, Freneau wrote, citizens had not only the privilege but the duty to criticize measures their government took. Since all power flowed from the people, the people had both the right and the duty to interpret and apply that power.[2]

Because such watching and criticizing of government were best done by groups, it was not surprising, wrote Freneau, that organizations for this purpose were coming into existence. There were in America, Freneau noted in the *National Gazette* of July 25, 1792, a few who

> seem greatly alarmed at an idea that has been lately started of *establishing constitutional societies* in every part of the United States, for the purpose of watching over the rights of the people, and giving an early alarm in case of governmental encroachments thereupon. Yet such societies seem absolutely necessary in every country, where the people wish to preserve an uncorrupted legislation. . . .

Freneau advocated forming such clubs to maintain popular interest in government and to sound the tocsin against governmental encroachments. Unless the
people were vigilant, he insisted, *"what is every man's business soon becomes no
man's business."* Citizens were like sleepers on a beach who could be overwhelmed by the incoming tide if not awakened by friendly monitors. These
societies would give notice of danger before it was too late, and so they should
be "denominated *Friends of the people*."[3]

It was not long before groups of this nature came into being. Most historical
accounts have treated these societies as of foreign, and particularly French, origin, and not as "indigenous phenomena." Their roots were in France and England, and even perhaps in Poland, Holland, and Prussia, but not in the United
States.[4] In 1942, however, Eugene P. Link published his *Democratic-Republican
Societies, 1790-1800,* in which he took issue with the view that the popular societies were not indigenous to the United States. While conceding that the Jacobin
societies of France were their immediate forerunners and that English patriotic
societies influenced them, he emphasized that their immediate predecessors were
America's own revolutionary and prerevolutionary popular organizations. Link
pointed to the Regulators in colonial North Carolina, who worked through associations of people and their militia companies, and especially to the Sons of Liberty, the influential revolutionary organization that led the opposition to Britain
after 1765 and played a decisive role in bringing about the repeal of the Stamp
Act, enforcement of the nonimportation agreements, and the boycott of English
tea. Other "Patriotic societies" also influenced the men who formed the popular
associations of the 1790s, including the Associators in Pennsylvania; the Whig
clubs in Boston, Baltimore, and Philadelphia; "The Society for the Preservation
of Liberty" in Virginia; the Sons of St. Tammany; and the Society of Political
Inquiries of Philadelphia. But, as Link notes, the Sons of Liberty provided the
most significant precedents for the Democratic-Republican clubs. Characteristic
of the Sons of Liberty were vigilance to check counterrevolutionary activities,
secrecy so that the members would not be easily identified, appeals to the rank
and file for action through discussion, and committees of correspondence. The
Democratic-Republican societies borrowed these organizational principles, a fact
that is not surprising when one realizes that in many cases the societies were under the leadership of former Sons of Liberty.[5]

Not only did Link deny the foreign origin of the popular societies, but he insisted that American societies influenced similar organizations in Europe. It was
the American Revolution that set this popular movement on foot, and from the
United States it spread to England and France. The committees of correspondence, introduced by the Sons of Liberty, were taken over from America by the
popular societies organized in England by the followers of John Wilkes and by
the Jacobin clubs of France.[6]

Most scholars today accept Link's emphasis on the American rather than foreign precedents of the Democratic-Republican societies. Moreover, it is also

clear that problems within the United States furnished a base for the existence of these clubs. The immediate sources of the popular societies go back to the day when revolutionary soldiers returned to their homes to find them mortgaged, their families in debt, and their government in the hands of wealthy merchants and landed gentry who were piling up their wealth by speculating in land, in soldier certificates, in treasury warrants, and in continental paper. Shays's Rebellion of 1787 was evidence that many common people felt that a new struggle was needed to preserve the cause of freedom for which they had fought during the revolutionary war.

It appears that most members of the popular societies were in favor of the new Constitution. This was particularly true of the mechanics and laborers, who were eager to halt the dumping of British goods in American markets, which was causing considerable unemployment. A bill of rights, they believed, would aid in preventing certain evils predicted by those opposed to the Constitution. Eager for a strong, central government, the mechanics and laborers joined with others in the community to push the demand for a bill of rights.

But provisions in a written document guaranteeing freedom of religion, press, speech, assembly, and petition to all were not sufficient of themselves. Whether the Bill of Rights was to be meaningful or to become a dead letter depended upon the plain people. The *Newark Gazette* stated the case accurately when it wrote on March 19, 1794: "It must be the mechanics and farmers, or the poorer class of people (as they are generally called) that must support the freedom of America."

For freedom was once again in danger. Hamilton and the Federalists were open in their determination to convert the new government into an agency for the wealthy. John Jay summed it up: "Those who own the country ought to govern it." The common people were entirely too ignorant to be entrusted with political privileges. The proper place for mechanics and laborers was at the workbench and for small farmers at the plow. Affairs of state were reserved for "the rich and the well-born."

With the able assistance of Alexander Hamilton, "the rich and the well-born" did nobly. Hamilton's funding program alone provided enormous profits for Federalist merchants and bankers who were paid by the government the face value of the soldiers' certificates and other securities they had purchased from farmers and laborers at one cent on the dollar. As the late Alexander Laing put it: "It was a device calculated to leave multitudinous veterans undisturbed in the poverty while it enriched eminent speculators who had persuaded them to part for a pittance, with their hitherto uncashable pay vouchers." Laing points out that James Madison was "pivoted into outright anti-Federalism by Hamilton's "cruel program."[7]

This lining of the pockets of "the patronage and paper men," roused feelings that were to find expression in the popular societies. So too was the fear that the existence of the Society of Cincinnati, an aristocratic organization of officers of the Continental army, indicated a desire on the part of the upper classes to establish a nobility in America, based on a hereditary officer group. Finally, the general government appeared to accept docilely English encroachments on trade and efforts to prevent American expansion on the frontier.

While all these factors combined to give mass support to the Democratic-Republican societies, the reverberations of events abroad were mainly responsible for their appearance. It was the French Revolution that rekindled democratic enthusiasms. It gave new life to the Revolution Society in England, long established to defend the principles of 1688. The Society for Constitutional Information, which appeared in 1781 in England to express sympathy for the Americans, developed a new scope and opened correspondence with the societies in Ireland, Scotland, and, a little later, Germany and France.[8] When Edmund Genêt came to America as the first minister from the Republic of France in 1793, he fanned into flame the spark of '76 and tied America into a world revolutionary movement, which the country itself had inaugurated.

"Within a week after Genêt entered Philadelphia," notes John Bach McMaster, "a few shrewd politicians who saw how strong the popular feeling was towards France determined to use it for political purposes. They accordingly made haste to form a club after the manner of the Jacobin clubs at Paris, drew up a Constitution and called themselves the Democratic Society."[9] Other historians have also insisted that Genêt was the sponsor, if not the overt creator, of the popular societies.[10] Yet the fact is that the first such society formed probably held its initial meeting in March 1793, some six to eight weeks before Genêt's arrival. This was the German Republican Society of Philadelphia, founded by Peter Muhlenberg, Henry Kammerer, and Dr. Michael Leib. Although Leib had formerly been a Federalist, he was on the way to becoming a leader of Philadelphia's Republicans. Kammerer, vice-president of the society, was one of the editors of the *Philadelphische Correspondenz,* in which the aims of the group were first published.[11]

"A Customer" wrote to Freneau about this new society, and called on the *National Gazette* for an English translation of its announced, and very worthy, aims. He also urged establishment of similar organizations in all parts of the country to preserve equality and combat aristocracy. "May the example of the German Republican Society prove a spur to the friends of equality throughout the United States."[12]

In a circular letter the German Republican Society reiterated the obligation of every citizen to assist in a republican government, either by actually taking part in it or by being alert to errors. Only constant action could keep alive the spirit of liberty. Political societies could give the attention and effort so needed to preserve that liberty—through education, observation, and public expression of opinions. They would thus provide for all the people additional protection against corruption and the infringement of political rights. In their circular letter, society members offered to communicate with other groups with similar principles that might be established elsewhere.[13]

In May or June 1793, the largest and most influential popular association, the Democratic Society of Pennsylvania, was formed. (Originally it was to have been called "The Sons of Liberty," but Genêt suggested the name that was adopted.)[14] The officers of the society were elected at a regular meeting on July 3, 1793; the president was David Rittenhouse, a man whose reputation for scholarship, integrity, and skill were well known, and the vice-presidents were William Coats and Charles Biddle. Although the society had agreed upon its principles, articles, and regulations on May 30, 1793, it did not decide to publish them until July 3, when it also approved a circular letter.[15] The circular letter urged the formation of similar societies, insisting that the need was urgent. The French Revolution was under attack by the "European Confederacy." If the French were defeated, the United States would not be permitted to enjoy "the honors of an independent and the happiness of a republican government." And the danger was not only from abroad; in this very country, wealth and "the seeds of luxury" seemed to have eclipsed "the spirit of freedom and equality." The letter called on Americans all over the country to "erect the temple of LIBERTY on the ruins of *palaces and thrones.*"[16]

William Cobbett, the cantankerous critic of these societies, insisted that the response to this appeal was limited; Americans, he said, "are phlegmatic, slow to act, extremely cautious and difficult to deceive."[17] Cobbett, however, was not entirely correct. Although a full national network of popular societies was never developed, they did spring up from Maine to Georgia. At least nine other clubs were formed before the end of 1793; twenty-three in 1794; three in 1795, one in 1797; and three in 1798. Indeed, Eugene P. Link lists forty-two such societies organized between March 1793 and 1800, when Jefferson was elected. And his list is not complete; it does not include the French Patriotic Society of Charleston, the French Society of the Friends of Liberty and Equality of Philadelphia, the Juvenile Republican Society of New York City, and the Tammany Society of New York City.[18] (Although the Tammany Society was originally a social and benevolent fraternity, during the 1790s, Republicans gradually gained control of the organization, drove out the Federalists, and turned it into a Republican organization.)[19]

The Democratic Society of Pennsylvania, largest in the country, had about 315 members.[20] In New York City Alfred Young found a membership of 100 to 200.[21] In Charleston Link found a membership of 114. In nearby Pendleton County, the Franklin or Republican Society publicly claimed 400 members.[22] Other societies were smaller; most may have had memberships ranging from 20 to 25.

William Cobbett derisively characterized the membership of the Democratic Society of Pennsylvania as a group of "butchers, tinkers, broken hucksters, and trans-Atlantic traitors."[23] Link, however, rejects the "swinish multitude" interpretation of the membership, although he notes that the bulk of the members (about 70 percent) were either craftsmen or of the "lower orders."[24] In a more recent study, Roland M. Baumann estimates that the society membership was much more diverse than Link indicates. Although craftsmen were the largest group among the members, their percentage was lower than Link indicated and the public officials and mercantile group was larger.[25]

Meetings of the New York Democratic Society, Federalists charged, were attended by "the lowest order of mechanics, laborers and draymen" and were purposely held at night to accommodate them. In his detailed study of the New York society, however, Alfred Young concluded that "its leading officers were merchants of wealth and some status, its lesser officers young lawyers, teachers and craftsmen, while its rank and file were men of the 'middling' and 'lower sort.' "[26] A study of the Tammany Society in New York City, which Cobbett said was made up of "about 40 poor rogues and about 3 rich fools,"[27] reveals that merchants, investors, doctors, lawyers, and editors were among its members but that "mechanics supplied the largest single group in both membership and leadership."[28]

The southern societies had their share of slaveholding planters and the western societies a fair percentage of wealthy landowners and land speculators in their ranks, but "the body of the clubs on the frontier was composed of small farmers, settlers, and rentees."[29] Although lawyers were anathema to Democrats everywhere[30] (and most lawyers were Federalists), a fairly representative number belonged to the popular societies.[31]

Many important leaders of the period belonged to these popular societies. Jefferson, Madison, Monroe, and Burr, it is true, never had any discernible official connections with the societies, but David Rittenhouse, president of the American Philosophical Society, was the president of the Democratic Society of Pennsylvania; Alexander J. Dallas, secretary to Governor Thomas Mifflin of Pennsylvania, drew up its constitution; and Israel Israel, well known in Philadelphia for his revolutionary war activities, was its treasurer. Other members of the Philadelphia society included Charles Biddle, James Hutchinson, Jonathan D. Sergeant, and Pierre S. Du Ponceau, all men of high standing in the community. Robert Goodloe Harper was vice-president of the Charleston society. Doctors Charles Jarvis and William Eustis were active in the Massachusetts Constitutional Society, and James Sullivan, attorney general of Massachusetts, was one of its earliest members. James Brown of the Democratic Society of Lexington, Kentucky, was Secretary of State, John Breckenridge was soon to become Attorney General, George Muter was chief justice of the highest court in the state, and Thomas Todd was later to fill a high judicial position.[32]

Of particular importance is the fact that numerous publishers opposed to Federalist policies were active in the societies. At least thirty printers have been identified as "almost certainly connected with these societies." These included Benjamin F. Bache of the *General Advertiser and Aurora* and Eleazer Oswald of the Philadelphia *Independent Gazetteer,* both members of the Corresponding Committee of the Democratic Society of Pennsylvania; Henry Kammerer of the *Philadelphische Correspondenz,* a founder and officer of the German Republican

Society of Philadelphia; Philip Freneau of the *National Gazette* and other papers and Thomas Greenleaf of the New-York *Journal* and the *Argus,* both members of the Democratic Society of New York; Aaron Pennington, of the *Newark Centinel of Freedom,* a leader of the Republican Society of that city; Robert Coram of the *Delaware Gazette,* one of the leading figures in the Patriotic Society of Newcastle, Delaware; John Bradford of the Lexington *Kentucky Gazette,* who suggested and organized the Democratic Society of Kentucky; and Matthew Lyon of the *Rutland Farmers' Library,* who was probably a member of the local society.

We can conclude that the Democratic-Republican societies represented a coalition of merchants, political leaders, landowners, slaveowners, professionals, small tradesmen, mechanics, seamen, and laborers and that within this coalition, mechanics supplied the bulk of the membership while the political leaders and professionals supplied the bulk of the leadership.

A contemporary referred to the members of the New York Democratic Society as "the heroes and the sons of the heroes" who had established independence. The same was true of the other societies. All had in their ranks a great number of former members of Sons of Liberty, of Committees of Safety, and revolutionary war leaders who sought to revive the spirit of '76. The need to do so was urgent. They perceived reactionary tendencies that had already appeared in American political life. Certain persons, for example, had been gradually "*royalizing* themselves" under the auspices of the federal government. Tunis Wortman, the brilliant and energetic young secretary of the Democratic Society of New York, developed this theme in an oration:

> It is a truth too evident to be disguised, that since the completion and final establishment of our revolution, the flame of liberty has burned less bright, and become less universal in its operation. The charms of wealth, the allurements of luxury, the thirst of gain and the ruinous system of speculation, have borne down like the irresistible flood upon us, and have threatened destruction to the most valuable elements of social life:—the desire of affluence and the love of ease, have absorbed every honorable and patriotic consideration; have rendered us supine and indolent, and have nearly banished from our minds the sentiment of public virtue, destroyed the ardor of liberty, and diminished our attachment to the sacred interests of our country.[33]

Jefferson's warning in his *Notes on Virginia* of the demise of patriotic ardor was frequently cited by the popular societies. Once the war was over, Jefferson had predicted, people would become so absorbed "in making money" that the government would forget the people and their rights, and, indeed, the people themselves would become indifferent and fail to maintain "a due respect for their rights. The shackles, therefore, which shall not be knocked off at the conclusion of this war, will remain on us long, and will be made heavier, till our rights shall revive, or expire in a convulsion."

It thus fell to the popular societies to reawaken the spirit of liberty from one end of the union to the other. Members of the Charleston club explained that the popular societies had but "one general purpose, that of watching narrowly public characters" to make certain that the liberties won a decade earlier would be preserved.[34]

Once organized, the societies met monthly; at elections or during times of political crisis, they met more frequently. New members were admitted at these meetings. Usually applicants had to be vouched for; the New York society, for example, stipulated no one could be accepted unless five members could testify that he was a "firm and steadfast friend of EQUAL RIGHTS OF MAN," and one-fifteenth of the members present might blackball a candidate. "Apostasy from Republican principles" was ground for expulsion.[35] Members were usually addressed as "citizen" and officers as "Citizen President." There were to be no titles. (The Charleston society forced the city council to do away with the titles of "Esquire" and "His Honor.")[36] In keeping with the belief that frequent changes in the administrative personnel were necessary to protect popular liberties, officers in every society were chosen for no longer than one year, and in at least one the chairmanship of the committee of correspondence was rotated monthly.[37]

The societies participated in local elections, either openly or sub rosa. They organized or joined in public celebrations and parades, particularly on July Fourth, and were credited in 1794 with having made that day "more universally celebrated" than it had been for "many years."[38] They honored July 14—Bastille Day—though not as fulsomely and with as many toasts and zealous republican addresses as on the Fourth of July. The societies were also involved in certain direct actions (such as equipping French privateers) that their opponents considered, if not illegal, at least extralegal.

A great part of the activities of the popular societies consisted of creating public discussions; composing, adopting, and issuing circulars, memorials, resolutions, and addresses to the people; and remonstrances to the President and the Congress—all expressing the feelings of the assembled groups on current political issues. Along with general addresses and resolutions critical of administration policies, the societies dealt with specific questions. In western areas they agitated against the English for holding the frontier posts and against the Spanish for closing the Mississippi; in the East, they hit at England for "piracy" against American shipping. They agitated in the Carolinas for a uniform currency and demanded adequate representation for the growing backcountry.[39] The societies strongly protested the excise tax. Almost to a man, they opposed the nomination of John Jay as envoy to England, and most of them denounced the treaty that resulted from his mission. They constantly lashed out against secret sessions of Congress and the state legislatures and demanded that legislators, executives, and judges abandon the use of "dark, intricate, antiquated formalities" and "obsolete phraseology" that only lawyers and classical scholars could understand. They made frequent addresses to their congressmen, and in the South and West, they expected to receive regular reports from their congressmen in return. Representatives who failed to render such periodic accountings of their stewardship might find themselves censured.[40] On the other hand, they regularly approved "Patriotic acts" by elected representatives.

The societies urged equal justice and a general diffusion of knowledge as essential "pillars supporting the sacred temple of liberty."[41] Since it was widely believed that every undemocratic governmental system sought to perpetuate ignorance, a primary purpose of the societies was to disseminate political information. They invariably proclaimed the right of citizens to assemble for that purpose and to make their sentiments known. In such fashion they could discharge their sacred "*obligation* to secure and transmit to posterity, unsullied and undiminished, the blessings of freedom" secured by the Revolution.[42]

"To support and perpetuate the EQUAL RIGHTS OF MAN" was the New York society's "great object," and toward that end they would "constantly express our sentiments."[43] To the Democratic-Republican societies, the "Equal Rights of Man" meant the right to freedom of speech, press, and assembly; the right to criticize governmental representatives and to demand of them an explanation of their public acts; and the right to publish their reactions in a free press. Typical of all the societies is this resolution from Washington, North Carolina:

> It is the unalienable right of a free and independent people to assemble together in a peaceable manner to discuss with firmness and freedom all subjects of public concern, and to publish their sentiments to their fellow citizens, when the same shall tend to the public good.[44]

The resolutions, addresses, and toasts of these societies and the orations of officers and members are of considerable importance in evaluating the reform sentiment of republicanism. The popular societies and their members crusaded to eliminate imprisonment for debt, "sanguinary, cruel and unjust" criminal laws, and capital punishment for a wide variety of minor offenses. They thundered against a penal system that kept people in jail for no crime other than poverty. They cited legal fees charged and argued that poor men unable to pay the fees could be sent to jail even though innocent.[45] In Kentucky, the Lexington Democratic Society sent a memorial to the state general assembly, urging it to give attention to the reform of the criminal code. Because many crimes besides murder were capitally punished, offenders who "might be reformed and restored good members to society" were executed. The memorial urged "a radical change" and the institution of a "new system" of criminal procedure. In an oration to the Ulster (N.Y.) Republican Society, Dr. Phineas Hedges listed a series of defects in the "comparatively happy land" the United States represented, which prevented it from attaining "a state of moral political perfection." The most important defect, as he saw it, was the fact that "the severity of the criminal code is a reproach to freedom and to justice."[46]

Since "both slaveholders and abolitionists were on the membership rolls" of the popular societies, any resolution favoring abolition would have "ruined what unity the societies had attained."[47] Hence it is not surprising that there is no record of a society ever having passed a resolution against slavery. However, several of the leaders and members were active in the abolitionist movement. Among them were Alexander McKim, president of the Baltimore Republican Society, who was also vice-president of the Maryland Society for the Abolition of Slavery. Archibald Buchanan of the same society was also an active abolitionist. George Logan, Peter S. Du Ponceau, Dr. James Hutchinson, and Absalom Baird were members of both the Democratic Society of Pennsylvania and the Pennsylvania Society for Promoting Abolition of Slavery. Other antislavery members of the societies were Robert Coram in Delaware, Josiah Parker in Virginia, and James Nicholson, Tunis Wortman, Samuel L. Mitchill, Melancton Smith, and Philip Freneau, all of New York City.[48]

In celebrating the 1794 Fourth of July, the members of the Republican Society of Baltimore—several of whom had just freed the slaves they owned—first attended a meeting of the Maryland Society for the Abolition of Slavery at the courthouse. They heard Dr. Drysdale, one of their colleagues, deliver a "learned oration on the abolition of slavery." Later that day, they participated in the Republican Society celebration. In this manner, the society's members made sure that the cause of "our great revolution and arduous struggle for our birthright (liberty) was not suffered to be forgotten—nor was the cause of humanity, in sympathizing with the unfortunate African, and in endeavoring to loosen his shackles, permitted to suffer." On the other hand, as we shall see, southern members of the societies were enraged when Jay did nothing to recover their slaves who had escaped to the British during the war or to obtain compensation for their loss of human property. Likewise, while Bache's *Aurora* kept up a running attack against Washington as a slaveholder, it said nothing about the fact that its hero (Jefferson) also kept black human beings as slaves.[49]

In his Fourth of July oration of 1795 before the Republican Society of Ulster County, New York, Phineas Hedges referred to the fact that "humanity" is "outraged by the infamous traffic and merchandise of the human species." The General Society of Mechanics of New York on that same Fourth of July toasted: "May the time soon arrive when men shall be ashamed to make their fellow creatures an article of commerce." Since the mechanics had to compete with slave labor, this stand is not entirely surprising. Nor was the fact that the Tammany Society in New York City, composed mainly of mechanics, included among its toasts a call for the "speedy abolition of every species of slavery throughout America."[50]

Whether blacks were members of any of the popular societies cannot be determined conclusively. To be sure, William Cobbett gleefully cited the case of a member of the Democratic Society of Pennsylvania, "a philanthropist, a true equality man," who resigned from the organization when it rejected a Negro whom he had proposed as a member. On the other hand, a Federalist attack on the True Republican Society of Philadelphia noted that a meeting of the society was marked by the presence of "Citizen Sambo," a reference to Cyrus Bustill, a leading Philadelphia black. Still, Tunis Wortman made it clear that though he was opposed to slavery, he did not think that blacks were the equals of whites and entitled to the same rights:

> We may sincerely advocate the freedom of black men, and yet assert their moral and physical inferiority. It is our duty to assert their liberties, but it is not our duty to blend our form and colour and existence with theirs. Education and habit, nay, nature herself recoils at the idea.[51]

Finally, although there were scores of resolutions adopted by the popular societies hailing and supporting the French Revolution, not one was passed supporting another revolution occurring at the same time—the black revolution of slaves in the French West Indies.[52] Similarly, while there were numerous resolutions adopted denouncing the Indian depredations against white settlements, not once did any of the popular societies concede that the Indians had any justification for resenting the practices of the white settlers on the frontier. Finally, while the societies regularly toasted "the fair daughters" of America, none were invited to become members. Like the Sons of Liberty, the popular societies were for men only.

Just as the societies included slaveowners and abolitionists, they had conservatives on religion and devoted Deists as members. To be sure, the Federalists branded all the club members "infidels," but although Elihu Palmer, David Denniston, and John Slidell of the Democratic Society of New York formed a Deistical Society, the Democratic Society itself annually joined with the Mechanic and Cooper Societies in celebrating American independence by a parade and a service in a church. Moreover, clergymen were often invited to deliver the Fourth of July orations.

Nevertheless, the appeal to reason and the view that natural knowledge was more reliable than revelation or miracles inevitably attracted members of the popular societies. Hence it is not surprising that most outstanding American Deists were associated with the Democratic-Republican societies or that the clubs played an important role in spreading the deistic doctrine.[53]

The spirit of reform characteristic of the Democratic-Republican societies manifested itself most clearly in the campaign to establish a free school system. The New York Democratic Society spoke for all popular societies when it declared: "Ignorance is the irreconcilable enemy of liberty."[54] Only an informed people could defend and preserve the liberties won in the Revolution. In the late eighteenth century, however, the mass of the citizenry lacked the opportunity to acquire a formal education. In 1787 Benjamin Rush foreshadowed the stand

the popular societies would take in an essay he published proposing that education be provided for the poor through a tax-supported system. Several years
later, a member of the Democratic Society of Pennsylvania called for implementation of the idea. "The rich," he emphasized, "can buy learning—it is a luxury.
But to the poor it is a necessity, and to them, O Americans, it is denied. Let this
reproach be wiped off." How? By requiring by law that "cities and districts of
the country . . . support free schools."[55] Or to put it in another way:

> In a republican government we are told that the supreme power derives
> from the people. But what sort of power will that be which flows from an
> ignorant people. The fact is, the power does not flow from such ignorant
> people; the enlightened and wealthy few alone possess the power. . . .[56]

When, asked an advocate of public education, will men who claim to be Republicans

> prove their republicanism by passing laws to establish free schools? Let
> the education of children become a common charge. If a man has prop-
> erty and no children, still he should be taxed to pay for the education of
> other men's children. . . . Let every state . . . divide its territory into proper
> districts, and establish at least one school in each. Make a beginning, and
> afterwards carry on the good work as fast and as far as possible.[57]

A leading exponent of this concept was Robert Coram, an English-born schoolmaster, publisher of the Wilmington *Delaware Gazette,* and a leader of the Newcastle, Delaware, Patriotic Society. Coram published a pamphlet in 1791, *Plan
for the General Establishment of Schools Throughout the United States,* in which
he observed that "most of the American legislatures are composed of lawyers
and merchants," not farmers or other workers. The reason, he said, was

> because the farmer has no opportunity of getting his son instructed, with-
> out sending him to college; the expence of which, is more than the profits
> of his farm. An equal representation is absolutely necessary to the preser-
> vation of liberty. But there can never be an equal representation, until
> their is an equal mode of education for all citizens. . . .

The solution was obvious: "Let public schools be established in every county of
the United States, at least as many as are necessary for the present population;
and let the schools be supported by a general tax."[58]

Coram's solution was endorsed by every one of the popular societies. The
"mother society," the Democratic Society of Philadelphia, voiced the common
viewpoint when it resolved in 1795 that "the establishment of public schools
upon proper principles, will ensure the future of independence and republican-

ism." It urged the government to act immediately.[59] That same year, in his
sermon to the societies of New York City, Reverend Samuel Miller insisted that
legislative aid to establish public schools was "so plainly and intimately connected with the welfare of all republics that neither proof nor illustration on the
subject are necessary."[60]

Several societies prodded their legislatures to act. The Delaware Constitution
of 1792 provided "for establishing schools and promoting arts and sciences."
But beyond that the legislature refused to go. In 1794 Robert Coram, Nicholas
Van Dyke, and Caesar A. Rodney were appointed by the Patriotic Society of
Newcastle to draw up a memorial to the legislature urging the establishment of
public schools "whereby the unfortunate children of indiegence and neglect,
may be educated and enlightened among the children of opulence and vigilance—
which is an essential means of preserving that equality so necessary to the preservation of pure Republican Government." The memorial complained that the
legislators had done nothing in respect to free schools. "There still remains in
the minds of many," the memorialists declared, "a torpor on this subject, as difficult to account for, as to excuse. . . . We cannot help lamenting the sad effects
of such listless attention to the first principles of society. . . . We cannot avoid
pressing the Lesiglature . . . to make some beginnings in this important business."[61]

Memorials and resolutions by the popular societies were to no small extent responsible for the passage of legislation in at least two states establishing funding
for public schools. The New York law of 1795 distributed a fixed sum annually
to each county over a five-year period "for encouraging and maintaining schools."
The Delaware act of 1796 "to create a fund sufficient to establish schools in this
state" declared that revenue from the sale of marriage and tavern licenses to the
beginning of 1806 should become "the fund for establishing schools in the state
of Delaware." The results of both laws, however, were disappointing.[62]

To the Democratic-Republican societies belongs the credit for the postrevolutionary demand for popular education. By means of correspondence committees,
the societies made public education a national issue. Even though no true general system of public education was established as a result of their efforts, the
founding of the U.S. public school system was the direct result of the work of
these societies. Moreover, at least ten colleges and academies were begun or
aided by the members of the societies.[63]

The Democratic-Republican societies looked beyond schools to the press as a
means to educate the public. In particular, they felt the need for their own press;
it seemed to them that "the greater part of the American newspapers seemed to
be lock, stock and barrel in the hands of the anti-democrats."[64] In the words of
William Manning, a poor, untutored Massachusetts farmer who had marched with
his militia company to the "Concord fite" on April 19, 1775, and was a staunch
Jeffersonian Republican: "A labouring man may as well hunt for pins in a hay-
mow as to try to collect the knowledge necessary for him to have from such
promiscuous piles of contradictions." Manning published his *Key of Libberty*

in 1797 in which he proposed a nationwide "Labouring Society," which would publish a weekly magazine that would go to every town in the country where "librarians" would make them available even to people who could not afford them. The magazine would be free of the triviality and biases that filled the existing "ruened Press," thus for the first time furnishing *useful* knowledge vital in a republic. The government, Manning thought, should support the magazine on behalf of the public welfare.[65]

Manning conceded that there was no lack of a press through which the people, organized in various associations, could express their views. He complained, however, that because of the number of papers and the frequency with which they appeared, it was necessary for "a labouring man . . . [to] read and studdy halfe his time, and then be at a loss to know what is true and what is not."[66]

There had, indeed, been a considerable increase in the number of newspapers published in the United States. In 1790 there were only about a hundred published in the United States; by 1800, the number had more than doubled.[67] Republican Manning may not have been so happy with this development, but neither were the Federalists. The Federalist *Gazette of the United States* complained in 1801 that in the previous decade

> *Republican* papers . . . sprung up in every town and village. Those men who, in their own country had been advanced to the rank of a Secretary to a seditious club, or *strolling player upon the stage,* could write and harrangue; while others could work a press or travel through the country and proclaim to the ignorant, that government is usurpation, that taxes are a robbery upon the poor to support the powerful, and that nothing but immediate opposition to their rulers can save them from the chains of slavery.[68]

In short, during the years that the popular societies emerged, there also emerged a press that guaranteed that their toasts, resolutions, manifestos, and memorials reached an audience much larger than the membership of the clubs themselves.[69] The New York Democratic Society paid for a supplement in the *New York Journal* of April 20, 1794, which gave in full the principles and constitution of the Associated Democratic Society of Chittenden, Vermont. Usually, however, the societies had their documents, speeches, and proceedings published in the press without cost.[70] When the Federalist *Mercury* began charging advertising rates in February 1795 for printing club resolutions, it was unusual enough to cause wide comment.[71]

To be sure, the circulation of the newspapers of the 1790s was limited by today's standards. The total number of copies printed annually was probably under five million in a nation of 5,308,483 in 1800—less than one copy per person per year.[72] The influence of the newspapers, however, was augmented through secondary circulation in coffeehouses and taverns. There was thus no absence of a

medium through which the Democratic-Republican societies could get their
message across to the people.

Scholars commonly state that, more than any other issue, the French Revolution and the developing United States-French relations helped to draw party lines
in the United States. Hamilton's financial policies and the question of just how
centralized the new government should be and which "interests" should wield
its power continued to concern the American people. But it was the French
Revolution and the crisis over foreign policy during 1793 and 1794 that integrated all other issues. These two issues, moreover, were the ones that enabled
the popular societies to build a following to challenge the Federalists. "No other
single event," writes one student of the political scene in the 1790s, "was more
responsible [than the French Revolution] for causing men to take stock of their
beliefs and choose priorities among conflicting values."[73]

Almost all Americans had sympathized with the French Revolution at its
outbreak, and from 1789 through most of 1792 enthusiasm mounted. France
had been America's ally and Britain's foe, and she continued to be looked upon
as the country's savior. Hence, the French Revolution and the proclamation of
a new French republic were enthusiastically received by persons of both parties,
and the French people's struggle against monarchy and aristocracy was compared
to the American struggle in 1776. The pamphlet war between Edmund Burke
and Thomas Paine helped to dramatize the issues in terms most Americans could
grasp. Paine's *Rights of Man,* an effective answer to Burke's reactionary attack
on the French Revolution, came off the press in London in February 1791 and
was quickly reprinted in the United States. The American edition featured a
preface by Thomas Jefferson in which he wrote: "I am extremely pleased to find
it will be reprinted here. . . . I have no doubt our citizens will rally a second time
to the standard of Common Sense."[74]

The news of the abolition of the monarchy in France on September 21, 1792,
reached America in the middle of December. And then, says Charles D. Hazen,
"began a year utterly without parallel, as far as I am aware, in the history of this
country. American citizens gave themselves up to the most extraordinary series
of celebrations in honor of the achievements of another country."[75] Three
months after the September 1792 massacres, Jefferson advised William Short
that 99 out of every 100 Americans were in full sympathy with the French Revolution and realized that "the liberty of the whole earth was depending on the issue in the contest."[76]

But in truth much was changing in 1793. Though Federalists were at first
sympathetic to the ends of the French Revolution, it was not long before their
hesitant approval turned to genuine fear and dismay at what they termed the
"violent excesses" of the new regime. "There is a difference between the French
and American Resolution," argued the Federalist *Gazette of the United States*
as early as January 16, 1793:

In America no barbarities were perpetrated—no men's heads were struck upon poles—no ladies bodies mangled, were carried thro' the streets in triumph—their prisoners guarded and ironed, were not massacred in cold blood. The Americans did not, at discretion, harass, murder, or plunder the clergy—not roast their generals unjustly alive.—They set limit to their vices, at which their pursuits rested. And whatever blood was shed, flowed gallantly in the field. The American Revolution, it ought to be repeated, was not accomplished as the French has been, by massacres, assassinations, or proscriptions: battles, severe and honorable, were fought, and the chance of war left to decide.

Republican enthusiasm for France, however, continued unabated. Republicans accepted the violence and disorder as necessary. Jefferson wrote to William Short in 1793 that he regretted the innocent blood that had been shed in the French Revolution but pointed out that it was necessary to secure liberty for posterity. "My own affections," he continued, "have been deeply wounded by some of the martyrs to this cause, but rather than it should have failed, I would have seen half the earth desolated."[77] When Federalists expressed horror at the execution of the king, "a Republican" asked, what was his death compared to the "millions that have suffered under the cruel yoke of despotism?" John Bradford, one of the founders of the Democratic Society of Lexington, editorialized in his *Kentucky Gazette:* "Instead of reviling the French republicans as monsters, the friends of royalty in this country should rather admire at their patience in so long deferring the fate of their perjured monarch, whose blood is probably considered as an atonement for the safety of many guilty thousands that are still suffered to remain in the bosom of France."[78]

In the midst of all this, France's new minister, Citizen Edmund Charles Genêt left for the United Stated on the French frigate *L'Embuscade.* On April 6, 1793, two days before he landed in Charleston, a British packet arrived in New York bringing news of the execution of Louis XVI and of the French declaration of war on England and Holland. Because the treaty of commerce and amity of 1778 with France stated that "the terms hereinafter mentioned shall be perpetual between the Most Christian King, his heirs and successors and said United States," there arose the question of whether the treaty was still in force.[79] Hamilton claimed that because of the king's death and because of alterations in internal conditions in France, "which render treaties that before subsisted between it and another nation, it is a plain dictate of reason that the latter shall have a right to renounce these treaties."[80] Jefferson, on the other hand, argued that "treaties between the United States and Louis Capet, but between the two nations of America and France, and the nations remaining in existence, though both of them have since changed their forms of government, the treaties are not annulled by these changes."[81]

To the Republicans of 1793 the answer to the question of whether the treaty of 1778 was still in force was clear: France had helped the United States when it needed aid, and it was only fair that the United States reciprocate. In his Fourth of July oration to the Republican Society of Baltimore in 1794, Archibald Buchanan urged Americans never to forget in their rejoicing over their independence the "former services" France had rendered them:

> Oh France.... At a time when the prospect was all gloomy around, and the benighted travellers seemed ready to sink with fatigue and desperation upon the earth, thy benevolence appeared, like a taper through the dark, to enlighten and to guide us; we were strangers and yet ye took us in; we were naked and ye clothed us; we were pursued by robbers and ye put arms into our hands for defence; we wanted money, and we found thee a benefactress; by thy assistance were our right defended; and by thy assistance, I repeat it again and again, by thy assistance, do we enjoy all our present blessings, and exist not the vile slaves of unlimited despotism? Can we then so soon forget thy former kindness, and be insensible to thy present sufferings? Sink us first, kind heaven, to the bottom of the sea! As Americans, we must feel every wound at which our earliest, dearest, only friend bleeds? As men we cannot but pray for your complete success. And spurn from you, my countrymen, those wretches who would seduce you into the opinion, no less dangerous than false, that this nation of heroes is but a horde of assassins, and would lessen the weight of that obligation you are under to the nation at large, by ascribing it entirely to the king.... Louis the sixteenth is now no more!... To his intervention, in our favour, I gratefully acknowledge myself and country, eternally indebted. But can we ever forget, that the blood which he sent to be spilt on our shores, was the blood of the people; and that the treasures which he used, in our defence, were the treasures of the people too! And can we, ever, ever forget the cause, the glorious cause, in which these same people do now fight; and shall we suffer our wishes for the life of a single man, to come in competition one single moment, with our wishes for the lives and liberties of millions? No, fight on,—fight on then, illustrious nation, to be true to the cause in which you have engaged, despise the censures of an unthinking world, and let philosophy, reason, and liberty prevail!

It was, moreover, in America's own interest to defend the French republic. Should England and the "combined tyrants" be successful in restoring monarchy to France, Republican America itself would eventually be subdued by the promonarchist European confederacy.[82]

While Americans were debating the extent of their commitment to the principles of the French revolution and of their obligations under the treaty of 1778,

Genêt arrived in Charleston. (Owing to delay in communications, no one, of course, knew that the Girondist-controlled government he represented had already been ousted from power.) Few diplomatic missions have left such a vivid imprint or have been so much discussed by historians. It is hardly necessary to relate in detail the oft-told story of how Genêt did not bother to present his credentials at Philadelphia; how enthusiastic and clamorous were the receptions accorded him wherever he went; how he was carried away by his public receptions; and how, ignoring the warning the government he represented had given him against straying from diplomatic channels, he immediately entered upon privateering and recruiting activities; how on April 22, 1793, after several days of deliberation in the cabinet, Washington issued the Proclamation of Neutrality; how Genêt challenged presidential authority by appealing to the "voice of the people"; how many Republican leaders came to realize that Genêt had become an "intolerable liability"; and how finally the story of Genêt's threatening an "appeal to the people," and his efforts in enlisting privateers and recruiting Americans against the Spaniards in Louisiana, led the administration in 1794 to demand the minister's recall.[83]

We can note, however, that authorities on Genêt and his mission have presented a number of versions to account for his downfall. The most popular one appears to be that Genêt came into disrepute through his own misconduct. Others have pointed out, however, that while the minister had considerable shortcomings as a diplomat and was certainly headstrong and arrogant, the Federalists, in their desire to destroy the Franco-American alliance, expanded hearsay into fact and exaggerated the real nature of Genêt's offenses.[84] Genêt himself contended that Jefferson led him on, always pretending friendship for France, to betray him as a scapegoat for party purposes. He later charged Jefferson with having promoted entertainments to impress him but would not attend a single event himself.[85] Another thesis is that Genêt probably was the Democratic-Republicans' cat's paw.[86]

While the mission ended in failure, the repercussions of the Genêt affair were of considerable importance in the formation of the first political parties in the United States. The popular societies became deeply involved in the debate over the French minister, and, while they suffered from Genêt's disgrace, their public activities in the cause he represented brought a more democratic strain into the political process, which had long been dominated by an elite leadership.

The Proclamation of Neutrality President Washington issued on April 22, 1793, declared the foreign policy of the United States to be one of neutrality in the wars of the French Revolution. Although many Republicans acquiesced in the proclamation, the Democratic-Republican societies throughout the country demanded the unhesitating fulfillment of previous treaty obligations to France and found the proclamation abhorrent, a pusillanimous truckling to Britain, despotically conceived and unconstitutionally promulgated. It represented the will of the executive solely; he had bypassed the nation's lawmaking body, unconstitutionally usurping its power.[87]

The popular societies were almost unwavering in their support of Genêt, even after many friends of France had deserted the minister. Several of the societies defended Genêt against the imputations of Federalist leaders that he was prepared even to use force to circumvent the provisions of the proclamation. On the other hand, the societies in some areas aided French plans for recruiting troops and arming ships for insurrections against Florida and Louisiana.[88] In the Carolinas they defended Stephen Drayton and Alexander Moultrie against prosecution for recruiting on Genêt's behalf.[89] At the same time, along the coast, they did their best to make sure that British ships did not violate the neutrality proclamation. In Charleston, they forced one English vessel to cease loading military supplies.[90]

The societies complained to the President and Congress of the feeble and abortive efforts of the federal government to secure for them their "natural and just rights" to navigate the Mississippi River, "which is withheld from us by Spaniards." Moreover, both individual citizens and the popular societies secured signatures to the remonstrance and transmitted them to their representatives in Congress.[91] At the same time the societies and others in the West took concrete steps to open the Mississippi by force. These actions were in conjunction with the expedition against Louisiana organized by George Rogers Clark with the aid and encouragement of Genêt and his agents. Clark wrote to Genêt that "the Democratic Society of Kentucky have made some advances in ammunition and Given all the encouragement in their power."[92] But Fouchet, Genêt's successor, terminated the expedition.

The resolutions and memorials of the Democratic-Republican societies made it clear that the French republic was to be defended at all costs. In part this was because France had become the scene of the new birth of the struggle for liberty and equality; in part it was because France had helped the United States in its own struggle for the same ends. But there was a more selfish purpose, and it was openly expressed—a desire for self-preservation, a desire to protect the hard-won rights of free men that neutrality seemed to endanger. Britain was the leader of the war against France, and, reasoned the societies, should it be successful, America's turn would be next. How could we expect tyrants to do anything but rejoice when they saw how little the free men of America were doing "to rescue their brethren in France from the iron hand of despotism"?[93] Was not Britain guilty of failing to evacuate the forts in the Northwest, in violation of the 1783 Treaty of Paris, of stirring up the Algerine pirates against American shipping, and of inflaming the Indians on the western borders? Could America afford to let Britain and its allies destroy the French Republic? Or as the Democratic Society of Wythe County in Virginia put it in its address "to the People of the United States" on July 4, 1794:

Shall we Americans who have kindled the Spark of Liberty stand aloof and see it extinguished when burning a bright flame in France, which hath caught it from us? Do you not see if despots prevail, you must have a despot like the rest of nations? If all tyrants unite against free people, should not all free people unite against tyrants? Yes! Let us unite with France and stand or fall together.

Benjamin Franklin Bache, editor of the Philadelphia *Aurora,* told his readers much the same:

Upon the establishment of overthrow of liberty in France probably will depend the permanency of the Republic in the new world. It is not very absurd to suppose that if complete success attends the arms of the combined powers, that they will endeavor directly or indirectly totally to extinguish the fire of freedom in every part of the globe; —hence this country is much deeper concerned in the politics of the European world than might appear to a superficial observer.[94]

Because the future of the American republic was linked, in the eyes of the societies, to the success of the French Revolution, support for France was proof of loyalty to America. "The man who is an enemy to republican government elsewhere, cannot be attached to such a government at home" was one way of putting it. The New York society declared: "We firmly believe that he who is an enemy to the French revolution cannot be a firm republican; and therefore . . . ought not to be intrusted with the guidance of any part of the machine of government." Several of the societies openly urged war on France's behalf. "The cause of France is the cause of the people of all nations," resolved the Pinckneyville group. French victory would mean "one great Democratic Society of the world."[95]

There was a revolutionary optimism in this world view. It rejected the view that human nature was essentially depraved, lacking in moral principle, and not to be trusted.[96] This had probably been true in the past when human nature had been shaped by monarchical despotism; but with the establishment of a republic in America all this was changed, and the rest of the world would follow its example. "Revolutions, may they never cease until the whole world be regenerated," was a toast frequently heard whenever Democratic-Republican societies gathered. The regeneration would encompass every aspect of society. In his *Oration on the Influence of Social Institutions upon Human Nature and Happiness,* Tunis Wortman called upon all who subscribed to "that monkish and dishonorable doctrine which teaches the original depravity of mankind"—a doctrine he labeled "a false and pernicious libel upon our species"—to envisage a society based upon "the ruling principle of Republics" instead of that of despotic monarchy:

When once that happy aera dawns upon the world, luxury, wealth, and sumptuous dissipation, will give place to the charms of public spirit, and the solid delights of a general and expanded philosophy: No distinctions will be known but those which are derived from a happy combination of virtue with talents, and such distinction will promote a generous emulation without degenerating into jealousy or envy. The arts of civilized life will then be esteemed and cherished: Agriculture and manufactures will flourish; commerce, unrestrained by treaties, and unshackled by partial provisions, will become as extensive as the wants and intercourse of nations. Philosophy, the sciences, and the liberal arts will advance in a continued and accelerated progression. Sanguinary punishments will then be forgotten and unknown. Persecution and superstition, vice, prejudice and cruelty will take their eternal departure from the earth. National animosities and distinctions will be buried in eternal oblivion.[97]

Much was at stake then in keeping alive the spirit of '76. Toast after toast was raised to the late revolution and to the memory of the "martyrs in defense of our National Sovereignty." Fourth of July orations sponsored by the popular societies reminded audiences of the sacrifices made to achieve independence. These orations were often published as pamphlets to take the lessons to a wider audience.

With vigorous voices, the popular societies condemned every attack upon domestic liberties, resisted every tendency toward aristocracy at home, and proclaimed their faith in popular government. Toasts to "the sovereign people" or to "the people—the only source of legitimate power" were frequent, as were toasts to a free press, to free speech, and to an uncorrupted electorate. There were also toasts to the victims of tyranny in England, Scotland, Ireland, Poland, and other countries, and to the idea that America must be the asylum for all such victims of tyrants.

As the Democratic-Republican societies advanced their defense of the French Revolution and communicated their position on popular government through the press, the Federalists struck out at the organizations. The societies replied in turn. The debate that resulted overflowed with rhetoric, but its significance lies in the fact that it introduced new concepts in American political ideology and hastened the growth of egalitarianism.

Federalists launched their attack by attributing the origin of the societies to Genêt and the French Revolution. They were "Jacobins," "Genêt begotten," "Genetites," and "Genêt's scouting party."[98] The clubs "were born of sin, the impure off-spring of Genêt," thundered Fisher Ames. Oliver Wolcott declared that "the clubs consist of hot-headed, ignorant or wicked men devoted entirely to the views of France."[99] The Reverend John Sylvester John Gardiner poetized in his *Remarks on the Jacobinad:*

At Pandemonium meets the scoundrel throng,
Hell in their heart, and faction in their tongue. . . .

Who are the men these caitiff chiefs command?
A Strange, unlettered, multifarious band—
Some with weak heads, but well-intentioned hearts,
Are simply dupes to Anti-Federal arts;
Who, viewing tyrant acts in useful laws,
Mistake foul Faction's for fair Freedom's cause.
The rest are foul progeny of dirt,
Who, for a pint of rum, would sell their shirt!
With heads of adamant, and hearts of steel,
The worst of passions, are the best they feel.
An envious, restless, swearing, drinking crew,
When sense ne'er guided, virtue never knew;
Some foreign ruffians, hireling tools no doubt,
French, Irish, Scotch, complete the "rabble rout."[100]

The attack continued. The "demonical societies," Federalists charged, were
disorderly, dangerous to liberty, "nurseries of sedition," "treasonably Franco-
phile, exclusive and secretive."[101] They were well on the road to becoming the
"tyrants of America." Their "real design was to involve the country in war, to
assume the reigns of government and tyrannize over the people."[102] They abused
any friend to energetic administration, and indeed set themselves up as extralegal governments. They attempted unduly to influence legislation. Truly virtuous people did not circumvent the legitimate institutions of government by resorting to popular agitation. By their attacks they weakened respect for all lawful authority and paved the way for anarchy.[103] They were "unlawful," concluded Oliver Wolcott, Jr., "as they are formed for the avowed purpose of a general influence and control upon the measures of government."[104] In short, the
societies were unlawful because the common people had no right to instruct their
representatives once they were elected. Or, for that matter, no right even to
concern themselves with political affairs. The Federalist elitist philosophy that
only the "rich and well born" should concern themselves with government was
summed up in the following verse:

Next, every man throughout the nation,
Must be contented in his station,
Nor think to cut a figure greater
Than was designed for him by Nature.

No tinker bold with brazen pate,
Should set himself to patch the State,
No cobbler leave, at Faction's call,
His *last,* and thereby lose his *all.*[105]

The very name "Democracy" was used as part of the Federalist attack on the popular societies. "Democracy" was carefully distinguished from "republicanism," and the former was equated with French Jacobinism. A poem entitled "Democracy," published in 1794, linked democracy with anarchy and lawless confusion. In editorials and articles the Federalist press reviled the word "Democrat" and coupled it with all that was seditious. Reserving the title of "republican" for themselves, the Federalists first sought to make the word "democrat" obnoxious to the people and then to tar the popular societies with the term.[106]

The Democratic-Republican societies, their members, and their newspaper supporters struck back, both by refuting charges against the clubs and by presenting their philosophy. They defied anyone to point out a single action of the societies that was contrary to the Constitution or inimical to the nation's interest.[107] To the charge that they were not republican but democratic, they answered that the two were "synonymous."[108] Some insisted that "democracy" was a better term because it implied equality and popular power more definitely than did "republic." "Monarchies have been called Republics—aristocracies are Republics," one member insisted. "But, sir, depend upon it, he that is not a Democrat is an aristocrat or a monocrat. . . . He that is not a Democrat, is a Tory in his heart."[109] It is certainly nor surprising that many of the Republican societies chose to call themselves "Democratic-Republican" societies.

To the charge that the societies were "leaders of factions" determined to overthrow the government, they answered they were nothing more than legitimate assemblies of people called together to discuss public affairs. The societies considered themselves a credit to a republic, which depended for its effectiveness on alert, well-informed citizens.[110]

Under a Constitution which expressly provides *"That the people have a right in an orderly and peaceable manner to assemble and consult upon the common good,"* there can be no necessity for an apology to the public for an Association of a number of citizens to promote and cherish the social virtues, the love of their country and a respect for its Laws and Constitutions; nor can it be derogatory to Freemen *in America* to declare their attachment to *Universal Liberty* and openly to profess a sacred regard to the great principles of *Natural Equality.*

After having set up a government, citizens ought not to resign it into the hands of agents—whither does this tend but toward despotism? We conceive that it is the right and duty of every Freeman, to watch with the vigilance of a faithful centinel the conduct of those to whom is intrusted the administration of Government, that they pass not the sacred barriers of the Constitution.[111]

To those who took umbrage at the societies as representing but the views of pressure groups, the answer was obvious. Let the critics similarly band together.

The privilege of organization, discussion, and petition was the birthright of every man.[112] "A CANAAN DEMOCRAT" regretted that the meeting place was inadequate to include all the liberals of that town in the Columbia County Democratic Society, but he welcomed others of like sentiments to form other Republican clubs, and indeed

> aristocrats Aristocratical Societies, and Monarchists Tory Societies, &c.
> and all freely discuss and publish as we do or as they might choose, that
> the views of each might be made manifest and bear the proper weight with
> an enlightened and orderly people. . . . We for ourselves prefer Societies
> because in them every grade and capacity can furnish something to the
> general stock of improvement, and because they tend to fraternity, con-
> sistence, and due order.[113]

Instead of "a discontented few, the remains of the anti-federal party," as the Federalists charged, the clubs were composed of a goodly number of true friends of the Constitution. (Many of its members had been Federalists in 1788, the New York society pointed out.) But these friends of the Constitution had learned that obtaining freedom was much easier than preserving it, and there was always the danger that the fruits of the American Revolution might be perverted to benefit a few rather than all. To prevent this, they had organized the popular societies for the primary purpose of "the promotion of useful knowledge and the dissemination of political information." Why should those in power denounce their effort? Thinking men should suspect and resent any effort to stifle freedom of inquiry. "Should all other societies be tolerated in a free country, and that, whose object is political information, be proscribed?" Only one reason could explain this: "That government must be unfit for freemen which cannot bear investigation, and that administration must be corrupt which hides itself in darkness. Truth fears not the light."[114]

One charge the societies proudly admitted: they were pro-French. "Yes, fellow citizens," replied the New York Democratic Society, "we take pleasure in avowing thus, publicly to you that we are lovers of the French nation, that we esteem their cause as our own." If this was "the language of treason, if this is the language of faction and sedition," then let the authorities "punish us for these, our open, our avowed principles, from which no earthly consideration shall ever tempt us to recede." Such a prosecution would only expose the accuser to the wrath of the people, for "he who is an enemy to the French revolution, cannot be a firm republican."[115] More soberly, the Democratic Society of Kentucky explained why it was pro-French:

> To the present age it has been reserved to witness renovating Revolutions.
> In America we fought not shelter, from the oppressions of one tyrant, un-
> der the talons of another. The Rights of Man, the principles of a govern-

ment formed to protect those rights, and ensure to our latest posterity, the blessings of freedom and equality, were the objects of our political deliberations. France has since caught the glorious flame! Long have her people been deprived of the rights bestowed by their beneficent Creator. At length they have arisen in their strength, and like inundation, have, at once, swept away their tyrants and their Gothic structures. May success and freedom reward their merits.[116]

But sober language did not protect the Kentucky Democratic Society from Federalist attacks. Writing in the *Virginia Chronicle* of July 17, 1794, "Xantippe" raged:

But in Kentucky you have a Democratic Society—that horrible sink of treason,—that hateful synagogue of anarchy,—that odious conclave of tumult,—that frightful cathedral of discord,—that poisonous garden of conspiracy,—that hellish school of rebellion and opposition to all regular and well-balanced authority.[117]

There was no way the popular societies could answer this type of paranoia. They simply expressed confidence that their fellow countrymen would understand that the organizations were formed to preserve the spirit of '76, and they were open to all friends of liberty. They had a right to exist, and those who denied that right were foes of all Americans who favored freedom. "Our caluminators," said the New York society, "are your enemies, as well as our own."[118]

In the late summer and fall of 1794 and through the early months of 1795, the popular societies faced a more severe challenge as Federalists grasped the chance to lay the Whiskey Rebellion at their door. The Whiskey Rebellion in the western counties of Pennsylvania is a familiar story.[119] Although the farmers had a wide variety of grievances, such as land speculation, trials held in remote federal courts, and lack of concern for their defense and navigation rights on the Mississippi, a tax on liquors was especially distasteful. The cost of shipping their farm produce in freight wagons to the eastern cities was prohibitive, and, as a consequence, their only recourse was to reduce their grains to a more portable form. To them, the excise was a tax on their livelihood. Moreover, since the tax was upon the process of distilling rather than upon the retailer or consumer, the people believed the government was discriminating against them to the benefit of those in the East who were better able to pay.

Opposition to the law passed on March 3, 1791, led to mass meetings over a two-year period. By late 1793 violence had repeatedly broken out against the property of local revenue inspectors, and, in November 1793, and inspector's house was burned to the ground.

While the objection to the excise law was long-standing, the immediate cause related to the practice of forcing westerners to travel to Philadelphia for trial. Actually, to remove this complaint of the protestors, Congress passed an act on June 4, 1794, that allowed state courts to try excise cases when the nearest federal court was more than fifty miles distant. However, the federal court in Philadelphia issued legal processes against seventy-five western distillers under the old law on May 31, four days before passage of the new act. The attempt to serve court processes commanding appearance at Philadelphia by Marshal David Lenox, in company with General John Neville, the local excise inspector, brought on the famous attack on Neville's Bower Hall home on July 17, 1794. At the inspector's request a small detachment of regular troops from the garrison at Pittsburgh had come to his aid, but they were compelled to surrender by the much larger attack body, a considerable number of whom were Pennsylvania militiamen. The leader of the militia, Major James McFarlane, who had fought in the Revolution, was killed in the conflict. Neville's house and the buildings on his estate were burned.

The not-unexpected insurrection in the western counties of Pennsylvania was precisely what Alexander Hamilton, father of the excise tax, had been waiting for. He had pushed for a military solution to enforce the excise as early as 1792, and in 1794 he again demanded its use. Hamilton had long been striving for a strong national government, and the insurrection to him was a major test. The new government had to prove that it could successfully crush organized resistance to its laws.[120] As Hamilton put it, the rebellion "will do us a great deal of good and add to the solidity of everything in this country."[121]

At first President Washington did not respond positively to Hamilton's call for force. Instead he permitted Governor Thomas Mifflin of Pennsylvania to pursue a plan for amnesty. In addition, the two men named five commissioners and instructed them to assess the situation by holding conferences with the so-called insurgents.[122] Events following the commissioners' conference moved swiftly. The state's plan of conciliation was undermined as the federal administration moved step by step toward military intervention. On August 7 President Washington issued the sharp proclamation in which he ordered the insurgents to disperse. He also asked for Mifflin's full cooperation.[123] In response, Mifflin issued a mild proclamation condemning unlawful combinations and calling the Pennsylvania assembly into special session to enact legislation to resolve the western crisis. On August 8 Mifflin ordered Josiah Himer, adjutant general of the Pennsylvania militia, to call his men into service. Four days later, in a letter to Washington, Governor Mifflin reaffirmed his intent to cooperate in enforcing the national laws.[124]

Between August 12 and 28 peaceful negotiations between the commissioners and the insurgents were held in Pittsburgh. Then, upon receipt of the commissioners' report asserting that only "physical force could reestablish complete peace in the west," Washington ordered the troops to put down the rebellion.

With Hamilton in command, the army moved forward. It actually encountered no resistance, and in the end, a few ringleaders were captured and brought to trial. Only two were convicted, and Washington pardoned them.[125]

This then was the Whiskey Rebellion. In July 1794 the first shots were fired in Washington County, Pennsylvania. On August 7, Washington as commander-in-chief ordered the militia to be gathered; and when negotiations with the insurgents failed, 15,000 men were ordered to march. The insurrection immediately collapsed.

Hamilton was attacked for having accompanied the troops to Pittsburgh. He replied in the fashion that had become common with him, declaring that he had "long since . . . learned to hold public opinion of no value."[126] But this did not mean that he would not try to make use of the Whiskey Rebellion to try to destroy the organizations that were expressing "popular opinion"—the Democratic-Republican societies. In a letter to Thomas Fitzsimmons, the Pennsylvania Congressman, on November 27, 1794, Hamilton conceded that "the opposition to the excise laws began from causes foreign to Democratic Societies" but added that it was "well ascertained by proof in the course of judicial investigations, that the insurrection immediately is to be essentially attributed to one of those societies sometimes called the Mingo Creek society, sometimes the Democratic Society." Hamilton went on to charge that the president and members of "The Mingo Creek, sometimes called the Democratic Society," were leaders in the two marches upon Neville's house. All this had been established by "good proof and information."[127]

In 1938 William Miller correctly pointed out that the Mingo Creek society was not the same as the Democratic Society of Washington County. Moreover, while conceding that some of the members of the Washington County society did take part in the insurrection, he argued that they apparently did not do so in their capacity as members of the club.[128] Eugene P. Link finds this approach labored and unconvincing and argues that while the evidence is not conclusive, there is enough to indicate the direct involvement of the "more radical leaders and members" of the Washington County society in their capacity as club members.[129]

The differing interpretations of the role of the popular societies on the scene in the rebellion—whether they were directly or only seemingly involved—will probably never be resolved for lack of definitive evidence. (Technically, for example, even the Mingo Creek society in the disaffected area itself apparently did not act as an organization.) What certainly can be said is that the sister societies throughout the country left no doubt where they stood.

The available evidence makes it clear that the societies were almost entirely silent about the excise tax before the insurrection broke out in mid-July 1794. Indeed, the only protest was made by the Democratic Society of Pennsylvania, and that was against a new excise on salt, coal, sugar, snuff, boots, shoes, spirits, coffee, and cheese.[130] When the news of the first shots fired in Washington

County reached the societies, they took steps to make it known that they could not condone actions that were not carried out through legal, constitutional means. While condemning the excise law as the cause of the rebellion and sometimes voicing sympathy for the rebels, they unanimously condemned resistance by force to the execution of laws legally enacted. No instance is known of a Democratic-Republican society publicly approving the revolt, and a number of them deplored it, stating that legally constituted government must be maintained.[131]

This is not to say that there was no difference of opinion on the question of using military force to suppress the rebellion. The Democratic Society of Pennsylvania, for example, at first tried neither to condone nor condemn the insurgents' acts. It confined itself to condemning the excise as the cause of the difficulty while still noting that it should be rescinded by constitutional means. When it learned of the failure of the peace party to get a favorable vote in the committee of sixty (made up of the insurgents) on the federal government's offer of amnesty, the club condemned the citizens of the western counties for their refusal to submit to the minimum demands of the government.[132] At this meeting, held on September 11, three resolutions were proposed to clarify the society's position. The first resolve praised President Washington and Governor Mifflin for "pursuing a plan of pacification with the western people." The second endorsed "the sentiment that the strength of the state ought to be exerted should the power of reason prove inadequate with the Western Citizens." The third affirmed that the westerners' intemperance had augured "an enmity to genuine principles of freedom, and . . . an outrage upon order and democracy."

The members of the society agreed with the first two of these amendments when they were presented to the society as a whole; however, the third caused a split among the members. President Blair McClenachan unexpectedly left his seat at the reading of the amendments, throwing the society into a disorder and stopping the proceedings. The Irish merchant and twenty-eight followers marched out of the meeting hall. Benjamin Bache took the president's place pro tempore, and the society voted (thirty to zero) to withdraw the third resolution. They then proceeded to pass the first two resolutions approving the mild and prudent action of the President of the United States and the governor of Pennsylvania in their nonmilitary attempts to pacify the western counties.[133]

The Hamiltonian attack on the Democratic societies on the scene of the insurrection was soon to be expanded by the Federalists into an all-out offensive against all of the clubs. Even before the Whiskey Rebellion, the Federalists had charged that the societies sought to foment rebellion against the government. Now they had the opportunity to make the charge stick, thus destroying the prestige and influence of the societies.

As early as August 6, 1794, President Washington privately stated that the insurrection was "the first formidable fruit of the Democratic Societies."[134] In his September 19 message to Congress, he made this accusation public. In his speech,

Washington charged that "certain self-created societies" had been responsible for the insurrection in Pennsylvania:

> ... And when in the calm moments of reflection, they [the citizens] shall have retraced the origin and progress of the insurrection, let them determine whether it has not been fomented by combinations of men who, careless of consequence and disregarding the unerring truth that those who rouse cannot always appease a civil convulsion, have disseminated, from an ignorance or perversion of facts, suspicions, jealousies and accusations of the whole government.[135]

With this the tremendous weight of Washington's prestige was thrown against the Democratic-Republican societies. The Senate promptly speeded a reply, which commended Washington for his efforts to quell the insurrection peacefully and for calling out the militia when peaceful efforts failed. It condemned "certain self-created societies" for having by their proceedings, "founded in political error," misled "our fellow-citizens in the scene of insurrection." After Aaron Burr made an unsuccessful attempt to have the paragraph dealing with the "self-created societies" removed, the report was accepted without debate.[136]

In the House, however, sharp debate took place on an amendment Fitzsimmons of Pennsylvania introduced, which included a reprobation of "these self-created societies" and charged them with having "stimulated and urged the insurrection."[137] The debate lasted three days, and party lines were drawn throughout. The Federalist position was symbolized by William Smith of South Carolina who declared that "if the committee withheld an expression of their sentiments in regard to the Societies pointed out by the President, their silence would be an avowed desertion of the Executive." He added that "he had no scruple to declare that the conduct of these people had tended to blow up the insurrection. . . . Every gentleman who thought that these clubs had done mischief, was by this amendment called upon to avow his opinion. That was the whole."[138]

The Republican response was that if the "self-created societies' had acted contrary to law, they should be prosecuted. But there was no need or reason for censure. The House, in short, should restrict its business solely to legislation.[139] However, James Christie of Maryland went further and defended the Republican Society of Baltimore by name—the only member of Congress to defend the societies by a specific example—and decried the House attempts to cast odium on such a fine body of men. That society, he declared, "was composed of a band of patriots, not the fair-weather patriots of the present day, but the patriots of seventy-five, the men who were not afraid to rally around the American standard when that station was almost concluded to be a forlorn hope. They were men who, with their persons and properties, had assisted to drive from the soil of America the present lawless disturbers of the world."[140] As for the charge that the societies were responsible for the Whiskey Rebellion, Christie pointed to the action of the Baltimore society as refutation:

> What was the conduct of this society when the first news of the late insur-
> rection reached them? Did they not in the most pointed manner discounte-
> nance any such proceeding? Did they not refuse to correspond with any
> society that aided, or in any manner abetted the insurrection? They did
> more. They offered their personal services to go and help crush this com-
> motion in the bud.

Christie asserted that "nine-tenths" of the members of the Baltimore society
had actually taken their muskets and marched in the field against the rebels. What
more was needed to prove that the members of the society were "the friends of
peace and order, and not the disorganizers that the present amendment would
make them"?[141]

The most significant speech during the House debate was made by James
Madison. Although he condemned the insurrection as a flagrant outrage and
praised the President's efforts to restore order without bloodshed, he found
Washington's denunciations of the societies a sign of danger for the Republic.
"The game," he wrote to Monroe, "was to connect the Democratic Societies
with the odium of insurrection; to connect the Republicans in Congress with
those Societies"; and to put Washington's prestige "in opposition to both."[142]
Madison told the House that "opinions are not the objects of legislation." The
people must reserve the right to express opinions. How far, he asked, will the
abuses of this reserved right go? Start criticizing the people for abuse of their
right and the censure could extend to liberty of speech and of the press. And
what of the people who were thus condemned by Congress? "It is vain to say
that this indiscriminate censure is no punishment. . . . If we advert to the nature
of Republican Government, we shall find that the censorial power is in the people
over the Government, and not in the Government over the people." He had confidence in the "good sense and patriotism of the people" and did not anticipate
that much damage could be done by the publications of the societies. "They
will stand or fall by the public opinion."

Madison concluded with a principle that became a key defense of the popular
societies: "The law is the only rule of right; what is consistent with that, is not
punishable; what is contrary to that, is innocent, or at least not censurable by
the Legislative body."[143]

The debate on Fitzsimmons's amendment finally produced a clause with all
mention of the societies deleted. It asserted the "greatest concern" over the fact
that there had been "any misrepresentation whatever, of the government and its
proceedings, by individuals and combinations of men" and that this had been
"credited" with having fomented "the flagrant outrage which has been committed
on the laws."[144]

For a short time, as the tempest about their role began to develop, the popular societies paid little attention to the accusations of their having fomented the insurrection. The Boston *Independent Chronicle* of September 18, 1794, even praised their self-restraint:

> With a continual yelping and barking are our Swindlers, Aristocrats, Refugees and British Agents making at the *Constitutional Societies*. But how gratifying must it be to the friends of *Constitutional* Government to observe these Societies proceeding in the paths of patriotic virtue with a composure and dignity which become men engaged in such important and timely services. Thus have we seen a noble mastiff proceeding on his way, without deigning even to cast a look on the impotent and noisy puppies at his heels.[145]

Four days later, the Newark Republican Society became the first to lash back at its Federalist accusers. Only men of "prostituted principles," said the Newark group, would blame the Democratic-Republican societies for the Whiskey Rebellion. The clubs upheld the Constitution and believed in the rule of the majority. Yet governments *could err,* and attempts to prevent inquiry into their conduct were as dangerous as armed uprisings against legitimate aspirations.[146]

The initial defense of the popular societies appeared before Washington's November address to Congress describing the rebellion as the evil fruit of "self-created organizations." It also appeared before the first returns in the 1794 elections revealed that the Republicans were victorious in a number of key areas. With the societies the spearhead of the Republican victories,[147] the Federalist clamor against the clubs reached unprecedented heights, and the societies defended themselves in lengthy addresses and resolutions. They insisted that they had had no part in fomenting the whiskey insurrection and challenged anyone to show evidence to the contrary. The opposition to the excise had arisen from the inception of the tax, and only deliberate dishonesty could portray the clubs as responsible. The societies had publicly condemned the disturbance, and members of the eastern organizations had been foremost among those who marched to put it down. Nor was it unlikely that the Federalists had secretly inspired the revolt in order to discredit republicanism or to show the need for a standing army. Certainly this was as logical to believe as holding the societies responsible.[148]

Once they set out their position, the societies and their supporters next moved to a defense of their constitutional rights. Spirited debates concerning the legitimacy of the societies were conducted in every community where a society existed. They countered Federalist charges of "self-created" and of "darkness and secrecy" the accusation that administration supporters opposed the right of free assembly for its critics. Were not the Society of the Cincinnati and the chambers of commerce "self-created," they asked? Did not Washington himself head "a certain self-created society" (another reference to the Cincinnati)? Had not the Constitutional Convention met in secrecy and usurped authority? Compared to it, the Democratic-Republican societies were "mere shadows of self-creation."[149] Examining the charge of "self-created," the Democratic Society of New York asked, "By whom, then, ought we to have been constituted?"

> Is it for assembling, that we are accused; what law forbids it? for deliberat-
> ing, for thinking, for exercising the faculties of the mind; what statute has
> deprived us of the right? for the publication of our sentiments? where is
> the constitution that is prohibitory?[150]

Societies called the charges leveled against them ridiculously contradictory. The societies were said to be secret, yet were blamed for too much publicity. They were too contemptible to be noticed, yet they instigated the rebellion. Some called them self-created, and others said Genêt created them. The *only* consistency in these accusations lay in the uniform Federalist opposition to the right of the people to express their view on their elected officials.[151] With bitter indignation the Democratic Society of Pennsylvania pointed out that "some of our temporary rulers . . . are striving to propagate an opinion that public measures ought only to be discussed by public characters." It continued:

> What! Shall the servants of the people, who, at their pleasure, may be
> stripped of all authority, if found to abuse it, dispute the right of their em-
> ployers, to discuss their public proceedings? Do they imagine, that all
> knowledge, public spirit, and virtue, exclusively are confined to themselves?
> Is it already an offense of the deepest dye to meet and consult on matters
> which respect our freedom and happiness? Should this be the case, our fu-
> ture prospects must be deplorable indeed! The liberty of the press, that
> luminary of the mind, as emphatically expressed, may be next proscribed,
> for, such is the nature of despotism that having made some encroachments
> upon the liberties of the people, its rapacious jaws are constantly extended,
> to swallow every vestige of freedom.[152]

Were Americans to be muzzled whenever they disagreed with the administration? A republican government must provide freedom of opinion; and until any group adopted violence as a policy, it was entitled to respect for its principles. When the President could condemn citizens for exercising their privilege of assembly, no man's liberties were safe.[153] "Why are these people so alarmed at these so-cieties?" asked the *Independent Chronicle*.

> Are they afraid to have measures of government considered by the citizens?
> Do they wish to keep all public transactions within a particular circle, or
> must a certain class of men who live *on* the government, be the sole dicta-

tors to Congress while the citizen who lives *by* the government, is to be totally excluded from even conversing in a social meeting upon matters on which his political happiness depends?[154]

The Chittenden Society of Vermont answered the accusations against the societies one by one: (1) They never called themselves "the people" and arrogated to themselves power accordingly; (2) they never violated U.S. neutrality, although they openly rejoiced at French victories; (3) they did not hold secret meetings; (4) they did not find fault with "every act of government," although admittedly they had been critical of some they believed merited opposition; (5) they were not antifederalists in the sense that they had opposed, or continued to oppose, the Constitution; (6) they did not stir up the Whiskey Rebellion; (7) they had opposed Federalist treachery to Genêt and were proud of it; (8) as societies, they considered themselves neither illegal nor useless. The Vermont society challenged detractors to disprove any of these assertions. Proud of the service record of its members, it asked its aristocratic opponents, "Where are your scars?"[155]

In a letter to Jefferson, Madison noted that the attack "on the essential and constitutional right of the citizen" initiated by Washington's castigation of the popular societies was not having the effect intended. Although the attack hit the societies sorely, few Republicans were persuaded by the official displeasure to turn against the clubs. On the contrary, they continued to see the societies as nothing more than legitimate assemblies of people called together to discuss public affairs. Such groups were a credit to a republic where good government depended upon an abundance of alert, well-informed citizens.[156]

While Hamilton's tax on whiskey and the insurrection against it dominated the scene in the summer and fall of 1794, his other excise taxes led to an urban rebellion at the polls, which promoted the growth of the Republican party. The Democratic-Republican societies led the protest against the new excise taxes, charging that they were detrimental to the growth of domestic manufactures and threatened ruin for mechanics and shipwrights, as well as manufacturers. This stand brought new members into the societies at the time they were being subject to furious Federalist attack, and it also paid off at the polls; in the 1794 congressional elections, the Republicans scored several victories in traditional Federalist strongholds. Clearly the impact of the attack on the societies from high places was not as effective as it was supposed to be.[157]

The societies distinguished themselves in the 1794 elections by organizing the voters and bringing out the Republican vote, influencing even those who had formerly stayed at home. Indeed, as one student has noted, the popular societies "introduced a new vigor into elections and the immediate effect was a marked increase in voting and general interest in public affairs."[158] Little wonder, viewing the scene after the official arraignment of the societies, Madison concluded that "on the whole the prospect is rather improved than otherwise."[159]

Federalists who believed that Washington's attack had left the Democratic-

Republican societies high and dry without a battle cry soon learned that they were mistaken. The new issue was Jay's Treaty.

The societies had stood almost as one in opposing the appointment of Chief Justice John Jay as special envoy to Britain in April 1794, condemning both the mission and the man. Their resolutions charged that the appointment violated the separation of powers theory upon which the Constitution rested, for a judicial officer was also acting in an executive capacity; that Jay was pro-British in his sympathies and had voiced hostility to the French republic; that Jay had already conceded that Britain had the right to hold the western posts; and that the appointment indicated an attempt on the part of the administration to bind the United States to the English system of government.[160]

Jay concluded his negotiations with England, and the Treaty of London (always referred to as Jay's Treaty) was signed on November 19, 1794.[161] It did not reach President Washington until March 7, 1795, a few days after Congress had adjourned, and it was not until June 8 that the Senate convened, prepared to consider ratification. From June 8 through June 24 the Senate debated Jay's handiwork behind locked doors. They ratified it (after deletion of the hated article, Section XII, which limited trade to the British West Indies to small seventy-ton vessels) by a vote of twenty to ten, a bare two-thirds majority. All Senators were enjoined to keep the treaty secret.[162]

But the terms leaked out. An abstract of the treaty was published by Benjamin Bache in the Philadelphia *Aurora* of June 29, 1795, four days after the Senate ratification. Bache then published the entire treaty in pamphlet form for $.25. Thousands of copies of the pamphlet were distributed, many by Bache himself with the hearty approval of Madison and Jefferson.[163]

The criticism of Jay's appointment by the popular societies was mild indeed compared with the outburst of their wrath over the treaty itself. The concealment of the treaty terms and the secrecy of the Senate discussions, a classic example of the governmental secrecy that the clubs had been denouncing from their inception, was in itself sufficient to arouse Republican anger.[164] But it was the unsatisfactory terms, which adversely affected American commercial interests, that gave the societies a common cause.

Jay had been instructed to secure British compensation for injuries to American commerce, to secure evacuation of the western posts, and to provide for British and American implementation of some of the provisions of the Treaty of 1783 that had not been honored. He was also empowered to discuss the terms of a commercial treaty. The treaty he signed, however, did not recognize the traditional American principle that free ships make free goods. The provisions he made on compensation for Britain's illegal ship seizures were so complicated that it appeared almost impossible for anyone to collect. By the terms of the treaty, the United States agreed to indemnify Britain for losses suffered at French hands in American waters and to prevent the French from outfitting ships in American ports or Americans from serving under the French flag. But on British impressment of American seamen, the treaty said nothing. It was also silent on compensation for slaves the British carried off during the war. The British promised to evacuate the western posts by mid-1796, but British fur traders were to retain rights equal to Americans.

These inadequate provisions enabled the Democratic-Republican societies in port cities like New York, Philadelphia, Baltimore, and Charleston, and in interior parts of South Carolina and other sections of the South where the treaty's failure to provide compensation for stolen slaves was especially resented, to excoriate the treaty as a surrender to Great Britain, a betrayal of France, an infringement upon congressional control of foreign trade, and an outright fixing of the United States within the British sphere. In a number of communities, July 4, 1795, was a day of mourning for the death of liberty on its birthday. Under the treaty, said the popular societies, Americans once again became British subjects. Jay was burned in effigy in several leading cities amid the acclamation of the gathered citizens, and copies of his treaty were then tossed into the flames.[165] The Republicans of Fayetteville, North Carolina, had the following item inserted in the local press:

> As it is in contemplation to burn the effigy of John Jay, and the treaty which he has signed, derogatory to the national character of America, tonight; and rumor tells us that persons inimical to liberty, who wish to subvert the ties existing between America and France, mean to try to repel the execution of this just action; It is hoped that the spirit which ever characterized the true friends to a democratical government will be prevalent on the occasion, and shew these satellites of anarchy that tar and feathers will be the recompense for their good intensions. Ca Ira, Ca Ira.[166]

The Franklin Society of Pendleton, South Carolina, adopted twenty-eight resolutions execrating the treaty. They condemned pro-English and anti-French measures, the misleading of Washington, the trickery of Hamilton and Jay, secret negotiations, British encroachments on trade, monarchical actions of certain Senators, unconstitutionality of procedures, and, as might be expected in a slave society, the failure to secure compensation for "the value of the Negroes and other property carried away, contrary to the seventh article of the treaty of 1783." The resolutions ended with a pledge to all other Republican societies to see that Jay was brought to trial.[167]

In the western areas, however, hostility to the treaty diminished and gradually disappeared. The recovery of the forts, even if belatedly, and the granting of substantial concessions to Americans who were trading with the British colonies of Lower and Upper Canada, made the document appear much less one-sided to westerners than it did to those in the port cities, and even their fear of war if Jay's Treaty was rejected resulted in a gradual diminution of opposition.[168] Consequently, the wrath of the Democratic-Republican societies over the treaty was never quite strong and persistent enough to keep President Washington from signing the document, even though the early massive public protests kept him in a state of indecision for weeks. He finally signed it on August 18.[169]

In September a number of the Democratic-Republican societies launched a petition campaign to convince members of the House of Representatives to withhold appropriations necessary to execute the treaty. Even Jefferson thought well of the idea. The ambitious project was to be directed from Philadelphia, and a number of leading figures in the Democratic Society of Pennsylvania, including Benjamin Bache, were among the directors. But others in the popular societies were convinced that the matter had ended when Washington signed the treaty; and they were right. The campaign to defeat Jay's Treaty was lost, and Bache himself conceded later that little would change until the direction of American trade changed:

> The influence which our commercial connections with England have upon our politics, is the chief cause of the alienation of our administration from France and predilection for Britain. And this cause will operate until the French can rival the British with their manufactures in our market; or until the agricultural part of our nation determine no longer to draw their politics with their merchandize from our commercial cities.[170]

When the societies lost their campaign against Jay's Treaty, they also lost some of their influence. Federalist papers exultingly printed "epitaphs," and in September 1796 the *Gazette of the United States* gleefully proclaimed that "the Demo societies are dead."[171] For corpses, however, a number of the Democratic-Republican societies continued to show a surprisingly active life years after they were supposedly interred.[172] The New York City group was active as late as 1799,[173] and while this was a longer existence than most, the fact that notices of meetings, celebrations, and resolutions of various societies continued to appear spasmodically until the close of the century, indicates that it had company.[174] The Democratic Society of Pennsylvania, the mother society, officially went out of existence early in 1796,[175] but it continued to play a role in the political arena by operating behind the scenes in election campaigns. The same appears to have been true of some other societies. Political activities in Philadelphia, Boston, and several other cities in 1800 were alleged to be organized by old members of the popular societies.[176]

In 1798 the Philadelphia *Aurora* noted with glee that on one day the Federalists proclaimed that the societies were destroyed root and branch, and on the next that they were about to overthrow the government.[177] In reality new societies were formed as late as 1798 to 1800; part of what has been called "the second wave of Jeffersonian societies," they were welcomed by Republicans.[178] Would they not, asked one writer, "be [more] a safeguard to our Constitution and liberties than standing armies and sedition laws?"[179]

The societies fought the Federalist program of increasing rapprochement with Great Britain, of open hostility toward republican France, and of attacks upon democratic liberties at home. The culmination of this program came in 1798 with the creation of a war hysteria against France and the enactment of the Alien and Sedition Acts.[180]

While the alien and sedition bills were under discussion in Congress in 1798, the Democratic Society of New York and Tammany led a parade of organizations on the Fourth of July. Tammany member George Clinton, Jr., gave the oration. In a vigorous indictment of the Tammany program, he spoke of the threat to the "constitutional privileges of the people," which always exists in a "state of war, or public danger." Recalling one of the slogans of the Revolution, he urged his listeners to "resist the first appearance of usurpation. . . . While with cheerfulness you obey the constitutional acts of the constituted authorities, evince to your country and the world, that you are resolved to *live free or die.*" Calling "popular indignation and the vengeance of heaven" to light upon "the unprincipled wretch that shall attempt to infringe" the rights of free speech and free press, he announced that the Constitution should be "the rallying point of all true republicans."[181]

When Tammany met that evening, it denounced attacks upon free speech and the liberty of the press as "High Treason against the majesty of a free people" and expressed the hope that the "Independent Yeomanry of America" would "detect and oppose the most subtle and daring attempts upon the constitution of our country."[182]

Outbursts in the Federalist press against the popular societies showed that the antidemocratic forces had not written off the Democratic-Republican organizations. "We meet them at every turn," raged a Bostonian in the *Columbian Centinel.* "We read their productions in every democratic newspaper. . . . They are the Ciceros of the mob. They harangue the gaping Mechanic and the admiring Truckman. . . . They are the vapors of putrefying democracy."[183] Federalists charged that the societies were functioning through the "dark and silent system of organized treason and massacre, imported by the UNITED IRISHMEN " and that they were linked to the plot to create an American "Illuminati" (a branch of the European secret order formed in Bavaria in 1776 to oppose despotism and superstition, but actually, according to conservatives, to develop a worldwide plot to destroy Christianity and all government).[184] They also charged that the societies were dominated by Jews and were part of a conspiracy of the "tribe of Israel" to control American politics. In attacking the Democratic Society of New York, James Rivington, a Federalist publisher, wrote that its entire membership seemed "like their Vice-President (Solomon Simpson) of the tribe of Shylock."[185] When Israel Israel of the Democratic Society of Pennsylvania ran on the Republican ticket for state senator in 1797, William Cobbett, the virulent anti-Republican editor of *Porcupine's Gazette,* charged that his candidacy was part of a Jewish plot to take over the state in the interest of the Jacobin societies.

He fumed: "Since the *Jews* obtained such a complete triumph over the Gentiles, it is said they have conceived the idea of imposing on us a *general* circumsision. Ah! poor Pennsylvania."[186]

The "true reason" for opposition to Israel, the *Aurora* insisted, was that "he is a *Republican.*"[187] In New York City, a member of the Democratic Society, signing himself "Slow and Easy," replied to Rivington's anti-Semitic attack on Solomon Simpson: "If by the word Shylock, you mean a Jew, from my knowledge of the Vice-President, I dare say he would think himself honoured by the appellation, Judaism being his religious profession, as Democracy is his political creed."[188] A similar answer was published by Benjamin Nones when he was attacked in an anonymous account of a meeting of the True Republican Society of Philadelphia and scornfully charged with being "the Jew" who was both a Republican and head over heels in debt. In his famous reply, Nones wrote that he was proud of being a Jew, a Republican, and poor. "I am a Jew, and if for no other reason, for that reason I am a republican," he asserted boldly.[189]

Just when the Democratic-Republican societies passed from the scene remains a matter of dispute. There is also controversy over the exact role they played in the political movement of the 1790s. Some historians emphasize that the societies took on the functions of a political party and were the formal machinery of the Jeffersonian movement, while others see them solely as pressure groups and as auxiliaries to the main party organization.[190] One thing, however, seems to be clear: the societies may not have provided the precise machinery for the Democratic-Republican party, but they certainly contributed the techniques of democratic expression that by 1797 had become characteristic of the Democratic-Republican movement. They did this through the circulation of public petitions, manifestos, memorials, and resolutions and through their patriotic celebrations and other meeting at the local level. They contributed, too, to the Democratic-Republican philosophy. It was they who brought most sharply to the forefront the principle that only public vigilance could frustrate the designs of those hostile to popular governments and who emphasized that every free state needed a watchful eye on the representatives to whom it had delegated authority. In contrast to the Federalist presumption that the people should be seen but not heard, the popular societies stressed the need for extensive popular participation in the governmental process. Moreover, they created the avenue through which the people could express themselves. As a center of Republican agitation and propaganda—from 1793 to 1795 especially, but even on to 1800—the societies did much to forge the sword that defeated Federalism and put Jefferson in the presidency.

NOTES

1. William Smith to Alexander Hamilton, April 24, 1793, Alexander Hamilton Papers, Manuscripts Division, Library of Congress.

2. *National Gazette* (Philadelphia), July 4, 11, 18, 1792.

3. Ibid., July 25, 1792.

4. William Miller, "The Democratic Clubs of the Federalist Period, 1793-1795" (Master's thesis, New York University, 1937), pp. 1-2. See also Charles Warren, *Jacobin and Junto, or Early American Politics as Viewed in the Diary of Dr. Nathaniel Ames, 1758-1822* (Cambridge, Mass., 1931), pp. 50-53; Charles Downer Hazen, *Contemporary American Opinion of the French Revolution* (Baltimore, 1897), pp. 195-196; Anson Ely Morse, *The Federalist Party in Massachusetts to the Year 1800* (Princeton, N.J., 1909), p. 74. For an earlier presentation, see George Gibbs, *Memoirs of the Administration of Washington and Adams* (New York, 1846), p. 134.

5. Eugene Perry Link, *Democratic-Republican Societies, 1790-1800* (New York, 1942), pp. 19-35. For the Sons of Liberty, see Philip G. Davidson, "Sons of Liberty and Stamp Men," *North Carolina Historical Review* 9 (1932): 38-56; Herbert M. Morais, "The Sons of Liberty in New York," in Richard B. Morris, ed., *The Era of the American Revolution* (New York, 1939), pp. 268-289; Richard Walsh, *Charleston's Sons of Liberty* (Columbia, S.C., 1959). For the Associators in Pennsylvania, see J. Paul Selsam, *The Pennsylvania Constitution* (Philadelphia, 1936), pp. 102-103, 138. For The Society for the Preservation of Liberty, see J. G. de Roulhac Hamilton, "A Society for the Preservation of Liberty, 1784," *American Historical Review* 32 (April 1927): 550-552. The society met in 1784 and resolved that "the surest mode to secure Republican systems of Government from lapsing into Tyranny, is by giving free and frequent information to the mass of people." Among its leaders were James Madison, James Monroe, Patrick Henry, the Lees, and John Breckenridge.

6. See Morais, "Sons of Liberty," p. 272; R. W. Postgate, *That Devil Wilkes* (New York, 1929), pp. 24-28; George Rudé, *Wilkes and Liberty* (London, 1962), pp. 39-43.

7. William A. Robinson, *Jeffersonian Democracy in New England* (New Haven, 1916), pp. 111-114; *New York Journal,* March 5, 1794; *American Daily Advertiser* (Philadelphia), January 3, 1793; W. R. Fee, *Transition from Aristocracy to Democracy in New Jersey, 1799-1829* (Somerville, N.J., 1933), p. 44; Philip S. Foner, *History of the Labor Movement in the United States* (New York, 1947), 1: 82-85; Alexander Laing, "Jefferson's Usufruct Principle," *The Nation,* July 3-10, 1876, 12.

8. Walter Phelps Hall, *British Radicalism, 1791-1797* (New York, 1912), pp. 124-138.

9. John Bach McMaster, *History of the People of the United States* (New York, 1921), 2: 109.

10. For a recent statement to this effect, see Alexander De Conde, *Entangling Alliance: Politics and Diplomacy under George Washington* (Durham, N.C., 1958), p. 252.

11. *Philadelphische Correspondenz,* April 9, 1793. Kammerer's signature did not appear in this printing.

12. *National Gazette* (Philadelphia), April 13, 1795.

13. Ibid.; *General Advertiser* (Philadelphia), April 15, 1793.

14. Meade Minnegerode, *Jefferson, Friend of France, 1793* (New York, 1928), p. 220; George C. Genêt, *Washington, Jefferson, and "Citizen" Genêt, 1793* (New York, 1899), p. 34.

15. Minutes, Democratic Society of Pennsylvania, Historical Society of Pennsylvania.

16. *General Advertiser* (Philadelphia), July 17, 1793; Minutes, Democratic Society of Pennsylvania.

17. William Cobbett, "A Summary View of the Politics of the United States from the Close of the War (1783) to the Year 1794," in *Porcupine's Works* (London, 1801) 1: 100.

18. Link, *Democratic-Republican Societies,* pp. 13-15. Miller, "Democratic Clubs," 45-46, lists twenty-six societies for the period 1793-1795.

19. Gustavus Myers, *History of Tammany Hall* (New York, 1917), p. 12; Alfred F. Young, *The Democratic Republicans of New York: The Origins, 1763-1797* (Chapel Hill, N.C., 1967); Peter Paulson, "The Tammany Society and the Jeffersonian Movement in New York City, 1795-1800," *New York History* 34 (January 1953): 72-75.

20. Roland M. Baumann, "The Democratic-Republicans of Philadelphia: The Origins, 1776-1797" (Ph.D. diss., Pennsylvania State University, 1970), p. 448.

21. Young, *Democratic Republicans of New York,* p. 394.

22. Link, *Democratic-Republican Societies,* p. 71; *City Gazette* (Charleston), June 30, 1794.

23. William Cobbett, *A Little Plain English Addressed to the People of the United States* (Philadelphia, 1795), p. 70.

24. Link, *Democratic-Republican Societies,* p. 72.

25. Baumann, "Democratic-Republicans of Philadelphia," pp. 448-551, and appendix, table 3., pp. 598-603. Baumann finds sixty-one members who cannot be identified; of the others, eighty-six were craftsmen; fifty-two mercantile and manufacturing; twenty-nine public officials; five gentlemen; three clerks; nineteen maritime; five doctors; nine lawyers; eight teachers; six financiers; nine innkeepers; and thirteen printers and scriveners. This is based on comparing the members listed in the manuscript minutes of the Democratic Society of Pennsylvania with the trade directories of Philadelphia for the years in which the society existed. My own study of both sources confirms Dr. Baumann's list. The occupations of those members of the society that can be identified are listed in the appendix to this book.

26. Young, *Democratic Republicans of New York,* pp. 394-395.

27. Cobbett, *Porcupine's Works,* 1: 129n.

28. Paulson, "Tammany Society," pp. 79-80.

29. Link, *Democratic-Republican Societies,* p. 73.

30. It is difficult to study a single Republican newspaper of this period without finding some expression of bitter animosity toward members of the legal profession.

31. Link, *Democratic-Republican Societies*, p. 85. For the fact that most lawyers were Federalists, see *Aurora* (Philadelphia), November 9, 1798.

32. Charles Biddle, *Autobiography of Charles Biddle, 1745-1821* (Philadelphia, 1883), p. 256; Thomas Coffin Amory, *Life of James Sullivan with Selections from His Writings* (Boston, 1859), pp. 258, 275, 297-298; Link, *Democratic-Republican Societies*, pp. 80-82; E. Merton Coulter, "The Efforts of the Democratic Societies of the West to Open the Navigation of the Mississippi," *Mississippi Valley Historical Review* 10(1924): 381. Donald H. Stewart, *The Opposition Press of the Federalist Period* (Albany, N.Y.), 1969, pp. 648-649.

33. *An Oration on the Influence of Social Institutions Upon Human Nature and Happiness, Delivered before the Tammany Society at Their Anniversary, on the Twelfth of May, 1796; by T. Wortman* (New York, 1796), p. 29.

34. Jefferson, *Notes on Virginia,* quoted in ibid., pp. 29-30; Link, *Democratic-Republican Societies*, p. 96; *City Gazette* (Charleston), October 8, 1794.

35. *Constitution of the Democratic Society of the City of New York* (New York, 1794).

36. *Daily Gazette* (New York), April 21, 1794.

37. *Spooner's Vermont Journal* (Windsor), April 21, 1794; *Gazette of Maine* (Portland), August 23, 1794.

38. Young, *Democratic Republicans of New York,* p. 411.

39. *City Gazette* (Charleston), February 30, March 19, June 25, 26, 1794.

40. *North-Carolina Gazette* (New Bern), April 19, 1794; *Independent Chronicle* (Boston), April 18, 1794; *American Daily Advertiser* (Philadelphia), August 2, 1794; *New York Journal,* September 13, 1794.

41. Resolutions, Democratic Society of Canaan, New York, in *New York Journal,* October 4, 1794.

42. Constitution, Baltimore Republican Society, in *Baltimore Daily Intelligencer,* May 24, 1794. See also *Independent Chronicle* (Boston), January 16, 1794, for the Massachusetts Constitutional Society, and August 28, 1794, for the Democratic Society in Portland, Maine; and *Kentucky Gazette,* August 24, 31, 1793, for the Kentucky Democratic Society.

43. *Constitution of the Democratic Society of the City of New York.*

44. *North-Carolina Gazette* (New Bern), April 19, 1794.

45. See *American Daily Advertiser* (Philadelphia), March 22, 1796.

46. *Kentucky Gazette,* November 16, 1793; *American Daily Advertiser* (Philadelphia), December 21, 1793; *An Oration Delivered Before the Republican Society of Ulster County, and Other Citizens . . . the Fourth of July, 1795, by Phineas Hedges, M.D.* (Goshen, N.Y., 1795), p. 14.

47. Link, *Democratic-Republican Societies*, pp. 153-154.

48. Young, *Democratic Republicans of New York,* pp. 516-517.

49. *Baltimore Daily Intelligencer,* July 7, 1794; James D. Tagg, "Benjamin Franklin Bache's Attack on George Washington," *Pennsylvania Magazine of History and Biography* 99 (1976): 210. For manumission of slaves by members of the Republican Society in 1794, see Link *Democratic-Republican*

Societies, p. 153n.

50. Hedges, *An Oration Delivered Before the Republican Society of Ulster County . . . ,* p. 15; *American Daily Advertiser,* (Philadelphia), July 10, 1795; minutes of the Society of Tammany or Columbian Order, Committee of Amusement, October 24, 1791 to February 23, 1795, Manuscript Records, Manuscripts Division, New York Public Library; *New York Journal,* December 6, 1794. For the effect of slave competition on antislavery views, see Young, *Democratic Republicans of New York,* p. 518.

51. Cobbett, "History of the American Jacobins," pp. 29-30; Tunis Wortman, *A Solemn Address, to Christians & Patriots, upon the Approaching Election of a President of the United States* (New York, 1800), p. 16; "An Observer," in *Gazette of the United States* (Philadelphia), August 5, 1800.

52. Duncan J. MacLeod argues that "the conflagration in the French West Indies" and the fact that Genêt was a member of the *Amis des Noirs* (Friends of the Blacks) caused "the collapse" beginning in 1793 of the Democratic societies of the South. But he offers no convincing evidence for the thesis, and his date for the supposed "collapse" is clearly wrong. See Duncan J. MacLeod, *Slavery, Race and the American Revolution* (London and New York, 1975), p. 92.

53. Herbert M. Morais, *Deism in Eighteenth Century America* (New York, 1934), pp. 130-132; Gustav A. Koch, *Republican Religion: The American Revolution and the Cult of Reason* (New York, 1933), pp. 120-122; Link, *Democratic-Republican Societies,* pp. 119-121; *New York Journal,* July 1, 1796. See also William Gribbin, "Republican Religion and the American Churches in the National Period," *Historian* 35 (November 1972): 61-74.

54. *New York Journal,* May 31, 1794.

55. Benjamin Rush, *A Plan for the Establishment of Public Schools and the Diffusion of Knowledge in Pennsylvania; to Which Are Added Thoughts upon the Mode of Education Proper in a Republic, Addressed to the Legislature and Citizens of the State* (Philadelphia, 1786); Benjamin Rush, "To the Citizens," *Independent Gazette* (Philadelphia), March 28, 1787; *Gazette of the United States* (Philadelphia), November 2, 1791; *Aurora* (Philadelphia), November 3, 1791.

56. "Extract" in *General Advertiser* (Philadelphia), May 16, 1791.

57. *General Advertiser* (Philadelphia), March 15, 1792.

58. Robert Coram, *Political Inquiries to Which Is Added a Plan for the General Establishment of Schools Throughout the United States* (Wilmington, 1791), pp. 93-103. For a discussion of Coram's educational philosophy, see Charles and Mary Beard, *The American Spirit* (New York, 1942), pp. 126-137.

59. *Federal Gazette* (Philadelphia), March 21, 1795.

60. Samuel Miller, *Sermon at the New Presbyterian Church* (New York, 1795), pp. 28-29.

61. John A. Munroe, *Federalist Delaware, 1775-1815* (New Brunswick, N.J., 1954), p. 175; *Delaware and Eastern Shore Advertiser* (Wilmington), December 27, 1794.

62. Young, *Democratic Republicans of New York,* pp. 524-526; Munroe, *Federalist Delaware,* pp. 175-176.

63. Link, *Democratic-Republican Societies,* pp. 166-171.

64. Foner, *History of the Labor Movement,* 1: 86.

65. William Manning, *The Key of Libberty* (Billerica, Mass.), 1922, pp. 66-71.

66. Ibid., pp. 71-73.

67. Thomas Isaiah, *The History of Printing in America* (Albany, N.Y., 1874), 2: 9.

68. *Gazette of the United States* (Philadelphia), August 10, 1801.

69. Donald H. Stewart, "Jeffersonian Journalism: Newspaper Propaganda and the Development of the Democratic-Republican Party, 1789-1801" (Ph.D. diss., Columbia University, 1950), pp. 24-27.

70. See, for example, *Connecticut Journal* (New Haven), October 9, 1793; *Baltimore Daily Intelligencer,* May 8, 1794; *City Gazette* (Charleston), March 18, 1794.

71. See *Aurora* (Philadelphia), February 9, 1795.

72. Bureau of the Census, *A Century of Population Growth from the First to the Twelfth Census of the United States, 1790-1900* (Washington, D.C.), 1909, p. 80.

73. Regina Ann Markell Morantz, " 'Democracy' and 'Republic' in American Ideology, 1787-1840" (Ph.D. diss., Columbia University, 1971), p. 102.

74. Philip S. Foner, ed., *The Complete Writings of Thomas Paine* (New York, 1945), 1: 243. The reference to *Common Sense* is, of course, to Paine's great pamphlet of that name published in January, 1776.

75. Hazen, *Contemporary American Opinion,* pp. 168-169. See also McMaster, *History,* 2: 89-95, and Bernard Fäy, *The Revolutionary Spirit in France and America at the End of the Eighteenth Century* (New York, 1927), chap. 4.

76. Thomas Jefferson to William Short, January 3, 1793, in Philip S. Foner, ed., *Basic Writings of Thomas Jefferson* (New York, 1944), pp. 611-612.

77. Ibid., p. 612.

78. "A Republican," in *New York Journal,* April 6, 1793; Huntley Dupré, "The Kentucky Gazette Reports the French Revolution," *Mississippi Valley Historical Review* 26 (September 1939): 173.

79. *Treaties, Conventions, International Acts, Protocols, and Agreements between the United States of America and Other Powers, 1776-1909* (Washington, D.C., 1910), 1: 469 (Art. I). For a discussion of the treaty, see Charles Marion Thomas, *American Neutrality in 1793: A Study in Cabinet Government* (New York, 1931), pp. 54-66.

80. Henry Cabot Lodge, ed., *The Works of Alexander Hamilton* (New York and London, 1904), 4: 375.

81. Paul Leicester Ford, ed., *The Writings of Thomas Jefferson* (New York, 1892-1899), 6: 220.

82. Pamphlet, 1794, Maryland Historical Society. See also declaration of the Charleston Republican Society in *Daily Repository* (Baltimore), September 18, 1793.

83. There is a vast literature on the Genêt mission. The following are especially useful: De Conde, *Entangling Alliance;* Harry Ammon, *The Genet Mission* (New York, 1973); Harry Ammon, "The Genêt Mission and the Development of American Political Parties," *Journal of American History* 52 (March 1965): 225-241; William Frederick Keller, "American Politics and the Genêt Mission" (Ph.D. diss., University of Pittsburgh, 1951); Albert Hall Bowman,

The Struggle for Neutrality: Franco-American Diplomacy during the Federalist Era (Knoxville, 1974). For a general summary of events during the mission, see John C. Miller, *The Federalist Era, 1789-1801* (New York, 1960), pp. 126-139; Dumas Malone, *Jefferson and His Times* (New York, 1948), 3: 68-131; Noble E. Cunningham, Jr., *The Jeffersonian Republicans: The Formation of Party Organization, 1789-1801* (Chapel Hill, N.C., 1957), pp. 54-66.

84. Link, *Democratic-Republican Societies,* pp. 191-192; Ammon, "The Genêt Mission," pp. 230-231.

85. Edmund Genêt to Thomas Jefferson, July 4, 1797, Genêt Papers, Manuscripts Division, Library of Congress. Minnegerode, *Jefferson,* pp. 230-233, is generally hostile to Jefferson but agrees with Genêt. However, Malone, *Jefferson and His Times,* 3: 121-123, discounts the thesis entirely. Still, it is worth noting that after it was charged that Jefferson had been unfriendly to Genêt, the Democratic Club in Grenville, South Carolina, changed its name to the Madisonian Society to honor James Madison rather than Thomas Jefferson. John H. Wolfe, *Jeffersonian Democracy in South Carolina* (Chapel Hill, N.C., 1940), pp. 79-80.

86. Maude H. Woodfin, "Citizen Genêt and His Mission" (Ph.D diss., University of Chicago, 1928), p. 07.

87. *Boston Gazette,* June 20, 1794; *Farmers' Library* (Rutland, Vt.) May 27, 1794; *American Daily Advertiser* (Philadelphia), July 29, 1794; *City Gazette* (Charleston), March 17, 1794; Hazen, *Contemporary American Opinion,* pp. 196-200.

88. Niels H. Sonne, *Liberal Kentucky, 1780-1828* (New York, 1939), pp. 28-29; *Kentucky Gazette,* August 31, 1793.

89. *City Gazette* (Charleston), February 20, 1794.

90. *American Daily Advertiser* (Philadelphia), August 27, 1793.

91. For the background, see Arthur Preston Whittaker, *The Spanish-American Frontier: 1783-1795* (Boston, 1927).

92. E. M. Coulter, "The Efforts of the Democratic Societies of the West to Open the Navigation of the Mississippi," *Mississippi Valley Historical Review* 11 (December 1924): 378-379.

93. *Independent Gazette* (Philadelphia), December 1, 1792.

94. *American Daily Advertiser* (Philadelphia), August 2, 1794, *Aurora* (Philadelphia), July 26, 1793. A recent study of Bache and the *Aurora* notes: "Bache never abandoned this view. His interpretation of European and American politics hung almost entirely upon the unwavering belief that France was the mainstay of liberty, equality, justice and progress. Accordingly, any impediment to France's success was seen as an impediment against the progress of all men." (James D. Tagg, "Benjamin Franklin Bache and the Philadelphia *Aurora,*" (Ph.D. diss, Wayne State University, 1974, p. 305.)

95. *National Gazette* (Philadelphia), June 19, 1793; William Jay, *The Life of John Jay* (New York, 1933), 1: 315-321. *State Gazette of South Carolina* (Charleston), April 29, 1794; *City Gazette* (Charleston), February 19, 1794; Eugene P. Link, "The Democratic Societies of the Carolinas," *North Carolina Historical Review* 18 (July 1941): 270-271.

96. For a discussion of the controversy over human nature, see Morantz, " 'Democracy' and 'Republic' in American Ideology," pp. 25-36; Robert Shal-

hope, "Toward a Republican Synthesis: The Emergence of an Understanding of Republicanism in American History," *William and Mary Quarterly,* 3d ser., 29 (January 1927): 49-70.

97. Delivered before Tammany, May 12, 1796, New York, 1796, pp. 24-25.

98. *Massachusetts Spy* (Boston), June 5, 1794; Young, *Democratic Republicans of New York,* p. 414.

99. Seth Ames, ed., *The Works of Fisher Ames* (Boston, 1854), 2: 150; George Gibbs, *Memoirs of the Administrations of Washington and Adams* (New York, 1846), 1: 134.

100. Rev. John Sylvester John Gardiner, *Remarks on the Jacobinad* (Boston, 1798), pt. II, p. 12. The reference to "Pandemonium" is to the Green Dragon Tavern where the Massachusetts Constitutional Society met. Ibid., p. 9.

101. Ames, *Works,* 1: 148; Gibbs, *Memoirs,* p. 179.

102. Hazen, *Contemporary American Opinion,* p. 204; "Manlius" in *Columbian Centinel* (Boston), September 3, 1794.

103. *Connecticut Journal* (New Haven), June 25, 1794.

104. Gibbs, *Memoirs,* 1: 179.

105. Quoted in Morantz, " 'Democracy' and 'Republic' in American Ideology," p. 148n.

106. Ibid., pp. 147-152.

107. "A Constitutionalist" in *Independent Chronicle* (Boston), September 4, 1794.

108. "Address to the Republican Citizens of the United States by the New York Democratic Society," *New York Journal,* May 28, 1794.

109. *Independent Chronicle* (Boston), January 3, 1793; Morantz, " 'Democracy' and 'Republic' in American Ideology," pp. 153-154.

110. *Independent Chronicle* (Boston), January 4, 5, 1794.

111. Ibid., January 16, 1794.

112. Ibid., September 4, 1794.

113. *Columbian Mercury* (Canaan, N.Y.), October 1, 1794.

114. *Herald* (New York), October 26, 1794; *Baltimore Daily Intelligencer,* June 14, 1794.

115. "Address to the Republican Citizens in the United States," *New York Journal,* May 28, 1794.

116. *Kentucky Gazette,* August 31, 1793.

117. Quoted in Link, *Democratic-Republican Societies,* p. 175.

118. *New York Journal,* May 28, 1794.

119. For a comprehensive study of the insurrection in Pennsylvania, see Lelan D. Baldwin, *Whiskey Rebels: The Story of a Frontier Uprising* (Pittsburgh, 1939). For a good analysis of what has been written on the subject, see Jacob E. Cooke, "The Whiskey Insurrection: A Re-evaluation," *Pennsylvania History* 30 (July 1963): 316-346.

120. Harold C. Syrett and Jacob E. Cooke, eds., *The Papers of Alexander Hamilton* (New York, 1961), 16: 84, 310-313, 316-317.

121. Quoted in Cooke, "Whiskey Insurrection," p. 326.

122. Harry Marlin Tinkcom, *The Republicans and Federalists in Pennsylvania 1790-1801* (Harrisburg, Pa., 1950), pp. 96-106.

123. John Alexander and Mary Wells Ashworth, *George Washington* (New York, 1957), 7: 186-190.

124. *Pennsylvania Archives,* 2d ser., 4: pp. 122-129.

125. Baldwin, *Whiskey Rebels,* pp. 260-264; Hamilton to Washington, November 11, 1794, in Lodge, ed., *Works of Hamilton,* 6: 64-65; Richard H. Kohn, "The Washington Administration's Decision to Crush the Whiskey Rebellion," *Journal of American History* 59 (December 1972): 580-581.

126. Lodge, ed., *Works of Hamilton,* 6: 64-65.

127. John Church Hamilton, *History of the Republic* (Philadelphia, 1864), 6: 123.

128. William Miller, "The Democratic Societies and the Whiskey Insurrection," *Pennsylvania Magazine of History and Biography* 62 (July 1938): 327n, 342-347.

129. Link, *Democratic-Republican Societies,* pp. 45-49, 146.

130. *American Daily Advertiser* (Philadelphia), July 7, 1794.

131. See *Woods's Newark Gazette,* September 24, 1794; *State Gazette of South Carolina* (Charleston), October 20, 1794; *Gazette of the United States* (Philadelphia), September 1, 1794; *Herald* (New York), September 4, 1794; *American Daily Advertiser* (Philadelphia), September 8, October 6, 1794; *Aurora* (Philadelphia), September 23, 1794; Young, *Democratic Republicans of New York,* p. 417.

132. Minutes, Democratic Society of Pennsylvania; Miller, "Democratic Societies," 331-332.

133. Minutes, Democratic Society of Pennsylvania; Bowman, *Struggle for Neutrality,* p. 232. Miller is in error in asserting that all three resolutions were adopted. "Democratic Societies," 332.

134. Washington to Lee, August 6, 1794, in Worthington C. Ford, ed., *The Writings of George Washington* (Washington, D.C., 1889-1893), 12:454. For an even earlier private attack by Washington, *see* Harold C. Syrett and Jacob E. Cooke, eds., *The Papers of Alexander Hamilton* (New York, 1972), 16: 259-260.

135. Ibid., 491, 496.

136. *Annals of Congress,* 3d Congress, 1794, p. 794.

137. Ibid., p. 899.

138. Ibid., p. 902.

139. See ibid., pp. 899-901, 902, 910.

140. Ibid., p. 908.

141. Ibid., p. 909.

142. Madison to Monroe, December 4, 1794, in Gaillard Hunt, ed., *Writings of James Madison* (New York, 1900-1910), 6: 220-221.

143. *Annals of Congress,* 3d Congress, pp. 912-914; Hunt, ed., *Writings of Madison,* 6: 222.

144. Ibid., p. 917.

145. *Independent Chronicle* (Boston), September 18, 1794.

146. *Woods's Newark Gazette,* September 24, 1794.

147. Miller, "Democratic Societies," 348.

148. *Federal Intelligencer* (Baltimore), February 11, 1794 (Republican Society of Baltimore); *Columbian Herald* (Charleston), December 24, 1794 (Republican Society of Charleston, South Carolina). See also Miller, "Democratic Societies,"

338-340, which has a summary of the arguments the societies used.

149. *Independent Chronicle* (Boston), December 8, 18, 1794; *Independent Gazetteer* (Philadelphia), January 17, 1795; *Federal Intelligencer* (Baltimore) December 2, 1794.

150. *New York Journal,* January 17, 1795.

151. *Woods's Newark Gazette,* December 10, 1794; *Independent Chronicle* (Boston), December 11, 1794; *Delaware and Eastern-Shore Advertiser* (Wilmington); *Federal Intelligencer* (Baltimore), December 11, 1794; *Independent Gazetteer* (Philadelphia), January 24, 1795.

152. Minutes of the Democratic Society of Pennsylvania.

153. *Independent Gazetteer* (Philadelphia), January 17, 28, 31, 1795; *Independent Chronicle* (Boston), January 12, 1795.

154. *Independent Chronicle* (Boston), September 15, 1794.

155. Ibid., February 26, March 2, 1795.

156. Irving Brant, *James Madison: Father of the Constitution, 1787-1800* (Indianapolis, 1950), pp. 419-420. For the view that Washington's attack practically spelled the end of the societies, see Miller, "Democratic Societies," pp. 187-189; Hazen, *Contemporary American Opinion,* pp. 207-208; McMaster, *History,* 2: 206.

157. Baumann, "Democratic-Republicans of Philadelphia," pp. 232-233; William Miller, "The First Fruits of Republican Organization," *Pennsylvania Magazine of History and Biography* 63 (1939): 141-143.

158. William A. Robinson, *Jeffersonian Democracy in New England* (New Haven, 1916), p. 10. See also George D. Leutscher, *Early Political Machinery in the United States: Philadelphia* (1903), p. 60.

159. Brant, *James Madison,* p. 420; Hunt, ed., *Writings of Madison,* 6: 225.

160. *City Gazette* (Charleston), April 18, 1794.

161. For a full delineation of the treaty, article by article, see Samuel Flagg Bemis, *Jay's Treaty: A Study in Commerce and Diplomacy,* 2d ed. (New Haven, 1962), chap. 13.

162. Ralston Hayden, *The Senate and Treaties, 1795-1805* (New York, 1920), pp. 75-83; Bradford Perkins, *The First Rapprochement: England and the United States, 1795-1805* (Philadelphia, 1955), pp. 31-32.

163. Madison to Monroe, December 20, 1795; Hunt, ed., *Writings of Madison,* 6: 258; Malone, ed., *Jefferson,* 3: 245.

164. *Aurora* (Philadelphia), June 25, 27, 1795.

165. *New York Journal,* July 8, 1795; *Aurora* (Philadelphia), July 7, 9, 10, 13, 1795; *Independent Gazette* (Boston), July 4, 8, 1795; *Federal Intelligencer* (Baltimore), July 24, 27, 1795; McMaster, *History,* 2: 221-222.

166. Link, "Democratic Societies of the Carolinas," p. 272.

167. *City Gazette* (Charleston), June 25, October 28, 1795.

168. Young, *Democratic Republicans of New York,* p. 467; Chilton Williamson, *Vermont in Quandary, 1763-1825* (Montpelier, Vermont, 1949), pp. 214-215.

169. Carroll and Ashworth, *Washington,* 7: chap. 10. Washington's decision to sign was also hastened by the Fauchet revelations. These dispatches seemed to indicate that during the Whiskey Rebellion of 1794, Edmond Randolph had

asked the French minister for funds with which to foment rebellion against the federal government. Randolph was Secretary of State in Washington's cabinet. For a defense of Randolph, see Irving Brant, "Edmund Randolph, Not Guilty," *William and Mary Quarterly,* 3d ser., 7 (April 1950): 180-198

170. Young, *Democratic Republicans of New York,* p. 458; Jefferson to Monroe, September 6, 1795; Ford, ed., *Writings of Jefferson,* 7: 28; *Aurora* (Philadelphia), October 9, November 18, 1795; George M. Dallas, *The Life and Writings of Alexander J. Dallas* (Philadelphia, 1871), pp. 330-335; De Conde, *Entangling Alliance,* p. 141.

171. *Gazette of the United States* (Philadelphia), September 1, 1796 and reprinted in *Republican Journal* (Dumfries, Va.), September 9, 1796.

172. See, for example, McMaster, *History,* 2: 206; Leutscher, *Early Political Machinery,* p. 62; Bernard Fäy, *The Two Franklins* (Boston, 1933), pp. 207, 221. For evidence that the societies were active much longer, see Link, *Democratic-Republican Societies,* pp. 13-15.

173. *New York Journal,* July 3, 1799; Link, *Democratic-Republican Societies,* pp. 202-203; Young, *Democratic Republicans of New York,* p. 398.

174. *Independent Chronicle* (Boston), January 21, 1796, January 30, 1797; *Argus* (New York), July 6, 1798; *Aurora* (Philadelphia), December 22, 1798.

175. *American Mercury* (Hartford), January 25, 1796.

176. Baumann, "Democratic-Republicans of Philadelphia," 232; Bernard Fäy, "Early Party Machinery in the United States: Pennsylvania in the Election of 1796," *Pennsylvania Magazine of History and Biography* 60 (October 1936): 375-390; *Boston Gazette,* November 3, 1800.

177. *Aurora* (Philadelphia), December 22, 1798.

178. *New York Journal,* February 24, 1798 (Constitution of the Republican Society of Stamford, Conn.); *Republican Journal* (Danbury, Conn.), March 26, 1798 (Norwalk, Conn., Republican Society). Link, *Democratic-Republican Societies,* p. 15, mentions also a society formed at Norfolk, Virginia, in 1798; and "Philo-Franklin," in the Newark (N.J.) *Centinel of Freedom,* August 12, 1800, says that the citizens of Orangedale, in that state, met five days earlier to form the Jeffersonian Society. See also *To the People of the County of Burlington, Republican Meeting, of Republican Citizens of the County of Burlington 20th September, 1800,* copy in New Jersey Historical Society.

179. *Norfolk Herald,* March 16, 1799; *Centinel of Freedom* (Newark, N.J.), August 12, 1800; Carl E. Prince, "New Jersey's Democratic-Republicans, 1790-1817" (Ph.D. diss., Rutgers University, 1963), pp. 22-23, 93-102.

180. The Alien Act gave the President authority to deport all aliens that he judged dangerous to the peace and safety of the United States. The Sedition Act was designed to protect Federalists from attacks in the press, and editors, writers, and speakers charged with attacking the government could be arrested. The requirement for naturalization was extended from five to fourteen years. The laws were repealed by the Jeffersonian-controlled Congress in 1801, and those imprisoned were released by Jefferson's pardon.

181. *An Oration Delivered on the Fourth of July, 1798, Before the General Society of Mechanics and Tradesmen, the Democratic Society, the Tammany Society or Columbian Order . . . by Geo. Clinton, Jun.* (New York, 1798), p. 14.

182. Paulson, "Tammany Society," pp. 77-78.

183. *Columbian Centinel* (Boston), July 25, 1798.

184. John C. Miller, *Crisis in Freedom: The Alien and Sedition Acts* (Boston, 1952), p. 45; Edward C. Carter II, "A Wild Irishman Under Every Federalist Bed: Naturalization in Philadelphia, 1789-1806," *Pennsylvania Magazine of History and Biography* 94 (July 1970): 331-346; Vernon L. Stauffer, *New England and the Bavarian Illuminati* (New York, 1918), pp. 140-142; Alan U. Briceland, "The Philadelphia *Aurora,* the New England Illuminati, and the Election of 1800," *Pennsylvania Magazine of History and Biography* 100 (January 1976): 3-36.

185. Morris U. Schappes, "Anti-Semitism and Reaction, 1795-1800," *Publications of the American Jewish Historical Society* 38 (December 1948): 114. See below for Simpson.

186. *Porcupine's Gazette,* October 16, 1797. See below for Israel.

187. *Aurora* (Philadelphia), October 9, 17, 1797. For an anti-Semitic attack on John Israel when he started his paper *Tree of Liberty* in Pittsburgh in 1800, see Russell J. Ferguson, *Early Western Pennsylvania Politics* (Pittsburgh, 1938), pp. 160-163.

188. *Argus* (New York), December 17, 1795; Schappes, "Anti-Semitism and Reaction," 117-118.

189. *Gazette of the United States* (Philadelphia), August 5, 1800; *Aurora* (Philadelphia), August 13, 1800. For Nones and the text of the scurrilous account of the meeting and Nones's reply, see below.

190. For the view that the societies operated as a political organization, see Miller, "First Fruits of Republican Organization," 118-143, and Donald H. Stewart, "Jeffersonian Journalism: Newspaper Propaganda and the Development of the Democratic-Republican Party, 1789-1801" (Ph.D. diss., Columbia University, 1950), pp. 802-803. For the position that they functioned only as pressure groups, see Noble E. Cunningham, Jr., *The Jeffersonian Republicans: The Formation of Party Organization, 1789-1901* (Chapel Hill, 1958), pp. 63-65.

2 | Democratic-Republican Societies of Pennsylvania

GERMAN REPUBLICAN SOCIETY OF PHILADELPHIA

To Friends and Fellow Citizens, April 11, 1793

To the EDITOR *of the* NATIONAL GAZETTE.

SIR,

   A German society has been established in this city, for republican purposes, and as a *hue and cry* has been raised against it by some who are both ignorant of its principles and its objects, and as a misrepresentation may excite prejudice in the minds of even *candid and republican* men, you are requested to give the enclosed circular letter a place in your useful paper[1]—As the objects of the society are sufficiently designated in the letter, it will be unnecessary to enter into any further explanation, either to satisfy the well disposed, or to shut the mouths of *snarlers:* It would be to the advantage of Pennsylvania and of the Union if political societies were established throughout the United States, as they would prove powerful instruments in support of the present system of equality, and formidable enemies to aristocracy in whatever shape it might present itself—May the example of the German Republican Society prove a spur to the friends of equality throughout the United States!

A CUSTOMER.

Friends and Fellow Citizens,

   In a republican government it is a duty incumbent on every citizen to afford his assistance, either by taking a part in its immediate administration, or by his advice and watchfulness, that its principles may remain incorrupt; for the spirit of liberty, like every virtue of the mind, is to be kept alive only by constant action—It unfortunately happens that objects of general concern seldom meet

53

with the individual attention which they merit, and that individual exertion seldom produces a general effect; it is therefore of essential moment that political societies should be established in a free government, that a joint operation may be produced, which shall give that attention and exertion so necessary to the preservation of civil liberty—The importance and truth of these reflections have operated upon a number of Germans in this city, they have therefore thought fit to associate themselves in a society under the name of the Germans to objects of government and education; it is high time they should step forward, declare themselves independent of other influence, and think for themselves—Ignorance not only excludes us from many enjoyments in life, but renders us liable to imposition, and to judge of an evil, and its extent we should have a mind cultivated by education, added to our own, or the experience of others; hence the necessity of instruction and information in a government where every citizen should be capable of judging of the conduct of rulers, and the tendency of laws—The society wishes to impress the importance and the advantages of education upon the minds of their brethren throughout the state—To be respected, men should be virtuous, but to be capable of fulfilling a republican duty and of serving our country, we should connect wisdom with virtue—There is a disposition in the human mind to tyrannize when cloathed with power, men therefore who are entrusted with it, should be watched with the eye of an eagle to prevent those abuses which never fail to arise from a want of vigilance—Jealousy is a security, nay it is a virtue in a republic, for it begets watchfulness; it is a necessary attendant upon a warm attachment to our country.

The society wish to call the attention of their countrymen to affairs of state; they wish to inspire them with jealousy to guard them against every encroachment on the equality of freemen. As the faithful administration of government depends greatly upon a judicious delegation made to offices dependent upon the people, it is a common duty to give this every attention; we shall therefore comprehend this in our plan, and we shall take the liberty, occasionally, to offer our opinions, and shall take a peculiar pleasure in receiving a free communication of sentiment from you on this subject. We think it proper to assign reasons why we have associated ourselves in a German society, and why we have chosen the German language, to conduct and communicate our transactions; a large portion of the citizens of this state are German, and many of them are wholly ignorant of the English language, and therefore ignorant of the most essential transactions of our government; it is but just, therefore, that information should be given them in a language which they understand, on those subjects which involve this dearest interests—Being, in common with your brethren of other nations, but one people, we wish not to make national distinctions, but in so far as necessity may require; a kindred in language will necessarily draw men together, for we are as naturally inclined to those with whom we can hold communion in our own, as are distant from others, who are incapable of social intercourse with us from an ignorance of their language—This will beget distinction, but as it is more the distinction of language than of nation, it will only remain until the English language shall become the mother tongue of every citizen in the state. Our situation is peculiar, and we must avail ourselves of those advantages, which our brethren, who are conversant in the English language can afford.

Thus we have in as concise manner as possible, pointed out the views of the society, and we hope for your concurrence and assistance in giving the Germans that station which their industry, their integrity, and their patriotism merit; any communications which you have to make, you will please address to the President of the German Republican Society of Philadelphia. As we have in our constitution provided for the admission of members at a distance by the title of honorary and corresponding members, you will please inform us if you wish to be considered as one of our body, that we may enroll you accordingly.

With your best wishes for your private as well as public happiness, we are—

By order of the society,

HENRY KAMMERER [2]

April 11.   Vice-President

National Gazette (Philadelphia), April 13, 1793

To Citizen Genêt and His Reply, May 17, 1793

Last Saturday, a committee, appointed by the German Republican Society of Philadelphia waited on M. Genet,[3] Minister Plenipotentiary from the Republic of France to the United States, with the following Address:

Citizen Genet, Minister Plenipotentiary from the
Republic of France, To the United States of America.

SIR,

The German Republican Society of Philadelphia congratulate you as the representative of *the people* of France, on your safe arrival in this city; We welcome you, with heartfelt joy, to this Land of Liberty, which your generous and gallant *Nation* contributed to make happy. We feel the liveliest sympathy for the distresses of our republican brethren, who are combatting the fell hosts of tyrants, in defence of their own natural rights, and the rights of mankind; and deplore, that a nation, from whom we are descended should be among the first in the conspiracy against Liberty. We see, with pain and horror, the confederation of all European despots against freedom—their united efforts to supersede the *general will* of France: but though foes encompass her brave sons, we trust, the arm, nerved to Liberty, will be invincible, and that the millenium of political happiness, is opening its prospects upon them. The combinations of the sovereignty of the people, are the only security for general liberty and happiness; and we flatter ourselves, these will be at length so well understood, as to fix the Rights of Man upon an immovable basis, and that the French nation will give an example to the European world, of rulers and ruled having but one object and one will— *The Good of Their Country.*

With our best wishes for the perpetual union and freedom of our respective republics, and for your full enjoyment of every blessing which can serve the glorious cause in which you are embarked.

We are,

With sentiments of republican affection,

Your friends,

By order of the Society:

HENRY KAMMERER, Pres.

MICHAEL LEIB,)[4]

Phila. May 17, 1793.   ANDREW GEYER)[5] Sec'ries.

———

To the German Republican Society of Philadelphia,

CITIZENS,

I have had the satisfaction of spending several years of my life among the people of Germany,[6] and during my stay with them, knew how to esteem and respect those individuals whom the absurd prejudices of birth and the disgraceful habits to slavery, had not entirely estranged from humanity. It was ever my opinion, that this great nation would enthusiastically rouse itself to vindicate and maintain with invincible firmnes, the sacred flame of liberty as soon as it could free itself from the encumbrances of its monstrous constitution:—That desirable event has not yet, however, taken place. The hosts of despots that have possessed themselves of the sovereignty of the German people, still continue to rivet their chains on them; I am convinced, however, that my opinion is well founded, notwithstanding, and that Germany will be free.

The republican sentiments that animate the hearts of all those I have had opportunity of seeing beyond the limits of their own unfortunate country, are a convincing proof to me, that this will be the case; and under such a view of things, so important to the sincere friends of humanity, I cannot express how much your address has excited my sensibility. I shall make your sentiments known to my fellow citizens and have no doubt they will receive with the most lively marks of satisfaction, the good wishes you have expressed for their success of their arms and the extension of their principles.

GENET.

American Daily Advertiser (Philadelphia), May 20, 1793

To the President and Members of the Democratic Society of Pennsylvania, February 20, 1794

To the President and Members of the Democratic Society of Pennsylvania.

FELLOW-CITIZENS,

The German Republican Society of Philadelphia, founded upon the same principles, and having the same general objects of public good in view as the Democratic Society of Pennsylvania, is of opinion, that the intentions of the two Societies can be better promoted, and a greater energy given to their exertions, by the establishment of a mutual correspondence, and a concurrent operation.

If any thing could have added to the impression which this society has already felt of the utility, nay the necessity of political institutions of this sort, the late clamour that has been raised against them would strengthen this impression, add to its union, and encourage its exertions. Why it should be deemed improper that political societies should exist among us, is not easy for an ingenuous mind to conceive; for any measure or regulation, which seeks to avoid the eye of the people's scrutiny, must create a suspicion, that less than public good is the object; for in a government where the people are supreme, where they delegate only to superintend their rights, who but they have a right to enquire, who but they ought to be satisfied, that their agents have done their duty? To recur to argument to substantiate a principle so evident is to suppose it doubtful; it is sufficient to say that this society is sensible of the benefits which result from political associations, and that it feels the right—a right purchased with the treasure, and the blood of our country.

Sensible of the tendency of republican governments to degenerate and equally sensible that this degeneracy is hurried by supineness, this society will heartily concur with you in any measures which shall be deemed proper to perpetuate the unpolluted principle of republicanism.

To prove to you the sincerity of our wishes, that the public good may be a common object with the two societies, we subjoin the following resolutions, for your concurrence.

Resolved, That it is the natural privilege of every free citizen, to give his sentiments on all public measures, and not only on those which have operation, but on those also that are pending.

Resolved, That this society highly approves of the resolutions proposed to Congress, by James Madison,[7] and that it entertains the most pleasing presage of the present majority of Congress.

Resolved, That as republicans, and friends to universal liberty, that this society views with concern, the attempts which are making to depress the French character in this country: That when we see men, insidiously endeavoring to produce an abhorrence of a principle, because the actors have gone to imagined excess? that when we see men, who, under the guise of patriotism, enter into a defence, nay a panegyric upon the perfidious, insolent, and tyrannical conduct of Great-Britain, every freeman ought to express his abhorrence of such dark policy, and declare, that the true and unbiassed American, has different sympathies.

By Order of the Society,

HENRY KAMMERER,

February 20th, 1794 President of said Society.

General Advertiser (Philadelphia), March 10, 1794.

To the President and Members of the Democratic Society of Pennsylvania, May 30, 1794

To the President and Members of the Democratic Society of Pennsylvania. Fellow Citizens!

I am directed by the German Republican Society of Philadelphia to forward to you the enclosed Resolutions. From them you will learn the sense this Society entertain of the Resolutions, which you communicated to us, on the appointment of Mr Jay, and on the Excise contemplated by Congress.[8] You will, also, see in them an approbation of your opposition to an unconstitutional and dangerous measure; and an intention to fraternize with you in every proceeding that shall have public good for its object.

By order of the Society:

May 30th) <div align="right">Henry Kammerer, Presid^t.
1794   )

German Republican Society,
May 30th 1794.

A letter from the Corresponding Committee of the Democratic Society of Pennsylvania, covering sundry Resolutions on the appointment of John Jay as an Envoy Extraordinary to the Court of Great Britain, and on Excise, were presented and read:

"Whereupon on Motion,

"Resolved, That this Society sincerely concur in the Resolutions communicated to them by the Democratic Society of Pennsylvania; and that they will, at all times, unite with that Society, in legal opposition to every measure, which shall affect our rights, or invade the Constitution of our Country.

"Resolved, That the foregoing Resolution be immediately transmitted to the Democratic Society of Pennsylvania, as a testimony of hearty approbation of their manly, spirited, and patriotic conduct."

By order of the Society:

Henry Kammerer Prest.

Manuscript Minutes, Democratic Society of Pennsylvania, Historical Society of Pennsylvania

Resolutions Adopted on the Resistance of Citizens in Western Pennsylvania, July 29, 1794

German Republican Society
July 29.

The following resolutions were proposed, adopted, and ordered to be published.

Resolved, as the opinion of this society, that every law enacted by the majority of the people ought to be submitted to, and that every opposition to the laws by violence is unconstitutional and dangerous.

Resolved, that this society highly disapprove of the resistance of the citizens of the western counties of Pennsylvania to a law of the United States,[9] as such hostility is contrary to the constitution of our country, and repugnant to every principle of liberty.

Resolved that as citizens who estimate the blessings of freedom, order and union we will, at all times, discontenance every attempt to resist the will of the majority by force, and will ever consider attempts of this sort, as subversive of the principles of a free government.

By order of the Society,

Henry Kammerer, President

Gazette of the United States (Philadelphia), September 1, 1794.

Address to the Free and Independent Citizens of the United States, December 29, 1794

At a full meeting of the Society, the following Address was unanimously agreed upon, and ordered to be published.

———

The German Republican Society of Philadelphia, to the free and independent Citizens of the United States:

———

FELLOW-FREEMAN,

A voice too loud not to be heard, calls upon us to address you. A just and an
honourable cause summons us at your bar, and we most chearfully pay obedience
to us, under the fullest persuasion, that reason, and not authority, is the scale by
which you measure the actions of men—The right secured to us by the late glorious struggle for liberty, and guaranteed by the constitution of our country, has
been exercised by us, and for this we have met with the most opprobrious denunciation. The right consecrated by our social compact, and held sacred by
every nation pretending to liberty, the right to speak and publish our sentiments,
has been called into question, and the legislature of the United States were about
to erect themselves into a tribunal of Censors, to deprive the freemen of America
of their birth right. An usurpation of power so flagrant, so contrary to the true
intent and spirit of our constitution, so repugnant to the principles of liberty,
could not have escaped your observation.—The most extraordinary fact in the
annals of the age could not have passed unperceived by you, that *patriotic societies were the objects of denunciations in the same year, in Great Britain, France
and the United States of America!!*

We have been charged with the authorship of the western insurrection, and
upon this unsupported assertion, an interdiction of the most dreadful kind was
to be fulminated against us. How true this charge is, we will leave to you to determine. The proofs are in your hands, and you are already competent to decide
upon them; for every act of ours which had relation to public affairs, has been
promulgated to the world. Let us call your attention to our resolutions in reprobation of the insurrection, and search in them for matter of crimination. Did
they arise from fear, as has been basely insinuated? What is to deter a freeman
from speaking his sentiments, when he is within the sale of the law! A thought
so foul is worthy only of the wretch who engendered it, and marks him a fit instrument of cowardice and treachery.

Are we the abettors of insurgents for supposing government can do wrong, for
disapproving an excise? Then is the freedom of opinion at an end,—then is that
august band of patriots, who combated against a British tyrant, a precedent for
disorder, for having declared to the people of Canada, that EXCISES WERE THE
HORRORS OF ALL FREE GOVERNMENTS.—But our declaration in disapprobation of the insurrection has been questioned as to its sincerity; for we have
been accused of wearing the masque of conspirators.—As well might we say
that our accusers wear the garb of patriotism, and are loud in favour of freedom the more certainly to effect its destruction.—As well might we say, that
the pretended friends of law and order had secretly fomented the insurrection,
that they might borrow another argument against republicanism, and be furnished with a stronger evidence in favour of a standing army, as that the patriotic societies were instrumental in disseminating sedition.—The language of
Pitt[10] (that satellite of despotism) was in praise of the glorious constitution of
Great Britain, and the liberty of Britons, even at the moment he was sapping

the citadel of personal security, the *habeas corpus,* and how near is its affinity with the late language of American legislature, when about to plunge a dagger into the bosom of liberty.

Our accusers have not been daring enough to say our institution was unconstitutional, how great then their absurdity in araigning us. By this they meant to dishonour us: but truth cannot be sullied by any contact with falsehood. If Democratic Societies are not proscribed by our social compact, why this congressional enquiry, why this denunciation? Was the national treasury in the freshet that it was necessary to find such a sluice for its abundance? Or did the denunciators, by a declaration of their opinions, expect to give a law to the United States? Here then rests the artifice—Men are the creatures of opinion, and it is by means of opinion alone that laws in all well regulated societies can and ought to be enforced. What is the common law of England and which has taken root in this country, but opinion? It is opinion alone that gives force to our laws; for we have not the physical power of a standing army to argue obedience to them. Thus then the representatives of the freemen of America designed to give an opinion which was to have the operation of a law, and by means of it effect the destruction of the freedom of speech. In this view of the subject say, fellow citizens, who are the conspirators against the liberties of the United States? Say, who mediate the destruction of our constitution, and seek to plunge us into all the horror of anarchy or of despotism? Say which is the self-created society, the one composed of citizens, under a constitutional sanction, or the one, delegated for the purposes of legislation, and usurping a censorial authority?

But self-created as we are supposed,[11] hereditary distinction has no place in our code, diplomas, with the insignia of nobility, adorn not our mansions, neither does birth give an exclusive claim to a place among us. We drain not the public treasury for disputations about diphthongs and particles—the public purse rewards us not for making handsome syllogisms or pretty metaphors. We have never stepped forth the champions of an enemy, who sought to enslave us, and dishonoured a friend on whom our political salvation depended. Principles and conduct so unrighteous cannot be imputed to us, though truth, as in the denunciations against us, were placed upon the rack.

Fellow-citizens, a bare view of the subject will show you that our enemies teem with absurdities.—At one moment we are said to be self-created, at another, the late minister of France is said to be our parent.—At one moment we are considered as obscure and contemptible, at another as a combination so formidable as to endanger the government.—At one moment we are supposed the abortions of society, at another as possessing influence and vigour to supercede the wisdom and strength of the nation. Dishonesty cannot be rendered so systematic as long to pass for truth; that cloven foot of falsehood must be seen at last, and such has been the fate of our accusers. In the convulsion of zeal and of exaltation they have unmasked themselves, and presented the bold front of conspirators against the inestimable liberty of opinion.

The right to association in Democratic Societies has been questioned by some;

but if we have not this privilege, by what constitutional text will other associations be justified? If we as a number have not the right to speak our sentiments, by what political logic will the right of an individual be defended? If many have not this privilege, few certainly must be deprived of it; for the right must be multiplied by the number which compose the society, up to the majority of the whole nation, who give law to the community. To deprive a number of this right will leave not a shadow of claim to one; for it is in direct contradiction to the principles of a free government that one individual shall have a right from which many are excluded. The principle recognized by our constitution, that the many are to govern the few, must be at an end, if this reasoning obtains; for the right of an individual to publish his sentiments, no one has yet been bold enough to controvert.

But admitting we are criminal, by what clause of the constitution expressed or implied was Congress metamorphosed into a body of tutors for our condemnation? The remedy for a trespass of the kind imputed to us is plainly pointed out by our laws, and to wander from it is an usurpation exceeding in guilt the crime with which we are charged.—Nay, so great is the advantage of government over us, that if we had been guilty, they had the power to translate us from the vicinage of the criminal commission, to any place favourable to their views.

If Democrats have been the instruments of the western insurrection, how will it be explained, that they were among the foremost to suppress it? Our brethren, the Democratic Society of Pennsylvania, could have made a quorum in the field, and they were among the number who received the commendations of the President of the United States.

Fellow-citizens, this subject is solemnly important to every freeman in the United States; for however some may disapprove our institution, all must unite in the support of the liberty of speech. It is but too obvious that an endeavor was made to wrest this right from us; how incumbent then is it on every one who values his freedom, to bend his attention to a subject so highly interesting.

All governments are more or less combinations against the people; they are states of violence against individual liberty, originating from man's imperfection and vice, and as rulers have no more virtue than the ruled, the equilibrium between them can only be preserved by proper attention and association; for the power of government can only be kept within its constituted limits by the display of a power equal to itself, the collected sentiment of the people. Solitary opinions have little weight with men whose views are unfair; but the voice of many strikes them with awe. To obtain a connected voice associations of some sort are necessary, no matter by what names they are designated. The checks and balances of government are inventions to keep the people in subordination, a reaction of some sort is necessary, therefore, to keep up the equipoise, between the people and the government. Whether these be town and township meetings, called to echo the pre-eminent virtues of administration, or whether they are associations of another kind, that approve or condemn as their judgment directs, they are alike legal, they may be alike useful and to interpose a veto to them is alike tyrannical.

It is the substance and not the shadow of things that we should regard, and if the substance meets our wishes, no matter by what sound it is conveyed to our senses. The bugbears anarchy and antifederalism, invented to stifle free enquiry, can no longer lead you astray; they have been so hackneyed, that, like worn out jades, they are no longer fit for service. To your judgment we now submit our cause, for it must ultimately rest with you whether liberty or tyranny shall reign among us, and whatever may be your opinions of our institution, you will do us the justice to believe, that we owe no greatness to our country's ruin. In defiance of every menace and denunciation, we are determined to remain firm at our posts, and never will we surrender the rights of freemen but with our lives.

By order of the society.

HENRY KAMMERER, President.

Attest, ANDREW GEYER, Secretary.

The printers in the United States who have not surrendered the freedom of the press are requested to give a place in their papers to the foregoing address.

Philadelphia Gazette and Universal Daily Advertiser, December 29, 1794

"A Friend to Religion" to the *Aurora,* January 1, 1795

For the AURORA

THE attack made upon the German Republican Society in the *Grubb Street Gazette,* by a couple of would be wits, should have passed without any further notice than contempt would inspire, had it not been for the flagrant outrage upon common decency contained in them. The awful scene which has occasioned the grin of *Monies* was too melancholy a kind to produce many proselytes to his fun; for it must be an abandoned and callous heart indeed, that could make itself merry over the ruins of such an edifice as the German Lutheran Church.[12] Every friend to the beauty and ornament of our city must regret the loss of so noble a building; and every mind impressed with sentiments of religion must be-moan the destruction of so valuable a temple dedicated to the service of the Deity. Can it be possible that things sacred should be sported with by such a buffoon without abhorrence! degenerate have we become indeed when a public paper shall be so debased as to admit into a ridicule of religious service, and the effusions of a diabolical transport at the destruction of a public place of worship! psalms ought to be sung for wretches of this kind if there could be any prospect, that by means of them his satannic majesty would be exercised.

A FRIEND to Religion

Aurora (Philadelphia), January 1, 1795

THE DEMOCRATIC SOCIETY OF PENNSYLVANIA, PHILADELPHIA

Principles, Articles, and Regulations, Agreed upon, Drawn, and Adopted, May 30, 1793

THE RIGHTS OF MAN, the genuine objects of Society, and the legitimate principles of Government, have been clearly developed by the successive Revolutions
of America and France. Those events have withdrawn the veil which concealed
the dignity and the happiness of the human race, and have taught us, no longer
dazzled with adventitious splendor, or awed by antiquated usurpation, to erect
the Temple of LIBERTY on the ruins of *Palaces* and *Thrones.*

AT this propitious period, when the nature of Freedom and Equality is thus
practically displayed, and when their value, (best understood by those, who have
paid the price of acquiring them) is universally acknowledged, the patriotic mind
will naturally be solicitius, by every proper precaution, to preserve and perpetuate the Blessings which Providence hath bestowed upon our Country: For, in
reviewing the history of Nations, we find occasion to lament, that the vigilance
of the People has been too easily absorbed in victory; and that the prize which
has been achieved by the wisdom and valor of one generation, has too often been
lost by the ignorance and supineness of another.

WITH a view, therefore, to cultivate the just knowledge of rational Liberty, to
facilitate the enjoyment and exercise of our civil Rights, and to transmit, unimpaired, to posterity, the glorious inheritance of a *free Republican Government,*
the DEMOCRATIC SOCIETY of Pennsylvania is constituted and established. Unfettered by *religious* or *national* distinctions, unbiassed by party and unmoved
by ambition, this Institution embraces the interest and invites the support of
every virtuous citizen. The public good is indeed its sole object, and we think
that the best means are pursued for obtaining it, when we recognize the following, as the fundamental principles of our association.

I. THAT the people have the inherent and exclusive right and power of making and altering forms of Government; and that for regulating and protecting our
social interests, a REPUBLICAN GOVERNMENT is the most natural and beneficial
form, which the wisdom of Man has devised.

II. THAT the Republican Constitutions of the UNITED STATES and of the
STATE of PENNSYLVANIA, being framed and established by the People, it is our
duty as good citizens, to support them. And in order effectually to do so, it is
likewise the duty of every Freeman to regard with attention, and to discuss without fear, the conduct of the public Servants, in every department of Government.

III. THAT in considering the Administration of public affairs, men and measures should be estimated according to their intrinsic merits; and therefore, regardless of party spirit or political connection, it is the duty of every Citizen, by making the general welfare the rule of his conduct, to aid and approve those men and measures, which have an influence in promoting the prosperity of the Commonwealth.

IV. THAT in the choice of persons to fill the offices of government, it is essential to the existence of a free Republic, that every citizen should act according to his own judgment, and, therefore, any attempt to corrupt or delude the people in exercising the rights of suffrage, either by promising the favor of one Candidate or traducing the character of another, is an offence equally injurious to moral rectitude and civil Liberty.

V. THAT the *People of Pennsylvania* form but one indivisible community, whose political rights and interests, whose national honor and prosperity, must in degree and duration be forever the same; and, therefore, it is the duty of every freeman, and shall be the endeavor of the Democratic Society to remove the prejudices, to conciliate the affections, to enlighten the understanding, and to promote the happiness of all our fellow-citizens.

Having united these principles, we adopt the following Rules and Regulations for transacting the business of the Institution.

ARTICLE I. The Society shall be co-extensive with the State, but for the conveniency of the Members, there shall be a separate meeting in the City of Philadelphia, and one in each County, which shall chuse to adopt this Constitution. A Member admitted in the City, or in any County, shall of course be a Member of the Society at large; and may attend any of the Meetings wherever held.

ARTICLE II. A Meeting of the Society shall be held in the City of Philadelphia, on the first Thursday in every month, and in the respective Counties as often and at such times as they shall by their own Rules determine. But the President of each respective meeting may convene the Members on any special occasion.

ARTICLE III. The election of new Members and of the Officers of the Society shall be by ballot and by a majority of the votes of the Members present at each respective meeting. But no new member shall be voted for at the same meeting at which he is proposed. The names of the members proposing any candidates for admission shall be entered in a book kept for that purpose. Every Member on his admission shall subscribe to this Constitution and pay the sum of half a dollar to the Treasurer for the use of the Society.

ARTICLE IV. The Officers of the meeting in the City of Philadelphia shall consist of a *President, two Vice-Presidents, two Secretaries, one Treasurer and a Corresponding Committee* of five Members; and the meeting of the respective Counties shall chuse a *President* and such other *Officers* as they shall think proper. The *Officers* of the meeting held in the City of Philadelphia shall be chosen on the first Thursday in January in every year.

ARTICLE V. It shall be the duty of the Corresponding Committee, to correspond with the various meetings of the Society, and with all other Societies, that may be established on similar principles in any other of the United States, and to lay all communications which they shall make and receive, together with such other business as they shall from time to time deem proper, before the Society at a meeting held within their respective Counties.

ARTICLE VI. It shall be the duty of the Secretaries to keep Minutes of the proceedings of the several meetings; and of the Treasurers, to receive and account for all monies to them respectively paid.

Principles, Articles and Regulations Agreed upon by the Members of the Democratic Society in Philadelphia, May 30th, 1793. Philadelphia, Printed by E. Oswald, No. 156 Market Street South, 1793.

Circular Letter to the Counties, July 4, 1793

Fellow Citizen:

We have the pleasure to communicate to you a copy of the constitution of the Democratic Society, in hopes, that after a candid consideration of its principles, and objects, you may be induced to promote its adoption in the county of which you are an inhabitant.

Every mind, capable of reflection, must perceive, that the present crisis in the politics of nations is peculiarly interesting to America. The European Confederacy, transcendent in power, and unparalleled in iniquity, menaces the very existence of freedom. Already its baneful operation may be traced in the tyrannical destruction of the Constitution of Poland;[13] and should the glorious efforts of France be eventually defeated, we have reason to presume, that, for the consummation of monarchical ambition, and the security of its establishments, this country, the only remaining depository of liberty, will not long be permitted to enjoy in peace, the honors of an independent, and the happiness of a republican government.

Nor are the dangers arising from a foreign source the only causes at this time, of apprehension and solicitude. The seeds of luxury appear to have taken root in our domestic soil; and the jealous eye of patriotism already regards the spirit of freedom and equality, as eclipsed by the pride of wealth and the arrogance of power.

This general view of our situation has led to the institution of "The Democratic Society." A constant circulation of useful information, and a liberal communication of republican sentiments, were thought to be the best antidotes to any political poison, with which the vital principles of civil liberty might be attacked; for by such means, a fraternal confidence will be studiously marked; and a standard will be erected, to which, in danger and distress, the friends of liberty may successfully resort.

To obtain these objects, then, and to cultivate on all occasions the love of peace, order, and harmony; an attachment to the constitution and a respect to the laws of our country will be the aim of "The Democratic Society." Party and personal considerations are excluded from a system of this nature; for in the language of the articles under which we are united, men and measures will only be estimated according to their intrinsic merits, and their influence in promoting the prosperity of the state.

From you, citizen, we hope to derive essential aid, in extending the Society and maintaining its general principles. We request therefore an early attention to the subject, and solicit a constant correspondence.

We are with esteem, your

Philadelphia, 4, July, 1793.   Fellow Citizens.

National Gazette (Philadelphia), July 17, 1793

Manuscript Minutes, July 3, 1793, to January 1, 1795[14]

July 3rd 1793

The Society met pursuant to their adjournment of the 20th June last.

Citizen William Cowels, vice President, in the Chair—

Citizens David Jackson, Alexander James Dallas,[15] Jonathan D. Sergeant, Elisha Gordon, Joseph D. Hamelin, and John Wigton.

Agreed the Constitution and paid each half a Dollar to the Treasurer.

The Minutes of the preceding Meeting were read.

Mr. Dallas from the Committee of Correspondence, reported a Circular Letter to be sent to the different Counties which was read and debated by paragraphs.

It was moved and seconded, That the word "Sir" be struck out throughout the Letter and the words "humble Servants" from the subscription thereof, and that the words: "fellow Citizens" and "fellow Citizens" be substituted in lieu thereof.

The amendment and the Letter so amended were agreed to.

On motion; ordered: That the Committee of Correspondence publish in one or more of the public newspapers of this City, the principles, articles and regulations agreed upon by this meeting, together with a list of the names of the officers thereof, and the circular Letter ordered to be sent to the different Counties.

Ordered that the same be also published in the German newspaper.

On motion, ordered that the Election of Citizens proposed as new members at the last meeting by members present be now gone into.

And it was accordingly proceeded.

It was moved and seconded to revise the mode of electing new members. After some debate, it was agreed to postpone the farther consideration of this business to the next meeting.

On motion; Resolved: That the Society meet again on Thursday the 8th instant. Adjourned. . . .

Thursday 2[d] January 1794

The Society met in Stated meeting agreeable to adjournment. . . .

The Society, agreeable to the four articles of regulations, went into an Election of officers, for the present year, when the following Citizens were duly elected.

David Rittenhause[16]   Presid[t]

William Coates ⎫
David Jackson ⎬   vice presid[ts]
A. I. Dallas   ⎭

Benjamin F. Bache[17] ⎫
Hugh Ferguson   ⎬ Corresponding Comm
Michal Leib   ⎬
Samuel Bryan   ⎭

Israel Israel[18]   Treasurer

Peter S. Deponceau[19] ⎫ Secretys. . . .
John Smith   ⎭

Citizen Dallas for reasons assigned declines acting as one of the members of the Committee of Correspondence

Adjourned to Thursday the 9th of January Instant

Thursday the 9th of January

The Society met in pursuence to a previous adjournment.

Citizen Coates Vice Presdnt in the chair

The vice President presented a letter from Citizen David Jackson which was read by the Secrety declining to Serve as a Vice President

Citizen Deponceau from the committee apointed on the 11th ultimo reported a Set of Resolutions which was read & are as follows

1st. Resolved, that it is one of the unalienable rights of freemen at all times to meet together in a peaceable manner, to discuss with temper, but with freedom and firmness all subjects of public concern, and to declare and publish their Sentiments to their fellow citizens, whenever they think they can thereby promote the general good. That as a consequence of this principle and from a Sense of the advantages which result to a community from such discussion, popular societies have been cherished—and incouraged in every free country, and never have been dreaded but by men, whose conduct or principles could not bear the test of public investigation.

2d. Resolved, that the democratic society, founded on the purest principles of civil liberty, and of respect and attachment to the constitution and laws of their country; unbiased by any party views, and actuated solely by patriotic motives, at a time when the most momentious concerns agitate the public mind, and call forth thro' every channel the expressions of the public sentiments, have thought it their duty to take these important subjects into their serious consideration, and declare their sense of them by the following resolutions:

3d. Resolved, that we view with inexpressible horror the cruel and unjust war carried on by the combined powers of Europe against the french republic—that attached to the french nation (our only true and naturel ally) by sentiments of the liveliest gratitude for the great and generous services she has rendered us, while we were struggling for our liberties and by that strong connection which arises from a similarity of government and of political principles, we cannot sit passive and forbear expressing our anxious concern, while she is greatly contending against a World, for the same rights which she assisted us to establish— that exclusive of the sentiments, so natural to every true american, the powerfull motive of self interest combines to connect us still closer to france; for when we see so many sovereigns, having different interests, and some of whom are natural enemies to each other, Confederate against a single Nation with no other avowed object than that of changing her internal government, we cannot believe that they are making war against that Nation solely, but against liberty itself. Impressed with this idea, we cannot help concluding, that if those lawless despots succeed in destroying an enemy in france so formidable to their tyranical usurpations, they will not rest satisfied untill they have exterminated it from the earth; it therefore behoves us, as we value our dear bought rights to give to a cause, so just in itself, and which we may so properly call our own, every countenance and support in our power, consistently with the laws of our Country.

4th. Resolved, that we ought to resist to the utmost of our power all attempts to alienate our affections from france and detach us from her alliance, and to connect us more intimately with great britain; that all persons who, directly or indirectly, promote this unnatural succession ought to be considered by every free american as enemies to republicanism and their country.

5thly Resolved, that our interest as well as our national dignity requires that the sentiments of the people of america should be manifested at the present important period, and that it should be known our faith not punic but american; that we are determined to abide by our national engagements, and preserve our national friendships; that a firm and manly conduct is the best calculated to secure to us the blessings of peace, while timid and wavering measures will expose us to numberless insults and outrages, and after a painful career of humiliation, finally draw us ingloriously into a war, which firmness and decision might have prevented.

6th. Resolved, that the conduct of the maritime powers at war with the french republic, in prohibiting the exportation of our produce to france and her collonies, and in seizing our vessels laden with provisions for that country, is a daring infringement of the established law of nations, and ought to be resented with a proper spirit.

7th. Resolved that we conceive we ought in the same manner to resent the outrageous conduct of great brittain [sic] in impressing our seamen, in seizing our vessels on the high seas, and detaining them in their ports on the most frivolous pretences, in stirring up against us the savage nations of africa and america, and in short in carrying on against this Country a covert and insidious warfare, which evinces her fear of our power, at the same time that it can leave us no doubt of her hatred and enmity.

8th. Resolved, that while america holds out the olive branch, and sincerely wishes to persevere in a pacific line of conduct, the world ought to be convinced, that she knows her rights, that she feels her strength, and that the same spirit which she has shewn in the acquisition of her Independence will be exerted with double energy in its defence.

9th. Resolved, that the friendly conduct of the french nation towards the United States forms a strong and lively contrast to that of the powers who are at war with her; that the proposition she has lately made of entering into a new commercial treaty with us, on a broad and liberal basis, and placing us upon the same footing with her own Citizens at home and in her colonies,[20] is an aditional proof of the warm attachment of the people of france for their american brethren; that such a treaty cannot but prove highly beneficial to this country in securing to it in the french colonies rich and abundant sources of trade, and constant and profetable market for its staple commodities.

10th. Resolved, that treaties solemnly entered into between sovereign nations ought to receive a fair and liberal construction, that the best interpretation, in doubtful cases, is that which we should have adopted at the time of signing the instrument.

11th. Resolved, that it is the opinion of this society, that the agents of foreign powers, acting in the name and under the responsibility of governments by whom they are delegates, are responsible only to their own sovereigns, for their official conduct in the countries to which they may be sent.[21]

Impressed with this political truth, we find ourselves called upon highly to reprobate all attempts that have been and may be made, by spreading false and calumnious reports, by indecent strictures and news paper publications and by others as unwarentable means to traduce and vilify a foreign Minister,[22] to excite suspicion against him in the minds of the people, and a jealousy in their public officers, with a view to render his cause unpopular and his situation amongst us irksome and disagreeable; and we cannot but see in such attempts the efforts of a foreign influence, acting in opposition to the nation whom that minister represents, and indeavoring to make the good people of the United States subservient to such hostile designs.

12th. Resolved, that tryal by jury ought to be held sacred and inviolate; that all attempts made by judges to overawe or influence juries in the exercise of their functions, and all publications made by any citizen, but more especially by persons in authority, tending to prejudge a cause and to influence the minds of the jury by whom it is to be tryed are infringements of that sacred right; that the danger is greater in proportion to the weight of authority which prejudge a cause and that every precedent of this nature ought to be strongly guarded against, particularly in criminal cases.

13th. Resolved, that the firm tone of our executive in demanding from the British government a fulfilment of the treaty of peace[23] deserves the approbation of every citizen who is interested in the dignity, independence and welfare of our country.

14th. Resolved, that we differ in opinion from those who imagine that the rulers of a republic may conciliate the favour of monarchs and despotic courts, by assuming the courtly forms, etiquettes and manners;[24] that republics are held in detestation by despotic governments, not on account of their manners but of their principles, and that nothing but interest or fear can prevent the efects of the hatred, while the mimicry of their absurd pomp by the citizens of a free commonwealth, serves but to make them despise those whom they before only hated.

Ordered that they be read and considered by paragraphs.

When the Secty had read the same they were unanimously adopted and Messrs M. Lein, Benj. B. Bache & I. Israel apointed a Committe to wait on the President of the Society in order to obtain his Signature & Superintend the Publication. . . .

Adjourned to thursday the 16th Instant at 6 O Clock P.M.

Thursday the 16th. . Jan^y. . 1794

The Society Met pursuant to adjournment

Citizen Coates vice president in the chair

Citezens John Harrison, Christian Shaffer, Jno. Meer, Stephen Girard, John Fimeton, Geo. Logan,[25] Mical groves each signed the Constitution and paid each fifty cents to the Treasurer.

Citezens I. Israel, M. Leib & B. F. Bache Members of the Committee appointed on the 9th Instant reported accompanied with two letters from Citezen William Barton & David Rittenhouse the latter of which is as follows, adress^d. to Citezen Bache.

Dear Sir

The Resolutions of the Democratic Society of the 9th Instant have my most Cordial approbation, but I think I cannot with propriety affix my name to them as Presedent because I was not present when they were agreed on. The Signature of the Chairman, for the time, or the secretary if attending, will I conceive be more proper. I am fully senceble of the disadvantage arising from the nonattendance of the Presedent and therefore thanking the Society with great Sicerety, for the honour they have done Me and wishing to promote its very laudable views; I must request them to accept my resignation, and to choose another in my stead.

David Rittenhouse

Whereupon Resolved that the vice presedent give notice to the members of this Society to Meet on Thursday evening the 23rd Instant for the purpose of choosing a President in the room and stead of Citizen D. Rittenhouse, and that said notification shall be accompanied with the late Presidents letter of resignation. . . .[26]

Citezen Dallas recalled his resignation of members of the Corresponding Committee ordered that he persue the duties Asigned to said Committee. . . .

Adjourned to Thursday 23rd Instant. . . .

Thursday 6th of March.

The Society Met in Stated Meeting, agreeable to Adjournment.

Citezen Israel Israel, in the chair. . . .

A letter was laid before the Society, Addressed to the Press[dt], from the German republican Society, accompenaed with Certain propositions in the following words: (See the annexed paper)[27] which was ordered to lay on the Table, for further consideration. . . .

The Society then went into the Consideration of the Propositions from the German Republican Society, and came to the following resolutions.

Resolved, Unanimously, that this Society heartily Concurs, in the resolution proposed by the german republecan Society, and that they will unite with them in any Measures, which will be Judged proper, to promote the Public Welfare. . . .[28]

Adjourned to Thursday the 13th Instant.

Thursday, March 13th 1794.

The Society met pursuant to Adjournment.

The President and Vice-Presidents being absent,

Citizen William Robinson was appointed Chairman, pro. tem. . . .

Citizen John Barker, from the Committee appointed at the last Meeting, on the subject of the Letter etc. from the German Republican Society of Philadelphia, reported a Reply to the same; which, by order, was read;—

On Motion, the said *Reply* was read the second time, by paragraphs; and, being amended, was adopted, as follows;

To the President and Members of the German Republican Society,

Fellow Citizens!

The Democratic Society of Pennsylvania, anxious for the public welfare, and zealous to secure that Freedom, which has been the offspring of our late glorious Revolution, will heartily fraternize with the German Republican Society of Philadelphia, in any measures that will perpetuate the blessing of a Free Government.

This Society has felt uncommon satisfaction, in finding so much zeal in their German brethern [sic], to guard against those encroachments, which all Governments endeavour to make, upon the People's rights. The despotism which Man too generally inclines to exercise, makes caution necessary—His disposition to avail himself of opportunities for domination, ought to beget an attention, that more should not be committed to him than necessity extorts; for, in the change of circumstances, the human mind is liable to revolutions, which self-preservation ought to observe with an eagle-eye, and prudence should never lose sight of.

Political associations, which have, for their object, the restriction of Government within Constitutional bounds, naturally excite the disaffection of those, whose principles and measures are the subject of enquiry and attention: but, in the pursuit of our own happiness, by moral and legal means, the obstacles that prejudiced Ambition interposes, should serve but as incitements to the attainment of the end. This Society, Fellow Citizens, can not but approve your firmness:— it rejoices, that you are not to be intimidated from the prosecution of a constitutional privilege, by the empty tho' noisy declamations of pretended Patriotism, nor the prescriptions of Aristocracy, under the masque of Federalism.—Let us *coalesce* in our endeavours against usurpation:—let perseverance be our common motto,—public good our bond of union,—equality our guide,—and liberty our banner, and we will strike opposition dumb, obtain an ample recompence for our labours, and transmit as far as our efforts can avail, an inheritance that will gladden the hearts of posterity.

The Resolutions which you forwarded to us, Fellow Citizens, have our hearty and unanimous approbation—They speak our sentiments;—they breathe our feelings.—That they might assist in declaring the public will, we have directed them to be published, with our Resolution of concurrence annexed to them—We trust this proceeding will meet your approbation.

Inclosed, are some Resolutions, which this Society, passed some time ago; our Circular letter to our brethern in the Country; and a copy of our Principles and Constitution.

Ordered, that the said Reply be transcribed, signed by the President, and attested by the Acting Secretary; and that the same, together with the several in-closures therein mentioned, be by the Secretary delivered to the President of the German Republican Society. . . .

The Address to the National Convention of the French Republic, reported at the last Meeting and postponed till the present, was

Adjourned to Thursday, the 20th inst. . . .

Thursday, March 27th 1794.

The Society met, pursuant to adjournment.

Citizen Israel, one of the Vice-Presidents, in the Chair. . . .

The following communications from certain popular Societies within the Union, were read, & Ordered to lie on the Table, to wit:

A letter, dated the 12th March 1794, from the President of the Republican Society of Charleston, inclosing sundry Resolves of that Society, and inviting a free communication of sentiments and information.

A letter, dated the 11th March 1794, from the President of the Democratic Society of New York, inclosing a copy of the Constitution, & a Resolution appointing a Corresponding Committee, and cordially inviting the friendly correspondence of the Society.———and

A letter dated the 22^d of Feby 1794, from the Corresponding Committee of the Democratic Society of Pinckney district in the State of South Carolina, inclosing a copy of the Constitution and Rules of that Society, and soliciting, among other things, to cultivate a correspondence through the medium of our corresponding Committee. . . .

On Motion, Resolved,

That the appellation, "Citizen", shall, exclusively of all titles, be used in the correspondences of this Society; that the usual formula at the bottom of letters shall be suppressed; and that all letters shall be dated from the Era of American Independence.

The Society now took into consideration the several communications from the popular societies of Charleston, Pinckney District and New-York; and, thereupon,

RESOLVED,

That this Society fully concurs in the sentiments expressed in the several Communications received from the popular Societies of Charleston, New-York and Pinckney district; and will heartily join and fraternize with them in every measure, that may tend to the advancement and support of Republican principles.

RESOLVED,

That the said Communications, together with this Resolution be published; and that the Committee of Correspondence be directed to forward the same, with their answers to the said Communications. On Motion,

RESOLVED, That a Committee be appointed to report a Set of Resolutions, expressive of the sense of the Society, on the present crisis of our National affairs:—

The Members appointed are, Citizens Bache, DuPonceau and Michael Leib. Adjourned. . . .

Thursday, April 10th 1794.

The Society met, pursuant to Adjournment,

The President in the Chair. . . .

It was moved, seconded and carried, That the Resolutions adopted at the last meeting, on the present state of our National affairs, be re-considered for the purpose of amending the same: whereupon,

By Order, the said Resolutions were read—

By special order, the said Resolutions were read, by paragraphs; and, after considerable debate, and several alterations and amendments, the same were adopted as follows:

At a time, when, notwithstanding the aggravated insults and injuries inflicted by Great Britain on our defenseless trade, our Representatives appear but half-rouzed to a sense of our distresses and the danger which menaces our Independence, and have shewn little of that energy and decision which the present crisis calls for; *The Democratic Society,* sensible of the importance of an expression of the public sentiments, at such a juncture, have agreed to communicate to their Fellow-Citizens, their feelings and opinions on the following *Resolves:*—They are the more encouraged to this from the attention bestowed on their former Resolutions, by their Fellow-Citizens in different parts of the Union; which, tho' reprobated at the time, by certain characters in this Country, as exaggerated and inflammatory, events have proved to have been consonant with political calculation and correct observation.

1. *Resolved,* as the opinion of this Society, That unequivocal evidence is now obtained of the liberticide intention of Great Britain, she having declared it thro' one of her satellites even to Savages;[29] that the successes of Freedom against Tyranny, the triumphs of our magnanimous French brethern over slaves, have been the means of once more guaranteeing the Independence of this Country; that their glorious example ought to animate us to every exertion to raise our prostrate character, and every tie of gratitude and interest should lead us to cement our connection with that great Republic.

2. *Resolved,* as the opinion of this Society, That the Proclamation of Neutrality by our Executive,[30] tho' we have every reason to believe it the offspring of the best motives, is not only a questionable constitutional act, but has eventually proved impolitic; and, being falsely construed by Great Britain as a manifestation of a pusilanimous disposition on our part, serves to explain the aggressions of

that nation; and that experience urges us now to abandon a line of conduct, which has only fed the pride and provoked the insults of our unprincipled and implacable enemy, it being derogatory to the honor, inconsonant with the interest, and hostile to the Liberties of our Country.

3. *Resolved,* as the opinion of this Society, That every infringement which a Neutral Nation tamely suffers upon her rights, inflicts a correspondent injury on the nation at war with the offending power; and that every aggression of Britain on our trade, which instead of being resented has even found advocates among us, has been a just subject of complaint against us by France,—especially as her West-India colonies need the supplies which were filched from us by the rapacity and piracies of Great Britain.

4. *Resolved,* as the opinion of this Society, That Great Britain has been waging war upon us in the most insidious and cowardly manner, and has wounded us in the only part enmity could make her utmost power felt.—Insidious, in as much as her orders to seize and condemn our property floating on the high seas, under the sanction of the Law of Nations, were transmitted directly and expeditiously to her commissioned pirates, and at the same time carefully kept out of those channels of information, by which we could have received intelligence of their unwarrantable intentions;—insidious inasmuch as they were so worded as to conceal their intentions by a studied ambiguity, which should give their friends among us an opportunity, by disputing their import, to keep the public mind the longer in suspence; but at the same time so accompanied to their islands, that their marauding colonies should not mistake their meaning:—Cowardly inasmuch as their wanton depredations have been exercised on property protected only by the Laws of Nations, feeble barriers when opposed to their lawless usurpations, and at a time when our Government was lulled into security by false assurances of friendship.

5. *Resolved,* as the opinion of this Society, That the farther instructions of Great Britain on the 8th of January,[31] while they still manifest a disposition to make the mandates of that court a law to us and the world, are only a temporary relaxation of their system of tyranny, dictated by fear in consequence of the successes of our brave Allies the French; and that the instructions, which exhibit strong evidence of their weakness and their fears, should teach us, that terror is the only logic which can be used to keep Great Britain within the bounds of justice and humanity, and within the limits of reason and of law; and that the present is the most auspicious moment to narrow the circle of her arrogance and presumption.

6. *Resolved,* as the opinion of this Society, That as the general system premeditated and pursued against the United States by Great Britain, beggars every outrage heretofore practised by nations pretending to civilization and the government of Laws, we ought to have recourse to any and every mode of indemnification within our power; that the moment of national embarrassment and decline is the most opportune to demand a fulfilment of national engagements; and

that, this being the present state of Great Britain, it would be a dereliction of the means, which Providence has put in our hands, not to avail ourselves of the present crisis to insist on a surrender of the western posts, and a full indemnification for all the injured which the United States have sustained from her; and that a firm, manly and dignified conduct in the present posture of affairs, will have a tendency to preserve the blessings of peace; while on the contrary, a continuance in a temporizing and pusilanimous conduct will bring contempt, disgrace, and perhaps chains upon us.

7. *Resolved,* as the opinion of this Society, That wisdom teaches, and our own experience has evinced, that to suffer an insult without resenting it is to encourage further injury: that if the voice of a class of men among us, was listened to, we might be stripped of every right with a view to nurse an artificial interest, distinct from that of the great body of the people; and that the whole of the credit which the resources of this country may command, is not to be put in competition with the least of our rights as a free and independent Nation.

8. *Resolved,* as the opinion of this Society, that the progress of British influence in the United States has endangered our happiness and Independence, that it has operated to make us tributary to Great Britain, and to endgender systems and corruptions baneful to Liberty.

9. *Resolved,* That we rejoice with our Republican Allies in their late glorious successes,[32] feel our hearts expand with pleasure at the certain prospect of the downfall of despotism; and that we entertain the most flattering anticipation, that the Sister Republic of America and France will have an inseparable relation and attachment—that they will ever be the temple of Liberty, the residence of the Arts, Sciences, Liberality and Humanity, and Hercules in the extermination of every monster of unlawful domination.

Three several Resolutions were now proposed to be added to, and to be held & taken as a part of the aforesaid Resolutions,—which were read, considered and adopted as follows.

1. *Resolved,* That this Society considering and believing that the general welfare of our country is involved in promoting necessary manufactures as far as is consistent with our situation in giving full employment and comfortable support to all our Citizens; it is expected that the members of the Democratic Society will have sufficient patriotism, to prefer and make use of the manufactures of their own Country; confident, that, by creating a demand for them we shall afford them that substantial encouragement and support particularly necessary at this time,

2. *Resolved,* That it be recommended to friends of Democracy throughout the United States, to take immediate measures for introducing the use of American, and excluding the use of British manufactures.

3. *Resolved,* as the opinion of this Society. That the language used by Lord Grenville, the English Minister, to Mr. Pinckney,[33] in asserting, that some evil-disposed person in the United States endeavored to excite disaffection to the

Government, is of a piece with the insolence of the British Ministry, at the same time that it conveys the highest compliment of patriotism, to those Citizens against who it is directed; that disaffection to the Government in the sense intended by him, is affection to our own country, a disposition to resist the outrages of that piratical nation, and maintain that sovereignty which flows from a Revolution in which we triumphed over Great Britain;—that his language insinuates a discordance between our Government and the People, highly derogatory to our administration, as it conveys the idea that the people were sensible of the oppressive conduct and wished to resist it, but that the government was disposed to remain passive under every circumstance of injury and dishonor.

On Motion, Ordered,

That all the Resolutions adopted this evening be transcribed signed and published; and that it be the duty of Citizens Bache, DuPonceau & Leib, the Committee appointed on the 27th ult^O., to arrange the same for, and superintend the publication. . . .

Adjou^d to the 17th inst.

make report to the next meeting. . . .[34]

April 17th 1794.

Certain Resolutions, on the subject of holding a Civic Feast, were presented to the Chair and read:

By special order, The said Resolutions were read, by paragraphs, and, being altered and amended, were adopted as follows:

RESOLVED, That this Society will partake of a Civic Feast to be hold in honor of the victories obtained by the Democrats of France, over the horde of Royalists and Aristocrats associated for the express purpose of expelling the Rights of Man from the world:—that seven Citizens be appointed to fix the time and place, to receive subscriptions, and to provide whatever may be necessary;—that all the Democrats in the City and neighbourhood be invited to join in the festival,[35] that each person set his name to a subscription list, and thereupon pay one dollar;—that three citizens be appointed to select proper Sentiments to be given on the occasion;—and that, if the fund be sufficient, Artillery be provided.

RESOLVED, That the German Republican Society be solicited to join us in the foregoing measure, and appoint Committees to concur in the management.

On Motion,

ORDERED, That Citizens Porter, Barker, Israel, Kerr, Smith, Ferguson and Groves be the Committee, [so] mentioned [on the] above Resolution, and

That Citizens Dallas, Leib and DuPonceau be the last mentioned Committee, for the purpose of selecting Toasts and Sentiments proper for the occasion.

The Society now adjourned to Thursday the 8th day of May next.

Thursday, May the 8th 1794.

The Society met, pursuant to Adjournment.

The President and Vice-President being absent, Cit[n]. John Smith was appointed Chairman pro tempore.

Agreeably to the order prescribed, the Minutes of the preceding Meeting were read.

Citizen Charles Kinney, who had been previously elected, subscribed the Constitution, paid to the Treasurer 50 cents, and took his seat as a Member.

The Secretary laid before the Society a letter from Citn Hay of New-York, inclosing a letter from the Chittenden Democratic Society through their Corresponding Committee, a Copy of their constitution and of the principles on which it is founded, together with several documents accompanying the same; and inviting a free communication of any intelligence that may be deemed essential to promote the mutual intention of the sister societies.

On Motion, the Society proceeded to the reading of the several papers mentioned above; and, after some time spend therein, the same was postponed, for the purpose of entering upon some more pressing business.

Cit[n] Leib, from the Corresponding Committee, reported an answer to the Communications from the Democratic Society of Washington county which was read and approved, as follows:

Fellow Citizens!

We rejoice that you have been awakened to the necessity of establishing an Institution, which shall add another organ to speak, and another power to protect the rights of the Freemen of America. To expatiate upon the benefits of Democratic Societies, will be but to burthen you with remarks which must have been already suggested by your own reflection & observation: we shall confine ourselves, therefore, to the immediate matter of the letter that you favoured us with.—As far as our efforts can second your just claims, you may be assured they shall be employed; and as far as any communications or information from us, can aid the cause in which we are jointly embarked, you may be persuaded, that neither zeal, nor industry shall be wanting.—Lest you should not have seen the principles and constitution of our Society, we take the liberty to enclose them:—They will express to you the leading characters, by which our proceedings are governed.—We shall make no apology for inclosing likewise, some Resolutions which this Society passed on the present state of public affairs.

It will scarcely be necessary, we hope, to assure you, of our good wishes for the prosperity of your institution, and of our inclination to engage in a free correspondence with you.

Philada 28th April 1794, the)   We are, your Fellow-citizens,
18th year of American   )   M. Leib, B. F. Bache, A. J. Dallas
Independence.   )   Corresp. Comm.

the final adoption of the System of Excise now contemplated by Congress.[36]

Ordered, That the said Resolutions be signed by the President and Secretary, or, should that be impracticable, by the Chairman and Secretary, and published without delay.

Adjourned to the 15th instant.

Thursday, May 29th 1794.

The Society met, pursuant to adjournment.

The President, Vice-Presidents and Secretaries being absent, Citn George Logan was called to the Chair, and Citn Benjamin Franklin Bache chosen Secretary protem. . . .

Citn. Leib, from the Corresponding Committee, reported a Copy of a Circular Letter to certain Societies established upon Democratic principles, inviting an union of efforts, for guarding and preserving the rights of Americans; which was read and approved in the words following, to wit—

Fellow Citizens!

The importance and solemnity of the present Crisis of our affairs ought to command our attention, and cement the Democratic interest of the United States. At all times ought the people to have a Solicitude in public affairs, but at no moment ought this Solicitude be manifest itself so much, as when the general interest of our Country seems to be made to bend to private considerations, and the principles of Freedom to be construed to serve the purposes of individual ambition. An influence dangerous to the Freedom of this Country, appeared to be gaining ground among us; to resist it was the object of our association, and to stifle it ought to be the most zealous endeavour of every well-wisher to the cause of Liberty. As individual resistance would, perhaps, be unequal to counteract the combination against the people, we earnestly invite you to join your efforts with ours in the preservation of those rights, for which Americans fought, bled and died.

We enclose the principles and Constitution under which we are associated, and shall take a pleasure in receiving yours and a free communication of sentiments from you.

Pha. May 20, 1794, 18th year of Am. Indep.—Geo. Logan   )
Benj. F. Bache) Corr. Com.
Michl. Leib

The same Citizens also reported another Circular Letter addressed to all the Democratic Societies in the Union, offering, for their concurrence & the Resolutions of this Society protesting against the appointment of John Jay, as Envoy Extraordinary to Great Britain; which letter was read and approved in the words following; to wit:

Fellow Citizens!

The importance of the subject of the enclosed Resolutions, has induced us to offer them to your consideration and attention.—To us, the subject appeared of so serious a nature, so injurious a principle, so dangerous in its consequences, that to pass it by in silence was to forfeit the character of the Society, and to abandon the motive which associated us.

Political evils are more easily, and certainly more safely prevented than cured: it behoves us, therefore, to guard our constitution with the most jealous care, and to protest against every encroachment upon it, that the evils of Despotism or a Revolution may be alike prevented. If, while our feelings are still warm with the contest against British usurpation, we tamely submit to have the citadel of our liberties undermined, we may soon expect, as the Revolutionary enthusiasm is fast on its decline, to submit to its explosion, with all the sang froid of men who had never tasted Freedom.

Shall We, Fellow Citizens, who have professed to be centinels on our Constitution and our Laws;—Shall we who have felt, and who know how to estimate the blessings of liberty:—Shall those who have assisted in that Revolution, the prize of which was to be free:—Shall they submit in silence to an usurpation, which attacks the essence of their rights and their security, and exposes them to all the calamities attendant upon the will of an individual?

Gratitude is a virtue when it does not operate to our own destruction; and, to let it smother wrongs, great as the one of which we complain, is a weakness unworthy of Freemen. If the weight of influence is already so great as to stifle the voice of our Representatives, it is high time to sound the alarm; and, we trust, there is yet virtue and independence enough in the American people, to rouse at the signal of danger, and to convince their Agents, that they have contended for Freedom against British Tyrants, and that it shall not be wrested from them by any power or influence upon earth.

If the Sentiments expressed in the inclosed Resolutions should meet your approbation, an evidence of your concurrence will add much to their weight, and a publication of them on your part increase their effect.

Philadelphia	)	Geo. Logan	)	
May 20th 1794,	)	Benjn. F. Bache	)	Correspond.
the 18th Year of American	)	Ml. Leib	)	Committee.
Independence.	)			

The same Citizen reported a draft of an Address to the Citizens of the United States, exhorting the adoption of Societies upon democratic principles at which was read—and

Ordered to lie on the Table.

The Report of the Committee of arrangement, considered in part by paragraphs on the 15th inst., and then postponed, was now taken up for further consideration.

It was moved, seconded and agreed, to reconsider a part of that report; which, being accordingly done, the report, with its several alterations and amendments, was adopted as follows:

The Committee, appointed to digest and arrange the unfinished business of the Society, submit the following Report.

That on sufficient proof being given to the Society, that any member has avowed or supported principles inimical to this Institution, or that he has been guilty of infamous conduct, he shall be expelled: But the person accused shall be notified of the accusation, before a decision be had thereon; and, if he requires, shall also be heard in his defence.

That on the Stated Meetings of January, April, July and October, each Member shall pay twenty-five cents to the Treasurer, towards a fund to defray the expences of the Society.

That every officer of the Society, who shall neglect to attend its Meetings for three months successively, shall be considered as having vacated his Office, and that another be immediately elected in his room, unless his attendance is prevented by sickness, or absence from the City and County of Philadelphia.

That every person who shall be elected a Member, and shall neglect to attend to sign the Constitution for three stated Meetings after his election; and that every person already elected who shall not have signed the Constitution three stated meetings after the adoption of this regulation; shall be considered as having relinquished his right of Membership; provided, that if any member elect shall either by letter, or by proxy, assign a satisfactory reason for his not attending to sign the Constitution; such reason shall be admitted in excuse, & entered on the Minutes of the Society.

That when any Committee has been appointed to prepare Resolutions for publication, they shall acquaint the Secretary as soon as they shall be ready to report; and it shall be his duty to give notice to the members that business of importance will be transacted[37] . . . meeting of the Society:—And no final decision shall take place on such Resolutions on the same evening on which they shall be introduced.

That no person shall become a Member of this Society who is not a Citizen of the United States; unless such person shall be approved by a Committee to whom the previous nomination be submitted.

That every Citizen of the United States, who is a member of any Society, founded upon similar principles with this within the States, shall be at liberty, on producing a Certificate of membehip, or being introduced by a member, to attend the Meetings of this Society; but shall not have the right to vote or take a part in the private business.

On Motion,

The other part of the Report of the Committee of Arrangement, being considered as a separate business, was ordered to be deferred for further consideration. . . .

Adjourned.

Thursday, June the 5th 1794.

The Society met at the German Lutheran Schoolhouse, pursuant to a public notification for that purpose.

The President, and Vice-Presidents being absent, Cit[n] Harlie was chosen Chairman pro tem. . . .

Cit[n] Leib presented a communication from the German Republican Society, in which they express their concurrence in the Resolutions of this Society protesting against the appointment of John Jay as Envoy Extraordinary to the Court of Great Britain, etc.[38]: which communication was read, and ordered to be recorded in the words following, to wit:[39]

Cit[n] Bache presented a Communication from the Republican Society of Newark, inclosing a copy of their principles and Constitution, and inviting a friendly correspondence and free communication of sentiments. And the said papers, being read, it was ordered,

That they be preserved among the records of the Society.

The Society now resumed the consideration of the Address to the Citizens of the United States respecting the adoption of Democratic Societies; and the same having been read, by periods, and amended, was unanimously adopted in the words following, to wit:

Fellow Citizens!

At this eventful period, when liberty and despotism seem in an equipoize in the balance of Fate, at a crisis, when a world is warring against the Rights of Man in a single community, and the peaceful Temple of Freedom is threatened in this Western hemisphere;—at a time when patriotism seems to be absorbed by ambition in the breasts of many among us, and there is cause to apprehend that the fruits of the late Revolution may be fatally converted to partial and not general good; . . . do The Democratic Society of Pennsylvania raise their voice to councel their brethern, the citizens of the United States. Strongly impressed with the belief, that it is much more easy to obtain freedom than to preserve it; as many nations have been, but few now are free, and as an uniform energy is necessary to the former, while a temporary struggle will produce the latter; they solicit the constant attention of their Fellow Citizens to their rights. In the enthusiasm of a Revolution every patriotic mind sympathizes in the general cause, and is alive to its Objects; but, in the calm which peace affords, attention to private concerns too often supersedes the interest in the general weal. This is a crisis when a common cause is buried in individual considerations, and the interest which belongs alike to all can find but few to support it; and it is in this state of things that ambition meditates and successfully executes its plans against liberty. As an awful stillness generally precedes a convulsion of the earth which carries ruin in its bosom; so does the lethargic calm of a republic presage convulsion & destruction to its frame. This state, Fellow Citizens, appeared to be advancing rapidly upon us; when the French Revolution gave a new impulse to America, and the American Citizens felt a new warmth reflected from the freemen of France. To cherish this feeling for our rights—to guard it against a dangerous slumber,—should be the wish and ought to command the exertion of every zealous friend to his Country. Associations of citizens for political purposes, keep attention alive; and in case of Governmental misconduct they may act with effect.—How desireable, then, that Societies, whose objects involve every thing dear to freemen, should be called into being in every quarter of our country! How desireable, then, that by means of them a preventive should be applied to anything which might rise up in hostility to our liberties; that by means of them a corrective should be applied to measures at enmity with our Constitution; and that they may prove an efficacious instrument to secure & perpetuate the glorious inheritance of the late Revolution! We invite you, Fellow-Citizens, to this duty:—we invite you to fraternize with us in a common cause; and give your aid, that the principles of a free Government may be handed down incorrupt to posterity.

If any incentive could be wanting to so important, so interesting a duty, the solicitude evidenced by certain characters among us, to bring political Societies into contempt, would give every requisite incitement; for, whatever calumny could invent, and sophistry devise have been played off against such institutions. They have been charged with a desire to dictate, nay to supersede Government; but how does this charge apply? Does an association of citizens to guard against encroachments upon their constitution, or be remonstrate against unjust measures, or to declare their sentiments on the state of their country, imply a desire to dictate or govern? Should this be true, every citizen who speaks or publishes his opinions, may be characterised as dictator or an usurper; and the right, guaranteed by the principles of freedom and our Constitution, dwindle into a charge of Treason against our Country! Are you aware, Fellow Citizens, of the implication and extent of this accusation. It tends to rob us of one of the most essential rights of Freemen, that of declaring our sentiments: for if a number, and a large one too, are not privileged to offer their opinions, who will be daring enough to say that an individual has this licence?

Has our Government become so sacred, that it shall be above enquiry? Has our administration the divine characteristic of kings—inviolability? Whence, then, the accusation against Democratic Societies?—The friend of liberty fears them not;—they are only dreadful to its foes.

That Government must be unfit for Freemen, which cannot bear investigation; and that administration must be corrupt, which hides itself in darkness. Truth fears not the light—it seeks not concealment—the strictest scrutiny but serves to make it the more regarded:—Surely the enquiry cannot injure a good Government, or a virtuous administration; for, like gold from the furnace, they must come out more pure after the ordeal. Falsehood only seeks the night; and it is Falsehood, which Democratic Societies wish to place upon the rack. Falsehood is their enemy, and seeks their destruction; but Truth is omnipotent— it must & will prevail.[40]

We invite you again, Fellow Citizens, to fraternize with us in the cause of liberty—to associate yourselves in political societies; for union and watchfulness will give us happiness and security; while division & supiness will hurry us into the arms of Tyranny. Let it not be said, that Americans had energy to contend for Freedom; but that they wanted firmness to preserve it; that they saw danger in British despotism; but that domestic domination carried no cause for alarm.— Let it be impressed upon your minds, as a truth, which past ages, and the experience of our own age will sanction, that vigilance is the best security, for the preservation of the Rights of Man.

Ordered, That the said Address be signed by the President, or one of the Vice Presidents, and attested by the Secretary, and published without delay. . . .

Adjourned to the 12th instant.

Thursday, June 12th 1794.

The Society met at the German Lutheran Schoolhouse, pursuant to adjournment.

The President in the Chair. . . .

Cit. Bache, from the Corresponding Committee, reported a copy of an answer sent by them to the Democratic Society of New York; which was read and approved in the words following, to wit—

Philada 1794 year
of American Independence.

Fellow Citizens!

We acknowledge, with pleasure, your communication of the 13th ult°:

Firmly impressed with the sentiment, that it is not enough for the people to have framed a Constitution on the Principles of Liberty and Equal Rights, and to have appointed their public servants with an eye to integrity and talents only but that continued vigilance is best calculated to preserve those principles in their purity, and is the best security against the encroachments of unlawful power;— We have formed ourselves into a Society, the objects of which you will find more fully detailed in the Constitution we inclose.

The clamour raised against this and similar institutions, by a certain class of men among us, is a convincing proof of the utility of them; and the opposition endeavored to be made to their acquiring respectability, should only serve to excite the redoubled efforts of the Republicans to support them.

Their utility will be greatly enhanced by acting in a measure in concert:— We, therefore, the Corresponding Committee of the Society, invite you to a fraternal communication of sentiments and intentions; of which, on every occasion worthy of your attention, we shall give you the example.

_____) Corresponding Committee
_____) of the Democratic Society
_____) established at Philad[a].

At this important crisis, we have tho[t] the expression of the public sentiments of peculiar importance, and have entered into sundry resolutions on the subjects which now engage the public attention, which we enclose.

Ordered, that the said answer be preserved among the records of the Society....

Cit. Dallas moved a Resolution, which was agreed to, in these words:

Resolved, That a Committee be appointed to prepare and report an Address to the Citizens of the United States; representing the material transactions of the General Government; and calling upon them to deliberate and decide, at the approaching elections, how far their Representatives are entitled to public confidence, by approving the good, and dismissing the bad.

Ordered, That Cit[s] Dallas, Leib, Bache, DuPonceau and Ferguson, be the Committee for the purposes expressed in the said Resolution.

It was moved, seconded and carried, That as inconveniences have arisen from the nomination of Committees by the Society at large, the President for the time being shall exclusively be empowered to nominate individually for the approbation of the Society all persons who shall hereafter be appointed on Committees.

Cit[n] Hardie offered a Resolution for consideration, which was read and adopted as follows:

Resolved, That the Democratic Society at Philadelphia, sincerely sympathize with the sufferings of Mess[rs] Muir,[41] Margarot[42] etc., who have suffered so severely in the cause of Liberty; and that a Committee be appointed to consider whether it be practicable to relieve them:—

Ordered, That Cit[s] Hardie, Swift and Israel be the Committee for the purposes contained in the said Resolution; and that they make report upon the subject to the next Meeting....

Adj[d] to the 19th inst.

Thursday, June 19th 1794.

The Society met at the German Lutheran Schoolhouse, pursuant to adjournment.

Cit[n] Israel, one of the Vice-Presidents, in the Chair....

The Committee, appointed to report a mode of celebrating the approaching Birthday of American Independence, submit the following:

Resolved, That such members of this Society as feel disposed to celebrate the next fourth of July,[43] by partaking of a frugal repast, shall subscribe an agreement; and, at the time of subscribing, pay into the hands of the Committee of Arrangement, hereinafter mentioned, the sum of One dollar.

Resolved, That each Member, so subscribing, shall be at liberty to introduce two friends, on their paying, each, the same sum of one dollar.

Resolved, That a Committee of Arrangement of seven members, including the President and Vice Presidents, be appointed, to make the necessary preparations, draw up a list of Toasts, fix upon the place and hour of meeting, give due notice thereof, and preside at the Feast.

On Motion, Ordered,

That Cit[s] Hugh Ferguson, Leib, Bache and Porter be the Committee above mentioned. . . .

Adj[d] to the 26th inst.

Thursday, June 26th 1794.

The Society met at the German Lutheran Schoolhouse, pursuant to adjournment.

The President in the Chair. . . .

Cit[n] Leib from the Committee appointed respecting the celebration of the 4th day of July next, reported, that it is impracticable to carry the Resolutions on the subject into the effect for the small price of admission therein specied—and

On Motion, the said Resolutions being re-considered,

It was agreed, That one dollar, the sum limited for the subscription of each person, be struck out, and the word two dollars inserted instead thereof.

On Motion,

Resolved, That the Committee appointed to arrange the said Festival, be directed to invite, in the name and on behalf of this Society; the German Republican Society, and the French Society of Friends to Liberty and Equality in Philadelphia, to unite with us in the public celebration of the day which gave America Liberty and Independence.

The Society took into consideration the various reports respecting the official conduct of the Executive of the Union and the Executive of Pennsylvania, relatively to a proposed establishment at Presqu'-isle-and

On Motion,

Resolved, That a Committee of three Citizens be appointed, in order to enquire into the causes of the suspension of an Act of this State for laying out a Town and Military Post at Presqu'-isle:[44]

Ordered, That Citizens Smith, Bache & Leib be the Committee for the purposes contained in the said Resolution; and that they make report to the next meeting.

The Committee appointed to enquire whether it be practicable to relieve the sufferings of Mess[rs] Muir Margarot etc., informed the Society that they are not yet prepared to report—and further time was granted. . . .

Adj[d] to the Stated Meeting

Thursday, July 3rd 1794

The Society met, in Stated Meeting, at the College (or University) in Fourth Street, pursuant to a public notification for that purpose. . . .

The President and Vice-Presidents being absent, Cit^n Bache was chosen chairman pro tempore. . . .

A letter, addressed to Blair McClenachan the Pres^t, from the Board of Trustees of the College, was read, granting the use of the southeast room on the lower floor, for this Society to hold its meetings at all times when the same is not occupied for the business of the Seminary. . . .

Adj^d to the next Stated Meeting.

Thursday, July 31st 1794.

The Society met in Special Meeting, at the University, pursuant to a public notification for that purpose.

Cit^n Israel, one of the Vice-Presidents, in the Chair. . . .

Cit^n Smith, from the Committee, appointed to enquire into the causes of the suspension of the Presqu'-isle establishment, made report upon the subject; which, being read and considered,

Resolved, That the Society will take no order upon the said Report.

Cit^n Leib presented to the Chair a Communication from the Republican Society of Baltimore, inclosing a copy of their Constitution; which was read—

Ordered That the same be preserved among the Records of the Society.

Cit^n Leib offered a set of Resolutions against such opposition to the Excise or any other law of the land, as is not warranted by the Constitution of the U.S.:—; which, on motion, were read: But, it appearing that, according to a Rule of Order, the said Resolutions could not be acted upon, till after the nominations for membership, it was

Resolved, That the Society will despense with the Rule, for the purpose of taking up the said Resolutions for a special reading—whereupon, by Order, the said Resolutions were read and considered by paragraphs, and almost unanimously adopted in the words following:

Resolved, as the opinion of this Society, that in a Democracy, a majority ought in all cases to govern; and that where a Constitution exists, which emanated from the People, the remedies pointed out by it against unjust and oppressive laws and bad measures, ought to be resorted to; and that every other appeal but to the Constitution itself, except in cases of extremity, is improper & dangerous.

Resolved, as the opinion of this Society, that altho' we conceive Excise systems to be oppressive, hostile to the liberties of this Country, and a nursery of vice and sycophancy; we, notwithstanding, highly disapprove of every opposition to them, not warranted by that frame of Government, which has received the sanction of the People of the United States.[45]

Resolved, that we will use our utmost efforts to effect a repeal of the Excise-laws by Constitutional means; that we will, at all times, make legal opposition to every measure which shall endanger the freedom of our Country;—but that we will bear testimony against every unconstitutional attempt to prevent the execution of any law sanctioned by the majority of the people.

On Motion.

Resolved, That the said Resolutions be published as soon as conveniently may be[46]—

Ordered, That they be signed in the manner heretofore pointed out. . . .

Adj[d] to the Stated Meeting

Thursday, August 7, 1794.

The Society met at Stated Meeting at the University.

The President in the Chair. . . .

A Committee from the French Society of Friends to Liberty and Equality, being admitted, presented to the chair a letter addressed to the President and Members of the Democratic Society; inviting them to join a public festival to be held on Monday next, in commemoration of the 10th of August, that glorious Epoch of French Liberty:[47]—Whereupon,

On Motion,

Ordered, That the President return the thanks of this Society to their French brethern, with an assurance that every attention shall be paid to so polite & friendly an invitation—Which was done accordingly—and

The Committee aforesaid withdrew.

The Committee appointed to translate into our language the Communication from the French Society of Friends to Liberty & Equality etc., produced their translation which was read—and

Ordered, That the Corresponding Committee answer the said Communication, in the same manner as others of a similar nature; and make report thereof to the next meeting.

The attention of the Society having been called to the subject of certain Resolutions entered into at the last meeting; and some disapprobation of the measure and apprehension of bad consequences, expressed by members not present when those Resolutions were adopted; a Resolution was proposed to the consideration of the Society; which was amended, and, for the sake of preserving unity and fraternity among the several Democratic Societies, was adopted in the words following, to wit:

Resolved, That a Committee be appointed to write to the Democratic Societies west of the Mountains, on the business entered into respecting the Resolutions come to last night of meeting, and that the communication, which the Committee may think proper to make, be submitted to this Society before it be sent to the westward.

Resolved, That the aforesaid Committee Consist of five persons; and that Cit^S Goodfellow, Dallas, Israel, Kerr and Porter be that Committee. . . .
Adjourned.

Thursday, Sep^{tr} 4th 1794.

The Society met in Stated Meeting at the University.

The President and Vice Presidents being absent, Cit^n Bache was chosen Chairman pro tempore.

Agreeably to the order prescribed, the Minutes of the preceding Stated Meeting were read.

But the Secretary having represented that , since the said Meeting, there had been handed to him the Minutes of a Meeting held on the 14th of August, tho' not duly notified, the Society called up the reading of those Minutes; and the same being approved as authentic, were ordered to be recorded, in the words following, to wit:

At a Meeting of the Democratic Society

August the 14th 1794

Cit^n William Coats, Vice President in the Chair.

The Secretary being absent, Cit^n John Smith was appointed Secretary pro tempore.

Citizen Israel Israel from the Committee appointed to draft a letter to the Democratic Society of Washington District, reported a draft of one which being amended was adopted as follows:

Friends and Fellow Citizens:

It is not without much anxiety that we now address you. Unacquainted with the true state of your affairs at this momentous period, we cannot express our sentiments with that promptitude and decision, which you have a right to expect from our regards to your particular interests and happiness, and our attachment to our common country.

We beg you to accept our condolence for the lives that have been already lost on the present unhappy occasion; and we sincerely hope that matters may be accomodated [sic] without the further effusion of human blood or the destruction of property.

With regard to the law which has given birth to so much general uneasiness, we have expressed our opinions so fully on a former occasion, that it is unnecessary to say much now: Indeed, fancy wants a figure, and language words, to convey our detestation of Excise-systems in this country. If examples were necessary to evince the iniquity of them we have only to turn our attention to those countries that have experienced their baneful effects. In every instance, poverty, wretchedness, slavery and corruption among the people, have been the invariable consequences. Nor can we imagine but the same causes will produce like effects in all ages and countries.

It is matter of surprize and indignation to us, that a system of taxation so oppressive should, in the very infancy of our Government have received the approbation of a majority of our Representatives. They certainly were no[t] sufficiently acquainted with the genius, situatio[n] and circumstances of their constituents. Without, however, considering the motives which led to the adoption of it; let us endeavour to apply a constitutional remedy to the evil, by obtaining a repeal of the law. In the meantime, Fellow Citizens, we earnestly reccommend [sic] prudence and moderation; with a sincere desire, that the Supreme Ruler of the Universe will so direct our affairs that this destructive Exotic may be speedily and peaceably eradicated from the American Code.

We enclose, for your information, a copy of the Resolutions, which were passed, on the 31st day of July last, in the Democratic Society, and which will naturally be interpreted to have a particular relation to the events that have recently occurred in the western counties of this State. That an occasion for passing those Resolutions should ever occur, we sincerely lament; but it was thought that the expression of our sentiments was not only necessary to manifest our impartiality and firmness, but to demonstrate that, in our opinion, the genuine principles of Democracy were perfectly compatible with the principles of social order. A considerable and respectable part of our society were averse from any declaration of our opinions at this crisis; though they approved of the abstract propositions contained in our Resolutions: but we trust that you will do justice to the purity of our motives; and that you will candidly consider that those Resolutions were passed upon general principles, and not with authentic information of your actual situation, or of the circumstances that have produced that opposition to the Government, which excites in our minds a serious apprehension for the event, and a fraternal solicitude for your safety and honor.

We shall be exceedingly happy to hear from you as soon as convenient— Accept our sincere wishes for your peace and happiness.

Ordered, That the Vice President, now presiding, sign the foregoing when transcribed by the Secretary pro tem.

Adjourned to the next Stated Meeting. . . .

Thursday, September 11th 1794.

The Society met at the University, pursuant to Adjournment:—
The President in the Chair. . . .

A letter from Cit^n James Marshel[48] was read, dated Washington the 27th August & addressed to Cit^n Coates, Vice President etc., acknowledging the receipt of the communications of this Society, respecting the late disturbances in the western counties, and giving an assurance that they should be laid before the

Democratic Society, as soon as the circumstances of that country would admit:—

Ordered, That the same be preserved among the records of the Society. . . .

Cit[n] Leib presented three Resolutions expressive of the sense of this Society of the conduct of the Executive of Pennsylvania at the present crisis & which, on Motion were read as follow:

Resolved, That this Society highly approves of the moderate prudent and republican conduct of the Governor of Pennsylvania in originating the plan of pacification with the western people; an appeal to the reason of freemen being more consonant with the principles of liberty, than the argument of immediate coercion.

Resolved, That we fully concur in the sentiment, That the strength of the State ought to be exerted, should the power of reason prove inadequate with the Western citizens; and that the manner in which the Governor has conducted himself, and the exertions which he is making for the honor of the State, the cause of republicanism, and the voice of the majority (the only legitimate authority) entitle him to the commendation of every well wisher to the cause of liberty and to his Country.

Resolved, That the intemperance of the Western Citizens, in not accepting the equitable and pacific proposals made to them by the Government augurs an enmity to the genuine principles of freedom, and that such an outrage upon order and democracy, so far from entitling them to the patronage of Democrats, will merit the proscription of every friend to equal liberty, as will exhibit a rank aristocratic feature, at [one] with every principle of just and rational government.

It was moved and seconded,

That the aforesaid Resolutions be taken up, by special order, for consideration; and when the question was put (30 members app[ear]ing on the affirmative side, and 29 on the negative) it was resolved in the affirmative and thereupon the said Resolutions were read the second time.

On Motion,

The Society now considered the said Resolutions by paragraphs:—and after an amendment the first and second were adopted. going[49] to the 3[d], an unusual warmth took place among some of the members, and the President suddenly and unexpectedly quitted his seat,[50] which threw the Society into a disorder that occasioned a suspension of the Proceedings—Whereupon, the Society called Cit[n] Bache to fill the Chair pro-tempore; and continuing the prosecution of the business before them, began to debate the 3[d] Resolution.—during this period the President and a number of members left the room for the Evening.—Afterwards the remaining members (who were 30 in number) cooly and dispassionately discussed the said 3rd Resolution; and thereupon the same was withdrawn.

It was then, On Motion,

Ordered, That the aforesaid Resolutions, as the same have been amended and agreed to, be signed by the Chairman now presiding and the Secretary, and published as soon as convenient, in the words following, to wit.

Resolved, That this Society highly approves of the moderate prudent and republican conduct of the President of the United States and the Governor of Pennsylvania in pursuing the plan of pacification with the Western People;[51] an appeal to the reason of freemen being more consonant with the principles of liberty than the argument of immediate coercion.

Resolved, That we concur in the sentiment, that the strength of the State ought to be exerted, should the power of reason prove inadequate with the Western Citizens; and that the manner in which the Governor has conducted himself, and the exertions which he is making for the honor of the State, the cause of Republicanism, and the voice of the Majority (the only legitimate authority) entitle him to the commendation of every well-wisher to the cause of liberty and to his Country. . . .

Adj[d] to the 18th ins[t]. . . .

Thursday, October 9th 1794.

The Society met at the University, pursuant to adjournment.

The President and Vice Presidents being absent, Cit[n] Purdon was appointed Chairman pro tempore. . . .

Agreeably to the order prescribed the Minutes of the preceding meeting were read.

Cit[n] Porter from the Committee appointed to draw up an address to the Patriotic Societies through the United States, made report; which was read.

On Motion, the Society went into the consideration of the same by paragraphs; which being amended was adopted as follows:

Fellow-Citizens,

Sensations of the most unpleasant kind must have been experienced by every reflecting person who is not leagued against the liberties of this Country on hearing and reading the various charges and invectives, fabricated for the destruction of the Patriotic Societies in America. So indifatigable are the aristocratical faction among us, in disseminating principles unfriendly to the rights of man—at the same time so artful as to envelop their machinations with the garb of Patriotism, that it is much feared, unless vigilence, union and firmness mark the conduct of all real friends to equal Liberty, their combinations and schemes will have their desired effect.

The enemies of Liberty and Equality have never ceased to traduce us—even certain influential and public characters have ventured to publicly condemn all political societies. When denunciations of this kind are presented to the world supported by the influence of character and great names,[52] they too frequently obtain a currency, which they are by no means entitled to either on the score of justice, propriety, or even common sense. Sometimes by a nice stroke of policy, or by a combination of some favorable circumstance, which the address of the Liberticide turns to his advantage, the imposition gains ground even with the best informed men. As the history of other countries as well as our own has taught us that this influence has too frequently given a death wound to Freedom, it is the indispensible duty of every man, who is desirous of enjoying and transmitting to posterity equal Liberty to guard against its pernicious effects.

Our society with others established upon similar principles in this and the different states were early viewed with a jealous eye by those who were hostile to the rights of man. It has ever been a favorite and important pursuit with aristocracy to stifle free enquiry, to envelop its proceedings in mystery, and as much as possible, to impede the progress of political knowledge. No wonder therefore that societies, whose objects were to cultivate a just knowledge of rational Liberty—to enquire into the public conduct of men in every department of government, and to exercise those constitutional rights which as freemen they possess, should become obnoxious to designing men. Accordingly, their shafts have been darted from many quarters. We have been accused of an intention to destroy the government. The old cry of anarchy and anti-federalism have been played off. The inconsistency of our adversaries is remarkable. At one time we were described as too insignificant to merit attention—too contemptable to be dangerous; again—so numerous and so wicked as to endanger the administration—so formidable as to be no longer tolerated.

Unfortunately, a favourable circumstance for the designs of aristocracy lately took place—we mean an insurrection in the western counties of this state. A number of people, dreading the oppressive effects of the Excise Law, were carried to pursue redress by means unwarrantable and unconstitutional. Passion instead of reason having assumed the direction of their affairs, disorder and disunion were the consequences. The executive, however, by marching an army into that country, *many of whom were members of this and* other political societies soon obliged those people to acknowledge obedience to the laws. Now to the astonishment and indignation of every good citizen, there are not wanting some in administration who are attempting to persuade the people in a belief, that the insurrection was encouraged and abetted by the wicked designs *of certain self-created societies*—that no cause of discontent with respect to the laws or administration could reasonably exist. Strange that such palpable absurdities are offered in the face of day. Is it not an indisputable fact, that the complaints of the western people, against the excise law, have sounded in the ears of Congress for some time before the existance of the present Patriotic Societies? Is it not equally true, that the general voice of America have considered their complaints as well founded? The Public opinion was ever indubitably manifested on any occasion, it was at the late election in this city, where the citizens exhibited a decided proof of their abhorrence of excise systems, even at the fountain head of aristocracy, by depriving of a longer seat in the public councils of this country, one of its supporters, and placing in his stead a man who is supposed unfriendly to that species of revenue—They indeed nobly and successfully exercised right of election, which certainly is the most proper and efficacious mode of address.

That man must have passed through life without much reflection, who does not know that in other countries as well as our own, aristocracy has ever been disposed to proclaim every real or imaginary delinquency on the part of the people, a reason for depriving them of their rights, and for strengthening the arm of government. In Europe we find, the present diabolical combination leagued against the rights of man, have endeavored to promulgate the abominable doctrine, that the swinish multitude are unequal to the task of governing themselves by reason of their deficiency in virtue and knowledge. Hence they claim a right to subjugate their fellow-creatures, and to compel them to relinquish those invaluable priveleges which they derived from the deity. Some of our temporary rulers seemed to have adopted the same righteous policy. They too are striving to propagate an opinion, that public measures ought only to be discussed by public characters. What! Shall the servants of the people who derive their political consequence from the people and who, at their pleasure may be stripped of all authority, if found to abuse it, dispute the right of their employers to discuss their public proceedings? do they imagine that all knowledge, public spirit and virtue are exclusively confined to themselves? Is it already an offence of the deepest dye to meet and consult on matters which respect our freedom and happiness? Should this be the case, our future prospects must be deplorable indeed! The Liberty of The Press, that luminary of the mind, as emphatically expressed may be next proscribed: for such is the nature of despotism, that having made some encroachments upon the liberties of the people, its rapacious jaws are constantly extended to swallow every vestige of Freedom. If we are thus, without a shadow of reason or justice to be filched of our rights—if we are not permitted to detect and expose the iniquity of public men and measures—if it be deemed a heresy to question the infallibility of the Rulers of our land, in the name of God to what purpose did we struggle thro' and maintain a seven years war against a corrupt court, unless to submit to be "hewers of wood and drawers of water" at home for surely foreign domination is not more grievous than domestic.

In this view of the subject Fellow-citizens, it may be proper to enquire, whether you are prepared to relinquish those invaluable privileges obtained at the expence of so much blood, and recognized by our constitution? Whether you are disposed to bend the knee to Baal? We trust and hope you will spurn at the idea. Let us then exercise the right of peaceably meeting for the purpose of considering public affairs—to pass strictures upon any proceedings which are not congenial with Freedom—and to propose such measures as in our opinion, may advance the general weel. Let us combat with Herculean strength the fashionable tenet of some among us, that the people have no right to be informed of the actions and proceedings of government. Nothing, surely, presents a stronger barrier against the encroachments of Tyranny, than a free public discussion—by this means the attention is roused—the sources of intelligence are multiplied and truth is developed.

Where then is the propriety of questioning this important privilege? Good Rulers will not shrink from public enquiry, because it is to their honor and advantage to encourage free disquisitions. It is to the policy only of a corrupt administration, to suppress all animadversions on their conduct, and to persecute the authors of them. If the laws of our Country are the echo of the sentiments of the people is it not of importance that those sentiments should be *generally* known? How can they be better understood than by a free discussion, publication and communication of them by means of political societies? And so long as they conduct their deliberations with prudence and moderation, they merit attention.

Among other rights secured to the people by the constitution is the right of election. This Fellow-Citizens, is certainly one of the most important. Political societies by combining the attention and exertions of the people to this great object, add much to the preservation of Liberty. Aristocracy will, as heretofore, preach up the excellency of our Constitution—its ballances and cheecks against Tyranny. Let not this however, lull us into a fatal security or divert us from the great objects of our duty. Let us keep in mind that supiness with regard to public concerns is the direct road to slavery, while vigilence and jealousy are the safeguards of Liberty.

We sincerely hope that Wisdom and harmony may attend all the deliberations in your laudable and patriotic society, and that those institutions may be the means, as we doubt not of securing and perpetuating equal Liberty to the most remote posterity.

It was, on motion.

Resolved unanimously that the address to the different Patriotic Societies be transmitted as soon as possible by the corresponding committees [in] conjunction with the committee who drew up the address, and that the same be signed by the President and attested by the acting secretary.[53]

On Motion,

Ordered, That a set of Resolutions be drafted in approbation of citizen James Monroe's patriotic and republican conduct at the court of France.[54]

And on Motion,

Ordered, That Citizens Goodfellow, Smith and Porter compose the committee for the above mentioned purposes.

Four Citizens were now proposed as candidates and entered in the nomination book, to be voted for at a subsequent meeting.

Adj. to the Stated Meeting.

Thursday Dec. 11th 1794.

The Society met pursuant to adjournment.

The President and Vice-Presidents being absent, citizen Taylor was appointed chairman pro tempore.

Agreeably to the order prescribed, the minutes of the proceeding meeting were read.

Citizen Nathaniel Prentiss who had been previously elected, subscribed the Constitution, paid the Treasurer fifty cents and took his seat accordingly

On Motion,

Resolved, as the opinion of this society that at this time when a party in the United States wish to alarm our fellow citizens and hold up to view as self-created and dangerous in a republic. That therefore it would be advisable to publish such testimonials as we have in our power.

Resolved that a committee be appointed to make such extracts for publication from our Journals as they may think necessary and report at the next meeting.

Whereupon,

Ordered That Cit^{ns} Porter, Booth, and Bailey compose that committee.

The Resolution approbating the conduct of Cit^{n} James Monroe's patriotic conduct, was read, and

On Motion,

Ordered That the same be read a second time by paragraphs, which was adopted after considerable amendments as follows, viz.

Resolved as the opinion of this Society that commendations for meritorious services is not unbecoming a free people that impressed with this sentiment we cannot avoid expressing our most cordial approbation of Cit. James Monroe the American Minister to the National Convention of France for his animated and patriotic addresses dated the 15th of August and 11th of September to that enlightened Assembly. They do indeed speak the sentiments of every genuine republican in this country; and will be echoed we have no doubt by every true friend to the rights of man.

Resolved as the opinion of this Society, that the sentiments contained in the letters of which Cit. Monroe was bearer to the National Convention of France and in his credentials meet the approbation of every friend to the honor of this country and the best interests of republicanism.

On Motion

Resolved That the said resolutions be published as soon as conveniently may be.

Ordered That they be signed by the President and attested by the acting Secretary.

On Motion

Resolved That Cit[n] Bailey be a committee for the above mentioned purposes
and also to wait on the President to obtain his signiture.

Cit[n] Caleb Hughes who had been previously nominated as prescribed by the
Constitution, was duly elected a member.

Two Citizens were now proposed as candidates, and entered in the nomination book to be voted for at a subsequent meeting.

Adj[d] to the 18th 1794.

Thursday Dec. 18th 1794.

The Society met pursuant to adjourment.

The President and Vice-Presidents being absent, Citizen Purden was appointed
chairman pro. tempore.

Agreeably to the order prescribed the minutes of the preceeding meeting were
read

The Committee appointed to draft an address to the citizens of the United
States reported, which, was read, and

On Motion,

Ordered, That the same be read [a] second time by paragraphs; which was
adopted as follows, viz.

The Democratic Society of Pennsylvania, established in Philadelphia, to their
Fellow Citizens throughout the United States.

FELLOW CITIZENS,

The principles and proceedings of our Association have lately been caluminated.
We should think ourselves unworthy to be ranked as Freemen, if awed by the
name of any man, however he may command the public gratitude for past services, we could suffer in silence so sacred a right, so important a principle, as the
freedom of opinion to be infringed, by attack on Societies which stand on that
constitutional basis.

We shall not imitate our opponents, by resorting to declamation and abuse, instead of calm reasoning, and substituting assertion for proof. They have termed
us anarchists; they have accused us of fomenting the unfortunate troubles in the
western counties of this State:—yet not a single fact have they been able to ad-
duce in support of the charge,—They have accused us of aiming at the overthrow
of the Constitution; and this also rests upon their bare assertion. Neither shall
we recriminate; though we might with at least as much plausibility assert, that
endeavours to crush the freedom of opinion and of speech, denote liberticide intentions. But We shall content ourselves with a bare examination of the question,

which has agitated the public mind; and refute the calumnies heaped on our Institution.

Freedom of thought, and a free communication of opinions by speech or through the medium of the press, are the safeguards of our Liberties. Apathy as to public concerns, too frequent even in Republics, is the reason for usurpation: but the communication or collision of sentiments, knowledge is increased, and truth prevails.

By the freedom of opinion, cannot be meant the right of thinking merely; for of this right the greatest Tyrant cannot deprive his meanest slave; but, it is freedom in the communication of sentiments, [by] speech or through the press. This liberty is an imprescriptable right, independant of any Constitution or social compact: it is as complet a right as that which any man has to the enjoyment of his life. These principles are eternal—they are recognized by our Constitution; and that nation is already enslaved that does not acknowledge their truth.

In the expression of sentiments, speech is the natural organ—the press an artificial one and though the latter, from the services it has rendered, has obtained the just appellation of Bulwark of Liberty; it would not be difficult to show that the former should be more prized because more secure from usurpation.

If freedom of opinion, in the sense we understand it, is the right of every Citizen, by what mode of reasoning can that right be denied to an assemblage of Citizens? A conviction that the exercise of this right collectively could not be questioned, led to the formation of our institution; and in the conduct the Society have held since their first establishment, they trust, no instance can be adduced in which they have overstepped the just bounds of the right, of which they claim the enjoyment.

The Society know the extent of their rights, and feel the obligation which their duty imposes. They never have, as has been weakly advanced, attempted to usurp the powers of Government; they never did attempt to substitute their wishes for law; and never expected that their opinions would have more weight than their intrinsic merit demanded. They felt themselves, as a portion of the people, bound by the acts of the legal representatives of the whole, and ready with their lives and fortunes to maintain obedience to the laws; but the observance of this duty did not deprive them of the right of questioning their policy:— they claim and will exercise all the influence which they can command, by the weapons of argument, over the minds of their fellow-citizens.

They are not unapprised of the excesses, which popular societies in a Sister Republic have been accused of: but, even admitting those accusations well-founded, from the abuse of such Institutions, it is unfair to reason against their use. Until our association leaves the field of argument, abandons the weapons of reason, and attempts violence on the constituted authorities, it must be respected for the sake of the principle on which it stands. If that principle is abused then the members become amenable to their country, and may be tried by a Jury of their fellow-Citizens.

To the scrutiny of such a tribunal, we are willing to submit: but no other department of Government has a right to limit us, in the exercise of the right for which we contend. The line between the use and abuse of the principle, must be drawn by considering the merits of each particular case; and it can be done only in a regular course of judicial proceedings—Any attempt, directly or indirectly by a Legislature, to limit the extent of the principle, is tyrannical, because it is an infringement on an imprescriptible right.

The impropriety of a Legislative interference attempted in a late instance, is still more glaring; as it there was meant to inflict a punishment by retrospection. Its absurdity was not a little heightened, by the advocates for the measure confessing that what they meant to punish was a Constitutional act. It was trivial in the extreme to pretend that "to denounce to public hatred" (and perhaps vengeance) a certain class of men was not inflicting a punishment on them. In fact the whole proceeding was so made up of contradictions and absurdities, that it was, happily, well calculated to defeat its own purposes. Indeed, any representative body, by attempting such an interference, would overstep the powers delegated to them by the people, and become, so far, a self-created Society of the most dangerous kind.

It may be asked, with some force, why certain anonymous publications containing the same sentiments which are condemned when expressed by Democratic Societies, were not denounced also?—Because the liberty of the press has been habitually held sacred; and it is known to all that a Jury are the only judges of its abuse. Republican Societies were a novel institution, and therefore deemed more open to attack:—but the good sense of the people of this Country enables them to see that the two institutions stand precisely upon the same principle; and that an attack on either is an infringement on a right second to none in a Freeman's estimation.

The late agitation on the public mind, occasioned by the Western Insurrection, has been taken advantage of, to cast an odium on popular societies, and been made the plea for their suppression. Let us examine whether this plea be well founded. This Institution is in no manner liable to the imputation. The Democratic Society of Pennsylvania, and, we believe, every similar institution, have ever held an open and manly conduct; and it is a fact, which recurrence to the publications this society have issued will warrant, that, on most subjects, it has not hazarded opinions different from those expressed by a very respectable minority at least of the House of Representatives of the United States: And is it probable, that the expression of those opinions by a contemptible junto, composed of ignorant and obscure men, as the Society is politely termed by some of its opponents, should produce an event, which is not in the most remote manner attributed to an expression of the same sentiments by a number of the Constitutional representatives of the people?

The fact is, that most of the people who, in the western counties, have been guilty of the outrage on the laws, which every good citizen must lament, are too ignorant to have been incited to those unwarrantable measures, by the circulation of the sentiments and opinions which the Democratic Societies have, from time to time, expressed on public men and measures. Their active opposition arose from feeling the burthen of the law, which till lately had been permitted to slumber, a dead letter, as far as they were concerned. Indeed, the great Luminary of the Anti-Democratic party has declared officially that the opposition of the Excise law dates from its existence; and it is well known that Democratic Societies were not thought of, till some time after the passing of that law.

But if freedom in the communication of opinion produced the event we lament, to what a deplorable situation is this Country reduced, that sentiments (in abhorrence of excise) which were supposed to have done honor to the old Congress, cannot now be uttered without causing the melancholy crisis, which we all deplore. In assigning that cause for the effect produced, is not too much assumed? is it not tantamount to a declaration, that the people in the western counties of this State are not fitted for the enjoyment of rational liberty? And in what manner is it intended to remedy the evil? Shall they be deprived of an opportunity of becoming better informed, by a free communication of thought? And shall they be made blindly to obey and bow submissive to the doctrine of passive obedience?

This Society might here rest their defence, if, indeed, they at all needed one, but they further can advance; That, far from being instrumental in fomenting the late disturbances, they early discountenanced those proceedings by a public declaration of their sentiments on the occasion, expressing in the warmest terms their abhorrence of an attempt to overturn by open violence the laws sanctioned by a constitutional majority. Neither did they stop here. Many members of this Association voluntarily stepped forward to maintain the legal authority, and joined those patriotic bands of Citizen-soldiers, who, by their readiness to take the field, have probably saved this country much bloodshed,[55] and given this important lesson to the world, that the spirit of Republicans, and their knowledge of the principles of civil liberty, give to their Government all the energy required to secure a due subordination to the laws.

Having taken this view of the subject, and exculpated themselves from the aspersions thrown on them, the Society are free to declare that they never were more strongly impressed with a sentiment of the importance of associations, on the principles which they hold, than at the present time. The germ of an odious Aristocracy is planted among us—it has taken root,—and has indeed already produced fruit worthy of the parent stock. If it be imprudent to eradicate this baneful exotic, let us at least unite in checking its growth. Let us remain firm in attachment to principles, and with a jealous eye guard our rights against the least infringement. The enlightened state of the public mind in this country, frees us, we trust, of all apprehension from bold and open usurpation; but the gradual approaches of artful ambition, are the source of great danger. Let us especially guard, with firmness, the outposts of our Liberties: and, if we wish to baffle the efforts of the enemies of freedom, whatever garb they may assume, let us be particularly watchful to preserve inviolate the freedom of opinion, assured that it is the most effectual weapon for the protection of our liberty.

Resolved, That the said Address be signed by the President and attested by the Acting Secretary: and that it be published.[56]

Resolved, That Citizens Morris and Bache be a committee to fulfil the objects of the foregoing Resolution.

Ordered, That the Secretary give public notice to the members of this Society that business of importance will be transacted at their next meeting.

Cit^{ns} Antoine Hubert and Joseph Poole, who had been previously nominated as prescribed by the Constitution, were duly elected members.

Adj^{d} to the Stated Meeting.

Civic Festival
on ye 1st of May 1794.

The Democratic Society of Pennsylvania, at their meeting in the city of Philadelphia on the 24th of April, 1794, Resolved unanimously That they would commemorate the successes of their Republican French Brethern in a Civic Festival on the first day of May 1794; and that to this Festival they would invite their Sister Society the German Republican, and all other citizens who harmonized with them in sentiment—To carry this Resolution into effect, seven Managers were appointed on the part of the Democratic Society—and three on the part of the German Republican Society—A Committee consisting of four were likewise appointed to prepare Toasts and Sentiments suited to the occasion—On the part of the Democratic Society, the following Citizens were appointed Managers, to wit, Israel, John Porter, John Barker, James Ker, John Smith, Hugh Ferguson and Michael Groves;—and on the part of the German Republican Society, Henry Kammerer, Andrew Geyer and George Forepaugh were appointed.—The Committee to prepare Toasts and Sentiments, were Alexander James Dallas and Michael Leib on behalf of the Democratic Society;—and Peter Muhlenberg on behalf of the German Republican Society.

On the first day of May, agreeably to the aforesaid Resolution of the Democratic Society, about Eight hundred citizens assembled at the Country Seat of cit^{n} Israel Israel, now called Democratic Hall, on the Passyunk Road;—among whom were the Governor of the State of Pennsylvania, the Minister[57] and other Officers and Citizens of the French Republic, and several Officers of the Federal and State Governments.[58]

The Flags of the Sister Republics marked and ornamented the seat of festivity.

At two oclock, the Company partook of a plain yet plentiful repast:—after which the following *Toasts* were drank, accompanied by universal approbation:

1. *The Republic of France;* one and indivisible:—May her triumphs multiply, until every day in the year be rendered a Festival in the Calendar of Liberty, and a Fast in the Calendar of Courts

2. *The People of The United States:*—May each revolving year encrease their detestation of every species of tyranny, and their vigilance to secure the glorious inheritance acquired by their Revolution

3. *The Alliance between the Sister Republics of the United States and France:* —May their Union be as incorporate as light and hear, and their Friendship as lasting as time.

4. *The Mountain:*[59]—May tyranny be chained at its foot, and may the light of Liberty from its summit cheer and illuminate the whole world.

5. *The Republic of Genoa.*—May every nation that values its Independance, disdain, like her, the solicitations, and resist the power, of Tyrants combined for the destruction of Freedom and Equality.

6. *The Great Family of Mankind:*—May the distinction of nation and of language, be lost in the association of Freedom and of Friendship, till the inhabitants of the various sections of the Globe shall be distinguished only by their virtues and their Talents.

7. *The Constitution of the United States:*—May its form and spirit be the invariable guide of all who administer it—May its authority never be prostituted, nor its departments illegally blended for the purposes of intrigue.

8. *The Men of the People—the Minority of the Senate and the Majority of the House of Representatives of the United States:*—May they on future as on past occasions, have wisdom to discover, and fortitude to resist, every attack upon the Constitution and rights of their Country, while they enjoy for their services the patriot's true reward, the love and confidence of their Fellow Citizens.

9. *A Revolutionary Tribunal in Great Britain*—May it give lessons of liberty to her King, examples of Justice to her Ministry, and honesty to her corrupt Legislature.

10. *The Armies of the French Republic;*—May they be invincible and unshaken, till, by their glorious efforts, Liberty and Peace exalted in the same Triumphal Car shall be drawn to the temple of Janus by the humbled Tyrants who have dared to molest them.

11. *The Extinction of Monarchy:*—May the next generation know kings only by the page of history, and wonder that such monsters were ever permitted to exist.

12. *Reason:*—May it successfully counteract the baneful effects of Executive influence, expose the insidious arts of Judicial sophistry, and preserve inviolate the purity of legislation.

13. *Knowledge:*—May every Citizen be so learned as to know his rights, and so brave as to assert them.

14. *The Fair Daughters of America & France:* May they ever possess virtue to attrack merit, and sense to reward it.

15. *The Democratic and Republican Societies of the United States:*—May they preserve and dessiminate their principles, undaunted by the frowns of powers, uncontaminated by the luxury of aristocracy, till the Rights of Man shall become the Supreme Law of every land, and their separate Fraternities be absorbed, in One Great Democratic Society, comprehending the Human Race.

Volunteers.

1. May every Free Nation consider a public debt as a public curse; and may the man who would assert a contrary opinion be considered as an enemy to his Country.

2. The unfortunate victims of British tyranny—the members of the Popular Convention of Scotland—May their fate recoil upon their persecutors; and may those who have sought an asylum in this country, find in every American a brother and a Friend.

3. The dispersed friends of Liberty throughout the world—May France be the rallying point where they may collect their scattered forces, and whence they may sally forth to the *destruction of all the tyrants of the earth.*

By the Minister of the French Republic:

May the principles of Reason be universal as they are eternal.

By the Governor of Pennsylvania.[60]

Peace, on their own terms, to the French Republic.

The Presidents and Vice Presidents of the Sister Societies presided at the Feast; the preparation for which do the greatest honor to the Managers.

After dinner the Citizens formed a double line in a lane which lead to the place of entertainment[61]

Resolutions Adopted on the Appointment of John Jay as Envoy to Great Britain, May 8, 1794

At a meeting of the Democratic Society of Pennsylvania, held at Philadelphia, on the 8th day of May in the year 1794, and of American Independence the Eighteenth:—[62]

RESOLVED, as the opinion of this society, that the constitution of the United States, that sacred instrument of our freedom which every public officer has sworn to preserve inviolate, has provided, that the different departments of the government should be kept distinct; and consequently that to unite them is a violation of it, and an encroachment upon the liberties of the people guaranteed by the instrument.

Resolved, as the opinion of this society, that, as by the constitution all treaties are declared to be the supreme law of the land, it becomes the duty of the judiciary to expound and apply them; to permit, therefore, an officer in that department to share in their formation is to unite distinct functions and tends to level the barriers of our freedom, and to establish precedents pregnant with danger.

Resolved, as the opinion of this society, that justice requires, and the security of the citizens of the United States claims an independence in the judiciary power; that permitting the executive to bestow offices of honor and profit upon judges, is to make them subordinate to that authority, is to make them its creatures, rather than the unprejudiced and inflexible guardians of the constitution and the laws.

Resolved, as the opinion of this society, that from the nature and terms of an impeachment against a President, it is not only necessary that the chief justice of the United States should preside in the Senate, but that he should be above the bias which the honors and emoluments in the gift of the executive might create; that it is, therefore, contrary to the intent and spirit of the constitution to give him a foreign mission, or to annex any office to that which he already holds.

Resolved, as the opinion of this society, that every attempt to supersede legislative functions by executive interference, is highly dangerous in the independence of the legislature, and subversion of the right of representation.

Resolved, as the opinion of this society that the appointment of John Jay, chief justice of the United States as envoy extraordinary to the court of Great Britain, is contrary to the spirit and meaning of the constitution:[63] as it unites in the same person judicial and legislative functions, tends to make him dependent upon the President, destroys the check by impeachment upon the executive, and has had a tendency to control the proceedings of the legislature, the appointment having been made at a time, when Congress were engaged in such measures as tended to secure a compliance with our just demands.

Resolved, as the opinion of this society, that after the declaration made by John Jay, that Great Britain was justifiable in her detention of the western posts,[64] it was a sacrifice of the interests and the peace of the United States to commit a negociation to him, in which the evacuation of those posts ought to form an essential part; that to abandon them is to put at stake the blood of our fellow citizens on the frontiers, is to give birth to a perpetual military establishment, and endless war, and all the oppressions resulting from excise and heavy taxation.

Resolved, That the above resolutions be made public, that they be immediately transmitted to all the democratic societies in the union, as a protest of freemen against the most unconstitutional and dangerous measure in the annals of the United States, and as an evidence, that no influence or authority whatever shall awe them into a tacit sacrifice of their sacred rights.

By order of the society,

J. Smith, Presid. protem.

Geo. Booth, Sec'ry.

General Advertiser (Philadelphia), May 10, 1794

Resolutions Adopted Opposing the Excise Tax, May 8, 1794

At a meeting of the democratic society of Pennsylvania, held at Philadelphia, on the 8th day of May in the year 1794, and of American independence the eighteenth:

———————

Resolved, As the opinion of this society, that the infant manufactories of this country, require the fostering care of government; and that those articles of domestic manufacture which are proposed, in a report to the House of Representatives of the United States, to be excised,[65] cannot bear the burthen; and that such a tax will tend to the ruin of many individuals and the impoverishing of the country.

Resolved, As the opinion of this society, that taxation by excise, has ever been justly abhorred by free men; that it is a system attendant with numerous vexations, opens the door to manifold frauds, and is most expensive in its collection; It is also highly objectionable, by the number of officers it renders necessary, ever ready to join in a firm phalanx to support government even in unwarrantable measures.

Resolved, That we cheerfully concur in the sentiments expressed by our fellow citizens at a general meeting this evening; and will join in any constitutional measures, to prevent the final adoption of the system of excise now contemplated by Congress.

By order of the society,

(signed) J. Smith President pro tem.

Geo. Booth, Sec'ry.

General Advertiser (Philadelphia), May 12, 1794,

Toasts Drunk at the Eighteenth-anniversary Celebration of American Independence, July 4, 1794

The 18th anniversary of American Liberty was celebrated by the Democratic Society, with other patriotic citizens, at Dally's hotel last Friday where, after a handsome repast, during which conviviality and mirth prevailed, the following sentiments were drank amidst the loudest applause.

1. The day; May the birth-day of our liberty be the only jubilee in the American calendar.

2. The patriotic band who broke the fetters of tyranny by the declaration of Independence; May they be honored as the apostles of liberty, who have proclaimed glad tidings to the universe.

3. The champions of liberty, the officers and soldiers of the late American army; May they ever live in the remembrance of those who enjoy the fruits of their ill-requited services.

4. The representatives of the people; May they never forget the source of their power and the end of their appointment.

5. Our allies and brethren, the Sans Culottes[66] of France; May the temple of liberty which they are erecting have the whole earth for its area, and the arch of heaven for its dome.

6. The patriots of Poland; May their oppressors be led in chains by them, and their future government be of their own choice.

7. The late victims of British tyranny: May they receive consolation in reflecting, that their sufferings accelerate the regeneration of their country.

8. Economy and simplicity: May the agents of freemen be known by their patriotism and virtue, and not by the flavor of their wines, the delicacy of their viands, or the sumptuousness of their equipages.

9. Governmental secrecy; May it be banished the land of freedom, and be hereafter known only to a conclave or a court.

10. Excise: May this baneful exotic wither in the soil of freedom.

11. Public debt; May it be considered as the Charybdis of republicanism and the Scylla of virtue.

12. The sovereignty of states; May it be guarded with the eye of jealousy, and maintained with republican firmness.

13. Agriculture; may the interests of our western brethren never be sacrificed for the aggrandisement of a mercantile junto.

14. Commerce; May the American flag form a British passport, and assert its rights under the law of nations.

15. Manufactures; May they speedily render us independent of a nation, once open, now our covert enemy.

Volunteers.

1. The Jacobin Clubs of America; May our citizens be impressed with this truth, that vigilance is the only preservative of freedom, and that implicit confidence in public servants is a stride towards slavery.

2. The army and navy of the French Republic; While they are contending in the cause of universal liberty, may the laurel of victory adorn their brows, and the cowardice of guilt confound their opponents.

3. Ruin to the combined despots; May their efforts to stifle the flame of liberty in France, serve only to kindle it in their own dominions.

American Daily Advertiser (Philadelphia), July 7, 1794

Resolutions Adopted on the Importance of Establishing Public Schools, March 19, 1795

At a meeting of the Democratic Society of Pennsylvania on Thursday, the 19th of March, 1795, the following resolutions were unanimously agreed to:

Resolved, as the opinion of this Society, That the only solid and lasting foundation of a republican government, is the affections of the people, arising from a conviction that it is calculated to promote the general happiness of its citizens, the great object of civil society.

Resolved, as the opinion of this Society, That the establishment of public schools upon proper principles, will be the best means of impressing every class of citizens in the community with a true sense of their rights, duties, and obligations; and, by diffusing a just knowledge of rational liberty, will improve, preserve, and perpetuate the blessings of independence and republicanism.

Resolved, as the opinion of this Society, That if the measure enjoined on the legislature by the constitution of the commonwealth be carried into effect in such a manner, as that the children of the poor may have equal opportunities with those of the rich, for the acquisition of political and other useful knowledge, it would greatly tend to call forth into public life such as may be the most useful to their country: and thereby bid fair to establish our liberties on the broad and firm basis of science, virtue and patriotism.

Resolved, as the opinion of this Society, That such of the members in the department of our government as have exerted or may exert their influence in promoting the important and desirable objects of a measure of this kind, will deserve well of their country, and be entitled to the warmest gratitude and support of the friends of liberty.

Published by order of the Society, March 21, 1795.

Attest, James D. Westcott, Secretary.

Israel Israel, Vice-President.

Aurora (Philadelphia), March 21, 1795

Letter from the Corresponding Committee to the Committee of Correspondence of the Democratic Society of the City of New York, March 25, 1795

CITIZENS,

There is a crisis in our affairs so mingled with circumstances flattering and inauspicious, that it demands all the attention, energy and union of the democratic interest. The attempt to prostrate the freedom of speech at the feet of government, has been happily frustrated; and the abettors of a project so daring, and so hostile in every principle of freedom, have involved themselves in the contempt prepared by them for democratic societies. The public mind sympathizes more the political associations at this moment, than at any period since their formation; and if this feeling is but properly improved, much good may be the result. Already have some of the high-toned deputies experienced the indignation of an insulted an [sic] injured people; and if the characters of others were as fully dilated, the democratic triumph would be complete.

If the avenues of information were as open to us as to those in opposition to us, the people would be made sensible of their wrongs, and be speedy in their redress: But the channels of intelligence are too generally directed by the government; and too many of the printers, instead of being the mirrors of the public sentiment, are the creatures and eulogists of administration. Were we for a moment to abstract ourselves from our local situation, and read some of the American prints, we should fancy ourselves in the meridian of London, so great is the analogy in the language, adulation, and tone between them. Every insignificant conception against democratic societies is echoed and reechoed, till it dies upon the ear; whilst any thing in their defence can scarcely find a channel to the public eye. The half-fledged ideas of "Germanicus"[67] are propagated with as much zeal as if they were our political decalogue; while the writers in favor of the freedom of enquiry cannot trace the puny heretic through his various mazes, for want of the same path. The press ought to engage the attention of our associations; and a remedy for the hardships, with respect to it, under which we labor, ought to be studiously fought for.

While we indulge in the pleasing anticipation of a change in the next Congress favorable to the genuine principles of freedom, our prospects suddenly darken by the permanent systems establishing at present. The excise, that horror of all free governments, that nursery of ministerial warriors, that tomb of liberty, is extending its roots in the vitals of our country; and, from its permanency, augurs clouds and darkness. Freedom never can be secure while this baneful spectre is permitted to haunt our land: To chase it away should be among the first objects of democratic societies.

We wish not to pass a hasty judgment upon public transactions, neither do we mean to pass sentence upon governmental measures which are not fully disclosed: but the treaty, said to have been concluded between Great-Britain and the United States, is of two [sic] high importance not to call for our attention.[68] Should our commerce, our western posts, and our national honor, be the price of a commercial treaty, we should abandon the stake we have in the government to be silent.

Although every mind interested in the welfare of our country feels a degree of agitation on this important subject, and is more or less disposed to decide from the information we have received, we will suspend any opinion until the treaty itself is before us; and if it contains principles in hostility with our interests and our rights, we trust the democratic societies will have but one sentiment on the subject.

We invite you citizens, to counsel freely with us; to unite in a common cause; and to give the aid which that common cause requires. We will receive your counsel, as fellow-citizens having but the general good in view; your union, as friends having the public happiness as our object; and your aid, as brethren having the good of the great family of our country as the end of our solicitude.

New York Journal, March 25, 1795

Notice of Dissolution, January 25, 1796

Stockbridge, January 19.

* * *

The Philadelphia *Democratic Society* has dissolved itself. As this has been considered the *Mother Club* in this country, there is reason to conclude that the various germs which have sprouted from that root of anarchy, will wither and die.

American Mercury (Hartford), January 25, 1796

TRUE REPUBLICAN SOCIETY OF PHILADELPHIA

Toasts Drunk at the Anniversary Meeting, May 7, 1800

Republican Festival.

On Friday the 3d of May, the "TRUE REPUBLICAN SOCIETY" [69] met at the Sign of Robin Hood, in Poplar-Lane, to commemorate their Anniversary—After their Election of their Officers, and ordinary business was completed, about fifty of the Members sat down to a handsome Dinner prepared for the occasion, and after Dinner they drank the following Toasts:

1. The Day [70]—may harmony, brotherhood, love, and attachment to the Rights of Man, characterize the True Republican Society—2 guns and 9 cheers.

2. The People, the Sovereign of the United States—may they never submit to be subjects or slaves—1 gun and 3 cheers.

3. The Constitution and the Laws—may they never be made a cloak for ambition, and an instrument of oppression—2 guns and 6 cheers.

4. Thomas Jefferson, the friend and favorite of the people—may the next election declare him the pilot of our political bark, that she may be conducted into the haven of peace and security [71]—3 guns and 9 cheers.

5. The Republicans of the United States—may they never be awed into surrender of their rights by the means of power, or seduced into an abolishment of them by the clamors or intrigue of the enemies of liberty.—one gun and 3 cheers.

6. The Republican cause throughout the world—may it take root in every soil, that peace, liberty, and justice may be extended to all men.—3 guns and 9 cheers.

7. *Thomas M'Kean*[72]—may the next election demonstrate, that patriotic and republican virtue are the qualifications necessary to constitute a governor of the people.—2 guns and 9 cheers.

8. The Republican Correspondence Committee—may success crown their actions, and the approbation of the people the certain and honorable reward of their patriotic endeavours.—2 guns and 6 cheers.

9. The Minority in the House of Representatives of Pennsylvania—may every lover of man's rights say to his representative, *"go and do thou likewise."*—2 guns and 6 cheers.

10. Knowledge—like the sun, may it pervade and illuminate every corner of our hemisphere.—1 gun and 3 cheers.

11. Reason—may it be substituted for prejudice, and become the only touchstone of moral and political truth.—1 gun.

12. Peace—May neither blind passion, nor inordinate ambition nor wicked and false speculations drive this first of blessings from our land.—3 guns and 6 cheers.

13. The memory of the illustrious Franklin—If Heaven permits such thing, may his spirit revisit our country, and lead us back again to the paths of political veritude.—1 gun and 3 cheers.

14. The Commonwealth of Pennsylvania—may she not change her view of virtue, liberty, and independence in asking for her governor an advocate of the British treaty.—3 guns and 9 cheers.

15. The Yeomanry of the United States—may their minds become as discerning as their hearts are honest, and they will not again become the dupe of the cry "Jefferson and war and win half a crown."—3 guns and 9 cheers.

16. Mankind, our country and ourselves.

The greatest harmony and cordiality prevailed, and the day was closed without giving birth to a single incident for uneasy reflection; for thus it always *is* with *True Republicans.*

Aurora (Philadelphia), May 6, 1799

Anniversary Meeting

At the Anniversary meeting of the True Republican Society, at Sagder's Tavern, in the Northern Liberties—the following Toasts were drunk:—

1. The day we celebrate.—3 cheers and one Gun.

2. All Societies founded upon principles of humanity and benevolence.

3. The people of the United States—Success to their exertions in the cause of truth and the rights of man.—3 Cheers and one Gun.

4. The Constitution of the United States—May the man in the faction who interprets it according to British rules, like Cain, have every honest man's hand against him.—3 Cheers and one Gun.

5. The Democrats of New-York—May their late triumph[73] invigorate and ensure success to their brethren of the United States.—3 Cheers and one Gun.

6. Thomas Jefferson—our next President, the man of the people.—6 Cheers and 3 Guns.

7. The people of Pennsylvania—May every effort in favor of the republican cause, be crowned with a success equal to that of the last election.—3 cheers and 2 Guns.

8. The minority in the Senate and House of Representatives of the United States—May their energy and firmness in resisting oppression, meet the grateful reward of an approving country.—6 Cheers and 2 Guns.

9. The memory of Benjamin Franklin Bache[74]—May his country ever retain a grateful sense of his services.

10. The friends of freedom throughout the world.

11. The Militia of Pennsylvania the natural and only safe protectors of the liberties of the Commonwealth.—6 Cheers and 2 Guns.

12. The Militia Legion of Philadelphia, and their Commandant—Having preserved the peace of our city against the lawless violence of the friends of order, may they receive the honors and the gratitude of every true lover of his country. —6 Cheers and 2 Guns.

13. Knowledge—May its rays like those of the Sun be universally diffused, and that the darkness of federal maxims may be discerned by every citizen in the community.

14. Ress & his conclave Bill—"Is there not some chosen curse, some hidden thunder, red with uncommon wrath in the stores of Heaven, to blast the man who owes his greatness to his country's ruin"—6 cheers and 3 Guns.

15. The American fair.

Aurora (Philadelphia), May 7, 1800

"An Observer" to the *Gazette of the United States*, August 5, 1800

MR. WAYNE[75]

Sir,

Actuated by motives of curioisity, I attended the meeting of Jacobins,[76] on Wednesday evening last, at the State House. Diverted at the consummate ignorance and stupidity, as well as self importance of these miserable wretches, I will endeavour to recount the various and singular transactions of this *wonderful* meeting, almost altogether composed of the very *refuse* and *filth* of society. To prove this my assertion (if proof be necessary) let it be known, that a large proportion of this meeting was men of the most infamous and abandoned characters; men who, are notorious for the seduction of *black innocence,*[77] who have more than once been convicted in open court of wilful perjury, and men who with sacriligious hands have imperious dared to tear down from the sacred desk, the emblems of mourning in honour of our beloved Washington—When persons of such character assume to themselves the order and regulation of a *government,* soon may we expect anarchy, confusion and commotion to ensue.

This meeting was opened by the *great big little* citizen of Market Street in the following style, "Fellow citizens, its most eight o'clock; an't it most time to commence the meeting, shall our worthy and Republican say—hem, Citizen B——r[78] take the chair." Aye, Aye, was the general response, whereupon from the *motley group* but pops little Johnny (Knight of the Thimble) and at his tail the lap stone boy, R. as his journeyman, Pshaw I mean his secretary. When seated, Barker loudly thumps his cudgel upon the table and with an audible voice proclaims order; "order Gent.—hem—Fellow Citizens, order, posi-ti-vely we cant *recede* to business without some order; Brother R—read the minutes of the last assemblage." Here secretary Vizze seating himself upon the table near the *Rush light* (for reader he has not very good eyes) after a great deal of coughing twisting and snuffing the candles, and a *little bit* of spelling here and there (having no doubt accustomed to the din of *Hammers*) bawled out in a most ridicullus and blundering manner the aforesaid minutes.) Cit. B——r—"The committee will report and *fetch* them on the table, and let Brother R——y read them order," (one thump of his cane) Citizen Printer "Citizen, the committee to whom was *deferred* the *composing* of candidates for the next election have reported—I mean do report the following report;

Here he handed the paper to B——r who in a half whisper asked if they had *put him in?*

The report was then read or rather spelt. It consisted of persons proposed as candidates for the Assembly, Select and Common Council.

Citizen F——n. Citizen Chairman, hem, I think citizen that the *motion* should be taken upon each of the *composed* candidates, separately, distinctly, and individually, that is, one by one.

Several. I second that there motion, I third it.

Citizen B——r. I believe that the citizen did'nt make any motion.

Several. Yes he did, I'm sarton of it. (one) yes I swear I'll *assedany* he did.

Citizen B——r. Did he, well there is so much noise here, I did'nt hear it. To secretary *Vizze;* keep your clack. Brother F——n make it agen, will you?

Citizen F——n. Citizen I was going to observe—that is I was about to observe—I say I moved—

Citizen B——r. Order, citizens, order, it is impossible.

A great noise—

Chairman what's the matter?

Citizen I——s——l. [79] Nothing only our friend Billy is a little gone.

Citizen B——r, (in a half whisper and shaking his head), Ah poor soul, I'm afraid that damn's gin will be the death of him; but come let us *reconnoitre* the business;—I think Citizen F——n was going to move—

Citizen Sambo [80]

Ah massa he be move *off* already; he go away wid broder Bully—oh here he come.

Citizen F——n. Motion—me—motion—oh—yes . . . yes . . . I was about to say. I say sir I was saying, that I thought it properest that the *motion* should be taken upon all the candidates together, that is separately, and then we'll know who's who; that is, who we like best.

Several, yes, yes, I second that, the question, the question.

Citizen B——r. As many as are in favor of agreeing to that motion will shew their assent by saying aye.

All—Aye, aye.

B——r. Those of the contra-ry opinion will show their *assent* by saying no— Here Vizze called the names of the candidates, and B——r took the question. But our hon. chairman was placed in rather an awkward situation. His name was on the list for Assembly man, and when Vizze cried out his name, he rose and said, "Fellow Citizens if you will put me in let me alone for *cutting out* business for *Aristoccats;* depend upon it; I shall be true to your dearest interests—As many of you as agree to *me*—that is I mean John *B——r.*

Citizen P——n. [81] Stop citizen, I think the secritary had better take that question.

Several. yes, yes, yes.

Vizze. As many of you here present as are intent to *collect* Mr. Col. John B——r, Esq. as your *Legislature* will be so obliging as to say no—aye I mean.

Members, Aye, aye, aye, huzza.

Vizze. Those who don't like to *collect* will say no.

One. No,—*Several.* Turn him out, turn him out.

Chairman. Order, order.

Citizen F——sher. [82] That is some damn'd spy of the aristocats—turn him out, turn out, hiccup.

Citizen B——r. As many as are agreed to citizen S——d will show their assent by saying aye.

Several. Aye, aye!

B——r. Those of the contr-ary opinion will make their *assent* know by saying no.

One. No.

Citizen P——n, suroeyn and regulator of streets &c., &c. What an't that ass done braying yet; I say hasn't that ass done braying yet.

Numbers. Throw him into the street, down with him.

P——n. Ah do and Ill take a draft of him, ha, ha, I say I'll take a draft of him, ha, ha, why you don't laugh, I say you don't laugh, ha, ha, (same), ha, ha.

Citizen F——n. Citizen Chairman, we have been grossly and *monstrously* insulted, and I move that when that fellow's found but—

Citizen F——r. I move—hic—you citizen to kick him now—hic.—

Citizen P——r. I approve of that motion, but I think we'd better stay till we find him out before we kick him, ha, ha. I say we'd better wait till we found him out, ha, ha.

Citizen F——N. I *prophet* that citizen P——n's been drinkin—hic—vinegar, he's so damn'd-hic-sharp to night, ha ha.—

The proceedings once more went on preety smoothly, till the name of Phillip O——r, one of the candidates for the Common Council was called by the Secretary. Citz. F——r then rose and said "Citizen Chairman, I hope that this citizen's name will be struck off the list—hic—My reasons for this motion are —hiccup—good, substantial and fair, cit. This man lives the same ward with our mayor—hic—Now we all know that that cursed aristocatic major of ours—hic—is an a—an aristocat—Now old Commodore Nic B——s—hic—is a deviling clever fellow, he'll—hic—always be a better pill to the aristocats—hic—I move therefore to strike out and insert B——s.

Citizen P——r. Citizen I second Brother F——r's motion with this amendment, that the question be divided. I think it properest to divide becase I think it much better to make a division.

Citizen F Oh curse your division, hic—we'd enough of it last night, we don't know how to do it, let's take it in a lump—hiccup.

Citizen B (in a pet.) P. Shaw if you cant divide, come to my school and I'll larn you.

Numbers. No, no, no division, no division.

This occasioned some desultory and very sultry debate; the question was then taken and lost.

Cit. P——N. Citizens I have had the honour of being *denominated* one of your candidates for the Assembly, but the Secreary in a *devert ney* passed over my name, and so the question hasn't been *put* upon me yet; I would fain hope it would now be taken as I want to go home, or I shall be lockt out.

Cit. F——r. That's one of R——s damned blunders, I wonder how they came to *chose* him clark.

The question was then taken and carried.

Cit. F——r. I move—hic . . . the *reading* of this here meeting be printed in the Aurora—hic—and that a suitable address be printed before it. (Carried) Several, adjourn, adjourn.

Cit. S——h. Who's to write the address.

Chairman. I am, to be sure.

S——h. No it would be properer for *some one body* else to write it because you know you are a candidate.

B——r. Well cant I write it, you fool, and not sign my name (SS——h) Oh yes)

Numbers) aye let B——r write it he knows how; he's a scollard.

Cit B——r. Citizens before we sojourn, I will remark that I know Republicans are always a pertty much *barrassed* for the rhino, but must *detrude* upon your ginerosity to night by exing you to launch out some of the *ready* for the citizen who provides for the room; I know Democrats hav'nt many *English Guineas* amongst them but I hope they have some *sipyenny bits* to might *at least,* and if they will *jist* throw them into my hat as they go along I shall be *defientially* obliged to them.*

Here I observed not a few gave an eleven penny bit and asked for a sipenny bit change, which they received. As for myself, I returned to my house as soon as possible, that I might enjoy my laugh, which be assured I did, and heartily too.

AN OBSERVER.

Citizen N—— the Jew.)[83] *I hopsh you will consider dat de monish is very scarch, and besides you know I'sh just come out by de Insholvent Law.*

Several. Oh yes let N—— pass

Gazette of the United States (Philadelphia), August 5, 1800

Benjamin Nones to the Editor of the *Aurora,* August 13, 1800

To the EDITOR.

Mr. Duane.[84]

I enclose you an article which I deemed it but justice to my character to present for insertion in the Gazette of the United States, in reply to some illiberalities which were thrown out against me in common with many respectable citizens in that paper of the 5th inst. when I presented it to Mr. Wayne, he promised me in the presence of a third person, that he would publish it. I waited until this day, when finding it had not appeared, I called on him, when he informed me that he would not publish it. I tendered him payment if he should require it. His business appears to be to asperse and shut the door against justification. I need not say more:[85]

I am &c.

B. Nones.

Philadelphia Aug. 11, 1800.

TO THE PRINTER OF THE GAZETTE OF THE UNITED STATES.

I HOPE, if you take the liberty of inserting calumnies against individuals, for the amusement of your readers, you will at least have so much regard to justice, as to permit the injured through the same channel that conveyed the slander, to appeal to the public in self defence.—I expect of you therefore, to insert this reply to your ironical reporter of the proceedings at the meeting of the republican citizens of Philadelphia, contained in your gazette of the fifth instant: so far as I am concerned in that statement.—I am no enemy Mr. Wayne to wit; nor do I think the political parties have much right to complain, if they enable the public to laugh at each others expence, provided it be managed with the same degree of ingenuity, and some attention as truth and candour. But your reporter of the proceedings at that meeting is as destitute of truth and candour, as he is of ingenuity, and I think, I can shew, that the want of prudence of this Mr. Marplot in his slander upon me, is equally glaring with his want of wit, his want of veracity, his want of decency, and his want of humanity.

I am accused of being a *Jew;* of being a *Republican;* and of being *Poor.*

I *am a Jew.* I glory in belonging to that persuasion, which even its opponents, whether Christian, or Mahomedan, allow to be of divine origin—of that persuasion on which christianity itself was originally founded, and must ultimately rest—which has preserved its faith secure and undefiled, for near three thousand years—whose votaries have never murdered each other in religious wars, or cherished the theological hatred so general, so unextinguishable among those who revile them. A persuasion, whose, patient followers have endured for ages the pious cruelties of Pagans, and of christians, and persevered in the unoffending practice of their rites and ceremonies, amidst poverties and privations—amidst pains, penalties, confiscations, banishments, tortures, and deaths, beyond the example of any other sect, which the page of history has hitherto recorded.

To be of such a persuasion, is to me no disgrace; though I well understand the inhuman language of bigotted contempt, in which your reporter by attempting to make me ridiculous, as a Jew, has made himself detestable, whatever religious persuasion may be honored by his adherence.

But I am a Jew. I am so—and so were Abraham, and Isaac, and Moses and the prophets, and so too were Christ and his apostles, I feel no disgrace in ranking with such society, however, it may be subject to the illiberal buffoonery of such men as your correspondents.

I am a *Republican!* Thank God, I have not been so heedless, and so ignorant of what has passed, and is now passing in the political world. I have not been so proud or so prejudiced as to renounce the cause for which I have *fought,* as an American throughout the whole of the revolutionary war, in the militia of Charleston, and in Polaskey's legion, I fought in almost every action which took place in Carolina, and in the disastrous affair of Savannah,[86] shared the hardships of that sanguinary day, and for three and twenty years I felt no disposition to change my political, any more than my religious principles.—And which in spite of the witling scribblers of aristocracy. I shall hold sacred until death as not to feel the ardour of republicanism.—Your correspondent, Mr. Wayne cannot have known what it is to serve his country from principle in time of danger and difficulties at the expence of his health and his peace, of his pocket and his person, as I have done; or he would not be as he is, a pert reviler of those who have so done—as I do not suspect you Mr. Wayne, of being the author of the attack on me, I shall not enquire what share you or your relations had in establishing the liberties of your country. On religious grounds I am a republican. Kingly government was first conceded to the foolish complaints of the Jewish people, as a punishment and a curse; and so it was to them until their dispersion, and so it has been to every nation, who have been as foolishly tempted to submit to it. Great Britain has a king, and her enemies need not wish her the sword, the pestilence, and the famine.

In the history of the Jews, are contained the earliest warnings against kingly government, as any one may know who has read the fable of Abimelick, or the exhortations of Samuel. But I do not recommend them to your reporter, Mr. Wayne. To him the language of truth and soberness would be unintelligible.

I am a Jew, and if for no other reason, for that reason am I a republican. Among the pious priesthood of church establishments, we are compassionately ranked with Turks, Infidels and Heretics. In the *monarchies* of Europe we are hunted from society—stigmatized as unworthy of common civility, thrust out as it were from the converse of men; objects of mockery and insult to forward children, the butts of vulgar wit, and low buffoonery, such as your correspondent Mr. Wayne is not ashamed to set us an example of. Among the nations of Europe we are inhabitants every where—but Citizens no where *unless in Republics.* Here, in France, and in the Batavian Republic alone, we are treated as men and as brethren. In republics we have *rights,* in monarchies we live but to experience *wrongs.* And why? because we and our forefathers have *not* sacrificed our principles to our interest or earned an exemption from pain and poverty, by the direliction of our religious duties, no wonder we are objects of derition to those, who have no principles, moral, or religious, to guide their conduct.

How then can a Jew but be a Republican? in America particularly. Unfeeling and ungrateful would he be, if he were callous to the glorious and benevolent cause of the difference between his situation in this land of freedom, and among the proud and privileged law givers of Europe.

But I am *poor,* I am so, my family also is large, but soberly and decently brought up. They have not been taught to revile a christian, because his religion is not *so old* as theirs. They have not been taught to mock even at the errors of good intention, and conscientious belief. I hope they will always leave this to men as unlike themselves, as I hope I am to your scurrilous correspondent.

I know that to purse proud aristocracy poverty is a crime but it may sometimes be accompanied with honesty even in a Jew. I was a bankrupt some years ago. I obtained my certificate and I was discharged from my debts. Having been more successful afterwards, I called my creditors together, and eight years afterwards unsolicited I discharged all my old debts, I offered interest which was refused by my creditors, and they gave me under their hands without any solicitations of mine, as a testimonial of the fact (to use their own language) as a tribute due to my honor and honesty. This testimonial was signed by Messrs. J. Ball, W. Wister, George Meade, J. Philips, C. G. Paleske, J. Bispham, J. Cohen, Robert

Smith, J. H. Leuffer, A. Kuhn, John Stille, S. Pleasants, M. Woodhouse, Thomas Harrison, M. Boraef, E. Laskey, and Thomas Allibone, &c.

I was discharged by the insolvent act, true, because having the amount of my debts owing to me from the French Republic, the differences between France and America have prevented the recovery of what was due to me, in time to discharge what was due to my creditors. Hitherto it has been the fault of the political situation of the two countries, that my creditors are not paid; when peace shall enable me to receive what I am entitled to it will be my fault if they are not fully paid.

This is a long defence Mr. Wayne, but you have called it forth, and therefore, I hope you at least will not object to it. The Public will not judge who is the proper object of ridicule and contempt, your facetious reporter, or

YOUR HUMBLE SERVANT,

BENJAMIN NONES.

Aurora (Philadelphia), August 13, 1800

REPUBLICAN SOCIETY OF LANCASTER, LANCASTER COUNTY

Constitution and Address, January 3, 1795

From the LANCASTER GAZETTE

(Republished by desire)

At a meeting of the REPUBLICAN SOCIETY of *Lancaster,* held in the borough, on the 3d of January 1795.

On motion, ordered, that the corresponding committee do publish, in the English and German newspapers of Lancaster, the constitution of the society, with the names of the officers thereof, and an address to the public.

Extract from the minutes,

JACOB LAHN, Secretary

CONSTITUTION.

At a period pregnant with the most important events abroad, and with alarming attempts of ambitious men at home, every reflecting mind must become sensible of its own situation, and attentive to those occurrences, wherein our welfare is concerned. Anxious for the undisturbed enjoyment of the great blessings, which we expected to reap from the progress of liberty, we are desirous to enquire into the feelings of our fellow citizens, and to communicate our own, in social and fraternal deliberations with them.

Moreover, remembering that we, as citizens of Pennsylvania, have a natural and constitutional right, in a peaceable manner to assemble together for our common good; to examine the proceedings of the legislature, or any branch of government, to communicate freely our thoughts and opinions; and to apply to those invested with the powers of government, for redress of grievances, or other proper purposes, by petition, address or remonstrance.

And, being convinced, that no freedom, either political or religious, can dwell, except with a virtuous, enlightened, and well instructed people; we the subscribers have, therefore, unanimously entered into an association, under the name of the REPUBLICAN SOCIETY of *Lancaster,* for promoting useful knowledge and political information, and for disseminating liberal and republican sentiments.

Having united in these designs, we adopt the following regulations for transacting the business of the society.

ARTICLES

1. The society shall be composed of independent citizens, residant in the borough and county of Lancaster; and shall meet in the borough on the first Saturday of every month.

2. The officers of the society shall consist of a President and Vice President, two secretaries, one treasurer, and a corresponding committee of as many members as the society may think proper; and be chosen, by ballot, on the first Saturday of January in every year.

3. The duty of the corresponding committee is to correspond with persons or associations in other places, and to lay all communications, which they shall make or receive, before the society.

4. It is the duty of the secretaries, to keep minutes of the proceedings of the societies, in a book provided for that purpose; and of the treasurer, to keep regular accounts of all monies by him paid or received.

5. It shall be the duty of the President (or, in his absence, of the Vice President) to convene the society, upon the request of any five members.

6. New members may be admitted into the society, by ballot, and a majority of the members present, in a stated meeting next following that wherein they were proposed.

7. Every member, on his admission, shall subscribe the constitution, and pay the sum of one dollar to the treasurer, and the sum of half a dollar at every annual meeting.

8. No member shall be expelled, but by ballot, and by a majority of the members present, in a stated meeting subsequent to that in which the motion for his expulsion was made.

9. One fourth of the whole Society shall be a quorum to transact business.

10. No article of this constitution shall be altered, but by a majority of the members present, at a stated meeting following that in which the alteration in writing was proposed to the society.

OFFICERS OF THE SOCIETY

George Moser, *President.*

Joseph Carpenter, *Vice-President.*

Christopher Mayer, *Treasurer.*

Jacob Lahn ⎫
James Gill ⎬ *Secretaries*

William Reichenbach,[87] ⎫
William Dickson,
Jacob Lahn, ⎬ *Corresponding*
Jacob Carpenter,[88]   *Committee.*
John Miller, Jun.
Frederick Steinman, ⎭

ADDRESS.

Fellow-Citizens,

In the above publication the society has a two fold intention. First, to exhibit in public view their design and principles; then to promote the extension and interest of the society. Whether it will have the desired effect last intended, we are not able to foretell.

On the one hand, it is easy to anticipate the clamour that will be raised by those whose ideas and sentiments, on this subject, differ from ours: For, experience has taught us that there are, in the bosom of the Republican State of Pennsylvania, many anti-republicans; some from principle; others, from prejudice; and more from private interest. These will endeavour to crush, if possible, this self-created association in its infancy; not so much by open opposition, as by secret calumny.

On the other hand, relying on the common sense of our plain and industrious Farmers and Mechanicks, in the county of Lancaster (that respectable class of the people) with whose interest the public welfare is naturally and strongly connected; we trust they will readily discern private views from the love of the common good; delusion from truth and reason; arrogance and ambition, from equity and humanity. They will easily discover the propriety of such an association, if duly supported; and its usefulness in collecting the sentiments of the people, when required to be known.

Thus, countenanced by popular favour, animated by the purity of our design, and supported by the great authority of the divine and triumphant rights of man; we hope to deprive from you, fellow citizens of the county of Lancaster, essential aid in extending the society, and maintaining its genuine principles.

We are,

With esteem

And Friendship, your

Fellow-Citizens.

American Daily Advertiser (Philadelphia), January 26, 1795

DEMOCRATIC SOCIETY OF NORTHUMBERLAND COUNTY

Resolutions Adopted Condemning the Legislature's Disfranchisement of Freemen of Four Western Counties, March 3, 1795

From the SUNBURY GAZETTE.

At a meeting of the Democratic Society of Northumberland county, held at Lewisburg on the 3d day of March, 1795—the following Resolutions were unanimously agreed to:—

First Resolved, That in the opinion of this society, the disfranchisement of the freemen of the four western counties by the Legislature of this state, was an illegal extension of power, and unconstitutional;[89] there being no proof suggested that those counties were in a state of insurrection at the time of the election: that their continuing to legislate in the absence of near one sixth part of their members, ought to meet the disapprobation of all who wish well to their country.

Second Resolved, That the five members of the legislature from this county, for their last virtuous and patriotic vote in support of the rights of the people, deserve well of their country; and that the committee be requested to inform them of this resolution.

Third Resolved, That in the opinion of this Society, the means used to procure to Peter Faulkner a commission for the peace at Lewisburg, was uncandid, and intended as an insult to the inhabitants of said town and neighbourhood—He the said Faulkner, nor any of the signers of his petition to the governor (except William Steedman) being residents of the town or district for which he is appointed; neither is he possessed of any property therein.

Fourth Resolved, That the German Republican Society of Philadelphia, the Democratic Societies of New-York and New-Castle, are entitled to the thanks of this Society, for their firm and judicious defence of the rights of freemen, against the insidious attacks of a designing or aristocratic party.

Fifth Resolved, That this society will at all times deem it a pleasure to correspond and cooperate with those societies, and any other civil associations, so far as their proceedings tend to the support of the constitution and laws of the United States, the freedom of speech and opinion, the investigation of public measures, and the conduct of the officers of government.

Sixth Resolved, That the foregoing resolutions be inserted in the Northumberland Gazette.

JOHN THOMPSON, President.

Aurora (Philadelphia), March 23, 1795

REPUBLICAN SOCIETY AT THE MOUTH OF YOUGH

Constitution, April 15, 1794

At a meeting of a society from the four counties at the house of Samuel Sinclair, at the mouth of Yough, April 15, 1794.

SAMUEL WILSON, in the Chair, and

MATTHEW JAMISON, Secretary.

Resolved, That the following be proposed as a constitution for forming a Republican Society, in each colonel's district throughout the four counties.

WE, the people of Colonel   district in   county, in order to form a speedy communication between ourselves and the citizens of Westmoreland, Washington, Fayette and Allegheny counties, and a more perfect union to ourselves and our posterity, do ordain and establish this constitution for the district of

ARTICLE I.

Section 1. All powers herein granted, shall be vested to a society of the district which shall consist of a president and council.

Sect. 2. The council shall be composed of members chosen every six months by the people of the several militia company districts. The electors of every such district, shall be entitled to a vote from 18 years old and upwards within the district. No person shall be a councilman, who shall not have attained to the age of 21 years, and shall not when elected, be an inhabitant of that district in which he shall be chosen. The number of councilmen shall not exceed one for every company district. The first captain's district one. The second captain's one, &c.

&c. throughout the militia's companies. When vacancies shall happen in the representation of any company district, the captain of said district shall issue notice of election to fill such vacancy.

Sect. 3. The society shall choose their treasurer, secretary and other officers; and shall choose deputies to meet the county or counties, out of the society or district, as they shall think proper.

Sect. 4. A majority of the members elected, shall constitute a quorum to do business, but a smaller number may adjourn from day to day, and may be authorised to compel the attendance of absent members in such manner, and under such penalties as they may provide. All fines shall go into the society's fund. They may determine the rules of their proceedings, punish its members for disorderly behavior; and with the concurrence of two thirds, expel members. The society shall assemble at least once in every month, and such meetings shall be on the Monday in each month, unless they shall appoint a different day.

Sect. 5. The society shall keep a fair journal of all its proceedings, and shall from time to time publish the same in writing to the militia captains of the district, for the use of their respective companies, excepting such parts as may in their judgment require secrecy.

Sect. 6. The secretary and deputies shall be rewarded at the discretion of the society. The president, council or deputies, for any speech or debate in society shall not be questioned in any other place.

No person holding any office of trust or profit under this state, or the United States, shall, while holding such office or trust, be admitted a president, councilman, or deputy in the society.

Sect. 7. The society shall have, from time to time, the laws of the United States, with the minutes of the house of representatives of Congress; the laws of Pennsylvania, with the minutes of the house of representatives of the commonwealth; together with any other book or books that may be thought necessary for the instruction of the society.

Sect. 8. The society shall have power, with the concurrence of the district and county, to nominate and recommend such persons as in their opinion will be capable to represent us in the government of this state and the United States. To hear and determine all matters of variance and disputes between party and party. To encourage able teachers for the instruction of youth. To examine into the conduct of their teachers. To introduce the Bible and other religious books into their schools. To encourage the industrious, and promote the man of merit. To make all bye-laws, which shall be necessary and proper for carrying into execution the foregoing powers, and all other powers vested by this constitution in the government of the Society.

Sect. 9. No money shall be drawn from the treasury but in consequence of appropriations made by the bye-law and a regular statement of, and accounts of the receipts and expenditures of all money shall be published from time to time, to the militia captains within the district.

Sect. 10. All matters in variance, and dispute within the district, shall be laid before the society; and no district, or citizen within the district, shall sue or cause to be sued before a single justice of the peace, or in any court of justice, a citizen, or citizens of the district, county or counties, before they first apply to the society for redress, unless the business will not admit of delay.

ARTICLE II

Sect. 1. The president shall hold his office during the term of nine months, and be elected as follows:

Each company district shall elect the president in the manner and form as they elect their councilmen. The electors shall meet in the bounds of their respective companies, and vote by ballot for a president, who shall be an inhabitant of the district; and they shall make a list of all persons voted for, and the number of votes given for each, which they shall sign and certify, and transmit the same sealed to the society. The society shall then open all the certificates, and the votes shall be counted; the person having the greatest number of votes, shall be the president, if such number be a majority of the whole number of electors; and if there be more than one having such a majority, and having equal number of votes, then the society shall immediately choose by ballot one of them for president.

Sect. 2. The society may determine the time of choosing the president, which day shall be the same throughout the several companies. No person shall be eligible to the office of president, who has not attained to the age of 25 years, and a residencer within the district. And in case of removal of the president from office, or his death, resignation or inability to discharge the powers and duties of the said office, the society may then declare what officer shall act as president, and such officer shall act accordingly until the disability be removed, or a president shall be elected.

Sect. 3. When the president shall receive any appointment to any office or trust or profit under this state, or the United States, he shall resign his office as president of the society.

The president and councilmen of the society shall be removed from office on impeachment for, and conviction of bribery or high crimes and misdemeanors. Nothing in this constitution shall be construed as to prejudice any claims of this state, or of the United States.

If any thing is found in this constitution that may require alteration or amendment in a future day; a convention shall be called for the purpose of making such alterations or amendments.

Resolved, That it be recommended to the several captains of the several colonels districts throughout the four counties, to call together on the second Monday of May next, all within their respective bounds, from the age of 18 years and upwards, at the place where they usually meet in company, and elect one fit person to represent them. And the men so chosen within each colonel's district, to meet in a committee for the district the Monday following, and form a society for their respective districts, upon the above or a more eligible plan, according as they shall think proper.

Resolved, That it be published in the Pittsburgh Gazette.

By order of the Society,

SAMUEL WILSON, *Chairman.*
Attest.

MATTHEW JAMISON, Sec'y
Pittsburgh Gazette, June 28, 1794

"Democratus" to the *Pittsburgh Gazette,* June 28, 1794

I AM much surprised that so little notice has been taken of what was done by the society which met at the mouth of Yough, and that the measures they recommended have not been adopted.

I am too well acquainted with mankind to suppose every one would agree to any one system either of a judicial or civil nature, but I hope there are few Americans who would adopt that British maxim taught by and supported by ecclesiastic authority, viz. that it is not for people of ordinary capacity to argue but to obey.

But there is one argument which I apprehend has considerable weight with some, and that is contained in article 1st, section 6th, of the constitution formed by the society, where it is said, that no person holding any office of trust or profit under this state or the United States shall be eligible to the office of president or councilman while holding such office—They think thereby militia officers are excluded, and if so they will not encourage the business at all, but will strive to hinder its progress.

There is likewise some other business made cognizable by the constitution which some do not seem to relish, particularly those who are of a litigious spirit, and like the people of Connecticut, are desirous of having every thing settled according to law; now it might not be proper to compel such to lay their disputes before the society, but only do business for such as please to lay it before them.

There is other business pointed out by the constitution to the society which none I have met with attempt to dispute the propriety of, viz, recommending fit persons to represent us in the government of this state and of the United States, examining into the conduct of the school-matters, &c.—Yet though it may be admitted the constitution requires amendment, it can be done at a future day, but having societies established upon such plan will no doubt be pleasing to every republican, and particularly so to

DEMOCRATUS.

Pittsburgh Gazette, June 28, 1794

DEMOCRATIC SOCIETY OF THE COUNTY OF WASHINGTON, WASHINGTON

Remonstrance to the President and Congress on Opening Navigation of the Mississippi River, March 24, 1794

Washington, March 24, 1794.

That part of the Democratic Society of Pennsylvania, in the county of Washington, having met in the town of Washington, for the purpose of electing officers, and for other purposes, adopted the following

Resolved, That the following remonstrance, on the subject of opening the navigation of the Mississippi river, be signed by the President, on behalf of this society, and forwarded to the President of the United States, to be by him laid before Congress.

To the PRESIDENT *and* CONGRESS *of the United States of America.*

The remonstrance of the Democratic Society of the county of Washington, in Pennsylvania.

Respectfully sheweth.

THAT your remonstrants are entitled by nature and by stipulation, to the undisturbed navigation of the river Mississippi, and consider it a right inseparable from their prosperity. That in colonizing this distant and dangerous desart, they always contemplated the free enjoyment of this right, and considered it as an inseprable appendage to the country they had sought out, had fought for, and acquired.— That for a series of years during their early settlement, their petitions to government to secure this right, were answered by its alledged weakness; and your remonstrants taught to expect, that the time was approaching fast, when both power and inclination would unite to establish it on the firmest ground. In this anxious expectation they waited, and to the insolence of those who arrogated its exclusive exercise, they patiently submitted, till the government of America had so strengthened itself as to hold out an assurance of future protection to all its citizens, and of redress for all their wrongs.

That protection has not been extended to us, we need only refer to our present situation, and that that situation has not been concealed or unknown to Congress, we appeal to its archives. We have, without ceasing, deplored to our degraded situation, and burdened you with our humble petitions and requests. But alas! we still experience; that the strong nerved government of America, extends its arm of protection to all the branches of the union, but to your remonstrants. That it is competent to every end; but that single one, by which alone it can benefit us; the protection of our territorial rights. It is competent to exact obedience, but not to make that return which can be the only just and natural exchange for it.

Long have your remonstrants been anxiously in quest of the obstacles that have stood in your way, to the establishment of this our right; and as long has their pursuit been fruitless. Formal and tardy negociations have no doubt been often projected, and have as often miscarried. It is true, some negociations were once attempted, that were neither *formal* nor *tardy,* and gave an early shock to our encreasing population and to our peace of mind; but your remonstrants are constrained to be of opinion, that the neglect or local policy of American councils, has never produced one single real effort to procure this right. Could the government of America be for ten years seriously in pursuit of the establishment of a grand territorial right, which was arrogantly suspended, and return to that quarter of the union to whom it was all-important, but an equivocal answer? We think it high time that we should be thoroughly informed of the situation on which your negociations, if any, have left this right; For apathy itself has grown hopeless from long disappointed expectations.

Your remonstrants yield not in patriotism to any of their fellow citizens; But patriotism, like every other thing, has its bounds. We love those states from which we were all congregated, and no event (not even an attempt to barter away our best rights) shall alien our affections from the individual members who compose them; but attachment to governments cease to be natural, when they cease to be mutual. To be subjected to all the burthens, and enjoy none of the benefits arising from government, is what we will never submit to. Our situation compels us to speak plainly. If wretchedness and poverty await us, it is of no concern to us how they are produced. We are gratified in the prosperity of the Atlantic states, but would not speak the language of truth and sincerity, were we not to declare our unwillingness, to make any sacrifices to it, when their importance and those sacrifices result from our distresses. If the interest of Eastern America requires that we should be kept in poverty, it is unreasonable from such poverty to exact contributions. The first, if we cannot emerge from, we must learn to bear, but the latter, we never can be taught to submit to.

From the general government of America, therefore, your remonstrants now ask protection, in the free enjoyment of the navigation of the river Mississippi, which is with-held from them by the Spaniards. We demand it as a right which you have the power to invest us with, and which not to exert, is as great a breach of our rights, as to with-hold. We declare, that nothing can retribute us for the suspension or loss of this inestimable right. We declare it to be a right which must be obtained; and do also declare, that if the general government will not procure it for us, we shall hold ourselves not answerable for any consequences that may result from our own procurement of it. The God of nature has given us both the right and means of acquiring and enjoying it; and to permit a sacrifice of it to any earthly consideration, would be a crime against ourselves, and against our posterity.

By order of the Society,

JAMES MARSHEL, President

(Teste)

W. M'CLUNEY, Secretary.

Resolved, That it be published in the Pittsburgh Gazette, that this Society is organized—and have adopted the foregoing resolutions.

Pittsburgh Gazette, April 5, 1794. The original is in the National Archives, AL, RG59, Miscellaneous Letters, 1790-1799.

H. H. Brackenridge to the *Pittsburgh Gazette,* April 5, 1794

To the *Pittsburgh Gazette*

Certain papers from a committee of the people of Kentucky on the subject of the navigation of the Mississippi, western posts, &c. having been transmitted to me amongst other persons of this town, I have charged myself with the making an arrangement to procure the sentiments of the people of this county, and propose that in each election district at the usual place of holding, there shall be a meeting on Saturday the 12th day of April, and a number of delegates (as many as the people think proper, the more the better) be chosen to meet at Pittsburgh on the Saturday following to make such resolutions on the subjects proposed, and on other subjects, that especially concern this country, as may be thought adviseable.

April 2, 1794.   H. H. BRACKENRIDGE.[90]

Pittsburgh Gazette, April 5, 1794

Officers of the Democratic Society to Brackenridge, April 8, 1794

Washington (in Pennsylvania) April 8th
1794

Citizen Brakenridge

On the 24th ultimo, a form of a Remonstrance drawn up by the Democratic Society of Kentucky, was laid before the Democratic Society of this place, by David Bradford, our Vice-President.[91] Several of the members were opposed to the adoption of the precise form, as inapplicable in all respects to the Washington Democratic Society, but rather suited the people of the Western Country generally, and in one particular, to the people of Kentucky only; however so earnest were a majority to remonstrate before the present session of Congress would rise, and others in order to convince the people of Kentucky that we feel ourselves the same people with them in many of the most important political considerations, the form so presented, was adopted and signed by the President of the society and transmitted under cover to the President of the United States and a duplicate thereof to Genl. William Irvine,[92] a member in the House of Representatives, for this State, in order to be laid before Congress, in case the President should omit laying the one presented to him before that body. You Sir, may assure the Democratic Society of Kentucky that the Democratic Society of Washington will be at all times happy in communicating to them, or receiving from them such communications as may tend to procure and establish both our and their national and personal Rights.

If this Letter should happily reach you, we shall be glad to know in future, where to address our communications for your Society. Yours for this may be addressed to Citizen James Marshal, President of the Democratic Society of Pennsylvania, in Washington County.

The officers of this Society are
    James Marshel—President
    David Bradford—Vice-President
    William McCluney—Secretary
    William Hoge—Treasurer[93]
    David Redick[94]
    Absolem Baird[95]
    Joseph Penticost[96]   *Corresponding Committee*
    John Marshal
    Gabriel Blakeney[97]

        we are Citizen President with Respect &
        Esteem your Fellow Citizens
            David Redick
            A. Baird
            J. Penticost
            J. Marshal
            Gabl. Blakeney

President
and Members of the
Democratic Society of Kentucky.

Innes Papers, XIX, Manuscripts Division, Library of Congress

Response to an Address from the Democratic Society of Kentucky, April 26, 1794

Pittsburgh, April 26.

At a meeting of Delegates from the different election districts of Allegheny county, in the town of Pittsburgh, on Saturday the 19th day of April inst.

THOMAS MORTON in the Chair,

WAS read, an address from the Democratic Society of Kentucky to the people west of the Allegheny and Apalachian mountains, on the subject of the free navigation of the Mississippi river, together with several papers respecting the conduct of Great Britain towards the United States, and which being taken into consideration by the meeting it was unanimously resolved,

That we accord with our brethren of Kentucky in their complaint, that this right has not been asserted by the United States hitherto in a manner consistent with the justice they owe to this part of the Union. We noted the proposition made in Congress some years ago of bartering it away for a time, in consideration of some advantages in trade to the sea coast settlements. It was asserted that a greater interest would result to the United States in general. But who gave a power to sacrifice a part for the whole? There has been yet no positive surrender of the right; but there has been what may be called a negative surrender; to wit, an acquiescence in our privation of it.

When we talk of this right, we mean not only that of descending the stream without toll, duty, or restriction; but the use of every port free upon its banks as a natural appandage of the river; and if those who inhabit these ports will not give the free entrance of them to the tenants in common of the right, it is an injury; under the maxim of municipal law and natural reason; "use what is yours, so as not to disturb others in what is theirs."

But we are far from wishing to possess these ports ourselves provided we can have the free use of them in the hands of others; and there is no nation in whose hands it is more our interest they should remain than in those of Spain, because that kingdom has gold and we have bread. We think this our mutual interest, elucidated and pressed with the Court of Spain, might before this time have led to a satisfactory adjustment; which unless it shall take place, we feel clearly that in no very distant period, it will be as impossible to keep the people from an invasion of the Mississippi banks, as to prevent the spring floods from rolling into that river. With respect to the expediency of such a revolution, we say nothing; but in case of continuing to occlude the navigation have no doubt of the justice of it.

By the meeting was next taken into consideration the conduct of our government in their acquiescence with the holding the posts of Niagara, Detroit, &c. by the administration of Britain, and the sense of the delegates being taken, it was resolved,

That the people of this country had hitherto themselves been disposed to acquiesce in this grievance, under the idea that the treaty on our part had not been fully executed; for we could not demand right until we were confident that we had done right. But in the mean time we could see no reason for not going near those posts with our establishments, and taking possession of the Lake, in order to have it in our power to restrain the Indian hostilities; for we have little or no idea that these can ever be restrained; but by having possession of these posts;[98] or by going near them without our establishments by the way of Presqu'Isle and Lake Erie; for it has always been known to us that the British are the source of the Indian dissatisfaction and enmity; they have furnished the scalping knife; they have urged its use against us; and nothing but our interposing ourselves between them and the hostile tribes can give or preserve peace. But the objection has been that a measure of this nature would give umbrage to Britain, and involve us in a war. The suggestion appeared sufficiently humiliating, and was a proof how abject a people could in a short time become, who had shewn themselves a few years before to be capable of brave and republican exertions. It was preposterous enough that the public treasury should be for years past wasted in chasing Indians as you would fugitive wild beasts, when by attacking the source of their hostilities the communication with Britain, a visible and tangible object, they would of themselves languish and like a serpent, without the heat of the sun, become torpid and motionless; but we are perfectly sensible that such has been the extreme ignorance of the sea-coast parts of the union with respect to our situation, that they either did not believe what we always asserted, to wit; that the British were the prompters of the Indian depradations; or such was their self-interest that they were not willing to credit it, least by restraining the conduct, a war might be incurred. It is perhaps fortunate for us that the spoliations of the British cruizers, and of the Algerine corsairs[99] has made them fellow sufferers with ourselves; dissolved the enchantment of mercantile attachment, and the bands of slavish fear by the sense of wrong; and wrought up, once more, the American mind to an energy and resolution which their honor demands, and their interest requires. War is beyond question a horrid evil, but the attacking an adversary who has made war, is reducing him to peace, by making war painful to him that he may cease to continue it.

At this juncture we have France to assist us, who, should we now take a part, will not fail to stand by us until Canada is independent of Britain, and the instigators of Indian hostilities are removed; and should we lie by, while France is struggling for her liberties, it cannot be supposed that her republic will embark in a war on our account after she shall have been victorious. It was for this reason that though we approved of the conduct of the President, and the judiciary of the United States, in their endeavours to preserve peace; and an impartial neutrality until the sense of the nation had been taken on the necessity of retaliation by actually declaring war, yet now that the Congress have been convened, and such just grounds exist, we are weary of their tardiness in coming forward to measures of reprisal.

But we have observed with great pain that our councils want the integrity or spirit of republicans. This we attribute to the pernicious influence of stockholders or their subordinates; and our minds feel this with so much indignancy, that we are almost ready to wish for a state of revolution and the guillotine of France for a short space in order to inflict punishment on the miscreants that enervate and disgrace our government.

Nevertheless we know that in the case of a war with Britain we are the most exposed of all parts of the United States, and we consider it as great dereliction of our interest that in the bill making provision for putting in a posture of defence several sea ports, there is a total silence of the port of *Presque 'Isle,* from whence it is well known the British would invade our country; and though we hear of vessels of war fitted out to protect against the Algerines, yet not a word of an armed vessel on lake Erie, to intercept the supplies of knives and axes to the Indian allies of Britain.

But it is hoped that our public councils will take advantage of these hints, and should a war take place with the British administration

Resolved, That we will submit to any direct tax, and possible service to give it a successful termination.

Resolved, That a copy of these resolutions be sent to the Members of Congress from this side the mountain, and to the Democratic Societies of Kentucky and Philadelphia.

Resolved, That these resolutions be inserted in the Pittsburgh Gazette.

THOMAS MORTON, Chairman

Attest.
W. H. BEAUMONT, Secretary.
Pittsburgh Gazette, May 17, 1794

Resolutions Adopted on the President's Proclamation of Neutrality, June 23, 1794

(Republished from the Pittsburg Gazette, by particular desire.)

At a stated meeting of the Democratic Society of the County of Washington, in Pennsylvania, held at the Town of Wilmington on the 23rd day of June, in the year 1794, and of American Independence the eighteenth.

Resolved, That on reviewing the conduct of the executive of the United States, we are under the painful necessity of censuring in sundry particulars, viz.

1st. The language of the President's proclamation, in which, instead of making it known that certain powers were at war, with whom we were at peace, and
that it behoved individuals to take no part until the body public authorised it,
he slides into the place of Congress, and undertakes to say what by the constitution they alone have a right to determine, viz, that it was our *interest and duty,*
as a people to remain neutral; which sentiment, even had it been constitutionally
expressed, we disapprove, and believe it was neither the interest or duty of
America to remain neutral; for if no connection had ever subsisted between the
people of France and America—if we had not been bound by every possible tie
of gratitude, the cause alone was sufficient to have interested us, and we believe
it to have been both the *duty and interest* of the American people to have supported it at all events. And we are of opinion that on issuing the proclamation
as a temporary notice to the public, it became the President to have convoked
the Congress, to decide the other point *whether peace or war was adviseable,*
the circumstance of Britain taking a part against France, being a justification of
him in that measure; nay, making it his duty, as an event in which the honor,
and even the existence of this republic was concerned.

2nd. The interfering at the time the Congress, roused to a sense of the national dignity and safety were brought at length, in spite of stockholders, and
British influence, evident in the speeches of some of the members, to deliberate
on measures of compulsion in obtaining reparation for the spoliations of our
commerce, the relinquishment of the posts within our territory, and a general
compliance with stipulated treaties, and the known laws of nations. And we not
only censure the interference as improper, but we reprehend the nomination of
a special envoy, as unnecessarily expensive, the minister already at the British
court being to the supposed competent, if at all qualified to be in the place, and
ought either to have been recalled or continued with all trusts; but we also reprobate the vesting Chief Justice Jay with a diplomatic mission, which to say the
least of it, was a great indelicacy towards the people of the United States, as if
there were such penury of virtue and talents that an envoy could not be found
equal to the trust, without accumulating offices in the person of one. Is it the
spark only that is already struck out, that can inflame; or the wave only that is
already roused, that can impel? Is there not fire still remaining in the rock, and
billows in the ocean? Amongst the great mass of the people surely numbers
might be found who occupy no office, and yet are capable of discharging any
trust at home or abroad. The revolution of France has sufficiently proved that
generals may be taken from the ranks, and ministers of state from the obscurity
of the most remote village. Is our president, like the grand sultan of Constan-
tinople, shut up in his apartment and unacquainted with all the talents or capacities but those of the seraskier or mufti that just happens to be about him.

But the nomination was equally exceptionable on the principle of being in violation of the constitution; the confounding of judiciary and diplomatic functions,
a principle which if countenanced and pursued would lead to an aristocratic en-

grossment of all offices and power in a few individuals. We are persuaded that no man but a Washington, fenced round as he is with the unapproachable splendor of popular favour, would have dared, in the very prime and vigour of liberty to have insulted the majesty of the people by such a departure from any principle of republican equality, and regard for the great charter of the constitution, by which the boundaries of office are distinguished and kept apart. It is still more our astonishment and regret, that notwithstanding these sentiments have been brought forward and expressed, and could not have escaped the observation of the President, yet has he persisted in a similar conduct by the nomination of Mr. Monroe, a senator, as minister to France. It is true the senator had resigned, but that was posterior to his appointment; and though it might have been understood prior to nomination, that he was to resign, yet we hold it degrading to the citizens, that it should be thought that no man can be capable of office, but one that is already thrown up, and is in some department. Attend to the nature of popular elections, & it will be found that amongst candidates, it is often a difficulty to determine the preference, and frequently a matter of accident to whom the majority of suffrages is given.—To suppose, therefore, that those whom the people have already sent forward to the house of representatives or the senate, are the only persons equal to judiciary or diplomatic trusts is a mistake, and ought to be corrected.

American Daily Advertiser (Philadelphia), July 29, 1794

To Mr. Scull, *Pittsburgh Gazette,* June 28, 1794

June 23d, 1794.

Mr. Scull,[100]

PERUSING this morning a bundle of newspapers sent me by a friend, my attention was principally attracted by the resolutions of the different Democratic Societies—having leisure on my hands, I entered into a consideration of their proceedings, and as resolves are now in fashion, I send you mine on that subject, not doubting but the sentiments of honesty and candour from an individual will be as well received as the inflammatory sophistry of those intriguing juntos.

Resolved, That the constitution of the United States is a great and wise regulation, well calculated to ensure equal liberty and political happiness; that it is the admiration and envy of the most enlightened and civilized nations who are looking up and flying to it as a refuge from tyranny and oppression.

Resolved, That the government of the United States has hitherto been in the hands of a virtuous and wise executive (whose integrity hath been rendered only more visible by the attacks of party) under whose direction and management we have grown into consequence and credit; from anarchy and poverty into respectability and a situation to be just.

Resolved, That any attempt to create causeless jealousy or mistrust, or to inflame the minds of the less informed in a government under the above circumstances, is inimical to its true interests and real happiness, and that the patriotism of such although arrogating the titles of *Democrats, Friends to Liberty,* &c. ought to be as much doubted, as the friendship of the savage who at the time he salutes you brother, applies either the knife or hatchet.

Resolved, That the members of those different societies, wherever they have appeared, have had in view their private interest and popularity and not the public's welfare, that in times of real danger few of them were seen in the field ready to encounter it; that they are national *bullies* breathing war and confusion, at the same time they have neither bravery nor patience to support themselves under its trials and hardships.

Resolved, That it is perfectly compatible with the dignity and wisdom of any government to do themselves justice by spirited remonstrance, and that war should be the *ultima ratio,* and dernier resort.

Resolved, That democracy which formerly meant that form of government in which the sovereign power is lodged with the body of the people, now means quite a different matter—it now means supineness, lethargy, and sometimes a little toryism in times of real and necessary danger; and violent threats, defiances, meetings, mobs, tar and feathers in times of peace—or now means abuse of the federal government formed by collective wisdom, and found expedient on a lengthy trial; it now means scurrility against the President (the best of men) and accusations against the superior officers, without supporting a single charge, &c. in short, it now means a thousand things of which Johnston never tho't, nor did it enter into the mind of Sheridan to conceive of.

Pittsburgh Gazette, June 28, 1794

David Reddick to Mr. Scull, December 25, 1794

Washington, Dec. 25, 1794

Mr. Scull,

Having learned by the speeches delivered by some members of Congress in that body, and from conversations with private gentlemen as well as those in public and important stations, that the Democratic Society of Washington has been charged with having contributed to the late disturbances, in this country,[101] and that the Society is therefore become in some degree obnoxious to government. It has been also said by ill disposed and false speaking men, that they have instead of pursuing the patriotic purposes of the institution, been engaged in electioneering schemes, to the dishonour and disgrace of their country, as well as to its injury. Now, Sir, I am conscious that the several charges are malicious and without true foundation; for the Society was only organized at last March court, to wit: on the fourth Monday in that month, that long previous to that date divers acts of outrage had been committed in opposition to the laws by tarring, feathering, &c., &c. that within about fourteen weeks afterwards the principal mischiefs were perpetrated, and if have not been very ill informed, the government is in possession of sufficient evidence that the dreadful deeds had long been determined on by people altogether unconnected with the Democratic Society. The other charge of electioneering is equally false; as no act of theirs, neither private conversation was ever had nor contemplated on the subject of electioneering in favour of any individual, and I believe that the members were as much divided on that subject at the late election, as if there never had been members of a Democratic Society. Indeed, one of the principal views of the constitution was to prevent the people from undue influence at elections, but, Sir, we have one or two men, especially in our country, who like a hog, loves to be dabling in muddy waters, and will always be charging the most virtious with crimes which they lament their own ill success in.—On the whole, Sir, as some indiscreet things have been done in the Society, for want rather of due deliberation than ill intention; and inasmuch as I am resolved not only to be a good citizen, but to avoid any thing which may tend to give umbrage, and more especially at this time when but small prospects of being useful in a society under suspicions in a country generally loaded with guilt, at a time when it becomes all to give every possible evidence of their attachment to the lately violated laws and government, I say, in consideration of these things, and with a solemn declaration in favour of the virtue and patriotism of a large majority of the members, I withdraw myself from the Society; and I do recommend to the Society to dissolve themselves entirely if they think as I do. Let me at the same time assure the members of the Society that I have a most cordial respect for a powerful part of those who compose it, and I shall be happy at all times to consult with them individually or with the rest of our countrymen on the best means of restoring this unhappy and dishonoured country to that respectable state in which it was previous to the late disorders.

I am &c.

David Reddick

Philadelphia Gazette & Universal Daily Advertiser, January 23, 1795

Democratic Society to Fellow Citizens of the United States, January 31, 1795

That part of the *Democratic Society* of Pennsylvania established in the County of Washington, to their *Fellow-Citizens* throughout the United States.

We have been accused of having been instrumental in exciting and fomenting the unhappy insurrection that has recently prevailed in this our country; were we to suffer this charge to pass unnoticed (however innocent we may be) it might be construed into a tacit acknowledgment of guilt.

Our accusers to establish the above charge, have brought forward insinuations without foundation—assertions without proof—abstract reasoning without principle, and *self-created* surmises unworthy of republicans. It is truly to be lamented that any of the representatives of a free people should be jealous of every thirty or forty of their constituents who may get together to exercise a constitutional right. The right of speaking, publishing and declaring sentiments (thro' the medium of the press or otherwise) is a right inseparable from republicans. For if one man in his individual capacity has a right to point out the errors of the government under which he lives, by the same parity of reasoning, fifty in their aggregate capacity have, subject, nevertheless, to the controlling opinions of their countrymen. To you, then, fellow-citizens, we make a just representation of our conduct, and to your candor and impartiality we appeal.

On the 24th of March last, this society was organized, and not before that time, have we known of a Democratic, Republican or any other political society, established in any of the counties of Pennsylvania, west of the Allegheny. At the first sitting of the society, we adopted a certain remonstrance, transmitted to us from Kentucky, on the subject of opening the navigation of the Mississippi; the adoption of this remonstrance met with considerable opposition, and was carried by a majority of two only; previous to this, it is true, certain transient meetings had been held in this county, particularly committees, or assemblages of persons to effect a repeal of certain laws of the United States, which, they declared in their opinion, were oppressive; but, can it be presumed that this society was either directly or indirectly concerned with those meetings in any scheme of opposition to government (if any such they had) when, at that time, we did not exist. For in no instance, nor at any time, have we taken the subject of any law into consideration; our doors never prevented the admission of strangers, and for the truth of the above assertion we appeal to every unprejudiced by-stander. At the second meeting of the society, on the 23d of June last, certain resolutions were adopted and published, none concurring with some executive acts; but we persuade ourselves that nothing will be inferred from these, in support of the charges exhibited against us. Subsequent to this second meeting and previous to the third, which was on the 22d of September, the principle outrages took place, and it may not be amiss here to inform our fellow-citizens, that a serious opposition to the excise law was abundantly manifested, (by insulting and holding in contempt the revenue officers) from the earliest promulgation thereof, which will fully appear by having recourse to the report of the Secretary of the Treasury, on that subject. These indubitable facts being premised, we confidently hope will be a sufficient refutation of every calumny, attempted against us, independent of all other considerations—and we assert that no subject such as that with which are charged, was ever spoken of by any member of the society, but on the contrary, as far as the situation and disposition of the country would admit, we have expressed our disapprobation of the violent measures which have prevailed.

It has been asserted, on the floor of Congress, in order to prove that we have been instrumental in fomenting the late insurrection, that some of our members were leaders in it; we admit, that a few of them (not more than seven) in their individual capacity,[102] were too deeply involved, but, suppose there had been twenty, is that any reason that the society should be stigmatized with being fomenters of the rebellion; with the same reason and propriety it might be asserted, that if a member of a corporate body should commit murder, that the corporation should be punished; or if any of the members of congress, in attempting to cry down Democratic Societies, should *commit* themselves, would it be reasonable that the other members of the same body should be held in contempt. We always have, and always shall consider ourselves amenable to the constitutional laws of that government from which we have the honor to derive the appelation; our institution we are resolved to continue; our government we are resolved to support; our public men and measures we are resolved to watch over; our sentiments to the world we are resolved to publish; and free communication of thoughts and opinions (one of our most invaluable rights) we are resolved to maintain; these resolutions we consider as the result of true Democracy, and perfectly compatible with our constitution.

Fellow-citizens, we feel ourselves constrained to (one or two words illegible, the papers having been chaffed in the carriage) the representatives of the American People an instrumentality calculated to render useless and inefficacious almost every patriotic association for the dissemination of republican sentiments—had success crowned their late efforts, might not even the illustrious *self-created* Society of Cincinnatus have trembled for its fate.

Here, then fellow-citizens, we rest our cause, and we trust, from a review of our conduct, we have proved our innocence to your satisfaction; and to the Supreme Ruler of the Universe we appeal for the rectitude of our intentions.

By order of the Society,
A. BAIRD, Vice President.

W. M'CLUNEY, Sec.
Jan. 13, 1795.

Aurora (Philadelphia), January 31, 1795

3 | Democratic-Republican Societies of New Jersey

POLITICAL SOCIETY OF MOUNT PROSPECT

Constitution, March 26, 1794

For the NEWARK GAZETTE

FOR the satisfaction of those who wish to join the Society, recently formed at Mount-Prospect, we publish the following particulars of our constitution.

1. This institution, established at Mount-Prospect, February the 14th, 1794, shall go under the denomination of a Political Society.

2. No man shall be precluded a seat in this society, merely on account of his religious or political principles; nor shall this constitution contemplate any distinction, except between virtuous and licentious characters.

3. No person of an immoral character who, at present does not, and for two years last past, has not punctually obeyed the good laws of this country, who, on examination, shall be convicted of having incurred, so many as four penalities a year, during the two years last past, shall be admitted as a member of this society; neither shall a notedly fraudulent person, nor any officer holding a commission, gained through intrigue or any unfairness, have admittance to membership, in this institution.

4. Admonition and expulsion are the only modes of punishment; but by virtue of mutual agreement, between the members, society shall ever have a right to advertise an expelled member, with his offence, in any public paper of this state: & in such case the society shall not be accountable.

5. This society shall never establish any mode of correspondence, with any other institution, which, or shall be formed on a party, less refined or less liberal plan, than this at Mount-Prospect.

141

Being prepared for business, we now invite all, within the limits of this parish, whose characters are coincident with our constitutional requisitions to join the society. Are several of you disposed to advocate an aristocratical or monarchical government? Where there is real opposition of sentiment, in a well regulated discussion, the righteous cause will probably shine with an additional lustre: Come forward then, with your arguments; we are more general than cowardly; liberty is yours, as well as ours; come on, and vindicate your cause, in the open field of reason; but we fear, their characters will exclude most men of your opinion.

The Society will hereafter meet the second Wednesday of each month, at in the afternoon; those who are absent an hour after, will not be allowed to speak on the subject: for two hours tardiness, they will be prohibited voting.

The following questions are to be debated, at our next meeting.

1. Whether they who treat the good laws of our country with contempt, are by the laws of reason and equity, eligible to the office of a representative in Congress, or State Legislature?

2. Whether a petition shall go forward at the next sitting of the legislature, against several licentious magistrates of the county.

Published by order of the society.

J. YEOMAN, *Secretary.*

Woods's Newark Gazette, March 26, 1794

REPUBLICAN SOCIETY OF THE TOWN OF NEWARK

Notice of July 4 Commemoration, June 12, 1794

NEWARK, June 12.

It will, no doubt, be a gratification to the friends of Liberty in this state, to be informed that preparations are making in various parts of the United States, to commemorate that eventful day (a day that ought never to be forgotten by such as can say we are Americans) (4th July) that gave to us Liberty and Independence. It is to be wished that a becoming observance be paid to the day in that place—Patriotic Society, with other Gentlemen of the town, we hear, have in contemplation.

American Daily Advertiser (Philadelphia), June 14, 1793

"Cato" to the *Newark Gazette,* March 12, 1794

For the NEWARK GAZETTE.

The following facts and observations arising on them relative to the meeting on Thursday evening last, at Mr. Seabury's Tavern, are submitted to the public.
The evening proving stormy, very few of those who intended forming themselves into a Society appeared, but the storm did not deter the enemies of the institution, from collecting all their force, & appearing at the place of meeting, with an intention, as it turned out in the sequel, to oppose the institution.[1] A person in favor of the institution, although he had reason to suspect the intentions of those assembled, undismayed by the vapouring menaces previously displayed, and unintimidated by the frowns of a rich and powerful combination, produced to the meeting a plan of a Society, which was to be denominated, *The Republican Society of the Town of Newark,* which he submitted to the consideration of the meeting with some introductory remarks; in which he laid it down as a political axiom, that no community could remain for any length of time happy and free, unless there should be a general dissemination of political knowledge among the people; he looked upon institutions peculiarly devoted to political enquiry, as best calculated to acquire and diffuse political knowledge among the members, he had chose the word *Republican* because that it was the government we lived under, and which he believed was best calculated to promote the happiness of society.
It was objected to the institution by one gentleman that it embraced objects too extensive for the capacities of a few persons in the town of Newark, who it could not be expected know as much as all the wise men in the United States, he confessed for his part that he had too much modesty to become a member of such an institution, where it would be necessary for him to give his opinion on subjects beyond his capacity; this assertion is the more extraordinary as it came from a man, no way remarkable for want of confidence in his own *political* opinions on other occasions, he was answered by the proposers of the institution, that he had political opinions of his own, and would not abandon his political interests without examining the conduct of those who managed them, this was replied to by a gentleman, that we wanted he said no other watch or check on the general government than Congress, who were our representatives; why the general government in particular was brought into view I know not, but that a government should become the only watch and check on its own actions in conformable to institutions, of which those who live under them make great complaint; another gentleman declared that his great object to the society was, that it was to be called *Republican,* and this appeared to be the substantial objection of all its opposers; the proposer lamented that the name of republican had be-

come so odious in this country. After considerable debate it was resolved in substance; That the town of Newark did not stand in need of a Republican Society, and that the author of the advertisement that proposed it, merited the censure of the meeting.

That a number of rich influential characters, possessing the most important and lucrative offices in the place, should assemble with all their dependants for the express purpose of preventing a number of persons from forming themselves into a society of the most inoffensive kind, and censuring the person who called them together, is a phenomenon of so extraordinary a kind, that it must alarm and astonish every thinking man. If societies are to be suppressed because they are republican, and men are to be proscribed because they promote republican societies, it is time to pause and look about us; it brings us to a crisis in our political affairs that dictates the enquiry, whether we have political rights, and if we have what these rights are, and whether they are to be wrested from us by the despotic exertions of opulence in office, aided by the influence of sycophantic treasury dependents, and the avowed enemies of the French and American revolutions, or whether we have spirit enough to maintain them against all invaders.

We may safely lay it down as a truth that needs no illustration, that to establish a government (let the principles be ever so pure) & then consecrate it as infallible, and prevent all enquiry into political concerns is the unerring road to oppression, for such is the frailty of human nature, & such the disposition of men, that should you give them an unlimited controul over your persons and properties, they will appropriate that power to their own benefit, shall we then without enquiry, consecrate their actions and say that they *can do no wrong*.

To declare that the affairs of government are too enveloped in mysterious intricacy as to be placed beyond the reach of common capacities, is as slavish a doctrine as ever disgraced the creed of the vilest minion of the most despotic tyrant, and is the source from which much oppression springs. But we are told that our rulers are men of our own choice. In private life if a man employs any agent to transact his business for him, he does not abandon all enquiry into the situation of his affairs, and the conduct of his agent, or if he does, the agent soon becomes master. To neglect all enquiry into the transactions of government, and the conduct of our public agents and then go to the poll and vote for a man to represent us; not knowing whether he has done well or ill is in the infallible way to destruction, the powers of government which nature entitles us to, and which we have acquired possession of with our blood, are weapons that will avail us little unless we learn how to use them; like edge tools in the hands of children, the chance is that we cut ourselves oftener than we use them to any good purpose.

To interdict a society instituted for no other purpose, than to acquire and diffuse among its members political knowledge, is what no government in America dare attempt, but for a few individuals clothed with no authority from the state for the purpose, to meet together for the avowed and express design of preventing other persons possessing equal rights with themselves, from forming themselves into a Republican Society, & fulminating censures against the promoters of it, is one of the most audacious acts of superlative impudence, that ever disgraced the annals of usurpation.

CATO.

Woods's Newark Gazette, March 12, 1794

"Republicanism" to Friends and Countrymen, March 19, 1794

For the NEWARK GAZETTE

Friends and Countrymen,

IT is not a strange matter to see the moneyed part of the people of America in general opposed to Republican Societies; the only reason is, because a great many of them have crept into offices, and jealous, least too great a share of political knowledge should be difused among the people, and of course, their conduct would be examined into, which they are doubtful will not stand the test, and of consequence they will be hurled from their easy situation; a change which they cannot think of undergoing, while there is a possibility of avoiding it. For this reason, they oppose the forming of Republican Societies, because it will have a tendency to enlighten the minds of the people.

The forming of Republican Societies has caused a great stir in many parts of America, amongst the tory part of the people; but in none more than it has in this place; the tories and the nobility have joined their efforts to prevent the forming of a Republican Society in this town; but (to the praise of the Republicans be it spoken) they have not succeeded.

It must be the mechanics and farmers, or the poorer class of people (as they are generally called) that must support the freedom of America; the freedom which they and their fathers purchased with their blood—the nobility will never do it—they will be always striving to get the reins of government into their own hands, and then they can ride the people at pleasure.

It stands the people in hand, who would keep up the spirit of freedom in America, to stir themselves up, lest while they are sleeping, the lamp of liberty goes out and they be left to grope in the dark land of despotism and oppression. Now is the time—every day you slumber gives strength to the enemies of freedom—they are waking while you are sleeping—trust not the enemies of the precious diadem—you have won in the field of battle, amidst blood and carnage to be the guardians of it.

It is said that we have a good constitution—let us know it well—let us see whether we have a good constitution or not; and if we have, let us see whether the administration is agreeable to it or not; if so let us endeavor to make each other as happy under such a constitution as possible, if it is a good constitution let us take care that neither ruler nor ruled infringe upon it!

A good constitution is like good wine, unless it is kept corked tight, it will degenerate. And it may be compared to a fountain, that if ever so pure, if the spouts are filthy, the streams will be corrupted. Let us therefore watch with attention and let us take great care that we do not pin our faith upon other men's sleeves.

Newark, March 18, 1794.   REPUBLICANISM.

   Woods's Newark Gazette, March 19, 1794

Resolutions Adopted on the Excise, June 9, 1794

At a Meeting of the Republican Society of the Town of Newark, held in the Society Chambers on Monday the 9th June, 1794.—The following Resolutions after being duly considered, were agreed to, and ordered to be published. [2]

RESOLVED,

AS the opinion of this Society that in a free country any act of government, or of any department thereof, cannot with safety, be placed beyond the reach of decent animadversion, that the freedom of the people in a great measure depends on a general circulation of the sentiments of individuals and societies relative to the transactions of government.

Resolved, That this Society recognize as a principal essential to liberty, the maxim long since established by an enlightened philosophy, that the three great departments of government, legislative, executive and judicial, should be kept distinct from, and independent of each other.

Resolved, As the opinion of this society, that to invest in one man, more than one important office at the same time would be introducing a precedent dangerous to civil liberty,[3] and establishing a practice which would be perpetually at variance with republican equality. That the judges of the superior courts either in the state of general government, ought not to be eligible to any other office; but should be independent of every other department of government that they may exercise the important powers committed to them by the people, unintimidated by frowns, & influenced by hopes of favor, or uninterruptedly by the multiplicity of offices.

Resolved, As the opinion of this society that the raising a revenue by means of excise, except in cases of eminent necessity, is incompatible with the spirit of a free people. Insomuch as to make it productive, it would become necessary to throw open the sacred doors of domestic retirement, and expose the persons of all ages and sex, to the ferocious insolence of the lowest order of revenue officers, which would have a tendency either to debase the minds of the citizens, and prepare them for slavery, or excite disgust against the government, and produce convulsions and the dissolution of society. Besides its being the most expensive mode of taxation is a sufficient reason for disapproving of it, experience having taught that the mode of raising a revinue by excise, takes more money out of the pockets of the citizens; and puts less into the public coffers than another— it having a tendency to corrupt the morals of the people, by opening another door to fraud and perjury, is in the opinion of this society, an additional argument against the adoption of an excise system of revenue.

By order of the Society,

MATTHIAS WARD, *President.*[4]
AARON PENNINGTON, *Secretary.*[5]

Woods's Newark Gazette, June 18, 1794

Resolutions Adopted Condemning Opposition of Citizens of Western Pennsylvania to the Excise, September 22, 1794

At a meeting of the Republican Society of the town of Newark, on the 22d Sept. 1794.—On motion, the following resolves were unanimously adopted:[6]

Resolved, As the opinion of this Society, that at no period of our political existence has the government stood so much in need of a public expression of the voice of the citizens in its support as the present—when the operations of its constitutional acts are arrested in their progress by the intervention of lawless and domestic violence.

Resolved, That this Society hold it as an essential ingredient in the Republican government, that the voice of the majority govern; that a deviation from this rule unhinges every principle of freedom, by setting up the will of the few against that of the many. That the conduct of our fellow-citizens in several counties of a neighboring state, is a flagrant violation of this important principle—the law which they have refused obedience to, having been constitutionally enacted by a majority of the representatives of the people. If they sincerely believed that this law was unjust and oppressive, they have fatally mistaken the remedy, by substituting force in place of reason, violence in place of arguments; and indecent menaces in place of temperate and manly remonstrance; thus under a pretext of defending their freedom, have they set at defiance the most rational and obvious principle of liberty.

Resolved, That we think it our duty explicitly to declare our sentiments, and say whether we will submit to the arbitrary and tyrannical voice of the minority, or whether we will pledge ourselves to the public to support the republican principles recognized in the Constitution which binds the inhabitants of the United States together. We, therefore, in the most solemn manner, embrace the latter— we look up to the general government as a wall of defence, and as a bond of union; to the state government as the impartial distributer of justice—the repository of domestic security, and the guardians of Civil Liberty. To these wise and well constructed governments, we have cheerfully confided our lives and our properties, and pledge ourselves to our country to support as far as in our power, their constitutional operations. Notwithstanding which we are aware that our governments are not infallible, but being under the controul of men, are liable to the weaknesses and infirmities incident to human nature, and therefore may DO WRONG. But as we have a legal, constitutional, and with all a peaceable remedy, to the evils that folly or even vice may cause, they ought to be submitted to, until such constitutional remedy can be applied.

Resolved, That in the opinion of this Society any attempts to prevent enquiry into the conduct of government, is as dangerous to civil liberty, as to raise in arms against its constitutional operations.

Resolved, That in the opinion of this Society, the late attempts to press on the minds of the people of the United States, a belief that the Republican Societies in the different parts of the union, have been instrumental in promoting the riots in the back parts of Pennsylvania—is not only an invidious calumny, but calculated to stifle enquiry into the conduct of government; by rendering odious and sus-pected those who have had virtue and public spirits enough to engage in it, that the man who would involve in the same indiscriminate censure a society of men, who, during the pendency of a law, should peaceably and quietly enquire into its propriety and utility, and a body of men who, after the law was constitutionally enacted, should raise in arms and oppose its execution, must either have a claim on our party for his ignorance, or merit our contempt for his prostituted prin-ciples.

Published by Order of the Society.

MATTHIAS WARD, Chairman,
AARON PENNINGTON, Sec'ry.

Woods's Newark Gazette, September 24, 1794

Resolutions Adopted Upholding Freedom of Speech, Writing, and Publishing, December 17, 1794

NEWARK, December 31.

At a meeting of the Republican Society of the Town of Newark, held at the Academy on the 17th December, 1794, the following resolves were adopted.

Resolved, As the opinion of this Society, that no country can be free, where the people have not a right to the freedom of speech and of writing and publish-ing their sentiments, concerning the transactions of government; and that a num-ber of citizens associating together does not destroy or weaken that right; that the different members of the government, are nothing more than the agents of the people, and as such, have no right to prevent their employers from inspecting into their conduct, as it regards the management of public affairs. That the freedom of opinion is a right inherent in nature, and never was intended to be surrendered to government. That if the government possess an uncontroulable power over the opinions of the citizens, a tyranny of the most despotic nature, may at any time be exercised, and the liberties of the people, laid prostrate at the feet of their public agents.—That the operation of public opinion forms one of the most important guards against a bad administration of government; to do away that operation and invest the public agents with the tremendous power of shackling the mind, would be at one blow sweeping away every substantial pillar on which the sacred temple of freedom is erected, and trampling that holy edifice with Goth barbarities in the dust, and with it the happiness of the great body of the people.

Resolved, As the opinion of this Society, that both justice and policy require, that every citizen either in public or private life, that hath done service to the public, should be respected and rewarded for such services, but no practice can be introduced into society of a more pernicious tendency than that of setting up an attachment to men above a veneration for principles.

Woods's Newark Gazette, December 31, 1794

4 | Democratic-Republican Societies of New York

DEMOCRATIC SOCIETY OF THE CITY OF NEW YORK

Constitution, 1794

CONSTITUTION, &c. OF THE DEMOCRATIC SOCIETY
of the City of New-York

PREAMBLE.

THAT all legitimate power resides in *the People,* who have at all times the natural and inherent RIGHT to amend, alter, or abolish the form of Government which they have instituted, is now considered a TRUTH so demonstrable, that to attempt to explain the intuitive principles on which the maxim is founded, might, in this enlightened age and country, be deemed superfluous. Under this conviction, We, whose names are hereunto subscribed, do declare, THAT to support and perpetuate the EQUAL RIGHTS OF MAN, is the great object of this Association: That to this grand point all our deliberations shall tend; to the furtherance of this glorious and important design, our views and exertions shall be solely directed; and to this end we will, with the moderation and obedience, inseparable from GOOD CITIZENS; in consistency however with the independence and firmness which ever characterize PATRIOTS, constantly express our sentiments as well of our PUBLIC OFFICERS, as their MEASURES. And in order more fully to secure the principles and objects of the Association we adopt the following

CONSTITUTION.
CHAPTER I.
Title of the Society.

THIS Association shall be called and known by the name of "*The* DEMOCRATIC SOCIETY *of the City of* New-York."

CHAPTER II.
Of the Officers of the Society, and their Respective Duties.

Art. 1. The officers of this society shall consist of a President, first and second Vice-Presidents, Treasurer, Secretary, and Deputy Secretary.

Art. 2. It shall be the duty of the President to preside over the meetings of the society; to call special meetings, when necessary; and to decide upon questions of order. He shall not vote with the society, except in cases by ballot; but shall have the casting vote when the numbers are equally divided: And shall also perform such other duties as may be imposed upon him by the constitution and laws.

Art. 3. The first Vice-President (and in his absence the second Vice President) shall perform all the duties of the President in his absence; but shall have no other privileges, except in common with the other members. An in case of the absence of both the Vice-Presidents, the society shall proceed to ballot for a President for the meeting.

Art. 4. It shall be the duty of the Treasurer to keep the funds of the society; to collect the dues; to pay the debts with the order of the President; and to enter its accounts in a book, to be provided for that purpose, and which is to be entitled the Book of Treasury Accounts.

Art. 5. The Secretary shall keep a minute of the transactions of the society, and read them at its next subsequent meeting; after which, if they are approved, he shall fairly enter them in the book of minutes. He shall enter and fairly transcribe all the laws of this society in the statute-book, and read them for public information whenever requested.

Art. 6. The President, Vice-Presidents, Treasurer, and Secretaries, shall respectively continue in office for the space of one year after their having been elected, or until the next general election.

Art. 7. The general election of officers shall be held on the first day of July in every year, unless it should happen to be Sunday, in which case such election shall be held on the following day; and all elections shall be by ballot.

CHAP. III.
Of Meetings and Business.

The regular meetings of this society shall be on *the last Wednesday in every month:* and twenty members shall in all cases be a sufficient number for the transaction of business.

CHAP. IV.
Of the Admission and Qualification of Members.

Art. 1. No person shall be admitted a member of this institution unless he is a firm and stedfast friend of the EQUAL RIGHTS of MAN.

Art. 2. No candidate for admission shall be balloted for on the same evening he is proposed, nor without at least five members of the society shall give positive testimonials of his patriotism and Republican principles.

Art. 3. All candidates for admission shall be elected by ballot; and if black balls from one-fifteenth of the members present appear against them, they shall not be admitted.

Art. 4. No more than one member shall be balloted for, or more than three members initiated at the same time.

CHAP. V.
Crimes and Punishments.

Art. 1. All crimes and offences against the peace, harmony, and good order of this society, shall be punished by removal from office, public censure, or expulsion, according to the degree or evil tendency of such offences or crimes.

Art. 2. No person shall be punished twice for the same offence of crime, and not until convicted thereof agreeably to law.

Art. 3. No crime shall be punished with expulsion in the first instance, except apostacy from Republican principles, or public infamy justly incurred.

Art. 4. No law of this society shall, by any construction in regard to crimes and punishments, have a retrospective influence: And no person shall be punished, unless in pursuance of a law previously existing and publicly promulgated.

Art. 5. All crimes not herein specified, and the punishments annexed to them, shall be ascertained and established by the statutes of this society, in pursuance nevertheless of this chapter of the constitution.

CHAP. VI.
Of Laws and Amendments to the Constitution.

Art. 1. All legislative powers are exclusively veiled in the great body of the society.

Art. 2. No alterations or amendments shall be made to this constitution, without the concurrence of two-thirds of the members present, nor unless one month's previous notice is given.

CHAP. VII.
Of Titles.

There shall be no TITLES used or allowed in this society, except those which are descriptive of some office actually held in it; to which title, so descriptive of office, the general name of *Citizen* shall be prefixed.

PRINTED by ORDER of the SOCIETY; At GREENLEAF'S Press,[1] 1794.

Also published in *New York Journal,* February 19, 1794; *Daily Gazette* (New York), February 20, 1794

"A Friend to Good Government" to Mr. M'Lean, February 21, 1794

(For the New-York-Daily Gazette)[2]

MR. M'LEAN,

Upon reading the constitution of a Society lately established in this city, entitled, 'The Democratic Society,' published in your paper yesterday, the following Queries struck me:

IS liberty in danger, either from the form or administration of the general government?

Or, is the government in danger from the excess of liberty?

Is America in so critical a situation, as to require the aid of new councils?

Is it necessary we should be in a revolutionary state, and try new projects?

Do the people require intermediary guides betwixt them and the constituted authorities?

Or, are they weak, and uninformed, after having performed wonders in legislation and arms—is a *restless* society necessary to their preserving it?

Are the members who compose this society, more virtuous or less ambitious than others?

Have they long given proofs of piety, patriotism, morality, and various other duties, that characterise good citizens?

Are these people organizers, or disorganizers; are they federalists or anti-federalists?

Do they associate to electioneer to effect, or to prevent others from doing it?

Above all, Mr. Printer, I ask, Are they chosen by the people? If not, as I know no other authority, I shall hereafter regard them as self-creators, as a branch, perhaps, of the Jacobin Society of Paris.

                                            A Friend to Good Government

New York Daily Gazette, February 21, 1794

"A Member" to the President and Members of the Democratic Society of the City of New York, February 22, 1794

For the NEW-YORK JOURNAL, &c.

To the Citizen President and Members of the DEMOCRATIC SOCIETY of the City of New-York.

CITIZENS,

The impertinent querist who appeared in M'Lean's paper of yesterday, under the signature of *A Friend to good Government;* and who has the audacious effrontery to call in question not only the moral character of your members, but also their patriotism, and the sincerity of their attachment to the interest and happiness of their country and fellow-citizens, with several other interrogatory hints, grossly characteristic of the sordid satellites of despotism—merits nothing from your body, or from any individual thereof, but silent contempt.

Although I am not a member of your Society nor personally acquainted with any of its members, yet having satisfactory information of the design of the institution, and of the patriotism of its members, I look forward with earnest desire, and certain assurance, to that more happy period, when your's, or one similar, shall extend itself, not only into every county of this state, but of the United States, and convince this *good government* querist, that *nineteen twentieths* of the people of these states are despiser of him and of his achievements.

A Friend to Rational Government,

For the NEW-YORK JOURNAL, &c.

A MEMBER of the Democratic Society, in answer to the QUERIST in Mr. M'Lean's paper of yesterday, informs him, That the *old whigs* in this city, observing of late the warm attachment of the old tories (who deserted their country, and joined their enemies, during her conflict with the British Dey) who are now enemies to our good allies, the French—I say, we, observing their attachment for measures and men in government that no patriot can approve of, suspect all is not right, and it behooves us, who purchased Liberty at the risque of life and fortune, to be *on our watch.* I hope this explanation will satisfy the *Querist;* if not, by calling at No. 244, Cooper-street, he may be further informed of the designs of the Society.

A Member

New York Journal, February 22, 1794

"A Federal Democrat" to Citizen Greenleaf, March 19, 1794

For the NEW-YORK JOURNAL, &c.

Citizen Greenleaf,

In your No. 2817, I have amused myself with the farcical new constitution of the democratic society of your city displayed in *great primer.* I must confess that the size of the type, and the pompous parade of chapters and sections drawn up in hostile array, prepared my mind for some wonderful revolution in the order of the day, as the immortal Paine is pleased to term the present era of the political world. But alas! in dissecting, analizing and sifting this monument of *human wisdom,* alias —, in every point of view; I find that I have waded beyond my depth, and that I cannot touch the bottom of this profound production. I request therefore that your Secretary, Citizen Wortman, will unfold the misteries contained in the body of this wonderful machine. Should he condescend to do this; I beg leave to state the following queries.

Does it comport with the genius of true Republicans to inflict a double punishment on public servants for the same crime? If your answer should be in the negative, why do you, in your preamble wish to lash "public *officers,* and their *measures*" with your displeasure? You profess to be a democratic society which should of right embrace the great mass of the people: but in chapter III, you say 20 members can do the business.

Is this Republican? instead of wishing, or aiming to embrace society, on the broad surface of a pure democracy, I insist and avow that your constitution is highly scarred with aristocratic S——k? to demonstrate this beyond the reach of doubt; be so kind as to glance your eye over part of the third, and all of the fourth chapter.

There we find bar gates, hedges and ditches to climb over before a citizen can get admission within your threshold; besides you have erected an eternal barrier to circumscribe your numbers within a small compass, as though you were afraid the misterious measures which you affect to have in view, should be too much known.

Is this characteristic of real Republicanism, whose basis should be candor, and wholly open to the view of the Sun? but not smothered in a dark corner grouping about in pursuit of an obscure object? no problem in Euclid can be asier demonstrated than this, or why do you say, that "no candidate shall be balloted for, on the same evening he is proposed," and that capricious 15th shall have it in their power to reject him, notwithstanding in the preceding article it is provided, that five members shall give previous testimony of his political principles? again, in a third chapter, you say your meetings shall be monthly, and the 4th article of the four chapter, you say not more than three members shall be admitted at one time.—What will this lead to? at most your society can only receive an acquisition of 36 persons in a year, out of which taking one year with another, death will cut down at least two of that number; so that it will require a period of 20 years to swell the number of your society to 680.

You talk of laws, punishments, and amendments to your constitution, with the same familiarity as though you were a legal, constituted body.

This, sir, in my estimation, is a breech of that decency, every worth member of the community owes society, and the constituted powers by which he is protected. From these remarks you will be led to pronounce me an aristocrat, and a high flying federalist; but sir, the truth lies here. Not one drop of aristocratical blood flows in my heart; I profess myself a pure, and unshaken Republican, and all my actions from infancy have given the most unequivocal proofs of this truth. I profess myself at the same time an uniform and a decided federalist, because I am certain that nothing short of a firm support of the federal government can save us from the compleat wretchedness and contempt; and I must in candor add further, that although attached to our present national government from its commencement, as our only hope and sheet anchor, I have never been without my doubts, but it would insensibly tend to draw within its vortex a greater seasoning of aristocracy than was congenial with the Republican genius of free Americans, and I shall never cease to exert my mite to lop off those exuberant breanches whenever they may be discovered, shooting forth from the great trunk of our constitution, and this we clearly find amply within our reach, without hazarding the peace of society, by establishing illegal and dangerous combinations within the body of well organized government.

A consoling door has been wisely left wide open in the very body of the constitution, and whenever experience shall point out palpable defects, the people (as has been already evinced in two instances) are sure to find redress in attaining amendments by assailing that door with their petitions and their wishes.—Where then lies our danger? And why would you hazard a great uncertainty for the most substantial blessing any nation ever yet enjoyed?

Should we be so ungrateful as to spurn the partial favours which the Supreme Being is pleased to bestow upon us, what can be expect in return, but that the vengeance of his unerring justice will descend upon our guilty heads?

A FEDERAL DEMOCRAT.

New York Journal, March 19, 1794

"A Member of the Democratic Society" to Citizen Greenleaf, March 22, 1794

For the NEW-YORK JOURNAL, &c.

CITIZEN GREENLEAF,

I OBSERVED a piece in your last paper, signed a *"Federal Democrat,"* who appears to be much displeased with the Democratic Society, because he has read their constitution and finds it (though very plain) too deep for his short sight; but if he stopped when had waded beyond his depth (as he expressed it) he would have saved you the trouble of printing, hundreds the trouble of reading, and myself the trouble of answering his foreign queries and impertinent observations. His first question is, "Does it comport with the genius of true Republicans, to inflict a double punishment on public servants for the same crime." To which I answer no, but that it is a duty we owe ourselves and our country to find out those who are guilty, and see that they are punished. He also appears very much troubled about the bars and gates to be got over before any person can get into the Society; but I can inform him, that true Republicans find very little trouble in getting over them. I think it a pity he had not gained a little more information before he attempted to write on the subject, for he (as he supposes) proves to a mathematical demonstration, that this Society cannot admit more in a year than thirty-six members. Now, to prove his ignorance, I will inform him, that it consists already of several hundred, and it has only been instituted two or three months.

He further observes, "You talk of laws, punishments, and amendments to your constitution, with the same familiarity as though you were a legal constituted body. This, Sir, in my estimation, is a breach of the decency every worthy member of the community owes Society, and the constituted authorities by which he is protected."

If this writer is not as ignorant of things in general as he is of the subject on which he writes, he must know that there [are] a great number of Societies in this city, who all have their constitution, laws, and punishments. Now I wonder that this writer and his brother anti-society men, have not before come forward to lash those daring men who are guilty of forming themselves into Societies such as the Agricultural Society, Commercial Society, Manumission Society, Tammany Society, St. George's Society, &c., and that they should yet have the assurance to question the right we have of forming a Democratic Society. For my part, I cannot see why we have not as good a right, nor why it is not as meritorious for us to establish a Society for the promotion and extention of Republican principles, and patriotism, as it is for others to establish Societies for the promotion of Agriculture, Commerce, &c. or for the St. George's Society to promote Aristocracy, by celebrating the birth-day of a tyrant. The truth, I believe, is the Democratic Society is only dangerous to Aristocracy, and her supporters, and the noise they make, are here dying groans.

A MEMBER OF THE DEMOCRATIC SOCIETY.

New York Journal, March 22, 1794

"A Federal Republican" on the Democratic Society of the City of New York, June 18, 1794

(Some OBSERVATIONS *upon the* "FEDERAL REPUBLICAN" *having been communicated for publication in this Journal, the Editor supposed it impartial and necessary to preceed it by the piece itself—which is as immediately follows:—)*
  To the Great and Mighty Democratic Society of New-York.
WHAT under heaven has frightened you just now, to come forward with a long vindication of your institution, and appoint a solemn deputation to wait on all the printers in town, requesting them to publish it? Have you discovered that public opinion is against you, that you are dwindling but into contempt, that the steady firmness of our government is like to defeat all your schemes; that elections do not go right; or what has given you a start just now? When the Christian religion was first promulgated, it was opposed; but, said one of its champions, "If this council or this work be of men, it will come to nought, if it be of God, ye cannot overthrow it." The same remark will apply to every new institution;

and one would think the Democratic Society, if their intentions are as pure as their professions are strong, and the excellence of their institution, as clear and as obvious as they pretend it to be, might hazard its existence and growth on *its own merits.* Depend on it, no really good establishment will need the aid of long laboured vindications, and formal deputations to printers. The people of America are not so stupid as to be unable to discover the benefits of your institution, if any such exist; nor do the printers in general wait for the ceremony of an invitation to publish what is really worthy notice. I strongly suspect you think yourselves on bad ground, and in need of support.

To answer every particular paragraph of your vindication, would require more time than I can spare, for a thing of so little consequence. Indeed your address to the admirers of the British constitution, needs no answer, for I am confident the number of such people is very small and of little weight in the scale of public opinion.

I believe there is no objection to the title of your society, if the society is in itself good. Names are very harmless things; but your recurrence to Johnson's dictionary for a definition of forms of government vindicates you to be young in the science; it is the business of *boys* to consult dictionaries for the meaning of words; men of intelligence have recourse to the things themselves which are to be defined, and there find their true distinction—And your opinion of Johnson's dictionary shows you understand its merits as little as you do the science of government. It is an idle business to cavil about the words *Democratic* and *Republican;* it is sufficient that the governments of America are *Representative;* that the constitutions and the laws of the country have clearly designated the mode in which the people are to be governed; and that in these constitutions, and laws, there is no authority given, for any number of persons to form private clubs, to establish a test admission—to exclude their fellow-citizens from these clubs—bind the members on admission by a solemn promise of secrecy—and then call themselves the people and censure the measures of government. If there is a constitution or law in the United States, that directly or by implication authorizes such associations, you are called on to name the article; you are challenged to specify the authority under which you act.

The fact is, your professions and your conduct are in perpetual hostility; your avowed principles and your proceedings are one chain of contradictions. Your darling theme is liberty and equality, a free press and the people's right to censure men and measures. In the principles we all agree, and we federal republicans, American whigs, practise upon these principles. We maintain the laws, which secure liberty—we obey the laws, which preserve equality; we lay no restraints on the press, but every man discusses the measures of government, as freely as you do, and I trust with quite as much decency. In all this business, we are open, public and avowed.

We have no clandestine meetings to manage opinions, to concert plans, and frame resolutions. We reprobate all such parties.

You, on the other hand, with the most solemn professions of being friends to equal rights, form yourselves into a private club; admit no person who cannot bring good evidence of agreeing with you in principle; that is, who is not of a party previously formed—and then, shut up from enquiry and contradiction, your debate, on public measures, in which your fellow-citizens are concerned as well as yourselves, and who are not admitted to the debate to offer their reasons for or against your opinions: here you deliberate and form resolutions; here you censure Representatives whom others have had a share in electing—You attempt to influence men and measures that I perhaps approve, and that without my consent.

This, far from being either liberty or equality, is a direct infringement of both.—It is an insult to our fellow citizens and a satire on every pretence to re-publicanism.—Republicanism is a disposition to promote the common good in securing equal rights by law. A republic (if I may be allowed to define it with-out the help of Johnson's Dictonary,[3] which is not before me) a republic, in the strict sense of the word (Res Publica) is a common-wealth; a government that has the public good for its object. Now is it possible that men who have the public good for their object, can wish to be private in their deliberations? Is secrecy a proof of patriotism, of a regard to equal rights, of love to your coun-try? Does it not rather furnish a well founded suspicion that not the public, but *private* good, the interest of a *party* is your object? Are not you the very men who lately clamored, about the opening the doors of the Senate? Did you not rail about the secrecy of their proceedings, and call that council cabal, a conclave, and I know not what hard names? One of your fellow Societies, I think that in Vermont,[4] has made the secrecy of the Senate, a ground of its establishment, if I mistake not; and yet at the very moment, you condemn that secrecy, you are forming a censorship over our Representatives, which is to be conducted with *close doors.* It is thus your principles and your practice are constantly at war with each other. Depend on it, whatever may be your efforts to strengthen your party in a few large cities, there is an immense and respectable body of firm fed-eral republicans in the country, farmers and mechanics of property and principle who look on you with a jealous eye; who watch your proceedings; who consider your institution, as arrogating a right that does not belong to you, and who are determined not to suffer your private cabals to assume an undue influence over their freedom, lives and property. You insinuate that "men in power have deep designs and machinations;" then name the men and name their designs. Deal not in innuendoes; those insidious daggers, which cowardice and meanness aim at the reputations of respectable men. Come forward like men; tell your fellow citi-zens who are the men and what the designs and machinations against our rights. —If there is corruption in administration, point it out plainly. I am an American citizen myself who have life and property and family at stake. I now call on you and every American citizen to disclose the danger if any awaits us. I love my liberty and property as well as you can possibly do yours.—We have all a right to enquire into the conduct of our public officers; and I now demand of you to renounce insinuation; to come forth with facts. Name the man in office, who has directly or indirectly betrayed his trust or formed a design against our liberties. I will be one of the first to arraign him; even were it the President himself, before the bar of public opinion; to try and condemn him. But if you do not throw off the mask of cowardly slander, and openly drag the offender to fight with his crimes upon his head all candid men will set you down as a band of dire calumniators, who merit what you really will have, the detestation of your fellow citizens.

You tell your opponents to call in their scouting parties and silence their trifling anonymous writers. Pray have you no anonymous writers, no scouting parties? Who writes all the abusive paragraphs against the supporters of our government—the federal men; the friends of neutrality? Who abuses the President, Mr. Hamilton, Mr. Jay, and other old patriots, whigs and the advocates of peace? Had you no scouting parties out at the late election? Did they not appear at every ward by relief or rotation? Did you not at some of your meetings just before the election, to avoid the charge of interfering with government as a society, adjourn the Democratic Society, and then, with most or all the members present, proceed to the nomination of candidates? If you did not employ this pitiful subterfuge report belies you.—Come forward then, disavow the least interference with governmental concerns; and tell your fellow citizens, you have rights and property to protect, whether all the members of your society have a legal vote for senators and representatives; tell them, whether in your secret council you do not treat of subjects which equally concern us all, and which therefore you have no right to conceal. But why do you talk of scouting parties? Is not your whole society, by your own confession, a scouting party, formed to keep an eye on men and measures? Have you not, either as a society, or in some other way, been taking pains to form a distinction between your fellow citizens? Was not the ostensible reason for the formation of your society, to ascertain your friends, as you call them, from your foes? Have you not a list of what you call aristocrats or tories, who are held up as odious men, and enemies to their country? Have you no federal native Americans, and old whigs of 1775, upon that list? Have not some of your members talked of taking off those proscribed characters at a general sweep? Have they not been indiscreet enough to say there would not be one aristocrat left, in short time? Have the laws of our country defined or designated an aristocrat from a democrat? By what rule do you distinguish one from the other? Have you any other standard to try men than your own opinions and prejudices? Who has subjected your fellow citizens to this tremendous inquisition into their sentiments.

Where is the law, natural, moral, or municipal, that authorizes this scrutiny, and the distinctions which it creates? Is this liberty and the equal rights, that a few citizens may lock themselves up and make out lists of proscription against their fellow freemen? And, this merely for opinion, without any overt act?

What is the design of such a list? Does it secure one right, one priviledge to you? Does it not engender hatred, prejudices, and faction? Is not universal toleration the glory of our government; and would you introduce a court of inquisition into this peaceful country? Come forth like men, answer these questions, and correct the public opinion, if wrong, on these and many other points interesting to public happiness.

Still farther, tell the public whether the late French minister was not the father of your clubs? Did he not, directly or indirectly, form the first society of the kind; that in Philadelphia or Charleston?[5] Did he not do this, at the very time he was privately issuing commissions to enlist men within the jurisdiction of the United States, for the purpose of making war on the Spanish dominions? Was not this a high misdemeanor, for which, in most countries, he would have hazarded his neck? Was it not a daring violation of our laws, and one that committed the peace of the country? Does not this same man, though out of office, continue in the country, protected by the laws? Does he never attend your meetings? Is he not intimate with some of your members?—Has he no influence in your councils? Whispers of this kind are abroad, and many good citizens wish to know the truth, so cautiously concealed from them. Come forward then, and convince the world of your friendship for the country, by a fair public avowal or denial of these things.

Come forward, and prove what your father hath asserted, and some of your society insinuate, that British gold has influence in our councils.

As to the only good purpose your society could ever answer even upon a liberal plan, that of spreading political information—I would only ask how you can gain valuable information, that is truth, with doors shut against every person whose principles are not, before his admission, proved to be the same as your own? You shut out every body, but your party, and discuss political questions. This must be a discussion indeed, like that at the City-hall last winter, with all the opinions & arguments on one side.

If this is a democratic way to gain information, it is certainly a very odd way and I am sure, has no example, except that of St. Peter in making orthodox Catholics, which was to sentence every man who would not be convinced, to be roasted to all eternity on the devil's grid-iron.

The writer of this is no tory, no British agent, no speculator. He is a native American, an old whig of 1775, a plebean, educated in the country on a farm, where his friends follow the plough for a living; he is not connected with an Englishman nor Frenchman on earth, and hopes he never shall be—He never owned a shilling in the funds and is under no influence but that of truth and integrity; a real lover to his country and its republican government. He knows the general opinion of the middling class of people about the country, and he knows that they generally reprobate Democratic Societies; considering them merely as Genet's scouting parties.

                                                  A FEDERAL REPUBLICAN.

New York Journal, June 18, 1794

"A Member of the Democratic Society of the City of New York" to a "Federal Republican," June 18, 1794

For the NEW-YORK JOURNAL.

To the person stiling himself a "Federal Republican," whose meek and christian attack upon the Democratic Society of New-York, made its appearance in the Minerva *on Tuesday last.*

New-York, June 13, 1794.

SIR,

HOWEVER strong your wish may be to the contrary, that a spirit of unanimity on the great political subjects which have agitated the minds of Americans for upwards of twelve months past, would prove highly beneficial, I dare assert no good man will attempt to doubt.

The Democratic Society of this city, on the 18th of May lst, in addressing such of their opponents as were natives of America, amongst many others of a similar nature, exhibit the following sentiment:

"Forgiving all injurious reflections against us, we most sincerely wish to unite with you in the strictest political friendship. Tell us what we can do without injuring our feelings as freemen, and we will go a great way indeed, to exterminate, forever, that spirit of discord and dissention, which has by far too long perplexed, and tormented the citizens of this state."

As *your* interrogatories to that Society are very numerous; permit me to ask *you* this one question:

Does any part of your address to them demonstrate the most distant wish to join in bringing about this spirit of reconciliation? Or does it appear penned for the purpose of producing a quite contrary effect?

Let candid, disapassionate, well-meaning men, of all parties, judge upon this very important point between them, and you; incited thereto by a love of peace, of good order, and of regular undisturbed government, they still most sincerely wish to meet their opponents with the olive branch, while, at the same time, you may assure yourself, if they compel them to the lamentable alternative, they stand ready to encounter their bloody flag.

You began your address with a contemptuous sneer, by asking what has occasioned their present fears; and, in the progress of your denunciations, declare, that there is an immense and respectable body of federal republicans in the country, who look on them with a jealous eye, and consider their institution as arrogating a high tone that does not belong to it.

That the middling class of people about the country, generally reprobate Democratic Societies, considering them only as Genet's scouting parties, that they are dwindling into contempt, &c.

The assertions, Sir, I declare to be false; you and I therefore are fairly at issue upon a matter of fact, which it will be criminal in either of us to evade substantiating as both of us have fairly acknowledged, that the public is greatly concerned therein. I will therefore propose, that you name the place within the state, not exceeding one hundred miles from this city, where the virtuous republican and labouring yeomanry shall be requested to convene on a certain day & hour, giving them at least two week's notice thereof, that their opinions may be the result of mature deliberation—that your numerous assertions shall then be laid before them, with such arguments in their support, as you, in your great wisdom, may think proper to display, allowing an equal right to another person to offer his arguments against them—that after a free & dispassionate discussion on each side, a division shall be had, & each person approving or reprobating your assertions, shall declare the same, by signing his name; and that the names on both side shall be exhibited to public view, in one of the newspapers of this city.

This, Sir, I assert, is bringing the matter to trial with very great advantage on your side, because you are permitted to chuse the place, and because, if your abilities are but in a small degree commensurate with your confidence and effrontery, they must greatly exceed those of your proposed opponent, who is conscios that his are very considerably beneath the point of mediocrity, being a plain unlettered Farmer, so destitute in the knowledge of even his mother tongue, as readily to confess that he ought not so much to be relied on, for an explanation of English, as Johnson's Dictionary.

It is on the striking goodness of the cause he offers to espouse, he solely depends for success.

His name is left with the Printer (Mr. Greenleaf) and will be delivered on your declaring yourself, in writing, to be the author of the piece alluded to, and that you are willing to risque the proposed trial.

Should you reject, after all your bickering, bullying, this candid mode of discovering the public opinion on the legality or illegality of the establishment of Democratic Societies, I shall leave the real republicans to determine, from what motives your very intemperate attack upon the Societies could possibly have been produced.

You attempt to ridicule the New-York Society, for their solemn deputation to the printers, and soon after for binding the members, on admission, by a solemn promise of secrecy.

In answer to the first, the many unmanly, insidious, and unbecoming attacks upon the Society, occasioned a wish in them to lay before the public, an undisguised statement of their principles (which you thought proper to entitle their long laboured vindications) and they appointed a deputation to request several of the printers of this city to give it a place in their papers, that none of their errors might be concealed from public censure; and yet you torture this open, ingenuous appeal to the public at large, into arrogating a right which does not belong to it.

In one paragraph they are highly blamed for being too earnest in arresting the public attention to an examination of their principles; in the next, they are severely censured for their secrecy.

Unless your vanity exceeds your insolence, I cannot help believing, that even you yourself must see, that the unprejudiced part of mankind will interpret this censure upon two points, so extremely opposite to each other, as a proof of your anxious desire to black up every avenue to that accommodation of political disputes, of which the Democratic Society appears so very desirous, and which, I again repeat, every good man must earnestly see accomplished. Their secrecy, Sir, which I do not approve of, I must firmly believe, arose merely from its being customary in other Societies; and, in support of this opinion, I dare to affirm, that in none of their books is there an observation on the subject of government, which has not been fully exhibited to public view.

You challenge the Society to prove their authority, either under the constitution or laws.

This is so self-evident a truth, that the Society would be disgraced by attempting to prove it.

Once more, Sir, you are at issue—If they are not constitutional—if they are not legal, it is the indispensable duty of their enemies in general, and you in particular, to quash them.

If they are so dangerous as you and some others of their enemies affect to believe, where has the justice—where the patriotism—where the love of good government, in you and your friends fled to? Why do you not bring some of their members to the bar of justice?

O fye! Jerry Sneak, you must certainly feel ashamed of this challenge, so often repeated, and constantly repeated in vain. The refusal implies, that you are destitute, either of spirit or patriotism, or that you are conscious of having advanced falsehood, for the support of which, to your great mortification, the good sense of a community, ever attentive to their rights, will preclude you from an appeal to them with any prospect of success.

On purpose to relieve you from this dilemma, and to afford you the consolation of reflecting on one patriotic deed in the course of your life, if it is by any means possible to rouse your palsied courage, I will go much farther than the Democratic Society has done, that you may attack me with a certainty of conquest, at least in your degenerate mind, & thereby prove that your actions have some analogy to your professions.

I dare the Legislature of the United States to pass a law prohibiting the Democratic Society in the city of New-York: Yes, Sir, I repeat it—they dare not even make the attempt. O! you seditious wretch, say you—O! you poor pusillanimous varlet, say I.—So he is truly a Jerry Sneak, who shrinks at supporting his professions by his actions. What! have you got a fainting fit? Take a little hartshorn, to ease your pain, to relieve your distressed heart. I will tell you why they dare not do it—Because, Sir, they have too much virtue—too much regard for our happy, our glorious, constitution, to attempt passing so base, so tyrannical, so unconstitutional, an act.

You farther say, that their avowed principles and proceedings, are a chain of contradictions. Take up once more the envenomed pen, and shew me one single link of this; I will then acknowledge the truth, or prove the falsehood of your assertion.

Though your baseness of heart may have smothered every sense of shame, yet respect for the community ought to have had sufficient controul over your pen, to have prevented such a long string of assertions and inferences, the greatest part of them being without so much as the resemblance of truth in their support.

You accuse the Society of admitting no person who cannot give good evidence of agreeing with them in principles; that is, who is not of a party previously formed.

I acknowledge the fact—and that you may, with more propriety, denounce our adequate punishment, I will, notwithstanding your equally furious and un-merited rancour, explain to you the nature of the party. Before member can be admitted, he is obliged to declare to the following purport:—That he is a friend to republican governments, in which are maintained the equal rights of man, and that he will ever defend those principles to the best of his abilities.

If, as you say, you really was an Old Whig of 1775; revert to your old princi-ples; and, if your moral character be a good one, you, perhaps, upon a humble ap-plication, a confession of your political misdemeanours, and a hearty promise of repentance, may have the honour of being admitted one of the party: Be not afraid, as our treatment of you in Society will be guided by the following obser-vation, made in holy writ, "There is more joy in Heaven over one sinner that re-pented, than over ninety and nine persons who need no repentance." You say a republic, in the strict sense of the word, is a commonwealth. It has not been un-common for the members of the British Parliament to state Great Britain a commonwealth.

Do you then mean, that the principles of the British government absolutely ought, or at least that they might, without destroying the original intention of our constitution, be adopted by the United States?

If you have given your explanation on purpose to pave the way for this propo-sition, God help the Democratic Societies, for they will certainly have to encoun-ter your farther wrath and indignation, as they cannot bring themselves to relish the principles of that government, even in its utmost purity; and the present practice upon those principles they equally despise and detest; and you, Sir, I cannot join with you in boasting, that I am not connected with any Englishman or Frenchman on earth, and hope I never will be. This is really the wish of a poor, pitiful, recluse, insolated mind. There are members of the Democratic Societies, who, while they abominate the principles of the British government, love, with a cordial affection, many of its admirers.

Learn, Sir, from such men in future, to distinguish between innocent error and intentional criminality. You ask, Have they not a list of what they call aristocrats or tories, who are held up as odious men and enemies to their country? I tell you, Sir, they neither have such a list, nor, to the best of my knowledge and belief, was there ever such a list even so much as spoken of in the Society; but though you have found out that "the laws of our country have not defined or designated an aristocrat from a democrat," the Democratic Societies take a pleasure in avowing (the offence given to all negative whigs, notwithstanding) that they will watch the conduct, and even the intentions, not only of the aristocrats and tories, but of all their adherents; and whenever they attempt to propagate their principles, in contradiction, either to those of the federal or state constitutions, will pursue every legal method to prevent their carrying their intention into operation; in which, were they to fail, they would recur to the good old method which produced the commemoration of the 4th of July, 1776. You ask a number of questions respecting the late French minister, Mr. Genet. He is not a member of the Society, nor ever attended it; nor, as far as I know and believe (you will take notice, I really cannot pledge my honor or veracity, through thick and thin, as you do) was he ever the means of influencing one act or resolution in it, either mediately or immediately.

On the other hand, I believe, I am safe in assuring you, that such of the Society as have the honour of his acquaintance, hold him in the highest esteem as a virtuous good man, and a *positive*, not a *negative*, Republican.

He may have committed errors; but, being such as flowed from an enthusiastic wish to serve his country, and that best of causes in which it is engaged, though the acrimonious malignity of your heart may have rendered them indelible there, they are long ago extinguished in the breast of every generous Democrat, by a consideration of the virtuous motives which produced them.

Having observed, that a number of your friends (I will neither call them aristocrats or tories) speak of your power at satire, and invective, with perpetual and undiminished rapture, and appear to esteem it the production of a man who possessed very eminent talents—willing to confide in their judgement, I will conclude with the observation which *Lord Mansfield*[6] made to the arch thief *Barrington*, upon his trial at the Old Bailey, "Do not continue to pervert the intention of providence; reform your manners; rectify your conduct, and convert your great talents in future, to honourable pursuits." That you may profit by this advice, go and do likewise, is, for your own sake, the sincere wish of

A Member of the Democratic Society of the City of New-York.

New York Journal, June 18, 1794

Toasts Drunk at a Celebration on the Recapture of Toulon, March 20, 1794

CELEBRATION.

The following are the PATRIOTIC TOASTS which were given at Corey's Hotel on Monday last, by a body of Joint French and American patriots, who there celebrated the glorious event of the RE-CAPTURE of TOULON.[7]

1. The people of the United States and their President. 3 cheers.

2. The People of France and their convention; may their cause be as successful as it is just. 3 cheers.

3. May the allied Republics of America and France, be bound together by the dissoluable ties of Liberty, Friendship, and Justice. 6 cheers.

4. An external abolition of all privileged orders, whether monarchical, aristocratical, or ecclesiastical. 3 cheers.

5. May virtue, talents, and patriotism, be the only qualifications, which may command the approbation of the citizens of America and of the world. 3 cheers.

6. May the people of all nations, kindreds and tongues, under the whole Heaven, be instructed in the Rights of Man, and ever be determined to maintain those rights on the principles of Justice, Benevolence, and Mercy. 3 cheers.

7. The people of the State of New-York, and the Governor thereof. 6 cheers.

8. May the present Minister of the French Republic pursue the interest of his country, with the same zeal and integrity as his predecessor citizen Genet. 6 cheers.

9. The fleets and armies of the French Republic; may success ever attend them. 9 cheers.

10. All true Republicans in Great-Britain and Ireland; may their shackles be removed, and their wounds be spedily healed; may their present venal and corrupt government be destroyed, and the gentle sway of Liberty established for ever. 9 cheers.

11. May the re-capture of Toulon by our brave allies (which we this day celebrate) be the prelude to the final extermination of traitors and tyrants throughout the world. 13 cheers.

12. Our captive brethren in Algies; may the protecting hand of our government be speedily extended to their relief, and may the insidious and persecuting government of Great-Britain, feel the shapes of reproach more strong than the sting of an adder. 9 cheers.

13. The heroes of France and America who have fallen victims to the cause of Liberty; may their names be written in indelible characters in the unspotted book of virtue, and may the trump of same, never cease to resound their glorious achievements.

14. May ignorance, bigotry and superstition be for ever banished from the

earth; may the crowns and sceptres of tyrants be melted in the furnace of a perpetual reformation; and may the genius of philosophy and liberty extend her wings over all the world to bless the children of mankind.

15. May virtue and true religion prevail over all the earth, and may the effect be peace, harmony, justice, and good will among all the nations of the world.

VOLUNTEERS.

1. Thomas Paine,[8] and all who are friends to the rights of man.
2. The Democratic Societies throughout the world.
3. Confusion to the politics of William Smith of S.C.[9] and all those who pursue his system of British measures.
4. Citizen Dugamiere and the Republicans that re-took Toulon.
5. The Mayor and Corporation of New-York.

ADDRESSES

Several congratulatory ADDRESSES and REPLIES, were spoken at this festival, expressive of joy at the glorious intelligence lately confirmed; of sincere wishes for the further *succeses* of our brethren and allies against all *despots,* and their minions—and of their *friendship* for *each other,* as *fellow-citizens of Republican nations.*

It has been difficult to *compute* the numbers of those Republicans who walked in the PROCESSION on this occasion[10]—the space occupied is said to have been *three quarters of a mile;* the streets were also lined with many known *Republicans.*

New York Journal, March 25, 1794

Ode on the Retaking of Toulon, March 20, 1794

ODE

On the re-taking of TOULON, addressed to the DEMOCRATIC SOCIETY of NEW-YORK.[11]
Written by Mrs. ANN JULIA HATTON.

> Hail! glorious day, with sacred joy survey'd
>   By men and angels; whose bright dawn
>   fortells.
> The fate of kings. No more by pomp betray'd
>   Shall man be bound in Pride's fantastic spoils

All hail! Democracy! whose fulgent light
   Shall chace the plague of tyranny away;
Whose wholesome laws, clear to the dimmest
    sight,
Shall rule the land with uncorrupted sway.

Hail! Band of Brothers! for the noblest ends
   Whom mighty Heaven approving, doth
     combine
To scourge the guilty; groaning nature's friends
   In whom soft mercy and firm virtue join.

Undaunted still each patriot passion feel,
   And still pursue the bright, the glorious plan;
On a firm basis fix the public weal,
   Nor cease till you secure the *Rights of Man.*

Down with the senseless pagentry of thrones!
   Rear'd at the dire expence of woe and war;
Of orphan's tears and widow's piercing groans,
   Wrung from the tortur'd bosom of despair.

Beneath the splenders of a diadem
   Fierce rapine, murder, desolation stride;
Blood stains the lustre of its brightest gem,
   And foul injustice swells the rank of pride.

Then be it yours, these evils to redress,
   To snatch the power from cruel despotice
    hands;
To crush that soul which would his kind oppress;
   And link the suffering world in social bands.

O! be it yours, in Mercy's school approve'd
   From tyrant wrong each groaning wretch to free;
From vice to strip the titles so much lov'd,
   And 'mongst mankind fix fair Equality.

From all its golden gates, Heaven hears the prayer,
   And seraphs, joyous, bail thé blest decree—
"My sons proceed, let virtue be your case,
   "And the exulting world shall soon be Free."

An authentic copy of the letter and resolve sent by the Democratic Society, on Monday morning to Mrs. Hatton.

Madam,

I have the pleasure of sending you enclosed a copy of a resolve of the Democratic Society of this city, expressive of their thanks on your addressing to them your handsome Ode on the subject of the recapture of Toulon. Be assured that this public mark of your attachment to the liberties and happiness of mankind will always place you high in our esteem, and the liberal philanthropy of your sentiments be ever remembered with approbation.

I have the honor to be,
> Madam,
>> Yours with respect,

JAMES NICHOLSON,[12]

President to the Democratic Society.

At a meeting of the Democratic Society of the city of New-York, at Corre's Hotel, in Broadway, March 14, 1794.—Resolved, that the thanks of this Society be expressed to Mrs. Hatton, for her polite favour in addressing to them her beautiful Ode on the re-capture of Toulon.

A true Extract from the minutes of the Democratic Society.

T. WORTMAN, Sec'ry.[13]

New York Journal, March 20, 1794

Address to the Republican Citizens of the United States, May 28, 1794

At a Meeting of the DEMOCRATIC SOCIETY *of the city of New-York, on Wednesday, the 28th day of May, 1794, and in the eighteenth year of American Independence, the following* ADDRESS *to the* REPUBLICAN CITIZENS *of the* UNITED STATES, *was, upon mature deliberation, unanimously agreed upon, and ordered to be made public:*

FELLOW-CITIZENS and REPUBLICAN FRIENDS,

Whereas sundry anonymous writers have advanced objections against this and other societies established upon similar principles, with a view of making them appear, at one moment dangerous, at another contemptible, we esteem it a duty incumbent upon us, not only to expose the falsity of the charges, but to demonstrate, as well the legality and propriety of such meetings, as also the advantages which the community will probably derive from them. In accomplishing which, we beg leave to observe—

In all nations wherever there has been an inclination in government, any principal part thereof, or in any particular class of the community, to subvert or abridge the Rights of the people, there never have been men wanting ready to sacrifice their time and their talents at the altar of expected power, at the shrine of anticipated greatness, who, with the apparent meekness of doves, but the real undermining subtlety of serpents, have industriously and infidiously wrote and harrangued, with devotional fervous, on the necessity of supporting government, on the evils, the terrible evils, of anarchy and confusion, on the villainy of designing demagogues, who, under the pretext of asserting the rights of the people, were engaged in schemes subversive of every principle of order, and perfectly destructive to those endearing bonds which link society together in peace, harmony, and friendship; and then, with affected candour, dwell upon the numberous blessings, the extensive advantages, which flow from a perfect union in sentiment between the government and the people; closing this delusive appeal to the passions by depicting, in the most lively colours, the horrid scenes which must, on the other hand, be the attendants of a civil war.

These have been the darling topics, the studied themes of a certain set of men, artfully obtruded upon the citizens of the United States for some time past; they well knowing, that there is more than an equal chance of preventing the people, by such general and specious observations, from attending to the deep designs and machinations of men in power, the great body of them being in easy circumstances, and lovers of peace, good order, and good government, equally enemies of the despotism of anarchy, as of the despotism of kings.

While *we* heartily join in the great advantages which arise from a perfect union between the people and the government, we firmly deny, that either the principles, regulations, or practice of this society, or any of the others alluded to, as far as our knowledge of judgment of them extends, can justify, in the smallest degree, any accusation made against them, or us, as sowers of civil discord and sedition, or as promoters of feuds and broils in the community; but that, on the contrary, we most sincerely wish for an union of sentiment throughout the nation, on the *real principles of the constitution,* and *original intention of the revolution,* and for a perfect and uninterrupted peace with all nations, upon safe and honorable terms; in support of which assertions, we now lay before you, our fellow citizens, such objections against our and other societies founded upon similar principles, with our justificatory answers thereto.

IT has been objected, that we have not stiled ourselves *Republican,* but *Democratic;* which signifies, as it is alledged, a government composed of the whole mass of the people, and not a representative government.

To this we reply—It is ever deemed a strong presumptive proof of a very bad cause, when its advocates attack their opponents with either false or flimsy arguments; and any one who will take the trouble of applying to Johnson's dictionary (admitted to contain the best explanation of English terms) will find, that the words Republican and Democratic are synonymous; and, therefore, that this accusation is absolutely false and groundless:—Besides, the author of the Federalist[14] (see vol. 2, page 20) generally supposed to be the present Secretary of the Treasury, and our opponents are universally his warmest friends, asserts, "That political writers have applied the term *Republican* to so many various forms of government, that it is left without any definite meaning at all."

Men of suspicious characters, men matured in intrigue and design, might alledge it was from a foresight of his being able, at some future convenient opportunity, to affix to the term Republican such meaning as he and his friends should find best to comport with their then wishes and intentions, that the first sentence of the 10th section of the 4th article of our constitution obtained its existence, which is, "The United States shall guarantee to every state in this union a *Republican form* of government;" for if the term Republican has no definite meaning, Republicans *form* must be still more indefinite.

It has also been objected, that we are *anti-federalists.* To this we reply—In the first place, we positively deny the charge, there being many, very many, members of these societies, who were warm advocates for the adoption of the constitution, from its first formation; But suppose there were none but those who, previous to the adoption thereof, *were stiled anti-federalists*—Reflect, fellow-citizens, what the nature of the objection would then be.

A convention was appointed in 1787, to amend the old confederation;[15] instead of amending which, agreeable to the intention and direction of their constituents, they thought it absolutely necessary to exceed their original powers, and proposed one totally new, to be adopted or rejected, as the people might think proper.

All parties agreed, that a new constitution was necessary, but those stiled anti-federalists said, Let us first make certain amendments, and then adopt it, because there is a risque of our not obtaining those amendments, which all parties think right, and we deem *indispensably* necessary. The federalists, on the other hand, declared in favor of the immediate adoption, alledging, that it contained within its own bosom the power of amendment.

This, fellow-citizens, we call on you to witness, was the only essential difference between the two contending parties at that time.

That amendments were absolutely necessary, as the anti-federalists insisted on, cannot now be rendered disputable, for they have been actually adopted in sundry important instances.—What, then, is the charge against the anti-federalists?

A matter of the utmost importance to the liberty and happiness of the people of the United States, was referred to themselves at large, in the year 1787; a division of sentiment took place throughout the states; in a legal point of view, those denominated anti-federalists, became the minority. The constitution was adopted in a different mode from what they proposed, and they are now, in

1794, by a certain set of their former opponents, branded with the disgraceful epithets of—Enemies to the constitution and government of their country. For what reason? Because they had the daring impertinence, the unpardonable audacity, the unprecedented effrontery, freely to declare their sentiments on a subject of equal importance to both parties, and left to the unbiased discussion of each person of every class and denomination.

If this is a true statement of facts on this particular point (and we call upon the enemies of the Democratic Societies to come forward and openly disprove it)—can you, fellow-citizens, who are true lovers of those principles for which we fought from 1775 to 1783—you who must wish to abolish every distinction, except *Republican* and *anti-Republican*—can you possibly permit yourselves to suppose, that those who exert every power, and strain every nerve, to rekindle the pernicious flame of discord and disunion from the sleeping embers of a once warm, but long since dead and buried, political dispute, can be the real friends of either your principles, your constitution, your government, or your-selves?

We will not insult common sense, by saying more in our vindication on this, which, of all our offences, is asserted to be by far the most heinous, and, of course, the least pardonable.

The third objection is, that we are leaders of faction, possess a turbulence of disposition, and intend to oversot the government.

To this we reply—General accusations, without any specific proof, being nothing better than idle declamation, can seldom be answered but by a general plea of, *Not Guilty.* Yet we will go farther.

We are so far from dreading, that we *eagerly court,* the most minute, the most strict investigation into our real characters, either as men or politicians; among such numbers we will not pretend to say that every individual will stand the test of enquiry; but it is the unequivocal wish of this, and we have no reason to doubt, that we are heartily joined therein by each of the other societies, that no one may remain a member, who is not a lover of genuine republicanism, a man of good moral principles, and strict honor, a friend to his country, and determined to defend it at the risque of every thing which is near and dear to him on earth.

We deny our being the camelions of accident, changing either our principles or practice, as fortunate or adverse events may turn up; nor are we the *minions of power,* inclined to disgrace the character of freemen, by sacrificing the delicate, the heaven-born principle of gratitude; those sympathetic emotions of friendship, so justly due to a nation contending for the right of enjoying the first principles of human nature, with a firmness and dignity on which angels must look down with admiration; principles which many of our enemies, while they have not virtue enough openly to advocate, possess, nevertheless, a sufficiency of either timidity or shame, not fully to disavow.

Yes, fellow-citizens, we take a pleasure in avowing thus publicly to you, that we are lovers of the French nation, that we esteem their cause as our own, and that we are the enemies, the avowed enemies, of him or those who dare to infringe upon the holy law of *Liberty,* the sacred *Rights of Man,* by declaring, that we ought to be strictly neutral, *either in thought or speech,* between a nation fighting for the dearest, the undeniable, the invaluable Rights of Human Nature, and another nation or nations wickedly, but hitherto (we thank God) vainly, endeavoring to oppose her in such a virtuous, such a glorious struggle.[16]

If this is the language of treason, if this is the language of faction and sedition, come forward, ye votaries of opposite principles, ye stoical apathists, who can set with folded arms, with sullen silence, with unmoved composure, while the house of your next neighbor, your former benefactor, *your only real friend,* is on fire, without affording even one single solitary bucket of water, to aid in quenching the raging, the wide spreading flame; ye secret abettors of tyranny and despotism, ye hermaphroditical politicians, come forward, we call upon you, bring us legal means, if such you can contrive, to the bar of justice, and punish us for these our open, our avowed principles, from which no earthly consideration shall ever tempt us to recede. But, be cautious! Could ye select, in this land of freedom, such an execrable groupe of judges and jurymen as condemned the innocent, the virtuous, the patriotic MUIR, our brethren, who we now address, would not only rise as one man, and, by every constitutional method, prevent the iniquitous, the unjust sentence from being put into execution, but would, if they failed therein, open the sluices of their justly provoked wrath, and crush forever the nefarious opposers of these principles; principles which they know, we know, and you *ought* to know, brought forth the most glorious epoch in the annals of our country, the ever memorable 4th of July, 1776.

We would not be understood to mean, that every man who opposes our societies, is an enemy to this country, or even an aristocrat in his heart; but we most firmly believe, that he who is an enemy to the French Revolution, cannot be a firm republican; and, therefore, though he may be a firm republican; and, therefore, though he may be a good citizen in every other respect, ought not to be entrusted with the guidance of any part of the machine of government.

The one moment we are denounced as a set of discontented, disappointed men, too insignificant to be worthy of notice; the next we are a restless, uneasy faction, who not only embarrass, but who will, if permitted to proceed, certainly bring about a revolution in our government.

Contradictory as these charges are, we will endeavor to vindicate ourselves from both—As to the first, we call upon our *enemies* to form amongst *themselves* a permanent political society in this city, under any name they please, let their number be equal to ours; we will reciprocally exchange the name of each individual member, and thereby give an equal opportunity to them, and to us, of discussing the characters, the opinions, the general conduct of each person composing the two societies, from the memorable 19th of April, 1775,[16] to the present moment; and thus place it in the power of you, our fellow-citizens,

to discover on which side the love country, and the true principles of republicanism, have been most prevalent.

If you, our opposers, dare not enter the lists with us in this open and unde-
signing proposition, call in your scouting parties, order your trifling anonymous
writers, your abusive hirelings, to be silent, and join us hand in hand in supporting those principles which *we practice,* and *you affect to profess.*

With respect to the second of these charges:—Are your interests our fellow
citizens so essentially different from those of the government?—Are the constitutional privileges of that government so incompatible with your rights, as to
render it an inevitable consequence that we should be their enemies, because we
are your friends? Are your public officers so conscious of having violated their
most sacred duties, and sacrificed your liberties, as to make it necessary that we
should oppose their measures because we have espoused your interests? Reflect
but a moment, and see what a dangerous, what a fatal concession would be involved in this charge against us. If the interests of our government are the same
with those of our fellow-citizens (and it is necessary for your safety that it should
be so) what possible motives can the friends, the advocates of the people have
in the destruction of the government and constitution of their country?

We have thus, we trust, to your satisfaction, fellow-citizens, vindicated ourselves from the charges which have industriously been propogated against us:
It yet remains to make a few observations as to the propriety of taking into consideration the measures of government, and to point out some of the advantages
arising from the establishment of popular associations.

To you who are admirers of the British constitution, and esteem it the emblem
of perfection, though you are citizens of these United States, and well-known to
be universally inimical to our principles, we give the following extract from the
late speech of an Irish patriot, Mr. *Curran,*[17] delivered before a corrupt bench
and a prejudiced and packed jury, for whose political damnation with all its attendant afflictions we most fervently *do,* and you most sincerely *ought* ever
to pray.

This great and good man *even in their presence,* has the honesty and firmness
to declare, "That it is the glory of the British constitution, that the people
derive a right to watch over the government, and to see whether abuses have
been committed by those entrusted with the administration of public affairs, and
that their liberties and properties be attended to as they ought:" Again, "It is
not only the right but the *absolute duty of the people,* to have a jealous eye
over the conduct of the government." And he farther says:—"Is it on the sacred
soil, sanctified by the liberty of a British constitution, that the people *collectively*
or individually, are to be prohibited from animadverting on the conduct of those
entrusted with the administration of their government?"

Tell us, ye whom we have lately adopted as our brethren—Have we generously
granted to you who have emigrated from Great Britain, or its dominions, every
privilege we enjoy ourselves in the freest country on earth, and do you, even be-

fore you have entered your teens in this country, wish in return, to deprive us of one of the greatest blessings of our birth-right? a blessing formerly claimed, and which we most sincerely hope will soon be regained in the country which gave you birth.

You certainly cannot be so ungenerous, so extremely ungrateful.—We will impute *your* opposition merely to your inattention to the principles of our government, and flatter ourselves with the hope that each day will gradually wear off your enmity, and that experience and time will at last render you our firm, our stedfast friends.

To you native Americans, who oppose us, we shall only say—Do you not blush at being so ignorant of the real essence of our constitution, as to object that the people of this country should enjoy a liberty asserted in Ireland, as an unalienable privilege under, and undeniable appendage of the British constitution? and this claim boldly and nobly insisted on, under the immediate direction of a despotic, tyrannical, time-serving bench; *a bench at the same time possessing more modesty than our opposers;* for they did not, even in the plenitude of their power, attempt to contravene the propriety of the claim.

Forgiving all injurious reflections against us, we most sincerely wish to unite with you in the strictest political friendship; but you cannot, nay we are certain you will not, on due consideration insist, that the first bond of that union on our part, shall be a deliberate and sacriligious surrender of one of our dearest Rights, an open acknowledgement that we do not enjoy an equal degree of freedom with the people of that nation, from whose tyrannical fangs many of you but a few years ago gravely assisted us in emancipating ourselves.

Tell us what we can do, without injuring our feelings as freemen, and we will go a great way indeed to exterminate forever that spirit of discord and dissension which has by far two long perplexed and tormented the citizens of this state.

We are sensible that you have all the agents from Great Britain, and lovers of the government of that country on your side, by which means you in a great degree direct our commerce and command our purses, but we cannot, notwithstanding, permit you to divest us of the privileges we enjoy under our constitution and laws; it would be improper in you to desire such a sacrifice.

And now, Republican fellow-citizens, we will close with shewing a few of the advantages which probably will arise from the establishment of such societies as ours.

Is the liberty of the press an advantage?

It would be treason against common sense to say that it is not.

Let us then see, what the learned gentleman, the author of the Federalist, whose authority will not be questioned by our opponents, says on the subject, see vol. 2, page 349. In proving that no possible evil could arise from the liberty of the press not being secured by the constitution, he says, "What is the liberty of the press? Who can give it any definition which would not leave the utmost latitude for evasion? I hold it to be impracticable, and from this I infer, that its security, whatever fine declaration may be inserted in any constitution respecting it, must altogether *depend on public opinion, and on the general spirit of the people,* and of the government; and *here* after all, as intimated upon another occasion, *must we seek for the only solid basis of all our Rights."*

If we must then, as this gentleman confesses, rest the only basis of our *rights* on the spirit of the people and the government, shall his friends and admirers come forward and say:—That the people, or any part of them, are not to meet for the purpose of examining and discussing whether there is, or is not, any infringement on those rights, and in a manly but decent tone express their opinions, and when necessary, *demand redress?*

But perhaps some of our sophistical opponents may observe, that the Federalist was written for the express purpose of obtaining an adoption of the constitution, and that many of the sentiments contained therein, were only designed to be applied to that very critical period, but buried in utter oblivion for ever afterwards.

For the honour of human nature, we are bound to think otherwise, but if our opinion is too favourable, the author can easily undeceive us.

In the meantime, we request him, or any of his advocates, to reconcile the above quoted expressions, with their opposition to the Republican and Democratic Societies established on this Continent.

Should they be silent, it must be deemed a tacit acknowledgement of their error, and if they favour us with a serious argumentative answer, they may rely on having a temperate dispassionate reply.

This mode of conduct, if pursued on their part, as requested and determined to be observed on ours, will enable you, our *Republican* fellow-citizens, to determine clearly and upon good grounds, Whether *they* or *we* are most your friends; and the friends of our joint country and government. Sarcastic wit, scurrilous ribaldry, general and unmeaning calumny, let it come from what quarter it will, we are determined to treat with silent contempt.

Another very important advantage to be derived from the institution of societies similar to ours, is the promotion of useful knowledge, and the dissemination of political information.

The character and worth of individuals ought ever to be estimated in proportion to the services they render to the community of which they are members. The active exertion of our talents, the industrious exercise of our abilities, is a debt we all owe to society from the first and most sacred principles of the social compact; and it is upon the strict and faithful performance of these duties, that the safety and public happiness of nations depend.

If then society possesses an absolute and unlimited claim upon the services of its members, it follows as a necessary consequence, that it is incumbent upon each individual, to use every exertion in acquiring a knowledge of the principles of government, and of the Rights and interests of his fellow citizens, that he may be the better qualified to support and maintain the one, and to protect and defend the other.

But it is in Republican governments,—governments instituted upon the only just and solid principle, to promote the universal good and welfare of the people, and not to further the wicked designs and crafty intentions of men in power,— governments in which *political* as well as *civil* liberty has established its salutary and happy, sent where the offices of state are equally open to every class and description of citizens, without any other distinction than that which arises from a superiority of virtue and talents—where no other empire is known than that of liberty,—no other sway acknowledged but that of law directly derived from the pure and flowing stream of justice and equal Rights—that it becomes a duty more particularly incumbent upon individuals, to require a perfect knowledge of the government and political institutions of their country, the administration of which they may one day be called upon to take an active share.

To the memory of illustrious characters, the ornaments of their age and country, who have spent their veritable lives in philosophical pursuits, and in making beneficial discoveries in science,—those who have invented or improved the useful or the liberal arts, public honours have been paid, and statues erected. The reason is obvious,—because they were useful members of society, and bene-factors of mankind. Is the study then of government, in which are involved the dearest interests of human nature, less serviceable or honourable than attain-ments in any other science? Is less honour or esteem due to the men who devote their time in pursuing the general welfare of their country? Let truth, let can-dour, let public gratitude decide.

Fellow citizens, without attempting to awaken your feelings, or sound the trumpet of alarm to your passions, we will now proceed to pourtray the incon-sistency of the enemies to our institution.

Public opinion agreeable to the assertions of their great champion, *is the foundation of all our liberties,* and constitutes the only solid ground-work of all our Rights. But how is this opinion to be formed? Is it to be the result of a careful and attentive deliberation, are you to hear and impartially weight the arguments on both sides of all questions, and decide as the scale of reason is found to preponderate? By no means, say our enemies, let the presses teem with publications in justification of every measure of the government, however im-politic or arbitrary: Let *Pacificus* and *Publicola*[18] distribute their aristocratic writings in every corner of the union, and gain eternal fame by underming the liberties of their country; Let us crush all societies and meetings of the people established for the purpose of disseminating political information: Let us tell the citizens, that public opinion is to be the evidence and safeguard of their rights: but let us mould that puplic opinion so as to make it congenial with our own interests.

Such is the sum and substance of the arguments of our enemies, when the clue is unravelled,—the garb of dissimulation removed, and the naked deformity of their assertions presented to the view. Attend for a moment with candour to the voice of men who are devoted to your interests—the first wish of whose hearts is the preservation of your Rights, your fellow citizens, embarked in the same cause, and cemented to yourselves by ties of the most indissoluble union, who have no sinister motives or private views to serve, and cannot therefore be suspected for an intention to deceive. Watch therefore, carefully watch the conduct of your public servants; examine the different motives by which they appear to be actuated; view all public measures throughout the whole connected chain of consequences, and diligently enquire, whether your supreme and universal good is the real object to be promoted.

If this, then, is found to be the case, if the conduct of your government is found to proceed from pure and disinterested motives, and not from views of personal aggrandizement and private gratification, reward it with all that a *free people* can bestow, your attachment and esteem; but by no means suffer your eyes to be closed by the baneful opiate of excessive security. If, on the other hand, the picture of your affairs assumes a darker shade—if the sable hue of your political atmosphere portends an impending storm, suffer not the dreadful cloud to approach too nigh; sound the alarm, then flock to the standard of common defence, and evince to the world, that the people of the United States are the only supreme soveriegn, and careful preservers, and saviours of their Rights.

Already, fellow citizens, you have doubtless observed the striking contrast between our sentiments, and the opinions of your opponents; You cannot but be well convinced, that the throne of despotism, the seat of oppression and tyranny, can only be founded upon the basis of ignorance and unlimited confidence; while the best preservative of Liberty is public knowledge and information: If, then, by the institution of our society, or of others similar to our own, we acquire a knowledge of one single political point, we benefit ourselves; if we publish it for your inspection, we render you a service the most essential.

Again—As ignorance is the irreconcileable enemy of Liberty so also is it the immediate parent of guilt; it poisons every pure fountain of morals in a state, and generates the greater proportion of crimes, that infest and disturb the peace of society; until at length, its contagious influence, flowing through every stream of example and imitation, has pervaded the most remote parts, the most obscure recesses of the political system, and banished every element of Virtue. Thus it is, that from want of information, the moral features of a state become distorted, and a large groupe of enormities are presented to the indignant reflection—It would, in the nature of things be impossible, that the evil should rest here, or government escape the dangerous infection; the symptoms of the malady too soon become evident; penal laws and capital punishments, the prison, the gibbet, and the rack are soon found to be the inseparable consequences, and inevitable additions to the natural evils that are attendant on Man. The association, then that is established to obtain a knowledge of our Rights, must also be calculated to instruct us in the nature and extent of our Duties.

Such was the pure, such the patriotic purpose for which the society that now addresses you was instituted. To obtain a more perfect knowledge of the fundamental principles of our own constitution; to diffuse political information; to form a more intimate acquaintance with the sacred and unalienable Rights of mankind; to cherish in our breasts the pure and holy flame of Liberty, and to cultivate the love of our country as the most noble of human virtues, were the great and ruling objects of its formation. Will you, then, our brethren, listen to the pitiful artifices of our calumniators, your enemies, as well as our own? Will you be beguiled by the insidious misrepresentations of those men who wish to banish us forever from your confidence? Will you consider it as criminal in us that we regard your own and our Rights, that we love our country, and adore Liberty? Too well we know your hearts to entertain for a moment the injurious idea. We will cease to wound your feelings even with the appearance of a doubt. Yes! our countrymen, we still recognize in you the saviours of freedom: We yet see in you that deep rooted enmity to tyrants; that settled detestation of kings and royalty; that determined, inconquerable spirit of independence which has hitherto rendered the American character first among the nations of the world.— How then could we suppose, that you, our fellow citizens, whose sentiments are so congenial, whose interests are so closely interwoven with our own, should become our enemies? Who so hardy to declare, that before the sons of fathers who so recently had conquered in our revolutionary war, have attained the years of manhood, before the blood that so lately streamed at Lexington, has mingled with the earth, the Republican Americans will oppose the institution of a society, intended for the promotion and preservation of Republican principles, or condemn the sentiments of Democracy, founded upon the Equal Rights of Mankind, as sentiments contradictory to their own.

We shall only add, That as this session of Congress has been remarkable for debate on some of the most momentous national concerns, it must be incompatible with the idea of a free government, not to suppose, that our legislature were desirous to know the sentiments of the people at large, whose voice, when it can be fully and clearly expressed, they ought implicitly to obey, if circumstances and events remain the same, as when that voice was given; and we know of no better mode of expressing that voice, that by societies whose members are composed of, and mingle with, every class of citizens; and who dedicate a certain portion of their time to that particular purpose.

The different Printers in the United States, are requested to publish the foregoing address.

By Order of the Democratic Society of the
City of New-York,

JAMES NICHOLSON, Pres.

Attest, T. WORTMAN, Sec.

Broadside, Library of Congress, Rare Book Department; Pamphlet, Newport, Printed by Southwick and Woodman, 1794; also published in *New York Journal,* May 31, 1794

Address to Joseph Priestly and His Reply, June 6, 1794

ADDRESS
of the Democratic Society of New-York to JOSEPH PRIESTLY,[19] L.L.
D. F. R. S.

Sir,

We are appointed by the Democratic Society of the city of New-York, a committee to congratulate you on your arrival in this country: And we feel the most lively pleasure in bidding you a hearty welcome to these shores of liberty and equality.

While the arm of tyranny is extended in most of the nations of the world, to crush the spirit of liberty, and bind in chains the bodies and minds of men, we acknowledge, with ardent gratitude to the great parent of the universe, our singular felicity in living in a land, where reason has successfully triumphed over the artificial distinctions of European policy and bigotry, and where the law equally protects the virtuous citizen of every description and persuasion.

On this occasion we cannot but observe, that we once esteemed ourselves happy in the relation that subsisted between us and the government of Great Britain—but the multiplied oppressions which characterized that government, excite in us the most painful sensations, and exhibit a spectacle as disgusting in itself, as dishonourable to the British name.

The governments of the old world present to us one huge mass of intrigue, corruption, and despotism—most of them are now basely combined, to prevent the establishment of liberty in France, and to effect the total destruction of the rights of man. Under these afflicting circumstances, we rejoice that America opens her arms to receive, with fraternal affection, the friend of liberty and human happiness, and that *here* he may enjoy the best blessings of civilized society.

We sincerely sympathize with you in all that you have suffered and we consider the persecution with which you have been pursued by a venal court, and an imperious, uncharitable priesthood, as an illustrious proof of your personal merit, and a lasting reproach to that government, from the grasp of whose tyranny you are so happily removed.

Accept, Sir, of the sincere and best wishes of the society whom we represent, for the continuance of your health, and the increase of your individual and domestic happiness.

JAMES NICHOLSON, President.

To the members of the Democratic Society in New-York.

GENTLEMEN,

Viewing with the deepest concern, as you do, the prospect that is now exhibited in Europe, those troubles which are the natural offspring of their forms of government, originating, indeed, in the spirit of liberty, but gradually degenerating into tyrannies, equally degrading to the rulers and the ruled, I rejoice in finding an asylum from persecution in a country in which these abuses have come to a natural termination, and have produced another asylum of liberty, founded on such wise principles as, I trust, will guard it against all future abuses; those artificial distinctions in society, from which they sprung, being compleatly eradicated, that protection from violence, which laws and government promise in all countries, but which I have not found in my own, I doubt I shall find with you, though I cannot promise to be a better subject of this government, than my whole conduct will evince that I have been to that of Great Britain.

Justly, however, as I think I may complain of the treatment I have met with in England, I sincerely wish her prosperity, and, from the good-will I bear both to that country and this, I ardently wish, that all former animosities may be forgotten, and that a perpetual friendship may subsist between them.

New-York, June 6.   J. PRIESTLY.

General Advertiser (Philadelphia), June 10, 1794

Resolutions Adopted on the Conduct of Citizens in Western Pennsylvania, August 20, 1794

At the meeting of the DEMOCRATIC SOCIETY of the City of New-York on Wednesday the twentieth day of August, 1794, and the nineteenth year of our independence, it was resolved that the following should be published as a declaration of their sentiments:

IT is the opinion of this Society, that the present situation of the United States is critical and alarming; and it is the indispensable duty of every citizen to use his utmost exertions to preserve public liberty, the first of all blessings, and to support the constitution of the United States, which has been adopted by the choice of the people.

2. This Society disapprove the conduct of their fellow citizens of the western part of Pennsylvania, in resisting, with arms and violence, the execution of a constitutional law, which however odious, had been enacted by a majority of the representatives of the people; because we conceive that a recourse to arms should only be the last resort in those melancholy times, when the memorials, and remonstrances of a majority of the people have proved ineffectual, or been treated with contempt.

3. It is also the opinion of this Society, that every lenient and conciliatory measure, consistent with the welfare of the United States, should be used with our western brethren before resort is had to that most dreadful of all alternatives, which can never be justified, but from principles of imperious, and urgent necessity, that of spilling the blood of the citizens, by the hands of each other; an alternative that must endanger the existence of all good governments, and be pleasing to kings and tyrants only.

4. This Society most highly approve of the prudent measure adopted by the executive of Pennsylvania in appointing persons to confer with our fellow citizens of Pittsburgh,[20] hoping, that by their own timely intervention, all disquietudes may be removed from the minds of our western brethren, and general harmony, fully and firmly re-established.

5. It is the decided opinion of this Society, that the mode of collecting public revenues by means of excises, is oppressive and dangerous to civil liberty, because, among a number of evils, they are partial in their operation, and productive of innumerable vexations, oppressions, and acts of violence in their collection: because they have generally been destructive to the internal tranquility of those communities, in which they have been established: because they create a dangerous and pernicious influence in government, by unnecessarily increasing the number of its officers, and subordinate dependents: because they tend to alienate the affections of the people from the government; and to excite those alarming jealousies, and dissentions, which can only end in opposition and resistance on the one part, and oppression on the other; and lastly, because in these United States we have every reason to believe they are immediately contrary to the wishes of the people, whose authority, in every free country, can only be supreme. And this Society, while they pledge themselves to use their unremitted exertions, by every constitutional means in their power, to obtain a repeal of those "immoral, oppressive, and expensive laws," do most earnestly recommend to their western brethren, an immediate and unanimous return to that state of order and tranquillty, which is the duty of all good citizens to preserve.

By Order of the Society,

DAVID GELSTON, *President*
JACOB DE LA MONTAGNIE,[21] *Sec.*

The several printers in this state, are required to publish the above in their papers.
New York Journal, August 27, 1794

Resolution Adopted on James Monroe's Address, November 5, 1794

Democratic Society—*New York.*

At a meeting of the Democratic Society of New York held at Citizen Hunter's hotel, on Wednesday Evening, the 5th November, 1794.

The Address of our Minister Plenipotentiary at Paris was read, and unanimously approved of, and on motion,

Resolved, That in the opinion of this society, the Address of Citizen James Munro, our Minister to the National Convention of France, is becoming the Representative of a free and enlightened people, and meets our warmest approbation.

Ordered, That the same be entered on the minutes, and published in two or more of the papers of this city.

Extract from the Minutes.

J. D. L. MONTAGNIE, Secretary.

Virginia Gazette and Richmond Chronicle (Richmond), November 21, 1794

Resolution Adopted on the Appointment of James Monroe, November 26, 1794

Democratic Society

New-York, 26th Nov. 1794.

Whereas this Society on the 5th inst. did resolve, That in their opinion, "the address of Citizen James Munroe, our minister to the National Convention of France, is becoming the Representative of a free and enlightened people, and meets our warmest approbation." And whereas, at that time, the letter of credit from the President of the United States to citizen Munroe, and the two letters of address from the Secretary of State to the committee of public safety of the French Republic, were not made public—It is therefore resolved, as the opinion of this Society, that the letter of credit of the President of the United States to our Minister Plenipotentiary at Paris, conveys the sentiments of every genuine republican and friend to the rights of man; especially when he expresses "the wishes of the United States for the happiness of our Allies, and of drawing closer the bonds of our emity."—Resolved, as the opinion of this Society, That the letters from Edmund Randolph,[22] Secretary of State, to the Committee of Public safety, dated 10th and 16th June last, declaring the good wishes of both Houses of Congress for the success and prosperity of the Republic of France, are evidences of the sincere affection and regard of the citizens of the United States, for their brave friends and allies who are now contending for the same liberty which they once assisted us to obtain.

By order of the Society,

Azarias Williams, dep. sec.

New York Journal, December 1, 1794

Circular Letter to the Democratic Society of Pennsylvania, 1794

CIRCULAR
DEMOCRATIC SOCIETY, New York
To The Democratic Society of Philadelphia

FELLOW-CITIZENS,

At this period, so important to the happiness and liberties of mankind, so interesting to the philosopher and the patriot, we have esteemed it our duty to address you upon subjects which you cannot but have contemplated with that virtuious enthusiasm that inspires the minds of American Freemen; with that anxious solicitude which must be attendant upon men feelingly regardful of their country's welfare.

The beneficence of Providence, as if, in pity of the sufferings and miseries of man, has already opened a new and brighter area to his view; that prospect which, but a few years since, seemed only portentive of approaching calamity, now kindly presages the establishment of general liberty and happiness, upon the firm foundation of KNOWLEDGE, and its attendant TRUTH.

The REVOLUTION IN AMERICA, however splendid it may appear in the historic annals of our country, whatever dignity it may confer upon our public character as a nation, like most other revolutions, arose from small, though by no means uninteresting, causes; originating from what we conceived to be abuses of the principles and administration of the British constitution: A mere change of measures, without any alteration in the political system, would have settled our disputes, and hindered our contest with that haughty and imperious nation. Convinced of our danger, by the cruel inflexibility and arrogant disdain with which our supplicating but manly memmorials were treated, by their severe and hasty determination to enforce the most rigid and unconditional submission to the supremacy of their parliament and government, and by the extent of their military and naval armaments, for the purpose of supporting their usurped authority, we then but plainly saw, that the security of our liberties, our prosperity, and even of our lives, was incompatible with our situation as DEPENDANT COLONIES of the British empire; and that resistance, in its origin barely designed to remedy the existing evils of a present oppression, extending itself in proportion as our knowledge and our views were found to expand, at length settled into a contest which terminated in the sovereignty and independence of America.

The same unbounded spirit of discovering enquiry which but so lately had extended itself to every department of human learning, soon began to dart its exploring eye into the nature and principles of that science which appears so intimately connected with the condition, the happiness, and the general character of man. It was not to be expected, that in an age of philosophical investigation, when the revolutions of the planets were surveyed, and their distances measured, when even the swift and subtle lightning was pursued, and traced to its hitherto hidden sources, that the errors and abuses of government, one of the plainest branches of moral science, should remain unnoticed and unknown. While the discerning pen of the moralist inculcated and traced the various duties arising from the necessary relations of beings, the vast distance which once appeared to separate the monarch from the peasant, by degrees grew more and more imperceptible, and at length totally vanished. The JURE DIVINO, title of crowned tyrants, once the constant theme and study of subtle schoolmen, and still more crafty ecclesiastics, established by mysterious comments upon a prostituted and perverted revelation, was reluctantly abandoned, and kings became necessitated to erect their superstructure of dominion upon the broader and more solid foundation of compact. Deprived of those formidable weapons, superstition and delusion, the diadem and tyara possess but a precarious existence, and the Rights of Mankind will be permanently established upon the tombs of their oppressors.

SUPERSTITION in religious creed, and DESPOTISM in civil institution, bear a relation to each other similar to that which exists between the children of common parents. The same principle which supports the one, tends to strengthen and invigorate the other; both are founded upon the degraded state of the percipient principle, and equally arise from a want of the powers, or the opportunities, of reflection. Sensible of the nearness of their relation, and the unity of their interests, the civil and ecclesiastical hierarchies, the CHURCH and the STATE, had pledged themselves to each other by vows of the most indissoluble fidelity; the articles of the treaty were solemnly ratified, and the object of the parties was, deception and plunder.

The PRIVILEGED ORDERS of modern Europe, essentially differed from those of any other country or period, both in their origin and in the general nature of their establishment. The patricians of ancient Rome, a name derived from an honorable but improper etymology, had real duties subjoined to their distinguished stations—to protect the poor dependant client—to furnish him with prudent advice in a moment of difficulty—to rescue him from oppression, and even to appear his advocate when summoned within the walls of the *forum contentiosum,* were all of them indispensable obligations, which the generous patron delighted in performing. The feudal nobility, possessed of territorial rights, which they granted to their vassals by subinfeudations, under a burthensome and precarious tenure, and accompanied with slavish and dishonorable services, were neither distinguished from their dependants by the charms of virtue, or the superiority of talents. EUROPE is indebted for her progress in civilization, and her proficiency in the sciences, to the exertions of the untitled commoner, and not to the labours or abilities of the privileged orders.

Deeply impressed with the importance, as well as the truth, of the sentiments, acquired amidst the toils and the hardships of the American contest, our French

auxiliaries, zealous and sincere in the cause in which they had engaged, returning
with honor to their native country, felt their patriotism kindle into indignation
at the view of her wrongs and misfortunes; inspired with that ardent love of
Liberty, which is felt by all who understand its principles, and have perceived
its salutary influence, those stern Republicans, who had so nobly fought in establishing the liberties and independence of a foreign country, could no longer
endure the insolence of a court, that had become proverbial for its intrigues, its
oppressions, its tyranny, and its cruelties. In less than seven years from the conclusion of that war, in which they had assumed so distinguished a part, the sentiments of the soldiery had pervaded the mass of the French nation, and we have
been the approving spectators of a revolution, that has implanted the sacred
Tree of Liberty in a soil, hitherto accustomed to the most baneful and poisonous
weeds of despotism.

While we perceive and rejoice in the astonishing increase of knowledge and
public liberty, yet are there causes which, even in this country, have proved
dangerous to their existence, or at least have retarded their progress. GOVERN-
MENTS have always an extensive influence in forming the character, the manners,
the habits, and the customs of a people; but when such habits and customs are
established previous to the formation of a government, its features and its genius
afford a faithful picture of national manners and prejudices. Educated under the
administration of the BRITISH CONSTITUTION, the American citizen too often
involuntarily feels a blind attachment to its principles. Led, by his earliest habits
of thinking, to entertain the most exalted idea of the purity of its maxims, and
the justice of its laws, his former associations retain an ascendancy in his mind,
and impede independence and originality of reflection. The same devoted attachment to his pre-conceived opinions, that so often has proved fatal to the
improvement of the sciences, will long retard our approach to that perfection in
government, which the progressive nature of man is capable of attaining.

Another important cause of our undue attachment to the principles and the
maxims of the English government, arises from our extensive intercourse with
that nation. Commerce, though justly celebrated as one of the greatest causes
of the present civilization, and refinement in manners, yet, by introducing the
corrupt principles and abandoned polity of foreign climes, often proves injurious
to the morals of a state. It is not only in our pecuniary concerns, but also in our
government, and in our laws, that we have experienced the unhappy effects resulting from our too intimate connection with Great Britain; a similarity in
language, and in habits, has given to its agents an ascendancy in our elections,
and *perhaps* of consequence in our councils, that is hard to be reconciled with
the honor, the welfare, or even the INDEPENDENCE of the United States.

The channels of commerce, when once established, are difficult to be removed;
the connection, the confidence, and the credit that subsist between merchants,
the predilection in favour of particular articles and manufactures, and even the
habits of intercourse itself, render the designation of the evil much easier than
the application of the remedy.

The emigration of foreigners, though one of the causes in which this country owes its astonishing increase in wealth and in splendor, yet when considered with a view to its internal prosperity, appears productive of some evil in its consequences. The great influx of British subjects, many of whom still continue to retain a deep rooted attachment to their much boasted constitution, as it tends to strengthen that commercial dependence, and to confirm and diffuse those prejudices and sentiments which have been considered as so dangerous, is far from being favorable to improvement in our political institution.

The plot of our political drama is by no means original, but has been copied with some degree of servility from the European stage. The character of the heroes bear a striking analogy, and the sentiments inculcated, are substantially the same in the copy as in the original—The excise laws, the system of funding, and that of stock-jobbing, considered as imitations, are unusually correct. The constituent unities, however, appear to have escaped the attention of the authors of the performance, as the sentiments and the moral do not appear suitable to the *times,* or correspond with the genius of REPUBLICAN POLITICS.

The fear of DISUNION, whether real or pretended, is another source to which may be attributed the defects in our political institution. Sensible of the attachment which binds the people of the United States to each other by kindred and endearing ties, apprised of their tender regard to that inviolate connexion which can alone secure the tranquillity and happiness of this country, advantage has been taken of the sincerity and ardour of those very sentiments which precluded the most distant probability of danger. The calamaties attendant upon disunion, the horrors of intestine commotions and civil broils, and the example of the Grecian confederacy, have often and artfully been urged as unanswerable arguments for the necessity of energy in our federal government.

Fellow-Citizens,

While we express to you our sincere attachment to the constitution of the United States, we yet avow the sentiment, that too much power is incompatible with the principles of republican government, that EXCESS OF ENERGY IS DESPOTISM.

Let the enemies of Democracy exert their insidious artifices to lesson us in the public estimation. Let them accuse us of being the friends of sedition and anarchy, and inimical to every system of order & legitimate government. Let them openly proclaim to the world, that we entertain views hostile to the true interest of our country; that we are endeavoring to erect our fabrick of greatness upon the prostrated ruins of its constitution. Unmindful of the clamour of a ministerial party, who would banquet upon the grave of public liberty, while we will constantly endeavor to displace such of our public representatives as shall be found unworthy of our confidence, we will continue to remain the unshaken supporters of our present representative government, in times when its pretended friends would shrink from its defence, or even grasp the sword for its destruction.

To preserve, to secure public liberty, is the most urgent duty that a freeman owes to his country. The preceding picture, though faintly and perhaps inaccurately drawn, must manifestly evince the necessity of union between the republican citizens of the United States, to counteract the pernicious tendency of those erroneous and dangerous principles.—Considered as a mean to effect this truly valuable purpose, the institution of DEMOCRATIC and other REPUBLICAN associations must appear an happy event in the political history of this country. Unawed by the frowns or the menaces of men in power, by the reproachful or malicious insinuations of the tools to party, or the sycophants of government, we trust, fellow-citizens, that you will feel it your interest to preserve those sacred rights which were purchased at the expence of so much blood; that you will esteem it an insuperable obligation to transmit them unimpaired as the fairest birthright of a grateful posterity.

TRUTH never shrinks from discussion, but ERROR is fearful of shadows. That government which feels a consciousness of exerting the despots of power, which is entrusted to it by its SOVEREIGN, the PEOPLE, for the public welfare, will always court an investigation into its motives and its measures. In order to promote that investigation, to unite by closer bonds of union the members of the various Republican Institutions throughout the United States, and to increase their active influence in furthering the welfare and happiness of their common country, we beg leave, fellow-citizens, to submit to your consideration the following propositions:—

I. That the members of each of the Democratic and Republican Associations shall respectively have the rights of membership and sitting in each.

Many are the valuable effects that, in all probability, would result from the adoption of this measure. The intercourse between our respective institutions would be facilitated and strengthened—we would all become acquainted with the principles and opinions of each other—our stock of general information would be greatly improved and increased, and the republican interest of the United States would be concentrated, and, by acting in unison, would be enabled to gain a redoubled vigour and activity. The private benefit resulting to individuals in acquiring friends and acquaintances in the different states, appears equally obvious.

Should this measure obtain your approbation, in order to prevent deception and imposition, it would be necessary to establish some general mode of proving membership, and we know of none better than a certificate, signed by the presiding officers of the respective societies.

II. Impressed with the idea, that our respective associations were established to promote the welfare of their country, by their active and industrious exertions, so as, by those exertions, they do not violate the principles and the spirit of its established constitution—We also submit to you the expediency of petitioning Congress, at their present session, for the repeal of the excise laws. Far as we are from approving of the too hasty and violent resistance of our brethren of the west of Pennsylvania, we still remain convinced, that the present system of excise, by its own arbitrary principles, and the undue power and influence it bestows upon the executive officers of the government, is inimical and dangerous to what we conceive and trust to be the principles of our present constitution:— We, therefore, earnestly recommend to you to promote and further memorials to our public representatives, upon this most important subject, in the various counties and cities in which your institutions are respectively established; not, indeed, as societies, but as individual citizens; and we pledge ourselves to you, should this measure obtain your approbation, that we will join our interest with yours, in its advancement, and procure the names of as many respectable citizens to be subscribed to such petition, as are found to agree with us in sentiment.

III. There is yet one subject, fellow citizens, that will doubtless awaken all your feelings into action—An American, and in slavery! not one consoling hand to lighten his chains—not one kind friend to administer relief, or drop a tear upon his grave. Is it policy, inattention, or insensibility that prevents our government from extending that protection which is the right of every citizen, to the unfortunate CAPTIVES OF ALGIERS. Whatever may be the fact, it is an indispensable duty in us to afford them that pittance of relief which is in our power to bestow. It appears from an estimate of Mr. Humphreys,[23] our minister at Lisbon, that 300,000 dollars would procure the release of our unhappy fellow-citizens. Large as this sum may seem, a great proportion of it might be raised by the voluntary contribution of our members, and the remainder, perhaps, be procured by the subscription of the citizens at large. Let us at least attempt it, and if we fail, we can console ourselves with this reflection, that we have made use of every exertion in the performance of so god-like a duty.

In all future exertions to promote, to the utmost of our power, the happiness and welfare of our country, we solicit your support; upon the subjects contained in this address, we request your speedy answer; and upon these and all other subjects that concern the public weal, we earnestly request a regular correspondence.

We are, fellow-citizens, with the most sincere wishes for your private happiness, and for the prosperity of our common country,

      Yours, &c.

(Signed)   Melancton Smith
             Wm Allum
             T. Wortman   *Committee of*
             Thos. Gilbert   *Correspondence of the*
                                      Democratic Society
         New York, December   *of the City of*
                                      NEW-YORK.
                                      1794.

Pamphlet, New York, 1794, copy in New-York Historical Society

Address to "Fellow Freemen," January 26, 1795

At a meeting of the DEMOCRATIC SOCIETY of the City of New-York, held at
citizen Hunter's Wednesday evening, Jan. 14, 1795, the following ADDRESS
was unanimously agreed to and ordered to be printed:
The DEMOCRATIC SOCIETY of the city of NEW-YORK, to their brethren, the
citizens of the UNITED STATES.

FELLOW FREEMEN,

The alarm has been given! a signal has been made! confidence hath fled, and
the sweets of security have given place to the apprehensions of danger! At the
seat of government a voice, loud, and imposing, has been heard, and already has
it reached the distant corners of the union! We have been charged with the commission of crimes the most aggravated, & some of the public functionaries have
become our accusers. We have been stigmated with habouring designs destructive to the peace, and subversive of the constitution of our country; and some
of the representatives of the people have listened to the accusation! To a call
so imperious and so powerful, silence would be a crime; inattention would assume the aspect of a total dereliction of character, and a criminal abandonment
of principles.

The privilege of a fair and impartial hearing is a right sacred to innocence,
and consecrated to the proservation of virtue. Painful as it at all times is, to
labour under the suspicions of guilt; when the imputation becomes strengthened
by men whose characters and station in life have wrested the public confidence
in their favour; when the imputation is openly avowed under the imposing sanction of their names, and impressed with the all powerful stamp of their popularity:
when the crime imputed is not only such as would prove injurious to the dearest
interests of their country, but even threaten destruction to all the elements of
social life, the powers of language become inadequate to describe the emotions
of the mind. Contemptible as we have deemed the artifices of our enemies,
much as we have despised their calumnies, we feel that the present ought not
to be passed over in silence, for the support of our reputation, for the preservation of our character, as PATRIOTS, as CITIZENS, and as MEN. We shall make our
appeal to the PEOPLE.

To you our fellow freemen, to you the people of the United States, the only
SUPREME SOVEREIGN of our country, you to whom all power, exercised for
social purposes, is responsible for the faithful fulfilment of its delegated trusts,
at this moment we address ourselves. At your august tribunal, devoted to the
preservation of public liberty, and consecrated to the guardianship of the laws,
we submit all the charges and evidences against us—feeling as we do, the rectitude
of our intentions, unconscious of criminality, or error, from the decision of that

tribunal, we have everything to hope and nothing to fear. By your determination therefore, by the voice of *justice* and of our *country,* we submit ourselves TO STAND OR TO FALL.

To begin, with the first, and most momentous accusation, our supposed instrumentality in exciting or fomenting the late *insurrection at Pittsburgh.*—But how shall we vindicate ourselves against a charge exhibited without testimony? Unsupported by the smallest shadow of evidence? So weak and futile, as scarcely to possess an attendant circumstance in its favour.

Ardent and sincere in our attachment to the cause of liberty, *your cause as well as our own,* we have exercised a right, the most invaluable to freemen, and dangerous to TYRANTS ONLY. No sooner had the existence of our institution been announced to the world, than certain characters, unfriendly to the principles of equal liberty, commenced an outrageous warfare of slander & abuse against us. Accusations the most groundless, and calumnies the most base and dishonourable, were heaped upon each other. Even the press, that hitherto faithful guardian of public freedom, through the industrious artifices of our enemies, became converted into a vehicle of abuse. Such has been the avidity with which certain writings and periodical publications have been circulated, as manifestly proves that their publishers and fabricators were actuated by more than ordinary motives, stimulated by incentives more lucrative than honorable, more beneficial to themselves, than productive of the prosperity of their country.

Still relying upon the purity of our motives and the justice of our cause, impressed with the most forcible conviction of the indulgent candor, and determined patriotism of our countrymen, we contented ourselves with submitting to public view a fair and accurate statement of the nature of our institution, and the principles by which we had been uniformly governed. Observing the strictest obedience, and regard to the laws and political institutions of our country, we remained satisfied with the consciousness of having deserved your friendly countenance and approbation.

Such was the history of our association, and proceedings, and similar was the conduct of the other patriotic institutions, when an alarming opposition to one of the laws of the union, took place in the west of Pennsylvania. At the commencement of the present sessions of Congress, the president of the United States, in his address to the public representatives, in some measure, attributed that insurrection to certain *"self created societies,"* whom he asserted to have assumed the *"tone of condemnation."* The senate, in their answer to that address publicly pronounced their acquiescence in the opinion.

The solemnity and publicity of testimony should always bear a just analogy to the extent, and enormity of the crime that is charged.—But of what conduct have we been guilty, thus to subject us to presidential animadversion, or senatorial proscription. The censure of the senate has been indiscriminate. But shall we be condemned without proof? It may be possibly urged, that our *sentiments are inimical to the law, which gave birth to the insurrection*—but does it from

thence follow, that we approved of the *mode* and *violence* of the opposition?
We expressed our disapprobation of the principles of an EXCISE, but in terms,
full as pointed; *we condemned all unconstitutional opposition to the law of our
country.* Nay, to render our assertions still less doubtful, the members of our
sister societies of the states from which the requisition was made, were among
the foremost to fly with alacrity, and promtitude to the standard erected for the
defence of the constitution.

Is our being "*self created*" reckoned among the charges of the proscription?
By *whom* then ought we to be constituted? If appointed by *delegation* we would
become the representative of the people, if *elected* we should become organ of
the general will. But are not all private associations established upon the foundation of their own authority sanctioned by the first principles of social life, and
guaranteed by the spirit of the laws? Was it thought *necessary* to obtain a *special
act* of legislative power for the *exclusive* creation of the SOCIETY of CINCINNATUS
of which our first executive magistrate, is, or was the presiding officer, or *is that
society* "SELF CREATED?"

Is it for *assembling* that we are accused? what law FORBIDS it? for *deliberating,*
for *thinking,* for *exercising the faculties of the mind.* What statute has DEPRIVED
us of the RIGHT? For the *publication of our sentiments,* where is the constitution
that is *prohibitory?* if our opinions are founded in political error, if they are
calculated to mislead, counteract their evil tendency by the *force of argument.*
Truth may be suppressed by violence, but it will ever triumph amidst freedom
of enquiry. Is it for *animadverting* upon the *conduct of government,* or for pre-
suming to *disapprove of any of the measures* of administration, that we are
censured? The government is *responsible* to its sovereign the people for the
faithful exercise of its entrusted powers, and *any part of the people* have the
right to express their opinions on the government.

But what possible danger has the government of this country, to apprehend
from the existence of popular societies? They have no interest but in common
with their fellow citizens, they are equally concerned in the preservation of law,
and the establishment of civil order, for upon that the safety of their lives, and
the security of their fortunes depend. They have pledged themselves as faithful
citizens, while they use their utmost endeavours to preserve public liberty, to
maintain inviolate the principles of the constitution, and their personal interest
is a surety responsible for their sincerity. They are not even suspected of being
the *advocates of a standing army* in time of peace; they never have used their
endeavours to *cherish a funding system,* to negociate *unnecessary* loans or to preserve a *public debt for ever;* for they derive not the smallest benefit from the influence which that system of measures, never fails to occasion. They indeed
hold their assemblages in the evening, the *private employments, and avocations
of their members, prevent them from assembling* in the day; they indeed *close
the doors;* of the rooms which they frequent, because they are not obligated to
hold their meetings in the public streets, and because *they have always claimed*

the valuable privilege of CHUSING THEIR COMPANY. They cannot surely be suspected of *plots* against the liberty, combination against the laws, or conspiracies against the constitution of their country. They are *too numerous* for the purposes of *conspiracy,* their numbers would become the means of inevitable detection.

It has frequently been asserted, it has even been maintained with in the walls of the HOUSE OF REPRESENTATIVES, That the existence of *popular assemblages,* must inevitably terminate in the violation of law & in the destruction of government. And why! because they PROMOTE ENQUIRY? because they produce INVESTIGATION. A good government and in danger from *associations of the people!* a constitution, the *conservation* and *security of the public interest,* and yet endangered by the very persons *whose welfare it so essentially promotes!* This is a contradiction too gross to be believed, a paradox too absurd to be credited. It was FREE INVESTIGATION that procured our emancipation from the destable yoke of British thraldom; it was FREE INVESTIGATION that established their liberty which now forms the enviable blessing and the boasted birth right of the American citizens. It was FREE INVESTIGATION that procured the adoption of the constitution of the United States, and IT IS FREE INVESTIGATION that must ever form *the only sure support* of that constitution, and constitute the only permanent basis for the preservation of the liberties of the people.

Fellow Citizens! we owe to you, we owe to the purity of our cause, a faithful portrait of our fundamental principles. We feel ourselves the determined friends of public liberty, but we are equally the enemies of licentiousness and anarchy. While we sincerely express our warm attachment to the most sacred rights of humanity, with you we are the steady advocates of law, and social order—Banish far distant then, the hated voice of calumny, and listen with attention to the sentiments we shall ever continue to inculcate.

CIVIL LIBERTY is the right of the citizen freely to dispose of his actions subject only to the restraint of the laws. It leaves us the compleat mastership over all our actions that are in themselves indifferent, and only recognizes coercion, when such coercion is necessary to restrain us from the commission of injuries.— Restraint commences, at that point, where the liberty of one individual is incompatible with the safety, or happiness of another—it is dictated by justice, and constitutes law.

Restraint from the commission of injuries being necessary for the preservation of individual safety, forms one of the fundamental objects of the social state. Personal security, protection from violence, and enjoyment of civic rights are claims of the citizen which society is obligated to guarantee. To give efficacy to these rights, society is vested with adequate powers, composed of an aggregation of the rights surrendered by individuals for the safety and preservation of the residuum. These powers constitute the sovereignty of a state.

Legislation is a power of the sovereignty exercised for the sole purpose of promoting the public welfare. It is a declaration of the general will, through the medium of organs appointed by the constitution. Laws thus pronounced, form a rule for the regulation of the conduct of the citizen, and obedience on the part of the citizen forms the stipulated price for the protection he receives from the laws. It being necessary for the *preservation* of civil liberty, that limits should be prescribed for the regulation of human conduct, it is equally necessary for its *security* that limits should be assigned to the law.

NATURE has placed the sovereignty of states in the individuals who compose them. *Tyranny,* which is ever founded upon artificial regulations, has vested it in the Monarch or the government. In *despotic communities* all the Magistrates are *inviolable,* and the powers of the government *unlimited*—In *Democracies,* whether strictly popular or representative, the public functionaries are *responsible to society,* for the due exercise of the powers with which they are entrusted.

In every free state the sovereignty is vested in the people, and each individual is at once a legislature, and a sovereign. From the impossibility of *personally exercising* the sovereign powers, has, arisen the necessity of REPRESENTATION. The security of public liberty, has annexed *responsibility* to the person of the *representative.*

In every constitution, the power that is entrusted to the government, *more than what is necessary* for the safety and welfare of society, approaches within the verge of TYRANNY. Every degree of coercion *more than what is indispensible for the purposes of general, and individual preservation,* is so far a DESPOTISM. The legislature at that instant becomes a TYRANT, and the people dwindle into SLAVES.

The LEGISLATIVE is the ONLY SUPREME POWER in a community, whose constitution is well organized—the EXECUTIVE, and JUDICIAL are functions *subordinate* to the legislative, still they are equally the *organs of the Sovereign power;* equally the *Representatives of the general will;* and equally AMENABLE TO SOCIETY, for the faithful discharge of their respective functions.

The same reason that renders it indispensable for the sovereign, to delegate suitable organs for the manifestation of the general will, renders equally impossible in its collective capacity the exercise of its revisionary powers. *The* RESPONSIBILITY *of* PUBLIC FUNCTIONARIES *presupposes a* RIGHT OF INVESTIGATION INTO THEIR PROCEEDINGS.—It is a right appurtenant to *individuals,* otherwise it would be incapable of exercise. It is a right appurtenant to *every collection of individuals*—because every association *must comprehend all the privileges,* and *properties* of the members of whom it is composed, and because it is a RIGHT, *not susceptible of* RESTRAINT *in the mode of its enjoyment.*

The social state is founded—in immutable justice, it has its origin in the virtues and benevolence of the human heart—it is the common parent that attaches its members to each other, by the endearing ties of common interest, and reciprocal affection—it creates a new relation between men, besides the general one of nature, pregnant with *duties:* and it affords *the necessary means* for their fulfillment.—In the bosom of SOCIETY, man acquires that KNOWLEDGE which is the source of the most exalted felicity, and forms his distinguishing characteristic—he enters into those tender connections which form the charm, and the solace of civilized life, and are sources of the most happy enjoyment. If fine, he becomes enabled to display, all the talents of the mind; to exert all the virtues of the heart. The GENERAL WILL, the supreme law of society, is the public good; Justice commands, Truth decrees, Virtue enforces, and Nature sanctifies the principle.

REPRESENTATIVES of the PEOPLE! *ye* to whom the voice of your country, hath *delegated* the precious trust *of preserving inviolate* her most inestimable interests; *ye* whom the constitution hath invested with the solemn authority of promulgating the general will, which always decrees the public safety—*Will* YE consent to become the assassins of the law, by destroying the most sacred rights, of the citizen *freedom of speech and opinion;* rights which are claimed under their function, and enforced by their authority? *Will* ye become the *first violaters* of that constitution through which you claim your delegated trust, by establishing yourselves into a *self elected authoritive tribunal* which it does not recognize by the *assumption of powers* which it *does not delegate;* by the exercise of authorities, which *it has not granted?*

What shall preserve public liberty, but the WISDOM *of an* ENLIGHTENED *people?* What shall support the law, unless their authority? Who shall become the guardians of the social welfare, who the conservators of the constitution, but the people themselves? How has it happened, that ATHENS and SPARTA, once the celebrated seats of LIBERTY, once the boast of philosophers, the price of Greece, and the envy of mankind, have fallen the devoted victims of OTTOMAN TYRANNY? Their *climate* is still the *same,* their *soil* equally fertile, and the *beams of the Sun equally luminous* and *splendid* but the WISDOM *of the* ATHENIANS *is extinct, and the* VIRTUE *of the* LACEDEMONIANS *has long been* EXPIRED—Why is it that over the extensive continents of AFRICA and ASIA not the smallest vestige of liberty, can be discovered however industrious the research? Is it because the *countenance* of the African has assumed a *sable garb?* because the *complexion* of the Asiatic passes through a *vast variety of shades?* Is it because the TURKE drink *Sherbet* or the waters of the Nile overflow? NO: the EMPIRE OF DESPOTISM,[24] *founded in* VIOLENCE *and maintained by FEAR, has established its only permanent security in the* ABJECT IGNORANCE OF ITS SLAVES. The physical force of society can *only* be exerted for its own destruction, *when its moral powers have become* TOTALLY DORMANT OR EXTINCT. Remember that Greece and Rome, and Britain, NOW ENSLAVED, *were* all *once free.*

And *ye* PUBLIC FUNCTIONARIES, the RESPONSIBLE SERVANTS and not the *masters of the people,* what can *ye* have to fear, from assemblages of your fellow-citizens? Have *ye* already formed the *rash attempt,* to violate the public constitution—and to ENSLAVE YOUR COUNTRY? for then, *and not till then,* can ye have grounds of apprehension from the exercise of popular societies. An attempt to enslave a people *yet enlightened,* would too evidently terminate, in the destruction of the conspirators, and cannot therefore be presumed—the insidious artifices of corruption may possess a momentary influence, but will shrink from the all-discriminating eye of a PUBLIC, *free, enlightened, omnipotent.* The throne of the monarch shall be prostrated to the earth—the oppressions of tyranny shall have an end—constitutions are susceptible of amendment—and laws are subject to alteration—*But the* LIBERTIES, *the* RIGHTS *of the* PEOPLE *are* IMMUTABLE, IMPRESCRIPTIBLE, *and* ETERNAL.

By order of the society,

DAVID GELSTON, *President.*

Attest.
Jacob De La Montagnie, Sec.

The Printers of the several newspapers in the United States are requested to publish the foregoing Address.

General Advertiser (Philadelphia), January 26, 1795

Celebration of the Anniversary of the French Alliance, February 6, 1797

New York February 7
Tuesday

On the sixth day of February, 1778, a treaty of alliance, offensive and defensive, was signed at Paris, between our country and the French nation—an alliance which afforded every kind of relief in the midst of our struggles against the tyrannical mandates of the British nation, by the aid of which, and the brave soldiers, and marine armaments thereby stipulated, we completed gloriously an eight years bloody war, and established our independence.

The 9th anniversary of this fortunate, this propitious connection, was yesterday celebrated at Hunter's Hotel in this city, by a large and respectable company of American patriots—in which civic festival they were joined by the Consul of the French Republic, and a number of other patriotic French citizens now resident in this city.

After the company had taken their seats, Mr. B. Livingston[25] addressed them on the interesting subject which they were met to celebrate, a copy of which we hope to obtain for our next publication.

At this festival brotherly love and social glee prevailed in the exchange of patriotic mutual good wishes.

The following TOASTS was drank, interspersed with various songs.

1. The people and constituted authorities of the United States.

2. The people and constituted authorities of France.

3. The ALLIANCE between France and the United States, founded on the basis of reciprocity—the keystone of our independence and the scourge of tyrants.

4. The standard of American liberty; may it never be untried in the wretched cause of the coalesced despot—*"Marseilles Hymn."*

5. Perpetuity to the union of these States; may they ever find their prosperity in an adherence to the principles of our late revolution.

6. The freedom of the press, the palladium of liberty.

7. The British treaty; may it be an awful lesson how to trust to the "justice and magnanimity" of those who ever have, and still do, seek the ruin of our commerce and the destruction of our liberty. DEATH SONG.—*"The sun sets at night."*

8. May the men who are anxious to involve our country in a war with the republic of France be the only soldiers to take the field against it.

9. The speedy establishment of a *Cartel* with Britain for an exchange at the rate of *forty* of our inveterate tories for *one* of the persecuted patriots.

10. May the *God of battles* lead on the soldiers of liberty to a decisive victory over the remainder of its opposing *slaves.* SONG—*"Ca Ira."*[26]

11. The memory of those patriots who have sealed with their blood the *magna charta* of freedom.

12. The Republican economy, instead of monarchical prodigality.

13. Republican federalism.

14. The law of nations founded on the principle of natural justice, may it be the only commercial treaty.

15. A speedy termination of all controversy between the republics of France and America—confusion to those who attempt to sever the ties which unite us.

16. External disappointment to all incendiaries, who, by secret designs, or open force, attempt the dissolution of the union.

By the Consul of the French Republic.

Republican Virtue; May it, both in America and France, be the ambition of the young and the consolation of the aged.

By Chancellor Livingston.[27]

May the present coolness between France and America produce (like the quarrel of lovers) a renewal of love.

By Citizen James Napper Tandy

The virtuous citizens of New York who, in despite of *British* influence returned their *faithful* Representative to Congress.

Towards the close of the festival, the following *Volunteer* was given by citizen Hulin, capt. of the Ranger.

"Puissent les deu governments, Francais and America, bien. S'ent endre pour le bonheur de peuple de leu nation respective."

Translation.

May the two governments, French and American, pursue such measures as will promote the happiness of the people of our respective nations.

The company dispersed at ten o'clock in the utmost harmony.

On account of the above celebration, a salute was fired from the cannon of the Republican sloop of war Ranger at noon, and at the setting of the sun; the Ranger being hove down, her guns, by permission, were formed into a battery on shore near the Belvedere house. Cap. Hulen and his officers, on this occasion, at the first salute, *entwined* the American and French flags, expressive of their desire of lasting unity and friendship between the two Republics.

Argus (New York), February 7, 1797

Notice of a Meeting to Draft an Address to Congress, June 13, 1798

At a very large & respectable meeting of Citizens, held at Martling's Tavern on Wednesday Evening, the 13th inst., agreeable to notice in the public papers, Solomon Simpson, in the Chair, Resolved Unanimously, That a Committee of five Citizens be appointed to draft a respectful address to our Representatives in Congress, to take effectual measures to prevent further depredations upon American commerce by the British Government, or any other nation.

Resolved, that Aaron Burr,[28] Doctor Mitchell,[29] David Gelston, John Broome[30] and Henry Rutgers[31] be the committee to draft an address agreeable to the above resolution.

Resolved, That the proceedings of the evening be published in all the Public Papers in this City, and that a general meeting of the Citizens be called in the Fields, on Saturday the 16th inst. at 12 o'clock, to hear the report of their Committee.

The meeting then adjourned to meet on Saturday, the 16th inst. at the above time and place.

New-York, June 14.   SOLOMON SIMPSON,[32] Chairman.

Argus (New York), June 15, 1798

NEW YORK TAMMANY SOCIETY

Minutes of the Committee of Amusement, October 12, 1792

Great Wigwam 12th Oct. 1792

being the 3d Century of the discovery of America—

Toasts

1st May the new world never experience the vices and Miseries of the Olde, and May it be an Happy Asylum for the oppressed of all Nations and all Religions.

2—May peace and Liberty ever prevade United Columbia.

3rd The Memory of Christopher Columbus.

4. De La Fayette and the French Nation.

5. May French Liberty Rise Superior to all the efforts of Austrian Despotism.[33]

6th. The 12th October 1792, the Commencement of the 4th Century.

7th The Rights of Man.

8th May this be the last Columbian Centuary Festival that finds a Slave on this globe.

9th Thomas Paine.

10th May the Duke of Brunswick be Burgoined.[34]

11th May the fourth Columbian Century be as Remarkable for Improving and Understanding the Rights of Man, as the first was for discovering, and the Improvement of Nautical knowledge.

12th May every friend of Science ever Venerate the Immortal Columbus.

13th May the deliverers of America never experience that Ingratitude from the Country, which Columbus experienced from his King.

14th May the Genius of Liberty as she has conducted the Sons of Columbus with Glory to the Commencement of the fourth century Gaind their fame to the end of Time.

Volunteer by the Grand Sachem.

Society of Tammany or Columbian Order, Committee of Amusement, Minutes,
October 24, 1791 to February 23, 1795, Manuscript Records, Manuscripts Division,
New York Public Library.

Resolutions Adopted to Celebrate the Recapture of Toulon, February 24, 1794

Last Monday evening the TAMMANY SOCIETY met according to their resolutions of the 24th ult. to celebrate the Re-capture of Toulon, and the other Glorious successes of the French arms over Tyranny and Despotism.—Entertainments being provided for the purpose, the following TOASTS were drank, given by the different Tribes.

New-Hampshire.

May the enemies of Liberty throughout the world experience a state similar to the Royalists in the Garrison of Toulon, on the 19th of December 1793.

Massachusetts.

May our country maintain an honora[ble] peace, or soon be engaged in a successful war.

Rhode Island.

May the flags of republican government ever fly in defiance of those who oppose them.

Connecticut.

Wisdom and firmness in the councils of the Union, and the support of all good Citizens to their resolutions.

New-York.

The President of the United States. (3 cheers)

New-Jersey.

May the Angel of death cover his cold mantle over all the enemies of Liberty. May the spirit of freedom proceed more quickly throughout the earth than light from the Sun, and may the universal empire of Peace be established upon a basis as lasting as the foundation of the world.

Pennsylvania.

An honorable peace and a firm republican government to the French.

Delaware.

May the dwelling of all the enemies of the Republic be assigned them in a place as rocky as their hearts and as feared as their consciences.

Maryland.

Citizen Fauchet, minister of the French Republic.[35] (3 cheers).

Virginia.

May the flame of Liberty never be extinguished by British engines.

North Carolina.

May all friends to freedom ever experience the good, flowing from the knot annexed to our national flag.

South Carolina.

May Americans ever manifest the same joy at the successes of the brave Republican Allies, as they have shewn this day, until the Universal Republic of Mankind are to see that their joy shall know no intermission.

Georgia.

May the commerce of America be as free as its air, and may the citizens of this country see the impropriety of importing British merchants as stock in trade.

Volunteer from the Grand Sachem.

Perdition and contempt to the tongue of calumny and malice that would divide at this period the friends of Liberty and Equal Rights of Man. (3 cheers)

During the evening's festivity, a number of Patriotic songs were sung and joy seemed to beam on every countenance on the glorious occasion.

At an early hour the Society adjourned with the peace and harmony which is characteristic of that band of brothers, the firm supporters of a Republican government, and friends to the equal rights of man.

New York Journal, March 12, 1794

Resolutions Adopted to Commemorate the 1783 British Evacuation of New York City, November 26, 1794

NEW-YORK, Nov. 26.

Yesterday the Tammany Society met according to adjournment, at Hunter's Hotel, in order to commemorate the auspicious day when the British evacuated this city.—After partaking of a cold colation, the following toasts were drank:

1. The United States of America; May they prove an asylum to the prosecuted throughout the globe.

2. The patriotic *Washington;* May his worth and eminent services be dear to Americans to the latest posterity.

3. May the pleasing remembrance of this auspicious day on which the satellites of George Guelph left our peaceful shores, excite in the breast of every true American the most pleasing sensations.—*Three cheers.*

4. May the glorious struggles for liberty in France tend to illuminate & renovate the world.

5. Kosciusko and the glorious advocates for liberty in Poland.[36]—*Six cheers.*

6. The State of New-York.

7. The Congress of the United States; May they possess Wisdom to contrive, Firmness and Patriotism to execute laws calculated to advance the best interest of their constituents.

8. The Rights of Man, the liberty of the press, and trials by Juries, to be the happy privilege of the citizens of America, from the Gulf of St. Lawrence, to the river Mississippi.

9. A speedy abolition of every species of slavery throughout America.

10. A happy amelioration of our penal laws, respecting criminal punishments and imprisonment for debt.

11. May the establishment of public Schools throughout this state be the favourite object of our next and every future Session of our State Legislature.

12. General Wayne and the western army.[37]

13. The Republican Sons of Tammany throughout the world.

14. May the Duke of York[38] continue swiming and falling *back* until he experiences the fate of Saratoga.—*Nine cheers.*

15. May the greasing of the flag staff be the last effort of the enemies of liberty in Amsterdam—*Six cheers.*

Volunteer from the Chairs.

Perpetual union of sentiment to the citizens of United America.

In return for the compliment paid to the Military, they gave the following toast:

May the Tammany Society continue as they hitherto have been, the firm supporters of freedom and the ready defenders of the laws—*Three cheers.*

The Militia Officers yesterday partook of an elegant entertainment at citizen Hunter's, after the ordinary business of the day was completed. The following toasts, interspersed with patriotic songs, were drank:

1. The Day.
2. The United States.
3. The President. 3 cheers.
4. The Governor of the State. 3 cheers.
5. The late American army.
6. Franklin, Adams and Jay; the American commissioners who signed the treaty of peace.
7. The French Republic. 3 cheers.
8. Kosciusko, and the Polish nation.
9. The memory of those who have fallen in the cause of Freedom.
10. The patriotic army under General Lee. 3 cheers.
11. The Corporation of the City of New York
12. Liberty and Humanity—May they be the order of the day in every government. 3 cheers.
13. The Militia of the United States.
14. The Agriculture, Manufactures, and Commerce of the United States.
15. The American Fair.

A display of FIRE WORKS on the battery concluded the ceremonies.

General Advertiser (Philadelphia), November 29, 1794

To the People of the United States Approving of the Conduct of the President of the United States, January 19, 1795

AT a meeting of TAMMANY SOCIETY or COLUMBIAN ORDER, held in Tammanial Hall on Monday evening the 19th January 1795.[39]

Resolved, That it is the opinion of this society, that the President of the United States, in using his best endeavors to support on all occasions the laws and constitution of these states, intitles him to the warmest thanks and fullest approbation of every lover of their prosperity and happiness.

Resolved, that a committee of three be appointed to draft an address to the citizens of the United States, and publish the same.

Tammany Society to the People of the United States.

FELLOW CITIZENS,

WE address you not alone, because it is now considered a question interesting to every patriot—How far the existence of political institutions of a nature like

ours has a friendly or a malign influence on public happiness. But attempts having been made to stain the character of this society, by originating therein measures hostile to the great interest of the community, it is proper that an open
declaration should be made of our views and sentiments.

We avow, then, our hearty and entire approbation of the conduct of the
President of the United States, in his late endeavors to discountenance certain
self-created societies; and we perceive from the irritation a consciousness of
merited censure has occasioned, in various parts of the country, that the appelation by which he chose to distinguish them, has been sufficiently discriminating;
the event presents him to us as the firm and independent patriot, the prudent
and sagacious statesman.

With him we love our country, *and* we are grateful to Heaven for its glorious
constitution of government. *Nay,* we are happy in its administration—trusting,
that at the helm, even among those who have been generally in opposition to
measures terminating in national prosperity and honor, are men distinguished
for their talents and for their integrity.

We hold this constitution as the great palladium of civil liberty, security of
peace and property to ourselves, and happiness to posterity, and are ready to
devote to its support our lives and fortunes.

It has within itself an active power of regeneration, which nothing can impede
but the madness of faction, or an extreme licentiousness or ignorance. Civil and
national liberty are to be carefully distinguished; the former is as excellent as
the latter is dangerous. The latter must be abridged in order to secure the
former—Civil liberty is wisdom and order; natural liberty is ignorance and anarchy. While the citizens of the United States are careful to educate their youth
in moral and political science, their liberties can not be greatly endangered;
nothing is wanting but information and virtue generally diffused. Inordinate
jealousy, which has often proved the bane of Republics, which with a jaundiced
eye those constituted authorities, which support the best interests of the community; engendering at the same time the polluted streams of faction, disappointment, ambition, avarice, falshood and disorder.

We claim it as the unquestionable right of citizens, to associate, to speak and
to publish there sentiments whether for or against the laws, but such associations
are only excellent as revolutinary means, when a government is to be overturned.
An exercise of this right, in a free and happy country like this, resembles the
sport of firebrands; it is phrenzy, and this phrenzy, is in proportion to the party
zeal of the self-created associations, to the secrecy of its measures, and the
permanency of its compact.

It *violates* this leading principle in republicanism, that rights are to be *equally*
exercised. It discovers under the garb of democracy the cloven foot of aristocracy.

It will be often seen to operate as a system of threat, illiberality, and sedition.
Ought it not be sufficient to the patriot, that the real wants and wishes of the

community, fairly and indiscriminately collected on particular occasions, are conveyed to that common center, wherein is collected, also the public wisdom sympathies and virtue. This society disclaims a factious or disaffected spirit; it cherishes American citizenship, as the highest civil dignity of man, it interferes not with the constituted authorities of the country unless it might be in the support of the laws. If there be well meaning men, in self created societies, who suppose they can legislate better than its representatives, this society can only pity their presumptuous delusion. But designing men, who would rise on the ruin of the tried friends of the people, ought to dread the public information.

No dark recess remains long obscured, misteries are soon disclosed under the brightness of our political day. We trust the reputation of Tammy Society will ever be preserved from measures founded either in honest delusion or political artifice.

By order of the society,

JONATHAN LITTLE,
GRAND SACHEM.

BENJAMIN STRONG,

Secretary.

The different Printers in the United States, are requested to republish the above.

New York Journal, January 21, 1795

"A Calm Observer" to "Federal Members of Tammany Society," January 31, 1795

For the Daily Advertiser
To the Federal Members of Tammany Society.

THE democratic members of your Society, having at your last meeting, endeavoured though in vain, to publish certain resolutions to counteract your excellent public address, it is submitted to your consideration whether it would not be fair, as there are pr——.t numerous among you to allow them one or two evenings to emit all their chagrin, unmolested and uninterrupted. Why not? The public know you are much divided in political matters, and you have been heard; now, let them speak.

They say, contrary to your address, that natural and civil liberty is the same thing.—They say, also, that a man should exercise all his rights—even to intoxication. But with respect to the father of this country. G. W. who your address approbates, they, as yet, say little:— let us hear them from Tammany-hall.

It would be a pity, after the pains they had taken to prepare their sentiments, in the Democratic Society, this week, that they should not be suffered to utter them to the world, next Monday night. "No dark remains long uncovered." Should it become necessary, you will herafter have it in your power to answer them, or to overrule any improper measure they may take.

Jan. 30.   A CALM OBSERVER.

Daily Advertiser (New York), January 31, 1795

Tammany Democratic versus Tammany Federal, February 4, 1795

NEW-YORK, Feb. 4
Tammany Democratic versus Tammany Federal.

Last monday evening, the Tamany society met and resolved, that whereas that society neither acknowledges political principles for its establishment, nor political objects for its pursuits, but is designed solely to connect American brethren in the indissoluble bond of patriotic friendship; and it militates against its constitution to intermeddle in political questions, and tends to interrupt its harmony; and whereas the address of the 19th Jan. was passed precipitately and in a thin meeting, and approves of the President's denunciation of self created societies, of which this society is one, thus becoming a party against the house of Representatives in Congress, the BEST friends of the rights of the people—the said address does not express the candid and deliberate sentiments of this society, and is therefore condemned as officious, inconsiderate, impolitic and unconstitutional; therefore resolved that said address does NOT express the candid opinion and deliberate sentiments of the Columbian order.

To give the public some just idea of the contradictory proceedings of the Tammany Society, as we understand them, it must be observed that the society is composed of persons of opposite politics. One part of the members are attached to the present government and its administration—the other consists of the Democratic Society.

We know not which is most numerous; but at the meeting when the first address was ordered, the Federal members were most numerous. The address roused the opposite party, who, at the next meeting, collected their strength to overthrow the former proceedings. Violent debates succeeded and some confusion; and the society dispersed without doing anything to effect. Last monday evening, we understand, the Grand Sachem and most of the federal members purposely neglected to attend, and left their antagonists masters of the field; when a counter address or resolution was passed by a large majority. We have given a fair statement of this business, as far as we have obtained information. If it is incorrect, we will readily amend it.

American Minerva (New York), February 4, 1795

"A Calm Observer" to "Federal Members of Tammany Society," February 9, 1795

For the Daily Advertiser.

TO THE FEDERAL MEMBERS OF
TAMMANY SOCIETY.

According to promise I shall now make two or three remarks on the curious publications of your democrats.

They in the first place take care to tell us they are very "large and respectable"—very good! They in the second place inform us, least we might suspect them, tho' so very respectable, that "their resolution and preamble were regularly moved and duly considered." But as simple democracies are not very apt to be very regular, not very duly to consider, all this is well enough.

They then go on to inform us that Tammany Society at one of its regular meetings, published an address which was signed, as all your public acts have heretofore been, except the present one no doubt they would be assiduous to put their names.

They then proceed—your "Society (they say) acknowledges neither political principles, nor political objects, being founded on a broad basis—but solely designed to connect American brethren in the indissoluble bands of patriotic friendship."

Such a heap of absurdities would disgrace a combination of Sweep Chimnies! What! no political principles, when there has been scarce a public day for this three or four years back but your sentiments, your toasts, your principles, and your objects have been in the most formal manner obtruded upon the public? What! have not your sermons, your pamphlets, and your orations, made our presses groan? What! have you not uniformly sounded the name of Washington abroad as your pride and delight?—But in the mind of your democrats this was no politics, until the hapless moment when he chastised certain self-created societies who assumed a tone of condemning the constitutional acts of the representatives of our country, "truly better-friends and firmer supporters of the rights of the people," than they are.

But they proceed to express their opinion that intermeddling in politics is contrary to the spirit of your constitution and tends to destroy harmony; and yet they directly after turn politicians themselves with a witness, and publish to the world as a political sentiment of their's, one of the most outrageous things I have seen. A thing equally false and ridiculous, viz. that the President of the United States and the Representatives, have been or are at variance. But this I suppose is for the purpose of restoring harmony among you—or is it for the more important purpose of creating uneasiness abroad? This consistency is truly laughable! But perhaps your constitution allows democrats and discontents to publish their political sentiments, while it forbids the happy Fed's from expressing their satisfaction and pleasure in the government of our common country.

In the next section of their preamble they tell us your meeting "was very thinly attended considering the importance of the business, and that you published your address notwithstanding the objections of a very respectable minority." A very important business truly, and a very respectable minority no doubt; but I suppose we may be allowed to conclude that the majority were at least equally respectable.

I think it indeed not unlikely that their meeting has been rather the most numerous since if I am not misinformed, the business had been considered a very important one, at no less than two previous meetings of the whole democratic world.

The next paragraph of their preamble is a curious one. They seem to think by approving of the conduct of the President you have condemned yourselves—and not only so but have roused against you "the resentment of all other self-created societies." Dreadful indeed! What, religious, political, medical, philosophical, mechanical, masonic? What, all other? Or do they only mean the democratical? Why yes I suppose they would have us to believe you a democratical club clipt of its feathers, that is silenced; no power to speak or write or publish; or meddle in politics; and yet at the same time would persuade us, and you, that the President denounced; the ghost of Tammany among other hobgoblins! ha! ha! ha!

In the last paragraph of this wonderful preamble they assume, as you know is characteristic, the tone of condemnation: The address "is therefore condemned as officious, inconsiderate, impolitic and unconstitutional."

And now as to the resolution itself. It is a short one: "Resolved, as the sense of the society, (that is not their own sense) that the address to the people of the United States, under the name of the Tammany Society, does not express the candid opinion and deliberate sentiment, of the Columbian Order," and so the Mountain is delivered of a Mouse!

And now, after all, we are left as much in the dark with respect of the real sentiments of your society as ever. You ought to be numbered. It is of the utmost importance to the public that it should be known, how many Fed's you have and how many Demo's, ha! ha! ha!!!

And lately I find the whole proceedings signed too by the secretary of the democratic society—How is this?

But how is this to end? The farce is to go on next Monday night I suppose, and then I would advise your democrats to publish an address to the public, as your sense, reversing all your senses. They may commence it with a pretty solid column of whereas's;—Whereas, whereas, whereas,—and then proceed. You approve of the President; they should disapprove and villify. You say that the men in administration who are opposed to you, are yet many of them of talents and integrity they should say all who are with you are aristocrats and tories.

You said that natural Liberty, as contrasted with civil, was dangerous; they should say natural liberty is preferable to civil. You said that societies formed to oppose a good government ought to be discountenanced; they should say it is the candid opinion of your society, that all societies should oppose governments or else hold their tongues. They ought then to conclude with a little about British influence—aristocratical spirit—growing monarchy—power—corruption—guardianship of the people, &c. &c. assuring us, that they were very large, very respectable, very deliberate, very regular, no way precipitate, &c. &c. and that you were all the contrary, &c. &c.

A calm observer

Daily Advertiser (New York), February 9, 1795

"Shade of Tammany" to Citizen Greenleaf, February 18, 1795

For The NEW-YORK JOURNAL, &c.

CITIZEN GREENLEAF.

As the proceedings of the Tammany Society have lately engaged somewhat of the public attention; and as their proceedings have been mistated, permit me, through the channel of your paper, to make some remarks on the same, taking in a piece which appeared in Child's paper of the 9th inst. signed, *A Calm Observer,* who has endeavored to misrepresent every circumstance, and which has a tendency to mislead the unwary and uninformed: It is a shame for men of genius too, to treat any subject with ridicule, when they cannot bring reason and truth as auxiliaries to aid their designs. If *fashion* and *party* is to be the order of the day, let this be brought home to those to whom it alone belongs, and not to those to whom it will not at all apply.

The address to the *Federal Members of Tammany Society,* by a *Calm Observer,* cannot be called a just and candid statement of facts, but is exaggerated in almost every instance and is a very *partial one.* If indeed, *ridicule* is admitted *as a test of truth,* he is right; if *reason,* he is wrong. But as that party have very unfortunately but little *reason* on their side, we must exercise some small flights of fancy and attribute it to the extreme mortification they feel, in being thwarted in all their measures. The address is in fact so paltry a performance as scarcely to deserve notice; but left impressions injurious to the society might be made on some who are unacquainted with the business, I shall make a few remarks on some parts of it exactly in his own way:

He commences his harrangue with "According to promise, I shall now make two or three remarks on the curious publication of your Democrats;" this, it appears was not a promise *extorted* from him, but a *voluntary one,* and without a single request from the public. Pray does this "Calm Observer" suppose that the public are such a set of block heads, as to need his comments to make the subject plain? this comes exactly to the idea which the Republican part of the community have, and still do entertain of these *high flying "fed's"* (to use their own expression) none but their *high mightinesses* forsooth can understand the drif of an *address,* either "religious, political, medical, philosophical, mechanical, masonic, or even democratical" or aristocratical. The *swinish multitude* must therefore pay attention and respect to all, which these *august well-born* think proper to alter, however ridiculous. This is *liberty* and *equality* with a witness, ha! ha! ha!

The largeness and respectability of the meeting, and the manner in which the resolution (for disapproving the address) was carried, he next endeavors to ridicule, but unfortunately for himself, has failed and the ridicule must recoil on himself alone.

"They then go on (he says) to inform us that the Tammany Society at one of its regular meetings, published an address, which was signed as all your public acts have heretofore been, except the present, by your Grand Sachem and Secretary."

The evening on which a committee for drafting the address was appointed, was not a *stated meeting,* as he asserts, the stated meetings being only once a month, viz. the first Monday. The address was indeed signed by their Grand Sachem and Secretary, but this (if I am rightly informed) they were not authorized to do, but very officiously undertook a duty which ought to have been done by the committee appointed for that purpose.

He then proceeds to the preamble, and makes a number of very *abusive and ungenerous* remarks, many of which I shall treat with a *silent contempt.*

"Your society (says he) acknowledges neither political principles, nor political objects, being founded on a *broad basis*—but solely designed to connect American brethren in the indissoluble bonds of patriotic friendship." It is here worthy of remark, that the writer very carefully leaves out a number of words, and presents us only with *disjointed sentences;* the society *does not* acknowledge political principles for its *establishments,* not political objects for its *pursuit,* that is, the *establishment* or the *immediate design* of the society, was not for the publication of *political addresses,* &c. but to promote natural friendship; to alleviate the distresses of their poor and afflicted members; to assist the fatherless; to wipe the widowed eye; and to unite its members being "American brethren in the indissoluble bonds of patriotic friendship," as appears from their public constitution.

"They are founded (he says) on a *broad basis;*" but he very carefully leaves out the next word, viz. "Of Natural Rights;" this he did not think proper to mention, because he could not deny it, and as he has not denied it I shall pass it by.

He proceeds with, "Such a heap of absurdities would disgrace a combination of sweep chimneys. What! no political principles, when there has been scarce a public day for these three or four years back, but your sentiments, your toasts your principles and your objects, have been in the most formal manner obtruded on the public." He does not here think proper to draw a line between the principles on which a *society is established,* and the principles of its individual members; for instance should the society of Black Friars (which is admitted by all to be established on principles of benevolence and friendship) determine to publish their sentiments on *religion.* Is it therefore to be concluded that it acknowledges religious principles for its establishment? No! The supposition is absurd. For there is not I believe a word of religion in their constitution, much less that they should publish on the subject; the same reasoning will apply to all other societies, and consequently to the Tammany, whose objects are sociability and benevolence. But let me ask this *wiseacre* whether he approves of toasts being published at all by any society? Whether the Tammany Society are not equally justifiable in publishing their toasts with the Sons of *St. George, St. Andrew* or any other *Saint* in the World? The reason why they have not the same right in the estimation of some people is obvious; because they breathe a *very different spirit;* were their sentiments exactly similar, no doubt in the opinion of *this writer,* they would be the very essence of *truth and sound reasoning.* What is it a *crime* for our citizens to publish their *toasts,* their sermons and their *orations?* It is immaterial what society; if so, we are indeed in a dreadful situation; *a certain faction* no doubt would be highly gratified, but our liberties would be departing from us, and it would be time to assume "a tone of condemnation."

"What (says he) have you not uniformly founded the name of *Washington* abroad, as your *pride* and *delight*." Yes! and he is still our pride and delight, when we consider him as the *Saviour of his country* in perilous times, and therefore entitled to our highest respect and veneration;—'But in the minds of your Democrat, this was no politics, until the hapless moment when he *chastised certain self-created societies.'* That this denunciation was the *immediate act of the President,* I never will *believe,* but on the contrary think, that he was prevailed on *contrary* to his better judgement, by certain *demogogues,* to do *an act* which the *event* has proved to be both *impolitic* and *unjust.* "No chastisement for the present seemeth pleasant but grievous, but they work out for *us* a far more exceeding and abundant weight of honor and glory;" this is freely exemplified in the change of sentiments which has taken place among our New-York Electors—witness the *last election for members to the House of Representatives in Congress,* this is a sufficient token of their opinions on the subject.

The Society do undoubtedly express their opinion, that "intermedling in politics is contrary to their constitution;" this is a fact—examine their public constitution, and you will find that if it is not expressed directly in words, it is so by implication at least; and that it tends to destroy harmony, is equally true, but as he has attempted no proof to the contrary, I shall pass it by.

"And yet (says he) they directly turn politicans themselves with a witness, and publish to the world as a political sentiment of theirs, one of the most *out-*

rageous things. I have seen a thing equally false and ridiculous, viz. That the President of the United States and the representatives have been or are at variance." And certainly it is high time to turn politicians, when a *faction* undertake to publish their private opinions, as the opinions of a society consisting of 500 members, without giving them notice of their intentions, and the opportunity of at least giving a vote on the occasion, and endeavoring to prevent the publication of opinions as the sense of the society, equally *disgraceful* as *false*, as the sequel has fully shown.. As to the *outrage* complained of the assertion is equally ridiculous and false; for it is well known to every person, except *infants, madmen* and *fools*, that the President did *denounce certain self-created societies,* and that the *House of Representatives,* ever jealous of the *rights of the people,* did not think proper to coincide with him in sentiment; but that on this subject they materially differed. Did it not employ their attention several days? and was not the result favourable to those *self-created societies,* among which number the *Tammany* undoubtedly is enrolled? who will be hardy enough to deny this? Let them consult the proceedings of that *house*—let them attend to their votes, and then let *truth* declare, and falsehood stand abashed.

He then proceeds to abuse and vilify the Democrats, as tho' they were about to sow diffentions, to destroy harmony, to overturn our "Happy government," to scatter about fire brands, arrows and death, and to destroy the world before them; this, however, being the *trick* of the *party,* and submitted in the place of reason, deserves only to be treated with that contempt which it so justly merits. It is however, not a little surprising, that these men do not see the impropriety of their conduct; for by exalting the power, the energy, the strength and respectability of the Democratic Societies, the *huge Colossus* of our country; they themselves, by their own account dwindle into mere pigmies; if they cannot therefore bring proofs, they had better remain silent—for instead of benefiting they injure themselves and their cause. We are content, that those who are stiled the "happy feds" should enjoy and publish too, their sentiments and their happiness to the whole world; but let them beware how they publish in future their sentiments, as the opinion of a society, which unfortunately they have disgraced and abused!

He next touches on the smalless of the meeting, the respectability of the minority against the first address, and the importance of the object all which he endeavors to turn into ridicule and which at a single glance must convince all that truth has forsaken them, and that they are obliged from the necessary of the case, to employ ridicule as their only weapon of defence.

Having made particular enquiries relative to the business of the society, I shall relate it exactly as it was mentioned to me. The number of persons present when a committee on the first address was appointed was 46; on a division, 31 voted in the affirmative; 15 in the negative; these 3, notwithstanding, the remonstrances of the minority, like a set of hot-headed men, determined that a committee should be appointed to draft and publish an address, as the sentiments of the society, without having first reported the same for the approbation of the society at another meeting; a compliance with which they knew would defeat their object and designs. The address which they published was brought in and read, which was at that time so far disapproved of by almost all present, that it was determined as above, to appoint a committee to draft and publish another; which committee, however, thought proper to adopt and publish the same address, of the propriety of which let every unbiassed man judge. At the next meeting of the society, held agreeable to a public notification in the newspapers (which notification, if I am informed right, was at the particular request of "your Democrats") there appeared a very large number of members, which 'the happy fed's' so much dreaded at the last meeting, and which appeared from the haste in cramming the address down the throats of members then present The resolution for disapproving of the address, was moved, and after lengthy debates, was carried on a division, by about 100 affirmatives, and 64 or 65 negatives; the negatives having previously rallied all their forces, and led them on to the contest. Having been completely beaten (which they themselves acknowledged) very few of them made their appearance at the succeeding meeting.

The respectability of the minority on the first evening this writer *dare not deny,* unless he insists that his "Happy Feds" are *indeed more respectable,* which will effectually establish their doctrine of *distinction of rank,* the *well born,* pitted against the *Swinish multitude.* This is liberty and equality with a witness, ha, ha, ha. He "thinks it not unlikely, that their meetings have been rather the most numerous since." This now, is all very *good,* and *very true* and very *just;* "and if I am not misinformed, says he, the business had been considered a very important one, at no less than two previous meetings of the whole Democratic world." This is not denied neither, but be it remembered, that they exactly followed the example set them by our "Happy Feds" in the first instance, whom it would be *unpardonable* not to imitate in all their *praise worthy actions,* particularly in using undue influence out of doors, for which they are noted. *The others* although they be *Democrats,* are as capable of receiving instruction as the "Happy Feds." ha, ha, ha.

"At two previous meetings of the whole *Democratic World.*" Why certainly this writer has turned Predestinarian without knowing it, for we may rest assured, that the whole Democratic world have never *at one time* been collected in the City of New-York: it must therefore, I presume, be the *elect* from among them, for in no other sense can a private meeting of 20 or 25 members be called *the world.* Respecting the importance of the business, it will be unnecessary, to say much, as no candid man will deny, that it is the duty of a society to contradict all false publications of their sentiments, which may have been done by a faction or a party.

"In this last paragraph (says he) they immediately assume the tone of condemnation." But, who, pray, do they condemn? Not the *constituted authorities,* but those *restless, meddlesome, officious members,* who have endeavored to bring them into disgrace and contempt. These are the men they justly condemn; and may such men ever be condemned, whose *folly* is more conspicuous than their *wisdom,* and their *party zeal* than their *honesty* and *honor.*

"And lastly I find (says he) the whole proceedings signed by the *Secretary* of the *Democratic Society.*" On this I shall only remark, that it is a *downright falshood;* and this sufficiently convinces me, that *this writer* did not himself know what he was about when writing his remarks.

But I quit the tedious subject; the remainder of his remarks are equally *groundless, insipid, ridiculous, and nonsensical;* and shall, therefore, conclude with observing to the *real republican members* of that society, that it is the wish and expectation of their opponents, that they will neglect and forsake the society, and leave the field to them—Some of them have so declared, but as you value your own honor, and the reputation of the association, adhere to it, punctually attend its meetings, beware of their craft and cunning, and give not again the "happy feds" an opportunity to tarnish your glory, and blacken your fame, wither through the influence of a few individuals or a host of them combined together. Your cause is good, forsake it not—if you do, you deserve not only the denunciation of a mortal, but the still more dreadful vengeance of the injured

New-York, Feb. 11, 1795.   SHADE of TAMMANY.

N. B. If Mr. Childs think proper to publish this answer to the *Calm Observer,* it is at his service.

New York Journal, February 18, 1795

Toasts Drunk Honoring the Victories of the French and Batavian Patriots, April 8, 1795

A NEW REPUBLIC BORN

On Monday last the Society of Tammany, assembled and commemorated the late auspicious *victories of the French and Battavian patriots,*[40] a number of patriotic songs were sung, and the following toasts were drank amidst repeated applauses.

1. *The Republic of France;* may she be as celebrated in the page of history for the wisdom and clemency of her councils, as she is distinguished by the invincible power of her arms.

2. *The new star in the East;* may it prove a conducting light to all the wise men who are entrusted with the regulation of the concerns of nations.

3. The glorious constellation of Republics, America, France, Switzerland, Genoa, and Holland.

4. May French political principles, pervade the mind of all honest men and French arms, conquer and humble all aristocrats.

5. The men who planned and executed the happy alliance between *America and France.*

6. *The Freemen of Poland,* whose hearts undismayed, still watch.

7. *Ireland;* may she gain by the energies of her arms, what has always been refused to the earnestness of her entreaties.

8. The immortal memories of Sydney,[41] and Miltons,[42] and Hampdens,[43] may the soil of Great Britain, once more become fertile in men like these, and *may the genius of universal emancipation, extend its happy influence to bless that now infatuated kingdom.*

9. The Legislature of the *State of New York;* success to their plans for the diffusion of knowledge, the surest basis of Freedom.

10. *The Legislature of the United States,* who in the reformation of their penal code have felt the ameliorating influences of freedom.

11. *The patriots of the world.*

12. May the torch of truth, be kindled by the sacred fire of Reason, may its light be as piercing as the Sun, and eternal as the heavens; may it never cease to brighten the altars of Liberty throughout the universe; and may the *last of Tyrants,* soon expire a devoted victim to the unceasing happiness of worlds.

13. May the Empire of Liberty, be that of philanthropy, and may the angel of grace record on its Altar, "PEACE ON EARTH AND GOOD WILL TOWARDS MEN."

Volunteer from the Grand Sachem.

May the patriots of France, convince the *Tyrants of the* world, that the establishment of the *Rights of Man,* and not plunder, is their object.

April 7, 1795
New York Journal, April 8, 1795

Celebration of the Anniversary of American Independence, July 7, 1795

NEW-YORK,
July 8

Saturday last, being the Anniversary of AMERICAN INDEPENDENCE, the same was celebrated by the TAMMANY SOCIETY of COLUMBIAN ORDER.—At 8 o'clock A.M. they assembled in their Wigwam, and walked from thence in procession to the Battery proceded by the Cap, the Emblem of Liberty, and the standard of the United States, which were borne by two brothers. Having there joined 2 other societies and the military, the whole proceeded, in grand procession, to the New Presbyterian Church, where an excellent and truly patriotic Sermon was delivered by the Rev. Samuel Miller.[44]

From church they returned to the Battery, where a *fou-de-joy* was fired by the legion under the command of Lieut. Col. Rutgers.

In the evening the Society again assembled when the following toasts were drank, viz.

---

1. The United States of America—May she never enter into any ALLIANCE which may have a tendency to smother the flame of Liberty, or to injure the Rights of Man. 3 cheers.

2. The President of the United States—May he never affix his signature to a treaty, on whose front is engraven,—"Destruction to Liberty & Commerce."[45] 3 cheers.

3. The patriotic Minority in the Senate of the United States—May they receive the thanks of a grateful people, for their determined, though unsuccessful, opposition to a treaty with Great Britain, which must terminate in the ruin of our commerce, and be the disgrace of our country. 6 cheers.

4. The House of Representatives of the United States—May they evince an undaunted firmness and true republican spirit when the rights and liberties of the people are invaded. 6 cheers.

5. The Republic of France—Unanimity to her Councils, perpetuity to her liberty, and a glorious and uninterrupted success to her arms—May the ties which unite her to the American Republic, be as lasting as nature itself. 3 cheers.

6. GEORGE CLINTON, our late worthy Governor[46]—May his meritorious conduct and decided patriotism ensure him the love and esteem of his fellow citizens and of all true republicans. 9 cheers.

7. Confusion to the Councils of the confederate despots, and dismay to their hosts—May they never be able to form a centre of union or of action. 3 cheers.

8. Our country—May it never be disgraced by unworthy and dishonourable concessions to despots or their minions. 6 cheers

9. The Militia of the State of New York. 3 cheers.

10. The memorable Declaration of Independence.—May it ever continue to be the boast of American freemen, and may they support it with their lives. 9 cheers.

11. Eternal union and concord between republics—May those of America and France be indissoluble, and may all who attempt a disunion, be treated as traitors. 9 cheers.

12. The memory of those patriotic heroes who have shed their blood, and offered up their lives, on the altar of Freedom to secure the liberties of America and France. 6 cheers.

13. All true Republicans throughout the world, who spurn at the idea of passive obedience and non-resistance—May success attend their honest wishes, and land them to glory, honour, and immortality. 3 cheers.

14. The citizens and corporation of the City of New-York. 3 cheers.

15. May the commerce of America be as free as its air, and may the citizens

of this country see the impropriety of *importing British merchants* as stock in trade.—6 cheers.

Volunteers from the Chair.

The Day, and all who honor it.

VOLUNTEERS

1. The Mechanic Society of the City of New-York[47]
2. The Democratic Society of the City of New-York

New York Journal, July 8, 1795

Toasts Drunk on the Fourth of July, 1799

TOASTS drank by the TAMMANY SOCIETY or *Columbian Order,* on the Fourth of July, 1799.

1. *America!* our Country! The mother of the doctrine of *equal rights*—May she refuse to nurse any other children, but the sons of freedom and may they ever be victorious.

2. The *President* of the United States—May he be as wise as a serpent, and as harmless as a dove.—3 cheers.

3. *Jefferson, the friend of the people.*—May the Declaration of Independence which he framed, secure him the confidence of his country; and may his honest and patriotic exertions in the cause of universal Liberty meet with success. 6 cheers.

4. A free and *uncorrupted* representation of the *People*—May no *sycophant* or *time server* ever obtain the suffrages of freemen.

5. Perpetuity to the *principles* of our late revolution.—May the death wound to tyranny be dated from that period.

6. A *tarry vest* and a *coat* of *feathers* to the slaves of monarchy, and all who oppose the freedom and happiness of the human race.—3 cheers.

7. Wisdom, virtue, and integrity to the councils of our nation.—May they keep a watchful eye on the fawning *Lyon,* and all his *whelps.*—3 cheers.

8. The honest yeomanry of our country. May they convince all incendiaries that they are *Americans,* and not the dupes of *British Renegades* of *American apostates.* 6 cheers.

9. The Martyrs to American Independence—May their patriotism be handed down to posterity, and their memorys honoured at every celebration of freemen.

10. May the *terrorists of our late election* who have threatened to deprive the *labouring poor of bread,* not only have their names registered; but (unless they repent) meet a like fate with *Robespierre*[48] their *progeniture.*—9 cheers.

11. The *War Hawks,*[49] however high they soar, may they *soon* be brought to

a level with *domestic fowl,* and be equally tame and docile.

12. The standard of American liberty. May it wave triumphantly in spite of the enemies of Republicanism, whether foreign or domestic.

13. The *Sons* of TAMMANY throughout the Union—May they never forget *the day* when the *Chiefs* and *Wariors* of the United American Tribes determined to *unburry* the *tomahawk,* rather than sacrifice their liberty; and declared Columbia free from a foreign and tyrannical yoke, and established the *grand wigwam,* whose basis is Liberty, Happiness and Virtue.

14. The *Benefactors* of the human family. As such, may the venerable Congress of '79 be remembered at each anniversary of our Independence, till the end of time. 3 cheers.

15. The *mechanic arts*—May they not only, be successful in supplying Manhattan with the cool and limpid stream, but find a passage from Erie to Ontario, and lead Champlain in triumph to the bosom of the deep.

16. The *American Mothers*—May they teach their sons to love liberty, and their daughters to hate tyranny and adore virtue.

New York Journal, July 6, 1799

JOINT ACTIVITIES OF THE DEMOCRATIC, TAMMANY, MECHANIC, AND OTHER SOCIETIES OF NEW YORK CITY

Celebration of the Eighteenth Anniversary of American Independence by the Mechanic, Tammany, and Democratic Societies, July 4, 1794

JULY 5.

Yesterday being the Anniversary of American Independence, it was celebrated in this city, with the most unanimous demonstrations of patriotism and festivity.

At Sunrise, a federal salute was fired from the battery, accompanied by the ringing of the City bells, which were repeated at noon and at 6 o'clock P.M.

The Legionary corpos of this city, consisting of the troop of horse, the Brigade artillery, and the Grenadier and Infantry companies, assembled at 9 o'clock A.M. and went through a variety of manouvres, in which they were reviewed by major Gen. Morris, commanding the Southern division, the exercises of this corpos, did great honor to themselves, and to Major Steddiford, who commanded them for the day, on their return from their grand parade, they paraded on the battery at noon, and fired a feude joye.

The different societies of the city, gave their several testimonies of mutual congratulations on this auspicious day.

The members of the corporation; the Mechanic, the Tammany and Democratic Societies, had reach their selective boards on this occasion; the Chamber of Commerce, Merchants and other citizens, partook of an elegant entertainment at Mr. Hyde's.

The Mechanic and Tammany Societies proceeded to the new Church in Ann-Street, where an excellent sermon was preached by the Rev. Dr. Pilmore and the declaration of Independence was read by Captain Francis Childs, who preceded the reading of the Declaration by the following observations.—

"Fellow Citizens and Friends!

It was on this auspicious day that the Representatives of the people of America, sired with the love of freedom, and their country, broke the base shackles of despotism, emancipated these United States from the tyranny of foreign domination; and in the language of pure Philosophy, and sublime Eloquence, declared that we were, and should continue *free! "This, fellow citizens, is the Record;"* and I esteem it a high honor, that, on this festive day, I have been chosen to recall them in this manner to your remembrance. Let me therefore crave your attention whilst I read this precious instrument, dictated by the wisdom, and enforced by the swords of our brave countrymen. May the truths which it contains sink deep in our hearts, and animate us all as with one soul, in the defence of our country—that we may convey to posterity the invariable privileges which, under the smiles of Heaven, we now enjoy!"

The Democratic Society and the officers of the militia proceeded to the new Presbyterian Church where the Rev. Dr. M'Knights delivered the appropriate and elegant discourse. The Declaration of Independence having been previously read by Capt. James Morris. After service the whole of the societies assembled in the Fields, and proceeded in procession to the battery, where the company dismissed under the feude joye fired by the Legion and by 3 cheers.

At three o'clock the officers of the Brigade, and of the Independent Regiment of Artillery, assembled at the old Coffee House, where they sat down to a handsome dinner provided for the occasion.—They were honored with the company of his Excellency the Governor, and Major General Morris.

The day was spent with great good humour, good order and happiness, and the following toasts drank under the discharge of artillery.

1. The *Day.*—May it ever be auspicious to the cause of Freedom; and may each returning anniversary bring some new blessing to our country.

2. *The United States of America. May* they be the abode of peace and of freedom, and may their prosperity evince to the world, that in the union of liberty and of law consists the respectability of the government, and the happiness of the individual.

3. Columbia's favorite Son, the *virtuous Washington.*—May he long live to en-

joy the richest meed which a Patriot can receive, "The affections of a grateful and a happy People."

4. *The Senate and House of Representatives of the United States.*—May their decisions be guided by wisdom, and the purest principles of patriotism and may they meet with the cordial support of their constituents.

5. *The People of France.*—May their exertions in the cause of Liberty terminate in a free republican government, and may peace and union with all their attendant blessings, crown them with political and individual happiness.

6. *The State of New York.*—Success to its agriculture, its commerce, and its Manufactures.

7. The Corporation of the City of New-York.

8. *The Heroes who have fallen in defence of American Freedom*—Taught by their great example may we learn, that in the sacred Cause of Freedom our fortunes and our lives are at the disposal of our Country.

9. The memory of our late respected Commander, Brig Gen. Malcom.

10. *The Rights of Man*—May they be clearly understood, and fully enjoyed.

11. *The Militia of the United States.*—May they be everfound the firm defenders of freedom, and zealous supporters of the laws.

12. *The great Family of Mankind*—United by one common nature may they feel and know that they have one common interest, "The happiness of each other."

13. *The Empire of Freedom.*—May its bounds be described by the circuit of the sun, and its duration be commensurate with time.

14. *The Fair of America.*—May they reward with their smiles the mind which respects and the arm which protects their important station in society.

15. *The Militia of this State.*—May the call of our Country beat the Reveille to every generous passion of our bosom; and the Tattoo to those which are selfish.—On our march thro' life, may we never forsake the Standard of Freedom and Republicanism: And at the evening of our days when death shall call his solemn Roll, may an unabated love for our country appear first on the Master, and the sign for its happiness be the *Evening Gun* of our lives.

The Governor and Major General having withdrawn, the following Volunteers were given:—

By General Alner.—The Governor of the State.

By Col. Bieker.—The *Maj.* Gen. of the Southern Division.

The Herald (New York), July 7, 1794

Celebration of the Nineteenth Anniversary of American Independence by the Joint Societies: The Democratic, Tammany, Mechanic, and Military, July 4, 1795

New-York, July 8.
AMERICAN INDEPENDENCE.

The 19th anniversary of this glorious aera, was commemorated with greater cordiality, and apparently more seraphic gratitude and patriotic ardor, than for many years past! The day was ushered in by the ringing of bells and firing of guns, which were repeated at full meridian, and at the moment the celestial orb of the universe settled behind yon western horizon.

The joint societies, viz. the Democratic, Tammany, Mechanic, and the Military, agreeably to arrangements, convened at their respective rendezvouses; they formed upon the battery at eleven o'clock, and moved in one grand procession, their respective insignia held high in view, through Pearl-street, and up Beckman-street, to the Presbyterian Church in the fields, where Mr. *Edward Livingston*[50] introduced the ceremony by reading the DECLARATION of INDEPENDENCE, after which the Rev. Mr. *Samuel Miller* addressed the throne of grace, and a piece of solemn vocal music was performed. Mr. *Miller* then delivered a most pathetic and patriotic discourse, which he had prepared at the joint request of the respective societies,[51] as a ground work for which he took these words from *Exodus* xii. 14.—"*And this day shall be unto you as a memorial*"—The discourse was handled in so ingenious and masterly a manner that it excited universal applause—the choice of the text was very pertinent; the words were spoken by the Lord unto the children of Israel, on the day of their freedom from the *Egyptian bondage.* The house was much crowded. A handsome collection was made for the school of the church. The ceremony finished here by chanting the following *Ode to Freedom,* composed by Mr. S. A. Law, upon the occasion:—

I
Behold a glorious theme
    Awakes the tuneful voice!
Triumphant *Freedom* swells the strain,
    And bids the world rejoice.

II
She speaks, and light divine
    Restless wings its way,
While desp'rate kings in concert join,
    To blast the spreading day.

III.

But ranc'rous kings must die,
    For Freedom's reighn's begun,
And lords and despots, trembling, fly
    Before this glorious Sun!

IV.

In radient pomp she comes,
    To bless the wretch that mourns!
The ransom'd captive leaps and sings.
    The slave adores and burns!

V.

And may her empire rise,
    And haste Immanu'l's reign!
With Halleluhahs to the skies,
    In one celestial strain,

The societies and military again formed before the church, and moved down Broadway to the battery, their line of march, in that ample street, extending beyond the *visual ken.* Here the military, with their usual dexterity, went thro' various evolutions and firings, closing with a tolerably well executed *feu de joy,* who, with the societies, after giving three cheers, were all dismissed, in the utmost harmony and good order.

The Cincinnati dined at Belvideer house, and made their annual election.

The military officers dined at the new Assembly room in William-street.

The merchants, with Governor Jay as an honorary guest, dined at the Tontine.

The Mechanics dined at Mechanic-Hall.

The Democrats dined at Hunter's Hotel; had for their guests, Mr. Miller, the consul of the French republic for N.Y., the consul of the French republic for Mass. and several other gentlemen. After dinner the following toasts were given, interspersed with patriotic songs, amid bursts of applauses—

1. The People of the United States—May they always possess wisdom to discern their rights, virtue to deserve and courage to maintain and defend them. 6 cheers.

2. The Federal Union—May it ever preserve the Liberties, promote the Happiness and secure the Independence of the contracting states. 6 cheers.

3. The President of the United States—May he comply with the unanimous wishes of every true friend of his country, by preventing Grenville's late treaty from becoming the supreme law of the land.[52] 3 cheers.

4. Mason, Burr, Butler, Brown, Bloodworth, Jackson, Langdon, Martin, Robinson, and Tazewell, the ten virtuous, wise, and independent Senators, who refused to sacrifice their country's commerce, rights, and honor, by adopting the

present impolitic and truly disgraceful treaty with Great-Britain.[53] 6 cheers.

5. May falsehood yield to truth, darkness to light, and the rays of the sun be permitted to visit and illumine the dark recesses of the Senate chamber. 3 cheers.

6. GEORGE CLINTON, our late worthy and patriotic Governor—May peace, health, and happiness crown the evening of his days, and may his past services be remembered with gratitude by his fellow-citizens. 9 cheers.

7. Revered by the memory of that illustrious Congress, who with unshaken courage, and magnanimous fortitude, amidst the alarming perils of the times, declared and maintained our national Independence—May future generations of American freemen never fail to pay them the tribute of affectionate gratitude, and justly hail them, the saviours and fathers of their country. 9 cheers.

8. The heroes of America, who so gallantly vanquished and triumphed over the mercenaries of the British tyrant—May they also meet with the merited reward of their honorable services; and when death, the common destroyer of the despot and the slave, has chilled the once genial current that invigorated them to action, may an eternal monument be erected to their memories in the grateful hearts of their countrymen. 9 cheers.

9. The FRENCH REPUBLIC, our best and faithful friend, who generously assisted us in the period of danger and calamity, and favored us with her smiles, when the rest of the world frowned upon our cause—May her present struggle against the barbarous coalition of tyrants be attended with glory and success, and may an approaching honorable peace secure to her the perpetual enjoyment of Liberty, Independence, and Happiness. 9 cheers.

10. The Republic of Holland, and a thorough reformation of the abuses in every government. 3 cheers.

11. The progress of education—May it cause a speedy abolition of every species of dangerous distinction, and render every American a patriot from principle. 3 cheers.

12. Enmity to tyrants—peace and good will to the rest of mankind. 6 cheers.

13. Our sister societies throughout the United States—May their steady regard of the constitution and laws of their country, their orderly submission to the will of the majority of the people, and their firm and invincible attachment to public liberty, ever continue to obtain the confidence and affection of their fellow citizens. 6 Cheers.

14. The American Fair, and the improvement of Female Education. 3 Cheers.

15. THE AUSPICIOUS DAY that rescued our country from the hated yoke of foreign tyranny, and gave us honorable rank among the nations of the earth; may its glorious events never be effaced from our memories—may the blessings it has conferred, be lasting as the globe we inhabit—and may each revolving year find us more united, more happy, and more free. 12 Cheers.

Mr. Miller retired at an early hour—after which the following volunteer was given from the chair.—

Rev. Samuel Miller, the virtuous and patriotic orator of the day.

On Saturday the 4th inst. Capt. Montaignie's Company of Light Infantry paraded on Broad-way, and, having joined the Legion under the command of Col. Rutgers, proceeded, with them, in front of the different Societies from the Bowling-Green, through Beaver, Broad, and Pearl-streets, to the Brick Meeting in Beekman-street, where a patriotic Sermon was delivered by the Rev. Mr. Miller. When the congregation was dismissed, they returned in the same order in which they came to the Battery, where they fired a *feu-de-joy,* in presence of the societies and other citizens assembled.

They then retired to partake of a handsome dinner prepared for them at the Hotel of Citizen Hunter, after which the following patriotic Toasts were drank:

1. The DAY—May it be remembered with gratitude by all who rightly estimate the blessings of Liberty and Independence. 3 cheers.

2. The People of America—May they continue to enjoy the blessings of Prosperity and Freedom, and may no calm of political supineness ever endanger the inestimable reward of a seven year's glorious struggle against *barbarity and despotism.* 9 cheers.

3. The Sons of France—May their united efforts be successfully directed to the establishment of Order and of Liberty; and may the *God of Battles,* who has hitherto upheld them through the uncommon events of a stormy revolution, continue *their stay,* until their enemies are convinced of the justice of their cause, and the power of their armies. 6 cheers.

4. The regenerated Republicans of Holland—May they never permit a second triumph of aristocracy under the mask of moderation. 3 cheers.

5. Citizens Washington, Jefferson, Madison, Clinton, and the whole group of worthies, who remain the decided friends of those principles which gave birth to the illustrious event which we this day celebrate. 6 cheers.

6. The departed heroes of the revolution—May their successful efforts, so precious and invaluable to freemen, be ever held in grateful remembrance. 6 cheers.

7. The Patriotic Societies throughout the Union—May their firmness and indefatigable zeal to perpetuate the liberties of our country, continue to be rewarded by every decided republican. 6 cheers.

8. May governmental secrecy, that sin of aristocracy, be forever banished our Republic. 3 cheers.

9. A standing army, the charybdis of republicanism—May the faction who have so long strove to saddle one upon the freemen of America, continue to experience disappointment in a measure so pregnant with *death to our Liberties.* 6 cheers.

10. The silence of the grave to those who raise their voices only for the degradation of their country—May this day's military display convince our enemies, that we have another *"resource"* preferable to *"the justice and manganimity"* of kings and courts, whose only rule of right is, the measure of their *power.* 6 cheers.

11. May the FAIR DAUGHTER of Liberty never give her hand to the vile *Son of Despotism,* but turn abhorrent from the unnatural alliance—May she remain a vestal in the temple of American Independence, and, like a wise virgin, keep in trim the brilliant lamp of HOLY FREEDOM. 9 cheers.

12. May the *cage,* constructed to coop up the American Eagle, prove a trap for none but *Jays* and *King*-birds. 9 cheers.

13. The TEN WORTHIES, who nobly strove in our national Senate. 6 cheers.

14. May our country never be in want of the patriotism and pen of the modern FRANKLIN. 6 cheers.

15. The flame of Liberty, kindled in the bosom of our country—May it continue to run rapidly through the nations of the earth, until ALL MANKIND become invigorated by its warmth, and enlightened by the splendor of its rays. 12 cheers.

———

Saturday last, being the Anniversary of AMERICAN INDEPENDENCE, the same was celebrated by the TAMMANY SOCIETY, or COLUMBIAN ORDER. At 8 o'clock, A.M., they assembled in their Wigwam, and walked from thence in procession to the Battery, preceded by the *Cap,* the Emblem of Liberty, and the Standard of the United States, which were borne by two brothers. Having there joined the other societies and military, the whole proceeded in grand procession, to the New Presbyterian Church, where an excellent and truly patriotic Sermon was delivered by the Rev. Samuel Miller. From church they returned to the Battery, where a *feu-de-joy* was fired by the legion under the command of Lieut. Col. Rutgers.

In the evening the Society again assembled, when the following Toasts were drank, viz.

1. *The United States of America*—May she never enter into any ALLIANCE which may have a tendency to smother the flame of Liberty, or to injure the Rights of Man. 3 cheers.

2. *The President of the United States.*—May he never affix his signature to a treaty, on whose front is engraven, *Destruction to Liberty and Commerce.* "— 3 cheers.

3. *The Patriotic Minority in the Senate of the United States*—May they receive the thanks of a grateful people, for their determined, though unsuccessful, opposition to a TREATY with Great-Britain, which must terminate in the ruin of our commerce, and be the disgrace of our country. 6 cheers.

4. *The House of Representatives of the United States*—May they evince an undaunted firmness and true republican spirit when the rights and liberties of the people are invaded. 6 cheers.

5. *The Republic of France*—Unanimity to her Councils, perpetuity to her Liberty, and a glorious and uninterrupted success to her arms—May the ties which unite her to the American Republic, be as lasting as nature itself. 3 cheers.

6. GEORGE CLINTON, our late worthy Governor—May his meritorious con-

duct and decided patriotism endure him the love and esteem of his fellow-citizens, and of all true republicans. 9 cheers.

7. Confusion to the councils of the confederated despots, and dismay to their hosts—May they never be able to form a center of union or of action. 3 cheers.

8. *Our Country*—May it never be *disgraced* by unworthy and dishonorable concessions to despots or their minions. 6 cheers.

9. *The Militia* of the state of New-York. 3 cheers.

10. The memorable *Declaration of Independence*—May it ever continue to be the boast of American freemen, and may they support it with their lives. 9 cheers.

11. Eternal union and concord between republics—May those of America and France be indissoluble, and may all who *attempt* a *disunion,* be treated as *traitors.* 9 cheers.

12. The memory of those patriotic heroes who have shed their blood, and offered up their lives on the altar of Freedom, to secure the Liberties of America and France. 6 cheers.

13. *All true Republicans* throughout the world, who spurn at the idea of *passive obedience* and *non-resistance*—May success attend their honest wishes, and lead them to glory, honor, and immortality. 3 cheers.

14. The Citizens and Corporation of the city of New-York. 3 cheers.

15. May the commerce of America be as free as its air, and may the citizens of this country see the impropriety of *importing British merchants* as stock in trade.—6 cheers.

Volunteer from the Chair:

The Day, and all who honor it.

VOLUNTEERS.

1. The Mechanic Society of the City of New-York.
2. The Democratic Society of the City of New-York.

On Saturday last, the 4th instant, the officers of the brigade, and in part of those belonging to the regiment of Artillery, dined together at the New Assembly Room, where the following toasts were drank, accompanied with martial music:

1. The people of the United States. 3 cheers.

2. The president of the United States. 3 cheers.

3. The officers of this State, civil and military.

4. Our late worthy Commander in Chief—May the important services he has rendered his country be forever remembered with gratitude by every Republican. 3 cheers.

5. The French Republic—May victory lead their VAN—Liberty, Justice, and Humanity be their MAIN COLUMN—and an honourable peace bring up the REAR. 6 cheers.

6. The Republic of Holland—May their army and navy be united with that of France, and maintain a superiority over the league of Despots. 3 cheers.

7. Republican principles—May they pervade the universe.

8. The militia of the United States—May their martial spirit prove an irresistible argument against the introduction of a standing army. 3 cheers.

9. The memory of departed heroes—May their glorious deeds ever meet their with *"honourable mention."*

10. The mayor and corporation of the city and county of New-York. 3 cheers.

11. A nearer connection between France and the United States—May the two Republics cultivate a more friendship intercourse, and receive into their friendship none but defenders of the Rights of Man. 9 cheers.

12. May liberty, peace and happiness, be the "Order of the Day" throughout the Universe. 3 cheers.

13. The American Fair. 6 cheers.

14. Gratitude to our Friends—and Forgiveness to our Enemies.

15. The DAY, and all who honour it—May each succeeding anniversary find our country more prosperous and happy. 6 cheers.

Volunteers.

By Col. Rutgers, the president—The *Patriotic Ten* in the Senate of the United States, who were opposed to the late treaty in its *present* form. 15 cheers.

By Col. Bicker, the vice president—May our present Governor's administration give as much satisfaction to the people, as that of our late Governor.

By Major Stagg—Major General Wayne and the Western Army. May they form a *satisfactory* and permanent treaty with the hostile Indians. 9 cheers.

At a Meeting of the Officers and Privates of Captain Snowdon's Company of Artillery, to celebrate the 19th Anniversary of Independence, the following Toasts were given:—

1. The United States; may liberty, fraternity and equality, remain the birth right of its citizens, and publicity hereafter characterize its councils.

2. Citizen George Washington; may he temper the austerity of power, with a simplicity of manner, that will unite with obedience, the reverence of love. Six cheers.

3. Citizen George Clinton, our late worth Governor; may he soon be restored to health, and long enjoy the fruits of his patriotic exertions in favour of the independence, liberty, and happiness of his country. Nine cheers.

4. American Commerce; unfettered by the influence of tyrants thro' the medium of secret negociations. Six Cheers.

5. The *virtuous minority of the Senate,* who refused their assent to a treaty destructive of the commerce and independence of their country. Nine cheers.

6. The French Republic; may the sword of justice, and the right arm of freedom which they have raised "Go forth, still conquering, and to conquer," till liberty makes the tour of Europe in a triumphant Carr. Three cheers.

7. The State of New-York; may her public servants never forget, that her people is the source whence they derive their authority.

8. The friends of freedom.

9. The New-York Regiment of Artillery; may every officer to be a *man,* and every man a *soldier.*

10. May the first rocket that is thrown this evening, illuminate the theatre of heaven, and angels shout in chorus to the birth-day of freedom. Six cheers.

11. May the genius of liberty stand centinel on the watch tower of independence, and forever hail America with, *"all's well."*

12. The militia of the United States; may they still prove the bulwark of liberty, and by their readiness to support the laws, supercede the necessity of a standing army.

13. The soldier's knapsack, wife and friend.

14. The American Fair; may their approving smiles ever cherish the soldier of freedom.

15. The Day, and all who honor it. Nine cheers.

There has never been known a greater harmony than existed on this glorious occasion—Polite and truly friendly deputations of congratulations on the return of this auspicious anniversary, were reciprocated by all the companies through the day, and no disturbance of any kind alloyed the general joy.

In the evening a brillant display of artificial fireworks was exhibited at the Bowling-Green, opposite the government house, by Col. Bauman, which occasioned so great a croud that it was not possible at nine o'clock to approach the place of exhibition by any direction.

Several transparent paints were exhibited in the evening the most brilliant of which was a full portrait of the President of the United States against the poles of the government house, fronting Broad-Way.

These words were illuminated in front of the Federal-Hall,
17—AMERICAN INDEPENDENCE—76.

The evening closed in the utmost harmony, and at eleven o'clock not a soul was seen in the streets.

Song Sung at the 19th Anniversary of American Independence
Commemorated by the Democratic, Tammany, Mechanic, and Military Societies

The Triumph of Liberty:
Or, The Rights of Man.
Tune—"Hearts of Oak"

Come, cheer up, my Countrymen, ne'er be dismay'd;
For freedom her Banners once more has display'd:
Be Stauch for your rights—Hark to Liberty's call,
For Freedom, dear Freedom, stand up and one all!

(CHORUS.)
With heart and with hand,
Swear firmly to stand,
'Till oppression is driven quite out of the land.

To redress all our wrongs, let Man's Rights be applied;
Truth and justice they shew, and by these we'll abide.
Luxurious pomp, which brings taxes and woes,
No more we'll maintain with the sweat of our brows.
    But with heart, &c.

The bold Rights of Man struck such terror and fear,
That stern proclamations in all parts appear;
But deter us they can't— for as friends we'll agree,
The state to reform—and we'll die or be free.
    Then with heart, &c.

So much tribute we pay, that we scarcely can live;
For the light of the sun, what a rent do we give!
To be told, "We are hapy!"—'Tis mere gasconade,
For we're burdened like slaves, and like pack-horses made!
    But with heart, &c.

Then to Freedom press forward, like men who are wise,
And accompany France out of bondage to rise;
And America's world—Let us with them agree,
And join the grand concert—TO DIE, OR BE FREE.
    Then with hearts, &c.

> To conclude—Here's success to honest TOM PAINE:
> May he live to enjoy what he well does explain.
> The just Rights of Man may we never forget,
> For they'll save Britain's friends from the BOTTOMLESS PITT.
>   Then with heart and with hand,
>   Swear firmly to stand,
>   'Till oppression is driven quite out of the land.

New York Journal, July 8, 1795

JUVENILE REPUBLICAN SOCIETY OF NEW YORK CITY

Toasts Drunk to Commemorate American Independence, July 4, 1795

On Saturday 4th July, the Juvenile Republican Society met, to commemorate American Independence. Several of its friends honoured the institution with their attendance. After the delivery of a suitable address by a member, the company partook of a dinner provided for the occasion. During the whole of the entertainment conviviality and an enthusiasm, resulting from the grandeur of the object, prevailed. The following are the toasts drank after dinner.

1. May all the nations of the earth be blessed in the enjoyment of religion without superstition. Liberty without licentiousness, and government without oppression.

2. The press—May it continue free, but never be conducted by those who through factious or selfish views would sacrifice religion, morality, or their country.

3. A cool head, a warm heart, and a strong arm to the defender of the Rights of Man.

4. Virtue, science, and Independence may they be the portion of every succeeding generation.

5. May the removal of tyranny, ignorance, and prejudice shortly produce a permanent and universal peace.

6. A speedy emancipation to the sons of Hibernia[54]—may they soon rank as a Republic amongst nations.

7. France—may her arms henceforth be as forceful in giving freedom to nations as in the influence of Holland.

8. Holland—may the unanimity and moderation which has characterized that infant Republic continue to excite other nations to follow her example.

9. Poland—may she shortly enjoy the blessings of Peace, Liberty and Independence as the reward of her arduous tho' unfortunate struggles.

10. May the recovery of their just rights, crown the exertions of British patriots with success.

11. Columbia—in the negociation and fulfilling of treaties, may she display the candor, firmness and fidelity which becomes a Republic.

12. The government of the United States—without possessing an influence capable of subverting the rights of the people, may it ever enjoy sufficient energy to enforce the execution of laws calculated to promote the general good.

13. Less respect to the consuming speculator, who wallows in luxury, than to the productive mechanic who struggles with indigence.

14. The sons of Columbia—may they henceforth feel as little inclination to become masters as they have heretofore for being slaves.

15. The Martyrs in the cause of American Independence—may the remembrance of their actions inspire us with a firm resolution to transmit to posterity that freedom for which they fought and bled.

VOLUNTEERS.

1. The exiled and suffering patriots of all nation.

2. Republicanism, may it pervade the globe.

3. May the torch of persecution be effectually extinguished by the cap of Liberty.

4. The Fourth of July.

5. The farmers, artists and mechanics of the United States, may they never be last in the defence of their country.

American Daily Advertiser (Philadelphia), July 10, 1795

REPUBLICAN SOCIETY IN ULSTER COUNTY

Resolutions Adopted on the State of Political Concerns, January 1, 1794

At a meeting of a number of Citizens of ULSTER COUNTY, *held at the town of* MONTGOMERY, *on Thursday the 20th of February 1794, for the purpose of forming themselves into a* SOCIETY, *to promote* POLITICAL KNOWLEDGE, *the following* CONSTITUTION *was unanimously adopted.*

ARTHUR PARKS, in the chair.

We the subscribers, sensibly impressed with the importance of civil and religious liberty as ensured by the constitution of the state in which we reside, and that—the United States, and convinced that a reciprocal communication of knowledge is the best mean to perpetuate those blessings, do firmly associate ourselves for the purpose of political information.

1st. This Society shall be known by the name of the REPUBLICAN SOCIETY in Ulster County.

2nd. It shall consist of an indefinite number of members, approved for their moral character and republican principles.

3rd. The officers of this Society shall consist of a President, Secretary and Treasurer, to be elected annually by ballot, or as often as either office becomes vacant.

4th. The business of the President shall be to preside and keep order, and upon an equal devision to have a casting, which in all cases shall be his only vote.

5th. The Secretary shall keep a regular journal of the preceedings of the Society.

6th. The Treasurer shall have the care of the funds of the Society, and shall at the expiration of his office, deliver a true account of all his receipts and expenditures, which shall be referred to a select committee, for their examination to report thereon,

7th. Two fifths of the members of the whole Society, shall form a quorum.

8th. The votes of three fourths of the members present collected by ballot, shall be necessary to admit a member.

9th. There shall be two stated meetings in every year, & special ones whenever a majority of the Society deem necessary.

10th. The meetings of the Society shall not be attended from apprehension of constraint, as no fines shall be imposed for non attendance.

11th. There shall be a standing committee, consisting of not less than five members to be elected annually by ballot, whose business it shall be to write and publish such things as the Society shall think necessary, and in the recess of the Society, whenever a majority of the standing committee shall think a meeting proper, shall notify the President, and it shall become the duty of the President to publish the time and place of such meeting, agreeably to the notice given him by the committee; and in case of the absence of the President, and in case of the absence of both, the majority of the standing committee shall have the power of themselves to call a meeting of the Society.

12th. All communications made by the members of the Society during their recess, shall be directed to the President, and at their next meeting communicated to the Society.

13th. Whenever a member shall be guilty of any disorder or immoral conduct, or shall openly contradict any acknowledged principle of Republican government, shall on the motion of any member, for the first offence be publicly admonished by the President, and for the second offence, unless he evidences, by his principles, or contrition for his immoral conduct, by the voice of the majority be expelled.

14th. There shall be a collection of Republican principles selected and arranged by the standing committee, which together with the Constitution of this Society shall be subscribed by every member as a condition of his admission.

15th. Whenever it is thought necessary to have a revision of the Constitution of a motion of any member, the question shall be put by the President, and if three fourths of the Society agree, the standing committee shall have power to immediately proceed to a revision of the Constitution, and if a majority of the Society approve of the said amendments, they shall become part of the constitution.

16th. The standing committee shall be the organ through which this Society communicates with other Societies of a similar nature.

17th. The funds of this Society shall be supported by voluntary contributions only.

(a true copy)
ELIAS WINFIELD, Secretary.

Resolved, That this constitution be inserted in the public prints, and that the Society meet the first Thursday in March, at 12 o'clock, at the house of Mathew Hunter in the town of Montgomery.

New York Journal, March 15, 1794

At a meeting of a number of citizens of the county of Ulster, in the state of New-York, held at the town of Montgomery, on the first day of January, 1794, agreeably to previous notice, to take into consideration the existing state of the political concerns of this county.

The following persons, viz., John Barber, Phineas Hedges, Charles Clinton, Elias Winfield, and George Clinton, jun. were appointed a committee to draft resolutions, expressive of the sense of this meeting. After a short retirement, the committee returned, and reported a number of resolutions, which being discussed, amended, and duly considered, the question being taken on each resolution, were unanimously adopted.

Resolved, as the sense of this meeting,

1st. That it is an inherent right in the people to assemble whenever they may judge proper, and with order and decency, to express their sentiments in their individual capacities, respecting their natural and political rights.

2d. That notwithstanding it is the interest of the United States, in the present contest, to remain in a state of neutrality, yet, as citizens of a free Republic, and friends to the Rights of Men, it would be a restraint inconsistent with the dignity of Freemen, to stifle our wishes and feelings.

3d. That the present efforts of the combined powers of Europe, against the Republic of France, are a most daring attack upon the sovereignty and independence of nations, and nothing less than a war of tyrants against the sacred Rights of Man.

4th. That the treaty of amity and commerce between France and the United States, is still binding in both nations, notwithstanding the change of government that has taken place in former, and the decapitation of Louis XVI.[55]

5th. That it is the duty and interest of the government of the United States, unawed by the menaces of the British court, and unbiassed by foreign influence, faithfully on their part to fulfill the said treaty, according to the true spirit, and meaning thereof.

6th. That although it has not, as yet, *"been convenient"* for the court of Great Britain to deliver up the western posts to the United States, yet we conceive their conduct in this particular, to be a violation of the treaty of peace, and that *it,* together with the seizure and depradations committed on American vessels, call loudly for the interference of the government of the United States.

7th. That the present unhappy misunderstanding between the President of the United States and the French Minister,[56] has given occasion to the enemies of freedom under the pretext of patriotism, to lead the Minister with the most indecent calumnies, to inveigh against the present measures of France, and to do all in their power to smother that generous spirit of freedom which glows in the breast of every true American.

8th. That every exercise of power, in any of the great departments of national government, which is not expressly delegated by the constitution of the United States, ought to be narrowly and critically examined, lest precedents create law, and although we entertain a high sense of the integrity of the President, it is our duty, as republicans, to presume every man fallible—we think, therefore, that the conduct of the President, in the suspension of citizen Duplaine, is a proper object of Congressional investigation.[57]

9th. That the revolution which has been effected in France, is the proper touch-stone whereby to discriminate the friends of liberty, and that every man who is opposed to the regeneration of France, is, in principle, opposed to the constitution of the United States, and would, were it in his power, saddle us with a monarchy or aristocracy.

10th. That Thomas Paine is entitled to the gratitude of every republican and philanthropist, for his invincible productions, in support of the liberty and dignity of man.

11th. That the late glorious success of the French arms,[58] affords us a subject of the highest joy and exultation, and inspires us with confidence to hope that, in the issue, the Republicans will have taken ample satisfaction on all their enemies, and will have leisure and peace to perfect and organize a system of government founded on the broad basis of LIBERTY and EQUALITY.

12th. That the chairman of this meeting cause the preceding resolutions to be inserted in the public prints.

JOHN NICHOLSON,
Chairman

Elias Winfield,
   Secretary.
   New York Journal, January 18, 1794

DEMOCRATIC SOCIETY OF CANAAN, COLUMBIA COUNTY

Constitution, March 8, 1794

CONSTITUTION
OF THE DEMOCRATIC SOCIETY OF THE TOWN OF CANAAN,
IN THE COUNTY OF COLUMBIA

The signers hereof, at this interesting crisis, have agreed on a political inter-course and association, for elucidating, as far as in our power, the Rights of Man, for the following and other similar reasons:

Because a powerful combination of Europe seem now desperately bent on the extermination of liberty: while in these States the growing establishment of pride, formality, inequality, political heresy, and a baneful and servile imitation of sovereign and corrupt nations, incompatible with freedom, justly awaken the solicitude of the true patriot.

Because the glorious revolutions of America and France, have now, more than ever, disclosed the true objects of society and free government, causing a politi-cal fermentation among nations, and making the present as the precious and peculiar season to give force and effect to reformation, principles and regulations, in favor of the equal Rights of Mankind.

Because, patriotic vigilance can alone preserve what patriotic valor has won: and the supiness of one generation, too frequently destroys the liberty, bought by the noble ardor of the preceding. It is, therefore, a necessary precaution for the patriots of these states to associate, animate and inspire the rising generation with sentiments, worthy the hearts of the heroes of the American revolution.

Because the political happiness of every enlightened people depends on their observance of the Democratical form of republican government, which is un-tenable without social union and communication, and we think, societies formed for political investigation the best mean, at present, of answering the desirable purpose.

And because the patriotic inhabitants of a principal city, in a neighboring state, have taken the lead and furnished us with noble precedent:

We, therefore, rejecting prejudice, religious, national and political, have formed our institution, so far as to embrace the interests of all true patriots, agreeable to the principles contained in the following articles, which we hold as unquestionable:

Art. 1st: That the people have the sole and inherent right, by their representa-tives, of making, and altering forms of government, and, in order to regulate their social interests, to secure their public and private happiness, as well as their natural and civil liberty, a republican form is the best which the wisdom of man has ever yet devised.

2. That the institutions of all free states are improveable, by amendment, and the officers under them amenable for their administration, and as all men are imperfect, therefore a free investigation of the constitutions we are under, and of the conduct of the public servants in office under them (as it is consistent with that full allegiance which we owe to the government of the United States and to that of this state, so it) is proper and necessary.

3. That all corrupt proceedings in elections, alluding by favors, detering by the threats, or abusing the character of candidates, are indecent and subversive of liberty.

4. That as our political weal much depends in the conduct of those in public trust; therefore, regardless of interest or connection, we ought to join in upholding by every lawful means in our power, such men and measures as [will] strengthen government, on the aforesaid principles, and, particularly, such men only as are haters of every species of deception, intrigue, and intricate policy; for virtue seeks no disguise; but corruption hides her guilt in a specious closed of artful intricacy.

5. That pomp, splendor, formality and the like, those attendants of vain equality! those auxiliaries of corruption and oppression! as they are the fruits of a contracted mind, so they tend to degrade the heart, by disseminating an idolizing reverence for things trifling, peurile and utterly foreign to merit, as being frequently the lot of the unworthy, and as often unattainable by the good and wise; and tending to introduce a disrelish for, and neglect of things plain, virtuous, useful and essential to freedom, which can only be upheld by frank honesty, prudence, oeconomy and sincere open dealing public and private.

6. That as the people in this, and every free state, form one joint, equal community, and as the political errors or misapprehensions of a part, must, consequently, injure the whole; therefore, it is the interest and duty of every one, and shall be the endeavor of this society and of each of its members, to cultivate the conciliation and friendship of all our fellow citizens, by renouncing, as far as in us lies, their prejudices against and indifference to a government of open justice and equal rights.

Having thus premised our motives, objects and principles, we adopt the following rules for prosecuting the business of the society.

1. The subscribers join, for the purpose aforesaid, in an association, stiled The DEMOCRATIC SOCIETY OF THE TOWN OF CANAAN, inviting the patriotic inhabitants of the other towns in this county to do the like, that so, by representation from each, a central society may as soon as convenient be found for the county of Columbia, to content, order and methodize the whole.

2. A meeting of this society shall be held the first Thursday in March next, and the first Thursday in every third months thereafter, at such places in this

town as adjourned to, or at such times and places as shall at any time be voted on adjournment; but in the recess the acting chairman shall, on the application of five members, notify one of the clerks to call a meeting at the place adjourned to, or if no place was adjourned to, at the place, where the last meeting was held, or on absence or inability of both, the chairman, and three members of the committee, on such application, may call a meeting.

3. No new members of this society shall be received but in pursuance of express invitation, by nomination voted in meeting. Every member whatever, on admission, to sign this constitution as a test of his sentiments and purposes, and in conviction of wilfully counteracting the intent thereof of the resolves of the meetings, or the proceedings of the officers in pursuance thereof, shall by ballot of a majority in meeting be expelled this society.

4. The officers of this society shall be chosen at least once every year by ballot, in meeting, and shall consist of two chairmen, two clerks, and a committee of two members; but in the absence or inability of both the chairmen, or of both the clerks, others may be occasionally appointed to act in their stead pro temp.

5. It shall be the duty of the committee to correspond with other societies or persons for forwarding the purposes of this society, in its name, and to transact such other business as the resolves of the meeting in the premises, shall assign them, and to report the same, with such other matters as they shall think proper, to subsequent meetings, or to the acting chairman, in the recess.

6. It shall be the duty of the clerks to keep the records of the society, and to warn meetings subject to their orders and instructions.

7. If other town or towns, county or counties, shall form like societies, their members shall occasionally be members of his society they allowing the members of this society the like privilege.

In meeting of the Democratic Society, of the town of Canaan, at the house of Jonathan Warner, Esq. in said town, on Tuesday the 11th of February, 1794, vote, that one of the clerks do cause the above copy to be published

Extract from the minutes

PHILIP FRISBIE, Chairman
JONATHAN WARNER ⎱ Clerks
MOSES YOUNGLOVE ⎰

New York Journal, March 8, 1794

Resolutions Adopted on the Need for Reform in Laws, Courts, and Juries, July 10, 1794

CITIZEN GREENLEAF

One of the Members of the DEMOCRATIC SOCIETY OF CANAAN, *in Columbia County, would thank you to publish the following proceedings of that Society, which were had in the 10th July last.*

Z.

RESOLVED, at the sense of this meeting, agreeable to the principles of the Constitution of this Society.

1. That equal justice, virtue, oeconomy, and a general diffusion of knowledge, are some of the principal pillars that must support the sacred temple of liberty:

And that a veneration of the equal, just and undisguised principles of the Constitution,[59] and of the public administration under it, or its different branches, is the only sure band of allegiance of the people of every free state.

2. That this state, recently emancipated from the tramels of monarchical sway, hath retained certain forms and usages subversive of these principles: which having been formerly disguised under the flowery wreaths of sophistry, and since recommended by habit and prejudice, have not yet sufficiently awakened the public attention: and which, being by no means sanctioned in the constitution, do yet demand the weeding hand of a patriotic legislature.

And as the best preventative against disorder, and the subversion of government, is the timely removal of grievances, and correction of errors:

And whereas this Society, ever devoted to the government of constitutions and of laws, is equally solicitious for the regular and constitutional correction of abuses:

Therefore,

3. Resolved, that this society will make application to the Legislature of this state, at their next session (and use our influence towards having such application generally made) for legal correction of the following particulars, viz:

1. Higher Salaries to certain officers.[60]

We conceive that posts of trust in a free state, ought never to be considered as places of emolument; or as rewards for past services: but as duties occassionally requested of citizens found worthy to be honored with public confidence, for which only a reasonable indemnification can be expected.

Because more than this might tend to excite the avidity of the avaricious for these offices.

Because it might probably tend sometimes to encourage in these offices a prompt formality and parade—inconsistent with that attention, promptitude, industry, and patience, essentially requisite to the dispatch of business in the important departments of the state: which might also by example tend to diffuse in the state a taste for pride, extravagance, and dissipation, degrading to the dignity of republicans—pernicious to morals, & subversive of the public weal.

And because justice, humanity, and sound policy, require, that the burden of public contribution on the people should in no case be lightly or unnecessarily augmented beyond the bounds of strict oeconomy.

2. Unequal designation of public recompence, particularly in the judicial departments, where some of the officers of the higher courts have very considerable salaries, while most of the officers of the lower courts, and the jurors of all, on whom falls a principal part of the business, are by no means indemnified for time, trouble, or expence.

This partial distinction was probably kept up in arbitrary states, as having a natural and certain tendency to depress the common people, and aggrandize the great, and thus to preserve that inequality which is a necessary auxiliary to every corrupt government; It must, therefore, be highly improper and dangerous in a free state, the energy of whose government solely consists in that confidence and cordial co-operation of any enlightened people, which equal justice to all can alone inspire.

3. The extraordinary delays of the decisions in our courts of civil justice especially in some of them, with no other apparent advantage to any than the accumulation of fees and costs—we think highly improper, and unjustifiable on the plea of the tardiness of the parties, since the parties might, with more justice, be obliged to attend or abide a more early and summary decision.

4. The dark intricate and antiquated, formalities as practiced in our said courts; the obsolete phraseology; the vast accumulation of books required; many of them written in dark ages and corrupt governments, among which ruling precedents are to be painfully sought out and substituted for law, appears to us, in this age and country of general and solid improvements and independent sentiments, highly irksome and degrading.—Tending to bewilder the parties as to understanding their own means of defence; and as to understanding the particulars charged against them in the bill of cost: as rendering the rules of administrative justice equivocal and its awards indecisive; and tending to exclude all but those of the law profession from judicial offices; or to perplex, embarrass and render them passive in attempting to officiate in them.

This policy manifestly suited the benighted ages and corrupt states whence it originated; where a mystical solemnity of forms impressed with a kind of magic have and reverence the stupid croud; where the prying eye of enlightened patriotism was justly dreaded by ruling corruption, as per most deadly foe; and where every science was to be perverted to answer his purposes. It must therefore be of a very pernicious consequence in a state like occurs, and might, we conceive, be effectually removed by a new code of laws and rules in plain English, full, concise, and unequivocal.

5. The pleadings of the attornies, agreeable to the present rules and usages of

our courts, are such as must frequently do violence to their own feelings, as insincere harrangues, partial representation and equivocation, must be a painful task to a generous mind, especially when, as frequently happens, an oppossite party present as seen to be heart wounded by it injured, and perhaps ruined. And will not this eloquence of licensed partiality, under the awful sanction of an established court—under the hallowed view of public justice—appear, in the artless eyes of simple virtue, a solemn mockery, and my example have a baneful effect on the borals of the audience.

This must also have suited the policy of the corrupt states whence it is derived, where the preservation of the government required that every channel of sincerity truth & virtue, should, under specious pretences, be corrupted, and their votaries brow beaten and depressed; and that an order of men should be reared up as fit instruments to fill their many high offices, who were hardened, unprincipled, confident perservering, insincere, crafty, eloquent, courtly and plausible.

This error, derived from corrupt states it must be acknowledge, the Republican virtue and magnamity of our courts, and of many of our attornies, hath hitherto greatly ameliorated; yet we can but consider it a dangerous and useless weed—an exotic in the soil of freedom, which ought therefore speedily to be plucked up.

4. Resolved as the sence of this meeting, that any court or jury is more competent, with the parties and witnesses, to award calmly, justly and unpartially, without partial pleadings of attornies, than with them; and more especially if the laws and prims of procedure were duly simplified by the legislature:

And that there are in this state far more actions of small consideration, tried by justice, juries, referees and arbitrators, without attornies or the formalities of the higher courts, than there are larger suits tried by them—that the former equally intricate and difficult, yet are decided with at least as much justice and impartiality, with far more brevity and conciliation of parties, and at a very striking odds of expence in time and money; and it is our sentiment that simple and concise modes for trying actions to the highest amount, might with equal advantage be established, unsullied by precedents and forms from barbarous ages, or by the pleadings of licensed partiality, either by methods similar to those now in use for trying actions under ten pounds (which we think will admit of great corrections touching juries* and some other particulars) or rather by some other mode still more simple, just, equal, cheap and easy; which the present age is unquestionably under better advantages by far to devise and establish than any age preceding.

*Query. might not compelling so many jurors all into one opinion by hunger and thirst, be well amended for a majority out of a jury of 3 or 5, and save them the cruel necessary of perjury?

And is it not unnecessary to call so considerable a number of men at once from their business by a venire?

New York Journal, October 4, 1794

Resolution Adopted on Opposition to the Excise Law in Western Pennsylvania, September 4, 1794

HUDSON, September 14.

At a meeting of the Democratic Society of the town of Canaan, on Thursday the 4th day of September, 1794, and in the nineteenth year of the independence of the United States.

Resolved, as the sense of this Society, that, whatever may be the sentiments relative to the excise law of the United States, we highly disapprove of that riotous opposition to the laws enacted by the constitutional powers of government, which at present exists in the western part of the State of Pennsylvania, as an improper and dangerous means to obtain redress of grievance.

Resolved, That the above resolution be signed by the chairman and clerk and be published.

Philip Frisbie, Chairman.
Moses Younglove, Clerk.

General Advertiser (Philadelphia), September 23, 1794

Address to the Patriotic Inhabitants of the United States, March 5, 1795

Political Miscellany

At a full meeting of the Democratic Society of *Canaan, Columbia County, and State of New-York, on the fifth day of March, 1795, the following* ADDRESS *was unanimously agreed on, and ordered to be published.*

To the PATRIOTIC INHABITANTS of the UNITED STATES OF AMERICA.
FELLOW-CITIZENS,

A YEAR has now elapsed since the formation of our society,—and the promulgation of its principles, in the course of which we have reason to congratulate you on the triumph of the cause of equal liberty, on either side of the Atlantic.

There are certain partial and ambiguous propensities of human nature, which even the best cannot always wholly resist, and from which arises this contest in the political theatre of man, whether the real object of government shall be *the general benefit of the community,* or *the emolument and aggrandizement of a few.*

Of these rival principles of state, the former cherishes general information and vigilance as its only prop; the latter promotes popular ignorance, and is supported by it.

Government, in the former, *courts* free inspection: in the latter it *demands* blind homage.

In the former the mild attraction of general interest secures allegiance, in the latter, fear, corruption and fraudulent artifice.

Economy and an open policy in fiscal arrangements are essential to the former; the imperceptible accumulation of popular burthens, and the complication of popular accounts, promote, by various ways, the dark designs of the latter.

The former is a source of virtue, enlightened simplicity, independence and social felicity; the latter of vice, imposition, popular inconnection, and servile depression.

As frequently the advocates for these opposite principles, have neither of them fully prevailed, many of the various forms of government are jarring, intermediate mixtures of the two kinds, in most of which the latter has the assendency, and in none of which anything but the attention of the people, can secure to them the benefits of the former.

No people, in the choice of a government, could ever wittingly prefer one in which the latter principle predominated; but few communities, at their constitutional establishment, have been so happily situated as to have their general interest *sincerely* attended to, even on points commonly understood and urged; this hath mostly been presented by too implicit a deference to precedent; and to the counsels of the celebrated and interested; and by a want of popular combination. Nor could the people; especially in darker ages, wholly distinguish their true interests thro' the ambiguities and artificual mists, in which for many centuries, policy hath involved a science naturally simple.

But the revival and the diffusion of letters ushered in genuine philosophy, whose keen eye pierced the *factious* cloud; unpriviledged orders peeped behind the veil of the monarchical, aristocratical and hierarchal *Sanctum Sanctorum:* Man gradually descried his rights, appreciated his dignity, and broke his fetters; usurpation and tyranny were constrained to adopt the *general interest* for the ostensible object of their government; though now more fruitful in profound devices to pervert this end by pompously formalizing and faltering science; by sanctioning fiction and insincerity; by giving countenance to effeminating and depraving luxury and pride; by nicer refinements on the old policy, to promote complication, corruption, and inequality; & by establishing mercenary standing armies, of the obdurate and abandoned of the people, on principles devoting them to a master's will; separated from the enjoyments and interests of social man, and opposed to his happiness.

But truth still wrought her way in fettered States; and against the oppressive and viciating reign of these obstructions, the patriotic Americans, at the late revolution, made a gallant and successful insurrection, in which most of the members of the Society took an active and zealous part, and the benefits of which we dearly prize, and firmly resolve to improve and defend; and also to cordially countenance, and second by our best wishes, the efforts for emancipation, made by our oppressed fellow men in every country, as becomes benevolent and sympathizing brethren among the various family of mankind.

Such were our objects, when we formed our institution; objects, which we then though peculiarly interesting, both on account of the struggles for *equal liberty* in France (which must deeply affect every patriotic and grateful American) and on account of its retrograde progress here; an event before anxiously apprehended in some from popular inattention among us, the sure harbinger (in every republic) of usurpation on the one hand, and servile ignorance on the other.

But the prospect brightens, and latterly we have remarked in these States, the growing advantages of growing research in eploiding the fatal imitation here of the corrupt policy of trans-atlantic monarchy and aristocracy—the natural consistence (in a free and enlightened state) between frank animadversion on the errors of administration, and perfect allegiance to government, while we beheld riotous opposition suddenly crushed.

We have seen aristocratical finesse detected and defeated, and the advocates of a powerful standing army, and for titular pomp, baffled and mortified.

In brief, we have seen corrupt artifice, in seeming apprehension, varying her ineffectual shifts to justify her dark policy in the face of day, and to oppose iresistible truth, and the growing prevalence of free enquiry.

In Europe we have remarked with delight, the progress of political morality and information, sapping the foundation of tottering tyranny and imposition.

We have there beheld *regenerated democracy,* rendered almost invincible a nation, before enervated and depressed; drawing forth to action her enthusiastic myriads, by the cordial attraction of *equal freedom* and *political truth;* bearing down the hosts of their combined foes, and trampling on their principalities and powers. Under the smart of treachery and adversity, driven for a while to desperate efforts and indefensible severity; but in prosperity, magnanimous and humane, through yet terrible to armed corruption.

In both hemispheres, the press hath more and more exposed the ancient abuses; exhibiting, in full view, the all-attractive rights of man, and hath so far awakened his attention to them, as to almost abash the wily advocates for corrupt precedent.

In fine, the splendid frippery, the pompous sophistry, with which the bands of slavery have been tinselled over are now found like a species of rotten wood; shining in darkness, but rayless filth by day; will 'a wisp may decoy the [be]wildered traveller by night, but the political day dawns, and the shadows fly away.

Let us, therefore, fellow-citizens, *be up and doing,* let us well improve the auspicious morning, each in his particular sphere and manner (whether as members of private associations for aiding the general good, or merely as members of the social whole) assisting in the prosperous work of investigating our rights, interests and duties, of guarding the purity of our government, and *supporting its constitutional authorities.*

That we may transmit to the *charge* and fruition of posterity, an unimpair patrimony of free government, whose administrators, by firmly prefering the general benefit of the people to every partial and opposite interest, may avoid the least occasion of fear, from growing disaffection or formidable insurrection: by constitutional, equal and disinterested agency, may render courtly finesse and intricacy unnecessary in pecuniary institution, or in fiscal, financial, or other policy; and by a respectful attention to the prevailing sentiments and wishes of their *sovereign,* may supercede every cause of apprehension from associations among their constituents, for free inspection and research; and thus ensure the true republican energy to government, from *the confidence of public zeal and prompt co operation of the people.*

By order,

PHILIP FRISBIE, *Chairman*

Moses Younglove, Clerk.

Independent Chronicle (Boston), March 30, 1795

Address by a Member to the Democratic Society on Jay's Treaty, September 3, 1795

CITIZEN GREENLEAF

Be pleased to publish the following Speech addressed to the Democratic Society of Canaan at their quarterly meeting on the 3d of September by a member. It was forwarded to you some weeks back, but has probably not come to your hand.
The first copy was received and ACKNOWLEDGED, but has been omitted from time to time for want of room.

October 2, 1795.

FELLOW CITIZENS,
The subject of the pending treaty with the British court,[61] hath undoubtedly excited the opposition and solicitude of the discerning disinterested and patriotic through the American union, notwithstanding what had been pretended to the contrary. I shall not, on this occasion, enter fully into a consideration of that alarming subject. But it may not be improper to notice some of the inconsistent fallacies and hostile designs, now become more apparent than ever in the pretenses and measures of some of the partisans and agents of that business, who perhaps have too much influence in our government.

Although the anti-republican objections and sophistical arguments in opposition to our political Societies for some time past, have been very little regarded by sagacious patriots, who readily detected the wolf lurking under the sheep's disguise, yet most of you may, perhaps, recollect that the objectors made pretense of founding their disapprobation on some of the Societies shutting the door at some of their meeting; and on the members being only received by vote, thus *selecting some to the rejection of others as good, while the subjects attended to, especially involved the interests of all.* That on this account our institutions tended to Partial and aristocratical assumptions of the free citizens at large, *making a part greater than the whole,* &c. Against secret counsels & governmental censure, was their chief cry, while those of the Societies, whose constitutions enjoined open counsels, and who had merely sought information, nor had ever passed any vote, or act of censure, equally with the rest, shared the lash of their acrimonious reprobation as Jacobin clubs.

This mock shew of guarding the rights of the people at large from partial assumptions imposed, however, on some honest citizens, who, inattentive to the tendency of other insinuations of this combination, obliquely inculcating the doctrines of unlimited confidence in *rulers,* of the baneful effect of popular influence of government &c. and, who, inattentive to their conventions and the like, suffered themselves in a degree to be fascinated by their syren songs.

But as few things are so evil as to be unproductive of any good, so the treaty before mentioned, stimulating the public mind, hath produced occurrences, furnishing a clue, by the guidance of which their labrynth of delusive artifice, is further explored and detected. The present opposition to the treaty is, by the citizens at large, in and out of office, members of the Societies, and unassociated zealous partizans for the constitution of our general government in its present form, and such as wish a legal correction of some parts of it. Patriotic citizens of all these descriptions, in large numbers, have openly and fraternally assembled in almost every quarter of the United States, for the purpose of petitioning the President to withhold his signature. These open unselected assemblages of citizens, warranted by the essential rights of freemen, and expressly guaranteed by the constitution of the United States might, by some, have been expected to meet the cordial approbation of these pretended zealots for the constitution, and for a free equal exercise of the rights of the people at large. But mark their increased horror and apprehension on this occasion: Their fervent deprecation of a measure so hostile to the constituted authorities of government and order, so pregnant with tumult, action, and anarchy! And their hackneyed and opprobrious epithets, of which they branded the numerous agents of it!

Thanks to S. T. Mason they had now no shift remaining to sanction their rooted, and hitherto disguised enmity to every assertion of the popular privileges and interest, but must stand forth in opposition to the natural and constitutional right of the people in general, *to meet, and petition;* they sighed at the idea of foregoing the mask by which alone they could fascinate the popular mind in any degree into their favour; but the anti-republican projects of attack they had been so long and so painfully maturing in ambush, they could not renounce; their consequent choice has divested them of their disguise, and exposed them openly to the detecting eye of every sagacious republican, while their mortified situation subjects them to embarrassments and inconsistent pretences, which plead their best apology for having so long and so strenuously struggled to preserve their veil of secrecy and disguise.

In saying this, my censure is not by any means aimed at all those who have been, in any degree, opposed to our Democratic Societies, or to this or that proceeding of theirs. Our institutions, like all others, are liable to abuse, need inspection, and may frequently deserve animadversion. And the purest patriots, as more or less warped by an attachment to this or that *person* or principle, may, undoubtedly, vary in sentiment concerning them, and also concerning the particular forms or proceedings of *popular assemblages in general, for communication of sentiment, and for petitioning.* My censure is merely aimed at those who betray a systematic opposition to the free exercise of that right in any form, who have varied their ground, and shifted their pretext in this opposition, as occasion and artifice required, and the investigation of whose drift and conduct plainly indicates this conspiracy to evade the inspection of the people, while they tap the foundation of their constitutional rights and speciously bind their hands.

On the particular grounds of such suspicion, I will mention a few—most of which do not appear to have been attended to in the public discussions, and some of which I have already hinted at.

In tracing the artifices of this party, we shall find, that aristocratic conspiracy is a *Proteus* of various shapes. They not only, as before mentioned, villify the popular societies under one disguise, and oppose assemblages of citizens for petitioning under another, but also ply a very art and fiction to dissuade and deter the people from the exercise of the rights of petitioning in any way, as well as from making any open declarations of their sentiment on any unpopular public measures, and then improve the advantage of that forbearance, to misconstrue the silence most of them into an approbation of the measure in question. That by this finesse, they may discountenance any final proportion of the people who shall presume to constitutionally speak for themselves the general sentiment in opposition, by opposing to them a nation of mutes in the character of approvers.

Instead of impressing the people with a sense of the necessity of a general dissemination of political information and virtue, without which, free government is untenable, their conversation, writings, and influence, teach us, that politics and government are sciences to intricate and profound as to render nugatory, and even ridiculous the attempt of common people, to acquire any useful knowledge of them, that patriotism and public virtue are mere fictions; that we ought to know no difference between one man or public agent, and another, as to his drift and sentiment in governmental or political concerns, otherwise than from his proving a fair and unfair dealer (in common business) humane or austere, &c.; that one form of government is just about as good as another for the body of the people; that it is idle to suppose the citizens at large can acquire or form any rational judgment on the merits or demerits of any constitution, treaty, law, or the like, otherwise than by acquiescing under the experiment of it with perfect silence and deference, and if then their crops turn out well, their avocations succeed, prices are as they would wish, taxes do not swell to such magnitude or assume such a *visible form,* that the pressure of their increase is *sensibly felt;* and if the rapid growth of general prosperity is not fully checked by such evidence, and such only, they are competent to judge the act in question an excellent one, and that every public measure is in its best possible train.

In excuse against the steady pursuit of the free equal principles of government, they frequently when pressed on plead the ignorance of the people, for, say they *the principles of the government must be more free and equal or less free and more unequal in proportion to the knowledge of ignorance of the people:* and as the real operation of all their endeavors on the people is to immerse them in ignorance and torpitude, this shews what kind of government they have selected to fit them for, and this evident maxim of their plea will thus explain. Why the genuine republican is ever anxiously endeavoring to differentiate popular atten- tion & knowledge, and why this counterfeit republican party and their allies, are no less sedulous to promote *popular inattention, indifference, and their offspring, ignorance.*

It appears an evident principle from the writings of the affecters of equality of rights and from the uniform experience of people of present and past ages, that *as the true object of government is to promote and secure the benefit of the community in general, and the greater possible degree of individual happiness and freedom consistent therewith, in favour of every citizen equally:* to this end it is essential that laws and public administration should harmonize as far as pos- sible with the general will; but as distinct and frequent opposite interests will naturally actuate citizens of different conditions, stations, &c. and as the selected and more or less dignified legislators of the public, will naturally be mostly taken from a rank or condition more elevated by wealth and power, than the people in general; they will, in consequence of that difference, as well as of their public office or trust, be tempted by a separate interest and bias, in a degree common to those of their own condition, station, &c. and consequently receiving no ef- fectual check, merely from them: in a greater degree opposed to the general interest, and therefore requiring a vigilent inspection of the people at large, as its only proper and efficacious check; and the public agent or representative ought, for the same reason, to be impressed with a sense of his responsibility to the people, by frequent returns of election.—Yet those pretended republicans, in contempt of every republican axiom, not only as I have before said, spurn such popular vigilence, in whatever shape as dangerous Jacobinical inquisition, but are also ever warm in the praise of certain leading politicians among them, who on secret occasions, have laboured hard to have our general government so con- stituted as to have the President and the Senate elected for life, and who, with the whole party have ever adhered to the principle that *those in public trust who farthest removed from the inspection, responsibility and interest of the people at large, should possess the highest and most permanent powers of government.* They have also, for their firm adherents and supporters, all the determined ad- vocates for [mo]narchy on either side of the Atlantic, while they themselves, in common conversation, say very little for or against the nature of monarchic government, and are ever leaning their attentions and attachments toward persons and to the neglect of principles. Not merely the office but the *person* of the public administrator is, in their eye, an object of such *devotion* and magnitude, as to nearly intercept their views from the lesser and less remote *objects,* the *rights and interests of the sovereign people,* from whose authority alone he derives his official existence; and *the constitution,* his subjection to which can alone give his agency legal force, for neither of these objects can they view in any other direction than behind him. Nor is their cautious taciternity less observable on the aristocratical principle of the expediency of a partial impulse, operating on the government and thwarting the general interest, which is the polar star of their politics, and which argues, that the people should be held subject to the government by deception, corruption, or force, rather than by the kind impulse of general benefit.

The ambiguity, obscurity, complication and secrecy which hath enveloped their operations and projects in other instances, are no less indicative of the hostility of their aim, as their cautious artifices can have no other object than the invasion of public inspection, which implies that the plans or measures so concealed or disguised, are against the general will and interest. The variety of their impositions attempted on the people, & the further instances of their duplicity, are too numerous now to be recounted yet too important to be all passed in silence.

Who can forget the democratical and limited constructions they gave the constitution of the United States in their writing and harangues, before its adoption (*"vesting in the democratic branch the sole command of both the public purse and sword, &c."*) and the very different constructions attempted to be given to it by the same men on several occasions since and at present. Their confidence at the mission of our late envoy, of our receiving, in confidence of his negociations, prompt reparation from the British King, their determination *in the possible case of failure,* to join hand in hand in an instant war against him, their subsequent confidence in the justice of our claims, and in the complete success of the negociations till very lately; and the sudden and astonishing change, at the promulgation of the treaty, of their *views,* convictions, apprehensions, and arguments; *views* which they can now scarcely pretend to deny, were the secret guide of their measures before. The profound policy of their various attempts to establish a powerful standing army under colour of preparing for active operations against an aggressing power, whereas it now appears they were predetermined not to use them against that only power, which appears perserveringly hostile to our rights and safety, and that the advantages they aimed at deriving from the proposed army must have been of a nature far less grateful to the freedom of the American people. The principle avowed only on urgent and proper occasions, but pertinaciously adhered to, and practiced on, by all the fraternity as far as cautious policy and the spirit of the times will admit. *That a national debt is a national blessing,* as affording (with other auxiliary establishments) the means and *cloak* of a happy influence in government, preponderating in favour of a privileged few, and imperceptibly counteracting the blind vulgar influence and interest of that many headed monster the people: and the officious promptitude of the same party, on several occasions, since their adopting this principle, and *practicing on it so far as to deeply involve their pecuniary interest in its protraction,* to outstrip all others in pretendedly providing for insuring and expediting the seasonable *redemption of our public debt,* by arrangements and appropriations, extending a controul over the economy of the public revenue for many years, very artificially constructed complex and obscure. While those of them who were more active in these expediting measures, were also the active and warm advocates of diverting large portions of the revenue to new and extraordinary channels of expenditure.

But time will fail me to enumerate instances of their impostures to mask the hostility of their operations, I therefore forebear.

The particular grounds of suspicion & alarm above mentioned, and many others having been publickly exposed in the late political controversies, will suggest themselves to the collection of the attentive republican, appear to have all arisen from one party, who, forming a powerful combination play into each other's hands, cling together and persevere. Such conpirations might have been expected, and ought to have been more vigilantly guarded against. The seeds of usurpation and oppression are sown among the better seed in every state, which naturally springing up, indispensibly require the weeding hand of an attentive and jealous people. To which consideration, it may be added, agreeably to the opinion of many, that some remains of the old bitter root of *partial government* not sufficiently eradicated at the formation of our constitution and modes of public administration, and since rankly shooting up and flourishing, begin to overshadow, choke and threaten the ruin of the wholesome republican crop. The wavering voice of many enlightened statesmen seasonably predicted and cautioned in vain against this, and the stable, the incorruptible Jefferson among the rest, who wrote during our revolutionary war "It can never be too often repeated (said he) that the time for fixing every essential right on a legal basis, while our rulers are honest and ourselves united, from the conclusion of this war we shall be going down hill, it will not then be necessary to resort every moment to the people for support; they will be forgotten therefore, and their rights disregarded. They will forget themselves, but in the sole faculty of making money, and will never think of uniting to effect a due respect of their rights; the shakles, therefore, which shall not be knocked off at the conclusion of this war will remain on us long, will be made heavier and heavier, till our rights shall revive or expire in a convulsion."[62]

Fellow citizens, is not the verification of these predictions advancing with amazing celerity? Do not the conspiring combination seem now redoubling their efforts, strengthening their alliances at home and abroad, and concentrating their plans to a degree which renders it probable they will, ere long, bring their operations to a focus? The important crisis is probably at hand, in which the ambitions and unwarrantable objects of a few aspirers is to be weighed against the liberty and happiness *of the free citizens of America,* when, I hope, we have reason to anticipate the guardian genius of human rights, will direct the balance.

New York Journal, October 14, 1795

5 | Norwalk Republican Society, Connecticut

Toasts Drunk at a Meeting, October 7, 1793

New Haven, October 7, 1793

This day, the Republican Society in this city assembled, and having dined in perfect conviviality, drank the following toasts:

1. GEORGE WASHINGTON.
2. The land we live in.
3. The mothers of liberty.
4. The cradle in which it has been and shall be nursed.
5. Our friends.
6. The Republic of France.
7. Citizen Genet.
8. The yeomenry of America.
9. Our commerce.
10. Our courts of justice.
11. The distressed of all nations.
12. Our brethren of Philadelphia—speedy relief and a perfect restoration of health to them.[1]
13. Peace and plenty to the whole earth.
14. Our University—may our legislators be its nursing fathers.
15. The American Fair—May their progeny be free and honorable to the latest generation.

Connecticut Courant (New Haven), October 9, 1793

Introduction to the Constitution, April 4, 1798

INTRODUCTION TO THE CONSTITUTION OF THE NORWALK REPUBLICAN SOCIETY

To support the Laws and Constitution of this and the United States, even at the hazard of lives if called thereto. To exercise the right of speech, and freedom of debate, recognized by the Constitution. To perpetuate the equal rights of man, to propagate political knowledge, and to revive the republican spirit of '76, are the great objects of this institution.

The history of nations whose governments are founded on constitutions in some measure republican, affords us melancholy proofs of the baseness of the human heart, so conspicuous in the attempts that have invariably been made by some intriguing, designing men, not only to distort, but even to violate the sacred *Palladium,* of both civil, and religious liberty, to answer sinister purposes of their own and have thereby, usurped authority, never delegated them by the people, the only source of all human authority.

History also furnishes instances sufficient to convince every rational mind, of the fallacy of an opinion too often credited, that a person can be placed in such an elevated situation as to render it impossible for him to do wrong; such a belief, has a tendency to produce an apathy in the public mind, which invites abuses; it is repugnant to common understanding; pregnant with mischiefs incalculable, and ought to be guarded against with the utmost precaution.

From these considerations, and from a review of what is taking place within the circle of our own knowledge, it must be evident, to the most inattentive observer, that the present crisis is an important one, and demands the attention of every friend to his country; and that it is the duty of all republicans, to be active and vigilant, no on can deny: and as strength consists in unanimity, we feel it incumbent on us to associate together, and for our own regulation adopt the following constitution:

(Here follows the articles.[2])

Bee (New London), April 4, 1798

6 | Democratic-Republican Societies of Massachusetts

THE MASSACHUSETTS CONSTITUTIONAL SOCIETY, BOSTON

Rules and Regulations and Declaration, January 13, 1794

THE
MASSACHUSETTS CONSTITUTIONAL
SOCIETY.
RULES AND REGULATIONS.

PREAMBLE.

WHEREAS it is the wish of the Subscribers to promote and cherish the social virtues, the love of their country, and a respect for its Laws and Constitutions; an attachment to Liberty, and above all a sacred regard to the great and essential Principle of EQUAL RIGHTS, which in their apprehension is the only just and legitimate basis of a free Government: They, therefore, for their mutual information and improvement, and for the general dissemination of those principles, do hereby associate and form themselves into a Society, under the following Regulations, by the name of The MASSACHUSETTS CONSTITUTIONAL SOCIETY.

ARTICLES.

Article 1. A President, Vice-President, a Corresponding Committee of fifteen members, with a Corresponding and Recording-Secretary, shall be annually chosen by ballot on the first Tuesday of November, and by a majority of the members present.

Art. 2. The stated meetings of the Society shall be quarterly, *viz.*—on the first Tuesday of November, February, May and August, at such place as the Society shall appoint.

Art. 3. All letters and communications addressed either to the President, Vice-President, Committee of Secretaries, shall be publicly read to the Society at their next meeting after such letters and communications are received; and the Society shall act upon them as they shall think expedient.

Art. 4. For the preservation of order and decency in all debates, every member that has any thing to offer shall arise and address the President. And no member shall speak more than twice on a subject without permission so to do from the Society, nor be interrupted while speaking unless to be called to *order,* which shall be determined by the President or presiding officer for the time being.

Art. 5. The Recording-Secretary shall keep a fair record of all transactions of the Society (excepting such as are expressly assigned to the Corresponding-Secretary). Shall notify the members in the public papers of each stated or *special* meeting. And in case of absence the President shall have power to appoint another member to act in the office of Recording Secretary for the time being. The Recording Secretary on the expiration of his office shall deliver to his successor all the books and papers belonging to the Society.

Art. 6. The Corresponding-Secretary shall forward all letters and communications *from the Society* and keep on file all letters and communications to the Society; and keep a fair copy of all communications, and correspondence to and from any public bodies, associations or individuals. On the expiration of his office he shall deliver up the Society's books and papers to his successor.

Art. 7. It shall be the Duty of the President, Vice-President, and Committee to correspond with other Societies that are or may be established on similar principles, in any of the United States, or elsewhere; to transact any business that may arise between the stated meetings, unless a majority of the members present should think it proper to summon the whole Society to consider on the subject. In this case the President, or presiding officer for the time being, shall have a turning vote.

A stated meeting of the President, Vice-President, Corresponding Committee, and two Secretaries, shall be at least monthly, and eleven members of the Committee shall make a quorum—and no business shall be transacted unless by the consent of seven members present at the meeting exclusive of the votes of the two Secretaries.

Art. 8. The President shall have the power to call a special meeting of the Society upon application of *two* members, and the doings of such meeting shall be equally as valid as at the stated meetings.

Art. 9. Every member shall keep a printed copy of the articles and regulations, with the names of the members. The assessments on the Society for all expences shall be settled at each meeting by the Recording Secretary, provided always that the occasional expence of the President, Vice President and committee at *their* several meetings shall be discharged by themselves without any expence to the Society at large.

Art. 10. That this Society may embrace the great objects of its institution, persons from any part of the Commonwealth may be admitted as members; and no person shall be admitted the same evening he is proposed, (unless a majority of the members present determine otherwise) but shall stand a candidate till the next meeting of the Society; and the name of the member who nominates a candidate shall be entered with the name of the candidate in the books of the Society. Persons admitted shall be by written balot and by two-thirds of the members present, and all members shall sign these rules and regulations or an acknowledgment to abide by and support them.

Art. 11. Should any member willfully neglect attendance for one year (unless on public service or at sea) after being duly notified, without, good reasons given, his name shall be erased, and he no longer considered as a member of this Society.

Art. 12. That if a member of the Society shall behave in any wise contrary to the rules *principles* and regulations of the Society, he shall be expelled there-from, if two-thirds of the members present think proper so to do.

Art. 13. The President, Vice President any one of the committee or any one member being seconded, shall have a right to propose, at any meeting of the Society, any question of political importance, for discussion at the next meeting of the Society, and the question so proposed shall be the subject of debate at such succeeding meeting.

Declaration, by the Society.

———————

UNDER a Constitution which expressly provides, *"That the People have a right, in an orderly and peaceable manner, to assemble to consult upon the common good,"* there can be no necessity of an apology to the public, for an association of a number of Citizens to promote and cherish the social virtues, the love of their Country, and a respect for its Laws and Constitutions: Nor can it be derogatory to *Freemen in America,* to declare their attachment to *Universal Liberty,* and openly to profess a sacred regard to the great principles of *natural Equality.*

That the People, upon having formed a government, are implicitly to resign themselves to the Agents and Delegates appointed by them, without any kind of attention to their own Liberty and safety, is a doctrine calculated to undermine the foundations of Freedom, and to erect on her ruins, the fabric of Despotism.

WE conceive, that as Citizens of the United States, we are individually interested in the measures of our General Government, and as members of the State, in those of the Commonwealth of which we are a part.

That it is the right and duty of every Freeman, to watch with the vigilance of a faithful centinel, the conduct of those, to whom is intrusted the administration of Government, that they pass not the sacred barriers of the Constitution.

Predicated on these principles, the Members of this Association have united, and agreed to meet in whole, or in such parts as may be expedient, to converse together for the purpose of gaining and communicating information on the affairs of their country, to express with decency and firmness, their sentiments respecting the measures adopted by their Delegates, and to offer their opinions with candour on matters of political concernment.

As Freemen we publicly declare, that we adore the cause of Liberty, wherever it may be in exertion; and our wishes and our prayers are fervently engaged against the Despots of the earth.

We are persuaded that the present struggles of the French People are directed to the subversion of Aristocracy and Despotism, and to the lasting improvement and happiness of the human race, as they are founded on the *Equal Rights of Men.*

With such objects in view, and on these principles, the particular *form* of administering their government in detail, we consider, at *present,* unessential: But on the accomplishment of the great objects of their Revolution, depends not only the future happiness and prosperity of Frenchmen, but in our opinion of the *whole World of Mankind.* Their success will put an effectual check to the progress of despotic ambition, while the failure of so great and gallant a nation, would encourage the Despots of the earth to aspire to the hope of extinguishing the Spirit of Liberty perhaps in every other part of the globe. When in addition to this, we recollect the generous assistance, which the French nation afforded us, in the day of our distress and danger, we cannot but with that the great Ruler of the universe had placed it within our power to reciprocate their friendship, by aiding them in the establishment of that Liberty, for which they are now bleeding with so much firmness, and magnanimity.

Published by order of the Society.

WILLIAM COOPER,[1]

President, *pro-tem.*

A true copy from the Society's Records.

SAMUEL HEWES, Rec. Sec.

Boston, January, 13*th*, 1794.

We have authority to say that 269 persons have actually signed the Books, and 63 more have been since admitted, on their respective applications.

Boston Gazette, January 20, 1794

Circular Letter to All Republican Societies in the United States, August 28, 1794

Boston, August 28.

At a meeting of the Massachusetts Constitutional Society held in Faneuil Hall the 14th instant, Voted unanimously that the Circular Letter reported by the Committee be sent to all the Republican Societies in the United States.

(CIRCULAR)

FELLOW-CITIZENS,

The Massachusetts Constitutional Society in Boston having appointed a committee to correspond with the Societies established on similar democratic principles with their own, it is with the highest satisfaction we embrace this opportunity to address you, on the objects and principles of our association.

At this important period when the despots of Europe are combined to destroy every vestige of republicanism, and to restore monarchy upon a more permanent basis, it behoves the friends of freedom in this country in particular, to associate for the purpose of defending their constitutional rights. We conceive it the duty of the people, to watch the conduct of those to whom they have intrusted the administration of their government: being agents for this important business, they are accountable to their constituents for their measures and whenever they deviate from the great objects of their appointment, the people ought to be assiduous in exercising their constitutional authority to remove them from office.

For this purpose, and in order that the people should obtain the best information on all political subjects, and act with *efficacy* in their measures, the institution of Republican Societies must be considered as the great bulwark to protect themselves against the artful designs of men, who are secretly endeavouring to destroy those fundamental principles of liberty and equality, on which are founded the happiness and security of mankind. Societies thus instituted serve to harmonize the public mind, by becoming sources of authentic information, by which means the people become equally guarded against the ambitious and designing views of men both *in* and *out of government*.

Information is the great source of political knowledge, and the great cement of Society: while this is diffused the liberties of the people will ever be secure, and none but the dishonest will endeavour to check its progress, or attempt to annihilate the organ through which it is conveyed.

Order and good government are the primary objects of the Constitutional Society, and we trust of every institution founded on Democratic principles;

and however their opponents may please to reflect on the tendency of such societies, or on the designs of their members, yet we trust nothing will ever be adopted by them, that shall endanger the happiness of the community, but on the contrary establish on a permanent basis the constitutional liberties of the people, and the peace and independence of our country.

We cannot refrain on this occasion to observe that on the successes of the French depend the happiness of the United States. The prosperity of this Republic is the constant theme that invigorates the minds of Americans. We consider their patriots as contending not only for their own liberties but for those of America, and the world of mankind—and should they be overcome (which God forbid) America must fall a sacrifice in the universal ruin; the citizens of the United States would be summoned to attend the funeral of their liberties and our children yet unborn would be arrayed in the garb of slavery, and forced to drag out a pitiful existence as Vassale to a banditti of tyrants.

We are Citizens, with every
   sentiment of respect, your
      brethren in one common cause,
         your most obedient humble servants.
(In behalf of the committee)

WILLIAM COOPER, P.P.
A true copy from record,
   SAMUEL HEWES, Rec. Secretary.
The Citizens Members of
   the Democratic Society
      Philadelphia. _____
      By order of the Society,

GEORGE BOOTH, Secretary

General Advertiser (Philadelphia), November 6, 1794

Address to Democratic-Republicans Throughout the United States, January 5, 1795

AN ADDRESS FROM THE
Massachusetts Constitutional Society

The follow Address of The Massachusetts Constitutional Society, *is respectfully inscribed to the democratic Republicans throughout the United States.*

Friends and Fellow Citizens:
MORE than a year has expired, since the rules and principles of our Association, and the sentiments we adopted on the existing state of public affairs at that

period, were submitted to the judgment of an enlightened public. No objection of weight having then appeared to that publication, we presumed that no exception could be taken to any circumstance attending the institution. But much speculation having been lately excited in many parts of the Union, by similar establishments, we have thought it expedient, to state at large the motives which induced us to assemble—the opinions we have uniformly held, and to reply to such objections as appear to us to be entitled to a serious refutation.

In order, however, that our sentiments may be clearly understood, in these interesting points, it will be necessary to recur to the celebrated declaration of the American Independence.

An object, in our estimation, the most resplendent of any, which, till the moment, the extended landscape of human affairs, had presented to the eye of political speculation.

Various were the ideas formed by the politicians and philosophers of either hemisphere on this singular expedient. In this country it was considered of indispensible necessity to ensure the intervention of *"foreign aid."*

By the nations of Europe, but particularly *France,* it was viewed as a circumstance highly favorable to that balance of power, which it has been the wish of the ablest statesmen of the last and present centuries, to preserve. In *England,* it was insidiously represented, and generally believed to be, the separate effort of unprincipled incendiaries, and of turbulent and aspiring demagogues, to encrease their consequences amidst the confusion of the times, and the wreck of empire. But among these supposed incendiaries, happily for the human race, were to be found, those great and illustrious politicians, who never viewed this event as a mere partition of territory, but embraced it as a fortunate occasion of exhibiting to the world a representative system of Government, established on the imperishable basis of a *perfect Equality of Rights.*

NOTWITHSTANDING the visible benefits which immediately resulted to America, from the adoption of this principle in the act of their national Independence the real importance of it to the world was never justly appreciated, until the French National Convention had erected an European Republic, in the same philosophical tenet. This sublime and unanswerable truth being thus established by the people of the United States as the foundation of all their future political institutions, the moment it was naturalized in France, formed the most eventful epoch of civil history. Till this period the art of Government has been but the study and benefit of the *few* to the exclusion and depression of the *many;* but from this auspicious moment, a new scene has opened in the Theatre of human affairs; and as a portion of the national sovereignty in every country which is really free, must be unalienably deposited in the breast of every individual, the existence of such governments in the purity of their original principles must of necessity depend on the actual information of all.

THE Society will readily admit the truth of a maxim, which has been often urged, that on *common occasions* the free and peaceful citizens of America, should be preserved wholly independent of the refined, but corrupt politics of European governments. But with all the deference that is due to those of a different sentiment, we are obliged to consider the contest, now pending in Europe, to be a striking exception to this principle. The present war is so singular in its objects, that it cannot be classed in any general description. It is not a war of religion, of territory, nor of personal pique or ambition. It is a war of *power* against *right* of *oppression* against Liberty, and of *Tyrants* against the PEOPLE. The other conflicts in Europe have stained that highly cultivated country with the blood of its inhabitants, but the present threatened almost their total extermination; for it is so much more sanguinary than those of any former period, that in our opinion, the combination of Kings against Freedom was intended to deluge every country with the blood of its citizens, who should dare to assume the right of forming a Constitution of Government "*to promote the general welfare,*" and "to secure the blessings of Liberty to them and their posterity." The final issue therefore of this last and illustrious revolution, will determine whether the spirit of *despotism* or *Liberty* shall hereafter assume a predominating influence.

IF these ideas are well founded, two conclusions must necessarily follow: 1st. That the political interest of France and America, at the present crisis, are "one and indivisible"—and 2dly, That no policy on the part of this country, whether temporizing or decisive, would have prevented the horrors of war from extending to it, had France been unsuccessful in her present struggle.

UNDER the influence of such impressions, and with the solicitude they were calculated to inspire, the Massachusetts Constitutional Society was formed, to converse with freedom the state of Liberty both in Europe and America.

It is true, that in the early period of our institution, the affairs of civil and religious liberty did not wear so agreeable an appearance as the present; but we were not discouraged by the circumstance; for we firmly believed, that "the vessel, which was charged with the liberty perhaps of two worlds, was not doomed to shipwreck." It is readily acknowledged that it was not in the power of unauthorized individuals to do much, but they might at least have the pleasure of convincing the democratic republicans in France, that there were many in America who had a sympathetic feeling for their sufferings. At a more favorable conjuncture, our professions might be cooly received. When the triumphal car of the Republic was ascending the hill of the capital, surrounded by the invincible legions of Liberty, we should have blushed to have waited 'till this interesting moment, to have testified our approbation. We were sensible that the professions of friendship which are systematically postponed to the hour of uncontested prosperity, are but of little value.

SINCE the origin of our institution, events have taken place, in a high degree propitious to the cause of democratic republicanism. We have seen the flag of the French Republic displayed in triumph from the straits of Calais to the margin of the Mediterranean; from the Pyrenian mountains, to the seas of Batavia. In the irresistable carreer of Freemen, we have observed the hitherto invincible order of the German phalanx broken and destroyed by the armed citizens of France.[2] We have seen with an ineffable delight the proud spirit of British maritime usurpation humbled, and even the sovereignty of the ocean contested with such determined courage, as to leave but little doubt of future victory.

In the calm and silent enjoyment of these political sentiments, the denunciation of the President of the United States appeared against *"certain self-created societies"* as having fomented the late insurrection in Pennsylvania. The charge is so indefinite in its language, that we are at a loss to determine whether all or which of the multifarious self-created Societies in the United States were intended to be implicated.—On the subject of the censure however, we have no scruple to declare our sentiments in the fullest and most unequivocal manner. In a free government like ours, where the right of periodical elections is guaranteed by the constitution on the principles of Equality to every description of citizens, a remedy is supposed to exist for every wrong without the necessity of resorting to any act of violence, against the law, which can scarcely be justified under any circumstances; and experience has demonstrated, that every such effort, which must be almost of necessity unsuccessful has only served on every other occasion, to extend the power of the government to the prejudice of the people, and the diminution of their rights. It must hence be apparent that this Society are opposed to every outrage of this nature, not only from principle, but policy; for it is impossible, that any system of social improvement can be embraced, either as to the government, or its administration, amidst that tumult of passions, which such commotions have a direct tendency to produce.

WITH as little truth have we been charged with the design to involve our country in war with Great-Britain. It is extremely difficult to conceive, that so large a portion of the community should be so lost to their own interest, safety and happiness, as to court the calamities and domestic distress attendant in a state of war. We are however ready to acknowledge, that we are among those, who believed, and are still of opinion, that decisive and energetic policy on the part of our government was best calculated to preserve the honor and peace of our country; and that the latter ought not to be enjoyed at the expense of the former. We have attentively observed the policy of the British Cabinet. She progressed or receeded from hostility against the United States in proportion in the success or failure of her arms against France, and in proportion to the spirit of submission or the disposition to retaliate, discovered on the part of the American government.—

When the President proclaimed us neutral, and every office of friendship and good neighborhood, consistent with that neutrality was excersised towards the British nation, in common with the other Belligerent powers,—when the arms of the combined forces were penetrating into France; when Toulon was treacherously surrendered, and the insurrection of Le Vendee[3] was formidable to the interior of the Republic, the orders of June and November issued from the

British Cabinet, licensing spoliations on our commerce;—the speech of Lord
DORCHESTER,[4] inciting the Indians to hostilities, appeared, and all their conduct indicated war. But when Toulon was recaptured; the rebels of the Le
Vendee suppressed; when the combined forces were driven back, and the arms
of the French Republic became every where successful, and when measures of
retaliation were contemplated and moved in Congress, almost with success,
Great Britain relaxed in her hostilities, and from fear and necessity has proferred
a disposition to remain in peace.

We have been called *Jacobins;* we think it unnecessary to reply to an imputation of this kind, until those who make use of this epithet are able to define
it. If to act under the Laws of our Country, to profess & feel an attachment to
her free and happy constitution; if to advocate the right of Free Enquiry and
Opinion, and to wish success to the cause of *equal Liberty* every where, compose
the character of *Jacobins,* we avow ourselves JACOBINS.

But if to oppose by violence the constituted authorities of our country; if to
pass high sounding eulogies on the oppressors of mankind, and to speak con-
temptuously of exertions in favor of Liberty; if to denounce the right of any
portion of the People, freely to enquire into, and openly express their sentiments
of public men and measures are traits in the *Jacobin* character, we detest the
appelation.

It is remarkable, that those who have so violently opposed every Popular
Society, instituted for the purpose of political information, have uniformly
taken for granted, what does not exist. They have presumed motives which
never operated—principles which were never countenanced, and objects which
have been invariably disclaimed by the Society;—Have we not a right to presume
in our turn, that the *designs* of such opposers would not be fully accomplished,
by the mere suspension of the Democratic Societies? This consideration alone
is sufficient to induce us to double our diligence in the progress of political
information.

We shall but pretend to offer our sentiment on the nature and administration
of the Government, with every possible mark of respect and affection, due to
our fellow-citizens in general. And if this inherent right can be annihilated by
the breath of legislative censure, or even by a law of the Government, we do not
hesitate to declare in our opinion, that however the *forms* of our Constitution
may be preserved, their sepulchral remains will only leave occasion to lament,
that the vital spirit which once animated them has taken its flight to some happier clime.

WM COOPER, President, *pro. tem.*

By order of the Society,

SAMUEL HEWES,
                Secretary.

Independent Chronicle (Boston), January 5, 1795

Report of a Meeting, December 1795

At a Meeting of the Massachusetts Constitutional Society in December last, the following persons—viz: John Avery Junr,[5] Perez Morton,[6] James Price, Calvin Fosdick, Charles Jarvis, Wm Dennison, Henry Bass, Samuel Ruggles, & Benjamin Austin Junr [7] were chosen a Committee for the ensuing year, to Correspond with all other Democratic and Republican Societies which are or may be established within this Commonwealth, the United States or elsewhere, for the purpose of supporting the general Rights of Man and the Liberties of their Country.—

Extracts from the Records
Sam! Hewes, Rec. Sec'y

N. B. Pleas to direct to Saml Hews, N^O 25. Marlboro Street. It will be necessary to give particular directions when any Communications are forwarded, as they may be intercepted without care is taken to make the conveyance sure

Portland Republican Society Papers, Maine Historical Society

Samuel Hewes to the Republican Society in Portland, Maine
January 22, 1796

Boston January 22^d 1796

Citizen,

I received the Communication of your Society of the 7th inst by Post—

I have not the satisfaction to return an answer in my Capacity of Secretary to the Constitutional Society, as they have not yet had your Resolutions laid before them, the next meeting will be the second Sunday in Feby next—

My own opinion is "that the alarming strides of British influence" requires all the exertions of the real friends to American prosperity to step forward & assert their rights—the present Crisis is big with events, & ever hour seems to be the *midwife* of some important transaction—Randolph's vindication[8] is up to the ,[9] that man has been most barbarously used, as you will see in his Vindication, which I have the honour to present to your Society—The insersion of "unlimited Confidence" in the report of the Committee of Congress in Answer to the Presidents speech, is well known to be a political stroke of great Madison's;[10] knowing the full strength of the house upon that subject, he was very willing that Sedgwick & Sitgreaves should be mortified in the result as you have seen in the conclusion on that subject—The Treaty will no doubt be before Congress in a short time—you may rely that the House will make no provision for carrying it into execusion—what follows—the British will not give up the *posts* & we shall be in a much worse perplexity, after all the parade & noise about a Treaty, than we were before—Capt McClannon the bearer of this will purchase several of Randolphs books at my request

Health & Fraternity
Saml Hewes[11]

PS—this town is in a distrest situation, Money is unusually scarce, produce has fallen 50 per cent—The whole tontin Company have shut themselves up & many tenderman are nearly ruined by it—Several merchants have the day 23th shut their doors; money is letting from 1 to 3 per cent *per week* Tom Paine & his blackguard army have been publickly condemned on the boards of the Theatre by Mr Nodykinson, to the great applause of a full house—

Portland Republican Society Papers, Maine Historical Society

REPUBLICAN SOCIETY IN PORTLAND, MAINE[12]

Notice of a Meeting, June 26, 1794

A meeting of the Republican Society will be held on Thursday evening next, at 6 o'clock, P.M. at the Republican chamber over Samuel Bryant's store, where all members are required to attend.

N.B. New members will be admitted at the above time and place.
July 24.

Gazette of Maine (Portland), June 26, 1794

Formation of the Society, July 12, 1794

We whose names are hereunto subscribed agree to form ourselves into A Society upon the strict principles of the Rights of man by the name of the Republican Society[13] & to meet on Thursday evening next To form such Rules Regulations &C as the majority shall think proper

Portland July 12th 1794

John Baker[14]	Henry Fitcomb
Joshua Freeman	Jne McLellan
C Robinson	Dan Mussey
Elliott Seering	James Kettell
Frank Hart	Isaac Hilton
Tom Colby	Alexand^r Wildrage
William Lowell	Wm Freeman

Joshua White	David Bradish[15]
Joseph Mc Lellan Jr	Saml Bryant[16]
John Motley	Moses Noyes
David Alder	

This may certifie that we whose names are under written have agreed to form ourselves into a Society upon the strictest principles of the Rights of Man By the Name of Republican Society—after Being fully Satisfied with the following Articles [being Voted as a Whole for Our Guide][17] which we are willing Strictly to adhere to with any othe articles the Society may think proper to add.

Portland Republican Society Papers, Maine Historical Society

Resolutions Adopted, July 17, 1794

Portland July 17–1794

At a meeting of the Republican Society of Portland, held at Portland on the 17th day of July 1794—

This Society contemplating the outrages already committed and those daming insults continued by the British Court, and the evil intrigues now practised by her agents and emissaries, to undertake and destroy the Liberty and happiness of America, the Laws of nations, treaties of peace and the Rights of Man, and holding it just & laudable to call the attenion of our fellow Citizens to the alarming situation of public affairs, doe hereby submit to their consideration the entertained of thos important circumstances and Resolved as follows.

Resolved

That the proceedings of the last session of Congress appearing to us alarming; in particular that of the discontinuance of the Embargo, and that it is the peculiar privilege of Citizens of the United States, to meet at all times and on all occasions peacefully to propose the best means for obtaining and preserving the public happines, & freely to investigate or censure or approve the conduct of all persons in Public employment, and to submit their opinions to the sense of the community:

Resolved, That this Society view with indignation the conduct of certain members in Congress, two of them Representatives from the District of Main, being convinced from the whole tenor of their actions, and votes in Congress they ar possessed of the basest and most dangerous principles, that far from being Republicansm they indifferent to the repeated Insulsts offered the American Flagg and the repeated Depradations committed on the prosperity of the Citizens of America; that in addition to such Depradations the Detention of the Western Posts, contrary to express treaty, supplies to the Indians our deadly foes. The Treaty devis'd and concluded by the British government to sett the Algerians upon our Commerce are to them but trifles when compared to the amazing advantage of the British influence.

Resolved. That every member of this Society equip themselves as speedily as possible with every implement of war compleat, and to be ready to oppose every Enemy to the Rights of Man, and good government.

Resolved. That Proclamations are intended only as Promulgations of Laws Constitutionally enacted, to inform the Citizens, who in consequence of the attention necessary to their various occupations may require such information or Proclamation may with propriety be made to give warning of the approach of any Public calamity or to announce to the People the Day and place of any Public act, but when any person or set of men in office instead of announcing only the Laws of the Land attempt by Proclamation to declare his or their own will and determination as the Sovereign Rule, binding on the People the Judges and the Courts of Justice, such an exercise of power is unconstitutional Tyrannical arbitrary, and in the highest degree dangerous, an usurpation of Sovereignty of the most Despotic nature and a direct attack on the Liberties of the People.

Resolved, That all Public officers are appointed under the Constitution, their Political creator & Ruler, and they are but Servants of the People.

Resolved, that Treaties solemnly made with nations who act with sincere friendship and profess zealously their faith towards us ought to be inviolably adheared to and guarded from infractions at every   ;[18] that the cause of France is our own that our Interest, Liberty and public happiness are involv'd in her fate, that we are bound to support her by every tye of principle and gratitude, as well as principle of self preservation, That for any man or set of men either in private or public, and particularly those to whom the welfare of our Community are intrusted to advocate doctrines of principles derogatory to the cause of France or her commerce with America, or in support of the base measures of the combined Despots of Europe, particularly that Piratical[19]   of British is a convincing manifestation of sentiments treacherous and hostile to the Interest of the United States, and well deserves the swift censure from all true Republican Citizens of America

Resolved, That this Society entertain a grateful sense & highly approve the conduct of all those members of Congress, who were disposed to support the dignity of the Republican Flagg.

Resolved, That this Society are determined to support the Rights of Man and a true Republican government, and oppose every Invador at the Risk of Life and Fortune.

Resolved, That this Society be disposed to assist and releave all distressed Republicans of what nation soever to the utmost of their abilities.

Resolved. That the foregoing Resolutions be printed in all the public newspapers for the Information of our fellow citizens, in order that they may take such measures as they shall deem most proper for their support. All true Republicans who wish to join this humane Society will apply to any member for admittance—

Portland Republican Society Papers, Maine Historical Society

Principles, Resolves, and Regulations Agreed Upon, August 1794

The Principles, Resolves, and Regulations, agreed upon by the members of the Republican Society in Portland, August 1794.[20]

Philosophy and reason have not only clearly developed to human nature the natural and civil right of man, but have opened the way for the most splendid aera in the annals of the world, by giving a strong and general turn to the human mind for the investigation of subjects that hitherto have been hid from vulgar sight in the grand arcana of state policy.

The effects of this light breaking forth on the world we have partly seen—it has already raised up and confederated a considerable part of the human race to assert and vindicate the almost annihilated rights and liberties of man, which we trust will be finally and gloriously established in justice and equality upon the universal ruin of despotism.

It is not for us to decide, whether in the order of sublunary affairs, mankind once possessing the full enjoyment of those rights, will ever revolve into that ignorance and stupidity, that darkness and slavery which throughout past ages have universally degraded the species—stamping them with a character directly the reverse of what nature and their proper faculties designated for them; such disquisitions we shall leave to the curious and the speculative.

This our common country has had its day of trial—the bloody conflict is past—and we have arrived at that propitious period when the nature of freedom and equality is practically displayed and universally acknowledged.—The patriotic mind will naturally be solicitous by every proper precaution, to preserve and perpetuate the blessings which Providence hath thus bestowed upon us. With a view therefore, to cultivate a just knowledge of rational liberty, to facilitate the enjoyment and exercise of our civil rights, and to transmit unimpaired to posterity the inestimable blessings of a free republican government, the Republican Society of Portland, in the District of Maine is constituted and established, unfettered by religious or national prejudices, uninfluenced by party and unmoved by ambition, this institution embraces the interest and invites the support of every virtuous citizen—the welfare of the whole being its sole object, we think the best means are pursued for obtaining it when we recognize the following as the fundamental principles of our association.

1st—That the people have the inherent and exclusive right and power of making and altering forms of government.

2nd. That the Constitution of the United States and of the state of Massachusetts being framed and established by the people, it is our duty as good citizens, to support them; and that we may effectually do so, it is likewise the duty of every freeman to regard with attention, and to discuss without fear, the conduct of the public servants in every department of government.

3d. That [in] the choice of persons to fill the offices of government, it is essential to the existence of a free republic, that every citizen should act according to his own judgment; therefore any attempt to corrupt and delude the people in exercising the rights of suffrage, either by promoting the favor of one candidate, or traducing the character of another, is an offence equally injurious to moral rectitude and civil liberty.

4th. The treaties solemnly made with nations who act with sincere friendship, and preserve zealously their faith towards us, ought at every resque to be inviolably adhered to, and guarded from infraction—That we consider the cause of France as our own upon the fate of which depends our interest, liberty, and public happiness—That we bound to support her by every tie of principle and gratitude, as well as self-preservation—That whoever cipher in private or public (more especially if entrusted with the interest of the public weal) advocates doctrines or principles which instead of drawing closer the bands of friendship, tend to weaken them between the two nations, thereby supporting the saguinary measures of the combined enemies of freedom, and abetting British piracy, manifests sentiments treacherous and hostile to the welfare of our country, and ought to be held up to public detestation. Actuated by these principles we have resolved.

1st. That esteeming frequent change of those men to whom we have given a delegated authority, very necessary towards the security of our right, we hold a long continuence in office incompatible with that security, as it strongly tends to give a peculiar turn and character to the individual, a forgetfulness of his duty and his constituents, highly injurious to the public good.

2nd. That it is the duty of every citizen by making the general welfare the rule of his conduct to aid and approve those men and measures which have an influence in promoting the prosperity of the commonwealth;—therefore, that those independent and worthy members of Congress, who in the last session voted in favor of the propositions brought forward by Mr. Madison, and who by their truly patriotic efforts laboured to uphold and give importance to the honor and dignity of an injured people, merit the most exalted approbation and applause of their country.

3rd. That we view with indignation the unmanly, undetermined, and mean conduct of many members on Congress, two of whom are from the Western part of the District of Main, for their opposition to measures which in their operation must eventually have given respectability to our flag, and to America.

4th. That at present we deem it unnecessary to enlarge upon the long and black catalogue of aggression, acts of depradation, and cruel insult committed by the British, that foe to our peace and the peace of mankind; under the wounds of whose malice so large a part of our fellow citizens are now languishing; flattering ourselves that satisfaction commensurate to our injuries will be given; but should unhappily disappointment be the result of a late mission, and our claims for justice be unsupported with energy and efficient coercion in defence of our national honour—we than will declare that the flag of stripes, the dignity, the honour of free America, are but a name, and deserve the contempt of the nations of the earth.

5th. That the discontinuence of the embargo was not only impolitic in itself, but highly greatful to the friends of Britain, and to every enemy to our national welfare.

6th. That we consider the appointment of a judicial character to an executive office, as a direct contravention of one of the fundamental principles of our constitution, and a most dangerous precedent.

7th. That wishing to hold up always to view the cause of humanity and charity, we propose to have a fund—as well to assist any our unfortunate foreign brethren who may have suffered in the cause of freedom, and may have fled to our shores for an asylum, as also those of our society who by the casualties of life may be reduced to distress.

8th. That there shall be no prescribed limitations to this society.

9th. A meeting of the society shall be held in the town of Portland on the first Thursday in every month, and the Chairman shall have power to convene the members on any special occasion.

10th. The election of the officers of the society shall be by nomination, and appointed by the majority of the members present at each respective meeting.

11th. The officers of this society shall consist of

A Chairman to be chosen monthly.

A Treasurer annually.

A Clerk annually, and

A corresponding committee of nine members monthly.

12th. It shall be the duty of the Clerk to keep minutes of the proceedings of the several meetings, and of the Treasurer to receive and account for all monies paid to him.

13th. It shall be the duty of the corresponding committee to correspond with all other societies that may be established on similar principles & to lay any communication or other business they shall deem proper before the society.

On motion, ordered, that the committee of correspondence publish in the public newspapers of this town, the aforesaid principles, resolves, and regulations agreed upon by this meeting. Extract from the minutes.

In behalf of the committee,

JOHN BAKER, Chairman.

Independent Chronicle (Boston), August 28, 1794

Toasts Delivered at a Meeting, January 11, 1797

PORTLAND, Jan. 11.

THE PORTLAND REPUBLICAN SOCIETY, met agreeable to adjournment on Friday evening, 30th Dec. last—After supper, the following TOASTS were given.

1. The Republicans throughout the globe—6 cheers.

2. The National Convention of France—6 cheers.

3. The Ten worthy members in the Senate, who opposed that infamous British Treaty—9 cheers.

4. Our worthy brothers in Congress, who followed their glorious example—9 cheers.

5. Citizen P. Adet[21]—may he support the Rights of Man, with courage, fortitude, and wisdom—6 cheers.

6. May the Wing of Liberty never loose a Feather—3 cheers.

7. Governor ADAMS[22]—May he live in free Boston once more purged of all enemies to the Rights of Man.—9 cheers.

8. May the American stripes retrieve their character, and teach desports humanity—3 cheers.

9. May the French arms succeed in their undertakings—on whom the liberties of man depend.—4 cheers.

10. May the spurs of the Republican Cock, prick every tyrant to the heart—9 cheers.

11. May the self-created sticklers for the British treaty repent of their folly and imprudence.—6 cheers.

12. May FISHER AMES and his confederates' imprudent and inconsistent speeches in Congress the four last sessions, cause the British influence to be as conspicuous to every true Republican, as their insult to our flag was in 1793.—9 cheers.

13. May every Speculator in the American funds be obliged to wait on the officers and soldiers, widows and children, barefooted to do them justice.—6 cheers.

14. May the three American Frigates stand fast.—6 cheers.

15. May all secret communications to both houses of Congress be made public.—9 cheers.

Independent Chronicle (Boston), January 30, 1797

7 | Democratic-Republican Societies of Vermont

DEMOCRATIC SOCIETY OF THE COUNTY OF RUTLAND, CASTLETON

Formation and Constitution, April 17, 1794

THE FORMATION
And Constitution of the Democratic Society, held
at Castleton on Thursday the 17th of April 1794.

In the 15th Article of the Bill of Rights of the Inhabitants of the state of Vermont, it is written, "That the freemen have a right to freedom of speech, and of writing and publishing their sentiments concerning the transactions of Government."—And in order the better to enable the freemen to improve their political talents for the good of community, the 22d article of the same declaration justifies the people's coming together, to consult the common good, instruct the Representatives &c.

The wisdom of the gentlemen to whom was committed the charge of framing the above articles evidently appears, by their clearly anticipating a necessity of not only leaving a door open for the correction of constitutional, but also of both legislative and executive errors;—We therefore have assembled to exercise the priviledges we claim an indulgence in, from the rights of human nature as well as said articles—and being so assembled do assume, as a name or distinction, the most compatable, by which we are actuated, that of the DEMOCRATIC SOCIETY of the COUNTY OF RUTLAND, declaring that we will by all legal means in our power strengthen and support the reins of the government under which we live, in its several branches, where it appears calculated to promote and maintain the peace, happiness and equal rights of its citizens.—And that, we will with equal energy detect, discountenance, and reprobate any public proceeding in any man, or set of men, which appear evidently repugnant to the purest principles of republicanism.

We have therefore agreed on the following articles as the rules and regulations of this Society.

Art. 1st. In order that all our disquisitions may be regulated by the strictest order, we will choose a President, to whom & by whose leave (first obtained) shall all addres's in our meetings be made; he shall have a casting, but no other vote, and shall have power on the requisition of eight Members, to call a meeting of the Society, giving at least one weeks notice thereof in a newspaper printed in this County, and shall sign all such orders and resolutions of the Society as they may think proper, and perform such other offices as may be consistent with his station.—We will also choose a Vice-President, who in the absence of the President shall perform all the duties of the President.

2nd. We will choose a Treasurer, whose duty it shall be to keep the funds of the Society, and render regular accounts thereof when required.

3r. We will have a Secretary, who shall record all orders and other transactions of the Society and shall publish such part of the doings thereof as shall be agreed by two thirds of the Members present.

4th. We will choose a Clerk, whose duty it shall be to obey the orders of the Society in meeting, and those of the President, Vice-President or Secretary, in such matters as concerns the Society at other times.

5th. Each Member of the Society on his admission shall sign the following declaration, to be read to him by the Secretary, viz——

"I do declare upon my sacred honor, that it is for the promotion of genuine republicanism, that I wish admission into the DEMOCRATIC SOCIETY in the county of Rutland, that I have no views but what derive from principles; and that I always will use my utmost endeavors for the exaltation of human nature, as well as for the support of rational liberty and the equal rights of man."

And no candidate shall be accepted as a Member unless five Members declare that they fully believe he will promote the original intention of the institution, and strictly abide by the aforesaid declaration.

6th. Every Member who shall be convicted of having wilfully counteracted the fundamental intent of the Society, or the proceedings thereof shall be censured or expelled, as two thirds of the Members shall determine.

7th. There shall be a corresponding committee of not less than three Members, of which the Secretary shall always be one; they shall correspond with such Societies as they may think proper, and deemed to be formed on principles similar to this, or with any individual, by a correspondence with whom they shall believe the Society may be benefited, subject to such further regulations and restrictions as any of the general meetings of this Society shall think proper.

8th. All general meetings shall be held at such time and place as the majority of the preceding meeting shall appoint.—But this shall not be understood to contravene the power lodged in the President, in the 1st article, nor to admit of the regular annual meetings, being on any other day but the fourth day of July (or in case of it being on Sunday on the Monday following.)

9th. The power of making all rules and regulations not inconsistent with, or repugnant to the true spirit, and intention of the foregoing, shall be vested in the general meetings only, in which the majority shall ever determine—Provided always that no alteration shall be made in the foregoing regulations, without the consent of at least two thirds of the general meeting, at which such alterations shall be proposed.

Published by order of the Society,

JAS. WITHERELL, *Sec'cy.*

Farmers' Library (Rutland), May 6, 1794

THE DEMOCRATIC SOCIETY IN THE COUNTY OF ADDISON

Constitution, September 9, 1794

CONSTITUTION
of the Democratic Society in the County of Addison.

WE, the undersigned, compact and associate ourselves into a Society, on the principles, for the reasons, and to promote the political ends expressed in the following articles, which shall be considered constitutional of our Society.

ARTICLE 1st. We make no apology for thus associating ourselves (altho' an inconsiderable body of citizens of the United States) to consider, animadvert upon, and publish our sentiments, on the political interests, constitution and government of our country; this is a right, the disputation of which reflects on political freedom, and wears an appearance peculiarly absurd, proceeding from the tongue or pen of an American.

ART. 2d. We declare the following, among others, to be some of our political sentiments, and principles of government, which, whether in an individual or associated capacity, we are bound, under the laws of reason and morality, to maintain and defend.—That all men are naturally free, and possess equal rights.— That all legitimate government originates in the voluntary and social compact of the people.—That no rights of the people are surrendered to their rulers, as a price of protection and government—That the constitution and laws of a country, are the expressions of the general will of the body of the people or nation, that all officers of government are the ministers & servants of the people, and, as such, are amenable to them, for all their conduct in office.—That it is the right, and becomes the duty of a people, as a necessary means of the security and preservation of their rights, and the future peace and political happiness of the nation, to exercise watchfullness and inspection, upon the conduct of all their public officers; to approve, if they find their conduct worthy of their high and important trusts—and to reprove and censure, if it be found otherwise. That frequent elections, directly from the body of the people, of persons, to important offices of trust, have an immediate tendency to secure the public rights, as less opportunities intervene for abuse of power; that compensations for public service ought to be reasonable (and even moderate, when the debts and exigencies of a nation require it,) and a reward only for actual service; that a public debt (and a financial funding system to continue the same) is a burthen upon a nation, and ought, by the oeconomical exertions of the nation, to be reduced and discharged; that an increase of public officers, dependant on the executive power,—a blending the distinct branches of government together, in the functions and offices of one man, or body of men;—a foolish copying of ancient corrupt and foreign governments and courts, where the equal rights of men, are trampled under the feet of kings and lords; and a standing army,—are all highly dangerous to liberty; and that the constitution, laws, and government of a country, are always of right, liable to amendation and improvement.

ART. 3d. We are convinced that the present political state of our country, calls for the rational, wise and vigilent attention of its citizens. The price which Americans have paid to obtain liberty and independence, as republicans;—the hope which wise and great men in Europe, have placed on our revolution, as eventual of a better understanding of the rights of men, and a more enlightened and equal policy and government, on which account many are emigrating from lands of tyranny and arbitrary power, to enjoy the freedom denied them in their native land; the confidence which the French nation, in their present unparalleled struggle with despotism, have reason to repose in us as their friends, from our alliance, but more from gratitude, and the goodness and greatness of their cause. The fate and happiness of the millions of the unborn posterity of America, to indeterminable ages;—our own happiness, and that of our immediate posterity; the progress of truth, reason, and humanity in the world, and that aspect on the political fate of all mankind, which a maintenance, or desertion of the principles of liberty and true republicanism at the present day, may occasion, are, with us (and we trust they are so, with our attentive American fellow-citizens in general) Interests and considerations of very great magnitude; they are such as forcibly induce us—to attend to our constitution, laws, and government; to dispose us to justify those popular societies, already formed in the United States, whose measures have been rational and temperate; and to determine for ourselves, that did we possess the happiness to believe and be satisfied, that our constitution and government, and the conduct of all of our public officers, were as perfect and faultless, as at the present time they could be: It would nevertheless become us, to endeavor to preserve and increase that happiness, by increasing our information, and attention to the important objects which have been mentioned. But, it is our DUTY not to conceal, that we have in a degree, at the present time, the unhappiness of considerations before us, which increase our obligations to national attention and solicitude, we possess a degree of serious concern, at—the state of our national debt—The expences of our government, and in the causes of those debates and divisions which have agitated Congress, particularly during their last session.

ART. 4. It shall be the objects of the business and pursuit of this society—to study the Constitution, to avail ourselves of the journals, debates, and laws of Congress—reports and correspondencies of secretaries, and such other publications as may be judged necessary to give information as to the proceedings of Congress and the departments of government and also of the conduct of individual officers in the discharge of their trusts, whether in Congress, or in the departments of the executive, or judiciary. And on information, we will speak; and upon deliberation, we will write and publish our sentiments. A steady zeal and firmness for the liberties of our country, and a strictly republican government, in pursuing our enquiries, & in passing our resolutions, shall be severely guided by that reason and temperance, which a sense of moral obligation, and the dread of ignorant popular convulsions, demand; and with that deference to the nation, the great body of our fellow-citizens, which our inconsiderableness of numbers and information may require: But, let no unfaithful servant of the public, or plotter of the ruin of his country's freedom, however dignified his station, hereupon, affect the contempt of independency of office, or flatter himself to escape censure with impunity.

ART. 5. We will correspond with other Societies, in this, & the United States, formed upon similar principles.

ART. 6. A Chairman, Clerk or Clerks, and Committee, or Committees, shall regulate and conduct the formal proceedings and business of this Society, from time to time, as occasion may require, under the direction of the Society.

By Order of the meeting.

(Signed)

ISAIAH GILBERT, *Chairman.*

Copy,

THOMAS TOLMAN, *Clerk.*

AT a meeting of the Societie held at Middlebury-falls, Aug. 21st, 1794, agreed that the Constitution of this Society, be published in the Farmers' Library, under the direction of the Committee for rules, and the Clerk of the society.

Adjourned the meeting of this Society, to the first Thursday in October next, then to be attended at the house of Citizen Samuel Mattocks, in Middlebury, at ten o'clock forenoon.

JOHN WILLARD,
WILLIAM SLADE,
EBENEZER WHEELOCK,   Committee.
JOEL LINSLY,
THOS. TOLMAN, *Clerk.*

Farmers' Library (Rutland), September 9, 1794

Resolutions Adopted Praising the Conduct of Members of Congress from Vermont, October 28, 1794

At a meeting of the Democratic Society in the County of Addison, held at Middlebury-Falls, October 2d, 1794, the following resolution was passed, viz.

RESOLVED, That this Society highly approve of the virtuous republican part, which the Senators and Members of the House of Representatives in Congress, from this state, have taken in the questions and debates on important and national propositions, since the accession of this state to the Union. The satisfaction of this society, in noticeing their public conduct, is proportioned—to their activity in business, and uniformity of action, which they have manifested, and to that sacrifice of private convenience, which they may in some instances have made, by tarrying the session entire; and beg them to accept the thanks of this society, accordingly

A circular letter, inclosing a copy of the above resolution to each member, is as follows:—

(CIRCULAR.)
Middlebury, Oct. 3d, 1794.

SIR, The citizens composing the Democratic Society in the county of Addison, having observed the public conduct of the Representatives of this state, in the Congress of the United States, approve of the virtuous and republican part which they have taken on interesting national questions, and as a testimony thereof, have passed a resolution, a copy of which, we have the honor and pleasure to enclose you. We trust that this will appear an evidence, that while the citizens composing this society, cannot conceal their concern for certain acts and establishments of Congress, which you have judged it your duty to disapprove, they are not disposed to indiscriminate censure, or to throw any weight into the scale of public licentiousness

We have the honor to be

Sir, your obedient humble servants & fellow-citizens,

Joel Linsley,
Thos. Tolman,   Corresponding
John Willard.   Committee.

To which the Hon. I. Smith returned the following

ANSWER.

The Members of the Democratic Society of the county of Addison.

GENTLEMEN, A Resolution of your society of the second of October, and this·day presented me by one of the members, expressing your approbation of the conduct of the Senators and Representatives of this state, in the Congress of the United States, (among whom I am included) has been productive of very agreeable emotions on my part. Next to an honest regard for the rights and interests of my constituents, and for this state, in connection with the rights and interests of other people & states within the union, has been my wish to maintain their good opinion. Your resolution is a respectable testimony, for my satisfaction on this latter point. Permit me, gentlemen, while I am flattering myself from this expression of your approbation, to encrease the pleasurable emotion, by indulging a hope and expectation, that meetings and deliberations of your societies, may not only not prove subversive or hurtful to public order and good government, but the real promoters of them.

I am Gentlemen, with sentiments of respect and
esteem, yours,

ISRAEL SMITH.[1]

Rutland, Oct. 13th, 1794.

Farmers' Library (Rutland), October 28, 1794

ASSOCIATED DEMOCRATIC SOCIETY OF THE COUNTY OF CHITTENDEN, COLCHESTER

Principles of Formation and Regulations, March 17, 1794

DEMOCRATIC SOCIETY.

The Principles of Formation, and Formation, and Regulations of the Associated DEMOCRATIC SOCIETY, in the County of Chittenden, State of Vermont.

As meetings of any part of the People, for the purpose of discussing with freedom, moderation, and a due degree of respect to the Governing Powers, all political questions, which they may deem proper to take into their consideration, will never be termed illegal, but by the natural enemies to the true spirit of Republicanism, and the Equal rights of man. It is unnecessary for us to demonstrate our undoubted right to form this association, to those, whose political friendship we wish to cultivate, and whose approbation alone, we are desirous to acquire; but, willing ever to reclaim from their errors, the few, who may attempt to doubt the principle of right, we refer them to the 6th, 13th, 18th and 20th Articles of the bill of rights prefixed to the constitution of this State, and to the 42d Article of the Constitution itself, which incorporates that whole bill of rights into its own body; and no man has (as yet) been bold enough to assert, that the Constitution of the United States, has deprived us of any of those natural rights, so fully manifested in her own.

It may however be incumbent on us, from a respect due to some few really virtuous Republicans, who while they fully acknowledged the right, seem to doubt the propriety of such Associations at present; to exhibit some of the general reasons and grounds whereon we have formed this; among which are the following:—

I. The open declarations in favor of Great Britain, not only our former, but *present* bitter enemy, and the undue influence, which it is said, she has acquired as well in our Legislative Councils, as with some of the first officers in our general government.

II. The unmerited abuse, with which the public papers have so often teemed against the Minister of our *only Ally*,[2] a nation who is gloriously, zealously, uniformly, and perserveringly (beyond example) wading through *oceans of blood*, for the mere purpose of obtaining permission to establish a government for herself, upon the same plain simple, and immutable principles of truth, on which the whole system of ours is founded.

III. The almost total inattention, (except in the Executive) which has been paid to the recovery of the Posts, agreed to be surrendered by the Treaty of 1783, on which surrender, not only the peace and prosperity of the Nation in general, but even *the very existence* of this country, may in some measure depend.

IV. The doors of the Federal Senate, being *always* shut, in contradiction, (as we conceive) to the true Principles of Liberty, as well as to the repeated wishes of a number of the States, signified publickly, by their respective Legislatures.

V. The construction of the Federal Judges, on the suability of States,[3] thereby effectually extinguishing their sovereignty, whilst the United States are placed under no such restriction.

VI. The alarming circumstance of eleven members of the Federal Senate, having voted in the negative, on a motion for laying before that body the correspondence between our Ambassador, at the Republic of France, with the Minister of that nation, for Foreign Affairs; as well as his correspondence with our Executive, and which motion was carried by a majority of two only.

From the above statement, as well as from many other circumstances, which have, for some time past, & still do, vehemently agitate the publick mind, we are clearly convinced, that it is the *duty* of the good Citizens to associate in such numbers, and under such regulations, and to pass such resolutions, as will best enable Congress to be fully acquainted with the real sentiments of the people; and thereby produce a perfect spirit of accord and unanimity, between our present Governors, and their fellow citizens, in whose power, though they must soon be placed for a continuance in, or discharge from their present dignified stations; yet perhaps, not sufficiently soon, to avert those evils, which a great part of the Community, are (at present) apprehensive of.

Whilst this sentiment of our own, excites us to form the present Association, it must receive great additional weight in the eye of the community, from the decided approbation of a man learned in the Law, and well known admirer of our happy constitution and government.

For some part of the approbation referred to, see Chipman's Principles of Government,[4] page 55, where, speaking of the advantage arising from the social sense being connected with *any society.* He says, "If it be not the Germ of every social attachment, it certainly gives strength to the attachment, *and vigor to patriotism itself.* It is a very necessary part of the social nature of man, and of great importance in Government."

Page 138, "An interest in the approbation of the Publick, and a strong sense of accountability to them, in all official conduct, is the greatest, or rather the only effectual security against abuses in those, who exercise the powers of Government."

Page 239, "Banish mystery from politicks, open every channel of information, *call for investigation, tempt a discussion of measures, and the public sentiment will be the best criterion of what is right, and of what is wrong, in government."*

Page 164, "In a Republic, the powers of government are supported, not by force, but by the sentiments of the people. It is necessary to cultivate a sentimental attachment to the Government."

Page 236, "The Governments of the several American States, as well as that of the Union, are of the *Democratic* Republican kind. We ought to know their principles, to study well their tendency, and to be able, both in theory and practice, *to exclude all foreign principles."*

We publish our opinions not from a confidence in our numbers, or importance; we cannot, but in a very small degree, claim dignified stations, to sanctify those opinions; but as virtuous individuals, zealously engaged in what we deem but services we can render to our country, determined to be influenced by principle only, and not by party, or party views:—At a distance from the seat of Government and news, we solicit the friendship and good will of all those who can give us information, especially of those societies, founded on principles similar to our own.—And we now, submit to the free and full discussion of every individual in the community, especially if he will come forward under his proper signature.

The Following REGULATIONS FOR OUR GOVERNMENT.

I. There shall be no officers in this Society, but a *President, Vice President, Treasurer, Secretary* and *Clerk.*

II. It shall be the duty of the *President,* to preside over all meetings:—to determine all questions of order, unless one eighth of the members present, shall signify their wish, that it may be left to the Society at large, in which case, a majority of the Society then present, shall determine. He shall have the casting vote on all occasions, when the members are equally divided but shall have no other vote. And shall, upon the requisition of five members, call a meeting, giving, at least, one week's notice thereof, in as publick a manner as can conveniently be done. He shall sign his name to all such orders and resolutions of the Society, as they shall require; and perform such other offices, consistent with his station, as they shall demand.

III. The *Vice President,* in the absence of the President, shall perform all his duties; but shall, on all other occasions, be deemed a mere member of the Society.

IV. The *Treasurer* shall keep the funds of the Society, and render a regular account of receipts and expenditures at each annual meeting, or whenever they are called for by the Society in meeting.

V. The *Secretary* shall record all proceeding of the Society in meeting, and for that purpose, keep two books: one for all such acts, regulations, and resolutions, as respect the publick at large; the other for such as respect the order or regulation of the Society only. He shall duly respect and obey all such orders of the society, as shall be perfectly consistent with his station therein.

VI. The *Clerk* shall obey the orders of the Society in meeting and those of the *President, Vice President* or *Secretary,* at all other times:—He shall be paid an adequate compensation for his trouble. All elections for officers shall be by ballot, they shall respectively hold their offices for one year, until the first annual meeting, unless three fourths of the Society determine otherwise. At each annual meeting all officers shall be ballotted for as at first.

VII. Each member, on his first admission to this Society, shall sign the following Declaration, to be read to him by the Secretary.

"I declare upon my sacred honour, that it is the promotion of real and genuine Republicanism, unsullied and uncontaminated with the smallest spark of monarchical or aristocratical principles, which has excited me to wish for admission into the *Associated Democratic Society* of the county of Chittenden. That I have no views but what arise from principles, not men. And that I will use my utmost exertions, in conformity with the Constitution and Laws of my country, to support the rational Liberty and Equal Rights of Man."

No candidate shall be balloted for as a member, unless three members will certify in writing, that they fully believe he will endeavour to promote the original intent of the institution, and strictly abide by the declaration ordered to be presented to him for signing.

VIII. Every member of this Society shall have a right to propose such resolution as he may think proper, but if the resolution respects the public at large, it must be in writing.

RESOLUTIONS.

1st. Resolved, That having in the preamble to our regulations, declared in general terms the apparent enmity of Great-Britain to the United States, it is our duty to demonstrate in a brief manner the truth of that assertion, and we therefore call up to public view—

Her non-payment for the negroes she robbed us of in direct contradiction to the treaty of peace.

Her non-fulfilment of that part of the treaty which stipulates the delivery of our posts.

Her ungenerous prohibitions in many instances with respect to our trade, especially in the West-Indies, which part of her colonies we conceive to be in our power, by proper regulations (attended we acknowledge with a temporary loss to ourselves), greatly to distress, perhaps utterly to ruin.

Her inhuman and disgraceful aid secretly given to the Indians, the better to enable them to scalp, torture and murder the innocent inhabitants on our frontiers:

The capture of many of our vessels on the most frivilous pretences.

Her haughty, disdainful, and even cruel treatment of many of our captured seamen:

Her violation of the modern law of nations, by denying the priviledges to the neutral bottoms of America, which she has for the present found politic to grant to Sweden and Denmark under similar circumstances.

Her impressing our seamen on many occasions:

Her unnatural, unchristian, though too successful efforts in setting on us her dearly beloved brethren, the blood hounds of Algiers:—In addition to this, we beg leave to be informed by her adherents in this country, what we have not to fear from such a government, in an hour of success (should an hour so unfortunate for mankind ever arrive) a government which tho' overwhelmed with distress of almost every nature, to which a nation is liable, the plague, famine, total and complete national bankruptcy, excepted, has wantonly plunged herself into a war in direct opposition to the cause of humanity, and pledged the blood of a large portion of her citizens for the destruction of France, under the frivolous pretext of aiding her allies the Dutch, who it has been plainly proved, are but little anxious about defending themselves.

This is the *pretext* of the *Government*—let us now see what the virtuous part of mankind, what the patriotic, and honest part of her own subjects, assign as the *real* reason which induced her to commence so bloody, so barbarous, so cruel, & so disgraceful a war.

Conscious of having lost the confidence of her best her firmest patriots, and

that she justly merited the stroke of heaven for her many and unparralled iniqui-
ties—The strong apprehensions of the down-fall of her own corrupt and mostly
government ay they, was the real source of her unchristian, diabolical and tyrannical resentment against that nation, from whose electrical machine of liberty
she was fearful some particle of Republican fluid, might glance to her own terri-
tories and create that degree of light which would bring clearly to view the errors and impositions which they have long been dupes of.

In this war she has spurned the offers of peace with contempt in contradiction to the will and repeated wishes of the best men in the nation; and it is not
only to be hoped for the benefit of the humane race, but expected from the
mercy and justice of providence, that a war commenced in dishonor, and continued with injustice, will terminate in disgrace and eternal infamy to the promoters of it.

Though she has so liberally lavished her blood and treasure in this unjust war,
has she not, in contradiction to her beloved and refined system of maintaining
the balance of Europe, over looked the unnatural aggrandizement of Russia?—
Winked at the robbery of Prussia, and suffered the dismemberment of Poland,
without a feeble effort to prevent it; without a sigh for this public and unprecedented act of villany, an act of too base a nature, too deep a dye, too black a
hue, too glaringly villanous to have been perpetrated by any but ROYAL ROBBERS.

Has she not disarmed the Irish volunteers, those brave and virtuous guardians
of her honor in a former hour of distress.

May the excessive tameness and submission of those, on many occassions,
manly sons of freedom be a warning to the people of other nations.

Has she not for many, many years, in contradiction to the true spirit of religion, both natural and revealed prohibited her Roman Catholic subjects & dis-
senters from enjoying the natural priviledges of citizens, tho' in her kingdom of
Ireland they compose nearly seven eights of the whole people—has she not in
contempt of the laws of uninformed nature, as well as of enlightened reason, and
the laws of God, forced Genoa and Tuscany from their state of neutrality—In
short, has she not spent very nearly one half of the last hundred years in shedding the blood of the human race.

From this short as well as faint sketch we call again upon her adherents in
this country to inform us, upon what new constructed, what possible principle
we can place any degree of trust, *any even remote* dependence upon her faith,
her honor, her justice or her humanity.—Americans are generous, they are un-
suspicious, but they cannot be so far the dupes of credulity and folly as to
imagine, that while she has treated her natural, her faithful children with such
ineffable contempt she will nevertheless be happy in piling unnumerable and
unbounded favors on the head of an ejected son, whom she has long branded
with the epithets of stubborn perverse and rebellious.

2d, Resolved, that, though we have given the above deformed but true and
unexaggerated picture of the British Government, we are still sensible that there

are some of her former subjects, who are amongst the number of our best citizens, and that even those of them who from an attachment to their former country differ from the real whigs of this, in political principles, ought in our opinion to be fully protected from either public or private insult to their persons or the smallest depradation on their property, as long as they behave with due respect to the laws of the land, and do not attempt to thwart the inclination of the great body of the people; but ought under no pretext whatever to be trusted in any office under government.

Let our generosity to others be great and extensive, but bounded by the necessary line of safety to ourselves and our dear bought rights.

3d, Resolved, that we have read with all the care and attention which their importance justly merits the Resolutions of the Democratic Society of Philadelphia of the 6th of January last, that we believe they speak the general language of the people, and deem them well calculated for the advancement of the true interest of every Republican in the United States, they therefore meet with our most hearty animated and sincere approbation, the first clause of the 11th resolution excepted, being in the following words, "Resolved, that it is the opinion of this Society that the agents of the so[v]reign powers acting in the name and under the responsibility of the governments by whom they are delegated, are responsible only to their own sovereigns for their official conduct, in the countries to which they are sent," Which is of such an obstruce nature, and depends so much on the laws and customs of nations that we do not esteem ourselves sufficiently well informed either to approbate or disapprove of.

4th. Resolved, That we esteem the uncontrouled freedom of speech in Congress as one of the greatest bulwarks of our constitution, and that therefore no individual member thereof should ever be attacked or censured for any expression used therein, unless absolutely subversive of the rights of the nation or the dignity of the house, or unless it should *clearly* appear that they were dictated by similar and wicked motives—even though his opinion and expressions may be very discordant from those of the people he represents; but we at the same time declare that all such members ought to be watched with a *scrupulously* jealous eye, and the greatest care taken that at the election they be prevented from the power of continuing their mischief by raising heats, and promoting disturbances in the community.

5th. Resolved, That the tryal by Jury is one of the first and dearest rights of freemen; that where the law and fact is combined, they have an undoubted power to determine on both, & that every attempt to deprive them of this valuable privilege, this master key to safety of life and property, ought to be held in the *utmost detestation:* Juries nevertheless ought ever to pay the greatest attention, the highest respect and difference to the charge given by the bench, reserving the right of differing from their opinion in the application of the law on the fullest, clearest, and most self-satisfying conviction only.

6th, Resolved, That having established ourselves as a Society on the firm foun-

dation of incontrovertible truths, (an adherence to our own rights and the constitution and laws of our country) firmness in the hour of trial, candor in dis-
quisition, freedom in expressing our opinions, and a general liberality of sentiment shall be eagerly courted in all our acts, and resolutions as our great supporting pillars.

7th, Resolved, That Lord Dorchester's reply to the speech of the Indians,
given at the Castle of St. Lewis, in the city of Quebec, on the 10th day of February last, contains expressions so injurious to the common feelings of humanity,
so inconsistent, we are certain with the sentiments of the people whom he gov-
erns, so defamitory to the government of the United States in general, and so
interesting a nature to the people of the country in particular, that it would be
improper to let it pass in silence, where therefore address him in the following
words:—

(The Address is to be inserted next week.)

THE PRINCIPLES
Of Formation, &c of the Democratic Society.
Continued.

MY LORD,

As the world has yet to learn, that nature has been *even* commonly bountiful
to your Lordship, in those endowments of the mind, which form the great, the
exalter, the finished character—we will neither flatter *your* vanity, nor degrade
our own good sense, by apologizing for the following sentiments, extracted from
us, either by the joint folly, and weakness of *your* head, or the unbounded
malignity and depravity of *your* heart.

You have once more, my lord, disgraced that nation, of which you are a member, by elaborately and deliberately calling forth, in support of an intended,
though unprovoked War, the infamous and shameful weapons of ferocious barbarism, *the Tomahawk and Scalping Knife;* weapons which are exploded in this
enlightened age, by all but the corrupt ministry of the deluded and oppressed
nation, (of which we once composed a respectable part) and the low, mean,
servile, crouching dependants of that abandoned ministry: We know, my lord,
that you are not accustomed to be addressed with this manly, this at present
necessary freedom; but recollect, that that whole correspondence you have
courted, are not the mean, the despicable sycophants of a still more mean and
despicable, though a higher exalted wretch than themselves: They are part of
those virtuous sons of liberty who, in their infant years, before ever they knew
their real strength, had twice defeated the vain glorious enemies of the boasted
conquerors of the world. They are men at the same time, who wish to cultivate
a good understanding, wish to live in the utmost harmony and friendship with
the numerous and truly virtuous part of the community, whom you have the

unmerited honor of governing; a community who, we are convinced, shudder at the barbarous ideas held forth in your very effectionate reply, to your beloved children of the *Tawny Tribes* and most sincerely blush for him, who they have too much reason to know is incapable of blushing for himself.

You will already have perceived my lord, that we do not intend to pay our worship to the *star or garter, the blue or red ribband, nor to the empty gewgaws of undeserved title;* they are too often conferred on those, who with more propriety should have graced a halter.

It is the noble virtues of the mind—the graces of benevolence—*humanity*—and the general goodness of the heart only, which shall ever draw forth applause from our Society.—your Lordship, therefore, will undoubtedly discover that we do not mean to *prostitute* the real intention of panegyric, by conferring any part thereof on you.

Neither will we stain our pen, by attempting to impress *your* mind with one sentiment of honor, but we will awaken that passion, which is the constant concomitant of cruelty, and therefore apply to your fear.

Are you, my lord, so far advanced in your pregnancy of *dotarism,* as to imagine that the people, under your immediate government, will join in your shameful, disgraceful, nefarious scheme.

Do you really suppose that they will be so far dupes to your proposed cruelty, as to resque their honor, their lives, their safety and their property—abandon every tenet of humanity, every principle of virtue, and join a band of lawless savages, who they well know, if the arm of the Union is but exerted, can be crushed in one campaign by the conquest we shall make in the city of Montreal, and the plains of Abraham, should your lordship, & the few adherents, you will then have, choose to measure the length of your bayonets with us.—We see your lordship smile at the term honor, being applied by us to the people under your government.

Yes, sir, we apply it with pleasure, because we are certain that a large, a very large proportion of them are justly entitled to the sacred appellation.

True it is, that you have endeavored to inoculate the whole with the spirit of your own genius—but you have failed.—Your lordship's venom, has as yet polluted but a small proportion of the community; and it is to be hoped for the honor of the human race that it will never do more.

What do you really imagine the honest, the virtuous the truly noble, the generous, the patriotic part of that nation, which unfortunately gave *you* birth, must think of your attempting to excite the cruel revenge and imbittered resentment of the savages of America, against their many friends and connections in the country.

Reflect on the sentiments of your virtuous kinsman, Lord Effingham; bring into contemplation the *possibility* of you meeting in an other world: ask your own heart what a look of disdain you must expect to receive from him, & recollect that tho' you are at present past blushing at the evil of your intention you will not then be, and trembling at the dreaded extent of your punishment.

The people of your government, sir, are well acquainted with our additional strength at present, when compared with what it was at the commencement of last war: a war in which your nation lost thirteen flourishing colonies, after sinking one hundred and twenty millions in the equally vain as wicked pursuit of bringing them to acknowledge their obedience in all cases whatever.

The reflection on these two well known facts, could you ever instill into their minds your own principles of barbarity, which *we* firmly believe to be impossible, must deter them from joining you in your proposed, wanton and unprovoked aggression; but should they, contrary to our expectations and wishes, voluntarily unite with your *beloved banditti,* who you well know by experience cannot be kept under any military countroul or regulation, it is true that we may possibly lose for a short time, some few of our possessions, as we know the feelings of those ruffians, whom you have so eagerly courted as your partners in robbery & murder, are too calous, too much resemble your own, to be moved with compassion, by the grey and hoary heads of infirm, but reverential old age, by that awe with which the human heart is naturally penetrated by viewing the pregnant wife, by (to all but you and them) the irresistable graces of the charming, the beautiful virgin, the pity claiming plaints of the innocent, the helpless babe; But sir, we comfort ourselves with this reflection, that in a short time thereafter, we shall certainly be masters of the movable property of our enemy, more than adequate to repair our burnt houses and fences, and as to our farms, we well know that you can neither carry them with you in your retreat, or dare to maintain posts, by which they will be kept under your jurisdiction.

In the last war sir, you was generally esteemed amongst the most humane of British officers; but there are some of us who then knew and often declared, that your *apparent* humanity was not the natural effusions of a tender heart, but the effects of a jesuitical, inveterate, diabolical, policy; the conduct you now pursue, evinces the truth of that opinion and assertion.

Shrinking, my Lord, as you certainly must, from the effects of this open inquiry into your heart, we think it highly probable that you will wish to shelter yourself under instructions received from your Court. Whether you have or have not received such instructions, is, to us, & ought to have been to you, a matter of very little consequence; ought at your advanced period of life, the desire for position, place, or title, to have been so very great as to have occasioned your sacrificing your honor as a soldier, your reputation as a man of humanity, or even the dignity of your station, by obeying the dictates of an abandoned ministry, long hated by the people over whom your king has appointed them to preside, and most heartily dispised & rediculed by the greatest part of the world, if they were contradictory to the dictates of your own conscience.—But you will perhaps, say that no *Lord* was ever known to sacrifice real solid interest, to unmeaning unsubstantial honor; or to yield up the weight of his purse to the feelings of his conscience. Judging from your own heart, this opinion is, perhaps, to your mind, my Lord, a very natural as well as a very weighty one, but the noble names of Effingham and Campden, will be handed down to posterity as an iresistable proof of the falsehood of the assertion.

Had your Lordship's heart & conduct thro' life, been in any degree similar to theirs, it is far from being impossible that in your later days, you would have been ashamed to have deviated from so rare, so lovely, & so honorable a pattern.

It may be asked what we can gain by this address to your Lordship:—we will tell you:—1st, It will demonstrate that we entertain a much higher opinion of the virtue, moderation, and humanity, of the people of Canada, than you do:—

2d. That we are really desirous of peace, if it can be maintained on honorable terms:—

3d. That we have some faint hope, tho' you have had neither virtue nor firmness sufficient to resist the first impulse of your heart, in favor of wanton, as well as unprovoked cruelty, you may nevertheless, even yet, feel ashamed of it.

5th. That should you be totally lost to that *least* of virtues—SHAME—your leicentious avowal of calling to your aid those savages, who will join you, is treated by us, with the utmost contempt—And lastly, that we may prevent you from tendering us any insiduous professions of your personal friendship, and thereby saddling an indelable disgrace upon our memory, in the eyes of posterity.

A true extract from the minutes:—Attest.

WM. COIT, *Sec'ry.*

Colchester, March 17th, 1794.

Farmers' Library (Rutland), April 23, 29, 1794

Letter of Judge Nathaniel Chipman, June 9, 1794

NEW-YORK, July 11.

TO THE PUBLIC.

Some time ago Judge Chipman of Vermont published a small tract, entitled— "Sketches of the Principles of Government," in which he has with great ingenuity and deep discernment, unfolded the genuine principles of our free representative constitutions of government. This book is sold by Mr. Fellows, in this city, and is highly deserving of perusal.

When the Democratic Club was formed in Vermont, the father of it very artfully called in the aid of Judge Chipman's book; trusting, no doubt, that the eminent character and talents of that gentleman, would help to prop the Institution and give it celebrity. How far he succeeded, will appear from the following letter from the author, which we are requested to insert.

Copy of a Letter from the author of SKETCHES of the PRINCIPLES of GOV-
ERNMENT, to his friend in this city, dated Rutland (Vermont) June 9, 1794.[7]

Dear Sir.

You have doubtless noticed the proceedings of the Democratic Society in the
county of Chittenden, in this state. I find they have been published with great
avidity in New York and Philadelphia. The fomenter of that society, and sole
author of their late productions, perhaps, you are apprized is not an inhabitant
of this state, but resides generally in the city of New York. What could have induced that gentleman to call in the aid of my name or my writings in support of
such associations is best known to himself. If you have not perused the book,
you might be led from the detached sentences there cited to believe that it contains the principles of anarchy, instead of the principles of government; principles
wholly subversive of a representative democracy. If you will give yourself the
trouble to read the passages there cited, in their connection, you will find that
they have been brought in by the head and shoulders and "with the strength of
Hercules," as a comic author observes on a like occasion.

I have, indeed, in treating of a representative democracy, asserted, that "an
interest in the approbation of the people, and a strong sense of accountability to
them, in all official conduct, is the greatest or rather the only effectual security
against abuses in those who exercise the powers of government." I have further
said, that "to render the public sentiment a more rational and more powerful
check upon every department of government, it is essentially necessary that there
be in every free state an effectual provision for the dissemination of useful knowledge." That "in a Republic, by which is intended a representative democracy,
the powers of government are supported not by force, but by the sentiments of
the people," that "it is necessary to cultivate a sentimental attachment to the
government." I still believe these principles to be just, not in theory only, but
in practice; yet I cannot discover that they express, or even remotely imply, an
approbation of self created societies and clubs formed for the purpose of censuring the proceedings of government in transitu, of anticipating the deliberations
of constitutional bodies, or dictating the measures, which those bodies ought
to pursue.

If, Sir, you will have the patience to read so long a letter, I will give you my
reasons for believing such societies not merely useless, but mischievous and a
very dangerous imposition. Simple democracies, in which the people assemble
in a body, to enact laws & decide on all public measures, have, from the earliest
ages, exhibited scenes of turbulence, violence and fluctuation, beyond any other
kind of government. No government has ever been able to exist under this form
for any length of time. Experience has evinced, that the people collected in a
body are impatient of discussion; that they are fatally incapable of reasoning;
but they are highly susceptible of passions. To those the more artful direct their
whole attention. By these every decision in the numerous and heterogeneous

assemblies of the people at large, is irresistably influenced. In a simple democracy, there can be no fixed constitution. Every thing is liable to be changed by the frenzy of the moment, or the influence of popular faction. In such a government, where all are immediate actors no accountability can exist; consequently, in no government, have there been instances of a more flagrant violation of rights, or a tyranny more cruel and remediless than that which has been exercised over a minority of the citizens, or against an unpopular individual. Many public measures, whether they regard the internal legislation of the state, or its conduct towards foreign powers, will often be, not a little complicated. Many of the people, for want of the means of information, for want of leisure, patience or abilities, will come forward wholly ignorant of the relative circumstances necessary to be known, in order to a just and proper determination; and I believe you will agree with me, that, on such occasions, presumption, passionate zeal, and obstinacy, are always in proportion to the ignorance of the actors. In such governments, the measures, will, of necessity, be frequently unjust, violent and fluctuating.

Such is not the government under which we live. Our national government and the governments of the several states, are representative democracies. This kind of government is calculated to give a permanent security to all the essential rights of man, life, liberty and property, the equal rights of acquisition and enjoyment, in a just compromise with the rights of all, which a simple democracy by no means secures. This kind of government is designed in its constitution to provide equally against the tyranny of the few and the tyranny of the many. The people have endeavored to place their delegated rulers in a constant state of accountability. This is the hinge on which American liberty turns. That the most perfect freedom of deliberation might be secured, the members of the legislature are, in their public conduct, made amenable only to the sentiments of the people, by the interest which they have in the approbation of their constituents. The executive is made accountable to the public sentiment, and is further amenable to a constitutional tribunal, for every violation of trust. The powers and duties of the several departments, are in many instances, limited by the laws of the constitution, by which the people have said to their rulers, thus far shall ye go; and no farther. Many things are left to their integrity and discretion, to act for the best good of the nation. Congress are, from their situation furnished with the necessary information relative to the present state of things, as they may affect the nation, whether internally or externally. All this is, in their debates, handed out, and circulated among the people, together with all the reasons for, and against any measure that could be suggested by the most mature deliberation. By these means, the people have in their power, sufficient information to judge calmly and rationally of the measures which have from time to time been adopted.

Proceeding in this way, I am persuaded that a representative democracy may secure to a people more civil and political happiness than any of the kinds of governments which have hitherto existed. Such is the state of things, that knowledge in the complicated affairs in civil society comes not by intuition. The means of information, and frequently, diligent investigation are necessary. The knowledge of the people will follow, but can rarely precede, a public discussion. They will generally approve or disapprove with judgment, but in dictating, are exposed to all the rashness of ignorance, passion and prejudice.

Our self created societies and clubs, as it appears to me, have a tendency, directly or indirectly, to introduce into the measures of government, all the precipitation, all the heat and ungovernable passions, of a simple democracy. Have we reason to believe that these self prounounced dictators, have a free access to the means of information, that they have been able more fully to comprehend the present circumstances, the principles and reasons which ought to direct public measures, than those to whom the people have confided that talk? Or even than their more peaceable and quiet fellow citizens? Certainly they have given us no unequivocal proof of either.

Their professed design has been to promote political knowledge; but wherever they have established themselves, they have assumed a dictatorial style in their resolves. Where any man, or body of men have refused their dictates, or presumed to differ from them in opinion, no length of meritorious services, no virtue or integrity of character, has been proof against their bold proscriptions. Like the demagogues of simple democracy they have applied wholly to the passions and jealousies of the people. They have assumed to speak the sentiments of the people, though, in point of numbers they are certainly a very inconsiderable minority. If their assertions have so far imposed on their national government as to direct its measures it is worse than the evils of a simple democracy. It is an engine to govern the majority by a minor faction. Nothing of this kind can happen in an assembly of the people at large. Is it, sir, supposed that the measures of Congress have, in their present session been influenced by means of these societies? I should be very unwilling to believe that the American government, which I had supposed to be an improvement on the wisdom of ages, had so soon submitted to the controul of a few self-authorized oligarchs.

If however these societies are unable directly to dictate measures to the national governments, they will still have a very pernicious effect. When once, though under the thickest clouds of ignorance, they have prejudiced a measure, and assumed to dictate it, unless they have more candour than most men, their prejudices will rarely yield to any light of conviction. This, as far as their influence extends, will, in a great degree, prevent the happy effect of the wisest and best measures. It is perhaps, of as much importance, in general, that the people should see and acknowledge the measures of government to be wise and good, as that they should be really wise and good. If there is a failure in either respect they will not secure the happiness of the people. It is of great consequence that the people, with the means of information should cultivate a disposition to judge with coolness and impartiality, and that legislators should endeavour to render the reasons of their measures plain and intelligible to the common sense of mankind.

I know that it is frequently said, that in a republic it is necessary to the maintenance of liberty, the people, should be jealous of their rulers. But I have never been able to persuade myself, that to be a good republican a man must imbibe prejudices, which is the necessary consequence of jealousy. That certainly is an unfortunate situation which renders candour dangerous, or jealously a species of virtue. In no government are rulers held more strictly and generally accountable than in our representative democracies. Their continuance in place depends constantly on a faithful discharge of their trust. Ought we not then, for a suspicious jealousy, to substitute a manly and rational confidence. This by no means implies a supine inattention to public men or measures; but it admits candour in the examination. If jealousy be a republican virtue, if it be necessary to excite suspicions among the people, to render them watchful of their liberties, it must be acknowledged that democratic societies have, in this respect great merit. —They will not surely think that the people ought to exempt them from suspicions and jealousies, because they are self-existent. Until their turn shall come, they may on their principles justify any, the most ill grounded and violent invectives against the members of the federal government, as purely intended to keep alive, among the people a necessary jealousy, a wholesome distrust of rulers. If by these means the people should be deprived of all the present blessings of government and the nation plunged into a long series of calamities, they have only to say, all this is the glorious price of liberty. They need not blush for their violent censures of the executive of the federal government: for an opposition to the measures of a foreign minister; those measures which were disapproved by his nation, and for which he was displaced with pointed marks of disgrace.

Notwithstanding what has been observed, I do not mean to insinuate, that such associations as our democratic societies are a crime animadverted upon by laws and restrained by constitution. The exercise of such a power would be more dangerous to liberty than the associations themselves. They must be left to rise or fall, solely by the good sense of the people. Nor would I insinuate that it can never be expedient for the people to assemble on occasion to petition for a redress of grievances, whether constitution or legislative. But it would be well if the petitions and representations of the people, unless when they come from known corporate bodies, were always to be signed individually, that it might appear how far they are expressive of the public sentiment. When they come forward from voluntary societies, there is often a deception. It is not known whether they contain ten or ten thousand individuals.

From these observations you will be convinced that I am no friend to such societies, and that my name ought not to have been brought forward as one who favored their principles.

The Herald (New York), July 14, 1794

J. M. to Nathaniel Chipman, August 5, 1794

For the NEW-YORK JOURNAL, *&c.*

CITIZEN GREENLEAF,

THE answer to judge Chipman, which will be handed to you with this, I am in conscience obliged to confess was first given to Mr. Bunne, the Printer of the Minerva, for publication, but his partner, Mr. Webster, after reading it (as my friend, who had the honor of conversing with that gentleman on the subject, informs me) refused to print it, alledging, *"that his paper should never be disgraced with such scurrility."*

In consequence of this unexpected information, I re-perused the piece with the greatest attention, but was unable to discover any thing scurrilous therein, unless giving the epithets very generally bestowed upon the French nation, and the Democratic societies, could be considered as such, which, indeed, leads me very warmly to suspect, that Mr. Webster must have had some other reason for his refusal, and more especially as it is said, that there have appeared a number of pieces and paragraphs in his paper, which stamps a believe, that he is an avowed enemy to both.

I wish Mr. Webster would condescend to inform me what is the *real* reason of his refusal, that I might hereafter have it in my power to avoid the *sin* of offending him, and which I could not well suppose I had already done, as in bestowing my epithets on the Democratic societies, I was only copying the example pursued in his paper on sundry occasions, particularly on the 5th of june last, where it is said, *"they are dwindling fast into contempt,"* and should they neglect doing what the writer *prescribes as their duty,* "that all candid men will set them down as a band of calumniators, who merit what they really will have, *the detestation of their fellow-citizens."*

Upon my word Citizen Greenleaf, if I did not tremble at the idea of my becoming the object of Mr. Webster's wrath and indignation, I should be much inclined to impeach him at the bar of the public, as guilty of open, downright partiality in this business.

As to the epithets given to the French nation, it must very evidently appear, that I only aimed at an *humble imitation* of some very great men, who I always supposed stood in the highest grade of Mr. Webster's respect and esteem.

The king of Great Britain, for instance, says (vide a late speech to his Parliament) "French principles are utterly subversive of the peace and order of all civil society."

The great Mr. Pitt[5] declares, in the same Parliament, *"that peace cannot be maintained with them* without the sacrifice of every principle of religion, morality, and justice."

And that first of all sober orators, *that inflexible, that unchangeable patriot* Edmund Burke,[6] before the same honorable body, calls them "rascals and assassins;" "a vile banditti of robbers and plunderers;" "merciless savages;" "men who have neither honor, honesty, or any virtue whatever, & in each of whose countenance assasination is depicted;" "the unbreached heroes of France, the outlaws of humanity, the *incommunicable* people, *who acknowledge no God but the sacred right of insurrection;* had no judges but Sans Culottes." In another place our incomparable orator terms them the "bare breeched corps;" and speaking of one of their leaders, still improving in the delicacy of his metaphors, he, with uncommon *refinement* of language, calls him the "Orator of the naked posteriors," &c.&c

Upon the whole, Sir, I am absolutely compelled to conclude, from Mr. Webster's aversion to scurrillity, that he is a gentleman of much more delicacy (especially *where the argumentative part of the subject does not suit him*) than Mr. Burke.

But on the other hand, between yourself and Mr. Webster, I am much afraid, that I am not placed in a very pleasant situation, for I have said so much in favor of the British government (to whom it is reported, you not a very warm friend) that I have also reason to suspect that you too will be offended.

Please, Sir, to accept my apology; it is briefly this, that no evil can arise therefrom, for no man, *in his senses,* who is acquainted with their present system can possibly believe me; as for those who are *out of their senses,* of whom, however, I must acknowledge we have rather too many among us, they never can be objects of your consideration; Besides you will be pleased to notice, that in my eulogium on that government, I was personating a person who was praying for the right of monopolizing the politics of a whole state, with a view of crushing the Democratic societies, and to maintain a consistency of character, was under the necessity of advancing a multitude of absurdities.

Yours, &c.

Westchester County, August 5, 1794   J.M.

Mr. Bunce,

FROM the good opinion I had inbibed of Judge Chipman's political principles and practice, I read, with great avidity, a letter *said* to be his, inserted in your paper of the 10th instant, on the subject of Democratic Societies in general, but more particularly respecting one in his own state.

From his pen, I expected sound reasoning and conclusive argument, such as his friends, and the enemies of these societies, would have pronounced irrefutable; for this I have waited, but waited in vain.

Before, however, I make my remarks on this as it appears to me very extraordinary production, I will, in justice to and vindication of that gentleman's character, take the liberty of suspecting that you have been artfully imposed on by your correspondent, as I cannot bring myself, *as yet* to believe that he is the author thereof, because among others, it is liable to the four following objections:—

1st. Because it establishes false premises, and, of course, draws therefrom false conclusions.

2d. Because it artfully conceals the truth.

3d. Because a great proportion of the letter is idly and childlishly, though very elaborately taken up in proving what none of the Democratic Societies ever attempted to deny.

4th. Because one of the most important sentiments therein, cannot in consistance with charity, be supposed to have escaped from the pen of so good a Republican, as the Judge has been generally esteemed.

Though I am inclined, from this principle to think that he is not the author, I esteem myself nevertheless at perfect liberty, without any apology, to address him as if he really was, because there can be no difficulty, on his part in stamping the certainty thereof in either way on the public mind; and I therefore request you to publish the following answer.

To Nathaniel Chipman, *Esq.*

Your letter dated the 9th of June last at Rutland to your friend in this city, on the establishment of the Democratic Society in Chittenden county, I have read with care and attention, and find it amongst others liable to the four objections already stated; in proof whereof, it will be necessary to make sundry quotations therefrom—You declare, that "there is only one sole author of their late productions"—This is absolutely and literally false. There was not a clause which did not undergo a discussion of two meetings; sundry propositions, made by different members were rejected, and sundry others amended.

In another place you observe, "they need not blush for their violent censures of the executive of the federal government for an opposition to the measures of a foreign minister: Those measures which were disapproved by his nation, and for which he was displaced, with *pointed marks of disgrace.*"

As to the first part of this sentence, you are called upon to point out an expression in all the proceedings of that Society at which your animadversions seem most pointedly leveled, which can, with all your ingenuity at the art of fiction, be construed into a censure of the "executive of the federal government." On the other hand I have collected the following information from authority which cannot be doubted—That it was proposed by one of the members while they were debating on that clause of the 11th resolution, of the Philadelphia society, of the 9th of January last, which censures the impropriety "of vilifying the French minister, by spreading false and calumnious reports, by indecent strictures and newspaper publications, and by other as unwarrantable means" to annex the following clause in addition to their approbation of the above censure. "We further declare, that in this censure flowing spontaneously from the honesty and simplicity of hearts zealously patriotic, we do not mean to include, in the smallest degree, *the conduct of the executive,* who in the unfortunate differences between him and the minister alluded to, pursued the only mode consistent with the true and mutual dignity of two such great, such friendly nations."

I know you, Sir, too well, to suppose you *entirely* destitute of candour, wen [sic] in this business, in which you have engag-[sic] with such religious warmth: To the remains of that virtue then, which, even in the extreme bitterness of peevish sentiment for disappointed expectation, you cannot, I am convinced, totally bereave yourself, I appeal for your own determination whether this looks, *as you have asserted,* like an inclination to bring forward *"violent censures of the executive of the federal government."*

True, this was not published in their proceedings, but that arose entirely from a determination to make no comment at all on that part of the Philadelphia resolution, as the President's conduct did not by any possible construction, appear involved therein.

Your observation, that "the late minister of France was displaced with *pointed marks of disgrace,"* was it even true, would speak very little indeed, in favour of either your charity, or benevolence.

A man, possessed of true greatness of mind, will not even wish for, *much less eagerly court,* an opportunity of triumphing over the unfortunate though he may be their enemy—But if your assertion is false, which I, *without any qualification* declare it to be, the expression must disgrace its author, until it is recalled, or proved to be true.

And as a proof of its falsity I will tell you, Sir, that he was not so much as recalled—The tenderness of the ruling power in France for the feelings of the first officer in this government was the cause of his dismission.

Again, speaking of the Democratic societies *you* say, *"wherever* they have established themselves, they have assumed a *Dictatorial* style in their resolves."

The Chittenden County society proves the falsity of this accusation, for they say "we publish our opinions, *not in a confidence of our numbers or importance."*

Is this, Sir, a *Dictatorial style?*

You declare the societies are formed for the purpose of censuring the proceedings of government in transitu, of anticipating the deliberations of constitutional bodies, of dictating the measures which those bodies ought to pursue, of assuming to speak the sentiments of the people." &c. &c. &c.

The 4th resolution of the Chittenden Society is:

"Resolved, that we esteem the uncountrouled freedom of speech in Congress, as one of the greatest bulwarks in our constitution, and that therefore, no individual member thereof should be attacked, or censured for any expressions used therein, unless absolutely subversive of the rights of the nation, or the dignity of the house; or unless it should *clearly* appear that they were dictated by sinister and wicked motives, even though his opinions and expressions may be very discordant from those of the people he represents.

But we at the same time declare, that all such members ought to be watched with a *scrupulously* jealous eye, and the greatest care taken, that at the next election, they be prevented from the power of continuing their mischief, by raising heats, and promoting disturbances in the community."

Does this look like dictating measures of government?

Much more might be said, in refutation of your insidious, unwarranted and unmerited charges, but as the *onus probandi* in support of them lies entirely on you, and you have rested the proof as yet on your mere ipse dixit, which you certainly deem by far too important, more is unnecessary; for it has been already made to appear, that the spirit of falsification must have gone abroad at Rutland *about the 9th of June.*

Thus far as to the 1st objection, of your having established false promises.

The second objection is, because you have artfully concealed the truth.

In enumerating the quotations, taken by the Chittenden Society, from your *truly* valuable book "on the principles of government," you have artfully concealed the most applicable of these quotations, which may be found in page 139 in the following words: "*banish mystery from politics, open every channel of information, call for investigation, tempt a discussion of measures, and the public sentiment will be the best criterion of what is right and what is wrong in government.*"

If this is not *an artful concealment on your part,* condescend, Sir, to inform the world, what you meant by the above quoted sentence; if you intended that "the investigation and discussion of public measures" should have been confined to the *bench* and the *law* only, you ought to have expressed yourself more explicitly; and if not confined to any particular members of the great community, on what possible principle do you exclude those who meet for this express purpose in societies stiled democratic? a purpose which you have so strenuously and forcibly recommended.

Be so kind as to answer this, with that honesty and candour which *I once* knew you to possess, and which, *for your own sake,* I hope in future you will ever be governed by.

The third objection is, because a great proportion of your letter is idly and childishly taken up in proving very elaborately what none of the Democratic Societies ever attempted to deny; "That simple democracies, in which the people assemble in a body to enact laws and decide on all public measures, have from the earliest ages exhibited scenes of turbulence, violence and fluctuation, beyond any other kind of government."

It is acting, Sir, with that impartiality and upwrightness which ought to be attendant on the proceedings of a judge, and ever will be on that of a good man, to take such uncommon pains as you have done, to *insinuate* that a certain part of the citizens of the United States harbour the intention of producing a simple democracy. For if this is not your meaning, I cannot conceive for what possible purpose you could have wasted so much ink, in demonstrating what appears self-evident to every Democratic Society on the continent. And if it is your meaning, surely you will not deem it impertinent to discredit your insinuation, until you bring something like proof to support it, and which I dare to affirm, it is not in your power to do.

The 4th objection is, because one of the sentiments, cannot be supposed to have escaped from the pen of so good a Republican as you have been generally esteemed, which is, *"it is perhaps of as much importance in general, that the people should see and acknowledge the measures of government to be wise and good, as that they should be really wise and good."*

This is the most hoodwinking maxim I ever saw come from a republican pen—a belief in this would be an effectual opiate to lull our cares, and dissipate every uneasiness which could possibly arise, from the strongest apprehension of the severest attack on our liberties, our lives, or our property.

This is acting the jocky with a witness; having got your brethren tackled in the political harness, you want them to put on blinders, that you and your favorites may freely use the whip without the possibility of their knowing it, till the stroke is first received. This is a ready way to be sure of preventing them from becoming restive, or quitting the road you wish to drive them in. One would suppose you had served an apprenticeship to the hitherto *unrivalled William Pitt.*

If we can be brought to suppose that all goes right, it is of equal importance as if it really did so! Have you satisfied your mind that this creed will be swallowed by your fellow citizens of Vermont, because sanctioned by the respectability of your name?

It might indeed be exhibited with propriety, as the great article of saving faith, in the creed of aristocrats and despots, for this would serve to silence the malevolent tongue of enquiry, and shut the inquisitive eye of patriotism.

Supposing, Sir, in your late character of district judge, under the influence of this your new invented maxim, you had been addressing a grand jury; would it not have perfectly comported with this doctrine to have said?

"Gentlemen of the Grand Jury,

"It is a duty incumbent on you, from your present honourable and very important station, to make due enquiry into all criminal acts committed against the laws of your country, into all grievances and nuisances under which your fellow-citizens labour, that from their nature are cognizable before this Court. But, gentlemen, it will be of "equal importance to your fellow-citizens in general, if, by your influence, you can persuade them that no crimes—No grievances—No nuisances do exist—Let me admonish you, gentlemen, that this transubstantiating *law of policy* be indelibly stamped on your hearts:—The grace of faith is equally meritorious, equally beneficial—equally necessary—equally important in politics as in religion."

The sensible, the thinking, the judicious freemen of Vermont—could treat such language with a hiss of contempt—and yet it is language which comports fully with this your new nostrum, your infallible cure for all political sores.

Thus far as the four objections I have stated—I will now beg your permission to make a few observations on some other expressions in your letter.

In one of your raving fits of declamation you declare the Democratic Societies to be "a mischievous, and a very dangerous imposition," in another you insinuate that they are "criminal," and yet, when the fit is over, and you get restored to the exercise of your former good sense, you boldly affirm, that "they ought not to be animadversed on by laws, or restrained by constitutions." It will, upon reflection, be difficult for you to believe, and therefore you ought to pardon the want of faith in others, that such inconsistencies were ever generated in your brain: For it would be ridiculing in your most satyrical and most contemptuous manner possible, the spirit and energy of Republican governments to suppose that any act committed under them "mischievous, of a dangerous imposition, and even criminal," ought not to be "animadverted on by laws, or restrained by constitution."

Another of your accusations is, that these Societies are self-created," are self-pronounced dictators.

I will do you the justice to suppose, that you clap this intended brand of sarcasm on them, not because they are Societies—but because they have impertinently intermeddled in *your strongly wished for department,* by avowing their opinion on some public principles, and some public measures.

But are they not as much interested in these principles and measures as you are? This you *must* answer in the affirmative.

And was not you, in the most extensive point of view, a self-created politician, when you wrote your "principles of government."

I am not inclined to flatter you by supposing that either Congress, the President, the Legislature of your own State, or your own Governor, petitioned you to do so.

Is it criminal then in fifty men to deliberate and give an opinion on *some* public principles and measures, while it is highly *laudable* in *one man* to write on the "principles of government *in general?*"[8]

If you think so, pray tell us from what principle of sound reasoning, from what code of law, from what author of consequence, you have extracted that sentiment.

I will now pause a little and consider, if I possessed the same degree of political knowledge, and equally wished, as you seem to do, for an exclusive right to be the only vehicle in the State of Vermont, through whom political opinions should be disseminated, how I should petition Congress on a subject equally eccentric and unprecedented.

May it please your Sacred Honours,

I have long viewed with deep and melancholy concern, the decreasing respect of your constituents for your truly honourable, infallible and sacred Majesties, but my apprehensions have of late been greatly increased, by a set of bold, dangerous and adventurous democrats, who, in contradiction to my most sincere wishes, and fervent exhortations, have dared to form themselves into a society, with this State, for the avowed purpose of prophanely, sacreligiously, and irrevently examining into your decisions, and, where unfortunately you differ in opinion from each other , not only contemptibly and scornfully (being contrary to my late promulgated Republican doctrine of submissive obedience) but ever openly and avowedly declaring to the whole world, which of you they think ought, and which they think wrong.

And, it may further please your Hight and Mighty Honours, amongst all the corroding and afflicting anxieties of my mind, there is none which penetrates my whole frame with so great pain and sorrow, as to see these vile, abominable, base, worthless, infamous scoundrels, these accursed *liberty* and *equality* democrats act and speak with such guarded caution that they are not so much as *reprehensible* as by any law hitherto enacted. And yet, may it please your Honours, *it is impossible to say,* that they may not at some future period, disturb the peace of the community, produce the utmost anarchy and confusion, nay, engender even a civil war (for they are a set of d——d uncivil fellows) should you only, in the purity of your hearts, and for the ease, benefit and emolument of yourselves, and some of your best friends, deviate materially, in the exercise of your power, from the original intention of what they call the constitution (for these fellows have the impudence to preach that all your deliberations ought to be limited thereby) or should you only, though with the most exalted view, and for the best and wisest purposes, disengage yourselves from the ill-fated alliance, and disgraceful connection which at present subsists between you, and that cowardly, dastardly, meagre, half-starved, restless, King Killing, ragamuffians, rabscallions, tatterdemalians, frog-eating sons of B——t——s, the French, and throw yourselves under the protection, and into the arms of that mild, wise, brilliant, flourishing, friendly, peaceable, virtuous, patriotic, rising empire, and immaculate government of *Great Britain,* whose *minister, from his uncommon and unprecedented devotion in favour of the Rights of Man,* demonstrated to the whole universe, past the possibility of contradiction, by his attempt to resque the unfortunate country of France from her present state of tyranny, and compel her to accept a government, which the people, for their own benefit, ought to believe to be a *really* good one. A minister, whose spirit and firmness in this heavenly contest, has secured, to himself and his nation, a name, which wondering millions for ages to come, will never mention but with amazement!!!

A minister, whose religious enthusiasm in this glorious cause, has urged him on even to risk (not the brains) but the head of a son of his beloved monarch. And yet, *wonderful to tell,* I can assure your honours, that there is not one member of the Society in this State, who has wisdom and discernment sufficient to discover the beneficent actions and intentions of Great Britain either towards the French or this country. Nay, (I blush as I write it) they madly and ignorantly prefer the principles of these French anarchists.

Now, therefore, may it please your sacred Honours, taking the above premises into your wise and Catholic consideration, and for sundery other good and substantial reasons, which your petitioner would rather whisper in your ears privately, than publish for the inspection, perhaps animadversion of these unhallowed democrats—Your petitioner humbly prays, that your Honours will be pleased to enact, that no person, within the State of Vermont (*your petitioner excepted*) shall hereafter be permitted to *think, speak, write* or *publish* any thing, in any manner whatever relative to, or connected with your honourable body, or any individual member thereof, until the present European war is happily terminated by Great Britain and the other combined powers, establishing a good, energetic, and permanent government for the *French Nation,* after such mode, form and fashion, as they, in their great wisdom, and disinterested generosity, shall deem best calculated for the preservation of the *royal dignity* of the rulers, and the due subordination of the ruled—"As it will be of equal importance to that then happy nation that they deem their government a good one, as if it was really so."

In hopes that many of your honours will view this maxim as a very important one, and therefore great the prayer of your petitioner (any objections made thereto by the Democratic Societies and other constitutionalists notwithstanding) your petitioner, as in duty bound, shall ever pray.

N.C.

Having read over my petition, I find it very defective in that respect which is ever due to the great lawgivers of the nation, whose dignity it is the duty & interest of every individual to maintain, but the nature of the petition being quite original, it became necessary to find new language for its introduction and support.

I shall only observe farther, Sir, that you have certainly on sundry occasions, given distinguished proofs of *candour,* both on the bench & at the bar; though in a fit of the spleen, you appear in your letter to have clapped a mandate on your pen, to stifle that amiable virtue; I will therefore hope, that in your future discussion of Democratic Societies, you will pay more attention to that good old adage, *"honesty is the best policy,"*—and rest assured, Sir, it is not because you differ in opinion from me respecting those Societies, but because, unfortunately for your own honour, in your objection against them you have deviated from the truth, & have there by apostatised from your former principles, that upon the present occasion I cannot consistently declare myself

Your Sincere Admirer.

New York Journal, August 9, 1794

To the *Vermont Journal,* **September 22, 1794**

COMMUNICATIONS
For the Vermont Journal

Judge Chipmann, in a letter published in the HERALD, a New-York paper, some time in July last, has asserted, that the Democratic Societies, are not merely useless, but mischievous and a very dangerous imposition.

A late writer in Mr. *Greenleaf's* paper, appears to be highly offended at this, as he deems it, injurious charge. No proof, however, is like a matter of fact. The late insurrection in the Northern counties of Pennsylvania, has proved beyond the possibility of contradiction, that the assertion is well founded. It is clear that more than nine tenths of the people are of the same opinion; and the Societies themselves have confirmed it, by their late but alas! too late attempts to prevent the pernicious effects of their former intemperate conduct. There is little probability that they will be able to *Resolve* into order that spirit of *frenzy,* which their inflamatory resolutions have been so instrumental in exciting.

It is certainly a very shocking consideration to any body of men, who have not sacrificed every particle of humanity to party rage, to have reason to believe that their conduct has in any measure contributed to the violent and untimely death of some of their fellow citizens,[9] and has been the means of forfeiting to the justice of their country the lives of many more. We have indeed from the mild spirit of our national laws, and the known humanity and discretion of those who are entrusted with their execution, good reason to expect that every lenient measure will be pursued, which can consist with the end of prevention—with the insuring of a rational and orderly submission to the laws which have been sanctioned by the authority of the people, on which depends the future happiness and safety of the country, and indeed our very existence as a nation. But should rigorous measures in some instances became unavoidable; should the severest necessities of our country, and the just requisition of the law, reluctantly drag some of our fellow citizens to an ignominious death, let not the disconsolate widow, the miserable orphan, and the aged parent, bereaved of his last support, too indiscriminately curse the *Democratic Societies,* as intended accessories to the dismal catastrophe. Many of the number know not what they did.

Could they have foreseen the fatal consequences of their measures, they would sooner have sacrificed their own lives, than thus to be the means of exposing the lives of their fellow citizens.

Spooner's Vermont Journal (Windsor), September 22, 1794

Resolutions, January 8, 1795

Resolutions of the DEMOCRATIC SOCIETY of Chittenden
county, state of Vermont.

January 8, 1795.

RESOLVED,

That this society, impressed with a deep sense of the numerous blessings which flow to the community, from the orderly and peaceable conduct of each individual, and from a due obedience to the constitutional laws of the majority, take the liberty of presenting the President of the United States with their unfeigned thanks for the lenient proceedings he in the first instance adopted, against the Western insurgents, by deputing commissioners to treat with them, and for the spirited and effectual measures he afterwards pursued, for enforcing a due submission to the laws: particularly, for his exemplary conduct in heading our brave, patriotic brethren, employed in that honourable though disagreeable task; many of whom, following his example, voluntarily sacrificed their interest and ease to that love for their country which the true spirit of republicanism will never fail to inspire.

RESOLVED,

That this society return, with the most lively sensibility, their warmest thanks to the forty seven virtuous representatives in Congress,[10] who, at a very late period, refused approbating the motion of censure upon part of their fellow citizens, for conduct which neither the constitution nor laws prohibit, and the dictates of reason warrant as just and laudable.

RESOLVED,

That in the opinion of this society, an unequivocal tribute of praise is not only due from them, but from each citizen of the United States to Mr. Baldwin,[11] for his wise, politic, and benevolent proposition, for adopting some effectual method, "to pour light on the transactions of government, into every corner of the country," and that the house of representatives, in appointing a committee to report on the subject, have given a fresh proof of the high confidence which the citizens of these states ought to place in the disposition and determination of the majority of that honourable body, to preserve unimpaired, in this happy land, that fair fabrick of liberty and independence which, but a few years ago, cost such an immense and invaluable profusion of blood and treasure to obtain.

We flatter ourselves that, in his pursuit of this desirable end, the repealing the law regulating the postage of newspapers will be brought into view, as one of the means.

RESOLVED,

That this society have read with exstatic pleasure, the whole of Mr. Munroe's and Mr. Randolph's address to the French National Convention, every sentence whereof we admit is truly expressive of the high esteem and unalienable attachment which the real friends and lovers of our government have had, and still do cherish for the republic of France, but in a particular manner the sentence in Mr. Munroe's, where he says, "Each branch of the Congress, conformable to the mode of deliberation established in it, has required the President to inform you of its disposition; in fulfiling the desire of these two branches, I am instructed to declare to you, *that the President has declared his own sentiments:*" Which conjoined to the following clause of Mr. Randolph's, "the President of the United States having committed this honourable and interesting talk to the department of state it cannot be more conveniently executed than by seizing this occasion to declare formally to the allies of the United States, that the cause of liberty, for the defence of which the Americans have lavished so much blood and treasure, is cherished by our republic with increasing enthusiasm, that wherever the standard of liberty shall be displayed, the affections of the United States will always be roused, and that the success of those who rise to assert the cause of liberty, will be celebrated by the United States and felt as if it was their own, and that of the other friends of humanity," must tend, unless they are deprived of every sense of shame, affectually and forever to silence the ungodly and seditious yelping of those lovers of Britain and slavery, those snarling anti-republicans, who have been so long fretting the public ear by their railing against the democratic societies, as the promoters of war from abroad and disturbers of society at home, because they cared (in contradiction to the wishes of those impious despisers of the sentiment of our law makers) faintly to intimate what both the President and Congress have since, in such explicit, unequivocal decided and elegant language, declared to be the opinion of the people of those states, on the subject of the present contest between the French nation and the powers combined against them.

Resolved, as the opinion of this society, that every act, contradictory to the laws of philanthropic hospitality, exercised against an individual of a foreign nation, is a breach of true religion. And therefore,

Resolved further, That every person belonging to the province of Canada, passing through this country, shall be treated by us, and each of us, with that politeness, civility, friendship and attention, which a stranger has a right to expect, and the generous mind will ever be happy in the opportunity of conferring; not withstanding we cannot avoid remembering that several of us, and of our fellow citizens, in our late intercourse with that country, have not only met with those delays and disappointments which the etiquette of their government renders unavoidable in many instances, but have, on sundry occasions, been treated with an insolent, imperious haughtiness, demonstrative that kings may confer power on men to whom heaven denies that dignity of mind necessary for executing it properly.

Resolved, That though it is the undeniable duty of every good citizen, to pay high respect, not only to the laws of Congress, but to every individual member thereof, traveling within that line of duty pointed out to them by the constitution of the United States, which ought in all their deliberations to be their unquestionable guide;—should certain members deviating therefrom, wantonly commence, and wickedly pursue an irritating attack, upon any part of their fellow-citizens, without assigning plain, pointed and specific reasons for their doing so, it is the unanimous and decided opinion of this society, that such members so, thereby, extinguished and annul every degree of that respect, which otherwise would be due to them, and therefore,

Resolved, That the address to Messrs. Tracy, Dexter, Sedgwick, Murray, William Smith, Ames and Dayton, members of the House of Representatives, of the United States,[12] complimenting them on their equally unsuccessful, as unconstitutional attempt to stigmatize a considerable proportion of their constituents, without the appearance of trial, prepared by a committee of this society, be read.

The committee accordingly reported their address, which being once read, was then deliberately discussed by paragraphs, and after sundry amendments, was agreed to in the following words:

To Messrs. Tracy, Dexter, Sedgwick, Murray, Wm. Smith, Ames and Dayton.

GENTLEMEN,

YOU have thrown the Gauntlet—You have wantonly, and against repeated advice challenged us to a trial of skill in the field of invective, slander, scurrility and abuse.

Was recrimination for unmerited, unprovoked injury and insult so illiberally heaped on us by you, one of our darling passions, we should undoubtedly hazard, with eagerness and avidity, all our stock of resentment, in that valuable branch of *indiscriminate* censure and reprobation, in the manufacturing of which, you have displayed talents and abilities which can be equalled but by very few, and exceeded by none.

But we will not indignify ourselves by imitating a conduct so unworthy of American Freemen—so unbecoming the character—so derogatory to the title of gentlemen.

We will not retort, by accusing you as the "*self created*" censors of men, who, in the scale of true patriotism, would far outweigh their accusers.

We will not accuse you of having spent a number of days, while enjoying a magnificent salary, in torturing language to invent expressions significant of your disdain and implacable resentment, against a part of your very paymasters, because they dared to exercise a right, vested in them by that constitution which we are determined to support, and which in your wild career of your phrenzied pursuit, for unrestrained despotic sway, the virtuous part of your colleagues did not, and as we trust, never will permit you to trample on.

We will not term you the leaders of a party, fonder of the British government than our own, though it is well known that there is not a man of that description on the continent, who does not most heartily pray for the success of your measures.

We will not term you the indiscriminate calumniators of the best friends to the ally of our Nation, fighting at this moment for that liberty and independence, which not only nature, but universal policy, demonstrates that ever nation ought to possess; and for their speedy and effectual attainment of which, in the most unlimited sense, we are determined to continue our most fervent wishes, our most ardent prayers, risquing, *with folded arms,* the tremendous effects of your threatened hostility and contempt, for this, in the eyes of many of your admirers, inexpiable sin.

We will not entitle you the Roberspierreans of congress, on account of your unconstitutional denunciations of thousands of your fellow citizens, without even the color of proof against them, without affording them any opportunity of defence, though we cannot avoid discovering a strong similitude between such proceedings, and those of the infamous and justly degraded tyrant.

We will not exhibit for the derision of your fellow citizens, MR. TRACY, your *delicate, sentimental and refined* metaphor of a SORE BACK'D HORSE.

Neither will we, on account of the sincere regard we have for your constituents, Mr. DEXTER, Make a single comment on your *extreme ignorance* in not knowing that there were no town meetings in the Southern states.

We would wish, Mr. SEDGWICK, was it possible, to conceal, even from Heaven itself, your sacrilegious comparison, when you say "the conduct of the democratic societies differ as far from a fair and honorable investigation, as CHRIST from BELIAL" but we will at the same time tell you that, though every impression of religion might have been obliterated from your mind, a regard to common sense ought to have prohibited you from drawing, in the sober moments of senatorial discussion, a comparison between Finity and Infinity; *You* are now however, the first professional man who, to gloss over a falsehood, has been guilty of an absurdity.

We will not ask you, who were your principal companions about the time Ticonderoga was ceded to the enemy in the late war; we will not ask, in what part of your body was concentered all that fire, which ought to have been exhibited against the open violaters of your country's rights in that hour of *real danger,* and which in the present moment of perfect security, blazes out in the front, against the Democratic Societies, with such apparently terrible, though, in reality inoffensive flame.

We will not require you to give a categorical account of your risques—your dangers—your wounds and your fears, during the late revolution. Was you under the necessity of answering such questions, with all their appurtenances, your face, brazen as it is within the walls of Congress, might be forced to the blush. Ignorant, despicable, and detestable as you are pleased to paint us, Mr. Sedgwick, we sometimes read an Almanac; in one of which we remember to have seen a maxim to this purport "He who is a *coward* in a good cause, during an hour of *adversity*, will ever prove a tyrant in a bad one, if he thinks himself *safe*"—As experience teaches fools, Mr. SEDGWICK, Be so good as to make the application.

Though you have been so imprudent, Mr. MURRAY, as to propose *"gibbeting the principles of the societies"* without any enquiry into them; as you have not like some of the others, insinuated a desire of abridging the rights of the people by one almighty fiat, so far should we be from improving upon your hint, that, was an attempt made, in our presence, to gibbet you, though only in effigy, we would use every legal means to prevent its execution.

We will not accuse you, Mr. SMITH of S. Carolina, of wilful falshood when you say, "if a revision be taken of their proceedings, (alluding to the Democratic Societies) it must be seen that they are calculated to *mislead, deceive, and inflame into acts of opposition to the laws*" But if your resentment against us, for our constant and determined opposition to the British government, on account of their piratical depredations against this country, as well as for their unprovoked attack on our only ally, in contradiction to the laws of Heaven, and the welfare of every independant nation, has not considered us beneath your notice or attention.—We request you to show one single act of *this society,* to which under the most forced construction, your unqualified construction can, with the appearance of propriety, be applied.

The gliding smoothness of your stile, the radient ingenuity of your arguments, have often given us pleasure, and extorted from us, in spite of your present principles, a most sincere wish, that you might never again be engaged in favor of a bad cause.

Though England was the place of your education, you should not forget, so often as we are afraid you do, that the United States is the place of your residence, and that your present power is entirely dependent on the people thereof. You are certainly master of a style which forces the attention, and captivates the passions, for your own sake therefore, as well as for ours, let your arguments hereafter be such, as will afford you an opportunity of shewing that you can likewise convince the judgment.

We will not tell the "tip toe" the "frowning into nothing" Mr. AMES, because it might raise the torrent of his daily increasing vanity, till it irrecoverably overflowed the banks of his *remaining* reason, that the numberless moongoverned flights which he has taken into the wild regions of fancy, added to the uncommon quantity of inflammable matter with which his brain appears to be overloaded, has procured him the honor, by way of distinction from all other moonarians, of being denominated, the ROYAL CONGRESSIONAL BALLOON.

Had you sir, even confined yourself within the limits of even decent *black-guardism,* we could in some measure have forgiven you, from the supposition that you was, in a certain degree, under the influence, ellegant, accomplished and amiable wife, whose opinions against republicanism, it is not unnatural to believe, were strongly rivetted at a very early period of her life, by the instructions of a Father, who contaminated the political principles, in the hour of his country's distress, of a great number of the inhabitants of the county of Hampshire in the state you at present so *worthily* represent.

Benedict Arnold had a wife likewise, strongly attached to the British government. Do not get into one of your strutting postures Mr. AMES, and call us a set of indelicate scoundrels, we pledge our honors, that it is not our intention to draw the butt of the comparison between the FEMALES of the two families. Mrs. Ames's discernment will convince her, that your unbecoming expressions, on the floor of Congress,[13] where "want of decency, is want of sense" has dragged us into the necessity of reminding your advocates and friends, that what has happened once may possibly happen again. From the bottom of our hearts do we declare our belief that she possesses, *in a moral point of view,* all those qualities we have already ascribed to her.

We will not accuse you Mr. DAYTON, of being much more guarded in bestowing praise, than in dealing out scandal, and yet there is great room for suspicion, when, upon the subject of the President's policy, with a firmness of which we highly approve, you sternly declare "you could not give your approbation to what you did not know" and yet in a very short time afterwards you take upon you to affirm, (though we will venture to say, with all due deference to your real merit, that you cannot establish *your* assertion by any reasonable proof) "That the Democratic Societies had produced the most mischievous effects in the western counties."

As we highly respect and unfeignedly esteem your general conduct in defence of the honor and dignity of our joint country, we are really sorry you should, thus erroneously, have adopted so unfavorable an opinion of our intentions and designs, as well as of their effects; We beg you to read *our* constitution and *our* different resolutions. We sincerely wish for your friendship, being determined we will ever support the real patriot, however inimical he may be to our society, in particular, as long as he advocates the honor of the nation, and the rights and privileges of the citizens at large.

But we will now gentlemen, proceed in our defence, upon the strong ground of reason and argument, and, whatever our present opinions may be of most of those members who have so indecently abused us, the love we bear to their constituents, the respect we have for the important and honorable station in which they are placed, our wish to evince our strict adherence to good order, and a due deference and veneration for government, will prove a compulsory preventative against using any language which the chastest delicacy can possibly be offended at, for truth will ever bear being rehearsed in very strong terms.

The President of the United States in his address to congress at the commencement of the present session, and in conformity we suppose with that clause of the constitution which requires "that he shall from time to time give to that honorable body information of the state of the union" after tendering a due degree of praise to *every description of citizens,* adds 'let THEM determine whether the insurrection has not been fomented by combinations of men who have disseminated from ignorance or perversion of facts, suspicions, jealosies, and accusations of the whole government.'

The President's original meaning, as to the persons alluded to by this expression, appeared to us, as it did to many others extremely ambigious; The answer of the senate, on their re-echoing the address left no doubt of their conviction that he meant the Democratic, Republican & Constitutional societies in the various states; The President whatever might originally have been his own meaning, certainly did not misunderstand theirs, and yet, in his answer to them, he says 'with a satisfaction which arises from an unalterable attachment to public order, do I learn that the Senate discountenanced those proceedings, which arrogate the direction of our affairs, without any degree of authority derived from the people.'

If this was a mere abstract proposition, no good man would attempt to deny the truth or propriety of the assertion; but if the president meant to designate all the democratic and other similar societies, as arogating this direction of affairs which he alludes to, we positively deny the truth of the charge. And, though our feelings are not capable of that degree of apathy, which could render us insensible to the many benefits this country has derived from his valor and predence, yet, such an ungenerous, unmerited crimination, without proof, without trial, of some thousand citizens, many of whom had a principal hand in fixing on his brow those laurels which have rendered him so conspicuous in the annals of the present day, convinces us, that the virtue of gratitude is not the growth of every soil, and that a long continuation in power is to apt to blunt that necessary moderation which ought to be its constant concomitant.

"No man liveth who sinneth not," saith the apostle—humanity is ever liable to error—the President therefore ought not to take it amiss if we do not deem him infallible; The charge we make against him is conditional: if we have misinterpreted his meaning, we most cordially and sincerely are ready to acknowledge our error, but, if his charge was intended against us, we call for it in such specific terms, as will enable us to convince the unprejudiced part of mankind, that he has been deceived.

Jealousy in the rulers will ever be the parent of discontent in the ruled, and we therefore *Court this fair discussion of* OUR conduct, & that of our brethren in the other societies, that a perfect good understanding may take place between the governors and governed of this yet happy country.

HE who has brought up this question, and withholds the effect of this requisition, will be the real fomenter of disturbance should any arise.

We will in the mean time, endeavor to enumerate the weightiest of the accusations, as far as they have come to our knowledge, alledged against the societies, either within the house of representatives, by some of the members of that house without doors, the adherents to the British government, or any other description of citizens.

(To be continued in our next.)

RESOLUTIONS *of the* DEMOCRATIC SOCIETY *of the County of Chittenden, State of* VERMONT, *Jan. 8th, 1795.*

ACCUSATION I.

They call themselves the people, and arrogate powers accordingly.—We are conscious of never having done so, nor do we believe that any of the other societies ever did—even sophistical triflers must admit, that the *onus probandi* lies on our opponents.—As to us in particular, we beg leave to quote the following clause in our original Constitution:

"We publish our opinions, not from a confidence in our numbers, or importance; we cannot, but in a very small degree, claim dignitied stations to sanctify those opinions, but as virtuous individuals, zealously engaged in what we deem the best service we can render to our country—determined to be influenced by principles only, and not by party or party views—at a distance from the seat of government and news, we solicit the friendship and good will of all those who can give us information, especially of those societies founded on principles similar to our own."

Has this, Gentlemen, the appearance of stiling ourselves the people? Or is this arrogating the direction of public affairs? No, gentlemen; but when a man or men chuse to relinquish that conduct, or those opinions which first made him or them the favorites of the people, to borrow Mr. Tracey's delicate metaphor,— they wince, on the appearance of enquiry, like "a sore-back'd horse."

Accusation 2. They have broke the President's Proclamation of neutrality, by constantly and publicly rejoicing at every success of the French, walking in procession with them on their festivals, and even entwining the colors of the United States with those of that nation.

The facts in this accusation we firmly believe many of the Societies have more or less commited; and with a degree of pleasure bordering on ecstasy, would our hearts and hands have intermixed with theirs, in every one of them, had an opportunity offered.—But are these facts crimes? Was the proclamation annuled when Mr. Munroe was commissioned as Ambassador to the French Republic? It certainly was not. Let us view then that gentleman's declaration on his first introduction, to the Nation Convention, amongst other expressions replete with sentiments of the most lively sensibility and tenderest friendship, he declares, by order of the President, as he asserts, "that we participate in their fate."—In what manner does Capt Barney address the Convention, when, by orders of our Ambassador, he tenders the American colors to that body, whom we are censured for reverencing?[14] He closes his speech with these words. "Henceforth suspended on the side of the French Republic, it will become the symbol of the union which subsists between the two nations, and last, I hope, as long as the freedom which they have so bravely conquered, and so wisely consolidated."—Those who assert that the facts charged against us in this accusation are criminal, ought to urge the impeachment of the President, Mr. Randolph, and Mr. Munro.—But perhaps there are some who still endeavor to maintain the force of the accusation, because we showed our inflexible friendship for that nation, in her present struggle, when it was by no means so certain, as at the time of Mr. Munro's mission, whether they would completely conquer their enemies—Let those frozen politicians, those unseeing adherents to good fortune, whose friendship depends totally upon success, triumph in their prudence, and condemn our too forward march to virtue and distress.—We wish not for the approbation of men, whose hearts are so callous to the dictates of humanity.—We would rather be the companions of retreating virtue, than of advancing villainy, had it even Royalty in its front, Aristocracy in both wings, and a groupe of treacherous, timid, half-made Republicans to bring up the rear.

Accusation 3. They keep their doors shut, admit no members but by ballot, who must engage to keep the secrets of the Society—and they hold their meetings after dinner, and sometimes at night.

We do not keep our doors shut—every person who pleases is at liberty to attend—the Societies in the cities are probably under the necessity of pursuing a different mode, from their being too numerous to admit strangers; and if they are to judge of the disposition of some of their enemies, from the Billingsgate language they frequently use, in the public papers, and which has lately been in great vogue elsewhere, it is natural to suppose that they would breed riots, on purpose to bring the societies into disgrace.—We neither do, nor ever did, exact of our members any promise of secrecy; nor do we know of any other societies that do.—The not admitting members but by ballot, is too puerile and trifling to merit an answer.—The accusation of holding our meetings after dinner, and sometimes at night, must have originated with some drunken debauched sot, who supposed, that like himself, the rest of mankind were seldom sober at those periods.—When our enemies deign to explain the nature of this accusation, we shall endeavor to afford them a rational answer.

Accusation 4. They find fault with every act of government.

The principal acts of government, which the Societies have generally disapproved of, as far as we know, are the Assumption business—the Funding system[15]—the Excise[16]—and the appointment of the Chief Justice of the United States as an Ambassador to a foreign nation;[17] on which last act, the Societies, coinciding in sentiment with a respectable part of the Senate, declared, in their

opinion, was an infringement on the Constitution, and therefore highly improper.—We should be glad to see (if it is within the bounds of possibility) the
arguments made use of in the protest of the minority of the Senate plainly and
clearly refuted, that we may have it in our power to prove that classes of American citizens know the proper distinction between firmness and obstinacy.—As to
the other acts, will you deny, Gentlemen, that a respectable part of our Representatives and of the people, have been as decidedly opposed to them, as the
Societies?—As to us, we have not yet ventured to give an opinion, because doubtful whether our fund of information was sufficient for that purpose.

Accusation 5. They are antifederalist.

We will, in the first place, answer for ourselves, that in the whole Society,
consisting of more than eighty persons, there is scarce a member who could,
either previous to, or since the adoption of the Constitution be, without falshood, distinguished by that appelation.—But though we are not antifederalists,
though we were once warm opposers to men of that description, we find so
many of them friends and supporters of government, upon true republican principles, that we not only most sincerely wish, that the term was obliterated from
the memory of every American, but are well convinced that it cannot be brought
so often into public view, and with such malicious inveteracy, but for some sinister and insidious purposes, for we even find men distinguished by that name, the
most violent opposers to British depradations and machinations of every nature,
and firm adherents to those principles on which our opposition to British tyranny
was first founded.—But still further, that none of our fellow citizens may any
longer be duped by this bugbear so artfully exhibited by Tories and Aristocrats,
we earnestly request them to reflect seriously what an *Antifederalist* really is.—
A Convention presented the form of a Constitution to the people, which they
were to accept or reject, as they tho't proper. This was a task of the most serious
nature which could occupy the minds of an enlightened community. Debates
run high; the people divided; in many states the numbers on each side were nearly
equal—the Federalists advocated the adoption of the Constitution, as handed by
the Convention; the Antifederalists insisted upon amendments, previous to the
adoption.—The Federalists in the State Conventions proved to be the majority—
the Constitution was adopted, and amendments soon after took place.—If this is
not a fair statement, gentlemen, do you be so good as to amend any error there
may be therein; truth is the only aim we have in this concise explanation, and if
this statement is true, must not those persons be the most envenomed enemies
to the happiness of the people at large, who are still endeavoring to blow up a
spark, for the purpose of rekindling that flame of discord, which had so nearly involved the community in such inextricable distress?—We request such of our fellow citizens as have hitherto permitted themselves to be deluded by a name, to
reason without passion or prejudice, upon the above observations, and let their
own good sense dictate afterwards, what the conclusion ought to be.—We will add
for your information, Gentlemen, that a recurrence to the debates in the Conven-

tion of this State, will evince its having been in the spirit of federalism inferior to none in the Union.

Accusation 6. They have promoted and fomented the Western insurrection.

Those who have brought forward this accusation, have guardedly avoided declaring in what manner they have been guilty of this most iniquitous act—whether negatively, by assigning reasons in support of the propriety of repealing the Excise law, or by some positive resolutions of all or any of the Societies. In the first case, every member of Congress, who has given his opinion against that act, since it passed into a law, is equally guilty with the Societies; why then are they not bro[ught] by impeachment to the bar of the Senate?—Sorry we are to think that th[ere] is even one man in the United States, so lost to the spirit and intention of the Constitution, as to criminate any set of men for expressing, in the strongest, while decent terms, their desire of having a law repealed, as long as they pay proper respect to it, during its existence.

We ask our enemies, have any of the Societies failed in this respect? In the second case we know, that a number of the Societies have disapproved publicly of the conduct of the insurgents; while none of our accusers, either in or out of Congress, have produced one single resolution, or even a clause of one, flowing from them, which could tend to commence to foment any resistance to Government.

It is said, indeed, that some individuals, members of some of the Societies, have promised succour to the Insurgents.—That may be true tho' no proof thereof has been exhibited; and if true, we have no knowledge of it. We will ask the gentlemen, however, who thought proper to make the assertion, and thereon to build the accusation, supposing it true, whether he would deem that man an orthodox preacher, whom he heard thundering out damnation against the twelve Apostles, because *Judas Iscariot,* who was one of them, had proved an arrant traitor? or, whether he would not instantly esteem him a man secretly undermining that religion which he affected to admire?—The application is obvious.

Accusation 7. The Charleston Society is condemned to Mr. *Ame's* most virulent censures, (we unfortunately have not his speech before us) because they wished to fraternize with the Jacobins of France, to who he ascribes all the massacres and murders, which have for some time past happened in that country.

The gentleman must excuse us, for doubting the truth of his assertion against that body of regenerated French Citizens, though joined in his calumiations of them, by the unhallowed howling of many royal mouths. In justifications of our want of faith, both of him and his royal friends, though he may emphatically entitle them, *"the lord's anointed,"* we present you, gentlemen, with the following speech of the President of the National Convention, of a very late date, to a deputation from those *Jacobins,* whom Mr. *Ames,* and his royal consorts, so warmly, if not so justly detest and despise:—He says,

"The Republic will never forget, what they owe to a Society, so honorably calumnated by Kings. The *Jacobins* have forcibly contributed to the overthrow of the throne, and at this moment, many of those generous friends of liberty cement with their blood the rights of the people which they have defended with their eloquence. These men are not the mere adherents of individuals; they loved only their country."

With men of this description, Mr. *Ames,* (and really the President of the National Convention ought to know their true character, as well as you can do) we shall ever glory in intermingling our sentiments, our friendship, and our love, should you, and every King on earth continue to lash them with all the malevolent virulence which vindictive impotency never fails to inspire.

You cannot, at least you ought not, Mr. *Ames,* to be surprised, at our observing, that the language you have used respecting the *Jacobins* of France, in contradiction to the opinion of the President of the National Convention, would have appeared much less uncouth, much more natural from the fawning sycophant of some crowned Tyrant, than from one, who avows himself the warm friend of the President of the United States.

Accusation 8. This Society is accused by Mr. Ames, "of having found fault with the unmerited abuse, with which the public papers so frequently teemed against Mr. *Genet,* the Minister of our only ally."

From the nature of this extraordinary charge, sir, you must either be an advocate for unmerited abuse; insist that all which was wrote against Mr. *Genet,* in the public papers, was founded on the justice, decorum, and propriety; or perhaps that no abuse given to the Minister of the French nation, pursuing with enthusiastic ardor, the instructions received from his constituents, could be deemed unmerited.—There is no other alternative which we can think of, sir—Take your choice, and we will then make our reply.

Accusation 9. "The Societies, though perhaps not strictly illegal, are at least useless, and will be more likely to produce evil than good."

We will acknowledge, gentlemen, that this accusation carries in its front more the semblance of truth, than all the rest added together; but let us examine whether it is more than semblance.—In the first place, Has it not been frequently asserted, by men who did not wish to conceal their names, that a proposition was made in that very Convention, which formed our present Constitution, that the Chief Executive should be a Monarch, and the Senate an established Nobility during their lives?—And are there not men who then formed a part of that Convention, and now enjoying the highest offices under the Constitution who did not oppose that proposition?—In the second place, By the very term, Representatives, it must be understood that the intention of their appointments is, for the express purpose of representing the real interests, sentiments, and opinions of the majority of their electors, as far as they can be positively known, and clearly discerned.—Have not the Representatives of the Nation been warmly, and very nearly equally divided, for sundry years[18] upon some subjects of the utmost[19] in a particular manner, Have not the members of Congress been spiritedly and zealously opposed to each other, ever since Great-Britain thought proper to declare war against our only Ally, and in her predatory excursions, to rob a number of our fellow-citizens of their property, and deprive them of their liberty; exciting in the most insidious manner, the Algerines to enslave, and the Savages of America to murder them?—Have not all the old enemies to the liberation of our country from British tyranny, religiously adhered to that class of men in Congress, of whom (Mr. Dayton excepted) you, gentlemen, as far as we know have formed, we will not add a respectable part?—Has not the pusillanimous, the dastardly Mr. *Sedgwick,* (names, which nothing but a plea of an intentional treacherous deserter of his country's rights, in the late war, can save him from) the tory connected Mr. *Ames,* and the British educated Mr. *Smith,* been the warmest advocates on the floor of Congress, in favor of all those measures, of which our old enemies have, in every instance been so enamored?—Is it possible that all those circumstances conjoined, should not give cause of suspicion to the sincere *Republican,* possessing still those feelings so warmly recommended to him by Congress, as his political guide in the years 1775, and 1776?

Have not you, Gentlemen, in all the various stages of the discussions on the important subjects above alluded to, been opposed by men whose firmness and stability in the hour of fiery trial, (generally speaking) rendered them admired, beloved, and revered by the virtuous part of their fellow citizens?—If these observations are not substantially true, Gentlemen, we ought to be reprobated for holding them up to public view:—Tell us therefore, what part you deny—and we will either retract, or evidence shall not be wanting to support our assertions.— If on the other hand they are true, blame us not for faintly imitating that mode of expression, and attack, when speaking of you, at which we are under the necessity of acknowledging, you have demonstrated yourselves to be greatly our superiors.

But to the point:—Under the whole of the above circumstances, was it not time to take such measures as were most likely to prevent the increase of those men's influence, of whose apostacy we had such presumptive proof?—Have not we, whose principles (generally speaking) have been tried and fully proved in the worst of times, an equal right to grant our support to your opponents, as every tory on the continent has to grant his to you and your friends?—We acknowledge that this society was formed, amongst others, for the express purpose, not as some of you have falsely and wickedly hinted, of *opposing government;* but of giving our whole weight and influence, in support of that body of our rulers (in their almost equally divided state) whose present sentiments and opinions correspond with their former expressions and actions; and who, we are convinced, are anxious for promoting the interest, and expressing the real wishes of the great body of the people.

If we effect our purpose, though even but in a small degree will not the virtuous part of our fellow-citizens, reap great benefit thereby?—If, on the contrary, we propagate sentiments contradictory to those of the great body of the people, we must as naturally as deservedly fall into contempt, and dwindle into insignificance.

Where was there the necessity of Congress, forming themselves (*extra officially*) into the grand inquest of the nation, some of them betraying their trust, and prostituting their stations, by an attempt to criminate without proof, and condemn without trial, a numerous and respectable part of their fellow-citizens?—Posterity will not believe, that, but for the firm opposition of forty-seven virtuous Members in the lower House, such a tyrannical wicked measure would certainly have disgraced the history of our independence, even before it had passed its nineteenth year.

As we do not suspect more than one of you, Gentlemen, being amongst the number of those, who merit the appellation of *"real friends of the people;"* we can be but little surprised, that you should wish such unbecoming violence, have endeavored to crush us.

But we affirm in the face of the world (and if this is sedition, bring us to trial, ye abettors of despotism) that we claim our existence as a Society, not as a matter of courtesy, but of right; a right which none but traitors to the majority of the people would attempt to prohibit us from.—We claim it from the original intention of the Constitution, and more particularly from the amendment thereof, which took place on the 4th of March 1789, declaring, "That Congress shall make no law abridging the freedom of speech or the press."—He who digeth a pit for another, often falleth therein himself.

In your chace after us, you have rode with fiery speed, hoping probably that your fine English coursers would either dash out our brains or overwhelm us with dust.—You have been deceived, your expectations have proved vain.—Inspect yourselves and see whether you or we have got most bespattered—remembering always, that it is much more difficult to brush out a stain on the heart arising from plain facts, than from palpable falshood, though affirmed with the impenetrable brass of a *Sedgwick,* or the supercilius vanity of an Ames.—You may possibly, Gentlemen, with a look of disdain (which men enjoying stations they never merited, can put on at pleasure) ask, Who are these, poor, groveling, insignificant *Democrats,* who dare thus to libel us?—(for, says Lord Mansfield, and dare these fellows dispute his authority? "the greater the truth, the greater the libel."—To show you that we wish to gratify you in every reasonable demand, we will tell you—We are eighty four citizens of the county of Chittenden, and State of Vermont, amongst whom are eight Members of the Legislature, all the General Officers of the county, the High Sheriff, the majority of the Bench, and of the Bar, except two, whom prudence has as yet prevented asking for admission.

You, Gentlemen, in contradiction to our real wishes, have compelled us to statement—attribute it, therefore, not to the vanity of any of us, but to the unparalelled arrogance of some of yourselves.

These are but a few of the men who, Mr. *Ames,* on the tip-toe of vanity and ambition, is of opinion can easily be frowned into nothing.

Rely on it, Mr. *Ames,* that a number of them are old soldiers, who esteem themselves perfectly secure from your threats, upon this almost never-failing maxim, "that an overbearing bully in the house, will ever prove an arrant coward in the field."—but perhaps, Mr. *Ames,* you will ask us, if we are ignorant that the best friends to the British *Lion* in this country, have for some years past, emphatically denominated You, Mr. *Sedgwick,* and Mr. *Smith,* of South-Carolina, the three *game cocks of Congress?*—We will admit that this may possibly be true; but as we have long differed from them in our opinion, on most political matters, you will be pleased to pardon us for acknowledging, that we are much more inclined to esteen you the three *dung-hill fowls* of the people; and with that idea we leave you all, Gentlemen, till by a new, unfought for, and unmerited provocation, you court us to come forward again; assuring you, that nothing but a second intemperate breach of the conditions of the following resolution, passed by this Society on the 27th of March last, shall ever prevail on us to forfeit the claim we have to the religious observance thereof, in its fullest latitude and intent:

"*Resolved,* That we esteem the uncontroled freedom of speech in Congress, as one of the greatest bulwarks of our Constitution, and that therefore, no individual member thereof ought ever to be attacked or censured for any expressions used therein, unless absolutely subversive of the rights of the Nation, or the dignity of the House."

Resolved—(that it be made public,)

That in consequence of a report being circulated, that certain members of this Society had endeavored to stir up an opposition to some of the laws of the Federal Government, a citation issued to bring them forward the 1st of November last; but unavoidable casualties prevented the evidences and parties from coming forward, whereby the Society were prevented from making an investigation of the grounds of the report agreeable to their wishes, and accordingly adjorned to the 3d day of February next, at the Court Chamber in Burlington, where it is requested, that those persons formerly called on as evidences, may appear, and give this Society an opportunity to convince the public, that they are resolutely and firmly determined to support the Laws of the United States.

By order of the Society.

STEPHEN PEARL, *President.*

Attext, WILLIAM COIT, *Secretary.*

Spooner's Vermont Journal (Windsor), February 9, 16, 1795; *Vermont Gazette* (Bennington), February 20, 27, 1795

8 | Patriotic Society of the County of Newcastle, Delaware

Declaration of the Political Principles and Constitution, August 30, 1794

DECLARATION OF THE POLITICAL PRINCIPLES OF THE PATRIOTIC
SOCIETY OF NEWCASTLE COUNTY, IN THE STATE OF DELAWARE

DECLARATION, &c.

As free Citizens, both natural and constitutional rights will entitle us to meet together in an associate capacity, and to consult for our common benefit.

In our associate, as well as our individual capacity, we have a right to deliberate upon and determine for ourselves, whether the transactions and administrations of Government be right or wrong; and to publish our opinions thereon.

We apprehend that associations are not more necessary for the cultivation of Arts and Agriculture, than for the improvement of Political Knowledge.

With a view, therefore, to cultivate and diffuse a just knowledge of Rational Liberty, and transmit the glorious inheritance of a free Republican Government unimpaired to Posterity,—WE, the Subscribers, unfettered by religious or national distinctions, unbiassed by party, and unmoved by ambition—the Public Good being our sole object,

DO DECLARE:

1st. That the PEOPLE have the inherent right and power of making and altering forms of Government.

2. That the Republican Constitutions of the United States, and of the State of Delaware, having been framed by the People, it is our duty to support them; and in order to do so effectually, it is both OUR RIGHT AND OUR DUTY, as well as that of every other Freeman, TO REGARD with attention, and DISCUSS with freedom, the conduct of the Public Servants in every department of Government.

3d. That we believe the infirmities of human nature often bias men in power, and induce them to exceed the rules by which they are limited.—It is therefore the DUTY of every good Citizen, to esteem men and measures, according to their

319

INTRINSIC merit; and to approve and aid such as have an influence in prompting the public good.

4. That in the Choice of Persons to fill the offices of Government, it is essential to the existence of a free Republic, That every Citizen should act according to his own judgment; and therefore, any attempt to corrupt or delude the People in exercising the Rights of Suffrage, either by promising the favor of one candidate, or traducing the character of another, is an offence equally injurious to moral rectitude, and Civil Liberty.

5th. That the People of the State of Delaware form but one community, whose Interest, Rights, and Prosperity are the same:—It is therefore the duty of every good Citizen, and shall be the constant endeavor of this Society, not only to remove prejudices, to conciliate the affections, to inform the understanding, and to promote the happiness of all our Fellow Citizens;—but to *detect* and *publish* to the world, every violation of our Constitutions, or instance of Mal-Administration.

CONSTITUTION OF THE PATRIOTIC SOCIETY OF NEWCASTLE COUNTY IN THE STATE OF DELAWARE

SECTION I.
Of the Title.

ART. 1. THIS Association shall be stiled, THE PATRIOTIC SOCIETY OF THE COUNTY OF NEWCASTLE, IN THE STATE OF DELAWARE.

SECTION II.
Of the Formation of the Society.

ART. 1. ALL Citizens of the County, who shall sign the Declaration and Constitution now agreed upon, and pay Fifty Cents, to the Treasurer—except Senators and Representatives of this State, and of the United States, and any person holding any office under this State, or the United States, during their continuance in office—other than Officers of the Militia, shall be Members.

ART. 2. The Society shall consist of a General Meeting of the Associators[1] within the County, and of Meetings of the Associators in every Hundred.

ART. 3. The General Meeting shall be held at Newcastle, four times in each year, to wit: On the last Saturday in the months of May, August, November, and February; and a majority of the Members convened at said Meeting, shall transact the business of the Society.

ART. 4. The Hundred Meetings shall convene and sit on their own adjournments.

ART. 5. The Hundred Associations may correspond with each other, and with the General Society; but public communications shall be made by the General Society only.

ART. 6. The doors of the Society shall be always open.

SECTION III.
Of the Officers and their Duties:

ART. 1. THE Officers of the Society, shall consist of a President, Treasurer, and Secretary.

ART. 2. It shall be the duty of the President, to preside at the Meetings of the Society; to call Special Meetings, when necessary; to decide upon Questions of Order; and to perform such other Duties, as may be required by the Constitution and Rules of the Society.

ART. 3. In case of the absence of the President, the Society shall appoint a President, *pro tempore,* who shall perform all the duties of the President, in his absence.

ART. 4. It shall be the duty of the Treasurer, to keep the Funds of the Society; to collect the Dues, and to pay the Debts of the Society, on the Order of the President; to enter its Accounts in a book to be provided for that purpose; and to perform such other Duties, as may be required by the Rules of the Society.

ART. 5. The Secretary shall keep a Minute of the Transactions of the Society—and a fair Record of such Matters, as they may judge worthy of recording; and perform such other Duties, as may be required by the Rules of the Society.

ART. 6. The first Election of President, Treasurer, and Secretary, shall be held on the last Saturday in August, One Thousand Seven Hundred and Ninety-Four; and afterwards, on the last Saturday in May, annually—who are to continue in Office for One Year: And which Election shall be always by Ballot; and a Plurality of the Votes of the Members present at said time of Election, shall constitute the Choice; any thing in this Constitution to the contrary notwithstanding.

ART. 7. The Hundred Associations shall have like Officers, with the same Duties, as those of the General Society.

SECTION IV.
Of Correspondencies, &c.

ART. 1. All Communications received by the President, or Members of the Society, shall be laid before the next General Meeting, that the Society may take order therein.

ART. 2. This Constitution may be altered or amended by the Society, at any future Meeting, if approved by Three-Fifths of the Members present—provided such amendment be offered for consideration, in writing, at the next preceding Meeting.

Signed by Order of the Society,

JAMES M'CULLOUGH,[2]

Done at Newcastle,⎫   President.
  August 30, 1794. ⎭

      Attest.

         J. BIRD,[3] Secretary.

Pamphlet, Wilmington: Printed by Adams and Smyth, 1794, copy in Historical Society
of Delaware

Resolution Adopted on the Establishment of Public Schools, August 30, 1794

Register of the Proceedings of the Patriotic Society,
Newcastle, August 30, 1794.

On Motion of Mr. Higgins, seconded by Mr. Rodney—
Whereas by our declaration of principles, we have pledged ourselves, among
other things, to promote the diffusion of knowledge among our fellow citizens:
Therefore, Resolved That this Society do recommend to their fellow citizens,
the establishment of schools throughout the State of Delaware, under direction
of Government, whereby the unfortunate children of indigence and neglect,
may be educated and enlightened among the children of opulence and vigilance—
which is an essential means of preserving that equality, so necessary to the preservation of a pure Republican government. And that a Committee of three be
appointed to prepare a Memorial to be laid before the Legislature of this State,
and report the same to our next meeting.
    The Committee are, Messrs. Coram,[4] Vandyke and Rodney.[5]
      Extract from the Minutes.
           J. Bird, Secretary

Delaware & Eastern-Shore Advertiser (Wilmington) September 2, 1794

Memorial to the Legislature on Schools, December 23, 1794

Patriotic Society

Newcastle, Delaware, December 23, 1794.

    The Committee appointed to prepare a Memorial to be laid before the Legisla-
ture, on the subject of Schools, now made their report—which is as follows.

To the Legislature of the State of Delaware, the Memorial of the Subscribers, freemen of the county of Newcastle, in the said state, respectfully sheweth:

THAT your Memorialists, deeply impressed with the sense of the inestimable benefits arising from a general and public system of education, calculated to extend to all the citizens of the State, are constrained to pray your attention to this important subject.

Your memorialists beg leave to suggest, that, although the necessity of some general system of instructing the people hath been long felt and universally acknowledged in most parts of Europe, as well as in the United States, although immense benefits have arisen from such institutions in Scotland and the New England states; although a constitutional provision for public instruction hath existed for some years in this state; although there is scarce a charge given to the Grand Inquests from the Courts of Justice of the United States which does not forcibily inculcate the necessity of public instruction; in short although the political horizon of the United States hath been long enlightened with so many luminous principles on this momentous subject which we would have thought must have darted into every mind, and expanded every heart; yet we are sorry to say, that those to whom the authority of making laws hath been hitherto delegated, have done nothing in the business; and there still remains in the minds of many, a torpor on this subject, as difficult to account for, as to excuse.

Far be it from us to presume to dictate to the Legislature, which at present we have the honor to address; yet we cannot help lamenting the fatal effects of such listless inattention to the first principles of society, which guarantees to every member of the community, the means of acquiring a knowledge of those duties, the performance of which is expected from them. By such inattention to fundamental principles, the bond of society becomes a rope of sand:—and the history of all nations abundantly testify, that no tears can wash away the fatal consequences, or the indelible reproach of such neglect.

As freemen, deeply interested in the happiness of our fellow citizens and anxious for the honor of our country we cannot avoid pressing the Legislature with our earnest solicitations, to take the premises into consideration, and to make some beginning in this important business:—being fully convinced that such government is happiest, and will be most durable, which is supported by citizens well instructed in all their social duties.

The said Memorial being read, and unanimously adopted, the Society earnestly recommend it to their fellow citizens throughout the State, to give their aid in endeavoring to effect the important and laudable design contemplated therein, by signing, and forwarding to the Legislature of the State, without loss of time, similar memorials.

Extract from the Minutes,

J. BIRD, Secretary.

Delaware & Eastern-Shore Advertiser (Wilmington), December 27, 1794

Circular Letter to Patriotic Societies Throughout the United States, n.d.

CIRCULAR.

The Patriotic Society of New-Castle county, in the State of Delaware, To the Patriotic Societies throughout the United States.

Fellow Citizens,

When we consider the causes for which we braved the Storm of British Tyranny, and the consequent success of our struggle in the cause of Liberty, it is with regret and indignation that we behold many influential Characters among us, hastening with giant strides back to those false principles, the opposition of which, has cost us so much blood and treasure.—In order therefore, to counter-act, as much as in us lies, designs of such baneful tendency, we have, from a sense of strict obligations of duty, associated ourselves for the purpose of expos-ing all indirect attempts upon our liberties; and of promoting and diffusing po-litical knowledge among us. And we conceive that the best means to obtain a just knowledge of the principles of Rational Liberty, & to diffuse the same, are by associations of discussion: such associations have been hitherto favourable to other sciences; for it has been well said, that the collision of opposite opinions, produces the spark which lights the torch of truth.

It is perhaps unnecessary, and would be tedious, to enter into a detail of all the inconveniences we labour under; it is sufficient to say, that we have not hastily exercised the right of publicly animadverting upon the conduct of con-stituted authorities: we have much to complain of in our State Government, and not a little in our political relation as Citizens of one of the United States. We are told that our State is indebted to the United States, in the sum of six hundred and twelve thousand dollars and upwards, and no officer in our Government can tell us how this happens. Here is certainly room for enquiry; and as individuals who expect to contribute a portion of this demand, it is somewhat interesting to us to know the true state of this debt.

Such, Fellow Citizens, is the general outline of the motives of our association: we now request your attention the vindication of our conduct, against the asper-sions which have been so unjustly thrown upon us, under the general description of Self-created Societies.

If we were aliens, totally insulated from all political connexion with the peo-ple of the United States, there would be some ground for the clamour raised against us. But, as we are Citizens of the United States, faithful to the con-stitution, and obedient to the Laws, we conceive that we have a full right to all the priviledges of other Citizens; and although we are not the whole of the Peo-ple, nor delegated by them, yet it ought not to be forgotten, that we are at least a part of the whole, and have full claim to the exercise of all the rights and previledges, guarranteed to us by the Constitution of our Country.

If indeed it can be seriously maintained, that the Citizens of the United States cannot legally exercise the right of censuring the conduct of those whom they have entrusted with authority, unless they exercise such right *Una Voce,* then is their boasted Freedom but a sounding brass, a noise without a meaning; and they have indeed fought and died in vain. Surely this spirit of tantalizing us with the exercise of Rights, the exercise of which is morally and practically impossible, proceeds from a vain, unprofitable, and dangerous source.

It is indeed incessantly suggested, that we are only acting under the mask of specious pretences; that our real designs are to overturn the government, and to introduce anarchy and confusion. But we equally despise and detest such unwarrantable insinuations. We can with conscious rectitude, affirm, that there is nothing contained in our constitutions or in our publications, warranting such censure. And we cannot but, deprecate, that more than inquisitorial spirit which passes by our overt acts, upon which only we can be judged, and assuming the province of the Deity, undertakes to condemn us for our secret intentions.

We should be sorry to shoot so wide of the mark with respect to the intentions of our adversaries, as they have with respect to what we are conscious is our intention; and what we hope is the design of all the political associations among us: yet we are strongly inclined to believe, that the uproar lately raised against self-created societies is nothing less than a masked battery levelled against freedom of opinion. But the enemies of liberty are not aware of the magnitude of the enterprize. The monarchy of France, the oldest in Europe, supported by an hereditary Nobility, the most numerous in the old world; by a clergy, possessing two thirds of the property, and ruling with unlimited confidence, and unbounded sway, over the minds and consciences of the people; a government where loyalty was the point of honor, consecrated by immemorial usage, and so deeply engraven on the hearts of all the graduated orders of the people, from the charriot to the plough; that the duration of this stupendous fabric, like the Pyramids of Egypt, seem to bid defiance to the corroding waste of time itself: yet it could not withstand the irrestable force of public opinion.

If the complaints of the self-created societies, are well founded, they will obtain from the public, and we hope also from the government, that attention which well founded complaints ought to receive; but, on the other hand, if those complaints should appear to proceed from a restless, wayward spirit, rather disposed to carp, than actually aggrieved, they will necessarily fall into well merited contempt, and consequent dissolution. Such must be the natural and peaceable issue of this business.

That the will of the majority should govern, is the definition of true rational liberty; and although a very good form of government may be very badly administered; yet we must never suppose, in theory, that the majority of the people can be misled or corrupted. Because the moment that we admit of such a supposition, we abandon the strong hold of freedom, the will of the many, and become subject to the will of the few.

We are disposed to treat this subject with candor, as well as freedom; we are therefore constrained to acknowledge, that in practice the majority may be deceived, and certainly are sometimes misled; yet this is an evil as unavoidable as death. It is morally and physically impossible to escape or avoid this evil, without encountering a much greater, and sanctional principles which are treason against the letter and spirit of our Constitutions. For if we abandon the strong hold of the many, we must subject ourselves to the government of the few; and what security can we have that the Few will not also be deceived?

What man then is there in the United States, who harbours a real sentiment of fear from the effects of Self created societies, who does not, at the same time, abandon the broad principle upon which all legitimate government is founded; to wit, the moral and physical capacity of the majority to govern in all cases?

For if the Self created Societies consist of the majority of the People, they are the nation; but if they do not consist of a thousandth part of the People; holding no delegated authority from them; possessing neither the Purse nor the Sword of the Nation; and violating no law by their associations; what danger can be apprehended from them? The real aristocracy, the few who wish to govern will reply, that the societies will become dangerous; that they will corrupt and mislead the people and instigate them to the subversion of the government. Here they unwarily drop the Mask; they tell you that it is not the societies they fear, but the people; who may be corrupted by the societies, and stimulated to overturn the government. If this is not expressly abandoning the fundamental principle upon which the Constitution of our government is founded, then it is difficult to determine in what dereliction of principle consists.

Who then best deserves the character of Friends to their country, to order, and to government? Those who support with firmness the Constitution, which has subjected the administration of government to the salutary restraint of temperate animadversion; or those who upon the first appearance of alarm, real or imaginary, desert the standard of the Constitution to rally round the officers of government.

What then is the amount of the late attempt to denunciate, and the reasoning of some in authority on this subject, but language to this purpose: "You, the majority of the people, have delegated to us the constituted authorities, the exercise of certain powers; in trust nevertheless, and for your special use and benefit. You have reserved to yourselves as a restraint upon our conduct, the right of publishing your opinions respecting the proper or improper execution of this trust reposed in us. But as this right is now usurped by clubs and used for the purposes of faction and sedition, and will be productive of anarchy and disorder, it becomes our duty as guardians of your welfare, to modify and restrain this right, and it behoves you to submit with respect & allegiance to such our determination." But a sensible and gallant nation is not at this time of day to be jockeyed out of her liberties by such sort of logick; which under the pretext of expediency, permits the government to assume powers essentially national, and to act in the double and inconsistent capacities of truster and trustee, government and nation. Surely the liberties of no people upon earth could stand for a moment against the exercise of such tremendous powers.

The right of the people to assemble and consult for their common good, has been questioned by some; to such we disdain any reply. Others acknowledge the right, but assert that the intentions of the clubs are to overturn the government, and that they therefore ought to be demolished. But it is indeed a hard case that because a few clubs have done amiss, that therefore the people of the United States must be abridged in, or deprived of, the exercise of the censorial power over the conduct of their own servants. It is a maxim as absurd as novel, that the abuse of a right by A. shall work the extinction of the right in B.

It is the rule of all double faced politicians to confound the constitution of government with its administration, and to set up the hue and cry of antifederalism, disorganizations, sedition, and insurrection, against every man who has penetration to discover, and honesty and firmness to expose the improper measures of government. Hence we have been stigmatized as disorganizers, although we have not even hinted that we desire an alteration, in the constitution; and thus even the good qualities of popular associations have with much art and dexterity been played off against us. We have been successful in pulling down a government, it is said, but not in putting up. In reply to such groundless calumny, for calumny it is, we may be permitted to observe, that all principles of organization necessarily involve in them principles of disorganization; to produce an organized body, something must be disorganized; and if the popular associations of America deserve any credit for disorganizing, they deserve no less credit for organizing, unless indeed it can be proved, that the Whigs pulled down the Colonial, and the Tories raised the Federal Government.

To assert that the members of the Popular associations of America, did not materially and essentially contribute towards the organization of the Federal Government, is a premature and indecent outrage upon the living testimony of the present age.

We have not been so much dazzled with the eclat of the exertions of the French Nation in the cause of freedom, as not to have perceived that even that glorious cause, has been stained with unnecessary cruelties. We are also sensible that those cruelties have been attributed wholly to popular societies; but as all the writers who have endeavored to support this charge, have been partizans of aristocracy, who, however they might be disposed to paliate the cruelties of kings, will abate nothing for the phrenzy of popular fermentations, when a long abused people are in the act of taking exemplary vengeance, by breaking their chains over the heads of their oppressors; so we cannot give full assent to the truth of their assertions. That country is too far distant, and the passions of men too violently agitated, to trace the miseries of France to their proper sources. It may not however be amiss to observe that at the time of the massacre of St. Bartholomew,[6] to the cruelties of which the pains of the guillotine are tender mercies, there existed no Jacobin Club: and that faction has run as high, and humanity has been as violently outraged, under the most despotic and monarchical, as under the freest and most popular governments.

As duplicity in the actions of men, entrusted with public confidence, deserves the severest reprehension, we are constrained to take some notice of the conduct of the Representative in Congress from this State. At the formation of this society, the said Representative was present, and a resolution was then entered into, in the following words: "Resolve, that every member present shall declare for himself, whether he approves of popular associations for the purpose of watching over the administration of public affairs, of aiding an upright, or opposing a corrupt administration, and guarding against all encroachments upon the security of property, or personal liberty;" which was unanimously resolved in the affirmative. After having thus sanctioned this association by his vote, the said Representative went to Congress, and voted for the indiscriminate censure of all popular societies.

Such, fellow-citizens, is the outline of the motives of our institution, and such the defence of our conduct. We meet with open doors, and we publish to our country and to the world every communication which we make to, or receive from other societies; and we are conscious of the rectitude of our intentions, so we trust that we will be permitted peaceably to continue our associations, whilst we respectfully submit to, and cheerfully support the Constitution and laws of our Country.

Signed by Order of the Society,

JAMES M'CULLOUGH, President.

(Attest.)

JOHN BIRD,
   Secretary.

Broadside, Historical Society of Delaware

Address to the People of the United States, January 8, 1795

THE ADDRESS OF THE PATRIOTIC SOCIETY OF THE COUNTY OF NEWCASTLE, STATE OF DELAWARE: TO THE PEOPLE OF THE UNITED STATES OF AMERICA.

Fellow Citizens,

At this crisis, when, whether man shall be freed from the trammels of tyranny, or her iron chains be riveted on him forever—is the great question of the day, we appear before your tribunal, upon the most important occasion of our lives; important to ourselves, because the legality of our associations, has been denied by the highest authority; but still more important to our country, because if that denial is warranted by law, our dear bought liberties are not only endangered, but completely annihilated.

Silence in us on such an occasion, might have been construed into an admission of a doctrine highly erroneous, and would have at least amounted to a species of treason against the rights of the community. Considering the subject therefore in this light, we should have thought ourselves unworthy of the greatest honor upon earth, the appellation of American citizens had we remained silent and inactive, while aspersions of the most serious nature were daily thrown out, upon us, from so respectable a source. To the decision then of a free and enlightened people, we cheerfully submit the fate of our institutions, after having candidly unfolded to them, the reasons upon which they are founded, and our views in forming them.

If we consult the lamentable annals of mankind, & cast our eyes back over the historic page we shall find this solemn truth recorded in large characters; that all governments however free in their origin, have in the end degenerated into despotism. The want of vigilance in the people, added to the want of wisdom and consequently of virtue, has been the great cause of promoting that natural tendency in all of them, arising from the imperfection of human nature itself, to slide gradually into the lap of slavery. Athens happy under the wise institutions of a Solon, notwithstanding every effort of that celebrated patriot, fell a sacrifice to the artful wiles of the tyrant Pisistratus.[7] Rome herself, after having nobly rescued herself from the hands of a Tarquin,[8] was enslaved by a Sylla.[9]

Deeply impressed with these sentiments, and taking into our consideration the rapid strides which in this early period of our government, have been made from the republican simplicity of the revolution; we were impelled from a duty we owed to ourselves and our country, to form an association whose express object should be, the diffusion of political knowledge among our fellow citizens. Societies for the promotion of the useful arts and sciences, are sanctioned by the experience of ages, and the numerous advantages which have flown from them to man; but of all the sciences that of government is doubtless the most useful, and the most necessary, tho' least understood; after a period of six thousand years has elapsed since the creation, this glorious science seems yet to be almost in a state of infancy, and therefore requires every citizen who is a friend to the rights of man, like a nursing father to cultivate it with a fostering hand, and with peculiar care and attention.

Conscious also, the vigilance was the only pavilion of security, against all encroachments of government on our rights, we determined to observe with watchful eyes every transaction of the officers of the people, and to publish our honest opinions of them to the world, accordingly as we thought them right or wrong. Every citizen, without distinction, who will support the laws and constitutions of our country, (for they are the basis of our institution, and the preservation of them on their true principles, the foundation of all our proceedings,) is freely admitted a member. We hold our meetings in the face of day, with our doors thrown wide open, that all who chuse may hear our discussions; the only secret we possess, being that of making every thing public.

Not suspecting that calumny herself, would have whispered a single charge against us, we were affected beyond measure, when we saw even the constitutionality of our association denied and every popular society throughout the continent denounced and branded with the disgraceful epithet of *"self-created."* Will it be believed by posterity, that a half a score of years had scarce passed away after an end had been put to the bloody contest for our liberties, before the most sacred of them all, the freedom of opinion was violated, and an attempt made to trample it under foot? It was this darling right that brought about the revolution, and nothing less than the free exercise of it, can transmit unimpaired to our children the inestimable jewel we possess. What were our wise and virtuous committees of safety and correspondence during the war, who laid the corner stone of our independence, in the real sense of the phrase but *self-created* societies: and shall we at this time of day, inpliedly stigmatize the characters of those instruments under heaven of our political salvation, by throwing an odium on societies of a similar kind?

The circumstances call to our minds, the proceedings of that tyrant under whose lash we were once so severely goaded. The memorable proclamation of May 1792, relative to the societies for constitutional information,[10] and the debates on that subject in Parliment, form such a contrast to the case before us, that they deserve to be briefly noticed. In the month of April, 1792, a society of the above description was instituted in London,[11] at the head of which were Messrs. Erskine, Grey and Sheridan, members of Parliament, which was joined by many of the most respectable characters, both in the commercial and literary world. Against this society, his *Majesty's* proclamation was levelled, and then the address was moved for in the house of lords, which was as usual an echo of the proclamation, the Marquis of Lansdowne,[12] after making a number of other eloquent observations, in favour of their constitutionality, proceeded and said,

"To go back no farther than the glorious Revolution, was not the chief means by which that great event was effected—the associations and publications? The same at the Hanover succession. The same in a variety of instances down to the year 1768, when the club of rights, openly wrote letters to all the Mayors and Corporations in the kingdom, inviting them to join in and further a reform in the constitution. At that hour, there were open assemblies of thousands in London, and yet no such measures were taken. So again, when his lordship and the present minister acted in unison: at that time it was one of the strong measures mutually agreed upon, that a moderate reform in the legislature as well as the executive branches, was become a measure absolutely necessary to preserve the constitution, by wiping off the rust and canker, and bringing it to its primitive beauty and splendor. At that period upwards of *thirty counties* were *associated* and regular meetings were held, to obtain the very object which the associated gentlemen now want to effect. There was then no proclamation issued to command the discontinuance of such associations; and if there had, it would have been useless, because highly unconstitutional."

And Mr. Fox,[13] speaking on this same topic in the house of Commons, delivered himself in the following masterly manner:

"We have read of religious persecutions; of the implacable oppressions of the Roman See; of the horrors of the inquisition of Spain; but so obdurate, so hard, so intolerable a scheme of cruelty, was never engendered in the mind much less practised, by any tyrant spiritual or temporal. For see to what lengths they carry this system of intellectual oppression: under various pretexts there have been tumults and disorders, but the true design was to overturn the constitution, so says the speech; and mark the illustration of the right honourable magistrate— (Sir James Sanderson the Lord Mayor of London, the mover of the address). "There have been various societies established in the city of London, instituted for the plausible purpose of merely discussing constitutional questions, but which were really designed to propagate these seditious doctrines." So then by this new scheme of tyranny we are not to judge of the conduct of men by their overt acts, but are to arrogate to ourselves at once the province and the power of the deity. We are to arraign a man for his secret thought, and punish him because we choose to believe him guilty? "You tell me indeed," says one of these municipal inquisitors, that you meet for an honest purpose; but I know better, your plausible pretext shall not impose upon me; I know your seditious design. I will brand you as a traitor by *my own proper authority*." What innocence can be safe against such a power; what inquisitor of Spain, of ancient or of modern tyranny can hold so lofty a tone? Now this, Sir, is the crisis which I think so truly alarming. We are come to the moment, when the question is, whether we shall give to the king, that is, to the Executive Government, complete power over our thoughts? Whether we are to resign the natural faculties to the ministers for the time being? or whether we shall maintain that in England no man is criminal, but by the commission of overt acts forbidden by the law? This I call a crisis more eminent and tremendous, than any the history of this country ever exhibited.—I know well that there are societies who have published opinions, and circulated pamphlets, containing doctrines tending if you please to subvert our establishments; and I say they have done nothing unlawful in this, for their pamphlets have not been suppressed by law. Shew me the law that orders these books to be burnt, and I will acknowledge the illegality of their proceeding; but if there be no such law, you violate the law yourselves in acting without authority. You have taken upon you to do that, for which you have no warrant, and you vote they are guilty. What is the course prescribed by law; If any doctrines are published tending to subvert the constitution in church or state, you may take congnizance of the act in a court of law. What have you done? Taken upon you, *by your own authority* to suppress them! To erect every man not merely into an inquisitor, but into a judge, into a spy, into an informer; to set father against son, brother against brother, and neighbour against neighbour; and in this way you expect to maintain the peace and tranquility of the country! You have gone upon the principles of slavery in all your proceedings; you neglect in your conduct the foundation of all legitimate government—*the rights of the people; the rights of man.*"

These manly arguments and observations delivered in a despotic clime, certainly apply with additional force in this free country, and are a complete answer to all the declamation and futile reasoning, of certain gentlemen on this subject, which to the honour of the age a virtuous Republican majority, in the House of Representatives, proceeding immediately from the people themselves, disdained to subscribe to and finally rejected the unjust and illiberal proposition, for sanctioning this first attack on the freedom of opinion in the United States. By their spirited conduct, in all probability, they have fixed an eternal barrier, that will forever prevent another's being made, and have erected a great sea mark by which our state pilots may avoid in future, the rock upon which they lately lay nearly ship-wrecked.

The language of the immortal Milton, a great authority in all learning, in his most eloquent address to the parliament of Britain on a similar occasion, ought not to be forgotten.

"Believe it lords and commons," says the venerable Milton, "they who counsel you to such a suppressing of opinions, do as good as bid you, suppress yourselves, and I will soon shew you how.

"If it be desired to know the immediate cause of all this free writing and free speaking, there cannot be assigned a truer than your own mild, free and humane government; it is the *liberty,* Lords and Commons, which your own valorous and happy counsels have purchased us; liberty which is the nurse of all great wits; this is that, which hath enfranchised, enlarged, and lifted up our apprehensions, degrees above themselves. Ye cannot make us now less capable, less knowing, less eagerly pursuing the truth, unless you first make yourselves, that made us so, less the lovers, less the founders of our true liberty. We can grow ignorant again, brutish, formal and slavish, as ye found us; but you then must first become that which ye cannot be, oppressive, arbitrary and tyrannous, as *they* were from *whom you have freed us.* That our hearts are now more capacious, our thoughts now more erected to the search and expectation of the greatest and exactest thing, is the issue of your own virtue propagated in us. *Give me the liberty to know, to utter, and to argue freely, according to conscience, above all liberties.*"

Various were the pretexts brought forward in Congress to induce a concurrence with the censure, every argument which the accuracy of long preparation could suggest was urged, genius herself tortured, ingenuity put to the rack, and appeals to the passions made, but in vain, the Representatives of a free people, impressed with the same sentiments of Milton, with the dignity and firmness of true Republicans, refused to subscribe, implicitly, to the opinion of the wisest and best of men, who has been justly stiled the pride of peace and the support of wars when contrary to their honest judgments, and have no doubt received the approbation of the illustrious Washington for this display of their genuine independence; for being so wise, his wisdom has taught him, less confidence in his own opinions, and that to err belongs to human nature.

We have been accused of being the origin of the western insurrection; but is it not known to the world, that the opposition to the excise, began with the law itself, and that many years ago while it existed under the government of Pennsylvania, numbers in that very spot which was the seat of the insurrection, were compelled to pay the penalty incurred by a non-compliance with the law? Are not these facts notorious from the official report on the subject, in the hands of everybody; and after all this, will it be seriously said, that the societies were the cause of that, which, there is conclusive evidence, existed long before they themselves had a being?

But even allowing, for argument sake, the contrary to be the fact, that the opposition to the excise arose since the birth of the present popular societies. We believe it has never been even asserted, that the societies themselves went farther in opposing the excise law, than they were fairly warranted by the constitution; but then it is said that their justifiable resistance to it produced the open opposition; now, granting this to be the case (which we totally deny) we would ask you, whether when the Legislature of a free country are so inattentive to the voice of their constituents, and so forgetful of their relation to them, as to pass a law which from its repugnance to the common feelings of their fellow-citizens, who have more than once declared it to be the *horror of all free states,* as that an honest constitutional resistance to it, which every citizen who sincerely thinks it wrong, is bound to give, will necessarily endanger it; who are to blame? Those independent citizens, who acted not only a virtuous but a laudable part, in constitutionally opposing a law, which they honestly thought improper; or that legislature spurning the maxims of a free government, enacted a law in such direct hostility with the great sentiments of the people? Certainly no man will hesitate a moment in declaring the blame should lay at their door; for we hold it, as a received opinion, that a representative, when it is indisputably clear, is bound by the voice of his constituents. We do not mean by these observations to justify the conduct of the greatest enemies to democratic government that ever existed, and who have given a deep stab to the cause of Republicanism; on the contrary we severely reprobate it, and are ready at any hour of our lives to lay them down in defence of the very first principle of our liberty and happiness, *that the minority shall submit to the will of the majority;* all we mean is simply to assert, that any individual citizen (and of consequence a society which is a collection of individuals) can never be blamed for a constitutional resistance to a law, which he believes from the bottom of his heart to be a bad one; and that if in consequence of his constitutional resistance, any unfortunate event should follow, the burthen of blame should lay upon the shoulders of that legislature who passed it, rather than on him, if it must rest upon either.

But we will go still farther, and admit that some of the societies have actually abused this constitutional right, which is not impossible for like all others it may be abused, and what then? Are we to argue from the abuse of a thing against the use it? If we were, nothing, not even the sacred scriptures themselves, those oracles of God, would escape our censures; for they too in common with all other blessings, are liable to be abused.

If we were once robbed of this palladium of our rights, this divine panacea for every evil in government, we should soon become subject to the will of a foreign tyrant, or to a much more to be dreaded faction at home; for a tyrant might be swept off with his supporters, while there was a spark of public virtue existing, by a rising of the people like a torrent in favour of their liberties. But a faction would go more artfully to work, they would corrupt the very source of society, they would degenerate the republican principles of the people, and the want of public virtue in a democratic government, is a loss which can never be repaired.

Fellow-Citizens, the *freedom of opinion* has been in every clime and country, the last liberty which the people have been able to wrest from power; uniformly power has resisted the propagation of truth; all other concessions it has been willing to make, but against the truths of reason, against the light of knowledge it has maintained an eternal war. Other liberties are held under government; but the *liberty* of *opinion* keeps governments themselves in due subjection to their duties. This has produced the martyrdom of truth in every age, and the world has only purged itself from ignorance with the innocent blood of those who have enlightened it. For this right we fought and bled seven long years; for this right, a Warren, a Mercer and a Haslet fell; and at the shrine of the freedom of opinion we are still ready to immolate our fortunes and our lives.

Resolved, That the foregoing address be published in *The Delaware and Eastern Shore Advertiser.*

(Signed)

JAMES MCCULLOUGH,
President.

Attest.

J. BIRD, Sec.

Wilmington, Ja. 8, 1795.

General Advertiser (Philadelphia), January 20, 1795

9 | Republican Society of Baltimore, Maryland

Constitution, May 24, 1794

CONSTITUTION
OF THE REPUBLICAN SOCIETY OF BALTIMORE.

AMONG the acknowledged truths, which attempts to explain cannot render more evident, we recognize the *right* of every individual to the enjoyment of happiness, and *the obligation* to secure and transmit to posterity, unsullied and undiminished, the blessings of freedom.—*This right,* derived from nature, and engrafted into the human mind with the first principles of existence, remains unaffected by the *social compact*—and *that* obligation, which is coeval with the right, exists immutably and eternally.—In that instant, when the *right* shall be impaired, or the obligation to preserve its attendant blessings, shall cease to be a moving principle thro' every class of society, the reign of tyranny commences.— It was from this cause that the human race degenerated from freeman to slaves— and without a greater degree of vigilance than has of late been manifested, the same people who *first supported* the principles, and cherished the enjoyment, of civil liberty, will be the *first* fitted for the views of tyranny, and the attacks of corruption.—The flame of liberty must extend or be extinguished:—Patriotism must support, and jealousy, the attendant of freedom, guard the altar on which it blazes, with incessant watchfulness.

The spirit of domination which has marked the course of the combined tyrants of Europe, excites a well grounded apprehension, that America is implicated in the fate of the French republic.

Impressed with these sentiments, we, the subscribers, citizens of the United States, solemnly pledge ourselves to each other, and to the world, that we will observe the constitution and the laws of our country—that we will support, maintain, and defend the cause of liberty, equality, and national justice—and, that we will oppose tyranny, corruption, and oppression, in whatsoever form they may be exhibited. It is for this purpose, we form ourselves into a society, to be called the REPUBLICAN SOCIETY OF BALTIMORE, and do hereby establish the following constitution and regulations for our government.—

CONSTITUTION.

I. The officers of the society shall consist of a president, vice-president, secretary, treasurer, a standing committee, consisting of the vice-president and six members, and a corresponding committee, consisting of four members and the secretary, to be elected by ballot, on the first Monday of June annually.

II. The president, or, in his absence, the vice-president, shall have a casting vote in all cases of an equal division of the society: shall preserve order, and decide all questions respecting the same: shall subscribe all public acts of the society; and whenever they may judge proper, or six members require it, shall call a special meeting of the society. All letters on the business of the society shall be addressed to him.

III. The secretary shall keep fair records of the proceedings of the society.

IV. The treasurer shall receive and apply the funds of the society under the direction of the president, or, in his absence, the vice-president, & standing committee.

V. The standing committee shall, during the recess of the society, attend to such business as will best promote the object of the association, and report the same to every stated meeting.

VI. The corresponding committee shall conduct the correspondence of the society, under the direction of the president, or, in his absence, the vice-president.

VII. All persons hereafter proposed as members, shall be balloted for at the stated meetings, subsequent to any meeting of the society, in which they shall have been nominated.—No person shall be balloted for as a member, unless thirty members, at least, be present, and four-fifths concur in his admission.

VIII. All members who, by the judgment of the society, shall be deemed unworthy to continue members, shall be suspended, dismissed, or expelled, by a majority of the attending members, being not less than fifty.

IX. The society shall meet on the first Monday in the months of June, September, December and March.

X. All propositions relative to the alteration or amendment of this constitution, shall be made in writing, and remain unacted upon, until the next stated meeting after that in which the same shall have been proposed;—and, if approved by two-thirds of the members present, shall be received as part thereof.

XI. That twenty-four members attending shall be competent to the ordinary business of the society. And in case of the absence of the president and vice-president, the society shall elect a president, pro tem.

A Meeting of the Republican Society of Baltimore, *will be held at* EVANS'S Tavern, THIS AFTERNOON, *at* 7'oclock, *to receive applications from such as wish to become members,—agreeably to the Constitution.*
Baltimore, May 24, 1794.

Baltimore Daily Intelligencer, May 24, 1794

To All Other Societies, n.d.

To all other Societies established on principles of Liberty and Equality, Union, Patriotic Virtue and Perserverance.

We, the members of the Republican Society of Baltimore, certify and declare to all Republican or Democratic Societies, and to all Republicans individually, that Citizen Joshua Barney hath been admitted and now is a member of our Society, and that, from his known zeal to promote Republican principles and the rights of humanity, we have granted him this our certificate (which he hath signed in the margin) and do recommend him to all Republicans, that they may receive him with fraternity, which we offer to all those who come to us with similar credentials.

(Signed) Alexander M'Kim,[1]
President

In testimony where of, etc.
George Sears,[2] secretary.[3]

Harper's Encyclopedia of the United States (New York, 1902), 3: 79-80; Benson J. Lossing, *The Pictorial Field-Book of the War of 1812* (New York, 1869), 88

List of Officers, June 14, 1794

List of the officers to the *Republican Society* of Baltimore
President, Alexander M'Kim.
Vice President, William Van Wyck.[4]
Secretary, George Sears.
Treasurer, Thomas Dixon.[5]
Standing Committee, Paul Bentalou, Thomas Rutter,[6] Thomas Johnson,[7] Solomon Etting,[8] John Stricker,[9] John Spear.[10]
Corresponding Committee, James A. Buchanan,[11] James Winchester,[12] Edward Johnston, William M'Creery.[13]
New York Journal, June 14, 1794

Celebration of the Fourth of July, 1794

Baltimore, July 7

Celebration of 4th of July

During the celebration of the day, the first cause of our great revolution and arduous struggle for our birthright (liberty) was not suffered to be forgotten—nor was the cause of humanity in sympathy with the unfortunate African, and in endeavoring to loosen his shackles, permitted to suffer. An elegant and learned oration on the abolition of slavery was delivered to the Abolition Society, at the court-house, by that distinguished friend to humanity, Doctor Drysdale.—

The Republican Society, after partaking in the duties and amusements of the forenoon, met at the Assembly-room at 5 o'clock, when an Oration was delivered by citizen Archibold Buchanan,[14] on the cause of the late contest with Great Britain. The Oration, whether considered with a view to its composition or delivery, was elegant and interesting, and does equal credit to the talents and patriotism of the author. After this, and the business of the day, they dined at Mr. Grant's, and spent the evening with a great deal of hilarity. The following toasts were drank:

1. The events of the 4th July, 1776—May the principles which gave rise to them be universal, and their duration eternal.

2. The events of the 14th July, 1789—May every oppressed people on earth imitate the conquerors of the Bastile.

3. The United States of America.

4. The republic of France, one and indivisible.

5. George Washington—May every country find a Washington, and every Washington an enlightened people.

(*cheers.*)

6. The patriots of Poland.

7. The national convention of France, and an emulation of their virtues by the American congress.

8. The militia of the United States.

9. The Agriculture of the United States—May it ever maintain its merited influence in our public councils.

10. Encouragement and protection to the commerce and manufactures of the United States.

11. May oppression ever meet effectual resistance.

12. The societies of the friends of the people, throughout the world.

13. Universal liberty and extinction of monarchy.

14. Complete satisfaction from Great Britain—or—WAR. (*cheers.*)

15. Existence, as lasting as time, and friendship as lasting as existence, between the republics of France. (*cheers.*)

Baltimore Daily Intelligencer, July 7, 1794

Resolutions Adopted on the Insurrection in Western Pennsylvania, September 4, 1794

BALTIMORE, September 4.

At a stated quarterly meeting of the Baltimore Republican Society, held at Mr. Grant's on Tuesday the 2d of September, 1794, the following resolutions were unanimously agreed to, viz.

Resolved, as the opinion of this society, that all attempts to oppose the execution of constitutional laws, by force, are improper, dangerous to freedom, and highly unbecoming good citizens.

Resolved, as the opinion of this society, that the attempt in the western part of Pennsylvania to oppose the collection of duties on distilled spirits merits disapprovation and censure, as its tendency is to prostrate all the just powers of government, and produce anarchy and civil war.

Resolved, as the opinion of this society, that every opposition to the said act, except that of remonstrance and application to the constitutional authority, is equally censurable and dangerous.

Resolved, as the opinion of this society, that the conduct of the President of the United States, as well in calling forth the militia to suppress so dangerous a spirit, as also first attempting an amicable termination by negociation, was wise, prudent, and constitutional, and therefore deserving of the approbation and support of this society.

True extract from the minutes.

Published by order of the society.

Archibald Buchanan, Sec. pro. tem.

General Advertiser (Philadelphia), September 11, 1794

Address to the Government and People of the United States, December 9, 1794

TO THE GOVERNMENT AND PEOPLE OF THE UNITED STATES.

_____

FELLOW CITIZENS,

The censure lately thrown out on all Popular Societies within the United States, comes from too respectable a source not to have attracted the public attention. In their particular conduct these societies are declared to be instrumental in promoting the late insurrection to the westward; in their general principles they have been deemed unfriendly to all law and government. No epithet, however harsh and indecent, that they have not been thought to deserve; no purpose, however dark and horrid, that has not been attributed to them. Eloquence, which might have adorned an Athens or a Rome, has been laboured to blacken their actions and their principles, and the "Rags and Fritters of Society" have been blown upon from one end of the continent to the other.

Such general and indiscriminate reproaches, should they have come from the meanest quarter, must naturally excite indignation in the breasts of the innocent; but coming from one which is supposed to combine the greatest wisdom and caution, as well as all the power of the nation, must further produce a desire to wipe them away. And indeed, to let them pass on unnoticed would, in the opinion of the Republican Society of Baltimore, be to subscribe to their own condemnations; and to merit those injurious appellations of the disturbers of public happiness, the incendiaries and the petty tyrants of society, the assassins of virtue and character that have been, so liberally, heaped upon them. And though, from a conscious propriety of their own views and conduct, they see no necessity for a public vindication of themselves; yet, respect to the rulers of their country, which, notwithstanding the assertion of some men, they have never lost sight of; to their own character which they value above life; to the good opinion of their fellow-citizens, which it is their pride, as well as interest, to revere; and to that constitution which they look upon as the noblest "safeguard of human rights" ever yet devised by the wisdom of man, prompt them to declare the truth, both as to the part they have acted respecting the late insurrection, as also the general reasons and principles of their institution.

First, that we should be thought to have, in any manner, contributed to the origin or support of an insurrection which we deplore as the most grievous dishonour that ever befell our country, affects us the more sensibly in that, at the very early period, we hastened, by resolutions inserted in the public papers, to express our entire disapprobation of it; and have since, by every means in our power, and many of us by obeying the call of the executive to arms, as has been, truly, observed by a worthy representative of our state, endeavoured to discountenance and to quell it. Well convinced of the inseparable connexion between law and liberty; and that the principle in our constitution which enjoins that "the will of the majority shall prevail" is not only the most "luminous" but the only practicable principle of rational freedom, we beheld with as much indignation, at least, as all others of our fellow-citizens, an attempt to violate both; and hesitated not a moment, unanimously and publicly to express it.—Did our accusers derive the sentiments they have, so confidently, imputed to us from these our resolution? It cannot be. Let them, then, declare to the people, who have a right to be informed, from some conduct of ours, or from what other source of information, they have! Is it from the report of the secretary of the treasury,[15] written with a professed view "to give the citizens at large full information on the subject of the disturbance?" We see nothing there to warrant the opinion, but, again, have omissaries from us been detected in the western counties of Pennsylvania, fomenting discontent and insurrections among the citizens? Have we, by letter or otherwise, exhorted them to persevere in opposition to the laws? Have we sympathized with them in the grievances, either real or pretended, which they affected to labour under? Have we, to this day, expressed an opinion on the law of excise, either one way or the other? To all these quotions, with our hands upon our hearts, and appealing to him who knoweth the secrets of all men, we positively answer no. Why then, has our conduct been represented as like that of so many crocodiles weeping over these very laws and that constitution which, inwardly, we were resolved to destroy? Was it because that, in this country, dungeons, chains and death awaited the man who would dare to express a disapprobation which he felt respecting the form or the measures of government.

Was it because that, if real grievances oppressed us, there was no other mode of getting rid of them then by the direful and precarious resort to civil war? Was it because that it would not have seemed wiser to seek reparation in the good sense and justice, than in the blood of our countrymen; to have tried them by petition before we provoked them to Rebellion? Was it because that, among us, the liberty of the press was interdicted, and liberty of speech reckoned sedition, that we should be under the necessity of pursuing the most lawful end by the most unlawful means, and of "meeting in the dark to perform incantations" against a law which we had an aversion to, or against a Constitution which we did not approve? It would look indeed, as if personal rancour or impatience of public security which, we thank God, is *yet* the natural and constitutional right of all our citizens whether individually or collectively, had no little share in the conduct of our accusers, or as if that the censure which, for aught we know, some other societies may have deserved, has, hastily at least, been extended to us. Let our fellow-citizens judge? On the opinions of men accustomed to think for themselves, chearfully, we rely; well assured that "strong assertions without proof" will not, readily, be credited against us, and that, even should they, we have, still, the consciousness left of not having deserved them.

With respect to the reasons and principles of our institution, that the public has not, before, been possessed of them, has been more owing to want of attention than of respect in us to their good opinion. When we contemplated the history of nations which has lost their freedom, some from ignorance, some from supineness and some from the intrigues and artifices of ambitious men, it appeared to us that a wise people could not exhibit too much care and activity in the preservation of that invaluable blessing. Among others which occurred, the establishment of a society, whose object it should be to study the laws and constitution of their own and other countries, to watch the operations of government and scrutinize the principles and conduct of men in power, appeared a very likely means of effecting that great end; as being well calculated to dispel ignor-

ance, to rouse supineness and to counteract ambition. A Nation which under-
stands its rights, will not be apt to neglect them, and a nation anxious for the
preservation of its rights will not, easily, fall a sacrifice to artifice or power.
Slavery has, ever, been the consequence of ignorance, and no people ever yet
lost their liberties till they had first, lost the knowledge of them. Now, how is
this knowledge more likely to be acquired and maintained then among a society
of men, who, to the constant habit of investigating their rights, adds, likewise,
that of applying them to all the proceedings of our public bodies; and who, enjoying the perfection of science, constantly combine principle with practice!
Now does it appear that politics is less a science or dependent on less steady and
inflexible principles than any other which is the object of human research; nor is
the idea of a school for acquiring a knowledge of the nature of laws and government more absurd than that of one for acquiring a knowledge of astronomy and
the mathematics. And if from the latter we may learn to trace the wanderings
of a planet, so from the former may we know the certain effect of certain laws
and government to a people! And shall societies, for the encouragement, of the
meanest arts among men, meet with the public approbation and encouragement,
while a society for the study of the noblest of all arts, of the freedom, the dignity and the happiness of man be deemed unworthy of regard. But if we believed that this institution would tend to beget a knowledge of our rights, we,
also, believed that this knowledge, in its turn, would beget a spirit of independence, both in sentiment and action, unfavourable to the admission of slavery.

The man, who, to the natural love adds the true knowledge of freedom will
not, easily, be deceived by forms and names which exhibit but the appearance
without the reality of what they have been: bare authority without truth of justice he will despise; and respect custom and prejudice no further than as they
appear to be founded in reason and nature. Habituated to consider himself as
equally entitled with all others, from the gift of his creator, to the enjoyments
of his life, his understanding, his property and his liberty, he will, before he re-
signs them to any man or set of men, be prompted to enquire by what right it is
they demand them. And this will, admirably fit him for promoting a third effect
contemplated by our institution—that of resisting the intrigues and violence of
ambitious men.

That there have been such men in all countries, history, but too well, convinces us; that there may be such in our own common prudence would prompt us
to suspect. Add that these men should have some other controul over them then
what barely results from the Constitution and the laws is an opinion derived from
experience, when we consider how Caesar by preserving the sacred names of Senate and Consul, had art to change the whole nature of government in Rome; and
how in succeeding times, the free Governments of Venice, Geneva, the United
Provinces and of several other countries of Europe have been changed the most
into Aristocracies and yet retained the name of republics.—The advances of ambition are often through the most secret ways; it has appeared under the different
masks of religion, of patriotism and even of scorn for public life.

There are instances of men who have ventured their health, their fortunes and their lives in the service of their country, that they might, afterwards, midst the stupid gaze of popular admiration, slide down, like molten gold, into its very vitals. There are instances, again, of others who setting out with the purest zeal for the Liberties of Mankind, have been corrupted in their progress and could never afterwards, be induced to lay down the authority which the gratitude of a Nation or the necessities of the times had entrusted to them. And it appeared to us that, added to those proceeding from the Laws, from a perfect freedom of speech and of the press, a Society of Men whose duty it should be to watch the proceedings of our public Officers, would form not the least respectable or effectual check to such men. In times of public necessity, this Society would sound the alarm, and, mixing among their fellow-citizens, rouse them to a contemplation and sense of their danger. And what though the alarm be, sometime, false, will it, for that reason, never be true?—What though Rome produced a Fabius,[16] did she not likewise a Cromwell? What though America has produced a Washington, may she not likewise a Dumourier?[17] And is it not better that one man should lose his place, or even his life than millions their liberties from the ever security of the people? Moreover the persecution of the good cannot last long. Popular frenzy will blow over and real virtue, like the sun, though it may be obscured, for a moment, with spots and clouds, will again reassume its seat in all its meridian heat and splendour, and though it should, even, set in darkness, it sets only to rise with greater glory, in an happier country!

These are the reasons which induced certain citizens of the Town of Baltimore to form themselves into a Republican Society. Whether they be substantial, or otherwise let, our fellow-citizens judge. For ourselves we declare that they appeared convincing to our Reason and binding on our Conscience. And if to these we add the warmest attachment to the Laws and Constitution of our Country; if we profess no principles of Government but in common with yourselves, and assemble only for preservation; if we exercise no unlicensed power; if we arbitrarily controul no Man's actions; if we touch no man's property; if we violate no Man's liberty; if we demean ourselves like peaceable and good citizens, we expect and demand to be permitted the enjoyment of our institution in peace; and only request that you will judge us by our actions. If these shall be deemed innocent we hope, at least, to pass without censure; if they shall be deemed otherwise, then will we expect, and we will be contented that you should "from us" if you please "into nothing."

Published by order of the Republican Society of Baltimore.

ROBERT MICKLE, Sec'ry
Protem. Dec. 9, 1794.

General Advertiser (Philadelphia), December 17, 1794

10 | Democratic-Republican Societies of Virginia

REPUBLICAN SOCIETY OF NORFOLK AND PORTSMOUTH, NORFOLK

Declaration of Sentiments and Principles, June 3, 1793

At a meeting of the standing committee of the *Republican Society* of Norfolk and Portsmouth, on the third of June, 1793.

Resolved,

That it is the opinion of this Committee, that the *Declaration,* comprising an exposition of the sentiments and principles upon which this society has been formed, be published in the Norfolk papers.

"Declaration.

"We, the undersigned citizens, declare as our unalterable opinion, that the blessings of a just, mild and equitable government can only be perpetuated by that pure spirit of republican vigilance to which (under favor of the the Supreme Governor of the Universe) we owe our perfect political ease, tranquility and happiness.

"That the inattention which many of our fellow citizens discover toward the dearest rights, privileges and immunities of freemen, is to us matter of serious concern and regret.

"That the excellence of a mild representative government (affording an example of the happiness of equal liberty) will excite jealousies in the minds, and be painful in the sight of tyrants and their abettors: it does therefore behove men, who are experiencing the blessings of freedom, to be ever on the watch to guard against the machinations of those enemies of mankind.

"That the imaginary security into which we have been lulled, by our remote situation from the combined despots of Europe, and other considerations, may have the most fatal tendency: if not to destroy our independence as a nation, at least to sap the foundation of that glorious fabric upon which our liberties rest; our free and excellent constitution.

"That it becomes Republicans at all times to speak their sentiments freely and without reserve; but more particularly at this alarming period, when we behold the Tyrants of the world combined, and every engine of despotism employed in making a grand effort to crush the infant spirit of freedom, recognized by our brethren of France; whose virtuous exertions (in a cause so lately our own) we cannot as men, and as republicans, behold with indifference, or contemplate without a mixture of sympathy and admiration.

"That it is a truth, not less notorious than it is to be lamented, that in the bosom of our country we have men whose principles and sentiments are opposed to all free government, and that such are just objects of suspicion.

"That strongly impressed with these sentiments, we have conceived it to be our interest, but more particularly our duty, to form this Association, for the purpose of strengthening the bands of Union, and of cherishing republican sentiments, manners, morals and affections."

Virginia Chronicle (Norfolk), June 8, 1793

Civic Festival for the Consul of the French Republic, February 8, 1794

NORFOLK, Feb. 8.
CIVIC FESTIVAL.

ON Wednesday last a number of Democratic Citizens of Norfolk and Portsmouth, gave a *civic entertainment* to the Consul of the French Republic, the Commanders and Officers of the frigates Normande and Ambuscade, the Captain of the Merchant ships in the port and a number of other patriotic citizens. This entertainment was given in order to congratulate our allies upon the success of the French Arms against the armies of despotism[1]—The morning was ushered in by firing of cannon, and a display of colors from the American and French shipping—At eleven o'clock the citizens repaired to the point in Portsmouth, and at twelve precisely fired a salute of fifteen guns, which was returned by the Normande frigate and the French Merchantmen—The Marseiles hymn was then sung—The ardour with which every countenance was animated, it is impossible to describe—The two republics being drank by every Citizen present, the company formed a procession; martial music in the front—An American Citizen bearing the Flag of the United States, a Citizen bearing the tree of Liberty; then followed the Citizens in ranks of four, two American Citizens and two French—in this order they marched to the county wharf, where boats were provided to convey the company to Norfolk—The boats following each other in exact line, decorated with flags, and the shipping meanwhile firing cannon had a most pleasing effect— The Citizens, forming as they landed, moved on in the same order. When arrived on the parade, they halted and the Marseilles hymn was again sung—It was here the scene became highly interesting—No language can convey the joy and fraternal affection which beamed in the eye of every *patriotic* French and American citizen— The air resounded with shouts *long live the Republic of France and America.* Crouds of citizens testified their joy and admiration by enthusiastic acclamations—The serenity of the day served greatly to encrease the grandeur of the scene. And what above all heightened the pleasure, was a large and beautiful assemblage of the fair at the doors and windows, whose lovely countenances were greatly animated, and showed that they partook in the happiness of the day—At 3 o'clock the company sat down to dinner at the Borough Tavern—After dinner the following Toasts and Sentiments were drank in the French and American language—viz.

1. The United States of America.
2. The Republic of France.
3. A perpetual alliance between the Republic of America and France, and may disgrace and infamy cover the man who attempts to disunite them, (3 times.)
4. The Congress of the United States.
5. The National Convention of France.
6. Citizen Washington, President of the United States.
7. Citizen Genet, Minister Plenipotentiary of the French Republic.
8. The Patriotic navies and armies of France, may liberty, peace and independence be the reward of their gallant services. (3)
9. The arm of Hercules to those who combat the Hydra of Despotism.
10. May the light of freedom which was kindled in America and reflected to France in a blaze, illuminate the whole, and lay despotism in ashes.
11. May the dominion of Kings and superstitution give place to the dominion of Laws and Reason.
12. Liberty to the oppressed, and the guillotine to the oppressors.
13. Galling chains to those who promote Algerine depredations. (3 times)
14. A general peace upon the solid basis of general Liberty.
15. The memory of those who have fallen in defence of American and French freedom; may their names ever dwell on the Frontispiece of the Temple of Universal Liberty. (3)

By the French Citizens,

Prosperity to the towns of Norfolk and Portsmouth.

During the entertainment a number of Patriotic songs were sung in the languages of the two nations—and about sunset the company parted, saluted by a discharge from the artillery of the Borough.

Upon the whole we do not recollect on any occasion, to have witnessed a scene so highly interest, nor do we conceive it possible that the affection which the good citizen of each nation bear to each other, was ever more fully demonstrated—Order and tranquility, the result of harmony pervaded during every part of the entertainment.

Independent Chronicle (Boston), March 17, 1794

DEMOCRATIC SOCIETY OF THE BOROUGH OF NORFOLK

Address to Friends and Fellow Citizens, June 9, 1794

(From the VIRGINIA CHRONICLE and GENERAL ADVERTISER.)

At a meeting of the Democratic Society of the Borough of Norfolk, associated in defence of the Rights and Liberties of Mankind, the following Address was read and approved.

FRIENDS and FELLOW-CITIZENS,

CONVINCED that it is the duty of every individual, to obey the laws of that country in which he lives, and from which he expects protection, obedience and protection being reciprocal—As Republicans of Norfolk, we have formed ourselves into a society,[2] and pledged our honors each to the other, that no effort on our part shall ever be wanting to assist the magistrate in the administration of justice, and the legal execution of the duties of his office—At the same moment we make this declaration, a declaration to which we are determined to adhere; still we claim an indefeasible right, a right adherent to the law of nature, freely to investigate the conduct of our rulers, and as freely to censure them when reprehensible—All power originated from the people, and there can be no legal authority, but by their consent—In a state of nature, necessity compelled mankind to enter into society, out of which all was anarchy and confusion, property was insecure, and the persons of the week, subjected to the insults and rapacity of the strong—associated for mutual preservation and protection for the orderly government of the whole, laws equally obligatory upon each individual, were necessarily formed, the execution of which was entrusted to those, who, for their virtue, integrity and wisdom, were adjudged by a majority of the society, the most proper persons for that purpose, and although mankind, by entering into the social compact, resigned to the society at large, all those natural rights which were necessary for the preservation and good of the society, the residue which was much the larger part, they still retained the power that be, being delegated, and originating from the people, to them rulers as such, must be amenable; and we claim a right, when those to whom power is entrusted, pervert it to the oppression of the people, to call them to an account, to reprimand, to displace and punish them for exercising that power which was delegated to them for the good of the community, to the destruction of their liberty and happiness—and although, to redress these grievances, every lenient and emolient remedy should be applied, yet if from the obstinacy and perverseness of our rulers, this should prove ineffectual, coercive applications would be justifiable—the affections of a virtuous and understanding people will ever be secured to rulers and magistrates, by an equal administration of justice, by consulting their good and making the happiness of their constituents the primary object of their attention, and the ultimate cope of all their wishes and designs. Under the government of such rulers, we should hear of no complaining in our streets, no murmuring among our citizens, because when the righteous are in authority, the people rejoice, everyone would get contented & happy under his own fig-tree, but when the wicked rule, they moan—with the most heartfelt concern we see, they have too great an ascendancy in our councils, for we see men at the head of departments, whose principles are repugnant to the right of man—we see others, even in a legislative capacity, who are unfriendly to their country, more attached to their own interest, and more influenced by lucrative motives than the good and happiness of their country—many of our brave and veteran soldiers, to whom, under God, we are indebted for our liberties, and who have baffled the artifice and foiled the attempts of a British Tyrant, have been necessitated to dispose of their hard earned wages, for less than an eighth of their value,[3] to those who would sacrifice the liberties of America, to the aggrandezement of their coffers—men who have so far imposed on the credulity of our countrymen, as, by their suffrages, to obtain a seat in the American Congress, and who by their wicked devices, have established a fund for the payment of money at six per cent which the necessities of our soldiers obliged them to dispose of for 2s in the pound—Thus will these congressional speculators, by establishing a fund to secure their debt, receive from one year's interest, nearly as much as the principal cost them—These are the men to whom the liberties of America are entrusted, men whose interest it is (and who are governed by interest) to oppose every measure which they may suppose would be injurious to their funding system—exclusive of these grievances, we are apprehensive that British influence has likewise got into our legislative departments, and that British politics are too prevalent among our superiors in rank, but not in principle; of this we have recent instances, in the tameness and dilatoriness, both of our legislators and rulers, in submitting to the indignities and insults offered to our flag, and the piracies, spoliations, and robberies, which are daily committed upon the property of our fellow citizens, contrary to the law of nations and every principle of equity and justice; indeed we cannot but observe, with the most pungent sorrow, the predilection manifested by the magistrates of this Borough, to the enemies of America: Enemies who have basely deserted from our standard, who have robbed our countrymen, who have treacherously slain our officers, who fought against us when contending for our liberties, who are daily fulminating their anathemas against America, who have the audacity to return to this land of liberty, and temerity to boast of their attachment to a British Tyrant—these men are cherished and fostered by our magistrates, and with inpunity suffered to boast of their villainy, whilst the sons of America manifest a true republican spirit, are menaced with imprisonment for resenting their conduct, and endeavouring to punish such atrocious miscreants— America now ranks as a nation, but such is the incapability of her councils, imbecility of her laws, and the want of energy in her government, that unless some alteration is speedily effected, she will be a derision to every wise and enlightened nation.—To endeavour a redress for these manifold evils, friends and citizens, we have formed ourselves into a Democratic Society, and we trust and hope, that all republicans throughout America will do the same, to whom we shall be happy at all times to communicate our sentiments, and with whom to keep up a friendly correspondence—Actuated by these motives, and influenced by these considerations, the safety of the people being the supreme law—we are determined, when our rights and liberties are infringed, to sound the alarm to our countrymen, not doubting but, with their assistance, we shall be able to decapitate and destroy that Hydrae, that many headed monster, which will ruin America if not speedily subdued by the people, the proper origin of all civil government, adopted unanimously.

Signed by order of the Society,

Norfolk, June 9, 1794   J. BARRACLOUGH, Sec'ry.

Virginia Gazette and Richmond and Manchester Advertiser (Richmond), July 3, 1794

DEMOCRATIC-REPUBLICAN SOCIETY OF DUMFRIES

Resolutions Adopted Condemning the Conduct of Representative Richard Bland Lee, June 7, 1794

At a meeting of the Democratic Republican Society of Prince Wm. (Prince William Co., Va.) held at the Court house of the said County on Saturday the 7th day of June 1794.

Present, Twenty two members

Resolved unanimously that the System of Politicks pursued in the present session of Congress by Richard Bland Lee[4] the representative for this district is such as in the opinion of this Society ought to meet the most pointed disapprobation of his constituents and that the said Richard Bland Lee as a public character is altogether unworthy of the future confidence of Good Republicans.

Resolved, (Eighteen member voting in the affirmative) that this Society conceives it the duty of every Friend to democracy when a person shall come forward as a Candidate for a post of Profit or honor if he has heard any such person deliver sentiments Antidemocratical to make the same public.

Resolved unanimously as the opinion of this Society that it is incompatible with the genuine principles of republicanism that offices of high trust and great emolument should be heaped on the same person.

Resolved as the opinion of this Society that it is contrary to the Spirit of the Constitution that the Judges of the Supreme Court should be permitted to accept offices emanating from and at the disposal of the President as it has a tendency to give the Executive and undue influence and to destroy the Independency of the Judges.

Resolved unanimously that as the chief Judge is by the Constitution to preside on an impeachment of the President the appointment of him to any additional office that may be in the gift of the President is peculiarly improper.

Resolved unanimously that as treaties are the Supreme Law of the Land it is improper that Judges be appointed to make such treaties for it has ever been held as a true principle in all republican Governments that it is improper for the same person to make and expound the Law.

Resolved therefore unanimously that for these reasons this Society disapprove of the appointment of John Jay chief Judge of the Supreme Court of the United States as Envoy extraordinary to the Court of Great Britain.

(Signed) Geo. Graham President

A Copy

Test. Jno. Williams, Secy.

Innes Papers, XIX, 124, Manuscripts Division, Library of Congress

Committee of Correspondence to the Democratic Society of Kentucky, June 9, 1794

To the Democratic Society of Kentucky
Dumfries June 9th 1794

Citizens,

We the Committee of Correspondence of the Democratic republican Society of Prince William in Virginia having Seen in the public prints your Constitution and part of your subsequent proceedings and most heartily concurring with you in your laudable endeavors to promote the general good of our Country do therefore propose that a Correspondence may henceforth be Carried on between us for the purposes directed by our Constitutions. We herewith, present you with a Copy of our Constitution and Sundry resolutions and proceedings which have resulted from our institution. It will at all times afford us satisfaction to receive from you any Communications which you may Deem expedient to make and to further as far as we can whatever may tend to the public good.

By order of the Committee

George Brooke Chairman.

Innes Papers, XIX, Manuscripts Division, Library of Congress

DEMOCRATIC SOCIETY IN WYTHE COUNTY

Address to the People of the United States, July 4, 1794

Wythe, Court-House, Virginia,
July 4, 1794.

The DEMOCRATIC SOCIETY met according to adjournment.

Citizen William Neelly, chosen Chairman for the sitting

Citizen John Montgomery, chosen Secretary.

On motion of Citizen Alexander Smyth;

ORDERED, That a Committee be appointed to prepare an Address to the people of the United States, and a Committee was accordingly appointed of Citizens Alexander Smyth, Daniel Sheffy, Jehu Stephens, Jesse Evans, Joseph Crockett, William Drope, and William Hay.

Citizen Alexander Smyth, from the Committee, appointed, reported an address, which being read, is unanimously agreed to.

Ordered, That the said address be signed by the Chairman, and published.

(The said Address follows.)

Address of the DEMOCRATIC SOCIETY in Wythe County, Virginia, to the people of the United States.

FELLOW CITIZENS,

It is a right of the people peaceably to assemble and deliberate. It is a right of the people to publish their sentiments. These rights we exercise, and esteem invaluable.

A war raging in Europe; a war of tyrants against liberty, cannot be unfelt by the people of the United States—It has roused our feelings. We have rejoiced when victory followed the standard of liberty. When despots were successful, we have experienced the deepest anxiety.—We have lamented that our good wishes were the only aid we could give the French.

Among the different powers combined against the Rights of Man, we have marked the British Nation the champion of despotism. With indignation we have heard their insolent dictates to the small neutral powers of Europe, to join in the subjugation of France. With sorrow we have seen every principle of Liberty hitherto retained by the people of Britain, violated by its present corrupt government; and their most virtuous inhabitants transported to foreign lands, or going into voluntary exile: But we hope these things will ultimately produce good, and that there still a latent spark, which by excessive friction, will kindle to a flame, and consume the rotten edifice of the British government, on the ruins of which another may arise, the basis whereof shall be justice, liberty, and equality.

While with anxious expectation we contemplate the affairs of Europe, it would be criminal to forget our own country. A Session of Congress having just passed; the first in which the people were equally represented, it is a fit time to take a retrospective view of the proceedings of Government. We have watched each motion of those in power; but are sorry we cannot exclaim, "well done thou good and faithful servant!" We have seen the nation insulted, our rights violated, our commerce ruined;—and what has been the conduct of Government? Under the corrupt influence of the paper system, it has uniformly crouched to Britain, while on the contrary our allies the French, to whom we owe our political existance, have been treated unfriendly; denied any advantages, from their treaties with us; their Minister abused; and those individuals among us, who desired to aid their arms, prosecuted as traitors. Blush Americans for the conduct of your government!!!

Citizens!

Shall we Americans, who have kindled the spark of liberty, stand aloof and see it extinguished, when burning a bright flame, in France, which hath caught it from us? Do you not see if despots prevail, you must have a despot like the rest of the nations? If all tyrants unite against free people, should not all free people unite against tyrants? Yes! Let us unite with France, and stand or fall together.

We lament that a man who hath so long possessed the public confidence, as the head of the Executive Department hath possessed it, should put it to so severe a trial as he hath by a late appointment. The constitution hath been trampled on, and your rights have no security. Citizens! What is despotism? Is it not a union of executive, legislative, and judicial authorities in the same hands? This union then has been affected. Your Chief Justice has been appointed to an executive office, by the head of that branch of Government; In that capacity he is to make treaties: Those treaties are your supreme law?—and of this supreme law he is supreme Judge!!! What has become of your constitution & liberties.

Fellow Citzens,

We hope the misconduct of the executive, may have proceeded from bad advice; but we can only look to the immediate cause of the mischief. To us; it seems a radical change of measures is necessary. How shall this be effected, citizens it is to be effected by a change of men. Deny the continuance of our confidence to such members of the Legislative body as have an interest distinct from that of the people. To trust yourselves to stock holders what is it, but like the Romans, to deliver the poor, debtor to his creditor, as his absolute property. To trust yourselves to speculators, what is it, but to committ the lamb to the wolf to be devoured.

It was recommended by the Conventions of some of the States, so to amend the constitution, as to incapacitate any man to serve as President more than eight years successively. Consider well this experiment. 'Tis probable the most certain way to purge the different departments, and produce a new state of things.

Believe us fellow citizens, the public welfare is our only motive.

WILLIAM NEELY, Chairman,

Attest,   John Montgomery, Sec'ry

American Daily Advertiser (Philadelphia), August 2, 1794

Toasts Drunk, July 4, 1794

The Republican Printers throughout the Union, are requested to publish this Address.

TOASTS drank by the DEMOCRATIC SOCIETY, At Wythe Court-house, the Fourth of July, 1794.

1. The United States of America—May they prefer their liberties to the end of time.

2. The French Nation—May their glorious struggle prove fatal to despotism.

3. The Congress of the United States—May the next election purge it of paper and aristocratical influence.

4. The National Convention of France.

5. George Washington—May he be actuated by republican principles and re-member the spirit of the constitution, or cease to preside over the United States.

6. The ever memorable 4th of July—May its return still rekindle the patriot flame in each American bosom.

7. The memory of the heroes who fell for American Liberty.

8. The Guillotine—May it have an attractive virtue to draw despots to it.

9. The Democrats throughout the world.

10. The Tree of Liberty—May it flourish on the ruins of Despotism.

11. The Republican Fair of America.

12. Perpetual union between the United States and the French Republic.

13. The Republicans of the British islands—May they cease to be governed by lunatics.

14. Thomas Jefferson.

15. Liberty, Equality, fraternity and union.

RESOLVED, That a subscription be opened for the purpose of procuring a number of pamphlets on the Rights of Men,[5] for the dissemination of Republican principles.

The sum of twenty-four dollars, and seventy-five cents being subscribed, Ordered, the same be applied as aforesaid by citizen Daniel Sheffy.

Teste,

JOHN MONTGOMERY, SEC'y.

American Daily Advertiser (Philadelphia), August 2, 1794

11 | Democratic-Republican Societies of Kentucky

DEMOCRATIC SOCIETY OF KENTUCKY, LEXINGTON, FAYETTE COUNTY

Resolutions Adopted Forming the Society, August 22, 1793

At a meeting of a number of Citizens of the town of Lexington, at the house of Citizen Robert M'Gowan, for the purpose of taking under consideration the propriety of establishing a Democratic Society in this place.

On Motion,

RESOLVED, That the Citizens here present, form themselves into a *Democratic Society* embracing the laudable objects of the Philadelphia Democratic Society.

RESOLVED, That Citizens William Murray, John Bradford,[1] James Brown, Thomas Irwin, Robert M'Gowan and Thomas Todd, or any three of them be a committee for the purpose of drawing Articles and Rules for the government of this society, and that they make report at the State-House on Wednesday the 28th instant, at which time and place the Citizens of the County of Fayette are requested to attend to assist in carrying those laudable principles into execution.

RESOLVED, That Citizen John Bradford, be requested to publish the proceeding of the Philadelphia Democratic Society, in his next Gazette, and also these proceedings.

By order of the meeting.

August 22, 1793.

Kentucky Gazette, August 24, 1793

Circular Letter to the Citizens of Kentucky, August 31, 1793

Lexington, August 31.

At a meeting of the Democratic Society, at the State house in Lexington on Wednesday the 28th day of August, 1793.

The Society proceeded to the election of officers when a majority of votes were in favor of

John Breckenridge,[2] Chairman,

John Bradford and Robert Todd,[3] Vice Chairmen,

Thomas Todd and Thomas Bodley, Clerks,

Alexander M'Gregor, Treasurer,

William Murray, James Hughes, James Brown, James Moore[4] *and Robert Todd,* a Committee of Correspondence.

ORDERED, That the Corresponding Committee be directed to write a Circular Letter to the Citizens of this State explanatory of the principles and objects of this Society.

Extracts from the Minutes,

Test.

Thomas Todd, } C.S.S.
Thomas Boller,

CIRCULAR
To the Citizens of Kentucky

FELLOW CITIZENS,

The *Democratic Society of Kentucky* are now organized and have committed to us the charge of developing to you their principles and objects.

They are impressed with the sentiments, that a Democracy by representation is the best mode of Government, which the wisdom of man hath devised, and that all just power can be derived only from the people; of concequence the people have the exclusive right of framing and altering their forms of Government. That in order to preserve the inestimable blessing of Liberty, from the open attacks of avowed tyrants, on the more insidious, tho much more destructive machinations of ambitious and intriguing men,—it behoves the people to watch over the conduct of their officers in every department of Government.

Experience has shewn, that, the hope of Impunity, has tended to the encouragement of crimes, in public, even more than in private life. The man, who virtue may not restrain from the breach of an important public trust, may be awed by the vigilant and piercing eye of his fellow citizens. This however would be insufficient to preserve pure and uncontaminated, the best of all possible Governments. We ought to be extremely cautious in the choice of men, who are to represent us in the exercise of the powers of Government. Their public characters ought to be examined with strictness and attention, free from party or religious prejudices, and unaffected by their occupation, fortune or connections. The attempt to influence the vote of a freeman, either by the wily arts of promised favor, or by base calumniation, ought to be spurned at with contempt and abhorrence.

These are, in the abstract, the principles of the society. Their objects are to disseminate those principles, and to conciliate affectionate sentiments towards each other among their Democratic fellow citizens. That those objects may be effected, they propose not only to discuss the proceedings of Government, but to examine into the conduct of its officers in every department. They will discuss and examine with candor, but with the firmness and freedom becoming citizens, zeallus for the liberties of their country.

The blotted page of history has recorded the fatal effects which the neglect of similar precautions has occassioned. Had the citizens of Athens been attentive to the conduct of their public men, the pitiful stratagem of Pisistratus would not have imposed upon his Country an odious tyranny. To recite every similar event which similar consequences would extend our letter beyond the bounds which we propose. Too numerous, indeed, are the instances, which in former times, a like inattention presents for our instruction. What were then called Revolutions, were only a change of tyrants; or if a moment of freedom intervened,—it was, as the transient beams of the sun, between two storms. To the present age has been reserved to witness renovating Revolutions. In America we sought not shelter from the oppression of one tyrant, under the talons of another. The Rights of Man, the principles of a Government formed to protect those rights, and ensure to our fellow citizens, and our latest posterity, the blessings of freedom and equality, were the objects of our political deliberations.— France has since caught the glorious flame! Long had her people been deprived of the rights bestowed by their beneficent Creator. At length, they have arisen in their strength, and like an inundation, have at once, sweptaway their Tyrants and their Gothic Structures. May success and freedom reward their merits!

Fellow Citizens, We invite you to form meetings in your several counties, to join and to correspond with the *Democratic Society of Kentucky*. To this society, the members of meetings in any County of this State, formed on similar principles, will have admission. They declare the Society co extensive with the State.

These principles and regulations we have been directed to announce to you; we doubt not that impressed with the justice and importance of those principles, you will give them your support.

Thus will you preserve the blessings of freedom and merit the gratitude of posterity.

William Murray,	Committee of
James Hughes,	Correspon-
James Brown,	dence for the
James Moore,	Kentucky De-
Robert Todd.	mocratic Soci-

Kentucky Gazette, August 31, 1793　　　　ety.

Proceedings of a Meeting, October 12, 1793

Lexington, October 12.

At a meeting of the Democratic Society in Lexington on monday the 7th instant; the following resolution was read and ordered to lie on the table untill the
next meeting, and to be then taken up for further discussion:

The Citizens of this Commonwealth having for a series of years been anxiously
hoping, that the free use of an all important right, which they receive from
NATURE, and which is now wantonly & cruelly controuled and abused, would
have been long since secured to them; and finding so far as they have been able
to gain intelligence, that this event so inseparably connected with their happiness as a civilized and free people, instead of approaching is receding;

"RESOLVED, That the free and undisturbed use and navigation of the River
Mississippi is the NATURAL RIGHT of the Citizens of the Commonwealth; and
is unalienable except with the SOIL; and that neither time, tyrany nor prescription on the one side, nor acquiescence, weakness, or non use on the other, can
ever sanctify the abuse of this right."

Kentucky Gazette, October 12, 1793

Resolutions Adopted on Free Navigation of the Mississippi, November 11, 1793

Lexington, Nov 16

At a meeting of the Democratic Society in Lexington, on Monday the 11th
of November, 1793

On motion,

The Society resolved itself into a committee of the whole, upon the subject
of the free navigation of the Mississippi river; and after some time spent in the
discussion of the subject, came to several Resolutions, which were reported to
the society, and unanimously agreed to as follows:

The Citizens of this Commonwealth having for a series of years been anxiously
hoping, that the free use of an all important right, which they received from
NATURE, and which is now wantonly and cruelly controuled and abused, would
have been long since secured to them.

Resolved, That the free and undisturbed use and navigation of the river
Mississippi is the NATURAL RIGHT of the inhabitants of the countries bordering
on the waters communicating with the river; and is unalienable except with the
SOIL; and that neither time, tyranny nor prescription on the one side, nor
acquiesence, weakness, or non user, on the other, can ever sanctify the abuse of
this right.

Resolved, that the inhabitants of the Western Country had a right to expect that the present Federal Government would before this time have taken effectual measures to obtain from the King of Spain an acknowledgment of their undoubted right to the free navigation of the river Mississippi; that they ought as free men highly interested in the event of that business to have received information of the causes which have hitherto delayed the negotiation; and that it was the duty of the Representatives of the people to have called upon the Executive of the Federal Government for an account of what had been done respecting it.

Resolved, that the inhabitants of the western country have good cause to suspect that the applications for the acknowledgment of this their just and invaluable right, have been feeble, and that the attainment of it is not wished for by a part of the United States.

Resolved, that under these circumstances, it is a duty which the inhabitants of the western country owe to themselves and their posterity, to demand of the Federal Government that they take such steps as will immediately put them into the free enjoyment of this their just rights; that to make this demand effectual, they should unite in an application for that purpose, and that to bring about concert in this application a proper communication ought to be opened between the different settlements in the western country.

4. Resolved, that there be a committee appointed to prepare an address to the inhabitants of the western country, inviting them to a correspondence on this subject, calling on them to unite in their efforts on this occasion, exhorting them to sacrafice all considerations to the attainment of this great object; and recommending it to them to be prepared to surmount all obstacles which may be thrown into its way either by pusillanimity, and an improper regard to local interests at home; or by the arm of power and tyranny abroad.

Resolved, That they also prepare in the name of the inhabitants of the western waters, a remonstrance to the President and Congress of the United States on this subject, stating (in the bold decent and determined language proper to be used by injured freemen, when they address the servants of the people) that we consider the feeble attempts which have been made by the executive under the present government, and the total silence of Congress on this important subject, as strong proofs that most of our brethren in the eastern part of America, are totally regardless whether this our just right is kept from us or not.

That we expect and demand from the government, that they take immediate and effectual steps to procure and secure to us the enjoyment of that right; that we apply to them and wish to be put into the enjoyment of this right through their intervention. Altho' we feel a conviction that we are strong enough to obtain that right by force, yet an attachment to the American union; love to our brethren; respect to the government, and a sincere desire of preserving peace and harmony, have determined us to pursue this mode of application through which we hope speedily and effectually to procure it, and that we shall

not be driven to use those means to effect it with which we have been furnished
by the God of nature.

Resolved, That it will be proper to make an attempt in a peaceable manner
to go with an American bottom properly registered and cleared into the sea
through the channel of the Mississippi; that we may either procure an immediate
acknowledgement of our right from the Spaniards; or if they obstruct us in the
enjoyment of that right, that we may be able to lay before the Federal Government such unequivocal proofs of their having done so, that they will be compelled to say whether they will abandon or protect the inhabitants of the western country.

Whereas the criminal laws now in force in this Commonwealth are in their
operation sanguinary, cruel and unjust, from the multitude of inferior crimes
which are capitally punished, whereby many offenders are liable to be destroyed,
who might be reformed and restored good members to society; And whereas the
experience of all ages hath shewn, that cruel and sanguinary laws defeat their
own purpose, by engaging the benevolence of mankind to withold prosecution,
to further testimony, or to listen to it with bias; and by producing in many instances a total dispensation and impunity under the names of pardon and
priviledge of clergy; when, if the punishment were only proportioned to the
injury, men would feel it their inclination, as well as their duty, to see the laws
observed, and the power of dispensation, so dangerous and mischievous, which
produces crimes by holding up a hope of impunity, so that men while contemplating to perpetrate a crime, would see their punishment insuing as necessarily
as effects follow the causes.

Resolved, That a committee be appointed to draft a memorial to the General
Assembly, requesting that a radical change be made in our criminal code, by
erecting a system, "whereby punishments may be proportioned to crimes, and
that such punishments be made as analagous as possible to the nature of the
offences:" and that said memorial when drafted, may be laid before the Society
for their approbation.

Kentucky Gazette, November 16, 1793

Address and Remonstrance to the Inhabitants of the United States West of the Allegheny and Appalachian Mountains, December 13, 1793

FELLOW CITIZEN.

The Democratic Society of Kentucky have directed us to transmit to you the
Address and Remonstrance which accompany this letter. The subject of those
papers is highly interesting to the Western People. We flatter ourselves that the
measures recommended in the Address will meet your approbation; and that you
will exert your influence to induce your neighboring fellow-citizens to give their
sanction to the Remonstrance.

The Remonstrance when signed, may be transmitted to the representative in Congress from your district, or to any other member of that body, delegated from the Western Country. It is intended that a decision upon this subject should be obtained during the present Session of Congress, and to effect this, it is necessary that the Remonstrance should be presented as soon as possible.

The inclosed Resolution of the Democratic society is one on which we are directed to request your sentiments; and should you aprove it we promise ourselves that you will assist in carrying it into effect.

> WILLIAM MURRAY,
> JAMES HUGHES,
> JAMES BROWN,
> JAMES MOORE,   *Committee of*
> ROBERT TODD,   *Correspondence*
>
> *December* 31, 1793.

To George Muter

"RESOLVED, That it will be proper to make an attempt in a peaceable manner, to go with an American bottom properly registered and cleared, into the sea through the channel of the Mississippi; that we may either procure an immediate acknowledgment of our right from the Spaniards; or if they obstruct us in the enjoyment of that right, that we may be able to lay before the Federal Government, such unequivocal proofs of their having done so, that they will be compelled to say, whether they will abandon or protect the inhabitants of the western country."

To the Inhabitants of the United States West of the Allegany and Apalachian Mountains.

Fellow Citizens.

The Democratic Society of Kentucky having had under consideration the measures necessary to obtain the exercise of your right to the free navigation of the Mississippi, have determined to address you upon that important Topic. In so doing, they think, that, they only use the undoubted right of Citizens to consult for their common welfare. This measure is not dictated by party or faction, it is the consequence of unavoidable necessity. It has become so, from the neglect shewn by the general Government, to obtain for those of the Citizens of the United States, who are interested therein, the Navigation of that River.

In the present age, when the rights of man have been fully investigated and declared, by the voice of Nations, and, more particularly, in America, where those rights were first developed and declared, it will not be necessary to prove, that, the free Navigation of the Mississippi is the natural rights of the Inhabitants of the Country watered by its streams. It cannot be believed, that the beneficent God of Nature would have blessed this Country with unparalleled fertility, and furnished it with a number of navagable streams, and that, that fertility should be consumed at home, and those streams should not convey its superabundance to other climes. Far from it: for if we examine the wise diversity of the Earth as to Climate and production, Lands, seas and Rivers we must discover the glorious plan of infinite beneficence to unite by this exchange of their surplus, various Nations and connect the ends of the Earth, in the bands of commerce and mutual good office. From the Everlasting decrees of Providence, then, we derive this right: And must be criminal either to surrender or suffer it to be taken from us, without the most arduous struggles. But this right is ours, not only from nature but compact. We do not mean to urge this, as if a compact could give an additional sanction to a natural right; but to shew that our claim is derived from every source, which can give it validity. The Navigation of the Mississippi was solemnly given and confirmed, by great Britain, to the Citizens of the United States, by the provisional articles entered into, at Paris, between the two Nations.[5] More than Eleven years have since elapsed, during which we have been denied the exercise of a right, founded upon such irrefragible grounds. What has been done by the former or present Government, during that period, on our behalf? In the former, we have been able to learn of no attempt to procure from the King of Spain, even an acknowledgement of our right. Repeated memorials were presented to Congress upon this Subject, but they were treated with a neglect bordering on contempt. They were laid upon the Table, there to rest in endless oblivion. Once indeed, we know, this Subject was introduced into Congress, under the former Government; but it was by an unwarrantable and disgraceful proposition to barter away our right. The Proposition was not adopted; the attempt being rendered abortive by the Spirited and patriotic opposition of a part of the Union. The time at length came, when the voice of the people called for a change in the General Government; and the present Constitution of the United States was adopted. We then flattered ourselves that our rights would be protected; for we were taught to believe, that the former loose and weak confederation having been done away, the new Government would possess the requisite energy. Memorials upon the subject were renewed, six years have passed away and our right is not yet obtained. Money is to be taken from us by an odious and oppressive Excise: but the means of procuring it, by the exercise of our just right, is denied. In the mean while our Brethren, on the Eastern Waters, possess every advantage which Nature or contract can give them. Nay, we do not know that even one firm attempt to obtain it has been made. Alas! Is the Energy of our Government not to be exerted against our Enemies? Is it all to be reserved for her Citizens?

Experience, Fellow Citizens, has shown us that the general Government is unwilling, that we should obtain the navigation of the River Mississippi. A local policy appears to have an undue weight in the Councils of the Union. It seems to be the object of that Policy to prevent the population of this country: which would draw from the Eastern States their industrious Citizens. This conclusion inevitably follows from a consideration of the measures taken to prevent the purchase of and settlement of the lands bordering on the Mississippi. Among those measures, the unconstitutional interferance, which rescinded sales, by one of the States to private Individuals, makes a striking object. And, perhaps, the fear of a successful rivalry in every Article of their Exports may have its weight. But if they are not unwilling to do us justice, they are at least regardless of our rights and welfare. We have found prayers and supplications of no avail, and should we continue to load the Table of Congress with Memorials, from, a part only, of the Western Country, it is too probable, they would meet with a fate, similar to those which have been formerly presented. Let us, then, all unite our endeavors in the common cause. Let all join, in a firm and manly remonstrance to the President and Congress of the United States, stating our just and Undoubted right to the Navigation of the Mississippi, remonstrating against the conduct of Government with regard to that right which must have been occasioned by local policy or neglect and demanding of them speedy and effectual exertions for its attainment. We cannot doubt, that you will cordially and unanimously join in this measure. It can hardly be necessary to remind you, that considerable quantities of Beef, Pork, flour, Hemp, Tobacco &c. the produce of the Country remain on hand for want of purchasers, or are sold at inadequate prices. Much greater quantities might be raised, if the Inhabitants were encouraged by the certain sale, which the free navigation of the Mississippi would afford. An additional increase of those articles and a greater variety of produce and manufactures would be supplied, by means of the encouragement, which the attainment of that great object would give to Immigration. But it is not only your own rights, which you are to regard. Remember your posterity have a claim to your exersions to obtain and secure that right. (Let not your memory be stigmatized with a neglect of duty). Let not History record, that the Inhabitants of this beautiful country lost a most invaluable right and half the benefits bestowed upon it, by a bountiful Providence, through your neglect and supiness. The present crisis is favourable. Spain is engaged in a war, which requires all her forces.[6] If the present golden opportunity be suffered to pass without advantage, and she shall have concluded a peace with France, we must then contend against her undivided strength.

But, what may be the event of the proposed application is still uncertain. We ought therefore to be, still, upon our guard and watchful to seize the first favourable opportunity to gain our object. In order to this, our Union should be as perfect and lasting as possible. We propose, that Societies should be formed, in convenient Districts, in every part of the Western Country, who shall preserve a correspondence, upon this and every other subject of general concern. By means of these Societies we shall be enabled speedily to know what may be the result of our endeavours, to consult upon such further measures, as may be necessary, to preserve Union, and finally by these means to secure success.

Remember that it is a common cause, which ought to unite us, that, that cause is indubitably just, that ourselves and posterity are interested, that the Crisis is favourable, and that it is only by Union, that the object can be achieved. The obstacles are great, and so ought to be our efforts; Adverse fortune may attend us, but it shall never dispirit us. We may for a while exhaust our Wealth and Strength, but until the all important object is procured, we pledge ourselves to you, and let us all pledge ourselves to each other, that our Perserverance and our firmness will be inexhaustable.

JOHN BRECKINRIDGE

Chairman

December 13th 1793.

Teste
Thomas Todd
Thomas Bodley } Clks.

Innes Papers, XIX, Manuscripts Division, Library of Congress

Remonstrance of the Citizens West of the Allegheny Mountains to the President and Congress of the United States, n.d.

TO THE PRESIDENT AND CONGRESS OF THE
UNITED STATES OF AMERICA.
The Remonstrance of the Citizens West of the Allegany Mountains.

Respectfully sheweth.

That Your Remonstrants are entitled by Nature and by stipulation, to the undisturbed Navigation of the river Mississippi, and consider it a right inseparable from their prosperity. That in colonizing this distant and dangerous desert, they always contemplated the free enjoyment of this right, and considered it as an inseparable appendage to the country they had sought out, had fought for, and acquired.—That for a series of years during their early settlement, their petitions to government to secure this right, were answered by its alledged weakness, and your Remonstrants taught to expect, that the time was approaching fast, when both power and inclination would unite to establish it on the firmest grounds. In this anxious expectation they waited, and to the insolence of those who arrogated its exclusive exercise, they patiently submitted, as to hold out an assurance of future protection to all its citizens, and of redress for all their wrongs.

That protection has not been extended to us, we need only refer to our present situation, and that that situation has not been concealed from, or unknown to, Congress, we appeal to its archives. We have, without ceasing, deplored to you our degraded situation, and burdened you with our humble petitions and requests. But alas! we still experience, that the strong nerved government of America, extends its arm of protection to all the branches of the union, but to your Remonstrants. That it is competent to every end, but that single one, by which alone it can benefit us; the protection of our Territorial rights. It is competent to exact obedience; but not to make that return which can be the only just and natural exchange for it.

Long have your Remonstrants been anxiously in quest of the obstacles that have stood in your way, to the establishment of this our right; and as long has their pursuit been fruitless. Formal and tardy negociations have no doubt been often projected, and have as often miscarried. It is true, some negociations were once attempted, that were neither *formal* nor *tardy,* and gave an early shock to our encreasing population and to our peace of mind; but your Remonstrants are constrained to be of opinion, that the neglect or local policy of American councils, has never produced one single real effort to procure this right. Could the Government of America be for ten years seriously in pursuit of the establishment of a grand Territorial right, which was arrogantly suspended, and return to that quarter of the union to whom it was all-important, but an equivocal answer?— We think it high time that we should be thoroughly informed of the situation on which your negociations, if any, have left this right; for apathy itself has grown hopeless from long disappointed expectation.

Your Remonstrants yield not in patriotism to any of their fellow-citizens: but patriotism, like every other thing, has its bounds. We love those states from which we were all congregated, and no event (not even an attempt to barter away our best rights) shall alien our affections from the individual members who compose them: But attachment to governments cease to be natural, when they cease to be mutual. To be subjected to all the burthens, and enjoy none of the benefits arising from government, is what we will never submit to. Our situation compels us to speak plainly. If wretchedness and poverty await us, it is of no concern to us how they are produced. We are gratified in the prosperity of the Atlantic states, but would not speak the language of truth and sincerity, were we not to declare our unwillingness, to make any sacrifices to it, when their importance and those sacrifices result from our distresses. If the interest of Eastern America requires that we should be kept in poverty, it is unreasonable from such poverty to exact contributions. The first, if we cannot emerge from, we must learn to bear; but the latter, we never can be taught to submit to.

From the General Government of America, therefore, your Remonstrants now ask protection, in the free enjoyment of the navigation of the river Mississippi, which is withheld from them by the Spaniards. We demand it as a right which you have the power to invest us with, and which not to exert, is as great a breach of our rights, as to withhold. We declare, that nothing can retribute us for the suspension or loss of this inestimable right. We declare it to be a right which must be obtained; and do also declare, that if the General Government will not procure it for us, we shall hold ourselves not answerable for any consequences that may result from our procurement of it. The God of nature has given us both the right and means of acquiring and enjoying it; and to permit a sacrifice of it to any earthly consideration, would be a crime against ourselves, and against our posterity.

Innes Papers, XIX, Manuscripts Division, Library of Congress

August Lachaise to the Democratic Society of Lexington, May 9, 1794

To the Democratic Society of Lexington

9th May 1794.

Citizens

Your most pleasing answer to my fortunate address has been handed to me by Citizen Campbell. The obliging & flattering things which it contains, have filled me with the most lively gratitude, & would increase my zeal, & my attachment to the interests of your Country if those sentiments were susceptible of an increase.

I have read with the same sensibility the report of your Committee & can not but applaud to the wisdom of the motives which have dictated it. I will communcate those two pretious pieces to the Executive Council. Although not official papers, they will not be the less favorably received, being the authentic proofs of all I will advance upon the favorable dispositions of the inhabitants of Kentucky, towards the French Republic, their sincere and continual prayers for the success of her arms, & the universal Joy which I have seen exprest in every quarter at the announce of her different victories.

Citizens, I go with the firm assurance that my Steps with the Constituted powers of the Republic will be crowned with Success.[7] Was I deceived in that hope, I have still the resource of making an attempt on the minds of the head men of the Trading & maritime Towns, & their patriotic Societies. Why should not I have the luck of that fanatic priest, whose name I have forgot, who preached in France & the other States of Europe for the Conquest of the Holy Land. Louisiana & its wretched inhabitants are assuredly more interesting than that barren Country: The Spaniards who defend the Mississippi are more worthy of Contempt than The Ottoman; & the French of the eighteenth Century, freed from the yoke of Despotism, Superstition, & religious fanaticism, burn with the Divine fire & sacred enthusiasm which Liberty inspires. Subscriptions will be opened & immediately filled up, & Thousands of brave patriots will present themselves for that suberb & truly Holy Expedition.

Citizens, Receive these new assurances of my zeal, activity, perserverance, & punctuality to inform you, as often as possible for every Circumstance relative to my Mission.

Salus in Patria

August Lachaise

Innes Papers, XIX, Manuscripts Division, Library of Congress

Letter to a Citizen, n.d.

Citizen[8]

Your address to the Democratic Society, has been received, and became the subject of their consideration: In that address you were pleased to signify your intention of visiting your fellow citizens in France, who are now gloriously engaged in the cause of Freedom, and the happiness of the whole human race. We regret our separation, and lament the occasion, tho we applaud the motive—and acknowledge it consistent with those sentiments of ardent affection so often intimated by you for your countrymen; and while we love the man that sympathizes with bleeding France, we admire the sublime virtue which is not checked by any distance, difficulties or dangers, from joining the standard of Freedom.

The impediments to the Scheme (in which you had been destined to act an important part) for removing the Shackles created by a Despot that prevent our uninterrupted use of the river Mississippi, our natural right, as well as a right obtained by cession, we do not take a retrospective view of, without receiving those impressions of concern, that naturally flow from a knowledge of Oppression and injustice, imposed on a people who have a right to be free, and altho' there have been obstructions to this first design contemplated, we are not yet without hopes, that the breave and generous Republic of France, of which you are a Citizen, will not lose sight of effecting the possession of it, and thereby extend from her bountiful hand, compleat happiness to us and to Millions yet unborn. We are the more solicitious for this event, as they are the only people on earth whose sensations of freedom, vibrate in perfect unison with our own, wherefrom we are flattered, that perpetual amity and affection will subject between us, without a transient cloud of dissatisfaction interrupting its reciprocity.

Accept Citizen our thanks for your friendly disposition towards our interests, and be assured, we wish you a safe and speedy passage to our friends and brethren in France, and that you may there act a distinguished part, in healing the wounds of your country, and substantiate the freedom thereof, either by your exertions within its own limits, or in any other quarter where the wisdom of her councils may direct.

RESOLVED that the corresponding Committee be requested to open a correspondence with such persons as they may think proper, residing within So. Western territory of the Virga Counties in the Western Waters, respecting the

navigation of the River Mississippi, in order to obtain the joint cooperation of
the citizens of that Territory in our attempt to obtain the free navigation of that
river, and that they communicate from time to time their correspondence on that
subject.

RESOLVED that our Members in Congress who are now within this State be
requested by the said commee to give such information to them as they possess
on the above mentioned subject.

RESOLVED that the commee. of correspondence, be directed to address the
Democratic Republican Society of Prince William in Virga. in answer to their
letter of the 9th of June last, assuring them of our perfect readiness to carry on
a correspondence with them, & assuring them also, that their resolutions inclosed
to us in their Sd. Letter, meet our hearty concurrence, & contain the sentiments
of true & undefiled Republicanism—And that the same commee. do communicate to them, such of the proceedings of this Society, as they may think fit.

No. 1.

RESOLVED that the commee. of correspondence be directed to address the
President of the Democratic Society of Washington county in Pennsylvania, in
answer to a letter from the corresponding commee—of said Society, dated the
8th of April last, assuring them of our strong desire & perfect willingness to open
a correspondence with them, on the subject of our unredressed Grievances, &
assuring them also, that being all equally fellow-sufferers we shall heartily cooperate with them in endeavouring to attain & secure their & our natural rights.
And that the said Commee. do communicate to them such of the proceedings of
this Society, as they may think proper.

Resolved that the Corresponding Committee be directed to inform the Democratic Society of Washington County in the State of Pennsylvania, that this Society concurs with them in their Resolutions relative to the Official Conduct of
the President of the United States adopted at their meeting on the 23d day of
June——1794——.

RESOLVED, That Jno Campbell, Jno Coburn, Robt Johnson, Robt Patterson
& James Smith

be a Committee for the purpose of requesting our Members in Congress now
within this State by letter or otherwise to attend the next States meeting of this
Society in Order that we may obtain certain information relative to the import-
and matters respecting this Country; more especially regarding the Negociations
that have taken place respecting the free use of the Navigation of the River
Mississippi, and in what State those negociations (if any) now rest, as also respecting such other public national matters as may be interesting to the good
people of this Commonwealth.

Innes Papers, XIX, Manuscripts Division, Library of Congress

Resolutions Adopted on Navigation of the Mississippi, May 24, 1794

On Saturday the 24th instant a numberous meeting of respectable Citizens from
    different parts of this State assembled in Lexington and after taking into con-
    sideration the degraded and deserted situation of this Country, both as to its
    commerce and protection; and coolly deliberating thereon, the following
    Resolutions were adopted:—
    Resolved,
    1. That the inhabitants west of the Apalachian mountains, are entitled by
nature and by stipulation, to the free and undisturbed Navigation of the River
Mississippi.
    2. That from the year 1783 until this time, the enjoyment of this right has
been uniformly prevented, by the Spaniards.
    3. That the General Government whose duty it was to have put us in possession
of this right, have either through design or mistaken policy, adopted no effectual
measures for its attainment.
    4. That even the measures they have adopted, have been uniformly concealed
from us, and veiled in mysterious secrecy.
    5. That civil liberty is prostituted, when the servants of the people, are suf-
fered to tell their masters, that communications which they may judge important,
ought not to be intrusted to them.
    6. That we have a right to expect and demand, that Spain should be com-
pelled immediately to acknowledge our right, or that an end be put to all negociations on that subject.
    7. That the injuries and insults done and offered by Great Britain to America,
call loudly for redress; and that we will to the utmost of our abilities support the
General Government in any attempt to obtain redress.
    8. That as the voice of all Eastern America has now called on the President of
the United States to demand that redress of Great Britain, Western America has a
right to expect and demand, that nothing shall be considered as a satisfaction,
that does not completely remove their grievances; which have a stronger claim
to satisfaction, both from their atrocity and continuance.
    Kentucky Gazette, May 31, 1794

Remonstrance of the Citizens of the Commonwealth of Kentucky to the President and Congress of the United States, May 29, 1794

A general meeting of the inhabitants of Fayette will be held in Lexington on
Monday the 29th inst. to deliberate on the foregoing Resolutions, & to remove
such doubts as may be in the minds of any respecting the same.

To the PRESIDENT *and* CONGRESS *of the* UNITED STATES *of* AMERICA:
THE REMONSTRANCE OF THE SUBSCRIBERS, CITIZENS OF THE
    COMMONWEALTH OF KENTUCKY, SHEWETH:

That your Remonstrants have observed with concern and indignation, the injuries and insults offered to the United States by the king of Great Britain. He has violated in important parts, that treaty of peace, the observance of which might have obliterated the remembrance of former injuries. He has, by means of his agents, supplied arms, ammunition, cloathing and provision to those merciless Savages, who have so long ravaged the Western Frontier of these States. He has interposed, unsolicited, and negociated truces for Portugal and Holland, with the Piratical States, in order to turn the rapine of those African Barbarians solely on the American commerce. His vessels of war, and the Piratical vessels of his subjects, by his orders, in violation of the law of nations, have despoiled the commerce, and insulted the neutral flag of America. He has made no compensation for the property of citizens of these States, carried away by his troops contrary to reaty [sic]. And, that we might escape no species of injury which could be heaped on the weakest and most despicable of nations, he holds within the territory of the United States, in defiance of treaty and of right, posts fortified and garrisoned by his armies.

That these injuries and insults call loudly for redress, and that we will, to the utmost of our abilities and in any mode that can be devised, support the General Government, in the firmest and most effectual measures, to obtain full satisfaction for all our wrongs.

That your Remonstrants, and the other Inhabitants of the United States West of the Allegany and Appalachian Mountains, are entitled by nature and stipulation to the free and undisturbed Navigation of the River Mississippi; and that from the year 1783 to this day, they have been uniformly prevented, by the Spanish King, from exercising that right. Your Remonstrants have observed, with concern, that the General Government, whose duty it was to have preserved that right, have used no effectual measures for its attainment. That even their tardy and ineffectual negociations, have been veiled with the most mysterious secrecy. That, that secrecy is a violation of the political rights of the citizen, as it declares, that the people are unfit to be entrusted with important facts relative to their rights, and that their Servants may retain from them the knowledge of those facts. Eight years are surely sufficient for the discussion of the most doubtful and disputable claim; the right of the Navigation of the Mississippi admits neither of doubt or dispute. Your Remonstrants, therefore, conceive that the negociations on that subject have been unnecessarily lengthy, and they expect, that it be demanded, categorically, of the Spanish king, whether he will acknowledge the right of the Citizens of the United States to the free and uninterrupted Navigation of the River Mississippi, and cause all obstructions, interruption and hindrance to the exercise of that right in future to be withdrawn and avoided, that immediate answer thereto be required; and that such answer be the final period of all negociations upon this subject.

Your Remonstrants further represent, that the encroachment of the Spaniards upon the Territory of the United States is a striking and melancholy proof of the situation to which one country will be reduced, if a tame policy should still continue to direct our councils.

Your Remonstrants join their voice so that of their Fellow Citizens in the Atlantic States, calling for satisfaction for the injuries and insults offered to America, and they expect that such satisfaction shall extend to every injury and insult, done or offered to any part of America by Great Britain and Spain; and as the detention of the Posts and the interruption to the Navigation of the Mississippi, are injuries and insults of the greatest atrocity and of the longest duration, they require the most particular attention to those subjects.

Your Remonstrants declare, that it is the duty of the General Government to protect the Frontiers, and that the total want of protection, which is now experienced by every part of the Western Frontier, is a grievance of the greatest magnitude and demands immediate redress.

Innes Papers, XIX, 113, Manuscripts Division, Library of Congress;
Kentucky Gazette, May 31, 1794

DEMOCRATIC SOCIETY OF KENTUCKY, PARIS, BOURBON COUNTY

Address to the Citizens of Kentucky, March 31, 1794

At a meeting of the Democratic Society of Kentucky, in Bourbon county, held at
Paris, March 31st 1794,

Resolved that Mr. Bradford be requested to give following address to the citizens of Kentucky, a place in his next paper.

Fellow-Citizens:

WHEN the period arrived that Kentucky was no longer to be considered as a dependent part of the State of Virginia, and when her collective wisdom was employed in framing a Constitution for her government, great were our hopes and expectations, from the known wisdom and experience of many members of Convention, that a more compleat form of Government would be devised, than that of any other State in the Union. As time had discovered many defects in almost every Constitution in the United States, which could not have been so easily foreseen when they were framed, we hoped these deficiencies would have been considered by our Convention, as so many Beacons set up for us, in order that we might avoid those Scyll's and Charybdises upon which they had unfortunately fallen.

But how exceedingly disappointed were our expectations when our present form of Government first made its appearance! And how fully hath its operation since, justified those fears and apprehensions which many citizens had of that *undue, aristocratical influence* which one branch of the legislature would attempt over the other! What jarring and discord took place between them at the first sitting of the Assembly, when affixing the salaries and fees of certain officers of government! And how dreadfully has the same spirit of dissension prevailed ever since, to the great injury of the Commonwealth! How often has our *immediate* representatives been urged, and, in some measure induced to augment what *they* thought was a compensation adequate to the services of those officers, notwithstanding the petitions and remonstrances of their constituents to the contrary! And when for these, and other reasons, the citizens, at the last general election, almost unanimously manifested a desire to alter our Constitution; and when in conformity with that desire, our immediate representatives brought forward a bill for the purpose of calling a Convention; how was it treated by the Senate? Was it not with the most *sovereign contempt?* Surely these things, and many others which your own observation must have pointed out to you, ought to engage the most serious attention of every freeman in the state. If our Constitution sanctions such conduct, or is the original cause of those evils, certainly it ought to be speedily amended. If an *aristocratical few* are possessed of such contemptuous boldness when our government is so young, as to trample upon, and despise the *sovereign will of the people,* what may we expect, if we supinely submit to their depredations on our liberties and property for a *number* of *years,* but that at last we shall be deprived wholly of the means of doing ourselves justice; or, at least, it will be more difficult. Now is the time for us to step forward with an intrepidity becoming freemen, and assert our rights.

Let each of us at the ensuing election, make choice of men to represent us who will use their utmost endeavors to obtain a new Convention. Let us write Convention on our tickets, that it may be clearly evinced to both branches of the Legislature that it is the wish of a great majority of the citizen. Let us unite in a remonstrance to the Assembly, stating our dissatisfaction with their former refusal to comply with our desire, and declaring our *determination* to obtain a new Convention; and if they still persist in refusing to comply, we know the last resource.

This plan we intend to follow in this county, and we expect the citizens of each county in the State to join us heartily therein; and we hope through unanimity, resolution and perseverance to obtain our wishes.

Signed, by order of Society,

WM. HENRY, President

Teste,
JOHN BOYD, clerk

Kentucky Gazette, April 12, 1794

Resolutions Adopted on Navigation of the Mississippi, June 16, 1794

Democratic Society for Bourbon County

Paris, June 16, 1794.

Mr. James Smith, from the committee of correspondence, presented a copy of sundry resolutions, of *a numerous meeting of respectable citizens from different parts of the state,* assembled at Lexington the 24th day of May last, tending to adopt measures for obtaining the use of the river Mississippi, and the reduction of the posts on the Western waters now occupied by the British; also a copy of a remonstrance to the President and Congress of the United States, on the subject contained in the resolutions. And the said resolutions and remonstrances being read, and some time taken up in deliberating upon each of them separately; resolved unanimously that the society do approve of all and each of the said resolutions, and remonstrances.

Resolved, that the members of the society respectively, do recommend it to the citizens of this county, to meet at the Court-House thereof, on Thursday the 19th inst. to take the said resolutions and remonstrance into consideration; and that Messrs. John Allen, Thomas Jones, James Smith and Richard Henderson, be appointed to present and read the said resolutions and remonstrance to the people, and to take their voice on the same; and if they are approven of, to recommend it to the people to elect two men in the bounds of every militia company in this county, to meet at the Court House thereof, as a county committee, agreeable to the 13th resolution.

Extract from the minutes,

JOHN BOYD, S.C.

Kentucky Gazette, July 12, 1794

12 | Democratic Society of Washington, North Carolina

Address to the Honorable Thomas Blount and His Reply, July 3, 1794

An address from the Democratic Society of Washington, North Carolina, to the honorable Thomas Blount, esq., representative in Congress from this district, on his arrival at this place.

Citizen:
We, the Committee appointed by the Democratic R. Society of Washington, for the special purpose,

Do congratulate you on your safe arrival in this place.—We return to you the unfeigned thanks of our society for your truly patriotic conduct in the late session of Congress.—May your laudable endeavours to promote the general good of our country be every crowned with success.

We wish you health and happiness.

By order of the Committee.

D. Jones, Chairman.

Washington,
July 3, 1794.

———

To the Chairman of the democratic society of Washington,

Citizen:
As nothing can be more pleasing to a man who reveres the republican form of government, and regards as he ought the opinion of his fellow-citizens, than the applause of the virtuous and well-informed men, when is conscious of having endeavoured to deserve it.

The approbation which the democratic society of Washington have done me the honour, through you, so fully and so agreeably to express of my conduct in the last session of Congress could not fail to afford me the highest satisfaction; and excite in me, the most lively emotions of gratitude.

I beg leave to reciprocate the congratulations, the thanks and the wishes of the Society, and through you, as chairman of their committee, to assure them of a continuance of my best endeavours to promote the general good of our common country.

I am, sir,
    With the utmost respect,
        Your most obedient servant.
            Thomas Blount.
Washington, July 3, 1794

General Advertiser (Philadelphia), August 6, 1794

Resolutions Adopted Condemning the Conduct of the People of Pittsburgh, September 6, 1794

At a meeting of the DEMOCRATIC REPUBLIC SOCIETY, of WASHINGTON, N.C. held at the Court House in said town, on Saturday the 6th of September, 1794, and of American Independence the 19th.

ORDERED, That the Society take into consideration the Address of Citizen McDaniel; where upon the Society entered into the following Resolutions—viz.

1. That in the opinion of this Society, that in a Republican Government, a majority ought to govern—That the constitution formed by the free consent of the people, ought to be obeyed—that the remedies pointed out by it, ought to be referred to.

2. That although excise systems are considered to be oppressive, we reprobate every measure taken to oppose them, which may be inconsistent with the government which has been adopted by the free voice of the people.

3. That the conduct of the people at Pittsburgh is highly reprehensible, and ought to be discountenanced by every friend to the constitution of this country.

4. That we will at all times legaly oppose every measure which may endanger the liberty of our country—and with equal firmness we will likewise oppose any unconstitutional attempt to prevent the due operation of the law.

                    D. JONES, Chairman
        Teste,   E. HOWELL, Sec'ry
American Daily Advertiser (Philadelphia), October 6, 1794

13 | Democratic-Republican Societies of South Carolina

REPUBLICAN SOCIETY OF SOUTH CAROLINA, CHARLESTON

Declaration of the Friends of Liberty and National Justice, July 13, 1793

Declaration of the Friends of Liberty and National Justice.

WE, the undersigned citizens of the United States, calling to our remembrance the recent league of sovereign princes against the republic of Poland, and the consequent dismemberment of that ill-fated state; and the present unexampled combination of almost all the European potentates against the French republic, are deeply impressed with an apprehension, that the utmost efforts of despotism will be exerted to annihilate all ideas of liberty, and even to eradicate (if possible) from the human mind, every notion of national justice: And if the present eventful European contest should terminate in the dissolution of the French republic, we have no doubt but the craving appetite of despotism, will be satisfied with nothing less than American vassalage, in some form or other. The interest of absolute power requires that the voice of liberty should be heard no more, and in the event of the overthrow of the French republic, the United States, then without an ally, may be forced to yield to European confederacy. And in as much as an aristocratic ambition has already manifested itself in the conduct, even of some Americans, and has lately been more strongly marked, by its whispers of dissatisfaction to the cause of France, and of mankind: WE do hereby declare, pledging ourselves to each other and to the world, that we, and each of us, will contribute to the utmost of our ability, towards the support of equal liberty and national justice, as well in respect to the French republic, as of the United States, against tyranny and iniquitous rule, in whatever form they may be presented, by any character or body of men appearing in these United States.

IN TESTIMONY WHEREOF, *We have hereunto set our hands,* A.D. 1793.
13th July

Stephen Drayton,[1] etc.

English translation of original in French in Edmund Charles Genêt Papers, Manuscripts
Division, Library of Congress

Toasts Drunk on a French Victory, August 29, 1793

CHARLESTON.

*On the arrival of the ship Carolina, from Charleston, we have the following
advices:—*

August 29. A number of respectable citizens met at Harris's hotel, on Tuesday last, to celebrate the victory gained, on the 1st of August, by the French
frigate Ambuscade,[2] commanded by captain Bompard, over the British frigate
Boston, captain Courtney. After dinner the following toasts were drank, and the
evening was spent with great hilarity and harmony.

1. Citizen Bompard, and his heroic crew: may liberty always have such gallant
defenders. (*Three cheers.*)

2. The president of the United States.

3. Citizen Genet, minister from the republic of France.

4. General Custine.

5. The memory of general Dampierre, and the heroes of every rank, who died
in defence of liberty.

6. The United States of America: perpetuity to their alliance with France.
(*Three cheers.*)

7. The national convention of France: wisdom and unanimity to their councils.

8. The army and navy of France.

9. May republicanism predominate throughout the world, to the utter destruction of baneful aristocracy. (*Three cheers.*)

10. May America never forget the services rendered her in her day of trial.

11. The rights of man.

12. The republican members of congress: a decided majority to their patriotic
measures.

13. May wisdom and gratitude influence the councils of the executive of the
United States, in their conduct towards the French republic.

14. The patriotic jury of Philadelphia who acquitted Gideon Henfield,[3] and
supported the rights of man. (*Three cheers.*)

Independent Chronicle (Boston), September 15, 1793

Discussion in the French Jacobin Society on a Petition from the Republican Society of South Carolina, October 1793

FRENCH JACOBIN SOCIETY—Oct. 1793

The Republican Society of Charleston, in Carolina, one of the United States of America, demanded of the Jacobin Club its adoption.[4]

Hautier, "We have spilt our blood for the establishment of America—I think that the Americans ought to do the same for us before we grant them adoption."

A Citizen. "Before engaging them to intermeddle with our war, it is necessary to understand one another, to come to an agreement with them. I do not see them, a more efficacious way for the previous re-union, than an adoption of their society."

Collot d' Herbois,[5] "Dispatches are received by the Committee of Public Safety,[6] informing it that America has permitted French vessels to sell in their ports, all English prizes which they may take. On a close examination of these dispatches, it appears, that although they carry official mails, they are not from the American government, but merely from a Consul of one of the Anglo American cities, who being nothing but a Commercial Agent, and not a political one, may very likely have written them from interested motives, rather than authentic authorization.

Nevertheless, we should not neglect the advantage which may arise from this request. I conclude that we agree to this adoption. Resolved."

French Paper.

Independent Chronicle (Boston), March 17, 1794

Manuscript Minutes, August 1793 to April 14, 1794

CHARLESTON,

August, 1793.

Fellow Citizens,

THE present state of Europe, where every power seems to be arming one against the other, must naturally lead the citizens of America to contemplate with pleasure, the happy situation they are in, both in respect to locality and as to their being independent of any power on earth. But after enjoyment of this pleasing reflection, the mind will as naturally be led to enquire, what could have given rife to such animosity as now exist between the contending parties: And how grieved will every true American be, when, on enquiry, he finds France, that great and enlightened nation, is contending amidst a number of powerful, arbitrary despots and tyrants, who oppose her in establishing her political freedom. That she is now fighting for the very cause in herself, which she so freely bled ten years past to establish, and did fully establish in this happy, this blest climate! Americans must be alarmed! The interest and perservation of France is that of America. If she is oppressed, if she is reduced to slavery, the fate of our land is decided. Those very powers who are now combined against France, will not suffer a vestige of liberty to remain; wherever they can reach to destroy it, they will; and *America* will next become their object. Such, among other considerations, have induced a number of worthy citizens of this metropolis, to meet and to form themselves into a society, which they have denominated *The Republican Society of South-Carolina.*

The declaration of the principles on which they proceed, are herewith inclosed and forwarded unto you; nothing doubting, but that the patriotism which made you risk both life and fortune in establishing the freedom of your country, will also determine you to use the same means, should it be necessary, to support and defend it.

The eyes of the republican patriot, must ever be watchful; and as many characters have crept in among us, who are not *with us,* their steps should be carefully watched, and their machinations developed: For, generally, it is far more easy to prevent, than to destroy an evil. In pursuing this salutary purpose, the Republican Society will ever hold sacred and unchangeable, the constitution of the land, and the laws of their country. It is not to contravene these, but to prevent infractions, and to preserve inviolate, their inestimable privileges that they have established themselves. A free communication of sentiments throughout this state, either from individuals, or from societies formed in different parts thereof, upon the same principles, will, and must conduce to support the intention; and as several states in the union, have established similar societies, a general communication will consequently take place throughout the whole.

We flatter ourselves, therefore, to receive from you, considerable aid in promoting so laudable an enquiry upon the genuine principles of its formation. And therefore, have to request you early attention to the subject matter, and a frequent and constant correspondence.

We are, &c.

S. DRAYTON, *President.*
J. BLACKE, *Vice-President.*
W. TATE, *Secretary.* [7]

Your letter of   J. KENNEDY, *Assistant Secretary.*   *Committee of*
correspondence,   D. A. HALL,   *Correspond-*
you will be pleased   G. CROSS   *ence.*
to direct to the   J. MARKLAND.
President of the
Republican Society.

WILLIAM MARSHALL,
FRANCIS HUGER
THOMAS B. BOWEN.   *Standing Committee.*
SIMON M'INTOSH,
CHARLES CROWLEY,
SIMEON THEUS, *Treasurer.*
DOMINICK GEOGHEGAN,
WILLIAM CUNNINGTON,
O'BRIEN SMITH.

Cotte S
  No. 4.

In the Republican Society-Thursday
  the 7 November 1793—
    Extract from the Minutes viz.
  Received as a present from the Consul of France[8] a copy of the New Constitution of that republic[9] by the hands of Citizen Cunnington,—which was received
as a mark of his respect for the Society, and it is ordered to be preserved among
the *Archives* of the Society—and this minute to be conveyed to the Citizen Consul
of France by Citizen Cunnington—
                    By order of the Republican Society
                              Benjamin Legane
                                              Secretary
                                              Pro Tem

Charleston South Carolina
November the 7. 1793 &
18 year American Independence

                              No. 5
              The Citizen Consul of the French Republic
                    Charleston South Carolina

Citizen Consul,
  I have the honor to enclose you the resolve of the Republican Society relative
to the Copy of the new Constitution of the Republic of France, which you were
pleased to present them.
  I take the liberty to acquaint you, that the principles and basis of the institution are *Universal Liberty, and the Right of Man!*

That the Society is composed of men—who collectively and individually rejoice in every fortunate event of the French Republic, in their glorious struggle
in the cause of

Patriotism and Universal Liberty ⎱
against   ⎰ !!!
The combined powers of Tyranny and Despotism

As a token of my individual respect for the French Republic, permit me to
assure you, my *ardent wish* is, that their arms may speedily be adorned with *the
most brilliant success,*—and that the Citizens of America; so long as the soil endures; may retain *a grateful sense* of the services rendered them in the hour of
need, and the blood freely spilt on their Plains, by their faithful ally!

I am, agreeable to my own idea,

Your Fellow Citizen,
and Brother Republican
M. Cunnington

Charleston   ⎱
November 8. 1793 ⎰

Citizen Consul Mangourit
    The Citizen Consul
        Of the French Republic
            Charleston South Carolina

Citizen Cunnington

Be pleased Citizen to receive a ticket for tomorrow's feast, one of the Society
who acts as Steward, receives it at the door—We have issued tickets to prevent
confusion as well as *intrusion;*

I think five Salutes from the Republic's Sloop of War, after we have begun our
Toasts will be sufficient,—unless Citizen Captain Branzon may choose to give an
extraordinary one, at day dawn;—this is left entirely to his judgment of the
propriety—a signal will be agreed upon; which will be made from the Hotel, that
the Salutes may be fired as the toasts are given—

I entreat you, accept of my Respects,
Citizen S. Drayton

Wednesday P:M:
12th February 1794

No. 8.

Citizen Drayton, President of the Republican Society established in Charleston, to Citizen Mangourit, consul from the French Republic.

Charleston the 15th February 1794.

Citizen Consul,

It is with cordial pleasure I act in this address from the unanimous Voice of the Republican Society established in this City: and I do now return you their acknowledgment, for the favor you confered on them at the Feast of the thirteenth Instant, in presenting to the Society a part of that horrid Fabric of cruelty and Espotism, which had for a number of years disgraced Humanity and humbled the spirit of Frenchmen in the Dust.

You have presented unto us, Citizen, a Memento which We shall always preserve, to keep alive in our hearts, the miseries that our Brethren the People of France, must have suffered while the diabolical tyranny of Kings and Priestcraft reigned over them.[10]

We shall likewise hold in pleasing remembrance the gallant and Patriotic part which, Worthy Citizen, you acted in the destruction of that Den of Slavery the Bastile, and from the Temple of which, you have brought this Relct of, where Religion, Virtue and humanity have been so often sacrificed to Injustice, Tyranny and every brutal impulse of the heart.

We will have engraved on this piece of Marble, the Cap of Liberty and equality triumphing over the Diadem of Roualty reversed and the prostitution and infamy of a debauched clergy: and there Shall be engraved thereon, the date of the destruction of the Bastile—and when presented by you to the Republican Society.

It shall remain with us as a sacred pledge from a generous Ally to a greatful People, whom they assisted in obtaining their political happiness.

We will preserve it to remind us, that it shall be our duty to destroy every species of Tyranny which may arise in whatever shape or form, to the disgrace of Mankind, and as far as We can, it shall be handed down to Posterity for the like purposes.

In the Name of the Republican Society established in the City of Charleston

S. Drayton President

Citizen Consul Mongourit

No. 10

Cottee B   Charleston 14th April 1794—

To Citizen M. A. B. Mangourit

Citizen

The Republican Society of this City having agreed to an address to be presented from them to the National Convention of the French Republic & having required of me as their President to transmit the same to the Convention[11]—I have to request of you worthy Citizen to take charge of it & present it in the name of the Society possessing every Republican virtue & holding the highest esteem for the greatest Republic in the World, the French

I anticipate the pleasure the Society with receive, when they shall know, that their address will be presented by a Citizen whose principles are just & whose whole Soul burns with the pure flame of Liberty—accept Citizen of my esteem & Regard

S. Drayton Pres.^t

Republican Society of South Carolina Papers, Boston Public Library, Rare Book Room

Toasts Drunk at a Meeting, February 13, 1794

Messeurs Printers.

THE following volunteer toasts being drank in the Republican Society, on the 13th instant, after the departure of the president, and not having found a place in your paper, you will oblige some of the members of said society by inserting them:

1. The republican and revolution societies and conventions of Britain and Ireland: success to their efforts in the cause of freedom and the equal rights of man.

2. May William Muir, of Scotland, (condemned unconstitutionally by arbitrary judges, by a corrupt and ungenerous jury) feel the generosity of virtuous republicans, by being brought to this land of liberty, if he should be banished by his ungrateful country to the utmost parts of the earth.[12]

3. The memory of the brave patriots of France who have fallen martyrs to liberty.

4. May the inhabitants of the whole earth very soon disavow all kings but the king of Heaven.

City Gazette (Charleston), February 19, 1794

Address to Citizen James Madison, March 12, 1794

Charleston 12th March 1794.

To Citizen James Madison, Representative from the Commonwealth of Virginia, in Congress.

Citizen Representative,

The patriotic principles which have distinguished your conduct in the House of Representatives of the United States in the present Session,[13] have attracted the particular attention of your fellow Citizens: and while they with indignation reprobate the contrary conduct of some other character, who have imposed on their Constituents by holding forth doctrines as contrary to the interest of America, as they are disgraceful; they with pleasure behold in you, Citizen, the firm Patriot & true Republican.

The Republican Society established in this City, who have for their basis, a pure love of their Country and a just respect for its Laws and Constitution, cannot withold giving a testimony of their approbation of the part you have acted in support of the Dignity of America by preserving her faith to her Allies and resenting the injuries she has received from an ungenerous and implacable Enemy. They therefore unanimously Resolved that, you should be addressed by letter conveying to you their opinion of your conduct; and it is with the highest pleasure and satisfaction, I do now in their name and in compliance with their Resolve, give you, Worthy Citizen, their plaudit: receive then this mark of their esteem, and continue to preserve that general approbation; by exerting your talents to save your Country from dishonour and ignominy which may be brought on her, either by the weakness or by the baseness of others.

> In the name of the Republican Society established
>> in Charleston—
>>> S. Drayton
>>>> Citizen President

Citizen James Madison

James Madison Papers, Manuscripts Division, Library of Congress

Resolutions Adopted Condemning the Conduct of Great Britain, March 14, 1794

At a meeting of the Republican Society of Charleston, held at Charleston, the 14th day of March, 1794:

This society, contemplating the daring outrages and diabolical machinations of the British court, and the vile intrigues now practised by her agents and emissaries, to undermine and destroy the liberty and happiness of America; and holding it just and laudable to call the attention of our fellow citizens to the alarming situation of public affairs, do hereby submit to their consideration the sense entertained of these important circumstances, and resolve as follows:

Resolved, That it is the peculiar privilege of citizens of the United States to meet at all times and on all occasions, peacably to pursue the best means of obtaining and preserving the public happiness, and freely to investigate and censure, or approve the conduct of all persons in public employment, and to submit their opinions to the sense of the community.

Resolved, That this society view with indignation the conduct of certain members in congress, one of them a representative from Charleston district:[14] being convinced, from the whole tenor of their actions and debates in congress, they are possessed of the basest and most dangerous principles; that far from being republicans, they are indifferent to the repeated insults offered the American flag, and the repeated depradations committed on the property of the citizens of America; that in addition to the insults and depredations, the detention of the western posts, contrary to express treaty, supplies to the Indians our deadly foes, the treaty devised and concluded by the British government, to set the Algerines upon our commerce, are to them but trifles, when compared to the prosperity of the funds in which, by their infamous speculations, they are become deeply interested.

Resolved, That it is our opinion war is inevitable; we cannot therefore be too early in making preparations; we therefore recommend that such other forts should without delay be erected, as will secure this state from depredations and insult; and that it is the duty of all good republican citizens, to provide themselves as speedily as possible with such implements of war as may be necessary for their defence.

Resolved, That proclamations are intended only as promulgations of laws constitutionally enacted, to inform the citizens who, in consequence of the attention necessary to their various occupations, may require such information; or, proclamations may with propriety be made to give warning of the approach of any public calamity, or to announce to the people the day and place of any public act: but when any person, or set of men in office, instead of announcing only the laws of the land, attempt by proclamation to declare his or their own will and determination as the sovereign rule, binding on the people, the judges and the courts of justice, such an exercise of power is unconstitutional, tyrannical, arbitrary, and in the highest degree dangerous, an usurpation of sovereignty of the most despotic nature, and a direct attack on the liberties of the people.

Resolved, That all public officers are appointed under the constitution, their political creator and ruler, and they are but servants of the public.

Resolved, That treaties solemnly made with nations who act with sincere friendship, and preserve zealously their faith towards us, ought to be inviolably adhered to, and guarded from infraction at every risque; that the cause of France is our own; that our interest, liberty and public happiness are involved in her fate; that we are bound to support her by every tie of principle and gratitude, as well as a principle of self-preservation; that for any man, or set of men, either in private or public, and particularly those to whom the welfare of our community is entrusted, to advocate doctrines and principles derogatory to the cause of France, or her commerce with America, or in support of the basic measures of the combined despots of Europe, particularly Great Britain—is a convincing manifestation of sentiments treacherous and hostile to the interest of the United States, and well deserves the severest censure from all true republican citizens of America.

Resolved, That this society entertain a grateful sense, and highly approve of the conduct of citizen Madison and those of his sentiments in congress.

Resolved, That the foregoing resolutions be printed in all the public papers, for the information of our fellow citizens, in order that they may take such measures as they shall deem most proper for their support.

City Gazette (Charleston), March 17, 1794

Resolutions Adopted Condemning the South Carolina Legislature, June 23, 1794

The printers of the City Gazette are requested, to publish the following resolves of the Republican Society of Charleston, at an extra meeting held at citizen Harris's hotel, on Monday evening, the 23rd instant.

UPON reviewing the proceedings of the legislature of this state, toward citizen Stephen Drayton, in their sittings of December 1793, and the resolves of the house of representatives respecting Alexander Moultrie and Stephen Drayton, in May 1794,[15] and convinced that the same are founded on principles and doctrines subversive of the political freedom of this country, therefore

Resolved, as the opinion of this society, that any attempt made by the representatives of the people, in their legislative capacity, to accuse, try, convict and condemn any citizen for any imaginary crime, is unjust, arbitrary, and in direct violation of the constitution of this state.

Resolved, That the freedom of debate, and the liberty of acting without external restraint, only be admitted to the representative of a free people, in their *legislative capacity;* but ought to be, and it is denied them when they assume to themselves the powers of the judiciary or the executive.

Resolved, That it is the opinion of this society, the house of representatives of this state, in certain proceedings of December 1793 and May 1794, have entirely departed from their duty, and in direct violation of the constitution, as expressed in the 2 d and 6 th section, article 9, of the same—and that the liberties, privileges and immunities of the citizens have thereby, in the persons of Stephen DRAYTON and Alexander Moultrie, been grossly and flagrantly violated.

Resolved, That the foregoing resolves be immediately published in the *Gazettes* of this city, and signed by the president, pro tempore.

Extract from the minutes,
SIMON MACINTOSH, President, pro tem.

City Gazette (Charleston), June 28, 1794

Resolutions Adopted Vindicating the Conduct of the Society, December 20, 1794

Charleston, Dec. 23.

At a meeting of the Republican Society, held in the city of Charleston, on Saturday, the 20th Dec. 1794, the following Resolves were unanimously agreed to:

Brought before the tribunal of our fellow-citizens throughout the United States, as being guilty of crimes in our opinion the most heinous, those of fomenting and supporting insurrections in the Western parts of Pennsylvania, and attempting to destroy the peace of our country, we pronounce it a duty we cannot dispense with, that we do vindicate our conduct by contradicting where we can, every false accusation which has been made against us, as a Republican society; and in the first instance, we do unanimously

Resolved, That we will never relinquish the right of freemen to investigate the acts of any man or men who are or may be placed in power; on the other hand, while we consider this as a right appertaining to the sovereignty of the people, we shall always conduct our investigations upon constitutional principles, and the pure love of our country; and unerring truth shall be our guide.

Resolved unanimously, That the accusations which have been alledged against this Society, in a public body, are unfair, ungenerous, and unfounded in truth: Unfair, as this society has been brought into public view, upon no truth having been produced to support the assertion; ungenerous, because it holds up a number of citizens to scorn, proceeding entirely from personal enmity, and resentment, and not from an apprehension of public danger; unfounded in truth, because this society puts its accusers to defiance to produce in evidence, one instance, where they have acted as fomentors or supporters of any disturbance of opposition which may have been intended or made against the general government of the United States.

By order of the Society,

S. MACKINTOSH,

President

Independent Chronicle (Boston), January 29, 1795

THE MADISON SOCIETY OF THE COUNTY OF GRENVILLE, GRENVILLE

Resolutions Adopted on the Officers of a Free Government, July 26, 1794

Charleston, July 26.

Greenville, July 4th, 1794. A numerous and full meeting of the Madison Society of this county, was held at the court-house, when the following resolutions were unanimously entered into, as expressive of their sentiments on public affairs.

RESOLVED, That it is the opinion of this Society, that all the officers of a free government ought to be divided as equally as possible among the citizens having respect to the necessary qualifications, an impartial distribution of them being a means of disseminating political knowledge among the inhabitants, and an excellent stimulus to men to acquire such qualifications. And that all combinations, or agreements, between any set of citizens, to acquire and hold an undue proportion of them, as it tends to destroy that equality among the inhabitants which is a leading feature in our government, and is contrary to the principles of a republican, ought by every virtuous citizen to be reprobated; and as the framers of the constitution, not apprised that such a thirst for power would at this very early day exist, having omitted to guard against its dangerous tendency.

Resolved unanimously,

That we will at the ensuing election, and all future elections, unite our efforts to exclude from a seat in the legislature, all persons who may, or have, during their being members thereof, accepted from them any appointment of honor, trust or profit.

Ordered, That the printers in Charleston be requested to publish the above resolved in their gazettes:—

American Daily Advertiser (Philadelphia), September 4, 1794

THE PALMETTO SOCIETY OF CHARLESTON

Toasts Drunk at a Meeting, June 28, 1794

At a meeting of the Palmetto Society, held at Foederal Point (vulgarly called Shue's Folly,) on the 28th June, 1794, a president was appointed for the day, and after an agreable repast, the following toasts were drank:

1. The 28th June, 1776.[16] May the event of that day be ever repeated when the sons of freedom combat against the slaves of despotism.

2. Major general Moultrue.[17] May every attempt to asperse his character be *sir peter-parkered.*

3. Colonel Motte. May the evening of his days be as serene as their meridian was bright.

4. The gallant officers and citizen soldiers whose brave conduct, on that memorable day, reflected such lustre on their country.

5. The memory of those patriots who, on that occasion, sealed with their blood, their attachment to the cause of liberty.

6. The United States. May republicanism cement their union, and aristocracy be banished from their shores.

7. The President of the United States. May the blossoms of the tree of liberty, which he so largely contributed to plan, never feel a blight under his administration.

8. The republican members of both houses of congress.

9. The republic of France. May her perserverance in the cause of liberty be eventually crowned with success, and animate the Sans Cullottes, throughout the world, to initate his bright example.

10. The venerable Doctor Priestly. May his patriotic sentiments ensure to him that fraternal affection in this country, which despotism has denied him in his own.

11. Muir, Palmer[18] and others, martyrs in the cause of freedom.

12. Major Pinckney.

13. General Wayne, and the western army.

14. Our distressed brethren in Algiers.

15. The patriotic fair of the United States.

Volunteer. The right of expatriation to all those who wish to quit our country.

City Gazette and Daily Advertiser (Charleston), June 30, 1794

THE DEMOCRATIC SOCIETY OF PINCKNEYVILLE

Resolutions Adopted Upholding the Cause of France, April 7, 1794

PINCKNEYVILLE, April 7.

On Thursday evening a numerous meeting of the Democratic Society of this district, was held at the court-house. A committee was appointed to draw up, and report the next evening, certain resolutions, expressive of the sentiments of the Society on the present state of public affairs. The meeting was very full the next evening, when the following resolutions were reported and adopted with great unanimity.

1st. Resolved, that we declare ourselves, unalterably, friends to the Rights of Man; to Rights emanating from nature, founded on equal liberty, and protected by equal laws; and enemies to tyranny, whether under the form of monarchy, aristocracy, or anarchy. One of our essential rights, we consider that of assembling, at all times, to discuss, with freedom, friendship and temper, all subjects of public concern, and to publish our sentiments to the world, when we think we can thereby promote the general good, and secure the blessings of social happiness.

2d. That the cause of France is the cause of the people of all nations; they are generally interested in her success; the americans particularly and immediately; that they are bound, by every principle of gratitude, honour and interest, to render her every assistance in their power, and to allow her every privilege to which she is intitled, by reason of the friendship between the two nations, the similarity of their principles of government, and existing treaties, which ought to be construed in the most liberal manner.

3d. That France, since her alliance with America, has uniformly acted towards us in the most open, generous and liberal manner, and is daily giving us new proofs, that one nation may have a friendship for another.

4th. That the present combination of European powers against the french republic, is a combination against the principles of civil and religious liberty; an outrage on the laws of God and nature, and tends to keep mankind in ignorance, stupidity, and abject slavery.

5th. That our state and federal governments, are essentially democratic; that all power is derived from, and revertible to the people; that men, by appointments to public offices, are not rendered honourable; that they are agents of the people during their continuance in office, and accountable for their conduct. We, therefore, consider all honourable titles of office, all affectations of etiquette, all mys-

tery and secrecy in government (where the public safety is not immediately concerned) not only frivolous, but beneath the dignity of republican, and subversive
of equal liberty.

6th. That laws and government are the expression of the general will of the
people; their representatives are the organ through which that will is expressed;
that it is the duty of their representatives to inform themselves of, and to express the sentiments of a majority of their constituents. We, therefore, view with
resentment, the conduct of one of our senators in congress, in opposing the
opening of the senate doors, contrary to the will of the people, and against the
express instructions of the legislature from which he received his appointment.

7th. That the conduct of Great Britain towards the United States, since the
late war, has been uniformly hostile, injurious and insulting. That she has not
fulfilled her treaty of peace, nor manifested any intention of doing it. The re-
tention of the Western Posts, supplying the savages with the means of carrying
on a war against the frontier inhabitants, and setting loose algerine pirates on
american citizens and their property, the assumed power of controuling our
commerce, and capturing and condemning our vessels, are proofs that the late
peace was only a cessation of arms, and not an abatement of enmity, or a reconciliation on her part; and that she pays no other regard to the laws of nations
and rules of justice, than such as are induced by motives of interest or fear.

8th. That war to any nation, is a great calamity, and ought by every prudent
measure, to be avoided, but is better than a dishonourable state of peace, and a
tame submission to plunder and aggravated violence unresisted. And we are,
sorry to find that the condition of the americans has gradually become more
humiliating and distressing in proportion to their defenceless situation, the strictness of their neutrality, and their moderation.

9th. That it is our opinion, that the ministers of the french republic, residing
in America, derive their appointment from *that nation;* that they have a right of
delivering their opinions freely, in matters concerning the two nations, and the
construction of their treaties, and ought not to be villified or abused. That the
legislative, executive, and judicial authorities of the United States are separate
and distinct. The judges of the United States are the only legal expositors of
treaties, where the letter is silent, or the meaning uncertain. We therefore consider the illiberal censure of citizen Genet's principles and opinions, concerning the
reciprocal rights and duties of the two nations, as unjust and base, and that the object of it is to bring him unmeritedly into contempt, to disunite the fraternal republics, and injure the cause of freedom in general.

10th. That citizen Genet, as far as we can judge from documents made public,
has acted in pursuance of instructions to him given by the executive of France,[19]
at the time of his appointment, and cannot be accountable for a change of measures in France since his appointment. It is our opinion, since his residence here,
he has always evinced by his conduct, a zealous attachment to the true principles

of liberty and equality, and has endeavoured to cement the people of the two nations, by the strongest ties of reciprocal interest and friendship.

11th. That population is the only true principle of representation among a free people. That wealth causes its own influence, and ought not to be directly represented. That the representation of the people of this state, in their general assembly, is not founded on that principle, or any other, of equality and just proportion, and ought to be reformed.[20]

12th. That the spirited conduct of our brethren and fellow-citizens in Charleston, by their late remonstrance and address to congress, on the subject of the spoliation made by the british, on american property, taken on the seas, deserves our highest applause and firmest support; and we declare that we are ready and willing (and we believe we speak the language of the whole people of this district) to submit to any inconvenience which may result from such measures as congress may think necessary to adopt, to secure to us a total independency as a nation, or a connection with others, on principles of the most reciprocal benefits.

Ordered, that the printers in Charleston and Columbia be requested to publish these resolves.

After the business of the society was finished, the evening was spent in social intercourse, and a mutual exchange of patriotic sentiments among the members, which fully evinced their warm attachment to the true principles of republicanism; and that they will be among the last people of America to forget aid afforded us in the dark hour of our distress, by our generous allies; of the tenders they have made us of lasting friendship and advantages, since they have raised up persecuted liberty on the ruins of crowns and sceptres.

South Carolina State Gazette (Charleston), April 29, 1794

THE FRANKLIN OR REPUBLICAN SOCIETY OF PENDLETON COUNTY

Resolutions Adopted on a Variety of Subjects, June 30, 1794

CHARLESTON.
SOUTH CAROLINA, 12th *June,* 1794

The Franklin or Republican Society of Pendleton county, in a meeting of the 31st of May, at the house of citizen capt. Moses Liddle, and agreeably to adjournment at Pendleton court-house this day—the following preamble and resolves were laid before the society, which, having been duly considered and digested, were agreed to, to wit:

ON reflecting on the late war between the United States of America and
Great-Britain, the bloody scenes rise afresh in our minds; the cruelties, the murders and wanton depradations committed by British tyranny for seven years in
this ill-fated country, can never be forgotten. Fathers and husbands are still living, who bewail their murdered wives and children; and orphans unhappily exist,
who early lost the protecting hand of their parents.

Under the will of an all-wise Providence, our councils and our armies effected
the great work of American independence. The wisdom of our senate directed
them to seek an ally in France; Americans and French join in martial band;
Britons and their detestable tyranny are made to flee our land; peace takes
place; agriculture flourishes, and nature resumes her smile once more in our
fields and plains. Britain, like Milton's devil, views our increasing happiness
with a malignant eye; she dares not wage war; to disturb our peace she takes
other means, not less effectual in being secret; British subjects become American
citizens; our towns are filled with their private agents; our councils are warped;
aristocracy takes root and thrives; equality and liberty totters. *Emboldened,*
Britain pursues the plan; she refuses to fulfill the treaty of peace; she disgraces
our flag; she piratically robs our merchants, imprisons our seamen, and prescribes our trade. Our councils, lost to national dignity, lost to patriotic virtue,
suffer these insults and depradations without resentment: the people cry for
war; our councils disgracefully negociate. Thus we are in danger from British
machinations, while in arms we would bid them defiance. Hence we anticipate
with horror the prospects which the present policies place to our view, and do
behold our posterity, borne down with chains and fetters, weeping over the
graves of their fathers who fell in establishing the freedom and happiness of their
country, and which was lost by the pusillanimity or the treachery of our
councils.

We, therefore, the undersigned, members of the Republican Society of Pendleton county, do thus pledge ourselves each to the other, and to the world, that
we will, to the utmost of our power, support the rights of mankind. We have
sealed our liberties with our blood, and we will not part from them but with our
lives: and do therefore enter into and subscribe the following resolves:

1. Resolved, That the cause of the French republic is the cause of *America,*
and it is a duty which gratitude demands from the people of the United States,
that they afford to Frenchmen every assistance within their reach.

2. Resolved, That it is the undeniable right of all freemen and citizens to form
societies, to consult among themselves, and to recommend such means as shall
appear best adapted to support public peace, and to promote general benefit.

3. Resolved, That the people never did, nor never can delegate a power which
they do not in right possess. The people have not a power to fix eternal slavery
on their posterity; therefore their representatives, in a legislative capacity, cannot
enact laws to arrest, confine and punish a citizen of America who may incline
to remove out of the limits of the United States, because it is contrary to the

law of nature, and in direct violation of the law of the land.—*Man is born free.*

4. Resolved, That the collecting of taxes, or other duties to be paid in money, in these remote countries, is oppressive and unjust; for it must be well known, that no article of our produce will discharge its own freight to market, whereby money is to be obtained. And therefore,

5. Resolved, That under these circumstances the seizure of property, and the sale thereof by the sheriff, is highly injurious and destructive to the laborious and honest farmer and his family.

6. Resolved, That it is the inherent right of every free man to vote and to elect the officers who are to command them in a military character; and he who dares to attempt a contravention of this right, forfeits all protection from this country, is a tyrant and a despot, and an enemy to the people.

7. Resolved, That citizen Madison, and the real patriots of the present congress, are entitled to our just praise and to our warmest thanks; and on the contrary, that we do abhor and reprobate every character who may have endeavored to establish monarchial principles, or may be influenced by private interest.

8. Resolved, That the foregoing resolves be made public through the channel of some of the gazettes of this state, to shew the fixed and determined opinion of the Franklin or Republican Society of Pendleton county; and also for the purpose of convincing those infamous characters, who, lost to all fear of shame, and prompted by some evil spirit, have attempted to overturn and destroy the *rights and privileges of the people,* and their proceedings, are disapproved of, and that the people will persist in the support of their liberties.

> CITIZEN SAMUEL LOFTON,[21] Chairman.
> CITIZEN EDW. TATE M'CLURE, Sec'ry.
> CITIZEN JOHN MILLER,[22] Corresp. sec'ry.

Citizens   *John Barton*   *James Sterrit,*
            Moses Liddle,[23]   *Thos. Lofton,*   Standing
            Eliah Moore,   *Joshua Sexton,*   committee.

N.B. The society consists of four hundred members.

City Gazette (Charleston), June 30, 1794

To Messeurs Freneau and Paine, September 25, 1795

For the CITY GAZETTE.
Pendleton County, Washington District,
September 25, 1795.

Messeurs FRENEAU [24] & PAINE,

   I KNOW the public curiosity has been on tip-toe to learn the manner in which
the frontier district of South-Carolina would receive the *celebrated* treaty of the
celebrated Jay—We did not burn his effigy—we are too dignified for such business—But were the *original* among us, I would not insure him but at a very high
premium.
   On the receipt of Jay's treaty, the plot being completely developed, my
"pulse beat high" indeed. I had attentively watched and marked every step in
our executive, from the moment of Jay's and King's diabolical attempt to ruin
us with France, by their imputation on the ambassador. I plainly perceived
things were not as they should be—But, after the open, the candid, the generous
manner in which Mr. Dallas had explained the conversation between Mr. Genet
and himself,[25] (the report of which did not warrant even a shadow of ground for
Jay's and King's representation) I then plainly discovered the cloven foot—the
whole of a base and wicked attempt to alienate us from our tried and best friends.
From this period, taking in the President's proclamation of neutrality, (from
which we may date all our distress and confusion) in a very particular manner
Mr. Madison's provisionary resolutions, and afterwards Mr. Jay's *marked* appointment—and I form my judgment—the conclusion from all which satisfied me, that
without some convulsive effort in the body-politic, the views we had so fondly
formed on the rising happiness and greatness of our infant empire, must vanish
like a dream. No man than myself ever entertained a more exalted idea of the
excellency of the character of the President—but on the appearance of his
proclamation of neutrality, notwithstanding the division in mens' minds, I did
not hesitate to pronounce, that *Washington had placed an extinguisher on his
head!*—From that moment, all things, interesting to us as a nation, went wrong—
but Mr. Jay's British Pandora box—his *friendly* treaty-crowned the whole! My
motto, written on the heart, is *Nil Desperandum.* All my hopes are founded on
an earnest expectation that the good sense of the Republic of France in particular, (of Holland, and of all the other states immerging from the chaos of slavery
and the dregs of monarchy) must be strikingly convinced and impressed with
these sentiments: *that the hearts of the whole people of America vibrate in strict
unison with their own—that the imbecility in our government, and the defect in
our constitution respecting forming treaties, a short time will correct—and that
we shall, altogether, form such an union as must give freedom and happiness to*

the whole world!—I say, on receiving Jay's treaty, a few of the most watchful
amongst us immediately flew together,—The result of our meeting was to wait a
few days in expectation of information from our fellow-citizens in Charleston—
but being disappointed, (we have since found by the neglect of the post) and our
patience exhausted, a meeting of the district was called.—We assembled on the
22d of last month—After discussing the treaty, general Pickens, general Anderson, the Rev. Mr. Reese, Mr. Calhoun, and myself, were appointed a committee
to take it fully into consideration, and to report thereon to the several brigades,
at the approaching reviews by the Governor.

Tuesday, Sept. 15th, was fixed for our first review, that of col. Moore's regiment. Unhappily, our much respected governor was prevented from attending,
by the present temporary sickness in our country—a kind of influenza fever—he
was consequently detained in Abbeville. Col. Moore's regiment went through
the several evolutions with much more exactness than could have been expected
from the shortness of their practice—The adjutant general expressed himself sur-
prized and pleased.—After passing the line, in review, gen. Anderson ordered the
regiment to form a column by the right, the right in front, when he informed
them that he was deputed by the committee chosen to consider Mr. Jay's treaty,
to communicate to the regiment a report of their resolutions, which having read,
and made several spirited and judicious observations, the question of adoption
and rejection were put—The approvers of the resolutions were to remain covered,
and when the word was given not a single hat moved. On the reviewing ground,
a Liberty-Tree was erected, with the Cap of Liberty, and the Colours of the
United States, and an inscription on its base expressive of the general detestation
of the treaty.—The utmost order was preserved throughout the day, with a little
exception—The people were thrown into the utmost ferment by a confidential
report of the President's having ratified the treaty—But on assurance of the *im-
probability,* by those who thought it *impossible,* the people were cooled—and the
whole terminated much to the satisfaction of the citizens in general—to the honor
of col. Moore, major Farrar, the brigade inspector, majors Hamilton and Nicholson, and the officers and men in general.

On the 21st, col. Martin's regiment was reviewed in the Fork of Keowee and
Tugaloo, (the governor not yet arrived)—Col. Manning declared great satisfaction at the promptness of their discipline, and the great order and regularity observed. At the close of the day, general Anderson ordered the men to form, as
before at col. Moore's review, and read to them the resolves prepared by their
committee, on the treaty of amity, &c.—They were received with the highest
approbation, and, to a man, adopted by the regiment.

Col. Clarke's, the third and last regiment, will be received to-morrow, the
26th: from which we have the best found for expecting no less proficiency in
military discipline and orderly conduct as citizens, than unanimity in reprobating the treaty, which the more we investigate, the more are we excited to new
emotions of rage and indignation. When (next week) the two reviews in Green-

ville county are over, and the sense of the district will then be taken, the resolutions will be sent to you for publication.

On the day following col. Moore's review, the Franklin Society met together, to express (more at large than could be possibly brought forward to the whole district) their sentiments of Mr. Jay's treaty—A copy of their proceedings I have in charge, as corresponding secretary, to convey to your press, with a most urgent request, that you will *immediately* give their resolves not only to their fellow-citizens in Charleston, but to those of the United States in general.

As ever, I remain, unalterably your's, &c.

P.S.—and a frightful P.S. it is!—We have, at the moment of sealing our letter, received THE RATIFICATION!!![26]—What DOTAGE!—what LUNACY!—*Our* mind, by restrospect and anticipation, had been somewhat prepared—We received the shock with less impression than might have been expected—The alternative (at least in our minds) was at hand—A CONVENTION of THE UNITED STATES, *to* ALTER *and* AMEND *the Constitution!*—This must, necessarily, lead to a DISSOLUTION OF THE PRESENT GOVERNMENT!—A government, which, in its now existing executive form, and particularly as it operates in forming and concluding treaties, has been discovered to possess, and actually exercised, an uncontroulable power, subversive of our dearest, inalienable rights, both as men and citizens; and highly dangerous to our honor and interest as an independent nation!—In the way proposed, we may, possibly, get rid of the most infamous of all infamous treaties—of Mr. Jay's manacles, of his fetters, of his shackles!

We are too much agitated at the present moment to advise, calmly—but possessing, as we know the United States do, wisdom and ability equal to the severe task imposed on us, we shall, *for the present,* remain quiet.

City Gazette (Charleston), October 28, 1795

Resolutions Adopted on Jay's Treaty, September 28, 1795

SOUTH CAROLINA—WASHINGTON DISTRICT.
SEPTEMBER 28, 1795.

THE Franklin, or Republican Society of Pendleton county, having by the watchful vigilance of their standing committee, on a most pressing question, been called together to give their opinion on a public measure—a right they will not tamely relinquish, nor resign but with their lives!—having taken into consideration the ruinous treaty *proposed* and signed by John Jay, the American ambassador, with his Britannic majesty—a treaty, as detestable in its origin, as contemptible in its event!—a treaty which can never be enforced but by the bayonet!—having fully weighed it in all its articles—and taking into view, that when the complaints of a brave and powerful people are observed to increase in proportion to the wrongs they have suffered!—when, instead of sinking into submission, they are roused to resistance! the time must come at which every inferior consideration will yield to their security—to the general safety of the empire!

There is a moment of difficulty and danger, at which British flattery and falsehood can no longer deceive, and simplicity itself can be no longer misled!—that period has at length arrived.

When we see a man improperly appointed to negociate one of the most important treaties, because not properly, nor constitutionally *advised*—that this man was the most improper, because his attachment to Britain, and aversion to France, were notorious!—and that he was altogether an objectionable character, because, (in admitting doubts to be started by Britain about our line, and to which *he* acceded!)—instead of shewing a thorough knowledge of his country— appears to have been wretchedly ignorant, and consequently either shamefully imposed on, or *corruptly* influenced!—who, instead of using that policy which should have "extorted from Britain, in her present state of humiliation, (and which could not be hoped from her justice)" a reparation of reiterated wrongs!— was the *first* man to propose to submit to a treaty, which, if adopted, must blast us in the opinion of Europe as the most pusilanimous nation that ever existed!— a treaty which, in all its hardened features, betrays insult and contempt!—a treaty, not only thus made odious, but which abridges in every respect our rights, and which sports with our just claims and interests!—We demand, that when such glaringly ruinous conduct *appears,* is *permitted,* is *sanctioned!* have not the people just grounds of complaint—would not silence be criminal?

Therefore resolved, That when a public measure dares not be arraigned, *"because it is the offspring of the highest character"*—then Liberty lies prostrate— then Despotism begins!—and heartily adopting the sentiments of our fellow citizens of Camden, (*at the same time reprobating denunciations against orderly associations*) with them we do insist, that it is both the duty and right of freemen, on all great, public occasions, in which the honor and welfare of the Republic is concerned, to come forward and declare their sentiments with freedom and firmness—that those who are entrusted with power, may be admonished to use that power *only* for the good of the people, who placed it, for that *especial* purpose, in their hands; and to teach them to be cautious how they violate the precious, the sacred trust.

Resolved, That on the appointment of John Jay as an *extraordinary* ambassador to Britain, we were *led to believe* that our rights would have been vindicated with firmness, a reparation of our wrongs obtained!—On the contrary, *even after the signing of a treaty of amity,* our flag is the *common sport* of Britain, and our sailor fellow-citizens and property at their mercy.

Resolved, that we were induced by *profession* to believe our administration sympathized in the cause of an ally, wrestling for liberty—a great and regenerated people, who cherish in their utmost purity those sacred principles which have laid the foundation of OUR *freedom in the blood of our dearest citizens!*—but that ally has been treated with *insincerity, even at the moment our inveterate enemy, and the foe of human happiness, has been invited to our bosom! and when British tyranny and baseness can leave not a doubt on a single unprejudiced mind that we are about to give that nation* A FOOTING IN LAW AMONG US WHICH WILL BE CONVERTED TO OUR RUIN!

Resolved, That By the constitution of the United States, all treaties are to be made *"by and with the* ADVICE *and* CONSENT *of the Senate"*—But the Senate, as such, were ignorant of the principle or basis of the treaty itself. We admit they were made acquainted with the appointment of Jay, but did not instruct him, nor were informed of his instructions. *He was instructed, or he was not!*—IF HE WAS! *we will drop the curtain!* If not, and acted *of* and *from* HIMSELF, we shall lament the want of a guillotine! For when was it ever *conceived* to be *possible* that America could entertain the absurd and dangerous idea of trusting any man, (but especially a Jay) to negociate with *such* a government as Britain—without *explicit* instructions!—The obvious construction of the clause in the constitution, which makes the advice of the senate necessary, has been given by the President himself, when a treaty was proposed by France. Mr. Genet was empowered to propose a treaty *"on liberal principles, such as might strengthen the bonds of good-will which unite the two nations;"* but on making his proposal to the executive, he was informed *"that the participation in matters of treaty, given by the constitution to that branch of government, would necessarily delay any answer to his friendly proposition, the Senate being then in recess, and not to meet again until the fall."*—In the negociations with Great-Britain, the Senate *was in session,* and yet were they called on to *advise?* Did they give instructions? They did not!—We allow this most interesting business was taken up in the Senate by our patriotic citizen Butler[27]—but, from a want of formality, he was opposed—and this important matter died away, because it was not *orderly!*—In the treaty also with the Creeks,[28] the President required the *advice* of the Senate *before* he began to treat, and actually laid the outlines of a treaty before them, previous to the negociation.

Resolved, That we consider it becoming in a high degree the duty of the house or representatives of the general government, to enquire into so bold an attack on the palladium of our rights—'tis impossible they can suffer so flagrant a breach in the constitution to pass unnoticed!—The President and Senate will certainly endeavor to reconcile their conduct to the wounded feelings of their fellow-citizens.

Resolved, That so far as is depending on his own integrity and good wishes to the United States, we are still willing to behold in Washington THE SAME GOOD AND GREAT MAN! But, is it not possible, at least respecting Jay's treaty, that he may have been wrongly advised?

Resolved, That it is highly probable our generous and brave ally, however well-disposed towards us, viewed with some emotion of indigation, at the least, the *uncandid* manner in which their proposition for a treaty was *received* and *rejected* by our government; and now find themselves under the necessity of calling on us to declare, *honestly* and *openly,* our intentions towards them— *whether we will adopt the first supreme of the land under the patronage of France or of England?* The period has at length arrived to know our ultimatum— the mask has been strippen of by Mr. Jay—and the majority of twenty in the Senate, we conjecture, will be cautious how far they pledge themselves to their constituents on the utility of an English treaty, provided France should show her disapprobation, or consider herself neglected.

Resolved, That admitting (what is insinuated by a member of congress for this state, the advocate and defender of British systems and British tyranny!) that the treaty proposed by France HE suspects could not be obtained on eligible terms, but at the price of joining with her in the war—we do insist, that at the time alluded to, the honor, the interest of America earnestly called on us to enter heartily into measures opposed to the dreadful league formed against a generous and natural ally, whose welfare *should* and *must* be *inseparable* from our own!—the moment Britain openly declared against France, should have been our signal for action!—the united voice of the continent proclaimed the general, the generous sentiment!—*but the grateful feelings of a whole people were sunk in the* TIMIDITY *of the government!*

Resolved, That (reflecting on the present interesting moment, when an eventual war with Britain may be reasonably expected from *a further discussion* of Mr. Jay's *friendly* treaty) we deprecate, with the strongest emotions of apprehension, *a difference between America and France!*—War with England, will be war with Spain!—our government knows it!—Even the *neutrality* of France, under the circumstances, can be anticipated but with very unpleasing sensations.

Resolved, That we view with surprize the industry used not to disclose the articles of Mr. Jay's treaty—AFFECTING *and* PRACTISING *all the secrecy of* MON- ARCHY, *so opposite to open and republican principles.*—Will it, dare it be contended, that the people have no right to ask, nay, to *demand* information on the posture of their affairs?—Secrecy robs them of this right, and makes *twenty* greater than the *whole.* Is this republicanism?—is this liberty?—Monarchs and conclaves make a *trade of secrecy—it suits their designs*—but neither monarchs nor conclaves are, as yet, in unison with the sentiments, nor the wishes of the American people. There is no authorized secrecy in *our* government, and to infer such a right from the practices of other nations, is a prostitution of republican principles. The constitution of the United States gives to the president and Senate the power of making treaties, but it communicates no ability to hatch those things in darkness. A treaty! which is to be the supreme-law-of-the-land! and yet the people not to be informed of the terms of this law until binding upon them! until the opportunity for amendment is past!—Secrecy and mystery marked the conception, birth, and parentage of this lump of abortion and deformity.—The president received the treaty in January, when congress were sitting, and did not submit it to the Senate till June!—when it was impossible any one legislature in the union could be in session to give the alarm!—The press alone had the glory of the discovery and reprobation of this horrid political monster!—It is also worthy of note, that on the 29th of said month (January) the president *approved* "an act of *congress* to establish an uniform rule of naturalization," and that a few months afterwards, the *senate* (ALONE) *approved* a treaty which renders said act null and void, in favor of "all settlers and traders (the rooted enemies of America) within the precints and jurisdiction (a large extent of country) of the Posts."—Should this treaty be ratified, 'twill be out of the power of congress to remedy its evils without hazarding a war—And it may with safety be presumed, that nine-tenths, at least, of the citizens of America, look with indignation and abhorrence on the inglorious attempt made by Mr. Jay, and his advisers, to *chain* fifteen independent states as a *dangling appendage to the crown of Great-Britain.*

Resolved, That insurmountable objections lie against the treaty, were there no others, while the value of the Negroes and other property[29] carried away, contrary to the seventh article of the treaty of 1783, and the loss and damage in blood and treasure sustained by the United States from the detention of posts, remain unsatisfied for by the British government—the amount of which should have been ascertained by the commissioner to be appointed to liquidate the claims of British creditors, and set off against the principal of their debt; for, as to interest, during the war, they have not the shadow of a claim.—No man entertains a doubt (even the British, not the governor of Canada himself, have been sufficiently hardy to deny it) that the Indians were excited to war against us—and that the supplies for their warfare were derived from a trade *authorized by the British government, and protested by these posts which of right were our's, and ought to have been used for our defence.*—This war has cost us, annually, calculating the loss of the fur trade depending on the Posts, above one million three hundred thousand dollars more than would have been sufficient for the defence of our frontiers if the Posts had been in our possession. Let this sum, and the amount of their piratical depredations, the whole continent says, be made a set-off with the British claims.

Resolved, That by the article regarding the West-India trade, nothing can be more evident than that Britain mediated to wrest from America the carrying trade, an immense share of which she has lately possessed, as appears by the astonishing increase of our seamen and shipping; but we trust 'twill never be forgotten that the protection of a free carrying trade was one of the primary objects for which the federal government was established.—Let not, then, our national government have the discredit of doing any thing by which the limits of our navigation may be fettered—Let us not concur with the British ministry in eminently promoting the British commerce at the expence of our own!—Not satisfied with the innumerable depradations on our shipping, the British government wants their real destruction by this insidious article, confining our vessels to seventy tons, mere boats, whilst they reserve to themselves the right of navigating in any size vessels they please, in the same pursuit of trade. By this deceptive article, we *alone* granted—have been prevented from exporting in our own bottoms any articles of West-India produce, and even of *cotton,* an article of our own growth, and becoming a very important one in this and the sister state of Georgia (even in our own district)—while the vessels of *Britain,* and *every other* nation, would be at liberty to export from American ports every article of West-India, and some of our own produce, to all parts of the world.

Resolved, That the adopters and warm advocates for this treaty must have regarded a favorite policy, a close connection with Britain and British systems, more than pecuniary benefit or national dignity; for, setting aside all reciprocity, no one advantage can we gain by any regulation in the treaty, distinct from a much greater to be obtained by the British nation.

Resolved, That the article restricting the subjects or citizens of either party from accepting commissions in the army or navy of any foreign power, is a gross violation of the natural rights of man—and, as such, should have been indignantly spurned at!

Resolved, That we join heartily in sentiment with the truly patriotic and staunch republican, the Chief Justice Rutledge,[30] that Mr. Jay should have demanded an *unconditional* relinquishment of the Western Posts *as a right*—until which had been granted, and until the British minister had given orders to that effect, Mr. Jay shou'd not have opened his lips about a treaty!—What amity could be expected from a government, at the instant of negociation forcing the tomahawk and scalping-knife into the hands of savages, to the destruction of great numbers of our immediate frontier fellow-citizens!—It was, truly, prostituting the dearest rights of freemen, and laying them prostrate at the feet of royalty.—In 1793, the executive pressed the demand of the Western Posts with a spirit becoming the representative of a nation of freemen—an ultimatum was required on the subject by December of that year—and how were we treated?— With a contemptuous silence, and fresh injuries heaped upon us—depradations on our property, as unwarrantable as the robberies of an Algerine, or the plundering of a savage!—And, were it possible to sully the name of the British government with an additional shade of infamy, the same would be afforded by the circumstance of their treatment to this country *involving in it the* BLACK *design of* STARVING *a people, whose only crime has been the* DEFENCE *of freedom!*—Such treatment, it was natural to imagine, would have roused us to retaliate—and the *immediate* representatives of the people, according with the sentiments of their constituents, made an attempt to extort redress by means of a provisional retaliation—But—in *one* instance the senate—in another the supreme executive, *checked* them in their honorable career—and the *energetic* portion of the government, with UNPARALLELED *weakness, humbly sued* for the friendship of a nation which ever treated us as foes—rejecting, at the same time, (*the better to secure her smiles*) the proffered amity of another nation, to which, in a great measure, we owe our existence as a free people, and which has also other strong claims to our gratitude and friendship.

Resolved, With that tried veteran and patriot, the venerable Gadsden,[31] That we consider all connections by treaties with Britain, equally impolitic and dangerous—Dangerous, because (whilst her government is monarchical and unregenerated) we shall insensibly give her such a footing amonst us, and consequently so great an ascendancy over our councils and governments, as may eventually sap our independence, and subvert our constitution!—And impolitic, because 'tis our interest, by the utmost individual and national exertions, (particularly our southern states) to arrive at an independent transportation of our commodities— to become the carriers of their own produce—for 'tis an alarming fact, established in the best authority, that by the almost constant wars in which Britain is engaged, (she having had in the last one hundred years forty-two of war, and fifty-seven years and nine months of peace, which is three of war to every four of peace)—and that by being so largely the exporters of our produce, she carrying two-fifths of the whole exports of the United States—the difference of freight, insurance, and charges, amounts, on an average of peace and war, to one million, three hundred and ninety-two thousand, eight hundred and sixty-seven dollars— taxed annually on our agriculture by British wars, during their continuance, and our dependence on British bottoms, and so much more than we should pay did we but raise our own shipping to be competent to the carriage of all our production—and that, besides this, many of our bulky articles, not bearing a war freight, cannot be exported—While Britain, then, is the carrier of two-fifths of our produce, our independence is incomplete, and ever will be, if we tamely suffer such negociators as Mr. Jay to form treaties with that nation, calculated to keep up a servile and ruinous dependence, by the immoderate, the excessive use of her manufacturers. Let us wear nothing but what is American—eat nothing, drink nothing, but what is American—this would soon raise the head of America—Let the people of Britain be driven to poverty and despair *by acts of their own government!*—and what would be the consequence?—An acquisition of tens of thousands of really useful citizens to the United States, which form the *natural asylum* to the people of the old world—to snatch them from a wretched existence, from slavery—to the enjoyment of plenty, happiness—to liberty!

Resolved, That we ever considered the appointment of John Jay as *extraordinary* as it was unconstitutional—extraordinary, because under the abilities of our then ambassador—a man, *in every respect,* justly possessing the confidence of the union—especially, as there is good ground for asserting, that major Pinckney's[32] energetic and firm representation had insured the immediate cession of our Western Posts—and a treaty, at least, as favorable as any nation could have expected from England.

Resolved, That roused at length into a sense of our danger, we pronounce for war, with all its horrors, rather than see our country approve of measures which will effect her annihilation—A treaty! to be bought at the expence of infamy!—

purchased at the loss of the affection of an ally, as generous in friendship as glorious in arms!—No! magnanimous nation! truly worthy of liberty! we will *cherish,* we will *respect* thy *opinion! we will not suffer thy esteem to be taken from us!*—we will prove to the world, and, above all, to the English government, that we will not be the dupes of their insidious policy—their craft—their ambition!—Oh, ye Jays of America, who boast of wisdom so exalted, penetration so profound—how is it possible you have not yet lifted up the veil which hides from your eyes the low sinister politics of the English government!—How is it ye do not see to what a degree it abuses ye!—and what a trick it has put upon the *"solemnity"* of your *solemn* ambassador!

Resolved, That the much-esteemed names of Langdon, of New-Hampshire; Robinson, of Vermont; Burr, of New-York; Brown, of Kentucky; Mason and Tazewell, of Virginia; Bloodworth and Martin, of North-Carolina; Butler, our fellow-citizen, of South-Carolina; and Jackson, of Georgia—the patriotic senators[33]—be held in our highest veneration and most marked esteem.

Resolved, That public report, not contradicted, fixes on Jacob Read,[34] *our unworthy senator!* corrupt motives for his acquiescence in a treaty which would have made his country infamous!—would have restored her back to Britain!—We therefore do not hesitate to declare him, (with his ninteen quondam condjutors) undeserving of any further public confidence:—And, guided by an opinion founded in a knowledge of human-nature, we do insist, that if not lost to *all* the fine feelings of the heart, 'twill be impossible they can withstand that immense torrent of opprobrium which will rush upon them—they must resign!—they cannot, in future, transact any public business!

Resolved, That as the power of finally making and ratifying treaties by the President and two-thirds of the Senate alone, has in the present case been proved to be of a most alarmingly dangerous nature—that our very existence as a free people had been at stake—that had not a good Providence influenced even the *twenty* of the Senate to reject *one* article, which *from necessity,* must arrest the hand of the President from signing it—we say, that had not that providential care, which we have so often experienced, interposed, we had been a lost, an undone people—without pity, and without friends!

Therefore resolved, That our members be earnestly called on, at the next meeting of the assembly, to propose an amendment to the federal constitution, so far as respects the power of making treaties.—That a President, and twenty senators, perhaps fourteen (for that number makes a quorum) shall have the sole power of making treaties, which must, necessarily, the supreme law—must be binding on every individual—which swallows up the sovereignty and independence of each state!—No!—the people now see the folly of giving such a power into the hands of fourteen men, which, at all times may supercede every existing law in the union!—'tis too much!—Without a disposition to judge uncharitably of men, we say 'tis possible twenty or fourteen men may be tempted, may be bribed to betray the precious trust reposed in them by their fellow citizens!—And we repeat, that as it is notorious Britain carries all her points by corruption—(look at Lord North's estimate during the American war; you will there find our million for contingents or secret service!—Has not France throughout her struggle complained she felt British corruption in her very vitals!—and shall America expect to escape her baneful influence!)—then 'tis *possible* that twenty or fourteen men may be led to sell even their country!—We therefore again urge it on our representatives, to bring forward an amendment, by which CONGRESS AT LARGE, AND CONGRESS ALONE, shall have the power of forming treaties—at least of *ratifying* them—We venture to pronounce the people will not be satisfied short of this—from one extreme of the continent to the other, this will be the universal language.—We know, in framing the federal constitution, the objection to giving the house of representatives this power, jointly with the Senate and President, was, *that negociations generally required the* GREATEST SECRECY, *and that was not to be expected from a large body*—Curse on such secrecy! it has undone our country!—An American assembly, aloof from the combinations of Europe, should have no secrets!—No government in the known world, like ours, ever gave such an extensive latitude as we allow to the President and Senate—even the most arbitrary kings never possessed any thing like it!—In France, under the old government, appearances at least were kept up; the king's edicts were never of force until registered in parliament—In England they proceed with diffidence in making treaties—far from being considered as legal, without a parliamentary sanction, the preamble always states that *"his majesty would endeavor to obtain a law for ratifying the treaty"*—Such is the language and conduct of monarchs—and what is our's?—we blush! we blush!

Resolved, That while we stigmatize the man, and execrate his conduct, (John Jay) we rejoice he has been made an instrument to draw forth the united voice of the whole people of America in detestation of his treaty!—We congratulate each other, that from this truly *marking circumstance,* our great, our generous ally, will form a proper, a true judgment of the disposition of the United States!—that she will distinguish between the people and a part of its government!—that they will see our hearts never ceased to beat in unison with their's!—Of all possible temporal evils which could ever fall upon us, we deprecate a difference with France!

Resolved, That we pledge ourselves to our brethren of the Republican Societies throughout the union, as far as the ability and individual influence of a most numerous society can be made to extend, that we will promote every constitutional means to bring John Jay to trial and to justice—He shall not escape, if guilty, that punishment which at once will wipe off the temporary stain laid on us, and be a warning to traitors, hereafter, how they sport with the interest and feelings of their fellow-citizens.

Resolved, That, every compliment is due to the watchful zeal of our fellow-citizens of Charleston—to the great ability shewn by their committee in their elucidation of the treaty—We warmly embrace and adopt their report—it demonstrates great moderation—but—with such provocation!—we would not have been quite so tender!

Resolved, That we heartily approbate the representation of our wrongs made by our own district (Washington)—it proves that we are neither defective in knowledge, nor deficient in duty—that we know our interests as citizens—that we feel a tender concern for the whole commonwealth of America—this we will teach as the first of principles to our children—that we will endeavor to impress upon them the nonsense and folly of involving themselves with the people of Europe, eternally cutting each other's throats—we will urge to posterity, that American need only *"be still"*—that let her markets be but well supplied, all Europe will be the buyers—that they cannot do without us—to have no connection with the old governments by treaties, no written agreements; for the omission of a comma may involve us in war!—In this happy, but envied situation, had a gracious Providence placed us; and, guided by these principles, we should have had no wars— But!—the demon of discord entered into a JAY, and flew to England to blast our rising hopes—*to involve us with compacts and treaties!*

Resolved, That in the investigation of this business, not to have discovered warmth—a warmth resulting from the glowing picture of danger which our country exhibits, by a tame submission in its government to the most flagrant and daring outrages!—would have betrayed a stoicism unworthy of the subject—unworthy of the sons of 1776!—And should it be considered that unnecessary asperity has discovered itself to a nation, of whom we ought and must be jealous while the crown is upon its present head, we wish to make known to the world, and to Britain and Ireland in particular, that we discriminate between the honest and the slavish parts of their people—between the two nations and their governments!—Yes, congenial and generous souls!—we know you always longingly anticipated our warfare and rank among nations, and ever participated in our distresses and in our happiness!—No!—'tis your government we hold in abhorrence! —a government, with one *exception,* singularized from all the nations of the world by the number and extravagance!—by the foulness and blackness of its crimes!

Resolved, finally, That the vice-moderator, the corresponding secretary, and secretary of the society, do sign the foregoing resolutions—and that they be generally printed, as expressive of our abhorrence and detestation of a treaty—which gives to the English government more power over us a[s] states, than it ever claimed over us as colonies—and which, if Britain had been left to her generosity, *she would have been ashamed to propose!*—a treaty, involving in its pusilanimity, stupidity, ingratitude, and TREACHERY!—to blast the rising grandeur of our common country—of our infant empire!

    SAMUEL LOFTON, Vice-moderator.

    J. MILLER, Corresponding secretary,[35]

    ED. TATE M'CLURE, Secretary of the society.

City Gazette (Charleston), October 28, 1795

Notes

CHAPTER 2 DEMOCRATIC-REPUBLICAN SOCIETIES OF PENNSYLVANIA

1. The writer had seen the circular in German in the *Philadelphische Correspondenz*, April 9, 1793, and sent it to Philip Freneau, asking him to print an English translation in his paper, the *National Gazette*.

2. Henry Kammerer was a printer of the German newspaper in which the circular appeared. He had also printed and distributed *Feast of Merriment, by Well-Fed Domine Double Chin, Esq.*, a pornographic anecdote about sailors that satirized the upper classes. He was a member of the Pennsylvania Assembly until 1794.

3. Edmond Charles Genêt (1763-1834), the first minister of the French republic to the United States, arrived at Charleston, South Carolina, on April 8, 1793, and reached Philadelphia on May 16 by way of Camden, Salisbury, Richmond, and Baltimore. His approach to the city was proclaimed with the ringing of church bells. That evening a Republican meeting was held at the state house, and a committee was appointed to prepare a formal address to Genêt on May 17. On that morning a select group of thirty citizens, members of the Democratic Society of Pennsylvania, marched three abreast from the state house to the city tavern to pay their respects. They presented a warm congratulatory address, and Genêt responded with an address of his own. Genêt also received a cordial address from the German Republican Society and from members of the French Benevolent Society, to both of which he also responded with an address.

4. Michael Leib (1760-1822), physician, Congressman, and Senator, was born in Philadelphia of German parents. He studied medicine under Dr. Benjamin Rush, was a surgeon in the Philadelphia militia during the revolutionary war, and served on several hospital staffs in Philadelphia after the war.

5. Andrew Geyer, a bookbinder, was also a member of the Democratic Society of Pennsylvania.

6. In 1780 young Genêt studied at Giessen and spent several months in Berlin studying law.

7. "Mr. Madison's Resolutions," as they were known, called for a strict system of reciprocal favors and retaliations against nations that assisted and restricted American commerce. The resolutions, directed against Britain, called for higher tonnage taxes on vessels of nations having no commercial treaty with the United States. Port restrictions were to be met in kind. If shippers were unable to obtain reparations, Congress was to reimburse citizens who suffered losses from foreign regulations that contravened the law of nations.

For the reply of the Democratic Society of Pennsylvania to this communication from the German Republican Society, see below pp. 73-74.

8. The reference to Jay is to John Jay (1745-1829), first Chief Justice of the Supreme Court, who had been appointed a special envoy to Britain. The reference to the excise is to the new tax on salt, coal, sugar, snuff, boots, shoes, spirits, coffee and cheese.

9. The reference is to the Whiskey Rebellion in 1794 in which west Pennsylvania farmers opposed the payment of the whiskey excise tax.

10. William Pitt the Younger (1759-1806), the British prime minister who held office from 1783 to 1801 and from 1804 to 1806.

11. The reference is to the accusation by President Washington in his message to Congress, September 19, 1794, charging "certain self-created societies" with responsibility for the Whiskey Rebellion.

12. The German Lutheran church burned down on December 26, 1794. "Nothing remains but the bare walls," wrote Frederick August Muhlenberg, president of the Corporation of St. Michaels' and Zions' Church. *Philadelphia Gazette and Universal Daily Advertiser,* January 7, 1795.

13. The Polish Constitution of May 3, 1791, the first codified constitution in Europe, included the principle of a "people's sovereignty," the constitutional separation of powers between the executive, legislature, and judiciary, and the responsibility of the cabinet to parliament. But Catherine II of Russia viewed the constitution as dangerous to her own autocratic rule, and she ordered her troops to invade Poland in 1792. As a consequence the constitution was destroyed by force.

14. The first sixteen pages of the official minutes of the Democratic Society of Pennsylvania in the Historical Society of Pennsylvania are missing, and some subsequent pages have also been torn out.

15. Alexander James Dallas (1759-1817), born in Jamaica, settled in Philadelphia in 1783 and became a member of the bar two years later. He supplemented his income from his legal practice by editing the *Pennsylvania Evening Herald* and *Columbian Magazine* and by preparing a volume of *Reports of Cases Ruled and Adjudged in the Courts of Pennsylvania Before and Since the Revolution.* In 1791 he was chosen secretary of the commonwealth of Pennsylvania by Governor Thomas Mifflin. Dallas was a member of the Committee of Correspondence of the Democratic Society of Pennsylvania and drew up its constitution. Appointed United States District Attorney for the Eastern District of Pennsylvania by President Thomas Jefferson in 1801, he served for thirteen years. Over the years Dallas became increasingly conservative.

16. David Rittenhouse (1732-1796), instrument maker, astronomer, and mathematician, was considered second only to Benjamin Franklin in scientific

knowledge in the United States. He succeeded Franklin as president of the American Philosophical Society. In 1795 he was elected a foreign member of the Royal Society of London.

17. Benjamin Franklin Bache (1769-1798), grandson of Benjamin Franklin and one of the most influential journalists of the 1790s, began his career in 1790 with the founding of the Philadelphia *General Advertiser,* known better under the name of *Aurora.* Active as a member of the Democratic Society of Pennsylvania, Bache made his paper practically the official organ of the movement. He was arrested in 1798 under the Sedition Act but was released on parole. He died during the yellow fever epidemic of 1798 in Philadelphia.

Bache was considered one of the three most influential members of the society by the Federalists. One of Fenno's writers satirized the three in a poem entitled "THE TRIO." The first stanza of the poem proclaimed:

> The leaders of the Demon frantic club,
> Who Congress with their condine labels drub,
> Are Doctors L——n, L——b, and F——B——e,
> These learned cacklers nightly take their stand,
> With leaathern bell, and goose-quill in their hand,
> Lord, how of rapes on Liberty, they preach.
> (*Gazette of the United States* [Philadelphia], June 25, 1794.)

The other two men satirized were Dr. George Logan and Dr. Michael Leib.

18. Israel Israel, an ardent patriot during the Revolution and a leading Jeffersonian in Philadelphia, was the son of Michael Israel, a professed Jew, and Mary Paxton, an Episcopalian. He appears to have participated in Jewish religious ceremonies early in his life, although he was brought up in his mother's faith. Israel was the target of an anti-Semitic campaign when he ran for state senator in 1797.

19. Pierre Etienne Du Ponceau (1760-1844), erudite lawyer and one of the most profoundly learned men of his day, was born in France. After a thorough religious and classical education, he arrived in the United States in December 1777 as secretary to Baron Steuben. Following some service in the revolutionary war, he became a citizen of Pennsylvania in 1781 and anglicized his name to Peter Stephen Du Ponceau. As an attorney in Philadelphia, he was recognized as the leading authority in the nation on international law. He was a member of the American Philosophical Society and the Society for Promoting the Abolition of Slavery.

20. In February 1793, France opened all its colonial ports to the United States and in May of that same year removed all restrictions on American vessels.

21. In the published version, the following phrase was added: "and that the governments of the nations in which they reside, are bound in honor and duty to protect their persons from insult, and their character from abuse."

22. The reference is to the Federalist campaign to discredit Genêt, especially the charge, which he denied, that he had threatened to appeal from Washington to the people.

23. The reference is to the fact that England, in violation of the treaty, held

the western military posts.

24. The criticism was of Washington for introducing ceremony into social and official circles. Washington defended himself against such criticism, insisting that because of the great number of people making demands on his time, he found it necessary to appoint definite hours to receive them. See Washington to David Stuart, June 15, 1790, in Worthington C. Ford, ed., *The Writings of George Washington* (New York, 1889-1893), II: 487-488.

25. George Logan (1773-1821), physician, farmer, Pennsylvania legislator, and United States Senator, studied medicine at the University of Edinburgh but did not practice in the United States after his return in 1790. He turned instead to the study of improved methods of farming and was a founder of the Philadelphia Society for the Promotion of Agriculture. He was a member of the American Philosophical Society and the Society for Promoting the Abolition of Slavery. Logan's secret mission to France during the X, Y, Z Affair was one of his most important political activities.

26. At its meeting on January 23, 1794, the Democratic Society elected Blair McClenachan, a merchant, as its new president.

27. No paper is annexed. But see pp. 57-58 for the communication referred to here.

28. See pp. 57-58.

29. England was charged with inciting the Indians against its former colonists.

30. On April 22, 1793, President George Washington signed the Proclamation of Neutrality declaring the United States neutral in the "state of war" existing between Austria, Prussia, Sardinia, Great Britain, and the United Netherlands on the one part, and France on the other, and warning "the citizens of the United States carefully to avoid all acts and proceedings whatsoever which may in any manner tend to contravene such disposition."

31. In January 1794, Great Britain issued an order-in-council instructing naval commanders and privateers to stop only such neutral ships as were engaged in trade between the French West Indies and France.

32. This refers to General Houchard's victory over the English and Hanoverians in the Battle of Honschoots on September 9, 1793, which broke a long chain of reverses for the French army.

33. Thomas Pinckney (1750-1828), appointed minister to Great Britain in 1791, was instructed to seek the liberation of American commerce from British restrictions and the protection of American seamen from impressment. His efforts to resolve these issues were not successful; most of his requests were ignored by the British Foreign Office.

34. The intervening pages are missing.

35. For the account of the civic festival, see pp. 102-104.

36. The intervening pages are missing.

37. The following word is illegible.

38. See pp. 80-81, 104-106.

39. This has been transferred to the section on the German Republican Society; see p. 58.

40. The paragraph that follows was written in the margin.

41. Thomas Muir, parliamentary reformer of Scotland, was one of the Glasgow

allies of the London Society of the Friends of the People at the meeting on October 16, 1792, to form a kindred society for obtaining parliamentary reform. Muir also attended the convention of delegates held at Edinburgh. He was arrested on January 2, 1793, on a charge of sedition, but he declined to answer the sheriff's call and was freed on bail. He then left for France. Upon returning to Scotland several months later, he was arrested for exciting a spirit of disloyalty and disaffection, of recommending Paine's *Rights of Man,* of distributing seditious writings, and of reading them aloud. He was tried before the high court of justiciary at Edinburgh, convicted, and sentenced to fourteen years' transportation. He was dispatched to Botany Bay along with Maurice Margarot and others. Muir's case aroused great sympathy in the United States, and the *Otter,* Captain Dawes in command, was sent out from New York to rescue him. They reached him on February 11, 1796, and after many adventures, Muir finally arrived in Paris on February 4, 1798. He died in Cantilly later that year on September 27.

42. Maurice Margarot was a Frenchman who arrived in London and joined the Constitutional Society of London in the spring of 1792. For some time he acted as chairman of the London Corresponding Society. He was arrested in 1793 and sentenced to fourteen years' imprisonment at Botany Bay. Among other charges, he was accused of attempting to secure aid from France in an English rebellion. He returned to England after a long exile.

43. For an account of the Fourth of July celebration, see pp. 106-107.

44. The Presqu'isle on the shores of Lake Erie had been purchased by Pennsylvania from the Indians who were represented by Cornplanter, the famous Indian chief. His followers, however, charged that the chief had been bought out with Yankee gold, and they never accepted the treaty. The federal government, hoping to allay the uneasiness of the Six Nations, had halted the settlement of the isle, but many Americans feared that Britain, having failed to relinquish certain frontier posts, planned to extend forts to Presqu'isle and thus control the whole northwest region.

45. The reference is to the Whiskey Rebellion.

46. They were published on August 9, 1794, and signed by George Booth, secretary.

47. The French Society of the Friends of Liberty and Equality was formed in Philadelphia in the spring of 1793, and its notice "To the Public" was published in the May 4, 1793, *National Gazette* (Philadelphia). The notice announced the opening of a subscription "to purchase flour and other provisions, to be offered as a donation, and sent to the republic of France." It was signed by P. Barriere, president, and A. C. Du Plaine, secretary. Both were also members of the Democratic Society of Pennsylvania. In 1793, Du Plaine was appointed vice-consul for the Republic of France to the states of New Hampshire, Massachusetts, and Rhode Island, but his exequator was revoked in the fall of that year by President Washington because of his involvement in the seizure of the *Greyhound,* a British prize ship captured by a French privateer in American waters.

For toasts drank by the French Society of the Friends of Liberty and Equality at a dinner in Philadelphia, see *General Advertiser* (Philadelphia), February 12, 1794.

48. James Marshel (1753-1829), was born in Ireland and settled in Cross Creek Township, Pennsylvania, before the Revolution. He served as captain of the militia and was justice of the peace in Westmoreland County. When Washington County was organized, he was commissioned as one of its presiding judges and became an influential member of the court. Marshel was deeply involved in the Whiskey Rebellion as one of the rebels. His political career ended as a result, and he moved to Wallsburg, Virginia, in 1795.

49. Illegible.

50. The reference is to President Blair McClenachan who left the meeting with twenty-eight followers.

51. Although the insurgents had been ordered to disperse by September 1, under threat of a militia call, Washington, in a final effort to restore peace without launching a military campaign, decided to send three commissioners to the west with orders to confer with the disaffected persons. The commissioners were instructed to inform the insurgents that although Washington was reluctant to use force, he would enforce the excise law by that means if necessary. He would also grant amnesty and forget past acts and uncollected duties if the recalcitrants would guarantee compliance with the law during the year 1794. He refused to commit himself on the issue of repeal, for that was the responsibility of Congress. On the question of trial in state or federal courts, Washington gave assurance that when convenient to the United States, Pennsylvania courts would be used if it appeared certain that these bodies would not be frustrated by local opposition.

Governor Thomas Mifflin (1744-1800) at first hesitated to support suppression of the Whiskey Rebellion and urged that the insurgents abandon their resistance. Later he called the legislature into special session and urged speedy action against the insurgents. At the same time, he appointed two men as commissioners to go west with those appointed by President Washington and, through them, promised complete pardon for past transgressions if the westerners would guarantee further submission to the authorities.

52. This is a reference to President Washington's September 19, 1794, message to Congress in which he charged that "certain self-created societies" had been responsible for the Whiskey Rebellion.

53. The address was published without any substantial changes in the *Delaware & Eastern-Shore Advertiser,* December 27, 1794. It was signed by Blair M'Clenachan, president, and Robert Baily, secretary. Some of the words that were illegible in the original manuscript have been inserted from the published address.

54. In June 1794, James Monroe (1758-1831) was appointed minister to France. On his arrival in France, he made a speech before the National Convention that voiced his own sympathies for the French Revolution. Indeed, Edmund Randolph, then Secretary of State, rebuked Monroe for "the extreme glow" of the speech. For the text of Monroe's address to the French National Convention, see *American State Papers, Foreign Relations Documents Legislative and Executive of the Congress of the United States,* Washington, 1883, 1: 673-674.

55. Several of the members of the Democratic Society of Pennsylvania marched against the whiskey insurrectionists.

56. The address was published in the *Aurora* (Philadelphia) of December 22, 1794, where it was noted that it had been agreed to unanimously.

57. The name Fouchet was written in.

58. According to the account in the *Pennsylvania Gazette,* May 7, 1794, the celebration of St. Tammany's Day, which took place on May 1, "deprived the general meeting of a number of true Republicans."

59. This is probably a reference to the Jacobins, or, in political terms, the Mountain.

60. Thomas Mifflin.

61. The account in the manuscript minutes of the society ends here. But the report in the *Pennsylvania Gazette* of May 7, 1794, continued: "and the President of the democratic society gave the fraternal embrace to the Minister of the French Republic amid the acclamations of the most animated joy of all the company.

"The citizens, then, some time being spent in the effusions of mirth, friendship and good humor, accompanied the Minister to town in a regular order of march, headed by music and the colours of the French Republic and accompanied by one of the companies of volunteer infantry of this city.

"They partook of some refreshments provided in the Minister's garden, and preserving their line of march through part of the city with perfect good humour and tranquility before the State House.

"The provisions which remained after the repast were distributed, agreeably to order, among the prisoners confined in the Gaol of this city."

When Federalist editor John Fenno condemned the civil festival, Bache of the *Aurora* replied that "had a fete been celebrated for the knights of the funding system, had the birthday of that blessing, a public debt, been the subject," the Federalists would not have attacked the proceedings. *Gazette of the United States* (Philadelphia), May 9, 1794; *Philadelphia Aurora and General Advertiser,* May 16, 1794.

62. In the introduction to the account published in the July 11, 1794, issue of *Woods's Newark Gazette,* there is the following: "The following are the RESOLVES alluded to in the Letter from the Republican Society of this Town, to the Democratic Society of Pennsylvania—published by request of the Society."

63. While he was Chief Justice of the Supreme Court, Jay was sent on the diplomatic mission to arrange a peaceful settlement of existing controversies with Great Britain.

64. The British occupation of the northwest posts was one of the key issues in the dispute between the United States and Great Britain.

65. The excise taxes objected to were those on salt, coal, sugar, snuff, boots, shoes, spirits, coffee, and cheese.

66. This refers to one wearing trousers, instead of the more aristocratic knee-breeches, and was identified with the most active supporters of the French Revolution.

67. "Germanicus" denounced the "self-created societies" in the Philadelphia *Aurora* of January 27, 1795.

68. The reference is to Jay's treaty.

69. The True Republican Society was organized in May 1797 by leaders of the Democratic Society of Pennsylvania. It was viewed as a continuation of the former society.

70. The day was May 1, Saint Tammany's Day.

71. The hope was fulfilled. Jefferson won the election of 1800 by the vote of the House of Representatives after a tie with Aaron Burr in the electoral vote.

72. Thomas McKean (1734-1817) was a Pennsylvania and Delaware political leader who held office in both states; he was chief justice of Pennsylvania from 1777 to 1799. A Federalist in politics he became a Jeffersonian after 1792 as a result of his dislike of Federalist foreign policy, his friendship for France, and his aversion for England. He was elected governor of Pennsylvania on the Republican ticket in 1799.

73. In the election of 1800 in New York City the Republicans carried the important Sixth and Seventh wards.

74. Benjamin Franklin Bache fell victim to the yellow fever in Philadelphia, September 10, 1798.

75. The *Gazette of the United States & Daily Advertiser* was known for many years as Fenno's *Gazette.* It had been established by John Fenno in 1798 and was continued by his son John Ward Fenno when the father died in 1798. It was purchased by Caleb P. Wayne with the issue of May 28, 1800. Wayne continued the Federalist policies of his predecessors.

76. The meeting was called by the True Republican Society of Philadelphia but was referred to in the *Gazette of the United States* as the Democratic Society. This is not surprising since most of the members of the Democratic Society of Pennsylvania were also members of the True Republican Society.

77. The barb about "black innocence" was probably directed at Benjamin Rush (1743-1813), president of the Pennsylvania Society for Promoting the Abolition of Slavery and a member of the True Republican Society as he had been of the Democratic Society of Pennsylvania. William Cobbett also attacked Dr. Rush and misrepresented his treatment of yellow fever during the epidemics in Philadelphia. Dr. Rush brought a libel suit against Cobbett and was awarded $5,000 in damages. Physician and outstanding American reformer of his time, Rush was active in many of the reform causes of the day.

78. John Barker, a tailor and a former member of the Democratic Society of Pennsylvania.

79. Israel Israel.

80. "Citizen Sambo" refers to Cyrus Bustill, a leading Philadelphia black.

81. John Purdon, a former member of the Democratic Society of Pennsylvania.

82. Thomas Felsher, a former member of the Democratic Society of Pennsylvania.

83. The reference is to Benjamin Nones (1757-1826), born in Bordeaux, France, who came to the United States in 1777 to enlist in the revolutionary army, Captured in 1781, he was banned from Charleston by the British commandant for refusing to obey orders. He went to Philadelphia, where he went into business as a broker and merchant. Nones became involved with the Sons of St. Tammany, the French Society of Friends of Liberty and Equality, the Democratic Society of Pennsylvania, the Pennsylvania Society for Promoting the Abolition of Slavery, and the True Republican Society of Philadelphia. Freeing his own slave in 1793, Nones often helped secure the freedom of other slaves,

persuading even French Jewish refugees from the 1793 slave revolt in Saint Domingue to free the slaves they had brought with them. An active and pious Jew, Nones was president of the Mikveh Israel Congregation from 1791 to 1799.

84. William Duane (1760-1835), was, according to Claude G. Bowers, "the most effective journalist of his time." He had been editor of the *Aurora* when it was being published by Benjamin Franklin Bache, and, on March 8, 1800, he became its publisher.

85. In the fall of 1799, Duane had been indicted under the Sedition Act, but he did not hesitate to publish Nones's letter in the *Aurora*. The letter was also distributed as a broadside on the streets of Philadelphia. The only known copy of the broadside is in the possession of Maxwell Whiteman in Philadelphia.

Morris U. Schappes calls Nones's letter "one of the profoundest utterances made by an American Jew." *Documentary History of the Jews in the United States* (New York, 1950), p. 92. For another discussion of the letter, equally complimentary to Nones, see Edwin Wolf II and Maxwell Whiteman, *The History of the Jews of Philadelphia from Colonial Times to the Age of Jackson* (Philadelphia, 1957), pp. 209-212. For a Federalist parody of Nones's letter, see "A Jacobin—Ironically," in *Philadelphia Gazette,* August 13, 1800. "I am a Jew—thank God for that," began the letter. "But I am no Democrat, thank God for that *also.*" However, in Charleston, a "Citizen JEW" inserted Nones's letter in the *City Gazette* of September 3, 1800.

86. The battle of Savannah in 1778 ended in December of that year with a British victory. From Savannah, Georgia was overrun.

87. William Reichenbach (1749–1821) was born in Prussia, emigrated to the United States in 1785, and after settling in Lancaster, Pennsylvania, was appointed professor of mathematics and German literature in Franklin college.

88. Jacob Carpenter (1740-1803) was a member of the Pennsylvania legislature for a number of years stretching from 1765 to 1801. He was three times elected treasurer of Pennsylvania. In 1800 Governor McKean appointed him clerk of the Orphans' Court of Lancaster County.

89. On January 2, 1795, the Pennsylvania Senate passed the following resolution: "That the elections of Senators held in the counties of Washington, Alleghany, Westmoreland and Fayette, during the late insurrection, were not constitutional, and therefore not valid." It then expelled from the legislature members from these four counties. Those who favored the expulsion argued that elections in that area of the state had been held during the Whiskey Rebellion, and were therefore unconstitutional and void. The vote in favor of expulsion in the assembly was forty-three for expulsion and twenty against. Albert Gallatin (1761-1849) led the opposition to the expulsion, but his efforts were in vain.

90. Hugh Henry Brackenridge (1748-1816) was a jurist and author who settled in Pittsburgh and with John Scull established its first newspaper, the *Pittsburgh Gazette,* in 1786. He was a leader of the Republican movement in the west and one of the founders of the Democratic Society of the County of Washington. Brackenridge was appointed justice of the Supreme Court of Pennsylvania by Governor McKean in 1799.

91. David Bradford was born in Maryland, son of James Bradford reputed to be an immigrant from Ireland. He was admitted to the bar of Washington

County and in 1783 was appointed deputy attorney general for the county. He was a fiery leader and popular in his own county, which elected him to the assembly in 1792. A successful lawyer, he bitterly opposed the excise tax on whiskey, led the resistance to the tax, and was the only one who was exempt from the government's general proclamation of amnesty. Never pardoned, he fled to Louisiana, then in Spain's possession, where he died.

92. William Irvine (1741-1804), a revolutionary soldier, was elected to Congress in 1793 from the Cumberland district of Pennsylvania. In 1794 he was active both as arbitrator and commanding officer of the state troops in quelling the Whiskey Rebellion.

93. William Hoge was important in Pennsylvania politics and was elected to Congress by the counties of Washington, Greene, and Allegheny in 1801.

94. David Redick, a native of Ireland, was active in western Pennsylvania politics. He was elected a member of the Supreme Executive Council in 1786 and represented Washington County in the Constitutional Convention of 1790. In the Whiskey Rebellion he supported the federal government, being one of the commissioners to wait upon President Washington when he was on his way out with the army. He resigned from the Democratic Republican Society of Washington County after the rebellion.

95. Dr. Absalom Baird (1758-1805), son of a doctor from Scotland who had come to America with General Braddock in 1755, studied medicine and served as surgeon in the Pennsylvania regiment during the War for Independence. After he moved to Washington, Pennsylvania, in 1786, he was commissioned justice of the peace and of the Court of Common Pleas. In October 1794 he was elected to represent Allegheny and Washington counties in the state senate but was refused his seat because the county was in a state of insurrection when the election took place. A new election resulted in his reelection, and he served as a member of the state senate until October 1798, when he was elected to the house of representatives. He was one of the original trustees of Washington Academy.

96. Joseph Pentecost was a leading lawyer in the County and also active in Masonic affairs.

97. Gabriel Blackeny was elected justice of the peace in 1793.

98. Back of the Indian depredations, according to the western frontiersmen, were the British.

99. Depredations on American commerce by the cruisers of Algiers led to the beginning of the American navy in 1794.

100. John Scull was co-founder of the *Pittsburgh Gazette* in 1786, the first trans-Appalachian newspaper. At first he was nonpartisan and printed many articles by Democrats, but in due time the paper became a Federalist organ in Pittsburgh.

101. Hamilton accused the Mingo Creek society of having been deeply involved in the Whiskey Rebellion and made it synonymous with the Democratic Society of Washington County.

102. One of the seven was James Marshel, president of the society.

CHAPTER 3 DEMOCRATIC-REPUBLICAN SOCIETIES OF NEW JERSEY

1. When the Mount Prospect, New Jersey, Political Society was formed, membership was declared open to all men of good character—a restriction designed to bar automatically those with aristocratic leanings. When an effort was made to set up a similar group in Newark, the Federalists moved to thwart the action. A group of administration supporters took advantage of the reduced attendance occasioned by the stormy night to seize control of the executive meeting and pass resolutions branding such a group "improper and unnecessary." But the furious Republicans finally succeeded in perfecting their organization. *Woods's Newark Gazette,* March 5, 12, 19, 26, 1794; Walter R. Fee, *The Transition from Aristocracy to Democracy in New Jersey, 1789-1829* (Somerville, N.J., 1933), pp. 40-41.

2. The resolutions were adopted in response to a communication from the Democratic Society of Pennsylvania.

3. The reference was to the appointment of John Jay as envoy to England while he was still Chief Justice of the Supreme Court.

4. Matthias Ward was a major in the local militia.

5. Aaron Pennington became editor and publisher in 1796 of the Newark *Centinel of Freedom,* the first really effective Republican publication in the state. His brother, William S. Pennington, was also active in the Newark society.

6. The resolutions were adopted after the society had been subjected to considerable criticism by New Jersey Federalists as part of the general offensive against the Democratic-Republican societies, linking them to the Whiskey Rebellion. See Fee, *Transition,* pp. 46-47.

CHAPTER 4 DEMOCRATIC-REPUBLICAN SOCIETIES OF NEW YORK

1. Thomas Greenleaf (1755-1798) was a printer and journalist who moved to New York City in 1785 and became manager of the *New-York Journal, or the Weekly Register.* He became part owner of the paper in January 1787, changed its title to *New-York Journal and Weekly Register,* and in November 1787 turned it into a daily paper, the *New-York Journal and Daily Patriotic Register.* Federalists destroyed his printing press because he opposed ratification of the Constitution as insufficiently democratic, but Greenleaf persisted in his anti-Federalism and became a champion of the rising Republican movement. He was a founder of the anti-Federalist St. Tammany's Society or Independent Order of Liberty and was one of its sachems in 1789. On May 11, 1795, he began to issue another democratic paper, *Argus, and Greenleaf's Daily Advertiser.*

2. The *Independent Journal,* begun on November 17, 1783, by Charles Webster and John McLean as a semiweekly, five years later became the *New York Daily Gazette,* with John and Archibald McLean as publishers. In 1789 John McLean died, leaving the paper to Archibald.

3. In 1747 Samuel Johnson published his *Plan of a Dictionary of the English Language.* The full dictionary was completed in 1755.

4. For the society referred to, see pp. 279-289.

5. The German Republican Society of Philadelphia was organized at least six weeks before Genêt's arrival.

6. William Murray Mansfield (1705-1793) was chief justice of the King's Bench from 1756 to 1788 and made important contributions to commercial law. He became earl of Mansfield in 1776 and served as speaker of the House of Lords.

7. On August 27 and 28, 1793, royalist counterrevolutionaries handed over the port of Toulon, a major French naval base and arsenal, to an Anglo-Spanish fleet. The British fleet seized more than seventy French ships, almost half of the French navy. The siege of Toulon, lasting from August 28 to December 19, 1793, enabled the young artillery officer Napoleon Bonaparte to win his first military reputation by forcing the Anglo-Spanish fleet, which was occupying the city and its forts, to withdraw.

8. Thomas Paine (1737-1809) was a great journalist and social reformer, author of the immortal *Common Sense,* which stirred great numbers of Americans into favoring independence from Britain. His *Crisis* papers continued to hearten Americans during the War for Independence. In 1789, while in England, he defended the French Revolution in his *The Rights of Man* (1791-1792), and when the pamphlets were suppressed and prosecution proceedings instituted against him, Paine fled to Paris, where he was made a French citizen and elected to the Convention. The fall of the Girondists led to his imprisonment, and upon his release from prison, he prepared *The Age of Reason,* which detailed his deistic beliefs and earned him the reputation of being an atheist.

9. William Loughton Smith (c. 1758-1812) was a Congressman from South Carolina whose pronounced Federalist and pro-British views led his political enemies in the spring of 1794 to burn him in effigy in the company of Benedict Arnold and the devil.

10. The account of the celebration in Greenleaf's *New York Journal* referred to it as a "grand and pleasing spectacle," the likes of which had not been seen in the city "for many years." "The respective flags of France and America joined together to denote the friendship and firm alliance between the citizens of the two republics, preceded the procession, the former borne by an American citizen, and the latter by a citizen of France; the sacred emblem of liberty was also carried in procession." The procession, "with a band of music playing Ca ira, the Marseilles hymn, the Carmagnole, and other patriotic tunes, proceeded through Broadway, Beekman street, Queen street, Broad street, and Beaver street, past the Government House to Corres' Hotel, where a large number of French and American citizens partook of an agreeable repast." The account concluded: "It is impossible to describe the pleasing satisfaction that appeared in every countenance: How delightful is that sensibility, which ever accompanies the pure emotion of friendship! But when that friendship is not barely confined to individuals, but

attaches whole nations together in the bonds of close alliance, the powers of language are too feeble to describe the scene with justice."

The March 4, 1794, New York *Daily Gazette* reported that nine-tenths of the men who organized the grand celebration were "members of the Democratic Society."

11. In its account of the celebration, the *New York Journal,* March 12, 1794, reported: "A beautiful *Ode,* written by Mrs. *Ann Julia Hatton,* of this city and addressed to the Democratic Society, was also read, and gave additional pleasure to citizens whose hearts are ever ready to expand at sentiments of patriotism."

12. James Nicholson (1763-1804) was a naval officer and member of a notable Maryland family who settled in New York after he retired as a naval captain and moved over from Federalism to become active in Republican politics. His house on William Street was the headquarters for New York Republicans.

13. Tunis Wortman (d. 1822) was the brilliant secretary of the Democratic Society of New York. A follower of George Clinton, he was named clerk of New York.

14. The *Federalist Papers* (1787-1788) were written by Alexander Hamilton (author of almost two-thirds of them), James Madison, and John Jay. The authors who styled themselves "Publius," supported ratification of the Constitution.

15. The original purpose of the convention that met in Philadelphia in 1787 was to amend the Articles of Confederation.

16. The battles of Lexington and Concord were fought on April 18 and 19, 1775.

17. John Philpot Curran (1750-1817) was a lawyer, statesman and champion of Irish liberties. He undertook the defense in the treason trials of the rebel leaders of the Society of United Irishmen—Wolfe Tone, Archibald Hamilton Rowan, and Lord Edward Fitzgerald.

18. The letters of Pacificus were written by Alexander Hamilton in 1793 to defend the right of the President to issue the Proclamation of Neutrality. The letters signed "Publicola" were written by John Quincy Adams in reply to the theories Thomas Paine advanced in *The Rights of Man.*

19. Joseph Priestley (1733-1804), an English chemist and Nonconformist minister, showed an early interest in the sciences and became one of the foremost chemists of his time. He was chosen foreign associate of the French Academy of Sciences and later became librarian of Lord Shelburne. His greatest achievement was the isolation and identification of oxygen. He became minister of the New Meeting Society in Birmingham and was noted for his voluminous and controversial writings on religious topics. He was also an ardent admirer of the French Revolution, and his well-known sympathy for the Revolution led a mob to burn his house, books, and all his private effects. He reached London safely. Then on April 7, 1794, in search of greater freedom, he and his wife sailed for America, arriving in New York on June 4. He was greeted in New York City by Governor Clinton, Bishop Samuel Provoost of the Episcopal church, and deputations from the Democratic Society, Tammany, the Associated Teachers, the Medical Society of the State of New York, and "the Republican Natives of Great Britain and Ireland." Priestley disappointed the societies

by refusing to endorse the organizations. The Democratic Society and Tammany invited him to join, but he made it clear he was "not to be a public or political character." Nevertheless, when he returned to New York from Pennsylvania, the Democratic Society arranged a lecture series for him. He spent his time in Northumberland, Pennsylvania, working at his laboratory.

20. Governor Mifflin appointed state commissioners to accompany those named by President Washington to meet with the insurgents, and, through them, he promised complete pardon for past transgressions if the westerners would guarantee further submission to the authorities.

21. Jacob De La Montagnie has been referred to as a Jew, but according to Dr. Jacob R. Marcus, director of the American Jewish Archives in Cincinnati, Ohio, the evidence does not sustain this conclusion. Dr. Marcus to author, March 13, 1975.

22. Edmund Randolph (1753-1813) succeeded Thomas Jefferson as Secretary of State and served from January 2, 1794, to August 19, 1795. For Randolph's letters, see *American State Papers, Foreign Relations*, 1: 674. (Both letters bear the date June 10, 1794.) Randolph advised Monroe during his negotiations with the French government but also rebuked him for his passionate defense of the French Revolution in his address to the French National Convention.

23. David Humphreys (1752-1818), minister to the Portuguese, was assigned the task of signing the treaty with Morocco. But before he could reach Algiers, peace between Portugal and the Algerines was signed, and when the Portuguese squadron left the Straits of Gibraltar, the Algerine cruisers seized American ships, captured American seamen, and held them for ransom. Humphreys finally negotiated a treaty with the Algerine states for the freeing of American prisoners.

24. *Montesquieu, Esp. des lois.* (note in original). *L'Espirit des Lois* (1748), the masterpiece of Charles Louis de Secondat, Baron de Montesquieu (1689-1755), discussed the relationship between human and natural law.

25. Henry Brokholst Livingston (1757-1823) had been a leader of the opposition to Jay's treaty in New York. An ex-Federalist, he became a strong Jeffersonian Republican. He was appointed Associate Justice of the Supreme Court by President Thomas Jefferson.

26. Ça ira, ça ira—"it will all come right in the end"—the words were made the subject of a stirring song, which, until the *Marseillaise* appeared, was pre-eminent among the revolutionists in France and the friends of the French Revolution elsewhere.

27. Robert R. Livingston (1746-1813), one of the committee of five who drew up the Declaration of Independence, was chancellor of New York State from 1777 to 1801.

28. Aaron Burr (1736-1836), revolutionary officer and political leader, practiced law in New York City from 1783 on, was state attorney general (1789), and U.S. Senator (1791-1797). He was one of the organizers of the Republican movement in New York.

29. Dr. Samuel Mitchill was a Columbia University professor and founder of the *Medical Repository*.

30. John Broome was a Republican follower of Aaron Burr.

31. Henry Rutgers (1745-1830), revolutionary officer and landed magnate, was involved in New York local and state politics and helped advance Jeffersonianism in New York City.

32. Solomon Simpson (or Simson) (1738-1801), a Jewish merchant, was the second vice-president of the Democratic Society of New York when it was established in 1794. In 1795 he became first vice-president and continued in that office in 1796 until 1797 when he became president. He was a pillar of the Congregation Shearith Israel, of which he had been the president in 1773 and 1776. When the majority of the congregation decided to leave New York rather than collaborate with the British occupation, Simpson went to Norwalk, Connecticut, and was an active patriot there. Returning to New York after the war, he again became president of the congregation, a post he held in 1787, 1790, and 1791. In 1794 and 1795 he held the elected office of assessor in the Second Ward.

33. In August 1791 the monarchs of Austria and Prussia issued the Declaration of Pillnitz, which appealed to the other European rulers to act together with Prussia and Austria on behalf of the French monarch. This interference in French internal affairs led inevitably to France's declaration of war against Austria, and in practice, against Prussia as well, on April 20, 1792.

34. On July 30, 1792, the Allied commander, the Duke of Brunswick, crossed the Rhine and faced the French army on September 20 at Valmy. After failing to break the French army, Brunswick called off the battle.

The reference to Burgoyne was to John Burgoyne (1722-1792), the British general who was forced to surrender at Saratoga in 1777.

35. Jean Fauchet was the minister who replaced Genêt.

36. In 1794 Tadeusz Kosciusko (1746-1817) led an unsuccessful uprising against the foreign powers (Russia, Prussia, and Austria) occupying Poland.

37. On August 20, 1794, Anthony Wayne (1745-1796) defeated the Indians at Fallen Timbers on the Maumee River near what is now Toledo, Ohio.

38. Frederick August (1763-1827), duke of York and second son of King George III of Great Britain, was the British field commander against the French. In conjunction with an Austrian force, Frederick's army scored victories over the French early in 1793, but he was defeated near Dunkirk in September 1793 and at Tournai in May 1794 and was then driven in retreat through Belgium.

39. The resolutions and the correspondence that follows resulted in a bitter split in Tammany that led to the withdrawal of the Federalist members. It began when the Federalist members rushed to put their organization on record in support of President Washington's position in his attack on the Democratic societies as being responsible for the Whiskey Rebellion. According to a Republican source, the address was adopted by a vote of thirty-one to fifteen and was then published in the press as an address to the public. The Republicans immediately answered the attack and in the process, won the debate and control of the organization. See Peter Paulson, "The Tammany Society and the Jeffersonian Movement in New York City, 1795-1800," *New York History* 34 (January 1953): 72-75.

40. In 1795 the United Provinces of the Netherlands became the Batavian Republic under the influence of the French Revolution and after conquest by French revolutionary armies. It lasted until 1805 when the name was changed

to Batavian Commonwealth, which was replaced by the Kingdom of Holland in 1806.

41. This is undoubtedly a reference to Algernon Sidney (1612-1683), the English Whig leader executed for allegedly plotting to overthrow the government of King Charles II. His *Discourses Concerning Government,* published in 1698, became a popular "textbook of revolution" in the North American colonies.

42. John Milton (1608-1674), great English poet and pamphleteer on behalf of religious and political liberty.

43. John Hampden (1594-1643), British parliamentary leader, famous for his opposition to King Charles I over ship money, a levy the king collected for outfitting his navy.

44. Samuel Miller (1769-1850), Presbyterian minister of New York and a leading opponent of slavery. He was connected with the Tammany Society, at whose request he preached a Fourth of July sermon in 1793. On July 4, 1795, he preached a sermon at the request of the Mechanic, Tammany, and Democratic societies, and the Military Officers. See the *New York Journal,* May 12, 1798, for praise of his National Fast Day sermon on May 9, 1798, in which he pleaded for real neutrality.

45. The reference is to Jay's Treaty.

46. In 1777 George Clinton (1739-1812) was elected the first governor of New York State. He served until 1795 when he refused to seek reelection again.

47. The General Society of Mechanics and Tradesmen was founded on November 17, 1785, with about thirty trades. At first the society took no part in politics. It was not incorporated until March 14, 1792, at which time it had more than 200 members.

48. Maximilien Isidore de Robespierre (1758-1794), leader of the Jacobins in the French Revolution, is associated with the use of terror and the guillotine to suppress opposition to the revolution. He was himself executed on the guillotine.

49. The "war hawks" refers to the war fever stirred up by the Federalists during the X, Y, Z, revelations and the "quasiwar" with France. Under cover of the widespread hysteria, the Federalists pushed through the repressive Alien and Sedition Acts.

50. Edward Livingston (1764-1836), New York lawyer and member of the House of Representatives (1795-1801), had previously supported the Federalists, but in 1794 he went over to the side of Clinton and the party of Thomas Jefferson.

51. Reverend Samuel Miller's sermon was published by Thomas Greenleaf at the request of the Mechanic, Tammany, and Democratic societies. In the course of his sermon, Reverend Miller reminded his audience that they (and all other Americans) had the duty "to WATCH OVER THE INESTIMABLE PRIVILEGES WE ENJOY, AND ENDEAVOUR TO TRANSMIT THEM, NOT ONLY UNTARNISHED, BUT HIGHLY IMPROVED, TO THE LATEST POSTERITY." He stressed too that "in order to the security and perpetuation of Liberty, . . . it is of the highest importance that there be a GENERAL DIFFUSION OF KNOWLEDGE among all classes of citizens. . . . Educate your children in the manners, the feelings, the principles, and manly ardor of Americans; and they will always be able and dis-

posed to trample down the risings of arbitrary power." Pamphlet, New York City, 1795.

52. The reference is to the treaty Lord Grenville and John Jay signed at London on November 19, 1794.

53. These were the ten Senators who voted against ratification of Jay's Treaty.

54. Hibernia is the Latin name for Ireland.

55. On August 10, 1792, a popular insurrection overthrew the monarchy. On December 11, Louis XVI was brought to trial, and on January 14, 1793, he was judged guilty by unanimous decision of the National Convention. The death sentence was imposed by a vote of 387 to 334, and the king was executed on January 21, 1793.

56. The reference is to Edmond Genêt, French minister to the United States.

57. This is a reference to the revocation of Duplaine's exequatur as vice-consul for the Republic of France by President Washington because of his seizure of the *Greyhound,* a British prize ship.

58. This refers to the victory of the French armies over those led by the Duke of Brunswick at Valmy in September 1793 and against the Austrians at Jemappes on November 6.

59. The Constitution of 1777 was still in operation.

60. For the annual salaries of the officers of the state of New York, see "An Act for the Support of Government," passed April 11, 1792, in *Laws of the State of New York Passed in the Sessions of the Legislature, 1789-96*, 3: 369-372.

61. The reference is to Jay's Treaty.

62. The statement appeared in Jefferson's *Notes on Virginia,* written during the War for Independence but published in Paris in 1785.

In his *Oration on the Influence of Social Institutions upon Human Morals and Happiness,* delivered before the Tammany Society on May 12, 1796, Tunis Wortman quoted Jefferson's words and commented that "his description of the spirit of the present times" had been "truly prophetic." However, he warned that it was up to the "people themselves" to make certain that "this unpromising picture should ever become realised." Pamphlet, New York City, 1796.

CHAPTER 5 NORWALK REPUBLICAN SOCIETY, CONNECTICUT

1. In the summer and fall of 1793, Philadelphia, then the nation's capital, was devastated by a terrible yellow fever epidemic. Within a period of less than two months, thousands in Philadelphia fell victim to the disease.

2. The articles were not published.

CHAPTER 6 DEMOCRATIC-REPUBLICAN SOCIETIES
OF MASSACHUSETTS

1. William Cooper was a leading Revolutionist and a close friend of Samuel Adams.

2. In the fall of 1794 the allies were in full retreat before the French revolutionary armies. The French defeated the Austrians and British.

3. Vendée was a coastal department in western France where a counterrevolutionary uprising emerged.

4. Guy Carleton, first Baron Dorchester (·1724-1808), was governor in chief of British North America between 1786 and 1796. On February 10, 1794, he delivered an address to a delegation of western Indian tribes to request British armed intervention against the United States. In his speech Dorchester told the Indians that the United States had no desire for peace and that the Indians and the king would soon be at war with the newly founded Republic. The speech became public and caused a sensation in the United States. The *New-York Diary* observed: "Let the citizens of America attentively peruse the speech of Dorchester—let them examine it with a critical eye.—let them read,—'From the manner in which the states push on, and act and talk, and from what I learn of their conduct towards the sea, I shall not be surprised if we are at war with them in the course of the present year; and if we are, a line must then be drawn by our warriors.' . . . We are now upon a precipice; our eyes should be open; preparations should be made, and every American should be ready to strike one decisive blow at our declared enemy!" Reprinted in *Aurora* (Philadelphia), April 3, 1794.

5. John Avery, Jr., was a close friend of Dr. Nathaniel Ames, the Republican brother of Federalist Fisher Ames, who lived in Dedham, Massachusetts.

6. Peretz Morton served in the revolutionary army.

7. Benjamin Austin served in the revolutionary army.

8. Edmund Randolph resigned as Secretary of State as a result of revelations through the British minister of intercepted communications of the French minister, Jean Fauchet, to his government. The implication in Fauchet's correspondence was that Randolph made improper revelations to him and indicated he might be influenced by French money. When Washington raised the issue, Randolph resigned and wrote an elaborate defense of his conduct, *A Vindication of Mr. Randolph's Resignation.*

9. Illegible.

10. Madison headed the committee to frame a reply to Washington's message favoring Senate ratification of Jay's Treaty. Sedgwick and Sitgreaves, two Federalist Congressmen, forced a passage into the reply affirming that the confidence of the President's fellow citizens was undiminished.

11. Samuel Hewes, a member of the Massachusetts Constitutional Society, furnished the Portland Society with news that evidently did not appear in that city's press.

12. Maine was then part of Massachusetts.

13. In his *History of Portland* (Portland, 1865), p. 606, William Willis writes of the society: "The leading members were John Barker, Major Bradish, Wm. McLellan, and Samuel Dunn, who held monthly meetings, at which suppers were furnished at a house in Free Street. The society maintained so rigidly the doctrine of routine in office, that they provided by the constitution that the chairman should be chosen monthly. The members of the societies continued to retain a warm attachment to France, notwithstanding the waywardness of her political course, and thought our government was bound by justice and the obligations of treaties to assist her against the armed alliance of kings against whom she was singly contending."

In his *Portland in the Past with Historical Notes on Old Falmouth* (Portland, 1886), William Gould does not mention the society, but he does cite the enthusiasm the people of Portland had for the French Revolution. Referring to a celebration on George Washington's birthday in 1793, Gould quotes the following toasts of the thirteen drank: "6th. Our great and glorious allies, the French; may their victorious struggle for liberty be attended with all the success that the stores of heaven can shower down.

"9th. The enlightener of the world, Thomas Paine. May the 'Rights of Man' be understood and speedily practiced by the benighted corners of the earth.

"13th. Brave Irishmen! May the sword of justice, once drawn, never be sheathed till they have obtained equal liberty and laws."

14. John Barker was one of those who petitioned the Massachusetts House of Representatives in 1787 announcing the formation of "an Independent Company" for the "defence of the State by the best means in their power" and seeking permission to establish the company and name it "The Cumberland Independent Company of Cadetts." James Phinney Baxter, ed., *Documentary History of the State of Maine* (Portland, 1916), 21: 267-268. Maine did not become a state until 1820.

15. David Bradish was also one of the signers of the petition to the Massachusetts House of Representatives.

16. Samuel Bryant was another signer of the petition.

17. Crossed out in the original.

18. Illegible.

19. Illegible.

20. Link notes the difference in the spelling in the original documents and the published statement of the Republican Society in Portland and points out that it reveals "the dependence of the democratic party upon some 'larned person,' like a printer, to assist in editing its materials for publication." Eugene P. Link, *Democratic-Republican Societies, 1790-1800* (New York, 1942), p. 59n.

21. Adet was the French minister to the United States. He was recalled by the Directory.

22. Samuel Adams (1722-1803) revolutionary patriot, was governor of Massachusetts from 1794 to 1797. He enthusiastically approved of the movement for the Democratic-Republican societies even though he had opposed all extragovernmental committees in Massachusetts at the time of Shays's Rebellion. The change was caused by his fear of Federalist domination, and he proclaimed Republican principles from the governor's chair. See *Independent Chronicle* (Boston), December 9, 1793, September 22, 1794.

CHAPTER 7 DEMOCRATIC-REPUBLICAN SOCIETIES
OF VERMONT

1. Israel Smith (1759-1810), a graduate of Yale University, was admitted to the Vermont bar in 1783 and began law practice in Rupert. Between 1785 and 1790 he served four terms in the Vermont legislature, and in 1791 he was elected to the House of Representatives from Rutland. In Congress, he supported the Jeffersonian cause, joining in opposition to Jay's Treaty. Throughout his career in Congress, he was identified with the Republican party.

2. Edmund Charles Genêt, minister of the French Republic.

3. The federal courts took jurisdiction of cases brought by individuals against the several states. This was bitterly opposed. The case, *Chisholm* v. *Georgia,* 2 Dallas 419, brought the matter to a head and resulted in the Eleventh Amendment to the Constitution of the United States, adopted January 8, 1798, which reads: "The judicial power of the United States shall not be construed to extend to any suit in law or equity, commenced or prosecuted against one of the United States by citizens of another State, or by citizens or subjects of any foreign State."

4. Nathaniel Chipman's *Sketches of the Principles of Government* was published in 1793. Chipman (1752-1843), a Vermont jurist, was a leading Federalist in the state.

5. William Pitt the Younger (1759-1806) was the prime minister who led Britain in the wars against the French Revolution.

6. Edmund Burke (1729-1797) was the leading British opponent of the French Revolution.

7. The "friend" was Alexander Hamilton. *See* Daniel Chipman, *The Life of Hon. Nathaniel Chipman, LL.D.* (Boston, 1846), pp. 395-401, and Harold C. Syrett and Jacob E. Cooke, eds., *The Papers of Alexander Hamilton* (New York and London, 1972), 16: 465-470. The letter is dated January 9, 1794 in the Chipman biography.

8. Chipman, *Sketches of the Principles of Government.*

9. *"Some persons were killed, and others wounded, in the* RIOTS *near Pittsburgh"* (note in original).

10. See *Annals of Congress,* 3d Cong. 2d sess. p. 914.

11. The reference is to Abraham Baldwin (1754-1807), the Congressman from Georgia during the years 1789-1799 who urged on the House of Representatives the necessity of more effectually carrying out the laws of the United States. See *Annals of Congress,* 3d Cong. 2d sess., pp. 951-953. Baldwin supported the Republicans, opposed Jay's Treaty, and worked with Madison in opposition to Federalist policies.

12. The men referred to represented the following states in the House of Representatives: Uriah Tracy, Connecticut; Samuel Dexter, Massachusetts; Theodore Sedgwick, Massachusetts; Wm. Vans Murray, Maryland; William Smith, South Carolina; Fisher Ames, Massachusetts; and Jonathan Drayton, New Jersey. All were leading critics of the Democratic-Republican societies in Congress. For a digest of their speeches on the subject of "self-created societies," see *Annals of Congress,* 3d Cong. 2d sess. pp. 901ff.

13. Fisher Ames, Congressman from Massachusetts, married Frances, third daughter of Colonel John Worthington of Springfield, Massachusetts, on July 15, 1792. Ames referred to Worthington as "the Hampshire tory of 1775." See Seth Ames, ed., *Works of Fisher Ames* (Boston, 1854), 1: 146.

14. When the French National Convention ordered an American flag to be hung up in their hall, Monroe sent one with a letter. The bearer was Joshua Barney, a ship captain who had served during the Revolution and who had accompanied Monroe to France. Barney delivered the flag and the letter, made a speech to the Convention, and received a commission in the French navy. A few weeks later, a French flag was ordered to be given to the United States.

15. The reference is to Secretary of Treasury Alexander Hamilton's proposal that the Congress pay the state debts that had been contracted during the American Revolution. By the Assumption Act of 1790, also known as the Funding Act, Congress appropriated $21.5 million to pay off the entire outstanding debt.

16. The reference is to the whiskey tax, although there was also opposition to the excise taxes on other commodities.

17. The reference is to Chief Justice John Jay.

18. Illegible.

19. Illegible.

20. Stephen Pearl is listed as a sheriff by W. S. Rann in his *History of Chittenden County, Vermont* (Syracuse, N.Y., 1886), p. 149.

CHAPTER 8 PATRIOTIC SOCIETY OF THE COUNTY OF NEWCASTLE, DELAWARE

1. The name "Associators" may have been taken over from the Associators of Pennsylvania, military associations formed at the time of the Revolution and composed of mechanics and artisans. The Associators took an active part in defending democratic rights and fully supported the Pennsylvania Constitution of 1776, the most democratic state constitution adopted during the revolutionary era.

2. Jas. McCullough is listed as a weaver in J. Thomas Sharf, *History of Delaware, 1609-1888* (Philadelphia, 1888), 2: 852; however, Eugene P. Link lists him as a poor farmer whose estate, after debts were paid, amounted only to $229. *Democratic-Republican Societies, 1790-1800* (New York, 1942), p. 92n.

3. John Bird is mentioned in Scharf, *History of Delaware*, p. 863, as a member of the committee of two "to purchase an engine" for the Union Fire Company of New Castle County. He has no other reference to Bird.

4. Robert Coran (1762-1796) was an English-born schoolmaster and publisher. His parents brought him from England to Charleston, South Carolina, when he was about three years old. His father turned loyalist when the American Revolution broke out, but the boy, then about sixteen years of age, enlisted in the South Carolina navy and later served with John Paul Jones, winning a citation for "gallant behavior." Captured by the British in 1782, he remained in a British prison ship until the close of the war when he went to Delaware and

established his home in that state. He kept a school, acted as a librarian for the Wilmington Library Company, edited and published the *Delaware Gazette,* and became associated with the leaders of the Republican movement in Delaware. Elected a member of the Delaware constitutional convention in 1792, Coram helped frame Article VIII, Section 12, which instructed the legislature to provide for "establishing schools and promoting arts and sciences." In 1791 he published his *Political Inquiries to Which Is Added a Plan for the General Establishment of Schools Throughout the United States.*

5. Caesar Augustus Rodney (1772-1824), born in Delaware, nephew of Caesar Rodney, signer of the Declaration of Independence, graduated from the University of Pennsylvania in 1798, and was admitted to the bar in 1793. Although a member of the Democratic Society of Pennsylvania, his political activities on behalf of Jeffersonian principles were conducted mainly in Delaware where he practiced law and from which state he was elected to Congress. When he moved to Delaware, he joined the Patriotic Society of Newcastle.

6. The Massacre of Saint Bartholomew's Day, the massacre of French Huguenots (Protestants), which began on August 23, 1572, in Paris. It is estimated that in Paris alone 3,000 were slain.

7. Pisistratus (early sixth century B.C.-527 B.C.) was the tyrant of ancient Athens who made himself despot in 560 B.C. During his reign of thirty-three years, he was twice exiled, once for a period of more than ten years and once for five years.

8. Tarquin was the name of two of the seven kings who, according to tradition, ruled Rome before the founding of the republic around 509 B.C.

9. The reference is to Lucius Cornelius Sulla (138 B.C.-78 B.C.), Roman general and dictator during the last century of the Roman republic's existence. After achieving a series of governmental reforms, he resigned in 79 B.C.

10. A royal proclamation against seditious writings was issued on May 21, 1792.

11. This was "The Society of Friends of the People." It was formed by a large group of advanced Whigs, although Charles Fox did not become a member because he disapproved of the organization. Its members were more moderate in their demands than those of the Constitutional Society and the London Corresponding Society. The Society of the Friends of the People desired to establish a genuine House of Commons and believed that reform could be effected by restoration rather than by the introduction of new measures.

12. William Petty Fitzmaurice Landsdowne (first marquess and second earl of Shelburne), usually known as Lord Shelburne (1735-1805), British statesman, minister for the colonies (1766-1768), and prime minister of England from July 1782 to February 1783. He helped negotiate the Treaty of Paris, which ended the War for Independence.

13. Charles James Fox (1749-1806) was a British political leader who long opposed the policies of George III and who was one of the few parliamentary supporters of the French Revolution. He contributed to the ending of the British slave trade and restoring rights to trial by jury in libel cases.

CHAPTER 9 REPUBLICAN SOCIETY OF BALTIMORE, MARYLAND

1. Alexander McKim (1748-1832), a strong supporter of Jefferson, was a member of the Association of Manufacturers in 1790 and the Committee of Health in Baltimore (1791), and was elected to Congress, serving in the House from 1813 to 1815. He was vice-president of the Maryland Society for Abolition of Slavery.

2. George Sears was one of the founders of the Library Company of Baltimore.

3. The seal of the Baltimore society was composed of a figure of liberty, with pileus, Phrygian cap, and fasces, and bearing the name of the society.

4. William Van Wyck was a merchant who settled in Baltimore in 1783.

5. Thomas Dixon was a member of the Baltimore Committee of Health (1794) and a delegate to the assembly (1801).

6. Thomas Rutter, sheriff and marshal, was elected justice of the Orphans' Court in 1803.

7. Thomas Johnson was a member of the Committee of Defence (1781) and a justice of the Supreme Court (1791).

8. Solomon Etting (1764-1847) was a Jewish merchant.

9. John Striker (1758-1825) was a merchant.

10. John Spear, active in the revolutionary war, was a leader in the Presbyterian church.

11. James A. Buchanan is listed as a banker.

12. James Winchester, revolutionary soldier, was elected a delegate to the assembly (1794) and elected to the senate in 1796.

13. William McCreery (1750-1814), a state senator, was elected to the U.S. House of Representatives but his seat was contested (1807-1809).

14. Archibald Buchanan, a member of the Committee of Observation (1774), was elected delegate to the assembly in 1798. Buchanan was a leading opponent of Negro slavery. He delivered the Fourth of July address to the Republican Society of Baltimore in 1794.

15. The reference is to Alexander Hamilton's report to President Washington reciting the facts that led to the crisis of the Whiskey Rebellion.

16. This is probably a reference to Quintus Maximus Cunctator Fabius (d. 203 B.C.) whose cautious delaying tactics helped Rome obtain time to recover its strength and take the offensive against Hannibal's invading Carthaginian army. Fabianism has come to mean a gradual or cautious policy.

17. Charles-François du Périer Dumouriez (1739-1823) was a general prominent in the 1789 French Revolution.

CHAPTER 10 DEMOCRATIC-REPUBLICAN SOCIETIES OF VIRGINIA

1. See p. 422 for the victories referred to.

2. It is not clear why the Republicans of Norfolk formed another society when one already existed in the city.

3. Included in the issues to be refunded under Hamilton's funding program were the certificates with which the revolutionary veterans had been paid. Large amounts of these certificates, along with other issues, were scattered throughout the hinterland. Eastern speculators, learning of Hamilton's plan, bought up at a cheap price securities that were soon to be paid for at a much higher value.

4. This refers to the position held by Richard Bland Lee (1761-1827) in Congress with regard to the Madison resolutions on commerce. In his speeches before the House of Representatives he upheld the Federalist view.

5. Paine's *Rights of Man* was published in the United States with a preface by Thomas Jefferson.

CHAPTER 11 DEMOCRATIC-REPUBLICAN SOCIETIES OF KENTUCKY

1. John Bradford was born in Virginia in 1749 and settled in Kentucky with his family in 1785. In 1787 he and his brother established the *Kentucke Gazette,* which continued under this name until March 14, 1789, when the name was changed to *Kentucky Gazette.* Bradford was a member of the House of Representatives of Kentucky in 1797 and 1802.

2. John Breckenridge (1760-1806) was born in August County, Virginia. Because of his father's early death, young Breckenridge worked to support his widowed mother and the rest of the family. He practiced law in Albermarle County, Virginia, from 1785 until he moved to Kentucky early in 1793. He was appointed attorney general for the state in 1795 and was later elected to represent Fayette County in the lower house of the legislature. He was successfully reelected until 1801, being speaker the last two years. He was also prominent and influential in the convention that framed the Constitution of 1799.

3. Robert Todd, one of the early settlers of Kentucky, was elected senator from Fayette in the first session of the legislature. He was a circuit judge for a long time.

4. Reverend James Moore came to Lexington from Virginia in 1792 at which time he was a candidate for the ministry in the Presbyterian church. Shortly after, he became connected with the Episcopal church and was the first rector

of Christ Church in Lexington. In 1798 he was appointed acting president of Transylvania University.

5. The reference is to the Treaty of Paris ending the War for Independence.

6. Spain was then at war with France.

7. August Lachaise (sometimes spelled La Chaise) was one of the men associated with Genêt's plans for conquering Louisiana and opening the Mississippi. For this purpose he corresponded with the Democratic Society of Kentucky. In one of his letters to the society, he pointed to the fact that the Louisianans were French and that "the honor, the glory, the duty of the National Convention is to grant them their powerful support." He added: "Every petition or plan relative to that important object would meet with the highest consideration. An address from the Democratic Society of Lexington would give it greater weight." Charles Gayarre, *History of Louisiana: The French Domination* (New Orleans, 1885), 3: 343-344.

8. This is most likely the society's response to Lachaise's letter.

CHAPTER 12 DEMOCRATIC SOCIETY OF WASHINGTON, NORTH CAROLINA

1. Thomas Blount (1759-1812), born in Edgecombe County, North Carolina, served as an ensign during the Revolution; he was taken prisoner and sent to England where he remained until the end of the war. Returning to his native state, he participated in the second North Carolina convention called to consider the ratification of the Constitution. A Republican in politics, he represented Edgecombe County in the state assembly and went to Congress in 1793, where he served in several sessions. As representative of North Carolina to Congress in 1794, Blount opposed increasing the naval and military forces of the United States. He approved of a resolution prohibiting intercourse between the United States and Great Britain, insofar as it concerned the articles of growth or manufacture in Great Britain and Ireland. He favored a bill providing for the payment of a certain sum of money that the United States owed France. He voted against raising additional regiments of infantry within the states of Georgia, South Carolina, and North Carolina and the territory south of the Ohio and Virginia. See *Annals of Congress,* 3d Cong. 2d sess. pp. 459, 477, 498, 602, 738, 741, 779.

CHAPTER 13 DEMOCRATIC-REPUBLICAN SOCIETIES OF SOUTH CAROLINA

1. Stephen Drayton, member of the Federalist family of Drayton, was a member of the Georgia Council of Safety in 1775, and in 1778 he was commissioned deputy quartermaster-general for the Southern Department of the Continental

army. He was a member of the Georgia State Society of Cincinnati and secretary to Governor William Moultrie.

2. Throughout most of 1793 France suffered serious military reverses so the victory of the *Ambuscade* was a cause for celebration.

3. Gideon Henfield was one of the two American sailors on the *Citizen Genêt*, a French privateer, arrested in Philadelphia and bound over for trial on the charge of violating American neutrality by serving on a French armed vessel and thus engaging in hostilities against a nation with which the United States was at peace. Brought to trial, Henfield was acquitted by the Philadelphia jury.

4. Although it is the Republican Society of South Carolina that is mentioned, it is the opinion of some scholars that it was actually the French Patriotic Society of Charleston that petitioned the French National Convention for membership in the Jacobin clubs. For the address of the French Patriotic Society of Charleston to the French National Assembly and to the Society of the Friends of the Constitution sitting in Paris, see *Diary* (New York), December 14, 15, 1792. In the *City Gazette* (Charleston), January 3, 1793, Theodore Gaillard is listed as president and Luby as secretary of the society.

5. Jean-Marie Collot d'Herbois (1749-1796) was a member of the Committee of Public Safety that ruled revolutionary France during the period of the Jacobin dictatorship (1793-1794).

6. The Committee of Public Safety was set up on April 6, 1793, during one of the crises of the Revolution when France was beset by foreign and civil war. The new committee was to provide for the defense of the nation against its enemies, foreign and domestic, and to oversee the already existing organs of executive government.

7. William Tate was a frontier leader who went to France in 1795 and joined the French army. Two years later he was a leader in the Fishguard bay incident, an attempt to aid Ireland in its revolution.

8. Michel Ange Mangourit was the French consul in Charleston.

9. The Constitution of 1793 was the most democratic in history thus far. It provided for universal manhood suffrage and the right of referendum. It declared that society owes a living to the poor, either by finding work for them or by giving them the means of subsistence. It made the provision of education an obligation of the state. But because of the disordered conditions of the time, the Constitution of 1793 was never put into effect.

10. Mangourit, the French consul, had given the society a stone from the Bastille, and members planned to engrave the cap of liberty on it.

11. The address of friendship to the French National Convention is not in the "Correspondence of the Republican Society of Charleston."

12. "One gentleman of the Republican Society then present said he would contribute one hundred guineas toward said expence" (note in original).

13. Among other things, "Mr. Madison's Resolutions," introduced in Congress on January 3, 1794, endeared Madison to the Democratic-Republican societies. See p. 412.

14. William Smith, Congressman from Charleston, led the attack on "Mr. Madison's Resolutions" in Congress.

15. Alexander Moultrie and Stephen Drayton had been called before the

state legislature for alleged violation of the law in recruiting for Genêt's projects.

16. On June 28, 1776, the committee appointed by the Continental Congress to prepare a declaration of independence brought in its draft. On July 2 a resolution declaring independence was adopted, and on July 4 the Declaration of Independence was agreed to.

17. William Moultrie (1730-1805) was a revolutionary general who resisted British incursions into the South during the War for Independence. After the war he served two terms as governor of South Carolina (1785-1787, 1792-1794) and was a state senator between those terms.

18. Elihu Palmer (1764-1806), the militant atheist and member of the Democratic Society of Pennsylvania, had been forced by an angry mob to flee from Philadelphia after he had preached a sermon against the divinity of Jesus.

19. This may have been a reference to that part of Genêt's instructions that cautioned him to be circumspect in his dealings with pro-French public officials. It was essential that he "scrupulously observe the forms established for official communications between the government and foreign agents and never engage in any move or proposals which might offend free Americans concerning their constitution which differs in many respects from the principles established in France." See Frederick J. Turner, ed., "Correspondence of the French Ministers to the United States, 1793-1797," *Annual Report of the American Historical Association for the Year 1903* (Washington, D.C., 1904), 2: 202-211.

20. This is a reference to the fact that the backcountry was not properly and democratically represented in the legislature because of the opposition of the upper classes of the seacoast area.

21. Samuel Lofton held the honorable position of sheriff.

22. John Miller, an English refugee printer, had sympathized with the colonists in the Revolution. While living in Charleston, he had helped establish a circulating library. Miller established the first paper in the up-country, *Miller's Weekly Messenger.*

23. Moses Liddle held large plantations and was deeply involved in land projects.

24. Peter Freneau was the brother of the poet and journalist Philip Freneau.

25. John Jay and Rufus King had published a detailed account in *Dunlap's American Advertiser* (Philadelphia) of Genêt's threat to appeal to the people over Washington's head, and, in the same issue of the paper, the editor inserted a notice that Alexander J. Dallas had allegedly heard Genêt make this threat and was preparing a statement. But Dallas's letter, which appeared on December 9, 1793, admitted that Genêt had spoken of an appeal, although he flatly denied that the French minister intended appealing to the people over the head of the President.

26. The reference is to the ratification of Jay's Treaty in Congress.

27. The reference is to the fact that Pierce Butler (1744-1822), although elected to the United States Senate as a Federalist, opposed Jay's Treaty.

28. The Creeks were a tribe of Indians living in Georgia, Alabama, and Florida.

29. Article VII of the Treaty of Paris provided for evacuation without "carrying away any Negroes or other Property" and required Great Britain to return

those Negro slaves who had escaped within British lines during the war and who were taken away on British transports when the troops left the United States. In lieu of restitution of their persons, a money compensation was to be given to their owners. However, Sir Guy Carleton maintained that the slaves were free men from the time they entered the British lines and were manumitted thereby; thus the treaty did not apply to them.

30. John Rutledge (1739-1800) of Charleston, South Carolina, was offered the post of Chief Justice of the Supreme Court in place of John Jay who was about to resign to leave for England. However, when Jay's Treaty became public, Rutledge bitterly attacked it in a public meeting in St. Michael's Church in Charleston, and, as a result, his nomination was rejected by the Senate.

31. Christopher Gadsden (1724-1805), leader of Charleston's Sons of Liberty and delegate to the Continental Congress where he advocated complete independence, voted for ratification of the United States Constitution in the 1788 state convention.

32. The reference is to Thomas Pinckney (1750-1828), U.S. minister to Great Britain (1792-1794).

33. These senators had voted against ratification of Jay's Treaty.

34. Jacob Read (1752-1816) served as a Federalist in the United States Senate from South Carolina from 1795 to 1801. He voted for ratification of Jay's Treaty.

35. John Miller, who wrote the resolutions, read them before the assembled militia companies at Pendleton that were gathered around a huge liberty pole.

Appendix A: Occupations and Professions of Members of the Democratic Society of Pennsylvania

Lewis G. Alleck	cabinetmaker	William D. Brown	lumber merchant
Robert Aitken, Jr.	printer	Samuel Bryan	general register
Robert T. Allen	silversmith	Thomas Bryant	cabinetmaker
Wm. Allen	health officer	James Burnside	clerk
Thomas Amies	shoemaker	Stephen Burrows	saddler
James Anderson	saddler	Dunkin Campbell	shoemaker
William Annan	doctor	William Campbell	marine captain
John Arrison	grocer	James Carson	teacher
Benjamin F. Bache	printer	Charles L. Carter	clerk
Robert Bailey	shopkeeper	Samuel Carver	carpenter
John Barker	tailor	Samuel G. Clendenin	printer
Wm. Barker	engraver	Wm. Coates	tanner
Peter Barrier	gentleman	Robert Cochran	printer
John Barron	clerk	John Connelly	merchant
William Barton	lawyer	Wm. Council	hatter
Daniel Beakly	carpenter	Louis Crousillat	merchant
William Belcher	marine captain	Alexander J. Dallas	secretary of the
William Bell	merchant		commonwealth
Charles Biddle	merchant-notary	James Darragh	weaver
Clement Biddle	broker-notary	Jonathan Davis	merchant
Thomas Biggs	instrument maker	Nathaniel Davis	innkeeper
Bohl Bohlen	merchant	James Depuglia	translator, Depart-
George Booth	gentleman		ment of State
James Boyd	printer	John Dougherty	tailor
James Boylan	merchant	Patrick Duffey	broker
Nathan Boys	city commissioner	A. C. Duplaine	teacher
William Bower	mariner	Michael Durrey	joiner
Michael Bright	flour inspector	Andrew Ellicott	surveyor
George Brown	tobacconist	Charles Erdman	printer
William Brown	marine captain	John Erwin	cordwainer

Oliver Evans	millwright	Samuel Jackson	shopkeeper
Jacob Everly	hatter	Jeremiah Johnson	painter
Ebenezer Ferguson	carpenter	Samuel Johnson	tanner
Hugh Ferguson, Jr.	merchant	Thomas Jones	tanner
Robert Fielding	coachmaker	William Jones	merchant
John Fimeton	carpenter	Lawrence Justis	carpenter
Samuel Findley	printer	Michael Kenedy	clerk
John Fogle	shopkeeper	Andrew Kennedy	merchant
Adam Foulke	grocer	John Kennedy	sailor
Edward Fox	auctioneer, notary public	Michael Keppele	lawyer
		James Kerr	coachmaker
George Fox	manufacturer	Charles Kinney	marine captain
Wm. Galt	gentleman	Charles Kirby	marine captain
James Gamble	marine captain	George Kitte	innkeeper
Jacob Garrigues	clerk	Jacob G. Koche	merchant
Glibert Gaw	chairmaker	John Langdon	carpenter
John German	marine captain	Michael Lawler	tobacconist
Andrew Geyer	bookbinder, county commissioner	John Lawson	marine captain
		Samuel Lea	chairmaker
		Michael Leib	doctor
Stephen Girard	merchant	John L. Leib	lawyer
James Glentworth	broker	Thomas Leiper	tobacconist
John Goodman	blacksmith	George Lesher	innkeeper
Elisha Gordon	shoemaker	Adam Logan	shoemaker
John Gravenstine	shopkeeper	George Logan	gentleman
Peter Gravenstine	shopkeeper	John Logan	laborer
Robert Griffiths	carpenter	Peter Lohra	broker, notary public
Jesse Grooves	bricklayer		
Michael Groves	bricklayer	Robert Lollar	marine captain
Matthew Hale	carpenter	Blair McClenachan	merchant
John Hall	gentleman	John McClenachan	merchant
Joseph D. Hamelin	teacher	John McElee	painter
Charles Harris	grocer	Wm. McFaddon	marine captain
John Harrison	shipwright	Robert McGee	lumber merchant
Wm. Henderson	turner	James McGlathery	carpenter
Jacob Hoffman	printer	Alex McKinsey	weaver
Edmund Hogan	printer	John McKissick	clerk
Anthony Hubbard	starchmaker	Patrick Maddon	tailor
Caleb Hughes	tailor	Solomon Marks, Jr.	broker
Robert Hunt	hatter	Richard Marley	shoemaker
Wm. Hunter	coachmaker	Thomas Marley	shotmaker
Henry Hyneman	harnessmaker	M. Martin	carpenter
John Irwin	merchant	Wm. Milnor	gauger
Israel Israel	innkeeper	Thomas Moore	saddler
John Israel	mariner	Cadwallader Morris	ironmaster
Samuel Israel	printer	Jacob Moser	tailor
David Jackson	druggist	James Muir	bookbinder

John Mullowny	merchant	Archibald Shaw	innkeeper
Jacob Nice	carpenter	Abraham Shoemaker	lawyer
Elihu Palmer	lawyer	J. Simonds	tailor
Rowland Parry	goldsmith	Wm. Skinner	painter
John B. Patterson	marine captain	John Smith	hatter
James Paul, Jr.	teacher	J. B. Smith	merchant
James Paxson	grocer	George Snyder	laborer
James Pearsons	city surveyor	John Spaid	painter
George Pfister	carpenter	Thomas Stephens	book importer
Abraham Phillips	shopkeeper	Peter Stewart	printer
John Pierce	ropemaker	John Stuckey	weaver
Joseph Poole	marine captain	John Swanwick	merchant
Samuel Post	button maker	Charles Swift	lawyer
Nathaniel Prentiss	cordwainer	Peter Sybert	sugar refiner
Richard Price	county commissioner	Wm. Thorn	carpenter
		William Thornton	doctor
James Prince	merchant	James Trimble	Assistant Secretary of Commerce
John Purdon	merchant		
John Rabhoon	breeches maker		
James Read	flour inspector	John Vallance	engraver
George Reed	tailor	John Vannest	tailor
George Rehn	brewer	John Vincent	shoemaker
David Rittenhouse	director of the mint	John Walters	painter
		William Watkins	tobacconist
Wm. Robeson, Sr.	carpenter	Bernard Webb	clerk
Wm. Robinson	justice of the peace	Thomas Webb	marine captain
		George Weckerly	brass founder
Caesar Rodney	lawyer, public official	John Wells	plasterer
		Samuel Wetherill	druggist
		John Wheeler	tailor
Edward Rowe	shipmaster	Charles White	merchant
Benjamin Rush	doctor	H. L. Widerhold	broker
John Salsbury	mariner	Benjamin Wiggins	innkeeper
Stephen Sayre	merchant	John Wigton	teacher
Charles Scrivener	printer	Isaac Worrell	merchant
J. D. Sergeant	lawyer	Anthony Wright	shoemaker
William Sergeant	lawyer	Malcolm Wright	coppersmith
John N. Seidel	currier	William Yard	grocer

Appendix B: Other Letters in the Contemporary Press on Democratic-Republican Societies

1. A Friend to Equal Right, *New York Journal,* March 30, 1791
2. A Subscriber in *American Apollo,* September 11, 1794
3. Leonidas in *New York Journal,* February 25, 1792
4. Letter in *Columbian Centinel,* August 7, 1793
5. Aristides in *Kentucky Gazette,* September 14, 1793
6. Argus in *Columbian Centinel,* November 30, 1793
7. A Republican in *Columbian Centinal,* November 30, 1793
8. A Democrat of 1777 in *Louden's Diary and Evening Register,* February 11, 1794
9. A Republican in *The Herald* (New York), February 7, 1794
10. An Old Whig in *American Mercury,* January 24, 25, February 24, 25, 1794
11. A Friend to Good Government in New York *Daily Gazette,* March 12, 1794.
12. Republican in *Pittsburgh Gazette,* April 26, 1794
13. The People in *Columbian Centinel,* May 24, 1794
14. Letter to Mr. Scull in *Pittsburgh Gazette,* June 28, 1794
15. Democratus in *Pittsburgh Gazette,* June 28, 1794
16. Order in *Columbian Centinel,* September 3, 1794
17. One of the People in *Columbian Centinel,* September 10, 1794
18. Letter in *Columbian Centinel,* September 27, 1794
19. Manlius in *Columbian Centinel* (Nos. I-IV), September 3, 6, 10, 13, 17, 1794
20. Deodatus in *Columbian Centinel,* October 11, 1794
21. Wm. Willcocks in New York *Daily Advertiser,* February 9, 16, 26, 1795
22. Agis in *New York Journal,* January 31, 1795
23. Democratus in *New York Journal,* January 31, 1795
24. Falstaff in *Vermont Gazette* (Bennington), February 27, 1795.

Appendix C: Constitutional Association of the Borough of Elizabeth, New Jersey

Monday evening, Jan. 19, the members of the CONSTITUTIONAL ASSOCIATION of the Borough of Elizabeth met for the choice of officers, Mathias Williamson, Jun. Esq. was chosen President;–Col. William Crane, Vice-President;–Col. Aaron Ogden, Secretary;–and William Shute, Esq. Assistant-Secretary. A Committee of Correspondence was also elected, consisting of twelve members, in which the foregoing officers were included as official members. The meeting adjourned;– the Corresponding Committee to next Monday, and the members of the Association, in stated meeting, to the Monday following. The objects of this association are briefly expressed in the following articles of incorporation, to which one hundred and thirty inhabitants have already subscribed.

I. To contribute what in us lies to the maintenance of those principles, which animated the heroes of the late war, and which are now happily incorporated in the present invaluable constitution of these United States.

II. To support all legal and constitutional measures of government.

III. To raise a barrier against those torrents of abuse which, from different quarters, for some time past, have been or may be unjustly poured forth against the present administration of our happy government.

IV. To lay a foundation for the bringing to a point such a portion of genuine republican influence as, under God, may promise a permanent protection to our present constitution, and to the many blessings we enjoy under it.

V. To form a bond of union, in which the subscribers do pledge themselves to each other, and to the union in general, at the risk of life and fortune, to use every legal and constitutional exertion for the preservation of that happiness which they now enjoy under the present administration of public affairs.

New Jersey Journal (Elizabethtown), January 20, 1795

At a stated meeting of the "Constitutional Association of Inhabitants of the Borough of Elizabeth," held at Elizabeth Town, on the first Monday in February, 1795–present one hundred members;–after free discussion, the following resolutions were unanimously adopted, excepting one dissentient to part of the third—the fourth—and eight resolutions;

RESOLVED I. That the present constitution of the United States, the foundation of our federal union, is entitled to the patronage and defence of every real friend to the peace and prosperity of our country, as well as to the good wishes of every friend to the liberties and rights of mankind.

II. That the rank which the United States hold among the nations, their well established credit, their growing commerce, the full demand for all agricultural property, their present state of amity and peace with all European nations, and in word, the general aspect of the riches and rising glory of our country, form a sufficient testimony in favor of the present administration of public affairs, and afford a full answer to all the calumnies of its enemies.

III. That George Washington, our illustrious President, hath continued to *deserve well of his country,* and especially by his late exertions in issuing, and supporting a proclamation of neutrality, by developing and frustrating the designs of a foreign incendiary, by his exertions to prevent a war with Great Britain, and by crushing the late insurgency without the shedding of human blood.

IV. That the *late* attempts to lessen the esteem of the President in the opinion of the good people of the United States, have been marked with design, and betray both a disregard to truth and to the public weal, and ought to be guarded against, as attempts, in the person of the President, to sap the foundation of our present political fabric.

V. That if the citizens of New-Jersey have ever acquired any fame, by a ready expression of their zeal for the public good, so far as the influence of this association extends, care should be taken that this good opinion be not forfeited by any forgetfulness of duty in time to come.

VI. That the peaceful enjoyment of our religious rights will, under GOD, be best maintained by a steady adherence to the principles of the confederation, in which the rights of conscience and religious opinion are equally secured to all.

VII. That the right hand of citizenship be extended to all citizens of these United States, disposed to meet us on the principles of our association, and of these resolutions—assuring all such that we will ever be happy to maintain a friendly correspondence with any bodies of citizens, who may judge it expedient to form themselves into associations upon similar principles, or to maintain epistolary correspondence with any reputable individuals, as corresponding members of this association, with whom it may not be convenient to be united in any associated body at home; and it is humbly recommended to any other associations formed or to be formed in connections, to adopt the same principles of correspondence.

VIII. That this association highly approve of the patriotic testimony of the Tammany Society of New-York, in their declaration of the 19th ult.[1] and hope that as their constitution bespeaks them friends to liberty and their country, they will never want courage publicly to avow and boldly to defend their constitutional character.

IX. That the idea this association entertains respecting the existence of their own or other similar associations, is pertinently expressed in the following declaration of Germanicus, No. 3. "The propriety or impropriety of self-created societies depends upon the propriety or impropriety of their principle, and especially as that principle is developed by their actions."

X. That the committee of correspondence take such measures for the promulgation of the principles and proceedings of this association as they may think proper, and that the public be informed that this association contemplates an associate existence no longer than while associations of a contrary spirit and practice shall appear; and, finally, our doors are to be considered as ever open, not only to the attendance, but to the arguments of any citizens of the United States, demeaning themselves, according to the rules of this institution.

MAT. WILLIAMSON, Pres.

AARON OGDEN, *Secretary*.

The dissentient member, alluded to above, embraces the present opportunity to declare, that no man entertains more exalted ideas of Washington than himself; that in the third resolution the expression, "developing and frustrating the designs of a foreign incendiary," (on which was founded his objection) is in itself true;—but it was *intended* to pierce the Democratic Societies—as the framer of the resolution chose in this manner to stab in secret—to endeavor by ambiguity of expression to acquire an unanimous vote, rather than *honorably, candidly,* and *clearly* bring forward the matter, that it might be fairly met—for these reasons he voted against it.

For the fourth resolution he saw no necessity. Was it abuse in the Popular Societies to say that the President *was fallible*—that he *might* be deceived—that, in their opinion, he was unconsciously laying a foundation for future despotism?— Was it abusive in them to point to the ruins of cities once free and flourishing, and warn Americans to beware of the causes of this calamity?—Did these things display malice? Malice works in secret—these things were done openly; malice resides only in unworthy bosoms—to these institutions many of the most respectable inhabitants of the country belong. Would you wish to know their names? Ask the encrimsoned heights of Bunker's Hill, and the gore-stained plains of Monmouth, and let these answer. It is not reasonable to suppose that such men as these would fawn upon the hand, which forges shackles for them.

New Jersey Journal (Elizabethtown), February 4, 1795

1. See pp. 205-207.

Bibliography

MANUSCRIPTS

Brackenridge, Hugh H. Papers. Darlington Library, University of Pittsburgh.
Brackenridge, John. Papers. Library of Congress.
Charleston Republican Society, Papers. Boston Public Library.
Democratic Society of Pennsylvania. Minutes. Historical Society of Pennsylvania.
Genêt, Edmund Charles. Papers. Library of Congress.
Hamilton, Alexander. Papers. Library of Congress.
Innes, Harry. Papers. Library of Congress.
Jefferson, Thomas. Papers. Library of Congress.
Madison, James. Papers. Library of Congress.
Portland Republican Society Papers. Maine Historical Society.
Tammany Society, New York City. Minutes. New York Public Library.

DISSERTATIONS

Baumann, Roland M. "The Democratic-Republicans of Philadelphia: The Origins, 1776-1797." Ph.D. dissertation, Pennsylvania State University, 1970.
Cohen, Beatrice. "The Democratic Society of Pennsylvania." Master's thesis, Temple University, 1937.
Keller, William Frederick. "American Politics and the Genêt Mission." Ph.D. dissertation, University of Pittsburgh, 1951.
Miller, William. "The Democratic Clubs of the Federalist Period, 1793-1795." Master's thesis, New York University, 1937.
Morantz, Regina Ann Markell, " 'Democracy' and 'Republic' in American Ideology, 1787-1840." Ph.D. dissertation, Columbia University, 1971.
Prince, Carl E. "New Jersey's Democratic-Republicans, 1790-1817." Ph.D. dissertation, Rutgers University, 1963.

Stewart, Donald H. "Jeffersonian Journalism: Newspaper Propaganda and the Development of the Democratic-Republican Party, 1789-1801." Ph.D. dissertation, Columbia University, 1950.

Tagg, James D. "Benjamin Franklin Bache and the Philadelphia *Aurora*," Ph.D. dissertation, Wayne State University, 1974.

Wheeler, William Bruce. "Urban Politics in Nature's Republic: The Development of Political Parties in the Seaport Cities in the Federalist Era." Ph.D. dissertation, University of Virginia, 1967.

Woodfin, Maude H. "Citizen Genêt and His Mission." Ph.D. dissertation, University of Chicago, 1928.

PRIMARY WORKS

Books

American State Papers. Miscellaneous. Vol. 1: *Documents: Legislative and Executive of the Congress of the United States.* Washington, D.C., 1834.

——. *Foreign Relations.* Vol. 1. Washington, D.C., 1832.

Ames, Seth, ed. *The Works of Fisher Ames.* Boston, 1854.

Amory, Thomas C. *Life of James Sullivan.* 2 vols. Boston, 1859.

Annals of Congress. Third Congress. Washington, D.C., 1794.

Austin, James T. *The Life of Elbridge Gerry.* 2 vols. Boston, 1829.

Biddle, Charles. *Autobiography, 1745-1821.* Philadelphia, 1883.

Brackenridge, Hugh H. *Incidents of the Insurrection in the Western Parts of Pennsylvania in the Year 1794.* Philadelphia, 1795.

Brackenridge, H. M. *Recollections of Persons and Places in the West.* Philadelphia, 1868.

Boyd, Julian P., ed. *The Papers of Thomas Jefferson.* Princeton, N.J., 1961.

Bureau of the Census. *A Century of Population Growth from the First to the Twelfth Census of the United States, 1790-1900.* Washington, D.C., 1909.

Carroll, John A., and Ashworth, Mary W. *George Washington: First in Peace.* Vol. 7 of Douglas Freeman, *George Washington.* New York, 1957.

Chipman, Daniel. *The Life of Hon. Nathaniel Chipman,* LL.D. Boston, 1846.

Cobbett, William. *A Little Plain English Addressed to the People of the United States.* Philadelphia, 1795.

——. *A Summary View of the Politics of the United States from the Close of the War to the Year 1794.* Philadelphia, 1797.

—— (Playfair). *The History of Jacobinism: Its Crimes, Cruelties and Perfidies.* 2 vols. Philadelphia, 1796.

Dallas, George M. *The Life and Writings of Alexander J. Dallas.* Philadelphia, 1871.

Earle, Thomas, and Langdon, Charles T., eds. *Annals of the General Society of Mechanics and Tradesmen of the City of New York.* New York, 1882.

Findlay, William. *History of the Insurrection in the Four Western Counties of Pennsylvania.* Philadelphia, 1796.

Foner, Philip S., ed. *Basic Writings of Thomas Jefferson.* New York, 1944.
————. *The Complete Writings of Thomas Paine.* 2 vols. New York, 1945.
Ford, Paul L., ed. *The Writings of Thomas Jefferson.* 10 vols. New York, 1895.
Ford, Worthington C., ed. *The Writings of George Washington.* 14 vols. Washington, D.C., 1887-1893.
Gardiner, Rev. John Sylvester John. *Remarks on the Jacobinad.* Boston, 1798.
Gibbs, George. *Memoirs of the Administrations of Washington and Adams.* New York, 1846.
Hamilton, John Church. *History of the Republic.* Philadelphia, 1864.
Hamilton, S. M., ed. *Writings of James Monroe.* 7 vols. New York, 1900.
Harper's Encyclopedia of United States History. New York, 1902.
Hunt, Gaillard, ed. *The Writings of James Madison.* 9 vols. New York, 1906.
Jay, William. *The Life of John Jay.* 2 vols. New York, 1832.
Johnson, Allen, and Malone, Dumas, eds. *Dictionary of American Biography.* 20 vols. New York, 1928-1936.
Johnston, Henry P., ed. *The Correspondence and Public Papers of John Jay.* 4 vols. New York, 1893.
King, Charles, ed. *The Life and Correspondence of Rufus King.* 6 vols. New York, 1894.
Lodge, Henry. *The Life and Letters of George Cabot.* Boston, 1877.
————, ed. *The Works of Alexander Hamilton.* 9 vols. New York, 1886.
Maclay, William. *The Journal of William Maclay.* New York, 1927.
Mangourit, M. A. B. *Memoire de Mangourit.* Paris, 1795.
Manning, William. *The Key of Libberty.* Billerica, Mass., 1922.
Meigs, William Ma. *The Life of Jared Ingersoll.* Philadelphia, 1897.
Morrison, Samuel E. *The Life and Letters of Harrison Gray Otis.* 2 vols. Boston, 1913.
Muhlenberg, Henry A. *The Life of Major General Peter Muhlenberg.* Philadelphia, 1849.
Pennsylvania Archives. Selected and Arranged by Samuel Hazard. Harrisburg, 1896, 2d ser., vol. IV.
Syrett, Harold C., and Booke, Jacob E., eds. *The Papers of Alexander Hamilton.* Vol. 15, New York and London, 1969; Vol. 16, New York and London, 1972.
Thomas, Isaiah. *The History of Printing in America.* 2 vols. Albany, N.Y., 1874.
Treaties, Conventions, International Acts, Protocols, and Agreements between the United States of America and Other Powers, 1776-1909. Washington, D.C., 1910.
Tuckerman, Frederick. *William Cooper.* Amherst, Mass., 1885.
Warren, Charles, ed. *Jacobin and Junto, or Early American Politics as Viewed in the Diary of Dr. Nathaniel Ames, 1758-1822.* Cambridge, Mass., 1931.

Pamphlets

Buchanan, Archibald. *Oration Composed and Delivered at the Request of the Republican Society of Baltimore, July 4, 1794.* Baltimore, 1794.
Clinton, George Jr. *An Oration Delivered on the Fourth of July, 1798.* New York, 1798.

Coram, Robert. *Political Inquiries to Which Is Added a Plan for the General Establishment of Schools Throughout the United States.* Wilmington, 1791.

Democratic Society of New York. *Address to the Republican Citizens of the United States, May 28, 1794.* New York, 1794.

———. *Circular. To the Democratic Society of Philadelphia.* New York, 1794.

———. *Constitution.* New York, 1794.

Democratic Society of Pennsylvania. *Principles, Articles and Regulations, Agreed upon by the Members, May 30th, 1793.* Philadelphia, 1793.

Fauchet, Joseph. *A Translation of Citizen Fauchet's Intercepted Letter, Number 10, October 31; 1794.* Philadelphia, 1794.

Hedges, Phineas. *An Oration Delivered before the Republican Society of Ulster County, July 4, 1795.* Goshen, N.Y., 1795.

———. *Strictures on the Elementa Medicinal of Doctor Brown.* Goshen, N.Y., 1795.

Linn, William. *The Blessings of America! Sermon Preached on the Fourth of July, 1791, at the Request of the Tammany Society.* New York, 1791.

Massachusetts Constitutional Society. *Constitution.* Boston, 1794.

Miller, Samuel. *A Sermon Delivered in the New Presbyterian Church, New York, July 4, 1795.* New York, 1795.

Moultrie, Alexander. *An Appeal to the People on the Conduct of a Certain Public Body in South Carolina Respecting Colonel Drayton and Colonel Moultrie.* Charleston, 1794.

Paine, Thomas. *The Rights of Man.* London, 1792.

———. *The Rights of Man.* Philadelphia, 1792.

Patriotic Society of the County of Newcastle, Delaware. *Declaration of Political Principles and Constitution.* Wilmington, 1794.

———. *Circular.* 1795.

Randolph, Edmund. *A Vindication of Mr. Randolph's Resignation.* Philadelphia, 1795.

Rush, Benjamin. *A Plan for the Establishment of Public Schools and the Diffusion of Knowledge in Pennsylvania; to Which Are Added Thoughts up on the Mode of Education Proper in a Republic, Addressed to the Legislature and Citizens of the State.* Philadelphia, 1786.

Warner, George James. *Means for the Preservation of Public Libertty. Oration Delivered in the New Dutch Church on the Fourth of July, 1797.* New York, 1797.

Wortman, Tunis. *An Oration on the Influence of Social Institutions upon Human Morals and Happiness. Delivered before the Tammany Society . . . , the Twelfth of May, 1796.* New York, 1796.

———. *A Solemn Address, to Christians and Patriots, upon the Approaching Election of a President of the United States.* New York, 1800.

Newspapers

Connecticut
   Danbury, *Republican Journal.*

Hartford, *American Mercury.*
Hartford, *Connecticut Courant.*
New Haven, *Connecticut Journal.*
New London, *Bee.*
New London, *Connecticut Gazette.*
Norwich, *Norwich Packet.*

Delaware
Wilmington, *Delaware and Eastern-Short Advertiser.*
Wilmington, *Delaware Gazette.*

Kentucky
Lexington, *Kentucky Gazette.*

Maine (then part of Massachusetts)
Portland, *Eastern Herald.*
Portland, *Gazette of Maine.*

Maryland
Baltimore, *Baltimore Daily Advertiser.*
Baltimore, *Baltimore Daily Intelligencer.*
Baltimore, *Daily Repository.*
Baltimore, *Federal Intelligencer.*

Massachusetts
Boston, *American Apollo.*
Boston, *Boston Gazette.*
Boston, *Columbian Centinel.*
Boston, *Independent Chronicle.*
Boston, *Massachusetts Spy.*

New Jersey
Elizabeth Town, *New Jersey Journal.*
Newark, *Centinel of Freedom.*
Newark, *Newark Gazette.*
Newark, *Woods's Newark Gazette.*

New York
Canaan, *Columbian Mercury.*
Goshen, *Goshen Repository.*
New York, *American Minerva.*
New York, *Argus.*
New York, *Daily Gazette.*
New York, *Diary.*
New York, *Herald.*
New York, *New York Journal.*

North Carolina
New Bern, *North-Carolina Gazette.*

Pennsylvania
Lancaster, *Lancaster Journal.*
Philadelphia, *American Daily Advertiser.*
Philadelphia, *Aurora.*
Philadelphia, *Federal Gazette.*
Philadelphia, *Gazette of the United States.*
Philadelphia, *General Advertiser.*
Philadelphia, *Independent Gazetteer.*
Philadelphia, *National Gazette.*
Philadelphia, *Pennsylvania Gazette.*
Philadelphia, *Philadelphia Gazette.*
Philadelphia, *Philadelphische Correspondenz.*
Philadelphia, *Porcupine's Gazette.*
Pittsburgh, *Pittsburgh Gazette.*

South Carolina
Charleston, *City Gazette.*
Charleston, *Columbian Herald.*
Charleston, *South Carolina State Gazette.*
Charleston, *State Gazette of South Carolina.*

Vermont
Bennington, *Vermont Gazette.*
Rutland, *Farmers' Library.*
Rutland, *Rutland Herald.*
Windsor, *Spooner's Vermont Journal.*
Windsor, *Vermont Journal.*

Virginia
Dumfries, *Republican Journal.*
Norfolk, *Norfolk Herald.*
Richmond, *Virginia Argus.*
Richmond, *Virginia Gazette and Richmond and Manchester Advertiser.*
Richmond, *Virginia Gazette and Richmond Chronicle.*

State, County, and City Histories and Directories

Adams, A. N. *A History of the Town of Fairhaven, Vermont.* Fairhaven, 1870.
Ashe, Samuel A. *History of North Carolina.* Raleigh, 1925.
Baxter, James Phinney, ed. *Documentary History of the State of Maine.* Portland, 1916.
Bevan, Wilson Lloyd, ed. *History of Delaware, Past and Present.* 4 vols. New York, 1924.

Boucher, John N. *A Century and a Half of Pittsburgh and Her People.* New York, 1908.

Butler, Mann. *A History of the Commonwealth of Kentucky.* Louisville, 1834.

Charleston (South Carolina) City Directory for 1793, 1794 and 1795.

Clark, Thomas D. *A History of Kentucky.* New York, 1937.

Clearwater, Alphonso T., ed. *The History of Ulster County.* Kingston, N.Y., 1907.

Conrad, Henry C. *History of the State of Delaware.* 3 vols. Wilmington, 1908.

Creigh, Alfred. *History of Washington County, Pennsylvania,* Philadelphia, 1882.

Delaware. *Biographical and Genealogical History of the State of Delaware.* Chambersburg, Pa., 1899.

Ellis, Franklin. *The History of Columbia County, New York.* Philadelphia, 1858.

Fraser, Charles. *Reminiscences of Charleston.* Charleston, S.C., 1854.

Graham, John A. *A Descriptive Sketch of the Present State of Vermont.* London, 1797.

Hardie, James. *The Philadelphia Directory and Register.* Philadelphia, 1793.

Headley, Russell, ed. *The History of Orange County.* Middletown, N.Y., 1908.

Hemenway, Abby M. *The Vermont Historical Gazeteer.* 5 vols. Rutland, 1923.

Johnson, Thomas. *Kentucky Miscellany.* Lexington, 1821.

Kerr, Charles. *History of Kentucky.* Chicago, 1922.

Marshall, Humphrey. *The History of Kentucky.* 2 vols. Frankfort, 1824.

Matthews, Lyman. *The History of the Town of Cornwall, Vermont.* Middlebury, 1862.

Moore, Maurice. *Reminiscences of York County, South Carolina.* N.p., n.d.

Newark. *The History of the City of Newark.* New York, 1913.

New York City Directory for 1793-1798.

Peter, Robert. *History of Fayette County, Kentucky.* Chicago, 1882.

Philadelphia City Directory for 1793-1795.

Rann, W. S. *History of Chittenden County, Vermont.* Syracuse, N.Y., 1886.

Scharf, J. Thomas. *The Chronicles of Baltimore.* Baltimore, 1874.

——. *History of Delaware.* 2 vols. Philadelphia, 1888.

——, and Thompson, Westcott. *History of Philadelphia.* 3 vols. Philadelphia, 1884.

Smith, H. Perry. *Addison County, Vermont.* Syracuse, N.Y., 1886.

Snowden, Yates, ed. *History of South Carolina.* 5 vols. New York, 1920.

Swift, Samuel. *History of the Town of Middlebury.* Middlebury, Vt., 1859.

Thompson, Zadock. *History of Vermont.* Burlington, 1842.

Tyler, Lyon Gardiner, ed. *Encyclopedia of Virginia Biography.* 5 vols., New York, 1915.

Vermont Register for 1795. N.p., 1795.

Waring, William. *South Carolina and Georgia Almanac for 1793.* Charleston, 1793.

Wilson, Erasmus, ed. *Standard History of Pittsburgh, Pennsylvania.* Chicago, 1898.

SECONDARY WORKS

Books

Adams, William F., ed. *Commodore Joshua Barney*. Springfield, Mass., 1912.
Ammon, Harry. *The Genêt Mission*. New York, 1973.
Austin, Mary S. *Philip Freneau: The Poet of the American Revolution*. New York, 1901.
Baldwin, Leland D. *Whiskey Rebels: The Story of a Frontier Uprising*. Pittsburgh, 1939.
Bassett, John S. *The Federalist System, 1789-1801*. New York, 1906.
Beard, Charles A. *Economic Origins of Jeffersonian Democracy*. New York, 1915.
———, and Beard, Mary R. *The American Spirit*. New York, 1942.
Bemis, Samuel Flagg. *Jay's Treaty: A Study in Commerce and Diplomacy*. New York, 1924.
———. *Pinckney's Treaty*. Baltimore, 1926.
Bernhard, Winfred E. A. *Fisher Ames: Federalist and Statesman, 1758-1808*. Chapel Hill, N.C., 1965.
Birley, Robert. *The English Jacobins from 1789 to 1802*. London, 1924.
Bond, Beverly Waugh, Jr. *The Monroe Mission to France, 1794-1796*. Baltimore, 1907.
Borden, Morton. *Parties and Politics in the Early Republic, 1789-1815*. New York, 1967.
Bowers, Claude G. *Jefferson and Hamilton*. New York, 1933.
Brant, Irving. *James Madison, Father of the Constitution: 1787-1800*. Indianapolis, 1950.
Brigham, Clarence S. *History and Bibliography of American Newspapers, 1690-1820*. 2 vols. Worcester, Mass., 1947.
Bowman, Albert Hall. *Struggle for Neutrality: Franco-American Diplomacy during the Federalist Era*. Nashville, 1974.
Brown, John M. *Political Beginnings of Kentucky*. Louisville, 1889.
Brown, Philip Antony. *The French Revolution in English History*. New York, 1924.
Brown, Stuart Gerry. *The First Republicans: Political Philosophy and Public Policy in the Party of Jefferson and Madison*. Syracuse, N.Y., 1954.
Brunhouse, Robert L. *The Counter-Revolution in Pennsylvania, 1776-1790*. Harrisburg, 1942.
Charles, Joseph. *The Origins of the American Party System*. New York, 1956.
Childs, Frances S. *French Refugee Life in the United States, 1790-1800*. Baltimore, 1940.
Clark, Allen Cullen. *William Duane*. Washington, D.C., 1905.
Clark, Harry H., ed. *The Poems of Freneau*. New York, 1929.

Clark, Mary Elizabeth. *Peter Porcupine in America; The Career of William Cobbett, 1792-1800*. Philadelphia, 1939.
Combs, Jerald A. *The Jay Treaty: Political Battleground of the Founding Fathers*. Berkeley and Los Angeles, 1970.
Cunningham, Noble E., Jr. *The Jeffersonian Republicans*. Chapel Hill, N.C., 1957.
De Conde, Alexander. *Entangling Alliance: Politics and Diplomacy Under George Washington*. Durham, N.C., 1958.
———. *The Quasi-War*. New York, 1966.
Dunbar, Louise B. *A Study of "Monarchical" Tendencies in the United States from 1776 to 1801*. Urbana, Ill., 1923.
Faust, Albert Bernhardt. *The German Element in the United States*. 2 vols. Boston, 1909.
Fäy, Bernhard. *The Revolutionary Spirit in France and America at the End of the Eighteenth Century*. New York, 1927.
———. *The Two Franklins: Fathers of American Democracy*. Boston, 1933.
Fee, Walter R. *The Transition from Aristocracy to Democracy in New Jersey, 1789-1829*. Somerville, N.J., 1933.
Ferguson, Russell J. *Early Western Pennsylvania Politics*. Pittsburgh, 1938.
Foner, Philip S. *History of Black Americans: From Africa to the Emergence of the Cotton Kingdom*. Westport, Conn., 1975.
———. *History of the Labor Movement in the United States*. New York, 1947.
Forman, Samuel E. *The Political Activities of Philip Freneau*. Baltimore, 1922.
Fox, Dixon R. *The Decline of Aristocracy in the Politics of New York*. New York, 1919.
Genêt, George C. *Jefferson and "Citizen" Genêt, 1793*. New York, 1899.
Gilpatrick, Delbert Harold. *Jeffersonian Democracy in North Carolina, 1789-1816*. New York, 1931.
Goodman, Paul. *The Democratic Republicans of Massachusetts: Politics in a Young Republic*. Cambridge, Mass., 1964.
Griffin, Joseph. *History of the Press in Maine*. Brunswick, Maine, 1872.
Hall, Courtney R. *A Scientist in the Early Republic; Samuel L. Mitchill, 1764-1831*. New York, 1934.
Hall, Walter P. *British Radicalism, 1791-1797*. New York, 1912.
Hayden, Ralston. *The Senate and Treaties, 1795-1805*. New York, 1920.
Hazen, Charles D. *Contemporary American Opinion of the French Revolution*. Baltimore, 1897.
Jacob, Rosamond. *The Rise of the United Irishmen, 1791-1794*. London, 1932.
Kilroe, Edwin P. *Saint Tammany and the Origin of the Society of Tammany or Columbian Order in the City of New York*. New York, 1913.
Koch, G. Adolf. *Republican Religion: The American Revolution and the Cult of Reason*. New York, 1933.
Kurtz, Louis. *The Presidency of John Adams: The Collapse of Federalism, 1795-1800*. Philadelphia, 1957.
Leary, Lewis G. *That Rascal Freneau*. New Brunswick, N.J., 1941.
Levy, Leonard W., and Siracusa, Carl, eds. *Essays in the Early Republic, 1789-1815*. New York, 1974.

Link, Eugene Perry. *Democratic-Republican Societies, 1790-1800.* New York, 1942.

Ludlum, David. *Social Ferment in Vermont.* New York, 1939.

Luetscher, George D. *Early Political Machinery in the United States.* Philadelphia, 1903.

Lyon, Elijah. *Louisiana in French Diplomacy, 1759-1804.* Norman, Okla., 1934.

McMaster, John B. *A History of the People of the United States.* New York, 1921.

McMurtrie, Douglas C. *John Bradford, Pioneer Printer of Kentucky.* Springfield, Ill., 1931.

———. *The Beginnings of the American Newspaper.* Chicago, 1935.

Main, Jackson Turner. *The Anti-Federalists.* Chapel Hill, N.C., 1961.

Malone, Dumas. *Jefferson and the Ordeal of Liberty.* Boston, 1962.

Mayo, Lawrence Shaw. *John Langdon of New Hampshire.* Concord, N.H., 1937.

Miller, John C. *Crisis of Freedom: The Alien and Sedition Acts.* Boston, 1952.

———. *The Federalist Era, 1789-1801.* New York, 1960.

———. *Sam Adams, Pioneer in Propaganda.* Boston, 1936.

Minnigerode, Meade. *Jefferson, Friend of France, 1793.* New York, 1928.

Mitchell, Broadus. *Alexander Hamilton.* 2 vols. New York, 1957-1962.

Morais, Herbert M. *Deism in Eighteenth Century America.* New York, 1934.

Morris, Richard B., ed. *The Era of the American Revolution.* New York, 1939.

Morse, Anson E. *The Federalist Party in Massachusetts to the Year 1800.* Princeton, N.J., 1909.

Munroe, John A. *Federalist Delaware, 1775-1815.* New Brunswick, N.J., 1954.

Perkins, Bradford. *The First Rapprochement: England and the United States, 1795-1805.* Philadelphia, 1955.

Peterson, Merrill D. *The Jeffersonian Image in the American Mind.* New York, 1960.

Pomerantz, Sidney I. *New York, An American City, 1783-1803.* New York, 1938.

Poole, William F. *Anti-Slavery Opinions before the Year 1800.* Cincinnati, 1873.

Postgate, R. W. *That Devil Wilkes.* New York, 1929.

Prince, Carl E. *New Jersey's Jeffersonian Republicans.* Chapel Hill, N.C., 1967.

Purcell, Richard J. *Connecticut in Transition, 1775-1818.* Washington, D.C., 1918.

Robinson, William A. *Jeffersonian Democracy in New England.* New Haven, 1916.

Rossiter, Clinton. *Seedtime of the Republic.* New York, 1953.

Rudé, George. *Wilkes and Liberty.* London, 1962.

Sears, Louis Martin. *George Washington and the French Revolution.* Detroit, 1960.

Selsam, J. Paul. *The Pennsylvania Constitution.* Philadelphia, 1936.

Sisson, Daniel. *The American Revolution of 1800.* New York, 1974.

Sonne, Niels H. *Liberal Kentucky.* New York, 1939.

Spaulding, E. Wilder. *His Excellency, George Clinton, Critic of the Constitution.* New York, 1938.

Speed, Thomas. *The Political Club, Danville, Kentucky, 1790.* Louisville, 1894.

Stauffer, Vernon. *New England and the Bavarian Illuminati.* New York, 1918.

Thomas, E. Bruce. *Political Tendencies in Pennsylvania, 1783-1794.* Philadelphia, 1938.

Thomas, Marion. *American Neutrality in 1793: A Study in Cabinet Govern-ment.* New York, 1931.

Tinkcom, Harry M. *The Republicans and Federalists in Pennsylvania, 1790-1801.* Harrisburg, Pa., 1950.

Tolles, Frederick G. *George Logan of Philadelphia.* New York, 1953.

Walsh, Richard. *Charleston's Sons of Liberty.* Columbia, S.C., 1959.

Whitaker, Arthur P. *The Spanish-American Frontier.* New York, 1927.

White, Leonard D. *The Federalists: A Study in Administrative History.* New York, 1948.

Williamson, Chilton. *Vermont in Quandary, 1763-1825.* Montpelier, 1949.

Wolf, Edwin II, and Whiteman, Maxwell. *The History of the Jews of Philadelphia from Colonial times to the Age of Jackson.* Philadelphia, 1957.

Wolfe, John H. *Jeffersonian Democracy in South Carolina.* Chapel Hill, N.C., 1940.

Woodbury, Margaret. *Public Opinion in Philadelphia, 1789-1800.* Northampton, Mass., 1920.

Young, Alfred F. *The Democratic Republicans of New York: The Origins, 1763-1797.* Chapel Hill, N.C., 1967.

Articles

Adelson, Judah. "The Vermont Democratic-Republican Societies and the French Revolution." *Vermont History* 32 (July 1964): 3-23.

Bowman, Albert H. "Jefferson, Hamilton and American Foreign Policy." *Political Science Quarterly* 71 (March 1956): 18-44.

Brant, Irving. "Edmund Randolph, Not Guilty." *William and Mary Quarterly,* 3d ser., 7 (April 1950): 180-198.

Bushey, Glenn Leroy. "William Duane, Crusader for Judicial Reform." *Pennsylvania History* 5 (July 1938): 141-156.

Brown, Wallace. "William Cobbett in North America." *History Today* 22 (October 1972): 683-691.

Carter, Edward C. "A Wild Irishman under Every Federalist Bed: Naturalization in Philadelphia, 1789-1806." *Pennsylvania Magazine of History and Biography* 94 (July 1970): 331-346.

Cooke, Jacob E. "The Whiskey Insurrection: A Re-Evaluation." *Pennsylvania History* 30 (July 1963): 316-346.

Coulter, E. M. "The Efforts of the Democratic Societies of West to Open the Navigation of the Mississippi." *Mississippi Valley Historical Review* 11 (December 1924): 376-386.

Davidson, Philip G. "Sons of Liberty and Stamp Men." *North Carolina Historical Review* 9 (January 1932): 38-56.

Dupré, Huntley. "The Kentucky Gazette Reports the French Revolution." *Mississippi Valley Historical Review* 16 (September 1939): 163-180.

Dutcher, Gregory M. "The Rise of Republican Government in the United States." *Political Science Quarterly* 55 (June 1940): 199-216.

Fäy, Bernard. "Benjamin Franklin Bache, a Democratic Leader of the Eighteenth

Century." *Proceedings of the American Antiquarian Society* 40 (October 1930): 277-304.

──. "Early Party Machinery in the United States." *Pennsylvania Magazine of History and Biography* 60 (October 1936): 375-390.

Gilpatrick, Delbert H. "The English Background of John Miller." *Furman Bulletin* 20 (1938): 14.

Gribbin, William. "Republican Religion and the American Churches in the National Period." *Historian* 35 (November 1972): 61-74.

Hamilton, J. G., ed. "A Society for Preservation of Liberty." *American Historical Review* 32 (April 1927): 550-552.

Kohn, Richard H. "The Washington Administration's Decision to Crush the Whiskey Insurrection." *Journal of American History* 59 (December 1972): 567-584.

Laing, Alexander. "Jefferson's Usufruct Principle." *The Nation* (July 3-10, 1976): 12.

Link, Eugene P. "The Democratic Societies of the Carolinas." *North Carolina Historical Review* 18 (July 1941): 259-277.

Meacham, Standish. "Priestley in America." *History Today,* 12 (August, 1962): 568-573.

Miller, William. "First Fruits of Republican Organization: Political Aspects of the Congressional Election of 1794." *Pennsylvania Magazine of History and Biography* 63 (April 1939): 118-143.

──. "The Democratic Societies and the Whiskey Insurrection." *Pennsylvania Magazine of History and Biography* 62 (July 1938): 324-349.

Paulson, Peter. "The Tammany Society and the Jeffersonian Movement in New York City, 1795-1800." *New York History* 34 (January 1953): 72-83.

Phillips, Ulrich B., ed. "The South Carolina Federalists." *American Historical Review* 14 (April-July 1909): 529-543, 731-743.

Reitzel, William. "William Cobbett and Philadelphia Journalism, 1794-1800." *Pennsylvania Magazine of History and Biography* 59 (July 1935): 223-244.

Schappes, Morris U. "Anti-Semitism and Reaction, 1795-1800." *Publications of the American Jewish Historical Society,* no. 38 (December 1948): 109-123.

Shalhope, Robert. "Toward a Republican Synthesis: The Emergence of an Understanding of Republicanism in American History." *William and Mary Quarterly,* 3d ser., 29 (January 1972): 49-80.

Smelser, Marshall. "The Jacobin Phrenzy: Federalism and the Menace of Liberty, Equality and Fraternity." *Review of Politics* 13 (October 1951): 457-482.

Tagg, James D. "Benjamin Franklin Bache's Attack on George Washington." *Pennsylvania Magazine of History and Biography* 99 (1976): 191-230.

Turner, Frederick Jackson, ed. "Correspondence of the French Ministers to the United States, 1791-1797," *Annual Report of the American Historical Association* (1903): 2: 7-110.

──. "The Mangourit Correspondence in Respect to Genêt's Projected Attack up on Florida, 1793-1794." *Annual Report of the American Historical Association* (1897): 569-579.

──. "The Policy of France toward the Mississippi Valley in the Period of

Washington and Adams." *American Historical Review* 10 (1905): 249-279.

Walters, Raymond, Jr. "The Origins of the Jeffersonian Party in Pennsylvania." *Pennsylvania Magazine of History and Biography* 66 (October 1942): 440-458.

Weiner, Raymond C. "War Scare and Politics, 1794." *New York Historical Association Quarterly* 11 (1930): 324-334.

Wheeler, William Bruce. "The Baltimore Jeffersonians, 1788-1800: A Profile of Intra-Factional Conflict." *Maryland Historical Magazine* (Summer 1971): 153-168.

Whittaker, Arthur Preston, ed. "Harry Innes and Spanish Intrigue, 1794-1795." *Mississippi Valley Historical Review* 15 (September 1928): 236-248.

Wiener, Martin J. "The Changing Image of William Cobbett." *Journal of British Studies* (May 1974): 135-154.

Young, Alfred F. "The Mechanics and the Jeffersonians: New York, 1789-1801." *Labor History* 5 (Fall 1964): 247-276.

Index

nounces disfranchisement of western counties, 122-123

Democratic Society of Pennsylvania: abolitionist members of, 12; Address to Citizens of the United States, 83-85; Address to Fellow Citizens Throughout the United States, 98-102; address to from German Republican Society, 57-59, 72-74; Address to the Patriotic Societies Throughout the United States, 93-96; answers charge that societies responsible for Whiskey Rebellion, 93-96; answers letter from Democratic Society of Washington County, 79-80; attacks aristocracy, 73, 96; attacks England, 75-78; attacks Federalism, 73; attacks Proclamation of Neutrality, 75-76; calls for defense of French Revolution, 7; calls for extinction of monarchy, 103; calls for revolution in England, 103; calls for upholding treaty with France, 7; celebrates Fourth of July, 86-87, 106-108; circular letter of, 66-67, 80-81; Civic Festival, 78; composition of, 42; condemns excise taxes, 29; conflict in over Whiskey Rebellion, 30, 92-93; constitution of, 412; corresponding committee of, 67, 79, 81, 85, 412; defends Democratic Republican Society, 85, 93-96, 98-102, 109; defends French Revolution, 69-70; defends right of Democratic-Republican Societies to exist, 68-69; defends right of people to associate, 68-69, 83-85, 99-100; defends itself against charge it is responsible for Whiskey Rebellion, 100-101; defends trial by jury, 71; denounces England, 75-78; denounces excise taxes, 79-80, 88-90, 91, 94, 99-100, 109; denounces Jay's Treaty, 109-110; denounces Whiskey Rebellion, 99-

100; dissolution of, 110; expresses sympathy for men who suffer for liberty, 86; favors American manufactures, 107; favors economy in government, 107; favors public schools, 14-15, 108; formation of, 7, 64-66; hails French victories, 78, 102-104; holds Civic Festival, 102-104; invites union of action, 80; letter to Democratic Society of New York, 85-86; letter to Democratic Societies, 74-75; letter to from Republican Society of Charleston, 74; leaders of, 8; membership of, 7; members of march against Whiskey rebels, 416; minutes of, 67-104; as model for other societies, 357; occupations and professions of members, 439-441; opposes appointment of Jay, 80, 81, 104-106; opposes public debt, 107; opposes secrecy in government, 107; opposes use of force against excise laws, 88-89, 90-91; permitted use of University of Pennsylvania, 88; and petition campaign against Jay's Treaty, 38; position of endorsed by other societies, 285; praises Governor Mifflin for role in Whiskey Rebellion, 82; praises Washington for role in Whiskey Rebellion, 71, 93; president of, 71-72; Principles, Articles, and Regulations, 64-66; receives letters from Democratic-Republican Societies, 79, 83, 88; regulations for membership, 82; replies to letters from Democratic-Republican Societies, 90-91, 108-110; supports American manufactures, 77; supports French Revolution, 7, 76-77, 83-84, 89, 97, 102-104, 106-108; urges formation of popular societies, 7; views public debt as a curse, 104; wants America to be asylum for oppressed, 104; welcomes Genêt, 411

activities of in United States, 18-20; attacks upon, 296-297; biographical sketch of, 411; called father of Democratic-Republican Societies, 23-24, 34, 162; conversations with Dallas, 398; defended, 35, 70, 167, 280; effect of arrival in United States, 6; instructions to, 437; plan to conquer Louisiana and open Mississippi, 435; replaced, 425; suggests name for Democratic Society of Pennsylvania, 7; supported by Democratic-Republican Societies, 236, 301, 311, 394-395, 402; toasted, 253, 347, 380; welcomed in Charleston, 411; welcomed in Philadelphia, 56, 411

Geneva, 342
Genoa, 103, 284
Geoghegan, Dominick, 383
George III, 425, 432
German, John, 440
Germanicus, 109, 417, 444
German language, 54
German Lutheran Church, 63, 412
German Republican Society: address to Democratic Society of Pennsylvania, 57-59, 72-74; address to free and independent citizens, 59-63; attack on, 63; defends right to associate, 61-62; defends itself, 59-63; denies responsibility for Whiskey Rebellion, 60-61; formation, 6, 53-55, 422; invited to join in Fourth of July celebration, 87; invited to participate in Civic Feast, 78; joins in Civic Festival, 102-104; opposes excise tax, 58-59, 60-61, 83; opposes Jay's appointment, 58-59; opposes Whiskey Rebellion, 59; praised, 122-123; supports French Revolution, 55-56, 57-58; welcomes Genêt, 55-56, 411

Germany, 56, 263, 411
Geyer, Andrew, 56, 63, 102, 411, 440
Gilbert, Isaiah, 277
Gilbert, Thomas, 191

Gill, James, 121
Girard, Stephen, 71, 440
Girondists, 103, 422
Glentworth, James, 440
Glorious Revolution, 330
Goodman, John, 440
Gordon, Elisha, 67, 440
Goths, 149
Graham, Geo., 351
Gravenstine, John, 440
Gravenstine, Peter, 440
Greece, 197
Greenleaf, Thomas, 9, 57, 203, 211, 240, 246, 294, 421, 426
Grenville, Lord, 77-78, 224, 427
Griffiths, Robert, 440
Grooves, Jesse, 440
Groves, Michael, 78, 102, 440
Guelph, George, 204

Hale, Matthew, 440
Hall, D. A., 382
Hall, John, 440
Hamelin, Joseph D., 67, 440
Hamilton, Alexander: accompanies troops to put down Whiskey Rebellion, 29; accuses Democratic-Republican Societies of fomenting Whiskey Rebellion, 420; at first denies that popular societies are responsible for Whiskey Rebellion, 101; attacked, 29; author of Federalist Papers, 173; author of "Pacificus" letters, 423; condemns Democratic-Republican Societies, 29; contempt for public opinion, 29; defended, 161; funding program of, 51, 434; on treaty with France, 18; plan of for assumption of state debts, 431; receives letters condemning Democratic-Republican Societies, 3, 430; report of on excise law, 138; report of on Whiskey Rebellion, 340-341; reports to Washington, 433; urges force, 28; welcomes Whiskey Rebellion, 28
Hampden, John, 217, 289, 426

J.B. McLachlan
A Biography

Yours in the Fight

J. B. McLac

J.B. McLachlan
A Biography

David Frank

James Lorimer & Company Ltd., Publishers
Toronto, 1999

James Lorimer & Company Ltd. acknowledges the support of the Department of Canadian Heritage and the Ontario Arts Council in the development of writing and publishing in Canada. We acknowledge the support of the Canada Council for the Arts for our publishing program.

This book has been published with the help of a grant from the Humanities and Social Sciences Federation of Canada, using funds provided by the Social Sciences and Humanities Research Council of Canada.

Cover: *Miners' Houses, Glace Bay*, c. 1926.   Canada
Lawren S. Harris. Art Gallery of Ontario, Toronto.
Bequest of Charles S. Band, 1970.

Canadian Cataloguing in Publication Data

Frank, David 1949-
    J.B. McLachlan: a biography

Includes index.
ISBN 1-55028-677-3

1. McLachlan, J.B. (James Bryson), 1869-1937. 2. Trade-unions – Nova Scotia – Cape Breton Island – History – 20th century. 3. Coal miners – Nova Scotia – Cape Breton Island – History – 20th century. 4. Strikes and lockouts – Coal mining – Nova Scotia – Cape Breton Island – History – 20th century. 5. Trade-unions – Nova Scotia – Cape Breton Island – Biography. 6. Coal miners – Nova Scotia – Cape Breton Island – Biography   I. Title.

HD6525.M32F72 1999   331.88'122334'092   C99-931788-1

James Lorimer & Company Ltd., Publishers
35 Britain Street
Toronto, Ontario
M5A 1R7

Printed and bound in Canada.

I believe in telling children the truth about the history of the world,
that it does not consist in the history of Kings and Lords and Cabinets,
but consists in the history of the mass of the workers,
a thing that is not taught in the schools.
I believe in telling children how to measure value,
a thing that is not taught in any school.

– J.B. McLachlan,
1925

Contents

Abbreviations in Text

AFL: American Federation of Labor
AMWNS: Amalgamated Mine Workers of Nova Scotia
Besco: British Empire Steel Corporation
CCF: Cooperative Commonwealth Federation
CLDL: Canadian Labour Defence League
GMA: General Mining Association
ILP: Independent Labour Party
IWW: Industrial Workers of the World
MLA: Member of the Legislative Assembly
MP: Member of Parliament
MWIUNS: Mine Workers' Industrial Union of Nova Scotia
OBU: One Big Union
PWA: Provincial Workmen's Association
RCMP: Royal Canadian Mounted Police
SPC: Socialist Party of Canada
TLC: Trades and Labour Congress of Canada
UMWA: United Mine Workers of America
UMWNS: United Mine Workers of Nova Scotia
WUL: Workers' Unity League

INTRODUCTION

Jim B. McLachlan, the leader of men;
J.B. McLachlan united them and then
Held high the torch of freedom for all,
And asked his fellow miners to never let it fall.

– Charlie MacKinnon,
"The Ballad of J.B. McLachlan"

When he took the platform in the crowded movie-house, there was a resounding shout from the back of the hall – "Drive 'er, Jim!" McLachlan removed his coat and rolled up his sleeves. His pipe issued a stream of smoke. He stood still at the centre of the stage, focusing the coal miners' attention on what he was about to say. Restlessly, he moved back and forth, his red moustache bristling with anger. To demonstrate the devastation of the company's wage reductions, he seized a glass of water from the table and, like a magician, spilled out the contents, as if from a child's full glass of milk. Next, to demonstrate the profits of the coal operators, he crouched down on the edge of the stage and followed an imaginary trail of silver dollars end to end, from Cape Breton Island to Vancouver Island – and back. Then McLachlan held his audience easily: with a plain tale of the family life the miners were sworn to protect, with the bitter memory of the "blood splashed over the coal" year by year in the mines, with blasts of condemnation against the companies who "ravaged the coal mines and robbed the coal miners." Finally, there was a hopeful prayer for the future: "Our movement is chained to a star, and both the grave and the womb of time are fighting with us."

Could anyone who lived through the Cape Breton labour wars forget Jim McLachlan? Fighting Jim? Our Jim? Or simply J.B.? A short, spare man in his fifties, his face and hands flecked with the coal dust and blue scars of the mines, in the 1920s James Bryson McLachlan hurled his whole person into the battle against the British Empire Steel Corporation.

Few contemporaries doubted the influence of McLachlan among the coal miners. A police report described him as "one bad man" and a "fiend": "If he is left to go on with his sayings it will lead to trouble, as he is able to lead the miners of Cape Breton around by the nose." And in 1924 President Roy Wolvin of the British Empire Steel Corporation pleaded with Prime Minister William Lyon Mackenzie King to keep McLachlan behind bars: "I have had much experience with this man's activities and I consider him a dangerously clever 'Red.' He has cost the coal mining companies of Nova Scotia many millions of dollars and the miners an equal amount ... He is the concentrated cause of past unrest in this district and with him away for a few years, possibly, his teachings may be forgotten."

There were also more favourable opinions. As an officer of the coal miners' union, McLachlan commanded strong support. A founder of District 26 of the United Mine Workers of America, McLachlan was elected secretary-treasurer in 1909; undefeated in union elections, he remained a union officer until his controversial removal in 1923. In politics he also attracted a following. Although McLachlan was never elected to the provincial assembly or the House of Commons, he should have been, for at the peak of his influence he was running up absolute majorities at the polls in the mining districts.

In the years after 1917, the Cape Breton coal miners established a strong union and a tradition of independent labour politics. If one man embodied these achievements, it was McLachlan. For some admirers he was a veritable "'Moses' of the very first type," the man who would lead the coal miners out of captivity. For others he was a symbol of a new day in the history of the coal miners: "It took a long time for us to wake up," recalled "Sandy Mac" in 1919, an old-timer of seventy years. "But we have alarm clocks all around us now and McLachlan is one of the noisiest of them all. Good luck to him."

The story of James Bryson McLachlan occupies a central place in the history of the Cape Breton coal miners, but the two stories are by no means entirely interchangeable. As Christopher Hill has pointed out, folk memory is apt to embody causes in individuals.[1] Closer to home, the Cape Breton sociologist John deRoche has reported his difficulties in gaining accurate information about McLachlan from a series of interviews conducted with older miners in the early 1980s. Did he support the United Mine Workers, or one of the rival unions? Did he die in prison, or shortly after? Was he a godless man? Was he a Communist? What those interviewed did agree upon was that McLachlan was the champion of the workers in general and the coal miners in particular. Almost half a century after his death he enjoyed lasting functional significance as a symbol of working-class struggle and achievement: "J.B. embodied goodness, generosity, courage, wit, farsightedness, just anger, sanctity, and martyrdom."[2]

McLachlan's life is indeed the stuff of which legends are made. In his own day the worker-poet Dawn Fraser sang his praises in an epic verse, "The Case of Jim McLachlan," which was serialized in the *Maritime Labor Herald* in 1924 at the time of his incarceration in Dorchester Penitentiary. McLachlan is portrayed there as the workers' hero and a martyr to their cause: "The day that Jim McLachlan fell / The workers should have tolled a bell."[3] More recently, McLachlan has been celebrated in "The Ballad of J.B. McLachlan," written and recorded by the local singer Charlie MacKinnon. This song has been widely heard, since it is featured in the repertoire of the coal miners' choir, the Men of the Deeps, and was recorded on one of their early albums. It presents McLachlan as "a tried and true champion of the working man" who "united the miners" and "held high the torch of freedom for all."[4]

By the 1990s McLachlan's prominence in local history was assured. A commemorative society raised funds for a scholarship and a monument in his honour. The eight-foot-high granite memorial was unveiled with much ceremony on Labour Day 1992 at one of the main corners in Glace Bay. One after another, local union leaders came forward to pay tribute to McLachlan and his legacy. Not to be outdone, even the editors of the Halifax *Chronicle-Herald*, no fans of McLachlan in his own lifetime, paid tribute to his vision, courage, and significance: "The monument to J.B. McLachlan is a tribute to the memory of a man who, powerful in his own time, remains a magnificent example to Canadians of all generations."[5] The comment in the *Cape Breton Post* put it more plainly, pointing out that in a province where the Westray mine had exploded earlier that year, the relevance of McLachlan had not disappeared into history, and he might still have the capacity to "set a few skeletons spinning": "It is important that the image of J.B. McLachlan not be rounded on the edges for the sake of official respectability. He had an outlaw quality which was essential to who he was and to how the labour movement developed in his time. Too complete a rehabilitation would be a violation."[6]

Although McLachlan's name has become better known, his story has remained relatively unexplored. As early as 1926, one of the pioneers of Canadian labour history, Eugene Forsey, visited McLachlan at his home in Glace Bay during the course of his research for a thesis on the coal industry. Even at that time Forsey recognized that McLachlan's life was one of the great unwritten chapters in Canadian labour history. He was, Forsey wrote, "a picturesque and fascinating figure": "The story of his work in organizing and maintained [sic] District 26 is one of the epics of Canadian Trade Unionism, and the miners will never forget his 'strenuous and splendid service.'"[7]

But in the years that followed, no concerted effort was made to search out the documentary sources and to place McLachlan's story in its social and historical context. The task has been long overdue. In the 1960s the appearance of Paul MacEwan's *Cape Breton Highlander* columns on labour and politics in Cape Breton whetted the appetite for local labour history and eventually resulted in the book *Miners and Steelworkers*. Another popular historian, John Mellor, later produced *The Company Store*. Despite the prominence of McLachlan in both books, neither should be described as a biography.[8] Meanwhile, academic historians were gradually making their way through the long and tortured history of industrial Cape Breton, producing theses and articles that introduced the larger context of the story.[9]

The present author was one of that generation of students who wrote about the history of the coal miners, and I can remember sitting in a seminar at Dalhousie University in the 1970s when Professor David Sutherland wondered out loud when we would finally have a big biography of McLachlan. It was a good idea. Much has been said about the problems of synthesis in labour history, and also about the challenge of making history accessible to the wider public. It seems clear that biography is one of the more interesting ways these aims can be accomplished.

In principle, the biography of a labour leader requires the same sympathetic and serious analysis we expect in studies of other public figures. But, in the biography of a working-class figure, the problems of evidence are often enormous. There is no large, single, convenient body of source material of the kind one often finds in the cases of prime ministers, writers, generals, and businessmen. Until recently, libraries and archives took little interest in the collections of labour organizations or union leaders. Much material has not survived, and much of the most useful remaining material is buried in other collections, such as the records of unions and governments, in the files of government reports, and in the columns of local newspapers. Although this is a book I would like to have written much sooner, it is fair to say that the process has demanded an extended tour through the sources. In the meantime, I have had the benefit of a long apprenticeship in the methods of social history, methods that have proved valuable in searching out and telling the story of McLachlan.

This book may be described as a study in social biography. All history, social or otherwise, ultimately reduces itself to the story of individuals and their times. It has been famously said that people make their own history, but not under conditions of their own choosing. It is doubtful that even Donald Creighton, the biographer of Prime Minister Sir John A. Macdonald, would have disagreed with such an orthodox Marxist statement, though Creighton obviously preferred to use terms such as "character and circumstance" where more theoretically inclined historians speak of "agency and structure." The approach has been best described by Nick Salvatore in the introduction to his biography of the American socialist Eugene V. Debs: "It is a traditional biography in that it emphasizes this one individual's personal and public life as far as the evidence allows. But the book is also a piece of social history that assumes individuals do not stand outside the culture and society they grew in and from."[10]

Accordingly, this book uses the methods of labour and social history to locate and explain the history of one man's part in the modern struggle for social, political, and economic justice. It is also a story of the coal miners, a story of Cape Breton Island, and a story of the radical tradition in Canada. No attempt has been made to parcel out McLachlan's life to the various subdivisions of social history, and the approach is largely chronological and narrative in organization. The source material is large and diverse, and I have had the benefit of cooperation and assistance from many archives and libraries holding relevant materials. Their assistance is much appreciated.

Many friends and colleagues have shared and encouraged my interests, including Judith Fingard, Craig Heron, Greg Kealey, Ian McKay, and Allen Seager. Nolan Reilly and John Manley shared work on topics of common interest. Don MacGillivray and Del Muise deserve much credit for their pioneering work in rescuing the history of industrial Cape Breton from neglect, and I am grateful for their friendship and assistance. Along the way I also received encouragement from Robert Babcock, John Laslett, and David Montgomery. Silver Donald Cameron supported the project at an early stage, and Ernie Forbes pushed me to complete it. James Lorimer was enthusiastic about publishing the results. Curtis Fahey edited the manuscript with skill, and Ward McBurney saw it through production with care and efficiency. My mother and father have been supportive from beginning to end. I am grateful as well to the Social Sciences and Humanities Research Council, which provided support for much of this research, as did the University of New Brunswick and its Department of History.

I have especially appreciated the opportunity to learn first-hand about Cape Breton labour history from individuals such as the late Joseph Nearing, Annie Whitfield, and George MacEachern. Special thanks must go to the daughters and sons of Kate and Jim McLachlan, who shared personal memories of their family life; the late Jean Robinson and J.B. McLachlan, Jr, were most helpful in recalling the early years before McLachlan became a prominent public figure. I am also grateful to Mary McLachlan Sanger for her encouragement.

McLachlan was a man of his times, but he had a vision of history and society that he believed was timeless and universal. He was not a man who spoke calmly or reasonably about the human consequences of economic development. He was tortured by the enormous social and human deficiencies of the capitalist system. He deplored the contradiction between the mighty capacity of production and the feeble progress of social justice. He was appalled by the distorted shape of human life and work under conditions of deprivation and disregard. What he had learned about the exploitation of the coal miners, first in Britain and then in Canada, he applied to the larger problems of capitalist society.

The coal miners had learned to defend their rights in one industry, and McLachlan was determined to do what he could to bring the same consciousness of their power to all workers. Labour radicalism, he believed, was a condition of intense anxiety on behalf of the working class. This is what made him an instinctive socialist and led him to associate the struggles of the coal miners with the cause of social revolution.

In the end, McLachlan was not a successful revolutionary, at least not by his own lights, and his vision of the liberation of labour remained unfulfilled. By the middle of the twentieth century, to be sure, the balance of power between labour, capital, and the state was changing: employers and governments were making concessions, and unions and workers were recognizing their responsibilities for the reform of society. Much was achieved, and the condition of the working class in Canada benefited from the standards and expectations articulated by McLachlan and his generation. It was not enough. From McLachlan's point of view, all of this was a preparation. The new world of industrial relations that emerged in the course of the twentieth century represented only a short-term accommodation between labour and capital. McLachlan did not doubt that the working class were the elect of history. He knew that their struggle would continue in the future as it had in the past.

No claim is made here that McLachlan's personal history was typical of the coal miners or of the working class as a whole, in Cape Breton or in Canada or elsewhere. His story was the response of one man to the specific necessities of his times. But this is also the story of a society that was struggling with the consequences of industrial capitalism and in which workers fought long and hard to enrich the meaning of democracy. This is a story that has been repeated again and again around the world, though never in just the same way or with exactly the same outcomes. McLachlan lived the dreams and frustrations of an archetypal working-class radical in the age of industrial capitalism. Because his vision of social justice and human solidarity was not a solitary one, limited by neither time nor place, his struggle to make a better world remains a permanent part of our own legacy.

BOOK ONE

TO REDEEM THE WORLD
1869-1916

But it is to you, ye Workers,
who do already work, and are as grown men,
noble and honourable in a sort,
that the whole world calls for new work and nobleness.
Subdue mutiny, discord, widespread despair,
by manfulness, justice, mercy and wisdom.
Chaos is dark, deep as Hell; let light be
and there is instead a green, flowery world.

– Thomas Carlyle,
Past and Present (1843)

CHAPTER 1

Scotland

If I'm designed yon lordling's slave,
By Nature's law designed,
Why was an independent wish
'er planted in my mind?

– Robert Burns,
Rules of the Lanarkshire Miners' Association (1879)

Ecclefechan

I n the green fields of southwest Scotland the white stone cottages of Ecclefechan stand bright in the sun. The River Annan flows by the edge of the village. A few miles away on Hoddom Hill, a sixteenth-century castle looks down on the rich farmlands.

Many threads of history run through this land. This is the border country where early battles of Scottish nationhood were fought by William Wallace and Robert Bruce at Stirling Bridge and Bannockburn. It is also the country of the covenanters, the religious radicals who defied the state during the counter-revolutions of the late seventeenth century, and of Robert Burns, the great people's poet whose lines were adopted by Lanarkshire coal miners in the 1870s. In the nineteenth century Ecclefechan itself was famous as the birthplace of Thomas Carlyle, the moral critic who warned against the degradation of human life in the age of industrial capitalism. In the year 1869 the village of Ecclefechan was also the birthplace of James Bryson McLachlan.

In the 1860s Ecclefechan was a small community of about 800 souls. The people of the village were mainly farmhands, shepherds, shop-keepers, and craftsworkers. The cotton weavers were an important occupational group in this community, and the clicking noise of their looms was a common sound on the cobbled streets. One of the leading craftsmen of the village was James Bryson. He had been born in Ecclefechan in 1803 and had worked as a cotton weaver most of his life. He remembered the stirring days when the Scottish weavers rallied to the Chartist cause and heard their leaders proclaim the rights of labour. With his wife, Agnes Scott, James Bryson had raised a family of four sons and four daughters. Still active in his older years, in 1873 he was a leading member of the Ecclefechan Cooperative Society. Handloom weavers such as James Bryson were proud craftsmen, but in the course of the nineteenth century their trade was destroyed by the power looms and factories of the industrial revolution. As women and children in the crowded milltowns provided more and more of the labour needed in the cotton industry, the Glasgow manufacturers lowered prices for the rural weavers. The logic of starvation drove tens of thousands of families out of the industry. By the 1860s James Bryson, too, had given up his trade and was finding work as a labourer on the farmlands surrounding the village.[1]

Another major theme in the history of workers in nineteenth-century Scotland was represented by a younger man, James McLachlan. He was born in 1830 in Maybole, a small town in neighbouring Ayrshire. His parents, Richard McLachlan and Mary Mollin, were among the hundreds of thousands of Irish labourers who fled their hunger-ridden homeland in the early nineteenth century and looked for better opportunities in the towns on the western shores of Scotland. In centres such as Maybole, families of Irish weavers worked fourteen and sixteen hours a day for six or seven shillings a week. Starvation, sickness, and death were common. In 1850 Mary Mollin died of consumption, the unremarkable nineteenth-century fate of poor people taxed by overwork and malnutrition. Richard died not long afterwards. James McLachlan, the second of their five children, survived and by 1861 was working as a cotton weaver in Ecclefechan.

There he soon met one of his neighbour's daughters, Esther Bryson. Twenty-five years of age in 1863, Esther had left her father's home some years earlier and gained her living as a farm labourer. In October 1863 Esther Bryson, the daughter of the aging village craftsman, married James McLachlan, the son of impoverished immigrants from Ireland.

The new family grew quickly. Their first son, George, was born in 1864, and three daughters, Mary, Jane, and Anne, soon followed. Their fifth child, James Bryson McLachlan, was born at 7 o'clock on the evening of 9 February 1869. Family tradition tells us that he was born in the small cottage originally built by Thomas Carlyle's father, who was a stonemason by trade. McLachlan himself repeated the story in later years, and it is clear that the association with Carlyle was meaningful to him. Like many working-class intellectuals of his generation, he was impressed by Carlyle's thunderous denunciations of the laws of political economy and his eloquent tributes to the dignity of labour. When McLachlan quoted a favourite passage, the words reminded him of their shared background and common inspirations.[2]

By April 1871 the family was no longer living in the village. James McLachlan had removed his household to the fields between Ecclefechan and Hoddom Hill, and they were still living there two years later. Conditions for the weavers had continued to deteriorate, and now the family shared the lot of the farm labourers. In return for their work, they received the use of a small dwelling with damp stone walls and a clay floor. Much of their pay came in the form of oats, barley, and other produce from the fields. It was a life of hard work and long hours, with little security and few hopes for advancement. With the addition of two more daughters, Agnes and Janet, this was a crowded household.

In contrast to the depressed conditions of the countryside, the early 1870s were a time of rapid growth in the industrial valleys of Scotland. From the shipyards, factories, ironworks, and coal mines of the Clyde, there came regular news of steady work and good wages. After ten years of struggle to provide for their growing family, Esther and James McLachlan left the broad skies and green fields of Dumfriesshire to seek a better life in the industrial north.

James Bryson McLachlan was four years old when the family left the countryside. One of his earliest recorded memories was of a return visit to Ecclefechan when he was eight years old. He remembered his grandmother, Agnes Scott Bryson, as a tall straight woman in a long cotton dress. She wore clogs – boots with wooden soles – and a tartan shawl over her head. "I used to think she looked just fine," he recalled in one of his few pieces of autobiographical writing more than half a century later. She rewarded him with apples, oatcakes, and cheese, and the young boy was eager to be able to help his grandmother: "You brae the sand for the floor, Jimmie, she would say." "Braeing the sand" meant going down to the brook and looking for a bank of soft yellow sandstone. He would then break it down with a hammer – "until it was almost as fine as brown sugar" – so that the sand could be sprinkled on the freshly swept floor. Sometimes, too, the floor would have to be patched with a shovelful of mud.

There was a boy's happy satisfaction in these chores, but McLachlan recalled a note of fatalism about the poverty of working-class life: "That floor at that time made me feel happy when it had been patched and sanded by Granny and I. Could I have listened to it talk, it would have said: 'Floors have always been mud-patched and sanded, and always will be.'"[3]

Newmains

Only a short journey through the uplands by the Caledonian Railway, the Black Country of Lanarkshire was a world apart. During the nineteenth century dozens of new coal and iron companies transformed the countryside. The throb of pit-engines broke the quiet along the River Clyde, stormy fireworks lit up the night sky, and black smoke streamed over the landscape. By the 1870s Lanarkshire was producing almost one million tons of iron and ten million tons of coal every year. By the turn of the century this production would double.

The Scottish coal masters had never displayed much concern for the conditions of the men, women, and children who produced their wealth. Until 1799 men and women had worked in the Scottish coal mines as serfs, bound to the coal masters for life in exchange for an annual fee. It was only in the 1840s that women and children were freed from their cruel work hauling tubs of coal on their hands and knees through the caverns of the mines. The coal masters' ruling principle was to buy labour as cheap as possible and sell coal dear. Only the doctrines of "coal trade Christianity" brightened the picture: "There must be rich and poor," one coal master insisted sanctimoniously in 1863. "There must be fortunate and unfortunate, for blessed purposes; for if there were no poor there would be no sweet and holy charity."[4]

In 1837 a successful English cotton manufacturer, Henry Houldsworth, launched the Coltness Iron Company, which grew to become one of Scotland's largest coal and iron producers. Under the rule of the new laird of Coltness, the small farming village of Newmains, located near the rail and coal towns of Motherwell and Wishaw, became a busy industrial centre. Brickworks, blast furnaces, railways, foundries, mills, and pitheads covered the fields. The Coltness Company constructed churches, schools, stores, and rows of company housing. By the 1870s Newmains was an industrial colony of about

2,500 people. Coal was in high demand in the early 1870s, and wages for coal miners rose to the enormous sum of ten shillings a day. When he arrived from the countryside, James McLachlan found employment as a labourer in the Coltness mines.[5]

For McLachlan, the landscape of childhood was now a much harsher one than he had known in Dumfriesshire. Stone and iron structures covered the flat treeless fields, and the air was clouded with smoke and dust. On the railway line that passed near their home, engines roared and rattled day and night. In the mornings the hoarse boom of an air-horn summoned their father to work.

The family took up residence at Leslie Place, one of the company rows of stone dwellings at the main crossroads in Newmains. Housing conditions in Scotland at the end of the nineteenth century were notoriously overcrowded, especially in the mining districts; most of the population of Scotland at this time lived in dwellings of no more than one or two rooms. There was no opportunity for a proper garden at Leslie Place, but his mother planted flowers in front of the cottage. There was no running water indoors, and open drains and outdoor privies were standard. Still, this was considered one of the better dwellings in the district, a row of two-storey apartments with wooden floors, windows, and at least two separate rooms. Another brother, John, was born in 1878, making for a family of two adults and seven children. Beds were built into the wall of the crowded household to accommodate the younger children.[6]

The McLachlan home had its share of misfortune. One of the sisters, Janet, suffered from a disabling bone disease – possibly rickets. Two children, Mary and Edward, did not survive childhood, perhaps falling victim to the scarlet-fever epidemics caused by the primitive water and drainage conditions of the district. Many years later McLachlan recalled the death of his younger brother as one of his first introductions to the tragedy of working-class life. McLachlan's recollections were reported by George MacEachern, a young labour organizer who visited the McLachlan home in the 1930s: "His parents were devastated, both were crying but, even as a small boy he gathered that a great deal of their distress was due to the fact that a proper burial, entailing as it did the buying of new clothes for the family to attend the funeral and the costs of the funeral itself would put them badly in debt. [McLachlan said:] 'It dawned on me that the loss of a son was overshadowed by financial worries. Working people didn't have the right to mourn their loss, the bills took precedence.'"[7]

As a boy McLachlan also became aware of larger, public tragedies. In 1877, when he was eight years old, Lanarkshire was shaken by one of those calamitous disasters that punctuate the history of coal miners in every part of the world. An explosion at Dixon's Collieries in Blantyre killed 207 men and boys. It was the greatest disaster ever known in the Scottish coal mines. Public meetings and resolutions condemned the unsafe conditions in the fiery pit, and the coal miners raised funds for the widowed and fatherless families. Memories of the Blantyre Explosion lasted long in Lanarkshire, and the story entered the folklore of industrial Scotland in a sombre melody.[8]

Other lessons were also close at hand. In every mining settlement there were older men and women who recalled the brutal conditions of the past and left a strong impression on young listeners. His back bent, his joints twisted, his voice hoarse with many freezings, the older miner embodied the wisdom of a lifetime. The Scottish miners' leader Robert Smillie recalled how one such boyhood encounter kindled a bright flame in his mind: "He convinced me, beyond all disproof, that our industrial system was cruelly wrong. And with the eagerness of youth and the high hopefulness of inexperience, I vowed to give my life to the betterment of the conditions under which, even then, the miner still dragged out a life which was no life for a man made in God's image."[9]

The high wages of the early 1870s did not last long in the Newmains and Wishaw district. By 1875 the miners' earnings had fallen to six shillings a day, still relatively high even after deductions for rent, coal, tools, doctor, and school fees had been subtracted by the company. But in 1877 wages fell to four shillings and in 1879 they dropped to three shillings a day.[10] In a time of falling wages, the family needed to increase its earning power. The oldest daughters began to take in sewing to add to the family income, and George, the oldest son, followed his father down to the coal mines at the end of the village. Soon it would be time for the family's second son, five years younger, to go into the mines.

It is unlikely that McLachlan completed more than three or four years of formal education. Although a new Education Act in 1872 required children under fourteen to attend school, there were numerous exemptions, especially for children who mastered their reading, writing, and arithmetic without difficulties. By one account McLachlan left school at the age of nine to work as a florist's helper, his pay for the week being one white rose.[11] McLachlan's own short statement of the transition from school to work reveals little but seems clear enough: "I went to school until I was ten, then I went to work in the mine." As one historian of education in Scotland has noted, nothing more was expected of miners' children: "Neither the accessibility of schools nor the presence of well-qualified schoolmasters could counteract the imperatives of poverty." In fact, McLachlan also continued to apply himself to his studies throughout his youth, but in this he was departing from the normal expectations for children of his class.[12]

No coal miner ever forgot those first days down the pit. A young boy usually began work as a trapper, a job that required him to open and close ventilation doors for the passing coal cars. Physically it was not demanding work, but those long hours alone in the dark easily awakened fears among the young boys. The rumble and clatter of distant sounds echoed through the tunnels of the mine and mingled with the smoke, dust, and gas in the air. Somewhere there was the sound of dripping water and the scarcely heard movement of layers of coal and rock. Sometimes the stillness was broken by an ominous creak of timbers or the scurrying of rats. The feeble stabs of light from his lamp did little to calm a boy's worries, for he knew how quickly he could be swallowed by the all-encompassing darkness. If his lamp went out, he could not relight it and was doomed to wait until he could hear once more the reassuring sounds of approaching men.

In time the strangeness of the mine dissolved. The young miner gained confidence as he learned to walk the dark passageways with a sure, rolling step, and to see and hear in the dark and silence. Coal dust, lingering gas, and smoke lost their menace as the miner learned to gauge the safety of the air by the flame of his lamp. He began to acquire a sixth sense, which enabled him to tell the meaning of a creak of timber or snap of the coal. From experienced miners he learned the skills of the trade: how to protect the roof of his working place with carefully set timbers, how to cut and shoot the coal safely from the jagged coal face, how to load the coal into a cart while crouching awkwardly under a low roof. McLachlan also mastered the skilled trade of the borer and shaft-sinker, the miner who built strategic passageways and opened air shafts in the mine.

McLachlan came of age in this underground world. The day's work, he learned, was relieved with the talk and humour of the pit. For the rest of his life, long after he had ceased to be a working miner, McLachlan could still sit down and trade pit talk with other men who had also served their apprenticeship in the mines. Although coal mining has often had a morbid image among outsiders, McLachlan came to know and participate in the strengths of this underground culture with its remarkable blend of individualism and solidarity. And, although he had given up school, he could often be seen carrying a book, hoping to find spare moments in the course of the day to do some reading. The pages of some well-thumbed volumes soon became smudged with coal dust.

His fellow workers appreciated the character and abilities of this serious-minded youth. According to D.N. Brodie, a long-time family friend who must have had the story from McLachlan, at fifteen years of age J.B. was appointed by the miners to his first elected office, as secretary of a miners' relief society, entrusted with the keeping of the group's books and records.[13]

The Modern Covenant

At home at 5 Leslie Place in the Coltness Company row, Esther McLachlan was the commanding presence. This was a rigid Presbyterian household, and she instilled a sturdy discipline in her children. The wooden floors were always swept clean of coal dust, and if there were potatoes to peel for the Sunday dinner, the work would be done on Saturday. Though strict, the family circle was also a close one. At Leslie Place there were always home-made toys for the younger children, and in the evenings it was common to hear their father read from Burns and from the Bible.[14]

Esther raised her children in the doctrines of the Reformed Presbyterian Church, a small dissenting church that traced its origins back to the turbulent times of the covenanters in the seventeenth century. Much of McLachlan's library from this period demonstrated a concern with his religious heritage as well as the practical application of religious ideology. The older titles included standard Protestant texts such as an edition of John Foxe's *Book of Martyrs*, originally published in 1563, and a copy of *The Select Practical Writings* of John Knox printed in 1845. There were also later volumes issued by groups such as the Scottish Reformation Society. As late as 1897, on the occasion of his twenty-eighth birthday, McLachlan received an inscribed copy of the proceedings of an international meeting of Reformed Presbyterian churches.

One of the treasured volumes in the small family collection of books was a 1744 edition of Alexander Shields, *A Hind Let Loose: or, an Historical Representation of the Testimonies of the Church of Scotland*. This book was originally published in 1687 at the height of the covenanters' struggle to preserve the democratic structure of the church against the efforts of the crown to create an established church controlled by the state. Shields introduced his discourse as a vindication of the "Wild folk of Scotland" presented by "a Lover of true Liberty," and he addressed himself "to all that are free born, and are not contented slaves mancipated in a stupid subjection to Tyrants absoluteness." This was a key text in the radical democratic tradition, for in it arguments about church government were extended to civil society. One historian has noted that in *A Hind Let Loose*, "the participatory and democratic values of Calvinism are mobilised to justify resistance to tyrannous government."[15]

McLachlan's attention was especially drawn to the story of Richard Cameron, one of the famous names among the covenanters of the southwest of Scotland. Following the restoration of the absolute monarchy under Charles II in 1660, the covenanters (named after the National Covenant of 1638, which they saw as an early form of social contract between God, the people, and the crown) resisted the establishment of a state-controlled church. Throughout the countryside of the Lowlands, they abandoned the kirk by the thousands and arranged prayer meetings in outdoor fields and barns. Cameron was one of the unauthorized field preachers who arranged rural conventicles – clandestine religious meetings – in Dumfriesshire and other strongholds of presbyterian support in the southwest. These practices were declared a crime against the state and a capital offence. As a result, the covenanters were hunted down by government troops and subjected to fines, incarceration, and banishment; many were killed in armed confrontations or executed by hanging or drowning following summary trials. At Sanquhar in 1680 Cameron and his associates disowned the king and declared war on him as a tyrant and usurper. Cameron was killed shortly afterwards in one of the battles with the dragoons, and the period of repression that followed is remembered as "the killing times."

Under the rule of William and Mary, moderates among the presbyterians accepted the compromises that established the Church of Scotland in 1690, but the Cameronians remained unreconciled to what they saw as the annihilation of true presbyterianism and eventually established their own church in 1743. In retrospect the covenanters' resistance to absolutism has been viewed as one of the stages that led to the creation of the limited, constitutional monarchy which is one of the legacies of the seventeenth-century revolutions. The Cameronians, writes the Scottish labour historian Willie Thompson, deserve respect as an instance of the "uncompromising stand of poor men and women in the face of arbitrary and ferocious state power."[16]

As a young man McLachlan also came under the influence of local middle-class social reformers in the town of Wishaw. These included Alexander Wilson, a medical doctor, and George Whittet, a Baptist minister, both of them associated with the ongoing evangelical revival in the industrial area. The coal mines occupied a vivid place in the evangelical imagery of the times – they were the woeful pit of bondage and torment: where else were grace and redemption more urgent?

At the individual level the religious revival had liberating effects, bringing books, study, and reading into the company towns of the industrial districts. Dr Wilson was responsible for presenting McLachlan with a Greek-English lexicon (inscribed partly in Latin) and other textbooks. This kind of classical study suggests that Wilson hoped to further the young miner's education and rescue him from the pit, perhaps for training in the ministry. McLachlan proved himself a good student well into his twenties. He grappled with sectarian controversies and texts on logic and grammar, and he devoted long hours to Bible study, marking notes and passages in the margins. In later years, when he had a public reputation as an atheist, McLachlan was apt to surprise – even astonish – clergymen with his knowledge of Scripture.

In the Newmains and Wishaw district the evangelical tradition was embodied in the person of George Whittet, who carried the gospel to the open-air meetings, company rows, street corners, and country fairs of the area for more than forty years.[17] His preaching impressed the young coal miner, and McLachlan joined the Wishaw Baptist Church. At twenty years of age, McLachlan was – by his own inscription in a copy of *The Student's Analytical Greek Testament* – "born again in the Parish of Cam-neathen [Cambusneathen], Lanarkshire, in the year 1889, on 4th September."[18] And in a copy of Albert Bower's *Notes, Explanatory and Practical, on the New Testament*, McLachlan wrote:

Either saved for
1st My goodness alone
2nd My goodness and Christ goodness
                 joined together
3rd For Jesus sake alone
The last alone suits me

Nothing in my hand I bring.

Among the Baptists McLachlan found a larger, more vigorous spiritual fellowship than could have been available in the small Cameronian sect of the Reformed Presbyterians. It was also in the Wishaw Baptist Church that McLachlan met Catherine Greenshields, whom he would marry four years later. McLachlan and his new brothers-in-Christ saw themselves as the heirs of an "ancient doctrine of martyrs, confessors, reformers and saints … against which the gates of hell cannot prevail." On the day McLachlan married Kate in 1893, Dr Wilson expressed his best wishes in these terms: "May your life and mine adorn our doctrine, may our example recommend our creed, and may we never give credence to any teaching, but that which is manifestly approved of God, and owned by the Holy Spirit."

In later years McLachlan said little in public about his religious upbringing. On occasion Kate would entertain visitors with accounts of his youthful piety, recalling how he was too strict to take a streetcar on a Sunday or to sing a hymn in church. McLachlan's immersion in theology and revivalism demonstrated the young man's search for a meaningful mission. In the modern era, he came to believe, the old cause of the covenanters faced a new challenge in the relationship between the workers and their masters. Like Keir Hardie, who joined the Evangelical Union as a youth and served as a lecturer for the Good Templars before his emergence as a miners' official in the 1870s and 1880s, McLachlan would also find his mission in the redemption of the working class. As a labour leader, McLachlan came to see himself as belonging to a tradition of unauthorized preachers that went back through the field meetings of the seventeenth century and deep into the Old Testament. In 1919 he wrote about this theme with much conviction in a remarkable essay entitled "The Ideal Preacher for the New Era in Life."[19]

Confirming the significance of McLachlan's religious background are the later observations of J.S. Woodsworth, with whom McLachlan, at the height of his influence in the early 1920s, shared some thoughts about his intellectual development. The key to McLachlan's personality, wrote Woodsworth, was contained in one word – "uncompromising": "He was raised in the strictest sect of the Reformed Presbyterians. The old covenanter tradition became part of his being." Woodsworth described McLachlan in a particularly meaningful phrase when he called him a "labor covenanter": "The high-souled, unyielding religious fanaticism of an earlier generation has not died out of the men of his breed but finds expression in new forms in our modern life. Persecution will break him and his kind as little as it broke the martyrs."[20]

Meanwhile McLachlan was acquiring practical advice that would serve him well in his public career. A small, well-studied volume by Gawin Kirkham, long-time secretary of the Open-Air Mission, instructed the reader in the arts and skills of public speaking. A preacher required both a call and qualifications, Kirkham explained, and an effective preacher must have the necessary physical and mental preparation for the task as well as appropriate inspiration. A methodical approach included cultivating habits of correct speech, physical stamina, abstinence, a good voice, a natural manner, ease in conversation, and general reading in fields such as history, biography, and natural science. In turn a speaker needed to appeal to reason, imagination, and affections – to Prove, to Paint, and Persuade. "Cold, formal, measured, precise preaching will not do," warned *The Open-Air Preacher's Handbook*. "Life, fire, and energy are essential, as the powder is essential to carry the shot." In the end the preacher's best preparation was personal conviction: "It is impossible for people to take fire from a preacher who is not himself on fire."[21]

The Coal Masters

On 8 March 1887 a young man rose to his feet in a Glasgow conference hall. Before him sat the sixteen members of the Lanarkshire Coal Masters' Association, the most powerful employers in Lanarkshire. Presiding over the assembly was the Lord Provost of Glasgow. It was an historic occasion, for this was the first time the members of the Coal Masters' Association had agreed to meet a delegation of coal miners.

The coal masters had come to the meeting reluctantly. It was a time of rising coal prices, and the coal miners were demanding a sixpence increase in wages. All over the county the miners were taking idle days and practising what they called the "wee darg," restricting their output to "a small day's task." Then in February they went out on strike. When the coal masters brought in strikebreakers, violent scenes erupted around the collieries. The coal masters had refused to meet officials of the newly formed Scottish Miners' National Federation, for which the thirty-year-old Keir Hardie was employed as the secretary, or to negotiate with any of the union officials; however, once the miners agreed to suspend their strike, the owners did consent to meet with a delegation of miners representing the different parts of the coalfield. One of the sixteen miners' delegates was an eighteen-year-old James McLachlan.[22]

"What was the conference meant for? It was to deal with the wages question." McLachlan began to speak in a clipped, forceful voice. "That is what the men understand in the Middle Ward of Lanarkshire district. The understanding of the men is that the wage question, and no other question is to be brought up and discussed at this conference, which it is hoped may ultimately prove of benefit both to masters and men." Instead, now that the coal miners were sitting with them in a meeting room, the coal masters were evading the wage issue and attempting to introduce a list of demands for uninterrupted work at the collieries and a complicated sliding scale to regulate wages in accord with coal prices. Robert Steele, a veteran Motherwell coal miner, had first spoken out at the meeting against this manoeuvre. McLachlan, for his part, proclaimed that "no conference whatever would have been arranged to take place unless the question of wages was to be dealt with – the struggle between capital and labour – a struggle which would not have occurred as at present but for the obstinacy of the employers." Already McLachlan spoke with the uncompromising voice that would mark his years as a union leader: he stood by the miners' original demands and would give no ground. Also of note was his defence of restriction of output, a traditional form of action among the Lanarkshire coal miners; years later he would encourage the same form of protest in the Cape Breton coalfields. And, finally, there were those telling references to a conflict between "masters and men," between "capital and labour"; in the confrontations to come McLachlan would see no cause to change this basic view of the wages question.

Three days later the conference resumed. The miners' delegates reported that their members were not prepared to guarantee six days of steady work every week. At some pits the men would agree to work no more than nine days in fourteen; at others they were willing to work eleven days in fourteen in exchange for the sixpence advance in wages. Meanwhile, the position of the coal masters had hardened. Andrew K. McCosh, manager of the huge William Baird and Company coal enterprises, presented a new code of work rules. The coal miners were to work six days a week, with idle days allowed only for injury or illness or at the company's requirement. Above all, no coal miner was to interfere with the amount of work performed by any of his fellow miners.

The code brought forth a storm of protest. "There is nothing binding on them," declared one delegate. "The binding is all on us." "Talk about a true born Briton," protested Robert Steele. "Mr. McCosh's idea seems to be that the slave trade of South America was the only system to be introduced in the mining districts of Scotland." McLachlan added his voice to the protest, too, defending the coal miners' freedom to regulate their own work: "It is well known that Mr. McCosh has been carrying out these principles with his own workmen. He has gone very far out of place in the way of direction ... There can be nothing done so long as these strenuous rules are put forward."

The conference ended in hostility. Bitterly, the delegates concluded that their good faith had been abused. In February they had agreed to end their strike and come to the conference; now their original demands for better wages were shoved aside and the coal masters were imposing new requirements. This was the first experience of the Lanarkshire coal miners in negotiations with their employers, and it helped condition McLachlan's wary attitude towards the coal masters he was to deal with in the years to come.

For McLachlan, there was also an element of hopefulness in the encounter. The coal miners had crossed swords with the most powerful men in the land and stood their ground. "You gentlemen have not all the intelligence on your own side," warned one of the coal miners as the conference broke up, "for although you may have a great amount of intelligence, we have some practical knowledge, and we will take care of that."

Although the Federation did not survive the defeat of 1887, this moment has come to be regarded as a turning point in the history of the Scottish miners. Within a few years the organization was revived, on a permanent basis. And, as Fred Reid has shown in his biography of Keir Hardie, the experience of 1887 strengthened Hardie's belief that the miners must mobilize their political power. It also brought him to the moment where he declared himself a socialist: "What we complain of is that the honest, industrious, sober toiler is kept from year's end to year's end with only one step between him and pauperism ... The remedy is a simple one, if only the nation had sense enough to apply it. Get rid of the idea that the capitalist is an indispensible adjunct of an industrial system and the problem is solved. Capital is a necessity, but not the capitalist ..." Reporting back to one of the last meetings of the Miners' Federation in 1887, Hardie signified that something new was under way among the coal miners: "Ours is no old-fashioned sixpence-a-day agitation. We aim at the complete emancipation of the worker from the thraldom of wagedom. Cooperative production, under State management, should be our goal; as never till this has been obtained can we hope for better times for working people."[23]

Unions had never been strong among the coal miners in Scotland, and periodic revolts had failed to give rise to lasting unions. In their important studies of the Scottish coal miners, Alan Campbell and Fred Reid have drawn attention to the role of the myth of the "independent collier."[24] This myth was rooted in the emancipation of the miners from serfdom in 1799, and it was reinforced by the skills required in their daily work. Most of all, the myth was the long-standing outlook of the self-improving, skilled collier. It was his belief that with proper understanding his employers could be persuaded to allow him and his fellows the wages, status, and respect to which they were entitled. In trade-union policy, Alexander MacDonald, the dominant miners' leader of the 1860s and 1870s, reflected this hopeful quest for a state of harmony between masters and men. In union policy it meant sliding scales to govern wages, restriction of output to govern the coal market, conciliation and arbitration to settle differences, and participation in the mainstream political parties; MacDonald himself even served as a Liberal Member of Parliament. The problem was that, in the context of the changes taking place in the nineteenth-century coal industry, this approach was a failure. Small operators had been replaced by large iron companies, with extensive technology and new ideas about work discipline. Large numbers of inexperienced labourers, often Irishmen and farmhands, had been recruited into the mines, undercutting the position of the traditional colliers. The new arrivals in the coalfields demonstrated support for shorter hours, safer conditions, and higher wages, but they had little enthusiasm for MacDonald's moderate approach to the improvement of conditions. By the 1870s and 1880s the world of the independent collier was in full-blown crisis.

McLachlan thus entered Scottish labour history at an important crossroads in the history of the coal miners. In the upheaval of 1887 we hear echoes of old and new in the Glasgow conference hall. McLachlan's protests against new work rules and his defence of restriction of output reflected old themes of the independent collier; but now these traditional values were being put to a new use: the miners' delegates refused to accept a sliding scale to govern their wages and continued to insist on their original demand for an increased wage. By the 1890s, when trade unionism reappeared permanently in the form of the Scottish Miners' Federation, a new generation of labour leaders was in control. Associated with names such as Keir Hardie and Robert Smillie, they were supporters of militant strikes, aggressive wage bargaining, an eight-hour law, state insurance, independent labour politics, and nationalization of the coal mines.

From Alexander MacDonald to Keir Hardie, from the outlook of the independent collier to the idea of working-class solidarity – this was the crucial transition in the rise of the coal miners' union in Scotland in the late nineteenth century. McLachlan participated in this change and its effects shaped his view of unionism. Like Hardie, he was never entirely cut off from the roots that nourished the myth of the independent collier. These would be apparent in his firm attachment to values such as temperance, education, and self-improvement. The values of self-help, Reid has noted, were a significant part of the radical democratic tradition, for they were "the means by which the workers would contribute to their own fitness for power."[25]

Soon Hardie himself would be making his own transition from pit to parliament and entering British history in 1892 as the first independent labour Member of Parliament and then as founder of the Labour Party. But for younger followers such as McLachlan, the world of the independent collier remained alive in the coal mines. The coal masters might dominate the world outside the pit, but the world under the ground, where the coal miners tested their skill and muscle against the seams of coal, remained the domain of the coal miners themselves. When they were too weak to bargain through unions and committees and legislatures, the coal miners could offer resistance on their own terrain, in the mine itself.

Years later, as a labour leader in the Nova Scotia coalfields, McLachlan repeatedly drew on this legacy of workplace regulation. In speeches, conversations, and writings he painted vivid pictures of the ways the coal miners exercised control over conditions of work in the Old

Country pits, even in the absence of union recognition. For the benefit of one of his sons, he recalled conditions at one of the mines where he had worked in his youth. The size of the "darg," the day's work, was strictly enforced by the coal miners. At the end of the day the men gathered at the pithead, where the amount of coal each man had sent to the surface was weighed and recorded on a board. If any man exceeded the agreed limit, the miners would prevent him from return-ing to the mine. At a time of deepening confrontation with the employers in the Nova Scotia coalfields more than a generation later, McLachlan advocated restriction of output and other tactics based on the workers' control of the workplace. In this way he was applying some of the residual wisdom of the nineteenth-century independent collier to the new condi-tions and circumstances of the twentieth-century struggle.[26]

Kate

Catherine Ferguson Greenshields was the daughter of a Wishaw stone-mason, one of the relatively successful skilled artisans of Gladstonian Britain. Thomas Greenshields, after completing his apprenticeship in the trade, was twenty-one years old when he married Jane Russell, eighteen, a coal miner's daughter employed as a domestic servant. Their first child, Catherine, was born on 22 March 1873. They had high hopes for their daughter, who was known to the family as Kitty. She was black-haired, slim, and beautiful. She received a good education and showed a love for poetry and theatre; Ibsen and Schiller were among her favourite writers. By the account of her oldest daughter, Kate had a love of farm life; indeed, when she married, the register identified her as a farm servant. Although her father had left the Wishaw Baptist Church in 1883, Catherine continued to attend. Here she took notice of the young coal miner James McLachlan, who seemed to be singled out by the minister and others as a youth of special promise.

In the Greenshields family there was some concern about Kate's attraction to McLachlan. The prospects of a coal miner were humble ones, and the family feared that Kate was marrying below her station. But the difficulties were set aside, and the young couple were married, according to the forms of the Baptist Church, at the Greenshields home on Kirk Road on 29 December 1893. The Reverend Whittet officiated. McLachlan was twenty-four years old and Kate (as he called her) was twenty. As is so often the case in the biography of a public figure, we know little about the terms of their personal relationship, except for occasional later evidence. For instance, there is the vivid romantic poetry McLachlan wrote during the last hours of his imprisonment in 1924 – "Just twelve more hours then grudging sun, It's Kate and me and heaven." And their children recall with feeling the love and companionship they saw in their mother and father in later years. One of the younger daughters later recalled: "I have yet to meet another couple who *loved* and *liked* each other as my father and mother."[27]

There was little security for the new family. Unlike his own father, who remained a labourer in the Newmains-Wishaw district to the end of his working life, McLachlan experienced frequent changes of location and employment. In the first eight years of their marriage, the young couple lived at almost as many different addresses, beginning on Caledonian Road, Wishaw. Each of their first four children was born at a new location. Their oldest daughter, Jean – named for Kate's mother – was born in the miners' row at Blantyre in 1894, the site of the famous explosion of her father's childhood. She was followed in 1896 by Esther and in 1898 by Catherine; one was named for McLachlan's mother and the other for Kate; both were born in outlying locations surrounding Newmains. In 1902 their first son, James Bryson McLachlan, Jr, was born in an industrial suburb of Glasgow. Forty years later, recalling his life as a young married man in Blantyre, McLachlan could still convey a sharp sense of his frustration at the poverty of the miner's life:

I grew up and got married, and we had a sweet little baby girl. The house we lived in had a brick floor. One did not need to mud-patch it. The bricks were yellow and ten inches square. My wife used to wash it every day and with soft chalk make nice little, what I called "whirlie-jigs," around the edge of each brick. All the wives in that miners' row did this. We were very happy, my wife and baby and I. But at night when we would sit by the fire, just the three of us, my happy feeling would go smash looking at the damned floor of yellow bricks and scores of white "whirlie-jigs." Why could I not get something better for those I loved?

Where the floors in his grandmother's house had spoken a message of acquiescence, in McLachlan's own home the floors voiced an accusation: "Now this brick floor was an agitator. It said to me, 'Look at your girl wife, pretty as a picture, kind beyond compare, and you give her yellow bricks and "whirlie-jigs" to raise your baby on!' That floor would stab me to the heart, making me fighting mad."[28]

As a young husband and father, McLachlan considered himself under special obligations to succeed as a breadwinner. Like most late nineteenth-century working-class men who aspired to the achievement of security and respectability for their family, McLachlan subscribed to a widely shared cult of masculinity. As the head of the family, the male breadwinner considered himself responsible for providing the essentials of food, clothing and shelter, and, as much as possible, the comforts and satisfactions of a good life. Although both men and women contributed to the success of the household economy, the division of labour between men and women ran to extremes in the mining community. The employment of women underground had been prohibited since the 1840s, and opportunities for paid work were limited in the coal towns. By the time of the First World War, the male-breadwinner norm had become what one historian of the family describes as "a pervasive and fervently held proletarian ideal throughout the developed capitalist world."[29]

McLachlan readily recognized the hard work of women in the home. In the farm households of his childhood in Dumfriesshire, men, women, and children all contributed to the family's livelihood by doing chores and working in the fields. Later in Newmains, his older brother George went into the mines and his older sisters set themselves up as dressmakers in the home. The same would happen in his own family when the children reached a working age. As a labour leader McLachlan later paid tribute to the woman of the coal-mining household as "the miner's financier," and in his scanty reminiscences he dwells with some eloquence on the work of his grandmother and mother while saying little of his father's work as a colliery labourer. Nevertheless, in the industrial context the responsibility for winning a family wage was a masculine one. Failure to fulfil this obligation threatened to expose the worker to doubts about his own manliness. Moreover, this ideal allowed workers to make an argument from a position of honour that conformed to the expectations of respectable society; as Wally Seccombe has pointed out, "unions put employers on the defensive and condemned the operation of the free labour market by the criterion of a higher value – the sanctity of the family – shared by all social classes." Under the conditions of economic growth and exploitation in the coalfields, this domestic ideal, like the myth of the independent collier, contributed to the cultural, even psychological, pressures driving workers such as McLachlan to seek a better share of the rewards of industrial life.[30]

In the coal mines McLachlan continued to accumulate the experience of the skilled collier. Here was a place where he was able to demonstrate his manliness as a mineworker, even if the economic returns were unsatisfactory. McLachlan's value as a coal miner was enhanced by the specialized skill he learned as a shaft-sinker. This was the man whose job was to open air-shafts and other passageways for new developments in the pit. Like a mole, the sinker burrowed, crawled, scraped, chiselled, and blasted his way through the layers of coal, clay, gravel, and stone. The sinker wore a special oilskin – a hat, cape, and shoulder pads made of thick leather – to protect himself against the seeping water and the cuts and bruises of the narrow workplace. There was nothing to protect the miner's lungs from the surrounding dampness and the dust in the air. These were arduous conditions, but the sinker's expertise was in demand in an expanding industry, and he enjoyed a respected place among the skilled mineworkers.[31]

For the Scottish coal miners, the most important struggle of the 1890s was the Great Strike of 1894. In June of that year the new Scottish Miners' Federation led tens of thousands of coal miners across Scotland on a strike against a one-shilling reduction in wages.[32] The coal masters maintained a stubborn silence, refusing to meet the strike leaders. The Liberal government in London, which had already disappointed workers when it failed to enact the eight-hour day, refused to help the miners. From the pulpit the coal miners heard blasts of disapproval. In the press editors claimed that the Scottish miners were the best paid in the world. From England mounted police arrived to protect strikebreakers and terrorize the mining towns. In the coal towns the pawnshops were crowded with coal miners' possessions, and soup kitchens opened up to help feed the hungry families. Sympathetic shopkeepers offered contributions, and from outside the coalfields there was financial help from the Miners' Federation of Great Britain.

As the strike wore on, it was learned that the English coal miners, who had gone on strike the previous year, had been awarded, through conciliation, a sixpence reduction in wages. The leaders of the Scottish Federation were tempted to settle for the same reduction. R. Chisholm Robertson, the federation's fiery secretary-treasurer, broke with Robert Smillie and the rest of the Scottish leaders; Robertson believed that, if the miners stood firm, the coal masters could still be forced to surrender.

In the midst of this turbulent situation we catch a brief glimpse of McLachlan at a meeting of the Blantyre area coal miners. The miners of this district were among the most militant strikers in 1894, and in September an angry public meeting denounced the leaders for proposing a compromise. A resolution expressed "general dissatisfaction" and reminded the miners' leaders that they were the servants, not the masters, of the coal miners. McLachlan spoke briefly. On his suggestion "it was agreed that the general dissatisfaction with the executive did not apply to Mr. Chisholm Robertson."[33] Again, this short glimpse confirmed McLachlan's uncompromising stand in labour matters. The episode also introduced McLachlan to a characteristic tension in the politics of trade unionism – the push and pull of the membership measured against the hesitation and ambition of the union leadership. Should union leaders pursue cautious policies, consolidating gains and preserving solidarity? Or should they push on from one success to the next one, appealing directly to the militancy and resourcefulness of the membership? It was something McLachlan himself would have ample opportunity to ponder from the position of a union leader in later years.

In the end, after seventeen weeks, the strike was lost. Only a few coal masters agreed to the federation's terms. Once again the coal masters had triumphed, but McLachlan had also seen the workers standing together in solidarity as never before. Like thousands of Scottish coal miners, McLachlan pondered the penny pamphlet published by Keir

Hardie, who was now attracting national attention as a Member of Parliament. In his "Friendly Chat with the Scotch Miners," Hardie drove home the lessons of the class struggle.

"Why have fifty mineowners power to starve 70,000 miners into submission?" asked Hardie:

> On one side were the miners, and their wives and children; on the other, fighting against you, were hunger, the masters, the law, backed by policemen and soldiers, the Government, the press and the pulpit. In the face of all these you fought a heroic battle, but the forces against you were too many and you had to yield. Now, why were the masters, the Government, the press and pulpit, all arrayed against you? There is but one answer. All these are controlled by the rich and you are poor.

The only solution, Hardie argued, was to eliminate the power of the rich over the poor, and this could be achieved only by united action of the workers, both industrially and politically. He concluded with a characteristic appeal:

> Don't forget your trade union. Nothing can absolve you from your duty to your union. Be a consistent member; pay your contributions regularly; loyally carry out the decisions of the union. But after you have done all this, carry your principles to their logical conclusion, by acting politically as you do industrially. It is foolish to form a union to fight the coalmasters, and then send one of these masters, or his friend, to make the laws for you. The class which makes the laws can do as it pleases. Your class has no say in making the laws at present, and so they are made against you.[34]

During his time in Blantyre McLachlan may also have come under the influence of a remarkable local miners' leader, William Small. A former shopkeeper, Small was regularly elected to the local school board and was well known as a supporter of adult education. In his home Small conducted classes on subjects ranging from literature and social reform to biology and chemistry; Sundays he held his "Communicals," featuring music, poetry, and visiting speakers. A member of the Social Democratic Federation, a supporter of unions and nationalization of the coal industry, Small remained also a deeply religious man and his Sunday meetings always opened with a Bible reading. He followed what he called the "Socialism of Jesus" and was wont to remark that the Sermon on the Mount and the Lord's Prayer contained all the guidance a true Christian life required.[35]

McLachlan did not see his own religious idealism and his trade unionism at this time as competing loyalties. To him it was plain that the mission of the religious idealist and the labour reformer was the same. Both causes aimed to establish the rule of justice and morality in society. As one contemporary recalled, "the Scottish labour movement was not founded on materialism. The instinct for freedom and justice which animated the Covenanters and Chartists also inspired the Nineteenth Century pioneers. Their teachers and prophets were Jesus, Shelley, Mazzini, Whitman, Ruskin, Carlyle and Morris. The economists took a secondary place. The crusade was to dethrone Mammon and to insist that the welfare of the community should take precedence of the enrichment of a handful."[36]

Given the family stories about their common birthplace in Ecclefechan, it is not surprising that McLachlan felt drawn to Carlyle's writings as an expression of his moral and social commitment. Although they did not accept Carlyle's nostalgic prescriptions for social renewal, his generation of labour leaders were impressed by the stern sermons against the rule of cash and Mammon in human affairs and drawn to the philosophy of heroic moral activity. In books such as *Past and Present*, which can be considered Carlyle's most extended hymn of praise to the nobility of work, they were inspired by the promise of labour as "a seeing rational giant: But it is to you, ye Workers, who do already work, and are as grown men, noble and honourable in a sort, that the whole world calls for new work and nobleness. Subdue mutiny, discord, widespread despair, by manfulness, justice, mercy and wisdom. Chaos is dark, deep as Hell; let light be and there is instead a green flowery world."[37] Here was a vision of purposeful activism that promised to bring light and order to the world of the colliery village.

For McLachlan there was no single moment of conversion or illumination when the details of his life's work stood clearly before him. From boyhood McLachlan had known the life of the coal miners, and in many respects he always would remain a man of the coal country. But Carlyle's call to redeem the world from the chaos of industrial capitalism gave McLachlan a mission invested with universal as well as personal significance.

Glasgow

There is some evidence that in the wake of the Great Strike of 1894 McLachlan was blacklisted by the larger coal and iron companies.[38] This would help explain the constant moves to seek out work at smaller, independent mines. In turn, victimization by the companies and the continual "tramping" for work would also help explain the decision to leave Scotland for the New World.

In the winter of 1899–1900 the McLachlan family was living in Ponfeigh, a tiny miners' village in the hills near the Ayrshire border. The family's next move was to Camlachie in the sprawling suburbs of Glasgow, Scotland's great industrial metropolis. From the damp cottages of a miners' row the family of five now resettled on the fourth floor of a Glasgow tenement. The entrance was on a narrow alley-way running between two streets. McLachlan still travelled to work in the pits surrounding the city, and in Camlachie the neighbourhood children crowded around to watch the unusual sight of a man returning home – black with coal dust from his day's work. At street level there was a bakery and stables. At the corner there was an ash-pit, and at night the homeless poor of the city would climb over the wall to sleep there. In the morning children ran through the streets calling out in shrill voices, "A piece! A piece! A piece!" Kate McLachlan knew the meaning of the cry. The hungry children flocked like birds to the street below her window, while she tossed down pieces of bread wrapped in newspaper.[39]

Like so many of the urban centres of the nineteenth-century capitalist world, Glasgow presented extremes of poverty and wealth. The public squares were decorated with fountains and surrounded by magnificent stone buildings. There were libraries and museums to be inspected. On occasion James and Kate would take their three daughters on an outing to the Glasgow zoo. On Saturdays McLachlan took Jean, their oldest daughter, through the bookshops, where they examined the bins of old volumes.

McLachlan was also watching current events. In 1900 he was disturbed by the British war against the Boers, the Dutch-speaking white farmers of South Africa. The Baptist Church took a public stand against the conflict, and one of the few politicians to question the war was Hardie, who denounced it as "a capitalist war" over control of the goldfields: "The British merchant hopes to secure markets for his goods, the investor an outlet for his capital, the speculator more fools out of whom to make money, and the mining companies cheaper labour and increased dividends." McLachlan acquired at least two books giving pro-Boer accounts of the conflict. He also collected newspaper clippings about British atrocities, including one that concerned the shooting of Boer prisoners and the subsequent execution by the British of two Australian lieutenants who claimed they were only following orders from the high command.[40]

On Sunday afternoons McLachlan was often attracted to Glasgow Green. In the shadow of Nelson's monument crowds gathered to hear wide-ranging debates about God and man, unions and politics, land reform and Irish Home Rule, astronomy and evolution, and other controversies of the time. One of McLachlan's favourite speakers was Harry Alfred Long. In his seventies, this venerable white-bearded gentleman, known as the "Protestant champion of Scotland," was still a colourful and popular speaker among Glasgow workers.[41] Like many concerned social reformers of the time, Long considered wholesale emigration a solution to the wretchedness of industrial Britain.

Long had undertaken tours of the overseas colonies and dominions of the British Empire and reported his findings in speeches and booklets addressed to the Scottish workers. "Would an average operative be better off in one of our fifty colonies than in the old land? No man can give an answer applicable to all cases. We can but generalise." Still, his generalizations painted a glowing picture. "This is certain," declared Long:

Squalor and abject misery is as unrealisable by born colonials as snow storms by Arabs or sandstorms by the Esquimaux. I hunted for black stereotyped poverty with diligence through thousands of miles of the Canadian Dominion, and so too through Queensland, New South Wales, Victoria and South Australia; but happily in vain. Haggard poverty is here, not there ... To the honest young labourer, and the intelligent craftsman, I unhesitatingly say, "Go." Not that all should; but those who are pinched, or expect to be; or are willing to sacrifice themselves for the sake of giving their children a better chance in life.[42]

General conditions in the coal industry also tempted McLachlan to consider emigration. In more than twenty years of work, he had found no economic security. The unions had remained weak after 1894, and new wage reductions were imposed in the mid-1890s. The coal miners still had not won recognition of the eight-hour day. In 1899 the coal industry adopted a formal sliding-scale system of wage adjustment, under which the miners' wages would rise and fall with changing coal prices. An unusually large boom occurred in the coal industry at the end of the 1890s, and there were increases in wages. But sceptics pointed out that under the sliding scale wages would never rise any faster than prices and therefore the miners could never win any real increase in their standard of living. Then, after 1900, the boom came to an end and a period of depression and unemployment settled over the coalfields. Wages fell and thousands of miners, recently drawn into the industry, were looking for other work. There was a notable increase in the number of Scottish coal miners signing up for the war in South Africa.[43]

For McLachlan, the selection of Canada was a chance one. He had considered Australia, and he and Kate were also attracted by the name of a hardrock mining town in the British Columbia interior, which was the object of a big boom at this time – Rossland, said the promoters, was about to become the new Johannesburg. In their Scotch brogue the McLachlans pronounced Rossland as if it was named for its roses, and, although they never saw it, the daughters associated the town with flowers. But when the decision to emigrate was taken, the destination instead was Nova Scotia.[44]

"He wanted to better himself," his oldest son has recalled. "He knew he had to go somewhere, and this is where he landed." The Canadian government at this time was accelerating efforts to attract immigrants, with substantial results: in 1901 there were 55,747 immigrants; in 1902, 89,102; and in 1903, 138,660. There was an official preference for British immigrants in Canadian policy, and expanding companies regularly advertised in the Old Country for experienced industrial workers. It is likely McLachlan was recruited by the Nova Scotia Steel and Coal Company, which had a record of employing substantial numbers of British miners; subsequently he received advances from the company to arrange for the family's passage to Nova Scotia.[45]

As often happened in the movement of working-class families, the father travelled ahead. McLachlan did not leave until after the birth of his son in February 1902. The fact that his name has not been located in the extensive passenger lists for the emigrant ships out of Glasgow and Liverpool in these years, adds credibility to the story that he secured the cheapest possible means of passage across the North Atlantic, probably on a tramp steamer, and consequently escaped official notice.[46]

After McLachlan had left, there was some conflict with the Greenshields family. Kate's mother and father hoped that their daughter would abandon the coal miner and return to the family home. Jean McLachlan, then almost eight years old, never forgot the hurtful scene. She resented the choice her mother was asked to make and proudly recalled her mother's reply: "I'd rather eat potatoes and salt with Jim McLachlan than have everything your money could buy me." Kate McLachlan sailed from Liverpool on a Cunard liner in the summer of 1902, with three daughters at her side and an infant boy in her arms.[47]

CHAPTER 2

Cape Breton

Blessed is he who has found his work;
let him ask no other blessedness.
He has a work, a life-purpose;
he has found it, and will follow it!

– Thomas Carlyle,
Past and Present (1843)

Sydney Mines

Cranberry Head sits low against the sky, a flat finger of land reaching out into the Atlantic Ocean. Around the peninsula the crashing waves have broken a jagged line of cliffs, where black bands of coal are plainly visible. The grey mists that roll in from the sea have added a salty taste to the coal smoke in the air. From the higher ground of Main Street there is a panoramic view of the colliery lands, surrounded on three sides by the ocean and presided over by the gaunt structures of the pithead installations.

After thirteen days at sea Kate McLachlan and the four children reached Quebec City and boarded the Intercolonial Railway for the long journey to Nova Scotia. The trains from the interior of North America came down the St Lawrence River, through the New Brunswick woods, across the farmlands of Nova Scotia, and over the Strait of Canso onto Cape Breton Island. They made their final stop at the terminal in North Sydney, where fishing schooners and coastal steamers docked along the waterfront. There the family was reunited, and, with the roaring sea on one side and the dark woods on the other, they drove on by wagon to their new home. Across the harbour in Sydney stood the slag heaps and brick chimneys of the Dominion Iron and Steel Company, the newest and biggest steel plant in the Dominion of Canada. To the young McLachlan children, the last few miles to Sydney Mines, located on the far north side of Sydney harbour, seemed an enormous distance through a wild and open country.[1]

Sydney Mines was a boom town at the turn of the century, and it was showing the effects of rapid development. In 1901 there were 3,191 people in Sydney Mines; by 1905 there were 6,000 people, 2,000 of them employed in the collieries; and by 1911 the population would reach 7,470. The roads and yards were rutted with mud and dirt, and water and sewer mains were under construction. Housing was in short supply for the new arrivals, and much of it, such as King William's Row which dated back to the 1830s, was old and shabby. Doctors feared outbreaks of smallpox, scarlet fever, and other contagious diseases; in 1909 the medical-health officer warned that the number of deaths from tuberculosis would continue to increase "while so many of our population live in unsanitary, ill lighted and ill ventilated houses."[2]

The McLachlans established themselves on Queen Street. They lived in one of two double dwellings made over from an old schoolhouse and then moved to Queen Street for the use of immigrant families. There were a few signs of improvements in the area during their time in Sydney Mines: in 1906 St Andrew's Presbyterian Church constructed a new building on Queen Street, and in 1907 the town added a plank sidewalk. Meanwhile, electric street lighting was being installed in the town; a street railway began service along Main Street and down Pitt Street in 1903, and in 1906 the Intercolonial Railway extended its line to the town. But to the McLachlan children, Sydney Mines still looked like a primitive frontier settlement because almost everything but the new post office and the town hall was built of wood instead of the customary brick and stone of British industrial towns.

Despite these misgivings, Sydney Mines was the oldest of the Cape Breton coal towns. In earlier centuries Spanish and Portuguese sailors had passed along these shores, French soldiers had taken coal from the cliffs, and Halifax merchants had opened shallow pits. Industrial development began in 1830, under the direction of a British company which received a grant of all the unexploited minerals of Nova Scotia and turned Sydney Mines into an outpost of the British industrial revolution. The General Mining Association (GMA) opened shafts to reach the deeper seams of coal, installed steam engines to pump water and lift coal to the surface, built company housing for the coal miners brought over from the Old Country, and constructed a railway to haul the coal to shipping piers at North Sydney.[3]

Beyond Sydney Mines, the whole province was living through an industrial revolution. The age of wood, wind, and water had come to a close in the Maritimes at the end of the nineteenth century; now the economic life of Nova Scotia was being refashioned by the new forces of coal, steam, and iron. Shipping, shipbuilding, and fishing had dominated the life of the southern and western parts of the province; now the northern and eastern sections were in the ascendant. Railway lines were linking a network of factory towns and urban centres, and the coal towns were central to this development. The Sydney coalfield itself extended down the coast past the Sydneys, through the New Victoria and Lingan area (later New Waterford), and into the Glace Bay district and the smaller towns beyond. On the west coast of Cape Breton Island, the Inverness coalfield was opening up rapidly with the construction of a new rail line to the Strait of Canso, where it connected to the Intercolonial Railway. On the Nova Scotia mainland there were two large and long-established coal districts in the northern counties. In Pictou County, the GMA had developed coal mines as early as it had in Cape Breton, and the mining towns there now included Stellarton, Westville, and Thorburn. And in Cumberland County, the building of the railways had helped create a booming coal industry in and around the town of Springhill. The state took a keen interest in these developments. In 1879 the adoption of the National Policy, with a specific policy of protection for the domestic coal industry, offered some compensation for the decline of the maritime economy and encouraged the entry of new capital into the coal industry. One result was the establishment of large new companies such as Dominion Coal, a Boston-based operation that took over most of the existing Cape Breton mines on the south side of the Sydney field in 1893. Meanwhile, some of the older provincial companies, such as Nova Scotia Steel and Coal, were also expanding. At the turn of the century the coal industry was at the centre of the province's development strategy, and the coal royalties accounted for as much as one-third of the province's revenues.[4]

In Sydney Mines a new stage in local history began in 1901 when the operations were taken over by the Nova Scotia Steel and Coal Company, the successful business which had built up the coal and steel industry in Pictou County. Now it was expanding its operations to Cape Breton Island to take advantage of the island's coal reserves and also to have better access to the iron ore at Bell Island in Newfoundland. Between 1900 and 1902 the company's annual coal production in Cape Breton more than doubled, reaching the total of almost one million tons. In

1904 Scotia, as the company was commonly called, even brought
Sydney Mines its own modest steel plant, prompting some citizens to
propose that the town's name be changed to Steel City or Stahlburg in
order to distinguish it from the better-known steel centre of Sydney
across the harbour. Men came to the coal mines and steel plants from
all parts of the Maritimes and Newfoundland. Like the GMA in earlier
days, Scotia recruited experienced mineworkers in England and Scotland and assisted them in bringing their families to the New World.

Along with other new arrivals, the McLachlans belonged to a vigorous enclave of British immigrants in Sydney Mines, and years later
McLachlan would be recalled as "one of the family" in Sydney Mines.
In 1911 almost 20 per cent of the population had been born in the
British Isles, a much higher number than in the coal and steel towns on
the south side of the harbour. Commenting on the influx of Old
Country miners, especially in Sydney Mines, one observer welcomed
them as "good workmen" and "good citizens." And, he added, "they are
unionists up to the hilt."[5]

The new immigrants helped each other make the transition to the
New World by banding together in self-help organizations of the kind
they had known at home. In Sydney Mines they established the Sons of
the British Isles Social, Literary and Provident Society; this group was
dedicated to the "spiritual, moral, mental, physical and social" improvement of their members. It pledged to provide support for new
arrivals as well as the sick, the unemployed, the destitute, and the
widows and children of members. In 1906 British immigrants also
formed the British Canadian Cooperative Society, which was organized
along the Rochdale principles of the Old Country and provided the
coal miners with an alternative to doing business at the company store;
the British Canadian eventually spread throughout the Sydney coalfield and became one of the most successful cooperative enterprises
in Canada.[6]

In one of his earliest published contributions to the Halifax *Herald*
during this period, McLachlan reported on the successful economic
activities of the British Canadian. He also defended the Sons of the
British Isles against charges of godlessness. Membership in this society,
he admitted, required no religious test; nor did it require a medical

certificate or allow applicants to be blackballed as did other fraternal orders. Instead, the society's objects required them "to look upon creed, color, nationality as links in the great chain that will eventually unite us into one common brotherhood."[7]

From the time of his arrival in Sydney Mines, McLachlan worked in the biggest of the Scotia mines, the famous Princess Colliery that stood below the town facing the ocean. The sinking of the Princess pit had taken eight years, and when it opened in 1876 it was one of the GMA's proudest achievements, widely known for the superior quality of the coal embedded in seams that ran deep under the ocean floor. The coal miners entered the pit first in a cage that dropped 690 feet down a shaft to the pit bottom. There they clambered into the wooden boxes of the riding rakes and coasted thousands of feet down sloping haulageways into the working sections of the mine. There was a heavy flow of water from the rock formations, and in 1902 Scotia installed a pump capable of lifting 500 gallons of water per minute. Ventilation could also be poor in the extensive underground workings, some of which were more than a mile from the pit bottom and 1,000 feet below the ocean floor.[8]

Despite the extensive machinery visible at the surface, the Princess was still an old-fashioned "room-and-pillar" mine where work was carried on much as in the Old Country. Production depended on the skilled handpick workers at the coal face, where the miners worked in a small, isolated space – known as a "room" – seventeen feet square and divided from the next room by a sixty-foot block – or "pillar" – of coal. The seams were relatively generous here, five to six feet in thickness; as a result, the men could usually work standing up. In their room the miner and his partner were responsible for cutting, shooting, and loading their coal, all the time keeping an ear tuned to the creaking timbers that held the shale and stone of the roof in place.

McLachlan's experience in the industry gave him a recognized place in the occupational hierarchy of the mine, and this in turn contributed to his emergence as a leader among the coal miners. Indeed, although he was still in his thirties when he arrived in Sydney Mines, McLachlan was by local standards a veteran of the coal industry. Child labour was accepted as a matter of course in the coal industry; in 1902 there were almost 800 boys employed in the Nova Scotia coal mines, about 10 per

cent of the workforce, and this number had increased to more than
1,000 by 1910. According to more detailed data gathered by a royal
commission in 1907, almost half the mineworkers at the Scotia mines
in Cape Breton at this time were under twenty years of age, and almost
three-quarters were under thirty.[9] The younger men readily turned to
experienced workers such as McLachlan for the benefit of their knowledge of the industry. Increasingly, the miners also looked to men such
as McLachlan for a new kind of leadership in union matters.

The Provincial Workmen's Association

Unions were not new to Cape Breton Island at the turn of the century.
The earliest managers of the GMA, Richard Smith and Richard Brown,
had complained about the independent ways of their colliers, and in
1900 Sydney Mines still remembered the upheavals of the 1860s and
1870s, when troops were sent up from Halifax to enforce wage reductions, put the coal miners out of their homes, and break their strikes.
"The Yahie Miners," a local industrial folk song directed at strikebreakers, dated from this period and was based on a similar north of England
song, "The Blackleg Miners."[10] When Robert Drummond, the first
grand secretary of the Provincial Workmen's Association (PWA), carried his organizing efforts to Cape Breton in the summer of 1881, he
found fertile soil for union ideas. In the space of eight days he was able
to establish eight Cape Breton lodges, including one at Sydney Mines.
"Arriving at Sydney Mines," he wrote, "it was found that the Union
contagion had spread, and Sydney Mines was not to be exempt from
its attack. A Union was formed without any opposition."[11]

   Most of the Cape Breton coal miners at the turn of the century were
new to industrial life. Many were the descendants of the Scots who had
come out of the Highlands two or three generations earlier; for several
decades they had been moving out of the backlands and outports of
the island and into the coal districts. Others came from Prince Edward
Island, New Brunswick, and mainland Nova Scotia or across the Cabot
Strait from Newfoundland. There were also Cape Bretoners returning
from western Canada and the United States, and immigrants from Italy,
Belgium, Poland, and the Ukraine as well as England, Ireland, Wales,

and Scotland. As in other parts of Canada, those coming from industrialized countries often played a leading part in the organization of unions. In their cultural baggage British immigrants in particular often carried ideas about the proper relations of labour and capital.

In the history of labour leadership in the coal industry in North America, it is notable that some of the most influential leaders were British immigrants. John Laslett has pointed out that the miners' unions in North America belonged to a transatlantic world of labour reform. Although local conditions differed, the home country experiences and perceptions of immigrant leaders played a part in shaping labour traditions in the New World. In the case of Nova Scotia, the three most significant leaders were immigrants from Scotland, but they had left home at different stages in the development of Scottish labour history and brought differing assumptions and ideas to the local situation.[12]

Robert Drummond, the founder of the Provincial Workmen's Association, had come out from Scotland as a young man to work in the mines. By 1879 he was employed as a company clerk in Springhill, when he was outraged by an unjustified reduction in the coal miners' wages. He took the side of the coal miners in their strike that year, and the result was the creation of a coal miners' union, the PWA, that became the most successful labour organization of its time in Nova Scotia. In 1888 Drummond even took the word back to Scotland, where he argued for the advantages of a centralized body such as the PWA over the "feeble, flickering uninfluential 'local unions'" of the Scottish coalfields.[13] In the pages of the *Trades Journal*, a newspaper established in 1880, Drummond promoted the image of the coal miner as a responsible and deserving citizen. In alliance with the Liberal politician W.S. Fielding, Drummond engineered a substantial body of legislation in the 1880s, including new safety laws and the right to vote in provincial elections. Drummond was less active in confronting employers over economic issues, but the individual lodges themselves often engaged in protracted disputes.

Like many early union leaders, Drummond believed that the colliers and the coal operators had fundamentally common interests. The key statement among the PWA's "Objects" was the first one: "to advance

materially its members by promoting such improvement in the mode
of remuneration of labour as the state of trade shall warrant or allow,
and generally to improve the condition of workingmen morally, mentally, socially and physically." Sharon Reilly has aptly described Drummond
as "the Alexander MacDonald of Nova Scotia," and the outlook of the
"independent collier" was probably never more succinctly stated than
in the motto adorning the PWA's badges and rituals: "None Cease to
Rise but Those Who Cease to Climb."[14]

Drummond's PWA fell apart in the 1890s, largely over the issue of
the truck system at the company stores. This was the system that
allowed the coal companies to hold back wages in order to pay off the
miners' bills at the company stores. There were sound economic reasons for introducing the credit system in regions and industries where
cash was scarce and work was seasonal, but the company stores also
gave employers a powerful opportunity to manipulate prices, exercise
favouritism, and extort profits. A common grievance among the coal
miners was that under the truck system they often received little or no
cash for their labour, thus compounding their dependence on the
companies. Coal miners had protested by organizing cooperative stores
and patronizing independent merchants. As the coal industry grew
more prosperous and less seasonal in the 1880s and 1890s, there were
growing objections to the company stores, both from the coal miners
themselves and from the local middle class. It was argued simply that
men deserved to be paid in the coin of the realm rather than in
allowances and stoppages at the company office. Indeed, payment of
wages in cash had been one of the main recommendations advanced
by the Royal Commission on the Relations of Labor and Capital when
it reported on labour conditions in Canada in the 1880s.

To the surprise of many PWA members, Drummond took a strong
stand against legislation to end the truck system in the coalfields. His
opposition was essentially ideological and was based on the values of
independence and manliness associated with the myth of the independent collier. Drummond argued that the coal miner, like any other
responsible citizen, must have the right to sign away his right to be paid
in cash: "What! are we men, or are we weaklings? Must we be guarded
like imbeciles lest we do ourselves harm?"[15] But Drummond was out

of step with the mood of the coal miners. The Cape Breton lodges broke into open revolt, some even took steps to affiliate with the Knights of Labor, and in 1898 Drummond was forced to step down as grand secretary. By 1899 there were only two or three lodges in good standing and less than one thousand members. Still, Drummond continued to be a public figure, for the provincial Liberal government had given him a lifetime appointment to the Legislative Council. Moreover, as publisher of the *Mining Record* he commented regularly on developments in the coal industry.

John Moffatt, who became grand secretary of the PWA in 1898, had been a spunky young Ayrshire coal miner when he was brought to Cape Breton in 1882 to work in the GMA coal mines. Almost at once he quarrelled with mine manager Donald Lynk at Lingan over the accepted hours of work; as he later recalled, "I told Mr. Lynk in the argument that he had brought people out from Britain to make slaves of them."[16] Moffatt then tried to organize a lodge of the PWA, but he was blacklisted and went to work in the coalfields of mainland Nova Scotia. He did not return to Cape Breton until after the formation of the Dominion Coal Company in 1893, which was opening up new mines on the south side of the Sydney coalfield. In the town of Dominion, Moffatt became a pillar of the community: a temperance man, church elder, school commissioner, and officer of Golden Rule Lodge of the PWA.

As grand secretary Moffatt faced the challenge of rebuilding the union out of the ruins of Drummond's association. It would need to be a union strong enough to stand up to the new consolidations, such as the Dominion Coal Company, which now dominated the industry. Moffatt initially had some success. In 1900 the PWA accepted a sliding-scale arrangement with the coal companies, and in a time of rising prices this resulted in several wage increases. By the time of the Grand Council meeting in September 1903, the PWA was experiencing a revival. Membership was close to 7,000 men, organized in 34 separate lodges, including several among factory workers, railwaymen, and retail clerks.

Among the new lodges were Thistle and Ingot, which had been organized by steelworkers at the giant new Sydney steel plant. Here the revitalized PWA faced its greatest test. In efforts to shore up the company's financial condition, in October 1903 Dominion Iron and Steel cut wages sharply and dismissed hundreds of workers. The following summer the steelworkers went on strike in an effort to win back these losses. The coal miners' lodges in Cape Breton took up collections at the pitheads and marched through the streets of Sydney to demonstrate their solidarity. Determined to reopen the plant, the steel company appealed to the government to send in the militia. The soldiers camped out at the steel plant, armed and ready to disperse pickets and protect strikebreakers. The PWA backed down.

Although the PWA requested the government to appoint a royal commission to investigate the situation, it received instead the attentions of the deputy minister of labour. The young William Lyon Mackenzie King, who was beginning to earn an international reputation for his expertise in solving labour disputes, helped negotiate an end to the strike. As was typical of many of King's efforts, it turned out to be a bleak defeat for the union. The wage cuts remained in place and the PWA was forced to accept the blacklisting of twenty-eight union leaders. Following this confrontation, many union members began to look for ways of strengthening their union.[17]

After Drummond and Moffatt came McLachlan. When he joined the PWA and began attending meetings at the hall on Main Street, Drummond Lodge was also going through a troubled time. In 1901 there had been only a handful of members and no delegates were sent to the Grand Council. In 1904 it was reported that one of the officers had absconded with the lodge's funds. But the influx of new coal miners into Sydney Mines was breathing life into the lodge, and recent immigrants such as McLachlan were beginning to play an active part in the meetings. In 1904 he and others voted to contribute more than $1,000 to the strike fund for the Sydney steelworkers.[18]

Ironically, Drummond Lodge, named after the founder of the PWA, was becoming known as a centre of rebellion against the traditional conservative policies and outlook of Drummond's organization. Drummond himself drew attention to the development in caustic comments in the *Mining Record*: "Some wise men from the east, in other words some recently arrived Scotsmen, have taken possession of the PWA lodge at Sydney Mines, and are trying to introduce some old, new fangled notions. Some of these base their claim, to be heard, on the fact that they have sat at the feet of Keir Hardie, whose strong and only prominent characteristic is his oddity. He may be a smart man in his way; he is decidedly outre. And so are his following."[19]

The reference to Hardie was provoked by a letter to the Halifax *Herald* a week earlier in which McLachlan, writing under the pseudonym "A Miner," supported political action to obtain state-sponsored old age pensions, as had been achieved in Britain. Neither doctors nor lawyers in Parliament had protected the interests of the miners, Hardie had argued, and McLachlan recalled some of Hardie's short early morning speeches to the coal miners as they made their way to the pits: "Mind your own business, men: no one can have so much interest in your affairs as you should have yourselves." Besides thinking about labour politics, the rebellious "Drummondites" were also proposing a constitutional amendment to provide for a general membership vote on the election of the grand secretary. "The PWA has been of great benefit to the working class of this province," McLachlan admitted; unfortunately, it was also the case that "to suggest that it needs modifying shall be to many like trade union heresy."[20]

After Drummond's attack on the lodge, McLachlan replied in kind. He described Drummond's accusation against "recently arrived Scotsmen" as both inaccurate (only one of the lodge offices was filled by a Scotsman) and irrelevant: "Neither do the members of Drummond lodge meet as Scotchmen, or Canadians or Hottentots, but as trade unionists, and they leave the appeal to men's prejudices about nationality, creed and color to be made by antiquated and discarded trade union leaders."

Drummond had also charged that Scotland had little to teach Nova Scotia about unionism. McLachlan's response summarized the achievements of the Lanarkshire miners following their great defeat in 1894 – since then the vast majority of the miners had joined the union, they had forced the coal owners to meet with them, and they had fixed a minimum wage, established an eight-hour day, and adopted a five-day week. Besides all this, they were sending young members to Ruskin College, Oxford, on scholarships, they were contributing towards the

cause of labour representation in Parliament, and they were maintaining hundreds of thousands of dollars in their strike fund. By comparison,
he charged, the PWA, with its 8,000 members, had little to boast about
after twenty-seven years – according to the last report of the Grand
Council, there was much spending on expenses and regalia for the
officers but only meagre benefits for striking members and a remarkably puny bank balance of only $1,613.22.[21]

When Drummond soon after stated that steady work at existing
wages should enable most miners to "make provision fit for a prince,"
this seemed to prove that the founder of the PWA was out of touch with
conditions. "Was he ever in a mining town?" McLachlan asked:

> I wonder what he thinks caused the deformed legs, the drawn-up
> shoulders, the fallen-in chest and the 'clanny blinks' on the work-
> ers of such a town? Did he ever stand at a pit mouth and watch
> the men come up, and notice how very few are two-score and ten?
> Before they reach that age they generally get a 'narrow place' in
> the graveyard. It is not steady work that causes such results, but
> oppressive work, filthy and abominable surrounding, vitiated air,
> and a continually long-drawn-out cannibalism that in the mad
> hunt for profits sucks the very life out of the mine worker.[22]

As McLachlan had predicted, the Drummond delegates to the Grand
Council meetings in September 1906 proposed numerous reforms to
the organization of the union. This included a reduction in the size of
the Grand Council, a secret membership vote on contracts, and a
general election of officers by the membership. One of the Drummond
delegates, James Dorsay, proposed that the Grand Council take steps to
initiate the eight-hour day in the mines – "voluntarily" and "without
the consent of the government"; the date for inauguration of the
eight-hour day was to be 1 May 1907, a day on which the PWA lodges
were to come out on parade and continue to do so on every first of May
afterwards. None of these proposals was successful, but the reformers
were gaining a hearing for their case for renovation of the PWA.[23]

Of all the proposals from Drummond Lodge, the most controversial
was an amendment to the statement of the union's "Objects" in Article

2 of the constitution. The reformers proposed that the original "Objects" be changed to read: "to advance materially its members by promoting such a mode of remuneration of labour as to do away with competition among the workers for jobs and to ensure to the workers the unrestricted enjoyment of the entire results of their toil, and generally to improve the condition of workingmen, mentally, socially and physically."

Compared to Drummond's original text, this was an aggressive statement. Where Drummond's constitution had sought to gain for the coal miners "such a mode of remuneration of labour as the state of trade shall warrant or allow," the reformers now proposed that the miners' goal should be identified as "the unrestricted enjoyment of the entire results of their toil." And whereas Drummond had proposed "to improve the condition of workingmen morally, mentally, socially and physically," the reformers entirely omitted "moral improvement" from the list. Indeed, the amendments also proposed that the whole fourth paragraph, which undertook "to foster habits of thrift, industry, economy, and sobriety among its members," also be deleted.[24]

Drummond himself never forgot the terms of this debate within the PWA. And McLachlan was no doubt uppermost in his mind when he wrote scornfully years later: "By some alien agitators the fourth clause of the Constitution, referring to thrift, industry and sobriety, has been violently assailed and the question asked: 'What has a trades union to do with thrift, industry, economy or sobriety?' Were I asked to re-write the Constitution over again, in the light of a long experience I might give the clause ridiculed the first, the most prominent place – in Article 2 – Objects."[25]

McLachlan counted himself an advocate of the dignity and self-respect of the individual coal miner. But the manly virtue of the breadwinner also required an economic foundation. His views on this debate are heard most fully in a letter published in the labour columns of the Halifax *Herald* in December 1906. Here he took up the case of the lowest-paid men in the coal mines as a test of the morality and efficiency of the industry and, by implication, of the union as well: "At this Christmas time, I want to put up a plea for a little more justice and mercy for the poor and heavy-ladened in this province who are known

by the unkindly name of 'cheap labor.'" Combining economic analysis
and moral exhortation, he constructed an eloquent plea on behalf of the
men whose "cheap labor" stood at the foundation of the coal industry:

> Let us take a man that earns $1.38 per day. On such a wage a man
> with a wife and family of say, five children, must work every day he
> can. Let the number of days worked in the year be 300. That would
> give him $414. Let us see how he lives, and how he fares, on such a
> wage, and ask, which of his instructors – preacher or politician, who
> generally tell this poor man that it is his own thriftlessness and lack
> of industry that keeps him poor – would step into his overalls for
> one short year in order to give him a practical lesson in thrift,
> industry and economy? Or, will either dare to say that they could
> teach this poor man any thing about these virtues?
>
> Three hundred days work at $1.38 per day gives $414.00. He
> spends on rent, each year, $30; coal and light, $16.90; insurance
> for seven persons, $19; taxes, $3.00; doctor, $4.60 ...

The list went on, relentlessly listing only the necessities – boots and
clothing, laundry soap, and school books – with nothing allotted for
"rum, church, theatre, politics, or trades unionism." "A daily paper for
himself, a few toys for his children, or fifty cents spent on a little present
for his wife, are luxuries beyond his reach." In the end there was a
balance of precisely $271.70 remaining to spend on food for the year.
"Or to each of this family of seven, $38.81. Or 10 1/2 cents to provide
for each of these seven, for each day of the year. Or three meals a day
at 3 1/2 cents a piece."

Such wages fell far short of the wage that trade unionists such as
McLachlan saw as the necessary economic foundation of family life.
Here, in the vivid form of a family budget, McLachlan was preaching a
Christmas sermon on public morality and political economy:

> As we approach December 25th, our minds turn to Him who is
> the greatest of all men who appeared on this earth. His greatness
> appeared in this, that He refused to rise above His people in
> material things, and taught emphatically that no man had a right

to ask other men to shoulder a burden that they themselves would not move with one of their fingers, and that those who were greatest ought to be servants of all. To teach economics of that kind is to preach the very antitheses of what is practiced to-day.

It is said that "God giveth to all men liberally, and upbraideth not." This province, on account of the "great need for cheap labour," cannot afford to treat the $1.38 man liberally, or can the preacher or the politician afford to let the poor man believe that his poverty is caused by anything else than his lack of industry and thrift.

"None Cease to Rise but Those Who Cease to Climb?" McLachlan had rejected the prevailing wisdom of the PWA. A philosophy of self-improvement and respectability offered no answer to the basic problems of the underpaid worker:

Not only is he robbed of the wealth that he creates, but is insulted by having free lectures thrust upon him about thrift and industry by trade union leaders and clergymen, who generally don't get out of bed in the morning for hours after this poor man is in the harness ... We trade unionists at least might refrain from asking this man to come into our union in order to get lessons on thrift and industry. We might leave to the men who never take off their coat the job of insulting this poor man, by asking him to do the impossible.[26]

Drummond, Moffatt, and McLachlan – each was influenced by the myth of the independent collier, but they responded in different ways. Drummond was the oldest of the three men, and his outlook most faithfully reproduced the ideal of the self-respecting, self-improving collier. Moffatt admired Drummond and his ideals, and, from confrontations such as the steel strike in 1904, he drew the cautious lessons of accommodation and conciliation. McLachlan himself was only five years younger than Moffatt, but he had left Scotland later, and in Cape Breton he recognized the familiar shape of the crisis of the independent collier.

McLachlan could see that the same changes that made this philosophy obsolete in Scotland a generation earlier were now being re-enacted in the New World. The rise of large, integrated coal and steel companies, the exceptionally rapid growth of the industry, the flood of new workers into the labour force – these all represented a challenge to the established outlook of the PWA. If it had ever been valid, the notion of an equal partnership between masters and men was difficult to recognize in Nova Scotia at the turn of the century. As a coal miner and trade unionist, McLachlan had already seen the future – the ideal of working-class solidarity.

"A Miner"

"The Spirit of the Lord is upon me, because He hath anointed me to preach Glad Tidings to the Poor." In the summer of 1905 McLachlan underlined these words in a volume entitled *From Bondage to Brotherhood: A Message to the Workers.* This is a text in the tradition of Thomas Carlyle and John Ruskin, offering guidance to "the social reformer and true religionist." The chapters echo the the moral critique of industrial capitalism: the degradation of productive labour trapped in the "House of Bondage" and the corruption of the "Charmed Circle" where the rule of Mammon is maintained by the prostitution of church and state. Against this stands the dream of what "might be": a free and equal brotherhood, the reign of love, a regenerated England, the "Land Beautiful." The author's "Message to the Workers" concludes with a clarion call for mass conversion: "The 'general strike' of the workers, the day when they shall follow the advice of Jesus, and 'Call no man Master,' now looms ahead of us ... If you workers so willed, the General Strike and General Cooperation would gain England for you in a week, and turn it into Paradise in a twelve-month."[27]

This was evidently another well-used item in McLachlan's book collection, for the margins are marked and the pages fall open to key passages. At this time it is clear that McLachlan was thinking about social issues primarily in moral terms that were rooted in religious tradition and amplified by writers such as Carlyle. In Sydney Mines, McLachlan was also extending his intellectual horizon. Through his reading of books published by the Charles H. Kerr publishing house in Chicago, he was becoming familiar with the kind of social criticism that placed emphasis on the class struggle as the moving force in history. McLachlan never abandoned the ethical socialism that he had come to know in Scotland, but he was sharpening it with the harder edges of an economic analysis based on the socialism of Karl Marx and his followers in the labour and socialist parties of the Second International.

During these years McLachlan made a sustained contribution to contemporary debates on the labour question in Nova Scotia through contributions to the Halifax *Herald*, the big province-wide daily newspaper that was eager to attract working-class readers. Letters from McLachlan and other contributors were often printed under headings such as "The Labor Herald" and "The Miners' Herald." By 1908 several of McLachlan's contributions were appearing above his own name, but in most cases he used the pseudonym "A Miner." His subject matter included local controversies over mail service, housing conditions, and other matters in Sydney Mines, and on one occasion he commented that his contributions were a kind of hobby: "I only write for fun and have to dig coal for a living."[28]

But there was a good deal more to his writing than this. In these letters in the provincial press, McLachlan was establishing his presence as a working-class intellectual of unusual ability and trenchant perception. In forceful language, and with reference to local conditions and controversies and appeals to authorities who included Carlyle and Burns, Adam Smith and John Stuart Mill, McLachlan was working out the moral and economic implications of his own developing philosophy of labour radicalism.

One of McLachlan's interventions in the *Herald* resulted in an interesting discussion of working-class intellectual life. This letter was published under a heading that challenged the PWA's claim to be advancing the intellectual life of the coal miners: "'Improve the Condition of Workingmen Mentally.' But What is the PWA Doing to Carry out That Plank in its Platform?" Here McLachlan proposed that every lodge maintain a small collection of books for the use of the members. In the proposal each lodge would appoint a librarian and set aside $100 for the nucleus of a library. This would give young miners constructive ways to spend their evenings: "A healthy environment can be created in every lodge room with good books, the *Herald* and other good newspapers, and good, healthy, honest

discussions on questions that are of vital interest to workingmen. This
would make the young miner leave the rum shop in a way that few
would dream of." McLachlan even suggested some relevant titles to fill
the bookcase – he singled out the works of Carlyle, Ruskin, and Tolstoy,
as well as Adam Smith's *Wealth of Nations* and Karl Marx's *Capital.* The
debates and discussions he proposed were both intentionally provocative
and relevant to the controversies within the PWA – "Should labor be
remunerated always as the state of trade shall warrant or allow?" and "Is
production for profit, or production for use, most likely to create a high
moral standing in a community?"[29]

The idea of the libraries was enthusiastically endorsed by the editors
of the *Herald,* who shortly afterwards offered such a collection of books
as the prize for an essay competition on the contemporary labour
question. The set questions for the competition were: "What are the
most pressing needs of labor in Nova Scotia today? And what is the
most practical and feasible way of obtaining those requirements?" The
prize – "a library of 50 to 100 of the best books of the day on all phases
of the labor question, in a handsome hardwood and glass case" – was
to be presented to the PWA lodge selected by the winning author. The
proposal was attributed only to "one of our most forceful contributors," but McLachlan himself was identified by name as one of the
authorities who would help select the contents of the library.[30]

Entries in the contest included a submission by McLachlan, which
was published as Letter No. 1. Among his themes were the defence of
freedom of expression and the necessity of political action for workers.
The essay can also be read as an early statement of McLachlan's belief
in education as the basis for working-class independence:

To my mind, the needs of labor in this province are much the same
as the needs of labor everywhere. The two most pressing are
education and independence of thought and action ...

The lack of independence in thought and action is, to my mind,
the towering calamity of workingmen. The need of old age pensions, eight-hour day, workman compensation act, and better
housing, are dwarfed into utter insignificance when compared

with the great need of workingmen being freed from the fear of offending their employers with their opinions and actions ...

Workingmen feel their economic bondage, and act accordingly, even though they sing about "Britons never being slaves!"

The most practical means to secure better education for the workers was to establish a system of universal, compulsory education to the age of sixteen, paid for by the state. And, McLachlan added, it must be "secular as to character – with the idea of the universal brotherhood of man substituted for the brutal jingo spirit that now pervades the text-books used in school. Better far for Canada to pay an army of teachers to put brains into her people, than to pay an army to blow the brains out of other people."

Abolition of the workers' fear of self-expression, McLachlan concluded, required workers to take "united political action" and "dictate how the wealth of their country may be spent." Ultimately this argument depended on an optimistic view of state intervention for the full protection of working-class citizenship:

It is the right and duty of the state to secure the well-being of each of its members.

The belated theory, that every man has the right to [do] what he likes with his own, is now being invaded on every hand.

In factories and mines, for the safety of life and limb, the state interferes with the internal arrangements and does not allow a man to do what he likes with his own.

As a natural sequence, it is up to the workers by their united political action to extend this principle of the regulation of industry by common rules, to the determination of how much education a worker shall receive, and also to the right of every man to earn a living who is prepared to work.

Meanwhile, the workers already had some good advice in the pages of the Halifax *Herald* itself: "The *Herald* is now pointing out how the workers of today may help to bring about a more rational mode of action in their trade unions – get a library and use it!"[31]

More than thirty contest entries were published in the pages of the Halifax *Herald* during the following months. In the end no outcome was reported, probably because the administration of the competition, which involved votes and discussions in the PWA lodges, proved impossible under the conditions of growing turmoil within the union.

Afterwards, McLachlan continued to contribute to the *Herald*, especially on the subject of the deficiencies of the PWA. In a continuing round of debates, he took the position that the PWA "has not yet started in to even play at trades unionism." For instance, McLachlan charged, few copies of the official reports of the Grand Council were distributed: "In this lodge are five hundred members, and we have received one copy of the report, so that if each member is allowed one day to go over this report some of us shall be reading ancient history when our turn comes." He went on to point out inconsistencies and irregularities in the financial statements. On another occasion McLachlan objected to the PWA's willingness to consider restrictions on the miners' traditional practice of suspending work following fatal accidents: "Surely the last shred of human rights was bartered away when the PWA even condescend to discuss this."[32]

Recent struggles by the much larger unions of engineers in Britain and printers in North America demonstrated that large financial resources were needed to fight the battles of labour today: "Could the PWA really give each of her members a one dollar bill without becoming bankrupt?" When another correspondent replied, under the name "Observer," with a defence of the PWA, McLachlan ridiculed the idea that a labour union could depend on "droll stuff" such as "backbone," "common sense," and "public sentiment": "I tell you 'Observer' that when a strike is on, it takes more than 'common sense' to satisfy the craving hunger of children, and 'public sentiment' is very poor stuff to feed a striker on. You see I tried living on 'public sentiment' once during a strike, and I found it the kind of feeding to put a point on a fellow's elbow." He followed this reference – probably to the 1894 Scottish miners' strike – with an interesting catalogue of other failures of "public sentiment": "Was not 'public sentiment' with the steel strikers? And they were beaten. With the Boers? and they were beaten. Against William Lloyd Garrison, and [they] hounded him to prison and very near to death? yet he came out on the top. Was it not 'public sentiment' that nailed

him to a tree, whom ages and nations have called 'The Son of God?'
No! No! 'Observer.' Give me the dollars and the fellowship and mutual
support of the millions of trades unionists on this continent."[33]

Above all, McLachlan's charges against the PWA focused on the
union's mistaken idealism about the relations of workers and employers and its complacency towards the plight of fellow workers:

> If anyone should get up in the PWA and propose that this organi-
> zation should join in the great international working-class movement
> that is demanding that labor shall receive all, and control all, it
> produces, you are generally met with the old stale platitudes, "The
> owners and this union have always got on well together" or "We
> don't care to have any outside interference" or someone yawns
> and wearily asks "what need we bother with the rest of the world,
> if there is no work for these fellows here, give them their cards and
> let them look for a job somewhere else."

Such attitudes were nothing but "mammon's gospel preached to wage-
earners by the PWA leaders," condemned in McLachlan's view on both
moral and economic grounds: "Christians, how long will you deny your
Master by serving mammon? Materialists, how long are you going to
sacrifice your true welfare to this brute dividend-hunting god?"[34]

The independence of working-class action was also McLachlan's
theme when he considered the enactment of the Industrial Disputes
Investigation Act in the spring of 1907. This new Dominion legislation
was the brainchild of the ambitious deputy minister of labour, Mackenzie King, and it was widely regarded as an exemplary piece of progressive
legislation that attempted to reconcile the claims of workers, employers,
and the public in labour disputes. In his critique McLachlan argued that
the origins of this law were to be found in the prolonged Lethbridge coal
miners' strike of 1906 that was finally settled when wintertime coal
shortages forced the government to intervene and arrange a settlement.
The new legislation was nothing less than a form of revenge for this
humiliation: "These gallant 500 Lethbridge miners gave the government
such a trimming down, that it determined to pass an act to take the wind
out of the sails of the trade unions."

According to McLachlan, the act's provision for the postponement of legal strike action, a provision that has become one of the cornerstones of twentieth-century industrial relations, could be interpreted as a legal formula for the disarmament of the working class:

> The act when read through might be thus paraphrased: This act guarantees to trades unionists the right, which your father won for you after many sufferings, and imprisonments, and martyrdoms, to fight unitedly tyrannical and oppressive masters, but on and after the 22nd day of March 1907 you shall not start any fight till you give your master thirty days to entrench himself, during which time you shall hand to your master your gun and cartridge-pouch, which your master shall empty at his leisure after which you can have your gun and pouch and the battle can proceed.

Under the new law, the minister of labour became a kind of "labor Czar," with the power to say when and where the act would be applied. Rather than assisting striking workers, McLachlan predicted, the compulsory features of the act would be used to limit the unions' freedom of action: "The real purpose of the government is apparent. They see the rising tide of democracy that threatens to sweep them from the power and wealth that they now enjoy, and they are starting in to stem the rising tide."[35]

Perhaps the most remarkable short essay published by McLachlan in the *Herald* during this period was written on the occasion of Burns Day in January 1908. "Where Would Robert Burns Stand Today in Labor Problems?" Here was a question that seized his imagination because, like his references to Carlyle, it reached deep into his own cultural background.

"When reading Burns one cannot but speculate on what would have been his political and theological whereabouts had he lived in this twentieth century," McLachlan wrote. "The greatest political question of this century is how to distribute the enormous wealth that the ingenuity of the last century enables the world now to produce." He went on to outline the shape of the twentieth-century labour question in terms that tell us much about McLachlan's perceptions:

Twenty years from now, the names, grit and tory, shall have given place to the names that shall designate those, on the one hand, who have acquired the wealth and capital, and have the right and privilege to hand out the jobs when, where and to whom they like, and just so long as they please. And on the other hand, a property-less wage-class who have no legal right to demand room to make a living on the planet, but have to humbly wait the pleasure of their economic masters before being admitted to the means of life.

There was no doubt where Burns would stand in this struggle:

Where Burns did take a stand on any question, it was invariably on the side of the oppressed. His sympathies were broad and international, and he dreamed of the time when "man to man the world o'er shall brothers be." I unhesitatingly believe had Burns been alive today he would have been the poet laureate of the international socialist movement.

Interestingly, much of McLachlan's discussion was devoted not only to discussing the "political whereabouts" of Burns but also to considering his "theological whereabouts." McLachlan was struck by the ways in which Burns had satirized and ridiculed the prevailing church and defended the free-thinkers of his time:

Burns' theological whereabouts, had he lived to-day, I question if it would have been anything different from what it was. It was a kind of a half agnostic, half universalist. Writing to Mrs. Dunlop, he says: "If there is another world, it must be for the just, the benevolent, the amiable and the humane. What a flattering idea, then, is a world to come. Would to God I as firmly believed it as I ardently wish it!"

The higher criticism and the tearing the old Bible to tatters would not have helped Burns or his like to settle the disturbing elements that enter into their religious opinions. The baffling questions are not answered either in or out of the Bible yet.[36]

Such references to theological and religious doubt were characteristic of a generation of social reformers who found that religious
tradition and established churches were failing to provide satisfactory
answers to the troubling issues of social reform. But they also gave rise
to accusations, and within a few years McLachlan was being publicly
accused of godlessness as well as socialism. Within the PWA McLachlan
took the view that religious rituals had no place in union proceedings,
a position that contributed to his reputation as a non-believer. "As
regards religion," wrote one of McLachlan's detractors in 1910, "Sydney
Mines knows that he is not a believer in the Christian faith. At one time
in Drummond Lodge, of the P.W.A., at the opening ceremonies where
a prayer is always read, he declared that there was no one to pray to."[37]

In McLachlan's view, however, the attraction of socialism was based on
principles of moral and economic justice, and it did not require anyone
to abandon religious belief. His own writings during this period, almost
as a matter of course, included appeals to the authority of the Creator and
the Son of God. Yet, for McLachlan, the appeal of organized religion was
less powerful than it had been in his youth, and there is no evidence he
took an active part in the Presbyterian or Baptist churches in Sydney Mines
during this period.[38] Perhaps he was becoming, like Burns, "half agnostic,
half universalist." Whatever the case, it was during these years in Sydney
Mines that McLachlan was becoming a socialist.

Socialism

In Canada the river of socialism ran in many streams. There were those
who came to socialism out of the great nineteenth-century crusades
represented by the Chartists, the Cooperators, the Abolitionists, and
the Knights of Labor. Others were moved by Christian socialism, by the
enlightened intellectual views of the Fabian socialists, by the utopianism
of experimental communities, or by the direct action of the syndicalists.
In Britain, socialism could be found in the independent labour parties
and in demands for public ownership of resources, associated with Keir
Hardie and the British Labour Party. There was also the Marxist socialism of Britain's Social Democratic Federation and of North America's
Socialist Labor Party. In the United States there was as well the socialism

of Eugene Debs's Socialist Party of America, founded on the extension of republican and egalitarian principles to economic life.

All of these streams contributed to the Canadian socialist tradition, but by 1905 a single organization had emerged as the most widely heard voice of socialism in Canada. "Labor produces all wealth, and to the producers it should belong," declared the platform of the Socialist Party of Canada (SPC): "The interest of the working class lies in the direction of setting itself free from capitalist exploitation by the abolition of the wage system, under which is cloaked the robbery of the working-class at the point of production." The "irrepressible conflict of interests" between capitalists and workers would culminate in a struggle for "possession of the power of government – the capitalist to hold, the worker to secure it by political action." Within a few years McLachlan counted himself among the several thousand comrades across the country who belonged to the Socialist Party of Canada.[39]

Socialist ideas were carried to the coalfields at the turn of the century both by new arrivals and by returning Cape Bretoners who had come under socialist influence in other parts of the Maritimes, western Canada, or the United States. Socialist groups existed in Glace Bay in 1904 and in Sydney Mines in 1905. Local socialists supported independent labour candidates who ran for the House of Commons and the provincial legislative assembly. Among the earliest visiting agitators were the teacher and journalist Henry Harvey Stuart of New Brunswick, founder of the Fredericton Socialist League (one of the local groups that entered the SPC) and, on another occasion, the Alberta coal miner Charles O'Brien, who would be elected to the provincial legislature as a socialist candidate in Rocky Mountain in 1909. There was sufficient concern among the local clergy, Catholic and Protestant alike, that a series of sermons and lectures were directed at the socialist menace in 1904 and 1905. But by 1906 the Halifax *Herald* was reporting on "the Startling Growth of Socialism in Cape Breton": "Now the subject is discussed all over the island, not only in English, but in French and good old-fashioned Gaelic."[40]

McLachlan's contributions to the *Herald* in 1906 already carried a socialist flavour. The earliest direct evidence of his immersion in socialist ideas is found in one of his 1907 letters to the *Herald*. Again, the occasion was a response to the mistaken views of Robert Drummond, writing in one of his "Rambler" columns in the *Mining Record* (which, McLachlan complained, was delivered to him by a neighbour "who appears to take a diabolical delight in afflicting me"). As usual, McLachlan charged, Drummond was guilty of deliberate thick-headedness in his inability to distinguish between socialism and its various caricatures. The "'dividing-up' bogey," often used to discredit socialism, was just another form of "rampant individualism" rather than an expression of "socialist collectivism." What socialists proposed to do when they came to power was very different: "They propose to take and use the earth, and machinery, to produce all the good things that men need in this life, without paying any rent, interest or dividend to any idle owning class." The benefits of economic life would, accordingly, be redistributed:

> They would take the children out of the mines and factories, and send them to school, and would at least double the number of teachers. Instead of giving teachers a shabby-genteel wage, they would make their profession the most honored in all the land. They would immediately raise the reward for "unskilled labor" to enable them to live pure, healthful and comfortable lives. They would at once reduce the hours of labor to eight each day, to be followed by the further reduction as the necessities and comforts of life would accumulate. They would sell the products of labor back to the workers at actual cost, only allowing for a percentage to pay for public services.

The underlying principle, McLachlan concluded was a moral one: "No able-bodied man shall be allowed to live on the labor of others."

All this, McLachlan argued, was no more than the working out of an historical logic: "When kings had divine rights, then king-law was the go. When the church ruled, then church-law was the proper thing. When landlords ruled, then laws were made for the benefit of land-owners. When capitalists rule, then the right thing is to make laws for their especial good. When the workers come into power they in their turn shall forget those that ruled before them. Then labor-law shall be all the push."

One common objection to socialism, McLachlan noted, was the question of how individual achievement, even genius, would be rewarded under socialism:

> I reply, just like the rest of creation. He shall get all he can use, and no genius ever yet went whining among his fellows for an extra dose of this world's goods. The greatest scamps on earth have always got the greatest material rewards. Compare Humphry Davy, Michael Faraday and James Young Simpson with Rockefeller, Harriman and Carnegie; Moses with Pharaoh, Paul with Nero, and Jesus with Brigham Young. How could you reward Francis of Assisi, George Fox or Leo Tolstoi? If any man gets all he can use, where is the sense in asking for more?[41]

This was McLachlan's first full-blown defence of socialism, but there was continuity with his earlier thinking: the same arguments for the education and elevation of the working class, the same universal vision of a standard of comfort and security, the same vindication of economic justice and moral rewards. The Old Testament had long since pronounced on the value of labour: "By the sweat of thy brow shalt thou earn bread." And Carlyle had repeated the revelation in modern terms: "We must all toil or steal, howsoever we name our stealing."[42]

What was new here? For McLachlan, socialism offered the appeal of a practical program of economic organization that would take the rewards of economic life out of the hands of the profiteers and redistribute the earnings to the producers. Instead of offering injunctions against idleness and appeals to fair-dealing, a socialist government would guarantee the achievement of economic democracy through the actual structures of production and ownership. Working-class hegemony would then produce its own legal regime and "labor-law" would take its place as the rightful successor to preceding codes of law. From this perspective, it was the workers' historic responsibility to take their place as the governing class.

From the evidence in McLachlan's collection of books it was also clear that he was reading a considerable amount of socialist literature during his years in Sydney Mines. One major source of reading material for Canadian socialists were the small cloth editions published by Charles H. Kerr, the socialist publishing house in Chicago. McLachlan's collection included at least nine Kerr editions. Among those which could be dated to his years in Sydney Mines were a text by the German social-democratic leader Karl Kautsky, *Ethics and the Materialist Conception of History* (1907), and another by the American socialist John Spargo, *The Common Sense of Socialism* (1908). There was also a 1908 Kerr edition by A.M. Lewis entitled *Evolution Social and Organic.* Other titles from this period included a 1904 edition of John Stuart Mill and a 1905 edition of Adam Smith, both of which he quoted from in a *Herald* letter in 1907, a 1905 edition of John Ruskin, and a 1907 history of the slave trade. A 1908 edition of writings and speeches by Eugene Debs was inscribed to him by Alex MacKinnon, one of the early socialists in Glace Bay.[43]

In the course of this reading McLachlan was also finding practical applications for Marxist theory. In the pages of the *Labour Gazette*, for instance, the monthly report issued by the Department of Labour, there was abundant material for analysis. In a short essay written in February 1908, McLachlan used this material to offer a brief statistical study of the significance of labour power in the Canadian economy.

He began by noting that in 1907 there had been a total of 149 strikes, involving 34,694 workers and more than 600,000 days of lost working-time: "If we suppose each of these strikers represented a family of three persons, that would mean that a city of well over one hundred thousand inhabitants walked around three weeks and produced not one of the articles that they daily required to use in order to sustain themselves. Men don't quarrel like this to provide themselves with holiday amusement. There was something at stake which appeared very real to these workmen before such a struggle could take place." McLachlan then turned to statistical reports on the income of Canadian wage earners: "I think those 34,694 strikers have some excuse for their fight when a cruel competitive system forces them to march through life along the edge of the chasm of poverty, and any small reduction in wages may at any time precipitate them into its woeful pit." He surveyed reports of the immense productivity of modern capitalism, concluding: "These things being so, I don't wonder at working men going on strike sometimes, but I do wonder at the modesty of the demands made."

But, as a socialist, McLachlan took his analysis beyond an endorsement of trade unions and wage struggles. The wage earner was not only the victim of unfair exploitation by capital; capital had also robbed the producers of their economic citizenship:

> The capital in its entirety was produced by the workers alone. All the capital in Canada is being continually renewed by the workers of Canada, and more, the workers alone are increasing it every year. Yet wage earners don't feel hurt that they have no vote to say where and for what purpose this capital which they are continually renewing and increasing shall be used. Without his voice or consent a wage earner's time is often consumed in creating what John Ruskin termed "illeth," as opposed to wealth.

Examples of unproductive "illeth" sprang to mind: "Every morning 4,250,000 men get out on the parade grounds of the world and practice how to stab and shoot other men," and "little girls shall have their time and energy consumed producing rouge and pomade to paint and grease those who drive a traffic in shame." And "those who own the capital today care not whether it be used in the production of wealth or illeth if the dividend is forthcoming." In the end the workers must challenge the very logic of capital and assert the morality of production for use over production for profit:

> What the working men of Canada want to do under such circumstances is not to strike for a few cents on an existence wage, but vote the entire means of life away from its present owners to themselves. Take the right to vote the men into the positions of superintending the carrying on of production. We could pay them better than present owners pay them, and would but be exercising the right in industrial affairs that you now use at the town council election. We also want the right to vote whether we shall consume our time and labor in the production of wealth or illeth.[44]

All of this study and discussion was also producing organizational results. In August 1907 the Cape Breton socialists formed a local of the Socialist Party of Canada. It is not known if McLachlan was among the thirty-one charter members of this original Cape Breton local. But his voice was heard in a debate on socialism at meetings of the PWA Grand Council in the fall of 1907, where he spoke in support of independent labour politics. "I am a socialist," W.J. MacKay stated, "but not of the cut-throat or bombshell type, but of the kind that would add to the world's wealth and not to the individual's. As workingmen we are not receiving that part of our labour which rightly belongs to us." A few minutes later McLachlan, in attendance as a delegate from Drummond Lodge, followed with a declaration of his own political position:

> I am dissatisfied with both parties and will not vote for either one. I believe that neither one has the interests of the workingmen at heart. And when the time to vote comes I simply stay at home. If either church or state depended on my vote, they could both go to wreck, for I would not support a party apart from the work-ingmen. I have only one view on the question. There is but one party for workingmen and all workingmen will sooner or later find their way into that party.[45]

By the time a separate Sydney Mines local of the SPC was organized in the summer of 1909, McLachlan had emerged as a leading figure among the local socialists. "I had a grand crowd at Sydney Mines," wrote party organizer Wilfrid Gribble following a visit there:

> Com. [Comrade] McLaughlin [sic] opened the meeting, which is always a great help. Gave them the best I had to give and they took it in fine style. I spoke till my voice squeaked and still they wanted more, so we had a song, the Red Flag. Still they stood, so gave them a short talk on the Party and how we are forming a local; told them they would be given an opportunity to join, but urged them not to unless perfectly clear about it. The application form was spread out on a box and twenty-five signed, a number of nationalities

being represented. It kept me busy striking matches so they could see to sign.

This "glorious night" continued long into the evening at the McLachlan home – "where Mrs. McLachlan treated us to a bountiful spread." Gribble came away impressed by the local comrades, finding "quite a number of well-posted men in Sydney Mines." In general, he noted that the members of the new Cape Breton locals organized in 1909 were "no sudden conversions, but men and women who have been merely waiting for the assembly to be sounded."[46]

"As for James B. McLachlan he is an avowed socialist of the socialist party of Canada, one of whose principles is the overthrow of trade unionism."[47] Such charges of anti-unionism were commonly made against labour radicals such as McLachlan. In theory the Socialist Party of Canada was a thoroughly revolutionary organization dedicated to the achievement of political power on behalf of the Canadian working class. Its main work was to educate workers for the coming struggle, and organizers such as Gribble maintained that under capitalism only "palliatives" were possible: "It is too late for reforms and it is too late for reformers."[48] But in practice the SPC was a highly decentralized organization. The Vancouver headquarters issued the *Western Clarion* and received reports, but in the individual branches local issues and local leaders determined the shape of their activity. While the party's revolutionary rhetoric discouraged middle-class social reformers from flocking into the ranks, it also helped guarantee the working-class character of its constituency.

Most of all, the ideology of "impossibilism" was limited by the fact that most of the party's membership was made up of working-class activists such as McLachlan, who were deeply involved in the struggle to promote unions in their workplace. McLachlan shared Keir Hardie's view, which he expressed at the meetings of the Trades and Labour Congress (TLC) in 1908, that dogmatic divisions between labourites and socialists did not help the larger cause. The ultimate aim was the socialist commonwealth, but the immediate objective was a strong union.[49]

The United Mine Workers of America

More than 400,000 members strong, the United Mine Workers of America (UMW) was the biggest union of its time in North America. In Nova Scotia the most far-reaching proposal of the reformers in the PWA was the idea that their union could be strengthened by joining the UMW. The idea had been discussed as early as 1901. On learning of the existence of the PWA in 1901, Samuel Gompers of the American Federation of Labor (AFL) and John Mitchell of the UMW had discussed the possibility of bringing the PWA into the international union. This approach was already proving successful in expanding the AFL's presence in Canada, as local unions were encouraged to join up with the international union in their trade. By 1902 the AFL unions were strong enough to take control of the Trades and Labour Congress.[50]

In Gompers's view, "the United Mine Workers of America make no distinction as to Canada and the United States. It seems to me that the miners' union referred to, as well as all unions of miners, ought to be a part of the United Mine Workers of America." Mitchell was in agreement but somewhat more cautious: "If there were any possibility of our organization obtaining jurisdiction over the miners of Canada without entering into a contest with the national union now established there, we would do so; but unless they would withdraw from the field or amalgamate, we would not care to spend any money in a fight with them for control, as we have a wide field yet remaining uncovered in the United States."[51]

Later that year the AFL organizer in Canada, John Flett, made an organizing tour of the Maritimes and took the opportunity to meet with John Moffatt. The suggestion of affiliation was reported to the Grand Council of the PWA in September, and, according to Flett, Moffatt "was instructed to procure full information, with the view of affiliating at an early date with their brethren across the line."[52] Although the UMW in 1903 authorized its officers to "open negotiations towards getting the Canadians connected with our organization," these early discussions produced no results.[53]

Still, the idea had been planted that the PWA could be strengthened by joining an international union. In August 1904 the PWA lodges in

Cape Breton even appealed directly to the UMW to contribute $10,000 to support the steelworkers in their battle against the Dominion Iron and Steel Company that year.[54] Although the UMW failed to send money to the steelworkers on this occasion, Nova Scotia coal miners continued to look to the UMW for support. One reason for the interest in the UMW was that the union had already entered western Canada, where District 18 was organized in 1903. Among the westerners there were more than a few Nova Scotia coal miners. One of them was Peter Patterson, a Scottish immigrant who had worked in Nova Scotia and then gone west to Alberta and British Columbia, where he became the international board member for District 18. In 1906 Patterson was sent to Nova Scotia "to try to get the miners of that field to affiliate with the U.M.W. of A." Patterson presented the case for the UMW to members of the Grand Council and was voted the thanks of the delegates.[55]

The following year the issue was again on the agenda at the Grand Council meetings. McLachlan, who attended for the first time that year as one of six delegates from Drummond Lodge, proved one of the strongest supporters of the UMW. "I do not feel that there is much force in the arguments produced against affiliations of this kind," McLachlan argued. "I am strongly in favour of international unions. There should be no dividing line between workingmen, and the more international we become, the greater power will we be able to exert." McLachlan's support for the UMW was not surprising, for it was based on the principled internationalism of socialist thought. He was perhaps also thinking back to the model of cooperation he had seen in Britain, where the Miners' Federation had extended support to the Scottish miners in 1894. In the course of the debate McLachlan seconded a proposal that a UMW organizer be invited to visit the individual PWA lodges "and inform them fully of the aims and objects and workings of their organization" in preparation for a vote on amalgamation with the UMW. The motion was lost.[56]

But there was always more to the crisis in the PWA than the single issue of international unionism. At the 1907 Grand Council, for instance, discussions continued to focus on such issues as the eight-hour day, weekly pays, death benefits, and general wage increases. McLachlan himself served on a five-man committee on wage increases, where he advanced the Drummond Lodge proposal for a minimum wage of $2 per day for all mine labourers.

The reform movement also continued to support proposals for improvement of the PWA. McLachlan spoke in favour of reducing the number of delegates to the Grand Council, a reform that the Drummond delegates hoped would make the PWA a more efficient organization. In McLachlan's words: "We have to consider this matter from a business standpoint. There are a certain number of items on the docket. We have a certain time to discuss these matters. If every member spoke once he could only be allowed a very short time. Our coming here in such large numbers seems to me to be a waste of time and money. Large delegations become unwieldy and time is coming when the delegation of the PWA must harmonize with its business." McLachlan also spoke on the proposal for the election of the grand secretary by the membership rather than by the council. "Drummond Lodge has discussed this matter on several occasions," McLachlan argued, "and we cannot see any reason why there should not be a general election throughout the association for this office. We are a democratic institution. Other associations have general ballots for such offices."[57]

Later that year McLachlan acted as a spokesman for the local miners when he gave evidence before a provincial royal commission on miners' relief societies and pensions. The subject was close to the heart of a man concerned about his obligations to family and fellow workers – the distress of the widows, orphaned children, and aged and disabled men of the coal communities. When the commission held hearings in Sydney, McLachlan appeared as a delegate representing the men at the Princess Colliery. As in other matters, his knowledge of Old Country conditions helped provide a standard of comparison for assessing local conditions.

As they existed, McLachlan pointed out, the relief societies that dated back to the pioneer days of the PWA in the 1880s were failing to meet the needs of the miners. Allocations were rarely adequate because the societies were financially weak and were anxious to conserve their funds for fear of big accidents in the future. But voluntary pithead collections were not an equitable way to provide assistance for the incapacitated man and his family: "Personally, I do not believe in such a system; it works out unfairly, and very often depends on the popularity of the man." While the various local relief societies might be strengthened by "amalgamating the weak and strong societies together, merging them all," McLachlan favoured more radical proposals such as an old age pension for all miners at the age of sixty. In addition, McLachlan argued, "there should be some provision made where a man leaves a widow; there is no provision now for that excepting what is done through the Relief Fund." McLachlan also advocated the creation of an emergency fund to assist the victims of major disasters. In this he made it clear that the costs of compensation must be seen as a necessary charge upon the coal industry: "My opinion is that any such Fund should be raised from direct taxation on the industry; I believe the industry should stand that."[58]

At the end of 1907 the UMW leaders were still hopeful that the PWA could be persuaded to join the international union as a single body. Certainly there was more support for the UMW than was apparent at the Grand Council meetings, and Patterson requested that organizers be sent into Nova Scotia at once. Yet an appeal to the UMW from the Springhill miners, who were locked in another of their recurrent struggles with the Cumberland Railway and Coal Company, received a mixed response. Some members of the executive board favoured a $1,000 contribution to the strike fund; the board approved a $500 donation, but the money was withheld when news arrived that the strike had ended.[59]

Meanwhile, inquiries about entering the UMW continued to reach UMW headquarters in Indianapolis, and in February 1908 President Mitchell appointed Patterson to return to Nova Scotia. At the same time, a group of conditions was approved by the board: individual PWA lodges would be permitted to enter the UMW without the usual charter fees, two organizers would be kept in the field, one of them to be a local person, and a separate district would be established once sufficient locals were organized.[60]

Patterson toured the coalfields during February and March 1908. These were the stormiest months of the year, and most of his time was spent in two of the largest coal towns, Springhill and Glace Bay. He met first with Moffatt and other officers, and then proceeded to visit the individual lodges. Delegates from the seven lodges working at the Dominion Coal Company mines attended a meeting organized by Ironsides Lodge. As an elected officer of Drummond Lodge and a UMW supporter, McLachlan probably travelled over to Glace Bay to attend this crucial meeting. There it was decided that votes would be taken in the lodges "and if in favor of the U.M.W. of A., that they would call a convention and turn the organization over in a body to the U.M.W. of A." Patterson was impressed by the amount of support for the UMW and wrote an optimistic report: "I believe that about two-thirds of the men of the P.W.A. were willing to turn over at once and many who will not be members as long as Mr. Moffett [sic] is in office would join us. I feel that there should be some one in that field and attend their convention and help to work up the feeling in the weak places but there may be some danger of a fight with the Dominion Coal Company for recognition but I think all the other companies will work with us without any trouble."[61]

During May and June 1908 there was optimistic correspondence about prospects in the Maritimes. "The movement has progressed so far that there is no doubt about having those men affiliated with our union," wrote the new UMW president, T.L. Lewis. He urged AFL Secretary Frank Morrison to ensure that Flett confined his efforts to organizing other trades in the Maritimes while the UMW proceeded with its cautious campaign to win over the PWA. Accordingly, Morrison cautioned both Flett and Paddy Draper at TLC headquarters and reported back to Lewis that "Organizer Flett is a capable and careful organizer, and is not likely to take any action that would interfere with the negotiations now pending."[62] As late as October 1908, Lewis was still pursuing the same strategy. Writing to a concerned union supporter in Cape Breton, Lewis observed that the UMW had refrained from organizing unorganized mines in Nova Scotia "for the reason that I thought it best to have the P.W.A. come over in a body and then work to have the unorganized mines brought into the Union ... So far as the P.W.A. is concerned, I have no desire to do anything that will divide the forces of organized labor in that section of the country."[63]

Meanwhile, McLachlan had an opportunity to demonstrate what could be achieved by bringing the coal companies to the bargaining table. In December 1907 members of the PWA lodges at the Scotia collieries had asked for an increase of 15 per cent in rates. When the request was refused, they applied for the establishment of a conciliation board under the Industrial Disputes Investigation Act. In June 1908 a board was appointed under the chairmanship of the Queen's University political economist Adam Shortt, who spent much of July 1908 in Cape Breton. Initially the company refused to participate in the proceedings, but Professor Shortt was able to convince its president to allow his officials to appear before the board. The coal miners themselves were represented by PWA Grand Secretary John Moffatt and a committee of three men from the northside lodges, of whom McLachlan was one.

Negotiations continued for almost two weeks, including two days for the inspection of conditions in the mines. In the opinion of Shortt, the proceedings "were conducted on the whole, with much moderation and with exceptional forbearance." In the end, on 1 August 1908, there was an agreement, which was ratified both by the president of Scotia and by a meeting of the subcouncil of the PWA. The agreement involved numerous adjustments, some involving increases and others reductions in rates. Wages for the lowest-paid men, who were earning as little as $1.25 and $1.38 per day, were increased to a minimum of $1.45. Rates for machine runners were reduced and those for falling stone were increased. Shortt observed that the changes helped establish "more equitable conditions throughout the collieries," and he praised "the very admirable spirit in which the committee representing the miners faced a very trying situation."

McLachlan could be pleased that the hearings had resulted in immediate gains for more than 200 of the lowest-paid men in the Scotia mines. He had also shown that an aggressive approach on the part of the coal miners was not doomed to failure. Despite his misgivings about the purposes of the Industrial Disputes Investigation Act, in this case the miners' use of the legislation had avoided a strike and even established a de facto form of collective bargaining. The company had been forced to back down and negotiate with its employees and, in the process, both sides had made some concessions for the sake of an agreement.[64]

It was an interesting episode. For, despite their differences on many issues, it appeared that PWA loyalists such as Moffatt and reformers

such as McLachlan could work together in the miners' interests. The
tide was beginning to turn in favour of the reformers, it seemed, and
McLachlan may have been tempted to believe at this stage that the PWA
was about to reform itself. Eagerly, he awaited the meetings of the
Grand Council in September.

Rebellion

By 1908 McLachlan was recognized as one of the leaders of the reform
movement in the PWA. He had served as a delegate to the Grand
Council and represented the miners at public hearings, and his voice
was also heard in the public press. Early that year he was elected as
recording secretary in Drummond Lodge, and later in the year he was
a delegate to the fateful September 1908 session of the Grand Council.
Throughout the year McLachlan watched in frustration as the campaign to reform the PWA ran aground on the stubbornness of the
entrenched officers.

The future of the PWA was the great controversy of 1908. The old
union was under growing pressure from agitation in the lodges. Indeed,
some lodges were already declaring in favour of the UMW. When a
special meeting of the Grand Council was called in Halifax on 21 May
1908, the PWA officers attempted unsuccessfully to ban "disloyal"
lodges from attending, and McLachlan objected that Moffatt arranged
for two hand-picked members from Drummond Lodge to participate
in the meetings. That session turned into a showdown between PWA
loyalists and UMW reformers, and there were repeated calls for Moffatt
to step down as grand secretary.

At this session the PWA reached a crucial decision – a referendum
vote would be held among the membership on the question of "putting
the PWA in better condition or join the UMW of America." The vote
of thirty-nine to five on this motion should not be interpreted as a
measure of UMW support in the Grand Council; indeed, reformers
such as McLachlan himself were not in attendance on this occasion.
But the decision to hold a membership vote was regarded as evidence
of a conciliatory spirit in the PWA and indicated a desire on both sides
to bring the issue to a head.[65]

When the vote took place in due course on 24 June, more than 5,000 ballots were cast: 2,860 for the UMW and 2,448 for the PWA. Support for the UMW was highest among the lodges in Cumberland and Cape Breton counties, while the Inverness and Pictou lodges had favoured the PWA. In the Sydney coalfield the vote was 1,888 for the UMW, 1,296 for the PWA. Overall, there was a margin of 412 votes for the UMW.[66]

The PWA officers were surprised by the strength of support for the UMW and refused to recognize the result. At Drummond Lodge, McLachlan found that the grand secretary declined to accept the bills for expenses in connection with the referendum. This was his first indication that the PWA planned to repudiate the referendum result.[67]

When delegates assembled in September 1908 at St Paul's Church hall on Argyle Street in Halifax, observers believed that the Grand Council was almost evenly divided between those pledged to support the referendum results and those determined to uphold the PWA. Almost at once a controversy exploded over the seating of delegates. According to the UMW sympathizers, ten of their delegates were denied accreditation; in addition, five questionable PWA delegates were seated. The excluded delegates were asked to withdraw from the hall, but they refused to leave and insisted on remaining in attendance, although denied voice or vote. The UMW supporters had won the referendum, but they were outmanoeuvered by the PWA officers and failed to control a majority among the delegates at the Grand Council meeting.[68]

The critical vote took place on the question of adopting the minutes of the May council meeting, which had authorized the referendum. In Moffatt's view, the May meeting had no authority to call the referendum; both the meeting and the subsequent June vote were illegal. It was a cynical decision, for it was obvious that if the PWA had won the vote, Moffatt would not have repudiated the outcome. The vote was twenty-eight for adoption of the minutes and forty-seven for taking no action on them. Then came a secret ballot on changing the constitution in order to allow dissolution of the PWA by a majority vote of the membership. When this produced a vote of thirty-two for dissolution and fifty-one against any change, the UMW faction protested that the ballot box was being stuffed since there were only seventy-nine eligible voters in the hall. A standing vote produced little difference – a count of twenty-eight for the constitutional amendment and forty-nine opposed.[69]

With this decision to overturn the results of the referendum, the fate of the PWA was sealed. McLachlan stood and began to read out a resolution regarding the June referendum and the subsequent actions of the Grand Council, but the minutes of the meeting are interrupted at this point.[70] As the Grand Council adjourned, the reformers protested that the rulings of the officers were biased and that the proceedings were "unfair and tyrannical" and did not conform to "the spirit of true unionism, principle and consistency." It was expected that locals of the UMW would be formed almost at once and that there would be court battles over division of the PWA's defence fund and other assets.[71]

In the end, the reformers' strategy of working within the PWA had ended in failure. After several years of attempts to reform the PWA and to bring about a peaceful amalgamation with the UMW, they had won the support of the majority of the coal miners. But the entrenched leadership of the PWA had refused to bow before this demonstration of reform sentiment. Perhaps the reformers had overestimated their own strength; possibly they should have prepared the ground by securing a constitutional amendment at an earlier stage. But certainly they had underestimated the resistance of the old guard in the PWA. The lines were drawn, and the UMW would not enter Nova Scotia without a fight.

Shortly after this last bitter meeting of the Grand Council, McLachlan had more pleasant duties to perform. Keir Hardie was now famous throughout the English-speaking world for his achievements in Parliament, where there were currently no fewer than twenty-nine Labour MPs. Now he was in Canada, indeed in Nova Scotia, to attend the annual meeting of the Trades and Labour Congress, which was held that year in Halifax. Following the Halifax meeting, Hardie made a visit to the Cape Breton coalfields, where he and his wife and daughter were hosted by the McLachlan family.

At the Halifax meeting, Hardie assessed the conditions of recent British emigrants with a critical eye and encouraged the TLC to keep British workers fully posted on industrial conditions in Canada: "There are agencies at work there to induce immigration to Canada by misrepresentation, and he strongly advised the appointment of a permanent agent on the other side to 'check every lie' of this sort." He also urged the TLC to become more involved in political action: "Labour must, said he, enter the political arena if it is to successfully combat the forces opposed to it." To the applause of the assembled delegates, who were locked in bitter debates between pure and simple unionism and doctrinaire socialism, Hardie urged socialists and unionists to overcome their differences: "While he was personally a Socialist and hoped for the triumph of Socialism at the earliest possible time, he desired most of all to effect a united trades unionism."[72]

Hardie's own account of the trip to Sydney Mines was brief: "We went to Cape Breton and saw something of mining life, and did not find the conditions attractive."[73] As it turned out, Hardie's visit was the occasion for a controversial episode that demonstrated one of the obstacles facing the local labour and socialist movement. In Sydney Mines, McLachlan and other supporters had arranged a Sunday afternoon meeting in St Andrew's Church hall. But when the advertised time arrived, the church elders appeared in force and barred the way. According to the account in the Sydney Post, "the arrangement was cancelled when the lessees learned the nature of the meeting to be a labor demonstration." As a result, the assembly was forced to move to an open field near Trinity Church on Queen Street, where Hardie addressed a big crowd from the back of a wagon. McLachlan acted as chairman for the meeting and "performed his duties in admirable manner." Besides introducing the speakers, who included British Columbia and Alberta UMW leaders Peter Patterson and Frank Sherman, McLachlan expressed his "disappointment in being shut out of the hall."[74]

When he stood to speak Hardie thanked McLachlan for the invitation and commented that, despite the difficulties in arranging for the visit, "my anxiety to see this part of Canada and my old friends induced me to come." Hardie went on to mention the official welcomes he had received from the provincial premier and local mayors elsewhere in Nova Scotia and was "exceedingly sorry that the managers of the hall where he was advertised to speak showed such a narrowness of minds." Most of Hardie's speech was devoted to a review of the progress of labour reform in Britain, especially the achievement of a minimum wage and the eight-hour day. In reference to the struggle between the PWA and the UMW, he repeated the same message of unity he had given at the TLC meetings: "No good results would come by sectionalism."

As for socialism, Hardie argued, it was "not irreligious as many think": "We are a brotherhood and worship one father. It holds that the lands of the country should not be possessed by private individuals but for the people." The speech was loudly applauded by the crowd. The local reporter, who described Hardie as "a gentleman of striking appearance and brimming over with sincerity," observed that "his remarks could well have been addressed within the sacred walls of any church on Sunday."[75]

It has been suggested that these events marked McLachlan's final breach with the established church. By one later reminiscence, he never returned to church after this episode: "He didn't break with the church; they broke with him."[76] Certainly the appeal of organized religion was in decline for McLachlan throughout this period, when his loyalties were occupied by the causes of organized labour and social reform. Meanwhile, Hardie's visit had reinforced McLachlan's view that the church was not the only obstacle facing labour reformers at this time. The weakness of the miners' union and of labour politics in Nova Scotia compared poorly with the developments in Britain. Hardie's visit vividly demonstrated the distance that separated the progress of labour in the Old Country from the backward conditions in Cape Breton.

CHAPTER 3

1909: Bend or Break

And when the strike is over we'll march in grand array,
And we'll ring ten thousand cheers for the U. M. W. A.
And the scab will go under like the man before the gun,
And the miners they will flourish when the dreary strike is WON.

–"Arise, Ye Nova Scotia Slaves,"
United Mine Workers' Journal,
5 May 1910

District 26

He stands at the far left of the photograph. It is an official occasion and he waits awkwardly at attention for the photographer. His sharp features are softened by bushy brows and a bristling moustache. For the moment the fire in his eyes is frozen by the camera. He looks out sternly and with assurance. This is James Bryson McLachlan, secretary-treasurer, District 26, United Mine Workers of America.

The winter of 1908 was a season of hopeful discontent in the Nova Scotia coalfields. In December the Springhill miners were the first to quit the Provincial Workmen's Association and reorganize themselves as a local of the United Mine Workers of America. At Sydney Mines McLachlan led 380 coal miners into UMW local 945, which received its charter on 8 January 1909. Other locals were chartered at Florence and Glace Bay, Bridgeport and Dominion and Dominion No. 6, New Waterford and New Aberdeen, Inverness and Port Hood, Chignecto and River Hebert, and Joggins and Westville. Originally the UMW had hoped to absorb the PWA as a single body and for this reason was reluctant to establish locals in Nova Scotia or approve the creation of a new district, but now the international union's cautious approach had been overtaken by events. Before the end of January 1909 there were twenty UMW locals in Nova Scotia.[1]

As PWA lodges began to disintegrate during the winter of 1908, Dominion Coal started to take action against the new union. In the pits managers singled out those who were known UMW men: drivers received the poorest horses for hauling coal and pickmen were banished to the oldest workings where earnings were low. At Dominion No. 6, one of the UMW strongholds, the mine shut down entirely until a small number of men rejoined the PWA. At meetings of the new locals, members reported the appearance of company police, detectives, and "spotters," some of whom were considered "just a little bit too fresh."[2]

The company's strategy was obvious, and McLachlan later described it in these words: "A system of victimization was put into force for the awful crime of becoming a member of the United Mine Workers, and resulted in a thousand men being locked out during our long Canadian winter." He further noted that "as soon as navigation closed in November, 1908, the Dominion Coal Company locked out one thousand men, and expected that zero weather and starvation would crush the spirit of revolt."[3]

Meanwhile, delegates from the UMW locals assembled at the YMCA building in Sydney on 2 March 1909 for the formal establishment of District 26 of the international union. McLachlan, together with four other delegates, served on the committee that prepared a draft constitution. The document began with a preamble largely borrowed from the parent organization:

> It must be conceded by all that coal has been a potent factor in the development of all other industries and has played an important part in spreading civilisation. Therefore, believing that those whose lot it is to daily toil in the recesses of the earth producing this most valuable commodity are entitled to a fair and equitable share of the wealth they produce, we declare the following to be the object of our organization:

> 1. to secure compensation fully compatible with the dangers of our occupation,

> 2. to establish our right to receive our pay in lawful money, to abolish the truck store system.

This was moderate language, radical only in comparison to that of the PWA. None of the objects listed in Article 1 was calculated to sound a note of alarm:

It is the aim of this union to improve the material, intellectual, and moral conditions of the toilers in and around the mines. We hold that these ends may be attained by securing better conditions in the mines, better compensation for the miners' labour, and by interesting them in the study of industrial and economic questions. We extend to all miners and mine labourers, without regard to race or colour, an invitation to unite with us that these ends may be attained.

To secure all necessary appliances for the preservation of the health and lives of the mineworkers.

To secure the enforcement of existing laws and when needed to secure the enactment of new laws in the interests of miners and mine labourers.

To demand that 8 hours shall constitute a day's work, and that all coal be weighed before being screened.

To use every honourable means of maintaining peace between ourselves and our employers, resorting only to a strike when all peaceable and lawful means of adjusting difficulties have failed.[4]

After the adoption of the constitution, there was the election of officers. Those elected were to serve for three months, until a general membership vote was arranged. In the discussion of Article 5 the delegates had examined the remuneration of officers cautiously. The president was to receive $90 a month and the secretary-treasurer $80 per month. It was proposed that other officers receive $4 a day for work in service of the district, but delegates reduced this to $3.50, which they considered "a fair average for a miner's wage, and considering that expenses were allowed in this connection, the remuneration was rather more than ample."[5]

As president of the new union, the delegates chose Dan McDougall. Two other names had been proposed for district president, but McDougall's election was unanimous. A big-hearted, gregarious Scotsman,

McDougall was an important recruit for the UMW, since he had originally been a strong supporter of the PWA. In Glace Bay, where he had worked since 1902, he was active in the Orange Lodge, served on the town council, and was the local union president at the Caledonia mine.[6] Meanwhile, the position of vice-president went to James B. Moss of Springhill. It was important to recognize the significance of the UMW stronghold in Cumberland County; Pioneer Lodge at Springhill was the largest single local in the district. Moss was elected by a large margin.

For the position of secretary-treasurer there were four nominations. Oliver Maddin of New Waterford and Michael Mullins of New Aberdeen withdrew, leaving William Watkins of Springhill and J.B. McLachlan of Sydney Mines. Both men were recognized as able local union leaders; both were known as supporters of the Socialist Party of Canada; both were British immigrants. The ballot produced twenty votes for Watkins and twenty-eight votes for McLachlan. The result gave the northside miners representation among the three main officers and probably also reflected the voting power of the more numerous Cape Breton locals.

For the McLachlan family, this was a time of change. For one, it was the end of McLachlan's life as a working miner. By the spring of 1909 all of the UMW officers, including McLachlan, had been placed on the blacklist and banned from working in the mines. McLachlan's election to one of the new union's full-time positions offered some economic security. On the other hand, because the post of secretary-treasurer carried considerable administrative responsibility, it would require McLachlan's presence at district headquarters in Glace Bay. As a result, in becoming a full-time union officer, McLachlan was also leaving the familiar surroundings in Sydney Mines. The family would be making a new life for themselves in Glace Bay.[7]

Glace Bay

Glace Bay was the biggest of all the Cape Breton coal towns – a sprawling community divided into a dozen neighbourhoods surrounding the individual collieries. The town took its name from the ice floes that blocked fishing boats in the small harbour in the springtime. Several companies opened coal mines in this area during the nineteenth century, but it was the arrival of the Dominion Coal Company that put Glace Bay on the map as the principal coal town on the south side of Sydney harbour. The population more than doubled from 6,945 people in 1901, when the town was incorporated, to 16,562 in 1911. There was an additional population of more than 10,000 people in the mining district that ran along the coast from Port Morien and Dominion No. 6 in the south to the booming New Waterford area in the north. To many observers, Glace Bay itself embodied the physical bleakness and social dependency of the early-twentieth-century company town. There were whole new neighbourhoods of company housing, and the town's first mayor was also the general superintendent of the company stores. Noted the *Canadian Mining Journal* in 1908: "Everybody in Glace Bay is either the servant of the Coal Company, or the servant of the servant of the Coal Company."[8]

Dominion Coal was the largest of the province's coal companies and belonged, like the Scotia company on the northside, to the new era of industrial capitalism in the coalfields. It had been created in 1893 by a merger engineered by a Boston financier, Henry Melville Whitney. Anxious to promote the coal industry and collect revenue, the province of Nova Scotia granted Dominion Coal low royalty payments and a ninety-nine-year lease of all the unworked coal reserves of Cape Breton Island. Under Dominion Coal, the Sydney coalfield expanded rapidly, and the balance of coal production in Cape Breton shifted to the Glace Bay district. Much of the output was shipped up the St Lawrence River on the company's Black Diamond line of steamers; after the turn of the century much of the coal production was also consumed at the installations of Whitney's Dominion Iron and Steel Company in Sydney. By 1909 the Boston financier had withdrawn from his Cape Breton interests, and Dominion Coal was under the control of an uneasy alliance of Montreal and Toronto financiers associated with the Bank of Montreal and the Bank of Commerce. In a few sharp words the reform-minded colliery doctor A.S. Kendall summed up the leading officers of the steel and coal companies at the time: "J.H. Plummer – an Englishman stubborn and cruel out of time and out of place in Canada even at that date. James Ross was a rich

Savage who arrived in Canada well equipped as an engineer but insensitive to needs of humanity."[9]

Leaving Sydney Mines for Glace Bay, the McLachlan family settled in a rented a house on Reserve Street, the main road leading into town from the smaller mining village of Reserve Mines. The McLachlan home was in a group of four houses, one of them occupied by the family of D.N. Brodie, an early Glace Bay socialist. He and Brodie would have a lasting association. Brodie had come to Glace Bay from Halifax a few years earlier to work as secretary for the YMCA there. By 1907 he had opened a small printshop on Union Street and in later years he would be known as the printer of local labour publications.[10]

There is more than one McLachlan family story of harassment by company police from this period. One of the younger daughters recalled that one night, when their father was not home, Kate heard noises at the back of the house: "A man was in the room and was searching about in father's papers. Mother was brave. She marched in, took this big man by the shoulders, and steered him out the door. And then locked the door."[11]

As secretary-treasurer McLachlan assumed his new duties with hopeful expectations. When fifty delegates from UMW locals assembled at a church hall in Sydney on 29 June, he read an optimistic report: "The growth of the new organization has been almost phenomenal when it is considered that it has practically all come about within the last six months." McLachlan reported that the union was "in a flourishing condition financially and otherwise," with approximately 6,000 members enrolled.[12]

But he also knew that District 26 faced difficult challenges. There was never any doubt that the coal companies were opposed to the UMW. The PWA's philosophy of industrial loyalism made the old union a safe choice for the coal companies, much to be preferred over the UMW. Shortly after the formation of District 26, the province's coal operators met in Truro to form a combination against the new union. They proclaimed publicly that the arrival of the UMW was "fraught with much danger to the Nova Scotia coal mining industry, and is likely to result in the loss of a large part of our trade to the Americans. It was further decided that the attempt of a foreign organization to control our mines should be resisted in every way possible." The cry of anti-Americanism was a predictable one, for Canadian workers across the country at this time were joining unions affiliated with the American Federation of Labor in large numbers. The PWA itself had never objected to the investment of American capital in the Nova Scotia coal industry, and thus it was easy for UMW leaders such as McLachlan to portray its opposition to American unionism as more self-serving than patriotic. For McLachlan, it was natural to regard the American coal miners not as "foreigners" but as brothers in a common cause – "the international solidarity of the working class."[13]

Meanwhile, the existing labour laws offered no help. Under Canada's emerging labour-relations system, there were no procedures for determining which union was to represent the coal miners. For their part, the PWA leaders asserted that, following the deliberations of a conciliation board, they had concluded an agreement with Dominion Coal in March 1908. This agreement did not expire until the end of 1909, and in the view of John Moffatt and the PWA leaders the coal miners were obliged to continue at work to fulfil their obligations.[14]

At the same time, District 26 was launching its own appeals to the Department of Labour. Under the provisions of the Industrial Disputes Investigation Act, conciliation boards were appointed to investigate charges of discrimination against union men at Glace Bay, Florence, and Springhill. At the hearings of the board concerning Scotia miners, where McLachlan appeared on behalf of the union, his old boss T.J. Brown, general superintendent of the Scotia operations, argued that the UMW was "a foreign corporation" that threatened the interests of the Canadian coal industry. McDougall, who sat as the union member on the board and filed a minority report, replied that the UMW was "an international organization"; its purpose was "to promote the welfare, advance the interests, bless the homes, and bring peace into the country where they locate." None of the boards recommended reinstatement of the men or recognition of the UMW. According to the majority report concerning Dominion Coal, issued in April 1909, "there were special circumstances which made the company's preference towards the PWA ... a natural and reasonable one." In vain the union had argued that "preference" for PWA men meant "discrimination" against UMW men.[15]

McLachlan was not surprised that Canada's labour laws had little protection to offer the UMW. In his view, the new law limited the workers' freedom of action and protected the employer: "As a matter of fact the act has taken away privileges from us that we did and should enjoy. It has not been beneficial to workingmen because it was never intended to be so." Before a "legal" strike could be called in a major industry such as coal, unions were required to make application for a conciliation board and go through a waiting period. But conciliation boards rarely sided with the union – such as the one at Scotia, where two judges wrote the unsympathetic majority report. Meanwhile, employers were fully entitled to ban unions and blacklist union members, hire strikebreakers, and make other preparations for a strike. And, if a company did decide to recognize a union, there was no guarantee that the favoured union would have the support of their employees.[16]

The PWA, McLachlan would always claim, had been voted out of existence. As far as the existing agreement with the coal operators was concerned, McLachlan argued that it was "between the employees and the company, and not with the PWA as such." Moreover, the discriminatory actions of the company had emptied the agreement of meaning:

Every man that was locked out for joining the UMW was locked out in violation of that agreement. The members of District No. 26 have always said, say so now, and will continue to say, that they are willing and anxious and ready to live up to every condition of the agreement until its expiration. But we demand that when the coal company violates the agreement that they should be prepared to meet us and adjust matters. This they have hitherto absolutely refused to do. We have had no and get no redress except "leave the UMW," and we will treat with you. Under such conditions what could we do? Every effort was made to make a settlement that men could possibly make. All the answer that came back to to us was leave the UMW and we will treat with you.[17]

From this point of view, the PWA had simply ceased to be a legitimate union when it refused to accept the outcome of the miners' vote in the summer of 1908.

In Glace Bay, meanwhile, Dominion Coal was fortifying its installations in preparation for a confrontation. Around the collieries the company erected fences, eight feet high, mounted with searchlights and barbed wire charged with 5,000 volts of electricity. Behind the fence, barracks were under construction for the use of strikebreakers. The PWA collaborated with Dominion Coal in arranging for the appointment of 625 special police, under the authority of the county council, to be used in the event of a strike. These special constables were to be drawn from a list which included both the general manager of the coal company and the grand secretary of the PWA.

In the course of the following year, some of McLachlan's hottest language was reserved for John Moffatt: "By birth a Scotchman; by adoption a Canadian; by nature a traitor; by profession a scab organizer; and by long and continued habit the arch-lick-spittle of the Dominion Coal Company." "The unique thing about this fight," wrote McLachlan, "is the transformation of a trade union called the Provincial Workman's Association, with a thirty years life behind it, into a scab organization that welcomes into its ranks imported strike breakers of every kind and description."[18]

McLachlan remained confident that the international union would live up to his expectations in the coming struggle. John Mitchell's early retirement as UMW president in 1908 was prompted in part by questions about his close ties with business and government. His successor, T.L. Lewis, had the backing of the substantial socialist membership in the UMW. "T.L." was not one to back away from a fight and proved to be a strong supporter of the new district. When he toured Nova Scotia in June 1909, Dominion Coal officials refused to meet him. Lewis warned that the companies' policy of non-recognition was unacceptable: "Unless the coal companies recognize the right of their employees to join any labour organization they wish and adjust the many grievances the men complain of, it will lead to but one result and that is a suspension of operations."[19] At a subsequent meeting of his executive board, Lewis outlined the Nova Scotia situation in detail, and the executive board authorized the spending of up to $25,000 a week to support the Nova Scotia coal miners in the event of a strike.

District 26 continued to invite the coal operators to meet with the UMW, but there were no replies. A final deadline was set by a district convention at the beginning of July. On the instructions of the convention, McLachlan sent a lengthy resolution to Prime Minister Sir Wilfrid Laurier denouncing the actions of the Dominion Coal Company in recruiting a special police force and putting up electrified fences: "BE IT THEREFORE RESOLVED, that this Convention with its delegates representing over seven thousand wage workers of the Province of Nova Scotia, place itself on record, as being strongly opposed to such uncalled for and barbarian actions on the part of said Company in a civilized country ..." The prime minister returned only a brief acknowledgement.[20]

On 5 July, Dominion Coal posted notices at the coal mines stating that the company was determined not to recognize the UMW and would continue to operate the coal mines with the aid of loyal men: "In order that this may be done, the company will extend all the protection in its power to the persons and families of men who continue to work, and in addition has called upon the civil authorities to afford full protection." Dominion Coal also claimed that a strike at this time would be illegal under the terms of the Industrial Disputes Investigation Act and would be regarded as an act of disloyalty by the company: "Every man going on strike ... will be treated as no longer in the employ of the company as regards house, house coal, or any other privilege they now enjoy."[21]

It was time to strike. In McLachlan's view, the UMW had exhausted the limited options under the existing industrial-relations regime. The imposition of a blacklist followed by threats of eviction and other reprisals forced the new union to demonstrate its support among the coal miners. "We could not possibly wait until another winter would come," explained McLachlan. "The UMW had provided for the thousand men that were refused work all winter. If we were going to fight at all for the right to belong to the trade union of our choice, we felt that the time had come, and on July 6 the strike was called."[22]

The Strike

Fourteen coaches long, the train pulled out of Halifax in the dark early hours of 8 July 1909. It was loaded with arms, equipment, two heavy machine guns, and more than 500 men and officers of the Royal Canadian Regiment, the Royal Canadian Garrison Artillery, and the Royal Canadian Engineers. The progress of the military train was slowed down by heavy rains as it was ferried over the Strait of Canso and then rumbled on to the stormswept iron bridge at Grand Narrows and along the shores of the Bras d'Or Lake. After a journey of sixteen hours, the train reached the heart of the strike zone in Glace Bay.[23]

As the sun rose over the ocean on the morning of 6 July 1909, crowds were already gathering at Dominion No. 2 and No. 9, the largest coal yards in Glace Bay. As men made their way past the fence, they were greeted with hoots and jeers. Recalled one eyewitness: "Men going into the pit yard were asked by the UMW pickets, 'You know what you are doing.'" One man was grabbed by a group of women who began tearing his clothes until he was rescued by the company police. G.H. Duggan, general manager of Dominion Coal, rode up and down the road on horseback. When he slapped a woman across the face with his riding crop, he was pulled off his horse and again the company police came to the rescue.[24] By the end of the day, when the strikebreakers reappeared, the crowd was estimated to be as large as 3,000 people, many of them hurling insults at the men who had gone to work. There were similar scenes on the second day of the strike. Men on their way to work were forced to run a gauntlet of shouts and yells, backed up by flying stones and eggs. Duggan and his special police were clouted with sticks and stones as they tried to keep the gates open for loyal employees.

True to the company's threats, Duggan appealed for troops. Military aid to the civil power was one of the more common peacetime uses of the Canadian armed forces before the First World War, and the militia had been called out to do strike duty on more than twenty-five occasions since 1867. To the dismay of the Dominion Coal Company, the local civil authorities in Glace Bay failed to endorse the request, as required under the Militia Act. Company officials were well represented on the Glace Bay town council, but, on the deciding vote of Mayor John

C. Douglas, the council turned down the company's appeal for soldiers. "I am strongly of the opinion that the citizens of this place, whether strikers or not, have no intention whatever of destroying any property of the company," wrote Douglas in response to the company's request, adding that "any unlawful acts committed were engendered by your force of constables as much as by the men on strike."[25] Duggan then directed his appeal to a more sympathetic ear, and at 10 p.m. on 7 July County Court Judge Duncan Finlayson signed the necessary requisition. In Halifax the troops had been standing by on the alert since the early afternoon.

The arrival of the troops had a large symbolic importance, for the presence of the army signified the arrival of the forces of law and order. With soldiers stationed at the individual coal mines, the collieries would be protected against violence, real or imagined. Strikebreakers would be escorted behind the notorious electrified fences. Union meetings and union leaders would be under constant surveillance. Strikers would be evicted from company houses and their possessions confiscated for back rent. In legal terms the troops might have been called out to maintain peace in the coalfield; in practice, law and order appeared to be on the side of the Dominion Coal Company. Consequently, those who would disturb the balance of power in the coal industry could stand only for lawlessness and disorder.

There was little doubt that the armed forces were prepared to take active measures against the strikers. On 30 July, UMW supporters marched in a parade from Glace Bay to the neighbouring coal town of Dominion, the home of John Moffatt and a PWA stronghold. Here the town council had favoured the calling of troops, and, when the UMW parade was announced, the town council had passed a by-law prohibiting parades without proper permits. As the parade proceeded through downtown Glace Bay, past several collieries and on towards Dominion, there were some 3,000 people in the line of march. President Dan McDougall, mounted on a white horse, led the way. Flags and banners were held high, and songs of the strike filled the air.

Along the boundary line between Glace Bay and Dominion there ran a small creek, crossed by a wooden bridge. On the far side of the creek, on a small height of land commanding the roadway, stood the Church of the Immaculate Conception. The soldiers were there in force, standing at attention with fixed bayonets. On the steps of the church the soldiers had mounted their guns. The parade stopped. A town councillor came rushing up to McDougall, breathless with information: "For God's sake, Dan, don't come any further. The soldiers have been ordered to shoot but to shoot low." The coal miners turned back.[26]

For McLachlan, another incident that took place on the same day in Glace Bay also demonstrated the rule of terror in the coalfield. Under the terms of its leases with tenants, Dominion Coal had the legal power to evict striking coal miners from company housing. The typical lease allowed only three days' notice. At Dominion No. 4, McLachlan described how soldiers and special police drove Joseph Peters out of his home at the point of a bayonet. Left behind, his wife and children were imprisoned in the building from 5 p.m. Friday night to 8 a.m. Saturday morning under the guard of two soldiers and two company police. This was cruel punishment for supporting the UMW, McLachlan protested; moreover, it was an offence against the self-respecting masculinity of the coal miner who wanted only to protect his wife and family:

If ever there was an attempt to hand over a woman to the lusts of men, it happened at Dominion No. 4 on July 30th. This story was not told to me by anyone. I saw it take place with my own eyes. I spoke to Peters on the street while a soldier walked with a naked knife on his gun between him and his wife, and the men who were around her house at the instigation of the Coal Company. The law? There is no law for striking miners in Glace Bay. Had that happened in Russia we would have all thrown up our hands in horror. It has happened to a man whose only crime is of being on strike. And the perpetrators of this crime will go free. I speak that which I do know, I testify that which I have seen.[27]

Whatever the claims of law and order, whatever the rights of private property and armed force, McLachlan was determined to demonstrate that justice and morality were on the side of the striking coal miners. The coal miners had gone on strike out of economic necessity and in defence of their union. In doing so they had struck a blow for the virtues of social responsibility and true manliness. McLachlan's declarations rang with the language of the independent collier who was defending his very right to call himself a man:

> The mine workers of this province are not only unable to provide themselves with the current necessities of life, but if they would hold their miserable jobs they must learn to keep their mouths shut at the dictates of the boss. The man who has the pluck to stand up among his fellows and advocate any trade union not approved of by his employer shall do so at the peril of having sentence of death by starvation passed upon him and his family. Our "captains of industry" who never tire in their hypocritical ravings about "individual initiative" demand that their every employee shall be docile, obedient and tractable to all their wishes, especially in regard to trade union.
>
> Bend or break is the doom of every manly man employed in or around the mines. The insatiable greed for dividends is grinding the manhood out of the Nova Scotia mine workers and has forced their wages away below that of any other of their class who make any pretence to organized effort on this continent.[28]

After the first month the conflict settled down into a long battle of endurance. McLachlan later described it as "the largest, longest, and bitterest strike of coal miners ever waged in Canada."[29] On 3 July the Dominion collieries had produced 11,085 tons of coal, and when the strike began the output dropped off sharply, to only 3,014 tons on 8 July. By 30 July, however, production had increased to 5,866 tons and in early September production exceeded 7,000 tons.[30] The union claimed that these figures were inflated and that the company was drawing on banks of coal accumulated prior to the strike. Nevertheless, the undeniable fact was that, with the protection of the army and the courts and the support of loyal employees and imported strikebreakers, the company was able to continue production.

As secretary-treasurer, McLachlan was in an excellent position to know the significance of the support provided by the international union. By September the UMW had spent more than $110,000 in support of the strike. Some international board members were alarmed at the slow progress and high cost of the strike. They argued that, if the strike could not be won before the end of the shipping season, the union should call it off and save the expense of supporting a failing strike through the winter months. Nevertheless, both President Lewis and Vice-President E.S. McCullough remained strong supporters of the Nova Scotia struggle and beat back attempts to have the Nova Scotia situation reassessed.

As a result, UMW money continued to flow into Nova Scotia throughout the winter. In December 1909, six months after the beginning of the strike, the UMW ledgers showed approximately 4,500 members on the books for District 26. Of these, only 316 members, employed at smaller companies where the strike was not in effect, were paying dues into the union treasury; the remainder were on strike and supported by the union. In January it was reported that 1,780 families had been evicted from company houses and were being looked after by the UMW. Evictions continued throughout the winter, and union lawyers were kept busy challenging the evictions and the confiscation of property for back rent. Those evicted from company houses were often accommodated in tents and in new buildings erected by the union. By May 1910 the bills for the Nova Scotia strike amounted to more than $800,000, most of which was spent on food, clothing, and shelter for the UMW members on strike.[31]

In his role as secretary-treasurer, McLachlan handled large amounts of money, and the family often feared for his safety as he made long, solitary walks through the winter snow to deliver union funds to outlying locals. McLachlan later estimated that the UMW spent a total of $1.5 million in Nova Scotia during the strike: "Each miner received, per week, $3.00 for himself, $1.50 for his wife, and 75¢ for each child or other dependent. They (the Union) also paid all doctor and hospital bills and the rents of all who were not living in Company houses; gave a clothing order every two months, and special order when a new baby came home. These last orders would run as a rule from $10.00 to $15.00. Then there were hundreds of cases in court, evictions and picketing, etc. These were all financed by the U.M.W. of A."[32]

Dominion Coal advertised far and wide for new workers to take the places of the UMW men, and here again the benefits of the international connection were visible. The union answered with its own

advertising campaign. A front-page notice in the *United Mine Workers'*
Journal warned: "A strike has been on in Nova Scotia and at these mines
since July 6 with every prospect of winning. Don't go there and try to
defeat your brothers who are fighting for the right to organize and
better conditions of employment." One Yorkshire miner, who had
arrived in Cape Breton without knowledge of the strike, escaped the
barbed-wire stockade in Glace Bay and declared: "No English miner
would come to Canada to break a strike. I am no Black-leg. Every miner
in England belongs to the union. I would rather be thrown into the sea
than break a strike."[33]

International solidarity was working the way it was supposed to
work. Under McLachlan's direction, the district office distributed tens
of thousands of circulars, notices, and pamphlets in Britain, Europe,
and North America. At one point, McLachlan learned of company plans
to import 1,000 miners from Belgium. He immediately telegraphed
Samuel Gompers of the AFL, who in turn cabled the secretary of
Belgium's labour federation about the Nova Scotia situation, "urging
him to take such steps as would prevent the miners of Belgium coming
to take the places of the striking miners there."[34]

But the union's campaign against strikebreaking also attracted reprisals
from the coal operators. On a Sunday night in September 1909, shortly
after returning home from church, union president Dan McDougall was
seized by private detectives, loaded on a train, and transported to Montreal. There he was charged with publishing a criminal libel against the
Dominion Coal Company. The evidence was an advertisement placed in
La Patrie, one of the French-language Montreal daily newspapers, advising
workers of the strike and warning them not to accept work as strikebreakers. With a steady flow of new immigrants and its notorious labour
exchanges, Montreal had a bad reputation as a recruiting ground for
strikebreakers for the Maritimes.[35]

Secretary-Treasurer McLachlan was summoned to court in Montreal. He was ordered to produce minutebooks and other union documents
and interrogated as to the duties and responsibilities of the union officers.
McLachlan did not deny that the union had issued posters informing
workers of the Nova Scotia situation, but he also stated that "he did not
know anything about the newspaper publication of two of the posters

produced in court." The presiding judge "considered it strange" that neither McDougall nor McLachlan could confirm the union's responsibility for the advertisement in *La Patrie* and agreed with the defence lawyer, the Cape Breton Conservative Member of Parliament J.W. Maddin, that this was a good question to refer to the jury. The legal manoeuvres dragged on for more than six months, and when the case finally came to trial in March 1910, the jury took only a few minutes to declare the union president not guilty. McDougall himself spent weeks behind bars and never fully recovered from the beatings he suffered during the ordeal.[36]

The persecution of McDougall inspired McLachlan to launch his own legal case by way of retaliation. On the train back from giving evidence in Montreal in October 1909, McLachlan completed the plans. If the law was a kind of theatre, this time Dominion Coal and other operators would be portrayed as the lawbreakers. In Halifax, McLachlan paid a visit to the stipendiary magistrate and swore out a lengthy complaint. The list of the accused began with President James Ross of Dominion Coal and constituted a who's who of the province's coal industry. The charge included, in the loaded language of the Criminal Code, that they "unlawfully did, amongst themselves, conspire, combine, confederate, agree and arrange" to limit production, reduce competition, and fix coal prices over the preceding nine years. These kinds of allegations played on public concern about high coal prices for coal as well as regional suspicions about the domination of the coal industry by outside interests. As a result of the extensive newspaper coverage, the public was treated to the unusual spectacle of seeing most of the head officers of the provincial coal industry sitting in the dim light of the Halifax police court as "prisoners at the bar."[37]

The preliminary hearings dragged on through the fall and into January while company lawyers such as Humphrey Mellish and E.M. Macdonald scrambled to limit the damage. At one stage they claimed that McLachlan had instigated the case "for purposes in connection with the strike"; the union lawyer complained about "slurs and insinuations cast at himself and his client": "It was out of place to bring in the religion and other professions of the person who laid the information." The hearings examined company managers and sales agents and heard extensive evidence regarding costs of production, coal prices, transportation, wages, and standards of living. In due course J.R. Cowans of the Cumberland Railway and Coal Company and Alexander Dick of Dominion Coal were committed to trial; the charges were not finally quashed until April when a grand jury threw out the indictment. Along the way the "coal conspiracy" case, as it became known, produced what one report called "a lot of sensational news for the public's edification as to why they are obliged to pay such high prices for coal."[38]

Meanwhile, the coal companies were still able to exploit the legal system to their advantage. McLachlan was among the more than sixty prominent UMW members named in a far-reaching injunction ordering union members to cease "watching and besetting" the properties of Dominion Coal. In the future the document would also serve as an unofficial blacklist to identify the men who would never be rehired in the province's coal mines. The union launched an appeal. Once more the case dragged on, and in April 1910 the injunction was sustained by the higher courts. And there was more: when the sittings of the Supreme Court began in Sydney in February 1910, there were more than thirty cases arising out of the strike, most of them on charges of riot, unlawful assembly, and assault.[39]

One dramatic illustration of the peculiar implications of industrial legality appeared in Inverness. A UMW organizer there, David Neilson, was arrested and charged under the Industrial Disputes Investigation Act for distributing food and relief to strikers. Because the Inverness strikers had failed to apply for a conciliation board before going out, they were judged to be engaged in an "illegal" strike. Neilson was convicted and fined $500 or two months in jail. The idea that the Industrial Disputes Investigation Act allowed judges to decide that feeding hungry strikers was an unlawful act was highly alarming to union leaders. The UMW appealed the case to the province's Supreme Court, which ruled unanimously in support of the law. Some years later McLachlan would recall this incident as proof that the act, for all Mackenzie King's famous rhetoric about peace and harmony, was nothing more than Canada's version of the notorious American Fugitive Slave Law that enforced the return of escaped slaves to their masters.[40]

For its part, the Liberal provincial government of George H. Murray, despite its reputation for progressive reform and its concern about the coal royalties that were the largest single source of provincial revenue, was not prepared to intervene in the strike. Sympathetic Liberal politicians from the coalfields, such as Cape Breton's Dr A.S. Kendall, feared that the coal companies would use the opportunity to eliminate all unionism from the mines. Kendall proposed the appointment of a royal commission to investigate a dozen different areas of concern, including such matters as the price of coal and the recognition of unions. The Conservative opposition also proposed a requirement for the compulsory recognition of trade unions, as did the Liberal member from Cumberland County, E.B. Paul. This was the kind of law that unions believed should be the logical corollary of the legalization of unions under the 1872 Trade Union Act. But all of these efforts were overwhelmingly voted down.[41]

Throughout the winter, troops continued to police the coalfields, and no other kind of intervention was expected from Ottawa. The Department of Labour had already conducted conciliation procedures and was now determined to ignore the dispute as best it could. One of those boards had been chaired by Nova Scotia Supreme Court Judge J.W. Longley, a former attorney general of Nova Scotia. Following the publication of his report, Longley urged Mackenzie King, who was now the minister of labour, not to respond favourably to appeals for intervention in the dispute; in time, he predicted, the fight would result in a "death blow" for the UMW. King was happy to accept such advice, believing that, once a dispute had been investigated by a conciliation board, any further action would only encourage labour unions to look for more government intervention in the future. King's deputy minister toured the coalfields in September 1909 and reported: "At Glace Bay the strike appears to be practically broken, though the production is still below normal, and many employees are receiving relief; the military force is likely to be retained for some time to come."[42]

As the end of the winter approached, McLachlan and other UMW leaders had some hope that the strike could be settled, particularly after the appointment of a new superintendent and general manager for Dominion Coal. "Press and pulpit rang with the praises of the new men," McLachlan commented. "For a few weeks all evictions were stopped. Men were let out on suspended sentences, honeyed words were now tried where brutality had failed." The troops were withdrawn from Glace Bay in early March, and both the provincial government and local clergymen made efforts to bring the two sides together. The UMW was prepared to make compromises and end the strike in return for an undertaking that all miners would be taken back without discrimination. Also, without recognizing the PWA or the UMW as such, the company would have to agree to "receive committees of their workmen to discuss and remedy grievances." But the basic position of the company had not changed since the beginning of the strike, and J.H. Plummer, the new general manager of the combined coal and steel company, pointed out that any meeting with UMW representatives "might be misunderstood and regarded as recognition of the association, which is contrary to our policy." In anticipation of the resumption of the shipping season, the company stepped up production at the mines. Strikers drifted back to work, believing that the sooner they returned the less likely they would be to suffer reprisals.[43]

The strike against Dominion Coal was ended officially by the district executive board on 28 April 1910. It was not, McLachlan claimed at the district convention in June, a complete defeat. "A year ago our members were walking the streets of Glace Bay because they were members of the U.M.W. of A. A year ago the Dominion Coal Company refused to meet any committee of its workmen other than one from the P.W.A. These two grievances caused a ten months' strike and both now are happily removed. The change is complete; the D.C.C. not only has ceased to lay off our members because of their membership in the U.M.W. of A., but now receive committees of our men when any local trouble calls for such."[44]

McLachlan was putting a brave face on the situation. This was not the victory for which he and the UMW had fought ten long months. Dominion Coal had conceded little. The PWA would continue to be treated as the union of its employees, and the activities of the UMW would be kept under close watch by company police and private detectives.

Meanwhile, at Springhill, where the UMW had succeeded in totally driving the PWA from the field, the battle continued for another full year. From Glace Bay, where the coal miners were divided and dispirited in the wake of the strike, McLachlan could only admire the determination of the Springhill men: "It is a regular object lesson to the mine workers of this province on the benefits of working class solidarity in action."[45]

Agitation

"It has been a grand time for socialist propaganda," wrote McLachlan in the pages of the Chicago-based *International Socialist Review* in 1910. "The local comrades have taken advantage while the miners were in a mood to think and have spread the literature of socialism amongst them, where, hitherto stoic conservativeism reigned, it is now fast becoming red. On the whole the fight has been good for us all."[46]

Some socialist agitators had been predicting the defeat of the strike from the beginning. Wilfrid Gribble, the itinerant organizer who had helped establish the Socialist Party local in Sydney Mines, left the area shortly after the beginning of the strike. He observed pessimistically: "The majority of the miners are in a state of fatuous confidence as to their success, and are just now unfitted to some extent for listening to the real thing. It will not be long before many of them will be disillusioned however and then will be the chance of Maritime comrades to see that the only hope of the workers is again expounded to them." In Gribble's view, trade unions were "no use to the working class, because they stood for the present system of industry."[47]

McLachlan saw no contradiction between his unionism and his socialism. Good socialists were also compelled to be good trade unionists. Proudly, he recounted one episode in which he visited a shack where a group of foreign strikebreakers were housed: "A U.M.W. of A. interpreter told them I was an officer of the U.M.W. They grinned and nodded; not one of them speaking a word of English. He then said, I was a member of Glace Bay socialist local. That did the trick, in a moment they were round me shaking my hand and the grins gave place to beaming faces."[48]

In place of Gribble, the Cape Breton socialists welcomed a steady stream of more sympathetic socialist agitators. These included H.H. Stuart and Roscoe Fillmore from New Brunswick and national figures such as Jimmy Simpson, the Toronto printer and socialist, who was also vice-president of the Trades and Labour Congress. From Glace Bay, Simpson filed reports with the Toronto *Star* and was instrumental in guaranteeing that the PWA was denounced and the UMW given a ringing endorsement at the annual convention of the TLC in Quebec City in September 1909.[49]

Another visiting radical was the legendary Wobbly, Big Bill Haywood, the veteran of the Rocky Mountain mine wars and founder of the Industrial Workers of the World. Haywood had been framed by Pinkerton agents on a murder charge in Idaho in 1907. The case, in which he was successfully defended by Clarence Darrow, made him one of the best-known labour radicals in North America. In October 1909 he began a speaking tour that took him through western Canada and on to Toronto, Ottawa, Montreal, and the Maritimes. In crowded theatres in Glace Bay and Sydney Mines, Haywood pressed home the message of "The Class Struggle" and predicted the coming overthrow of the capitalist system: "He told the workers that they must achieve their own emancipation. They need not look for some kindly savior to do it for them." He also delivered the message of industrial democracy, giving "a very different idea of unionism from that held down there in the past – that of making the union an industrial school in which the workers study and develop themselves in such a manner that when the Socialist Party has achieved political emancipation, the industrial union would be prepared to efficiently and economically man and administer the means of production."[50]

McLachlan's own philosophy of action at this time was rarely formulated in explicit terms; it simply assumed that, under the influence of socialist leaders, the experience of class conflict would in due course bring about changes in class consciousness. In making the case for a strong union, McLachlan propounded a basic economic argument that applied his reading of Marxist economic theory. In this cause he enlisted the detailed official evidence of government publications, with every piece of information credited to a specific page and volume.

Driving home each statistical conclusion with a flourish, he presented a lesson in political economy that illustrated the separation of the working class from the fruits of their labour. For the year ending in September 1908, McLachlan reported, the Dominion Coal Company had raised 3,816,958 tons of coal and in doing so employed 5,486 men and boys: "That was well over 695 tons of coal per employee. The Dominion Coal Company sold that coal at $2.32 per ton, which means that for every man and boy employed in and around the mines the coal company realized $1,612.40, and out of that amount only had to pay back in the shape of wages, an average of $429 to each of their employees, leaving a profit from the product of each employee's labor of $1,183.40."

The only weakness in McLachlan's analysis, it seemed clear, was the underdeveloped class consciousness of the coal miners:

> You get such wages not because your employer cannot afford more, but because through fear of the boss or through utter indifference about your own welfare, you stay out of the only trade union which is able and willing, with your support, to get you more ...
>
> Is it not a fact that many of you have allowed yourselves to be divided from your fellows by the henchmen of the employers, the leaders of the so-called Provincial Workmen's Association, an organization that was voted out of existence June 24, 1908, and reorganized and financed by the men who are robbing you, for the very purpose of dividing the strength of the mine workers of Nova Scotia so that the robbery of you may continue.

In the end, McLachlan concluded, the purpose of the struggle was not only to defend the rights of labour but also to challenge the rule of capital: "You hold your present jobs not because your employer cares whether you get a living, but because he can make profit out of your life. Profit is the end for which you are employed at all. The kind of life you live is only an incidental matter with your boss. Get into an organization, man, that exists for no other end than to get the highest possible wages for your labor for you and so make your life happier and your home brighter."[51]

As early as October 1909 the Cape Breton locals of the SPC had resolved to contest the next provincial election. McLachlan was one of the three candidates considered in May 1910, but he placed second to Alexander MacKinnon, a Cape Bretoner who had learned his socialism in the United States under the influence of the Socialist Party of America and become a founder of the Socialist Club in Glace Bay in 1904. Through night-school study he had worked his way out of the coal mines and was employed as the town engineer for Glace Bay. He may have been a less flamboyant speaker than McLachlan, but MacKinnon was considered "the backbone of the movement in Cape Breton" and an effective speaker with a talent for "making puzzling things plain."[52]

MacKinnon carried the socialist banner in the provincial election of June and again in the Dominion election of September 1911. His vote was small on both occasions, 713 in the provincial election and 223 in the Dominion election. Many miners obviously preferred to vote for well-known local politicians such as John C. Douglas, A.S. Kendall, and J.W. Maddin, all of them critics of the coal company and friends of the UMW during the 1909 strike. Yet the socialists saw elections mainly as opportunities to conduct "clear-cut revolutionary propaganda." They were satisfied that they had campaigned on "the only vital and real issue before the workers of this country as well as the world," namely "Socialism versus Capitalism." Small as it was, the socialist vote was sufficient to split the anti-government vote, producing an unexpected defeat for the Conservative candidate in one of the country's major industrial centres.[53]

Socialist agitation continued after the end of the strike. In April 1912, a time of great discouragement for the UMW cause, the Glace Bay local reported fifty-nine members and in the next four months recruited an additional forty-two members and sold $200 worth of literature. Indeed, the circulation of *Cotton's Weekly*, Canada's most popular socialist newspaper, increased steadily in the years following the strike. *Cotton's Weekly* was never intended as an official party organ and more than anything it reflected the eclectic socialism of its editor, a young Eastern Townships lawyer, William Ulrich Cotton, who was influenced by the example of Julius Wayland's *Appeal to Reason* in the United States. In the pre-war years *Cotton's Weekly* achieved a circulation of more than 25,000 copies a week. Cotton considered the Nova Scotia struggle a significant one and almost every issue during 1909 and 1910 contained news, editorials, letters, or poetry about the coal miners' struggle. Local socialists seized the opportunity to distribute a "live propaganda paper." In December 1910 more than 300 copies were distributed in industrial Cape Breton, and by October 1912 the local circulation was close to 400 copies.[54]

Cotton himself was among the visiting socialist agitators who made their way to Glace Bay during the course of the strike. According to Paul MacEwan's account, Cotton framed his message to the coal miners in explicitly religious terms. His *Sermon to the Working Class* was especially meaningful to McLachlan. It began with a Biblical quotation (from *Proverbs*) that years later would be hammered in stone on McLachlan's tombstone: "Open thy mouth, judge righteously, and plead the cause of the poor and needy."[55]

Defeat

The battles of 1909 ended in defeat. Even the stalwarts in Springhill were forced to bring their struggle to a close in May 1911. District 26 still remained in existence, but for the UMW loyalists these were discouraging years. The district officers operated under strict instructions from the international office: "Under no circumstances must new Local Unions be formed, if as a result of doing so, it would involve the men in strike." The UMW agreed to continue paying the salary and expenses of the president and secretary-treasurer, but, wrote the new UMW president, John P. White, in 1911, "the Organization is in no position financially to take care of any campaign of organizing that will result in the financial support of the men affected."[56]

Although the status of the district was under constant review, the arrangement lasted for almost five years, and McLachlan had the benefit of a steady income. He was paid at the standard organizer's rate of $3.50 a day, plus an allowance for expenses. This was no more and probably less than he might have earned as a working miner. But it was steady income. After 1909 McLachlan was too well known to the coal operators to be employed in the industry anywhere in Nova Scotia.

One after another the veterans of 1909 retired from the scene. McDougall stepped down as district president in 1911. He was replaced by William Watkins of Springhill and in 1912 by another Springhill veteran, C.A. Bonnyman. In August 1910 McLachlan was one of eight delegates from District 26 who attended the UMW convention at Indianapolis. There he heard complaints from delegates about the large amounts of money being spent in Nova Scotia. He did not attend subsequent conventions but remained on cordial terms with the international union officers. James D. McLennan of Glace Bay continued to represent Nova Scotia at the international level, but his energies were often absorbed in American issues; on one occasion he was preoccupied with conciliating a dispute between Polish and Lithuanian coal miners in Pennsylvania. Increasingly after 1909, the UMW cause in Nova Scotia became associated with McLachlan.

In April 1911 McLachlan and the district officers made yet another attempt to achieve recognition of the union. The union's scale committee issued an invitation to the coal operators to meet in Halifax to discuss wages and conditions in the coal industry, once more without success. A printed circular reported the union's continuing aims, which included increases of 10 per cent for handpick miners and higher increases for men earning $1.75 or less. They also wanted recognition of the UMW and the eight-hour day. For the benefit of the public and the coal miners alike, the circular, signed by McLachlan and the other members of the scale committee, drove home the lessons of the strike:

> To the general public of Nova Scotia we would point out that the laws of this country guarantee to all the right of free association; but the Coal Companies have, on pain of dismissal and other forms of persecution, denied to their employees the right of taking an active interest in the organization of their choice.
>
> The millions of money spent on useless and costly law suits, a dangerous and privately controlled police force, and on an army of unscrupulous spies, together with other unnecessary expenditure to crush the aspirations of employees whose only desire is to

organize for their mutual benefit, would, if paid in wages, more than cover all the demands made above without increasing the cost of coal one cent to the consumer.[57]

The campaign failed, for none of the coal companies responded to the invitation to negotiate with the UMW.

During this period, the Dominion Coal Company police force made a business of following union leaders through the streets and presenting themselves in force at scheduled union meetings. "For two years I practically could not go down the street without being followed by a policeman employed by the company," McLachlan later recalled. "You could not hold a meeting without the policemen coming in." The company's harassment was amply documented when McLachlan obtained a circular issued in November 1910 by the chief of police for the Dominion Coal Company. In a list of instructions policemen were told to maintain "strict watch" on developments among the coal miners. They were to report any collections of money among the coal miners for any purposes, to watch "foreigners" "so that any one who owes company money do not escape without paying their bills," to file reports on meetings of the pit committees and any local controversies, to keep close watch on the movements of all U.M.W. officers, and to "try and induce all workmen to abandon the U.M.W."[58]

Union meetings took place under constant threat of disruption. The most sensational case came at a meeting of local 550 at McDonald's Hall in Glace Bay on 23 April 1911. There were about 150 men in the hall and McLennan was holding forth, over the constant interruptions of a half-dozen rowdies who were evidently drunk. The worst was a man named Connolly. McLachlan, who was chairing the meeting, warned the heckler to wait to say his piece until the speaker finished or he would be compelled to send for the town police to remove him from the hall. Connolly refused to quit and, according to the local newspaper, "assumed a belligerent attitude and dared anyone present to put him out."

At this stage the local union secretary, Fred Beal, a slight man in his twenties, picked up his cap and announced that he was going for the town police. Before Beal could leave, one Michael Murphy stepped forward and knocked him down into some empty seats. To everyone's astonishment, Beal came up from the floor with a gun in his hand. In the scuffle that followed, four shots were fired. Two of them went through the window, another lodged in Murphy's stomach, and another shot went through the heart of a man named William Bryant. The meeting ended in a stand-off – Beal holding off the crowd with his revolver while friends of Murphy and Bryant threatened to tear him limb from limb. McLachlan and "some of the older and more cool-headed present" helped to keep the peace until the police arrived. Then Beal surrendered himself into custody.[59]

Bryant had been shot dead on the spot, and the wounded man died in hospital shortly afterwards. Subsequently, the local union officer Beal was charged on two counts of murder. The first case went to trial at the sitting of the Supreme Court in Sydney in June 1911. As chairman of the meeting and an eyewitness, McLachlan was called to give evidence. According to McLachlan, Murphy had continued to attack Beal even after he produced the gun and threatened to use it. McLachlan remembered putting his hand on Murphy's shoulder, trying to stop him from striking Beal again, but he was pushed away. Murphy then knocked Beal's head into the window. When Beal fired his first two shots out the window, Murphy struck him again. Then Beal began shooting and McLachlan took cover behind a desk. When the case went to the jury, there was a speedy verdict. Beal was acquitted on the grounds that he was acting in self-defence.[60]

To McLachlan's despair, the shooting reinforced the idea that UMW meetings were unsavoury, even dangerous, events. Worst of all was the sensational revelation some time later that Beal himself was not an ordinary miner but a paid employee of the Thiel Detective Agency in Montreal. He had infiltrated the local for the purpose of disrupting union activity.[61] Reporting to union headquarters at this time, McLachlan observed that local 550 was "continually infested by paid agents of the Coy [Company] some of which got into office during the winter months. Twice they stole the money of the Local. Once they stole the books. If an honest union man took office next day he would have his lamp stopped and either had to leave the Local or the Country to get work." Following the shooting affair, McLachlan added, "the clergy interfered when we might have done some good, and 'bound every man over in the name of God not to attend any U.M.W. meetings.'" The episode cast a shadow of doubt and gloom over the UMW in Glace Bay.[62]

Despite plans to build a new union hall in Glace Bay, there was little evidence that the coal miners were prepared to rally around the UMW in large numbers again. In the fall of 1911 McLachlan secured a report of the PWA's October Grand Council meeting, at which plans for a new two-year agreement with Dominion Coal were discussed. The district issued a public protest against the PWA's method of making contracts without submitting agreements to the miners. But turnouts at the UMW meetings were disappointing. In Glace Bay the locals had difficulty renting halls for meetings. When McLachlan and other officers put up posters, company police tore them down. At Reserve Mines the local officer who hired a hall was sent out of the mine and the hall was locked up. At one meeting at Bridgeport, every man attending had to walk through a line of company police and mine officials to reach the hall. The following day, all but one of the audience had his lamp stopped at the mine and lost from one week to six weeks of work. Months later one UMW loyalist, Alf Brenchley, was still unable to get work anywhere in the province. At the Dreamland Theatre in Glace Bay on 30 October, an army of company police and officials waited at the entrance to discourage attendance, and although all the mines were closed that day, the audience amounted to less than 300 people.[63]

The PWA contract was "grossly unjust," McLachlan believed, but there were few protests from the coal miners, and he concluded that "there was not much hope of seeing the organization grow for some time." On 1 January 1912 McLachlan wrote a forthright analysis of the district's condition, setting forth the obstacles to organization and offering no false hope of immediate success. By virtue of its size and control of the market, Dominion Coal was able to keep smaller producers in line. The proprietor of the Maritime Coal and Railway Company at Chignecto had been willing to make an agreement with the UMW, but he feared that Dominion Coal would drive him out of business. McLachlan described other similar cases, and reported that the sales agent for one smaller company stated that "neither his coy nor any other coal Coy in N.S. dare show the least favor to our organization on pain of having their trade taken by the Dominion Coal Coy." "Under these conditions,"

McLachlan concluded, "the first men that want to be organized are the employees of the Dominion Coal Coy, and they are the most completely terror stricken of all the men I have ever seen, and it is just here where Moffatt and his damned agreement gives the appearance to the outsider, that the Company and men have met and come to an arrangement satisfactory to both parties. We are not now, and I am unable to say when, we will get these men into the organization."[64]

By early 1912 there were only four locals in good standing in District 26, with less than 400 members in total. UMW President John P. White was not optimistic about the Nova Scotia situation, and in making his gloomy analysis he was guided in part by his correspondence with McLachlan. "The strike in Nova Scotia caused the expenditure of a vast sum of money," White told the UMW convention in January 1912, "and it seems to me could not be a success in view of the fact that the miners were not united. There is an organization there known as the Provincial Workers' Association, and it is claimed it acts in conjunction with the coal companies. When this strike was ordered it was the concensus [sic] of opinion of those competent to judge that if it was not won in two months then it could not be won at all, yet it was allowed to continue for nearly two years without any hope of final success ... I am convinced more than ever that there will be very little success achieved in Nova Scotia unless means can be found to eliminate the dual organization which has proven so disastrous to the United Mine Workers."[65]

There were some occasional signs of progress to report. During 1912 and 1913 new members were signed up in Inverness and in Pictou, where four new locals were in existence in 1913. At one stage there was word of a bizarre behind-the-scenes plot by prominent Liberals to win over one of John Moffatt's leading supporters within the PWA in order to free the organization from the control of the Moffatt clique. In October 1912 there was a successful meeting in Glace Bay to report, the first since the previous May: "one of the best we had in the Glace Bay district during the last 18 months, several men getting up in the meeting and expressing themselves about the need of organization, and that is something that never took place for a long time. Up to the present no one has lost his work for attending that meeting." But none of this added up to the breakthrough that was needed, and the district membership continued to decline.[66]

McLachlan and the UMW cause continued to enjoy support from the Trades and Labour Congress. McLachlan attended the 1911 meetings in Calgary and was appointed to the provincial executive for Nova Scotia. At the annual convention of the American Federation of Labor in 1911, meeting in Atlanta, Georgia, the PWA was thoroughly denounced as "an outlaw organization" and "a band of traitors" "who by their action are helping to retard the work of the bona fide trades unionist and who by co-operating with the thugs and detectives of the employers are placing themselves on a plane lower than that of the meanest scab or strikebreaker." When TLC President J.C. Watters visited Cape Breton in 1912 he was shocked by the presence of company police at every stage of his visit, from arrival to departure: "Special police were in evidence on every occasion and shadowed me as if I were a criminal." In their annual interview with the prime minister and the minister of labour that year, the TLC executive devoted a lengthy part of the session to exposing the "system of espionage" practised by the company police and called for a royal commission to investigate conditions in Cape Breton. "The men there," Watters informed Prime Minister Robert Borden, "are living in sort of little Russia and have no freedom whatever."[67]

Despite the defeat, McLachlan was earning a reputation for his organizational abilities. In 1913 he was invited to add his voice to an organizing campaign among workers at the railway-car plant in Trenton, Nova Scotia. "Trade unionism is growing everywhere, as its advantages are becoming more generally known," McLachlan told a meeting of car workers at the Orange Hall in New Glasgow. Typically, his speech underlined the importance of the workers' own efforts and propounded his basic economic message: "Some say these unions are organized by agitators, but such is not the case. Men are becoming better acquainted with their own possibilities and are only seeking their rights; man's producing power stands at a certain figure, suppose it is $10.00 then if the 'boss' gets $8.00 the workman gets but $2.00 and so the more the worker gets the less the owner gets so he of course struggles against any change." The union campaign was successful, but McLachlan's satisfaction must have been tempered by the cutting remarks of the local newspaper: "If Jimmy B. has been unable to accomplish anything for the coal miners it should be obvious to all that he can do considerably less than nothing on behalf of the Trenton men."[68]

The arrival of the war in August 1914 dampened McLachlan's hopes for any progress on the labour front. "The war has spoiled, for the present, any little movement that appeared among the men during the last three months," he wrote a few weeks after the beginning of the war. "We have had several very good open-air meetings, the best in four years. The mines were working just about half-time and over-crowded at that, and men were less afraid to be seen at the meetings, but now the war fever has got them so bad that their own interests are neglected. The reaction is going to set in pretty early, and we may then be able to do a little more than keep the District alive."[69]

During this period there were also signs of internal dissension within the ranks of the UMW loyalists in Nova Scotia. Much of the controversy surrounded James D. McLennan, the brawny coal miner who had served as the district's representative on the international executive board since 1909. McLennan had been closely allied with T.L. Lewis, and on Lewis's departure from the presidency McLennan was responsible for present-ing a gift of furniture on behalf of the international membership at the 1911 convention. But in 1912 officers of local union 945 at Sydney Mines raised questions about the status of McLennan's union membership and requested that he be removed from office. As secretary-treasurer, on the request of the international office, McLachlan reported that McLen-nan's dues were fully paid up and, despite apparent irregularities, there was little cause for alarm: "It has been our experience, in this District, that it was not always possible to comply with the strict letter of the law, but we have lived up to the constitution as nearly as we could, under the abnormal conditions prevailing here."[70]

Then in 1914 McLachlan himself was embroiled in an embarrassing feud with McLennan. In a letter to Kent Foster of Springhill, McLennan announced that McLachlan was a "traitor" to the UMW cause. The brunt of the charge was that McLachlan was conspiring to encourage "a man named Sylvie Barrett" to stand against him in the next election for international board member. Silby Barrett was a young Newfound-lander who had gone from the fishing boats to the coal mines as a young man. After working in Ohio he had been converted to the union cause, and by the time he settled in Glace Bay in 1908 he was a strong UMW supporter. Unschooled but possessed of a flamboyant personality and a salty wit, Barrett came under McLachlan's influence and McLennan saw him as McLachlan's protégé. McLennan charged that McLachlan had called an irregular local union meeting to ensure Barrett's nomination. He also claimed that Barrett was being promoted by coal company officials. The letter containing these allegations found its way into McLachlan's hands. McLachlan wrote formally to UMW headquarters requesting that action be taken against McLennan on the ground that McLennan had circulated "a false and slanderous statement about me, inasmuch as in the said letter he says, that I am a traitor to this Organization."[71] When he subsequently appeared before the international executive board, McLennan failed to expand on the subject; it seems likely that in writing to Springhill McLennan was trying to muster support against a forthcoming challenge to his position within the district. For his part, McLachlan was apparently convinced that McLennan's time had passed. In promoting Barrett, a feisty young Newfoundlander who belonged to the latest generation of coal mine recruits, McLachlan was looking to the future.

The whole matter was discussed by the international executive board in December 1914. The president was empowered to appoint a committee to investigate the charges against McLennan, but no action was taken. Instead, the board decided to close the books on District 26. In a time of retrenchment and economy for the union, the outlying districts in Nova Scotia and Vancouver Island, where the union had spent large sums and lost spectacular battles, seemed unnecessary liabilities. At the December board meeting a Committee on Retrenchment advised that the charters of the districts 26 and 28 (Vancouver Island) should be revoked as of 1 January 1915. There was much discussion, especially by the Canadian representatives, McLennan of Nova Scotia and David Rees of British Columbia, and the recommendation was narrowly voted down. The recommendation came up again at the following board meeting in February 1915. Again McLennan defended the district's record and pointed out that it would be possible to economize by cutting off salaries to himself and the district officers without revoking the charter. His argument carried some weight, but nevertheless the vote was fifteen to eight in favour of revoking the charters of the two failed Canadian districts.[72]

Two days after the meeting President White wrote a brief formal letter to McLachlan conveying the decision of the board: "You will note that commencing with April 1st the charters of Districts Nos. 26 and 28 will be surrendered to the International Union." The door was closed with some regret and, White hoped, not permanently shut: "I believe the local unions in Nova Scotia will maintain their affiliation about as well with the district charter removed as they have done in the past – at least until such time as there can be an active campaign made in that field – for we will have the opportunity to keep in touch with the local unions and take advantage of any situation that might arise when opportunity presents itself."[73]

Steele's Hill

For McLachlan there was no going back into the coal mines. The 1909 strike identified him permanently with the UMW cause in Nova Scotia. The deputy minister of labour, in his report on the conflict, had explicitly named McLachlan – "a former employee at the Sydney Mines" – as one of the four principal "Leaders in the Agitation." Under the circumstances, no coal operator could doubt that McLachlan was an undesirable employee. As Eugene Forsey later wrote of this period, "Mr. McLachlan had been one of the prime movers in the trouble, and the operators did not forget it."[74]

During these discouraging years the McLachlan family moved to a small farm on Steele's Hill, an elevated area of Glace Bay close to the woods on the back boundary of the town. The property consisted of a home and six acres of land. From Steele's Hill it was just possible to see the shining surface of the ocean beyond the city streets below. The nearest colliery, Dominion No. 11, was only a short distance down Dominion Street, and at night the land on the hill sometimes trembled with the sounds of machinery and underground blasting.

The evidence suggests that the family moved here as early as 1913, when they began paying for the property at a rate of $10 per month.

According to the local land records, they finally acquired the property (from a widowed coal miner by the name of John J. Morrison) in August 1917. The purchase price was a substantial sum of $1,850, and the McLachlans were obliged to take out a mortgage for the remaining portion of the price, a debt that was discharged by August 1919. Interestingly, both the purchase and the mortgage were contracted in the name of Catherine McLachlan, with J.B. signing the purchase only as a witness. McLachlan took some pride in this acquisition of a small property. It was "just an ordinary working class house," he later told a royal commission, but in his view it was better than any company house in the whole town: "I would not give my place for a row in Dominion No. 2, an entire row. They are up there among engine ashes and open drains and sewers."[75]

Like defeated union organizers in other North American coal towns, McLachlan was locating the means to support his family on the margins of the industrial community. With a garden and a few cows, the McLachlans were converting themselves into a farm household. Kate had always had a fondness for country life – it was one of her parents' complaints – and the family now dedicated themselves to making a living from the farm. They grew potatoes and cabbages in the fields and kept chickens and geese; at one stage they had fourteen cows in the barn. In their milk wagon McLachlan and his sons made regular rounds through the streets of Glace Bay. Often they found that the coal miners were unable to pay in cash, and the McLachlans were satisfied to receive payment in other forms. On collection days, recalled the oldest son, they would have to make a second trip to transport the bales of hay, buckets of jam, clothing, and other payments for the eggs and milk.[76]

In making the move to Steele's Hill the McLachlans were confirming their roots in Cape Breton. McLachlan had received news of his mother's death, at the age of sixty-five, in 1903; two years later his father's death, at the age of seventy-three, confirmed his separation from the land of his birth. Meanwhile, his older sisters, Jane and Anne, had both emigrated to Winnipeg, as did his younger brother John, who enlisted in the Great War and never returned from the battlefields of France. At some time after his mother's death, McLachlan attempted to arrange for his younger sister Janet to join him in Nova Scotia; however, Janet suffered from a disabling bone disease and, under the medical restrictions of the time, she was considered an unfit immigrant and prohibited from entering Canada.[77]

As their older children began to come of age, this land on Steele's Hill remained the centre of family life. In addition to the four older children born in Scotland, there was now an additional son, Thomas, and four daughters, Eva, Elsie, Barbara, and Mary. McLachlan was remembered by several of the children as "a real Scots father," a strict and loving presence who treated the children with respect and expected them to show respect for their neighbours. In the family circle the father read the Bible aloud, and the children took their turn presenting memorized verses; one of the younger daughters remembers being paid five cents a verse to memorize passages from MacAulay's *Lays of Ancient Rome*. During this period McLachlan also acquired a number of standard collections for the instruction of the family, including in 1914 an eleven-volume *Foundation Library for Young People*. The children were also reading classics by Walter Scott, Robert Louis Stevenson, Jules Verne, and Jonathan Swift.[78]

Tom McLachlan, who was born in 1908, recalled that his father set them an example by his own application: "He never stopped studying; he was always reading up on something" – "and he would teach us about these things: about Scottish history back to the beginnings and about astronomy for instance." Like many self-educated workers, McLachlan was subscribing to courses from the International Correspondence Schools of Scranton, Pennsylvania; his studies included mathematics, history, economics, and Greek.[79]

McLachlan remained fascinated by the effective use of language. An English-Italian dictionary in his collection was undoubtedly useful in communicating with one of the groups of European immigrants in the mining district. At one time he tried to teach the whole family the new universal language that was fashionable in the early twentieth century, Esperanto. He also continued to train himself as a public speaker and acquired a five-volume *Book of Public Speaking* that included models of the art of rhetoric. There is a frequently repeated family story that McLachlan's favourite place to practise his elocution was at the back fence in the cabbage field, where the silent audience before him would offer no interruptions.[80]

Books in McLachlan's collection give evidence of his interests at this time. Several volumes revealed his own efforts to reconcile his theological knowledge with natural science. These included Edward Clodd, *Pioneers of Evolution from Thales to Huxley* (1909), and J.J. Welsh, *The Popes and Science* (1911). He was also reading about Canada, and his collection included a 1909 edition of J.G. Bourinot's standard text on the Canadian political system, *How Canada Is Governed*, as well as an exposé of Canadian business, Gustavus Myers's *History of Canadian Wealth*, which was published by Charles H. Kerr in 1914. Dan Cochrane, one of the Glace Bay socialists, gave him a copy of C. Osborne Ward's classic *History of the Ancient Lowly*; Alfred Nash, another comrade, provided a copy of Gustavus Myers's muckraking *Great American Fortunes*; Jules Lavenne, a Belgian socialist who became a leader of the Springhill miners, supplied an edition of Émile Vandervelde, *Collectivism and Industrial Evolution*. In a 1910 Kerr edition of Friedrich Engels's *Origin of the Family, Private Property and the State*, McLachlan marked out for special attention a section dealing with prostitution, monogamy, and the breakdown of the family under conditions of capitalism.

McLachlan's socialism had withstood the challenge of the war, and when a provincial election loomed in 1916 it was his turn to come forward as the socialist candidate. Under the title *Working Class Politics*, an election leaflet advanced the claims of "James B. McLachlan, The Workers' Candidate": "Of the nine candidates eight are running as candidates of the Old Capitalist Parties. One man, James B. McLachlan, has been nominated by the Socialist Party to contest the election in the interest of the working class alone." Little was said about the personal qualities or qualifications of the candidate himself, the election leaflet stating only that "the Socialist candidate is a working man, unable to leave his work for campaign purposes." Despite his identification with the cause of the coal miners, the ballot listed McLachlan as a farmer by occupation.[81]

The leaflet contained merely one brief reference to the cataclysm of the war, and it was presented as part of the argument for working-class power:

The workers being in the vast majority could take charge of the law-making machinery of the country tomorrow if they chose. To do this by political action is the only way open to them. You know that it can be done. You feel in your heart that it must be done some day soon, unless the workers wish to be crushed into slavery again. If the workers of Europe had done this five years ago, this war would have been impossible. Unless it is done very shortly similar collapses in Human Society will be inevitable.

As in past campaigns, the socialists concentrated on a single large theme – the education of the workers for the eventual possession of political power:

It should be as plain as daylight that before we can have the enactment and enforcement of working class laws we must have administrators, legislators and judges, who have the working class point of view, who have been elected to office under the auspices of a working class party and who are pledged to obey the mandate of a well disciplined working class organization. Once the workers organize politically, they can have any laws passed that they choose and which will at once place them in possession of the means whereby they make their living.

As usual, objections to socialism were also answered. The Socialist Party, it was underlined, was "purely a Political Organization" which did not seek to "interfere in any way with anyone's personal views on Art, Science, Religion, etc." Socialism was portrayed simply as "the coming civilization" under which "industry and politics shall both be managed democratically": "Men of thought and education, clergymen, lawyers, bankers, captains of industry, know that the principle of Socialism is sound, that it eventually must come. They are waiting, many of them, hoping that the workers will awake and redeem the world from the chaos of capitalism. Only the worker seems to be asleep and unaware of the power in his hands. Will you help to awake him?" The socialist campaign thus placed a "working class candidate" squarely against the "capitalist politicians."

The campaign effort was a modest one, limited to a few streetcorner speeches and the distribution of publicity. One observer later recalled the election in these words: "While on 'the black list' McLachlan ran for the local house as a labour candidate. He had no organization, no polling agents and the day of the election he was around town delivering milk to his customers. He lost his election deposit."[82]

When the ballots were counted, McLachlan finished in last place. In the mining districts he received 561 votes, mainly in areas where he was personally best known: 108 votes in Sydney Mines and 304 in Glace Bay. He also received 242 votes in the steel town of Sydney and an additional 235 votes in other parts of the county. His total of 1,038 votes represented a modest advance of several hundred over the vote Alex MacKinnon had received in the 1911 provincial election.[83]

In retrospect, one revealing feature of this election was the complete marginalization of McLachlan in the newspaper reports of the contest. The Sydney *Post* contained not a single report or editorial comment on his campaign, and none of his votes was included in the reports of election returns. According to the highly partisan *Post*, the "Workingmen's Ticket" consisted of the three barristers and one merchant representing the Conservative Party. Except for the custom of publishing sample ballots to advertise the party ticket, it would be impossible to know from the pages of this newspaper that McLachlan was even a candidate.[84]

At the time of the 1916 election McLachlan was nearing fifty years of age, a veteran of more than three decades of class struggle. True to his understanding of the laws of social development, he remained confident that revolutionary changes in the condition of the working class were in the making. The time would come, but when?

The 1909 strike left an enormous legacy of defeat for the coal miners. Their divisions were too great and their solidarities too weak to overcome the resistance of employers and the indifference of governments. In the end even the international union had abandoned the Nova Scotia coal miners. Nor, as McLachlan's first election campaign revealed, was there any considerable progress to report in the cause of labour politics. In the view from Steele's Hill, high on the land above Glace Bay, there was little to suggest that this sprawling company town would soon be the site of one of the most protracted class struggles in Canadian history.

The view from Hoddom Hill, Ecclefechan, Dumfriesshire, Scotland: the birthplace of James Bryson McLachlan, 1869.

Newmains, Lanarkshire. The family lived in company housing here, where J.B. McLachlan entered the coal mines at the age of ten.

Keir Hardie. Coal miner, union organizer, socialist, and Britain's first Labour Member of Parliament, Hardie was an early influence on McLachlan. Hardie visited McLachlan in Nova Scotia in 1908.

High Street, Wishaw, Lanarkshire, late 19th century, where McLachlan courted Catherine Greenshields. They married in 1893.

Installations of the Nova Scotia Steel and Coal Company, Sydney Mines, Nova Scotia. McLachlan worked here after his arrival in Canada.

Dominion No. 1. In the early 20th century the Nova Scotia coal industry supplied almost half of the coal produced in Canada. The coal royalties accounted for a substantial part of the province's revenue.

In the first decade of the 20th century there were as many as 1,000 boys employed every year in the Nova Scotia coal mines.

"None Cease to Rise But Those Who Cease to Climb." The Provincial Workmen's Association, established in 1879, articulated the ideal of the self-improving independent collier.

The United Mine Workers of America, established in 1890, presented a vision of brotherhood and solidarity for the coal miners.

Company housing. Only employees in good standing could rent company houses such as these. Rents were deducted from their pay. Workers who went on strike were subject to eviction.

Company stores. Dominion Coal operated company stores like this — also known as the "pluck me" stores — until the time of the 1925 strike, when the stores were raided and burned.

Company police. Dominion Coal maintained a large police force to protect company property and keep out unions.

Military aid. The most common peacetime use of the armed forces in the early 20th century was to protect property and break strikes.

The executive of District 26, United Mine Workers of America, 1909. Front row, left to right: J.B. Moss, Dan McDougall, J.D. McLennan. Back row: J.B. McLachlan, Charles Bond, Murray Graham, Ernest Bond.

Delegates to a United Mine Workers of America meeting, 1910, including J.B. McLachlan (top left).

William Lyon Mackenzie King (left), the famous rebel's grandson, a future prime minister of Canada, here shown as an industrial relations consultant (with John D. Rockefeller, Jr., 1915).

SAMPLE BALLOT

VOTE FOR THE
LIBERAL - CONSERVATIVE CANDIDATES

Mark Your Ballot as Shown Below:

1 — ROBERT HAMILTON BUTTS — of Sydney Mines, in the County of Cape Breton, Barrister-at-Law. — **X**

2 — DANIEL A. CAMERON — of Sydney, in the County of Cape Breton, Barrister-at-Law.

3 — JOHN C. DOUGLAS — of Glace Bay, in the County of Cape Breton, Barrister-at-Law — **X**

4 — NEIL FERGUSSON — of Marion Bridge, in the County of Cape Breton, Merchant. — **X**

5 — DAVID J. HARTIGAN — of New Waterford, in the County of Cape Breton, Physician.

6 — DANIEL C. MCDONALD — of Sydney Mines, in the County of Cape Breton Town Clerk.

7 — FINLAY MCDONALD — of Sydney, in the County of Cape Breton, Barrister-at-Law. — **X**

8 — JAMES E. MACLACHLAN — of Glace Bay, in the County of Cape Breton, Farmer.

9 — MICHAEL THOMAS SULLIVAN — of New Aberdeen, in the County of Cape Breton, Physician.

A sample ballot, 1916. The socialist candidate, McLachlan, is listed here as a farmer. The ballot recommends the straight Tory ticket in the four-member constituency. In the next provincial election in 1920 all four seats went to Labour and Farmer candidates.

BOOK TWO

THE ECONOMIC GOSPEL
1916–22

From Moses and Jesus
and Marx and Carlyle,
one outstanding theme runs thru all their teachings,
however much the language employed
may have differed.
The sins which all of them
denounced most fiercely
were economic sins,
and the mission of all of them in life
was to deliver the oppressed.

– J.B. McLachlan,
1919

CHAPTER 4

The Miners' Union

And they shall build houses and inhabit them;
and they shall plant vineyards and eat the fruit of them.
They shall not build and another inhabit,
they shall not plant and other eat;
for as the days of a tree are the days of my people,
and mine elect shall long enjoy the work of their hands.

– *Isaiah*, 65:21–2,
Strike Bulletin (Winnipeg),
23 June 1919

The United Mine Workers of Nova Scotia

All through the fall of 1916 and into the winter, the daily reports of the Dominion Coal police force began with the usual heading – "The Collieries and works were policed and watched during the day and night by our regular officers and watchmen." The most important news collected by the company police in these months was the appearance of a new group called the United Mine Workers of Nova Scotia (UMWNS). It had no official connection with the international union – except for the name and the fact that the organizers, including McLachlan, were familiar veterans of the old District 26. The struggle against the Provincial Workmen's Association was on again. But this time it was taking place under the unusual economic conditions created by the wartime economy.

As the killing continued in the fields of Europe and the machinery of war entered its third year, the coal mines at home were working at capacity. From the beginning of the war, heavy enlistments had been causing labour shortages in the mines. By 1916 it was estimated that 25 per cent of the employees of Dominion Coal had left the coal mines and joined the armed forces. Under wartime conditions the coal industry was booming: Nova Scotia coal supplied the industrial fuel for the province's steel plants and munitions works as well as for railway transport, ocean shipping, and naval patrols. Meanwhile, wartime inflation was taking its toll: prices were rising, and the miners' pay was not keeping up to the cost of living. There was little labour unrest in Canada in the first two years of the war but by 1916 and 1917, like workers in other parts of the country, the coal miners were pressing for wage increases. Those who had not forgotten the defeat of the UMW were also pressing for recognition of their union.

McLachlan was optimistic. Writing to Indianapolis in October 1916, he reported on the first big public meeting of the United Mine Workers of Nova Scotia: "The Casino Theatre, Glace Bay, was packed; four, or five hundred men unable to get inside thirty minutes before the advertised time for meeting. They also had a committee wait on the Premier of this Province, and he strongly advised them to push their demand for a 30% increase, and to organize in the U.M.W. of A., and that he would use his good offices to protect and assist them in every way in their efforts." McLachlan noted that the PWA had signed a new agreement with Dominion Coal for the next two years carrying only a 6 per cent increase: "Should the men here make a success of their present efforts, it will mean the tearing up of the PWA contract and the hardest blow that organization ever received."[1]

Steadily, the UMWNS was growing: by January 1917 nine locals had been organized, and another six were in place by June. Already the UMWNS was asking for a 25 per cent increase in wage rates. Then it was applying for a conciliation board under the Industrial Disputes Investigation Act. In April, McLachlan and other leaders were in Halifax, putting pressure on the provincial government. For months there had been rumours that the provincial government had a grudge to settle with the coal company – "that some of the people connected with the Coal Company did them dirty during the last Election" and Murray "is now going to get after them."[2] Premier George Murray did attempt to bring leaders of the UMWNS and PWA together – but, according to Silby Barrett, "at that time the P.W.A. officers did not appear to be in any mood to listen to either the Premier of this Province, or your representatives and nothing whatever came from this effort." Then there was an unsuccessful attempt to have the legislative assembly debate a bill authorizing a plebiscite among the miners on a choice between the PWA and UMWNS, with the winning union to receive the check-off of union dues "by law without any discretion on the part of the employers."

The turning point came at the end of April 1917. As in 1909, the road to union recognition led directly to confrontation. When the UMWNS threatened a one-day strike for Monday, 23 April, local newspapers accused McLachlan of sabotaging the war effort in the coalfields. McLachlan was gambling that a short stoppage demonstrating the new union's strength would succeed in getting the government to intervene. He was right. On 19 April there was word from Ottawa. The minister of labour, T.C. Crothers, was prepared to appoint a royal commission to investigate the unrest in the coal industry. On the Saturday before the strike deadline, the coal miners crowded into local moviehouses to hear the news and decide whether to call off the strike.

On stage at the Casino Theatre in Glace Bay, McLachlan hailed the appointment of the royal commission as a victory for the coal miners: "The politicians promised a great deal but gave nothing. Now the battle is fought and won, not at Ottawa nor at Halifax, it was won by you men who got the commission and can get any laws you wish … The only friends you have are yourselves. Organize, depend more on yourselves and the U.M.W. will do something …" In the meanwhile, McLachlan urged, the miners would remain united and delay any strike action: "We can get what we want without taking the idle day. We are going to cooperate with the commission. We don't want to prejudice these men against us." At stake was the future of the United Mine Workers in the coalfields: "All should join and help kill the P.W.A. That organization has been running since ten years and has got you nothing. You miners must see that John Moffatt has betrayed you, and you will be betraying your families if you don't hold together. Now is your best opportunity to organize. One hundred per cent of the men must be got into the U.M.W. this summer."[3]

In McLachlan's view, the royal commission presented an unusually favourable opportunity. The members included three prominent Halifax men selected by Premier Murray. The chairman was the recently appointed Supreme Court Judge Joseph Andrew Chisholm, a Liberal loyalist well known for his edition of the writings of Joseph Howe. The former Dalhousie University president John Forrest, a Presbyterian minister, was considered an energetic and progressive-minded educator. And the third member was the veteran Halifax longshoremen's leader, John T. Joy, known as the father of workmen's compensation in Nova Scotia. Joy was one of the coal miners' allies in lobbying the provincial government earlier that year and, according to McLachlan, he was "the best labor man in the province." The commission quickly recommended a large wage increase for the coal miners and then turned its attention to the problem of the rival unions. Joy acted as a go-between in negotiations between officers of the two organizations, and the result was a merger agreement.

On 12 June 1917 the two miners' organizations met in separate conventions in Sydney, each agreeing to dissolve on 1 July 1917 in favour of a new union to be called the Amalgamated Mine Workers of Nova Scotia. Six provisional officers were appointed – three from each side – to conduct the union's business until the founding convention. The nominees from the UMWNS included Silby Barrett, Robert Baxter, and McLachlan; old animosities still ran deep, however, and one of the PWA veterans, Stephen B. MacNeil, refused to serve on the same executive as McLachlan. Nevertheless, with a brave valedictory report, John Moffatt and the PWA were retiring from the scene: "To us as members of a most successful Labor organization the call of our Country has come, bidding us fall into line, close up our ranks and join forces with our Brothers for the common good of all. A patriotic duty never confronted any member of our loyal association without a hearty response, no matter how great the sacrifice."[4]

For his part McLachlan regarded the outcome as the final defeat for an organization that had long since lost its legitimacy as a labour union: "The old P.W.A. is gone for ever and the men who had been its chief officers for the last twelve years have been given official jobs with the Dominion Coal Company." Writing to UMW headquarters, he reported that the Nova Scotia coal miners were now organized "to the last man" with 10,000 coal miners united in the AMW – "I may also state that our union has the check-off and complete recognition." Another 3,000 men, mainly in Inverness and Pictou Counties, belonged to directly chartered AFL unions and could be expected to join the coal miners "when we go into the U.M.W. of A." Looking ahead to the founding convention of the AMW, McLachlan was already anticipating that the AMW would enter the UMW. He asked for an indication of how such an application would be received. UMW President John P. White made no commitments, but as the date of the convention approached, McLachlan renewed his appeals: "We expect to join the Trades and Labor Congress of Canada, and in the event of the way not being clear for the U.M.W. of A. to take us in, we could stave the matter off for the present by saying Congress was enough for us now. I would like to see the men here back in the Mine Workers, and if anything can be done along that line I would be very pleased to hear from you at an early date."[5]

The establishment of the AMW was a triumph of persistence for McLachlan and his supporters. Defeated in the original contest against the PWA, in the end they had won out, and they had done so without a single day's strike. This time there was no ambiguity about the transfer of authority. The AMW inherited the membership and property of the PWA, as well as a wage agreement arranged by the Chisholm Commission in May. But the new union was obviously built on the legacy of District 26. In October it was Dan McDougall, the first president of the old District 26, who was called upon to preside at the opening of the founding convention of the AMW.

All of the principal officers of the new union were men associated with the UMW cause, and all were elected by huge majorities in a general vote at the end of September. As president there was Silby Barrett, the young Newfoundlander whom McLachlan had taken under his wing and, it was said, taught how to read. As vice-president there was Robert Baxter, another Lanarkshireman, somewhat younger than McLachlan, who had also started his working life in the pits of the Old Country and come to Cape Breton at the turn of the century. McLachlan himself was returned as secretary-treasurer, with 4,713 votes in his favour against 1,659 for his nearest opponent. At the end of the year he reflected briefly on the significance of the election: "On September 27th the ordinary every-day miner had, for the first time in the history of trade unionism in Nova Scotia, a ballot placed in his hand and he was allowed to say by his vote who should be the officers of his union. The result was simply glorious for the radicals."[6]

The passing of the PWA marked the end of an era in local labour history. Reporters were impressed by the novelty of the occasion. There were no more secret handshakes and ceremonial passwords, and the meetings were open to the press. "In the old days we had secret meetings, and those outside of our ranks imagined we plotted and planned all sorts of dark deeds," McLachlan explained to a reporter, "There is no advantage in trying to do things secretly. We propose no action of which we have any reason to be ashamed."[7] To the assembled delegates and to the members of the union, McLachlan expressed his thanks for the confidence they had placed in him as secretary-treasurer: "Great as had been the troubles and calamities of the past it had taught us much and the present convention of miners, he had no hesitation in saying, was the finest ever gathered in Nova Scotia. The organization had been built to go ahead and would go ahead. He was confident that the old stubbornness that used to prevail had given way and he believed the miners should swear to themselves never to be again divided."[8]

There was much business to transact at the founding convention, but underlying all the resolutions and reports was the fact that the old debates about the place of unions in economic life were being resolved in favour of the radicals. In place of the "loyalist" views of the old PWA, the AMW in its new constitution endorsed a "rebel" vision of the place of workers in industrial society:

Whereas, a struggle is going on in all nations of the industrial world between those who labor and those who appropriate the wealth resulting from social labor. This irrepressible struggle over the distribution of the proceeds of labor is ever bringing more and more strength to the working class and imposing upon it ever greater duties and responsibilities; And, believing that all rivalry, whether between individual workmen or organizations, can bring to them only disastrous results: –

We therefore declare it to be our irrefutable duty to join hands and forces to form all miners and mine laborers in Nova Scotia into a trade union for the purpose of securing to its members the social value of their labor and procuring such legislation as they may require from time to time.[9]

The AMW document reflected McLachlan's understanding of the purposes of unionism. Unions were needed both to protect the rights of workers from day to day and in the long run to advance their interests in the class struggle. The first paragraph echoed the vocabulary of the Wobblies, the revolutionary industrial union that was determined to build the structure of a new society within the shell of the old. The second paragraph took its language from the UMW and a constitution that had evolved out of the struggles of North America's largest industrial union. In McLachlan's view the two purposes were inseparable. Only a strong union that was successful in defending the workers' everyday interests could fulfil its ultimate responsibilities to history.

As the union advanced from one success to another, winning recognition and establishing collective bargaining in the coal industry, McLachlan would be acclaimed to office or re-elected by large majorities every year. No longer an outsider agitating for reforms in the conduct of union affairs, McLachlan was entering a new stage in his public career. While Kate and their older children looked after the milk business at the little farm on Steele's Hill, he was meeting and corresponding with company managers and cabinet ministers as well as fellow union members; there were hearings, interviews, negotiations, more meetings – his agenda was filled with the daily business of the labour bureaucrat in the age of industrial legality. It was more than enough to keep a union leader busy and, perhaps, to suggest that the effective administration of day-to-day union business was a sufficient achievement for any one union leader.

But unlike many successful union leaders of his time, McLachlan considered the establishment of unions only a partial victory in the class struggle. There could be no lasting peace in the class struggle. Under conditions of industrial capitalism, the achievement of industrial legality, with all the trappings of union recognition and collective bargaining, was an important victory for the working class. It showed that the balance of power was changing in the workers' favour. But this kind of victory was only provisional. The inauguration of a workers' democracy was still somewhere in the future.

For McLachlan, there was never any doubt of the final outcome. From his office in Glace Bay, he watched in anticipation, knowing that around the world the working class was also on the move. In Britain and the United States the miners' unions came out of the war with large expectations about the prospects for industrial democracy; on the European continent there were revolutionary upheavals in Russia, in Germany, in Italy. Meanwhile, in Canada union membership more than doubled between 1916 and 1921, and events such as the Winnipeg General Strike in 1919 demonstrated that the class struggle was accelerating.

Most of all, McLachlan's faith was also a faith in history. As a Calvinist who had also become a socialist, he believed that the working class were the elect of history. In a moment of inspiration in 1917, shortly after the restoration of the miners' union and the revival of independent labour politics, McLachlan foresaw the inevitable triumph of the workers' cause: "Our movement is chained to a star, and both the grave and the womb of time are fighting with us."[10]

The Amalgamated

In that summer of 1917 John McKay was an officer of one of the new AMW locals. A shot-firer in No. 12 colliery, New Waterford, McKay was a well-respected citizen of the town, forty-five years of age, the father of seven children. When the day shift started at 7 a.m. on 25 July 1917, there were 270 men at work in No. 12 colliery. About thirty minutes later there was the sudden sound of a loud boom. At the sixth, seventh, and eight levels of the pit, the roof, walls, and ground shook. A rushing wind carried clouds of dust and coal and bits of broken timber out to the landings.

All day and long after dark, anxious crowds waited at the mouth of the slope until the final rake arrived with the bodies of the dead. A total of sixty-five men and boys died in the mine that day, including John McKay. In a small park on Plummer Avenue in New Waterford a monument erected by the miners' union lists the victims of the explosion. In age they ranged from boys of fourteen to men of sixty-five. By place of birth they were Nova Scotians and Newfoundlanders, Germans and Austrians, Russians and Italians. But it is the image of John McKay, the local union leader, that stands on the top of the monument, surveying the troubled landscape of the company town.[11]

Mine disasters have often been regarded as part of the natural order of things in the coal industry, one of the inevitable costs of production in such a dangerous industry. But the New Waterford explosion was different, and much of the difference was defined by the presence of the new union. Though hundreds of men had died in the Cape Breton coal mines – more than 500 in the preceding half-century – most of those coal miners had died in smaller accidents, crushed by falling stone and coal, struck and run over by runaway boxes, trapped by cables and ropes, burned and gassed in fires and explosions. There had been major disasters on the mainland, including the one at Springhill in 1891 that killed 125 men and boys, but the New Waterford explosion was the largest single disaster ever to strike the Cape Breton coal mines. Moreover, it had taken place in wartime, under the pressure of demands for high productivity. Somehow a spark had ignited gas in a mine that was considered relatively safe. At a coroner's inquest several miners testified that ventilation in No. 12 was bad and high levels of gas were often encountered. The jury's verdict concluded that there was "gross irregularity" in the operation of the mine, that this had allowed gas to accumulate, and that unspecified mine officials were guilty of gross neglect. A provincial inquiry into the explosion, which included union representatives, also recommended that better ventilation methods be followed at the coal face.[12]

This was not enough for the coal miners assembled at the AMW convention in October. New Waterford delegates brought forward resolutions demanding the dismissal of three mining officials and the cancellation of their mine certificates. Furthermore, unless the men were dismissed by 15 November the AMW threatened to remain idle every Wednesday and Saturday until they were removed. McLachlan, who had supported the demands and was now writing letters to convey them to the authorities, soon ran into objections. "Every knave in Waterford crept + crawled to these officials," he noted, "and howled their little heads off about 'finding men guilty before being tried.'" McLachlan argued that the union resolutions said no more than "both the coroner's jury and the special commission but had the courage of its conviction and refused to sidestep and hedge."

Meanwhile, with this kind of encouragement from the union, a grand jury in New Waterford approved criminal charges. The Dominion Coal Company was indicted for "causing grievous bodily harm." Two company officials, No. 12 mine manager Angus R. MacDonald and district superintendent of mines Alexander MacEachren, and one pro-

vincial official, deputy mines inspector Michael McIntosh, were charged
with manslaughter. The cases eventually came to trial in Sydney a year
later. The presiding judge was Humphrey Mellish, a new appointment
to the Supreme Court (and, like many Nova Scotia lawyers, a former
solicitor for the coal company). He ruled that there was not enough
evidence to allow him to send the case to the jury.[13]

As a union officer responding to the disaster, McLachlan was determined both to pursue the immediate interests of the miners and their
families and to raise issues of control and management in the industry.
Accordingly, he assisted the miners' widows and dependants in making
their claims and appealing the unsatisfactory allowances provided
under the Workmen's Compensation Act. John McKay's widow Elizabeth, for instance, received $35 a month to support their seven children.
First in October and then again in November, McLachlan appealed to
Prime Minister Robert Borden, using relatively temperate language, for
supplements to the compensation allowances: "I can very well understand that your time has been fully taken up with the affairs of the
country, during these strenuous months, and little time to devote to
matters of this kind ... The women affected are asking me all the time
if anything is going to be done and I would like to be able to give them
a definite answer." Months later the Dominion government authorized
an additional $10,000 in payments to the families, and the union
officers received credit for successfully pressing the case.[14]

Meanwhile, McLachlan was insisting that the administration of the
Coal Mines Regulation Act was "a veritable farce":

> The miners of Nova Scotia have had continually dinned into
> their ears that "we have the best mining laws in the world," and
> when those who profess to see such excellency in these laws are
> asked how it comes that the death rate in the mines of Nova
> Scotia is so comparatively high, they wriggle and twist and
> side-step any direct answer. The answer is this: the Coal Mines
> Regulation Act is not enforced, and is not intended to be
> enforced, excepting in cases where it suits the coal companies
> when they want to get rid of what they are pleased to call a
> "kicker." The opinion is openly expressed that the Government

Mines Inspectors are as subservient to the coal companies as the last trapper-boy that was hired on.

One of the principal objectives of the AMW, McLachlan wrote at the end of 1917, was to ensure that the Coal Mines Regulation Act was "enforced in its entirety." The only certain way to make sure it was enforced was for the local unions to take the power in their own hands and appoint their own committees to carry out regular inspections. Only a few days later, on 23 January 1918, another disaster struck the coalfields, this time in an explosion at the Allan Mine in Pictou County. It was the second major calamity in six months. This time eighty-eight lives were lost. For McLachlan, blood on the coal was the coal miners' supreme sacrifice in the coal industry. It was part of the coal miners' enormous investment in the industry and, for coal miners around the world, it helped set the price of their labour.[15]

In that first year of the AMW, McLachlan emerged as the district's most important officer and, more than any other district leader, came to personify the miners' union. From headquarters in Glace Bay it was McLachlan who arranged meetings, spoke to the press, and responded to local concerns. More than the limited statutory provisions of the Mines Act, the miners' agreements on rates and conditions made up the accumulated legislation that governed the working life of the coal mines. In visits to local union meetings, McLachlan filled up his notebooks with detailed information about conditions, wages, allowances, and grievances. This was the stuff of daily union business, to be rehearsed in hearings, negotiations, and agreements.

McLachlan's correspondence with the local unions made him an invisible presence throughout the district. His letters and circulars were read and discussed at the weekly local union meetings, and local minutes and resolutions contained frequent references to "Brother McLachlan" and "Our Provincial Secretary." In the month of August 1917 alone, for instance, McLachlan wrote to the Springhill local (which he had visited the previous month) on several occasions – to offer copies of the AMW constitution at $5.00 per hundred, to request appointment of a delegate to hearings on workmen's compensation, to ask the local to express its views "on the eight hour day matter," and to explain a controversial reorganization of the district office.

In return, every local union had its own demands on the district office. In 1917 the Springhill local was writing McLachlan about wage rates – "it is time for a general increase"; in 1918 the local complained about McLachlan's failure to achieve a satisfactory conclusion to a local grievance over interpretation of the contract with Dominion Coal – "we protest and authorize him *not* to enter into the next contract for our district until our present contract is carried out"; on other occasions the local invited McLachlan to provide further explanations of district policies or to contradict statements reported in the press. This was part of the natural push and pull of relations between local union and district office. McLachlan's performance of his duties was obviously judged satisfactory in the local, for in both 1917 and 1918 he received its nomination for secretary-treasurer.[16]

Under the prevailing wartime conditions, union officers were often called in to consult with the Dominion fuel controller. In 1918 McLachlan's correspondence with union locals contained numerous references to the war effort and efficiency in production. When the conscription controversy heated up in May 1918, "labour volunteers" were invited to participate in the registration process. Later, McLachlan wrote to point out that union members joining the army or navy were exempted from paying dues and were entitled to full membership on their return. In August, workers were asked to file reports with their checkweighman – the miners' elected representative at the surface of each mine – giving reasons for leaving the pit early or without getting all their coal away. When McLachlan wrote the Springhill local in November 1918 encouraging workers to participate in "a system of producing more coal," the local response was to ask "who pays the committee appointed to deal with more production of coal?"[17]

An additional sign of McLachlan's rising influence was his appointment to a royal commission. This was another hastily improvised commission named by the Dominion government to investigate labour unrest in several steel-making and shipbuilding establishments in the province. Within a month of their appointment in April 1918, the commissioners filed reports on six separate disputes. As the labour representative, McLachlan had hoped to be of some help in bringing about union recognition in these industries, but the results were disappointing. The most he could achieve, he reported, was to raise the wage scale sufficiently so that the lowest paid workers could receive "at least a living wage." The report received bad reviews in the labour press and was considered "very barren in its recommendations: Not a great deal was gained through the efforts of this 'august tribunal' outside their own fat fees, and what surprises us the most is that the whole commission was unanimous in its decision." The radical union leader C.C. Dane, an Australian boilermaker who was building unions in the metal trades in Pictou County, denounced McLachlan's "remarkable acquiescence" in signing the report. This was the one and only time McLachlan served on a royal commission, though it was not the last time he would be attacked for endorsing settlements that fell short of the most militant expectations.[18]

From this evidence it would be misleading to conclude that McLachlan in 1918 was a compliant labour leader whose only aim was to discipline the labour force in the interests of wartime cooperation. Instead, he took every opportunity to turn the arguments about low production into a critique of capitalist administration of the industry. When complaints about the threat of coal shortages began to circulate early in the year, McLachlan observed that low production was the fault of bad management by the coal operators – old pumps in one mine, conflicts over coal leases in another section, experienced coal-cutters doing the work of horses in another. Production could also be increased at least 100 tons a day, he argued, if about fifty members of the company police force – a perfect example of "a non-producing class" – were also put to work in the mines. And like other wartime labour radicals, McLachlan defied the "idle coupon clippers" to give up their unearned profits – amounting in the coal industry in 1916 to "seven mighty millions of dollars" – and let the government take control of the industry for the sake of the war effort. "The miners here will dig coal like slaves for their country," McLachlan pledged. "But not one cent's worth of wealth shall be produced by the miners of Cape Breton, with their willing consent, for idle profit takers."[19]

One provocative proposal at this time threatened to raise the spectre of racial divisions among the coal miners. In the early months of 1918 the Dominion fuel controller proposed that coal production could be substantially increased by importing large numbers of Chinese labourers. The idea of "coolie labour" in the coal mines aroused vocal protests. The prejudice against "Asiatic labour" was well-entrenched among Canadian workers, who feared that such "alien" workers would work for low wages and undermine existing standards. As union vice-president Robert Baxter told a public meeting in Glace Bay, "slowly but surely the Chinamen would work the white men out of jobs." Meeting with the fuel controller, the union officers proposed a more acceptable alternative – that the union itself would recruit as many as 1,000 labourers from Newfoundland to work in the mines. Such recruits were to be paid union wages and guaranteed return fare home. There were already substantial numbers of "Cape Breton Newfoundlanders" in the coal mines – among them the AMW president himself, Silby Barrett – and the union was confident that labour standards and class solidarity could be protected under such conditions.

McLachlan himself had worked hard in the past to reduce racist and nativist reactions in the interest of class solidarity among the coal miners. Under certain conditions he considered the recruitment of Chinese labourers, but he did so in a way that presented a challenge to the employers' agenda. McLachlan's alternative amounted to an experiment in workers' control of the industry. "Speaking for myself solely, and not for our organization," McLachlan told reporters,

it is my opinion that if in the future it becomes necessary to import coolie labor for Nova Scotia coal mines, the miners should demand that the mine where such labour is employed should be handed over completely to the union, and that the union should control such a mine absolutely. If the government only "wants coal" and does not want to import coolies to lower the standard of living of Canadians, then they won't object to this and to let the union reap any financial benefit such labor may create instead of such money going to a corporation.[20]

The biggest confrontation in 1918 came over the union's struggle for the eight-hour day. In the coalfields of Britain and the United States, the eight-hour day was widely regarded as the appropriate working day for unionized coal miners. In the spring of 1918 McLachlan insisted that 9,000 unionized miners in Nova Scotia were waiting for the provincial government to endorse their claim by enacting legislation: "The miners have been looking forward to the day when the government would recognize that their condition was such that it was imperative that their hours of labor be reduced in the interest of their physical well-being." More than anything else, the eight-hour day would be a sign that the Nova Scotia coal miners were entitled to the same standards as coal miners in other jurisdictions. While lobbying the legislative assembly for enactment of the amendment to the Mines Act, McLachlan was also prepared to concede that the eight-hour day need not take immediate effect under wartime conditions.

But from the beginning, McLachlan had warned that the provincial legislature could not be trusted to enact the miners' reforms. Instead, the miners might have to demonstrate their latent power to regulate conditions in the mines themselves:

We remember that miners elsewhere had to introduce an eight hour day themselves and continue to work the shorter day for years before it became the law of their country. We certainly shall avail ourselves of our own native ability to introduce the shorter working day if circumstances demand that from us. Our faith in the politician is limited, very. We understand exactly that working class laws are like the score kept at a cricket match, recorded after a run has been made in the field. We will make the run alright and the politicians in Halifax can suit themselves as to when they will record it.[21]

All of the union's amendments to the Mines Act (including those for changes in safety and ventilation procedures) were turned down at the spring session of the legislative assembly. It was time for action, and McLachlan led the union in a one-day work stoppage on 8 July 1918. The day passed quietly and without incident in the coalfields, but respectable opinion was scandalized by this "organized idleness" in the midst of the war effort. In his defence of the strike, McLachlan was not constrained by the ethics of wartime patriotism:

> Because of this idle day there were columns of editorials weepingly written and buckets full of crocodile tears shed by the troglodytes of the press because fifteen thousand tons of coal was being lost, and that coal would have made ever so much steel and shells for the "boys at the front," etc.
>
> Lost? Listen, one hundred and fifty miners lost their lives in the coal mines of Nova Scotia last year because the Government of this province failed to air the mines properly ... It is awfully nice to be a patriot but if being a patriot means having one's name bracketed up along with some of the men that compose our local Government and the troglodytes who write about matters of which they are wholly ignorant, then here is one who absolutely refuses to be a patriot.[22]

Amid all the alarms and confusions of wartime, McLachlan was making it clear that the coal miners' agenda included substantial improvements in the rights of workers. The coal miners' strike was a local instance of a tide of labour unrest that was beginning to alarm the Dominion government; by October all strikes would be legally prohibited for the duration of the war. Meanwhile, the campaign for an eight-hour law would be renewed again and again in subsequent years. McLachlan was right in his prediction that the eight-hour day would be won independently by the coal miners, for it was accepted in their contracts with the coal operators in 1919. But it did not appear on the statute books of Nova Scotia until 1924.

The second annual convention of the Amalgamated Mine Workers, meeting for six days in Sydney in late November 1918, was a celebration of the new union's strength. The eighty-six delegates in attendance represented thirty local unions across the Nova Scotia coalfields. They listened with satisfaction as the officers reported the union's successes. Wherever the AMW was organized, President Barrett proudly reported, organization of the work force was almost 100 per cent successful. In some of the coal towns the union had had to turn away fishermen, truckmen, and retail clerks – and even the wireless operators at the Marconi station in Glace Bay – who all wanted to join the miners' union. The only substantial gap in the union's success was in Inverness and Pictou Counties, where the miners were independently affiliated to the American Federation of Labor and hoping for the return of the UMW to Nova Scotia.

As for the union's wage campaigns, they too had been successful – in the face of rising prices, the union had already won two general increases on the wage scale, 12.5 per cent for men on tonnage rates and 24 per cent for men on daily wages, and then an additional 20 per cent six months later. In preparation for a new round of negotiations, the wage-scale committee prepared a detailed rate schedule, including a minimum rate of $4.25 a day for underground labour and increases of 25 to 35 per cent on other rates. The union would continue to pursue the eight-hour day, with no change in the wage scale; but whether the law was enacted or not, the miners voted to introduce reduced hours unilaterally on 1 May 1919. They would push too for the inclusion of miners' diseases and better rates under the compensation act, for better ventilation and drainage in the pits, and even for the election of mine inspectors by a vote of the miners in each district.[23]

Preoccupied with conditions in their own industry, the coal miners were also aware that they were meeting only a few days after the arrival of Armistice Day. With the war at last over, delegates called, for instance, for the removal as soon as possible of the teams of interned "enemy aliens" working under military discipline in the mines, to make way for returned men after demobilization.[24] Another resolution, anticipating "a grave social and economic situation affecting the existence of the workers" at the end of the war, instructed the union officers "to petition the Dominion government to nationalize all industries and their operation for benefit of the country instead of for private enrichment." A special committee was appointed to prepare a statement "embodying demands to safeguard the interests of the working class during period of reconstruction."

On the final day of the convention, the committee returned with an extended Reconstruction Report, which was read to the hall by machinist George Bagnell. It was an eclectic document, beginning with a short preface listing a variety of concerns – better housing in the coal towns, elimination of the shacks and unsanitary buildings, introduction of Dominion-wide prohibition, nationalization of the coal mines, repeal of the wartime orders-in-council suspending the rights of free speech, association, and assembly, and abolition of the provincial Legislative Council and the Senate. This was followed by a series of resolutions under headings such as "The Prevention of Unemployment," "Unemployment Insurance," "The Complete Emancipation of Women," "The Maintenance and Protection of the Standard of Life," "National Finance," and "Agriculture and Rural Life." The text for the construction of a new democratic social order was borrowed from the policy statement "Labour and the New Social Order," adopted that summer by the British Labour Party, a document that would be regarded as the blueprint for social democracy in Britain for the next several decades. For emigrant coal miners such as McLachlan and the union vice-president, Robert Baxter, political developments in the Old Country continued to have importance. Interestingly, there was one minor modification in the excerpts the miners adopted, a change that was in accord with McLachlan's views on wage standards: where the British document stated that "when peace comes, the standard rates of wages in all trades should, relatively to the cost of living, be fully maintained," the AMW version stated instead more simply that such rates should "be raised."[25]

During the six days of meetings, McLachlan followed the proceedings with satisfaction. Occasionally he was called upon to explain the accounts, read correspondence, or address the future of the union's relations with the UMW. His financial report showed the union in excellent condition – total receipts of $32,173.95 for the year and a balance of $16,217.39 in the bank. A proposal to increase the pay of the president and the secretary to $200 per month was voted down; instead it was agreed that the officers would be entitled to the same rate increases they won for the members. The AMW, McLachlan later reflected, "was probably the best union that the miners of this province ever had." Above all, this was a union that "responded splendidly to the wish and decisions of the rank and file."[26]

McLachlan must have been somewhat chagrined when the delegates approved the insertion of a prayer in the union ritual: "Guide us, direct us in our business transactions, grant to bless our entire organization and grant that the words of our mouths and the meditations of our hearts may be acceptable in Thy sight." The use of religious rituals in union business was something he had objected to in the days of the PWA. But at last, McLachlan reflected, the coal miners were on the move. They were taking care of their present interests aggressively, and they were determined to take care of the future. The coal miners were learning the lesson he had spelled out from the earliest days of the AMW: "In unity there is strength, and while we do not subscribe to the doctrine that 'might is right,' yet we do know from experience in Cape Breton that 'right' gets a pretty raw deal when there is no 'might' behind it."[27]

The Miner's Financier

"Wives, Mothers, Sisters and Sweethearts of Workmen, Attention." In 1917, as part of the AMW's first wage campaign, McLachlan launched a contest addressed to the women of the coal towns. Women were invited to write him and explain how they would maintain a family of two adults and five children on a daily wage of $3.50. It was a brilliant tactic, for no one knew the economic needs of the mining household better than the woman who managed a household budget.

When in 1917 McLachlan notified the coal companies that the union was ready to discuss a new wage agreement as soon as possible, he was acting on the instructions of a full day's discussion at the AMW convention that October. The report of the wage-scale committee contained proposed daily rates for sixty different kinds of labour in and about the mines, as well as tonnage rates for hand-pick miners and machine-runners. There were allowances for a dozen different conditions, including timbering the roof, clearing fallen stone, and pushing boxes. In addition there were rates for machinists, blacksmiths, electricians, hostlers, railway men, coal trimmers, and the many other trades covered by the miners' union. At the end of the day, members of the new union expected substantial increases, running about 30 per cent in most classifications. For what was still a ten-hour day, the proposed rate for general underground labour was $3.50 a day. Men working at the coal face were to receive at least $5.00.[28]

In response to McLachlan's appeal, letters arriving at the union offices gave detailed family budgets and informed commentary on household finances. McLachlan arranged for a series of the letters to appear in the pages of the new Sydney labour newspaper, the *Canadian Labor Leader*, where the columns provided ample food for thought in the miners' homes during the Christmas season. "I think the statement I have given," wrote one woman, "will show that only by the greatest economy and some privation can a family of seven live at the present time on $3.50 per day, and that is without taking into consideration lost time or sickness which would incur greater expense."

In the family budgets they prepared, the women concentrated above all on the cost of providing the basic needs of food, clothing, and shelter. Rents on company housing were relatively low, but the standard of warmth, comfort, and repair was often the subject of complaint. The wear and tear on a miner's work clothes were a heavy expense, and the dangers of sickness and accident led women to include substantial expenditures on insurance policies. The family diet was heavy on potatoes, flour, and rolled oats and it skimped on meat and fruit. One budget pointed out that numerous items were omitted from her calculations: salt, pepper, ginger, yeast, molasses, lard, onions, kettles, pans, dishes, blinds, curtains, bedclothes. "Of course," she added, "I cannot think of wall paper, paint or door rugs, neither can my man think of smoking or using tobacco in any form." Other women did include tobacco for the men and school supplies for the children as necessary spending, but pointed out they were omitting other items: cigars, drink, carfare, nickelodeons, picnics, races, newspapers, books, stamps, candy, presents, the costs of entertaining visitors or buying a musical instrument. "What a surprise," concluded one miner's wife at the end of her calculations, "his weekly income won't cover the food bill and house rent alone, let alone all the rest of life's necessities. There is two ways out of it. Eat less or earn more."[29]

McLachlan was more than satisfied with the results of the contest. The letters had documented the coal miners' case for an improved standard of living in extraordinary detail, gaining public sympathy for the miners' wage proposals and recognition for the women's contribution to "the economic side of housekeeping." Of course, he knew that the contest was an imprecise exercise. Women often met family needs out of gardens and by keeping occasional cows and chickens, and some households had more than one wage earner, including the young men beginning to work in the pits and the young women who worked as domestic servants, clerks, teachers, and telephone operators. But McLachlan was pleased to see that the women had written on a note of optimism, listing their requirements hopefully, all but certain that their standard of living must improve in the coming years. In January 1918 he pronounced the contest a success: "These letters prove that but very few are overpaid, and receiving more money in their pay envelopes than can be used to advantage."[30]

At the same time, McLachlan had made the point that the miner's wife was the hero of the household, struggling to make ends meet with limited resources. In the course of the wage struggles to come, he would often pay tribute to the miner's wife as "the greatest financier in the world." Although substantial numbers of young women were employed in a large mining town such as Glace Bay – including his own daughters – McLachlan focused his attention on the importance of the women who worked in the home. Like most of his contemporaries among labour leaders, McLachlan shared in the patriarchal view that it was the responsibility of the male wage earner to secure a wage adequate to support a family. That responsibility was part of the sacred obligation of a husband to his wife and children.

The letter-writing contest strengthened support for the union among the women of the coalfield, but it was also a challenge to the miners to live up to their responsibilities as family men. While acknowledging the significance of women's work, McLachlan was also implying that men had an obligation to secure the financial rewards necessary to support the family economy, and to do so they would have to support their union at least as strongly as their women did. This particular breadwinner version of the cult of masculinity, one that recurred again and again in McLachlan's speeches, had the additional advantage that it conformed to prevailing public attitudes about male responsibility. Masculine virtue was not just a form of middle-class privilege, this discourse implied, it was also a reasonable expectation within working-class

culture. Far from being a threatening form of male self-assertion, like
the roughness and rowdiness often associated with working-class stereo-
types, the coal miners' wage agitations had the eminently responsible
social objective of protecting the stability of family life.[31]

This effort to advertise the economic needs of the miners' families
was one part of the union's campaign to make substantial improvements in the miners' standard of living at the end of the war. At a time
when prices were rapidly rising, only an aggressive wage strategy would
protect the miners from falling behind and allow them to make some
lasting gains. By the summer of 1917 the miners' real wage rates had
fallen about 10 per cent below the level that prevailed in 1914 – which
itself was little different from the rates that existed in 1910 or 1900.
There was a general advance on the rates on 1 January 1918 and another
one on 1 July of the same year. These revisions in the wage scales were
proving the worth of the union. A surface labourer in the Nova Scotia
coal industry who earned $2.24 a day in 1917 was paid $3.25 in 1920;
the daily rate for a skilled underground miner was $2.94 in 1917 and
$4.50 in 1920; the average earnings of men on tonnage rates increased
from $4.63 in 1917 to $6.55 in 1920. Incontrovertibly, the miners' wages
were going up, but so were prices. In the face of rising prices, gains in
wage rates were not sufficient to bring about permanent improvements
in real wages.[32]

In 1920 a detailed new wage schedule was negotiated under the
supervision of a conciliation board appointed by the federal government. The board was chaired by Clarence MacKinnon, principal of the
Presbyterian divinity college in Halifax, who was well known as an
advocate of social reform. The miners' representative on the board was
the former TLC president J.C. Watters, one of McLachlan's frequent
allies; he was employed by the Dominion fuel controller in the later
stages of the war and was now resident in Inverness. The MacKinnon
Agreement was the product of six weeks' intensive work in which the
union leaders and mine operators negotiated directly with each other,
with only occasional intervention by the board. According to the board's
report, the proceedings were marked by an "amicable and conciliatory
spirit" and "everyone was deeply anxious to secure an equitable adjustment of the difficulties and to stabilize industrial conditions as much

as possible." The final wage schedule covered more than 300 classifications of work in and about the mines. The agreement provided a
"generous advance in the rate of pay and brought it up to the increased
standard of living."[33]

To McLachlan's surprise, the MacKinnon Agreement received a
surprisingly rough reception in the more militant union locals, where
the general increase in rates was considered too moderate. After a
stormy six-hour session of the Caledonia local, a reporter commented
that "the most surprising part of the imbroglio is the repudiation of
Baxter and McLachlan;" along with Barrett this was the triumvirate that
had ruled the miners since 1917 "without anyone raising serious
objection to their methods." Under attack in the locals, McLachlan
vigorously defended the agreement. In his view, the most important
gain in it was the "levelling up" of rates paid at different collieries for
the same work; this was a bargaining objective endorsed by the union
convention in 1919. At a public meeting in Glace Bay, McLachlan
underlined the priorities of class solidarity: "Many of your fellow
workers throughout the Province are not being paid as high as you and
if you are embued with the real spirit of unionism you will assist the
under man to get something on a par with yourselves." He also pointed
out that the settlement contained an escape clause that allowed for
future adjustments. Although the agreement was expected to last for
twelve months, one clause provided that it could be reopened by either
party "should there be any change in the cost of living or any disturbance in economic conditions."

In more general terms McLachlan also argued that acceptance of the
agreement was an important test for the union. Unlike the coal miners
in the United States, where the latest agreement was imposed by a
government board, this one was freely negotiated and "gives us approximately what we asked for." After several weeks of recrimination
and belligerency in the locals, McLachlan succeeded in turning the tide.
By late February most of the locals had voted to accept the settlement.
In the view of the Halifax *Herald*, the acceptance of the MacKinnon
Agreement was a "big personal victory" for McLachlan.[34]

That struggle underlined one of the tensions that often exists between
radical union leaders and militant union members. In McLachlan's view,

the wages question was always important. Indeed his homespun explanations of the differences between nominal, real, and relative wages would become famous among the coal miners during the wage struggles that followed in the coming years. But wages were only one element in the larger balance of power between workers and employers. In an early explanation of the AMW's objectives in 1917, McLachlan attached as much significance to shorter hours and improvements in conditions as he did to wage increases: "As to wages, this union knows that these are a result of competitive conditions, and if we work for, and attain the other things we set out for, the wage rate will settle itself largely. On the whole the miners of Nova Scotia have every right to expect a vast improvement in the conditions under which they have to toil in the years to come."[35]

In other pronouncements during these years, McLachlan left no doubt that he continued to subscribe to a labour theory of value and that as a socialist he could not rest content until the birthright of their labour was restored to the working class. But McLachlan's underlying strategy during the years immediately after the end of the war accepted the main premise of industrial legality – the installation of a strong union presence in the relationship between workers and employers. Moments of strategic opportunity would arrive in the future, and McLachlan was confident that the workers then would be in a position to strike hard for the full rewards of their labour.

The United Mine Workers of America

The United Mine Workers of America loom large in any history of unions in twentieth-century North America. By 1920 the UMW was the largest single union on the continent. For tens of thousands of workers, both within and without the organization, the UMW stood for the ideals of social and economic democracy. Skilled and unskilled, black and white, immigrant and native-born – all were welcome to join in the struggle to extend the rights of labour. The UMW boasted a strong socialist presence, including senior officers such as Frank J. Hayes, who became president of the union in 1917 when John P. White accepted an appointment to a government fuel board. Ten years after the ill-fated 1909 strike, the UMW continued to have a high reputation in Nova Scotia.

One of the first items on McLachlan's agenda in 1919 was the resurrection of District 26. From the very beginning of the Amalgamated Mine Workers, there was an enormous sentiment in favour of a return to the UMW. "The big trouble I had in convention," McLachlan later recalled, "was they accused me of not doing enough to bring the thing about; I was always getting into trouble over that."[36] The international union moved slowly and with some caution. In November 1917 McLachlan was pleased to learn that the UMW had appointed a committee to look into the Nova Scotia situation. Two months later their report was a favourable one, pointing out that the AMW enjoyed full recognition from the coal companies. The weakness in the district was that wages were "far below" the standards in the main American coalfields, or even in British Columbia, although wages had already increased in 1917 and there were "splendid prospects for another substantial increase." In the case of the directly chartered AFL miners' locals in Pictou and Inverness, the UMW noted that the miners preferred to belong to an international union rather than join the AMW, another factor in favour of reinstituting District 26. The main concern at UMW headquarters, however, was whether the coal operators would oppose the return of the international union. Accordingly, the Nova Scotians were asked to "get a clause inserted in their agreement permitting them without any opposition from the coal operators to be members of the U.M.W. of A."[37]

The coal operators were already anxious about the gains the unions were making and were reluctant to accept the UMW. In particular, McLachlan found that the general manager of Dominion Coal, D.H. McDougall, was hostile to the acceptance of the UMW. Writing to a federal official, he described McDougall's response in these terms: "As far as he knew the Dominion Coal Company had spent some millions of dollars to keep the Mine Workers out of Nova Scotia in 1910 and they had not changed their attitude."[38] In more general terms, the president of Dominion Coal, Mark Workman, had complained directly to the prime minister about the government's "kid-gloved diplomacy" in handling labour matters in the coal industry: "Unfortunately, this policy has resulted solely in labour realizing its power, and has given rise to a desire to take advantage of the situation by imposing exceedingly burdensome demands."[39]

For once the worried coal companies did not receive the usual sympathetic hearing in Ottawa. Again, the critical factor was the unusual significance of coal in the Canadian economy. From 1917 to 1920 the problems of fuel supply were under the special authority of the fuel controller, C.A. Magrath, whose main concern was to avoid any interruption in the fuel supply during the last years of the war and the difficult period of adjustment that followed. To maintain order in the energy market, Magrath continually used the authority of his office to settle conflicts of all kinds, including labour disputes. In the Maritimes, Magrath relied for advice on the former TLC president James C. Watters, a coal miner who had long counted himself a UMW supporter. In 1918 Watters travelled widely in Nova Scotia, exercising a mandate to adjust local disputes and keep Magrath informed about conditions in the industry.

As fuel controller, Magrath, a western businessman and surveyor by background and a former Conservative MP, had a progressive's suspicion of the coal companies and saw it as part of his mission to protect consumers and workers against excessive costs and profits in the industry. In one letter to Minister of Labour Gideon Robertson, he expressed the view that many union demands were justified: "Men must be given wages to enable them to live properly. The employers, in many instances, doubtless feel aggrieved because the men have demanded what they believed they were entitled to in the past few years ..." In general Magrath had a favourable opinion of the union leaders and later recalled: "In that Nova Scotia field in those days there was no harmony between the Company and the employee. Probably that was true throughout the district. My experience with the Miners' Committee, namely, Messrs. McLachlan, Barrett and Baxter, was most satisfactory. In looking back now, I have nothing but commendation for their behaviour during the war."[40] Under such circumstances, the coal companies could expect little sympathy from Ottawa. Although Robert Borden's government was not noted for sympathetic policies towards organized labour, under wartime conditions the coal industry was an exception. McLachlan was able to exploit the opportunities, and both the fuel controller and the minister of labour assisted the coal miners in reaching an accommodation with the coal companies.

At last, in February 1919, McLachlan was able to report to UMW headquarters that the ground was prepared for the return of the UMW to Nova Scotia. His formal application for a charter was addressed to President Frank J. Hayes on 26 February, only a few days after the conclusion of a joint conference of coal operators and union officers in Sydney. There the main obstacle to affiliation had been cleared when the operators agreed to accept the UMW's standard eight-hour day.[41] At the same time, the operators also insisted on a carefully worded statement to reassure them that the Nova Scotia coal industry would not be threatened by the application of American standards. Specifically, it was stated that the desire for reunification "does not arise from any intention to make the wage rates and working conditions of Nova Scotia conform to those obtaining in the other districts of the United Mine Workers of America." In addition, it was agreed that "the local districts will receive complete autonomy" and that "the limitation of Nova Scotia in regard to outside competition in the sale of coal are [sic] recognized by the incoming United Mine Workers of America, and will be borne in mind in the future." On this basis, the operators had agreed to accept the return of the UMW – "if that should be the wish of the majority of the mine-workers."[42]

This was exactly what was needed, according to Robert Harlin, one of the international officers who met with the Nova Scotia union leaders and then with the coal operators in Montreal in January: "Of course I had not forgotten our last experience with the Nova Scotia miners. I told the meeting in Montreal that we did not propose to spend any money in Nova Scotia, that we had nonunion fields in the United States that needed our attention." Meeting with the coal operators, Harlin reassured them that "it was not the intention of the United Mine Workers of America to go into Nova Scotia for the purpose of creating dissention and causing a strike." While the UMW was prepared to accept the return of the Nova Scotia coal miners, it was clear there were still hard feelings in Indianapolis about the costs of the 1909 strike.[43]

But McLachlan was prepared to overlook any ambiguities in the UMW's attitude. The reunion with the international union was unavoidable, for among the coal miners the vote in favour of the UMW was nearly unanimous. With the restoration of the district charter in 1919, the defeat of 1909 was avenged. The enabling agreement with the operators, which appeared to limit the international union's objectives in Nova Scotia, was obviously a general one which would not restrict District 26 from pressing its own causes with all the resources at its command. The operators might choose to interpret the provision for "complete autonomy" as a policy of restraint and exclusion in respect to Nova Scotia. McLachlan was prepared to see it more optimistically, as a mandate for independent action.

As a labour radical, McLachlan had no special fears at this stage about the influence of the international union in local affairs; the international president to whom his application was addressed was a popular leader usually associated with the socialists within the UMW. In fact, Hayes was virtually incapacitated by alcoholism at this time and about to be displaced as president by John L. Lewis, a more conservative-minded labour bureaucrat than his predecessor. Lewis had come out of Iowa and Illinois, an ambitious young coal miner of Welsh background. He was not well known to the union membership, for he had risen to the top through a series of administrative appointments. He became acting president in 1919 and then president in his own right in 1920, barely forty years of age at the time. Lewis came to dominate the miners' union, and much of the American labour movement, for the next three decades. He is remembered in labour history more for his part in promoting industrial unionism in the 1930s than for his administration of the UMW. As McLachlan and others soon discovered, Lewis had little sympathy for labour radicals within the UMW.[44]

1919

In Canadian labour history the year 1919 is known as the great year of labour unrest. In 1919 there were more strikes and more workers on strike in Canada than in any previous year in Canadian history. Much of the unrest was associated with the Winnipeg General Strike, which shut down one of the country's major cities for six weeks. There were sympathetic strikes in other towns, especially in the west, and a variety of strikes over issues of union recognition and wage rates erupted all across the country. There was even an impressive local general strike in Amherst, Nova Scotia. Accompanying all this was the domestic Canadian version of the red scare that blamed the labour unrest on "Bolshevism" and "OBU tendencies."[45]

In the Nova Scotia coal industry, 1919 was a relatively quiet year. There were no major strikes. Wage conflicts, most of them arising out of the ever-increasing cost of living, were being settled without disruption of production. Union recognition had been established in 1917 and survived the end of the war unchallenged. Even as the Winnipeg General Strike was ending in disastrous defeat in June 1919, McLachlan was still successfully leading the coal miners in their search for an effective strategy and tactics of radical unionism.

Before the end of the year, McLachlan's activity attracted the attention of the Royal North-West Mounted Police, whose mandate was now extended to cover state security in all parts of the country. Under their new name, adopted in 1920, the Royal Canadian Mounted Police would consider labour unrest to be one of the principal threats facing Canada. In the view of the RCMP, the main cause of labour unrest was the subversive activity of labour agitators; accordingly, the force maintained substantial files on labour leaders whom they regarded as dangerous. A file on McLachlan was started in October 1919 after he was identified in reports originating in western Canada as a correspondent of the western labour radicals and a frequent recipient of "O.B.U. and Bolshevik literature." Reports would continue to be deposited in this file for the rest of his life. One of the earliest documents contained background information on McLachlan passed along by the Dominion Police from their own earlier records: "He is looked upon as an Agitator of the worse type, and seems to be fearless in expressing his sympathies with Bolshevism, although up to the present, he has been careful to keep within the law."[46]

While the completion of affiliation to the UMW was still under way in the spring of 1919, McLachlan's attention was turning to the west. In Winnipeg the issues at stake were collective bargaining and union recognition, and when local unions appealed to fellow workers for support, some 30,000 supporters came out in sympathy. In the beginning it was a remarkably orderly test of strength between capital and labour. Workers holidayed, picnicked, and listened to speeches. But in the following weeks stubborn employers and a repressive government turned the dispute into a violent confrontation. The turning point came with the raids on the homes of the strike leaders and, a few days later, with the police charges on Main Street on Bloody Saturday that left two men dead. Subsequently, the Methodist minister and social reformer J.S. Woodsworth, acting editor of the *Strike Bulletin*, was arrested on charges of seditious libel for his commentaries, which included relevant quotations from the Old Testament prophet Isaiah on the abuse of wealth and power.

For McLachlan, this was the class struggle unfolding much as labour radicals had predicted. Soon after the defeat of the strike in June, McLachlan secured a $500 contribution from District 26 for the defence of the arrested strike leaders. In July he accompanied the Winnipeg labour leader Fred Tipping on a speaking and fund-raising tour through the coal towns. McLachlan's own speeches at these meetings drew special attention to the notorious new Immigration Act amendments that had been rushed through Parliament in early June; these permitted the deportation without trial of British-born immigrants – a category that included not only most of the arrested leaders but also McLachlan himself. He lectured at length on the subject, not neglecting to point out that the amendments were supported unanimously by Parliament, including the Cape Breton Liberal MPs: "Every Statute Book in Canada was delved into yet no item of it had been violated by the Winnipeg strikers, so the Governments made one in forty minutes and this hellish work was supported by D.D. McKenzie and the Liberals." In August the district convention adopted a resolution calling for the repeal of the amendments on the ground that "the said Bill is designed for the express purpose of crippling the labor movement of this country by rendering its active members liable to imprisonment or deportation."[47]

McLachlan recognized the requirements of solidarity, and in September, after the strike leaders were refused bail and reincarcerated after their preliminary hearings, he was calling for a national general strike in their defence – a "gigantic strike embracing every industry under union control." On 9 September questions were asked in the House of Commons about what was called "the McLachlan threat."

Two days later, when the strike leaders were finally granted bail, the defence committee telegraphed McLachlan to report the victory. Subsequently, McLachlan took charge of local sales of "Liberty Bonds" in support of the Winnipeg strike leaders. The trials continued until April 1920, resulting in the conviction of seven leaders on charges of seditious conspiracy; they received prison terms ranging from six months to two years. In response to an appeal from Winnipeg for protests, McLachlan campaigned for a one-day strike on 1 May, the international day of working-class solidarity: "These men were railroaded to jail and denied the right of a fair trial and convicted of crimes manufactured in Ottawa." The "holiday" took place without incident, but the newspapers were not slow to blame McLachlan for this "inexcusable attempt to exert pressure on the authorities." In the Halifax *Herald* staff cartoonist Donald McRitchie caricatured McLachlan as a mad "Queen of the May" – a music hall dancer in a frilly dress labelled "SYMPATHY FOR WINNIPEG REDS."[48]

In the wake of the Winnipeg strike, the Dominion government had attempted to repair some of the damage by proceeding with plans for a National Industrial Conference. This event was expected to present a more constructive image of reconciliation and cooperation between capital and labour. In a kind of "industrial Parliament" delegates representing business and labour would meet in the Red Chamber of the Parliament buildings to discuss plans for more enlightened industrial relations. The appointment of the seventy-nine labour delegates, however, was fully controlled by the leadership of the Trades and Labour Congress. The TLC leadership in turn was now dominated by the international craft unions, symbolized by the election of Tom Moore of the carpenters' union as president at the 1918 meetings in Quebec City. The TLC leaders were determined to demonstrate the moderation and sanity of organized labour, even if this meant limiting representation at the conference. McLachlan strongly objected to "the handpicking of delegates" by the TLC leadership: "Such a conference held where all labor unions in Canada including the One Big Union are not allowed to select their own representatives, cannot by any process of reasoning be said to represent organized labor in Canada." Although Robert Baxter, who had replaced Barrett as president of the miners' union, had already been invited to participate, a resolution from the executive board of District 26 announced that the union was refusing to take part in the conference unless all unions were given representation.[49]

McLachlan's protests earned him his first rebuke from John L. Lewis, now installed as acting president of the UMW. In this exchange Lewis reminded McLachlan that UMW members were prohibited from belonging to dual organizations such as the OBU. In addition, Lewis warned that the union constitution "by the same token would prohibit accredited representatives of our organization from giving aid and comfort to such organizations." McLachlan's reply took exception to Lewis on the ground that the TLC leaders were "usurping" the union's right to choose its own delegates. "Personally, I feel that the international Union would be going beyond its jurisdiction to interfere in any shape or form with purely legislative matters in Canada," McLachlan added, "We must at all times be at absolute liberty as far as the international union is concerned to cooperate with all the workers of Canada."[50]

By the fall of 1919 McLachlan had identified himself as one of the leaders of the opposition within the TLC. In 1919 the rise of the revolutionary One Big Union presented a challenge for the existing house of labour. The OBU was the organization of western labour radicals who had broken with the TLC and formed their own rival union centre. Its message of industrial unionism and social revolution was often associated in the public mind with the Winnipeg strike, although the OBU was not offically organized until after the strike. Instead of leading the coal miners into the OBU, McLachlan favoured a strategy of rebuilding the TLC itself around a more militant and radical program. His hope was that eastern and western delegates would unite in support of a radical platform.

On his departure for the annual meeting of the TLC in Hamilton, McLachlan was optimistic: "I can say for the miners that we want the Trades and Labor Congress remodelled. We want the Congress to have more power, to wield a greater influence among labor in Canada than it does." He argued that the TLC should endorse a reconstruction program focusing on issues such as unemployment and housing. Furthermore, the TLC should be prepared to engage in direct action, including general strikes, in order to protest violations of workers' rights such as those demonstrated in the case of the Winnipeg strike.

In Hamilton the radicals went down to defeat. Their resolutions were not accepted and their candidate for president, former TLC president J.C. Watters, was also defeated. The defection of large numbers of western allies into the ranks of the OBU had left McLachlan and other radicals with a shortage of supporters inside the TLC. One of the results for District 26 was that President Baxter, who had supported much of the radical program, was dropped from the official slate for the TLC executive and also went down to defeat. On his return from Hamilton, McLachlan did not conceal his disappointment. The meetings were "pretty much of a failure," he told reporters. "The congress never touched the vital things that are concerning labor; the things that are keeping the world in turmoil. It was a case of suppression, suppression and suppression all the time." Representation from the Maritimes was small, and the few western delegates in attendance "were never given an opportunity of expressing their views." Meanwhile, McLachlan charged, the Moore machine did everything it could to widen the gap between east and west. The large turnout of delegates from the international craft and railway unions in Ontario and Quebec was obvious in the voting results. What McLachlan did not know at the time was that in advance of the convention the Canadian Reconstruction Association, a powerful business lobby group, had spent some $50,000 to strengthen the attendance of the moderate faction. When the story began to come out a year later, McLachlan threatened that District 26 would stop paying its per-capita tax to the TLC.[51]

The defeat of the radicals at the TLC left McLachlan's strategy for strengthening that organization in disarray and the search for radical allies unfulfilled. Meanwhile, the issue of the OBU dogged McLachlan all through the later months of 1919 and into 1920. He was widely believed to be sympathetic to the radical new union. In Nova Scotia police informants expected McLachlan to come out unequivocally for the OBU and cause a split with the UMW similar to the one that existed in District 18 in Alberta.

Early in 1920 McLachlan was in regular correspondence with union leaders in western Canada. According to one letter to a miners' leader in Alberta, McLachlan's impression was that the conflict between the OBU and the UMW there was like "the old struggle between us and the P.W.A. being enacted over again only 'more so.'" He invited the westerners to appeal to the Nova Scotians for support in their conflict with the UMW: "It is only a matter of time until the miners here throw in their lot with the men out West. I predict the break will come the first time the International Union tries to dictate to N.S. miners in matters of wage contracts, or who they may join up with in Canada, in direct action, such as Winnipeg affair or your wage contract." This was as close as McLachlan came to endorsing the OBU. Much of this correspondence was intercepted by the police, and for the benefit of his superiors in Ottawa, the RCMP commanding officer for the Maritimes, Inspector C.D. LaNauze, counted McLachlan as the local agent of the OBU: "He is a fiend and will stop at nothing to gain his ends, that is to rule and control the O.B.U. in Eastern Canada."[52]

A showdown took place at the UMW district convention in Truro in April 1920. McLachlan predicted in advance that the meeting would be "some hummer," with representatives both from the international union and from the miners in District 18 in Alberta, which had been suspended for its support of the OBU. Inspector LaNauze instructed one of his undercover men to attend the Truro meeting, but the police agent found it difficult to gather intelligence. He found that McLachlan's room at the Learmont Hotel was "always guarded when there was anything going on inside, so it was quite impossible to hear any of the conversation that took place." Moreover, delegates had been warned by McLachlan "to keep their mouth shut on the train and in the hotels." But the anticipated alliance with the OBU did not materialize. Although several telegrams were received appealing for support in their struggle with the UMW, no OBU delegates arrived at the meeting, apparently because of a general shortage of funds and the existing state of crisis in the western coalfields.[53]

Instead McLachlan himself delivered a stormy speech charging conspiracy between the coal operators, the government and the international union to prevent the coal miners of the east and west from making common cause. Somehow, McLachlan charged, his correspondence with the deposed leader of District 18, P.M. Christopher, had "very mysteriously" reached the hands of the minister of labour, Gideon Robertson, who in turn not only warned McLachlan personally against the OBU but also alerted John L. Lewis of the UMW in Indianapolis. Again, McLachlan stopped short of endorsing the OBU unconditionally. As noted in the report of his speech by the police agents present in the hall:

> He said he did not agree with all the O.B.U. leaders, but that he did to a great extent. He said that the men in the West were being crushed by the rottenest government that ever held power in this country. He said that if these men are going to be crushed in the West he did not care whether it was the U.M.W., the O.B.U. or I.W.W. were fighting their battles, I am with them. I will not let the International officials nor the Government muzzle me when I talk to the laboring men. If I cannot express my views in this organization I will do it outside.

McLachlan held forth for nearly an hour and at the end of his oration was cheered solidly for almost five minutes. Clearly he had stolen the opposition's thunder. When his former protégé Silby Barrett, now the international board member for the UMW and a staunch ally of union headquarters, charged that McLachlan was "working underhanded in favour of the OBU," the accusations fell flat. A police report subsequently observed: "McLachlan came back from the fight at the Truro Convention over the O.B.U. a Hero in the eyes of his friends. He is pictured as a victim of spies of the government, who steal his letters and hand them over to the Minister of Labor." The police also concluded, however, that the exposure of McLachlan's correspondence "has been a decided shock to him, and he is endeavouring by every possible means to square himself with the government and the officials with the U.M.W. of A., and not be exposed in his underhanded O.B.U. tendencies and propaganda."[54]

During the following months the OBU threat seemed to evaporate. On 7 June McLachlan's RCMP file noted – "To date J.B. McLachlan did

not have anything to say along O.B.U. lines ..." And on 12 August –
"The O.B.U. is dead as far as McLachlan is concerned ..." Indeed by
November the police could report that "McLachlan appears to have
quite given up his OBU tendencies + is now fighting tooth + nail for
the U.M.W. of A." Despite the anxieties, McLachlan never came out in
support of joining up with the OBU. Until the time of the Hamilton
TLC convention, McLachlan hoped the TLC itself could be reconstructed. Following the defeat of the radicals, he obviously considered
the strategy of making common cause with the OBU, either by affiliation or by statements of solidarity. But he also recognized that an
alliance with the OBU would bring down the wrath of the international
union. And it would certainly cause a split among the coal miners –
who had just completed more than a dozen years of struggle, under his
leadership, to win recognition of the UMW. Then, too, it was becoming
clear in the spring of 1920 that the OBU was not going to replace the
TLC as the voice of organized labour in Canada; even in the western
coalfields the OBU was unable to carry the day without opposition. As
Inspector LaNauze observed, with growing respect for his tactical
judgment, McLachlan was "far too wise to break way from his present
position as Secretary Treasurer of District #26."[55]

This was not to say that the RCMP now considered McLachlan no
more of a threat. If anything, the police concluded, he would not be
vulnerable to easy attack. He was, LaNauze had caustically noted in
June in a detailed assessment for the commissioner in Ottawa, "an out
and out Glasgow socialist." Arrest and deportation under the Immigration Act amendments of 1919 were distinct possibilities, LaNauze
observed. But McLachlan's support among the coal miners ran from
40 to 60 per cent in the various districts, and for this reason, assuming
suitable evidence could be collected, "any attempt to deport him might
lead to upheaval in the labour circles." There was a greater possibility
that he would be defeated by more "fair minded" candidates in union
elections later in the year.[56]

As it turned out, McLachlan's position among the coal miners was
so strong that no candidate was prepared to challenge him for election
as secretary-treasurer. And Silby Barrett, who had taken a stand against
McLachlan at the Truro meeting, went down to an unexpected defeat.

The balance of power was shifting decisively into the hands of the radicals. Barrett's successor as international board member would be a radical local leader from Westville, Dan Livingstone, who also had a reputation for "OBU tendencies." In short, the radicals were in control, and McLachlan himself was now recognized, according to police reports, as "king among the coal miners."[57]

The Ideal Preacher

Who was this McLachlan? At the offices of the Halifax *Herald* the cartoonist Donald McRitchie was confounded. Was McLachlan anything more than a responsible labour leader, bringing overdue order and justice to labour relations in the coal industry? Or was he really a mad revolutionary, intent on overthrowing the established order? Or perhaps he was just a canny opportunist, ready to follow every turn in the road?

In the course of one year the same man who was caricatured as a mad "Queen of the May," dancing in sympathy with the Winnipeg reds, was also portrayed as a thoughtful and responsible union leader concerned about the fate of his people at the hands of a royal commission. But there was never any doubt in McRitchie's mind that McLachlan was the central figure in the unfolding drama in the coalfields. One elaborate effort, at the time of the unrest over the MacKinnon Award in early 1920, attempted to portray the complexities of internal union politics in Shakespearean terms. McLachlan was depicted as an assassinated Julius Caesar – murdered by the ingratitude of radical miners who considered the latest settlement too moderate. Silby Barrett (as Brutus) stood by with a bloodstained dagger while Robert Baxter (as Mark Anthony) pronounced the funeral oration.[58]

McLachlan had survived that crisis with his reputation intact, and for many coal miners the success of their union was embodied in McLachlan's leadership. One old-timer, who had memories going back to the days before Dominion Coal, considered McLachlan the symbol of the enormous changes that had taken place in working-class expectations since the 1880s and 1890s. "I worked for Dave McKeen for 80 cents a day and had to take my hat off everytime I saw him and go to church twice on Sunday to hold my job and that job was only good for the summer," "Sandy Mac" told the Glace Bay writer Stuart McCawley in September 1919. "We lived in the Monkey Row, in two rooms, got porridge and fish and an egg or two once and a while and voted how we were told. It took a long time for us to wake up, but we have alarm clocks all around us now and McLachlan is one of the noisiest of them all. Good luck to him."[59]

Despite his record of pragmatic compromises, such as the MacKinnon Award, McLachlan's radical views were no secret to the coal miners. His reputation went back to the days of the PWA and the SPC before the war; it was only a few years since he had run as a socialist candidate in the 1916 provincial election. In office as a union leader, McLachlan was advancing his version of industrial democracy by testing the limits of industrial legality. He was prepared to advocate the use of "direct action" on selective occasions such as the one-day strike for the eight-hour day in July 1918. Again, the miners followed him in demonstrating support for the Winnipeg strike leaders, first in the threatened general strike in September 1919 and then in the one-day protest in May 1920.

McLachlan was also out to achieve radical reforms in the administration of the coal industry. After the mine disasters of 1917 and 1918, in union resolutions the coal miners supported McLachlan's demands for the election of government mine inspectors by the coal miners themselves, a proposal that amounted to a form of workers' control in the government of the coal mines. Beyond this there was the vision of working-class ownership of the industry, a position that had been endorsed as union policy since 1918. "Jimmy is radical," a writer in the *Eastern Federationist* observed in the summer of 1919, "and so are the majority of the people of the civilized world today. They are not all outspoken in it, many are and Jimmy is one of them; hence the notice he is attracting."[60]

A few surviving fragments from one of McLachlan's notebooks, apparently from 1917, give a glimpse of some of the elements in his philosophy of labour radicalism. There, among his notes on local conditions, rates and grievances, statistical extracts and calculations, are several reflective notes on historical and economic themes, probably based on his current reading. In the jumble of notations, local detail intersected with overarching historical themes. It was the kind of material an experienced speaker could be expected to draw upon in public speeches.

In one note, McLachlan commented on the early days of the industrial revolution and the response of the Luddites: "When the machine was first introduced the workers wrecked them. They were on the wrong track because of the cheaper production. I would rather [be] standing in with those wreckers when they are condemned than be bracketed up with the weaklings who tamely submitted, but the shoe is on the other foot today. We can produce cheaper without capitalism." Another passage introduced the distinctions between different relations of production: "Let me draw your attention to three kinds of Labor, first Slave labor, where the Laborer does not seem to get anything at all for his Laborpower, second Serf Labor, where the Laborer works three days on his land and three days for his Lord on his Lord's land. Here it is open and apparent that the workers give three days Labor for nothing. Then wage-Labor, where the worker appears, but only appears, to be paid in the full product of his Labor. All three classes actually perform 'necessary' labor and 'surplus' labor."

One longer entry was headed "Dull times, their cause and cure" and contained several striking observations about the position of the working class:

The working class are disenherited [sic] and alienated by act of Parliament from the means of wealth production – from the means of life.

You men require to have access to the coal mines in order to live.

If you don't believe that you have been alienated, and have neither right nor title to earn a living, just say something to offend the, [sic] or go out, a bunch of you, and try to start a mine or a railway of your own.

This alienation results in the working class having to sell themselves to the men who do own the right and title to operate the mines, railways and factories, etc.

The sale of your labor is made under the same market conditions, as boots, coals or beef. In a word your alienation has resulted

in transforming you into a commodity, an article of trade subject
to all evils and very few of the benefits of a competitive market.

There was little personal reflection here on the role of the labour leader.
The closest perhaps was a short inspirational passage about Napoleon
crossing the Alps: "Napoleon when addressing his ragged and famish-
ing army, these were his words: – 'Soldiers abundance courts you in the
fertile plains below, (the plains of Italy) are you deficient in constancy
and courage?' They were not." This kind of language, characteristic of
turn-of-the-century socialist writers such as Robert Blatchford, offered
a powerful mix of economic and ethical arguments. McLachlan's version of labour radicalism continued to owe as much to the moral force
of socialism as it did to Marxist economics.[61]

He addressed these themes most directly in a remarkable piece of
writing composed in the spring of 1919. The occasion was an essay
contest sponsored by the Halifax *Herald* on the subject of "The Ideal
Preacher for the New Era in Life." McLachlan interpreted this topic
brilliantly as a statement of the radical social gospel and the responsibilities of the modern labour leader.[62]

"It is not to be assumed that all the 'Preachers' have always been
attached to the Church." Beginning with that challenge to customary
assumptions about clerical authority, McLachlan delivered a sustained
sermon of his own on the decline of the established church and the rise
of the working-class movement:

> Whether we like it or not, the rise of the working class and the decline
> of the Church are the direct results of the work of the free and
> unattached "Ideal Preachers." From Moses and Jesus and Marx and
> Carlyle, one outstanding theme runs thru [sic] all their teachings,
> however much the language employed may have differed. The sins
> which all of them denounced most fiercely were economic sins,
> and the mission of all of them in life was to deliver the oppressed.
>
> "I have surely seen the affliction of my people, which are in
> Egypt, and have heard their cry by reason of their taskmasters, for
> I know their sorrows and I AM COME DOWN TO DELIVER THEM."

Such has always been the mission of the "Ideal Preacher" and he invariably found himself in direct and deadly conflict with the owning and ruling classes of society.

Moses must have been an awful radical: his immediate purpose was the emancipation of a number of work people who were making bricks, and he goes to interview the king on the matter, and the king was anxious to compromise, but Moses talks to that old king just like a member of the I.W.W.

"If you refuse to let my people go, BEHOLD TOMORROW I WILL BRING," etc, anything from locusts to the death of your boy. No squeamishness in that proclamation, but a decisiveness and sure-footedness that must have enthused those brick-makers.

Nor was Jesus who was the flower of all preachers, different in this respect from Moses, but he contended with the rich from first to last.

What was true of Moses was also true of Jesus and his followers, and the modern-day preacher was confronted with the same choices:

Their gospel was an economic gospel that dealt with the affairs of men right down here on this earth, and the preacher that is going to be listened today, amid the turmoil and welter of a head-on collision between two economic classes – the exploited and the exploiters – must have a message of hope for the one, and not for the other. He must stand either for the supremacy of things as against the supremacy of man, or the supremacy of man as against the supremacy of things.

No more dramatic moment can take place in the life of a preacher than in making his decision on the question. For him it is the day of judgment. He is deciding on a reverence for caste and privilege; for vested rights and oblivion. Or he decides to grasp the torch flung to him from the dying hands of heroes and martyrs and join the world-wide crusade for the emancipation from all exploitation of the propertyless working class.

Here was a reading of the social gospel with a radical economic edge. In 1919 and 1920 this was the kind of sermon that could have been heard in the labour churches that constituted the radical wing of the social-gospel movement. It was the message of social salvation as interpreted by a veteran of the working-class struggle. Jesus and Marx belonged to the same tradition of struggle for human emancipation and social justice, and the mission of the preacher today was to advance the same cause under modern conditions, within or without the church.[63]

All this for McLachlan was much more than an exercise in biblical interpretation and theological explanation. He was speaking here to the heart of his own personal philosophy of labour radicalism. Here in concentrated form was McLachlan's vision of his own place in world history. From the "ancient lowly" of early history to the latest battles of the Wobblies, modern socialism drew its inspiration from the universal struggle for progress and justice. He was thinking not only of Moses and Jesus, and of all the celebrated early prophets, apostles, and martyrs in religious history, but also of the printers who undermined the authority of church and state across Europe, the persecuted field preachers of seventeenth-century Scotland, the scientific discoveries of Galileo and Darwin, the social teachings of Carlyle and Marx, and the practical politics of his old mentor Keir Hardie. Under modern conditions the "ideal preacher" was the working-class leader, and McLachlan's prescription was a confession of his own faith.

His words rang with the language of moral dedication and personal commitment. He had long since learned the elementary truth, he wrote – "the world do move." The world was still moving, more rapidly than ever since 1914, and the mission of the modern preacher was to work for the ancient cause. He must do so with righteousness and passion, guided by reason, experience and conscience. He must act with an unshackled mind and a granite will, uninhibited by the opposition of church and state. He must work "like a Trojan" as if the salvation of the world depended on his efforts, but he must also know that the future of light, freedom, and justice was assured – and would arrive "even if he had never been born."

This was the challenge of the times, and McLachlan was prepared to meet the demands. All his skill, his energy, and his time, he wrote, were dedicated to "the heaving, throbbing surge of the disinherited" – "keeping them on the narrow path that leads to the land where they shall 'call no man master'": "'He stirreth up the people,' for which he may get hanged some day, but if he gets his way the disinherited will refuse to remain disinherited."

CHAPTER 5

Working-Class Hero

The emergence of an industrial legality
is a great victory for the working class,
but it is not the ultimate and definitive victory.
Industrial legality has improved the working class's
standard of living but it is no more than a compromise –
a compromise which had to be made and must be supported
until the balance of forces favours the working class.

– Antonio Gramsci,
L'Ordine Nuovo (Turin),
12 June 1920

On the Road

J.B. McLachlan was sitting, elbows on the plain wooden table at the front of the room. He was checking his watch, lighting his pipe, shuffling his papers, looking over the resolutions as the meeting hall filled with delegates. History was unfolding, and McLachlan was watching with satisfaction.

One of the newspaper reporters present in the hall was listening as McLachlan made his preparations. He could hear the union leader humming quietly, under his breath. "Hear the Battle Cry of Freedom, / How it swells upon the air ..." It sounded like one of the popular marching songs from the war against slavery. But there was also something unfamiliar, something the reporter did not recognize. The words from "Just Before the Battle, Mother" were mixed in with new ones: "If we work for bread and lodging / While the sun is high and warm, / It would cause us sundry dodging / Through the winter's cold and storm ..." And then – "We must have the all that's in it – / In the labor that we sell; / For you cannot tell what minute / It may start to rain like hell ..."[1] For labour reformers, the struggle against slavery was a regular reference point, and this was the latest Wobbly version of the old Civil War song. For McLachlan, as he hummed the words under his breath, it seemed to be a kind of prayer in the battle against wage slavery.

There was much for McLachlan to consider as he went about the administration of union affairs in these years. It has been said that the natural terrain of collective bargaining leads towards an accommodation between labour and capital, as each of these partners in industrial society accepts common rules under which they are prepared to compete for advantage. From this point of view, the acceptance of the union agreement represented a fundamental reform of the capitalist system and provided a democratic solution to the inherent instabilities of the

labour-capital relationship. Accordingly, many labour leaders have regarded union recognition as the ultimate achievement of organized
labour, the reform that makes all other reforms possible. A more
skeptical perspective has suggested that, even with the benefit of widespread union membership and statutory protection for unions, the
rights of workers and unions have remained limited by the concentrated power of capitalism and by the legal structures that support it.
In this view, the achievement of "industrial legality" represented only
a temporary peace, a form of historical compromise between labour
and capital. In one form or another, the struggle continued, and it was
up to labour leaders to do their best to reconcile the demands of
industrial legality with the goals of industrial democracy.[2]

A full-time union officer in early-twentieth-century North America
spent much of his life on the road. For McLachlan there were local
meetings, district conventions, and international ones, meetings of the
Trades and Labour Congress and the American Federation of Labor,
meetings with coal companies and cabinet ministers, sometimes in
Sydney or Truro or Halifax but more often in Montreal or Ottawa.
There were long days and nights of railway travel. On the trains there
were dining cars and smoking lounges, sleeping cars with crisp white
sheets and black attendants. In the train stations there was the cosy
atmosphere of barber shops and cigar stores. Along the way, billboards
and news-stands advertised the gospel of material wealth and conspicuous consumption. In far-off cities there were spectacular skyscrapers,
luxurious public squares, handsome rooms, and posh hotels.

It was a world of affairs far in social distance from the coal miners'
life and work. For members of the small elite who belonged to the
bureaucracy of labour in the early twentieth century, this was the brass
ring of opportunity, and labour history holds many examples of the
ambitious union leader who was seduced by the attractions and opportunities of office. But McLachlan had no interest in imitating the living
standards and cultural habits of the travelling salesman, union road-
man, or corporation lawyer. His most acute feeling when attending a
meeting at one of the big railway hotels in Montreal, McLachlan later
recalled, was one of physical discomfort:

The floor in this hotel seemed to jeer and laugh at me as I walked over it. If I walked on its carpets my feet sunk up to the shoe-tops. If I walked on the sides, where the carpet did not cover, I would slip and stumble and slide as if I walked on polished glass. This floor sure was class-conscious. It seemed to shout out at me: "Can't you see you're out of your element! Feet black and dirty from the coal mine should not walk here. I am for the gentle feet of idle men and fine women which are never soiled by labor." This floor, too, made me mad. Oh, if the miners from Glace Bay's wind-swept shacks could only have one walk over this floor, how it would make them fighting mad![3]

Although devoted to raising the standard of living in the miners' homes, McLachlan was known as a man of modest tastes. His satisfactions came from the comforts of family life and the rewards of service to his class.

At home at Steele's Hill, McLachlan's oldest children were themselves beginning to enter the workforce. His oldest son, James Bryson McLachlan, Jr, had been driving the milk team for several years, but in 1919 he hired on as an apprentice at the machine shop in Glace Bay. His father tried to warn him that he wouldn't have any more money in his pocket by going to work as a wage labourer, the younger man has recalled: "'You'll get trimmed. Work for yourself.' And he was right." One of the older daughters, Kate, was working as a milliner in a downtown hat shop; within a few years she would be married and become the mother of two boys of her own. The other children helped with the chores around the small six-acre farm. Now that McLachlan was back at work in the union offices, there was less need to maintain the milk business that had seen them through the hard times. But McLachlan still enjoyed working in the barn and the field. The younger children fondly recalled his frustrations in trying to protect the potato patch or stop geese from eating the oats. Around the house McLachlan was always a teacher for his children. They recalled memorizing lines of poetry and looking up Greek myths for him in one of the household encyclopedias. Tom McLachlan, who would go into the mines at the age of sixteen and eventually become a president of District 26 himself, recalled his father as "a great student" and "the best of teachers": "He taught me all the dangers of the mine and all the dangers of the boss. I was well taught."[4]

Any assessment of McLachlan cannot be separated from the ethical force of his reputation. There were many stories about his otherworldliness when it came to material possessions. When any of the children needed money, he would reach into his pocket and allow them to take anything that was in his hand. Sometimes he would come home without any money, having given away everything in his pockets in the course of the day. One night he came back without his shoes – he had given them away, he explained, to a man who needed them more. On another occasion he loaned his horse and wagon to a young man who was in need of transport to move his household from Glace Bay to North Sydney. The man was a total stranger, but McLachlan was happy to help and supply two days' provisions for the horse. McLachlan also enjoyed a reputation for incorruptibility, and more than one story circulated about the times he was offered bribes to give up union affairs. In those days every promising labour leader was offered some kind of bribe, recalled P.M. Nicholson, an early labour organizer in Sydney and one of the founders of the Cape Breton Independent Labour Party in 1917; but McLachlan "would never take a penny." As a union officer McLachlan was paid "a reasonable salary" by the union, he added, "but not a fraction of what he was worth." Then, too, there was the story about the time an operative was hired to take McLachlan out in a rowboat and throw him overboard. It was said that the man had been hired and paid in advance, but when the time came he could not bring himself to commit the crime. Stories like these cannot be easily verified, but their circulation confirms the place McLachlan had come to occupy in the coal miners' imagination.[5]

Searching for the chinks in McLachlan's armour, his detractors could identify only the allegation of godlessness. Again and again he would be accused of being a blasphemist, a non-believer, and an atheist. Such charges went back to the days of struggle in the PWA and continued throughout the length of his public life, surfacing especially in the form of warnings from the churches at election time. In June 1920 Inspector LaNauze of the RCMP claimed that McLachlan had "no religion" but that he received support from the Protestants, partly because of his willingness to defy the Catholic Church.[6]

Such was McLachlan's notorious reputation that visitors to his home expressed surprise to hear grace said before dinner. Yet this was a home where the father read the Bible to the family on Sundays, much as his own mother and father had read to him in his childhood. His Bible remained a well-used text, and his public declarations often contained Biblical allusions. Further, when confronted with a document at the time of his arrest in 1923 requiring him to identify his religion, McLachlan gave the answer Presbyterian. Annie Whitfield, a miner's wife who counted herself one of McLachlan's followers, never doubted that McLachlan was religious: "He never said anything against religion, he knew when to hold his tongue. Not like me, I was always in trouble with the priests."[7] Indeed, McLachlan made little effort to defend himself against clerical attacks. True to his mission of working-class emancipation, he believed that the success of an independent working-class outlook depended on allowing workers to make their own judgments about leadership.

Independent Labour

The idea that workers should be represented by members of their own class was not a new one in Canadian politics at the end of the Great War. Socialists and labour leaders had been arguing the case for at least twenty years, and they had watched the rise of the Labour Party in Britain with considerable excitement. Beginning with the election of Arthur Puttee in Winnipeg and Ralph Smith in Nanaimo at the turn of the century, several labour candidates were elected to the House of Commons and some to provincial legislatures, but the successes had been modest ones. In Nova Scotia the occasional independent labour candidates presented little threat to the established party system. Then, suddenly, the old party system seemed to be falling apart. When angry union members protested wartime policies, local labour parties sprang up all across the country in 1917, and at the end of the war a tide of labour unrest and rural discontent caused more waves in the political world. Meanwhile, Canadian political democracy was coming of age, as the vote was extended to women in most provinces and property qualifications were finally removed for all citizens entitled to vote.

The new face of politics was soon visible in the results of provincial and Dominion elections. In Ontario the labour and farmer members elected in 1919 formed Canada's first Farmer-Labour government. In Winnipeg in 1920 four of the arrested 1919 strike leaders were elected to the Manitoba legislature, and in Alberta the United Farmers swept to power the following year. In the 1921 Dominion election the Conservative Party, the old party of Sir John A. Macdonald and the National Policy and the party that had run the war, went down to its worst defeat since Confederation. The Liberal Party, badly fractured by the war, returned to power with Canada's first minority government, presided over by William Lyon Mackenzie King, a man who considered himself one of the new breed of labour-relations experts. The House of Commons after 1921 also included a substantial contingent of farmer and labour representatives, among them such pioneers as Agnes Macphail, the first woman Member of Parliament, and J.S. Woodsworth, the veteran of the social gospel and now famous for his arrest during the Winnipeg General Strike.

In the coalfields there were great expectations for the success of labour politics. Much had changed since 1916, when McLachlan had run for office as a socialist. The Socialist Party itself was in disarray at the end of war and had virtually ceased to exist in the Maritimes. As a result, the rivalries between socialists and labourites that had distressed visitors such as Keir Hardie before the war were no longer important, and socialist advocates of working-class politics participated readily in the new labour parties. In McLachlan's view, a working-class presence in politics would be a logical extension of the success of the miners' union. Indeed, the unexpectedly strong resistance of the provincial government to an eight-hour-day law demonstrated the need for labour to exert more influence in politics.

Fresh from the first meetings of the Amalgamated Mine Workers, the coal miners came out in large numbers to the founding convention of the Cape Breton Independent Labour Party in Sydney in November 1917. There they elected McLachlan as president of the new labour party and the union vice-president Robert Baxter as treasurer. The ILP program included traditional progressive reforms such as proportional representation, abolition of the Senate, and public ownership of utilities, but it also included more specific labour demands – minimum wages, the eight-hour day, higher salaries for teachers, restrictions on child labour, better inspection of mines, and investigation of industrial accidents. Members were required to sign an application pledging to work only for candidates nominated by the ILP. While the program was less uncompromising than that of the old Socialist Party of Canada, the new party's constitution also supported the advancement of the class struggle. The party's "objects" were stated in unmistakeable socialist language: "To give expression politically to the hopes and aspirations of the working class alone and by use of the ballot to establish working class ownership and democratic management of all social means of wealth production and distribution at the earliest possible date."[8]

The ILP soon showed its appeal, especially among the coal miners. In the Dominion election in December 1917, the notorious "Khaki election" in which Robert Borden's Union government manipulated the franchise in order to win an endorsement of conscription, the labour candidates were the miners' Robert Baxter and John A. Gillis, a leader of the steelworkers in Sydney. They received more than 3,600 votes each, one of the more substantial labour votes in the country. The labour vote was strongest in the mining districts of the constituency, where Baxter and Gillis outpolled both their Liberal and Unionist opponents and won 37.66 per cent of the vote.[9]

Shortly afterwards, the power of labour politics was more fully demonstrated in the coal towns. In 1918 and 1919 labour candidates captured control of the town councils in Glace Bay, New Waterford, and Dominion; in 1918 a labour candidate, James Ling, was elected mayor of New Waterford, and Dan Willie Morrison was elected as a labour mayor in Glace Bay in 1922. This amounted to a small revolution in the coal towns, and during the course of the 1920s local government was dominated by labour councillors who demonstrated both class consciousness and community patriotism in their administration of local affairs. The working-class presence in local government was felt on a whole range of issues, including the use of company police and the taxation of company properties. The company town was giving way to the labour town, one more sign of the changing balance of power in mining society.[10]

McLachlan followed these developments from a distance. For him the success of the coal miners' union was the necessary foundation for all efforts to enlarge the house of labour and extend working-class influence. In June 1918 he resigned as president of the Cape Breton Independent Labour Party, though he remained on the executive as honorary president. Meanwhile, the labour party, like the expanding labour movement itself, was making room for a growing number of capable new labour and political leaders. McLachlan's replacement as president was a relatively well-to-do farmer and marine pilot from South Bar, a farming and fishing area on the shore road leading from the steelworks in Sydney to the mining district. Although most of the ILP locals were in Sydney and the surrounding coal towns, the selection of Arthur R. Richardson was a sign that the party was cultivating an alliance between labour and farmer interests in the county.

At this stage McLachlan was content to concentrate his own efforts on the industrial struggle and let the progress of labour politics follow its own course. During the harried summer of 1919, when McLachlan was preoccupied with the Winnipeg strike, the UMW, the OBU, and the TLC, he did not even attend the ILP convention; accordingly, he did not participate in the debate over an attempt to restrict party membership to working-class voters; it is not clear whether McLachlan would have supported this amendment, which did not succeed, but it is interesting to note that Richardson was replaced at this meeting by John Watson, a coal miner and labour party stalwart from Dominion. McLachlan also played a relatively small part in the organization of a provincial Federation of Labour in March 1919 which, among other things, supported the establishment of a provincial labour party. He attended the Halifax meetings as a delegate from the AMW local at Sydney Mines, but although nominated as vice-president, he declined to stand for office.[11]

The provincial Independent Labour Party of Nova Scotia finally came into being in April 1920, just in time for the election that took place in July. Across Nova Scotia that summer there were ten ILP candidates, an additional two candidates (one of them a woman) sponsored jointly by the ILP and the Great War Veterans Association. Another sixteen candidates were nominated by the United Farmers of Nova Scotia. On 27 July 1920 this third-party alliance made an explosive entry into Nova Scotia political history. Their candidates captured 32.3 per cent of the provincial vote and elected eleven members, five of them labour members. Although the Liberal Party was again returned to power, as it had been without interruption since 1882, the party system was thrown into disarray by the results. The Conservatives won only three seats.[12]

In the weeks before the 1920 provincial election, McLachlan's speeches articulated the logic of working-class politics. When he was invited to speak in support of striking workers at the Halifax shipyards that summer, more than 1,600 people crowded into the market building in Halifax to hear the miners' leader. McLachlan brought the Halifax workers a message of moral and financial support in their struggle for union recognition, but at the same time he urged them to prepare for political action:

> What is needed is political action by the workers to the end that their own representatives, members of the working class, are elected to parliament and all public bodies. This will be the next big move of the working class, and every worker must become conscious of his own power and educate and acquaint himself with social and economic questions, so that when the time arrives for Labor to take over the administration of public affairs the great bulk of the people will be ready to advance into the great cooperative commonwealth.

By the end of the summer the Halifax workers had gone down to defeat. The new manager of the shipyards, J.E. McLurg, had simply blamed the whole strike on "Bolshevik agitators" and refused to negotiate with the union. A few years later, as vice-president of the British Empire Steel Corporation, commonly known as Besco, McLurg would also become a notorious symbol of corporate intransigence in the coalfields. In this atmosphere of union weakness, the labour candidates in Halifax were badly beaten.[13]

Back in Cape Breton it was a different story. The local candidates included two labour leaders – the machinist Forman Waye from Sydney Mines and the carpenter Joseph Steele from Sydney. The third candidate was the Glace Bay coal miner Dan Willie Morrison, a longtime UMW supporter who had demonstrated his patriotism by serving in the war. He was nominated both by the war veterans and by the ILP. The fourth candidate was Arthur R. Richardson, who had served as president of the Cape Breton ILP; he was nominated by the United Farmers and also endorsed by the ILP. In Cape Breton County, a four-member constituency, this combined labour-farmer-veteran ticket swept the field. Each of the four candidates received more than 9,000 votes and all were elected by substantial majorities. Together they took 53.6 per cent of the vote across the whole constituency, and in the mining district they received 64.9 per cent of the vote. Beyond Cape Breton, another labour MLA, a coal miner, was elected in Cumberland County, and in Pictou County the labour candidate, a steelworker, came within a few dozen votes of election. For any skeptics, this was a powerful demonstration of the potential of labour politics. It was, of course, notable that the successes came only in areas where there was already a strong union presence. Moreover, in Cape Breton the ILP had skilfully made alliance with the farmers' and soldiers' organizations and avoided the dangers of religious and ethnic division. Still, despite the province's reputation for patronage politics and tradition-bound voting, the 1920 campaign demonstrated that a labour party could wage a successful political campaign and that large numbers of workers were prepared to vote along class lines at election time.[14]

McLachlan played only a modest part in this campaign. His name was put forward by supporters in Glace Bay, and when delegates were polled at the ILP nomination meeting in June, McLachlan came out at the top of a list of eighteen potential candidates. He declined to stand for nomination, however. When a reporter from the Sydney *Record* asked McLachlan to comment on the selection of labour candidates, he answered reassuringly: "They are good sensible chaps, not red firebrands – like me. This with the characteristic McLachlan twinkle." A week later McLachlan gave a spirited speech on behalf of the labour campaign at the veterans' nomination meeting in Glace Bay. He singled

out Dan Willie Morrison, the labour and veteran candidate, as one of
the early UMW supporters in the battles against Dominion Coal and
concluded with an attack on capitalist influence on lawmakers and
governments. His review of local history and current battles, wrote
one reporter, worked up the audience "to the highest pitch of interest
and enthusiasm."[15]

Had he chosen to accept a place on the labour ticket in 1920, McLachlan undoubtedly would have been elected to the provincial assembly that
year. But he was prepared to wait. His main concern in the summer of
1920 was the problem of getting the coal companies back to the bargaining table and, in order to do so, he was waiting for the government to
appoint a royal commission to review the coal miners' living and working conditions. For McLachlan, the economic struggle continued at this
time to take precedence over political action. Possibly, too, he was
listening to supporters who wanted to hold the miners' champion in
reserve and send him to Ottawa in the next Dominion election.

The Montreal Agreement

"Sooner or later the Merger and the Miners will have a trial of strength;
the exact date cannot be predicted." This observation was recorded in
RCMP reports in September 1920, and it proved to be one of the more
astute observations concerning industrial unrest in police files.[16] For
most of the year an ambitious alliance of industrialists and financiers
had been organizing to take control of the entire Nova Scotia steel and
coal industry in the name of a new holding company, the British Empire
Steel Corporation. Chief among the movers and shakers in these manoeuvres was Roy Mitchell Wolvin.

In photographs Roy Wolvin appears a mild-mannered captain of
industry, the kind of man whose experience was mainly in the offices
of accountants and directors. He would always remain a remote presence, arriving occasionally on the scene in his private railway car but
for the most part operating the coal industry from offices in the Canada
Cement Building a thousand miles away in Montreal. In the next few
years he would come to be known among the coal miners as the man
who embodied all the wickedness of capitalist development.

Wolvin's road to Cape Breton had begun on the Great Lakes. Born in St Clair, Michigan, as a young man he won a reputation as an expert in the shipping trade. When he was still working out of Duluth, Minnesota, in 1902 the twenty-two-year-old American was already known in Halifax as "one of the shrewdest shipping men on the lakes" and was praised for his efforts to improve the capacity of the St Lawrence canal system. His interest in Canada was firmly planted when he organized the Montreal Transportation Company and began working closely with J.W. Norcross of Canada Steamship Lines. Their interests were drawn further downstream in 1918, when he and Norcross organized Halifax Shipyards, reawakening local dreams of making Halifax a centre for steel shipbuilding. Wolvin was soon impressed by the enormous resources of the east coast coal and steel industries, which he expected could help support his shipping and shipbuilding enterprises, and he began to buy into Dominion Steel. In alliance with a blue-ribbon London-based group of shareholders, who had visions of using Canadian resources to shore up British industry after the war, Wolvin took over Dominion Steel in the spring of 1920.[17]

There was no fair sailing for the $500-million merger. Wolvin's grandiose plans aroused alarm among a number of veteran Montreal and Toronto directors. In a showdown at the annual meeting in June 1920, he succeeded in removing the opposition from the board. But throughout the summer and fall of 1920 the original plans were relentlessly criticized in the British and Canadian financial press. It was charged that the Besco merger was nothing more than a "huge watered stock promotion job" in which a number of dubious companies belonging to Wolvin and Norcross would be supported by the profitable coal and steel operations. The post-war speculative boom collapsed in the summer of 1920, and Wolvin later calculated that Besco had "missed the boat" by only a few weeks. Besco was reconstructed on a less unacceptable basis in 1921. Dominion Steel (which itself included Dominion Coal and was the largest company in the province) was joined with the extensive properties of the New Glasgow-based Nova Scotia Steel and Coal Company; also added to the merger was Wolvin's still unproven Halifax Shipyards. Critics still charged that some $19 million in watered stock was created by the merger – an unwarranted inflation of the paper value of the corporation. They also complained about another form of inflation in that a large block of common stock was translated into preferred shares. The result of these entirely legal financial manipulations would be increased and unrealistic pressure to pay dividends on the existing operations.[18]

In due course McLachlan would become an effective critic of the merger and the implications of its watered stock. In McLachlan's eyes, Wolvin presented the perfect image of the pin-striped financial buccaneer of the early twentieth century – cool and calculating in his business decisions, callous and indifferent about their human effects. Wolvin's corporation would be ridiculed as the British *Vampire* Steel Corporation, and Wolvin himself would be nicknamed Roy the Wolf. For the moment, however, McLachlan had little to say about these corporate manoeuvres. One of his few allusions to the construction of the merger in the summer of 1920 was a comment to the effect that consolidation movements were just as important to workers as they were to capitalists and that the union was "showing the new corporation" that the coal mines were completely controlled by union men.[19]

The miners' union was already rocking the boat. While Wolvin was attempting to float the new merger, District 26 was trying to bring the coal companies back to the bargaining table. The reason, McLachlan explained, was that since making the new agreement at the beginning of the year the coal operators had sharply increased the selling price of coal. The increases were substantial and ranged from sixty to eighty cents a ton. In the union's view, this fell very much in the category of an "economic disturbance" as defined in the MacKinnon Agreement. McLachlan explained that the 1920 agreement was a one-year contract with "a trick": "That clause about economic conditions is the finest that was ever written into a miners' agreement anywhere." Under capitalist business conditions, circumstances were always changing: "The ordinary course of business constitutes a change in economic conditions. If flour rises a cent that is a change in economic conditions. If stocks vary half a point that is a change in economic conditions. If sugar drops, that is a change in economic conditions. In other words, the clause means that every contract containing it is only good for four months, unless both parties to the contract agree to take a broad view and play the game." Alfred Tonge, general superintendent of Dominion Coal, did not deny there had been an advance in coal prices, but argued that this was caused by necessary repair, by the high cost of materials, and by the cost of the January wage agreement itself.[20]

For the rest of the year the miners and the operators were locked in a stalemate. No meetings took place until June. The MacKinnon board reconvened briefly in Halifax at the request of the Department of Labour. When that failed to produce any results, the government announced in early July the appointment of a royal commission. This was exactly what McLachlan wanted – an opportunity to expose existing working conditions and advertise the miners' expectations. Under the chairmanship of E. McG. Quirk, a conciliation officer for the Department of Labour, hearings took place during July and August. The union officers were determined to put on an impressive display of oratory and argument before the commission.

They presented an extended list of particular grievances – complaints about the distance the men had to push boxes loaded with coal, bad ventilation at the coal face, inadequate air pressure for machinery, and a shortage of cars for getting out the coal. There were also complaints about the condition of company houses, the water supply, and the high levels of infant mortality in the coal towns. During the course of the sessions at Glace Bay, McLachlan insisted on taking the commissioners down a mine to witness working conditions and on a tour of local neighbourhoods to inspect housing. "Are we making unreasonable demands when we ask that we get $1.00 increase?" McLachlan demanded. "We are the men who dig this coal, swallow the dust and endure the bad air and have 2 1/2 miles then to take it out. If the community pays more for their coal because of our increase then it is the fault of the dealers and not of the miners."

Throughout the hearings the union leaders argued their case both on economic grounds and on moral grounds. It was much too easy, they argued, to reduce the miners' case to a simple demand for another $1.00 a day for men on daily rates, 24 cents on the tonnage rate, and a 25 per cent increase on other rates. As Robert Baxter informed the commission, the time had passed when "anything was good enough for a Coal Miner": "We have learned a lesson as the helots of Sparta learned theirs, but we are of too great numbers and too great intelligence to be squashed."[21]

As secretary-treasurer, McLachlan also presented the union's case in statistical form. He prepared an impressive typewritten graph entitled "Price of Coal, Labor and Living," which was formally entered in evidence as Exhibit 12. Once again he was presenting himself, with some credibility, as an expert on the coal question. This document showed that some wage rates had gone up 114 per cent between 1909 and 1920, but that in the same period the selling price of coal had gone up 180 per cent and food prices had gone up 164 per cent. It was true, McLachlan explained, that a shiftworker who was paid $1.75 a day in 1909 was now earning $3.75, but the improvement in wages was only an illusion: "That increase looks a great big increase, 114% increase, but the man's real wage is not when he goes down the street with his wage, his real wage is what he can bring back to his family. In 1909 his real wage was higher than today."[22]

McLachlan was also careful to make the argument that the miners were not to blame for the high coal prices consumers were paying. He presented data demonstrating "the very unequal and unreasonable division of wealth created by the Coal Trade." In Halifax some coal dealers were delivering coal to local customers at $12.50 a ton, which amounted to a "criminal margin" of $4.25 a ton on the wholesale price of $8.25 for a ton of coal at the Halifax docks. Meanwhile, the cost of producing a ton of coal at the pithead, using an average of "nine typical Coal Mines in Nova Scotia," was running about $4.30 a ton. Accordingly, the miners' wage demands were not only affordable but "ultra-conservative." Again employing the masculinist rhetoric of the labour leader, McLachlan added: "This Commission could only consider us the very weakest kind of men, did we, for one moment, appear to be satisfied with one cent less than our demand calls for."[23]

At one stage in the hearings the coal operators complained about high levels of absenteeism and low productivity among the coal miners. This was McLachlan's opportunity to make the angry retort that shorter working time was a matter of life and death:

The miners of Nova Scotia work as steady as the miners in any other country of the world; I know some of the Operators said that if they would work like the men in any other country they would get along much better. I have worked in the old country and I was at a convention where it was decided that never again would the men work more than five days a week, we had been working three days a week. Did you notice the difference in the death rate between Nova Scotia and Great Britain? The death rate in Britain was the lowest. If a man works to the end of his shift he is very tired and accidents usually happen at the end of his shift when his energy has been sapped. Mines cannot be kept safe for six days and they should not be worked for six days.

McLachlan had already presented his data on fatality rates per 1,000 men employed, which showed Canadian and American rates in 1911 to 1918 to be substantially higher than those in other countries – Great Britain, 1.30; Prussia, 2.35; France, 1.21; Belgium, 1.06; Austria, 1.43; India, 1.21; South Wales, 1.06; United States, 3.76; Nova Scotia, 3.75; British Columbia, 5.39. "If there is any reason for paying something for dangerous work," he added, "then these men have a claim." But in all their calculations of working time the operators made no allowance for such things as sickness and death: "Miners are just like other people, they get sick and their families get sick and things of that kind yet these men come along and present a list of absenteeism and say these men could work 26 days in the month and never a word about sickness or death and scores of men have been killed in the mines."[24]

The coal miners waited impatiently for the report of the royal commission, so impatiently that McLachlan found himself restraining his followers from immediately tying up the mines and going on strike. At public meetings he warned against unauthorized local strikes – "what they call 'a holiday strike,'" as a police report put it. The same report explained: "He laid great stress on this point and made it very clear to all concerned."[25]

When the royal commission finally did report in September, there was strong language that seemed to accept much of the miners' argument about social conditions in the coal towns. These were described as "with few exceptions, absolutely wretched" and the report concluded that "such conditions have a deterrent effect on the miners' ability to produce coal and are a menace to themselves and families." The report also recommended big wage increases for the miners, as much as 55 cents a day – the union had asked for $1.00 – as well as substantial increases on rates for tonnage and other work.[26]

There were also some less attractive features in the report, most of all a provision to use compulsory arbitration to settle future disputes and a controversial sliding scale to regulate wages according to the amount of coal produced. These features were not acceptable either to radicals such as McLachlan or to the international union. Compulsory arbitration was anathema to union leaders, who regarded it as a betrayal of the right of collective bargaining. Furthermore, they worried that any kind of sliding scale would deprive the miners of the benefit of improvements in mining methods and new machinery and eliminate most of the new wage increases within a year. After all, the royal commission itself had concluded that low productivity was due at least in part to poor living conditions and inferior equipment.

On this issue, McLachlan was strongly supported by John L. Lewis at UMW headquarters, who wrote him that "I particularly agree with your expressed attitude pertaining to the sliding scale arrangement." Lewis also wrote directly to the deputy minister of labour in Ottawa to make the case that a sliding wage scale presented no solution to the problem of raising production levels: "By implication at least this provision of the award of the Royal Commission asserts that the responsibility of low per capita production rests entirely with the employees."[27]

But the international union was not prepared to endorse a strike in Nova Scotia. Lewis offered little hope of support and encouraged McLachlan to seek a negotiated agreement with the coal operators. Indeed he pointed out that the new British Empire Steel Corporation "would prove to be a formidable adversary in the event of a strike and the resources of our organization would be severely taxed to enter into a contest with a corporation with such financial influences behind it." Soon the man behind the merger, Roy Wolvin, was also making his presence felt at UMW headquarters. Later in October, Lewis explained to McLachlan that he had received a worried long-distance telephone call from Wolvin in Montreal: "He stated that he was anxious to learn whether or not his company had an agreement with the United Mine Workers and if there was any intention on our part to carry it out. It was difficult to understand him on the telephone at this distance, but I assume that he was referring to the agreement made last winter, which he contends has not yet expired."[28]

By this time the union locals were said to be "up in arms" over the report and, with the encouragement of the union leaders, had already voted down the royal commission's settlement. When none of the major coal operators agreed to meet for negotiations at the middle of October, the union made arrangements for a strike vote. This now seemed to be the only available course of action, McLachlan reported to Lewis on 15 October: the operators were refusing to engage in any negotiations, insisting that the royal commission award be accepted or rejected without any changes, and "there is nothing in sight to indicate that the operators and the representatives of the miners can find a common ground on which to meet and unless some outside influence interferes to bring us together a strike seems inevitable." McLachlan predicted that 95 per cent of the men would vote to strike.

"Why are we voting for a strike?" McLachlan asked at union meetings. "We are voting for a strike because the operators have been dodging us since last March." This would be the new union's first strike, and McLachlan was determined that it would be an effective one. Not a wheel would turn, since every single union member would be withdrawn from work, including enginemen, piermen, pumpmen, and firemen. "If you come out on strike, come out with the determination that you will not go back hungry or whipped," McLachlan told cheering supporters, "Make the fight short and sweet and go back into the mines when victory has been won."[29]

Suddenly Ottawa stepped in, alarmed about the prospect of a coal famine during the coming winter. It was "like a bolt from the Heavens," one police report noted, and McLachlan and Baxter left in a great rush on an overnight train for Montreal to meet with the coal operators. They had expected a quick resolution of the crisis, but in fact the showdown was postponed for two more weeks. The summons had come from the minister of labour, Gideon Robertson, who was himself a former international vice-president of the Brotherhood of Railroad Telegraphers; he understood union politics well and, particularly since the time of the Winnipeg General Strike, he had no fondness for labour radicals such as McLachlan. In this delicate situation Robertson recognized the value of having a representative of the international union on hand for the showdown, preferably John L. Lewis himself. Lewis excused himself but arranged for John P. White, the former president, who had been responsible for the original accord with the coal operators in 1919, to represent union headquarters.[30]

For several days in early November McLachlan and Baxter sat with White at the Windsor Hotel in Montreal. The small group of men across the table included Roy Wolvin and a handful of senior presidents and managers of the coal and steel companies in Nova Scotia. It was "a very hard fight," White recalled later, "although friendly in every respect." Robertson and senior officials from the Department of Labour watched anxiously. In the end there was a four-page agreement, carefully initialled on each page by the company and by the union officers. There was little in the way of grand rhetoric in the agreement: "It was deemed expedient in the interests of peace and harmony that something should be done to improve the existing labor situation." Reporting back to Lewis, White gave the agreement his endorsement: "I know everything has been secured for the mine workers of this field, that it was possible to be had, and a strike here with the conditions such as they are at the present time, would spell disaster to your Union and destroy the organization entirely." McLachlan and Baxter, he added, had also endorsed the agreement and would do their best to have it ratified by the coal miners.[31]

The Montreal Agreement, as this document came to be known, contained a tough prescription for industrial legality. There were the same improvements in pay for the miners that the royal commission had recommended: tonnage rates were increased ten cents a ton, contract rates 12.5 per cent, and daily rates 55 cents. The most controversial elements of the royal commission award were dropped, but in this contract for the first time the union was explicitly recognized as the partner of management in maintaining stability and efficiency in the mine operations. A new series of clauses spelled out management's authority to direct work in the mines. There was to be no discrimina-

tion against union members, but the right to hire and discharge workers was exclusively in the hands of management. The "duties and
limitations" of the miners' pit committee were spelled out. Local disputes and grievances were to be adjusted by local mine committees,
district officers, or, if necessary, arbitration by an outside party. Most
important in the light of frequent local strikes throughout the coalfield,
there were to be no strikes of any kind during the course of the agreement:
"No stoppage of work shall take place owing to any dispute arising at any
mine under the jurisdiction of District No. 26." The agreement itself was
to run to the end of November 1921, both sides agreeing to meet in
Halifax twenty days before the expiry of the agreement.[32]

Back in the coalfields there was a stormy reception for the agreement.
McLachlan and Baxter were denounced as traitors, and union locals
called for their resignations. McLachlan took it in stride, agreeing that
the contract was "a big disappointment to us all." But in Montreal he
had discovered that a strike under existing conditions was likely to fail.
In Montreal, he explained, he had seen that economic conditions were
changing – unemployment was rising and local workers were accepting
reductions. It was also clear that the international union was not going
to support a strike. And as for the government, Robertson's deputy
minister had declared that "the government would not tolerate a strike
of the coal miners in Nova Scotia at this time, and in the event of a
strike taking place, that the government would send here the North
West Mounted Police."

The coal miners had little choice, McLachlan told reporters: "It will
be just like the barren gospel if the men reject the agreement. There is
nothing left but to accept the terms, any other action would be placing
themselves on a barren desert. The agreement is the best they can
get under the present circumstances." But, he also added, "if Baxter
and I made fools of ourselves in Montreal, we are not going to run
away from it."[33]

McLachlan did not feel the full force of the opposition until delegates
from throughout the district assembled in Truro to decide on the
agreement. The attack was led by Dan Livingstone, the Westville miner
who was said to be sympathetic to the OBU. Livingstone gave McLachlan and Baxter a taste of the kind of angry rhetoric they themselves had

used against leaders of the PWA in the past: "Now we find two lions with their claws up in their wool and their fangs sheathed ... All this slobbering about what rejection of the pact will mean to wives, mothers and babies show that argument for the pact is weak." Other delegates were more concerned about the new clauses that seemed to weaken the union's presence in the workplace – How would the union be able to insist on the employment of union members? Would the miners still be able to quit work in dangerous conditions? What would happen to the adjustment of local grievances in the hands of arbitrators?[34]

This was an unfamiliar position for McLachlan – a labour radical pleading for restraint. After a long summer of agitation, he was asking the delegates to suspend their expectations and even give up some customary rights. Was this going to be the price of getting a contract in the new age of industrial legality? McLachlan made no attempt to defend the new management-rights clauses, except to remind the delegates that the pit committees would remain the miners' first line of defence. But he was firmly committed to his judgment about the changing economic conditions. The post-war speculative boom was coming to an end and the coal industry in particular could expect to suffer from excess supply and overproduction. McLachlan already had a good sense of the enormous drop in prices that would take place in the course of the next year: "We are on a toboggan slide and being irresistibly drawn by conditions. Three months from today you cannot make a good agreement. You may criticize Baxter and McLachlan and your wife can't buy groceries with that. You can take the 55 cents home and she can buy something with it. I'm going to take my responsibility for this agreement, and if you turn it down now, then in three months I'll take credit for making a worse bargain." Most of the evils in the contract, McLachlan added, had been exaggerated, and one important provision was being overlooked: "Now we have the operators locked into a pledge to meet with us at the end of contract. That is something we never had before. It took a lot of work to build up District 26, but the biggest fool in the district can tear it asunder in two weeks."[35]

The delegates were not convinced, and the vote went heavily against him, seventy-five to twenty in favour of rejecting the Montreal Agreement. But instead of calling for an immediate strike, the delegates agreed to let the union officers take the agreement to the membership. Leaving the Truro meetings, McLachlan would probably have agreed with RCMP Inspector LaNauze, who summarized the situation in these words: "The situation has now reached its most critical point and no matter what points are under discussion the real question at stake is, *Will the Miners stand by their organization or will they drift towards disorganization.*"[36]

Again, the fight was on, and McLachlan felt the force of the discontent among the coal miners. At a meeting of the New Waterford locals, McLachlan and Baxter were interrupted with hisses, jeers, and cat calls. A shower of eggs rained down from the gallery. Indignantly McLachlan defended himself against charges of selling out: "I never received a cent from any person, with the exception of the wages which I have been paid." Later McLachlan asserted that he had never before in his life as a union leader attended a more hostile meeting. He charged that the egg-throwing incident was part of a scheme to break up the union, and he blamed the local leadership for failing to keep order: "When I was a boy I would have liked one time to have thrown eggs at a platform speaker, but the older and saner men in the hall would have booted me out had I done it." The effect of the episode was to arouse sympathy for McLachlan and Baxter. An editorial in the Sydney *Post* praised the union leaders for their pluck, and several locals passed resolutions deploring the incident.[37]

In the end the Montreal Agreement was accepted in a general membership vote, 6,499 to 4,490. The vote was a tribute to McLachlan's personal credibility among the coal miners. As one veteran had argued during the debates, McLachlan had laboured long and hard for the miners' cause and brought back more than one good agreement in the past. Meanwhile, in early December McLachlan was re-elected to office, unopposed.[38]

Again McLachlan had escaped easy classification as an irresponsible labour radical. The debate on the Montreal Agreement seemed to reinforce his image as a pragmatic and responsible industrial statesman. After all, he had been able to hold the miners in check and avert a national crisis in Canada's fuel supply. One police agent found the transformation of McLachlan impossible to accept and even alleged that McLachlan was responsible for buying eggs for the boys who disrupted his meeting in New Waterford: "This man is as red as he was one year ago ... he has done wonders in the eyes of the public to stave off a big coal strike; the same public one year from today shall be the same as they were a year ago, denouncing him from every corner of the Province of Nova Scotia."

Another police agent who was shadowing the union leaders that month retrieved a torn-up letter from a hotel waste-paper basket and pieced together the following statement in McLachlan's unmistakeable handwriting: "I agree with you that the old craft idea has had its day, and must be replaced by something more comprehensive, whether that be the O.B.U. or some other form of industrial organization." The conclusion, the agent noted, was that McLachlan "is still the same sly and crafty agitator ... he still needs to be watched."[39]

Fuel Supply

The coal industry was one of the riddles of the Canadian political economy. Every industrial economy needed coal. This was the lesson of the industrial revolution: Britain, France, Belgium, Germany, the United States – in every case the success of industry was founded on the power of coal. Until well into the twentieth century, railways, factories, and cities all depended on an ever-expanding supply of coal. When Canada also went down the industrial road, the importance of coal was widely recognized. At the time of Confederation, coal was important enough to inspire dreams of industrial empire in the Maritimes, and when the National Policy of tariff protection was constructed in the late nineteenth century, the developing coal industry was also protected by a tariff against imported coal. The industry had grown, and by the early twentieth century it was firmly planted, both in the Maritimes and also in Alberta and British Columbia. But there was one thing unique about the structure of the coal industry in Canada – there was no coal industry in the heartland of the country's industrial economy, in Ontario and Quebec. The coal supply for central Canada initially came partly from the Maritimes, but by the early twentieth century more and more of the requirements for the industrial economy came from the coalfields of the United States. Even though high levels of tariff protection remained in place for most manufactured goods, the Dominion government failed to maintain equivalent protection for coal.

That was the conundrum of the coal industry, and it placed the Nova Scotia coal industry in a permanently vulnerable position. As long as coal remained the principal source of industrial energy, there would be a large domestic market. But as long as American coal supplies were available for export to Canada, there would be competition for coal in central Canada. And it would be possible for Nova Scotia coal to compete for a share of the market in central Canada only as long as the price of Canadian coal could be kept low. This kind of rivalry between regions within North America was one of the historic reasons for keeping down the level of wages for coal miners. The logic of market forces in the coal industry in early twentieth-century North America left out only one factor – the coal miners.

At the end of the Great War, the Canadian energy market was in disarray. Wartime conditions had destroyed the market for Nova Scotia coal in central Canada. Exports to Quebec were virtually decimated and they were almost completely shut out of Ontario. In 1920 this "acute fuel area" – as experts called the energy market of southern Ontario and Quebec – was still almost entirely dependent on imported supplies. Almost 14 million tons of bituminous coal alone was imported from the United States, but shipments from Nova Scotia into this territory amounted to less than 300,000 tons. Coal experts worried whether Nova Scotia would ever regain its position in the Montreal market. Meanwhile, it was becoming clear that the American coal supply was not dependable. During wartime the coal market had been managed by the Dominion fuel controller, who besides promoting labour peace and union recognition in the Nova Scotia coal industry also succeeded in ensuring allocations of coal for central Canada from the United States Fuel Administration. The removal of wartime controls changed the situation abruptly. Strikes in the American coalfields raised the alarming prospect of coal shortages in central Canada.[40]

Such anxieties prompted an upsurge of interest in a "national coal policy" to promote the use of the domestic fuel supply. The ideal of national self-sufficiency in fuel attracted considerable support, in both the producing and the consuming provinces. After a difficult winter in the coal industry, with producing provinces complaining of lack of markets and consuming provinces alarmed about shortages, in March 1921 the House of Commons named a committee to enquire into the problem of Canada's fuel supply. It was a committee dominated by Ontario and western MPs, but the interests of Nova Scotia coal would not be neglected. Three of the ten members were from Cape Breton – two longtime Liberals, D.D. McKenzie (Cape Breton North and Victoria) and A.W. Chisholm (Inverness), and one Conservative, John C. Douglas (Cape Breton South and Richmond), the former mayor of Glace Bay, who saw himself as a staunch defender of the local coal industry.[41]

Since the days of the Provincial Workmen's Association, the coal miners had counted themselves as supporters of protection for the coal industry. By protecting the market for Nova Scotia coal, the tariff also protected the employment of coal miners. At the end of the war, the new miners' union continued to express support for a stronger tariff on coal. In 1919, for instance, District 26 called for the extension of the standard 53-cent tariff to stop the entry of slack coal for industrial use at cheaper rates.

Also in the summer of 1919 McLachlan was telegraphing protests to Prime Minister Borden on behalf of idle men at Sydney Mines who objected to the purchase of cheap American coal by the Canadian National Railways. Borden replied that the CNR was buying as much Nova Scotia coal as the companies were able to transport with the limited shipping available. But McLachlan objected that the market for wartime shipping had disappeared and "our men justly feel the importation of American coal ought also to have ended." Some mines were operating only three days a week and miners returning from the war were unable to get work: "To buy 'cheap' American coal while our own people go in want or go short is a down right shame that ought to be corrected at once."

Expressions of support for the domestic market belonged to the traditional politics of protectionism, but McLachlan's protest also sounded a more radical note that was consistent with the changing balance of power that was taking place in coal-mining society. There was no gesture of loyalism towards employers or governments in the protest from the miners of the Jubilee local: "The power of endurance of hungry men is only very limited when the common call of nature forces them to take action themselves to relieve their necessities and any such action taken is no breach of the moral law however much it may be at variance with the laws made at Ottawa and Halifax." The insistence here was on the coal miners' right to full employment at their work and the moral duty of the government to make public policies to satisfy this demand. For McLachlan, protectionism was not about protecting the industry in the abstract or the coal operators in particular but about protecting the employment of workers.[42]

This distinction was most obvious when he and other union leaders appeared before the parliamentary Fuel Supply Committee in May 1921. The witnesses included representatives of producing companies and provinces, distributors, engineers, sales agents, and technical experts. Originally there was no plan to include the miners' unions – but District 26 had "requested a hearing" and "volunteered" to appear before the committee. McLachlan was determined to give the Members of Parliament full exposure to the labour point of view on the coal problem. Once more the union leaders appeared as recognized authorities on the industry, not just the advocates of the miners' special interests. For the better part of two days the committee members sat in Room 425 of the House of Commons and listened to the union leaders from District 26 – Baxter, McLachlan, and the new district vice-president, W.P. Delaney. Despite the importance of the coal trade to western miners or to the railway workers, no spokesmen for other unions appeared before the committee. But for the Nova Scotia coal miners, these hearings involved fundamental issues concerning the future of their industry.[43]

From the start Baxter conveyed a sense of the urgent situation in the coalfields that winter. Although consumers might be suffering from high prices and fuel shortages, the coal miners were suffering from lack of sufficient employment. At Dominion Coal many miners had been working only two days a week: "Our case is that we have had a very hard depression in Nova Scotia. The depression has caused considerable idleness, and the idleness has caused considerable deprivation amongst the miners and their families down there." In the face of this downturn, the coal miners insisted that wage reductions were no solution to the difficulty and were determined that existing rates be defended. Indeed, the much-abused Montreal Agreement now became a standard of achievement to be defended. In a context of falling prices, the existing rates promised a higher standard for the miners. At the end of the hearing, Delaney put the union's position in these words: "Our fight is to try to increase the standard of living of the miners, and what we have really been doing in the past has been following up the cost of living; we have never passed it, we never had the chance to pass it, and if there was such a thing as a decline in the cost of living, and we could maintain our wage rate for a certain period, it would be that much in favour of increasing or raising the standard of living of the miners."[44]

McLachlan's own evidence began with a detailed review of wage settlements in recent years, including the new Montreal Agreement. Wages had gone up considerably since 1909, mainly of course since 1916, but as usual he warned the committee that wages had not kept pace with the rising cost of living in the same period. All through this period prices had been increasing more rapidly than wages, and the men were falling behind in their struggle to raise the standard of living. This distinction between nominal wages and real wages was crucial to the miners' case against future wage reductions: "Now, it may be said that as the cost of living came down – and I think Mr. Wolvin made some statement to that effect – that if the cost of living came down naturally the wages should come down. Now, there is not the same argument when the cost of living comes down for making a change in the wages. It is absolutely different."[45]

To explain the distinction, McLachlan treated the committee to one of his more popular economic expositions, which was based on the recommended family budgets in the Department of Labour's own monthly *Labour Gazette*:

I want to take one item – that of milk. They allow six quarts of milk for a family of five. Now presumably the people who drafted that said "Here is a standard of living which the worker should have; six quarts of milk a week." If we put that at seven, it means

this, that the baby gets four-fifths of a pint of milk a day. That is
what they said. That is the allotment for a working man's family.
If the cost of living goes up just a few points, it means these people
are in distress. If, on the other hand, the cost of living goes down
a few points, it may mean that the baby will get a full glass of milk
instead of four-fifths, and I want to say that Mr. Wolvin or any
other man who lives as he lives, who comes to the miner, and says
that because the baby is getting a full glass of milk instead of
four-fifths, the cost of wages should come down, he cannot
be a wise man to do it, and it is not a wise man who says that
the cost of living is coming down, and therefore, your wages
should come down.[46]

In many respects, McLachlan's testimony was similar to the evidence
he had given before the royal commission the previous summer. He was
determined to show that the coal miners were not to blame for any coal
shortages or high prices in the energy market and deserved a chance to
benefit from the hard-won increases in wage rates they had achieved.

The distinction that was of most interest to the committee members
was the one that addressed the margins of profit that were available to
the coal operators. In 1909 the price of bunker coal in Halifax was
running $3.75 a ton; in 1919, amid rumours of coal scarcity, Dominion
Coal was obtaining $10.50 for the same coal. Prices went as high as $14
and $15 a ton in the spring of 1920 as a result of a coal strike in the
United States: "In other words, the operators made a raid on the public
and collected money simply because there was the belief that coal was
scarce." Without using such technical terms as nominal, real, and
relative wages, McLachlan was prepared to argue that in the years since
1909 the wage rate had gone up 110 per cent, the cost of living 149 per
cent, and the price of coal in some cases as much as 200 per cent.[47]

McLachlan's testimony also demonstrated that the coal miners had
a distinctive point of view on such questions as "the efficiency of coal
mines": "When we speak about the efficiency in the coal mines, that is
from the miner's standpoint, we talk about it from our own view, as to
the efficiency of a mine. The efficiency of a mine does not necessarily
mean the getting up of coal. We want to see the mines in such an

efficient condition that the men's lives will be safeguarded first."
Canada's record for coal mine safety, however, was "very bad and
notorious." According to recent data from the Bureau of Mines in the
United States, for the years 1911 to 1918 the number of fatal accidents
per thousand men each year was 3.76; in Britain the same rate was 1.3.
"In other words a man has a three times better chance of losing his life
in the United States than he has in the coal mines of Britain. That shows
that the British coal mines are being run efficiently." The Canadian
coalfields did not show up well in this comparison – 5.39 in British
Columbia, 3.75 in Nova Scotia. Consequently, the Nova Scotia record was as bad as the American, and almost three times worse than
the British.[48]

Pressed by John C. Douglas, McLachlan agreed that he was objecting
most of all to the non-enforcement of mining laws in Nova Scotia: "I
do not believe there was ever an operator, nor an official of the operators, convicted of any offence in Nova Scotia ..." As an illustration,
McLachlan described conditions in the No. 24 mine. The ventilation
there was inadequate, but since the mine inspectors had found no
explosive gas they failed to shut down the mine. There was not enough
oxygen for the men to breathe, and everyone knew it: "They were
coming out with their legs doubled up and they were walking like
drunken men. They were vomiting, and the men complained about it."
The result was that the mine was closed down for a week and the men
put out of work "as a sort of penalty because the men complained." For
McLachlan, this was an arresting local example of the non-enforcement
of regulations: "If that had been in Britain that man would have been
arrested and tried for failing to have sufficient ventilation passed to
these workmen, and convicted."[49]

Chisholm, the Inverness MP, was particularly alarmed by this account and recommended that the unions "make an exhibition" of one
of these cases of non-enforcement: "If labour unions would take up
these things, the law is there." When he asked for more information,
McLachlan was ready to oblige: "I have worked myself in a place in No.
1 mine of the Nova Scotia Coal Company, and if three men walked into
that place and started to breathe in it with three lamps, one or two of
the lamps would go out for the lack of oxygen. A man cannot dig coal

in a place like that." To complete the picture, Douglas and Chisholm both wondered who should be alerted first when air was bad, the mine manager or the mine inspector. McLachlan had no easy answer, since he had little confidence in either source of authority: "Well, I suppose we have not a great deal of faith in the inspector; that is the trouble ... and we have not a great deal in the management."[50]

Expanding on the same theme of "efficiency" in coal operations, McLachlan also described the unacceptable housing conditions which existed throughout the coalfields, with the exception of Cumberland County where there was little company housing. In the rows of company housing in New Aberdeen, for instance, overflowing outhouses made health conditions hazardous: "Now, we say that if you want to get the best out of a man, you want to give him the best home possible. The miners down there are not averse to paying for a good home. They want good homes. There has been a nursery tale peddled throughout this country about the miners getting cheap coal and cheap rent. The miners of Nova Scotia are living in the dearest houses in Canada." All of these conditions, McLachlan argued, had to do with efficiency – safety, ventilation, housing, and health: "These are things I am pointing out that lower production, lessen a man's efficiency, and of course lessen production."[51]

In the same category came the recent introduction of "checkers" into the mines: "These men go around the mines, and they have nothing to do in the way of manual labour at all. They keep tab on how much you are doing and how much the other man is doing through the mines, and because these men are in there, the production per man is being lowered and they are very irritating to the men themselves." The company police were another class of employees who were adding to the inefficiency of industry: "They are non-producers in the true sense of the word." New police were being hired every day, McLachlan complained. It was only about a year since the old company police force had been disbanded, but under Wolvin's new management the corporation had reinstituted the force – a sign that seemed to threaten a return to the old days of surveillance and harassment.[52]

Time was running short. It was almost 2 p.m. on a Friday afternoon, and the Commons was about to resume sitting. At this stage the acting chair of the committee, J.A. Maharg, a Saskatchewan MP, proposed that McLachlan's testimony be concluded. Douglas objected, knowing McLachlan had more to say on the subject of coal prices. Accordingly, the committee met again on Saturday morning, when McLachlan's final theme was "to say a little about the Coal Company's earnings."[53]

This time McLachlan's text was the annual report of Dominion Steel and its subsidiaries, which included a statement showing net earnings for the years 1916 to 1920 inclusive. After all expenses, taxes, depreciation, and other costs were taken into account, the net earnings were $3.9 million for 1916, $9.5 million for 1917, $8.5 million for 1918, $6.4 million for 1919, and $3.2 million for 1920 – for a total of $31,840,133.97. In short, the Dominion companies had a record of more than $31 million in clear profits over the past five years: "We say that this Coal Company – I do not like to refer to any person's war record; men have made great sacrifices; but if this is a sacrifice during the war, then lots of business men in this country would be glad to go in for a lot more sacrificing; if this is shooting up business, then lots of people would like to have their business shot up."

Even with a $17-million reserve fund, the coal and steel companies seemed intent on launching an attack on both the consumers and the coal miners. With that kind of profit-making record, was it fair for the companies to hold up the public for higher prices or to hold up the miners for wage reductions? By reducing working time over the past winter, McLachlan charged, they were losing more money than they could have made by banking the coal for future sale: "They were suggesting to the men in the most forcible language they could use that we should 'come across,' and beg for them to give us work at the lower wage."[54]

As far as the costs of producing coal were concerned, McLachlan reminded the committee that during the war the company books were inspected by government-appointed auditors as a matter of course. The Dominion fuel controller then fixed a price for coal that allowed the companies a 10 per cent return on invested capital: "With that ten per cent, they should be able to do the thing just as reasonably as they have been doing it and make money." McLachlan then provided a copy of the coal costs and prices submitted to the royal commission the previous summer, and he estimated that the current cost of producing coal was still very low, probably little more than $5.00 per ton. But he encouraged the committee to obtain its own information: "We have not any method of finding out the costs, and if this Committee wants the costs, there is only one source of getting the information, unless you want guesswork, and that is to get the cost-sheets."[55]

The miners' evidence received some modest national attention. A Canadian Press despatch reported briefly on the "shocking" living conditions in the coal towns and the economic mysteries of the coal industry. Back home McLachlan's estimate of real production costs played well, at least in the pages of the Sydney *Post*: "There are few persons acquainted with mining conditions in this county who will seriously contend that this estimate is too low." Allegations about price-gouging by the coal companies were a popular theme, and one of McRitchie's cartoons in the Halifax *Herald* had congratulated the committee for roasting the companies over the coals.[56]

But the last weeks of the hearings were taken up with a frustrating effort to obtain accurate information on production costs and pricing policies. On 14 May the committee repeated its earlier call for the companies to divulge information about costs. At Douglas's insistence, the committee voted to summon senior officers of the Dominion and Scotia coal companies to appear before the committee with their "original cost sheets from 1912 to date."[57]

Only one of the company officials obeyed the summons, D.H. McDougall, a veteran of the Nova Scotia coal industry and now vice-president of the new British Empire Steel Corporation. Unlike Wolvin, he had extensive experience in the industry. A mining engineer by training, he had served as general manager of Dominion Coal and also as president of Nova Scotia Steel and Coal in the years before the merger. When he appeared at last before the committee on 25 May, McDougall brought none of the "original cost sheets" demanded by the committee. He argued that production costs from the individual mines would not be helpful, since they included only expenditures on labour and material at the collieries, without provision for many of the other costs of operation. As far as the "final costs" were concerned, however, the company was not prepared to make them public: "We have always regarded our costs as sacred." There was of course nothing to conceal, he added, but no other operator had produced similar accounts for the committee and it would be unfair to require Besco to do so alone. Meanwhile, McDougall's testimony also hinted at what was to come for the coal miners. He estimated that at least 75 per cent of the cost of production in the coal industry was the cost of labour, and as the corporation struggled to pay its costs and reconquer its markets, it seemed likely that the miners' wages would be under attack: "We have got to produce cheaper coal in Nova Scotia, and we must find a way of doing it."[58]

The hearings of the Fuel Supply Committee ended in disarray. Douglas charged that the coal companies were in contempt of the committee for failing to produce the cost sheets and argued that their non-compliance be reported to the House of Commons. He was over-ruled, and the hearings were adjourned.[59] The idea of a "national coal policy," a theme that was raised repeatedly at the hearings and had been one of the original inspirations for the committee, produced uncontroversial proposals – the situation should be monitored by the Dominion government, transportation and storage facilities should be improved, Canadians should be encouraged to use Canadian coal wherever possible, and the production of hydro-electricity should be encouraged. It was a cautious report that suggests how little resonance the old principles of the National Policy now had in Canadian political debate. And the committee's final report had nothing to say about the miners' wages or the companies' profits.[60]

The *Maritime Labor Herald*

In April 1921 McLachlan was reading a book by Upton Sinclair, the famous American muckraker who had exposed the meat-packing industry and the conditions of working-class life in Chicago in *The Jungle*. In *The Brass Check* Sinclair addressed himself to the study of journalism. In America, Sinclair argued, there was no such thing as a free and impartial press. The newspaper industry was just another servant of capitalism, and stories about unions and strikes – as shown by the distorted reports of such events as the Ludlow Massacre in 1914 – were filled with prejudice, slander, and rumour. The "brass check," Sinclair wrote, was the "'price of

a woman's shame'" in a house of ill-fame; the money in the pay-enve-
lopes of American journalists was "in its moral implications and in its
social effect, precisely and identically the same."[61]

In his copy of the book, McLachlan noted the passage where Sinclair
quoted John Swinton, editor of the New York *Tribune*, to the effect that
journalists were nothing more than "intellectual prostitutes." The journalist's business was "to destroy the truth, to lie outright, to pervert, to
vilify, to fawn at the feet of Mammon, and to sell his race and his
country for his daily bread": "We are the tools and vassals of rich men
behind the scenes. We are the jumping-jacks; they pull the strings and
we dance. Our talents, our possibilities and our lives are all the property
of other men."[62]

Out of such discontents came the idea of the labour press. Like
independent labour politics, the rise of the labour newspaper was
founded on the idea that in order to participate fully in public life the
working class required organizations and institutions of their own. Just
as labour candidates could advance the workers' cause in politics, labour
newspapers would report the activities of unions and champion the
causes of labour, simultaneously educating supporters and informing
public opinion. Canada's first labour newspaper, the *Ontario Workman*,
emerged out of the struggle for union recognition and the nine-hour
day in 1872; dozens more local labour newspapers followed across
the country, though many of them were short-lived. In Britain Keir
Hardie invested much effort in the *Labour Leader*, which became a
weekly in 1894.[63]

In the Maritimes, Robert Drummond had moved swiftly to establish
the *Trades Journal* in 1880 to spread the message of the new miners'
union, the Provincial Workmen's Association, and it continued to
publish until 1898. Later there would be the *Eastern Labor News*,
established in Moncton in 1909 and supported by affiliates of the
American Federation of Labor around the region. There were also the
small weeklies published by local "entrepreneurs of protest" such as
Bruce MacDougall, who supported local unions and other labour
causes in the pages of his *Plain Dealer*, *Free Speech*, and *Vindicator*; his
unexplained death in a Sydney hotel in 1910, while supporting the early

struggles of District 26, had helped feed local suspicions about the suppression of independent journalism.[64]

In 1917 the resurgence of the miners' union and labour politics in Cape Breton was accompanied by the birth of a local labour press. The *Canadian Labor Leader* was edited by a Sydney union organizer, P.M. Nicholson, who had previously written a labour column for one of the daily newspapers. The board of directors included representatives of the AMW and the ILP as well as the Sydney Trades and Labour Council and the British Canadian Cooperative Society. At its peak the paper boasted a circulation of 4,200 copies per week. The *Canadian Labor Leader* helped account for the strong showing of the labour candidates in 1917 and also provided assistance in union campaigns; one of the highlights, for instance, was McLachlan's famous family-budget contest for the women in the coal towns. The *Labor Leader* followed in 1919, and it vigorously articulated the expectations of workers and veterans at the close of the war; this paper was published by a sympathetic Sydney entrepreneur and endorsed by the Cape Breton ILP, but the *Labor Leader* had a smaller circulation than its predecessor and contained less of direct interest to the coal miners. In August 1919 District 26 endorsed the *Eastern Federationist* in Pictou County "until such time as the district will decide to put in a plant of their own."[65]

The idea of a newspaper supported by the coal miners was discussed repeatedly at union meetings, and McLachlan was soon immersed in the plans to establish a weekly, or even a daily, labour newspaper at Glace Bay. In the fall of 1921 the *Maritime Labor Herald* was incorporated as a limited share company, complete with a set of by-laws. The total capitalization was set at $75,000, with shares valued at $5.00 each. Besides McLachlan himself, the four provisional directors included D.N. Brodie, one of his comrades from the days of the SPC and also the proprietor of a local printshop, and two well-known Glace Bay coal miners active in local labour politics, Ronald McInnis and Dan Willie Morrison, the newly elected labour MLA. The by-laws provided that 60 per cent of the shares in the company were to be held by labour unions. This requirement ensured that the *Maritime Labor Herald*, unlike newspapers operated by well-meaning "friends of labour," would remain under union control.[66]

From the beginning, plans for the *Maritime Labor Herald* were ambitious. The title suggested the possibility of expansion beyond the coalfields. Early discussions forecast an eventual daily newspaper, which was provided for in the by-laws. An invitation to take up the editorial chair was sent to J.S. Woodsworth, who had briefly edited the *Strike Bulletin* in Winnipeg in 1919. It appears that Woodsworth initially accepted the invitation to come to Glace Bay but later declined, probably because he had reached a decision to run for election to the House of Commons in the coming election. The organizers then approached a veteran of Canadian radical journalism, William Ulrich Cotton, former publisher of the socialist newspaper *Cotton's Weekly*.[67]

Cotton accepted the position, and the first issue of the *Maritime Labor Herald* appeared on 14 October 1921, announcing itself as "a paper devoted to the interests of labor": "We are a working class paper in working class dress and right on the job fighting the battle of the working class." The pages of these early issues showed the evidence of Cotton's experienced management – eight pages crammed with local news and letters, resolutions from the union locals and reports from conferences, learned editorials, occasional verse and humour, dispatches from a labour news service, union cards and notices, and ample local advertising.[68]

By the time the newspaper began publishing, McLachlan had accepted a nomination for the Dominion election on the Farmer-Labour ticket for Cape Breton South and Richmond. He had no formal position at the newspaper, but his influence was everywhere. McLachlan regularly filled front-page columns with his own hard-hitting writing. For the first issue he wrote a trenchant attack on the control of politics by "big business and frenzied finance": politicians such as Arthur Meighen and Mackenzie King were "but corporals working under a general staff composed of Bank Presidents, railway owners and captains of industry." Then he was reviewing the wage struggles of recent years, denouncing Wolvin's management of the coal industry, championing the miners' independence, defending himself against charges of godlessness, and accusing his opponents of manufacturing slanders and falsehoods. In the pages of the *Maritime Labor Herald* McLachlan was the working-class hero, loyally supported by the editor for his conduct of union business and praised as the labour candidate destined to represent the coal miners in the House of Commons.[69]

The *Maritime Labor Herald* was exactly what McLachlan had long wanted – a newspaper owned and controlled by the working class. Week in and week out it would take on the endless challenge to agitate, to educate, to organize. "This is the workers' paper, and stood with the workers when they needed it so much," he wrote following the end of the 1921 election campaign. "Every one must rally to its support and push up its circulation until each working class family in Nova Scotia becomes a subscriber." By the early months of 1922 circulation had increased to more than 6,000 copies a week, giving the *Maritime Labor Herald* more readers than some local daily newspapers. This proved to be the paper's peak circulation, but the *Labor Herald* maintained a circulation of some four to five thousand copies in the following years. Although the newspaper never did succeed in attracting a wide readership in other areas, the *Labor Herald* remained a vocal exponent of the class struggle in the coalfields. Roy Wolvin would denounce it regularly as one of the principal causes of the labour unrest in the coal industry. And McLachlan, who eventually served as the newspaper's last editor, never gave up his fondness for the paper he came to regard as "the child and champion of the workers."[70]

Member of Parliament

When McLachlan came to Parliament Hill in the spring of 1921, he was already thinking about the next election. When the Fuel Supply Committee adjourned on the Friday afternoon, McLachlan took a place in the steep seats of the visitors' gallery of the House of Commons. Down below he could see some of the old party warhorses such as George Foster and W.S. Fielding going through their paces. This was the last session of a discredited Parliament elected under questionable wartime procedures in order to put conscription into effect. This afternoon the minister of justice was introducing amendments to the Criminal Code, including one to provide for the whipping of juvenile convicts and one to make the possession of bombs illegal.[71]

By this time both parties had new leaders on the front benches. Borden had stepped down as prime minister in 1920, to be replaced by his minister of justice, Arthur Meighen. This was the man who had been one of the strongest advocates of conscription during the war and one of the architects of labour's defeat in the Winnipeg General Strike. Meanwhile, after the death of Sir Wilfrid Laurier in 1919, the Liberals had chosen William Lyon Mackenzie King as their new leader. King had been minister of labour at the time of the 1909 strike and was of no help at all to the United Mine Workers when the army was sent into the coalfields. Out of power he had spent recent years cultivating his reputation as a labour expert – which included advising John D. Rockefeller on how to avoid unions in the Colorado coalfield after the notorious Ludlow Massacre.

As far as McLachlan was concerned, these political leaders were no friends of labour. In the coming election the leaders of the old parties would face unprecedented opposition from farmer and labour candidates in every province. They would stand exposed as the enemies of democracy and the agents of big business. Already there was a Farmer-Labour government in Ontario, and the United Farmers had swept to power in Alberta. Was it just possible, McLachlan wondered, that Parliament Hill would now become the seat of a workers' and farmers' government for the whole of the country?

Back in Cape Breton during the summer of 1921, Inspector LaNauze of the RCMP reported an upsurge of activity by the Independent Labour Party. Local meetings were raising money for the new labour newspaper and also preparing the ground for the Dominion election. In a speech at Sydney Mines, A.R. Richardson, MLA, was predicting the election of a Labour-Farmer government in Ottawa. McLachlan was also there on the platform, and at similar meetings he "strongly advocated the use of the ballot in support of the Independent Labor Party to get better conditions and change the Government." Once the campaign was under way, a police agent reported much talk about the threatened wage reductions and dissatisfaction with the present economic system among the coal miners: "I had conversations with the local miners, and they strongly believe and state that 'labor would come to power in this election, and that the miners themselves would control and run the mines.'"[72]

McLachlan had been touted as the prospective labour candidate long before the election, and by early October he seemed assured of the nomination. Cape Breton South and Richmond was a two-member constituency, but instead of running a second labour candidate along with McLachlan, the labour party was intent on cooperating with the United Farmers in offering a joint Farmer-Labour ticket, as they had done with so much success in 1920. At the joint meeting where the candidates were chosen, McLachlan had little difficulty winning the labour nomination.[73]

Meanwhile, his running mate was chosen with an eye to attracting rural votes and perhaps also allaying some of the anxieties about McLachlan's radicalism. Born in rural Richmond County in 1882, Edward Charles Doyle attended St Francis Xavier University and the Maritime Business College. As a self-employed carpenter, Doyle belonged to the class of rural producers who were not easily accommodated by simplified versions of the class struggle. The decision to run a joint ticket in Cape Breton South and Richmond was an important one. The Canadian population was still half-rural and half-urban, and labour candidates could have no hopes of forming a government on their own. Given the realities of the Canadian class structure in 1921, the working class could come to power only by making alliances, and in his speeches during the election campaign McLachlan regularly referred to the prospect of a Farmer-Labour government.[74]

The Doyle-McLachlan ticket was soon denounced by the Sydney *Post* as a bizarre "Agrarian-Socialist" combination: "The so-called labour candidate is a socialist and the professed agrarian a wool-dyed grit who is a carpenter by trade." Worst of all, warned the *Post*, this team represented "a conspiracy of treason to the basic industry of Cape Breton." This was a reference to the the most common attack on Farmer-Labour cooperation in 1921, the charge that the farmers' support for lower tariffs could not be reconciled with the protectionist needs of Canadian industry. McLachlan replied directly to this charge in his public meetings by arguing that the real difficulty was to separate legitimate protection from the manipulation of tariffs and prices by the big interests. All the farmers wanted, McLachlan argued, quoting from a copy of their published platform, was that "every claim for tariff protection by any industry should be held publicly before a special committee of parliament." There was nothing here for the coal miners to fear, but a Farmer-Labour government would certainly force the coal operators to reveal some of the mysteries of their costs and profits: "We will say: 'Here is a government that is joined with the working class and they are determined that you shall produce your cost sheets and ascertain whether that trade requires protection or not.'"[75]

McLachlan had much more to say about protectionism. His views were a mix of muckraking rhetoric and working-class politics and were most fully reported in an account of an election meeting in the UMW hall in New Waterford on 7 November. It was "the greatest political meeting ever held in the town of New Waterford," according to the reporter, who threw up his hands in despair of recording the deluge of facts and figures presented by the labour candidate:

> He proved the good that protection did to the workingmen by showing how the combined manufacturing concerns in Canada, for one year, paid to over five hundred thousand men and women and children in wages millions of dollars less than they received in net profits themselves, and how the protectors of the people had handed hundreds of millions of dollars in cold cash out of the government treasury and millions of acres of the most valuable lands of Canada to Railroad companies and other friends, together with other numerous privileges, so they were well protected and provided for in their old age, but when the toilers of the soil, mines and workgates asked for protection in the form of old age pensions, widows and orphans allowances, then all protection talk stopped at once. Their protection for workmen was to provide them with lots of long hours of hard labor and short rations and at last ground enough for burial.

This kind of working-class critique of protectionism went over well, and the reporter concluded that there was no doubt how New Waterford would vote in the election: "The spirit and determination to overthrow the old regime was clearly felt and shown by the tremendous cheers the speakers received."[76]

The old party candidates in this election were a formidable group calculated to appeal to a variety of local loyalties. All of them were well-educated native sons of Nova Scotia and lawyers by profession. Among the Tories, John C. Douglas had a record of union sympathies and, as a Member of Parliament, defending the coal industry; his running-mate was R.S. McLellan, a Sydney barrister who had started his working days in the Glace Bay pits and considered himself a friend of the working class. Among the Liberals, George W. Kyte was a senior politician from St Peter's, Richmond County, who had first been elected to the House of Commons in 1908. The other Liberal was William Carroll, who proved to be the most dangerous adversary. Carroll had been elected as an MP in 1911 and earned a favourable press when he signed up for overseas service as a private in 1916. He had returned to Glace Bay with the rank of lieutenant and was appointed a crown prosecutor for Cape Breton County. Defeated by Farmer-Labour votes in the 1920 provincial election, Carroll plunged aggressively into the Dominion election.

When there was a suggestion that miners and steelworkers might protect their interests by voting for a ticket of McLachlan and Douglas, McLachlan would hear none of it: "I want to make it plain that old party candidates may throw their partner to the wolves to save their own hides, but for myself I want to say that I would rather a thousand times go down to defeat with Doyle than win with the best Grit or Tory that ever lived. I am far asunder from any Grit or Tory as the poles and every vote for any of the old party candidates is a vote against all that the Independent Labor Party and its candidates stands for." The following week McLachlan argued that, although Douglas could be considered a friend of the coal industry, he could not be trusted as a friend of the coal miners. As a lawyer Douglas had done very well by the coal miners at the time of the 1909 strike: "John was a 'leader' of the miners here one time. He had a wage of $250.00 a month for 'leading' them. The miners had money to burn at that time and Oh, Lordy, how the lawyers worked them fore and aft." By the time the strike was over the union had been stripped of its last dollar. Since then Douglas had acquired an interest in a small coal mine in New Campbellton and now he had the distinction of being "the only operator in all Nova Scotia and New Brunswick who has failed to either pay the Royal Commission's Award or the Montreal Agreement."[77]

Meanwhile McLachlan had learned that Carroll was stumping through Richmond County and denouncing McLachlan as a man who "did not believe in a God." He replied in the *Labor Herald* in a front-page letter to Carroll: "Now Billy, when you told the people that about me, you were a liar and a dirty character assassin." Would Carroll – "a smart lawyer like you" – try to defend himself against such a charge – "publicly calling you a liar"? If anyone was guilty of un-Christian behaviour it was Carroll – one of the lawyers who had done the dirty work for the Dominion Coal Company of evicting miners from their homes during the winter of 1909–10: "Did you tell the people at St. Peters how much money you made that winter helping to throw helpless women and children into the storm?"[78]

"What are Mr. McLachlan's religious views?" Even the *Maritime Labor Herald* asked the question. "We do not know and we consider it a matter which is not one for our curiosity, as it is a question between Mr. McLachlan and his Maker. However, there is one test which is given us and that is, 'By their fruits ye shall know them.'" Apply this test to McLachlan, the editor advised – "in his home life, in personal morality, in his dealings with his fellow men, and in the faithfulness to the convictions he holds as to what he believes is for the welfare of his fellow citizens of this constituency." Apply that test and McLachlan would not be found wanting. Yet the religious issue continued to haunt McLachlan and was kept alive by *The Casket*, the Catholic weekly which had a long record of warning voters against labour candidates. Two weeks before the election, *The Casket* published a long inflammatory attack on the *Herald*'s defence of McLachlan: "We know nothing about Mr. McLachlan's beliefs; but if he does believe in God, he is unfortunate in his champion." Cotton's attempt to defend McLachlan was denounced as the work of an unbeliever and ignoramus, and McLachlan stood accused by association with such an immoral venture: "Why have you taken a thousand words to make Mr. McLachlan's position worse than you found it; since your ignorance and vicious folly, and shallow rationalism will be taken as your representation of his views?"[79]

Besides godlessness there was an even more sensational charge – that McLachlan was engaged in a secret conspiracy to betray the coal miners after the election. Rumours of an impending wage cut had been circulating for months, and it was well known that the operators wanted to reduce wages at the end of the Montreal Agreement, which had been extended to the end of December. McLachlan confronted the issue from the beginning of the campaign, accusing Roy Wolvin of threatening to shut down all the coal mines and steel works in Nova Scotia unless the union accepted a reduction in wages. Such threats only demonstrated how the wealth of the country under capitalism was held hostage by corporate power: "Has this man, Mr. McLachlan asked, got sufficient power that he can shut off the living of those thousands of the men and the steel and industrial workers of Nova Scotia? He says he has, and I believe him. Where does he get that power? From those who talk about protection. They have handed over holus bolus to this corporation title to all means of wealth protection [production], and, as far as the miners and steelworkers are concerned, the means of livelihood."[80] On the face of it, it seems strange that McLachlan should be repeatedly accused throughout the campaign of making a secret deal to accept wage reductions. Those who knew him found it stranger still that he should be accused of accepting a bribe to do so. McLachlan had certainly been accused of selling the miners short at the time of the MacKinnon Agreement almost two years ago and again at the time of the Montreal Agreement twelve months past. But no one had ever accused him of betraying the miners for personal gain. And in any event the outcome of those confrontations was that McLachlan, along with the other union officers, had been forced to defend his position in open debate and to win the miners' approval of the settlement.

But the rumours did not stop. When the Glace Bay *Gazette* reported that Carroll had taken up the charges at meetings in the heart of the coal district, McLachlan again relied on the *Maritime Labor Herald*. It was the final issue of the newspaper before the election and McLachlan put his reply as strongly as possible: "A couple of weeks ago I had occasion to publicly call Carroll a liar. If he is correctly reported above then I wish to say he is again lying." Carroll's statement was "a lie from top to bottom and from end to end." The denial could not be more categorical: "When he said I consented to accept ANY reduction he LIED." Noting that the charges had not been reported in the Liberal newspaper, the Sydney *Record*, McLachlan deduced that the Liberals were plotting to spring this "lying propaganda" two days or less before the election, when McLachlan would be unable to reply effectively; on the other hand, the Tory newspaper, the *Gazette*, had let the cat out of the bag because it wanted to discredit both Carroll and McLachlan.[81]

Carroll persisted. In the days before the election the charges against McLachlan became the main attraction at Liberal meetings, where Carroll was still claiming that McLachlan "had gone down on his knees" and made a deal with the coal operators. At a rambunctious meeting in Reserve Mines on the Friday before the election, about one hundred men and women stormed into the hall and demanded that Carroll produce evidence or retract his charges. Carroll did not back down and challenged McLachlan to appear on the same platform to hear the proof of his treachery.[82]

The stage was set for one of the most dramatic public meetings in McLachlan's public career. As dark fell in Sydney on the Monday night before the election, a swelling crowd gathered outside the Lyceum Theatre. By 6 p.m. George Street was packed to the centre of the road. When the doors opened at 6.45 p.m. every seat was taken within ten minutes and the audience crammed into the aisles and stairways. At 7.40 p.m. McLachlan arrived at the rear door, where he was greeted by Carroll with an exaggerated show of courtesy which, a reporter noted, McLachlan did not seem to appreciate: "Mr. Carroll stepped forward and tended a hand to his opponent, which act the latter did not appear to altogether relish but with as good grace as possible met the other's courtesy."[83]

The band played a march, and the meeting was called to order at 8 p.m. by Arthur MacLellan, secretary of the steelworkers' union. He appealed to the audience to give both candidates a fair hearing. But before the chairman could launch the debate, Carroll was already on the attack, accusing McLachlan of stating in the *Maritime Labor Herald* that the Liberal candidate had refused to meet him in the Lyceum

Theatre. MacLellan interrupted to explain that the agreement was that
the discussion was to be restricted to the charges against McLachlan.
Applauded from the stands, Carroll persisted: "I claim I have a right to
get a reply from Mr. McLachlan as to whether he did make that
statement." Amid shouts of "Answer! Answer!" from the auditorium,
McLachlan replied: "He's only trying to draw a red herring across
the trail."

Carroll began by defending himself against charges that he had acted
as a company hireling at the time of the 1909 strike. In response to
McLachlan's claims that he had, as a solicitor for Dominion Coal in
1910, participated in the eviction of miners from company houses
during the strike, Carroll indignantly charged that McLachlan was "a
falsifier of the truth." He also challenged McLachlan to produce the
original copy of a telegram he was alleged to have sent to Premier
Murray regarding the sending of troops to Cape Breton at the time of
the strike. Turning to McLachlan he demanded dramatically, "Have you
got it?" McLachlan was still sitting quietly and replied only "You have
the platform."

The audience was growing impatient, and there were shouts from
the auditorium for Carroll to get on with his charges: "Produce your
proof and you will get a vote from me." Carroll plodded on, obliging
the audience by repeating his charge that, as reported in the *Post*,
"McLachlan had entered into a tacit and secret understanding with
Dominion Coal Company officials for a wage reduction of 31 1/3 per
cent." "That is a clear cut, distinct and specific charge," Carroll added.
"If it is false Mr. McLachlan has his remedy." But still Carroll was not
producing anything in the way of proof. He went on to refer to a
closed-door meeting in Halifax with company officials in 1920. In
addition, he charged, McLachlan had spent $1,450 of the miners'
money on expenses. And to this he added an accusation that McLachlan
had distributed only nine copies of a report to one union local, instead
of the required 500 copies.

At the end of Carroll's thirty minutes, there was little for McLachlan
to answer. Much of Carroll's attack, he pointed out, was unrelated to
the charges that the meeting wanted to hear about. And those charges
had been changing throughout the campaign. What kind of bribe had

McLachlan been given, and just when and where did McLachlan "go down on his knees"? And just where were the reductions? The Montreal Agreement had already been extended for a month, without any reductions. The only recent meeting with the coal operators was in November, and McLachlan was only one of nine officers who were present at the time. There had been no discussion of wages that day, and no negotiations. And when negotiations were finally undertaken, any settlement would be referred back to the coal miners for their approval – something that never took place in the days of the Provincial Workmen's Association. None of this was answered.

McLachlan took one more jab at Carroll's phantom charges. At the rowdy Friday night meeting in Reserve Mines, Carroll had said that a certain David Ryan of Thorburn, a former vice-president of District 26, was his inside source of information about McLachlan's treachery. Now McLachlan read out a telegram from Ryan stating that he had never communicated with Carroll. Better still, if the audience wanted to hear from Ryan, he was present on the platform and could speak for himself. The audience was cheering as McLachlan pointed his finger at Carroll and drove home his response to the charges by slowly spelling out the word L-I-A-R.

Then Ryan came forward and spoke briefly in support of McLachlan, denying that he had had any communication with Carroll. The showdown seemed all but over, and the chairman invited Carroll to give a final ten-minute rebuttal. Now Carroll strode to the front of the stage and, to McLachlan's astonishment, began to read out a letter describing McLachlan's "underhanded methods": "He is in league with Coal Company officials. He has agreed to get the U.M.W. to accept a cut of thirty-three and a third per cent after the company make a cut of somewhere about forty-five or fifty-five." The letter was dated 12 October 1921, it was addressed to one Donald McIsaac of Glace Bay, and the author – Carroll claimed – was none other than David Ryan. According to the *Post* reporter, McLachlan sat in his chair examining a copy of the letter and "appeared to be absolutely dumbfounded" by this new piece of evidence.

The meeting ended in chaos. Had Carroll at last "produced the goods"? McLachlan and Ryan were on their feet arguing with the chairman, while Carroll was preparing to leave the hall for another election meeting. The band struck up a closing number, and the Lyceum emptied. McLachlan and Ryan would make their responses at union meetings and in the pages of the *Maritime Labor Herald* where they would state that the letter was an unabashed forgery. They would swear out affidavits and seek legal opinions about taking Carroll to court. Local unions would demand that Carroll and McIsaac be charged with uttering forged documents. But for the moment the damage was done. A widely distributed special edition of the Sydney *Record,* which must have been prepared before the Lyceum meeting actually took place, reprinted the letter and reported that Carroll's charges against McLachlan had been substantiated. The *Post,* which supported the Tory candidates, denounced the debate as "a disgraceful exhibition of mudslinging." McLachlan was singled out for particular attention: "The mine workers of Cape Breton especially owe it to themselves and their union to relegate to private life a leader who now rests under the shadow of a dishonourable charge, or at least until such time as he is able to clear himself."[84]

"One campaign is over," announced the *Maritime Labor Herald* after the election. "Another Campaign Is On." Despite all the last-minute political skulduggery, McLachlan had collected an impressive total of 8,914 votes. The Doyle-McLachlan ticket together polled 16,798 votes, 32.63 per cent of the total. As elsewhere across the country, the Tories went down to defeat and finished in third place. But there was no escaping the fact that the Liberals had managed to secure a victory. The Liberal candidates had won 40.62 per cent of the total vote, and the margin of victory over McLachlan was only 1,473 votes. The Nova Scotia Liberals greeted Carroll's victory as a notable triumph: "You had a hard fight," E.H. Armstrong wrote Carroll, "and you acquitted yourself like a hero. I did admire the rapier thrusts you gave your doughty opponent, McLaughlin [sic]. It did me good to see the way you handled him. Your victory was one of the finest in the country."[85]

Narrow as the margin of defeat was, McLachlan interpreted the outcome as a failure of working-class solidarity. The old parties had operated up to their usual standards, he commented in the *Maritime Labor Herald,* but the workers had defeated themselves by failing to maintain unity: "Every defeat the workers ever sustained was the direct result of the foolish and criminal divisions within their own ranks ... All the lying powers of the lawyers running on the Grit and Tory Tickets were devoted to create suspicion and division in the ranks of the workers during the last week of the election and evidently they were successful to a degree which was fatal to labor." Now that the election was over, he wrote, the duty of the hour was to prepare for the next test of strength, whatever it might be – wages, working conditions, or elections: "We must work, work until it shall become impossible to split the ranks of labor."[86]

In the wake of the election, and for years after, it was widely believed that the sensational charges against McLachlan had cost him election to the House of Commons.[87] But this was too pessimistic an analysis. A close study of the returns shows that McLachlan's support in the mining district could not have been greatly damaged by the various charges directed against him. In the mining district McLachlan swept the polls with absolute majorities. The Farmer-Labour ticket led the balloting in Reserve Mines (with 64.4 per cent of the vote), and the same was true in Dominion No. 6 (57.0 per cent), New Waterford (58.3 per cent), and Dominion (63.1 per cent). In Glace Bay the Farmer-Labour candidates captured 54.9 per cent of the vote, and in the three principal mining wards the vote was particularly high: 63.5 per cent in Caledonia, 74.97 per cent in Passchendaele, and 75.12 per cent in New Aberdeen. In the mining district as a whole McLachlan and Doyle received 57.12 per cent of the vote. The Tories came in second place and the Liberals third. Even in Sydney itself, where Carroll may have enjoyed greater credibility, the vote went narrowly in favour of the Farmer-Labour ticket. But in 1921 this vote was simply not sufficient to win election in Cape Breton South and Richmond as it was then constituted. The returns demonstrate that McLachlan was defeated by the unfavourable vote in the rural parts of the constituency, not by lack of support among the coal miners or in the larger industrial community.[88]

Indeed, the most important weakness in the election strategy was the failure of the Farmer-Labour campaign in Richmond County. This was the largely rural farming and fishing district of southwest Cape Breton Island, much different in economic and social structure from the coal and steel towns of Cape Breton County. Richmond County had had its own Member of Parliament before the redistribution of 1914, a gerrymander that diluted the industrial vote in the old riding of Cape Breton South. Following the 1921 election, Doyle did not hesitate to blame the defeat on "unscrupulous and self-seeking politicians" who "from end to end of the campaign slandered McLachlan throughout Richmond County." The most vicious attacks, he pointed out, had been ineffective in the areas where the real McLachlan was known and appreciated: "The returns from Cape Breton show that the more intimately McLachlan was known the higher was his majority. His home town, Glace Bay, composed of all classes and all creeds, gave McLachlan three votes to the one his traducers received."[89]

McLachlan also found himself defended in the pages of *The Casket*. In 1921 Joe Wallace had been one of the unsuccessful labour candidates in Halifax. A graduate of St Francis Xavier University and a former Laurier Liberal, Wallace worked as an advertising copywriter and journalist in Halifax; in the years at the end of the war he had been moving rapidly to the left and was closely associated with labour causes. Like McLachlan, he would become one of the first Maritimers to endorse the Workers' Party. Wallace would become known as a Communist and as a poet, but he would also remain a practising Catholic. In an angry letter to *The Casket* in January 1922, Wallace castigated the Catholic newspaper for the part it had played in attacking labour candidates in the recent elections: "It worries me to think that the working class of this province are apt to consider that in the hour of their agony the Catholic Church, through you, joined up with the capitalistic parties of Nova Scotia to divide and despoil them."[90]

A week after the election, McLachlan also suffered some embarrassment in the election of the new district executive when, a supporter from Sydney Mines noted, "the very same ammunition was used" against him. For the post of secretary-treasurer McLachlan received 4,588 votes against 3,642 votes for Kent Foster of Springhill. Foster was a local leader in Cumberland County who, as early as the spring of 1920, had been warning UMW president John L. Lewis about McLachlan's radicalism and putting himself forward as a potential opposition candidate: "The only thing is to keep a sharp watch on McLachlan until then [the district elections] and run a good man against." McLachlan was returned to office with a comfortable margin, but the results indicated some anxieties among the membership about McLachlan's leadership. In 1919 and 1920 McLachlan had been unopposed, and it was Baxter and Barrett who encountered difficulties in gaining re-election. This time the other members of the "Big Three" did better than McLachlan. Robert Baxter, as president, received a total of 5,713 votes against 2,704 for P.G. Muise of New Waterford; and Silby Barrett was returned as international board member with 5,383 votes against 2,855 votes for Dan Livingstone. The unfortunate David Ryan, one of six candidates for vice-president, received only 491 votes against William P. Delaney, who was re-elected with 4,164 votes.[91]

Although he was not elected to Parliament, no one could deny that McLachlan was the coal miners' choice. It is clear that in 1921 he could have won the old Cape Breton South constituency as it had existed before 1914. Probably he also could have won the seat in a straight two-way race. The defeat was particularly galling to McLachlan since he had secured more votes than were needed to win election in the other Cape Breton seats: in Cape Breton North and Victoria, D.D. McKenzie had gone back to Ottawa on the strength of 7,399 votes, and in Inverness the Liberal Alexander Chisholm had won with only 4,650 votes. It was also true that the only two labour candidates elected in Canada in this election were returned with fewer votes than McLachlan: J.S. Woodsworth was elected in Winnipeg Centre with 7,774 votes and Bill Irvine was elected in Calgary East with 6,135 votes. This was a hard lesson in the structural limits of political democracy as it existed in Canada in 1921.

It is tempting to speculate on the national implications of McLachlan's defeat in 1921. This was one of the more important elections in Canadian history and marked the emergence of a substantial third force in national politics in the form of the Progressive and Labour MPs elected that year. McLachlan could certainly have added a strong Maritime voice to this group, which consisted mainly of Ontario and western MPs. Under King's leadership, the Liberal Party artfully manoeuvred many of these new MPs into supporting portions of the Liberal program, and the Liberal Party gradually emerged as the dominant governing party of the twentieth century. Had he been elected, McLachlan would have joined Woodsworth and Irvine in Parliament and given the small labour and socialist group – both were ministers – a stronger working-class orientation. Despite their differences in background, Woodsworth and McLachlan had a comradely respect for each other that would be seen on several future occasions. Woodsworth would later become the founder of the Cooperative Commonwealth Federation, which during the 1930s remained a parliamentary party with relatively weak links to organized labour; McLachlan, on the other hand, would become a prominent member of the Communist Party of Canada and one of the most influential radical labour leaders in the country. Closer collaboration between these two men might well have had considerable influence on the political history of the Canadian left in the 1920s and 1930s.[92]

In the space of a few years McLachlan had gone from being a marginal candidate to being the dominant political figure in the coalfields. Yet the fact that McLachlan's failure in 1921 was described at the time and remembered as a defeat may have served to undermine his prospects of success in subsequent elections. In capitalist democracies one of the purposes of the parliamentary system is to contain social conflict by demonstrating the existence of democratic choice within the political system. In this case the miners ignored the unscrupulous attacks of the local establishment on their candidate and rallied to McLachlan's support, but the miners' popular choice was thwarted by the deficiencies of the electoral system. Among the coal miners, McLachlan's defeat probably helped to weaken interest in electoral politics and increase the appeal of direct action as a method for defending their interests.

CHAPTER 6

1922: Class War

*Revolution is impossible
without a change in the views
of the majority of the working class,
and this change is brought about
by the political experience of the masses,
and never by propaganda alone.*

– V.I. Lenin,
Left-Wing Communism (1920)

The Miners versus the Merger

There is movement in the early winter sky. Along the ocean shores, forest and field are bending under the threat of snow. The colours stand out strongly in the harsh grey light. The bare trees are touched with rust and purple. In the towns the walls and chimneys are beginning to creak and shudder in their winter voices. The sky is moving and the light is shifting. The clouds are dark, as if stained by the black dust of the coal mines. Soon the north wind is bearing cold needles of rain, and heavy flakes of snow are sprinkling the mounds of coal in the colliery yards, warnings of the winter storms to come. Then the sky yawns in a lazy movement, the wind retreats, and the sun once more stretches a warm promise across the land.

Almost a thousand miles away, on 16 December 1921, the union leaders were sitting in a well-upholstered hotel room at the Windsor Hotel in Montreal. This was the first day of negotiations for renewal of the previous year's Montreal Agreement, and the union leaders were prepared for a struggle. McLachlan, Robert Baxter, and Vice-President W.P. Delaney made an impressive team, a local journalist had remarked earlier in the year: "With 'Bob' Baxter the canny president, and 'Jim' McLachlan the hardhitting secretary, 'Billy' Delaney the diplomatic vice-president makes a cabinet of labor that is always on the job and very wide awake."[1]

Across the shining mahogany table sat the senior officers of the British Empire Steel Corporation, whose head office was located only a few hundred yards away in the Canada Cement Building across the square. The company spokesman was the big red-haired Cape Bretoner, Dan Hugh McDougall. McLachlan watched him attentively. Here was a man who seemed to embody the virtues of working-class self-improvement. McDougall had started his working life in the coal mines in the 1890s at thirteen years of age, took correspondence courses and went to night schools, and eventually qualified as a mine surveyor and civil and mining engineer. By 1904 he was an engineer on a New York railway line; in 1907 he was managing the iron ore mines at Bell Island, Newfoundland; later he returned to Cape Breton as a manager of mining operations. By 1918 McDougall had become president of the Nova Scotia Steel and Coal Company. At the time of the merger, which he strongly supported on the ground that it would promote greater efficiency in exploiting the undersea coal resources, McDougall was appointed vice-president of the British Empire Steel Corporation. Since then he had become known in business circles for his energetic efforts to advance the efficiency of mining operations and keep the peace between "warring factions" within the consolidation.[2]

Now McDougall leaned back in his chair and pushed a sheet of paper across the table to Baxter. On the typed sheet of paper was a list of seventeen issues the union wanted to include in the discussion. No rate increases were proposed – the last item on the list was simply a renewal of the wage rates contained in the Montreal Agreement. But McDougall was returning the list without any comment. He was refusing all of the union proposals.

The following day the men returned to the table, and now McDougall made the announcement that started eight long months of open class conflict in the Nova Scotia coalfields. Besco, McDougall announced, planned to reduce the miners' wages. This came as no surprise, for the corporation had been threatening to do so for some months. In the light of falling prices, the union was content to settle for renewal of the existing rates. The surprise was the size of the cut – cancellation of the Montreal Agreement, plus a further reduction of 25 per cent in the wage scales. In all, this was a reduction of one-third in existing rates. Union leaders immediately pointed out that it was bad enough to eliminate all the gains of recent years and take the miners back to wage levels that existed before 1914. But as McDougall rose from the table and looked down at the union leaders, he emphasized that the company's proposal "did not leave room for cross-fire or barter."[3]

The sessions ended without agreement, and as secretary-treasurer of the district McLachlan now rushed into action. Under the familiar bureaucratic procedures, his first step was to apply for a conciliation board under the terms of the Industrial Disputes Investigation Act. In applying for a conciliation board the union leaders were following the rules of industrial legality, but they were also pursuing a strategy of delay. In Montreal, for instance, they had offered to drop all of their demands in return for renewal of the Montreal Agreement for a further four months. This would avoid the possibility of a disadvantageous winter-time strike and also bring the timing of the Nova Scotia dispute in line with the expiry of the general UMW agreement in the United States. The request for conciliation was granted as a matter of course on 24 December, and the union at once named James Ling, the labour mayor of New Waterford, as their representative. When the corporation refused to name a member, the government appointed a Halifax businessman who had previously represented the operators. The chair was given to a Toronto businessman, Ulrich E. Gillen, and the hearings of the Gillen board opened in Halifax on 17 January.

Meanwhile, notices of the wage cut were posted at the collieries on 19 December, to come into effect at the end of the month. McLachlan protested that this was a violation of the act – the conciliation board had not yet started hearings, much less filed a report, and the Industrial Disputes Investigation Act required a process of investigation and delay before conditions of employment could be changed. The text of the act, section 57 in particular, seemed plain enough on this point: "Employer and employees shall give at least thirty days notice of an intended change affecting the conditions of employment with respect to wages or hours; and in the event of such intended change resulting in a dispute, until the dispute has been finally dealt with by a Board ... neither of these parties shall alter the conditions of employment with respect to wages or hours ..." The new Liberal minister of labour agreed. James Murdock pleaded by telegraph with Besco president Roy Wolvin to show "reasonable adherence to obvious spirit and letter of statute." For his part, McLachlan took the case to the Supreme Court of Nova Scotia, where he won an injunction prohibiting the immediate implementation of the new scale. Justice Benjamin Russell, a former

MP and law professor who was one of the older members of the bench, took the view that thirty days' notice and a conciliation board report were required – "a condition precedent to the change coming into effect." For once it seemed that where changes in conditions threatened the status of the coal miners, the famous procedures of bureaucratic investigation and delay could be used to the advantage of the workers.[4]

But to McLachlan's dismay, this favourable court order was swiftly overturned by a panel of three other Supreme Court judges. Chief Justice Humphrey Mellish, who wrote the decision, was familiar to McLachlan from his days as a company solicitor in the "coal conspiracy" of 1909 and as a trial judge in the No. 12 manslaughter cases in 1917. Now Mellish (who was appointed to the bench in 1918) ruled that, under the meaning of the Industrial Disputes Investigation Act, the wage reductions did not constitute an "intended change" in "conditions of employment." Since the Montreal Agreement expired on 31 December, Mellish explained, "it was obviously contemplated by both parties that the conditions of employment should be open and unsettled." In this nice piece of logic, there could be no assumption that existing rates and conditions would continue beyond the end of December. On the strength of this ruling, handed down on 10 January, the announced reductions went into effect immediately, in time for the first pay day of the new year.[5]

"What a funny, funny thing the law is," commented McLachlan in the pages of the *Maritime Labor Herald*. The language of the act was "so plain that you would think a baby might understand it," and the miners had patiently waited for the opportunity to put their case before a conciliation board. Even though "the first fundamental principle underlying the whole act" was at stake, the operators had "ploughed ruthlessly through the heart of it." Their way out of the "legal noose" of section 57 was endorsed by Justice Mellish in terms that left no mystery about the rule of law: "What right had working men to gain any advantage by playing the game according to the rules set down by the flunkies of capitalism? The rules are not made for the benefit of the workers, but for the advantage and benefit of the owners of this country."[6]

Winter

Winter was always the hardest season for the coal miners, something that was often difficult for outsiders to understand. After all, coal was surely in high demand during the coldest times of the year. But companies such as Dominion Coal, which shipped large quantities of coal to the St Lawrence market, could afford to limit operations during the winter freeze-up because they were selling from reserves stockpiled during the shipping season. And if markets were uncertain, or wages high, the companies could afford to wait until the opening of navigation in the spring.

In Cape Breton some collieries had been closed since late November, and most others were on broken time. Following the first pay at the new rates, local merchants in the coal towns reported slow sales, and the daily press ran headlines announcing "Starvation Imminent at Collieries." Union locals dug into their savings and distributed relief to their members. This year there was an unaccustomed mood of resentment. McLachlan's proposal that a special levy be placed on the union's working members to raise more funds for relief ran into objections that the government, not the union, should be assuming responsibility for the alleviation of unemployment.[7]

The company stores were another customary source of relief in hard times. For almost a century the stores had been advancing supplies and goods on credit, often at inflated prices, and then charging the balances back against the miners' paysheets. The spectre of perpetual debt was a common objection to the system; so, too, was the paternalism of the managers, who had the authority to deny credit and limit goods and quantities to individual customers. At the New Aberdeen company store on Saturday, 21 January, an unemployed miner, with nine children and an ill wife, was refused credit. When headquarters refused to extend him credit, the man ordered the manager aside and helped himself to the food supplies. Other miners followed suit, demanding that the manager take note of the quantities. This was not so much a raid on the store as an insistence on the traditional right to credit in hard times. But after the store closed in the evening, the resentment turned violent. A crowd attacked the company police with snowballs, broke windows, and looted the building. The following night a crowd of several thousand men and women surrounded the store. The company police fired in the air and then retreated as hundreds of men emptied the store and adjoining warehouse.[8]

While these skirmishes were taking place, the machinery of conciliation was slowly creaking into action in the meeting rooms of the Board of Trade in Halifax. At stake in the discussions was an unusually clear-cut debate between a "living profit" for the employers and a "living wage" for the workers. The corporation spokesmen pointed out that wages were the largest single item in the cost of production. For this reason a reduction in wages was essential in order to sell coal at profitable returns in the existing markets. The union leaders, for their part, objected that a reduction in wages was not the only way to reduce costs. The first charge on the earnings of the industry, they argued, should be the the coal miners' standard of living, not the profits of the coal operators. The representative of the international union who was present insisted that the district officials not present a formal offer to accept a reduction, on the ground that this was contrary to international policy; privately, he informed John L. Lewis that "in my opinion they will be compelled to take a reduction of from 15 to 20 per cent."[9]

McLachlan prepared a barrage of documents for presentation to the conciliation board. First there was Roy Wolvin's address to the last annual meeting of the board of directors of Dominion Steel. According to Wolvin, "our labour is as loyal and efficient as in any other coal mining community in the world" and if wages were to come down "the income of the wage-earner should maintain approximately an equal purchasing power." Then there was McLachlan's estimate of annual earnings for a man paid at $2.44 a day, the new minimum rate put into effect on 1 January. How would earnings of barely $700 a year be used to provide food and supplies for a family of five? The city of Toronto, according to Ontario government reports, spent more to provide for the needs of inmates in its local prisons and reformatories. Then McLachlan filed a Dominion Steel financial statement showing net earnings of more than $7 million for the year ending in March 1921, and a 1920 Besco financial statement showing a surplus of more than $26 million. He also included detailed statements of rates paid under the Montreal Agreement and, for comparison, the considerably higher rates paid in the mines of District 18 in western Canada. Finally, he submitted a statement of fatal accidents in the Nova Scotia coal mines: over the years from 1908 to 1920, an average of 3.89 men per 1,000 employees; or, if the operators preferred, a cost of 6.82 men per 1,000,000 tons of coal production. In all this the message was clear: it was neither just nor necessary for the coal miners to serve as "economic cannon fodder" in the war for corporate profits.[10]

The Gillen board was unable to reconcile the coal miners to reduced wages. The majority report accepted the company claim that a substantial wage reduction was necessary to reduce production costs and compete in current markets. Their decision was based to a large extent on a confidential statement of production costs for the last three months of 1921. Ling objected in a minority report that the financial statements covered an unreasonably short and slack period and that the evidence constituted "masked and unverified testimony." Although Ling was prepared to accept some reductions in the scale, he refused to accept the majority report, which proposed only a small modification of the cuts already implemented. If they were enforced, stated Ling, the new wage rates "shall condemn thousands of men, women, and children, engaged in the mining industry of Nova Scotia, to live in a state of semi-starvation." There was no real controversy among the coal miners about the Gillen Award; on 10 February they voted 468 in favour and 10,305 against the recommendations.

After this spectacular failure at conciliation, would there be new negotiations? Would there be a strike? What kind of concessions would the company make? What kind of support could the coal miners expect from the international union? These were the questions before the miners' delegates when they assembled for a district convention in Truro in late February. To strike was not an attractive choice because the district treasury was already depleted by the payment of relief funds over the winter. Even with the mines operating, there was widespread hardship, and a strike would bring more deprivation. The international union was bracing for a coming fight to maintain the $7.50 daily wage rate in the American fields and was reluctant to commit resources to an early battle in an outlying district.

By all accounts the dominant figure at the Truro meeting was John P. White, the former international president who had helped negotiate the return of the UMW to Nova Scotia in 1919. With him White brought an ambiguously worded telegram from President Lewis which encouraged the miners to reopen negotiations but held out little hope of strike support. Although the UMW had adopted a policy of "no backward step" on wages, Lewis had little interest in fighting the battle in Nova Scotia and suggested the miners "decide for themselves whether they should accept any proposed scale or the alternative of going on strike." On his way to Truro, White had stopped off in Montreal to meet with Besco officials and secured a statement that they were willing to reopen talks on the basis of the Gillen report and a $3.00 minimum daily wage. Although this offer was rejected as "unsatisfactory," the delegates agreed by a thirty-eight to twenty-seven vote to send their officers to Montreal for one more round of talks.[11]

Back in Montreal the union leaders found McDougall and Wolvin almost as inflexible as in December. Besco would sign an agreement including the Gillen rates and a $3.00 minimum wage – but this was the same offer the delegates had rejected in Truro. Furthermore, the company insisted that the contract would expire in November 1922, thus setting the stage for a re-enactment of the same fight all over again the following winter. In their hotel room the officers debated their dilemma. White pointed out that he and Dan Livingstone, the district's international board member, were bound by the "no backward step" policy of the union and could not participate in the decision. The remaining officers were divided equally – four members (including Baxter) in favour of signing a contract; four members (including McLachlan) opposed. The deadlock was finally broken when one of the board members changed his vote in order to give President Baxter a majority. Baxter glumly made his way back to the table to place his signature on the waiting provisional agreement, alongside the names of Wolvin and McDougall. White reported the successful outcome back to Lewis: "It has been a very hard fight" but the executive board was recommending adoption of the agreement and "every one is hopeful that the miners will approve it."[12]

News of the settlement was greeted with relief back in the coalfields, but as it became clear that the changes were minute ones, the contract came under attack. The division in the union leadership was now visible. Baxter saw it as his responsibility to advise an unpopular course of action. He defended the contract as the best obtainable under the circumstances: a strike could not be won and might destroy the union entirely. In the past McLachlan had also used his influence to restrain his followers – including, ironically, the campaign for approval of the Montreal Agreement itself in 1920. But now he was opposed. Hostile critics even charged that McLachlan, still smarting from the charges that he had made a secret deal to support a wage cut, was giving in to "personal grudges and vanity."[13]

McLachlan did not sign the executive statement of 3 March recommending approval of the contract, and in the week before the miners' vote he began to speak out publicly against it. If ever the coal miners were ready to defend their gains, this was the time. He reflected with some satisfaction on the changes in the miners' outlook over the past dozen years: "Since the year 1910 much water has run under the bridge, and very many of the slave virtues have been shed by the miners of Nova Scotia. Humility and self-abasement in the presence of the 'rich and great' have gone from them forever." The wage cut remained unacceptable, he argued, and the corporation, after modifying its original position more than once, would do so again if the miners continued to resist: "Four times has the British Empire Steel Corporation crawled since December last, and the miners of Nova Scotia hold the trump cards that will bring them victory if they have the iron will to play them effectively."[14]

The vote on 14 March was not a close one. The coal miners rejected the agreement by a seven-to-one margin, 8,109 votes to 1,352. In doing so they were endorsing McLachlan's view that something must be done to defend the miners' standard of living and that something could be done. In the five years since 1917 McLachlan had led them from expectation to achievement on a whole range of issues, including hours and conditions and wages and, above all, respect for the power and solidarity of the coal miners. Now they were confident that their union could force even the most obstinate of employers to bend. But if something could be done, what was it? What were the miners' trump cards?

Ca'canny

In 1931 the *Scottish National Dictionary* defined the word "ca'canny" as a verb meaning to be moderate and proceed warily. It was now in general use, the entry continued, as a description of "the trade-union policy of limiting output." A recent example was quoted from the authority of Ramsay MacDonald, the one-time Scottish labour leader and Britain's first Labour Party prime minister: ca'canny tactics were "a magnificently organised system of passive resistance."[15]

Even in the age of industrial legality, wage disputes are not decided solely across the bargaining table. They are also decided by the amount of "force" at the disposal of either side, and in 1922 the coal miners located a remarkably forceful tactic to demonstrate their opposition to the wage reduction. Restriction of output was a well-established weapon of retaliation among workers, organized and unorganized alike, a tactic constructed out of the implicit forms of workers' control in the workplace. In so complex an industry as coal mining, the idea of what constituted a "normal day's work" – what the Scots called the "darg" – was a matter of customary practice, and in the case of disputes it was not unusual to see the normal "master's darg" replaced by the "wee darg." McLachlan was familiar with this practice from his days in the Lanarkshire mines, and when the necessity arose he seized the opportunity to apply the old tactic to new circumstances.[16]

As early as February, McLachlan provided a public defence of restriction of output in his response to the ruling of Justice Mellish on the Industrial Disputes Investigation Act. According to Mellish, there were apparently no recognized "conditions of employment" in the coal industry as of 1 January; everything was "open and unsettled." This kind of judgment was a "two-edged sword," McLachlan explained, for it applied as much to the quantity and quality of work as it did to the amount of money an employer might pay:

> Since January 1st, 1922, the employer has without the consent and against the wishes of his employees given just so much money in wages.

Since January 1st, 1922, the employee may give in return for this one sided wage arrangement just so much work and of such and such a quality as he wishes to give without in the least taking his employer into consideration.

If the shearing sword handed down by the Justices of the court of Nova Scotia enables the coal companies to cut wage rates in half because "no new arrangement" has been come to; then no one can have any just complaint if each coal-cutter, driver, landing-tender, road-maker, etc., uses this same shear-sword to lop off some of the quantity and quality –

Here was the explosive, unintended logic of Mellish's judgment, McLachlan concluded, adding an ironic stage whisper of advice: "Well you need not go around blabbing about it, keep it quietly to yourself."[17]

Before the coal miners rejected the new agreement on 14 March, the idea of "striking on the job" had become the tacit alternative to normal strike action. McLachlan later claimed that striking on the job started in January at two of the most important Glace Bay mines: at Dominion No. 2, which had a normal capacity of 3,000 tons a day, production was "pulled down to a point between 800 and 1,000 tons per day"; and at the Caledonia Mine the output was reduced from 1,800 to 600 tons a day: "Here at this mine the boss gave the men the credit of having 'striking on the job' down to a perfect science." By the time of the Truro convention at the end of the month, the reporter for the Halifax *Herald* was predicting that the convention might officially adopt what he called "Fabian tactics" – "a practice that is being carried on (and with no great amount of advertising) in some of the Cape Breton mines today." He added that striking on the job "had spontaneous growth, arising with the men themselves as their method of expressing dissatisfaction with the wages now in force."[18]

All this local resistance suddenly acquired new significance when the coal miners voted down the agreement on 14 March. Two days later McLachlan issued a rousing circular addressed to the officers and members of all local unions in District 26. It amounted to a declaration of war: "War is on, a class war. On the one side you have the British Empire Steel Corporation out to invade the homes and living of our people, to pay dividends on 'stock' which do not represent one dollar of real money. On the other hand you and your fellows have voted to defend that living to the last ditch." He then quoted examples of the desperate conditions in the coal towns: in the past week three children had died at Dominion No. 4 for lack of milk; at another mine the mother and father were facing prosecution because their unclothed, shoeless children failed to come to school; another miner was doing two years in penitentiary for "stealing" a bag of flour from the company store. McLachlan's appeal was a call to arms against those responsible for such conditions – "a class of stock gamblers who have an insatiable greed for money and utter lack of the milk of human kindness."

The plan of attack was directed at the profits of the company:

War is on, and it is up to the workers in the mines of the British Empire Steel Corporation to carry that war into the "country" of the enemy. There is only one way to fight this corporation and that is to cut production to a point where they cannot any longer earn profits. Every contract man who voted against acceptance of the wage agreement last Tuesday should at once cut down his production to a point where he can get about the same wage as the low paid men in the mine, and at the same time see to it that every day paid man takes the full eight hours each day to land his reduced output on the surface.

McLachlan was treating the conflict as a form of military exercise, and his rhetoric referred back to the field of battle: "Up men and in your well organized thousands attack them. Action and not words count now."[19]

Respectable opinion was outraged by McLachlan's formal endorsement of the slowdown strike. The local press called on the coal miners to "preserve their reputation for honesty and square dealing." One Halifax newspaper described it as a "monstrous proposal" and denounced McLachlan for "sabotage" and "reckless and desperate counsels," adding that "it is some satisfaction at least that it does not emanate from a native of this province."[20]

Among the coal miners there was a more measured response, although there is only fragmentary evidence of the impact on production in the mines. In the daily newspapers there were reports of individual men or groups dismissed for participating in the "underproduction campaign," and individual mines were singled out as exceptions to the alleged general pattern of "satisfactory" production levels. On 26 March four Glace Bay locals formally endorsed the policy, as did a joint meeting of New Waterford locals on 2 April. A police report from Springhill stated that the town was a stronghold of "the McLachlan policy."[21]

Joseph Nearing, a young coal miner who worked at the No. 5 colliery in Reserve Mines (and later became a prominent "McLachlanite"), has recalled how the policy was put into effect at his workplace. It was agreed in the local union meeting that, instead of loading ten boxes, the men would load only six boxes of coal per shift; meanwhile, the driver "took his time" and the shiftman "worked with his coat on": "There were only a couple of mines in the district that were kind of slow in endorsing this slowdown, but before it went into effect too far the whole district endorsed it, and they had it going for months. And the company hollered. They were getting hurt."[22]

Again the leadership of the union was divided. Within the district executive meetings a bitter clash took place over McLachlan's unauthorized circular letter. Baxter and those who had supported the new contract opposed the strike as an illegitimate tactic. But with Baxter presiding over the meeting, McLachlan and his followers secured a narrow endorsement of the policy. As a result, on 23 March, McLachlan was able to issue a short official statement reporting that the executive had endorsed "a policy of cutting down the production of coal in all the coal mines of the British Empire Steel Corporation."

There was nothing obscure about the reasons: "We demand that a living wage, for the men who do the actual work in and about these coal mines, be the first charge against this industry, and our people are going to refuse to live from hand to mouth like a stray dog in order that the fruits of their labor may be used to pay dividends on huge blocks of watered stock and idle steel works." And there was nothing, McLachlan added, underhanded or dishonest about the strike: "To all the world we proclaim our fixed intentions and our wage demands knowing that no honest man can refuse us his whole-hearted support."[23]

In the more radical Glace Bay locals there was impatience with the divided leadership of the union. The Phalen local even endorsed a proposal to suspend the usual practices of the union and appoint McLachlan a "dictator" to lead the miners "for the period of the war upon the operators." The proposal was endorsed by three additional locals before it was abandoned, on the ground that McLachlan "refused to countenance the move."[24]

As the constant repetition of the miners' case against reductions suggested, McLachlan's strategy at this time was also directed at public opinion. In addition to appearing at meetings throughout the coal-fields, McLachlan made time to travel to Halifax, where he received loud applause at meetings organized by the Independent Labour Party and local unions. While it is difficult to assess the impact of the slow-down strike on production levels and costs at the coal mines, McLachlan was satisfied that the campaign was having its desired effect elsewhere. In late March he twice addressed open letters to the newly assembled Members of Parliament in Ottawa, pleading for government intervention in support of the coal miners. Not only was the existing regime of industrial legality in a shambles, McLachlan pointed out, but the prevailing conditions threatened worse disorder. It was a calculated plea for the state to apply pragmatic compassion in support of social order.

McLachlan's first letter, circulated on 20 March to all members of the House of Commons, summarized the general conditions in the coalfields: the confrontation between desperate poverty and an irresponsible corporation. "Whether you take action or not, ten thousand mine workers in Nova Scotia who have no money, nothing but their naked hands to defend themselves and their hungry families with, shall use every means that can occur to the heart of desperate men to resist this invasion of their homes and living." The restriction of output was only one means of resistance, he added, for "a thousand other things will suggest themselves to men who are hungry." In his second letter, on 27 March, McLachlan warned that the corporation was "carrying on a deliberate system of starvation on hundreds of families." Would the government stand by helplessly "until open revolt takes place?"[25]

The minister of labour, James Murdock, also entered the fray. Murdock was a man of McLachlan's generation, a year or two younger, and like him a British immigrant, although one who had come to Canada as a child of three. He was also a union man. As a former vice-president of the Brotherhood of Railroad Trainmen, Murdock belonged to one of the international unions of skilled workers that had long dominated the Trades and Labour Congress. From the perspective of Prime Minister King, Murdock was the kind of "safe and sane" trade union leader who could be trusted to harmonize the interests of labour and capital. The Liberals recruited Murdock as a candidate for the 1921 election, and although he went down to defeat in his Toronto riding, the new government named him as minister of labour and found him a safe seat where he was returned by acclamation in a by-election. Murdock was only the second union man to serve as minister of labour (and the first in the Commons), and he was determined to prove his mettle.[26]

The opportunity arrived in the form of McLachlan's manifesto of 16 March, "War is on, a class war," which received wide circulation in the newspapers and appeared on Murdock's desk in the form of a clipping from the Ottawa *Journal*. Upon reading it Murdock composed a telegram inviting McLachlan to state that the published statement was without foundation and urging him to repudiate the policy it contained: "You will, I think on reflection agree with me [that] any strength which organized labour possesses at the present time is the result, not of underhanded and dishonest methods of undercutting, or, as it is sometimes called, sabotage, but of straight and honest dealings, each worker giving the best that is in him for the wages agreed upon." McLachlan welcomed the opportunity to reply, and the furious telegraphic duel that followed can be read as an informative study in the contrasting perspectives of conservative and radical labour leaders in the 1920s.

McLachlan at once rejected the term sabotage and reaffirmed the legitimacy of a policy that aimed to reduce production and profits for the employer:

This tactic as a method of retaliation for a highly unjust encroachment on the wages of their workmen and an invasion of an already too slender living I have proclaimed openly and in the face of day and there is nothing dishonest about it, you to the contrary notwithstanding.

I have preached this with the blessing of my friends and amid the curses of my enemies. I have preached it to individuals, to tens, hundreds, and to thousands. I have done it on land and on sea, in mines, halls and in churches, on the hillsides of Nova Scotia and in her busy streets, and Mr. Minister what are you going to do about it?

I shall do it again this week knowing that a miner has a perfect right to work with his coat on if he wants to.

From here McLachlan launched into an attack on Murdock's own record as a union leader. A little more than a year ago Murdock's union had been involved in a strike of railway workers at the Sydney steel works. Murdock himself, McLachlan charged, had advised union men on the Intercolonial Railway to boycott steel company shipments, even to the extent of diverting cars with perishable goods into the woods. That, McLachlan charged, was "sabotage from top to bottom, from start to finish." What kind of innocent or hypocrite was Murdock, and how could he allow himself to be manipulated into delivering lectures on behalf of the British Empire Steel Corporation? The coal miners' slowdown strike was "effective and within the law," and in the absence of any wage agreement, the coal miners were simply refusing to "strip themselves naked to the waist to give the best that is in them as you put it."

Murdock angrily rejected McLachlan's charges against his own record and denied that he had any sympathy for the corporation. But as far as union policy was concerned, Murdock refused to accept the legitimacy of the "so-called passive strike methods": "In my judgement it is un-British, un-Canadian and cowardly to pretend to be working for a wage rate while in effect declaring to the world that only partial, grudging service will be given. My experience has been that men quit like men and walk off the job when unwilling to work for wage rates or conditions offered and the advice you give would place you and those who accept such advice surely in some other class."

Murdock's hectoring response seemed unlikely to temper feelings, but McLachlan's final words turned attention away from their disagreements on union tactics and towards the urgency of taking action to discipline the corporation:

> Your government is young and surely yet uncorrupted by this corporation which you call one of Canada's tragedies. The starvation of ten thousand mine workers in Nova Scotia gives your government right now ample justification to appoint a commission at once which shall tear wide open the rotten heart of this corruptor of public life and starver of the workers of Nova Scotia. If you and your young government have the courage of your convictions you shall appoint a commission now and give it this man's job of cleaning up this corrupt tragedy.[27]

As the debate between Murdock and McLachlan subsided, the government faced more pressures. A delegation of mayors from the coal towns arrived in Ottawa to press the case for a government investigation. When this was turned down, the two labour MPs – William Irvine of Calgary and J.S. Woodsworth of Winnipeg – launched a debate in the House of Commons on the plight of the coal miners. Woodsworth contributed a sympathetic exposition of the miners' case; as a student of society and sometime longshoreman, he informed the House that restriction of output was "a natural, recognized mode of procedure" both in the business world and in the workplace. Even the former prime minister, Conservative leader Arthur Meighen, joined the discussion and scolded the government for not reopening the miners' case. From the Senate, Murdock's Conservative predecessor as minister of labour, Gideon Robertson, who had tangled with McLachlan over the Winnipeg General Strike and the National Industrial Conference in 1919, warned that it was a mistake to refer to Nova Scotians as cowards: "They were not cowards in 1914, and they have not been since, and nobody is going to talk to them in that language." When Progressive leader T.A. Crerar suggested that the Gillen board be sent back to study conditions in the coalfields themselves, the government was facing a united opposition in a minority house and finally yielded.[28]

McLachlan was enthusiastic about the outcome. Now the conciliation board would be forced to look beyond the corporation's claims and study "the cost sheets of the miners, and those cost sheets were hungry, shoeless, coatless women and children." The Gillen board would tour the mining towns "even if he had to buy Gillen a pair of hip boots to wade through the muck." Behind the scenes things were more complicated. In Halifax E.H. Armstrong, commissioner of public works and mines, complained that he had not been consulted and that the government was "compromising with a serious menace" and encouraging "open defiance of law and order." From Montreal, Besco President Roy Wolvin wired "serious objections" to the prime minister and predicted that more uncertainty would bring "disastrous results." Privately King reassured Wolvin that the promise to reconvene the conciliation board was "conditional on certain requirements being met." What this meant became clear on 4 April, when the union executive board called off the strike on the job.[29]

This was a small victory, but McLachlan believed it was significant. Even if their tactics were controversial, they had marshalled the support of the mining community against the corporation; and in Parliament they had precipitated a debate that attracted sympathetic attention to their cause. To accomplish this the coal miners had drawn upon an elementary form of workers' control over production – the ability to work as vigorously or as inefficiently as circumstances warranted. An informal device of passive dissent was turned into an organized tactic of resistance. By taking the fight into the workplace, the miners had shown unexpected resourcefulness in the struggle. At the very least they had won the right to have their case examined more generously. There was more to come.

Red Summer

Early on a summer morning in June, McLachlan was working at union headquarters when a stranger walked into the outer office and asked to see him. The visitor spoke in a pleasant voice, with a marked English accent, and gave his name. McLachlan took a look around the corner and saw a fair-haired man of no more than average height, dressed in a light summer suit like an ice-cream salesman. Could this really be the emissary from the Communist Party of Canada whom McLachlan had invited to visit the coalfields? McLachlan was doubtful and sent word to ask the visitor to wait in the lobby of the hotel. Meanwhile, he despatched an urgent telegram to Toronto asking for a description of the notorious Communist Party organizer Tim Buck.

After a few hours there was confirmation – right down to the second-hand suit contributed by a party member – and McLachlan went over to the hotel to greet him. As Buck recalled the encounter, McLachlan was "a little fellow, even smaller than I, but with an enormous mustache and talking with the most guttural Scotch brogue that you can imagine." McLachlan was full of apologies: "I'll tell you the truth, I'd never seen you. I'd read about you, and I thought you looked like John L. Lewis."[30]

In the history of the Canadian left, the years immediately after the Great War were a time of disruptions and new beginnings. In 1918 a dozen radical organizations were banned under the War Measures Act, and the old Socialist Party of Canada itself barely survived. Much of the energy of labour radicals went into local and provincial labour parties and new organizations such as the One Big Union. Meanwhile, for many radicals around the world, the Russian Revolution was opening a new chapter in world history. Under the revolutionary conditions that existed in Russia in 1917, a small group of radicals known as the Bolsheviks had launched the world's first workers' republic. For all the efforts of labour and socialist parties in other countries, none had yet succeeded in capturing state power, and this accomplishment gave the Russian Marxists a great deal of moral authority in the socialist world. When the Bolsheviks organized the Communist International in 1919, with the stated object of promoting the world revolution, various local revolutionaries competed for the privilege of forming sections of the movement.

In Canada a small group of twenty-two radicals met in May 1921 in a barn near Guelph, Ontario, where they formed the Communist Party of Canada and affiliated to the Communist International. This underground group remained little more than a paper organization, but by the end of the year plans were under way for a more broadly based

Workers' Party of Canada. This was officially founded at a four-day meeting at the Toronto Labour Temple in February 1922. Like previous Marxist organizations in Canada, the Workers' Party of Canada carried a revolutionary message. Its platform predicted "the overthrow of capitalism and capitalist dictatorship by the establishment of the working class dictatorship and of the workers' republic."[31]

But by the summer of 1921 the Communist International had reached the conclusion that the tide of revolution was receding and the collapse of capitalism in other countries was not imminent. Communist parties around the world were instructed to undertake the long hard work of preparing the working class for future struggles. This retreat into a kind of revolutionary pragmatism had the full endorsement of the Bolshevik leader, V.I. Lenin, whose 1920 pamphlet, *Left-Wing Communism: An Infantile Disorder*, addressed a cautionary message to radicals in the capitalist democracies. This text, with its prescription for a strategy of immersion in existing struggles of the day, found reflection in the agenda endorsed by the Workers' Party. Whatever the frustrations, for instance, elections were an opportunity to articulate grievances and expose the limits of political democracy. Breakaway organizations such as the OBU were condemned, and the existing unions were seen as the institutions where workers could be united under radical leadership and prepared for the struggle against capitalism.[32]

In Canada most of the early leaders of the Communist Party and the Workers' Party (the distinction was abolished in 1924) were skilled workers and British immigrants – men with a good deal of experience in union matters and labour politics. The best known of the party leaders was undoubtedly the chairman, Jack MacDonald, a young Scottish immigrant who worked as a pattern-maker and was vice-president of the Metal Trades Council at the time of the Toronto General Strike in 1919. MacDonald was also active in the Independent Labour Party and received more than 7,000 votes in the Ontario election that year. By 1920 he was disturbed by the defeats suffered by labour and by the frustrations of electoral politics and was increasingly attracted to the Bolshevik example of undiluted revolutionary politics. Tim Buck was a machinist who joined a union in England at fifteen years of age, emigrated to Canada at nineteen in 1910, and subsequently became a member of one of the smaller radical groups, the Socialist Party of North America. Like MacDonald, he was also moving to the left at the end of the war. When the Workers' Party was established, Buck was given responsibility for work among the unions, and in the spring of 1922 he quit his job at a Toronto machine shop and went on the road.

No Maritimers participated in the first meetings of the Workers' Party of Canada, although radicals such as Roscoe Fillmore and Joe Wallace were soon showing an interest and joining up. McLachlan was also in contact with the Toronto-based radicals that spring, for the party's new newspaper, *The Worker*, which began to publish in March 1922, contained a contribution by McLachlan in its edition of 1 May 1922 under the title "Nova Scotia Miners Versus British Empire Steel Corporation." Reviewing the recent events in the coalfields, McLachlan claimed a place for the miners in the Canadian revolution: "When the final conflict comes for the uprooting of the cursed system that is starving out people in a land of plenty, the mine workers of Nova Scotia shall take an effective hand in that conflict." According to Buck's reminiscences, McLachlan had written and even applied to join as soon as he received word of the founding of the Workers' Party. He had also invited Buck to make a speaking tour, and it was agreed he would come to Nova Scotia in June after he completed a trip to the west.[33]

But before Buck, there was Joseph Knight, who can be identified as the first of the Communist agitators to visit the coal miners in the 1920s. Knight arrived in the spring of 1922 as a spokesman for the Canadian Friends of Soviet Russia and the Soviet Red Cross. The years of war, revolution, invasion, and civil war in Russia had taken their toll, and the country was suffering from extensive drought and crop failures. The famine-relief campaign was an international one, supported by various respectable relief agencies and even enjoying the patronage of the prime minister. Two representatives of the Save the Children Fund had already toured the area before Knight's arrival. Knight spoke with special authority, because he had just returned from an extended trip to Russia. His lectures in local theatres were illustrated with a collection of lantern slides, and his appeals for funds were mixed with favourable accounts of the Russian social experiment.[34]

There was more to this visitor than first met the eye, for Knight was a veteran labour radical who had helped organize the OBU in 1919. An English immigrant, he was an Alberta carpenter who was active in Edmonton labour politics and the Socialist Party before the war and then as an OBU organizer in the west as well as in Ontario and Quebec. When OBU secretary R.B. Russell declined the invitation, Knight took his place and in the summer of 1921 made his way to Moscow as a representative of the OBU. There he attended the first meetings of the Communist International's new trade-union federation, the Red International of Labour Unions. On his return, Knight was a convinced supporter of the Communist policy that radicals should work in the mainstream unions. He was unable to persuade the OBU to join the Red International and soon moved on to join the Workers' Party.[35]

Little is known of Knight's contact with McLachlan at this time. He must have briefed McLachlan and other local radicals on the policies of the Red International and the Workers' Party, in much the same way MacDonald and Buck and others were doing in their recruiting tours across the country. Knight was also in a position to convey some of the excitement of his trip to the centre of the world revolution. It seems likely that he collaborated with McLachlan in preparing a telegram, dated 27 April, which McLachlan addressed to Lenin himself as head of the Soviet government: "Will Russian people guarantee repayment when possible of fifteen million dollar distress loan by Canadian government; Loan to be spent in Canada for purchase of wheat seed and food for Volga, to be distributed under the Nansen agency?" Remarkably, some weeks later there was a reply, addressed to McLachlan in Glace Bay and signed by one of Lenin's deputies. According to the press reports, McLachlan was expected to launch a national campaign to support the distress loan.[36]

Besides Knight, there was also a visit from J.S. Woodsworth, who had so effectively defended the miners in the House of Commons that winter. His accounts of activity on Parliament Hill were being published regularly in the *Maritime Labor Herald* that spring, and Woodsworth received a ready welcome. On a Sunday afternoon he addressed a large audience in Glace Bay, reviewing the events of the Winnipeg strike and thanking the Cape Bretoners for their support. He also described the growth of the OBU and socialism in western Canada and the need for more labour Members of Parliament, adding that "he found in Eastern Canada the working class more conservative." Radical changes in the political and economic system were in the works, Woodsworth concluded, "and he predicted that within the next few years the working class would take control of Canada." Woodsworth was followed on the platform by McLachlan – who flourished copies of some confidential Dominion Coal cost sheets and, according to the police report, "expressed his intention that he would do everything in his power to wreck Coal Corporation out of existence." Then came Cape Breton labour MLA Forman Waye, who had introduced a bill for public ownership of the coal industry in the recent session of the provincial assembly.[37]

This visit by Woodsworth seems to have been the first time that he and McLachlan had met. It was the beginning of a relationship that never became a close one, for the two men were at this time moving in different directions. Following his experience in the Winnipeg General Strike, Woodsworth had turned his attention to electoral politics. In the minority Parliament that opened in 1922, Woodsworth had some hope that an election would be called within the year, and he believed that the election of McLachlan would be a significant addition to the labour group. But McLachlan's own attention remained focused on labour struggles, not electoral politics, and he was foreseeing new forms of action and alliances to advance the class struggle.

Typical of McLachlan's rhetoric at this time was his appeal for "one united front" among all the opponents of capitalism. According to one report despatched to the RCMP commissioner in Ottawa by Inspector LaNauze in early June, "J.B. McLachlan dealt forcibly with the great need of a strong labor organization with one united front from coast to coast; he said that all workers must fight the Capitalists until the workers get control of the industries, and have abolished all private profit and interest; he said that there was no hope for the workers under Capitalism for better living conditions." The appeal for "one united front" was the current language of the Communist International, but it is also interesting that McLachlan interpreted it loosely enough to claim that the distinction between the OBU and the Workers' Party was not important at this time: "Comrades Brothers! We must stand together upon one united front; we

must establish a strong labor organization to fight the Capitalists class."
According to the police report, he also added: "I don't care what the
name of this organization will be, OBU or the Workers Party."[38]

In the midst of all this agitation, the prospects for a conciliated
settlement of the miners' wage dispute were not strong. Under the
Industrial Disputes Investigation Act, there was no provision for a
board to rewrite its report. When members of the Gillen board refused
to proceed, the prime minister was forced to appoint a new board to
examine the dispute. If anything, the challenge facing the board was
even more difficult than in January. Resistance to the wage reduction
had now become a symbol of all the miners' objections to the corporation. Meanwhile, both the success of the strike on the job and the
eruption of a large general strike in the American coalfields to defend
the "no backward step" policy helped convince the miners that the wage
reduction could be defeated. The claims that wage reductions were the
only means of cutting productions costs were not accepted, and in May
Besco reinforced the miners' scepticism by publishing an annual report
that showed profits of more than $4.4 million between April and
December 1921. All this was grist for McLachlan's mill, and issues of
ownership and control in the coal industry were widely debated among
the coal miners. At several collieries, resolutions called for cancellation
of the corporation's coal leases and operation of the mines by the
province. The *Maritime Labor Herald* published a plan to remove
capital from control of the industry and "hand the mines over to the
UMW to operate under provincial supervision."[39]

When a new conciliation board was appointed at the end of April, the
union named a politically ambitious young coal miner-turned-lawyer
from Inverness, Isaac D. MacDougall, while the corporation selected a
New Brunswick lumberman as their representative. The guiding hand in
the board's work was the chairman, D'Arcy Scott, a former mayor of
Ottawa. Scott took his board members into the coal towns, held public
meetings, and went down the pits, effectively giving the impression that
the miners were receiving more sympathetic consideration. McLachlan
himself appeared at the hearings in Glace Bay, where he received stormy
applause when he declared that "the miners are going to get a living out
of this industry and there will be no peace until they do." His statement

to the board demanded a report on the watered stock in Besco's capital accounts and disclosure of the salary and expenses drawn by Wolvin as president of eight individual companies: "Unless and until the public mind can be satisfied with a complete knowledge of these things it will never endorse any encroachment on the living of the mine workers."[40]

In the end there was no agreement. The majority report, signed by the chairman and the employer's representative, offered a review of living and working conditions, including a scathing denunciation of the state of company housing and an attack on the company store system. On wages, it held the line and proposed exactly the same rates the corporation had offered in Montreal at the end of February – and which the miners had rejected so conclusively in March. For his part, MacDougall objected, on behalf of the miners, that the scale would not provide a living wage for many workers and echoed McLachlan's logic when he concluded that "dividends should be sacrificed before the worker should be compelled to accept less than living wages."[41]

To workers already disposed to look for alternatives to capitalist control of industry, the failure of the Scott board only encouraged the search. If a "new code of morality" was needed to rule the coal industry, as one of the union spokesmen had argued before the Gillen board, then the Scott board had not discovered it. "How can we stop the struggle going on continuously between capital and labor?" asked the *Maritime Labor Herald*. "There is only one way to do this, and that way is to put an end to the separation between capital and labour. To do this, the capitalist must cease to be a capitalist, and labour must own and control the capital."[42]

No vote was held on the Scott Award. Some observers predicted a resumption of striking on the job or the start of a full-fledged strike. But the union leadership remained broken by the divisions of February and March. Baxter was reported "silent and reticent and will not utter a chirp favourable or otherwise," and McLachlan was said to be "up a tree measuring the dimensions of the industrial horizon." All eyes were on the union's annual district convention, which was set to convene two weeks after the Scott board's recommendations were released.[43]

On 20 June the miners' delegates crowded into the local hotels in Truro and walked through the tree-lined streets to assemble at the county courthouse. From the chair Baxter read a message of greetings from John L. Lewis, who stated that the American coal miners were currently "fighting a gallant fight with the greatest determination to win" and extended best wishes "for a meeting that will enunciate constructive policies." Baxter himself presented an extended report, which included a vindication of McLachlan's innocence of the notorious charges from the time of the 1921 election – that he had conspired to bring about a wage cut. He concluded with an appeal to avoid the temptations of breaking with the existing union and joining some other organization:

> Has there not been sufficient evidence in the experience of the past? To fully demonstrate that the successful methods are those that go doggedly on, if labor institutions are faulty (as they no doubt are) then mend them. Some say the process is too slow. It may be so, but I venture to say that there is no other way. All our failings are human failings, the same whether in one society or another. The antitoxin for such, is education. It is the duty of them that have a desire to rectify and up-lift the under dog, to teach us the error of our ways, from within not without, as a change of name won't change the individual. Democratic institutions are never better than the members that compose them.[44]

Baxter's report was persuasive on many points and may well have helped weaken any resurgent interest in the OBU. But he could not escape the accumulated resentment against his conciliatory policy during the winter months. On the third day of the convention a resolution of censure was directed against the officers who had not resisted the wage reduction strongly enough and thereby, it was charged, were responsible for the poor outcomes of the two conciliation boards. Tim Buck, who was in attendance at the meetings, listened in fascination as the miners carried on a semantic debate as to whether the wage cut of January 1922 was "accepted" or "received." McLachlan argued that "the men had not accepted the wage-cut, although they had received the low wages under protest." An attempt to table the motion of censure failed by sixty-six votes to fifty-three and, after much bitter debate and with only half the delegates voting, the motion was carried by a vote of thirty-five to twenty-eight. That night all the district officers tendered their resignations, setting the stage for a new election on 15 August. Supporters of both sides looked forward to a "straight fight between the Baxterites and the McLachlanites."[45]

It was still business as usual in the convention, and dozens of additional resolutions were debated, many of them regarding local conditions in the mines, the repair of company housing, the election of mine inspectors, and the introduction of old age pensions. Also under consideration were a loan of $5,000 to the *Maritime Labor Herald*, an endorsement of McLachlan's proposal for a famine-relief loan to the Soviets, a resolution to make May Day, the international day of workers' solidarity, a district holiday, and a proposal to replace the territorial basis of representation in Parliament with one based on occupation.

Then, on the morning of 24 June, all business was suspended to hear Alex McKay read an extended report prepared during the week by the policy committee. This proved to be possibly the most controversial document in the entire history of District 26, not so much for its practical implications as for the revolutionary rhetoric that captured the imagination of the coal miners.[46]

The document began with the familiar claim that a "super-abundance of wealth production in coal" was the prime cause for the idle time, wage reductions, and poverty experienced by coal miners throughout North America – such was "the pretty state existing among coal miners in Nova Scotia as a result of the efforts of 'captains of industry' to run the coal business." The Scott board had provided no solution: "Like a vaudeville actor, he was sent among us with his part in the show cut out for him; among us he went through his little stunts, made his bow and like a vaudeville actor, left us." The Scott Award was "hardly worthy of a minute's consideration by this convention" and ought to be rejected.

Although McLachlan was not identified as a member of the policy committee, the text carries the mark of his theatrical prose, complete with the satirical thrusts at "captains of industry" and "vaudeville actors" and the appeals to patriarchal responsibility and anti-slavery imperatives among his followers. In the words of the policy report, there were only two choices available to the coal miners:

(a) accept the present conditions with all their humiliation and poverty, and repudiate the sacred obligations which every sire owes to his son; or

(b) reject and fight with all the power that is in us the present conditions and make one bold attempt to hand down to our children something better than a slave's portion.

All this was in the nature of a preamble, to be followed by several more specific statements, but could there be any doubt that the miners would choose the second alternative?

First, the committee proposed, the miners should pledge to accept no contract for less than the 1921 rates. To adopt this policy was to define the actual size of the "living wage" the miners demanded. Silby Barrett, once a McLachlan protégé but now very conscious of his position as the international board member for District 26, proposed an amendment stating that the district would harmonize its wage policy with that of the international union. The vote was forty-one in favour of the amendment and seventy-four against. This was the only roll-call vote on the clauses of the policy report, and it was probably an accurate gauge of the relative support of radical and moderate factions at the convention.

Next came a more general appeal to "create one united front of all the workers in Canada," an invitation to be extended first to the coal miners of the west. Under such agreements between bodies of organized labour, "joint action" could be taken "to secure for the workers of this country a living, such action to be taken either with or without the consent of the Government." Here was a vision of coordinated working-class action, along the lines of the alliances McLachlan had supported at meetings of the Trades and Labour Congress in 1919. Such a campaign could be expected to precipitate open class conflict, and there was accordingly an appeal for allies for the working class: "To all soldiers and minor law officers we appeal, and when you are ordered to shoot the workers, don't do it. When you are asked to arrest the workers, don't do it. When you are asked to spy on the workers, don't do it."

The final two points became the most notorious of the resolutions. One was a short, emphatic declaration of opposition to the capitalist system: "That we proclaim openly to all the world that we are out for the complete overthrow of the capitalist system and capitalist state, peaceably if we may, forceably if we must, and we call on all workers, soldiers and minor law officers in Canada to join us in liberating labour." The language here owed something to the new rhetoric of the Workers' Party ("the complete overthrow of the capitalist system and capitalist state"); it also carried echoes of the Chartist debates of the 1830s about "moral force" and "physical force" ("peaceably if we may, forceably if we must"). Here was a fusion of nineteenth-century radicalism and twentieth-century revolutionary sentiment consistent with McLachlan's political lineage.[47]

The other resolution was a proposal that District 26 apply for membership in the Red International of Labour Unions and send a delegate to its next international meetings. An amendment asked that the district coordinate its action with the miners in District 18 in the west, and a subsequent resolution (which Barrett opposed) named McLachlan to travel to the west for this purpose. Interestingly, Buck has claimed no credit for the Red International resolution – in his memoirs he stated that McLachlan had not shown him any of the resolutions beforehand, nor had Buck mentioned the Red International at all during his visit. Nevertheless, affiliation to the Red International was among the union policies adopted by the Workers' Party in February, and in a well-received address to the convention Buck congratulated the miners on their decision.[48]

In his memoirs Buck also recalled a subsequent conversation in which he explained his misgivings about the resolution to McLachlan:

He was shocked. "What sort of a Communist are you? Why, we'll never get anywhere until we have all the unions in Canada affiliated to the Red International of Labour Unions."

I said that so far as North America was concerned, it's rather a distant objective and a matter of fraternal propaganda. "Now, for example, if we had sent fraternal greetings ..."

"Greetings! I can get greetings even from John L. Lewis."

Buck had not expected such revolutionary results to emerge out of his first trip to Nova Scotia – "'Oh, my goodness,' said I to myself, 'the fellows in Toronto are going to hold me responsible for this.'"[49]

"A Real Red-Blooded Canadian Strike"

All year long John Moffatt, the former grand secretary of the Provincial Workmen's Association, watched events with increasing alarm about the influence of his radical nemesis McLachlan. In early August, Moffatt, as the local correspondent for the *Labour Gazette*, reported his concern to the deputy minister of labour: "Workmen here are in a very ugly mood, it might be well to be prepared for the worst ... I am of opinion the leaders will be unable to control their followers."[50]

In the United States the coal miners were still on strike, and Barrett had returned full of enthusiasm for the progress of the lengthy strike there. He also reported that John L. Lewis was "opposed to miners in District 26 continuing to work without a contract." When Baxter and Barrett scoffed at "the reds with yellow streaks down their backs," McLachlan retorted that it made "good industrial logic" to strike during the peak shipping months at the end of the summer. Although there was still no promised support from the international union, the miners were more confident about their prospects of fighting a strike in the summer months. One enthusiastic meeting even planned to send a schooner to haul potatoes from Prince Edward Island and catch cod in the Gulf of St Lawrence. The coal miners had voted – 96 per cent, said Robert Baxter – to go on strike on 15 August for the 1921 rates.[51]

There was a final consultation with D.H. McDougall on 12 August, when he arrived back from a week in Montreal with a final offer for the coal miners. That Saturday afternoon he met with the union leaders, who turned down his proposal to raise the minimum daily rate to $3.15. They met again in Sydney all day Sunday, in a meeting that lasted after midnight. This time the union leaders returned with a minimum rate of $3.25 and equivalent raises in other rates.

This seemed to be an acceptable compromise, and Baxter was pleased to be able to telegraph the prime minister that a last-minute agreement had been reached. Telegrams went out to the union locals announcing that the strike was cancelled. On the morning of 14 August Mackenzie King sent his congratulations. But before the day was out Baxter had a correction: "Many thanks for your kind words of appreciation, but sorry to inform you that men have repudiated our actions and advices. We are now on strike."[52]

Moffatt was right about the mood of the coal miners. They had been waiting for the showdown for many months, and it was now too late to call off the strike. Furthermore, the union executive lacked authority among the membership; its mandate was expiring within hours, and the miners were preparing to elect a new slate of officers on 15 August. McLachlan later recalled the scene on 14 August: "When I walked down the street in the morning, the whole mass of the miners was there charging us with breaking the arrangement, which we actually had done. The arrangement was to strike for the 1921 rates."

Some four to five thousand men assembled on the ballgrounds in Glace Bay to take the union leaders to task. Baxter and McLachlan could barely make themselves heard above the crowd. The miners were "sick of voting," noted one reporter, "They wanted action." Baxter and McLachlan were escorted back to the union office with instructions to send out telegrams confirming that the strike was on. Recalled McLachlan: "There was no question about whether you would send out that wire or not. Mr. Wolvin would have sent it out that day if he'd been at that meeting."[53]

In spite of the contradictory messages from union headquarters, there was remarkably little uncertainty about the strike among the union membership. Throughout the province on Sunday and Monday the coal miners made final preparations to shut down the mines, and the strike started at midnight on Monday as originally planned. The initiative had clearly passed from the union officers to the local unions. It was, said the Halifax *Citizen*, "the most unique strike in Canada's history" – "a solid strike, with leaders ordered to take orders from the rank and file or get off the job." Dalhousie University professor H.L. Stewart, who toured the strike zone for the Halifax *Herald*, later singled this out as one of the remarkable features of the strike: "The rank and file have taken the management out of their leaders' hands."[54]

The other notable feature of the strike was the withdrawal, in most cases, of the maintenance men who were responsible for the operation of pumps, fans, and other equipment in the collieries. The threat of rising water levels and accumulations of gas raised the spectre of damage to the mines. Although the district made no formal decision regarding the "100 per cent strike," the policy had been openly discussed since July as the most effective guarantee of the miners' success in the coming strike. Like the strike on the job, this was another tactical application of the workers' latent control of production. Corporation officials denounced the "100 per cent strike" as "an insurgent move by men who have overridden law and order."[55]

McLachlan emerged unscathed from the last-minute confusion surrounding the calling of the strike. In repudiating their leaders on the eve of the strike, the miners were expressing a determination to continue resisting the wage reduction through direct action, the policy most closely associated with McLachlan during the course of the year. As they gathered around the collieries on 15 August, the miners were also casting their votes for a new district executive, and the results showed a marked preference for McLachlan and the radical leaders who had dominated the June convention.

Baxter and his allies went down to a heavy defeat; Baxter himself received only 1,695 votes against 7,170 votes for the new president, Dan Livingstone, the Westville radical and former international board member. McLachlan was re-elected with 6,192 votes, a margin of almost 4,000 over the 2,250 votes for the former district vice-president, W.P. Delaney, who had allied himself with Baxter. Most of the other positions were also won by supporters of McLachlan. Alex S. McIntyre, a radical from the hotbed of the Phalen local, became vice-president, though a second ballot was needed to determine a majority in that seven-way contest. Another McLachlanite, Alex M. Stewart, defeated Barrett for the seat on the international board, although the international union initially refused to recognize the vote.[56]

As in 1909, armed force was the coal operators' main response to the outbreak of the strike. When the union leaders failed to call off the strike on 14 August, Wolvin informed the prime minister that military protection was needed. As in 1909, the mayor of Glace Bay – on this occasion the labour mayor and MLA Dan Willie Morrison – rejected requests that he sign a requisition for troops. But, as in 1909, the sympathetic county court judge, Duncan Finlayson, complied and within hours troops from the Halifax garrison were embarking by train for the strike zone. The first soldiers arrived at Glace Bay on the afternoon of 16 August and occupied the grounds of Dominion No. 2 at New Aberdeen. By the end of the week they were reinforced by the Royal 22nd Regiment from Quebec City and additional forces from Ontario. In all, more than 1,200 troops were assembled, amounting to about 25 per cent of the permanent force of the Canadian army in 1922.[57]

If the company expected the soldiers to protect the mines from damage by manning the pumps, they were disappointed. Apparently under strict orders, the soldiers remained under canvas at No. 2, accepting occasional jeers and exchanging conversation with curious onlookers. Professor Stewart was impressed by the complete lack of disorder: "It is a remarkable and gratifying fact that – apart from the great breach of UMW discipline involved in the calling out of the pumpmen – the order preserved by a leaderless multitude has been so perfect. No looting, no drinking, no rioting!"[58]

There were resolutions of protest against the soldiers at local meetings, and in Ottawa the prime minister tried in vain to turn back the flood of protests. The district commanding officer was instructed to refrain from "active measures ... likely to precipitate trouble." Requests for more troops, for British warships, and for an airplane squadron were all denied. In Halifax, E.H. Armstrong was being exhorted to raise volunteers and seize control of the mines from "Mclachlan and his band of reds." On 18 August he announced the creation of a special 1,000-man provincial police force to go into the coalfields and patrol the mines.[59]

In the midst of all this turmoil McLachlan took some pleasure in the successful shutdown and sent a satisfied rejoinder to the minister of labour, James Murdock: "When we were striking on the job in order to secure a living you said it was un-British and un-Canadian and that red-blooded Canadians did not practice such, but quit like men and walked off the job. Today we have a real red-blooded Canadian strike in strict accordance with your definition and walked off the job one hundred per cent." Not content with making the point, McLachlan added another thrust at the former labour leader. With all these soldiers pouring into the district, was the government looking to "sanctify the crushing of this peaceful red-blooded Canadian strike?" Was Murdock

really prepared to go so far in support of his master Mackenzie King –
"the factotum of John D. Rockefeller, the saint of Ludlow?"[60]

The eruption of the strike was also causing anxiety for the international union. On 15 August, McDougall lodged a complaint on behalf
of the corporation. First, the union officers had failed to cancel the
strike, and then the men had placed the mines in dangerous condition.
None of this was in accordance with the usual policies of the union,
claimed McDougall: "We protest against strike action after we had
concluded agreement with district executive, and we further protest
against withdrawal of men necessary to preservation and protection of
mines." Lewis also received a similar urgent message from Murdock,
urging him to support a settlement that would avoid "irreparable
damage" to the mines. In reply Lewis could only inform them that
Baxter, McLachlan, and Barrett had all been advised that it was the
union's policy that "necessary men be furnished to protect property so
long as strike breakers were not used."[61]

But Lewis was getting no satisfaction from the union office in Glace
Bay. On 16 August, Barrett, somewhat belatedly, reported: "McLachlan
ticket elected strike declared in district men out one hundred percent
advice of executive not heeded." Any further communications, added
Baxter on 17 August, should be directed to the new district president,
Dan Livingstone, who was taking up his duties immediately. Meanwhile, McDougall reported to Lewis that the pumps had stopped in all
the Dominion mines. He also took special exception to a statement by
McLachlan in an "alleged interview" in the Sydney *Record*. According
to this story, McLachlan objected to Murdock's appeal to Lewis in
statements such as: "I want to say that a few drowned mines have no
bearing on the question at issue here" and "I can say that his revulsion
of feeling over a flooded mine or two won't have much effect on the
miners. We started out to tie up the coal mines of the British Empire
Steel Corporation and we don't propose at this time to change our
policy." Surely, McDougall demanded, such statements were not consistent with union policy?[62]

Suddenly the "100 per cent strike" had given the coal miners a
tactical advantage in the year's protracted struggle, and McLachlan had
no intention of retreating without making some gains. The expected

concession came soon enough in the form of intervention by Nova Scotia Premier George H. Murray, who was staying at his North Sydney residence when the strike began. While Armstrong prepared his "army" in Halifax, Murray invited McLachlan and Livingstone to a meeting. On Friday, 18 August, they concluded an agreement to restore maintenance work in the mines if the operators reopened negotiations for better terms. McDougall signified his consent, and maintenance work resumed on the following Sunday and Monday.

It was still heavy going. McDougall and Murray found themselves pleading with Wolvin in Montreal. For his part, McLachlan insisted on recruiting the engineer of the 1920 MacKinnon Agreement, the Reverend Dr Clarence MacKinnon, principal of Pine Hill Divinity School, to oversee the settlement. Four days later there was a settlement: the basic daily rate would be $3.25 and most rates were restored to the level of the old MacKinnon Agreement. Again, the outcome fell short of the 1921 rates; but since the original reduction in January had placed the scale 25 per cent below the 1920 rates, this was a measurable gain; in addition, a variety of substandard rates were eliminated, and the new agreement was expected to last for sixteen months, a full year longer than the company had offered on the eve of the strike. On 31 August the miners approved the new wage schedule, 7,768 in favour, 2,920 against. Two days later the troops began to evacuate the coalfield. Then, after a few last days of an uncustomary summer vacation and a celebration of Labour Day on 4 September, the coal miners went back to work.[63]

McLachlan must have had ambivalent feelings about the result of the strike. The agreement had failed to win the 1921 rates and was concluded in the presence of an armed occupation and in the midst of a great deal of criticism of the coal miners' tactics. And, although much of the original wage reduction had been eliminated, the final settlement in September and some of the lower rates were not considerably different from those he and other leaders had endorsed on the eve of the strike in August. Most of the miners' success was due to the long resistance of the previous eight months. The coal miners had shown that the corporation could be forced to back down, and they had demonstrated their ability to carry out a successful strike, without violence or disorder.

In a public speech on 4 September, reported by an RCMP informant, McLachlan described the strike as a "temporary success for the miners." The strike on the job and the 100 per cent strike were "effective blows" against the corporation, he stated. He also attacked the government for using troops during the strike and "declared that the present Government only care to save the property of the Coal Company, some old pieces of iron and pumps from flooding ... when our miners and their families starved last winter, the Government took no interest in us." To this assessment, Inspector LaNauze added a notation of grudging admiration for McLachlan's success in bringing the year's confusing struggles to a successful conclusion: "McLachlan is now more firmly ensconsed in power than ever before as he has a complete radical executive. He said little in public in the recent negotiations but had he used his influence to swing the miners against the offer of the Corporation, I believe the strike and attendant trouble would still be in existence."[64]

McLachlanism

"Nova Scotia has passed through a crisis simply bristling with dangerous possibilities," commented a reporter in the Halifax *Herald* at the end of the 1922 strike. "Had the negotiations broken down, or had the proposition resulting therefrom been rejected, there is no man in this province capable of saying what might not have resulted ..."[65]

Such fears indicated a new level of anxiety about the condition of labour relations in the province. During the course of the year the coal miners had broken many of the accepted norms of industrial legality. They had refused to accept the economic logic that when prices went down wages should follow. They had questioned the competence and morality of their employers and refused to believe that the coal industry could not pay a living wage. They had voted down concessions and repudiated leaders and taken their case to conciliation boards, and when these approaches failed they had taken control of the workplace in tactics such as the strike on the job and the 100 per cent strike –

evidence of a "physical force" trade unionism that was at least as threatening as all the radical resolutions about overthrowing the capitalist system.

Among the union leaders in office at the beginning of the year, only McLachlan had survived. Even Robert Baxter, who was known as an honest and capable union leader with a goodly fund of common sense, had gone down to defeat. McLachlan had triumphed by promising his followers that a radical, even revolutionary, union strategy could defend the coal miners in the short run and offer them hope for the future. Despite all the radical rhetoric surrounding the year's agitation, the miners' short-term objectives in 1922 had remained limited to the original goal of restoring the 1921 rates. Now the coal miners' new "red executive," as it was called, faced a significant challenge. McLachlan's record of tactical success since 1917 had brought him to the peak of his influence among the coal miners, and his opportunities to pursue a strategy of radical trade unionism were unparalleled. As Inspector LaNauze observed at the end of the year, "This agitator is at present in a stronger position than ever in Cape Breton; his present aspirations appear to be both political and revolutionary."[66]

McLachlan's pragmatic political instincts had told him to consent to a settlement of the strike in August, and he already knew from experience the importance of exercising caution in dealing with the international office of the UMW. By the middle of September it was apparent that McLachlan had abandoned plans to go to Moscow for meetings of the Red International. He was under pressure from his new comrades in the Workers' Party to attend – the coal miners were one of only two unions in Canada to endorse the International (the other was the Lumber Workers' Industrial Union) – and the party was eager to demonstrate its success in attracting working-class support. According to a police report, McLachlan resisted on the ground that "it would be foolish for him to leave Nova Scotia at the present time, as the radicals have only just obtained control of the executive." In the end, the Canadian delegation included only Jack MacDonald and Maurice Spector, both of them party leaders in Toronto.[67]

McLachlan was also concerned about relations with the international union. At the time of the June convention, Barrett had forwarded the full text of the radical resolutions to Lewis by telegram. Subsequently, Baxter reviewed the year's events for Lewis and advised him that "our men are in a vindictive frame of mind, and any propaganda with a tinge of red is very acceptable to them; our district is in jeopardy and something should be done to harmonise it with the policy of our union." Barrett urged Lewis to name a commission to investigate the district.[68]

For his part, Lewis seemed content to wait. His only significant action was the decision to disallow the election of Alex Stewart as international board member – on technical grounds – and confirm Barrett in the office for the remainder of his term. McLachlan, meanwhile, wrote to ask what stand the international might take in the event of District 26 affiliating to the Red International. The Red International, McLachlan added, was "absolutely opposed to all dual unionism," including the OBU in Canada and the Wobblies in the United States. Lewis responded with a request for information, stating that the matter would be placed before the international executive board in due course.[69]

The signing of the 1922 agreement was delayed for several weeks and not completed until 10 October. Difficulties developed when the coal operators presented draft versions of the contract that included a variety of clauses concerning managerial authority, of the kind that had been controversial when the Montreal Agreement was signed in 1920. This included the management's right to hire and fire and a restriction on the shutdown of collieries in the case of fatalities. McLachlan took the view that none of these clauses could be included in the agreement: the miners had voted on the rates alone, and no other issues were discussed in the negotiations or presented to the membership. "Their mandate to sign," he said "extended only to the particular matters set forth in the Sydney agreement." This was an unexpectedly rigorous adherence to the forms of industrial legality on the part of McLachlan, but the operators were forced to concede the point and sign the abbreviated agreement. The year's events had demonstrated the importance of autonomous action by the coal miners, and the absence of restrictive conditions from the new agreement preserved the miners' freedom of action. In the early months of 1923 McLachlan specifically pointed to the absence of conventional "no stoppage of work" clauses as an opportunity for the coal miners to close the mines without breaking the contract.[70]

McLachlan was also showing interest in a long-term strategy of labour education. In the fall of 1922 colleges in the Maritimes were discussing a plan for federation of the various local denominational institutions into a single university, a proposition supported by the Carnegie Corporation with a promised grant of $3 million. In Glace Bay a newly organized Workers' Educational Club named McLachlan to represent its interests in the discussions, suggesting that he be accepted as a delegate from a Glace Bay labour college "in process of formation."

In Antigonish Father Jimmy Tompkins, vice-president of St Francis Xavier University and a vigorous advocate both of adult education and of college federation, also welcomed the idea of including a labour college in the new university and sent McLachlan words of encouragement. In response, McLachlan explained that "our Labor College is just a dream as yet" but that "some day in the near future it may develop into a school." Seventy-two members were already enrolled in the Glace Bay Educational Club, and he hoped to see similar clubs opened in other industrial centres. In addition to holding weekly lectures, the clubs were attempting to open small libraries. Tompkins was pleased to hear this report, and he sent a copy of McLachlan's letter to Dr W.S. Learned, who was coordinating the Carnegie efforts to promote college federation in the Maritimes. Tompkins described McLachlan as "a very clever fellow and very *red*. If we can swing the Labor Party into line we shall make the Government wake up. These people are well organized and enthusiastic."[71]

By the end of October, in addition to the Friday public lectures, the club was running three courses, including one by the editor of the *Maritime Labor Herald* on effective writing and another by McLachlan on "effective unionism and methods of labour advance." There were discussions about hiring two or three teachers and establishing short programs of two weeks or terms of three or six months' duration. Support might be provided in part by levies on the union membership, and graduates would receive training to become union officials, public speakers, labour investigators, and members of legislatures. As it evolved,

McLachlan hoped the college might be organized "on lines similar to the Ruskin college at Oxford."[72]

Ultimately, the Carnegie plan failed to win acceptance among the existing universities, and Tompkins himself was sent into exile as a parish priest at Canso. It was still some years before the university was prepared to embrace the causes of adult education and social action that came to be known as the Antigonish Movement. But had the Carnegie plan succeeded, the new university might well have included a labour college dedicated to the education of the working class. The episode is notable for the common importance that the different parties to the discussions assigned to education. McLachlan had been advocating a form of labour education as an integral part of union activity since the days of the Provincial Workmen's Association, and he was confident that education in history and economics was a preparation for the class struggle. Others believed that education would weaken the influence of radicals among the working class. Tompkins had for some years held the view that the Catholic Church should take greater interest in labour issues, in part, he explained in 1920, because "the Labor element in our Industrial centres is getting out of hand and their leaders are a bad sort." A similar opinion was expressed in the pages of the *Canadian Mining Journal*, where it was hoped that a labour college might promote "civility, tolerance and citizenship among miners, not Red ideas."[73]

In October the embryonic labour college in Glace Bay sponsored a visit by J.S. Woodsworth, his second of the year. In addition to speaking at the high school and in other towns in the industrial area, Woodsworth addressed a large audience at the Savoy Theatre in Glace Bay. He congratulated the coal miners on the success of their strike but warned that industrial action was not enough: "The recent strike showed that the miners were 100 per cent organized industrially. The Sydney steelworkers were also organized industrially. But more was necessary. Political action was needed." The coal miners had learned the same lessons as the Winnipeg workers – that the courts and the military were controlled by the government, and therefore it was necessary for labour to "go into politics." In this, education was also important – "for we must know the aims that we desire to see brought about" – and just as John Knox had educated Scotland, it was time for workers to educate themselves. This meeting took place in the shadow of the Chanak Crisis, in which the issue was the possibility of Canada becoming involved in a British military effort in Turkey; with Woodsworth's encouragement, the meeting passed anti-war resolutions denouncing British imperialism and demanding a referendum vote before Canada committed itself to another foreign war.[74]

There was little here for McLachlan to disagree with, and in his own speech he gave vigorous support to Woodsworth's anti-imperialism: "The working class are not going to kill the working class of Turkey. They are our comrades in oppression and we want them to be our comrades in liberation, and we are not going to have weeping women because men are dying in Asia." As for working-class strategy, McLachlan made no criticism of Woodsworth's endorsement of political action and labour education, but he continued to emphasize the importance of industrial action. This, he insisted, was one of the lessons of the 1922 strike:

We have found out where the power lies. It lies with the miners, with the transport workers, with the steelworkers, with the workers in the basic industries.

We find doctors and lawyers and clergymen and members of parliament and the other classes can take a holiday for months and nothing is said. But when the workers with the hobnailed boots and copper riveted overalls quit for a few hours, they say that you have the nation by the throat. Now if you have the nation by the throat when you quit work, the power lies in you. They have borrowed power, you have inherent power ...[75]

What allies were there for radical unionism across the country? One of the assumptions underlying the resolutions adopted by District 26 during the summer was that there was a body of radical opinion in organized labour that required coordination and direction. Accordingly, on behalf of District 26, McLachlan was soon canvassing the country for allies. In an appeal circulated to hundreds of local unions, McLachlan proposed an agenda for joint action by all existing unions. At a time when the house of labour was increasingly divided into rival federations and groupings – some radical, some industrial, others national or regional – this was a plan to set aside differences and "come together for united action." There was, McLachlan stated in his message, "a latent and as yet an undeveloped power in our present organizations as they exist in Canada today." At the very least this was an appeal to unions to rise above institutional rivalries and focus their attention on advancing the class struggle.

The basis for common action was to be found in the crisis facing workers all across the country: "The terrible scourge of unemployment, the slashed wages, the aggressiveness of the employing class all cry aloud for a united front." The credibility of capitalism as an economic system was at stake: "Can capitalism continue to employ and hence feed the workers of this Country? Let us put it to the test." The proposed platform was a radical one, but not necessarily revolutionary; the idea originated with the miners' union of Porcupine, Ontario – local 145 of the International Union of Mine, Mill and Smelter Workers – which in response to the resolutions emanating from District 26 submitted what the *Maritime Labor Herald* described as "a conservative labour platform." The demands were limited to a list of measures to guarantee the economic security of the working class – full wages for the unemployed, a minimum wage based on the cost of a family budget, a five-day week, and a six-hour working day. All organizations pledging to support these demands were invited to appoint one member to "a joint committee of action." In McLachlan's vision, this "central council" would have the authority to "institute any means that in their judgement shall result in the realization of the fulfillment of these demands."

The appeal envisaged "one united front of all workers," organized around common goals and directed by a "central council." Here, McLachlan believed, was a constructive strategy for Canadian workers and one that was more specific in its proposals than the highly rhetorical declarations from the summer meetings. Local unions were instructed to return endorsements to McLachlan at the District 26 offices. The idea of "one united front of all workers," presumably ready to mount coordinated protests and even a general strike, was not a new one in labour history. It was there in the Chartist debates about a "sacred month" in the 1830s and in the struggle for the eight-hour day in North America half a century later; it could also be seen in the functioning Triple Alliance in Britain in recent years, where railwaymen, engineers, and miners collaborated in advancing common demands; and it resembled, too, the proposal for joint action McLachlan had proposed to the TLC in 1919. Yet, as one of the publications of the Department of Labour hastened to point out, it was also a plan that did not have the support of the Trades and Labour Congress and was "in line with the principles of the Workers' Party of Canada."[76]

McLachlan was the most prominent trade unionist recruited by the Workers' Party in the 1920s, and much depended on his success as a working-class leader. McLachlan's own well-tested sense of strategy seemed to be confirmed by his contact with international communism. From the evidence in his reading materials, it is apparent that McLachlan at this time was reading Lenin's influential *Left-Wing Communism: An Infantile Disorder*, with its arguments for tactical flexibility, especially in non-revolutionary situations. The temptations of dual unionism and syndicalism were to be avoided as symptoms of impractical enthusiasm. Instead, Lenin's prescription called for the construction of alliances while awaiting the inevitable revolutionary crisis. This document was regarded as one of the key texts of international communism in the early 1920s and was widely circulated in North America.[77]

For much of the year McLachlan had controlled the rhetorical discourse surrounding the miners' struggles. It was a battle of the patriotic family men of the coal mines against an invasion of their homes and an assault on their livelihood. The enemy were a band of corporate stock gamblers for whom the welfare of the coal miners and their community was a minor consideration. At stake in the struggle were the miners' claims for recognition of their manhood and their citizenship. McLachlan himself stood revealed not only as a preacher of the economic gospel but also as a master tactician.

To some observers, a new balance of power seemed to prevail in the coal industry at the end of 1922. The Halifax *Herald* was optimistic that the period of "industrial war" and "mutual suspicion" was coming to an end. As part of the new disposition, it would be necessary to accept McLachlan as the legitimate leader of the coal miners. In a commentary in the *Canadian Magazine*, Professor Stewart warned observers that "a limit should surely be set to the recklessness with which quiet folk are calling one another Bolshevists, just as they called one another Jacobins a hundred years ago." Even as McLachlan was becoming identified with the revolutionary left of the 1920s, he had not lost his reputation as a man of sincere motives and ethical convictions that were consistent with the principles of the social gospel. Among the books from this period in McLachlan's collection was a pocket edition of the New Testament presented to him by a well-wisher in Dartmouth on 29 November 1922: "To James B. MacLachlan, Labor-Leader and lover of workingmen, as a token of appreciation; and as a help in becoming better acquainted with the Carpenter of Nazareth. The world's greatest labour-leader, the supreme lord and lover of men ..."[78]

But in other accounts, McLachlan was increasingly villified as an outrageous radical, and the rhetoric of demonization was itself threatening to become an obstacle to the fulfillment of his strategies. Earlier in the year the editor of the Halifax *Chronicle* had singled out "McLachlanism" as a principal cause of the labour unrest: "A self-seeking mob is usually more or less easily swayed by a reckless 'man with a mouth.'" The following month the *Chronicle* added: "His very name is coming to make the hair of our heads stand up like quills upon the fretful porcupine. Soon, local mothers will be intimidating their wayward offspring with 'Be good now, or J.B. McLachlan will get you.'" The marginalization of McLachlan was also endorsed from the pulpit at St Anne's Church in Glace Bay, where Father A.M. Thompson warned that trade unionism was acceptable to the Catholic Church, but only under the leadership of "people of sound mind" – "not irresponsibles whose sole aim was to further the cause of Bolshevism, socialism and to keep the country in continual turmoil." Meanwhile, the aging Robert Drummond, founder of the PWA, had watched the year's events in discouragement; his *Mining Record* held out no hope for conditions of mutual trust in the coal industry "before the spit fires are extinguished and the 'reds' exterminated."[79]

Robert Baxter. A fellow Lanark-shireman to McLachlan, Baxter was a union pioneer and president of District 26 at the time of the 1922 strike.

Silby Barrett. A Newfoundland fisherman's son, Barrett rose to influence in the miners' union, first as a follower of McLachlan, then as a follower of John L. Lewis.

The United Mine Workers of Nova Scotia in June 1917, prior to the creation of the Amalgamated Mine Workers of Nova Scotia.

"The Same Old Flivver." Union officers McLachlan and Baxter of District 26 try to get results out of a royal commission, 1920.

"Now a smile, then a tear" – McLachlan quoted Burns in his ambivalent response to a royal commission report in 1920.

Robert Baxter, J.B. McLachlan and Silby Barrett in a cartoonist's vision
of the Shakespearean complexities of union politics in 1920.

"Queen of the May." McLachlan's support for the Winnipeg strikers gets a bad review from Halifax cartoonist Donald McRitchie.

J.S. Woodsworth, Labour MP. A Methodist minister charged with seditious libel for his part in the 1919 Winnipeg General Strike, Woodsworth was returned to the House of Commons in 1921. He hoped McLachlan would be elected to join him as a Labour Member of Parliament.

Roy Wolvin was the president of the British Empire Steel Corporation, and became known locally as "Roy the Wolf." He considered McLachlan "the concentrated cause" of labour unrest in the coal industry.

James Murdock, Mackenzie King's Minister of Labour. In 1922 he denounced the miners as "un-British, un-Canadian and cowardly."

The American union establishment in the 1920s included John L. Lewis, President, United Mine Workers (centre), Samuel Gompers, President, American Federation of Labor (right) and AFL Secretary Frank Morrison (left).

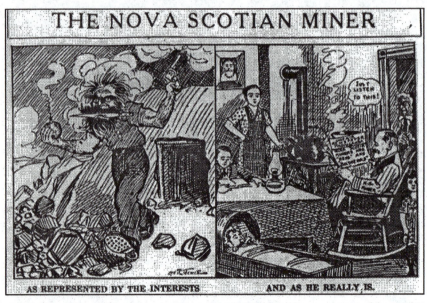

THE NOVA SCOTIAN MINER

AS REPRESENTED BY THE INTERESTS   AND AS HE REALLY IS.

As Halifax *Herald* cartoonist Donald McRitchie demonstrated in 1922, caricatures of the coal miners ran to extremes.

BOOK THREE

CRIME AND PUNISHMENT
1923-25

Sedition ... is when you protest
against the wrongs inflicted on working men;
when you protest against the resources of the province
being put in the control of men like Roy Wolvin;
when wage rates are forced on you without your consent.
These things will be given back to the working class
and their wrongs will eventually be redeemed.
If you say that strongly enough,
you are liable to get into jail for sedition.

– J.B. McLachlan,
1924

CHAPTER 7

Thermidor

Listen, my children, and you shall know
Of a crime that happened long ago,
In the dark and dismal days of old
When the world and all was ruled by Gold,
When the earth was a rich man's institution –
That was before the Revolution …

– Dawn Fraser,
Echoes from Labor's War (1924)

May Day

H ere they come around Senator's Corner, under a red banner big enough to block the whole of Commercial Street. People are standing on the sidewalks, hands in their pockets, wearing caps to protect themselves against the icy rain that has started to fall. Children are watching, pointing. There in the front row are the familiar figures of the union officers, the men who triumphed at Truro last year and brought the coal miners through the long strike: Dan Livingstone, Alex McIntyre – and Jim McLachlan, the miners' secretary, smaller than expected, walking with the rolling gait of a man from the pits, big moustache dripping with rain, his eyes twinkling as he marches past.

The red flag is carried by Tom Bell, a Communist organizer lately arrived from Winnipeg. The flag is truly huge, twenty feet by twelve, embroidered in gold thread with the words "Long Live Communism." Other banners carry slogans such as "Workers of the World Unite" and "The World for the Workers." Then, row after row, comes the so-called army of the revolution, miners from the surrounding coal towns. They are joined by a contingent of steelworkers who have come out for the day from Sydney. It is not much of a picnic for them so far, as they walk through the patches of snow and puddles on Commercial Street. But the parade continues, and later in the day there will be large crowds at the public meeting at the Alexandra Rink.[1]

At the turn of the century May Day was one of the strongest traditions of international socialism, rooted in the folklore of springtime. First celebrated as an international day of working-class solidarity in 1890, May Day was the historic proof that the workers of the world were prepared to unite in a common cause. In District 26 the 1922 convention had voted to observe May Day as an official holiday. For McLachlan, marching through the streets of Glace Bay under the red banners, this was a declaration that the coal miners were joining the ranks of a world movement.

All winter long, visiting speakers had travelled through the coal towns carrying the message of the class struggle. Labour Member of Parliament J.S. Woodsworth had toured Nova Scotia in October, but most of those who followed were associated with the more radical Workers' Party of Canada, to which McLachlan now belonged. In December, for instance, there was the war veteran Trevor Maguire, freshly convicted of sedition for a speech in Toronto's Queen's Park. Then in January came H.M. Bartholomew, who was considered one of the party's best propagandists; he stayed on in Sydney to help organize the steelworkers, lecturing them on the interlocking directorships of the British Empire Steel Corporation and also denouncing the British Empire – "on which the sun never sets and wages never rise."[2]

McLachlan himself went on to Toronto, where he attended the second annual convention of the Workers' Party in February 1923. There he found the organizers pleased with the achievements of the party's first year of activity, which had managed to recruit a membership of some 4,000 people. The party's appeal in Nova Scotia was one of the chief causes of satisfaction; according to the industrial organizer, "among miners and railroaders, our success has been remarkable." The earlier underground Communist Party now seemed unnecessary, and in any event the Communist International was advising its member organizations to build a "united front from below" by coming out openly as revolutionary organizations. After a long debate, plans were made to abolish the distinctions between the so-called open "A" party and the underground "Z" party: "The year's experience has proved, without possibility of contradiction, that open 'Z' activity is the only practicable method of carrying our message to the masses with any measure of success."[3]

No Maritimers had attended earlier party meetings, but now District 1, as the region was designated, seemed to hold great promise. At the opening of the meetings there were twenty delegates present, three of them from Nova Scotia. McLachlan held credentials both as a delegate from the Glace Bay branch of the Workers' Party and as a non-voting fraternal delegate from District 26. His importance was recognized when he was elected one of the five presiding officers for the convention and given a place on an enlarged party executive. There is no record of McLachlan's part in the debates over the party's future, but it is clear that he impressed observers as an agitator of the first order. According to one letter, probably by Tim Buck, McLachlan "had a great time, gave interviews to the reporters, shocked them all with his ideas about strikes etc, spoke in the Labor Temple, The Globe Theatre, and raised hell in general."[4]

In Toronto that month there was also discussion about building an alliance with miners in western Canada. Party leaders were anxious to have McLachlan travel to the Alberta coal towns for May Day meetings. McLachlan himself was enthusiastic about visiting District 18, where the coal miners also faced their own problems with the international union. He was disappointed that none of the western miners, some of whom he knew as former Nova Scotians, were present at the convention. But for the moment he was returning to Cape Breton, where there was so much to be done. As one correspondent reassured the western-ers: "Jim McLachlan is figuring on taking his trip through your District this spring, he has already been given a months leave of absence by the district executive board, and would have been in Alberta for May-Day, but for the fact that Alex Howat is spending the whole month of May in Nova Scotia starting with May-Day, and Jim wants to be there."[5]

The First of May was a day for building solidarity across borders, and for the occasion Alexander Howat seemed an appropriate choice as a visiting speaker and guest of honour. Howat was the controversial coal miners' leader from Kansas who was leading opposition to John L. Lewis inside the UMW. For his defiance of new labour laws in Kansas restricting the miners' right to strike, Howat had been tried and jailed by the state authorities and removed from office as district president by Lewis. Howat was an obvious ally for District 26 within the UMW, and McLachlan was eager to introduce the coal miners to a sympathetic representative of international solidarity. Several locals voted money to support the trip and Howat's visit was heavily advertised.[6]

The advance billing for May Day also aroused local anxieties. In early April a clergyman in New Aberdeen advised the premier of Nova Scotia that "foreign agitators" such as Howat should be stopped at the border: "It will help the sane and sober element of the miners to shake off the incubus of the 'Red' rule ... It is vain to think of accomplishing anything by the presence of the police if such men are given the freedom of the country and allowed to go through the mining districts holding meetings in the interest of revolution. The most effective way to head it off is to debar them from entering the country. Now is the time to act." Howat never reached Glace Bay. He was taken off the train by immigration agents at McAdam Junction, New Brunswick, and refused admission to Canada. McLachlan held Besco president Roy Wolvin personally responsible for the interference: "In the Federal Government one of your Directors, Mr. Gouin, is minister of Justice, and your own Mr. E.M. McDonald has considerable authority with the Cabinet and, I believe, [is] slated for Minister of Militia, and with these facts in mind the miners here believe that what you say 'goes' with the Federal Government."[7]

On the First of May, few miners appeared at work and most of the pits were idle. For the Sydney *Post*, "the May Day parade was nothing but a failure" and included only 1,300 marchers, few of them "born and bred Cape Bretoners." But the *Maritime Labor Herald* pronounced the day a great success and claimed as many as 4,000 marchers in the parade. At the public meeting at the Alexandra Rink, with Mayor Dan Willie Morrison in the chair, an audience of thousands heard performances of "The Internationale" and "The Red Flag" and listened to a long list of local speakers, including some in Ukrainian. McLachlan ended the event with a rousing speech:

All Hail May Day! The day of all the 365 days in the year when the world's Workers throw off their boss for a few short hours; leave mine, mill and factory, and take time to look back over the road over which they have travelled in the battle and struggle for bread; the day in which to draw inspiration from victories won, and above all to learn well the lessons purchased so dearly by bitter defeats ...

This May Day we shall celebrate a Labor movement which really moves in spite of Labor officialdom ... Only a few short years ago the miners of Nova Scotia were on their knees, afraid of the boss, while he kicked them in his contempt. The miners were reasonable then; today they are off their knees, and stand erect and organized, drilling and disciplining themselves for the day when they shall be in the saddle ...

The workers of this land are our comrades and brothers, the capitalists of this land our robber enemies, the complete solidarity of the former is our hope, the complete extermination of the latter our aim.[8]

All this activity attracted attention beyond Cape Breton. Reports of alarming developments in the Maritime provinces circulated widely. A New York magazine, for instance, announced that the Maritimes were becoming almost unrecognizable: "In a comparatively brief period the Maritime Provinces of Canada were transformed from a staid and prosaic territory into a hotbed of Communism, where incendiary speeches, violence and sabotage prevail with no interference from the civil authorities of the affected districts." Among the "Reds of Eastern Canada," McLachlan was identified as "the chief firebrand."[9]

Moscow and Indianapolis

The spectre of the Red International haunted UMW headquarters at the Merchants' Bank in Indianapolis. All through the winter of 1923 discussion of District 26 occupied a prominent place on the agenda of the international board meetings. There was the issue of irregular elections in 1922 and the seating of the board member for District 26. There were unpaid assessments levied on the district for support of the 1922 strike in the American fields. There was the problem that Nova Scotia had accepted a reduction in wages in 1922, contrary to the stated "no backward step" policy of the UMW. But most of all there was the Red International.

At this time President John L. Lewis was carefully consolidating his control of the union and grooming his own image as a business-minded union leader. The price of labour peace, however, was acceptance of the union contract, and Lewis was determined to demonstrate that his union was devoted to the maintenance of this form of industrial legality. As David Montgomery has shown, the 1920s was a significant moment in the history of labour in North America, when many of the democratic ideals of labour radicalism and workers' control were submerged by the gospel of business unionism and industrial legality. It is notable that two of the most influential twentieth-century American labour leaders served their apprenticeship in the UMW under Lewis. Among Lewis's chief lieutenants were secretary-treasurer William Green and vice-president Philip Murray; Green would become head of the American Federation of Labor and Murray would later lead the Congress of Industrial Organizations (CIO). In the 1920s Murray and Green were schooled by Lewis, and the Nova Scotia case was a prime lesson.[10]

The plan to join the Red International of Labour Unions was one of the radical ideas endorsed at the June convention in 1922. It had been a flamboyant gesture, but the union leaders in fact pursued a cautious policy, writing to request a ruling from Lewis on the district's right to join the Red International. McLachlan wrote first on 15 December 1922 and then with additional information on 2 January 1923. He pointed out that the Red International was opposed to dual unionism and had even requested the Industrial Workers of the World and the One Big Union to join the AFL. He also pointed out that, although the AFL itself had withdrawn from the International Federation of Trade Unions, formed in 1919 and based in Amsterdam, the Trades and Labour Congress of Canada, exercising its autonomy, continued to belong to that body and District 26 should enjoy similar rights to join an international organization. McLachlan sent Lewis a copy of the proceedings and constitution of the Red International and even invited him, in a comradely way, to scoff at the suspicions of governments: "I trust this book shall reach you alright. I do not forget that my 'Democratic' government on the north of the line and your 'Democratic' government to the South still ration out to us the ideas that we should read and hear, and both have flunkies enough in their employ between here and Indianapolis to destroy the book before it reaches you."[11]

The book arrived in Indianapolis without incident and on 8 January Lewis opened the meetings of the international board with the controversial documents in his hand. The Nova Scotia issue was debated for the better part of the day. District 26 President Dan Livingstone was present for the meeting and for one long afternoon was questioned by members of the board, which still included Silby Barrett. Reports of dissension in District 26 were greatly exaggerated, Livingstone claimed, and he assured the board that the district would comply with the international's ruling on the Red International. But the long cross-examination left no doubt that Livingstone, and probably other district leaders, were revolutionaries: "I told your International President when I came here first that I was a radical. I am a radical yet. I have been a radical since I was that high. I have seen the beast of capitalism in all its horrors before I was nine years old. I hate the capitalist class of this and all countries, and I would kill capitalism tomorrow. I challenge the function of the International Board to curtail my efforts in freeing myself and the class I belong to."[12]

A few days later Vice-President Philip Murray presented the board with a long report. The Red International was denounced as "an outgrowth of the One Big Union" and was said to have for its purpose "first – control, and afterward the destruction of the bona fide trade union movement." Moreover, it was said, the organization "not only sanctions, but in fact urges the workers to resort to street uprisings, mob demonstrations, violence, or any other method that they may deem expedient for the accomplishment of their purpose." The constitutions of the Red International and the UMW were found to be in contradiction. Accordingly, the Red International should be considered a dual organization, and no unit of the UMW could be permitted to affiliate. Members who did join, like those who belonged to the Ku Klux Klan and other prohibited organizations, were liable to expulsion from the UMW. District 26 itself was ordered to withdraw its application, and the alternative was spelled out: the district would be suspended and the international union would assume direct control of local affairs. The report was adopted quickly and, on Barrett's suggestion, it was agreed that copies of the report be mailed to all local unions in District 26. It was also given wide publicity in the pages of the *United Mine Workers' Journal* and the *American Federationist.*[13]

Back in District 26 the union leaders saw no choice but to comply. On 2 February McLachlan reported briefly to Lewis on the meeting of the district board: "A motion was passed that we comply with the decision of the International Executive Board." The following day, however, McLachlan gave notice that the decision would be appealed to the next UMW convention. The district was backing down, but not without some extended words of protest: "Upon examination of your committee's findings, District #26 Executive Board desires to point out that the Red Labor Union is not for the purpose of destroying the trade union movement, and the International Executive Board was utterly unable to quote anything from the 'Red Labor Union' even remotely hinting at such a proposition. The statement that the Red International is an outgrowth of the O.B.U. is amazing and has no foundation in fact." Then, after citing the program of the Red International, McLachlan went on to remind the UMW that passages describing the class struggle could be easily confirmed by recent episodes in the American coalfields:

> This section describes events in the past which have arisen out of the oppressive economical conditions which the workers found themselves in, and which again they shall find themselves in in the future. Does the Executive Board not remember Logan and Herrin? We hail with delight the march of the United Mine Workers into Logan County, and the gallant attempt they made to free their brothers from the thug and gunmen of capitalist class. With joy we hail the Mine Workers of Herrin who rose in their might and wiped that district clean of the gun-flunkies of capitalism, to condemn such men is to side with the most virulent oppressors of the workers in America.

As for upholding collective agreements, here, too, the UMW was promoting a too-narrow interpretation of the meaning of industrial legality:

> The "sanctity" of contracts has become of late years a vanishing quality. Where is the mine worker who in his every day toil does not find his employer continually interpreting the contract to his own financial advantage, if not openly violating it? Where was the

"sanctity" of the mine workers' contract in 1921 when the opera-tors refused absolutely to abide by the clause in the contract providing for a joint conference, and thus brought about five long months of struggle and starvation for the workers? Has not the International Executive Board violated their pledged word and agreement drafted at Sydney, N.S. February 22nd, 1919, when they deny the right of "complete autonomy" to District No. 26 and refuse the miners of Nova Scotia the right to strengthen their economic position by linking up with the workers of the world?

For the moment, however, District 26 was withdrawing its application to the Red International, mindful of the threat that the autonomy of the district would be suspended: "Remembering Kansas and District #18, and how these Districts were split into fragments, we are prepared to retreat from almost any position, rather than give anybody the opportunity to smash our solidarity. The onus for splitting this District shall never rest on this Executive Board."[14]

McLachlan still signed his letters to Lewis with customary fraternal greetings, but this was the language of opposition. At UMW headquar-ters, District 26 was now firmly identified not only with the Red International but also with the internal opposition to Lewis. The Red International was a highly visible symbol of difference, but what was at stake was a challenge to the Lewis vision of the UMW as a business-minded union under the authority of a chief executive officer. Like other parts of the union, District 26 was on a collision course with Indianapolis. The activities of Howat and other dissidents were closely followed in Nova Scotia, and a Conference of Progressive Miners was organized in early June in Pennsylvania, with two Nova Scotia delegates in attendance.[15]

McLachlan had also appealed to the Red International itself, sending them a copy of the UMW statement condemning the Red International as a dual union. In April he was able to submit a reply from Moscow, and in an accompanying letter he urged Lewis and the UMW to correct their views: "After reading this letter, I feel sure that both you yourself and the International Executive Board shall feel that they were in error when you stated that the purpose of the Red International of Labor

Unions is, 'first, control, and afterward destruction of the bona-fide trade union movement.' The statement that the Red Labor Union is an outgrowth of the O.B.U. was a most pitiable reflection on the intelligence of the leaders of our great organization ..."

Pointing out that the OBU was not formed in 1918 but in the summer of 1919, McLachlan charged the UMW leaders with an embarrassing ignorance: "Men who are unacquainted with the current labor history of their own country certainly are not in a position to discuss the current history of the world movement." If such a mistake could be made about the OBU, it was also possible that their view of the Red International was distorted: "I do not know whether you will be prepared to take the word of the men who have written the enclosed letter that the R.I.L.U. is not a dual union, but is strictly opposed to dual unionism."[16]

None of this was convincing, and it was clear that the international union would continue to undermine the district leadership. Silby Barrett made no secret of his own ambitions at this stage and told the Sydney *Post* that he fully expected the district officers to be removed and himself to be placed in charge.[17] Lewis followed a more cautious strategy and dispatched a five-man committee of investigation to Nova Scotia which discovered not only "a splendid feeling of loyalty to the United Mine Workers" but also "ample evidence of the machinations of the red outfit of Moscow." Barrett must have been disappointed to find that in some ways this was also a conciliatory report which recognized that the influence of the radicals in District 26 could not be easily challenged. The committee recommended that Alex Stewart be seated as board member, implicitly recognizing the validity of the elections in August 1922. New elections were ordered for July 1923, but this was not an alarming condition since district elections were already set for August 1923.[18]

Restoration of the 1921 wage rates, the committee found, had wide support, and it even made efforts to convince Besco to reopen the contract. At a four-hour meeting with company officials, the UMW emissaries argued that Nova Scotia was the only district where wage reductions were forced upon the miners in 1922 and that there was no justification for a continuance of the exceedingly low wage standards.

McLachlan pressed the case with his own special vigour and listed a series of individual "punctures, tears and rents" in the contract: "This 'sacredness of contract' only holds good for the Coal Company when it is to their financial benefit."[19] The meeting was a failure, however, and the committee concluded that "little hope can be entertained for reopening the contract unless the British Empire Steel Company makes a change in policy."

There was an extended debate on District 26 at the international board meeting, and the committee's report was adopted. Vice-President Murray argued that the report did not go far enough: "Some definite step should be taken toward punishing the members in District 26 who were responsible for the present condition of affairs there." Meanwhile, Stewart replaced Barrett as international board member, but not before Lewis delivered an extended lecture on the requirements of "loyal support and loyal service." It was clear that Lewis subscribed to his own version of democratic centralism and regarded the board member as an agent of the international union more than as a representative of the district. Indeed, Barrett himself, now occupying no elected position, would continue to serve Lewis in Glace Bay as an international representative. After considerable discussion, given that annual elections were already expected to take place in August, a proposal to send a committee to Nova Scotia to supervise new elections was withdrawn: "It was felt by the Board members that the autonomy of the District should not be interfered with in connection with their election."[20]

This was not everything that Lewis wanted, but he was able to secure consent for a stiff message to the District 26 convention, already in session at New Glasgow. It was a provocative telegram, which not only conveyed the board's decisions but also requested the convention to exclude unsuitable candidates from the next election: "There is no room in the United Mine Workers for men who seek to hold office therein for purpose of enhancing the welfare of an aggregation which seeks the control and later destruction of our great Union." Delegates were invited "to exercise their moral force to purge our Union in that field of its open and secret enemies."[21]

News of the board decisions reached New Glasgow on 19 June, where the district convention was already in session. The delegates must have been pleased by the report. Stewart was to be seated as their international board member. There was also obvious support for regaining the 1921 rates, even if the district officers were being blamed for the reduction of 1922. As for the Red International, it would no longer be an issue, since the application "has been withdrawn and shall not be made again until consent of International Union has been obtained." Lewis's attempt to disqualify the district officers from running in new elections was denounced in a message endorsed by a unanimous standing vote of the convention. The eligibility of candidates for office, the delegates declared, would continue to be governed by the normal provisions of the union constitution: "This convention declares that it shall firmly stand by the principle that in District 26 we shall defend freedom of thought, whether expressed by tongue or pen, and cannot consent to enact special rules to debar any members running an election in this District because of their belief, and this convention is amazed at your request to violate ideals upon which our great Union has been built."[22]

But relations with Indianapolis and Moscow were not the main themes of the New Glasgow convention. Above all, the delegates wanted to restore the 1921 rates, the symbolic standard of post-war achievement and the goal for which the international union itself had fought "no backward step" in 1922. Unanimously, they voted to inform Wolvin that they were determined to secure the restoration of the 1921 rates, even at the cost of repudiating the existing agreement. Just as the corporation had refused to abide by the existing rates in January 1922, now the coal miners would no longer abide by the present contract. McLachlan explained: "When our people were hungry you remember your action in January, 1922, flouting the law of this country and slashing the men's wages without warning. The miners of Nova Scotia have not forgotten those cruel days."[23]

After receiving this warning, Wolvin at once sent a telegram to Lewis, quoting McLachlan's words and reminding Lewis that the UMW contract remained in force until January 1924: "Please telegraph earliest possible if your organization approves telegram herein quoted, which proposes to violate contract now in effect. Would like answer in time reply McLachlan." Wolvin followed up with phone calls to Lewis as well.

What would Lewis do if the district broke its contract? Lewis played his cards close to the chest: "That was a matter upon which he could not make an expression at that time." But Lewis also informed Wolvin flatly that "the United Mine Workers of America had never repudiated a contract."[24]

At the same time, Lewis put the district on notice. He informed Livingstone by telegram that the convention's action was "an unwarranted violation of traditional and consistent policies of United Mine Workers which believes in integrity of contract and strict adherence to its provisions by all parties ... No district of United Mine Workers has ever repudiated a joint agreement after it had been accepted by membership affected and International Executive Board cannot permit District twenty six to take ill-considered action which will violate every rule of honorable joint relationship and bring our union into public disrepute." Moreover, Lewis warned, under the UMW constitution no district could engage in a strike without the sanction of the international office. Meanwhile, as a sign of reassurance, Lewis also sent a copy of the telegram to Wolvin's office in Montreal. The Besco president replied with enthusiasm: "Permit me to say that your action is the one which I fully expected the United Mine Workers to take, but taking it in the vigorous manner which you have, it is very much appreciated."[25]

Would the district uphold the UMW standard and go on strike for the 1921 rates, or would it accept the limitations of the existing contract and work at substandard rates until 1924? It was a test of priorities for the coal miners and of the principle of industrial legality for the union. These were issues sufficient to bring about a full-scale confrontation between Glace Bay and Indianapolis, and it would be put to the membership of District 26 in a strike vote at the beginning of July. As the delegates clambered aboard their trains and returned home from New Glasgow, events in Sydney were already touching off another explosion in District 26.

Steel

In 1907 Sir William Cornelius Van Horne painted a fine oil portrait of the steel plant. Van Horne – general manager and then president of the

Canadian Pacific Railway – was a member of the board of directors of
Dominion Iron and Steel as well, and the point of view is predictably
proprietorial. The night sky and the harbour waters are illuminated
with the fire and heat of industry. The mills and furnaces sit in a low,
gloomy light. There is no evidence of the thousands of workers who
toiled below, seven days a week, often twelve hours a day, for wages as
low as fifteen cents an hour. "Steel is the backbone of Sydney," wrote
H.M. Bartholomew in the *Maritime Labor Herald*: "The long rows of
ugly chimneys belching forth torrents of smoke and fire bear witness
to the fact (of which the papers are so proud) that Sydney is a town of
steel." But the imagery of industrial progress was supported by
another reality: "Under this small forest of chimneys toil the slaves
of steel – chained, by grim necessity, to the chariot of a brutal,
relentless corporation."[26]

In the winter of 1923 the chimneys of the steel plant grew cold and
silent as the steelworkers once more launched a struggle for recognition
of their union. Their demands were simple: an eight-hour day, an
increase in pay, and, above all else, recognition of their union. They had
been defeated several times before over the past two decades, but this
time, the organizers believed, it would be different. "Every day in every
way," organizers boasted, "we are getting stronger and stronger." By
February the union claimed support from more than 60 per cent of the
steelworkers. Suddenly, without notice, a walkout started in the nail
mill on 13 February and spread rapidly through the plant. A union
leader by the name of Sid "Hambone" McNeil had been fired for
disobeying orders and the incident at once became a test of the
union's strength.

The strike was on. The union claimed that 3,000 men walked out,
but company officials placed the numbers much lower, 600 at first, later
1,200. The strikers organized themselves in paramilitary style, working
eight-hour shifts on the roads and gates surrounding the plant, con-
sciously following the example of the miners the previous summer.
Highways and roads were blocked by pickets and barricades. Trains and
trucks were being stopped and searched. Officials and other loyal
employees were virtually imprisoned in the plant and even food supplies and mattresses were not being admitted. At the coke ovens,

strikebreakers were chased out of the plant and other strikebreakers were "serenaded" by the crowds and escorted home. The company police were swamped by the crowds and the Sydney police chief was being restrained by city councillors sympathetic to the strikers. By the fourth day the company was reeling from the effects of the strike. Wolvin complained bitterly to the minister of labour that there had been no notice and no negotiations preceding the strike and now the company was being held up for ransom. All of this was taking place in sub-zero weather. The plant itself was starting to freeze up and the coke ovens were in danger. From Montreal, Wolvin warned that if the strike did not end soon "the plant might be so seriously damaged that manufacture of steel might never be again undertaken there."[27]

Throughout the strike, the coal miners waited in the background, but it was obvious that they were planning to join the battle. A Montreal newspaper commented that efforts to unite the miners' and steelworkers' unions had created "something like a local OBU, and the attitude of the union leaders has been more aggressive in consequence." "Shall union coal make scab steel?" That week McLachlan appealed to the coal miners to make common cause with the steelworkers, again pointing out the virtues of a united front: "What a fine thing it would be for miners, steel workers, railwaymen, and those employed in the British Empire Steel Corporation's steamers to join hands in this fight and wrest from this Corporation a decent Canadian living for every man employed in these industries." As for those who claimed that the miners were under contract and could not go on strike, McLachlan pointed out that the current contract was not the same as the controversial Montreal Agreement of 1920:

> There is no "stoppage of work" clause in this contract. In the old Montreal Agreement such a clause did exist but the Company hypocritically with the assistance of Union Officials interpret that clause to mean that the Company could stop work for any reason and throw the men idle, but the men could stop work for no reason. This present contract has no such provisions in it. All that the contract calls for is for a stated wage for a stated amount of work. The company may lay you men idle as they are doing

without breaking this contract. On the other hand you men could lay the company's mines idle without breaking the Contract.[28]

The coal miners did not act, for at the end of the week Besco General Superintendant W.H. Bischoff sent for the executive of the steelworkers' union. As Forman Waye, who was then an officer of the union though not a Besco employee, later recalled, Bischoff "promised us if we got the men back to work they would give us full union recognition." On paper, however, the company had promised much less than this: only to reconsider the case of Sid McNeil. Still, the union leaders believed that the strike was a victory. The union had shown its power and the company had been forced to negotiate with the union leaders. Celebrating their victory, steelworkers marched through the streets late into the night.

The steelworkers had gambled that all this would be enough to bring the corporation to heel, but they were wrong. On 21 February the company completed its investigation of McNeil's dismissal and confirmed that he was being fired for insubordination. Then came arrests on warrants sworn out by the chief of police: by the end of March more than thirty steelworkers were charged with trespassing, intimidation, theft, and unlawful assembly for their activities during the strike. The blacklist at the plant grew longer. In June the corporation's board of directors once more rejected union recognition and gave Wolvin a vote of confidence. Forman Waye later compared the events to the conclusion of Wat Tyler's Rebellion in 1381: "When the King went out of London to meet his rebellious subjects, he promised them that all their wrongs would be righted and when they dispersed to their homes he had them all hanged ... Needless to say, once we got the men back to work the management forgot their promises and began to figuratively hang the steelworkers separately, until it all culminated in the July strike."[29]

As far as Wolvin was concerned, the real cause of the strike was to be found in an exotic factor called "Cape Breton Bolshevism." Following the defeat of the February strike, Wolvin made one of his rare personal appearances in Sydney in order to attend a meeting of the Board of Trade. No reports of his speech were published, but it was the talk of the town throughout the month of March. Wolvin had issued an ultimatum to the local business community: "Drive the radicals out of Cape Breton, or he would withdraw his capital from this Island and allow the grass to grow on the streets of Sydney." A second meeting of the Board of Trade three weeks later resulted in a public resolution against "Cape Breton Bolshevism."[30]

"The whole resolution breathes the spirit of Mussolini without having the open courage of Mussolini behind it," charged McLachlan. He now seized the opportunity to issue a public letter to the prime minister, signed also by Paul McNeil, secretary of the steelworkers' union. Here they provided their own definition of "Cape Breton Bolshevism":

"Cape Breton Bolshevism" consists in the working class of Cape Breton employed in the Steel Works and the Coal Mines exercising the right handed down to them by their British forefathers to walk off the steel plant to the very last man employed and to walk out of the coal mines and leave the Directors of the British Empire Steel Corporation to care for these plants as best they may. This right is being exercised in Cape Breton because of the fierce exploitation of labor carried on by the British Empire Steel Corporation.

They concluded with a call for a "thorough investigation" into Wolvin's "suppressed speech," but the main message was one of defiance: "We are writing this to inform you and your Government that Ten Thousand working men in Cape Breton are accepting the challenge of the Sydney Board of Trade and are inviting them to start in now and drive out the humblest 'Bolshevik' in our ranks."[31]

The controversy was brought to the floor of the House of Commons by J.S. Woodsworth, but the prime minister's response is not recorded. As an authority on industrial relations he could not fail to recognize a classic contest between the rights of capital and the rights of labour. According to King's theories of industrial relations, only an "impartial umpire" in the form of an interventionist government could restore harmony in such situations. Was it perhaps time for another conciliation board or even a royal commission? An official of the Department of Labour paid a desultory visit first to Wolvin in Montreal and then to Sydney. In Montreal he learned that there would be no eight-hour day in the steel plant and no union recognition, though there would be a small increase of wages effective almost at once. Then in Sydney he met with the steelworkers' leaders, who insisted that the time for investigations had passed: "The matter can only be settled by Mr. Wolvin, and that by accepting the terms of our demands." From McLachlan and Livingstone, who were also in attendance, he learned that "the Miners' Union was to a man with the steelworkers in this fight." McLachlan underlined the message: "He wanted it understood that the men would recognize their opportunity, and would not fritter away any time in dealing with Royal Commissions or a Board; that they would take advantage of their opportunities."[32]

King was not a politician to act where action could be avoided, but the provincial government preferred to make "every preparation necessary to preserve law and order." The new premier of Nova Scotia, E.H. Armstrong, was a south shore lawyer who had sat in the legislative assembly since 1906; he had served as commissioner of public works and mines since 1911, although it was said unkindly of him that he did not know the difference between a steel plant and a coal mine. He became premier on George H. Murray's retirement in January 1923, and one month later the steel strike had taken him by surprise. This time he was ready for trouble. In expectation of another eruption at the steel plant, a provincial police force was mobilized and stationed in Sydney, where it became known locally as "Armstrong's Army." If he had any doubts, Armstrong was pleased to receive an encouraging message from his predecessor, ex-premier Murray: "I am glad to see you are taking no nonsense from the 'reds.' That is the proper attitude, even if a political issue were created."[33]

The steel strike did not materialize on 1 April as expected, nor even on May Day. But before their departure from Sydney in May, "Armstrong's Army" carried out a series of raids in quest of what was described as "literature of a seditious nature." Riding into Glace Bay on the evening of 14 May, a squad of provincial police performed a hurried search of union offices. They failed to find any literature of the desired type but were able to seize the red flag which had been the object of much attention in the May Day parade two weeks earlier. The following night, the police also visited several residences, and a squad of 12 policemen arrived at McLachlan's home on Steele's Hill armed with a warrant for the arrest of Malcolm Bruce.

Among the Workers' Party crowd, McLachlan was particularly impressed by Bruce. A Prince Edward Islander by birth and a carpenter by trade, Bruce was a veteran of the Rocky Mountain mine wars, where he had known Big Bill Haywood. Back in Canada, Bruce joined the Socialist Party, the One Big Union, and then the Workers' Party, and in 1923 he was editor of *The Worker*. The police arrived on horseback at Steele's Hill that night, armed with guns and flashlights, looking to arrest Bruce for seditious remarks he was alleged to have made at a public meeting at the Savoy Theatre in downtown Glace Bay. McLachlan later described the episode in comic terms: "In the searching of my home, my wife suggested to the police that 'Malcolm might be in the sixty-egg incubator beneath the bed.' The incubator was hauled out and Bruce duly searched for. They looked in hand-grips, in a churn, in drawers, between the pages of books, and inside private letters – for Malcolm Bruce."

By this time, Bruce had already left town on the train, unaware that the police were looking for him. When he reached Toronto and learned the news, he turned around and came back to Glace Bay. Then, as McLachlan told the story, he waited to be arrested:

He arrived in Glace Bay on Saturday morning and hung around town for two days waiting for an officer to take him. He couldn't find anybody to do it. He couldn't break into jail. He finally grew tired of waiting for somebody to arrest him and he went and presented himself to the magistrate ... The great manhunt for a week for Bruce was over, the show a complete flop. Bruce was back in Glace Bay, and worse still, he was again holding meetings bigger than ever. Everybody wanted to see and hear the man whom the whole police force of Nova Scotia had been hunting.

As for the charges of sedition, McLachlan dismissed them with a joke. "How many miners will be ready to swear that Bruce didn't make the statements attributed to him?" a reporter asked. "Almost the full of the Savoy theatre," McLachlan replied.[34]

Still, there was no doubt that the attorney general's office was serious about hunting down the reds. At Steele's Hill the catch of the evening was a copy of the constitution of the Red International. This reading material was forwarded directly to the attorney general, Walter J. O'Hearn, who was already planning legal action against McLachlan at this stage. O'Hearn was studying the precedents to be drawn from the prosecution of labour radicals in Winnipeg in 1919. "Book found possession McLachlan filled with sedition," he telegraphed Premier Armstrong. "Will peruse 1919 amendment and King vs. Russell in Ottawa before advising you."[35]

Sympathetic Strike

From a distance the coal banks were nothing more than huge mountains of rock, dark and dull in the open air, often covered with drifts of snow. All winter it was common to heave coal into storage piles in the colliery yards to wait for the opening of the shipping season and eventual shipment to the industrial markets. These broken coal piles represented huge accumulations of labour power, stored energy, and potential profits. And, although they seemed to be inert, the coal banks were also living and breathing bodies of rock. When exposed to the air and sun at the end of winter, the ancient organic matter began to take on a life of its own. As currents of air ran through the storage piles, hot spots erupted here and there. The temperature could be measured regularly with iron rods, and with proper attendance, heat was allowed to escape through the cone. In fact, the coal bank was a kind of man-made volcano, and there was always the danger of combustion, even a conflagration.

As the bright summer days of 1923 arrived in the skies, and the woods at last grew green and bushy, industrial Cape Breton was nearing the point of combustion. Defeated and betrayed, the steelworkers' union had grown in numbers and was determined to keep pressing the union cause. The coal miners were standing by, preparing to strike for the 1921 rates and ready to aid the steelworkers as well. Malcolm Bruce considered that McLachlan's influence was supreme among the coal miners and observed that he had never seen such militant spirit among miners since the heyday of the Western Federation of Miners.[36] In Montreal, Roy Wolvin waited in his offices in the Canada Cement Building. In Halifax, Premier Armstrong and Attorney General O'Hearn watched for signs of trouble. Farther away in Atlantic City, John L. Lewis also waited for news from Nova Scotia.

When the directors of the company once more turned down the union's call for recognition, the steelworkers announced a strike and started to shut down the plant on the morning of 28 June. This time they were confident of success. According to police reports, the union now claimed support from 2,800 of the 3,500 workers and "the spirit of the union members is said to be excellent ... McLachlan and his associates are confident that a 100% organization will be effected in a short time."[37] The shutdown began with the familiar rowdy scenes at the plant gates. Crowds of pickets blocked traffic and stopped strike-breakers from entering the yards. At night masked men broke into the plant and dragged workers out of the boilerhouses and coke ovens. Attempts to read the Riot Act were met with howls of derision and flying stones. This time there was no delay in bringing outside forces onto the scene. The first soldiers arrived from Halifax on 30 June. They set up their tents on company property and erected machine guns and search lights at the plant gates. The provincial police were also reassembled and they arrived in Sydney on Sunday 1 July, under the command of an elegant officer with a swagger stick, Colonel Eric McDonald.[38]

That evening at about 7.30 p.m. a squad of sixteen mounted provincial police charged through the pickets at the plant gates. Swinging their clubs, they tried to drive the strikers into the long narrow underpass below the railway tracks. Instead the men scrambled up the embankment onto the tracks, where the horses could not follow. The police charged on towards the upper end of the tunnel and headed up Victoria Road into Whitney Pier. They attacked all pedestrians who came in their way. Men, women, and children were chased off the streets, many of them escaping into yards and homes. One eager horseman galloped onto the verandah of a hotel after his victim. News of this extensive demonstration of police violence spread throughout the industrial district and the events were soon common knowledge. A short report in the RCMP dispatches that week described the events as candidly as could be expected in a police report:

"On Sunday night the Provincial Police charged the crowd through the subway and Victoria Road, with the result that quite a number of strikers and other people were injured ..."[39]

As the news circulated through the surrounding coal towns, the coal miners crowded into protest meetings to proclaim their support for the steelworkers and demand the withdrawal of troops and police. There was a twenty-four-hour pause while the union officers presented these demands to the company. Then the sympathetic strike was under way. Throughout the coalfields, work stopped at midnight on Tuesday 3 July and some ten thousand coal miners were once more on strike. On Wednesday morning the scenes at the mines resembled those of the previous summer. The horses had been removed from the pits and pickets moved in to control the mines. Coal was dumped on the tracks to prevent trains from moving out of the yard. Only a handful of officials were allowed in to operate the pumps and fans. In the pit yard at No. 2, the largest single mine, the great coal bank was smouldering in the heat. Sparks and smoke were starting to rise into the still air. The miners watched impassively as a small group of volunteers worked to limit the fires.

There is no evidence that McLachlan was personally present in Sydney on 1 July, but he was soon at the centre of the fray. He spoke at the union meetings in Glace Bay on 2 July where demands for the withdrawal of troops and police were approved. First he piloted the strike plans through the union executive. Then he weathered a stormy meeting with company officials, who were demanding the union help control the fire on the coal bank at No. 2. McLachlan's reply became notorious among company officials, who claimed he said, "To hell with the property of the British Empire Steel Corporation." McLachlan's own version of the statement was more qualified and phrased in characteristic language: "If the men, women and children were to be placed in the scales against the interests and value of property, then to hell with your property."[40]

As the sympathetic strike began, the miners themselves were also voting, narrowly as it turned out, to support a strike of their own for the 1921 rates. With these events under way, McLachlan could see that the class struggle was again advancing surely enough. For a few minutes he thought back to 1919, the year when Canada had come as close as ever to a country-wide general strike, and he told western miners that the way to help Nova Scotia was "to strike every man from Vancouver to Sydney."[41]

But for the time being it was necessary to ensure that the miners were honouring their pledge to the steelworkers. On the morning of 4 July McLachlan composed the fateful, passionate letter to the local unions of District 26 that would become the central document in his trial:

To officers and members of Local Unions:

Brothers: This office has been informed that all the Waterford, Sydney Mines and Glace Bay sub-districts are out on strike this morning as a protest against the importation of Provincial Police and Federal troops into Sydney to intimidate the steel workers into continuing work at 32¢ per hour. On Sunday night last these Provincial Police in the most brutal manner rode down the people at Whitney Pier who were on the street, most of whom were coming from Church. Neither age, sex or physical disabilities were proof against these brutes. One old woman over seventy years of age was beaten into insensibility and may die. A boy nine years old was trampled under the horses' feet and his breast bone crushed in. One woman was beaten over the head with a police club and gave premature birth to a child. The child is dead and the woman's life is despaired of. Men and women were beaten up inside their own homes. Against the brutes the miners are on strike. The Government of Nova Scotia is the guilty and responsible party for this crime. No miner or mine worker can remain at work while this Government turns Sydney into a jungle; to do so is to sink your manhood and allow Armstrong and his miserable bunch of grafting politicians to trample your last shred of freedom in the sand. Call a meeting of your Local at once and decide to spread the fight against Armstrong to every mine in Nova Scotia. Act at once. Tomorrow may be too late.[42]

It was at once a report from the secretary-treasurer and a call to arms. The letter was both an explanation of the causes of the sympathetic strike and an attempt to spread the protest, especially to the mainland coalfields. And it was vintage McLachlan: the brutality of the police and the corruption of the government were presented as a challenge to the very manhood and natural rights of the coal miners.

As usual with district correspondence, a stencil was prepared and copies of the letter, over McLachlan's official signature, were placed in the mail to the locals. Another copy, addressed to Besco vice-president D.H. McDougall, the senior company official resident in Cape Breton, was taken personally by union president Dan Livingstone and delivered to the company offices in Glace Bay.[43]

To this declaration there was a swift and unexpected response from Halifax. It was the opportunity O'Hearn wanted. On 6 July Sydney police chief J.B. McCormick received a telegram from the attorney general informing him that warrants had been issued in Halifax for the arrest of McLachlan and Livingstone. The charges were described as "unlawfully publishing false tales whereby injury or mischief was likely to be occasioned to a public interest, namely the government and provincial police of Nova Scotia, contrary to Sec. 136 of the [criminal] code." With a carload of provincial police following them, Chief McCormick and his deputy drove to Glace Bay and located their quarry at the union offices. When they learned the policemen's mission, McLachlan and Livingstone were "greatly surprised" but agreed to accompany the police to Sydney.

The following day Chief McCormick and his Halifax counterpart placed the prisoners in a car and transported the two men over the winding roads along the shores of the Bras d'Or and through St Peter's to Point Tupper at the Strait of Canso. There they boarded the night train for Halifax. At the end of the journey there is a blurred newspaper photograph of the strike leaders entering the Halifax County jail. McLachlan is striding purposefully, a bowler hat on his head and a grip case in his hand. He looks as if he is late for an important meeting. The turn of events was unanticipated, but there is no air of defeat in the scene.[44]

For the rest of the month the union leaders were preoccupied by legal battles in Halifax. When they came before the stipendiary magistrate on

8 July, the crown argued that the prisoners were men of considerable public influence and "opposed allowing these men to be at large at the present time to go back to Cape Breton and continue to do acts to the injury of the public." The union's lawyer, John A. Walker, made the obvious objections: the offence was a relatively minor one and bail should be granted as a matter of course. And, in any event, the case was transparently weak: the warrant stated that the offence was committed in Halifax, but it was a matter of common knowledge that the accused were three hundred miles from Halifax at the time of the alleged crime. Nevertheless, bail was denied and the preliminary hearing was adjourned. Meanwhile, the defence lawyers scrambled to apply for a writ of habeas corpus. Finally, on 13 July, Justice J.A. Chisholm of the Supreme Court of Nova Scotia, who had served on the famous Chisholm Commission in 1917 and was one of the justices without previous ties to the coal companies, set bail at $2,000 each. Even then, at O'Hearn's insistence, there was another hearing on 24 July, at which time bail was continued. Then the preliminary hearing resumed on 2 August.[45] In and out of custody during these weeks, the union leaders were kept busy by the various legal proceedings. The sudden arrests and the confusion that followed had succeeded in removing McLachlan from his place at the centre of the storm.

The Byng Agreement

Julian Hedworth George Byng, nicknamed Bungo during his schooldays at Eton and given the title Baron Byng of Vimy and Thorpe-le-Soken for his part in the Great War, was named as governor general and commander-in-chief of the Dominion of Canada in the summer of 1921. It was not a surprising choice, for Byng had commanded the Canadian Corps during its heroic days on the Western front. A punctilious soldier with a record of service in India, South Africa, and Egypt, Byng had also proved a popular commander with his troops, impatient with political interference and not slow to promote able Canadians or listen to the lower ranks. The capture of Vimy Ridge in 1917 had brought Byng his title and had won the Canadian Corps its reputation as a fighting force. As governor general Byng was conscious of the limited powers of the office, but he did not hesitate to make candid comments about social problems of the day. On one visit to Montreal he lectured upper-class matrons about the poverty and squalor of the city's slums and on another occasion, speaking to Calgary businessmen, he quoted John Ruskin to them on "the licentious luxury of the rich."[46]

In the summer of 1923 the governor general was making his way by train on an extended tour of the Maritimes. This visit was timed to coincide with the 150th anniversary of the landing of the famous Scottish immigrant ship, the *Hector*, at Pictou. There would be bands and parades, honour guards to inspect, and a monument to unveil. There would even be a re-enactment of the vessel's entry into port, although as it turned out the tides prevented the boat from arriving on time.[47] Prime Minister King had already written a speech for the occasion but was sufficiently embarrassed by the turbulent labour scene to cancel his own plans to participate in the Pictou celebrations. Instead he went to Toronto to receive an honorary degree, and then on to Harvard to give the commencement address. But, to the prime minister's annoyance, the governor general himself became involved in the strike.

The senior politician at the celebrations was E.M. Macdonald, a portly Pictou County MP who, after years of service on the back-benches, was appointed minister of national defence in April 1923. Macdonald viewed the event as a "tremendous home-coming of Pictonians" and relished the long list of distinguished visitors and the impressive agenda of ceremonies. The strike of the coal miners was far from his mind and he was somewhat annoyed to find the industrial crisis interfering with his enjoyment of the occasion. Yet, for Macdonald, business and politics had mixed well over the years. Much of his career as a lawyer had been spent representing the interests of Dominion Coal, and, Macdonald later reminisced fondly, "it is doubtful whether any counsel were ever so amply and comfortably provided for as were the counsel of the Coal Company." In 1909 he had helped defend Dominion Coal against McLachlan's charges of conspiracy among the coal operators, and as recently as 1921 he had accompanied Roy Wolvin to England on company business.

The night before the governor general's train arrived at Pictou, Macdonald was unexpectedly called out to meet him at Scotsburn, a small station nine miles up the line from Pictou. There they paced the wooden platform as Byng explained that he had been asked to receive a delegation from the strikers. Macdonald considered the whole proposition improper from the beginning and, after some busy hours coding and decoding telegrams, the following morning he presented Byng with a telegram from the prime minister giving the same view. Byng was "very much disappointed," Macdonald recalled. "Though he was cordial and pleasant in regard to the whole matter, yet he had evidently made up his mind that he was going to receive the deputation in any event."[48]

The vice-regal railway cars stopped at Pictou for two days of festivities, and it was here that Byng sat down face to face with the union leaders on 17 July. Fresh from jail, McLachlan and Livingstone edged their way into the long narrow drawing room of the railway car and sat uncomfortably on the overstuffed furniture. Two other men were also present: Senator John Anthony McDonald of Shediac, the Amherst businessman who had originally approached the governor general about the meeting, and Dan Willie Morrison, the Glace Bay mayor and labour MLA. At the end of the conversation the men shook hands. The governor general and the mayor of Glace Bay shared a drink. The two union leaders, both teetotallers, watched. Press reports described the meeting as one of "the highest importance as it affects the present deplorable industrial situation ... No statement was given out by any present, beyond the assurance that some very important developments might be expected as a result of the deliberations." That evening the governor general went on to a glittering naval and military ball in his honour.[49]

The governor general's tour continued on into Cape Breton, where the visitors glimpsed the impoverished conditions of the industrial community and viewed the peacetime army patrolling the scene. In one of the coal towns they were presented with an eloquent letter appealing to Byng to "use your influence to give the mine workers a fair fighting chance for a decent living." In Sydney they toured the strike-bound steel plant and later attended a huge public reception, where a bodyguard of striking steelworkers helped them through the cheering crowds. Baron and Lady Byng came away impressed by the loyalty as well as the poverty of the local population. Years later Lady Byng vividly remembered this part of the trip and wrote: "I never saw a more wretched lot of hovels or a more complete lack of any attempt at social service for the employees."[50]

For their part, the union leaders came away from the meeting in the railway car believing that they had reached an agreement to end the strike. Under the "Byng agreement" as they called it, the armed forces would be withdrawn at the same hour the miners returned to work. They expected this could be done within twenty-four hours. Later, a royal commission would be appointed to investigate the steelworkers' grievances. According to McLachlan's subsequent account, Byng had invited the strike leaders to meet with him in an effort to settle the strike: "The arrested men were bailed out, and met Byng, the Governor-General, and agreed with him that the miners would return to work, commencing to do so at the same hour the soldiers and the mounted police would take train out of Cape Breton. Again the struggle took on a look that brought cheer to the workers and dismay to Besco."[51] Morrison's version of events was similar: if Livingstone and McLachlan could guarantee a return to work "simultaneously with the withdrawal of the troops," Byng would advise the provincial and federal governments to withdraw the troops.[52]

Prime Minister King had his own reputation as a mediator of labour disputes and he was not eager to have this dispute settled by his governor general, particularly one who had gone to Nova Scotia against the government's wishes at a time when King had cautiously cancelled his own trip to the province. There are more than a few hints here of a rehearsal for the full-blown crisis over the authority of prime minister and governor general in 1926 to be known to history as the King-Byng crisis. E.M. Macdonald (who was not present in the railway car) later claimed that the governor general had only clarified the union's position and had not actually concluded any agreement. In his view, Byng was guilty of trying to help the union leaders "save their face." Similarly, according to Byng's biographer, the prime minister later complained of "unconstitutional interference in the affairs of the country by the Governor-General."[53]

But these misgivings about the governor general's intervention seem to have been second thoughts, a week after the events. During the time Byng was actually in Pictou, the prime minister was prepared to overlook constitutional ambiguities in favour of an end to the industrial crisis. On the day of the meeting with the union leaders, King telegraphed Macdonald that he was prepared to offer the appointment of a royal commission in exchange for a return to work. The following day he added that, if the strike could be ended on such terms, "no time should be lost in agreeing to them." From King's perspective, the appointment of a royal commission was a vastly better alternative than the perpetual maintenance of troops in the coalfields. Personally he was highly embarrassed about the use of federal troops in the strike – for the second time in two years. Although Premier Armstrong remained sceptical, King was determined to have an investigation of the causes of industrial conflict in Nova Scotia. In its own way the federal government was slowly moving to bring about an end to the industrial crisis. It appeared that the prime minister was prepared to accept an agreement, if not to endorse Byng's role in bringing it about. All that was needed was time for King to make the settlement his own. But time was growing short, and the Byng agreement did not last more than a few hours.[54]

In fact McLachlan had almost succeeded in engineering a symbolic victory for the coal miners. A settlement had been within reach, McLachlan later explained: "The strikers were on the eve of victory when President John L. Lewis of the international 'jumped in'" to play his part in putting down the miners' revolt. "If he had not taken this action," McLachlan continued, "the following night would in all probability have seen the men back at work and the soldiers withdrawing from the district – a victory for the workers."[55] According to McLachlan, the governor general was disowned by the government, and Wolvin had appealed to Lewis "to play his part in smashing the Byng agreement." Lewis at last complied, and the two union leaders were now greeted with a sensational writ of excommunication from their own union. As McLachlan explained it, "This was as much a message to the 'fool' Byng as it was to the men in jail."[56]

"Evil Genius"

This was the hardest blow – not the rough and tumble of the battle against the coal operators and the steel companies, not the lectures of newspaper proprietors or the sermons of the clergymen, not the persecution over the years by police and courts. This time it was his own union, and it was striking a mortal blow at the man who had done more than any other to build the UMW in Nova Scotia. In a few minutes McLachlan was stripped of office. He would never again enjoy the same influence among the coal miners, and the union itself would never fully recover from the crisis.

At the beginning of July, John L. Lewis was ensconced in a suite of rooms on the fifth floor of the Ambassador Hotel in Atlantic City, where he was negotiating an important agreement with the anthracite coal operators. When he learned of the Nova Scotia strike, he began sending off inquiries to District 26, but since Livingstone and McLachlan had just been arrested there were no replies. Finally, on 11 July, he received a brief report from Alex Stewart, who had just arrived at the district office in Glace Bay: "District is out in protest against use of armed forces used against workers and arrest of president and secretary of district. Men are determined to stay out until troops are withdrawn and release of officers." A further letter on 14 July underlined that the strike did not involve wages or contracts, but a protest against the use of armed force in industrial disputes: "It is purely a question for the Canadian workers to settle. For years the use of armed force in industrial disputes have [sic] been fought by the workers here. The present strike here is part of that struggle. The miners here are solid on this issue. The District Executive has repeatedly guaranteed that the miners will return to work immediately the troops are withdrawn from the District."[57]

Lewis took steps to stop the threat of a sympathetic strike in western Canada, where Drumheller miners were already walking off the job. When Lewis learned that District 18 president W.A. Sherman was calling labour bodies together to plan a sympathetic strike throughout the west, he at once warned that the strike in Nova Scotia was "a pure violation of the existing contract between the miners and operators in that field" and that any sympathetic action in their support was ill-advised: "I seriously doubt the wisdom of your course. You are starting something wherein you may find later difficulty in stopping." The danger was contained, and on 13 July the executive board in District 18 voted against sympathetic action.[58]

Throughout these events Lewis received regular advice from Silby Barrett in Glace Bay. On 6 July Barrett boarded the train for Atlantic City to make a personal report to Lewis. There they discussed plans for the appointment of Barrett as a provisional president of a provisional district and Barrett returned to wait in Glace Bay while Lewis completed arrangements. There is a mysterious message on 15 July from Lewis to Barrett: "Party with whom I conferred after your departure has promised full co-operation. Our plans will go through as outlined except that there will be few days delay." Given Lewis's concern about industrial legality, it seems likely he was seeking assurances from Wolvin that there would be an orderly transition to the provisional district. In particular, he needed assurance that the company would maintain the union contract and pay union dues directly to the provisional officers. Lewis was satisfied with the results and later sent Barrett a copy of a telegram from Wolvin. According to Lewis, Wolvin had reported that "the managers of the subsidiary coal properties of that company agree to transact all business with the accredited representatives of Provisional District 26 and refrain from making payment of any monies under the check off arrangement to other than representatives designated by you." Meanwhile, in Glace Bay, Barrett was growing impatient. On 16 July he urged Lewis to act at once: "Would suggest that district charter be revoked tomorrow men are anxious to return to work I am afraid if we don't act immediately that men will break away from organization."[59]

For Lewis himself, events in District 26 were becoming a distraction which threatened to undermine his credibility, and he said as much in one of his telegrams: "Situation district twenty six is doing serious injury to United Mine Workers in anthracite conference here and elsewhere ..." Later, when he presented his actions for approval by the international executive board, Lewis explained that he had been placed in a difficult position in the anthracite negotiations, where the interests of 158,000 workers were at stake: "The press was belaboring the organization for asking this recognition on the one hand, while in Nova Scotia there was widespread defiance of contract obligations ... The matter became bigger than District 26 ..."[60]

Finally, on the night of 17 July, Lewis issued his injunction. The injunction took the form of an official three-page letter to district president Livingstone. It was carefully composed, designed largely for its value as public propaganda, and copies were released for publication in the Wednesday morning newspapers. He began by briefly reviewing the course of the strike, from the corporation's formal protest on 5 July to the district's refusal to end the strike on 11 July. This, Lewis charged, amounted to a failure to observe a contractual agreement or to accept the instructions of the international union.

From here Lewis moved on to a sweeping attack on the mad revolutionaries of District 26:

> I am not unmindful that it is probably a fruitless task to attempt to reason with you in the midst of your mad adventure, yet in your sane moments you must recognize that the course you have been and are now pursuing violates every tenet of your organization. It ruthlessly tramples upon every rule of conduct of our union and constitutes a departure from its every tradition. Your deliberate breach of the existing contract between the operators and miners of Nova Scotia is indefensible and morally reprehensible. Your assault upon the laws and institutions of your Provincial and Dominion Governments cannot be countenanced by the United Mine Workers of America. The official statement of the District Executive Board that the strike was for political purposes is illuminating and gives additional proof, if such was needed, of your true intent. I have in mind that you are a self proclaimed revolutionist. I am familiar with the constant intrigue between yourself and your evil genius McLachlan and your revolutionary masters in Moscow. I can recall the sentiments which you enunciated at a comparatively recent meeting of the International Executive Board at Indianapolis when with the cold ferocity of a five year old defying its Mother you announced you were a

believer in revolution by force. No doubt the present strike in
Nova Scotia corresponds with your idea of a revolution against
the British Government and is in pursuance thereof.

In consideration of these strange facts, the International Union
feels warranted in intervening for the protection of its membership and to permit the discharge of its properly assumed
obligations. You may as well know now as at any time in the future
that the United Mine Workers is not a political institution and
cannot be used to promote the fallacious whims of any political
fanatic who seeks to strike down the established institutions of
his Government. Neither can it be used to sustain officers of
perverted business morals or individuals suffering from mental
aberration such as yourself and the aggregation of papier-mache
revolutionists who are associated with you.[61]

For all these reasons, the charter of District 26 stood revoked,
effective immediately. All officers, from Livingstone and McLachlan on
down, were removed from office. District 26 ceased to exist and was
now replaced by a provisional district under a provisional president,
who would be assisted by a team of staff members who were already on
their way from Indianapolis. The message left no doubt that this was a
fully considered assault on the labour radicals in District 26. No reply
was expected. Indeed, Livingstone, to whom the telegram was addressed, did not receive the message until late at night. Among the first
to be officially informed were Wolvin and Barrett. Much shorter telegrams were sent to all local unions within District 26 informing them
of the creation of a provisional district under the authority of Barrett
and inviting them to comply with the new regime.

The action came on the very day that McLachlan and Livingstone
were meeting the governor general in the railway car. The timing of
Lewis's action was crucial and McLachlan was convinced that it could
not have been coincidental. Was there a conspiracy to rob the union
leaders of the victory they already held in sight on 17 July? McLachlan
certainly believed so. He believed that Lewis was drawn into the picture
that day through the agency of Besco. According to McLachlan, the
villain of the piece was E.M. Macdonald – "your own Mr. E.M. Mac-

donald" he had called him in a letter to Wolvin earlier that year. Hovering around the governor general's entourage for two days, and relaying messages back to the prime minister, Macdonald was in a position to know what was in the wind and sabotage the prospective agreement. Then, according to McLachlan, Macdonald "got in touch with Roy Wolvin in Montreal, who in turn got into communication with J.L. Lewis, the traitor, who sunk the knife into the backs of the workers."[62]

The coincidence was staggering, and it prevented McLachlan from claiming victory in the form of the Byng agreement. But in Atlantic City Wolvin's regular appeals for intervention were welcome. Lewis had been considering drastic action for several months. The corporation and the international union were working independently towards a common goal. There is certainly evidence that Wolvin was in communication with Lewis up to and including the final day, when he fully expected Lewis to take action. This was the final push. On the morning of 17 July, Wolvin telephoned Minister of Labour James Murdock and informed him that Lewis was about to depose Livingstone and McLachlan from office. Murdock was taken by surprise, and the prime minister was probably also unaware of what was about to happen; Byng must have known even less. Even at this late moment, Murdock urged Wolvin to bow to the inevitable and recognize the steelworkers' union. Wolvin replied sharply: "We can't do that."[63]

Lewis had delivered a crushing blow. The strikes fell apart. The steelworkers drifted back to work, their union broken once more. It would be another fourteen years before they finally achieved recognition of their union. That would require the enactment of Nova Scotia's historic Trade Union Act in 1937, one of the major turning points in Canadian labour history. Meanwhile, in the summer of 1923, the miners gathered on the ballfields and in their union halls and voted to return to work, their causes a failure. The coal miners were accustomed to confrontations with the company and the state, but not such a devastating attack from the headquarters of their own union. The district leaders had been labelled as heretics and cast out of the union, where they were now to be devoured by their enemies.

The revolution was barely under way, but the Cape Breton Bolsheviks had been beaten back and the forces of repression were in the ascendant. Had the radicals tried to carry the revolution too far and too fast? McLachlan did not think this was the case, and he made brave replies at his own meetings: "You miners of Nova Scotia have committed a great crime by becoming solidly organized. For that crime no government press or international union can forgive you. The enemies of the workers, the corrupt politicians, the bought press and Roy Wolvin are trying to befog the issue. The real issue, the one we are fighting for, is to have the armed forces of the state withdrawn from this peaceful island and to help the steelworkers to secure a few more cents to buy grub." As for Lewis himself, the international union leader was "simply an office boy for President Wolvin."[64]

For McLachlan, the events of 1923 were a watershed. He and his followers were suddenly overwhelmed by events, outmanoeuvred and overpowered. Men armed with injunctions were taking over the union headquarters, and McLachlan himself was charged with crimes against the state. A front-page cartoon in the *Maritime Labor Herald* supplied a graphic analysis. A Cape Breton striker stands with folded arms looking down at the barrel of a gun trained on him. The gun is marked INTIMIDATION and it is held by a hand labelled BESCO. Three fingers of the hand are also named, one for the federal government, another for the province, and a third for the Lewis machine.[65]

CHAPTER 8

The King v. McLachlan

Away, false teachings of my youth,
It's now a crime to speak the truth;
This man of law has so decreed
That it's a base and foul deed
Well meriting the dungeon cell
For anyone to boldly tell.

– Dawn Fraser,
Echoes from Labor's War (1924)

The Law Courts

The sun stood high over the harbour in Halifax on 17 October 1923. It was a fresh fall day, and a few seagulls climbed high in the breeze above Citadel Hill. Down below, the streetcars drove a halting course through the city streets, creaking their way up the hill on Spring Garden Road and past the Law Courts. This mid-Victorian public building, with its classical façade, was one of the city's landmarks. But over the years the stone walls had been blackened by the smoke of the city. The vermiculated stonework looked like it was being eaten by worms, and the carved stone heads over the front entrance presented a menacing welcome. The Halifax County jail was conveniently attached to the side of the building, destroying the original symmetry of the architecture.

Inside a carpeted chamber the Supreme Court of Nova Scotia was in session. The glass chandeliers rang as the judge pronounced his final observations in a sharp, peppery voice. In a few minutes a jury of twelve men would file out to consider their verdict in a case involving three counts of seditious libel, each punishable by up to twenty years in prison.

Appearing for the crown was the attorney general of Nova Scotia, Walter J. O'Hearn. A strong Liberal of Irish and Catholic background – his father was principal of St Patrick's Boys' High School – O'Hearn had served as stipendiary magistrate and registrar of deeds for Halifax before he entered the government. As a young lawyer, he had won a reputation as a "surprisingly resourceful opponent, with a knowledge of legal small points" and was considered to be "full of professional daring and initiative." It was unusual for an attorney general to prosecute a case personally, and in the present trial O'Hearn had good opportunities to show his courtroom skills. In his address to the jury he declared the case to be "the most important that had come before the courts of Nova Scotia in recent years." There was no doubt in his mind that this was a political trial, involving nothing less, as he put it, than "the principle as to whether or not the doctrines of Soviet Russia should flourish in Nova Scotia." O'Hearn had entered the provincial government only a few months earlier, in December 1922, and now he added, "I determined when I assumed the office I now hold that I would lock horns with men of this nature." Years later this case would be remembered as the "cause célèbre" of his career.[1]

Leading the defence was an equally prominent public personality, Gordon S. Harrington. Barely forty years old, a diffident figure with a military bearing, Harrington was a Halifax man who had gone to Cape Breton in the boom years at the turn of the century. He started a law practice in Glace Bay and served two terms as town mayor. In wartime he gained a reputation as one of the more efficient staff officers in the Ministry of Overseas Military Forces, the government department that did much to assert the independence of the Canadian war effort; Harrington eventually served as deputy minister in the chaotic days of demobilization, when Canadian soldiers rioted in their mudsoaked camps in the countryside. He left the army in 1920 with the rank of colonel, planning to devote his time to practising law and fishing on the Mira. His political ambitions had been awakened, however, and now Harrington was helping to rebuild the Nova Scotia Conservative Party. His instincts told him that there were good reasons to take on a case with so many political implications. The trial, he told the jury, had been "a nauseating, abominable fizzle." In the alleged seditious remarks, the accused was "only voicing the opinions of the thousands he represented among the miners of Cape Breton." The parallel to be remembered, claimed Harrington, was the trial of Joseph Howe in the same city on similar charges almost a century earlier, a trial that helped expose the corruption of the local establishment and vindicate the rights of free speech. He reminded the jury that Howe had won an acquittal, which was no more and no less than "the fate the prisoner in this case deserved."[2]

Presiding over the court was Supreme Court Justice Humphrey Mellish. This was a judge who relished his authority on the bench and, one lawyer later recalled, "ruled over his court as would an Emperor." Juries were never in doubt of his views, for he was known to take a lively part in the proceedings below, often piping in with shrill comments and questions. Mellish had more than a passing knowledge of the Cape Breton scene and was described in 1924 as "an outstanding corporationist on the bench." Like many Nova Scotia lawyers, he had done work for the coal companies on various occasions, and at the time of the trial his former law partner, Hector McInnes, was also serving on the Besco board of directors. As a judge, Mellish had already tangled with the coal miners on at least two occasions. Shortly after his appointment in 1918, he had tried the controversial case in which the coal company and several officials were charged with manslaughter after the New Waterford mine disaster. Mellish's law firm had helped prepare the defence and, when it came to trial, he did not hesitate to direct a not guilty verdict. Then, in January 1922, Mellish delivered the interpretation of the Industrial Disputes Investigation Act which allowed Besco to bring in wage cuts without delay.[3]

The case of *The King* v. *James B. McLachlan* would take its place in the history of political trials in Canada and serve to illustrate the broad applications of a loosely defined offence such as sedition. The principal evidence against McLachlan was his official statement promoting the sympathetic strike in July 1923. By McLachlan's standards, this was not the most inflammatory of his public statements over the years, and it would require a broad construction of the term to interpret the specific statements it contained as a form of sedition. But political offences depend more on the context of the surrounding events than on the contents of the charges, and much more was at stake here besides the rights of freedom of speech. As Kenneth McNaught has pointed out, a political trial is defined by the overt confrontation between the forces of change and the forces of continuity. In this case the age of industrial legality was still very much in its infancy; although unions were legal, they had few rights under the law. At a time when the law allowed the easy use of armed force in industrial disputes and offered no support for workers seeking union recognition, the prosecution of McLachlan came as a challenge to the extension of union organization among industrial workers in Nova Scotia. This was all the more threatening to

the establishment in the case of a would-be revolutionary union leader
such as McLachlan.[4]

"Fighting Jim"

The case was before the country long before the trial began in Halifax
in October. At the end of August, McLachlan had embarked on a long
journey across the country, accompanied by Forman Waye, the steelworkers' organizer and labour MLA. Their final destination was
Vancouver, where the annual meetings of the Trades and Labour Congress were taking place in September. Along the way they would take
the story of the Cape Breton events to the workers of Canada.

The two labour leaders made an effective team. McLachlan's rousing
descriptions were complemented by Waye's cool observations. In Toronto,
for instance, where they addressed a public meeting at the Labour Temple,
McLachlan gave a dramatic rendition of the events leading to his arrest:

> But, mark you! The soldiers weren't bad fellows. Ach, it was the
> police! ... Those policemen were brutal. They clubbed boys and
> women. I tell you, it doesn't matter whether we were right or
> wrong, we weren't going to stand there and see women clubbed.
> And that is why they arrested me. I wrote a letter telling how they
> had clubbed an old woman of 70 into insensibility, and how
> another woman gave premature birth to a child after being
> clubbed. They charged me with spreading a false tale, seditious
> libel and seditious conspiracy ... Oh, they say they will let me off
> with forty years.

Then Waye followed with observations on the blacklisting of hundreds
of steelworkers and the political significance of the struggle: "It has
been said that the steel workers are good fellows and that the miners
are bolsheviks. But this is obviously ridiculous. The miners and steel
workers have a complete understanding. The only difference is that the
miners are a 100 per cent organization ... And everyone in Cape Breton
County knows that the British Empire Steel Corporation owns the
government of Nova Scotia, body and soul."[5]

Although deposed as a union official, McLachlan arrived at the TLC meetings armed with credentials from at least six local unions and was seated as a delegate. He spoke only once during the proceedings: "As usual his words were firey [sic] and created a storm." As he had done at public meetings across the country, McLachlan accused the international union of betraying Canadian workers. The radical delegates introduced resolutions demanding greater autonomy for Canadian unions, and the case of District 26 was cited as one of the arguments for a more independent labour movement in Canada: "It is evident that had Canadian Labor complete autonomy in so far as strike action is concerned, withdrawal of the troops last July would have been a foregone conclusion." A long debate followed. Radicals called for a more powerful labour congress in Canada while more conservative unionists defended the existing structure of international unionism. In the end a substitute resolution confirmed the TLC's support for international unionism; still, the roll call vote of 120 to 53 revealed a substantial minority body of support for the radicals. Later in the day the delegates also endorsed a less controversial resolution on the Nova Scotia situation, directed at the Canadian government rather than the international union. This one simply protested the use of military forces during industrial disputes.[6]

Although McLachlan was returning from Vancouver to face serious charges in Nova Scotia, J.S. Woodsworth observed that he did not seem to be worrying about the outcome: "Indeed he impresses one as being largely indifferent to his own personal fate. Perhaps that is why he is so popular among the miners." For one of his newspaper columns following the TLC meetings, Woodsworth prepared a sketch of McLachlan, which was widely published in Canadian newspapers in the weeks before the trial. "This dour-faced Scotsman – so different from the ordinary run of men," Woodsworth wrote, was today "one of the most hated and best loved men in Nova Scotia – a man to be reckoned with in the years to come." It was an observant profile, based on their several years of acquaintance and conversation, and contained sympathetic details of his personal and family life. The red firebrand, Woodsworth pointed out, was a veteran trade unionist and a benevolent family man. He went on to identify McLachlan's radicalism as the authentic product of the working-class experience and the Scottish democratic tradition. The uncompromising McLachlan, with all his good will and fighting spirit, could best be understood as a "Labor Covenanter": "Whether or not we agree with his methods, we must recognize that he goes forth as to a holy war."[7]

The tour was a financial success. In Montreal, Toronto, and Winnipeg, fundraising was coordinated by local defence committees which raised hundreds of dollars for the Nova Scotia Workers' Defence Fund. Collections were taken in the streets and squares and at public meetings in Toronto, Montreal, Winnipeg, Brandon, and Edmonton as well as smaller communities. Donations also poured in from individual union locals and labour councils across the country. From Vancouver alone there were donations from the longshoremen, lithographers, civic employees, lumber workers, carpenters and joiners, tailors, electrical workers, blacksmiths, granite cutters, railway workers, operating engineers, street railway workers, hotel and restaurant employees, and the Japanese Workers' Union, as well as local branches of the Wobblies and the Workers' Party. The largest single contribution of the campaign came in the form of a $1,000 donation from the miners' union at Nordegg, Alberta. By the end of September the fund had raised $6,431.58 and ultimately the contributions would total $11,582.80. The funds raised were distributed to support the families of arrested and blacklisted steelworkers and to help pay the legal expenses in connection with McLachlan's trial.[8]

Yet these weeks travelling the country by railway coach also reminded McLachlan of the weaknesses of Canadian labour. In Vancouver, McLachlan had spoken in the debates at the TLC convention but he was not invited to deliver a major speech. The place of honour instead went to one of the leaders of the Miners' Federation of Great Britain, Frank Hodges, a Welsh miner who was himself a vigorous advocate of public ownership in the coal industry.

In Canada in 1923 the house of labour was still very much in disorder, divided over issues of jurisdiction, policy, and strategy: craft against industry, American against Canadian, conservative against radical. Membership was continuing to fall from the high points of 1919 and 1920, and the prospects for common action were weak. Had the days of solidarity passed forever? Was Canadian labour permanently in retreat?

There had been no general strike in support of the miners and steel-workers in the summer of 1923, and in Cape Breton the radicals were no longer "in the saddle" as they had been in 1922. At the beginning of October "Fighting Jim," as the reporters were now calling him, returned to Nova Scotia to stand trial.

Sedition

In the months after McLachlan's arrest in July 1923, Attorney General O'Hearn watched carefully as the criminal charges against McLachlan made their way through the courts of Nova Scotia and were forwarded for trial at the fall term of the Supreme Court in Halifax. In September defence lawyer John A. Walker attempted to have the trial removed to Sydney, where the court would also be sitting to consider criminal cases that fall. Walker argued that a trial in Halifax would impose heavy expenses on the defence and that it was proper for the trial to be held in the place where the alleged offence was committed.

That was something the crown could not allow. O'Hearn appeared in court to insist that the trial must be held in Halifax because the initial charges in the case were based on the publication of McLachlan's letter in the Halifax *Morning Chronicle.* Furthermore, O'Hearn argued, in recent months at least eighteen cases related to the industrial conflict had been thrown out by local juries and there was a danger that a trial in the industrial area would be too favourable to McLachlan. Among those cases was his own attempt to try Malcolm Bruce for making seditious utterances at a public meeting in Glace Bay in May; the case proved a disaster and the charges were dismissed by a local court in June. O'Hearn's arguments prevailed, and on 2 October a Halifax grand jury returned true bills in the charges against Living-stone and McLachlan.[9]

As the trial date approached, O'Hearn continued to manage his strategy with the utmost care. First, it was decided to proceed separately against McLachlan. Although Livingstone was a well-known union personality, and counted himself aggressively among the radicals, the Westville miner had been union president for less than a year and was not closely identified with developments in Cape Breton. Livingstone's case was held over to February 1924, then to October 1924, and ultimately never prosecuted. As a result, the full attention of the court in October 1923 was focused on the man whose name was synonymous with the cause of labour radicalism in Nova Scotia.

O'Hearn also arranged to revise the original charges. Originally the union leaders were arrested under Section 136 of the Criminal Code for "publishing false news." The indictment presented in court in October was a more serious one. Under Section 132 McLachlan was charged with "a seditious libel concerning His Majesty's Government of and for the Province of Nova Scotia and the Provincial Police established under the laws of the Province." The indictment then cited the "seditious matter" in full, namely, the text of McLachlan's circular letter of early July. The revision of the charges made the offence a substantially more serious one. Offences under Section 136 were punishable by a term of one year's imprisonment, but charges of seditious libel were punishable by up to twenty years' imprisonment. This penalty had been greatly increased from two years under Criminal Code amendments made at the time of the Winnipeg General Strike in 1919.[10]

There was another advantage in changing the charges from "publishing false news" to "seditious libel." Under the charge of sedition, the case focused not on the truth of McLachlan's statements but on his intentions. It was an important distinction, and when the trial began on 15 October, O'Hearn explained the crown's case in these terms: "The issue is not whether the statement published is false or true. There are many things which are true but cannot be published. It is not the question of the truth of the statement, but a question of whether it was said with the intention of creating dissatisfaction and disturbance."[11]

The trial lasted two and a half days, and most of the time was taken up by O'Hearn's presentation of the prosecution's case. The crown called twelve witnesses, several of whom described the disorderly scenes at the steel plant in some detail. Captain D.A. Noble, head of the company police force, stated that rioting continued at the steel plant gates continuously from Thursday when the strike began until Sunday night. Colonel Eric McDonald, commissioner of the provincial police, described the scene on his arrival on Friday 29 June: "The crowd outside the gate seemed to have control of all that part of the town, and the local police or steel company's police were not able to appear on the street." Mining engineer Walter Herd underlined the need to control access to the plant, stating that damage to the coke ovens could cost $2 million in repairs. The witnesses went on to describe the efforts of the provincial police to, in McDonald's euphemism, "send the crowd home." Sydney police chief J.B. McCormick reported that there was "practically no trouble" afterwards.

The weight of the prosecution's case focused on McLachlan's opinions and actions. The book taken from Steele's Hill in May was entered as an exhibit. The published minutes of the 1922 district convention were also placed on record, and excerpts from the radical resolutions were read to the court. Colonel McDonald reported that in negotiations with company officials on 3 July to avert the sympathetic strike, McLachlan had uttered the following words: "To hell with the property of the British Empire Steel Corporation." Then, by calling the union's office secretary, it was established that McLachlan had indeed authored the circular letter of 4 July. This point was confirmed by Andrew Merkel, the Canadian Press correspondent in Halifax who had verified the authenticity of the document with McLachlan before filing his report. Two union members from Pictou County were called to testify to the receipt of the letter by union locals in that part of the district. And the news editor of the *Morning Chronicle* testified that he had published the document – under the safely worded headline, "Miners are duped by the circulation of false statements" – in the 6 July edition of the Halifax newspaper.

The defence called no witnesses of its own. When the prosecution witnesses began to give evidence regarding events in Sydney, Harrington objected. If the truth of McLachlan's statement was not an acceptable defence, then evidence of the events should not be allowed. O'Hearn replied that the purpose was to show "general industrial disorder" since "seditious intention shall be judged from the times in which the thing was done." Judge Mellish ruled in agreement. Harrington then objected that some thirty witnesses would be needed to present the defence's view of the events. As the defence was unable to bear the cost of bringing witnesses from Cape Breton, he would be bound to move for a change of venue. Mellish replied sharply to this claim: "You are objecting to the evidence on the ground that you have not witnesses to meet it; I rule that is a bad ground; that is the short end to that."

Despite the lack of defence witnesses, Harrington and Walker were able to draw out some relevant evidence in the cross-examination of the crown's witnesses. It was shown that the proposal to join the Red International had been subsequently withdrawn by the district. In cross-examination of Colonel McDonald, Harrington was able to offer a corrected version of the statement attributed to McLachlan on 3 July: "If you put the women and children of the miners in one scale and the property of the Dominion Coal Company in the other, then I say if it is between the two, it is to hell with the property of the Dominion Coal Company."

It was also established that McLachlan himself had not been present at the riotous scenes in Sydney, but that there was subsequently "quite a bit of talk" about the actions of the police, including hearings by the Sydney police commission. Harrington was thus able to show that McLachlan's account of the events was not without foundation. Indeed, he introduced into the record the name and address of the pregnant woman whose assault by the police was referred to in McLachlan's letter. Harrington also elicited evidence that conditions at the steel plant gates were relatively peaceful most of the day on Sunday, 1 July, and he alleged that the provincial police were determined to, in words he attributed to Colonel McDonald, "put on a show about eight that night at No. 4 gate." As well, Harrington managed to imply that before charging down the street the provincial police might well have "passed the rum jar copiously around."

Then there was the extraordinary testimony brought forth by Walker's cross-examination of Andrew Merkel of Canadian Press. Merkel himself was well on the way to becoming a legend of the local newsrooms, a big lively Maritimer who churned out romantic regional poetry on the office mimeograph machine in between writing the grim dispatches that delivered news of the region's struggles across the country in the 1920s.[12]

For the prosecution, Merkel's testimony was an embarrassment, for he went out of his way to explain the very indirect route by which

McLachlan's letter had reached Halifax and appeared in the press there, thus providing the original basis for his arrest on charges of "publishing false news." Arriving in Sydney on 4 July, Merkel went to the offices of the Sydney *Record*, a daily newspaper known for its sympathies for the steel company and the Liberal government. There F.W. Gray, the assistant to Besco vice-president D.H. McDougall, handed him a typewritten copy of McLachlan's letter. This copy was apparently prepared from the text Livingstone delivered to the company offices earlier in the day. This was the first time Merkel had seen the letter, and, he recalled, "Mr. Gray suggested I put it on the wire and distribute it." Merkel called McLachlan on the telephone to confirm that the letter was authentic and then filed his report. The document appeared the following day in the *Morning Chronicle* and other newspapers.

O'Hearn re-examined the witness, but Merkel firmly maintained that the document was not published in the press until after it was released by F.W. Gray. In his final address to the jury, Harrington underlined the significance of this testimony: "If McLachlan is guilty for sending this letter to the locals of his union, why is not F.W. Gray of the steel company not also guilty for having it published? ... Why aren't there more people in [the] dock besides McLachlan?"

The proceedings came to a close on 17 October, when Judge Mellish delivered his charge to the jury. Nowhere in the Criminal Code, he explained, was the meaning of sedition specifically defined. Section 132 simply stated that "seditious words are words expressive of a seditious intention. A seditious libel is a libel expressive of a seditious intention." For the benefit of the jury, Mellish quoted one text on English criminal law, which defined sedition as including "all those practices, whether by words, deed, or writing, which fall short of high treason, but directly tend to have for their object to excite discontent or dissatisfaction; to excite ill-will between different classes of the King's subjects; to create public disturbances, or to lead to civil war; to bring into hatred or contempt the sovereign of the government, the laws or constitution of the realm, and generally all endeavours to promote public disorder."

Mellish qualified this sweeping definition by also reading Section 133 of the Criminal Code, which listed the kinds of social criticism not to be considered seditious: "No one shall be deemed to have a seditious intention only because he intends in good faith, (a) to show that His Majesty has been misled or mistaken in his measures; or, (b) to point out errors or defects in the government or constitution ..." The judge was being careful, but in fact he was overly cautious. He was apparently not aware that this permissive section had been removed from the Criminal Code in 1919, although he was certainly aware of the "more modern" penalty for sedition – up to twenty years' imprisonment – enacted at the same time.

Then Mellish turned to the case at hand. There should be no question as to McLachlan's responsibility for publication of the letter, he informed the jury, for distribution of the document to union locals "in itself was a publication." As for the appearance of the letter in Halifax – where there were no union locals and McLachlan had not sent any copies – this presented no problem: "I don't think it unreasonable to say that when a document of that kind once became distributed in the way McLachlan intended it should be distributed that he would naturally expect it would be published all over Nova Scotia and get into the newspapers also." In giving this direction, Mellish was endorsing two of the basic premises of the prosecution's case – that McLachlan was the "publisher" of the offending document and that one of the several places of publication was Halifax.

Was the document itself seditious? Mellish had few doubts: "It is capable of a seditious construction, I may tell you, gentlemen; and the next question for you is, whether it was intended that the construction should be put upon it." To answer that question, Mellish continued, it was relevant to consider the reasons why it was being urged that the military and the police be withdrawn from Sydney:

> You are told by counsel for the defence that the police were there to break the strike. Was that the purpose for which the police were there? Or were the police there to maintain order? What interest had the Glace Bay miners in having the police removed from Sydney? ... Was it to give the strikers a free hand to do as they had been doing before? That is a question for you to consider, as to whether this document was intended to operate and incite people

against law and order, – the orderly government of the community by the executive of the people.

Finally, the judge advised, in determining McLachlan's guilt it was also fair to "consider his opinions, and those of the party whom he represents." For the benefit of the jury he quoted excerpts from the radical resolutions of June 1922 and drew attention to the "seditious literature" found in McLachlan's home.

Thus instructed, the jurors retired to consider their verdict. They returned one and a half hours later to pronounce the prisoner guilty on all three counts. It was not a surprising result. It confirmed the enormous social distance that separated Halifax from Cape Breton. And the judge had virtually directed a guilty verdict against a man regarded as the personification of Cape Breton Bolshevism.

For their part the defence lawyers had offered a highly technical defence, based on objections to the rulings of the trial judge and the hope of a successful appeal. There were objections to the form of the indictment and an irregularity in the selection of the jury, as well as the admission in evidence of the copy of the constitution of the Red International collected at McLachlan's home in May. Although sworn statements were gathered in Sydney, confirming the accuracy of McLachlan's descriptions of the events of 1 July, they were not offered in evidence. Indeed, during the trial Harrington was surprised that the judge admitted so much evidence about conditions in Sydney. As expected, at the end of the trial Harrington placed a formal motion for a change of venue, on the grounds that "there is no possibility of the defendant getting witnesses here."

Harrington's biggest mistake was his willingness to accept the view that truth was no defence in a case of seditious libel. Although Harrington had drawn the parallel with the trial of Joseph Howe, he failed to recognize that Howe easily evaded such restrictions by insisting on the importance of clarifying his motives and intentions, which he then proceeded to do in one of his most famous speeches. As Murray Beck has observed, Howe argued that when he published his own charges "he was thinking in terms, not of tempting others to a breach of the peace, but of restoring and preserving the peace." It was an argument that could have been made in McLachlan's defence as well. In a contemporary comment on the McLachlan case written for J.S. Woodsworth, O.D. Skelton, then dean of arts at Queen's University and soon to become a senior civil servant in Ottawa, questioned the view, too easily accepted by the defence, that "under the English law truth is not justification for a seditious libel": "It is my impression, however, that this old rule has been considerably modified by statute in England, and I should think court precedent is also against such a mediaeval interpretation."[13]

In turn, Harrington's emphasis on a technical defence left no place for the famous platform abilities of McLachlan himself. Certainly the most remarkable aspect of the trial was the muted behaviour of the prisoner. During the proceedings McLachlan sat in uncharacteristic silence, arms crossed, pipe clenched firmly in his mouth. He spoke only once during the trial. This was to interrupt O'Hearn's final address to the jury. When the attorney general claimed that a red flag had been seized at his home, McLachlan interjected briefly, "There was no red flag; he never said it."

The Cape Breton poet Dawn Fraser would later celebrate McLachlan's attitude as one of "lofty scorn." One reporter found that McLachlan seemed to be maintaining "an air of sang froid" throughout the entire proceedings, apparently not troubled by the prospect of an adverse outcome: "The worse [sic] he looked for, apparently, was disagreement by the jury." But for all the talk of parallels with Joseph Howe, the missing element was the articulate personal defence of the accused. At least one contemporary report on the trial noted that McLachlan's failure to plead his case, as Howe had done, was a major miscalculation: "Had McLachlan done the same thing, the miners declare the verdict would have been different." Yet it is difficult to imagine McLachlan silent against his will. Family members recall that McLachlan seemed to be certain of his conviction. Perhaps he was simply preparing his family for the worst possibility. An additional explanation is that McLachlan recognized that the case was very much a political one and that the Halifax courtroom provided poor terrain for the kind of defence he needed to make. Whereas Howe in 1835 had faced a jury of peers and acquaintances who might be expected to listen with some sympathy to his case (and they acquitted him in ten minutes), the Halifax jury was not one of McLachlan's usual audiences. Indeed, as the subject of frequent demonization in the press over the past several years, McLachlan must have seemed a dangerous outsider to many of the citizens of the capital city.[14]

Many years later the junior defence attorney in the trial, John A. Walker, reminisced briefly about the case. Walker himself was a Cape Bretoner from the Lake Ainslie district who was a protégé of Father Jimmy Tompkins during his days at St Francis Xavier University. In 1919 he came to Halifax, where he practised law and, after 1925, served in the Conservative provincial government. More than fifty years later, Walker's observations on the case were summarized as follows: "He believes McLachlan was guilty and defended him because 'a man's liberty was at stake.' He does not think McLachlan had a fair trial. The jury was prejudiced against him, and this may have been true of the judge too. He does not think McLachlan would have been convicted in the Cape Breton area if the case was tried there. He was tried in Halifax because that's where he was charged." As for McLachlan's attitude? "McLachlan did not speak in court and did not want to. McLachlan didn't know how the case would turn out, but was not surprised or hurt when it went against him."[15]

Had the trial taken place in Cape Breton, before a jury of local residents and industrial workers, McLachlan undoubtedly would have insisted on a vigorous personal defence. The defence lawyers might also have entertained greater hopes of success in Cape Breton, where Harrington did win an acquittal for the Communist leader Jack MacDonald on another sedition charge in November. It may be excessive to claim that McLachlan's lawyers exploited the McLachlan case to prove the iniquity of the Liberals and promote the fortunes of the Conservative Party, but it is difficult to avoid the conclusion that they failed to present the most effective possible defence. Barry Cahill has concluded that one of the failures of the defence was its obsession with the Joseph Howe analogy, which was understood at the time as a case of libel rather than sedition. The more relevant case was Fred Dixon's acquittal on charges of seditious libel arising out of the Winnipeg General Strike. Dixon achieved this result by confronting the political implications of his case and performing his own "triumphant emulation of Howe." The defence was so effective that Woodsworth, charged with the same offence, was never brought to trial. In short, writes Cahill, "Harrington persisted in the attempt to achieve for his client what McLachlan perhaps could have better achieved for himself." Whether McLachlan had second thoughts about deferring to his lawyers is not known. On the evidence of later speeches, especially those following his release from jail in 1924 and before a royal commission in 1925, McLachlan could certainly have presented a speech to rival either Howe or Dixon. Whether he would have been acquitted is another matter.[16]

McLachlan appeared for sentencing on 31 October. Walker made a strong plea for leniency and urged that the prisoner be given a suspended sentence. O'Hearn again appeared in person and argued that McLachlan had been convicted of "a very serious offence against the law of Canada" and, whatever McLachlan's personal qualities, the conviction "generally speaking, was designed for the purpose of impressing the community."[17] Mellish then pronounced his sentence: two years in Dorchester Penitentiary on each of the three offences, the sentences to run concurrently. It was far from the maximum possible sentence then in force, but it was the maximum which would have been allowed prior to the Criminal Code amendments of 1919.

As expected, there would be an appeal in the case. Walker at once applied for bail pending the outcome of the appeal. The application was decided by Chief Justice Robert E. Harris. Again McLachlan came before a man who personified the class structure of justice in Nova Scotia. Among other qualifications for the bench, Harris was the former president of Eastern Trust and the Nova Scotia Steel and Coal Company; he was described by one contemporary as "most unprogressive, with the mind of a slave owner."[18] Bail was denied, and McLachlan was returned to the Halifax County jail to begin serving his time.

Prison

In cell no. 1, Halifax County jail, McLachlan was growing accustomed to his new role as a political prisoner. When the Halifax Communist Joe Wallace visited him in early November, his spirits were high and he entertained his guest with caustic comments on the capitalist system: "The only difference between jail and job is that here I am separated from my wife and family. Under capitalism all the workers are in jail all the time. And lots of them haven't got the security of shelter and food that is offered in a penitentiary."

He also shared some reflections on the rewards of the radical labour leader and the temptations of the labour bureaucrat: "You cannot permanently bring peace to the workers under capitalism. To retain the confidence and maintain the interests of the workers you have to lead them from struggle to struggle. But if you get out of line with the other sections of the working class army, your head is lopped off. Faced by this dilemma, you can easily understand why so many trades union officials who start as militants end as bureaucrats, bleeding instead of leading the workers."

There was, he said, returning to one of his recurrent themes, a great parallel to be remembered between the modern labour leader and the early Christian martyrs: "New ideas are born in stables and brought up in jails. Whenever a new cause is struggling its way to recognition its adherents frequently have to die for it. In the early days of Christianity many clergymen were dragged to the Coliseum. How many of them are in jail today for an ideal?"[19]

McLachlan's appeal was finally heard on 17 December, with Chief Justice Harris presiding over a court of criminal appeal. The defence presented arguments based on eleven points of law, all of them of a technical nature – the improper admission of evidence, the court's lack of jurisdiction, and the prisoner's inability to make a full defence. McLachlan remained behind bars while the judges began a leisurely Christmas break to consider their decision.

McLachlan's spirits were buoyed up by "a host of visitors" and "a vast number of Christmas and New Year gifts and messages from all sections of Canada and the United States and some from England." Among the greetings was a short message from the coal miners' legendary Mother Jones: "You are behind the bars for a holy cause. Courage, my brother, and do not falter! The brave and true die only once. Cowards and traitors die often, and, oh God, they have some horrible deaths at that!"[20]

Among the letters McLachlan received in time for Christmas was a short note from Louis McCormack, the provisional officer who had replaced him as secretary-treasurer of District 26. It contained a cheque in the amount of $200, McLachlan's unpaid wages for the month of July 1923. McLachlan would never cash the cheque. He dated it "County Jail, Halifax Dec. 25th 1923" and returned it with a blistering endorsement on the back: "This check, issued by traitors, who Judas like pretend to kiss the Nova Scotia miner on the cheek, while daily they run a dagger to his heart's core, may be cashed by anyone that can take blood money."[21]

From these weeks in the Halifax jail there are also two surviving letters home to Steele's Hill, both written to his daughter Eva. These are written on a cautious note of humour. On December 28: "I got a lot of cards, letters, telegrams and presents at Xmas. I got four boxes of cigars and I have lost count of the candies and fruit. It's great to be in jail, people go dippie over you. However, don't you try to get in until I get out ..." As far as the appeal went, McLachlan had ambivalent feelings: "I care if I do go to Dorchester, [but] it would never be half so hard for me, as taking a favor from the crew who want me there, and then I shall come out some day and be able to keep telling them what I think of that particular 'British institution' and you know it is sedition to [be] saying anything harsh about our 'great British Institutions.'"

And on 29 December, again to Eva:

Your letters did me good while I was in here and I'll tell you why. I never had very much reverence for institutions of the rich and great including their jails, one way to wear off the sharp edge that these institutions are intended to have on us is to scoff at them and scorn them and your letters helped me to do this very thing with this great British institution, the Halifax County Jail. How I like to mock it and those who have me in here. You see when they put one in here you are expected to whine and cry to get out, then they are pleased, their institution is "working" according to them, but when they find you mocking it and them; well that's sedition, and they get awfully sore about sedition.[22]

The decision of the appeal court was handed down on 8 January 1924. On one point the appeal judges agreed with the defence: in the light of Merkel's revealing evidence on how the letter reached the pages of the *Chronicle*, the conviction on the charge of publication in Halifax was set aside. On the other two counts the conviction was upheld. The judgment conveniently overlooked the fact that the questionable Halifax charge had been used to justify holding the trial in Halifax in the first place, and that the unfavourable venue for the trial had played a critical part in the case.[23]

There was one more legal avenue. On 29 January Walker applied for leave to appeal the case to the Privy Council, and on 16 February this was granted. Justice Russell noted that at least one significant point of general interest was at stake in the case: "the use that may be made of books or documents found in the library of a suspected person."[24] But the question never was submitted to the Privy Council. As far as McLachlan was concerned, the courts had lived up to his expectations. Further appeals could be based only on misplaced illusions about the nature of British justice.

On his departure from Halifax he had scathing observations about the crowded facility attached to the Law Courts. One section of the jail was "a veritable fire-trap." The diet consisted of bread and tea twice a day, without sugar or milk. There was soup for dinner six days a week and salt herring on Sundays. The occupants lived in a condition of enforced idleness, with no opportunities for exercise or improvement. Prisoners were likely to leave jail with their health undermined, and younger inmates would have "a schooling in life and crime that could not have been secured in any other way": "No man can leave the county jail as good a man as when he entered. No matter how strong his character ... A term in the county jail has no reformatory effects, its results on the contrary are destructive."[25]

From the casual filth and disorder of the Halifax County jail McLachlan now entered one of the Victorian strongholds of the Canadian penitentiary system. Dorchester Penitentiary rises grimly over the marshy grasslands of the New Brunswick border, a dark stone fortress sitting on a hill at the end of a long winding road. The penitentiary was one of the public works brought home to Westmorland County by Albert Smith during his days in the Dominion cabinet in the 1870s and originally opened in 1880. In 1919 the superintendent of penitentiaries was proposing that Dorchester be closed down, but in 1924 it still remained one of Canada's largest penal institutions, housing more than 200 inmates. With two large wings of cells, a huge dining room, a dozen workshops, a library, two chapels, residences for the guards and warden, barns housing more than 200 head of cattle and swine, and a farm of several hundred acres, the prison was said to be "to a large degree self-supporting" and "a complete town within itself."[26]

Daily life in Dorchester was officially governed by a code of 219 regulations which had not been revised since 1899. The routine was announced by a series of clanging bells, from the morning roll call to the "retiring gong" in the evening. Prisoners were required to treat prison staff "in a respectful manner" and "obey their orders without comment or hesitation." They were forbidden to hold "unnecessary conversation" with other inmates. Prisoners were allowed to write one letter home each month. Family visits were restricted to one in two months, subject to satisfactory behaviour. All inmates were required to attend religious services administered by the Catholic or Protestant chaplains, unless exempted by the warden. To assist in the work of reformation, they were permitted to use carefully selected prison libraries. For violations of the regulations, the warden was authorized to exact a variety of punishments ranging from the forfeiture of light, writing, tobacco, and library privileges through to solitary confinement, bread and water diets, hosing, and flogging.[27]

Despite the attitude of defiance celebrated by his followers, this was a difficult time for McLachlan. There was the public humiliation of being transported in chains in a public railway car. Then on arrival he was bathed, photographed, fingerprinted, and dressed in the prison garb appropriate to his new identity as convict no. U-908. Moreover, to conform to prison regulations, McLachlan's hair was clipped short and his face was shaved clean of his famous moustache, which never grew back in the same bushy vigour of his prime. At fifty-four years of age McLachlan was not a young man and no longer as robust as he once had been. At Dorchester the prison doctor noted no ill effects on his file: "Health is good, further confinement not likely to prove fatal."[28] However, McLachlan would leave jail a visibly older, weakened man who had lost more than twenty pounds in weight during his confinement. His children were convinced that their father never fully recovered his health afterwards and that those winter months in the damp and cold of the jail cells contributed to his final fatal illness.[29]

There was also the more subtle humiliation applied by progressive reformers who exerted growing influence within the penitentiary system. In 1924 Dorchester's acting warden, Major G.T. Goad, was known as an advocate of prison reform, more interested in reforming than punishing prisoners. Goad objected, for instance, to having his staff administer whippings and floggings ordered by the courts. He probably agreed with McLachlan's critical comments on the county jail, for he preferred to see his charges employed in the prison workshops and exposed to the good influences of chaplains and teachers. Occasionally the prisoners at Dorchester were also rewarded with visits from the Salvation Army Brass Band of Moncton, who once delivered "a message of cheer and gladness" that lasted for two hours while the prisoners remained locked in their cells. The prisoners were also expected to prepare their own variety shows, and when a new concert and lecture hall was completed in 1924, Warden Goad planned to have entertainments at least once a month, including demonstrations of singing and dancing by the inmates. The movie bill at Dorchester in 1924 included recent W.S. Hart and Harold Lloyd films, as well as Charlie Chaplin's *The Immigrant* (1917).[30]

Still, McLachlan appreciated the contrast with the Halifax jail. There was exercise in the yard and halls of the prison, and chores to be done in the kitchens, shops, and barns. In the prison workshops McLachlan worked with the shoemakers, helping to keep the books and learning something about the making and mending of shoes. Although reading material was carefully monitored in the prison library, he was still able to read some of his treasured books. When he arrived at Dorchester on 9 January, he was carrying a new copy of Thomas Carlyle's *Sartor Resartus*. His oldest daughter, Jean, had saved up the wrappers from Surprise Soap and sent away for a new copy to replace her father's well-worn edition of this favourite book.[31]

In the prison yard at Dorchester there was some curiosity about the older prisoner, and McLachlan was apt to find a humorous side in the

conversations. According to one story, another inmate asked McLachlan why he was in jail:

"Sedition," said Jim.
The prisoner drew back in amazement and awe.
"Is that something to do with women?" he whispered!
"Sometimes," said Jim.
"How many times did you do it?"
"Dozens," said Jim.[32]

Liberation

The movement for McLachlan's liberation began within hours of
his conviction. While Wolvin was telegraphing his congratulations to
O'Hearn, the coal miners were protesting the verdict. According to the
Post, "the general opinion seemed to be one of regret over the outcome
of the trial." In Glace Bay, Mayor Morrison found the verdict "a most
disagreeable surprise" and a meeting of the Phalen local in Glace Bay
declared, "We can only judge that he was found 'guilty' because he was
a devoted fighter for the interests of the miners of Nova Scotia
against the corporation which exploits them." At this stage there was
still hope that McLachlan would receive a suspended sentence, and
a number of union locals in the Sydney Mines area passed resolutions appealing for leniency.[33]

The announcement of the sentence at the end of October unleashed
a flood of letters, telegrams, and petitions, and the defence of McLachlan became a national cause, a modest instance of common action by
workers across the country. One of the first resolutions to arrive at the
offices of the minister of justice in Ottawa came from a public meeting
of the Labor Church in Edmonton, Alberta, on 4 November. There
followed dozens of protests from individual locals, labour councils, and
public meetings in all parts of the country: from the coalfields of
Alberta and British Columbia, from machinists and garment workers
in Montreal, from railway workers in Moncton and Halifax, from
labour councils in Calgary and Montreal. In London, Ontario, railway
workers described McLachlan's conviction as "a travesty of our com-

mon right of free speech." Steelworkers in Hamilton denounced the
Nova Scotia arrests as "a frame-up on the part of someone to break the
morale of the strikers and to drive the men into submission." From
Calgary the officers of District 18, UMW, protested the sentence as
"vicious": "We desire to point out that the representatives of labor in
the Winnipeg Strike of 1919 were sentenced to one years imprisonment
for a far more serious charge."[34]

The campaign for McLachlan's release intensified after the appeal
was denied and he was transferred to Dorchester in January. A common
resolution sponsored by the Nova Scotia Workers' Defence Committee
and endorsed by public meetings in Cape Breton called either for his
release or for a new trial to take place in Cape Breton, "which is his
home and where his honesty and integrity are known and an impartial
verdict can be given by unprejudiced fellow citizens." The same resolution was approved by other groups across the country and sent on to
Ottawa both by radicals such as the OBU's R.B. Russell on behalf of the
Winnipeg Central Labour Council and by craft unionists such as Percy
Bengough on behalf of the Vancouver Trades and Labour Council.

The Nova Scotia Workers' Defence Committee continued to provide
support for the dependants of imprisoned strikers and other victims
of the 1923 strike: "It becomes the imperative duty of every worker to
give unstintingly for the support of these helpless little children who
are deprived of their bread by the decision of the court." As Christmas
approached, the benefit picnics and baseball games of summer gave
way to new appeals. The committee issued so-called Defence Stamps
which sold for ten cents each and showed a man in chains and
the slogan "Release the Nova Scotia Strikers." In Sydney Mines a
defence concert was held in the Strand Theatre on 13 December;
the hall was filled almost to capacity and there was "not a dull
moment" in the entertainment.[35]

Resolutions from the municipal governments in the coal towns and
in Sydney also appealed for McLachlan's release. In Dominion, once a
stronghold of the old PWA, the town council offered a glowing testimonial to the character of the prisoner: "Whereas the said McLachlan
has for many years been a peaceable and law abiding citizen of Cape
Breton County and held in high esteem by all who know him for his

honesty and integrity and we believe he will conduct himself as a law abiding citizen if returned to this community be it therefore resolved that we respectfully request the Honorable the minister of Justice for Canada to order the release of the said McLachlan and permit him to return to his family and friends in Cape Breton."

There were also petitions from individual public figures, some of whom were well known to the prime minister. From his retirement in Oakville, Ontario, Phillips Thompson, the veteran labour radical of the 1880s who had influenced William Lyon Mackenzie King and other university students in their youth, wrote directly to the prime minister: "It would be much to be regretted should Canada follow the bad example of the degenerate republic across the border, with its judicial frame-ups, its scores of political prisoners and its brutal suppression of free speech."

Woodsworth took up the case with special vigour. He was in a strong moral position to plead McLachlan's case; he, too, had been charged with seditious libel during the Winnipeg General Strike. Now, as a Member of Parliament with considerable influence over the fate of King's minority government, Woodsworth was in an effective position to arouse public interest in the case and exert pressure on the government. Throughout the winter of 1924 the McLachlan case was a staple theme in Woodsworth's speeches. In January he spent a week touring Nova Scotia and pleading McLachlan's case in local halls. At the Savoy Theatre in Glace Bay, Woodsworth delivered an extensive review of "capitalist laws used to bind and gag the labor movement." He drew the obvious parallels with Winnipeg and pointed out that McLachlan's conviction only increased his qualifications to sit on the workers' behalf in the House of Commons: "If he should by any chance serve out his time in Dorchester it may chance that as in the case of three of the Winnipeg seditionists the day he leaves jail he may take his seat in Parliament." And then again there was the parallel with Howe:

Joseph Howe fought against the Family Compact which stood in the way of political democracy. In these days our great corporations have developed an autocratic power that is more dangerous to the democracy of our time than the Family Compact was to that of our grandfathers. All honour to the man who had the courage to stand up and defy those who are threatening the fundamental liberties of British subjects. McLachlan is in the penitentiary because he remained true to the workers. Will the workers remain true to McLachlan?[36]

In Ottawa the TLC's executive council also advanced the case for McLachlan's release at its annual meeting with the Dominion cabinet on 13 January 1924. The appeal was far from an endorsement of McLachlan or his views, but his imprisonment, King was told, "made heroes of that type ... and threw discredit upon the more rational leaders of the labor movement."[37] The danger of making McLachlan a working-class hero was also appreciated by the editors of the Toronto *Globe*, who rejected a letter on the McLachlan case in forthright terms: "We do not care to print your letter which makes a hero of MacLachlan."[38]

There were also protests against the release of McLachlan. The Cape Breton Liberal MP George W. Kyte, one of McLachlan's rivals in the 1921 election, expressed his concerns to the prime minister: "If he is liberated now, without having served any portion of his sentence, it will be accepted by his friends as an admission on the part of the Government that his trial was unfair and his conviction illegal." The Employers' Association of Manitoba, supported by the Winnipeg Board of Trade, warned that any such action "would have a most injurious effect on this country and result in further acts of sedition and lawlessness and disobedience to the authority of the State."

Besco President Roy Wolvin himself also offered some words of advice to the prime minister:

I certainly do not want any man in prison that does not belong there but I feel that our courts are the means provided to decide such matters and that the Supreme Court of Nova Scotia recently in refusing his appeal must have acted wisely.

I have had much experience with this man's activities and I consider him a dangerously clever "Red." He has cost the coal mining companies of Nova Scotia many millions of dollars and the miners an equal amount. Some leaders in this district today will say with bravado to let him come back but I do not agree with them. He is the concentrated cause of past unrest in this district and with him away for a few years, possibly, his teachings may be forgotten.[39]

Concerned about the movement for the release of McLachlan, O'Hearn met with the solicitor general in Ottawa to argue against clemency: "It is not in the interests of peace and order in the community that he should receive any clemency while he maintains his present defiant attitude." The interview could not have been satisfactory. The solicitor general of the day was E.J. McMurray, a young lawyer elected as the MP for Winnipeg North in 1921. He was named to the cabinet in 1923 as a western representative, in part to help balance the appointment to cabinet of E.M. Macdonald, the Nova Scotia MP who had played a minor part in the drama of the miners' struggles in July 1923. Interestingly, McMurray had participated as a defence lawyer in the trials arising from the Winnipeg General Strike. As solicitor general, McMurray placed no obstacles in the way of McLachlan's early release.

Indeed, preparations for McLachlan's possible release on parole began remarkably early, within a week of his sentence at the end of October. Initially the McLachlan file was a matter of some confusion at the Department of Justice, where it was mistakenly believed first that McLachlan had been sent to Dorchester and then that he had been released on bail pending his appeal. Officials were also surprised to find that he had been tried in Halifax rather than Sydney. They clearly had not been following the case closely, since the objection to holding the trial in Halifax was one of the main elements in the defence case. Until McLachlan was finally transferred to Dorchester, however, petitioners were informed, the solicitor general would not be in a position to consider any recommendations for parole.

As soon as McLachlan's appeal failed and he was delivered to the penitentiary, the Department of Justice requested a report from the trial judge concerning the case. Judge Mellish filed a report supporting the jury's verdict and defending his own handling of the trial: "I gave the accused a light sentence, perhaps unjustifiably so, but partly at least for the reason that the peculiar nature of this offence is such that it is desirable that the judiciary should not have the appearance, much less the disposition, of being inimical to labour."

At the time of McLachlan's arrival at Dorchester in January, the prison population included six participants in the 1923 steel strike. These workers had been rounded up in the wake of the strike and charged with a variety of offences, including rioting and "being unlawfully masked at night." In November 1923 they were tried and convicted in county court, without a jury, before Judge Duncan Finlayson in Sydney, and each received a sentence of two years. They, too, had received the support of the Nova Scotia Workers' Defence Committee, and by this time plans for their release were well under way. Judge Finlayson himself had written in their support: "They are not bad men but were unfortunate enough to be recognized and apprehended from out of the thousand others, most of whom were as bad as those apprehended." Parole for the first of these prisoners was approved on 12 January and for the last on 30 January 1924.[40]

At Dorchester, Warden Goad, somewhat to his own amazement, was also completing a report for the Remission Branch of the Department of Justice barely two weeks after McLachlan's arrival. From the point of view of a progressive reformer, this was hardly enough time to pronounce on the rehabilitation of a criminal. Besides, in Goad's view, recommendations for parole should not originate in Ottawa but with the staff of the penitentiaries who were in the best position to judge their progress. At the annual meeting of prison wardens in September 1924, Goad would second a resolution stating that "the unequal treatment and unfair discrimination accorded inmates in this respect is detrimental to the discipline of the institution and militates against the work of reformation."[41]

McLachlan's case, however, was obviously not a typical one, and on the file Goad noted only: "Conduct so far good. Has not been here long enough to gain remission." Was the prisoner's conduct satisfactory? "Yes Good." Was he likely to lead a moral and honest life on his release? "I cannot say."

The final recommendation was prepared by the chief of Remission Branch on 27 February 1924 with the following assessment: "This man had not been previously convicted of wrongdoing and ordinarily had a good standing in the community where he was resident. His offence was one which was committed in times of grave unrest in the community and the abuse of free speech could not in the circumstances be overlooked." With the endorsement of the solicitor general, the recommendation went forward to Rideau Hall the following day, where the document was stamped "Approved." It was signed with a flourish by the man who had failed to deliver a peace agreement to McLachlan and the coal miners in the summer of 1923: "Byng of Vimy."

Anticipating McLachlan's imminent liberation, Dan Livingstone, the codefendant whose case would never be brought to trial, wrote McLachlan a short letter on 3 March 1924 containing instructions to phone Westville immediately on his release. Livingstone would meet the train and "your thousands of friends in N.S. will give you a real welcome home." The letter was received in the warden's office on 4 March and passed along to McLachlan.[42] There is a popular story that McLachlan delayed his departure for twenty-four hours in order to finish making a pair of shoes for a fellow prisoner in the prison workshop, and the warden's correspondence confirms that McLachlan elected "at his own request" to remain at Dorchester until Wednesday, 5 March.

For a few hours before his release McLachlan was still alone with his thoughts. Throughout his imprisonment his letters home and his conversations with visitors featured humour and defiance. But now that the ordeal was ending he would allow himself to record a measure of his own personal anguish. His thoughts were of Kate, and in a few lines he wrote out the distilled emotion of a lifetime. Alone in his cell McLachlan turned over Livingstone's greetings and on the back wrote:

Thou laggard sun across the sky you loafed the whole day through,
And now jay-faced upon the hill you keep my cell in view,
A wag I always found you when I want[ed] most your light,
Across the sky you always plunged in your most headlong flight,
But now above the wooded hill you stand staring through my bars,
For heaven['s] sake go hide yourself and let God hang out the stars.

It was ever thus with you, thou sun, when I would Katie meet,
You would hurry like some wild war horse a-down a burning street.
When from Katie I was parted, you would lounge and loaf and play,
And stretch the hours both broad and long, along each joyless day,
Just twelve more hours and I'll be free from this my prison cell,
But there jayfaced you gaping stand, all to prolong my hell,
Just twelve more hours and the days are o'er that from Katie I've been
    riven,
Just twelve more hours then grudging sun, It's Kate and me and
    heaven.[43]

Return

McLachlan stepped off the Maritime Express at Truro on the afternoon of 5 March. Kate was there to meet him. They left for Cape Breton the following evening. On the way there was a stopover in New Glasgow, where Livingstone had arranged a "triumphal reception" from the Pictou County miners.

It was a late and rainy evening when McLachlan appeared before his first public audience in more than four months. The Academy of Music was packed to the doors when he appeared on stage, "and the building fairly rocked with applause." The cheering coal miners found McLachlan's fighting spirit undiminished by his stint in jail, and he entertained the audience at length with the details of his trial, ridiculing his persecutors, doling out equal measures of scorn for John L. Lewis and Walter O'Hearn. Then he explained the true nature of his crime: "Sedition, said Mr. McLachlan, is when you protest against the wrongs inflicted on working men; when you protest against the resources of the province being put in the control of men like Roy Wolvin; when wage rates are forced on you without your consent. These things will be given back to the working class and their wrongs will eventually be redeemed. If you say that strongly enough, you are liable to get into jail for sedition."[44]

Obviously unreformed, McLachlan left on the midnight train for another hero's welcome in Cape Breton. The next morning he was met by huge crowds at the railway station in Sydney and given a rousing reception at the steelworkers' hall on Charlotte Street. Then he boarded the electric railway car for Glace Bay, where several thousand people were waiting to welcome him home. According to police reports, two brass bands and cheering crowds accompanied him through the slush-filled streets of Glace Bay to a public meeting at the Savoy Theatre. The theatre was packed to capacity and there was so much shouting and cheering that the police had difficulty writing down his remarks. In short, the police noted, "He has returned 'quite' the conquering hero."[45]

It was an emotional return and McLachlan was moved by the enthusiastic reception:

How generous the workers are. No greater honor could have been done to a man than was done me at New Glasgow. I was only a few hours out of the Pen., and the miners from all over Pictou County gathered at midnight to give me welcome. They filled the largest hall in New Glasgow, many of them walking six miles in the rain at midnight. A like welcome was given me at all the mining towns along the Railway, and when I reached Glace Bay the people blocked the street. All of this, while it made me feel glad, yet made me feel I was accepting far more than I deserved.[46]

That night in New Glasgow, McLachlan had delivered the first torrential instalment in his defence speech. There would be much more in the weeks to come. He would even return to Halifax to give the speech he had not given in court, this time before a sympathetic crowd in a Dartmouth labour hall presided over by friends such as Joe Wallace. There was a wry and spirited flavour to his account, and McLachlan masterfully embroidered the absurdities and scandals of the story.

"When I look back on the trial it rather amuses me," he began. "The reasons given why I should go to jail were strange indeed." From the beginning, he confessed, he had difficulty keeping track of the charges against him, and he challenged the audience to calculate the number of years he was facing: "Since 1919 the Government in its wisdom had changed that law and amended it so that it was a penalty of twenty years for each count. I had three against me, and I had sent out 35 of the letters ..."

But in the end the charges were clear enough: "Ultimately they simmered down to one charge with three counts, the charge of sedition":

That was something new in Nova Scotia. I know you know exactly what that is. I had published a letter denouncing the Armstrong Government here for sending thugs into the City of Sydney and beating up men and women. That actually took place. They rode up the avenue that Sunday night and old men and old women, men and women, and boys and girls; age, sex, disability didn't appeal to those brutes. They beat one old Italian woman up, she had her head split open, and in one hand she had a string of beads and in the other a prayer book and they say to say these things against an arm of the Government is sedition. So much the worse for them. I would be ashamed of myself if my old mother had reared me to this time of life and I refused to revolt against a thing like that. I am proud of that.

Having fully repeated the offending seditious matter, McLachlan went on to paint a theatrical portrait of the trial, with a satirical emphasis on the personality of the attorney general:

I sat in the dock and saw the Attorney General going through the Court Room with his mind made up to get me, and the twelve jurymen, and the old judge on the bench. A fellow gets a little nervous when that thing takes place. I was very anxious not to miss anything of the reasons why I should be sent to jail, and I will give you some of the reasons the Attorney General gave to the jurymen – the reasons given to bring in a conviction against me; and they did it …

He said to the jury – and the twelve men were just as agitated as I was and a little more, he says "When I took over the office of Attorney General I determined to lock horns with this man McLachlan." If he had horns on, I didn't, and I don't believe that was a good reason to give to the jurymen why I should go to Dorchester; and he strutted through the Court Room bellowing

like a bull and tossing his legal horns in the air – and that was one
of the reasons he gave.

And he says to these twelve men, my father and my mother both
came from the south of Ireland and I love the British Constitution.
If the good St. Patrick chased all the snakes out of Ireland and one
of the horned variety had to become the Attorney General of Nova
Scotia why should I go to jail for that? I could see he was bent on
getting me to the pen, no matter what happened. A man from the
South of Ireland who turns around and casts reflections on the
race he sprang from, a traitor to Ireland, he gives his treachery to
Ireland as a reason why I should go to the Penitentiary; and so
they put me in jail.

But this was more than a speech in McLachlan's own defence, for it
culminated in a lengthy indictment of the stock gamblers and political
flunkeys who were responsible for the sorry state of the coal industry
in Nova Scotia. Roy Wolvin was attacked for his patronage of politicians
in Newfoundland and newspapers in Halifax: "If it costs $43,000 to buy
a Newfoundland Premier, how much does it cost to buy a Nova Scotian?" As for the matter of contracts, his acute sense of responsible
manhood provided a standard of comparison: "Talk about sacred
contracts! There is one sacred contract. When you take a woman to
the altar and promise and swear to love and support her, that is a
sacred contract. I will break any contract to keep that one. That is
what counts."

Then McLachlan went on to review the familiar catalogue of grievances against Besco: the watered stock and the punitive contracts, the
unenforced safety regulations, and the regular dispatches of police:
"You can't have peace where the workers are betrayed and where the
contract gives the boss the right to bully the men and the employers lie.
You will have war to the knife and that is what is happening in Cape
Breton … When men are betrayed, when men are being bullied and
broken and bled you cannot have peace; and that is all they are doing
it for, to get cheap coal for Wolvin so that he may pay dividends on
watered stock." As long as such conditions prevailed, there would be
no peace in the coal industry.

Already, McLachlan noted, there were calls for his return to prison, most notably from high-placed individuals such as Raoul Dandurand, a member of the Senate who, like several fellow Senators, happened also to be a director of Besco: "They want me in jail, not because I am saying things that are true but because what I say jeopardizes the profits made out of the blood and sweat of the working classes in Cape Breton, out of the children and out of their homes, so they may get their dividends. What kind of peace do they want?"

But his release, McLachlan was pleased to say, was the achievement of the workers of Canada and was guaranteed by them, not by governments and corporations: "I want to thank you for the protests and resolutions that were made on my behalf; that is the reason I am here, because of what the workers did, not because of the generosity of the King Government or O'Hearn or any of those men. I am not indebted to them, but to the working classes I am indebted for the freedom I have today ... I am glad to get out because the workers got me out."[47]

McLachlan was returning to the class struggle unrepentant, possibly even courting a return to jail. The ticket-of-leave was not a pardon but a form of conditional release which allowed a convict to remain at liberty on good behaviour. Under the terms of his release McLachlan carried a passbook which would be regularly stamped and signed by the local police in Glace Bay until the formal expiry of his sentence on 30 October 1925. The formal conditions of release included the blanket requirement to "abstain from any violation of the law." Yet in the weeks and months after his release almost all his speeches and writings repeated the substance of the seditious libel for which he had been convicted. At one public meeting, for instance, an informant recorded a detailed stenographic report, and the most offensive passages were carefully underlined and studied in the premier's office. McLachlan was running a calculated risk. There would be no reprisals against him, for as far as McLachlan was concerned his release was a political act, a special concession by the state to the workers. For McLachlan, his liberty was guaranteed not by the rule of law but by the support of his class.

On his return to Steele's Hill, McLachlan was uncertain about the future. Some of his feelings are recorded in a letter to Woodsworth.

McLachlan continued to address Woodsworth respectfully as "Comrade Woodsworth" and thanked him fully for his efforts in securing his release. For the moment, McLachlan wrote, there were large meetings to address: "After that I shall have to settle down to some regular job." Already he had been approached by the directors of the *Maritime Labor Herald* about assuming the editorship of the paper. He confessed some uncertainty about taking on the newspaper: "At first I refused because I did not think that I was able for the job, now I think I am going to take that job. What do you think? Should I take it?"[48]

The other issue facing McLachlan on his return to the coalfields was the future of the UMW in Nova Scotia. McLachlan had led the coal miners into the UMW, first in 1909 and then again in 1919. In order to take his revenge on Lewis, would he now lead the coal miners out of the international union, perhaps into the OBU? Or would he lead a fight against Lewis inside the UMW?

On the night of his release from Dorchester, such thoughts were high in McLachlan's mind: "John L. Lewis thought he was putting McLachlan out of the Labor movement. You cannot put a man out of the Labor movement. Some men are in it and some men are on its back. I am in the Labor movement, and the Mine Workers cannot put me out of it. I was born in it, lived for it, and will die in it. John L. Lewis is on its back."[49]

CHAPTER 9

1925: Standing the Gaff

Rise like lions after slumber
In unvanquishable number;
Shake your chains to earth like dew
Which in sleep has fallen on you —
Ye are many — they are few.

– P.B. Shelley, "What is Slavery?"
Maritime Labor Herald, 21 February 1925

The Editor

In November 1924 the winds came hard from the north and west. They blew up a storm along the shores, knocked down fences in the yards and coated the landscape in a salty frost. By January the coal towns were locked in deep snow and a winter chill that was the worst in years. There was an interval of warm weather and sunshine for several weeks in February. Then came the storms of March – cold rains and raging winds that battered the coal towns and in their wake left no hope of an early spring.

No one ever forgot the winter of 1925. All the turmoil of 1923 had solved nothing, and during 1924 the provisional regime in District 26 collapsed in confusion. There was a financial controversy, an unpopular contract, and the threat of a rival union. Meanwhile, McLachlan was out of jail. And six months later, after more than a year of supposed purification, District 26 was back on its feet, once again under the leadership of the labour radicals.

Under the familiar pressures of the Canadian coal market and the corporation's financial embarrassments, Besco's condition was steadily worsening. Once again the coal operators were announcing wage cuts, and the coal miners were challenging the justice and logic of a corporate-survival strategy that condemned them to permanent poverty. The 1925 strike is still remembered as the saddest, most difficult struggle in the history of the Cape Breton coal miners.

A journalist who visited Glace Bay at the end of 1924 on behalf of *MacLean's Magazine* sought out McLachlan for an interview. It was almost an afterthought in his survey of local conditions. The "reds," claimed Norman Reilly Raine, were more or less in retirement since the failure of the 1923 strike – but it was difficult to resist his own curiosity about the famous leader of the Cape Breton coal miners. He found

355

McLachlan upstairs in an old building opposite the railway station in what seemed to be a club room for the local radicals. The walls were painted a dull red and held pictures of Marx and Lenin as well as a large revolutionary poster from Italy. There were piles of old newspapers on the floor and a few rough wooden tables and chairs, some of them occupied by men who nodded a sociable greeting.

McLachlan welcomed the visitor brusquely – "What do ye want?" – and instructed him to sit down and have a smoke. Raine observed with some disdain that McLachlan was "a short, bow-legged little man, with a face lined and pitted with years of struggle, keen eyes beneath shaggy brows, a straggly red moustache, a soiled collar much too large for him and a wrinkled suit rather the worse for wear." A few minutes later McLachlan sat down. He warmed to his conversation with the reporter, and there was an appealing twinkle in his eye as McLachlan explained that he did not expect to be quoted accurately in a capitalist magazine. Raine came away finding "something decidedly likeable" about McLachlan. It was easy to see that McLachlan should not be underestimated: "He is a man with plenty of hard, common-logic beneath his communistic nonsense, and he is a clever and resourceful fighter." Raine's strongest impression was that "regardless of his views, McLachlan is basically sincere in his concern for the welfare of the working man."

As the reporter left the hall, McLachlan called after him with a forecast of the renewed class struggle – and a reminder that he was ready for the fight: "The company's goin' for tae try another wage cut in the spring, but mark ye, bye, the miners of Cape Breton'll be flat on their backs afore they'll tak'it! Mind that!"[1]

In March 1924, when McLachlan returned to Glace Bay, the *Maritime Labor Herald* announced that he was "returning to finish his work." Although invited to take charge of an organizing campaign among the Sydney steelworkers, McLachlan was not prepared to leave so much unfinished work among the coal miners. Apart from accounts of his adventures in the legal system, McLachlan's speeches in March and April 1924 were filled with militant rhetoric about the betrayals of the international union and the forthcoming struggles against the corporation. There was even talk of reviving McLachlan's strategy of 1922, the strike on the job, as a means of resistance. A police report noted that McLachlan was "as active and as radical as ever, and a foe to the British Empire Steel Corporation." Another report in May indicated that the unpopularity of the international union and the weakness of the provisional executive "gave more power and popularity to J.B. McLachlan, and his influence becomes more powerful every day." The miners were "in a fighting mood" and "more determined than ever to elect J.B. McLachlan to the district office."[2]

But as long as the district remained under suspension, there was no means of returning McLachlan to office in the UMW. Although the radicals had lost their appeal to the international convention in January 1924, there was still hope of making common cause against John L. Lewis with dissidents in other UMW districts. The radicals' strategy at this time was a temporizing one – to keep up pressure for restoration of the district's independence within the UMW and resist the attractions of groups such as the One Big Union. In this they were following the united-front strategy endorsed by the Communist International.

At the national convention of the Workers' Party of Canada, held in the Labour Temple in Toronto in April 1924, McLachlan was welcomed as a hero of the class struggle and elected to the party's Central Executive Committee. The Nova Scotia situation received prominent mention in a letter from the Executive Committee of the Communist International, a kind of report card from Moscow on the performance of the Canadian party. The campaign for McLachlan's release from penitentiary won a positive assessment, but there was also some criticism: "It could and should have been more intensified and broadened," up to and including a one-day general strike. In addition, the party was cautioned to uphold the united front in the coalfields of Nova Scotia and Alberta: "It is possible that the miners of District 26 and District 18, because of their defeat at the recent convention of the United Mine Workers of America, may slide back into a secessionist mood and contemplate splits, but you should spare no efforts to combat all these attempts. The miners should be made to understand that this would mean to play into the hands of the reactionaries, since there is nothing that would please them more than secession at the present time."[3]

Such comments assumed that the Communist Party of Canada (the name of the Workers' Party was abandoned at this convention) was in a position to exercise direct influence on local events in Nova Scotia. But as Tim Buck pointed out in his report on industrial policy, the party leadership had played little part in the conduct of the 1923 strike – "the strike was called almost spontaneously, and almost every move that was made was learned of by the Central Executive through the medium of the capitalist press ..." This was evidence of "the immaturity of our party, and the complete lack of the close cooperation between District and Center so essential to successful action on a large scale." The party's influence in Nova Scotia depended mainly on "a group of very sincere revolutionists occupying positions of leadership," and Buck expected to see a renewal of the struggle in the coming months: "Comrade McLachlan is very active since his release from Prison, and the sentiment throughout the District is strong for a fight." All this discussion impressed McLachlan with the significance attached to the Nova Scotia situation; given the problems of "looseness and localism" identified by Buck, he was also reminded of his own ability, as the leading light among the Cape Breton Communists, to influence local events.[4]

On his return to Glace Bay, McLachlan settled down to his new position as editor of the *Maritime Labor Herald*. The departure of the former editor, the Communist organizer Tom Bell, was reported on 12 April, with a note that "Tom's job is being partly filled by J.B. McLachlan." Bell was known as a hot-headed, hard-drinking rebel, not the kind of model of revolutionary virtue McLachlan preferred. A month later McLachlan, listed on the masthead as vice-president, had settled in as editor and was placing his personal stamp on the contents of the newspaper. The same slogans continued to appear on the front page – on one side of the title a quotation from Karl Marx: "Workers of all countries, unite! You have nothing to lose but your chains, and a world to win"; on the other side a brief political platform supplied by the Communist Party: "We demand: A Labor Party, Industrial Unionism, Nationalization of Industry with Workers' Control."[5]

Interestingly, the installation of McLachlan as editor even received notice in the pages of the *Financial Post*, the influential business newspaper, which paid him a backhanded tribute: "The fact that Jim McLachlan has recently taken over the editorship of the Herald will not lessen its dangerous qualities. McLachlan has an uncanny faculty of putting his finger on the sore spot and pointing the moral in words few and succinct." In response, McLachlan gave his own informal statement of purpose in a front-page statement: "The *Maritime Labor Herald* is openly the avowed enemy of capitalism and the capitalist class. We do our damndest in every issue to help drive the plundering crew from place and power and put them to work to earn an honest living."[6]

McLachlan's voice could be heard most clearly in the editorials, where he commented on each stage of local developments and preached a message of perpetual preparation for the class struggle. In general, the pages of the *Maritime Labor Herald* presented a mix of labour news and political agitation, local and international, all of which confirmed the existence of a working-class culture of resistance. There were controversies over safety conditions in the collieries, the salaries of company officials, and the balance sheets of the corporation. There were reports on the activities of local unions, labour parties, educational clubs, and branches of the Women's Labour League. There was a lively sports page, much of it written by Dawn Fraser, who also presented excerpts from his labour verse. From Ottawa there was J.S. Woodsworth writing about politics; from Toronto, Rebecca Buhay wrote on "Woman's Place in History"; from Halifax, Joe Wallace supplied essays on the relationship between communism and Christianity and on the record of the British Labour government.

There was also McLachlan's mordant sense of humour, which could be a redeeming quality even in the eyes of his detractors. For labour radicals, Samuel Gompers, founder of the American Federation of Labor in the 1880s, was an arch-enemy who for decades divided and weakened the working class. When Gompers died in 1924, McLachlan's comment in the *Maritime Labor Herald* was sometimes remembered as a response to an actual invitation to the funeral: "Sam Gompers, after serving the master class faithfully for forty years, is dead. We shall be unable to attend his funeral, but heartily approve of the event."[7]

In September, McLachlan's career as a newspaper editor was interrupted by a fire on the premises of the *Maritime Labor Herald*. The blaze started at the back of the cellar, where a door was left open. The building was badly damaged – the roof was burned and the offices were soaked – but not beyond repair. The circumstances were suspicious. The fire took place only a few days after the *Herald* published a bulletin reporting the removal of the provisional officers, and it was widely considered to be an act of retribution for the newspaper's part in trying to win back local control of the union. But the *Herald* did not miss a single issue, and McLachlan regarded the rapid recovery as a small triumph. When the newspaper celebrated its third anniversary the following month, there were front-page greetings from both J.S. Woodsworth and Tim Buck, and a rhyming set of verses from Dawn Fraser greeting the "child and champion of the workers" with a reference to the recent fire: "Yes the Bosses felt your power, / And they got some slave for hire, / One dark night while you were sleeping, / For to set your crib on fire."[8]

But for all the satisfactions of bringing out a successful weekly newspaper, the editor's chair left McLachlan seated at a distance from the action – and he waited with impatience for the next round of the struggle. One police report in 1924 noted his sense of frustration: "McLachlan sits in the Maritime Labor Herald every day, but is very sad and grouchy."[9] Although his restraint was tested, McLachlan continued to count himself a supporter of the united-front strategy and was prepared to keep pushing for the restoration of District 26. Indeed, when the One Big Union attempted to attract the miners away from the UMW in the summer of 1924, McLachlan's personal prestige helped convince local radicals that this was not the road back to power.

One Big Union

In the heady days of 1919 and 1920, as many as 70,000 workers signed membership cards and joined the One Big Union. At that time the OBU was a hopeful symbol of radical industrial unionism, embracing the philosophy of class struggle and proposing a new structure of labour organization to replace the existing unions. But the OBU was unable to capitalize on its moment of opportunity, and the house of labour remained more divided than reconstructed. Leaders such as R.B. Russell and William Pritchard were preoccupied with their trials in the wake of the Winnipeg Strike, and by the time they were released from prison at the end of 1920, the organization was in decline. Winnipeg remained a relative stronghold for the OBU, but elsewhere support was falling.

By 1922 veterans such as Joseph Knight and Malcolm Bruce, influenced by Lenin's critique of "leftism," were finding a new home in the Workers' Party. Meanwhile, the *OBU Bulletin* had worked out a spectacularly successful marketing strategy by running a weekly lottery on soccer and baseball games, and eventually on weather predictions as well, until the contest was shut down by the courts. But the union's organizing campaigns never succeeded in restoring membership to the promising levels of its first years.[10]

McLachlan's attitude towards the OBU was always ambivalent, and in 1919 he had opposed the OBU strategy of working outside the TLC and the international unions. His own successes as a union leader within the structure of the UMW gave him no reason to join a breakaway movement that threatened to divide the coal miners. But in 1923 news of the miners' betrayal by the international union reawakened the OBU's hopes of success in Nova Scotia, and in 1924 they directed special attention to the opportunities in the coalfields.

The most flamboyant of the OBU organizers to come to Nova Scotia in 1924 was Ben Legere – a Massachusetts stage actor who achieved some celebrity as the star of a touring melodrama (about an American scientist and a Hawaiian princess) called *The Bird of Paradise*. While performing in Calgary in 1919 he was caught up in the local labour agitation and arrested for making a speech attacking Tom Moore of the TLC. After he was bailed out by OBU supporters, Legere pledged that he and his wife – a Hollywood movie actress – would volunteer two months of work for the union every summer. Apart from having a theatrical background, Legere was also an experienced labour organizer; as a Wobbly he participated in the famous "Bread and Roses" strike of the textile workers in Lawrence, Massachusetts in 1912 and organized support for arrested union leaders; the following year he went to jail for his part in another textile strike in New York; in 1920 he worked for a pioneering industrial union in New England, the Amalgamated Textile Workers of America. Legere's attraction to the OBU was more than quixotic. He was dissatisfied with disunion and bureaucracy in organized labour and saw the radicalism of the OBU as the logical successor to that of the Wobblies; Legere was particularly impressed by the OBU plan to organize workers on a community basis rather than by craft or industry alone. His enthusiasm for the OBU was so strong that he led a breakaway from the textile union in 1921 and established a local chapter in Lawrence. Although the OBU expansion into the United States failed, for a short time in the early 1920s, writes one historian, "Lawrence served as the centre of the OBU in eastern North America."[11]

As it turned out, Legere spent more than six months in Nova Scotia attempting to build another base for the OBU in the east. Arriving in June 1924, his first report back to the *OBU Bulletin* drew a gloomy picture of confusion and discouragement among the once-militant coal miners: "The progressive, militant, and fearless organization of District 26 has either crawled into a hole or faded away." The misguided strategy of working for reform inside the discredited international union was "emasculating" the coal miners, and the radical leaders seemed to be more interested in gaining union offices than leading the struggle: "What good is there in a district election when we're still under the dictatorship of John L. Lewis? Of what use is it for sheep to talk vegetarianism and pass resolutions on it if they leave the wolf in control of the fold? There is only one way out it: organize on the outside in a class union based on the class struggle, controlled by the rank and file of the workers, embracing the class conscious revolutionary workers of the world. The One Big Union is such a one." In his attack on the local radicals, Legere was careful not to mention McLachlan by name. But he made it clear that the blame for the coal miners' weakness must be directed at "some of the self-styled Lenines and Trotzkys of Canada, representing the Workers' Party in this district."[12]

Despite Legere's attacks on his political position, McLachlan was still prepared to appear on a platform with the OBU organizer. On a rainy August evening in Wentworth Park, McLachlan joined in support of the OBU's organizing drive among the Sydney steelworkers. From McLachlan's point of view, the failure of the steel strike had left the steelworkers defenceless and without organization, and there was a considerable difference between a policy of sowing division among the coal miners and one of bringing organization to the steelworkers. The *OBU Bulletin* welcomed McLachlan's message of support for the steelworkers and his advice for the local struggle: "Go down and picket the steel plant and take out every maintenance man and show the British Empire Steel Corporation that if they are going to starve you, they can look after their own property." A report in the Sydney *Post* found McLachlan "in his usual fighting trim" and classified Legere as "only a second McLachlan."[13]

McLachlan's response to the OBU that summer was measured but sceptical. As early as June, he worried that the OBU threatened a re-enactment of the long schism between the UMW and the PWA that had held the miners back for so many years. He had no objection to OBU activity among the steelworkers, who were desperately in need of organization; but he attacked the OBU campaign among the coal miners on the ground that this was causing an unnecessary split: "We can fight better from within than from without. Winnipeg and Cape Breton at least point in that direction, and Soviet Russia proves it to our mind beyond the shadow of a doubt. We have been through a ten-year split in Cape Breton and we have no stomach for a like experience." In response to an OBU invitation to collaborate in organizing the coal miners, Alex McKay responded on behalf of the Glace Bay Communists that their position had been adequately explained in the *Maritime Labor Herald*: "We feel that if the OBU can start an organization among the Steel Workers it will keep any organizer on the job for the next few weeks, and as the miners are already organized we don't believe a meeting between us would help the present situation any." When McLachlan appeared at an OBU meeting himself, he spoke to a mix of hisses and cheers. He was, he said, prepared to give Comrade Legere credit that he "does not know much about the industrial condition of Nova Scotia." But a strategy of leading the Stellarton miners into a separate struggle against Besco was doomed to defeat: "The OBU has nothing to offer them and in one month the OBU will be a thing of the past."[14]

At the end of the summer, the *OBU Bulletin* announced that the OBU was making rapid progress. In Sydney a General Workers' Unit was organized, led mainly by steelworkers such as Emerson Campbell who had belonged to the old craft union in 1923. The OBU also attracted supporters among the coal miners, including one of the influential radicals in New Aberdeen, Joseph MacKinnon, who was expelled from the Communist Party as a result. OBU general secretary R.B. Russell, the famous veteran of the Winnipeg Strike who had served two years in penitentiary, also arrived to take on Communist spokesmen such as Malcolm Bruce in public debates. But except in Pictou County, where miners' units were formed in Stellarton, Thorburn, and Westville, the achievements were limited. Legere himself ran into legal difficulties when he was arrested on 15 September; he was held for deportation hearings on the ground that his prison record had placed him in violation of the Immigration Act. Legere was soon out on bail and eventually won his case. By this time Lewis had finally given up on the complete purification of Nova Scotia and announced the restoration of District 26. When Legere appeared at the doors of the District 26 convention in November, armed with credentials from the OBU locals in Pictou County, he was refused admission.[15]

As the struggle against Besco was renewed in the winter of 1925, it was clear that the OBU could be no more than a supporting actor in the conflict. By March, Legere was in New York City, looking for work in the theatre. The reinstatement of District 26 robbed the OBU of its strongest argument against the international union. Legere could reflect with chagrin that his vigorous campaign had indirectly helped bring the Cape Breton reds back to power in the miners' union; presumably Lewis feared the reds he knew less than those he did not. In any event, with the beginning of the strike in March, the public rivalry between the UMW and the OBU was suspended. "The division of the workers into two organizations is not affecting the solidarity of the strike," wrote Legere. "The present leadership is intrusted to the officials of District 26 of the U.M.W., presided over by J.W. McLeod of Glace Bay." In the pages of *The Nation*, a widely read American newsmagazine, Legere's account of Nova Scotia conditions predicted a difficult struggle: "The men have been half-employed and half-hungry for years; the U.M.W. has withheld approval of the strike and relief for the strikers. But the alternative to victory now is misery through an indefinite future, and the men and their families will hold out as long as their strength endures."[16]

The Restoration

To the disappointment of John L. Lewis, Silby Barret was not a success as provisional president of District 26. Installed in office in the summer of 1923, Barrett was unable to win back support for the international union among the coal miners. When the 1922 contract expired in January 1924, the miners went out on strike, and Barrett scrambled to negotiate a new agreement. Although the coal operators had demanded a 20 per cent reduction in the wage scale, they proved surprisingly accommodating in negotiations and agreed to small increases in the rates. At the same time, almost as compensation for the radical implications of the previous agreement, the controversial clauses regarding managerial authority, omitted in 1922, were restored. And a new clause banned the withdrawal of maintenance men during strikes. In addition, union locals were prohibited from contributing to the support of the *Maritime Labor Herald.*

The strike lasted almost four weeks – but the settlement never received the expected endorsement from the union membership. When the agreement finally came to a vote on 6 March, the miners rejected the contract by a substantial margin of 5,395 to 3,200. At union headquarters Lewis received news of this setback without comment. But at its April 1924 meeting the international executive board concluded that, despite the rejection of the agreement by the members, the February agreement "must be considered as being valid until the date of its expiration."[17]

Disappointed in Barrett's failure to attract the loyalty of the coal miners, Lewis claimed to be "utterly astonished" at his spending habits and demanded a complete investigation into district finances. Secretary-Treasurer William Green announced that the financial reports from District 26 were "astounding": "It never occurred to me that any representatives of the International Organization, working under its jurisdiction, would use money in such a lavish and indefensible way." Barrett's offence was that he had failed to resist demands for support from the striking miners and had issued orders for a total of $104,319.90 without proper authorization from the international office. As a result, Barrett was forced to submit his resignation. And to repair the financial damage, the district was ordered to levy a special weekly assessment to pay off the debt.[18]

This was industrial legality with a vengeance. After all, the 1924 strike was very much in accordance with union policy – no backward step, no work without an agreement, no inappropriate picketing. In tendering his resignation, however, Barrett assured Lewis that he remained "a staunch supporter of the policies of the United Mine Workers of America and will be ready and willing at all times to go down the line with these policies." Lewis had mixed feelings about Barrett's resignation and acknowledged that "the situation in Nova Scotia is indeed badly muddled." As William Houston, the international representative from Pennsylvania who was appointed to replace Barrett as provisional president, reminded Lewis, Barrett had a long record of loyalty to the UMW: "He has fought this radical element in here in and out of season and has incurred the enmity of all of this so-called Red faction as no other man has in this District."[19]

The radicals watched Barrett's departure with amusement and some restraint. Should the coal miners refuse to pay the special assessment, on the ground that the debt was the result of "the blundering mismanagement of the appointed officers"? From Toronto the Communist Party leaders advised McLachlan to follow a more cautious strategy – by all means denounce Lewis and his shameless repudiation of obligations to District 26; but the situation should also be exploited to make some political points: "The miners of District 26 have no desire to see local tradesmen suffer for credit extended during a struggle against Besco, and are willing to meet the debt on one condition. That is that District Autonomy be restored, Elections be held, and the Workers who pay, be allowed their say ..."[20]

Lewis was also aggravated by the progress of the OBU agitation during the summer of 1924. The inroads in Pictou County were especially alarming, since the local unions there were preparing to hold votes on joining the OBU. Meanwhile, a "Council of Action" representing the local unions in District 26 was calling a convention for early October, and it was difficult to predict what decisions it might make. There was also the prospect of a renewed wage struggle when the existing contract expired in January 1925; if the coal miners had failed to support Barrett, it was even less likely they would support a provisional president from Pennsylvania in making a new agreement.

In addition, an embarrassing legal situation was developing in Nova Scotia. There were good grounds for Lewis to be concerned about the legal status of the provisional district, since an earlier Nova Scotia court judgment in 1923 had found that there was nothing in the UMW constitution empowering the international president to appoint provisional officers. So far the various radicals had failed to take advantage of this ruling, which had given them an unexplored opening for resistance through the instruments of industrial legality. But now OBU supporters in Cape Breton and Pictou County were planning to apply for a court injunction challenging the authority of the provisional officers. As Lewis was busy consolidating his power over the international union by the increasingly frequent use of provisional officers, he had no wish to risk an extended court challenge over the issue, especially in a jurisdiction where his legal position was uncertain.[21]

Lewis was in a hurry. At the end of the summer he finally decided to cut his losses in District 26, even at the price of allowing the "reds" to return to power. Instead of waiting for the next meeting of the international executive board (which would not take place until January), Lewis informed the board by mail that the district's debts had been paid off and the union contract upheld. A few days later he was able to convey detailed instructions for restoring autonomy to District 26 "at the earliest practicable date." All records of the provisional district were to be returned to international headquarters, and arrangements were to be made for a district convention and the selection of interim officers.

But there was one important restriction on the district's freedom in the instructions approved by the board: "All individuals whose offices were vacated by the executive order of July 17, 1923" were ineligible for offices of any kind in District 26. It was a condition the radicals failed to anticipate. The *Maritime Labor Herald* published a special edition to announce the news, and – after recovering from the unexplained fire on the premises – claimed that Lewis was retreating from the district because he had learned Besco was planning to bring in "the huge wage cut which they proposed in December 1921."[22]

The restoration came swiftly. Delegates to a special convention at Truro on 29 September elected a temporary executive. Robert Baxter stood for president but received only fifteen votes against fifty for John W. McLeod. Also elected were Joseph Nearing as vice-president and Alex A. McKay as secretary-treasurer. All three of these officers were from the Glace Bay district and all counted themselves followers of McLachlan; Nearing and McKay were members of the local branch of the Communist Party and McLeod, at least according to later claims, had promised to join the party. When a full membership ballot was held on 3 November, all of the candidates endorsed by the *Maritime Labor Herald* were elected. Even if McLachlan and McIntyre and other reds were banned from union office, it was proof that the radicals had not lost their influence.[23]

When a district convention assembled at Sydney on 17 November, McLachlan entered the hall to cheers. He was introduced as "an old fighter for the miners," and when asked to speak he delivered a rousing attack on Besco. At a subsequent session the miners passed a resolution of support for the deposed officers, demanding that they be given employment before a new contract with Besco was considered. Another resolution authorized payment of wages and expenses to the deposed officers for the month prior to their removal in 1923. The officers of the provisional district were all denounced as traitors to "the true principles of Unionism."[24]

All of this must have pleased McLachlan, even if it seemed to assign him more to the district's past rather than to its future. At the same time, his conduct of the *Maritime Labor Herald* came in for a round of criticism. A resolution from the Caledonia local complained that under McLachlan's editorship the newspaper was becoming a "communist organ" and called for a shareholders' meeting to discuss the paper's editorial policy; the local had circulated its concerns to all local unions before the convention and there was considerable debate before the motion was finally defeated. Some speakers argued that "only certain opinions were expressed now"; others argued that the *Herald* was "the best fighting Press that we had in the District." McLachlan did not participate in the discussion. He had already given his reply in a response to the Caledonia local which was presented to the convention.

If locals chose not to support the newspaper, that was unfortunate; but McLachlan refused to modify his editorial policy: "There is only one way to bring matters up, that is to remove from office the present editor. He is not built in such a way as to be able to express other peoples' ideas. All he claims is that he has ideas and opinions of his own and gives expression to these."[25]

The main business before the November convention was the impending struggle with Besco, and again it was clear that the radicals controlled the agenda. The wage scale and policy committee presented a review of conditions which concluded that "the miners of Nova Scotia are facing the worst crisis in their history." Since the early summer several collieries had closed, and most mines were working only two or three days a week; as a result, the coal miners had "less work than at any time in the memory of the present generation" and "the annual earnings of the miners of Nova Scotia have been reduced by fifty per cent during 1924." Already they were taking up collections and sending petitions, resolutions, and delegations to governments. None of this was solving the problem, and the immediate future was bleak. With the arrival of winter the coal operators were expected to propose a huge cut in rates and shut down at least half of the coal mines.

McLachlan's familiar message of resistance by direct action was still very much alive among the coal miners. Clause 4 of the report contained an explicit endorsement of the 100 per cent strike as an effective and legitimate weapon for the forthcoming struggle: "The workers must learn to use such weapons as are in their hands; the power to throw in jeopardy the properties of the Coal Companies by calling one hundred percent strikes and leaving those properties to the mercy of nature and the elements." Clause 6 went on to specify that any more shutdowns at the mines or attempts to reduce wage rates should be regarded as the signal for commencement of a 100 per cent strike. In the debate on the report there was no opposition to the 100 per cent strike; after all, one delegate pointed out, the company "always asked for maintenance men if a strike is in force but they never make any provisions for the women and children of the strikers." But there was concern about how the international union would respond, and some delegates urged consultation with UMW headquarters. Other cautious delegates proposed a referendum vote before a 100 per cent policy was implemented.

After several amendments, the policy statement, adopted by a vote of forty-five to thirty-eight, endorsed the principle of the 100 percent strike as "the only effective method of conducting a strike if such is necessary to fight against wage reductions." This appeared to be a firm endorsement of the tactic, but it was actually a modification of the more aggressive policy proposed by the committee, which established the 100 per cent strike as the mandatory policy. As it stood, the final decision to apply this sanction was left in the hands of the district executive.[26]

The Resistance

"Which shall it be?" In early January the front page of the *Maritime Labor Herald* boldly contrasted the prospects for the coming test of strength between the coal miners and the corporation. A 100 per cent strike meant falling slopes, frozen pipes, railways blocked with snow: "Besco property dipped in red hell – and a won strike." Anything less meant well-fed horses for the corporation, starvation for the miners' children: "protection for Besco property while stripping the backs of the miner's family – and a lost strike."[27]

With such dramatic appeals leaping off the pages and his editorials often in capital letters, McLachlan was sounding a call to arms. Besco, McLachlan declared again and again, must be destroyed. A ramshackle corporation held together by a desperate crew of stock gamblers, it had never deserved the miners' trust nor was it a worthy custodian of the province's natural resources. There was nothing in heaven above or earth below to justify starving workers for the benefit of dividends on watered stock and financial greed. This was the British *Vampire* Steel Corporation, its villainy personified in the presidency of the chief plunderer, Roy the Wolf! It was time for the coal miners to drive the thieving gang out of the province and into oblivion.

But did the coal miners have an alternative? For many observers, the answer was to be found in the replacement of Besco by a more reputable business organization. But McLachlan's alternative was the more radical one of public ownership and workers' control. This was the panacea that the union had been advancing since the end of the war, and it was also the strategic solution to the coal question advanced by the Miners' Federation of Great Britain and by the opposition to Lewis in the UMW. As in 1922, McLachlan was determined to carry the battle into the enemy's territory. In the early months of 1925, articles by Joe Wallace and Tim Buck in the *Maritime Labor Herald* elaborated on the importance of nationalization of industry. McLachlan's editorials appeared under declarations such as "Let the Miners Run the Mines" and "More Power to the Mine Committees." The mine committees constituted an "embryonic form of workers' control" in the pits. And just as the coal miners were managing successful local businesses such as the British Canadian Cooperative Society and running municipal governments in several towns, he argued, they were capable of managing the coal industry as well.[28]

Responsibility for conducting the struggle rested in the hands of the district executive led by John W. McLeod. A generation younger than McLachlan, the new president of District 26 was still old enough to be a veteran of the 1909 strike. Born at Long Beach, Cape Breton, in 1887, he had gone to work as a driver at Dominion No. 6, one of the UMW's early strongholds. After the defeat of the union in 1909, McLeod went west and worked in the coal mines at Estevan, Lethbridge, and other locations. Back in Nova Scotia he showed studious habits and, by attending night school, earned certification as a mine manager. Although he worked as an official for several years, at the end of the war McLeod returned to the coal face and took his place as one of the local union leaders who gave the miners' union its special vigour as a workers' institution. McLeod owed his election to the radicals – but he also received a favourable review from the Sydney *Post*, which described him as "well endowed with the qualities of conscience and intelligence, and such being the case he is unlikely to allow himself to be stampeded into a false or untenable position."[29]

Although the 1924 contract expired on 15 January, McLeod was reluctant to call an immediate strike. But when the company requested a conciliation board, the union refused to participate or name a member, on the grounds that its scope was too limited and past conciliation boards had failed to result in "a fair and impartial investigation of the matters which underlie our difficulties with this Corporation." The union statement, which sounded as if it was written by McLachlan, called instead for a full investigation into the affairs of the corporation: "The Country at large knows that this Corporation was conceived in iniquity and brought forth in deceit. Its pap was watered stock and puffed inventories, and it suckled heartily ... Its assault on our wages comes with annual monotony, and will continue until we are starved below the point of resistance."[30]

Meanwhile, the worsening conditions in the coalfields were attracting national attention. Woodsworth launched an emergency debate on the situation in Parliament on 24 February. His exposition started with accounts of the existing privation and agitation in the coalfields, which Woodsworth had visited yet again in January. He continued with resolutions from local meetings and civic officials, along with a reading of Shelley's "What is Slavery?" from the front page of the *Maritime Labor Herald*. All this was to remind members of Besco's shabby record and the starvation conditions endured by the miners and steelworkers under its control. At the very least, Woodsworth argued, "we should look at the matter from the standpoint of the welfare of our citizenship at large, and emphasize more particularly the humanitarian side of the question."[31]

At this stage McLeod was still hopeful that a moderate strategy could succeed. The conciliation board had never completed an investigation; it was dissolved when word arrived from London that a constitutional appeal against the Industrial Disputes Investigation Act had decided that the legislation itself was outside the powers of the Dominion government. McLachlan welcomed the demise of Mackenzie King's "pro-slavery law" with a reminder of the ways it had been used against the distribution of relief to the coal miners during the 1909 strike.[32]

In any event, McLeod preferred the idea of a royal commission with its much broader sweep of investigative authority. At a district convention in February he convinced delegates to support a four-month agreement at existing rates, pending the completion of an investigation by a royal commission. For his part, Premier E.H. Armstrong was prepared to appoint a royal commission – on the condition that both sides agreed in advance to accept its recommendations. The union objected to the compulsory element in the proposal; the corporation preferred to limit the discussion to wages and also protested that there was no need for a complete investigation into the company's affairs.[33]

Then came an unexpected act of aggression. On 2 March, Dominion Coal posted notices announcing the suspension of credit at the company stores at New Aberdeen, Caledonia, and Dominion No. 6 – all areas where the locals were strongholds of union militancy. This was a policy of starvation, McLachlan protested in the pages of the *Labor Herald*. Even the normally complacent Premier Armstrong was shocked and complained that the whole purpose of the company stores was to carry the miners over periods of slack work; "your action cannot be explained or understood," he telegraphed Wolvin in frustration. The union charged that the company was bent on wrecking the coal industry by starving the miners into accepting a wage cut. Denouncing the shutdown of the stores and the slow time at the mines as a lockout, the union announced a complete stoppage of work.[34]

A few hours before the strike deadline, McLachlan was providing a report of the situation in a letter to Woodsworth: "Besco cut off all credit to all miners who are idle, that affected about 2500 families. Their jobs gone, their little bit of credit gone, left the men no alternative. The utmost gloom is settling over the mining towns and many of the men are talking the most desperate kind of talk." McLachlan also expressed concerns about the situation in the mines, where the company was preparing for a long shutdown: "The coal company is taking the horses and the pumps out of the mines and the local government is allowing this dismantaling to take place without one word of protest. No. 10, 11 + 12 mines shall be cleaned of anything that would be a loss to the company and the flooding this time is being done by company."[35]

The strike started at 11 p.m. on 6 March, and the tie-up was complete. Maintenance men also walked out, but company officials were permitted to continue essential operations at the mines. Even before the strike started, relief committees were at work distributing supplies to the most needy. That winter the struggle for survival dominated the life of the mining communities. "Up to this week," wrote the Reverend F.A. McAvoy, the Glace Bay Baptist minister, "the miners and their families have been living from hand to mouth, in many cases on the verge of starvation"; in the worst cases he found children wearing

clothes made from cement and flour bags and families living on little
more than black tea, molasses, and soup bones. The scale of the need
was immense, and some weeks later McAvoy estimated that a total of
31,986 people were receiving relief in the mining districts.[36]

Shortly after the beginning of the strike in March, Canadian Press
reporter Andrew Merkel paid a visit to Besco vice-president J.E. McLurg,
one of Wolvin's longtime, hard-bitten business partners. In the interview McLurg expressed the view that conditions were "getting better
every day they stay out." He went on to agree that the confrontation
could be compared to a card game: "Poker game nothing. We have all
the cards ... Let them stay out two months or six months, it matters
not; eventually they will have to come to us." Crowning it all was a
colloquial insult that became one of the most memorable statements
in Cape Breton labour history: "They can't stand the gaff." That made
headlines in both the Sydney *Post* and the *Maritime Labor Herald*.
McLurg's remark was regarded as an offensive slur on the character of
the long-suffering people of the coalfields. The phrase "standing the
gaff" became a rallying cry of the strike.[37]

One sympathetic visitor to the coal country at this time was Agnes
Macphail, the country schoolteacher in Grey County, Ontario, who in
1921 was sent to Ottawa by the United Farmers to become Canada's
first woman MP. After a tour of inspection through the coal towns in
March, she gave a harrowing report on local conditions in the homes
and neighbourhoods she visited. Her account emphasized the poverty
and hardship of the men, women, and children, as well as their pride
and determination. Members of Parliament, she charged, "have no idea
how deep the resentment is, how intense it is, and how quiet it is. These
people are not broken; do not ever think that. They feel that they have
not got justice anywhere. Whether they are right or wrong I am not
saying, but that is their feeling, and after all it is this kind of feeling that
makes such a situation as exists there now a very dangerous one."[38]

When Macphail asked to meet somebody "really red" – "the redder
the better" – she was sent to see McLachlan. Like Woodsworth before
her, she came away from the visit impressed by him as an intelligent
man with a respectable home life and a worthy ambition, even if he was
given to flights of rhetoric:

He is endeavouring to break the bonds, he is endeavouring to save a little money to buy a plot of ground and a home, he is endeavouring to get some culture. He has a beautiful family, a rosy-cheeked wife with a rolling Scotch tongue. And he is a man who has always stood for good citizenship. When I think of some of the things said by those who call themselves "good" citizens, I wonder really where we are going. Of course, these men say wild things. Naturally they do. They say awful things. But no one could blame them. Anyone who went to the same place and lived through the same conditions would, I am sure, say the very same awful things.[39]

All through March and April, John W. McLeod besieged John L. Lewis with requests for aid. At the end of March, McLeod was optimistic about the course of the strike: "The men are orderly and quiet. There is no picketing, and everywhere we are receiving sympathy and material assistance ..." Although the district had only $12,000 on hand at the beginning of the strike, sympathizers were already contributing a good deal of support. In Glace Bay a Citizens' Relief Committee was conducting a "scientific and systematic buying and distribution of relief." The tide of public opinion seemed to be running with the coal miners this time, and there was sympathetic attention from well beyond the coalfields. Newspapers such as the Halifax *Herald* and the Ottawa *Citizen* organized appeals and raised some $20,000. There were bundles of supplies from Winnipeg. There was support from the Red Cross, from town councils, and from hundreds of individuals and organizations across the country.[40]

McLeod's appeals on behalf of District 26 received unexpected support from the TLC president, Tom Moore, who was usually known for his hostility to labour radicalism of any kind. Following a tour of the coal area, Moore encouraged Lewis to provide support to the strikers. In a confidential letter on 27 March he explained that "Communistic influences" were less important than in previous years: "McLachlan and his Communist colleagues were being skilfully but nevertheless effectively placed in the background." There remained traces of his influence in the union's formal adoption of the "one hundred per cent

strike." But in practice, Moore reassured Lewis, the union leadership
had modified the policy by allowing clerical staff to carry out maintenance work and by providing the necessary power supply for operation
of pumps. Indeed, the executive had "watched very carefully at all times
to see that no actual damage occurred." In general, Moore argued,
there was much public sympathy in Canada for the coal miners and
the international union would do well to join in contributing to their
relief. "The men are just being weaned away from their ideas of 'Red'
affiliations," added Moore, "and lack of support from the international will be distorted and capitalized by the 'Red' element to destroy
the confidence in the international affiliation being of real value to
them in a crisis."[41]

The association between relief and respectability was brought to a
head by a controversy over a $5,000 donation from Moscow. The offer
came in the form of a telegram to McLachlan stating that the Red
International of Labour Unions and the All-Russian Miners' Union
were in full sympathy with the Nova Scotia miners: "On with the
struggle against exploitation and oppression. Long live the international solidarity of the working class." McLachlan welcomed the
donation and took responsibility for inviting it. His original proposal
was that the Soviet government, which was buying more than a million
barrels of Canadian flour, arrange to contribute a carload of flour to
the relief effort in Nova Scotia. Instead, the Soviet agents directed his
request to the Russian miners' union, which then arranged for the
donation through the Red International. To McLachlan's consterna-
tion, the Citizens' Relief Committee in Glace Bay rejected the contribution,
on the grounds that "its acceptance would be construed in certain
circles as Russian propaganda, and would result in diminishing contributions throughout the Dominion." This action provoked resolutions
of outrage from several local unions, and after holding the funds in
trust for several weeks, McLachlan delivered the money to union
headquarters, where the district executive accepted the contribution
without controversy.[42]

McLeod was still trying to make some inroads at UMW headquarters. When he wired Lewis at the Waldorf Astoria in New York on 8
April, he reported that the corporation remained firm in its refusal to

negotiate, and he feared that public contributions were beginning to fall off after the first month. An announcement of UMW support, he added the following day, would help turn the scales in favour of the union. Lewis paid a short visit to the province, while in the pages of the *Maritime Labor Herald* McLachlan asked embarrassing questions. For six years the miners had supported the international union and paid dues and assessments of about half a million dollars. When was the union going to support the Nova Scotia miners? "Is he and the United Mine Workers of America here for the money they can drag out of this province and to keep the miners in subjection to brutal Besco?" Finally, on 22 April, Lewis announced that the union would provide support of $5,000 per week. When McLeod responded that $5,000 was entirely inadequate, Lewis agreed to increase the amount to $10,000.[43]

For much of March and April, McLachlan was not well – "confined to his house with pleurisy, and his vitality is very low," stated a police report, "McLachlan has really not been a well man since his release from Dorchester Penitentiary." Apart from his contributions to the *Maritime Labor Herald*, McLachlan played little part in the desultory progress of the strike. When he appeared at an open-air public meeting on the ballfield later that month, it was noted that he was still recovering and did not speak long. He was obviously concerned about the slow progress of the strike, and he repeated his tactical advice – previous strikes had been more successful "because they had used the 100% strike against the Corporation, thereby forcing the Corporation to pay a living wage." This time the executive was "acting alone": "The Capitalist press praises the miners for their quietness and good order, but we can get nothing with quietness – we must get together as in the old days, and get that fighting spirit and solidarity which can sweep the miners to victory."[44]

At the end of April, McLachlan's public voice was almost entirely silenced, this time by another attack on the offices and printshop of the *Maritime Labor Herald*. A fire took place in the empty building early on a Monday morning, shortly after the appearance of the issue of 18 April. This time the entire building burned to the ground. It looked like an act of arson, and damages were estimated at $25,000. The newspaper was in no condition to recover from the blow, and for the remainder of the year the *Herald* was no longer a factor in the struggle. "They burn down the Labor Herald right this time," McLachlan observed in a letter. He was doubtful the value of the plant could be recovered or the paper even reopened under his editorship, for the newspaper had been unable to buy insurance: "Every company told us we had 'too many enemies.' This is four times I have been burned out since 1922, and three times raided. If the Herald does start up again, I guess they will have to get someone in my place, if fires are to be averted. At present I am fixing things up around home and digging in the garden, but it is awfully slow and quiet work."[45]

The enforced shutdown of the *Maritime Labor Herald* left McLachlan with little voice in the day-to-day progress of the strike. He addressed public meetings – such as the May Day celebrations in Sydney Mines. He also continued to dispense advice to local leaders, but with disappointing effect. During a visit to Glace Bay for the May Day meetings, the Communist Party leader Jack MacDonald – known in Glace Bay as Moscow Jack – observed that the party's role in the direction of the strike was extremely limited. He noted that some of the party members on the executive were young and relatively ineffective. The secretary-treasurer, Alex McKay, claimed that he had no time to attend party meetings; he was "lost to us," noted MacDonald, and indeed was a good candidate for expulsion from the party. As for McLeod, he had never been a member but "was considered close to us and promised, before his final selection, to join up." But instead of relying on the advice of veterans of the labour wars such as McLachlan, McLeod had virtually abdicated leadership of the union to the district's legal adviser (and McLachlan's unsuccessful defence attorney in the 1923 trial), Gordon Harrington: "The officers went to him for advice. He attends their board meetings, drafts all statements and has the officers sign same." Harrington was "undoubtedly playing the Conservative game" and "does all possible to prevent the adoption of a militant policy."

At a party strategy meeting, MacDonald and McLachlan, along with the union vice-president Joseph Nearing, urged the adoption of a more aggressive strike strategy – the 100 per cent strike – but without success. "The official policy of the board is no picketing," MacDonald observed, "as this would mean soldiers in the district. The board is still of the opinion that the strike can be won with the present policy. So far there is no break in the ranks of the men, but starvation is beginning to have its effect and I am afraid that a break will take place soon."[46]

As the conflict entered its third month, McLachlan had similar views on the dismal course of the strike. Relief supplies for the miners were falling off badly, he wrote to Tim Buck in Toronto on 4 May: "Last week neither butter nor meat, it looks as if the District executive are going to sit around till the last dollar is eaten up. There are no mass meetings, no picketing, nothing but begging, and being respectable. I do not think the strike can last two more weeks." In the end, the outcome was likely to be a complete collapse of the union: "There is no doubt in my mind but the present trouble here is going to see the end of the U.M.W. of A. in Nova Scotia. The men are simply 'fed up' with the Lewis machine."

Much of the problem, in McLachlan's view, was the weakness of the union leadership: "The present executive was elected by the left wing and now we are all cursing ourselves for doing it. They have failed completely and repudiated everything we stood for, and now it looks very like a lost strike, and they are going down to defeat not as battlers but as beggars, and without one thing to look back to with pride." Unfortunately, the coal miners were still showing too much good behaviour: "That sense of loyalty that one finds in the rank and file to 'their elected officers' has held them back from action that would have brought better results than we are having."[47]

Three weeks later there was little to add. McLachlan could say only that "the strike continues to drift" and that Besco was "in no hurry to get the men back into the mines." Maintenance work at the mines was being looked after by company officials, and the union leadership refused to keep them out on the ground that this was against the international union's policy. Lewis meanwhile was limiting his relief contribution to about $10,000 a week: "The strikers are simply quietly starving."

Unless there was a change in strategy, McLachlan feared that the strike was going to come to a miserable conclusion. The UMW could not survive, he warned Buck: "I feel sure that Besco is done with the checkoff, and may try to establish 'company unions.'" This in turn would lead to a period of renewed union rivalries: the OBU was still "a real danger here and may be able to upset all our plans"; indeed, the OBU had offered to finance a new newspaper under McLachlan's editorship if he would only "see things right" and support the OBU. Following the death of the UMW in Nova Scotia, it would be important to "keep the men organized in some fashion" and wait for the organization of a new Canadian miners' union. In the meantime, the desultory conflict continued, and McLachlan predicted that it was only a matter of time before the corporation invited the miners to start back to work without a union at all: "The test in this fight may come any day that Besco cares to blow the whistle."[48]

11 June

It was still winter in Cape Breton on the 24th of May in 1925 – a small blizzard covered the mining district with thick flakes of snow. This was an unusual occurrence even in a land of late springs. It was one more sign that the winter's troubles were not ended. Three months earlier the coal miners had gone out on strike for many causes – against wage reductions, against shutdowns and underemployment, against the company stores, against the priority of capital and the complicity of governments. Across the country the coal miners had won sympathy for their suffering and support for their defiance. They were "standing the gaff."

But would the strike ever be settled? As in other coalfields across North America, the coal operators in Nova Scotia were convinced that the miners' union could be permanently driven out of the industry. There had been no negotiations since the beginning of the strike, and the corporation insisted that it would not meet with any officers who were Communists.

At the end of May the company offered separate settlements to the men at the Princess Colliery at Sydney Mines and also to the miners at the OBU stronghold in Stellarton; they were asked to accept the wage reduction and give up the union check-off. In both cases the offer was refused. McLeod understood that the survival of the union was at stake and, in the hope of salvaging an agreement, offered a major concession. If the corporation would not meet with the union, the miners were prepared to submit the whole dispute to arbitration by an outside authority. Two names were put forward, neither of them likely to be accused of communistic tendencies – the minister of labour, James Murdock, and the Reverend Clarence MacKinnon, chair of the successful conciliation board in 1920.[49]

That was the union's last, desperate attempt to secure a peaceful settlement. When it was turned down, McLeod could no longer resist the pressure to adopt more aggressive measures. In May, union locals in the Glace Bay district were already stepping up the pressure and preventing company officials from entering the collieries. At New Aberdeen, pickets dumped coal on the rail tracks, cutting off the delivery of coal to the power station; as a result, the operation of pumps and fans at two mines had to be discontinued. Although the continuation of peaceful picketing was endorsed at a district convention that month, the union leadership announced on 3 June that it was finally introducing the policy of 100 per cent picketing at the mines.[50]

The adoption of these tactics was clearly associated with McLachlan, even though he did not seem to be visibly in command of events. And even at this moment in the unfolding drama, there was room for humour. A story circulated that week that McLachlan had died, and a senior company official was asked if he had heard of McLachlan's demise. One local correspondent reported the anecdote (under the column heading "Today's Best Story") as follows:

"Well," said Mac brightening up somewhat. "That's good news to me. I'm darn glad his [sic] gone."

We were surprised and said so, "That's a very nasty thing to say Mac. We thought you were Irish and an Irishman dearly loves an enemy, besides it isn't usual to allow spite to follow a man beyond the grave."

"Oh," said Mac, "I hadn't the slightest ill feeling towards J.B., as a matter of fact I rather liked him, still I'm glad he's gone. You see it has been more or less taken for granted that J.B. and I would reach the same 'place' eventually. I'm not feeling any too well myself at present, but my mind is easy now, no matter what happens: J.B. is sure to have all the maintenance men out on strike before I get there."[51]

It was a grim kind of humour that seemed to verify McLachlan's significance in the ongoing struggle.

Hidden in the woods several miles beyond the town of New Waterford, Waterford Lake was a favourite site for family picnics as well as the location of an important company installation. Under a tall smokestack a big brick structure at the edge of the water contained the boilers and pumps that supplied power and water to the collieries and the town. As long as the power plant continued to function, there would be water in the town and electric power at the collieries. In the debates over the 100 per cent strike, what was at stake was control of operations such as this one. In 1925 the power plant continued to function without interruption for the first several months of the strike, in conformity with the moderate version of the 100 per cent strike applied by the union leadership. But at 7 a.m. on 4 June, after the announcement of the new 100 per cent policy, the union men at Waterford Lake walked out. When company officials refused to leave, a band of several hundred men descended on the site later in the day and drove them out. The shutdown broke off water and power supply to the town of New Waterford. The company rejected the mayor's proposal for an emergency pumping station. A union committee was mobilized to keep the hospital supplied from local wells.

One week later, early on the morning of 11 June, the company sent out a special force to recapture the power plant at Waterford Lake. It was a rainy night, and the air was heavy with the dampness of early spring. A special train puffed in slowly through the dim dawn light along the branch line from Victoria Junction. On board were more than fifty men, company officials and company police, as well as a carload of pit ponies. Arriving at the lake, this force easily took control of the power plant from the small number of union men on hand. At 8 a.m. a patrol of company police, many of them mounted on horses from the mines, rode into New Waterford boasting that the power station was now in their hands. As word spread through the town, hundreds of men gathered on the ballfield to assess the situation. From there they began to march the several miles out to Waterford Lake, joined by more men and boys as they headed out along the railway tracks through the woods.

By the time the front ranks of the coal miners reached the lake, they were followed by a huge crowd; estimates vary from 700 or 800 people to as many as 3,000. When they arrived in a clearing by the lake and approached the fence surrounding the power plant, the company police began to shoot. The coal miners believed they were firing blanks to scatter the crowd, and they stood their ground; many of the men were war veterans accustomed to being under fire. Then the police rode forward on horseback brandishing night sticks and firing their revolvers. The unarmed men fought back barehanded, attacking the police with stones and sticks and pulling them off their horses. Several miners were hit by the gunfire and fell to the ground. Others were kicked and felled by horses. Gilbert Watson took a bullet in the stomach. And another union man – holding the reins of a horse and helping to unsaddle a policeman – was shot dead.[52]

It was William Davis. At thirty-seven years of age, William Davis belonged to the generation of coal miners who had grown up with the UMW in Nova Scotia. A skilled worker who was active in his union, a member of the Oddfellows Lodge and the father of a large family, Davis was the kind of man who embodied the virtues of working-class respectability and responsibility that were so important to McLachlan. Before coming to New Waterford, the Davis family had worked in Springhill, and before that they had come from England; one of William's older brothers, Thomas, had gone to his death as a fourteen-year-old boy in the famous Springhill disaster of 1891. Now, after decades of struggle to establish the rights of collective bargaining and unionism in the coalfields, a union man defending these rights was shot down by company police. Nothing had changed in the ultimate price the corporation demanded in support of property rights.[53]

After the shooting ended at Waterford Lake that day, the men swarmed into the power station, ripping out the main board and shutting down the pumps and boilers. Police and officials who did not escape into the woods or across the lake were marched into town and placed in the town jail. On the following nights, company stores in all parts of the coalfield were raided and emptied of their goods. Company stores and colliery buildings went up in smoke throughout the district, and property damage was later estimated at $528,625. The company stores, those symbolic institutions of the days of corporate control and working-class dependence, never reopened after the 1925 strike.

For the Davis family, the death of their father was a terrible tragedy. The coroner's jury found the cause of death to be "a bullet wound fired from a gun in the hands of a policeman of the British Empire Steel Company force." In New Waterford there was an enormous outpouring of grief and respect for the slain miner – the procession through the streets was four people wide and a mile long, the largest funeral the town had ever seen. For thousands of coal miners and their families, William Davis came to represent the spirit of determination and resistance that ran through the long weeks of the 1925 strike. At a subsequent district convention, 11 June was declared Davis Day, and the date is still marked throughout District 26.[54]

Once again in 1925, as so many times before, order had to be restored, and the Canadian army returned to the coalfields. As a gesture of conciliation, the union suspended the 100 per cent strike and allowed maintenance work to resume at the mines. The minister of labour and the prime minister himself took their concerns directly to a meeting of the Besco board of directors. All this seemed to indicate that the strike had reached a turning point, and, just possibly, there would be at long last a settlement of some kind. But the corporation still refused to make an agreement.[55]

Meanwhile, a provincial election campaign was giving local Conservative politicians an opportunity to denounce the Liberals for betraying the rights of labour. "The Cape Breton miners are our own kith and kin, our own flesh and blood,'" charged Gordon Harrington, now emerging from the union backrooms as the candidate in Cape Breton Centre, "and every Nova Scotian should resent this attempt of a reactionary government to drive them hither and thither like 16th century serfs." In Cape Breton East, John C. Douglas charged that the Labour Party had become "a party of Communists, with its directorate at Toronto, but its real heads abroad in Moscow." Then he accused the Liberals of "disregard for the rights of labor" and promised a rapid settlement of the strike. Party leader E.N. Rhodes, an Amherst businessman and former speaker of the House of Commons, called for a thorough investigation of Besco. The Conservatives won a sweeping victory, taking all of the Cape Breton seats and forty of the forty-three in the province. This put an end to more than four decades of Liberal rule in Nova Scotia.[56]

Even after his victory, Premier Rhodes was for several weeks frustrated in his efforts to engineer a settlement. In the end he arranged for a six-month contract to take effect until a royal commission completed a full investigation of conditions in the industry. Under the terms of the Rhodes settlement, the coal miners accepted a reduction of wages back to the level of the 1922 agreement; and as the price of their cooperation, Besco received a 20 per cent rebate on provincial coal royalties for the duration of the contract. McLeod was relieved to have an agreement at all, particularly one that recognized the status of the union and maintained the union check-off; he was also pleased with the decision to appoint a royal commission. This was the solution he had proposed in February, before the beginning of the strike. On 5 August the coal miners voted 3,913 to 2,780 to accept the agreement – the turnout was small, but this was the first time the miners had endorsed a contract in almost three years. The troops remained on hand in the coalfield until work resumed at last in August.[57]

During the final stages of the strike, McLachlan was at home at Steele's Hill, still in poor health and far removed from the action. He was sick at heart as he looked down from Steele's Hill on the nights after 11 June and watched the light of fires at the company stores and collieries in the town below. There were sounds of shouting and confusion in the night air as crowds of men, women, and children surrounded the company store at nearby No. 11 and emptied it of goods. Later in the month the surface installations at No. 11 also burned to the ground; there was even a rumour that McLachlan had started the fire himself although, as his oldest daughter has recalled, he was not even well enough to leave home at the time.[58]

McLachlan's police file contains only two entries for the month of June 1925. One stated that McLachlan went out of his way to caution immigrant workers not to take the lead in the crowd actions: "Let the English miners start first: one foreigner might spoil the whole miners' movement, because the foreigners will be blamed, as usual for all troubles in Cape Breton." The other reported a conversation in which McLachlan regretted that the miners were subdued by the return of the armed forces: "If it were not for the soldiers, the miners could crush 'Besco' in two weeks."[59]

From McLachlan's point of view, the temporary settlement was a sad end to a sorry struggle, scant reward for the months filled with deprivation and defiance. In the outcome of the strike there were no rewards for the radicals – the *Maritime Labor Herald* was destroyed, the influence of the Communists in the union was in decline, and in the provincial election all the labour MLAs elected in 1920 were defeated. It was true that the union had survived, and it had even won the half-hearted support of international headquarters. Against its will, the corporation had been forced to maintain union recognition. Indeed, from a longer historical perspective, the historian of District 26, C.B. Wade, has described the 1925 strike as a successful struggle to confirm union recognition: "The strike was lost, in terms of the immediate issue; it was won, in terms of establishing the union: after 1925 all serious efforts to destroy the union were abandoned." Many other districts in the UMW in North America were losing everything during these years, and the survival of the union and its contract in District 26 were in themselves achievements of significance in the context of the times.[60]

But for McLachlan the 1925 strike was a failure of leadership; from the beginning the coal miners had shown too much restraint and relied too much on the good will and sympathy of the general public; they had been forced to pay the price in starvation and suffering. A decisive confrontation between the coal miners and the corporation could not be avoided, but it came too late in the day and with tragic results. In the end, the union leaders had given up the initiative and settled for compromises. Once more the day of reckoning was postponed.

Instead of entering into an era of public ownership and workers' control, the coal mines ended the summer of 1925 under the joint management of the corporation and the armed forces. At one colliery in Glace Bay the commanding officer of the Royal 22nd Regiment, Georges-P. Vanier, presented a small photo album to the mine manager J.R. Dinn; the inscription described Vanier and Dinn as "The Two Managers."[61]

Wolvin or McLachlan?

So far the revolution had not arrived in Cape Breton – nor had it arrived anywhere else in North America. In Germany the revolution was defeated, in Italy the Fascists had come to power, and in Britain the Communist leaders were being arrested and charged with seditious conspiracy. Within the UMW, the various dissidents and radicals, with all their talk of union democracy and nationalization of coal, had been defeated by the Lewis machine, and the whole union was falling into decline. In Cape Breton the local radicals had been unable to control the course of events during the year's catastrophic strike. In an interview at the end of 1925, McLachlan estimated that by this time there were no more than fifty to seventy-five Communists in Cape Breton – "although there are perhaps a couple of thousand sympathizers, who are partially imbued with Communistic ideals."[62]

Obviously, the prospects for radicals were not what they had been in 1917 and 1919, or even in 1922 and 1923. McLachlan took a philosophical attitude to the change in opportunities. In his interview with a visiting magazine reporter, McLachlan expressed a wry appreciation of the peculiar difficulties facing revolutionaries in Canada. Even with half a million supporters, there could be no successful revolution in Canada: "That country to the south would crush us in a week if we were able to establish ourselves in Canada. But it is coming. Some day there will be a revolution in the United States and in Great Britain, and we want to be ready." "But," he added with a smile, "the trouble with us Communists is we look too far ahead."[63]

Although struggling to recover his health and sidelined by the course of events in 1925, McLachlan continued to see himself as a revolutionary. In September, along with Joe Wallace of Halifax, he travelled to Toronto to attend the Fourth National Convention of the Communist Party. The campaign for nationalization of the coal industry, Tim Buck reported, "had met with great response" and was widely accepted among the coal miners. In Nova Scotia the coal miners had fought "one of the most brilliant struggles in trade union history."

That was a description that McLachlan could hardly have recognized, except as a tribute to the endurance and solidarity of the men and women of the coal country. Buck added that the coal miners now faced the challenge of "provocative interference by a capitalist government in trade union affairs"; this was a reference to debates about the future of union recognition and abolition of the check-off that would be among the issues considered by the royal commission investigating the coal industry. Much of the attention in Toronto centred on developments in Alberta, where the radicals had been forced to abandon the UMW and form a new organization, the Mine Workers' Union of Canada; it was hoped that the Alberta story of collapse and disintegration would not be repeated in Nova Scotia. However, McLachlan's only reported comments at the convention referred back to the sacrifices the coal miners had made in the 1925 strike. As he often did in praising the solidarity of the working-class community, he singled out "the wonderful work that had been done by the women, during the critical times of the working class struggle."[64]

As the fall months arrived and another winter loomed, there were more battles to fight. One of them was an election. In early September, Parliament was dissolved and a Dominion election was called for 29 October. For McLachlan, elections provided an opportunity for propaganda and a moment to measure the balance of forces in the class struggle. Although the strike was over and the coal miners were back at work, political action represented a continuation of the struggle by other means.

For McLachlan personally, this must have been an appealing contest. After the frustrations of his defeat in 1921, here was the opportunity to win a public vindication against the scurrilous charges of disloyalty to the coal miners that were advanced at the time. There was also the personal encouragement from Woodsworth, who had regularly urged the coal miners to send McLachlan to Ottawa to take his rightful place as a labour Member of Parliament. A revision of electoral boundaries in 1924 even seemed to bode well for McLachlan. The old two-member ridings had been dissolved and the new constituency of Cape Breton South was centred on the southside coal towns and on the city of Sydney, areas where McLachlan had led the polls in 1921. Perhaps the only missing element was the failure of the sitting member, William

Carroll, to stand for re-election. McLachlan would thus not have the satisfaction of bringing him down.[65]

In McLachlan's election publicity the contest was portrayed as a straight fight between the archetypal capitalist and the working-class hero: "Wolvin or MacLachlan, Which Will Win?" Wolvin's shadow lurked behind all the lawyer-politicians nominated by the old parties: "Of course Wolvin doesn't dare come right out into the open. He'd be licked to a standstill if he did. So he acts through lawyers instead. Vote for a member of your own class – selected by you, tested by you, and proved firm in the fire of struggle."[66]

But the greatest challenge facing labour candidates in 1925 was not Wolvin or the Liberals. Instead it was the reinvigoration of the Conservative Party as a spokesman for regional rights. This new Conservatism shrewdly combined a recognition of the rights of labour with a sense of regional grievance against the federal government on behalf of local industries. It was a potent formula and represented Tory strategy in Cape Breton at its most effective: the old class politics of the National Policy, with the implicit alliance of labour and business around the cause of industrial progress. Using this formula, Tory politicians did their best to attract the labour vote.[67]

The new face of Nova Scotia Conservatism had already been revealed during the summer provincial election, when the successful Tory candidates included figures such as Gordon Harrington and John A. Walker, familiar names from McLachlan's trial in 1923. The Conservatives lost no time in applying the lessons of provincial politics to the Dominion contest in Cape Breton South, where Finlay MacDonald pledged that protection for the coal industry was the greatest single issue in his campaign: "I will get an increased duty on foreign coal or my seat in Parliament will be vacant." In this local version of Maritime Rights, the Tories were careful to distinguish support for protectionism in the coal and steel industries from support for the existing corporation.[68]

And although their party was led by the notorious Arthur Meighen, whose government had broken the Winnipeg General Strike in 1919, the Conservatives were also portrayed as better friends of the worker than the Liberals. After all, the Liberals were the ones who had sent the troops into the coalfields and McLachlan to the penitentiary. A front-page *Post* editorial addressed to the coal miners denounced the Liberal government in ringing terms: "No Government within the memory of men now living has shown less sympathy or more callous indifference towards the miners of this province in their struggle for improved working conditions than that headed by Premier W.L.M. King for the past three and a half years."[69]

While the King government and the local Liberal candidate L.D. Currie – "a stop-gap nominee" – were castigated for their inadequacies, very little was said in the press of the labour candidate, except to predict that he was certain to lose his deposit. At one Glace Bay meeting, Tory speakers appealed to the miners to ignore the "long debates on purely extraneous issues served up to them by the communist and government candidates." By directing much of their attack on the Liberals and virtually ignoring the labour candidate, the Conservatives attempted to portray McLachlan's candidacy as an irrelevant effort. On the eve of the election a front-page editorial appealed to voters to "ignore party and class considerations and unite to give the protectionist candidate an overwhelming majority at the polls tomorrow."[70]

When the results came in, the Tories had prevailed. Finlay MacDonald won Cape Breton South with a large majority. In the mining district McLachlan made a strong showing, placing second and receiving 30.55 per cent of the vote. But he led the polls in only a few locations – Dominion No. 6 and three wards in Glace Bay – and his vote was less than half what it had been in 1921. Overall, McLachlan received 3,617 votes; this gave him third place, with 20.46 per cent of the vote.[71]

To some observers, the 1925 campaign was one of McLachlan's more cautious efforts. According to the *Post*, "'J.B.,' many felt, was far too mild and easy going – not at all radical enough in his views to suit even his most enthusiastic supporters."[72] Perhaps McLachlan's relatively passive campaign was a reflection of his own physical exhaustion; perhaps, too, it was inevitable, given the divisions in the union leadership and the absence of a local labour newspaper to spread the word. Certainly, the campaign had shown that the Tories were able to control the language of public discourse in this election, successfully turning the attention from class conflict to regional protest. It was the same throughout the Maritime provinces in 1925; the Liberals lost seats everywhere and the Maritime Rights Tories won twenty-three of the region's twenty-nine seats in the House of Commons.

The 1925 election gave McLachlan his second defeat in a contest for the House of Commons. But the appeal of a labour candidate in Cape Breton South was still an obvious factor in local political calculations. And when King's minority government collapsed in 1926 – and Meighen's effort to form a government also failed – the country was back at the polls in September 1926 for the second time in less than a year. This was the occasion of the famous King-Byng crisis, when the prime minister claimed that the governor general's exercise of constitutional authority was an affront to Canadian autonomy.

In Cape Breton South the labour question remained the more significant issue, and the Liberals feared the nomination of a strong labour candidate there. As a result, Mackenzie King approached Woodsworth with a plan for cooperation. The proposition was that, in order to ensure a two-way fight and a Conservative defeat in Cape Breton South, there should be no labour candidate in the constituency. Indignantly, Woodsworth rejected the scheme. Instead, it was the Liberals themselves who should step aside: "If there is any constituency in Canada in which there should be a Labor representative it is Cape Breton South." King accepted the rebuke, and as a result the prospective Liberal candidate withdrew from the contest.[73]

He may not have recognized it at the time, but this was one of McLachlan's best opportunities to win election to Parliament – a two-way fight in a constituency centred on the industrial district. But on this occasion McLachlan did not stand for election. The labour nomination went instead to Dan Willie Morrison, the former labour MLA who since 1922 had been the labour mayor of Glace Bay. In a two-way fight against the Conservative candidate, Morrison won a bare majority in the mining district (50.6 per cent), but his support in Sydney and other parts of the constituency was not sufficient to win the election.[74]

Would McLachlan have done better, both in the coal towns and elsewhere, on the strength of his prestige as a veteran of the class struggle? In a two-way contest, McLachlan had a good chance of winning the polls in the coal towns, perhaps not as triumphantly as he had done in 1921 but the prospect of a majority was strong. That was of course also to assume that the Liberals did not renege on the deal and field their own candidate against McLachlan at the last minute. Certainly the steelworkers in Sydney owed McLachlan a debt of support from the time of the sympathetic strike in 1923; they were more likely to vote for a famous labour martyr than for the current mayor of Glace Bay.

But McLachlan expressed no public regrets about his failure to contest the 1926 election. He seemed to accept the fact that the defeats of the last several years had brought the class struggle to a low ebb. For their crimes of revolutionary ambition, the working class, like McLachlan, were still suffering their punishment.

MINEWORKERS FROM ALL PARTS OF PROVINCE GATHER AT NEW GLASGOW

Delegates from District 26, UMWA meet to plan strategy in 1923; McLachlan is seated sixth from the left in the third row.

Strike duty, 1923. Military encampment at the steel plant, Sydney, 1923 at the time of the coal miners' sympathetic strike.

The strike leaders are brought to Halifax. Union president Dan Livingstone (far right) and McLachlan (second from left) are accompanied by their lawyer John A. Walker (second from right) and Sydney police chief J.B. McCormick (left) at the Halifax police station, July 1923.

STRIKE BREAKING IN CAPE BRETON

Intimidation by the British Empire Steel Corporation, as represented on the front page of the *Maritime Labor Herald*, 4 August 1923.

Eric McDonald, commander of the provincial police – "Armstrong's Army" – who were responsible for the police riot during the Sydney steel strike in 1923. That event produced charges of sedition against McLachlan.

John L. Lewis of the UMW on the platform at a union meeting, 1923. Lewis was determined to establish his personal control over the international union in the 1920s.

In October 1923 McLachlan was sentenced to two years in Dorchester Penitentiary following his conviction on charges of seditious libel.

Attorney-General W.J. O'Hearn, who promised to "lock horns" with McLachlan. He led the prosecution at the 1923 sedition trial.

**"Let Them Stay Out---
It Matters Not"**

J.E. McLurg, Vice-President, British Empire Steel Corporation, famous for his words at the onset of the 1925 strike: "They cannot stand the gaff!"

LEST WE FORGET!

"Lest We Forget." No work at the mines, no credit at the stores – the beginning of the 1925 strike, as seen by the Halifax *Herald* cartoonist.

"Let the Miners Run the Mines." The bootleg pits opened during the 1925 strike could be seen as an embryonic form of workers' control.

The Waterford Lake Power House. The struggle for control over the coal mines came to a violent climax at Waterford Lake on 11 June 1925, when William Davis was shot by company police.

Women in Winnipeg prepare bundles of supplies for the people of the Nova Scotia coal country, 1925.

"The Two Managers." An album page from the summer of 1925, inscribed by Georges-P. Vanier, commanding officer of the Royal 22nd Regiment (and future governor-general) to J.R. Dinn, mine manager at the Caledonia colliery, Glace Bay.

BOOK FOUR

EDUCATION FOR ACTION
1925–36

Well, the revolutions is
like the North wind,
they come somehow,
of their own accord,
and I don't know how they come,
but they come, that's all,
they come out of conditions.

– J.B. McLachlan,
1925

CHAPTER 10

McLachlan versus Wolvin

The bosses couldn't stand the gaff –
Oh, let me write their epitaph!

– Dawn Fraser,
"Cape Breton's Curse, Adieu, Adieu" (1926)

The Duncan Commission

Wolvin and McLachlan – the two men face each other in a crowded chamber at the county courthouse in Sydney. Small tables have been pushed together to make a large horseshoe of a council table. The officers of the miners' union occupy the tables to the left – John W. McLeod, Joseph Nearing, Sandy McKay, Bill Hayes, D.R. McNeil. The company officers are ranged against them to the right – Roy Wolvin, J.E. McLurg, H.J. McCann, Alex S. MacNeil, Walter Herd. Around them are experts, lawyers, advisers, including the veteran mine manager T.J. Brown, now serving as deputy minister of mines and as secretary of the commission. Public attendance is limited to less than twenty seats, and all the available places are taken. Several reporters watch with interest. A woman stenographer sits on the judge's dais, recording the proceedings.[1]

These were the sessions of the Royal Commission on the Coal Mining Industry in Nova Scotia, the long-awaited investigation agreed to by company and union at the end of the 1925 strike. The names of the commissioners had been announced in early October – a British coal expert, an Ontario businessman, and a Nova Scotia university president – and the formal terms of reference were issued at the end of the month. The hearings lasted through much of November and into December. Before the report was released in January 1926 the commissioners had toured coal mines, visited miners' homes, and reviewed company records. And they had listened to testimony from more than 100 witnesses.

By Wednesday, 18 November, the sessions were in their eighth day. The miners had introduced their case with a prepared statement by the union president, John W. McLeod. In the following days the union presented thirty-six witnesses, all of them coal miners prepared to testify to local conditions. The miners' case was introduced by the union president, who questioned his own witnesses and later cross-examined those presented by the company; the corporation's case was led by none other than the Besco president Roy Wolvin himself, who also cross-examined the testimony of the miners.

"Wolvin or MacLachlan: Which Will Win?" The 1925 election contest was over, but this was more than a sequel. Each man regarded the other as the archetypal villain of the local class struggle. This was the much anticipated confrontation between capitalist and communist, Roy the Wolf versus the Cape Breton Bolshevik. At 10 a.m. McLachlan was standing ready at the miners' table, alert and wary. He knew he was on hostile ground here. As one observer noted, McLachlan was on edge, "all set for nooses, traps and such."[2]

Across the table Roy Wolvin watched without expression, his glasses glittering in the light. As head of the company, Wolvin had a formal standing before the inquiry: at this stage he was leading the questioning of the miners' witnesses, and later he would lead the presentation of the company's case. McLachlan, however, came before the commission as no more than another witness; he would not be presenting other evidence, and he would not be cross-examining Wolvin or other company spokesmen. But this was his day in court. In fact, he would testify for the whole day Wednesday, and again the next morning, for a total of eight hours.

Originally there was no plan to include McLachlan among the witnesses, but as the hearings progressed, the union vice-president, Joseph Nearing, insisted that McLachlan should also be called. Unlike some of the other union officers, Nearing continued to count himself a McLachlan loyalist. He was, wrote one reporter, "a Communist disconcerting to the popular idea of what a good Communist should be, for he neither drinks nor smokes and is a devout Catholic." Nearing has recalled that he intervened directly with the one Nova Scotia commissioner, Father H.P. MacPherson, to arrange for McLachlan's appearance. It was also agreed that the two other members of the "Big Three" among the union leaders of the early 1920s, Robert Baxter and Silby Barrett, would come before the commission, and they had done so on the previous day. The appearance of McLachlan — advertised in one newspaper as "the stormy petrel of past struggles" – generated unusual excitement.[3]

As he waited to begin, McLachlan was amused to note that all of the commissioners boasted titles – *Sir* Andrew Rae Duncan, *Doctor* and *Father* H.P. MacPherson, and *Major* Hume B. Cronyn, *KC*. They seemed to get along well. When questioned by reporters, the commissioners spoke appreciatively of each other, in line with the atmosphere of congeniality they wanted to promote at the hearings: "They seem to fit each other like paper on the wall."[4] But for McLachlan the proceedings would be like another trial, with the commissioners sitting in judgment as a court of appeal.

Looking to his left, McLachlan regarded the chairman of the commission sitting at the head of the council table. Although visibly younger and physically smaller than his fellow commissioners, Duncan gave an impression of "restrained power." Everyone deferred to him. Of late, Duncan had made a reputation for himself as an expert in the regulation of the coal industry. In Britain he had served as coal controller in 1919–20 and then was named chairman of the Advisory Committee of the Coal Mines Department. For his services he received a knighthood in 1921. Duncan had a genial appearance and his style was polished. By training he was a Glasgow barrister, but he liked to remind people of his Ayrshire roots and show a common touch in his dealings with witnesses. During a motor tour of Glace Bay later in the month, Duncan would even pay an unannounced visit to McLachlan's home at Steele's Hill, although McLachlan turned out to be absent. Duncan's public image at the time of the hearings was enthusiastically captured by the local correspondent in the *Canadian Mining Journal*: "He is a fairly young man bubbling over with good nature and has a strong spice of Scottish humour in his make-up. He is very approachable and one would say very companionable."[5]

It was well known that Duncan had been appointed to head the commission on the recommendation of the British government, which was asked by the provincial government to provide assistance in "obtaining someone of outstanding worth who will carry the confidence of the public." Gordon Harrington, McLachlan's former defence lawyer and now the minister of mines in the Nova Scotia government, had asked for "somebody of the standing of Sir John Sankey, Sir Richard Redmayne, or Lord Askwith." Sankey was a senior judge who had headed a British royal commission in 1919 that recommended in favour of nationalization of the coal industry; Redmayne was a distinguished coal expert, the long-time inspector of mines for the British government; Askwith was Britain's most experienced labour-relations expert and industrial conciliator.[6]

Duncan was certainly a more junior candidate than any of these individuals. Moreover, there was even an element of deception in the presentation of Duncan as an impartial outsider. At the time of his appointment, Duncan was the vice-president of the Shipbuilding Employers' Federation, a post he had held since 1920 – and indeed the only particular employment listed for him in *Who's Who* for 1925; this made him, indirectly at least, an associate of the British financiers and industrialists who had supported the creation of Besco in 1920, several of whom still sat on the board of directors. Nor did Duncan have an entirely neutral political record – he had run for Parliament as a Liberal candidate in Scotland in the 1922 and 1924 elections, and on both occasions he had been defeated by Labour candidates.[7]

The second commissioner, Father Hugh Peter MacPherson, was already a familiar figure in Cape Breton. Born near Antigonish, he had served as a priest in rural Cape Breton during the early years of his career. In 1906 he was named president of St Francis Xavier University at Antigonish. Although passed over for appointment as bishop, MacPherson continued to serve as university president for three full decades. Premier E. N. Rhodes regarded him as a "splendid choice" for the commission. Originally Rhodes had considered appointing three university presidents to the commission – those of Acadia, Dalhousie, and St Francis Xavier – but in the end there was only MacPherson. According to Rhodes, MacPherson could be expected to demonstrate "a sympathy and understanding that will infuse the work of the commission and render it something more than a cold analysis of the situation." McLachlan had reason to view MacPherson with more scepticism: as a union leader and labour politician, he had been subject to frequent, often vitriolic, denunciation by clerical authorities in recent years and expected little sympathy for his point of view from the Catholic Church.

Whatever his personal sympathies, Father MacPherson was known to be a survivor who preferred to work behind the scenes. It was only a few years since he had been unable to do anything to protect his second-in-command, the redoubtable Jimmy Tompkins, when his experiments in educational and social reform were ended by the bishop. MacPherson played a limited role in the hearings. He asked few questions at all, and none of McLachlan.[8]

The third commissioner, Hume Cronyn, was a businessman from London, Ontario – general manager of the Canada Trust Company, president of Mutual Life Assurance Company, president of a mortgage company, vice-president of another. Upon close inspection, Cronyn was recognizable as a pillar of the Ontario establishment – his grandfather an Anglican bishop, his father like himself a lawyer, his mother the sister of former Liberal leader Edward Blake, his wife the daughter of a London industrialist by the name of John Labatt. Cronyn was described in the press as "a strong imperialist" and "a keen student of events and of practical economy" and had recently enjoyed some success in arbitrating a business dispute in Toronto. Premier Rhodes had known Cronyn for years and was pleased to consider him "one of the outstanding business men of Canada." The nature of Cronyn's business activities, however, had given him little contact with organized labour, and in any event he could not be expected to accept any of McLachlan's hostility to capitalist enterprise. In his youth, as a student at the University of Toronto, Cronyn had served in the Queen's Own Rifles and helped put down the rebellions of Gabriel Dumont and Louis Riel and their Cree allies in the North-West in 1885; later he served in the militia as a major in the 7th Fusiliers. Despite his Liberal background, Cronyn had come to the aid of the Borden government in 1917 and was elected as a pro-conscription MP in 1917. For McLachlan, this also meant that Cronyn had an objectionable record as a supporter of the government that brought in conscription, prohibited strikes, and rushed anti-union laws through Parliament.[9]

From McLachlan's point of view, the royal commission hearings did not offer a particularly sympathetic audience. He did not challenge the commissioners' credentials – no one did – but, given their background, he could not hope to convert the commissioners to his analysis of the class struggle.

Nor could McLachlan expect that his evidence would attract the kind of wide attention he had formerly received in the newspapers. Although more than 4,000 pages of evidence would be collected, there was remarkably little newspaper coverage of the hearings. From the beginning Duncan had insisted that this was to be a "full and open" inquiry, but reports of the proceedings were to be limited to official daily summaries authorized by the commission.[10]

"The Cause of Your Unrest"

McLachlan began his presentation slowly. There were some preliminary questions by Duncan, and McLachlan responded with the shortest of answers to the question before the commission: "The immediate cause of the unrest in Nova Scotia is the merciless exploitation of labour by the British Empire Steel Corporation, and their attempts to pay dividends on acres of idle steel works, idle mines, and watered stock."[11]

From here he continued with a detailed review of local labour history. It was all there – the long march from the early days of District 26, the 1909 strike, the blacklists and evictions, the troops in the streets, the union meetings with company police at the door and spies in the hall. He reviewed the recognition of the Amalgamated Mine Workers in 1917 and the miners' affiliation to the United Mine Workers in 1919. Most of all, step by step he reviewed the wages question, the small increases of 1917 and 1918, the struggle to level up the lowest rates, the constant vigilance against sharp practices by managers and operators, the bigger wage gains of 1920, and the defence of their gains in the years that followed.

In the course of his evidence McLachlan referred to an array of documents on the table before him. Again and again he read out relevant excerpts – the 1919 agreement to accept the UMW, the high wage rates for Alberta miners and the low ones for Nova Scotia miners, the cost of living as published in the *Labour Gazette*, the changes in the selling price of coal. This was McLachlan in his usual command of the case, taking his audience through the financial statements, annual reports, and newspaper clippings. Once he paused to apologize for not having the text of the MacKinnon Agreement of 1920 on hand – "I have not a copy; they burned down the Labour Herald a couple of times and most of my gear is gone, but I can remember what it was."

Once more he rehearsed the unending struggle between the bloated corporation and the impoverished coal miners:

But here is what the gentlemen on the other side say: we have 101 millions dollars of capital to pay dividends on; the physical assets behind that are idle, steel works like Sydney Mines, acres of junk and rust; idle steel works in New Glasgow; half-idle steel works in Sydney, idle coal mines; abandoned; with fancy bank heads that no man that knows anything about coal mining would ever have put there or squandered their money on. And these men look at this little girl's milk glass and they say; "One fifth more of milk is in there." Snatch the glass from the baby to pay dividends on junk and watered stock. There is the cause of your unrest. That is what they did in cutting the men's wages. [12]

There it was – "the cause of your unrest" – "$19,000,000 of water, wine for the operators and tragedy for the workers of Cape Breton." In 1921 Dominion Steel was able to pay $2,226,300 in dividends on common shares, but the capitalist appetite was still not satisfied: "In December of that year they wanted to cut the miners 37 1/2 % and told them there was going to be no cross firing or bartering." [13]

Much of the story revolved around the Montreal Agreement of 1920, or most particularly the refusal of the operators to sign a new agreement at the end of 1921. Without reference to the agreement's provisions for future negotiation, without even the recourse to a conciliation board, the operators had insisted on a substantial wage reduction. Those meetings at the Windsor Hotel in Montreal in December 1921 marked the end of the short-lived period of industrial legality in the coal industry. That was the signal for the miners to defend their wage rate through direct action – the strike on the job, the confrontation with the minister of labour, the 100 per cent strike, and finally the agreement in August. It was a simple agreement, McLachlan underlined, contain-

ing none of the restrictive provisions of the Montreal Agreement –
"They were very glad to sign up any old agreement by August 17, I can
tell you that. There was no question about stoppage of work or anything
else then, and they signed up this agreement, not a word in it about
stoppage of work ... We deliberately drafted that thing so that it would
not be a breach for to go on strike."[14]

Across the room, Wolvin was listening carefully all morning, taking
occasional notes, impatient to begin his cross-examination. When
McLachlan consulted a small red book and began to read from it,
Wolvin interrupted:

– Might I ask, Mr. Chairman, what that book is he is reading from?
– It is the Minutes of District 26 Convention, 1922.

Later in the morning, when McLachlan told the story of a coal
miner's wife who was denied credit for "luxuries" – apples and
cranberries – at the company store, Wolvin interrupted a second
time: "Is this really evidence?"[15]

McLachlan's formal presentation stopped short in 1923: "That is as
far as my connection with the union goes. When that strike occurred
in 1923 I got canned, in several different ways." But his intention this
morning was not to dwell on the betrayals that ended his career as a
union officer. Instead, he was answering the terms of the inquiry with
the story of an inept and arrogant corporation that was driving the coal
industry into ruin, that was unwilling to observe the requirements of
industrial legality, that was unable to provide the miners with good
wages or steady work. Such conditions were the cause of the unrest.

For the remainder of the morning, union president McLeod led the
questioning, underlining several of the themes in McLachlan's presentation. He took McLachlan again back to the "early, struggling days" of
the miners' union, with ample reference to the company police, spies,
and detectives who followed, harassed, and spied on union men and
disrupted union meetings. There was the notorious shooting, by an
undercover detective, at one union meeting, McLachlan recalled, and
then too there were the unexplained fires at the *Maritime Labor Herald*
– "two fires inside of a year" – and the second one, the one that put the

newspaper out of commission for most of the 1925 strike, came only forty-eight hours after Wolvin had told the Halifax press that "he was out to do his dirtiest."[16]

McLeod also returned to the issue of the steel plant, and the operators' frequent argument that low wages for the coal miners were made necessary by the low prices for coal at the steel plant. This was an essential part of the union's critique of Besco – that despite everything the coal industry was actually profitable, but the miners' wages were being asked to bear the costs of other parts of the corporate empire. McLachlan gave a measured response: "I believe that the coal mines have been carrying the steel works and the Halifax Shipyards and everything else. There is where the revenue came from." And, McLachlan agreed, the coal miners were in no position to provide the commission with direct information on the profitability of the coal mines.

But when McLeod followed up by asking whether this, surely, was the main purpose of the present inquiry, McLachlan did not rush to endorse this view. He could not agree that the miners' standard of living should be governed by the profitability of capital:

Well, I suppose the men want to know these things, but what the men are principally interested in is getting enough to live on. I don't suppose the great general bulk of the men would care if they made a hundred million dollars, if their wages was good, and they would not care if they lost a hundred million dollars if their wages was bad. That would not satisfy them. What the men want is to get a living. I believe the men's living should be the first charge on that industry. The very first thing, a good substantial wage for these men. These men put a lot into these mines, more than the company put in.[17]

This was a distinction worth pausing on, and here Duncan leaned forward across the head of the table to pursue the point:

Duncan – Do you say Mr. McLachlan that the wages should be the first charge on the industry?
McLachlan – Aye. I think so. Yes. That is my position.

Duncan – And so long as the men get that, they do not care what happens?

McLachlan – No, I am speaking broadly of the mass of men. There may be an odd man here and there would inquire into the circumstances, but the great broad mass want a living out of it, and to tell these men that the Company is not making money, or not paying, that means nothing to them. That means nothing to the ordinary man. What does he care about that. He forgets that. What he wants is a living out of it.

Duncan – Even though it be a first charge, I imagine that the extent of the wage would depend upon the measure that the first charge could bear. Would not that be so?

McLachlan – The wage, to be satisfactory, it must satisfy the demand. To be satisfactory. No matter how widespread your depression is, or how keen and widespread the competition is, that is nothing to the ordinary workman. That is not an excuse for him. All he sees is his day's work and the pay. You may say the reparation coal from Germany to France or Britain is a factor in the competition, but that is too far fetched for him. "All I know is that my weekly bill costs me $25 and I have only $20 to pay it."[18]

Wolvin versus McLachlan

That was the end of the morning session. After a one-hour break, the commission reassembled at 2 p.m. McLachlan was on edge. All morning Roy Wolvin had been listening, waiting for his turn to cross-examine the man he had long regarded as "the concentrated cause" of local unrest. McLachlan sat tensely as Wolvin raised himself out of his chair and stood at the table. Peering across at McLachlan, Wolvin began with the casual authority of a crown prosecutor:

Wolvin – Mr. McLachlan, what is that button you wear in the lapel of your coat?

McLachlan – The button of the Italian Communist Party.

Wolvin – Are you an Italian?

McLachlan – No, not exactly, no.[19]

From here Wolvin went back through McLachlan's personal history. His unconcealed purpose was to establish that McLachlan was a long-time union officer, far removed from the ordinary mineworker and probably embittered by his loss of employment:

> Wolvin – During your period as an officer of the United Mine Workers of Nova Scotia, and the Amalgamated Mine Workers, did you work at the mines?
>
> McLachlan – No, sir.
>
> Wolvin – Did you work in the mines since you left Sydney Mines in 1909?
>
> McLachlan – No, sir.
>
> Wolvin – What have you done? Have you done anything besides giving your services to organized labour from 1909 till 1923 when you severed your connection with the United Mine Workers?
>
> McLachlan – No, unless worked a little around home, that is all.

And what had McLachlan been doing since then, since 1923? McLachlan answered sharply:

> McLachlan – I was mending shoes three months up in Dorchester and three months in Halifax at the time you wired the Attorney-General congratulating him on putting me in jail. I spent three months playing forty-fives.
>
> Wolvin – The time I wired congratulations.
>
> McLachlan – Yes.
>
> Wolvin – That accounts for six months.
>
> McLachlan – Yes.
>
> Wolvin – You came back into this district when?
>
> McLachlan – In March, I think, 1924.
>
> Wolvin – Have you had any means of support since then?
>
> McLachlan – I worked on the Labor Herald.[20]

Naturally, Wolvin's reading of the history of labour relations differed significantly from McLachlan's. Although Wolvin would be able to present his own version of events at a later stage in the inquiry, he took the present opportunity to correct McLachlan's testimony. The 1919 agreement, he argued, identified Nova Scotia as an "inferior" field, where lower wages were justified. In 1920 the provisions for reopening the MacKinnon Agreement, he argued, must have been part of McLachlan's strategy for promoting unrest in the district. And, contrary to McLachlan's claim, no dividends were ever paid on common stock in 1921. In Montreal at the end of 1921, Wolvin argued, the company was prepared to listen to reasonable proposals. When the company had finally signed a contract in 1922, it had received little help from the union officers.

With all this on the record for the benefit of the commission, Wolvin returned to McLachlan and his unforgiving attitude to the corporation in 1922:

Wolvin – And did you feel as if you wished to extend no mercy whatsoever to them?

McLachlan – Oh, I don't know that I was overflowing with mercy, no.

Wolvin – That is not one of your failings, is it?

McLachlan – Well my friends say it is, my enemies say it isn't.

Wolvin – Not overflowing as far as Corporations are concerned.

McLachlan – I don't know that I would extend very much mercy to the British Empire Steel.[21]

There was even a short lesson in economics for McLachlan, on the ground that during the time he was engaged in producing and selling milk, he was obliged to act as a capitalist:

Wolvin – What was milk selling at when you went into the business?

McLachlan – 10¢ a quart.

Wolvin – What was it selling it at when you went out of the business?

McLachlan – 12¢.

When McLachlan and other milk producers raised their prices, wasn't that a conspiracy?

> McLachlan – Well you can call it conspiracy if you like. We agreed to raise it.
> Wolvin – Did you conspire to take the children's food away from them?
> McLachlan – We conspired to get a little more for our own.
> Wolvin – "My own first" is that your motto?
> McLachlan – No, that has not always been my motto, they would be better off if I had done that.[22]

Later Wolvin needled McLachlan again on his personal finances, wondering how he was supporting himself. Was he drawing pay from the *Labor Herald*? – No, not since it burned down in April. Wasn't it true he was selling tombstones? – No, he wasn't involved in that business.

> Wolvin – Are you a capitalist?
> McLachlan – Well, no, not exactly a capitalist.
> Wolvin – What are you living on?
> McLachlan – What am I living on?
> Wolvin – Yes?
> McLachlan – I am living on my two boys and two girls. They are working.[23]

The sparring continued for the rest of the afternoon. Everything was contentious, and McLachlan gave little ground, often retorting in brief bursts. Were the coal miners' wage increases to McLachlan's personal credit? – "Oh, bless you, no." Did the company's so-called spies go around disguised in long whiskers? – "Some of them do." Wouldn't McLachlan run the steel plant about the same way as Wolvin? – "Probably a lot better."

By the time Wolvin returned to the burning of the *Maritime Labor Herald*, mentioned earlier in the day, McLachlan was ready to attack:

Wolvin – You don't think it was because I said I was going to do my dirtiest that it burned.

McLachlan – Well, Mr. Wolvin, you said here yesterday that you payed this higher rate in 1924 because you was getting value for it. The value consisted of the maintenance men, and what these men that were negotiating with you could do to suppress the Labor Herald. It was worth money to you, you said. How much? If I may ask you a question?

Duncan interrupted, separating the two fighters like a referee in a boxing match, but within minutes they were again scowling at each other:

Wolvin – Do you believe that I said in Halifax that: "I would do my dirtiest"?

McLachlan – Well, I don't know. The statement came out in the Press anyhow.

Wolvin – You have met me quite a few times. Do you think I would say anything like that?

McLachlan – I have heard you say some very foolish things.

Wolvin – Do you think I would be too clever to say anything like that?

McLachlan – No I don't.

Again Duncan interrupted: "He is not going to pay you a compliment, Mr. Wolvin."[24]

In his questioning of McLachlan, Wolvin was determined to show that the union leader was an unreasonable radical and that much of the unrest could be attributed to his irrational expectations. He turned now to an exploration of McLachlan's peculiar political views. It was only a short time since the Workers' Party had been dissolved and renamed the Communist Party of Canada, but McLachlan pretended to be amused by Wolvin's confusion about the complexities of radical politics:

Wolvin – What is "the workers' party of Canada"?

McLachlan – Which worker's party now?

Wolvin – The party known as that. Is there a Workers' Party in Canada, a political party?

McLachlan – I don't know of any.

Wolvin – What party do you belong to?

McLachlan – I belong to the Labor party. And I am a member of the Communist Party of Canada.

Wolvin – Is there an organization in Glace Bay known as "The Workers' Party"?

McLachlan – Not that I know of.

Wolvin – You are a member of the Communist Party?

McLachlan – Yes.[25]

Wolvin pressed on, determined to demonstrate McLachlan's hostility to private enterprise in the coal industry. McLachlan made no effort to conceal his views:

Wolvin – Do you believe in the nationalization of mines?

McLachlan – Well, now, there are so many schools of nationalization, I suppose I do.

Wolvin – Which school do you belong to? Do you believe in bringing it about by revolution?

McLachlan – I believe in the nationalization of mines with workers' control. For instance, I believe as to that mine at No. 6, if there is nobody else will work it, instead of keeping the men standing idle and starving, they should be working it.

Wolvin – What is the doctrine of the Communist Party in connection with that?

McLachlan – The doctrine of the Communist Party is that it is wrong to keep men wandering around the streets idle while somebody else acts like the dog in the manger and keeps the mine idle. Let the men make what they can out of it.

Wolvin – What is the remedy?

McLachlan – That is the remedy for the worker.

Wolvin – For the worker to take charge of the country?

McLachlan – Yes.[26]

Wolvin was making headway, but he wanted more than a declaration of faith. He also wanted McLachlan to declare that he was an outright revolutionist dedicated to overthrowing the established order by force:

> Wolvin – Are you looking forward to the time when the workers will take charge of the country?
> McLachlan – Yes. Evidently they have not charge now. The question implies that.
> Wolvin – Are you still working to that end?
> McLachlan – Still working to that.
> Wolvin – To the end that the workers will take control of Canada?
> McLachlan – Oh, yes, I hope so.
> Wolvin – Do you believe that this should be brought about peaceably and if not done that way, by force?
> McLachlan – I believe that the conditions will get so bad and the employing class will become so reckless – as they are in every country – that the workers will be forced to rise and defend themselves.
> Wolvin – Have you openly preached these Communist doctrines and policies?
> McLachlan – Oh yes, openly.[27]

Now Wolvin turned to specific instances of Communist activity. The Trade Union Educational League? – It had never existed in Cape Breton. Communist Sunday schools? – McLachlan had never attended one. The Red International? – McLachlan supported it. Who were all the directors of the *Maritime Labor Herald*? – He could not name them all. Did he receive $5,000 from Russia for relief of the miners in 1925? – Yes, McLachlan had received it. Had he received any other money from Moscow? – "Not a cent."[28]

Next Wolvin turned to the 1923 strike – an improper strike, a political strike, a strike in violation of contract. In Wolvin's view, this event represented the most extreme violation of industrial legality by the radicals. He also wanted to dwell on 1923 because it was the occasion of McLachlan's defeat, his repudiation by the international union and his conviction by the civil authorities.

What caused the strike? He let McLachlan answer: "It was called because a bunch of Provincial policemen, many of them drunk, rode up one of the streets in Sydney on Sunday night and beat up a number of men, women and children. That is what precipitated that strike." Wolvin responded by reading into the record McLachlan's circular letter of 4 July 1923, the one containing the seditious libel that formed the basis for his conviction. The bitterness was still there in McLachlan's responses:

Wolvin – Do you remember that?
McLachlan – Yes.
Wolvin – Will you ever forget it?
McLachlan – Oh yes. A minor detail in a man's life.
Wolvin – Was that one of the main reasons you went to Dorchester?
McLachlan – One of the main reasons.

Cooperatively, McLachlan went on to add the details of his arrest, explaining that the letter had been delivered to the company for its information and then turned over by company officials to the provincial authorities. Somehow it also ended up published in the Halifax newspapers. To McLachlan this looked like a conspiracy to arrange for his arrest – "that is how they treated a letter received from the miners." Wolvin did not take the trouble to deny McLachlan's charge:

Wolvin – The arrest was followed by conviction was it?
McLachlan – Followed by conviction, as you know.
Wolvin – I just want to be sure, and the Commission does not know these things.
McLachlan – Followed by a congratulation from yourself.
Wolvin – I think I sent some telegrams of congratulation.[29]

"Pop! Pop!" wrote one the reporters at the end of the day, "Like the smack of bullets shoot the questions and the answers of these two men who in their persons embody all the drama of the moment."[30] But the afternoon was growing late. As far as McLeod was concerned, McLach-

lan had already said enough. The commissioners had been exposed to
the face of labour radicalism and anything more was superfluous;
indeed, too much more, McLeod probably feared, might well damage
the miners' larger case. He was ready to bring the examination of
McLachlan to an end. Wolvin objected, stating that there was still much
ground to cover. At 4 p.m. he requested an adjournment to the next
day, and on that note the session ended. McLachlan had been giving
evidence for five hours.[31]

The North Wind

They returned to the fray at 10 a.m. the next morning, and once more
the two antagonists settled down to a wordy war of manoeuvre. Again
Wolvin was constructing his own defence. Besco was a good corporate
citizen and paid substantial taxes – as much as $150,000 a year – to the
province of Nova Scotia. It was not true that the corporation was full
of "dead wood" – Halifax Shipyards, for instance, was paying its own
way. And if anyone thought unions like the UMW were necessary for
the production of coal, there was an instructive situation in the Crowsnest Pass, where many coal companies had given up on the radicals in
District 18 of the UMW and were operating without the trouble of
union recognition.[32]

Wolvin also wanted to get one of McLachlan's more notorious
statements on the record, the claim that McLachlan had told the
company to "go to hell." That was during the hot days of the 1923 strike,
when the enormous coal pile at the surface of No. 2 mine was beginning
to overheat and was in danger of catching fire. Under normal circumstances, men working on the coal bank would turn the coal pile to cool
it down, but this was one more example of McLachlan's reckless
disregard of property rights:

Wolvin – When that bank was on fire and Mr. McNeil asked you
     for men to turn it over, what answer did you make?
McLachlan – Mr. McNeil did not ask.

It was not the first time McLachlan was tripping up Wolvin on details. It had happened the previous day, in a confusion between two different men with the same last name. It was one way of demonstrating that Wolvin was an outsider, unfamiliar with the management of the coal operations. But Wolvin was not unnerved:

Wolvin – Who asked you?

McLachlan – Dan H. MacDougall.

Wolvin – What did you tell him?

McLachlan – I told him what I said here, Take care of the children and we will take care of your coal, and your pumps and everything else, and he refused.

Wolvin – Did you tell him to go to hell?

McLachlan – No I did not tell him to go hell, I told him the bank could go to hell.

Wolvin – It was going, was it, at the time?

McLachlan – Well I hope so, I know there was a number of children going in that direction.[33]

Today, Wolvin could see that McLachlan was still wearing that Italian button – a hammer, a sun, and a sheaf of oats – and could not resist drawing attention to it again. As on the previous day, Wolvin was determined to demonstrate that McLachlan had no interest in the promotion of class harmony. For his part, McLachlan had no objection to presenting himself as a proponent of class struggle. Whereas Wolvin portrayed the industrial unrest in the coal industry as an unacceptable attack on the rights of property, McLachlan understood it as the latest local instalment in a universal struggle against injustice.

Now Wolvin was displaying a news dispatch from Minneapolis and quoting from a statement about Communist propaganda among children. Was McLachlan a promoter of this kind of "education for action"? Was that same kind of thing going on here?

McLachlan – Oh no, that is a garbled statement, I knew when you read it.

Wolvin – Could you make a better statement than that?

McLachlan – I think I could.

The problem with that clipping, McLachlan replied, was that it was a piece of "yellow press nonsense put in for the purpose of frightening the crowd."

Wolvin – You do not believe in education for action?
McLachlan – Not what is implied there.
Wolvin – How do you believe in education for action?
McLachlan – I believe in telling children the truth about the history of the world, that it does not consist in the history of Kings and Lords and Cabinets, but consists in the history of the mass of the workers, a thing that is not taught in the schools. I believe in telling children how to measure value, a thing that is not taught in any school.[34]

Next Wolvin was holding up a copy of the *Maritime Labor Herald* from early 1923 and quoting from one of McLachlan's published exchanges with John L. Lewis. What he wanted to highlight was an extract from the program of the Red International:

Wolvin – Do you support that doctrine that you quoted there?
McLachlan – I certainly support every working class effort where oppression has put them into that position where they are being reduced to starvation and slavery. I approve of that rather than approve of abject silence and submission. Just as I hail and approve the deeds and memory of one Wallace who slew and cut to pieces the oppressors who came to Scotland from England. We are proud of that thing. I am proud of the men of Logan when they refuse to submit to be beaten and despoiled. And I am proud of the men of Herrin.

The references to the UMW coal miners of Logan County, West Virginia, and Herrin, Illinois, probably meant little to Duncan, but the chairman, who was widely described as a man with a pride in his

Scottish heritage, could not let the reference to the eleventh-century hero of Scottish nationhood pass without comment:

Duncan – Do you know anything of Wallace, Mr. Wolvin?

Wolvin – I think I remember reading of him, Mr. Chairman.

McLachlan – No, he knows nothing about him. I suppose he won't appear any greater in your eyes, Mr. Wolvin, on account of me endorsing him.

Wolvin – Endorsing?

Duncan – Endorsing Wallace.[35]

From the table Wolvin now picked up a clipping of one of McLachlan's speeches from 1922, from the days when McLachlan was in office, again to demonstrate the notorious view that revolutionary upheavals could be justified and even encouraged. For the benefit of the commission, Wolvin read McLachlan's words:

– "These arise out of conditions. They come about when conditions are right and cannot be made to order. There is no more use you shouting against them than there is in shouting against the North wind. When they do occur they must be used for the permanent advantage of the working classes and not indulged in blindly." Did you say that?

This was perhaps as close as McLachlan ever came to proclaiming a philosophy of revolution. Like other radicals schooled in the Marxism of the Socialist Party of Canada before the war, he did not claim to be able to make a revolution of his own accord. Instead, revolutions arose out of the natural course of events under capitalism, and it was up to the revolutionaries to live up to their historic responsibilities and provide the leadership that was needed.

But before McLachlan could reply, there was a brief interruption from the miners' lawyer, A.D. Campbell. Should McLachlan be required to answer? Was Wolvin somehow trying to entrap McLachlan? Duncan reassured Campbell that McLachlan's testimony came under the protection of the Canada Evidence Act.

Following this exchange, McLachlan responded to the question in this way:

> McLachlan – I want to say this, Mr. Chairman, that street upris-
> ings and all that, raiding the stores, that these things arise just
> as I said there; from the oppression, from the economic condi-
> tions which the workers are subjected to. No man can go out,
> I could not go out in Sydney and say to the crowd, "Let us raid
> a store." As I said, they are like the North wind, they are a
> terrible thing, but it is useless complaining against the North
> wind.
>
> Duncan – According to this article, I gather you say that circum-
> stances make these things. No one can create them artificially
> or suppress them artificially?
>
> McLachlan – Yes, circumstances made the Great War. We could
> deplore it, but it grew out of circumstances and it could not be
> helped.
>
> Wolvin – Do you believe that when they do occur they should be
> used for the permanent advantage of the working class?
>
> McLachlan – I believe that every move in working class life should
> be used for the benefit of the working class. Whether foolish or
> wise.
>
> Wolvin – Revolution if necessary?
>
> McLachlan – Well, the revolutions is like the North wind, they
> come somehow, of their own accord, and I don't know how
> they come, but they come, that's all, they come out of condi-
> tions.

McLachlan was saying something here not unlike what Bill Pritchard, the western labour radical, had said: "Only fools try to make revolu-tions, wise men conform to them."[36] But this was not exactly what Wolvin wanted to hear:

> Wolvin – Do very many men work continuously, year after year,
> to bring them about?
>
> McLachlan – Year after year?

Wolvin – Year after year to bring these revolutions about?

McLachlan – Many men work year after year pointing out that conditions are driving men in every country towards that at the present time.

Wolvin wanted more and continued to bait McLachlan. Was he doing anything more than working towards revolution? Yes, he was. But wasn't it true that all his activities were directed towards that? "Oh, my own activities don't amount to very much."[37] Was there ever any article published in the *Maritime Labor Herald* under his editorship designed to allay the unrest in the coalfields? Could he identify even a single one?

McLachlan – Can I? I point to them all and say they were calculated to do that. There will be no end to this strife, Mr. Wolvin, until the workers have enough to feed and clothe themselves and have the terrific fear of unemployment taken away, and that is what the Maritime Labor Herald has in view.

Wolvin – Have you ever said that there would be no end to this unrest and strife until the workers were in control?

McLachlan – That is about when they will get enough to do them, not before that, never a day before it. With all due deference to this Commission going to bring peace, they are not going to do it.[38]

The exchanges continued to bristle with hostility. Wolvin quoted more extracts from McLachlan's speeches and writings, including his endorsement, in January 1925, of the current District 26 executive as "a triumph for the left wing." Did McLachlan support John W. McLeod? – "People accuse me of doing it in the Press." Did McLachlan ever disagree with the contents of the *Maritime Labor Herald*? "At times." Did he attend Communist Party meetings in Toronto in September? – "Yes." Did the recent election flyer with the heading "Wolvin or McLachlan. Which Will Win?" have his approval? – "It did not have my disapproval." Did he know the song "The Red Flag"? – "Yes." And "The Internationale"? – "Yes. Well, I am not strong on songs at all."[39]

Again, Wolvin wanted to know more about schools. Were children in Glace Bay being called together and taught communism?

McLachlan – Well, I would hardly say Communism. It is rather a big subject for a child, but there have been little schools off and on, not at all regularly.

Wolvin – Have there been little schools in Waterford?

McLachlan – Let me finish my first answer. Called together off and on, and certainly it wasn't Communism that was being taught to the children. It was something very elementary, such as I pointed out yesterday, that the current history of this world does not consist of dates, and kings and things of that kind. Working class history. How they lived, how they made their bread, and how they were suppressed. How there were jailed, that those were the important things, not how some king happened to get a hold of a throne. That does not matter anything to a working class child.

Wolvin – What else are they taught? You have only given part of it?

McLachlan – That is about the gist of it.

Wolvin – Do you teach them there is no God?

McLachlan – Don't teach anything at all about religion.

Wolvin – You don't?

McLachlan – No sir.[40]

The fireworks came a few minutes later, when Wolvin quoted a statement attributed to McLachlan:

Wolvin – Did you ever remark at one of those meetings: "I attended the class a few Sundays ago and the children are getting along fine and I tell you it will take more than Dr. Gillies or Father MacAdam to pull the wool over their eyes."

McLachlan – No, sir. I never made such a statement in my life.

On McLachlan's objection, Duncan asked Wolvin for the source of this statement. Wolvin replied that it came from "an indirect source." As far as McLachlan was concerned, he denied the statement entirely. Wolvin was inventing evidence in order to inflame opinion on religion, that most sensitive of local subjects:

> McLachlan – The impression was going abroad that somebody with some responsibility had made that statement, whereas it is nothing only a statement written with lead pencil on that piece of paper this morning, manufactured for the occasion. The thing that causes the unrest and resentment.
>
> Duncan – Don't let us have a speech about it at the moment, Mr. McLachlan.
>
> McLachlan – I want to say that that is the kind of double dealing stuff that these men put over.
>
> Duncan – Your explanation is on the notes, Mr. McLachlan.
>
> Wolvin – I will have that question withdrawn.
>
> McLachlan – Nobody only a coward would do that. I am going to tell him.
>
> Duncan – You have already told him.
>
> McLachlan – You bet I am going to tell him. A dirty, double dealing cowardly thrust, that is what it is.[41]

One of the last documents Wolvin read into the record was the lengthy writ of excommunication issued by John L. Lewis in July 1923. In Wolvin's view, this statement confirmed the fact that, as far as organized labour was concerned, McLachlan was an outlaw. When Wolvin asked him to verify that this was the telegram he had received, McLachlan had difficulty answering. Duncan intervened:

> Duncan – Was that telegram received by you?
>
> McLachlan – I want to say that this is a copy of a despicable lying telegram, a treacherous thrust of a traitor to the working class kicking a man when he was down and in jail.
>
> Wolvin – The question is, that is the telegram?
>
> McLachlan – That is the traitor's words.
>
> Duncan – It is a telegram from the President of the International Union.

McLachlan – Yes, I want to put it in my own way.[42]

The Remedy

That was the end of the confrontation with Wolvin, but before McLachlan was excused from the hearings, there were additional questions
from the commissioners. Cronyn questioned him on working conditions in the collieries and social conditions in the coal towns, and
McLachlan replied amply. But the discussion still kept returning to the
priority of wages.

Wouldn't more cooperation between employers and workers be
possible? McLachlan had a considered response:

> This cooperation works out to the benefit of the other man all the
> time. You can all cooperate with anyone if you meet them on equal
> footing. Isn't that right. If you are my employer and you hold in
> the hollow of your hand my means of living, and you come to me
> and say; now the market is so bad I must cut your wages. Well, I
> look at the market, and I look at the cut wage, and I look at the
> idle men on the outside, and I say; Yes, boss, we will cooperate, we
> will cut the wage. But in my soul I am saying, I am cooperating
> because I have to. You cannot get a worker honestly to say he is
> cooperating when he knows the wage he is accepting is not feeding
> and clothing and sheltering his family. No matter what the market
> condition is outside, whether the coal trade is paying or not, it is
> nothing to him. It is nothing to his family. He cooperates because
> he has to. He is economically bound.[43]

These were important distinctions. As McLachlan recognized, the
proceedings were structured around assumptions that he himself did
not share. The questions that were important to Wolvin, and also to the
commissioners, were the ones that charged McLachlan with violations of
industrial legality: the strike on the job, the withdrawal of maintenance
men, the endangerment of property, the reopening of agreements, the
political strike. And when he was not in contempt of industrial legality,
McLachlan could also be indicted for excessive zeal in promoting

industrial democracy – by calling for nationalization of industry and workers' control, by trying to attach the miners to organizations such as the Workers' Party and the Red International, and by supporting the *Maritime Labor Herald*.

From this perspective, Cronyn and Duncan both wondered whether more power should be placed in the hands of the union officers. They focused on the conduct of union affairs in 1922, when McLachlan was leading the coal miners through their first great battle against Besco. Were they really free to ignore the usual expectations in 1922? McLachlan had an answer. Yes, since the decision of Judge Mellish announced that "there were no conditions of employment. There is what the Judge said."[44]

And what about the breach of executive solidarity in February 1922, when McLachlan disowned a provisional agreement signed by the president:

– Normally it would not be done, would it?
– Normally it would not, but the question might be very vital, you know. It might be a violation of a principle that a man had advocated and everything like that.[45]

And what about striking on the job that year – was that normal? It was, McLachlan agreed, "a new policy in this district."[46] And the repudiation of the agreement in August 1922 by crowds of men on the ballfield in Glace Bay – was that normal? No, McLachlan agreed, that was "extraordinary entirely."[47]

And, Duncan wanted to know, what of the charge that McLachlan had abused the conciliation process, using it to gain publicity and play for time? From the time it was enacted in 1907, the Industrial Disputes Investigation Act had been used for exactly that purpose, McLachlan explained, to delay strikes and to exert moral pressure on public opinion. Certainly unions should be permitted to use it for their own purposes, to delay wage cuts and to put their case before the country. But, Duncan wanted to know, was that using the law of the land for a worthy purpose? In the light of his long experience with conciliation, McLachlan did not consider his answer particularly controversial: "No, I don't think it was what you would call a very worthy purposes, but like everything else that organized labor is doing it is sometimes not very worthy, but they have no alternative. Here is this wage going down. There are no other methods, any means to stop it."[48]

In the final exchanges, Cronyn and Duncan both pressed McLachlan to elaborate on "what we might call partial cures." They were particularly interested to hear that McLachlan's expectations of the commission were limited:

> Cronyn – And as I take it, the remedy for the whole trouble was nationalization under workers' control.
> McLachlan – Well, of course, that is the remedy.
> Duncan – But you are not expecting that from us?
> McLachlan – No, I don't expect that next week or next month. But there are one or two practical things that could be done and could be suggested to this Commission. That water ought to be squeezed out of it, every last drop ...[49]

But Cronyn insisted on returning McLachlan to the issue of nationalization. Would there be any compensation to the owners? "No, I would never agree to a cent for them. Never agree to any such a thing. The workers have put too much into these mines; three lives in every thousand. That is more than all the millions they put in, over a period of years. They have put their filthy money in; the workers have put their blood in it. Not a cent."[50]

But short of public ownership, what could McLachlan recommend? What else could the commission recommend by way of "what we might call partial cures"? His answers were, first, to squeeze the water out of the corporation; and second, to reduce the working day, increase employment, and improve wages:

> McLachlan – Here is the contradiction. The more wealth and coal that is produced, the richer the operators are in wealth production and control, the poorer chance the miner has for a living. If we would go to war with somebody and murder millions of men, we would all have lots of work and a good time. Why not pray for war?

Duncan – You do not want us to recommend that I am sure?

McLachlan – A good war would be all right but no, I don't want that. That is not the way to cure it. There is only one cure. Cut down the hours and raise the wages so that the workers as a whole can buy back a little more than all the things they produce. That is the only cure.[51]

Whether McLachlan was right or not to have so little faith in the capitalist system, his testimony served the purposes of the inquiry by amply demonstrating the depth of the bitterness between the corporation and the union. For his part, McLachlan could leave the hearings with some personal satisfaction. He had met Wolvin and stood his ground. The commissioners, and the union officers too for that matter, had heard an articulate statement of the radical expectations of the 1920s, edged with the bitterness of McLachlan's sense of betrayal. Much of it the commissioners could not accept, but they could not deny McLachlan's influence in setting the terms of the struggle.

The official summary of McLachlan's evidence released by the commission was less than ten paragraphs long and conveyed little of the contents or the drama of the occasion. In an unofficial comment, a report in the Sydney *Post* counted McLachlan the champion in the confrontation with Wolvin – Wolvin had received "a series of solar-plexus retorts which probably impressed Besco's President with the truth of the proverb concerning the client of the man who becomes his own lawyer."[52]

McLachlan himself was less restrained, and in the following weeks the story of the hearings was the main theme in his speeches at public meetings. At the Strand Theatre in Sydney and at the Russell Theatre in Glace Bay, McLachlan was "in fighting trim" as he regaled audiences with his own account of his "passage of arms" with Wolvin. There was laughter as McLachlan ridiculed Wolvin and applause as he repeated his own favourite replies.

There was nothing peculiar about the situation in Nova Scotia, McLachlan declared, for capitalism was crumbling around the world and the coal miners had their place in the international struggle that followed: "I hail with delight the uprising of all oppressed, whether it be in India, in Ireland, in Egypt or in any country in the world where the working class marches against its tyrants."[53]

The Report

The hearings continued for the rest of the month and into December, with the final sessions ending in Halifax on 23 December. Wolvin himself was one of the last witnesses to appear before the royal commission. There he confirmed the company's unwillingness to continue collective bargaining in the coal industry. The UMW had failed in its responsibility to inspire "confidence and cooperation" between workers and employers, and if union recognition was going to be continued, he warned, it would have to take place without violations of contract, without Communist union officers, and without the check-off of union dues: "I am opposed to assisting in the collection of funds for a body whose object is to secure possession of our corporation's property."[54]

The lengthiest testimony, however, was that of the district union president. McLeod gave evidence for several days and enjoyed considerable success in convincing Duncan that he was a more acceptable union leader than a man such as McLachlan. There was only one direct reference to McLachlan in McLeod's testimony, and it was a word of praise for his conduct of union affairs in wartime: "I think history will write down Mr. McLachlan as a better patriot than some of the profiteers that were honored in more than one way for services to their country."[55]

Certainly he did not spare the corporation, either in his formal presentations or in his testimony. Consistently, McLeod argued that Besco was a corrupt corporation that was out to destroy the union. But McLeod also made it clear that his agenda did not include nationalization of the coal mines. When pressed by Duncan, the union leader failed to endorse public ownership of the industry as a solution: "It is a subject that men talk about perhaps, well, flippantly, perhaps that is not the correct term, but they have not a proper understanding of what it really involves. The nationalization of coal mines is a subject that has not come under examination by any competent body in Nova Scotia, as far as I know, and in older coal producing countries it is practically a new subject yet. I think there is not very much to be gained by witnesses talking about nationalization or any subject on which they are not informed."[56]

This declaration distinguished McLeod sharply from McLachlan, who – Duncan reminded him – had called for nationalization without compensation. As Duncan was also well aware, McLeod was misrepresenting the international debate on nationalization. In the case of the Miners' Federation of Great Britain, its arguments for public ownership, as articulated by socialist intellectuals such as Sidney Webb and R.H. Tawney, had already swayed the Sankey commission in 1919. Now the British miners were preparing the renewed campaign for public ownership that would culminate in the British General Strike in the spring of 1926.

Duncan's appreciation of McLeod was further strengthened when the union leader arranged for him to meet privately with the international president of the UMW. In December, Duncan took a short trip to New York, to see off his wife who was returning home to Britain before Christmas. On 10 December, Duncan held a friendly three-hour meeting there with John L. Lewis, who found him to be congenial company: "I was profoundly impressed with the manifest sincere fairness exhibited by him and observed with pleasure the practical workings of his well-trained mind." McLeod in turn later reported to Lewis that Duncan was "tremendously impressed" by their encounter. As a result, McLeod expected, "some constructive recommendations will likely be offered."[57]

The commission's final report was completed with little delay, for Duncan was fully aware that the coal miners were working under a temporary six-month contract that expired in February. The report commented on a wide range of problems in the industry, ranging from minor grievances in the mines to the financial management of the corporation. Company police, company stores, and company housing were singled out for criticism; so, too, were the factionalism of the union officers and the editorial policies of the *Maritime Labor Herald*. Not a single word was said about public ownership or other forms of industrial democracy.[58]

In its attempt at even-handed judgment, the Duncan Report fully endorsed neither the company nor the union. The "recurring strife and friction" were attributed to two evils – on the one hand, "the opposition which the operators have offered to the men's desire to organize themselves in the U.M.W.A."; on the other hand, "the introduction of Communistic theories and aims into ordinary industrial relationships." The salvation of the industry was to be found neither in the replacement of the international union by a company-representation plan, as Wolvin would have liked, nor in the nationalization of the industry with workers' control, as McLachlan wanted. Instead, the future of the industry rested in the formula of industrial legality: open acceptance of the miners' union by the operators, and more responsible behaviour on the part of the union leaders.

There was no direct reference to McLachlan in the report, but there was no shortage of criticism of the conduct of union affairs under his leadership. In general, the union had failed to "settle down into a well-ordered organization." There was too much factionalism among union leaders, and under a system of annual elections, its leaders were lacking in "continuity, knowledge and personal responsibility." All this was made worse by what the report described as "political complications" – "trade union activity and industrial negotiation were being confused – and even on occasions overridden – by the political and social theories and aims of avowed Communists working within the Union." Propagandistic publications such as the *Maritime Labor Herald,* supported by union funds, were "making well ordered and amicable relationships within the existing order of industry impossible." In short, the commissioners concluded, they accepted the operators' view that as far as "amicable relations" and "good will and understanding between themselves and the men" were concerned, the radical leadership had caused "fundamental difficulties."

In the meantime, McLachlan had been busy nursing the *Maritime Labor Herald* back to life. When it reappeared in January 1926, McLachlan was featured in a weekly front-page column under the title "Our Point of View." Not surprisingly, one of his first topics was the Duncan Report. Would the Duncan Commission succeed in bringing peace to the coal industry? McLachlan was more than sceptical: "If it does, we replied, its members ought to be canonized and the Commission made a permanent institution to do that which has never been accomplished before – bring peace out of the murderous contradictions created by capitalism." The Duncan Commission was not the first commission to look into the coal industry – other commissions had tackled the coal miners' troubles in Britain, in the United States, and in Germany, all with similar lack of success. It is tempting to speculate whether Sankey, who had allowed himself to be persuaded of the benefits of nationalization in Britain in 1919, might have written a different kind of report, but the recommendations of the Sankey Commission had been long since abandoned by the British government. Indeed, McLachlan's commentary pointed to that example: "It was a classic of its kind, and the miners licked their lips in joyous anticipation of the good things that Commission was going to bring to them, and today, instead of the cooing dove of peace it's the strident roar of an ever-growing class conflict that is heard all over what once was 'Merry England' until the blighting hand of Capitalism rested on it."[59]

With the publication of the Duncan Report, the bubble finally burst. According to McLachlan, ever since the end of the 1925 strike, the miners' expectations had been rising. Even if radical solutions were not on the agenda, there had been hope that the new provincial government and its royal commission would take steps to guarantee steady work – six days in summer and five days in winter – and at the wage rates that existed before the 1925 strike. "To secure fairly steady work at half decent wages," McLachlan declared, "the miners would vote tory, or do anything else that promised relief from the grinding life that they had been forced to live since Besco had been created."[60]

At last McLachlan was also ready to comment publicly on the membership of the commission itself. True to form, he charged, all working-class influence was barred from the commission. It consisted of "a real live 'Sir' from England, a clergyman and an insurance promoter." And true to form it was acclaimed by the press as "utterly unprejudiced." With each day of the hearings, the miners' expectations of what the commission, this "utterly unprejudiced" commission, was going to accomplish continued to rise. Duncan himself had turned out to be "a kind of an industrial Doctor Hornbrook who can rattle off the names of your troubles, their cause and cure just like A, B, C." But in the end the inflated bubble had to burst, and when the report finally came down, it was a long and wordy document meant to "bewilder the miners with a shower of words."[61]

The Duncan Report – "stripped of the sawdust" – was nothing more than a long-winded endorsement of the rights of capital: "What the miner wanted to know was how he was to get enough to live on; what the report tells in three pages of ordinary newspaper is how the coal industry can be made profitable for Besco." According to the report, the 1925 wage reduction had been more than appropriate and the miners' long struggle to "stand the gaff" had not been justified. And why was the commission prepared to render this negative judgment on all the miners' suffering and struggle? "This commission answers that they had examined the financial position of the corporation and that settled the question for them."[62]

The future would be much the same. Returns on capital would be the first charge on the industry. In the language of the report, future rates were to be determined "by the ability of the coal industry to pay." That in turn was to be decided by accountants, "so that wage variation can go into effect without discussion or friction." In other words, McLachlan charged, the miners were asked to give up their hard-won rights to a team of accountants.

While the report deplored the influence of Communist teachings and tactics, McLachlan argued that the findings could also be read as an endorsement of the radical strategies of previous years. For one, the report stated that, in light of the relatively healthy condition of the coal operations, the miners were justified in resisting the wage reductions in 1922: "But it was exactly in that year that the miners put up an effective fight by striking on the job and finally calling their first hundred per cent strike. By these tactics they raised their wage by over eighty cents per day." And the report also stated that wage reductions in 1923 would have been justified: but that was the year the radicals were in control and trying to restore the higher 1921 rates – and Besco did not dare to reduce wages at that time.[63]

As for the corporation, it was dealt with lightly – scolded for not paying a higher price for coal used at the steelworks, but not for the $54 million worth of watered stock injected into the corporation over time. That was passed over with the indulgent comment that such practice was "not uncommon in Canadian companies." Or to put it another way, McLachlan paraphrased the conclusion: "This particular brand of murdering the working class is so common that it can no longer be considered a crime, and therefore could not, or at least should not, cause any trouble here."[64]

But what, then, was the cause of the strife? Why was there all this trouble around the coal mines? Why was there no peace between the miner and employer? The answer was nowhere to be found in the Duncan Report:

> The operators run the mines to make profit, the miners dig coal to make a living, and these two ends just won't jibe under present conditions. The miners want a living, the operators want profits. Which of these two "wants" should receive the prime and first consideration? The commission, this unprejudiced commission, has left no doubt on that question. Profits come first, and these must be maintained even if the present low standard of living of the coal miners has to be reduced still further.

The heart of the whole report, in McLachlan's view – "the heart of the trick that is about to be played" – was in section 16 of the recommendations. Here the commissioners outlined a formula for, using the language of the report, "the automatic regulation of wage fluctuations at stated intervals ... in the light of the ability of the coal operations to pay." In other words, McLachlan concluded, "capital is not supposed to suffer any deficits, but it's all right to reduce your standard of living."[65]

At the District 26 convention in February 1926, the miners were divided. To McLachlan, the acceptance of any agreement based on the Duncan Report would be a violation of union principles: "To accept the award was to hand over all the functions of the union to some professional accountant whose say-so would determine their wages and who would never once have to appear before the miners to give an account of his actions." The only alternative was to wait for a strategic moment – a harbour full of ships waiting for coal cargoes – to bring on a successful strike, even a 100 per cent strike, and secure their demands.

Under McLachlan's influence, the policy committee reported against signing any contract that included wage reductions. For two days the issue was debated. McLeod argued for acceptance of an agreement based on the Duncan Report. The miners had fought long enough – four big strikes, four commissions of investigation, four visitations of soldiers and police. In his view the miners were weary and weakened and a policy of caution would serve them best. In the end the roll was called and, by a vote of fifty-seven to thirty-five, McLeod carried the day. Even this did not settle the new agreement, for in a referendum the miners voted four to one against the new contract. A modified agreement, specifying no increases or reductions for six months, was narrowly accepted by a second vote in March.[66]

By this time, McLachlan argued, nothing could save Besco. The corporation, he claimed, was already "standing on the edge of a cliff" – a metaphor he happily attributed to Sir Andrew Rae Duncan. It was only a matter of time before it was pushed over the edge or fell off of its own accord. Even with a two-year agreement that was supposed to guarantee peace in the coalfields, Besco was incapable of surviving. As the corporation's share values fell steadily on the stock market in the following months, McLachlan observed that "the bluffers are being found out by their own class, just as the workers have found them out long ago."[67]

In the short run, observers judged the Duncan Report a qualified success. Its prescription for industrial legality was accepted – narrowly, and at least as much out of exhaustion as out of conviction. But the preservation of the union contract, along with the check-off of union dues, were notable achievements by the standards of the industrial anarchy that prevailed in the North American coalfields in the 1920s. Most of the coal miners in the international union had suffered substantial defeats in the course of the decade, and under the conservative leadership of Lewis they had been unable to defend their contracts. The outcome in Nova Scotia had been more favourable for the union, and much of the credit was due to the radical leadership which had mounted such a long war of resistance. But even in Nova Scotia the radicals were no longer in control of the district, and indeed the international union in 1926 had adopted a constitutional amendment banning all Communists from holding membership in the UMW.

None of this was a recipe for lasting peace. The Duncan Commission did not succeed in restoring stability to the coal industry, to its markets, or to its management. Besco's fortunes continued to decline. The banks refused further financing, and Dominion Iron and Steel went into receivership. Wolvin held on to the wreckage but was eventually forced to step down as Besco president. The discredited corporation was subsequently superceded by a reorganized Dominion Steel and Coal Corporation (Dosco) under the control of Herbert Holt and his financial associates at the Royal Bank of Canada. Wolvin remained active in the shipping and shipbuilding industries and later became chairman of the board of Canadian Vickers.[68]

The three royal commissioners passed on into history. Hume Cronyn soon retired from business and public life; one of his sons became a well-known stage actor. Father MacPherson served another decade as a university president; in retirement he occasionally reminisced about his service on the commission, writing Duncan fondly about their days "questioning and instructing the Cape Breton miners."[69]

For several years Sir Andrew Rae Duncan continued to enjoy popularity with Canadian governments. On behalf of the Dominion government he chaired the Royal Commission on Maritime Claims later in 1926. He would also return to Nova Scotia to conduct a second investigation into the coal industry in 1932. At home in Britain, Duncan went on to serve as chairman of the British Iron and Steel Federation, chairman of the Central Electricity Board, and director of several finance and industrial corporations, including the Bank of England and Dunlop Rubber. In 1940 he was elected as an MP for the city of London and served in economic portfolios in Winston Churchill's cabinet. Within the wartime coalition government he opposed the increasing influence of the Labour Party ministers in economic matters; one of them accused Duncan and others of behaving like "very sinister capitalists." One British historian has classified the later Duncan as "an affable monopolist."[70]

Back in Cape Breton, McLachlan remained ready to fight another day. However, as Besco disintegrated in the summer of 1926, falling circulation forced McLachlan to close down the *Maritime Labor Herald*.

One of his last columns was a commentary on the defeat of the British General Strike that spring, but his observations on the ebb and flow of unionism among the coal miners in the Old Country could also be taken as reflections on the course of local events: "One day beaten and broken, their organization would recede but never, never quite back to the point from which the flow had started. Next day the flow would set in and always reach a higher point than ever touched before. One day a heartbreak, the next the birth of a new hope ..."[71]

CHAPTER 11

Grand Old Man

Arise, ye prisoners of starvation!
Arise, ye wretched of the earth,
For justice thunders condemnation,
A better world's in birth.

– "The Internationale"

"Old Jim"

Spadina Avenue, Toronto. It's a jumble of factories, warehouses, shops, and homes, an industrial neighbourhood sprawling around the widest street in the city. In November 1928 McLachlan sat in a small photo studio. The shutter opened and closed, recording an image of three generations. By McLachlan's shoulder stood Max Shur, a short, powerful man with silver moustache and twinkling eyes. He was a leader of the Industrial Union of Needle Trades Workers, a fluent speaker in English and in Yiddish, and one of the organizers who was making this area known as Red Spadina. At McLachlan's knee stood a young boy with a bright eager face, almost three years old. His mother had named him Jimmie, in McLachlan's honour, and Annie Buller was proud to tell McLachlan that he already "uses his fists as you do on the stage."[1]

At fifty-nine years of age, McLachlan was now regarded as a celebrated veteran of the class struggle. Here on Spadina Avenue in 1928 he was playing the part of a guest of honour on the eleventh anniversary of the Russian Revolution. For the occasion a celebration was planned for one of the biggest halls on the street, the Standard Theatre, located at the corner of Spadina and Dundas Avenues. For immigrants from tsarist Russia, who made up so much of the local working class around Spadina, the 1917 Revolution had been a great inspiration. It had also attracted new immigrant radicals into the Communist Party; indeed, in the 1920s most of the party's membership consisted of Finnish, Russian, Ukrainian, and Jewish members, many of whom spoke little English. McLachlan was a shrewd choice of speaker for the event, as party organizers were eager to introduce these immigrant workers to some of the heroes of the domestic Canadian version of the class struggle.

The meeting almost did not take place, for the Toronto police were cracking down on subversive public meetings, especially those taking place in foreign languages. On Sunday morning the city police chief, Brigadier-General Denis Draper, attempted to cancel the theatre's permit. The police backed off when A.E. Smith of the Canadian Labour Defence League – and a former Methodist minister who, like McLachlan, had found his way to the Communist Party through the social gospel – promised that the proceedings would be entirely in English.[2]

That night McLachlan treated the audience to a dramatic rendition of the class struggle in Nova Scotia. In mischievous defiance of the police, his speech was amply thickened with guttural "Scotchie talk," and one policeman noted that "it was difficult to understand him at times." McLachlan was followed briefly by Max Shur, who gave a short, spirited talk in Yiddish, again driving home their defiance of the police. The police report commented that McLachlan's speech "contained nothing new nor interesting," but the packed house cheered enthusiastically and a collection of about $250 was taken. McLachlan's performance was repeated a few nights later at another popular Spadina location, the Alhambra Theatre.[3]

Annie Buller, one of the Communist Party's formidable women organizers, was delighted with McLachlan's presence in Toronto. "The movement in Canada has very little life in it," she had written to Glace Bay a year earlier. "It seems to be at a low ebb. Still the vanguard has to keep going regardless of the obstacle in our way." For her and for many party members, McLachlan personified that sense of determination and she did her best to make him welcome in Toronto. Following the visit, she sent a short note of appreciation to his family at Steele's Hill: "I can speak for the comrades here that we were delighted to have comrade J.B. as he succeeded in making some of us feel much younger and in general put a little more pep into us. If he did nothing else than that, he certainly succeeded." McLachlan himself seemed to enjoy the trip to "Toronto the Good," as he called it. After spending a week with Annie Buller and her family in Toronto, on the return trip he stopped over in Montreal to visit old friends from Sydney Mines.[4]

McLachlan's Toronto meetings marked the beginning of a series of free-speech fights in the halls, parks, and streets of the city. At one meeting a tear-gas bomb would be thrown and the audience would respond with a singing of the Internationale. There would be numerous raids and arrests, trials and deportations. In 1931 eight party leaders, including Tim Buck, would be charged with belonging to an unlawful organization under Section 98 of the Criminal Code, legislation originally enacted in 1919; most of them received prison terms of five years. All this helped bring the Communist Party unprecedented national prominence. Just as the Great Depression arrived in full force, official persecution placed the Communists squarely in the public eye. Repeatedly, the party would call on McLachlan to lend his presence to events where he could be seen as a symbol of working-class resistance.

By contrast, on the eve of the Great Depression conditions were more quiet in Cape Breton. The May Day celebrations were the smallest in years and gathered only small handfuls of supporters. The local Communists were reduced to no more than a dozen in number. Mine managers were weeding out the troublemakers in the pit, and company police were preventing them from selling *The Worker* at the mines.

As for the union, there seemed to be little fight left in District 26. In the summer of 1927 the district officers received a rough reception for their wage proposals, which delegates to the district convention turned down by a four-to-one vote. At the same time the delegates also defeated an attempt to remove the May Day holiday from the union constitution. McLachlan compared the meeting of the district convention to "a rather sleepy and grumbling giant that was too tired to battle, but would give an ugly growl at any attempt to further degrade and humble him." "District No. 26 is pretty dead," he observed, "but beneath the surface one can find if one looks for it the old spirit of battle."[5]

When one of the local seats in the provincial assembly fell vacant and a by-election was expected, McLachlan anticipated the contest with a kind of grim pleasure. "I have not been feeling well all winter and so was not at the Labor Party convention," he wrote Buller in February 1927. "However they nominated me without my consent and if an election is held I am praying the gods that it shall take place in the summer months. I would like to have one more real fight with the hated crew before I kick the bucket and the warm weather would suit me best. I don't believe that we have the ghost of a chance to win the seat, as things stand at present, but there is a splendid opportunity for some wholesome propaganda."[6]

There was personal tragedy for McLachlan in these years. In 1927 his daughter Kate suddenly took sick and died after a short illness. Kate was their second-oldest daughter, one of the four children who had come across the Atlantic to the New World. A lively, popular young woman, she was also the mother of two young children. McLachlan was badly shaken by her death, and friends were moved by the agony of his loss. It would be several years before McLachlan could speak in public about his private grief, and when he did so he still spoke in despair: "We have seen a mine blow up and our comrades brought out in roasted and bloody fragments; we have seen the North End of Halifax swept with a hurricane, leaving the battered and mangled bodies of men, women and children clothed in a winding sheet of ice. We have helplessly watched the girl we loved have her lungs eaten, fade, fail and die. If these forces are guided by intelligent, infinite love, then tell us what malignant hate could do to wring and break our hearts more effectively?"[7] He and Kate took charge of their daughter's two young boys, and it was obvious that McLachlan cherished his grandchildren. Together they spent long hours tramping through the woods and fields around Steele's Hill.

Nor was Kate in the best of health in these later years. Her legs were weak, and she often had difficulty standing. There is a family story from this period about a day when Kate was waiting on a downtown corner when McLachlan came marching down the street in yet another of the small Communist demonstrations of those years. She stepped off the curb and marched with him. "It was a brave thing to do in any event," recalls one of the grandchildren, "but especially in her condition."[8]

Among the younger miners McLachlan was now referred to as "Old Jim." On Saturdays the young radicals would come up to Steele's Hill to hear him give lessons on political economy and class struggle: "The British Empire Steel Corporation buys and sells – buys labour power and sells coal – and any union that's worth its salt as a real collaborating outfit will do its best to see to it that its lord and master is given every help to buy in the cheapest market and sell in the dearest. This is exactly the work that the present officers of District No. 26, U.M.W.A. are filling in their time doing."[9] Gradually McLachlan seemed to be adjusting to his status as a veteran and recovering some of his strength. At the end of 1927 one visitor reported that "Old Jim" was "very quiet at present but he seems to be in the best of health and so is his family."[10]

In the summer of 1928 there were small signs of renewal in union matters when John W. McLeod came up for re-election as president of District 26. Against him the radicals nominated the veteran labour politician, Dan Willie Morrison, who was still mayor of Glace Bay. As a labour mayor, Morrison had used municipal powers to challenge the company and support the union, most notably in refusing to call out troops during the 1922 strike. In the strenuous contest for the presidency of District 26 in 1928, Morrison won by a substantial margin. McLachlan's supporters regarded this as a victory for the left, and the defeated McLeod, who shortly afterwards took a senior position with the company, denounced Morrison as being under the control of the Communists. This was far from the case, and the correspondent for the *Canadian Mining Journal* was closer to the mark in describing Morrison as a man "possessed of ability and tactic."[11]

The provincial government never did call a by-election in Cape Breton East that year, and the seat remained vacant until the provincial election in September 1928. Then, the constituency boundaries seemed to favour the election of a coal miners' candidate in Cape Breton, since the mining areas were all lumped together in Cape Breton East. To McLachlan's dismay, the Conservative Party continued to claim that they were the great defenders of the coal miners. In this they were aided by the declarations of McLeod, who came out denouncing "Communist plots" and supporting the Conservatives in the election. More discouraging still was the resurgence of the Liberals, even in the old labour strongholds of Caledonia and New Aberdeen in Glace Bay. McLachlan received 2,589 votes, a substantial vote, but he and Forman Waye, the other labour candidate, finished in third place, behind both the Conservatives and the Liberals. It was his fourth defeat in an electoral contest, and he would not run in the Dominion election of 1930.[12]

Mine Workers' Industrial Union

Confusing signals were coming out of Communist Party headquarters in Toronto in the first years of the Great Depression, and McLachlan soon found himself involved in running battles with the party leadership. At this time the Communist Party was going through one of the turning points in its short history. A major change in direction was approved at the meetings of the Communist International in the summer of 1928. The prosperity of the 1920s, the Sixth Congress predicted, could not last. Within a few years the capitalist economy would lurch into another period of economic crisis. This would mean an upsurge in the class struggle, and revolutionaries around the world were expected to prepare themselves for the challenge. In particular, more effort would be devoted to denouncing moderate reformers and propounding revolutionary policies. Whether the change in policy was an astute assessment of current trends or a product of internal rivalries within the Soviet establishment, this "left turn" had a powerful effect on the political tactics of Communist parties around the world.[13]

The message could not have sounded especially original to McLachlan. Even if the class struggle was not at its peak after 1926, the coal industry in the 1920s had shown little evidence of capitalist stability. This was equally true in Britain and the United States. And in Canada the whole image of North American prosperity during the 1920s was contradicted by the Maritime provinces, which continued to be devastated by industrial depression, unemployment, and outmigration. Then in 1929 the wheat-crop failures and the stock-market crash began the years of economic crisis that would be known as the Great Depression. For McLachlan, there was little that was unfamiliar about the economic crisis, except that this time it ravaged most of the world, thus confirming Marxist predictions about the inherent instability of the capitalist system.

McLachlan played no visible part in the internal party struggle that accompanied the change. In November 1928, however, he must have been in attendance at the meeting of the Central Committee at which Maurice Spector, the party's young intellectual, was expelled for failing to report fully on the new approach after his return from meetings of the International. Certainly McLachlan could not have disagreed with the resolution on trade-union policy, which stated that "the 'international' unions are rapidly degenerating into semi-company unions."[14] McLachlan was absent from the national convention the following summer – there were no official delegates at all from Nova Scotia. At this meeting the longtime party leader Jack MacDonald was vigorously assailed for being out of step with the new direction in the Communist International, and there was a long debate on the dangers of underestimating the capitalist tendency to war and crisis. Following the convention, his confidence shaken, MacDonald resigned his post, making way for Tim Buck and a number of younger leaders to take control of the party.

McLachlan was content to accept the outcome of these internal struggles with equanimity. He had known Buck since the heady days of 1922 when he first joined the party, and so far McLachlan's sense of revolutionary pragmatism had not prevented him from accepting the party's leadership. On matters such as the temptations of the OBU and the need for united action among Canadian workers, McLachlan had been in agreement with most of the party's positions. Now, if Buck's opinions on international unions had shifted, McLachlan could reason, it might in part be due to his experience with the UMW in Nova Scotia. After all, Nova Scotia was constantly referred to in party debates as an example of the party's miscalculations and lost opportunities, real or imagined. Defending himself at the 1929 convention, MacDonald had even made a pointed reference to Buck, who was responsible for labour strategy: "I am prepared to take my share of the blame, but am certainly not allowing other comrades to hold themselves holy on this question."[15] As far as denouncing inadequate unions that were taking a pro-capitalist position, McLachlan had few rivals in the field. Every reader of *The Worker* was familiar with his views on the evil spirit of class collaboration embodied in the ideas of John L. Lewis, for whom McLachlan could spare no rhetoric in his denunciation: "the loud-mouthed shouting for peace in the industry; the solemn-faced cant about sticking to the constitution; and the pet doctrine of the arch-traitor, Lewis, the sacredness of contracts."[16]

Before the year was out, the Communist Party had a new trade-union policy. It was to be directed by a tough, energetic organizer by the name of Tom McEwen, who sometimes also used his father's surname, Ewen. Like McLachlan, he was a Scotsman, in this case from a rural fishing village in the northeast, Stonehaven. Orphaned at an early age, he apprenticed as a blacksmith and came to Canada as a young man in 1912. He became active in the Communist Party in Manitoba and Saskatchewan and arrived in Toronto in 1929 as the party's new industrial director. There McEwen headed up the provisional executive of Canada's new "revolutionary trade union centre," to be known as the Workers' Unity League (WUL).[17]

Prospects for the new union strategy seemed especially good among the hard-rock miners of northern Ontario and the coal miners of Alberta and Nova Scotia. Organizers expected that a new Mine Workers' Industrial Union would be one of the strongest elements in the WUL. In November 1929 party organizer Jim Barker arrived in Glace Bay. From his headquarters in a rooming house on King Edward Street, Barker launched plans for the new miners' union. A group of supporters from the Glace Bay locals issued a call for a special convention to establish "a real fighting Mine Workers' Industrial Union, with all power in the hands of the rank and File!" McEwen typed out a stirring set of greetings on behalf of the WUL and arrived in town, clothes tattered and torn from riding the rails, but complete with charter and membership cards for the new union.[18]

After more than three years of silence, there was also a new voice for labour in a publication launched by the Cape Breton radicals in December 1929. The *Nova Scotia Miner* announced that the days of peace in the coalfields were coming to an end and that the time had arrived to renew the class struggle. The first issue sold out quickly – in two hours flat said the *Miner* – and in January the paper stepped up from bi-monthly to weekly publication. Officially the newspaper was published by "The Progressive Miners of Nova Scotia" or by the "District 26 Left-Wing Committee," and the business management of the paper was handled by Murdoch Clarke, one of the young reds from Caledonia. For most readers, what mattered was that this was McLachlan's newspaper and the editorial content was under his control. The familiar McLachlan style was there again: the corporation's vaunted profit-sharing plan was yielding 2¢ on a $13.00 pay sheet – "Not enough to pay the first installment on a canary's breakfast!" As for the union itself, District 26 had become a "dues-collecting machine" for John L. Lewis and a "wage-cutting tool" for the company. In fact, the coal miners had little or no union and the time was ripe for the creation of a "real fighting union."[19]

The founding convention of the Mine Workers' Industrial Union of Nove Scotia (MWIUNS) in March 1930 proved a disaster. When McLachlan was invited to chair the meeting, some delegates questioned whether "the propaganda directed against the Communists would be detrimental to the success of the new union." The objections were overcome by a vote of twenty-two to five, but in a brief opening speech McLachlan felt a need to defend his record: "From 1908 to 1923 he had been elected every time upon the basis of his record as a fighter in the interests of the miners, and was still their elected representative." Later he also intervened in the debate: "We are not here to build a Communist Party," McLachlan pleaded, but to build a new union: "In 1920 you worked regularly – now you work three or four days a week. Capitalist rationalization will get worse, and you will be forced to fight and before you can fight it is necessary to have an organization capable of fighting."

But the wrangling was dispiriting and, looking over the hall, McLachlan realized that there was sparse timber there for the construction of a new union. On paper there were twenty-nine delegates from local unions with a membership of more than 4,000 miners, but only twelve of the delegates were official representatives of their locals. Moreover, the delegation from Westville, which included Dan Livingstone, the former president of District 26, opposed the new union and strongly favoured an endorsement of another new group, the Mine Workers' Union of Canada (MWUC). The MWUC had emerged as an alternative to the UMW in western Canada and was affiliated to the nationalist but much less radical All Canadian Congress of Labour (ACCL).

When it finally came down to a vote, the MWIUNS was approved by a vote of twenty-seven to five. But McLachlan could see that the new union would be an artificial creation. When McLachlan was nominated as provisional president, there were again objections from a minority on the ground that his name "would have a deterring effect on the development of the new Union." McLachlan declined the nomination:

"If he goes back into office, it will be with the vote of the rank and file." It was an uncomfortable outcome for the radicals who had planned the new union, but nothing they could say would change McLachlan's mind.[20]

Then came the reprisals. Almost immediately the six coal miners who had issued the convention call were expelled from the UMW and, at the union's request, their lamps were stopped at the mines. This meant they would not be permitted to work. McLachlan was outraged. The change in leadership did not seem to have made a difference, for Dan Willie Morrison was prepared to accept the punishing discipline of the international union. By this action, McLachlan charged, the union leadership had now joined the army of Herod: "The Herodian army of baby-fighters and baby-starvers, which slouches in black, dismal array down the ages, has had an accession to its ranks, in the shape of the Executive Board of District 26 U.M.W. of A."[21]

But McLachlan was not optimistic about winning this battle. The inexperienced party organizer, Jim Barker, was all for calling a general strike in support of the blacklisted men. McLachlan did not agree. According to Barker, McLachlan argued that the blacklists were "an attempt at provoking us into action" and that the union was too weak to carry out an effective strike. In the spring of 1930 McLachlan was certain that a strike was a hopeless adventure that could not succeed. Accordingly, Barker reported, "as a result of his support to the theory of 'Strikes are only effective on special occasions,' the enthusiasm of the Left Wing members was killed." He predicted "a bitter struggle" before the new union could be established.[22]

By May the divisions were running deep. After announcing that the coal miners were "solidly united" in their determination to "smash the bonds of the UMW machine," Barker went on to denounce the lethargic condition of the local party. In the *Miner* Barker was proclaiming an imminent strike and also pledging that there would be a Communist Party candidate in the coming election. By this time McLachlan had lost all confidence in the party organizer. When asked, on behalf of the party, to run in the 1930 Dominion election, McLachlan gave what Barker called a "blank refusal." McLachlan had also withdrawn his name as editor of the *Nova Scotia Miner*. Without McLachlan's endorsement, the paper would have few contributions and little credibility among the coal miners. A last issue appeared on 7 June 1930.[23]

Going over Barker's reports in Toronto, Tim Buck had harsh words for his old comrade: "Old Jim seems to have embarked on an open campaign against every Party decision." What was particularly alarming to Buck was McLachlan's preference for an "independent union" without international affiliations either to Indianapolis or to Moscow. "In other words," Buck wrote about the Cape Breton Communists, "the propaganda barrage of the bosses on Moscow is too much for them, and so they take the easiest way out by asking that the Party change its line to conform to the R.C. church and the Glace Bay Gazette. *This we will never do.*" In dealing with McLachlan, Buck wrote, there could be no exceptions and there was no room for sentimentality: "The lessons of the past few months should convince you that more attention should be directed towards trying to develop some of the younger elements who are not saturated with this demagogy and sentiment and who will constitute a much firmer base for carrying the Party programme in N.S." The correct strategy would be to continue the "split and build" approach and call a conference of the new industrial union at the same time as the next District 26 convention. He admitted, however, that there was neither the money nor the support to achieve this, and Barker was advised to continue gathering support for opposition within the UMW.[24]

McLachlan was plainly offended by the party's highhanded approach. His opposition probably cost him the opportunity to represent the Nova Scotia coal miners at international meetings in Moscow in 1930. The WUL was authorized to invite a representative of the coal miners to attend the Fifth World Congress of the Red International in July, which would be followed by a meeting of the International Committee of Revolutionary Miners. The WUL sent the appropriate invitation to Nova Scotia and McLachlan might reasonably have expected to be appointed as the representative. It is clear from Buck's correspondence with Barker that, in passing over McLachlan, the local organizer was following instructions from Toronto. Buck had written Barker: "It would be damned foolishness to send a man to the USSR who can drop the work of the Party unceremoniously when his pet feelings have been hurt a little. This is why I am now firmly convinced that the practice of sending people to the USSR to various Congresses, etc, to 'save them' should be unconditionally dropped. I think Jim has placed himself in this category."[25] Although a meeting to select a delegate was advertised, none was held, and it was decided that the young Murdoch Clarke should go in his place. McLachlan subsequently wrote directly to Moscow to complain about the method of selecting the delegate: "Where or how such appointment was made – I know nothing." This was a source of embarrassment for the American miner heading up the international committee in Moscow; Pat Toohey attempted to reassure McLachlan that he was still regarded as the unquestioned spokesman for labour radicalism in Nova Scotia.[26]

The whole series of events brought McLachlan close to a break with the Communist Party. It was a constructive opposition, however, for McLachlan was not at this time in disagreement with the party's general policy; what he most objected to was the disregard of local conditions. Some party leaders appreciated the distinction and McEwen was prepared to admit some of his own errors of excessive expectations. At the international miners' conference in Moscow in September 1930, McEwen delivered a self-critical report on the Nova Scotia episode: "We made serious mistakes, we built the movement around a few individuals, instead of winning the rank and file of the miners, now we have practically no influence at all." Another Canadian party leader, Thomas Rankin, drew similar conclusions: "We must not make the mistake as we did before of jumping in and laying down a rigid bolshevik rule saying to the miners, 'accept this or go back to the reformists.' It was this policy that was responsible for our abject defeat last summer in Nova Scotia. Let it not happen again."[27]

The year ended with a kind of vindication for McLachlan. Barker left Glace Bay in disgrace. "I am the most hated individual in Nova Scotia," wrote Barker. "I am compelled to move, whether the Centre permits it or not. You may think that this is sarcastic, but I can assure you that as far as I am concerned it's a grim reality."[28] By the end of the year the so-called "split and build" strategy was abandoned in favour of a more gradualist "united front from below." Certainly there was a growing interest in the WUL among the coal miners, and individual members were being recruited among the miners. But this could not be considered sufficient support for launching a rival union. Like the leaders of the OBU in the 1920s, the Communist leaders had also drawn the conclusion that the radical cause in Cape Breton could not flourish without McLachlan's support.

McLachlan pressed his grievances at the party's Central Committee meetings in Toronto in February 1931, claiming that the party's union policy was misguided and the most successful effort of the local activists, the *Nova Scotia Miner*, had been "murdered" by the party. McLachlan won his case. In the formal resolutions it was agreed to abandon the goal of starting a new union: "The work in the Nova Scotia fields must be strengthened by the building up of WUL opposition groups in the UMW, which should coordinate their activity with the work of the revolutionary union in Alberta." For the moment there would be no dramatic upheavals in Nova Scotia.[29]

Better than most, McLachlan knew that revolutions could not be induced solely by the will of the revolutionaries. The ground must be prepared, and to do so the *Nova Scotia Miner* would be revived, this time under McLachlan's personal control. When it came off the press again on 6 June 1931, after almost a year's suspension, McLachlan happily reported that the paper was a great success: by ten o'clock in the evening "we were five bucks to the good after paying all expenses."[30]

"Udarnik"

"The question that I must settle within the next two weeks is if I don't sow now I sure cannot reap in the fall ... However time will force me to decide whether it is to be Steelshill [sic] or U.S.S.R. for me this summer." In the spring of 1931 McLachlan was pondering whether to buy seed for his farm or make plans to travel. The investment in seed was the farmer's most important annual expenditure, and like any small struggling farmer, McLachlan knew that springtime was the season for making decisions. The idea of a personal odyssey to the land of socialism was planted years earlier, at the time District 26 made application to the Red International in 1922. A few years later Annie Buller continued to encourage his thoughts in that direction: "I should love to see you get to that land of hope. You I am sure would feel at home."[31]

All through the 1920s the Soviet Union had been the land of socialism, and McLachlan's trip would fulfil his hopes of seeing the promised land. Many of the leading Communists had already visited on official occasions: among them, Jack MacDonald, Maurice Spector, and Florence Custance had attended the Fourth Congress of the Communist International in 1922, Malcolm Bruce and Tim Buck the Fifth Congress in 1924, and MacDonald and Spector the Sixth Congress in 1928. Tom McEwen had gone to the congress of the Red International in 1930, and several of the younger party leaders had attended training schools there. Closer to home, Roscoe Fillmore, the veteran Maritime socialist, had witnessed the May Day celebrations in Petrograd in 1923 and spent the rest of the year working as an agricultural expert. More recently, Annie Whitfield, a miner's wife and Women's Labour League activist from New Aberdeen, had visited as part of a women's delegation led by Becky Buhay in 1930. McLachlan looked forward to his turn. Now that he was reconciled with the party leadership and his judgment had been confirmed in Moscow, the time was ripe.

At the time of the party meetings in Toronto early in 1931, he and Buck discussed a plan to arrange for a group of fifty skilled coal miners to live and work in the land of socialism. McLachlan was to travel ahead as an emissary to make arrangements for this move.[32] Over the next few months, they exchanged comradely letters and kind regards, and much of their correspondence concerned McLachlan's travel plans. The idea was for McLachlan to visit the mining areas on behalf of a group of young miners, mainly of Ukrainian and Russian origin, who intended to emigrate from Cape Breton. Early in April, McLachlan wrote, asking for news. "The boys are continually after me," McLachlan wrote, "and now they insist that I go without waiting for any reply. Of course that is entirely out of the question. I cannot go just as a private individual. It would only result in blank failure of the entire project." Buck could report only that he had received a cable to the effect that "the matter was being attended to" and he expected there would still be several months more to wait: "Unfortunately there is still a tremendous lot of red tape to wade thru [sic] in these matters." He advised McLachlan to proceed with the plans for his summer's work, at least to the end of August. Again in June, McLachlan wrote that, from his reading of Soviet reports, coal mining seemed to be "the one backward spot in the five year plan": "It does seem strange that it should take so long to put the powers that be in touch with a bunch of young active and skilled miners, who, one would think, they would be glad to get a hold of. However from this distance we may not understand just what's what. Keep us informed of any news you may get."[33]

By September 1931 it was common knowledge in Glace Bay that McLachlan would soon be travelling to Russia. The trip was described as a fact-finding tour. As secretary of the local branch of the Friends of the Soviet Union, McLachlan would be promoting the general purposes of that organization, which was to encourage a sympathetic body of Canadian opinion towards the Soviet Union. He may also have had some responsibility for planning a larger Canadian workers' delegation to be sponsored by the organization at a later date. In Glace Bay, collections were taken up in the union locals and in the streets to help pay his costs. At one miners' meeting, McLachlan collected questions concerning conditions to be investigated, and at least two local unions in Glace Bay provided McLachlan with official letters of introduction.[34]

In early October McLachlan sent in a passport application. In it he described himself modestly as a farm labourer and stated that he was planning a trip to Germany. The police would be watching. At the time, RCMP Commissioner J.H. MacBrien wrote personally to request a copy of McLachlan's photograph from the passport office. Six copies were prepared and distributed to RCMP officers at Halifax and other points.[35]

McLachlan sailed from New York on 23 October on board the passenger liner *S.S. Westernland.* In a few vivid letters he observed the desolation of travel in the midst of the Depression. At Sydney the ticket agent sold only six through tickets to Halifax: "A berth? I could sell you a carfull." Lumbering across the rough seas of the North Atlantic, McLachlan noted that less than 10 per cent of the passenger space was filled. He mused sadly on the "cheap pitiful little efforts" to create a party atmosphere on board the ship. The firecrackers and toy hats and balloons held little appeal; fortunately, he soon located more suitable company:

Capitalist introductions are great, and futile. The fool's supper is over, and you go on deck to smoke and forget, if you can, the sad get-together enacted below. You watch the eternal stars and the infinite roll of the sea, when your watch is ended by a "Halloabo!" and your heart warms – it is a worker talking. In a minute you have told each other where you're from, where you're going, and in an hour you have discussed the breadlines in Detroit and New York and the bum relief handout in Cape Breton. The unemployment, the helplessness of Bennetts and Hoovers to either end or mend it. Soviet Russia, the Five Year Plan, the chances of capitalist intervention in the USSR are all discussed. Our get-together on deck has grown to a couple of dozen.

Now McLachlan was in his element, listening sympathetically to the war-torn English veteran who had tramped his way from Parliament Hill in Ottawa to Fifth Avenue in New York and was now being deported to his land of birth – "ragged, penniless, homeless and jobless." With the moon riding high, the new friends and comrades debated the coming revolution, "the final working-class 'get-together'" – the bricklayer from Pittsburgh believed the break would come in the United States this winter, where the breadlines were a mile long; the fireman from the stokehold advised them all to watch Germany closely, where the working class was better organized. Encounters such as these gave McLachlan heart and confirmed that he was "leaving the old to visit the new": "While miners, railroad men and seamen starve under capitalism, the workers of Soviet Russia are daily adding fresh victories to their credit ... They are building a new world, the workers' world of Socialism, and I am going to see it!"[36]

Details of the trip are sketchy. Part of his time was spent with an American workers' delegation which arrived in Moscow in early November and included several black workers, seamen, and steelworkers as well as one coal miner. There is a surviving clipping from a Soviet newspaper showing portraits of McLachlan and three other visiting foreign workers – one from Toronto, one from Pennsylvania, and another from Saxony. In the broad streets of Moscow, McLachlan stood in awe as a detachment of one thousand Red Army soldiers marched past singing: "We follow them like a kid and strain our ears to try and catch some word that would give us an idea of the song. We got it – one word only, the last word of each verse, and we thrilled. It was drawn out, and sounded like this: 'Pro-la-tar-iate.'"[37]

For McLachlan, the highlights of the visit came during the three weeks he spent in the Donbas, examining conditions in the largest of the Soviet coalfields. There he made detailed observations of conditions and was awarded the honorary title of "udarnik" – a term roughly translated as "model worker" or "hard hitter" – for his service as a champion of the working class.

Returning to Moscow, McLachlan wrote an article for the English-language newspaper, *Moscow News*, edited by the American Anna Louise Strong, which compared coal-mining conditions in the Donbas with those in Canada. The conclusion was that Soviet mines demonstrated "the best working conditions in the world." Describing the rapid expansion and mechanization of the industry, McLachlan underlined the essential contrast between the West and the Soviet Union in the purposes of the work:

In capitalist countries the word "rationalization" has become a word of terror to the workers. It means creating wealth for the capitalists for which they can find no market. It means huge masses thrown out of work, longer bread lines, more starvation, and a bitter experience for millions of workers, filled with utter hopelessness. Rationalization in the Soviet Union is very different. It means that the workers in the mines and factories are creating more products for themselves – resulting in higher wages, better working conditions, better homes, more cultural opportunities.[38]

McLachlan recognized the existence of material shortages in Soviet society, but the shortage of writing paper and unpainted houses could be turned to instructive purposes: "The capitalists of France and England are very angry because of the shortage in the Soviet Union, not of writing paper and house paint, but of landlords and dividend takers, and so are preparing for war on the Soviet Union." Like other sympathetic observers, McLachlan saw the Five Year Plan as a kind of war of economic independence, in which the comforts of life could not be placed first: "The question history presented to them was; Shall we bend all our energy to having pretty painted houses and an abundance of fancy writing paper, or shall we build great steelworks, oil wells, factories and productive farms to grow bread first, and then, and then only, make provision for the less essential things? They decided on the latter course, hence the shortage of things that are not a pressing need."[39]

In a short autobiographical essay written a few years later, McLachlan included a description of his visit to the home of an older woman in the Donbas. Her son worked in the mines, but her husband had been murdered during the civil war in 1919. "It was a fine worker's home," he wrote, "clean and neat with lots of light and flowers growing in the windows." When he tried to explain to the old woman where Canada was, she asked if the miners' homes in Glace Bay were as good as hers: "I told her that as far as space was concerned I thought they were as well off as she was, but she had a very much better constructed and more comfortable home." The woman then pointed to a row of pig-houses and said: "I lived there all my life till after the Revolution. Those huts had mud floors. But look at the fine wooden floors I have now." For McLachlan, this story was a measure of working-class achievement, to be contrasted with the mud floors of his own childhood: "What a floor that was! How it talked to me of victorious struggle. This widow of a miner murdered in the class struggle was so proud of her floor. It was holy ground, made sacred by the blood of a struggling triumphant working class, where peace at last could live."[40]

Little is known of the return trip. It is possible McLachlan stopped over in Britain for a few days, even to visit the scenes of his youth in Lanarkshire. All that survives is a clipping from a London newspaper, dated January 1932, to indicate his passage. He arrived at Halifax on 13 January and stopped over briefly there with his old comrade Joe Wallace. Then, after an absence of three months, McLachlan was back at Steele's Hill on 15 January. For all the grandchildren there were sets of wooden dolls, and the smallest child received the largest dolls.[41]

Soon McLachlan was ready to report publicly on his trip. For two Sundays at the end of January he addressed large public meetings. At

Khattar's Theatre in Sydney there were between 750 and 800 people in attendance on 24 January, and another large audience crowded into the hall at Central School in Glace Bay the following Sunday. The speeches he delivered on these two occasions were virtually identical.

He began with the historical premises of 1917 and 1919: the Russian Revolution and Lenin's plans for socialism, the Treaty of Versailles and the plans of the four western leaders, who "promised the workers peace for evermore and contentment for all." McLachlan had not had such large audiences in Cape Breton for several years, and his speeches were skilfully prepared, this one structured around the metaphor of a growing tree:

When I was a lad, workers, my father used to say that when you plant a tree, do not go back next day and dig up the roots to see if the tree is growing. Come back in fifteen years and then see for yourself whether the plant has grown.

Now, Workers, these four mighty statesmen planted a tree. It is twelve years and more since that time. Let us see which of these trees gave out the best fruit. In the Capitalistic countries, we see unemployment on every hand and misery and starvation walk side by side. These four men prophesized no more war. What do we see on every hand? Every nation is spending millions to build up its war-machine, while the workers are suffering. This, workers, is the fruit of the tree that these four men planted.

I have just arrived from the Soviet Union and I will endeavour to show you the fruit of the tree that Lenin planted.

Most of McLachlan's speech was devoted to a detailed picture of conditions in the mines, the kind of observations which would be most revealing to coal miners. The contrast with local conditions was striking. Here at home there was bad ventilation, unsafe work, out-of-date machinery, one or two shifts a week, mines closed down. In the Donbas there was progress:

New mines were opening all the time and the demand for workers increasing every day. The machinery is the last word in modern

> efficiency and the mines are absolutely safe. The timbers are of a quality never used over here and they are placed side by side to avoid down falls. In all the time I visited, I did not see one hang-over or rotting and broken timber. The ventilation is of the best and there is no danger of men falling for lack of good air. The passage-way from the mine to the washroom is heated by steam, so that no sweating men could freeze on their way, as they do here.

And the currents of good air in the mines, McLachlan joked, were "strong enough to blow a Halifax Herald right out of your hand."

In the mines, he continued, there were two classes, "employees" and "workers": "The employees are those working in the offices and are the lowest paid while the men in the pit, the drivers and loaders, etc. are workers and they employ the employees ..." There was an age requirement of eighteen for working in the mines. Women worked in the mines operating switches and earned about eighty rubles a month. A doctor at the mines received the smallest wage, less than a beginning miner and sometimes less than half the pay of a skilled miner. Most miners, he estimated, received wages high enough to enable them to save about 20 per cent of their wages. And at "production meetings," McLachlan observed, "the workers had all the say." In the Soviet economy the coal miners were the heroes of the Five Year Plan. McLachlan was obviously impressed by the vision of a society in which the coal miners were recognized as the pioneers of industrial progress.

McLachlan's other principal theme was public morality. He encountered random examples on every hand: fares passed safely hand to hand through a crowded trolley car, long honeymoons for newlyweds, continual warnings against alcohol, and no drinking permitted in the army. The temperance campaigns were founded on education rather than enforcement, on the principle that "you cannot take people's habits away from them but that you have to educate them to it by means of education, propaganda and a material change of interest." In the schools children "were not taught 'how many wives Henry the fourth had'"; instead "they were educated on the lines of laborism. They could tell you of the different revolutions and what caused them."

And there was no such thing as unemployment: "In Canada there were 600,000 unemployed. In Russia none. No one was out of work, [every] man or woman could get employment." The status of religion was especially important to McLachlan's audiences, for in the 1930s the prevailing view of the churches towards communism was extremely hostile. From his hotel window, McLachlan reported, he could see twelve churches. At Easter and Christmas the churches were busy but at others times not. As for the priests, they worked in the pits shovelling coal, and those who did not work took up collections around the mines on pay day.

Each example was driven home with effect. "Can you imagine that being done here?" McLachlan asked, and the answers came back in ripples of laughter through the audience. The conclusions were obvious: "The reasons for this, workers, is that no Capitalists pocket the profits in the Soviet Union. The profit over there is used to better the worker's conditions and not to swell the pockets of some profiteer as it is here ... On the one hand you have misery, want, starvation, disease and death. On the other hand you have peace, bread, contentment and life."

McLachlan had little or nothing to say of Stalin or Stalinism. As in the case of many older radicals who had become socialists well before the Russian Revolution, McLachlan's admiration was reserved for Lenin, "the planter, the greatest man that has ever lived." There was, he said, a universal message in his example of leadership: "One of Lenin's sayings and I venture to add that in 10 years every child on earth will be learning his sayings by heart, was that you cannot change the customs and habit of a people by decree or law, but by propaganda and education."[42]

McLachlan had obviously travelled to the Soviet Union more than ready to be impressed. His impressions were shaped by a revolutionary's reading of the importance of the Soviet achievement, and his conclusions were always marked by the sharp contrasts between the crisis of capitalism and the promise of socialism. In this McLachlan's response was similar to that of other contemporary visitors who were not Communists. J.S. Woodsworth, who also travelled to the Soviet Union in 1931, returned with what his biographer calls "a sober yet optimistic evaluation"; in the press Woodsworth compared the progress of socialism to the work of a sculptor: "a great idea emerging from a rough block of marble." In the case of the Donbas, a reporter for the Toronto *Star* who visited the same coal mining area as McLachlan a few months later conveyed an identical impression of rapid expansion and mechanization in the coal industry and similar details of dramatic improvements in working-class life.[43]

In general, Western observers who were critical of capitalism found a great deal to admire in Soviet civilization in the early 1930s. Newspapers carried the reports of prominent visitors, such as George Bernard Shaw, who, also in 1931, reported enthusiastically on "the land of hope" – "an atmosphere of hope and security for the poorest as has never before been seen in a civilized country on earth."[44] Interestingly, a police informer attending one of McLachlan's first speeches in Glace Bay after his return did not find McLachlan's observations unusually controversial for the times and noted that "he said nothing that would impress me that he was a Communist if I were a stranger to him."[45]

Things had not gone well for the Communist Party while McLachlan was out of the country. The party leaders arrested in August had gone to trial in November. Under Section 98, they were all convicted. Buck, Bruce, McEwen, and others were sentenced to five-year prison terms. Following an appeal, the men started to serve their time in Kingston Penitentiary in February 1932. The prosecution was in part a product of government paranoia and in part recognition of the effectiveness of the small numbers of Communists in organizing workers in the early years of the Depression. There is no evidence that the arrest of McLachlan was considered in the original round-up of party leaders in August, but his absence from the country did prompt authorities to consider action against "the well known agitator J.B. McLachlan, who at present is in Russia."

In January 1932 RCMP Commissioner MacBrien and other government officials received a request that McLachlan be stopped at the Canadian border. The appeal came from a prominent businessman by the name of D.W. Clark, president of the Anglo-Canadian Wire Rope Company, who made a strong case against McLachlan: "I do not think that this man should be allowed to enter Canada at all under any circumstances. If he cannot make a living in Glasgow then he should not be allowed to make a living in this country instigating the people to open rebellion." MacBrien forwarded the request to the Department of Immigration and Colonization, but his recommendation was not a strong one by the standards of the day: "There can be no doubt about the bitterness which this man displayed several years ago. Of late he has not been so active partly because Communism has become less popular among the miners. However, he is still a strong Communist, and is concerned in the publication of the *Nova Scotia Miner*." The deputy minister replied on 1 February, pointing out that since McLachlan was a British citizen by birth and a long-time resident of Canada, the legal basis for excluding him was weak. Nevertheless, he was prepared to add, "it seems that he is a man whose activities during his residence in Canada would justify any action taken to exclude him, provided these bring him within the law." Instructions were issued to immigration officers to "be on the lookout for him, so that he may be subjected to a thorough examination, should he seek to return, and the regulations strictly applied."[46]

By this time it was too late to take any action to exclude McLachlan. As the RCMP soon discovered, McLachlan had returned to Canada ten days earlier and was in plain view on the public platforms. Originally it was reported that McLachlan would be undertaking a speaking tour following his return, leaving on a cross-country trip to Vancouver after resting for two weeks at home. The tour never did take place. Although McLachlan would often refer to the Soviet example in his speeches, the most urgent tasks were the local ones precipitated by the latest mad crisis of capitalism.

McLachlan versus Bennett

Ottawa, August 1932, the dog days of a hot, sweltering summer in the capital city. More than 500 delegates to the Workers' Economic Conference crowded into an old red-brick garage on Gladstone Avenue. There they sat on plank boards in an improvised conference hall. At night they bedded down on the floor on two inches of sawdust covered with canvas bags. Among those in attendance there were almost 100 delegates from the National Unemployed Workers' Association. Others represented more than fifty different organizations. Together they claimed to speak for a quarter of a million Canadians familiar with the soup kitchens, breadlines, and work camps springing up across the country. To reach Ottawa many of these delegates had crowded onto old trucks and boarded freight cars. Some were on the road more than three weeks, and hundreds, it was charged, were taken off the trains at gunpoint. One group of delegates from Verdun marched by foot along the highway from Montreal. For two days the hot dusty hall was filled with "stirring speeches and enthusiastic applause."[47]

As a union leader McLachlan had attended hearings and conferences in Ottawa before, but this time there were no deep carpets, marble floors, and plush chairs. At the "workers' 'Chateau Laurier,'" as the improvised conference hall was nicknamed, McLachlan was called upon to preside over the first day's sessions. He took the chair amid "thunderous applause." Men and women who knew his name and history were eager to shake hands with the famous veteran of the labour wars. When the time came to select a group of delegates to wait on the prime minister, McLachlan was enthusiastically voted onto the delegation. Observed *The Worker*: "It can be truly said that J.B. McLachlan is the Grand Old Man of the Revolutionary Labor Movement of Canada."[48]

The theatre of the event appealed to McLachlan. The Workers' Economic Conference was timed to coincide with the Imperial Economic Conference, at which Prime Minister R.B. Bennett was meeting with fellow premiers of British Empire countries. As the Depression headed into the worst months of the decade, the contrast between the two conferences appealed to the imagination and underlined the different solutions for unemployment placed before the Canadian people. Bennett was arguing for imperial trading agreements, to defend the Canadian market and "blast our way into the markets of the world," at best a long-range solution. The radicals were calling for a plan of non-contributory unemployment insurance, a standard cash relief of $10 a week plus $2 for each dependant, union wages for relief work, the seven-hour day, and the five-day week. For A.E. Smith, the Workers' Economic Conference was a kind of workers' Parliament which foreshadowed Canada's socialist future: "These seven hundred workers sat down for hours in an orderly business conference, and discussed with intelligence and deliberation the problems of action regarding unemployment and the needed remedy, the capitalist system and its replacement. It was a marvel. The man in overalls in the old garage excels the lords in the parliament."[49]

On 2 August the delegates spilled out into the streets for a march on Parliament Hill. As they gathered on Market Square the demonstrators were attacked and dispersed by police. The marchers reassembled in a nearby park and gave "stout resistance" to the police. Cheering and shouting, the procession continued on towards Parliament Hill, followed closely by the police. Within sight of the Parliament Buildings, the marchers stopped for more speeches. By this time the crowds of marchers and onlookers numbered in the thousands. Detachments of police, on foot and on horseback, lined up to face the marchers. Before they could continue on to Parliament Hill, the police attacked. According to *The Worker*, "men, women and children were brutally beaten with sticks and clubs." The fighting left at least one policeman and two demonstrators badly injured. Some fourteen workers were arrested. It was, *The Worker* concluded, a "brutal exhibition right under the shadow of Parliament where the Imperial Conference is taking place."[50]

But for McLachlan, the highlight of the conference was a second, more peaceable, assault on Parliament Hill. On earlier occasions Bennett had often refused to meet protest delegations, but this time he sent word for a delegation to meet him in his office. The group selected consisted of six men and one woman, most of them associated with local organizations of the unemployed across the country. George Winslade, secretary of the National Committee of Unemployed Councils, placed the conference's demands before the prime minister, concentrating on the call for cash relief and unemployment insurance. Bennett replied that the statement was "very extreme in places" and turned his attention to other members of the delegation.

McLachlan was the senior member of the group, and the prime minister certainly knew who he was. The tall, portly Bennett, awkward in his stiff shirt and tailored suit, shook hands with McLachlan as if they were old friends and referred to him familiarly as Jim. But Bennett's congenial manner went unappreciated. According to *The Worker*, McLachlan proceeded to fire "disconcerting questions" at the prime minister while Bennett sat at his desk and responded with "platitudinous generalities." Some of the exchange can be reconstructed:

McLachlan – Mr. Bennett, we put it to you. What would you do
    if you had no work, your wife and children had no food, the
    rent was unpaid and you were in debt? What would you advise
    us to do?
Bennett – The people of this country [are] too generous and kind
    hearted to let any needy family starve.
McLachlan – When you see, down in Nova Scotia, people getting
    a meal on Wednesday; perhaps a meal on Thursday, and no
    food on other days, just waiting for pay-day or no pay-day, we
    have to do something.
Bennett – You want relief until things get better?
McLachlan – They can never get much better in some parts of
    Nova Scotia while capitalism lasts.

That was a provocation, and Bennett turned to the offensive, lecturing the delegation like a schoolmaster instructing small children.

McLachlan interrupted at least twice. When Bennett rejected appeals for the release of Buck and the other party leaders in Kingston Penitentiary and warned that those who break the laws must pay the penalty, McLachlan broke in with a reference to a recent financial scandal, "reminding him of the irregular release of the swindling brokers who were let out of jail by his administration before their sentences were served." Then, when Bennett turned his attention to the Soviet Union and referred to "Russian dumping" and "unfair labour conditions," McLachlan jumped in again: "Ye no can tell me lies about the Soviet workers, Mr. Bennett. I spent six weeks in the mines with them in the Soviet Union! ... Although only one sixth of the world is under the workers' management, this part, which is Russia, has paved the way for the rest of the workers of the world to follow. And follow they must if they want to enjoy the fruits of their labour." There ended the interview with the prime minister.[51]

Out of that visit, McLachlan told more than one tale. Back in Cape Breton, he regaled audiences with accounts of his encounter with the prime minister, including how Bennett had started out by shaking his hand. The story is told that at one public meeting in Glace Bay the chief of police pushed through the crowd and interrupted: "That's a lie, McLachlan, Mr. Bennett wouldn't shake hands with the likes of you." McLachlan stopped, took off his coat, rolled up his sleeves and raised his hand in the air: "Smell it man, it stinks yet!"[52]

As for the Imperial Economic Conference, McLachlan announced afterwards, it was a failure "because of the grasping methods of the sharks who attended it." By contrast, the Workers' Economic Conference was a grand success, and next time there would be 5,000 delegates: "Bennett was scared of mass action on the part of the workers and that is why he is surrounded by police all the time. Although Bennett jailed some of the leaders of the labour movement such as Tim Buck and Malcolm Bruce, he would die of fear if the workers of Canada should show a united militant front and demand their rights ... The capitalistic system is rotting away and only needed a push by the workers to send it to oblivion where it belongs."

From Ottawa it was straight on to Montreal, where the long-delayed First National Congress of the WUL took place for three days. Here McLachlan found more evidence that the class struggle was gathering strength. The idea of a revolutionary trade-union centre had been little more than propaganda for more than two years. With 130 delegates in attendance it was now a reality. A constitution was adopted and the WUL was formally proclaimed as the Canadian section of the Red International of Labour Unions. McLachlan opened the meetings "with a rousing speech on the importance of the Congress at this time."[53]

Finally, McLachlan escaped from the hot summer days of Ontario and Quebec, back to the cool breezes off the Atlantic Ocean. After his return to Nova Scotia, McLachlan spoke to diverse audiences, including members of the Universal Negro Improvement Association in Glace Bay. He plunged into efforts to organize unemployed workers and helped lead a local delegation to Halifax. There were also the campaigns to defend the arrested party leaders, including Buck and McEwen, still sitting in Kingston Penitentiary. And then there was the weekly edition of the *Nova Scotia Miner*, where McLachlan continued to hammer home the urgency of the class struggle. It was time for the coal miners to be on the move again.

The Red Union

Once more in 1932 the Nova Scotia coal miners were in revolt against the UMW. It was the outcome of a year that started with rough surprises for the coal miners. Although they had expected wage increases in a new contract, the union leaders conducted secret negotiations with Dominion Steel and Coal to renew the existing contract. Even this was not acceptable to the new company, which was supposed to have a better sense of responsibility than the unlamented Besco. Dosco had prepared a program of wage reductions and mine closures that alarmed the entire population of the industrial area. The provincial government had stepped in quickly and announced that Sir Andrew Rae Duncan would return to chair a second royal commission on conditions in the industry. As in 1925, Duncan heard dozens of witnesses at public hearings. But he already knew the shape of the troubles well enough, and by the end of February 1932 he had completed his work.

A secret police report that month, passed on to the prime minister by the RCMP, warned that semi-starvation conditions existed in the coalfields. The industrial situation was serious, and the release of the Duncan report was likely to produce an explosion: "The mentality of the colliery worker is cross, has been cross for three years, and he is trying to keep cool and keeps hoping, and can be depended upon to carry on to the last moment of discussion and voting. But when he sees that there is no hope for food, he is likely to get mad and when he does he will make himself felt. I have been a spectator in every strike in the colliery districts for the last 32 years, and at no time were the conditions leading up to trouble so bad as they are now."[54]

To McLachlan it was no surprise that Duncan endorsed the company's plan for reductions and shutdowns. Some coal miners would be "reallocated" to other collieries, but 2,500 men – almost one in every five miners in the province – would lose their jobs. "What must the miners do now?" From his editorial chair at the *Nova Scotia Miner* McLachlan proclaimed that it was time to fight: "They must at once set up in every local union committees of action charged with the duty to prepare in detail for a 100 per cent strike to resist any further wage cuts ... These years should have hammered home to your inmost soul that under capitalism the working class has but two courses to follow ... crawl or fight."[55]

The UMW leadership was not prepared to lead a fight. Dan Willie Morrison and Alex McKay were getting along well with international headquarters, where there was no encouragement for a strike. And as far as cutbacks in the the coal industry went, they also seemed to accept the economic arguments of the corporation. But when the vote on the new contract was held on 14 March, the miners turned it down by a poll of 5,841 to 4,698. This was a relatively close vote, and the opposition was concentrated in the Glace Bay district, but it was a victory nonetheless, and the results showed that the radicals did have considerable support. The UMW leaders refused to authorize a strike and called a special district convention instead. There the policy of the leadership was again voted down. Then the radicals asked for a vote on "whether we stay in the UMW of A or revert to a provincial organization." As president, Morrison ruled that request out of order.

With that, the revolt was under way, and to McLachlan's sense of irony it must have seemed very much like the old struggle of the early District 26 against the officers of the PWA when they, too, had refused to accept the members' desire for reform of the union. Several Glace Bay locals began by voting themselves out of the UMW, and by June they had founded a new union, to be called the Amalgamated Mine Workers of Nova Scotia (AMW). For the rest of the summer the AMW gathered strength. Three more Glace Bay locals voted to join the new union, as did the miners in two New Waterford locals, Sydney Mines, Stellarton, and Inverness. By the end of the year the Department of Labour reported that the AMW had 7,801 members in 21 locals. Later, one local UMW leader commented wistfully that the AMW had attracted the most militant local leaders: "All the fighters have gone over to the A.M.W.; we have all the respectable ones, probably too respectable to fight."[56]

The new union adopted a suitably revolutionary constitution, proclaiming the principle of the class struggle: "Modern society is divided into two classes: those who produce and do not possess and those who possess and do not produce. Alongside of this main division all other classifications fade into insignificance. Between these two classes a continual struggle always exists." The union also adopted an ambiguous statement, perhaps designed to calm fears that it was primarily political in its ambitions: "This organization shall always remain a purely workers' organization and shall as far as possible be kept free from all political interference or anything which tends to disrupt the ranks of our organization. The business of the organization shall be confined to looking after the industrial business of the members."

There was as well a cautious regard for the dangers of bureaucracy. In operation, this would be a "rank and file" union: the supreme power of the union was in the referendum vote of the membership. There was even an expressed hostility to the ideal of industrial legality: no lawyers were to be engaged in connection with the making of agreements, the settlement of grievances, or the internal work of the union. The check-off of union dues itself was regarded as an unnecessary compromise with the companies, and the union planned to finance itself with dues collected directly from the membership. In a gesture of continuity with the radical times of the early 1920s, the union set aside May Day and Davis Day as constitutional holidays.[57]

It was widely believed that the new union took its orders from McLachlan, and it was certainly true that the new union was heavily promoted by the *Nova Scotia Miner*. Many of the leaders, such as Joseph Nearing, John Alex MacDonald, and Robert Stewart, saw themselves as followers of McLachlan. Also, both of McLachlan's sons were involved in the new union: Tom McLachlan, a working miner at Dominion No. 11, was a member of the committee that recruited delegates to the founding meeting in June 1932; and James B. McLachlan, Jr, his older son, became secretary of the AMW local at the Glace Bay machine shops. There was even a kind of historical symmetry expressed in the very name of the new organization: the AMW carried the name of the old union McLachlan had brought into the UMW in 1919, and now it would bring the miners back out of the discredited international organization.

McLachlan took no official part in the new union, but he delivered formal greetings and addressed the opening session of the founding convention in September 1932. Fresh from the meetings of the WUL in Montreal in August, McLachlan believed that the AMW might join the local struggles to a national movement:

> The miners of Nova Scotia must get into this militant Canadian labor struggle and discard for ever their narrow, stupid provincialism. There is no better way of doing this than by having the very best and most aggressive young miners appointed to local and district offices. Young miners who understand that the class war is world wide, and who are prepared to give their best to the greatest movement on earth and join up the forces of the miners of Nova Scotia with the marching millions who are out for the complete overthrow of the present rotten system.

Although the Workers' Unity League delivered "warmest revolutionary greetings" to the AMW, there was no official representative in attendance, and the AMW never did affiliate with the WUL.[58]

The AMW gained a reputation as a "red" union, but it was clear that, unlike the failed efforts to construct a radical union in 1930, this organization arose out of a major local struggle in the coal industry. Leadership had passed to a new generation of radicals whose actions did not depend on orders from Moscow, Toronto, or Steele's Hill. Some of McLachlan's reflections on the AMW can be heard in an interview which he later gave to the Dalhousie University professor H.L. Stewart. McLachlan's assessment made a point of discounting both the nationalism and radicalism of the union. "According to Mr. McLachlan," Stewart noted, "The A.M.W. does not owe its origin to any anti-American feeling, and the Cape Breton supporters of it are not moved by the Canadian nationalistic enthusiasm so apparent in the All-Canadian Congress party. Nor do the rank and file of its supporters feel any inclination to Communism." Instead, the AMW had emerged mainly out of other causes: "disgust with the record of financial corruption among U.M.W. leaders" and "indignation at the way in which free speech and free choice are crushed at a U. M. W. convention."

For Stewart's benefit, McLachlan spared no details in his description of UMW conventions:

"Gunmen" are placed at strategic points, "stewards" chosen for their prizefighting prowess, and those who come intending to express themselves in opposition to the ruling powers are silenced by the machine. Conventions are packed by the discretionary power of the president in the matter of "exonerating" or refusing to exonerate locals for failing to comply with requirements. Great numbers of non-existent locals are represented, and credentials are thus counterfeited. The President's salary has been pushed up from $3,000 to $12,000. Many protests, which would be made by locals really independent, are stifled by the Resolutions Committee. While it is unfair to suggest that Cape Breton Unions have paid into Indianapolis more than they got out of it, and while a great deal of valuable service has in the past been rendered by the U.M.W. to the Labor cause, it has also to be borne in mind that much of their expenditure in Cape Breton has been for shameful corruption, and that their dictatorial ways have become altogether intolerable to Canadians.

As for the AMW, McLachlan had no doubt that the new union enjoyed the support of most of the coal miners: "If there could be a quite free and genuine vote by ballot, the A.M.W. would have a majority of the mineworkers of Nova Scotia." But what reason was there to think that a local union would not develop its own vices like those of the UMW? McLachlan regarded the AMW with some detachment, and rather than give a long exposition of the virtues of rank-and-file control, this time he simply jested: "It would be on such a restricted scale, for example having so much less money at command, that it could not develop such 'gigantic' wickedness as was seen at Indianapolis."

Stewart expressed doubts as to whether Nova Scotia unions would ever be subject to much control at such a great distance from Indianapolis. But McLachlan knew from his own experience that, as it had done before, the international union would not hesitate to intervene in local conflicts to enforce a spurious industrial legality:

Thus "a mere sycophantic agent of capitalism (such as John L. Lewis)" can always find in the very complicated agreement usual between Company and workers some clause which he can pretend to think has been violated by the men. He can serve his real employers by paralyzing the union unless and until it does as it is told. This actually happened, according to Mr. McLachlan, in an amazing case in 1923, when the officers of the U.M.W. District #26 were suspended because of the sympathetic strike to aid the striking steelworkers in which they engaged – contrary, as alleged, to their agreement. J.L. Lewis acted impetuously, unaware that the agreement signed by District #26 had no clause in it of the kind he assumed to be there.[59]

There was reason for McLachlan to be optimistic about the AMW. Not since 1909 had a breakaway movement erupted so swiftly and with so much success. But, as before, the biggest challenge was how to transform this support into recognition by the coal companies. Even if most miners supported the AMW, there was still nothing in provincial or Dominion law requiring employers to recognize the union chosen by their employees. As Premier Murray had done in earlier days, Gordon Harrington – the old UMW adviser and since 1930 the province's Conservative premier – turned down the union's requests for a government-supervised vote. The only alternative seemed to be a strike for union recognition. It was not a decision to take lightly, for these were the worst years of the Depression. But the AMW's opportunity had never been greater, and if the radicals were going to succeed in driving the UMW out of the coalfields, there was no alternative.

Would the AMW strike for recognition, just as the old District 26 had been forced to do in the struggling days of 1909? In the summer of 1933 the AMW was plunged into its first major crisis. Delegates to the AMW convention in May 1933 threatened to launch a district-wide strike unless the company immediately recognized the union's grievance committees at the individual mines. The union leaders were more doubtful about the prospects for success and failed to distribute strike ballots. Meanwhile at Sydney Mines – where the mines were now in receivership and in the hands of the Eastern Trust Company – the operators had demanded a 25 per cent reduction in wages. Sydney Mines was probably the AMW's greatest stronghold, and local miners were prepared to go on strike against the wage cut. The issue was popular and would allow the AMW to demonstrate the extent of its support across the province. With the assistance of Bob Stewart, the union secretary, the men at Sydney Mines issued a strike call, directed to all coal miners, both AMW and UMW, throughout the province. The UMW leaders were alarmed at the prospect of a test of strength between the two unions, but insisted that all UMW loyalists must observe the conditions of their contract and remain at work.[60]

McLachlan saw this crisis as a test for the AMW, and despite Stewart's best efforts, the AMW seemed to be failing. The truth was that the AMW leadership was divided. More moderate leaders, such as the AMW vice-president Clarie Gillis, opposed the strike, at least until a membership vote could be held. In June, McLachlan argued that the AMW had "reached the parting of the ways," and in the *Nova Scotia Miner* he denounced the vacillations of the leaders: "The strike can be won because your foes were never before so weak as they are today. There is no power in Nova Scotia today equal to that united power of the 12,000 miners of this province ... This week will see the AMW crown itself with fighting working class glory or bury itself in a coward's grave."[61]

A week later McLachlan was bitterly disappointed: "Last week was a black week for the miners of Nova Scotia. Shilly-shallying officers made it so. Only Bob Stewart came out boldly for the only logical line of action open to men who are true trade unionists. What kind of a union man is he who at this time of day requires 'time to consider whether he will fight a wage cut'? Such a nut does not yet know the first principles of militant trade unionism."[62]

In due course the strike vote was completed in the locals and ran heavily in favour of a strike, but meanwhile the provincial government stepped in to avert the crisis. There would be some government assistance to the coal company, with the result that the wage cuts for the lowest-paid workers would be limited to 15 per cent instead of 25 per cent. McLachlan refused to believe the outcome was a successful compromise – "the men were deserted and defeated by the rank indifference of their fellow workers" – and he predicted that wage cuts would follow throughout the industry. Worst of all, the AMW had backed down in its first test of strength. Later, the union fought a number of small

strikes at individual pits, usually against wage reductions and dismiss-
als, but it never did launch a strike for recognition.[63]

The UMW leaders were relieved. "No Strike All Mines Working
Situation Good In Our Favor," Alex McKay had reported to Indianapolis when it was clear that the strike would not take place, and once the
compromise was announced UMW officials rejoiced over the AMW's
failure: "The AMW should certainly not get very far after agreeing to
reductions at that place. It seems that every report is just increasing the
number of indictments against that particular aggregation."[64]

By this time it must have been obvious that the AMW did not march
under McLachlan's command. Indeed, by the end of the summer
McLachlan's misgivings about the AMW were prompting him to think
the unthinkable about the future of the AMW and the UMW. In a
remarkable editorial in the *Nova Scotia Miner*, McLachlan reflected on
the parallel shortcomings of both unions: "Whatever differences exist
between these two bodies of men, there is at least one question that
ought to unite them, and this is the question of wages." In the past year
both unions had disgraced themselves by failing to fight wage reductions: "The Amalgamated Mine Workers were too weak to fight, they
said. What a shameful excuse! The United Mine Workers had a contract,
they said, and could not fight. What a traitors' excuse!"

Out of this experience McLachlan seemed to be giving up on the idea
that the AMW could ultimately carry the day. The class struggle was
more important than the conflict of unions, and McLachlan's comments were dropping the separate rancour towards the UMW and
appealing instead to the members of both unions with a case for united
action: "What are both unions going to do in the future about the Coal
Company's continual attack on the wages of the miners? The miners'
wages can be saved and increased if only both unions come out boldly
and fight all wage cuts ... The rank and file must demand that a united
fight must be made against all wage cuts."[65]

"Vote for Yourself!"

These events seemed to restore McLachlan's fighting spirit, and when
there was a provincial election to fight in the summer of 1933 he

entered the fray with enthusiasm. To his amusement, the leaders in this election were familiar old adversaries. Gordon Harrington, now Premier Harrington, had been McLachlan's defender in the great trial in 1923 before his entry into government in the 1925 election. The fresh face of Liberalism in the province was that of Angus L. Macdonald, a young Cape Bretoner and law professor from Dalhousie University who, at the time of the trial in 1923, had been one of O'Hearn's assistants in the prosecution. Macdonald had taken over the leadership of the Liberal Party in 1930. From McLachlan's point of view, none of this made any difference – both parties stood for the discredited capitalist system.

In Cape Breton East, a constituency now limited to the town of Glace Bay, McLachlan led a vigorous campaign. There were outdoor meetings and radio broadcasts, and the theme was "Vote for McLachlan and You Vote for Yourself!":

We, like you, are just plain working folks upon whom has descended all the misery of idle time, low wages, sometimes no wages at all, and are going short of enough to eat and clothes to wear. The ruling class will not and cannot get the workers out of their present misery; the old parties don't even propose any way out and certainly don't propose any adequate amount of relief. We are banded together for the purpose of using the United strength of the working class, both inside and outside of Parliament, to get more work, more wages and more of the comforts of life. We have no illusions that these can be secured without a great struggle, hence we ask you to join us and vote for our candidate who is pledged by his word, and above all by his life's work among the working class, to the following platform ...

The "Bread and Butter Platform" listed a program of working-class demands – protection against evictions, old age pensions at age fifty, union rates for relief work. If elected, the "Workers' United Front" candidate was pledged to accept no more than "working class wages" for his service in the provincial house, and to "vote against all laws not for the direct benefit of the working class as a whole and for all laws which are in their interest and for their benefit."[66]

The highlight of McLachlan's campaign was a large public meeting in McRae's Arena in Glace Bay. About 1,000 people crowded into the building. The meeting was chaired by AMW vice-president Joseph Nearing; other speakers included the ex-Wobbly Sam Scarlett, now an organizer for the Canadian Labour Defence League, and A.A. MacLeod, a young Cape Bretoner who was making a name for himself as a journalist in New York. According to press reports, McLachlan was "in fighting trim and went after both grits and tories." He pronounced the Liberals to be unchanged, "always ready to grab a gun to help the bosses take wage cuts from the workers." The Conservative government was denounced for "keeping up the financial record of the province by paying insufficient relief." McLachlan's campaign ended with an outdoor meeting behind the post office, a territory familiarly known as Red Square.[67]

On that final night McLachlan was also able to carry his message into hundreds more homes with a broadcast on the local radio station CJCB. It was a vintage McLachlan speech, filled with fierce rhetoric attacking the cruel commands of capitalism and the unsavoury record of the capitalist parties. At election times, he observed, the parties entered into a competition of scoundrels: "Many a youth during the last month took his first drink of rum, handed to him by a grit or tory politician. Rum is splashing all over Cape Breton." Throughout the talk McLachlan drove home a constant appeal to the virtue and responsibility of the mothers and fathers in his audience: "Where families are growing up and the children leaving school, it is only to be scattered to the four winds in the vain hunt for jobs that can never be found ... Vote Tory or Grit if you like, but look your boy in the face and tell the very truth about what you have done to him ... When you have voted, look your girl square in the face; she will know the heritage you have voted her."[68]

During these early years of the Great Depression, Canadian voters were throwing out governing parties with some consistency, and Nova Scotia in 1933 was no exception. As usual, both the Conservatives and the Liberals exploited memories of the industrial conflict. This time the Liberals seemed to make the better case, and a new government was

formed by Angus L. Macdonald and the Liberal Party. In Cape Breton
East the contest between the Liberal and the Conservative candidate
was very close. On election night the Liberal L.D. Currie was declared
the winner by a margin of only four votes, and a recount later gave him
a margin of twenty-three votes over his Conservative opponent. McLachlan polled 1,737 votes, 18.47 per cent of the total vote. It was more than
enough to remind the old parties that the working-class vote was significant in this constituency. McLachlan led many of the polls in Wards 3 and
4, and his total vote in Glace Bay had doubled since the previous election
in 1928. In *The Worker* the vote was optimistically described as "a sweeping
victory for the miners of Glace Bay, and a stern warning to the ruling class
that the working class of Glace Bay are closing in on them every day."[69]

An embarrassing factor in the election was the appearance of Dawn
Fraser as a candidate. This was the writer of popular verse who had
once worked for the *Maritime Labor Herald* and celebrated McLachlan
as the working-class hero. In this election Fraser stood as a candidate for
the newly established Cooperative Commonwealth Federation (CCF).
Under the leadership of J.S. Woodsworth, the CCF was supposed to be
the new party of workers, farmers, and socialists – representing a
distinctive Canadian socialism which had more in common with the
British Labour Party than the Bolshevik Revolution. For McLachlan,
the CCF had no relevance at this time. At best it was a well-meaning
but misguided movement; at worst it threatened to divide the working-
class vote.

When Woodsworth campaigned in Glace Bay that summer, McLachlan attended the public meeting and came away with a harsh review of
his old friend. "The big thing in life for Mr. Woodsworth is the CCF,"
he wrote, "and he thinks the main thing in the life of the ordinary
worker is to vote for CCF candidates ... He talks very much about 'the
common people' but never about the working class as a class. If the
workers are of any use at all in his scheme of things it is as voters –
voters for the CCF. Their strikes are folly, their demonstrations are
useless, and their 'demands' senseless." During this visit Woodsworth
found it awkward to explain why the CCF was running a candidate
against McLachlan when there were other local ridings where the old
parties were competing without any challenge from the left. Fortu-

nately, McLachlan concluded, the damage was minimal since Fraser received only 297 votes.[70]

For McLachlan, the vote was a limited instrument of democracy, only one of the weapons available to workers, and this was the obvious contrast between Woodsworth's parliamentary socialism and McLachlan's revolutionary socialism. During the election campaign McLachlan had defended himself against the charge that he considered the ballot a useless instrument: "'McLachlan does say that the workers cannot be and shall never emancipate themselves through the ballot.' Yes, that's true. He also tells the workers that partial strikes won't emancipate them, nor protest meetings against the jailings of the victims of lying stool-pigeons, nor can trade unions emancipate them. Yet McLachlan is in favor of all these activities of the working class, just as he is in favor of their casting a working class ballot at every opportunity."[71]

Again, at a meeting following the election, McLachlan commented, in words memorable enough for the police to record them in quotation marks: "Elections don't mean anything: the elected candidates only have delegated power while the people have the inherent power." The report continued: "McLachlan declared that he had faith in the honesty and courage of the workers of Canada. When these workers see that there is no hope for them and their families under capitalism, they will arise and take control of the country."[72]

CHAPTER 12

Time and Tide

Nae man can tether time or tide.

– Robert Burns

Agitator

J.B. McLachlan – Agitator." The police were still keeping a close eye on McLachlan, and in February 1934 his file was being rapidly updated. He was described as "one of the most widely known radicals in Canada for a number of years." There followed a hostile summary of his current activities: "He spends his evenings at Rukasin's hall with the 'United Front,' or unemployed and is always making speeches. He is a great reader, keeps posted, hates Woodsworth and the C.C.F., and both the political parties. He is a fluent speaker, is a mob leader, witty, sarcastic, and yells, with a Lowland Scotch burr that is worth hearing."[1]

McLachlan was aging. In 1934 he was sixty-five years old, and his pictures show a noticeably older man, his features thinning, greying. But the historical record for these years shows little sign of weakness or inactivity. If anything, McLachlan was more occupied, more vigorous, more optimistic than he had been for years. In the darkest years of the Great Depression, the workers' revolt was accelerating. Unemployed workers were on the march; new unions were getting organized; workers were fighting back; there was much talk of unity and solidarity and socialism. This was McLachlan's last long campaign, and out of the struggles of the 1930s there would come lasting changes in the rights and freedoms of the Canadian worker. But history would not unfold as he expected nor deliver all the results McLachlan wanted.

For many workers in the 1930s, McLachlan was now highly visible on the national stage of Canadian labour history, where he was often greeted as one of Canada's working-class heroes. At WUL meetings in September 1933, for instance, which he did not attend, McLachlan was acclaimed as national president. The delegates' testimonials were delivered to him in Glace Bay by Sam Scarlett, who, like McLachlan, was a

Scotsman who had come to North America shortly after the turn of the century. A machinist by trade, Scarlett was also a star football player. As a member of the Industrial Workers of the World in the United States, he was convicted in the mass trials in Chicago in 1918 and sentenced to twenty years in jail. Subsequently deported to Scotland, Scarlett immigrated instead to Canada, where he worked as a Wobbly organizer before joining the Communist Party. In the WUL campaigns of the 1930s, Scarlett was one of the toughest and most popular fieldworkers, especially among the western coal miners and the unemployed. For his part in the Estevan miners' strike in November 1931, when three miners were shot by the RCMP, Scarlett received a one-year prison sentence (as did Annie Buller). When he visited Glace Bay, to present McLachlan with a watch and a flattering set of official greetings, Scarlett's Glaswegian accent rang warmly in McLachlan's ears: "In every working class district and in every mining camp in Canada, McLachlan's name stood for a militant forward movement and was a symbol of hope and inspiration to every worker in Canada."[2]

That winter McLachlan could not avoid thinking about the fate of his comrades serving time in Kingston Penitentiary. As New Year's Eve approached at the end of 1933, Tim Buck, Tom McEwen, and other Communist leaders continued to serve their five-year sentences in Kingston Penitentiary. Moreover, Buck had received an additional nine months for allegedly participating in a prison riot in October 1932. Even the smallest gestures of support gave McLachlan some comfort. Sitting at home with a checkerboard on his knee, he drew up a defiant telegram addressed to Malcolm Bruce, the Prince Edward Island-born radical who had been a regular visitor at Steele's Hill in the early 1920s: "Your unconquerable spirit drives on and on tens of thousands of working men and women to live and work for your liberation and the great day." McLachlan was delighted when his ten-year-old grandson added his own name to the list and donated ten cents to help pay for the telegram. In short order they had collected fifty names and McLachlan was happy to report that the personal message had become a mass greeting.[3]

This was no time for McLachlan to rest, and in 1934 he spent much of the year on the road to Montreal and Toronto. At the end of June he presided at the opening of the ambitiously named National Miners' Conference. For McLachlan it was an historic event, the kind of meeting he had dreamed of for years – an assembly bringing together delegates from the coal miners of west and east, as well as representatives from the hard-rock miners and smeltermen of British Columbia, northern Ontario, and Quebec. The plan was to build a Canadian miners' federation in which the divisive Canadian particularities of craft and industry, distance and region could at last be joined in class solidarity. It was even hoped that iron-ore miners from Newfoundland would come into the federation. The meeting produced little more than a set of hopes and resolutions, but McLachlan stood front and centre in the group portraits of the delegates, proud to help in launching the campaign. He took no formal office in the organizing committee, however, which was led by John Stokaluk of the Alberta-based Mine Workers' Union of Canada as chairman and Bob Stewart of the Amalgamated Mine Workers of Nova Scotia as vice-chairman. High praise for the new generation of leaders was to say that they were "leaders of the McLachlan type."[4]

McLachlan expanded on the federation idea later, in reply to questions from Professor Stewart of Dalhousie University. The National Miners' Conference, McLachlan explained, was "the first meeting of all the miners of Canada." The purpose was to build a union of coal and rock miners, with autonomy for the member unions, "along the same lines as the British Miners Federation." And in the context of the Great Depression, McLachlan did not hesitate to add, "it shall be built on the lines of the class struggle as distinct from class collaboration. There are about seventy-five thousand miners in this country with less than one-third of them organized in any union. It is a big job we have set out to do." Whether the new union would become part of the WUL could be decided later. For the time being, the radicals were satisfied to work from within existing unions:

I know this "looks terrible" to many people. Poor simple folks! Is this not true of every political party and all Capitalist organizations from day school to church? The difference between us and them is we are more honest about it, our people are more devoted in their work, and a great deal more self-sacrificing, and hence their work stands out. The other side has money and can buy up their "borers from within" wholesale. We have no money, but a superabundance of – if you like – "fanatical" devotion to a movement.[5]

Then, in the summer of 1934, came the news that several of the Communist leaders were being released from jail. McLachlan received the news at the train station in Montreal, and at Queen's Park in Toronto he was one of the speakers before a crowd of 5,000 people who welcomed Sam Carr, the first to arrive home from Kingston Penitentiary. Soon there was more good news, and on 14 July McLachlan telegraphed home: "A glorious twelfth. Bruce, [John] Boychuk and [Tom] Hill just arrived here. Great workers' demonstration demands unconditional release of McEwen and Buck." The prisoners came out of jail in weakened health, but like McLachlan before them, they remained defiant. At another meeting, this one with about 1,500 people in attendance at the Standard Theatre on Spadina Avenue, McLachlan praised the work of the Canadian Labour Defence League and the Workers' Unity League in gaining the release of the "class war prisoners."[6]

The release of the prisoners, halfway through their sentences, coincided with the Communist Party's Seventh National Convention, which McLachlan attended in Toronto that month. At this time the party claimed 5,500 members, little more than in its first period of popularity in the early 1920s. However, the campaigns for causes such as unemployment insurance and the repeal of section 98 of the Criminal Code (the 1919 legislation under which the Communist leaders were convicted) had raised the party's profile considerably, and expectations were running higher than ever. Communist policies were summarized in a long manifesto entitled "Towards a Soviet Canada," which boldly proclaimed that communism was the only answer to the crisis of capitalism. Reform-minded political parties such as the CCF and trade unions affiliated with the TLC and the ACCL were denounced: at best they were ineffective; at worst they were agents of capitalism.

These July days in Toronto lifted McLachlan's spirits. He enjoyed the reunion with old comrades, and his faith in the inevitable triumph of his class was renewed: "What a holiday! How kind the gods were to us. We lived and fed and revelled for one whole week with the best and bravest of Canada's working class. We could not go to sleep at night, not till we stuck our thumb to our nose as we looked toward Ottawa and said: 'Bennett, the Communists will win!'"[7]

In one campaign after another these were hopeful days for Canadian labour radicals. By 1934 the WUL was no longer the paper organization the Communists had launched five years earlier. Besides sympathetic independent unions such as the AMW, the WUL affiliates had a membership of between 30,000 and 40,000 workers. In the divided house of labour the WUL had established a strong presence for the cause of industrial unionism and radical politics. Indeed, in the depths of the Depression in 1933 and 1934 the WUL was responsible for the largest strikes of the year, especially among lumber workers and garment workers, and it was racking up a reputation for success among unorganized workers.[8]

The day-to-day affairs of the WUL were run from a small office on Queen Street in Toronto, originally by Tom McEwen and then by Jim Litterick and Charlie Sims – all of them, like McLachlan, British immigrants. McLachlan's main function was to preside at national meetings and of course to act as a public spokesman. When a Toronto newspaper reported that AFL leaders were growing alarmed at the growth of the WUL and planned a campaign of "public exposure," McLachlan eagerly challenged AFL leaders to a public debate: "If there is anything we love better than a battle, it is two battles – one against labor fakerdom, and one against its masters, the robber gang who live upon the exploitation of the working class."[9]

Simultaneously, under the direction of the capable A.E. Smith, the Canadian Labour Defence League became widely known. Across the country local supporters defended radical workers arrested in local free-speech fights and unemployed immigrant workers slated for deportation. The league also took up the defence of the arrested party leaders and appealed for the abolition of section 98. In a sensational trial in early 1934 Smith himself had been charged with sedition for his defence efforts – and his unexpected acquittal by the Toronto jury seemed to mark a turning point in the acceptance of the radical left in the 1930s.[10]

Similarly, the emergence of a national campaign against war and fascism was also gaining wider support for the left. In the hands of A.A. MacLeod, the Canadian League Against War and Fascism took shape rapidly during the summer and fall of 1934. By October, MacLeod had organized a national conference with more than 500 delegates and observers in attendance; they came from organized labour – including members of the TLC and ACCL – as well as both the Communist Party and the CCF. Like McLachlan's campaign for a national miners' federation, these efforts were among the earliest indications of the party's success in adopting a less isolationist position towards other groups on the left and anticipated the more formal united-front policies adopted in 1935.[11]

McLachlan poured his efforts into these new campaigns. When he returned home to Nova Scotia at the end of July, a local group against war and fascism had already been launched at a meeting on the shores of the Bras d'Or Lake at Kempt Head, Boularderie Island. McLachlan spoke at a subsequent meeting in the Casino Theatre on Victoria Road in Sydney in early August. For his text that day he took a radio broadcast from the previous evening marking the twentieth anniversary of the outbreak of the Great War. Again McLachlan demonstrated his ability to breathe meaning into a homely illustration:

> The suffering portrayed of a grandmother who lost her son, husband and daughter-in-law was real and true and took place in millions of homes throughout the world. But the ending, which told of the grandson being promoted and receiving good pay was a lie and is only being used by the "Master-Class" to pave the way for another war. Young men and women of today face a black future and cannot enjoy the happiness which should be theirs. Instead of good jobs, these young people are found in "slave camps," "soup kitchens" and on the streets, where they are compelled to go under this present system. McLachlan next spoke of existing conditions in Europe and explained the contradictions

existing in the capitalistic system, which forced these conditions to arise. The scarcity of markets in which goods can be dumped had caused a crisis which the "master-class" seek to cure by wars, and as a result, Democracy has been thrown out and Fascism ushered in in its place.[12]

At the end of the summer, McLachlan was back on the train. In Montreal there were more meetings in support of the Miners' Federation. Then it was on to Ontario, where he made a speaking tour for the Canadian Labour Defence League during October. When McLachlan returned home at the beginning of November, it was in time to celebrate the release of Tom McEwen from Kingston; McEwen gave Glace Bay audiences a vivid account of his two and a half years in jail, including a first-hand account of the prison riot during which eleven shots were fired into Buck's cell. Later that month Buck himself was finally released, and in due course he, too, would appear in Cape Breton to acknowledge local support.[13]

All through these rounds of activity, week in and week out, McLachlan and his followers continued to publish the *Nova Scotia Miner* with impressive regularity. The front page now featured a distinctive symbol, a miner's pick and shovel crossed on a rising sun, and every issue carried the revolutionary slogan of the *Communist Manifesto*: "Workers of the World, Unite! You have nothing to lose but your chains." In November they celebrated the 200th issue. McLachlan recalled that the newspaper had started with $200 in donations and had survived without advertising and with only rare appeals for donations. The secret of survival, he boasted, was the paper's loyal weekly following among readers and especially among those who contributed freely of their labour: "Shop papers, such as the Nova Scotia Miner, can continue to live, only if workers give their time and labor in getting out the paper – for nothing. Not cash donations but free labor getting out and selling the paper at the mines every pay day, gave the Nova Scotia Miner its life of 200 issues." Two weeks later McLachlan made a more sombre appeal, warning that there was a danger the newspaper would be forced to suspend publication and urging friends to renew their support. The appeal appeared to meet with success, and the *Miner* continued on into the new year without interruption.[14]

Despite the vehement rhetoric published in the *Miner*, the newspaper had become an accepted part of the local scene in Cape Breton and suffered few legal difficulties. The one exception was a libel case brought against the paper by the proprietor of a rooming house, who was asking for $2,000 damages as a result of "uncomplimentary references." The case was heard in court in Sydney for a full day in April 1935. This time McLachlan was a successful defendant and won a not guilty verdict from the jury.[15]

Still, the year ended on a sour note for McLachlan. During November and December he was again embroiled in a dispute with the Communist Party organizer for Nova Scotia. A police report in November 1934 stated that the Cape Breton Communists were "divided into two camps at the present time" and McLachlan was refusing to accept the authority of the organizer. Another report two weeks later stated that McLachlan and three of his local followers had been expelled from the party but added that "McLachlan is not going to take [deletion] dictation in a quiet manner but will fight to the end. Many of the Communists in Cape Breton are behind McLachlan and are beginning to dislike [deletion] dictatorial ways." McLachlan had charged that the party organizer for Nova Scotia was engaged in an extramarital affair.[16]

This was not the first time McLachlan had applied moral tests to party organizers. He expected leaders to be models of responsible behaviour, which he defined in accordance with his own well-developed sense of the responsible masculinity of the husband and father. When the case was appealed to party headquarters in Toronto, McLachlan prevailed, and a new organizer was appointed. There appeared to be no lasting damage, and a few months later McLachlan was again heavily engaged in party activity. In March 1935 he accepted nomination in the Dominion election. Although technically the party was still illegal under section 98, McLachlan and others would run openly as Communist Party candidates.

The Amalgamated Mine Workers

Home in the coalfields, McLachlan watched the rivalry between the UMW and AMW with flashes of enthusiasm and frustration. Launched on a flood of hope in 1932, the AMW had so far failed to drive the UMW out of the district. To McLachlan's disappointment, the new union had not launched a strike for recognition at a strategic moment of opportunity in 1933. Although the AMW was strong enough to engage in local strikes over wage reductions and discrimination, it never succeeded in gaining formal recognition from the companies or replacing the UMW as the miners' union. In fact, the AMW was a reluctant dual union which never abandoned the hope of uniting all the coal miners in one organization. It was a point of pride with the AMW that it spoke for all coal miners, and much of its time was devoted to trying to implement slogans such as "the united front from below" and "unity in action."[17]

To McLachlan, it seemed that the AMW was settling in for a protracted struggle on the difficult terrain of industrial legality. At the end of 1933 the rivalry between the two unions entered a new stage as both sides struggled to win advantage under the provisions of the Coal Mines Regulation Act. So far, the provincial government had refused to hold a vote to determine the coal miners' choice of unions. Premier Gordon Harrington remembered the rivalries of the 1909 strike and agreed that the solution must be found in unity. But, as he explained to AMW vice-president Joseph Nearing, he had no intention of assisting in healing the split: "There is only one cure for it and that is amongst yourselves."[18]

The election of the Liberals in the summer of 1933 gave the AMW leaders new hope of assistance from the state. The new premier, Angus L. Macdonald, invited the officers of the two unions to meet jointly in Halifax with a view to uniting the miners in one organization. The immediate cause for the meetings was the eruption of a bitter local dispute over a wage reduction at Stellarton, one of the closely divided communities where both unions claimed to represent the miners. In Halifax, Premier Macdonald tried to cajole the UMW officers into meeting with officers of the rival union. They were suspicious, and the international board member for District 26, William Hayes of Springhill, believed that Macdonald was unduly sympathetic to the AMW. When Macdonald brought the AMW leaders Joseph Nearing and Bob Stewart into his office, the UMW delegation stormed out: "Before going we told the Premier what we thought about them allowing those fellows in on our meeting and the Premier was quite put out about it and tried to get us to stay but we kept going."

At once the AMW officers pressed their advantage, informing the premier that they were prepared to abide by the results of a government-sponsored referendum vote; indeed, they told reporters that they would submit their resignations in advance of the result "so that the miners of Nova Scotia may have the union and officials of their own choice." At the same meeting the premier also pledged to enforce the collection of union dues on the basis of individual signed membership cards submitted by the AMW. Earlier in the month the Nova Scotia Steel and Coal Company had agreed to deduct union dues for the AMW in the Sydney Mines district, where virtually all the miners belonged to the AMW, and the government's promise to enforce the card count throughout the district gave the AMW new hope. There was nothing new about the arrangement – it was already written into the Coal Mines Regulation Act – but the premier's promise to enforce the legislation was considered to be a promising concession for the AMW. Even without a referendum, the AMW would now be able to demonstrate its strength in numbers by presenting signed cards. On their return from Halifax, Stewart and Nearing urged members to take advantage of the law: "We should get our cards signed and get the checkoff and this will be the referendum vote that the UMW CANNOT stop."[19]

McLachlan watched these events with misgivings. His objections focused on the ambiguities surrounding the check-off of union dues. In September, when AMW leaders proposed a campaign to gain the check-off, McLachlan had published a sceptical commentary in the Nova Scotia Miner: "All history is against the check-off. The best unions, the unions which did most for their membership, never had the check-off, and never once had the fool's dream that the boss would make a good union dues collector." Even a model union such as the AMW, he warned, could be threatened by a "hand-in-glove relationship with the

boss through the check-off." Although the AMW was in an extremely
weak financial condition, barely able to pay a single officer, McLachlan
refused to accept the AMW's claim that the coal miners would not pay
their dues directly to the union without the check-off: "Let the AMW
show by working class deed that it is out to fight for the miners, and the
miners will, unasked, flock into its ranks." Again in January, McLachlan
was warning against the strategy: "We are against the check-off even
for a good union." And in March: "The check-off, in our view, is bad
in any form, and nothing more nor less than an attempt of the boss to
gain certain control over union affairs."[20]

Despite his reservations about the quest for industrial legality, McLachlan had no doubt that the AMW enjoyed the support of the coal miners.
He still welcomed the prospect of a referendum: "If there could be a
quite free and genuine vote by ballot, the A.M.W. would have a majority
of the mineworkers of Nova Scotia."[21] But there would be no free vote
between the AMW and UMW in 1934 or at any time afterwards. The
UMW would never give its agreement, and without this the provincial
government would not hold a referendum in the coalfields. Instead, the
government encouraged the two unions to submit signed check-off
cards to the company offices indicating each miner's preference of
union. Then, at the spring session of the legislature in 1934, the
minister of mines, Mike Dwyer, introduced amendments to the procedures. The most important change was that, after the cards were
counted on 15 November each year, the individual coal companies
would be permitted to grant the check-off to a single union favoured
by "the larger or largest numbers of employees in or about all mines
operated by said employer."[22]

The legislation was widely promoted as an effort to end the division
between the two unions. Although a new card count was provided for
every twelve months, it was hoped that the first vote would settle the
divisions and the union in the minority would withdraw from the field.
McLachlan gave the law a more sceptical reading than most observers:
"All the bunk used by the Grits about passing the amendment in order
to heal the split in the ranks of the miners was just so much hypocritical
talk." Instead, he charged, the amendment was a recipe for company
unionism since it allowed the companies to determine which union to

designate as the "official union." And that decision would be based on the company's advantage: "Not numbers but servility is the determining factor with them. But numbers and determined united action on the part of the miners can say what union is going to do business for them. The question that the new law has raised for the miners is the question of whether a Company union has to be set up or a miners' union."

A careful reading of the legislation shows the basis for McLachlan's concern. The key provision in the law was not mandatory but permissive, and the company would still have a great deal of discretionary power; regardless of the results, the companies would be in a position to decide whether to continue the check-off for one union or for several. Furthermore, although mine inspectors would be present at the card counts, the entire process would take place with minimal government supervision. There would be no secret ballot: each individual miner would submit a signed card indicating his preference for a union, an obvious recipe for discrimination against those who favoured the "wrong" union. To McLachlan, the arrangement forgot too much local labour history – as if there had never been a history of discrimination against miners belonging to the "wrong" union.

Thinking back to the days when the old UMW had finally replaced the Provincial Workmen's Association, McLachlan suggested that there might be some lessons there: "The Company wants a docile union, but it not only must be docile to the Company, it must also be able to prevent any effective revolt inside the ranks of the miners, and it is just at this point the AMW must wage its battle and prevent any agreement made by the company union being put into effect. This is the very point on which the old PWA perished – it failed to put over the contract it had signed with the company. The miners forced the company to tear up that contract and from that moment the old PWA became useless to the Coal Company. It had to recognize the new militant union. This can be done again by the same determined miners, if they go after it and end any company union set up through Dwyer's new law."[23]

McLachlan's warnings about the dangers of industrial legality were taken to heart by AMW leaders, and the union's hopes did not ride exclusively on the card count. The slogans of "unity in action" and the "united front from below" received McLachlan's enthusiastic encouragement when they were translated into action in smaller local strikes. In a dispute on the face at No. 2 mine, for instance, men from both unions successfully walked out to secure the reinstatement of one miner. At every opportunity AMW leaders appealed to UMW members simply to ignore their leaders and make common cause with other miners by forming joint grievance committees and delegations on local issues. This was the kind of local united action specifically encouraged by the Miners' Federation of Canada which McLachlan so strongly endorsed.

Shortly before the card count, AMW president John Alex MacDonald echoed McLachlan's cautions against excessive confidence in the process: "All miners should know that the Dwyer Bill was not passed to give 'just one union' the checkoff. What the Bill intends is to hamper the work of the AMW. Whether the UMW gets the majority or not, they will be paid the checkoff. If the AMW loses the count the company will not be 'obligated' to deduct dues." MacDonald warned that the company and the province were in league to smash the miners' union: "They hope to cripple the AMW financially and at the same time, using the tradition that a union is not a union unless it gets the checkoff, place the AMW in such light in the eyes of the miners that they would be easier to win for the UMW of A."[24]

McLachlan had not suspended his disbelief, but as the day of the count approached he encouraged the miners to give a resounding demonstration of support for the AMW. His appeal was most strongly addressed to the undecided miners who were sitting on the fence: "Be a man among men and get an AMW card and join the miners' struggle for bread and union liberty." He reminded miners that even as the vote approached the cards were being stacked against the AMW: "The coal company is the 'returning officer.' Only the cards the company hands out will be counted, and only the simple and foolish believe that the company will hand over all the cards signed in favor of the AMW." For this reason it was necessary to bring out a resounding demonstration of strength in support of the AMW: "Remember, you are fighting a robber boss, a corrupt racket, and a rotten, double-dealing government. This vile trinity will stop at nothing to falsify the vote and defeat the miners' union."[25]

When the first results were counted, the AMW showed "surprising strength," according to the Sydney *Post-Record*, and threatened to win the contest. But more cards were counted the following day – which was, claimed the AMW, contrary to the act – and the final result gave the UMW a small margin of victory across the province, 6,604 to 6,066. Local AMW leaders reacted with anger, charging that hundreds of AMW cards had not been counted and that UMW cards had been submitted on behalf of dead men, police officers, mine officials, and men who had not worked in the pit for years. Nevertheless, in the Sydney coalfield the AMW had won a clear majority over the UMW, 5,009 to 4,156, and it was the vote at smaller companies on the mainland which had given the UMW its margin of victory. But as McLachlan had warned, the card count by the companies was not the same as a referendum among the coal miners. The results would be applied not pit by pit or district by district but company by company. When the votes were distributed in this way the UMW came out of the count with majorities at six of the province's coal companies, including Dominion Coal, where the AMW had won Glace Bay but lost New Waterford; the AMW had majorities at only two companies, both in the Sydney Mines district.[26]

Two weeks after the vote, Professor Stewart of Dalhousie University again wrote McLachlan, who offered the professor guidelines for reinterpreting the results "to get a true picture of the strength of the A.M.W." "No doubt but the miners' card vote was a surprise," he said. "If you want to get the real eyebrow lifter, compare the total vote cast with the total number employed in and about the mines of Nova Scotia." With these and other discrepancies taken into account, McLachlan's revised estimate of the results gave the AMW 6,312 and the UMW 5,572. Also, McLachlan underlined the significance of the AMW majority in Cape Breton and in the most important producing mines: "The beauty of the vote is that the A.M.W. got the key men in the industry, while the U.M.W. strength was shown to be in the machine shop, shipping piers and construction men and such labor."[27]

The plain truth was that there was no breakthrough for the AMW. Appeals to the provincial government and to the courts gave no satisfaction, and appeals for an "undivided common front" were turned down by the UMW. The only comfort for the AMW was that twelve months later, again on 15 November, another card count would be taken. The results then were almost unchanged, 7,221 for the UMW and 5,754 for the AMW. It was another pyrrhic victory, since once more the AMW had won a majority of the Cape Breton miners but lost the check-off in all places except Sydney Mines. Again the AMW claimed that the count was riddled with irregularities. During the year the union had also added the charge that the minister of mines had helped campaign against the AMW during 1935 in areas such as Springhill where organizers were beaten and blacklisted; at one stage in 1935, bitterness against the Liberal government was so extreme that at an AMW convention correspondence from Angus L. Macdonald was voted "to the wastebasket."[28]

McLachlan was heartened by the union's large votes and by the evidence of united action in local disputes. But he agreed that the AMW's adventure in industrial legality was ending in frustration. The only remedy he knew was in the class struggle: "'Recognition' that is 'given' is worth nothing to you miners. The UMW has that now. Recognition that is won in spite of the boss is the only kind of recognition that is any benefit to the working class."[29]

The Last Campaign

"VOTE FOR YOUR CLASS!" "ELECT A WORKER TO PARLIAMENT!" These were the appeals on behalf of McLachlan in his final effort at the polls in 1935. This time, as one of the country's leading labour radicals, he would run as a candidate of the Communist Party. In 1935 the party's membership was growing rapidly – it would reach 9,000 in October 1935 and 15,000 two years later – and the Communist Party wanted to establish a national presence in this election. Earlier that year, the Communist Willie Gallacher had been returned to the British House of Commons from West Fife – a coal mining constituency in Scotland that was considered one of the so-called "Little Moscows" where the Communist Party enjoyed substantial local support.[30]

The choice of Cape Breton South, the only riding contested east of Montreal, was a predictable one, and McLachlan was the obvious candidate. The campaign platform ranged widely through the program of the left in the middle years of the Great Depression – unemployment insurance, the six-hour day, public works, the prevention of war. But the appeal was also a personal one in which the voters were invited to pay tribute to McLachlan for the deeds of a long career. McLachlan was advertised as "Nova Scotia's outstanding fighter for the working class. Over 45 years in the labour movement."[31]

McLachlan's own expectations in the campaign were limited. He had already run five times for provincial and federal legislatures without success. But, with the frustrations of the AMW campaigns fresh in his mind and a feeling that the local class struggle was not keeping pace with national events, McLachlan was not reluctant to enter the battle. His fighting spirit was sharpened that spring by the latest in the long list of mine disasters in the coalfields. Seven men were killed in a gas explosion at the Allan Shaft in Stellarton in April – the same badly ventilated pit where eighty-eight men had lost their lives in 1918 and another four in 1924. It was a reminder of how little priority was assigned to the protection of human life in the coal industry, warned McLachlan: "Governments won't help – their function is to keep you in subjection while the boss robs you." He denounced the investigation as a "mock inquiry" which shamefully blamed a "faulty shot" for the disaster. There was less concern about human lives in government reports than about horses and timber and brattice: "These things all cost real money to the boss, but dead miners are fearfully cheap and easily replaced, and are treated accordingly."[32]

From the earliest stages, McLachlan's campaign was under police surveillance. At the nomination meeting in March 1935, it was noted that McLachlan was campaigning on a "straight Communist ticket." McLachlan told his audience that other reformers were "all anxious to keep the Capitalist system by patching it up, while the Communist Party is the only party which wishes to abolish the capitalist system." At another public meeting in April, McLachlan "condemned the madness of the present capitalistic system, which forces millions of workers to starve while a few rich parasites live in luxury ... [I]n 1848 Karl Marx foretold everything that is happening to day and he was right. On every side can be seen the Bennetts and Ramsey [sic] McDonalds running around bewildered, not knowing which way to turn or what to do next to combat the rising militancy of the working class."

In May about 600 people turned out at the Strand Theatre in Sydney to hear Communist Party leader Tim Buck, on his first trip to Cape Breton since his release from jail, speak in support of the local candidate. McLachlan accompanied Buck with a blistering attack on Prime Minister Bennett and concluded: "The Communist Party of Canada is the only Party in Canada which has a plan and solution to cure the present misery and suffering of the Canadian masses. The Communist Party of Canada stands for the complete overthrow of the capitalist system and the forming of a Soviet Government of the Workers for the Workers."[33]

McLachlan was impressed by the well-organized effort mounted on his behalf. Donations came in from old comrades around the province, and at the height of the campaign there were daily local collections in support of the election effort. The final accounts showed contributions of $1,027.02. Apart from the $200 deposit, the main expenditures were for printing bills, radio time, hall rentals, and train fares. Thousands of copies of the election program were distributed door to door, and besides Buck there was a steady stream of visitors – Roscoe Fillmore, who was now running a popular gardening business in the Annapolis valley; Arthur "Slim" Evans, the hero of the On-to-Ottawa Trek, which had just been halted in a bloody police attack at Market Square in Regina on 1 July; A.A. MacLeod of the Canadian League Against War and Fascism (who would become one of the first Communist members of the Ontario legislature in 1943). One police report observed laconically: "The movement is gaining a lot of strength."[34]

McLachlan was especially pleased with the presence of the experienced, battle-hardened organizer Annie Buller – "She was, as one worker put it, 'like an army with banners.' How the folks loved Annie!" McLachlan credited her with galvanizing the local campaign into exceptional efforts and giving special attention to women voters: "Some people can do the job but it is useless sending a miner to do a carpenter's job," he later commented. "You cannot fit a square peg into a round hole. There are people who can build the women's movement down there. We want to look for the person who can do that job. Comrade B. is the person who can do it."

One election flyer published under Buller's influence was addressed directly to the women of the mining area and underlined the class interests of working women – "whether they work in a factory or at home." As mothers of schoolchildren deprived of the necessities of life and as mothers of youths condemned to the prospect of twenty cents a day in relief camps, women knew the hardships of the economic crisis: "The women have carried the crushing burden because the rich refuse to pay to save the country from poverty."

Forcefully, Buller defended McLachlan against the predictable charges: "The capitalist representatives cannot point to one thing that McLachlan did which was not in the interests of the common people and so they try to confuse the women by introducing the red bogey and religious issues." The charges of anti-Catholicism were contradicted by the struggle against fascism in Germany: "It is the hard-pressed Communists who make common cause with the catholics in resisting the brutal imposition of barbarism by Hitler." In short, Buller urged, "the women in Cape Breton South will do their own thinking, make up their own minds as to who stands by them, who fights their battles, who is out to save their youth, who helps the unemployed, who fights for wage increases and to improve the lot of women." According to McLachlan, Buller "made inroads which were not made for years. By her radio talks and work she put my vote a considerable amount higher ... [I]f Comrade B. had been down two weeks earlier I would have got 1,500 votes more."[35]

Certainly McLachlan was receiving attention in the churches, and this would again be a factor in the results. There was little evidence here of the social Catholicism of the Antigonish Movement, represented by populist priests such as Jimmy Tompkins and Moses Coady. Efforts to marginalize, even demonize, McLachlan were as apparent in this campaign as they had been at the time of his strongest challenge for office in 1921. On the Sunday before the vote, the parish priest in New Aberdeen devoted three successive services to "the moral aspects involved in the exercise of the electoral franchise." Parishioners were advised that, while the church did not normally interfere in party politics, it was necessary to do so on this occasion in order to counteract "the poison of communism" and "the chief propagandist of this diabolical creed in Nova Scotia": "This man is not so much to be judged by his fair fantastic promises as by the simple fact that he is the blatant champion of the Moscow anti-God front."

Similarly, a Liberal election advertisement warned that "Communism means the taking away by force of the private property of the people" and that "no matter what the private feelings of the Communist candidate may be and no matter how he may be regarded as a labor man, as a Communist candidate he must stand for the introduction of the Russian system in Canada and all that it means." The editor of the Glace Bay *Gazette* also took pains to explain that McLachlan's campaign should not be taken at face value:

Speakers for communist candidates in this election try to create the impression that communism in Canada is something different from communism as exemplified in the government of Russia. But they cannot thus dissociate themselves from Moscow for election purposes ... it is useless for platform and radio speakers to attempt to deceive the electors with statements concerning its good intentions as regards the churches and social and economic changes. There is no reason to suppose that its methods in Canada would differ from those of Moscow.

Indeed, warned the *Gazette*, "the election of one communist to the parliament of Canada would be hailed throughout the world as a sign that this anti-christian, anti-social cult had achieved a palpable success. It would have added significance if that result were to occur in Cape Breton."[36]

At the polls McLachlan's vote surprised many observers. As the *Gazette* commented, "McLachlan was expected to poll a large vote but even his most ardent supporters did not expect him to come within 100 votes of the leading candidates." Similarly, a police report noted that "McLachlan did much better than was anticipated and got good support around Glace Bay."[37] But the worst nightmares of local notables were not fulfilled. In Glace Bay, McLachlan won the lead in the principal mining areas – Wards 3, 4, and 5 – and came close to winning the town; he was initially reported only ninety-seven votes behind the Liberal victor, but the final results gave McLachlan 2,570 votes in Glace Bay against 2,704 for the Liberal candidate. In the mining area as a whole, McLachlan remained in third place, polling a total of 3,906 votes, 25.8 per cent of the total. Once the final results for the whole constituency were tabulated, McLachlan had a total of 5,365 votes, about 19 per cent of the total. It was a secure finish in third place.[38]

After the meagre results of the last few election campaigns, McLachlan was pleased with the outcome. "Our own folks are great," he wrote in the *Nova Scotia Miner*, and he gave thanks to his supporters: "There are no people like our own people, the workers and toilers. What splendid and heroic things they do when duty calls!" Although the Communists had been able to buy local radio time during the campaign, McLachlan was denied the opportunity to broadcast a message of thanks to his supporters on the local station CJCB.

The "suppressed radio speech" was printed in the *Nova Scotia Miner* with a brief note by McLachlan: "The powers that be who never stop yapping about 'freedom of speech' refused to allow me to talk to the workers and thank them." In his comments McLachlan reviewed the results in detail. The majorities among the coal miners in the Glace Bay district were splendid victories, and the success in mobilizing the votes of women and youth was especially encouraging. New Waterford was a "weak spot," he acknowledged, and in Sydney the most urgent need was to build the steelworkers' union before better political results could be expected. But in the areas of weakness he attached no blame to the workers: "The message we have for the working class is not an appeal to prejudice, but to their class interests and their working-class reason. It takes time to learn our lesson, and it takes real organizational work to get our message to the workers ... The working class are honest, and if they don't vote for us in the large numbers they should, it is because we fail them and fail to smash the false teaching and false promises of the master class and capitalist politicians." In all, McLachlan came out of the campaign charged with optimism about the future of the local class struggle: "The fruits of victory from this election are waiting all around us to be gathered up, and it would be a crime on our part if we failed to consolidate all the forces: the miners of both unions, the women and the youth, who fought so well and unitedly about these coal mines to give the Communist candidate such a splendid victory at the mines."[39]

In some contests that year the rivalry between the Communists and the CCF was a feature of the 1935 election that underlined the divisions on the Canadian left. In Winnipeg North, for instance, Buck competed for the working-class vote against A.A. Heaps of the CCF – who had been the sitting member there since 1925. According to the Communists, the absence of a CCF candidate in Cape Breton South in 1935 was a concession to the superior appeal of McLachlan and the efficient organization of his supporters. However, as McLachlan observed at the time, the CCF had no real presence in the area – "We had the CCF" – and the few active members supported the Communist campaign.

Still, the labour vote in Cape Breton South was divided by another factor. The UMW district president, Dan Willie Morrison, stood in this election for the Reconstruction Party, a new party founded in the summer of 1935 by H.H. Stevens, a disaffected former Conservative cabinet minister who doubted R.B. Bennett's dedication to social reform. Morrison's nomination in September, six months after McLachlan entered the contest, could certainly be regarded as an effort to divide the labour vote. Morrison cut into traditional areas of Conservative support and also appealed to UMW loyalists and non-Communist labour leaders associated with the AMW such as Clarie Gillis. In the end, Morrison polled 5,008 votes, finishing behind McLachlan in fourth place.[40] The combined vote of McLachlan and Morrison would have been sufficient to place the outcome of the election in doubt. Given the divisions between the AMW and the UMW locally and the rivalry between the CCF and the Communists nationally, a united labour ticket was unlikely in 1935. But the results underlined yet again the potential for the election of a workers' Member of Parliament in this area. That possibility would not be realized until the time of the next Dominion election in 1940.[41]

In McLachlan's case it is impossible to separate the personality from the politics. Many workers were voting for McLachlan in recognition of his long career in defence of the workers' interests. They were not necessarily voting for a "Soviet Canada," a slogan that was no longer promoted by the party in 1935; much of McLachlan's publicity simply described him as "the people's candidate." But those who voted for McLachlan were clearly endorsing the region's most famous, even notorious, advocate of the class struggle. McLachlan had received the largest vote of any of his election efforts since 1921, and the election helped shore up his faith in the future triumph of his class. His characteristic comment remained the same as in previous elections: "The campaign is over, but the class struggle is still going on."[42]

The United Front

The class struggle continued, but in 1935 it was also changing shape. Following the October election, McLachlan travelled to Toronto to attend some of the most important meetings in the history of the Canadian left. In November 1935 the Communist Party of Canada and the Workers' Unity League formally adopted a new strategy. The policy of the united front had already been approved at the Seventh Congress of the Communist International in the summer of 1935. Seven years earlier the International had propounded a set of revolutionary policies suitable for the anticipated acceleration of the class struggle. Now the International was endorsing a change of course that would be known as the united front – a policy of alliances to increase the unity of the working class and oppose the rise of war and fascism. Instead of denouncing other parties on the left, Communists would attempt to establish working alliances with them; and instead of promoting separate radical unions, Communists would unite with existing labour organizations.[43]

The endorsement of the united-front policy in Canada has sometimes been described as an example of the party's willingness to make abrupt changes in policy upon the receipt of the latest orders from Moscow. But there was nothing sudden or unexpected about the change in party line that year, and it enjoyed support among the party membership. From the frustrations of isolation it was an attempt to return to the mainstream of the labour and radical movements in Canada. By 1935 the Communist Party's most successful efforts were those in which it took up genuinely popular causes such as the fight for unemployment insurance and industrial unionism, the On-to-Ottawa Trek, and the free-speech fights. As the clouds of war again appeared in Europe and Asia, the threat of war and fascism was never far from the minds of these working-class internationalists. The 1934 slogan – "Canada is Ripe for Socialism" – now gave way to the rallying cry of 1935 – "Toward a Canadian People's Front."[44]

McLachlan was sympathetic to the new policy and welcomed its formal acceptance. Already in February 1935 he and Tom McEwen, on behalf of the WUL, had launched an appeal to unite organized labour in Canada in "one all-inclusive labour union federation." This was a far-reaching proposal that envisaged cooperation even with the most conservative of the national unions in Quebec and the railway brotherhoods in the AFL. It can be regarded as one of the early domestic versions of the united front which preceded the decisions of the Communist International in July 1935. The WUL appeal was for a form of unity in common action or by merger of the existing federations; it was to be achieved on the basis of a program of union democracy and militant struggle. These principles were similar to those of an earlier united-front appeal which McLachlan had advanced in 1922, and they remained central to McLachlan's view of the united front in 1935.[45]

Later in the year, following the meetings of the Communist International and the circulation of key documents such as Georgi Dimitrov's speeches, McLachlan's views remained consistent. Dimitrov was a prestigious figure: a Bulgarian Communist charged with burning down the Reichstag in 1933 and then acquitted in a sensational trial, he became a spokesman for the causes of anti-fascism and the united front; in 1935 he was general secretary of the Communist International. In the pages of the *Nova Scotia Miner* McLachlan published an excerpt from one of Dimitrov's speeches underlining the principle that the united front was a form of "unity in action" and the importance of maintaining independence even when entering into short-term and long-term agreements for joint action. Besides, Dimitrov had stated, "The chief stress in all this must be laid on developing mass action locally, to be carried out by the local organizations through local agreements."[46]

These would be McLachlan's touchstones in the events that followed, even as he endorsed the united front at meetings of the party's Central

Committee in Toronto in November 1935: "The basic conditions are a threat of war and fascism and a continual threat of the worsened condition of the working class. These are the conditions under which we have got to go out from this plenum and hunt for every ally we can get, and build up this great united front we are talking about."

In an extended report to the Toronto meeting, McLachlan returned to an analysis of the results of the 1935 election. There were good reasons for optimism. The defeat of the Tories, in both the Dominion election and in provincial elections, showed a "big sweep towards the Liberal Party." But, he warned, "we must not interpret that as an endorsation of liberalism. It is not an endorsation. It is a vote of vengeance against Bennett and his 'Iron Heel' policies. We must emphasize this everywhere." Accordingly, there was much to be done:

What does this mean? This means that the huge masses are moving. There are other people besides the Communists who are fishing in troubled waters. We heard about Aberhart and McBrien and Stevens. All of these people see their opportunity, and unless we do something, they certainly will do it, and we have to run a neck-to-neck race with these people, to get leadership of the people who are discontented with the old parties. That is going to be our chief task, amongst the women, the youth, among the farmers and the general workers throughout the country.

Then McLachlan turned to the issue of trade-union policy. In Nova Scotia this was above all the question of the AMW. The election campaign, he argued, was a practical example of the united front in action: "The election did more for wiping out that split among the miners than any other effort during the last two years." There were probably as many of his campaign workers from the UMW as from the AMW. Out of that experience working side by side came a remarkable document signed by equal numbers of members from the two local unions at the No. 11 mine in Glace Bay. They had called for a convention representing members of the two unions to begin uniting the miners in one union, and McLachlan heartily approved of the movement: "The meeting was to take place the night I was leaving. I know in No. 2 it was endorsed, at Victoria and Sydney Mines it was endorsed and they are for endorsation in Waterford on this united front movement. At every place they were all sending delegates to ascertain if they can lay the basis for one union of miners in Nova Scotia."

Would this mean returning to the UMW or would it mean, as McLachlan hoped, "one union that would be a Nova Scotia union"? Was it possible simply to ask the miners to return to the UMW? To McLachlan the answer was clear: "You cannot walk down and get into a miners' meeting down there with a cut and dried proposition and say: 'You ought to all go back into the U.M.W.A.'" The reason was simple enough: the existing UMW officers had fought long and hard to blacklist AMW miners and so, before any reforms could take place, there must be first a change in officers. "It may be that if the miners were united and these officers eliminated that it would not be such a very hard job to get them into the Mine Worker Union or the A.F.L., but that requires considerably better work, and it would be wrong to go there now in the face of the split in existence, and then attempt to unite the miners in the U.M.W.A. and precipitate a new question among them." In short, the reunification strategy should be pursued without haste and from the bottom up, and in due course one could expect a united union and militant policies among the coal miners. His report ended on a note of caution: "With patient work unity will be advanced."[47]

The outcome of the discussion was no surprise. The Central Committee pronounced itself in accord with the decisions of the International and undertook to "quickly proceed with the reorientation of its tactical line in accordance with the changed international situation and the concrete development of the situation in Canada." All signs pointed towards "a people's front" and a new emphasis on promoting unity in labour struggles. The underlying tension in the discussions was never resolved in the meetings. For some of the party leaders, the next step was obvious: "The cause of trade union unity will receive a tremendous stimulus by the rapid development of the unification of the two most important sections of the trade union movement, the Workers' Unity League and the American Federation of Labor." But from McLachlan's perspective, this was not the only way to construct a united front. It could also be done more cautiously, and it could be done without loss of independence or principle. This was the view McLachlan now took to the meetings of the WUL.

"We stretch out our hands in solidarity to every worker. Let us work out this united front of labor together brothers and sisters." Again McLachlan served the WUL as the symbol of struggle and unity. The cover of the latest issue of *Unity*, the WUL's magazine, featured a portrait of McLachlan – looking older and more feeble than in his most familiar portraits – and quoted his appeal. When the almost 150 delegates assembled they had McLachlan's statement in their hands:

> History demands of us, of the working class, and especially of members of the Workers' Unity League unions, that we stretch out our hands in solidarity to every worker who is willing to struggle in defence of such democratic rights as we have and for all-round better conditions of life.
>
> This congress of the Workers' Unity League must work out a program for unity of the scattered forces of labor in Canada. Out of two millions of working people in this country only some three hundred thousand are organized, and organized in four different federations. The great rank and file in all of these unions are showing a willingness to fight against a further lowering of wages, and for adequate unemployment relief, for real insurance and against reactionary laws, such as Section 98 and the hounding of the working class by orders in council.
>
> Can this congress draft such a program that will help to unite the workers of Canada? That's our task and we shall try. We shall honestly and sincerely, for this congress, present to the working class of Canada a program of unity.
>
> Not an iron-clad and fixed program of unity that cannot be changed, but a program of unity open to amendment and discussion from any section of workers in Canada who have come to the conclusion that the workers of this country must struggle unitedly for a better life. It is in this spirit that we stretch out our hands to every section of our hard-pressed brothers in every town and city saying let us work out this united front of labor together.[48]

It was a strong statement, fully in accord with the policy of the united front. But the wording was careful. McLachlan had not neglected to underline the importance of a negotiated unity, based on common demands and adapted to local situations. In McLachlan's view, this would be the only worthwhile kind of unity, not "unity at all costs" but the kind of unity he had always preached – "unity in action."

In these last days of the WUL, few of the 150 delegates doubted that the time had come to "show the way ahead." Existing unions would be drawn together, and organizing efforts would be extended among farmers and youth, women and French-Canadian workers, and in major industries such as textiles, auto, and steel which were not yet organized into unions. "Patiently and persistently," urged Tom McEwen, the WUL would lead the way towards "the bulwark of a single all-inclusive federated body of Canadian trade unionists." Under his guidance the delegates unanimously adopted a resolution entitled "The Road to Trade Union Unity." Each union would "take up the question of unity in its own industry and on the basis of the concrete conditions prevailing in each industry, strive to establish one union of all workers in such industry." The Dominion Council of the WUL would provide "guidance to its affiliated unions and help them to achieve unity in the speediest fashion."[49]

McLachlan's own account also conveyed a spirit of optimism about the new strategy:

They came from Cape Breton Island, down by the Atlantic Ocean; from Vancouver Island, over on the Pacific Ocean – 3,500 miles apart. Needle trades workers from old Quebec and Ontario rubbed shoulders with loggers and miners from Alberta, British Columbia and Nova Scotia. Food workers, steel and metal workers, fur dressers and dyers, furniture workers, cooks, waiters, housewives, domestic servants, dressmakers, textile workers, window cleaners, agricultural hands, shoemakers, loggers, nickel miners, gold miners, coal miners and coal handlers and truckers – their delegates were all there. They exchanged experiences. They worked in committees together. Sometimes they disagreed. Most of the time they agreed. The Convention was like a blacksmith's forge – the sparks flew as we hammered out the policies by which to unite and organize Canadian Labor.

He described the agenda for Canadian labour in a series of broad challenges. How to organize the great majority of unorganized workers – "Shouldn't we all get together to give a hand to the 1,700,000 Canadians who are yet untouched by trade unionism?" How to help prevent a new world war – "Shouldn't all Canadian unions get together to enforce working-class sanctions against the bandit Mussolini?" There was more, including the hope of a common "United Labor Legislative Program" presenting demands to the Dominion government jointly with the TLC and the ACCL. McLachlan could even foresee a new political party to unite the working-class vote in future elections – "And why can't we cooperate, brothers and sisters of other trade unions, to lay a foundation for a broad people's political party?"

"My firm opinion is that we grappled with these life-or-death questions in a proper way," McLachlan wrote after the convention. "We are prepared to go more than half-way to unite with our brothers and sisters ... We realize, more keenly than ever, that unity is the lifeline of Labor." This would be the last national meeting of the WUL, but he concluded the proceedings with no sense of defeat or despair. McLachlan remained certain that he was on the right side of history and quoted an old Scottish proverb to underline the urgency of the moment:

Time and tide wait for no man ... and neither do the reactionaries who would like to continue the avalanche of wage cutting or the reactionaries who'd like to establish Fascism here in Canada! We fighters for trade union unity have no time to waste!

The day will dawn, sooner or later, when the workers of Canada shall be united solidly in one mighty federation of labor unions. We want that day to be as soon as possible ... When the history of Canadian Labor is written I'm pretty sure that our efforts to hammer out correct policies at the Third National Convention of the Workers' Unity League will be recognized as a worthwhile contribution. They are good policies. Let's roll up our sleeves and put them into practice from Cape Breton Island – way across the Dominion – clean to Vancouver Island.[50]

McLachlan ended these weeks in Toronto still the grand old man of the class struggle. He was even re-elected president of the WUL. If he had doubts about the road ahead, he was not articulating them publicly. McLachlan returned to Nova Scotia identified in *The Worker* as "the foremost exponent of industrial unionism – one industry, one union – among the miners of Nova Scotia."[51]

"Unity in Action"

His confidence did not last. In the six months after the Toronto meetings, McLachlan was perturbed by the loud note of urgency coming out of Toronto. History was moving more rapidly than he expected. At the October 1935 meetings of the AFL, John L. Lewis delivered his famous blow to the jaw of the carpenters' union president, William Hutcheson. The next month Lewis was leading other dissident leaders in forming the Committee for Industrial Organization. These events accelerated the drive for industrial unionism in North America. They also created new opportunities for labour radicals who supported the idea of a united front. In a few short months the old points of reference – the craft unionism of the American "Separation" of Labor, the treacherous personality of John L. Lewis – seemed to be forgotten in the rush to endorse the ideal of trade-union unity.[52]

Unity was needed immediately, Joseph Salsberg had argued at the WUL meetings: "not ten years from now, not bye and bye – but as speedily as is humanly possible!" Salsberg himself had been a leader of one of the red unions in the garment industry and was a popular personality in the neighbourhoods around Spadina Avenue in Toronto; he would be one of the Communists elected to the Ontario legislature in 1943. Like many of the new generation of labour radicals in the 1930s, Salsberg counted himself an admirer of McLachlan – indeed, in a kind of tribute to McLachlan, he liked to be known to his supporters as "J.B." As the party official responsible for trade-union policies, Salsberg was determined to press hard for the rapid completion of the united front. But, unlike McLachlan, he described the strategy in the simplest terms: "We favor merging with A.F. of L. unions in most industries ... we favor organizing the unorganized workers in A.F. of L. unions wherever possible."[53]

To McLachlan this sounded too much like a policy of "unity at all costs," the very thing he had cautioned against in the Toronto meetings. Although dismayed by news of how easily some of the radical unions were coming into the fold of the AFL, in the early months of 1936 McLachlan had better hopes for the coal miners. Ever since the AMW had failed in its key tests of strength, McLachlan had been doubtful it could ever replace the UMW entirely, but now the campaign for trade-union unity opened new possibilities. Was it too much to expect that the coal miners could be reunited in a new union, independent of the UMW and suitably equipped for internal democracy and militant struggle? The AMW itself might have to disappear, but McLachlan believed that the radicals at this stage were in a position to bargain from strength.

In Cape Breton, steps towards unity had actually started months earlier, with meetings of local unions from both sides of the split in November 1935. At the beginning of January 1936 the AMW executive board approved a list of eight propositions for discussion at joint meetings of the locals of both unions. The aim was "to build one united miners' union in Nova Scotia which is pledged to struggle for a better life" and the emphasis throughout was on "complete democracy inside the union." A few weeks later the AMW secretary-treasurer, Robert Stewart, was reporting "a good start on unity in the ranks of the miners, we have been able to get a joint meeting at every mine." Joint committees of the two unions had been established at all the mines, and soon they would come together at the Arena Rink in Glace Bay to push the unity movement forward.[54]

Behind the scenes Stewart was obviously being coached by McLachlan. The key statement in the process, the proposed joint report for the committees, for instance, was drafted by Stewart, who passed it along to McLachlan – "I gave it to the old man to to put the finishing touch on it." McLachlan's role was not publicly acknowledged, however; it was necessary to maintain the principle that the movement was a rank-and-file initiative.[55]

One passage, which carried a note of nostalgia for the heyday of radical unionism, was undoubtedly McLachlan's work: "We all agree that the split was caused to win back for us our old tradition of fighting power in the world labor movement. It must now be agreed upon that this will make us a fighting machine that will stand solid to fight the operators of Nova Scotia who have taken advantage of our divided ranks." The proposed steps towards a merger also owed something to McLachlan, for the radicals hoped to repeat the successful formula of 1917, when McLachlan had engineered the amalgamation of the old PWA and the early UMW into the original Amalgamated Mine Workers: a joint convention of the two unions would be held, with equal representation from each union at each mine; the officers of both unions would then step down in favour of provisional officers; this would be followed by inauguration of a new union, under a name that was still to be determined.[56]

When Annie Buller arrived in late January in the middle of a snowstorm, she stayed at Steele's Hill and went over the situation with McLachlan. Officially, she was on a trip to organize labour clubs for women, but it must have been clear to party leaders that she was one of the Toronto-based organizers who had McLachlan's confidence. Buller was impressed by the local progress and sent in an optimistic report: "The men in my opinion are working very well and moving in the right direction. The basis for a mass meeting as well as for a convention is being laid."[57] In general it seems clear that the local radicals were acting independently in hammering out the details of the merger, again confirming McLachlan's belief that the construction of the united front would be the result of local agreements. At this stage, Stewart and Buller also discussed with McLachlan "a proposition about the old man." This could well have been a proposal to put McLachlan's name forward for an official role in the anticipated meetings or even an honorary office in the new union.[58]

There was an anxious undercurrent in this strategy. It was not certain how the UMW would respond to the initiative. UMW officials would be coming in from Washington "to look the situation over,"

Buller noted: "If our people work well I think that we can speed things up in a very short time. Silby would like to see some of the old leadership including Dan cleaned out but of course his idea would be to get John L to do the housecleaning. That of course has its dangers for us and of course our line must be that the miners here have their elections and appoint the people that they want." The best local strategy, Stewart agreed, was to move quickly: "We are trying to get the mass meeting arranged before all them cowboys get back from Washington, so that we will have the foundation laid and a convention proposed and then they cannot very well buck it." All this reflected McLachlan's thinking. It is less likely that McLachlan could accept the more or less positive assessment Buller and Stewart attached to McLachlan's sometime comrade, subsequent enemy, Silby Barrett, who was now counted as an ally in the struggle for unity.[59]

The reconciliation advanced steadily in the following weeks. At the beginning of February a committee of fourteen miners was chosen by the locals of the two unions at the Glace Bay mines, and this unity committee began meeting regularly. The proceedings proved surprisingly harmonious to local observers, a welcome relief after four years of fierce rivalry. At one of its first meetings in February the committee accepted the plan for a joint convention of the membership of the two unions in order to "unite the miners of the province into one union"; the only real controversy was whether a representative of the UMW international office should be invited to such a meeting, and this was voted down.[60] By early March there was a short five-point agreement – "to organize a Union to fight for higher wages rates, the enforcement of the Coal Mines Regulation Act and for increased compensation for injured workmen." Little more was said, except that the union would have complete autonomy and that final decisions on contracts and officers would be in the hands of the membership.[61]

At this point, however, McLachlan's strategy was abandoned. No joint-membership meeting was organized; nor was the unity committee able to convince the UMW locals to accept simultaneous conventions of the two unions as in 1917. Instead, the committee brought together the officers of the two unions. They remained in conference for a long four-hour session at the end of March. The unity committee was thus

presiding over an accommodation between the two labour bureauc-
racies, and in the end this was the meeting that decided the course
of events.

When those sessions were over, Stewart announced, on behalf of the
AMW, that his union was satisfied with the proposals advanced by the
unity committee. On the part of the UMW, however, Morrison was
making no concessions: "We have our district and our international
constitutions and we are not going to depart or deviate from them." As
far as Morrison was concerned, those interested in unity could join the
UMW: "To those who saw fit to leave the UMW, he said, the door was
ever open for them to return." Morrison's hard line on constitutional
continuity was unexpected, and Stewart objected: "He did not think
the men were assembled today to discuss the respective merits of each
union but to merge the two of them and make one out of them. He
scoffed at the 'open door' offer of the UMW heads and claimed there
were men in the mines today who would never return to the UMW."

The debate ran back and forth, much of it around the question of
whether District 26 already enjoyed autonomy within the international
union. On this point McLachlan's name was invoked – not as the most
memorable example of the international union's betrayal of the district, but as the union officer who in 1919 had insisted on the original
provision for district autonomy within the UMW. According to Morrison's interpretation of local labour history, that provision was still in
effect: "The international has never interfered with us, but gave us
generous assistance whenever called on."

There was a fundamental weakness in the radical strategy, and the
UMW leaders seized on it with a vengeance. For all their experience with
the UMW, the desire for unity was overwhelming and most of the
radicals were prepared to suspend their suspicions. In the end, Stewart
himself agreed that the AMW was prepared to pay the price of unity:
"We are giving up more than you fellows; we came out on a principle
and will go back on one." Clarie Gillis, one of the AMW delegates on
the unity committee, spelled out the implications of their position most
clearly: "The men had reached a crossroad now and the only logical
thing to do was to go back into the UMW, the other road was impossible.
Go back into the UMW, he advised, and make it a fighting organization."

The meeting ended with a unanimous endorsement of the unity committee's recommendations. Morrison made it clear that "he would have to be satisfied that there was nothing in the proposal that was conflicting with the international or district constitution of the United Mine Workers of America." Although the newspaper headlines celebrated the achievement – "Rival Unions Agree on Terms of Merger" – the key decision of this long-awaited reconciliation was that the agreement would now be forwarded to John L. Lewis for consideration.[62]

This was McLachlan's last attempt to lead the coal miners, and it was failing. There was little McLachlan could do to control the course of events. He had championed the cause of local democracy in the construction of the united front, and now it was necessary to submit to the consequences. It was true that the rank-and-file meetings and the unity committee had produced an unfortunate outcome. But in his comments in the *Nova Scotia Miner* McLachlan framed the issue in terms of union democracy: "If there is one thing the miners of Nova Scotia are fighting, and have led all the workers in Canada, is their struggle against this shoving the rank and file into a corner." Even a return to the UMW was not totally unacceptable to McLachlan, provided suitable terms for a merger could be reached. Readers of the *Nova Scotia Miner* were reminded yet again to support a principled basis of unity: "The miners of Nova Scotia should unite on the basis set forth by the unity committee, with Lewis if they may, without him if they must."[63]

McLachlan was dismayed by how rapidly the discussion of unity was transformed into a discussion of the terms for readmission of AMW members to the UMW. In his view, one of the causes for this development was the ambiguity of advice coming out of Communist Party headquarters. Even among those radicals who were not members of the party (and Stewart at least was still a party member), the opinions of the party, especially as conveyed through its publications, were a factor in framing local decisions. At the end of January, Stewart had expressed his confusion over the contradictory messages on party trade-union policy contained in the current issue of *Unity*, which included statements by J.B. Salsberg and Charles Sims: "Who is right? you or Joe? Listen Charlie, is there two of you there who are of the same mind on unity?"[64]

In particular, Stewart, who was probably reflecting discussions with McLachlan on this point, stated that it was misleading to focus so much on the AFL convention of 1935, "leaving the impression that we only started after they had decided at the A.F. of L. convention." After all, Lewis himself admitted that the AFL was guilty of "25 years of unbroken failure" on the issue of industrial unionism. "The first thing we will find the workers asking, is why should we go back then, this we will have to be careful of. Tell me who is right, you or Joe. Boy listen, I have been reading articles in the Worker and our other papers and it is looking like we are sending them back without any kind of democracy. We should stress the policy, we will agree to amalgamate on fighting for higher wages and better conditions."[65] In the *Nova Scotia Miner* McLachlan objected to patronizing comments in the WUL magazine and in *The Worker* on the Nova Scotia situation and argued that "it is useless to say that Lewis will not agree to such proposals. Lewis can be whipped into line." McLachlan also continued to publish reports concerning the negotiations between the Lumber Workers' Industrial Union and the United Brotherhood of Carpenters and Joiners, examples that showed how other unions were also attempting to negotiate from strength in establishing conditions for unity.[66]

For McLachlan personally, the most galling feature of the whole process was the miraculous transformation of Lewis during the last months of 1935. This dramatic turn to the left by Lewis coincided with the adoption of the united front and obviously spoke to the opportunities available for union expansion at the end of the Great Depression. Still, the rehabilitation of Lewis did not sit well with many Canadian radicals, especially among the coal miners; one Alberta coal miner wrote to the WUL magazine to complain at the beginning of 1936: "It was a bombshell to me to see John L. Lewis as one of the star contributors for 'Unity,' both in the November and December numbers." Accounts of the UMW international convention in Washington reported that Lewis now stood in the vanguard of "progressive industrial unionism," and his speeches were reprinted in the party press; by June, Lewis was being acclaimed as the "fighting leader" of the new flagship of industrial unionism in North America, the CIO.[67]

McLachlan's established judgment of Lewis was repeated in the title of one article in the *Nova Scotia Miner*: "Everything Charged Against AFL by Lewis He Does in UMWA – Only More So." Now McLachlan was not repudiating the cause of trade union unity or the idea of the CIO, but he insisted that Lewis – of all people – could not be trusted to defend union democracy: "No man on earth is good enough, just enough, or wise enough to have such power over the democratic rights of men, and no man on earth except a swollen, impudent, aspiring fascist would accept such power even handed to him on a gold plate." Specifically, he pointed out that Lewis was no friend of independent political action – he had threatened to withhold a promised contribution of $100,000 from the United Automobile Workers unless the union repudiated its recent decision to support a labour party in preference to endorsing President F.D. Roosevelt for re-election. Nor could McLachlan ignore the fact that Lewis had forced a roll-call vote at the UMW convention to give himself as president the independent power to depose district officials, a power he had of course exercised since the early 1920s but, apparently, without sufficient authority.

In the last surviving issues of the *Nova Scotia Miner*, McLachlan continued to repeat his basic message concerning Lewis, whom he regarded as the dictator of a once democratic union: "To lower the flag of trade union democracy now in the face of the flushed and victorious Lewis would be treachery to all who suffered in the past. We are for unity, but not as beaten and conquered slaves who actually kiss their chains to get into the UMW."[68]

Step by step, the miners were returning to the UMW. And what was worse, they were returning empty-handed. It was clear that the international union was not prepared to be governed by the outcome of the local negotiations in Nova Scotia. Indeed, the UMW would do no more than absolutely necessary to absorb the AMW membership. "As far as the A.M.W. is concerned here, there is no activity at present on their behalf," District Secretary-Treasurer A.A. McKay, himself a former "McLachlanite," wrote complacently to Washington at the end of March 1936. "It appears that the men who were members of the A.M.W. would like to return again to the U.M.W. en masse, and within a short period a large number of those who left the organization will again become members of the U.M.W."[69]

This was a deliberately misleading report on the outcome of the negotiations and the discussions that month, but it helped elicit the desired response from Lewis. Soon afterwards Lewis responded to the unity agreement of March 1936 in cautious terms, commending it as "meritorious and constructive" but noting calmly that all policies and procedures must be in accordance with the UMW constitution. Indeed, all local arrangements would be subject to his personal approval. In the interim he was delegating the authority to a two-man commission consisting of his trusted local lieutenants, Dan Willie Morrison and Silby Barrett, both long-time adversaries of McLachlan.[70]

These were alarming signs and several key AMW leaders, including former president John Alex MacDonald, who had been a key member of the unity committee, announced their dissatisfaction. But it was too late to call a halt to the process and at a meeting on 26 April the AMW voted itself out of existence. Locals from the Sydney Mines district did not attend this final meeting and continued on independently until 1938. By this time the original local agreement containing guarantees of local autonomy and internal democracy had been replaced by a set of guarantees that were modest in the extreme: AMW members would be accepted in the UMW without initiation fees or penalties and would have all the rights and privileges of members. And there was an unexpected kicker: a group of former AMW leaders were asked to sign pledges of loyalty to the international union; according to Clarie Gillis, this was a sign of "bad faith" on the part of the UMW, and Joseph Nearing pleaded in vain with Barrett to "come together for the good of the district and bury the hatchet." Barrett refused, and to humiliate the radicals further, he vowed that under no conditions would he ever accept the admission of Robert Stewart into the UMW. With these arrangements, subsequently approved by the international executive board, the road to unity was completed.[71]

Looking back over this strange course of events McLachlan was appalled. He had championed the process of joint action by the local miners, and he believed he had been loyal to the principles of the united front. Even if the ideal of an entirely new union was not realistic, it was not worth surrendering the prospects for reform of the UMW. The opportunity to guarantee union democracy and local autonomy in a reorganized union had been abandoned. Probably it was unrealistic, too, for McLachlan to believe that he could control the course of events from behind the scenes. But the last thing he expected was total capitulation to the UMW. As the events unfolded, the AMW had stumbled from one concession to the next and completed its dissolution with no guarantees of any kind for the future of the miners' union.

For McLachlan, the road to unity had ended in unnecessary and inappropriate compromises. The tactical priorities of the party and the intransigence of the UMW had left the Nova Scotia miners little choice. The enormous rhetoric in support of trade-union unity was widely supported by the coal miners, and it was not possible to turn back. The coal miners would struggle on, once again inside the UMW. As for McLachlan, he was outmanoeuvred by the international union. And he believed, too, that he was forsaken by his party.

"The Sad March to the Right"

McLachlan could not be reconciled. He watched in despair as the coal miners returned to the fold and the UMW exacted its revenge on the radicals. His discontent became an issue at local Communist Party headquarters. With the restoration of District 26 virtually accomplished, party leaders were anxious to put an end to the controversies about reunification. The *Nova Scotia Miner*, still recognized as the voice of the radicals in the coalfields, was expected to fall in line.

During these months, party leader Tim Buck was writing directly to McLachlan to criticize his continuing attacks both on Lewis and on Woodsworth. But McLachlan could not be persuaded to lay down his arms. George MacEachern, a young steelworker from Sydney who admired McLachlan as the heroic veteran of the local class struggle, has recalled McLachlan's last appearance at a party meeting. To MacEachern, who had led a successful campaign to organize the steelworkers and was now bringing his union into the CIO, McLachlan suddenly seemed to be out of step with the times:

I remember Jim at the last meeting of the party district bureau. I must have been sitting close to him because I was able to whisper to him. When the party organizer Bill Findlay charged him with causing confusion among the miners with his articles in the *Nova Scotia Miner*, Jim didn't answer very much but he was grumbling. I know he was upset. He admitted that what he was writing was bound to cause confusion. I said, "Well why don't you tell the meeting that you'll try to get the paper in line with the needs of the miners, and give up these continual attacks on John L. Lewis that were untimely anyway." He studied that for a while and the only answer he gave was, "Oh, to hell with it." He got up and shuffled around, back and forth, and snorted, and after a while he left for home. I didn't see Jim to talk to him from that date.[72]

Shortly afterwards McLachlan resigned from the party. His departure was noted on his police file as early as 25 May 1936, but McLachlan did not make a public declaration. From Toronto, Tim Buck, who had originally recruited McLachlan into the party back in the red summer of 1922, wrote expressing the view that McLachlan's break with the leadership could not be based on any real political differences: "Needless to say, we feel that your action can be based upon nothing less than a misunderstanding of the political line of the comintern."[73]

McLachlan responded to Buck in a personal letter written at Steele's Hill on the night of 13 June 1936. It was a detailed and emotional letter spelling out his reasons. He sat rigidly at his desk, with a few letters and clippings scattered before him, and pounded out the letter on his old typewriter. His daughter Eva vividly remembered the night. She understood the significance of the occasion and asked her father if she could keep a copy of the letter.[74]

In two and a half long, densely typed pages, McLachlan took up an explanation of his withdrawal from the party. He strongly rejected Buck's claim that he had failed to understand the decisions of the Communist International in 1935. On the contrary, wrote McLachlan, "I can assure you that I have paid the greatest attention to the line laid down by the VII Congress, specially the part dealing with trade union work, and have read everything I could get my hands on. I am absolutely

convinced, that in the 'Nova Scotia Miner,' I am following the line laid
down by the party. On the other hand, I firmly believe the party in
Canada has gone badly to the right."

These were strong charges, and McLachlan began by ridiculing the
party's unprincipled application of the party line: a union in Toronto
had been advised to leave the WUL and granted disaffiliation "*because
the boss did not like the W. U. L.*"; and in the Mine Workers' Union of
Canada in the west party members supported a resolution to lay off
miners over fifty years of age on the ground that older men "could not
produce as much coal *as the boss had a right to expect.*"

Then he returned to the heart of the dispute: the Amalgamated Mine
Workers of Nova Scotia. According to McLachlan, information about the
democratic process by which unity was being negotiated in Nova Scotia was
"deliberately suppressed" by the party. In the pages of *Unity*, events in
western Canada were held up as a model: "The miners of the west were
putting over 'stirring events' while Nova Scotia was doing nothing." And
when *The Worker* did publish a dispatch distributed by a labour press
agency, which briefly reported the terms of unity desired in Nova Scotia, a
final few lines were added stating "*that no one, however expected that Lewis
would ever grant these points.*" Such deliberate efforts to misrepresent the
situation in Nova Scotia were nothing more than a form of betrayal:

You know, Tim, what would happen to a soldier who would
preach such hopelessness, and spread despair and defeatism in the
very middle of a fight, as these three fearful added lines were
intended to do. He would have his useless brains blown out. Again,
the very manner in which the "Worker" sometimes characterizes
the objections of honest workers to the methods used to bring
about unity shows how far to the right the draft had become. It
was said these workers "got off a lot of hot air." "That they were
blowing off steam, etc."

At the same time, McLachlan's ancient enemy Lewis was to be the
subject of "frantic attempts to say as many nice things as possible about
a traitor and scoundrel." But Lewis, McLachlan warned, could not be
trusted as a supporter of industrial unionism or much else: "Lewis is a

wrecker and would wreck that industrial union rather than see it take
a political working class stand." Lewis's personal history was too well
known to be repeated, but in its rush to embrace Lewis the party was
also forgetting its own well-established critique of labour bureaucrats:

> The party's statement in the 'Clarion' of June 6th says: 'We must
> be on the most friendly and brotherly relations *with all trade
> unionists.*' Such a statement is pretty good theology worthy of a
> Methodist Conference, but in the trade union movement where
> the labor lieutenants of the boss have assumed the role of dictators
> on a prince's income extracted from poverty stricken workers,
> one, if honest to his class, must use whatever power he may have
> to expose and fight the scoundrels. The 'Nova Scotia Miner' is
> blamed for telling the miners the truth about Lewis. I refuse to
> deceive them either by my word or by my silence in regard to his
> dictatorship, his robbery or his treachery.

This preference to build unity from the top down rather than from
the bottom up showed more than anything else "the extent the party
has gone to the right." In all this there was a principle at stake, McLachlan insisted: "The core of true unity is found in the plain demands of
the great rank and file, whatever these demands may be, the core of the
activity of the party has been the wishes of the top leadership."

Finally, McLachlan scolded Buck for stating that the party would not
continue to support the *Nova Scotia Miner*. The paper, McLachlan
claimed, had never depended on party support: "The party never put
a cent, in its life, into the paper, but over and over again the paper has
given money to the party." He referred back to the controversy in
1929–30, when the party representative "did his best to destroy the
paper." Now he heard the same disparaging talk again in party meetings: "In 1929, party leaders here said I was too old and out of date and
should be out of the movement. In 1935 my age was given as a reason
why I should be dropped and today the talk both here and in Toronto
about ending the Nova Scotia Miner is just the same old story in
another form to try and silence me. I am not going to be silenced, the
paper won't die, nor am I getting out of the movement."

As McLachlan went back over old ground, bitter feelings rose to the surface: "As I look back over the years, it appears to me now that I was always more or less of a misfit in the party. I was always under a kind of humiliating supervision." The party had watched him closely at the time of the OBU controversy in 1924–25 and "accused me, to others, of trying to get into the OBU and had high party officials in other countries write me about this 'crime.'" Successive party organizers had also conspired against him: "To get me out of the movement was the one consuming ambition of Barker while he was here. You know that history pretty well. Luck thought I 'should be shot' if there was no other way of silencing me. Bill Findlay being more humane only tries to liquidate the 'Miner' so as to silence me for the good of the party." All this added up to a pattern of efforts "if not to get me out of the party, at least to silence me."

It was a difficult letter to write, and there was a subdued note of anguish running through these lines. Buck is referred to repeatedly in a reproachful first person – "You know, Tim …," "Tim, I can remember …," "Now, now, Tim …" McLachlan ended on a stern note of regret for the party and comrades he had known: "I refuse to follow the party in Canada in its sad march to the right in order to secure its blessing for the Nova Scotia Miner, and I am not going to give up my activity in the working class movement while I live. Therefore, in order not to embarrass the party further, I resigned from it completely, as Comrade Finlay informed you. This matter is settled and ended insofar as I am concerned." McLachlan finished the letter and signed his name "With Deepest Comradely Regrets."

Months later there was one final scene in McLachlan's departure from the party. This took place in September at a public meeting at McRae's Arena in Glace Bay. Some 500 people had come out to hear a speech by the visiting British Communist MP Willie Gallacher. As a member of the Executive Committee of the Communist International, he was a spokesman for the united front, and according to the local press, Gallacher's speeches during his tour of Nova Scotia focused mainly on the united front and the struggle against war and fascism.[75]

But in Glace Bay the highlight of the meeting was an emotional exchange concerning McLachlan's resignation. Undoubtedly Gallacher had been briefed on local conditions. In response to questions about McLachlan, he replied that McLachlan was not expelled from the Communist Party but "left of his own accord." This assertion was disputed by several members of the audience and the uproar continued for several minutes. Then McLachlan, who had been watching quietly from his seat, asked permission to speak. The audience listened respectfully as he came forward and addressed his last public meeting.

There are differing accounts of what McLachlan said, but the fullest report of his speech is contained in police reports of the meeting:

> McLachlan declared that at a recent National Conference of the C.P. of C. it was decided to organize and lead the working class movement by taking up the main demands of the workers. In Cape Breton the miners wanted complete autonomy which John L. Lewis would not grant but reserved to himself dictatorial powers. McLachlan said that he knows John L. Lewis is a skunk as he and several others have been tramped into the mud by Lewis. McLachlan said that he was partly thrown out of the party because he would not support Lewis and he partly left the party so as to have greater freedom to express himself. For this reason Bill Findlay and local party members killed the "N.S. Miner."
>
> McLachlan declared that he loved the C.P. of C. and would die for it, but he would not accept orders contrary to his beliefs and feelings. McLachlan was heartily applauded by the crowd present.
>
> Gallagher answered McLachlan. He said that a Communist while disagreeing with a Party decision must loyally carry it out if the majority votes for it.[76]

For the first time, this speech confirmed publicly what McLachlan had written to Buck months earlier. The issue was not a simple one. It was true that McLachlan "had had his fill of the Communist Party," but there is little evidence that he was undergoing what some writers have described as a "conversion to a milder form of socialism through the Co-operative Commonwealth Federation."[77] Instead, he was criticizing the Communist Party from the point of view of an uncompromising revolutionary socialist. On his side, McLachlan claimed the virtues of consistency and principle. Far from endorsing the CCF, McLachlan was accusing the Communist Party of giving up too much and steering too far from its true course. McLachlan could not follow the party in such a "sad march to the right," and for this reason he was forced to step aside.

Bend or break? A bureaucratic unionism, a politics of compromise – all of McLachlan's experience told him that these were not the forces to lead the disinherited to their emancipation. His covenant could not be broken. Now he had explained his reasons to his people. He had not betrayed his class and he had not abandoned the struggle. McLachlan did not wait for the meeting to adjourn, and for the last time he walked through the assembled crowd and out of the hall.

McLachlan (left) faces Wolvin at the hearings of the Duncan Commission in 1925; seated between them are the commissioners Hume Cronyn, K.C. (left), Sir Andrew Rae Duncan, and Father H.P. MacPherson.

Three Generations: McLachlan, Max Shur (a needle trades union organizer) and Jimmie Buller (son of Annie Buller) in Toronto, 1928.

McLachlan (left) on the *S. S. Westernland*, 1931, en route to the Soviet Union. Others are not identified.

Eight Communist leaders were arrested in 1931 and sent to Kingston Penitentiary. From left: Matthew Popovich, Tom McEwen, Tom Hill, John Boychuk, Michael Gilmore (charges were dropped in his case), Sam Carr, Tom Cacic, and Tim Buck. Malcolm Bruce is not in the picture.

McLachlan (seated, left) with Malcolm Bruce (centre) and Sam Scarlett (right). They were among the best known labour radicals in Canada during the Great Depression.

Catherine (Kate) Greenshields McLachlan (1873-1939).

N<u>o</u> 498

ELECT A WORKER TO PARLIAMENT

HIGHER WAGES

SHORTER HOURS

REPEAL SECTION 98.

RELEASE CLASS
WAR PRISONERS

J. B. McLACHLAN
COMMUNIST CANDIDATE FOR CAPE BRETON SOUTH.
Nova Scotia's outstanding fighter for the working class. Over 45 years in the Labor movement.

"Elect a Worker to Parliament." Promotional material on the 1935 election campaign – from McLachlan's RCMP file.

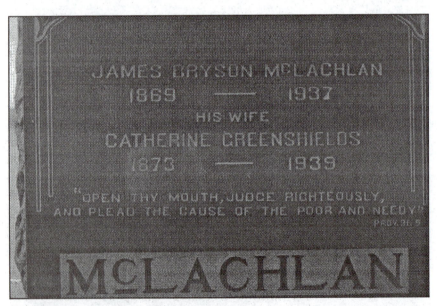

Greenwood Cemetery, Glace Bay: "Open thy mouth, judge righteously, and plead the cause of the poor and needy."

EPILOGUE

Open thy mouth, judge righteously,
and plead the cause of the poor and needy.

– Proverbs, 31:9

Out of the smoke and darkness of the meeting hall, he stepped into the street. It was still daylight. There was a salt breeze in the air and a clear sky. He looked thoughtfully up the road, where a train of coal cars was creaking across the level crossing. Sounds carried crisply in the cool air, and for a moment he thought he heard bagpipes sounding in the wind. The couplings jangled, the iron wheels pounded and crackled on the frosty rails, somewhere in the background there was a ringing bell. The sounds were almost musical in the air, and he shook his head in wonder, watching for signs of a band. The train gathered speed. The sounds drifted away. There was a ringing in his ears and the pressure of burning smoke in his chest.

Then he passed through the streets of Glace Bay, through the streets where soldiers had rolled barbed wire during the strikes and mounted police had dragged men out of their homes, past the scenes of street-corner speeches and marching parades, past the union offices and the company buildings. He walked on past the churches where priests had denounced him and the moviehouses where he answered them. He continued on past the dull stockpiles of coal, the black gold that was the currency of the industrial revolution and the cause of so much heartbreak and so many struggles for his people.

McLachlan was moving slowly now, making his way home to the old farmhouse on Steele's Hill where he could command a view of the silent hills and fields above the town. He walked past the small shops and homes of his fellow citizens, past the heavy work clothes snapping on the lines in the wind, past the women watching from their windows and the children peeking around the corners at the old man marching up the hill. He was walking home to Kate, home to their daughters and sons and their neighbours, home to his favourite horse Queenie, home to the roses he loved to cultivate, home to a sunlit room on Steele's Hill. He was walking out of the anxious struggles of the past and into the everlasting present of history.

There he died, on 3 November 1937, in the bright windowed room on the side of the old farmhouse. For some time McLachlan's declining condition had been obvious to friends and family. His face was thinning, his lungs were choking, he was coughing coal dust. After his death newspapers spoke of "two years of lingering illness" and stated that "an incurable illness numbered his days on earth." McLachlan's death certificate stated his age at sixty-eight years, eight months, twenty-four days but gave no cause of death. A more specific observation was made by D.N. Brodie, one of McLachlan's oldest comrades from the days of the Socialist Party, who was a regular visitor to his bedside during his last months. Less than a week before his death Brodie wrote an urgent letter to J.S. Woodsworth concerning McLachlan's rapid deterioration: "I presume you have heard of his illness during the past year, but probably are not acquainted with details. He contracted severely bronchial trouble while in Dorchester Penitentiary some years ago for which the doctor has been treating him ever since. The past winter it developed into T.B. He is in a dying condition and may not last more than a few weeks."[1]

The funeral took place on Sunday afternoon, 7 November. The room where McLachlan died was banked to the ceiling with flowers and wreaths sent by virtually every union local in the district, as well as from the steelworkers in Sydney, other unions, and individual friends, comrades and supporters. Hundreds of people passed through the house in single file to pay their respects. Then his closest friends and family assembled for a short service. Prayers were offered by the Reverend C.R.F. McLennan of Knox United Church. He was followed by the Reverend William T. Mercer, pastor of St Luke's United Church at Dominion No. 6, who had served as the labour candidate in that summer's provincial election. Mercer pronounced McLachlan "an honest and sincere man of upstanding qualities" whose religious views were often misunderstood: "His home-loving qualities and close affection for his family were attributes of the deceased, well known to all ... Such qualities bespoke the man he was. Though riches could have been his for the taking, he took the harder but more Christian course – the field of labour for his fellow man." McLachlan was described as "a champion of his class" and a man who "held ideals for the betterment of mankind like those of Him who went about Palestine doing good for women and children."[2]

Then the funeral procession, a mile long, carried McLachlan slowly down the hill and through the streets of Glace Bay. At the head was the coal miners' brass band from Dominion No. 6. The eight pallbearers were old friends and veterans of the local struggles: George Milley, Walter Davis, John Fortune, Alex J. McNeil, Alex McKeigan, Wesley Bond, M.A. MacKenzie, and D.N. Brodie. More than 500 miners followed on foot, and they were followed by almost 100 cars. The procession moved down the road from Steele's Hill, down Highland Street past the miners' homes, through the centre of town, past Senator's Corner, then back along Union Street and up the hill to Greenwood Cemetery.

At the graveside there were further prayers, and the band played two verses of "Nearer My God to Thee." As the family gathered around and watched, the casket was lowered into the ground, covered with flowers. There he rested, a few feet from his daughter Kate who had died so full of promise ten years earlier. In this high, secluded location on a green hillside overlooking Glace Bay, there is a measure of calm. But the Old Testament words on the polished stone remind us of the stormy life that is commemorated here: "Open thy mouth, judge righteously, and plead the cause of the poor and needy."[3]

In the pages of *The Steelworker*, the Cape Breton labour weekly published by M.A. MacKenzie that continued the traditions of McLachlan's newspapers, D.N. Brodie paid tribute to McLachlan's character and abilities and his unshakable dedication to the workers' cause. It was the kind of informed, thoughtful assessment that was rarely heard in the public press in McLachlan's own lifetime. His contributions were historic – the struggle to build the miners' union and bring the benefits of industrial unionism to all workers, the campaigns to win political influence for labour and to educate workers to their responsibilities. Brodie also singled out McLachlan's remarkable ability to plead the workers' cause, in print, on the platform, and in the small exchanges of personal interaction: "He knew the workers' thoughts, struggles, needs and aspirations, and could appreciate and present their case from his own personal experience."[4]

More followed, as those who had stood with McLachlan in various battles attempted to explain the significance of the man they had known. Alex S. McIntyre, the district vice-president in the days of the red executive in the early 1920s, described McLachlan as "a real friend of the common people and a lifelong crusader in the cause of the working class": "I never knew a more clean living, honest or sincere man. He was continually aflame with a sense of the social injustice under which the workers were laboring, and with an ever-burning zeal he strove to improve their condition." Forman Waye, the steelworkers' leader who fought alongside McLachlan in the 1923 strike and other battles, described him as "the greatest exponent of the cause of labor in the Maritime Provinces": "I came to know him as a friend whose word was his bond, as a man who was utterly fearless in fighting the tyrants who exploit the poor; and who possessed a brilliant and analytic brain that was tireless in labor's cause." A tribute signed "Coal Digger" identified "J.B." above all as a great educationalist: "The education the workers got, rank and file, whether they know it or not, during the past 30 years, will gain for them in the future as in the past, many concessions." There was even a young man's poem of farewell and dedication: "You bore the blows for us, / Forever singing of the dawn to come; / Lashing the foe to fury with the sword of truth, / You gave no ground ..."[5]

In the pages of the Communist newspapers, such as *The Worker*, McLachlan was treated with respect: "Old Jim is gone. That grizzled old fighter who was hated and feared by the coal barons and the multimillionaires is silent and dead. His memory will be evergreen to those who fought shoulder to shoulder with him in labor's cause. When labor's history is written the name of dear J.B. McLachlan will occupy an honored place. He was a fighter for Socialism. He was an irreconcilable enemy of all those who were against the people." The *Daily Clarion* said much the same: "His great personal gifts would have brought him material ease and comfort a dozen times over if he had quit his class. But they would never have brought happiness to a heart so stoutly proletarian as Jim's – and Jim was never turned aside by bribes or frightened back by threats. A great worker, a great Canadian is gone."[6]

The labour poet Joe Wallace, who counted McLachlan as one of the influences in his own conversion to socialism at the end of Great War, described McLachlan as "the greatest Nova Scotian since the days of Joe Howe, perhaps of them all." The comparison made sense to Wallace, because he saw McLachlan as a man who struggled in his own time to extend the meaning of democracy, just as Joseph Howe had done in the early days in Nova Scotia; and both had suffered persecution by the authorities of their time. Wallace concluded with a personal recollection: "There are sand-and-sea swept roads that we will never again travel together while I drink in his salty phrases; halls where I will never again hear his voice speaking through smoke to the men and women he loved with his whole life. Jim McLachlan is dead. To some that means the passing of an almost legendary fighter in the ranks of the working-class. But to thousands of us it means in addition the passing of a dear friend."[7]

There remained difficulties arising from McLachlan's break with the Communist Party in 1936. At the funeral there was no official party representation, and a wreath from party headquarters was turned away. In the party press there were brief allusions to the late differences. *The Worker* said only that "Jim joined the Communist Party in 1922 and until stricken down with his fatal illness was an active leader of the revolutionary movement"; on the west coast, the *People's Advocate* said a little more: "He agreed with the party's policy of trade union unity but could never reconcile his political beliefs with his personal hatred of President John L. Lewis of the UMWA."[8]

In the meanwhile, had McLachlan abandoned his revolutionary views and endorsed a more moderate form of socialism? The evidence for this is not convincing, particularly in the light of the nature of McLachlan's criticism of the Communist Party, which was that the party was too moderate in its course of action at this time.[9] In his letter to Woodsworth the week before McLachlan's death, Brodie (who became a CCF MLA in 1941) noted that McLachlan "spoke of you very highly + wished he could see you again. Of course that may not be possible but I wish you could find time to write him a little letter. He would appreciate it. Whatever differences you may have had in the past – it means nothing to poor Jim now and I know he feels badly over it."[10] It is difficult to see this as anything more than a statement of personal regret, as observed by an old comrade. In addition, there are the observations of the Reverend Mercer, who officiated at the funeral; he recalled McLachlan as "a righteous man, but a Communist." During their encounters, their conversations had focused on matters of human justice and the social gospel, and Mercer recalled McLachlan presenting him with a pamphlet entitled *The Carpenter of Nazareth*. At the time of Mercer's campaign for the provincial legislature as a labour candidate in the summer of 1937, McLachlan expressed personal support – "but did not become involved for fear of hurting me, by having me associated with a Communist."[11]

Did McLachlan die in defeat? In his lifetime McLachlan could not rest easy when the outcome of so many struggles was uncertain and the revolution had not arrived. But the world was moving. The miners' union, for all its troubles, was permanently established in the coalfields, and employers in the future would not dare to challenge the miners' right to union representation. And the cause of industrial unionism, pioneered by the coal miners, was at the time of McLachlan's death gaining ground everywhere in North America. This was labour's giant step forward. In the next dozen years, hundreds of thousands of Canadian workers, millions in the United States, would join unions for the first time and win the benefits of union recognition. Ironically, the best-known leaders of this new upsurge in labour militancy included men such as John L. Lewis and Silby Barrett who had counted themselves among McLachlan's sworn enemies in the 1920s.

In Nova Scotia, the steelworkers, led by young union leaders who saw McLachlan as an inspiration, forced the provincial government to introduce the long-awaited Trade Union Act that promised workers the right to join a union and be represented by a union of their own choice. This was the first law of its kind in Canada, and over the course of the next dozen years other provinces – and in 1944 the federal government itself – would bring in similar provisions. The arrival of industrial legality, as McLachlan had warned more than once, was not the end of labour history, and it carried its own dangers of bureaucracy and complacency; but it was a victory nonetheless. What the coal miners had won for themselves in the long labour wars of the early twentieth century was now becoming the democratic right of all Canadian workers.

In political influence, too, the working class was beginning to come into its own, and industrial Cape Breton became known as one of the strongholds of working-class politics in Canada. Although Mercer's own campaign did not succeed in the summer of 1937, in subsequent elections the coal miners were victorious in electing labour candidates to the provincial assembly and Dominion Parliament. In 1938 District 26 of the United Mine Workers was the first union in the country officially to endorse the CCF, and the party quickly benefited from this alliance with the coal miners. Coal miner Clarie Gillis, a former officer of the "red" Amalgamated of the 1930s, was elected as a CCF Member of Parliament in 1940 – the first CCF MP elected in eastern Canada. This was the local outcome of the united front that McLachlan had championed in his own political career, and, though party labels changed over the years, the political tradition still remained vigorous half a century later in the 1990s.

There was no doubt that the balance of power in Canadian society was changing. In the decades that followed McLachlan's death, working-class voters supported major social reforms, among them unemployment insurance, family allowances, old age pensions, and medicare. These provisions for the security of families and individuals are now counted among the rights of all Canadian citizens. For radicals of McLachlan's generation, these reforms were based on the idea that there is a shared responsibility for the social and economic welfare of the community. There were even modest advances in the direction of economic democracy, with the appearance of a form of public ownership in the coal and steel industries in the 1960s. This took place in the shadow of underdevelopment and decline in the coal industry, and there was no transformation of the local economy. It was not the triumph of workers' control, and the available state support turned out to be an inadequate form of reinvestment. Yet, for all their defaults and disappointments, innovations in public ownership, such as the rise of the coal miners' cooperatives and credit unions, demonstrated the importance of reconciling economic development and public responsibility. These communitarian social principles, bigger than the interests of any individual or corporation, now have deep roots in the Canadian political tradition, even as they face challenges from those who would undo the progress of the past century.[12]

To be sure, the Canadian revolution had not arrived, at least not in the form that McLachlan had envisaged. Uncompromising, irreconcilable, McLachlan championed a cause that did not end in his own lifetime, and we may sympathize with the frustration of a man who was still waiting for the fulfilment of a dream of human liberation and social justice. But McLachlan was more than a dreamer, and most of his achievements were the outcome of a pragmatic labour radicalism that never lost sight of the ultimate goal of social transformation. "The world do move," he had written in 1919, and one day the disinherited would refuse to remain disinherited. Like other revolutionaries before him, he had reached the conclusion that power concedes nothing without a demand, and that numbers weigh in the balance only when united by organization and informed by knowledge. He knew, too, that in history individuals do make a difference, and McLachlan had long since identified his own mission in the service he rendered to the coal miners and to his class.

On that November day in 1937 a small boy watched as the funeral procession passed by his streetcorner. He was watching his grandfather – his "Poppa" and his namesake – travel to his final resting place. The young James Bryson McLachlan remembered it as a sad day, for he always had wonderful memories of his boyhood visits to Steele's Hill – the inspections of the barn and the fields, the lunches of fresh bread and milk and mushrooms, the warm hugs from his grandmother, and through it all the half-humorous, half-serious conversations with his grandfather.

This young McLachlan went on to spend much of his life in England as a teacher, and it would have pleased his grandfather to know that he maintained an abiding interest in literature, history, and philosophy. Half a century after his grandfather's death, the grandson shared his meditations on McLachlan's historical significance in terms that bear repeating:

I like the idea of John the Baptist. By which I mean, that although John knew full well that he wasn't the Saviour, he also knew full well that what he was saying pointed out the only way through which salvation could be found. So it was with Gorbachev, so it was, I think, with Poppa & Hardie. None of them could, in themselves, achieve what they most dearly wanted to achieve, but they pointed to the only way by which workers could improve their lot: through unionisation & acquiring political power.

And they were right, and they were successful to this degree: there doesn't exist a single democratic country in the whole world that would dare not to look after its citizens' health & education & old age, that doesn't have at least some pretense to providing a minimum wage, that doesn't have factory acts that look after workers' safety & so on. I know of nothing that illustrates more clearly the power of the democratic system than the claim that I have just made. What's more, I marvel that these things were achieved within my own lifetime ...

I cannot believe that the democratic process could have achieved such power if it had not been for the work like Hardie's & Poppa's. The Labour movement & the progress of democracy are very tightly intertwined indeed, so that it is, to my mind anyway, impossible to conceive of the progress of the one without the progress of the other.

History almost compels the appearance of certain sorts of people. For instance, in Athens in the 5th Century BC, people were giving up their freedom willingly to their leaders. Along came a man who taught other men to think for themselves. That was Socrates, & the world honours him to this day, though his own fellow citizens finally condemned him to death. In the 1st Century AD, a young man looked upon the fossilised form that his religion had turned into & spent 3 years preaching against it up & down what is now Israel. For his efforts, he was crucified. In medieval France, a young girl looked upon how her people were being oppressed by the English & encouraged the French armies to fight against them & win. She was burnt at the stake ...

I am not in the least suggesting that Poppa, or even Keir Hardie, were as great as Socrates or Jesus or Joan of Arc. That they were of the same mould, however, I am sure. They were the "village Hampdens," the men of local fame. Every movement needs its disciples to propagate the word, & Poppa was certainly one of them.[13]

All this is to say that James Bryson McLachlan was a man who answered the challenges of his times. He entered history at a time when industrial capitalism was refashioning the world with its contradictory discourse of development and exploitation, prosperity and suffering, wealth and poverty. For all its achievements, so many of them fuelled by the power of coal, the industrial revolution failed to reward the working class in any way commensurate with their contribution to economic development. Under existing conditions, the wealth produced by the coal miners disappeared in the smoke and sweat of the coal country, leaving behind a ravaged social and human landscape. The world was still not redeemed from the chaos of capitalism. McLachlan was never reconciled to such a contradiction, and with all the force of his personality, he answered in the language of resistance, solidarity, and liberation.

That such a leader should emerge among the coal miners is not all that surprising. Economies based on the alienation and depletion of natural resources raise the issues of exploitation and reinvestment with special urgency. And as the historian E.P. Thompson has written, the coal miners have always been "a special case" in modern history. They have shown a stubborn difficulty in accepting such simple economic propositions as the market regulation of wages and the survival of the fittest as appropriate social ethics. Instead, they have attached great significance to such old-fashioned ideas as justice, fairness, and cooperation in human affairs and the priority of labour as a source of value. From this perspective, their history is not so much a reservoir of traditionalism and conservatism as an accumulated supply of stored cultural energy.[14]

In the world of the present it is often difficult to make out the record of perseverance, resourcefulness, and imagination that sustained those who went before us. But if the writers of history are at their work, those energies can be seen, burning still, and moments of cultural transmission and illumination will take place. Then we shall be in a position to recognize that the so-called "special case" of the coal miners is also the general case of the working people as a whole, and that the messages of empowerment and transformation that the coal miners have been delivering for the last 200 years are addressed to all citizens of the modern world. Like the coal miners, McLachlan was also a "special case," and for this reason his place in history is assured.

Notes

Abbreviations in Notes

AMWNS: Amalgamated Mine Workers of Nova Scotia
AO: Archives of Ontario
ARLOC: Annual Report on Labour Organization in Canada
BI: Beaton Institute of Cape Breton Studies
CLL: Canadian Labor Leader
CMJ: Canadian Mining Journal
CPC: Communist Party of Canada
DUA: Dalhousie University Archives
ELN: Eastern Labor News
MLH: Maritime Labor Herald
NAC: National Archives of Canada
NLS: National Library of Scotland
PANS: Public Archives of Nova Scotia
Post: Sydney Daily Post
PWA: Provincial Workmen's Association
SRO: Scottish Record Office
TLC: Trades and Labour Congress of Canada
UMWA: United Mine Workers of America
UMWJ: United Mine Workers' Journal

Introduction

1. Christopher Hill, *God's Englishman: Oliver Cromwell and the English Revolution* (Toronto, 1970), 270.
2. John E. deRoche, "Making History: A Sociological Study," in Shannon Ryan, comp., *Report of the Fourth Annual Meeting of the Atlantic Oral History Association* (St John's, 1982), 163-73.
3. For the most recent edition, see Dawn Fraser, *Echoes from Labor's Wars: The Expanded Edition* (Wreck Cove, N.S., 1992), 20-30.
4. John C. O'Donnell, *"And Now the Fields are Green": A Collection of Coal Mining Songs in Canada* (Sydney, 1992), 108-11.
5. Halifax *Chronicle-Herald*, 9 September 1992.
6. *Cape Breton Post*, 5 September 1992. Meanwhile, McLachlan was also being recognized as one of the giants of Canadian labour history; he joined a select group of labour pioneers inducted into the Canadian Labour Hall of Fame in Toronto.
7. Eugene Forsey, *Economic and Social Aspects of the Nova Scotia Coal Industry* (Toronto, 1926), 87. Forsey has noted that this edition of his MA thesis did not have the benefit of his editorial attention before publication and contains a variety of technical errors.
8. Paul MacEwan, *Miners and Steelworkers: Labour in Cape Breton* (Toronto, 1976); John Mellor, *The Company Store: James Bryson McLachlan and the Cape Breton Coal Miners, 1900-1925* (Toronto, 1983).
9. Among the earliest of these works were Donald Macgillivray, "Industrial Unrest in Cape Breton, 1919-1925," MA thesis, University of New Brunswick, 1971; and David Frank, "Coal Masters and Coal Miners: The 1922 Strike and the Roots of Class Conflict in the Cape Breton Coal Industry," MA thesis, Dalhousie University, 1974. In a class by itself was the manuscript by the research director of the coal miners' union, C.B. Wade, "History of District 26, United Mine Workers of America, 1919-1941" (1950); this pioneering work has remained unpublished. For a sampling of local history, including a bibliography, see Kenneth Donovan, ed., *The Island: New Perspectives on Cape Breton History, 1713-1990* (Fredericton/Sydney, 1990).
10. Nick Salvatore, *Eugene V. Debs: Citizen and Socialist* (Urbana, Ill., 1982), xi.

Chapter One

1. Basic biographical information in this chapter was assembled from census manuscripts, parish records, directories, and birth, marriage, and death registers at the Scottish Record Office, H.M. General Register House, and the National Library of Scotland, Edinburgh. Conversations and interviews with Mrs Jean Robinson and Mr J.B. McLachlan, Jr., both of whom were born in

Scotland, furnished essential information and clues. The volumes in McLach-
lan's personal library, which I examined with the kind permission of Mrs
Robinson, contained useful inscriptions and notations. See also H.E. Spragge,
Hoddom Castle and the Western Gateway to Scotland (Annan, n.d.), and *Rules of
the Ecclefechan Cooperative Society Limited* (Lockerbie, 1873), FS5/368, SRO.
General information is also drawn from Thomas Johnston, *The History of the
Working Classes in Scotland* (Glasgow, 1922); Anthony Slaven, *The Development
of the West of Scotland, 1750-1960* (London, 1975); and T.C. Smout, *A Century
of the Scottish People, 1830-1950* (London, 1986).

2. The story was repeated in biographical sketches by McLachlan's contemporaries: see J.S. Woodsworth, "'Jim' McLachlan, Labor Covenanter," *Post*, 1 October
1923, and D.N. Brodie, "J.B. McLachlan," *Steelworker*, 7 November 1937. For
evidence of Carlyle's influence on the early Scottish labour movement, see W.
Mary Dunning, "Memories of Ecclefechan," *Labour Leader*, 16 June 1911, and
Smout, *A Century of the Scottish People*, 249.

3. "Floors That Have Talked to Me," *Always Ready*, vol. 1, no. 2 (March 1934), 19.

4. Johnston, *The History of the Working Classes in Scotland*, 330.

5. For the local history of this district, see John L. Carvel, *The Coltness Iron Com-
pany* (Edinburgh, 1948); George McAlister, "Wishaw and the Parish of
Cambusneathan," in George Thomson, ed., *The Third Statistical Account of
Scotland* (Glasgow, 1960), vol. 8, 315-49; and Robert Duncan, *Wishaw: Life and
Labour in a Lanarkshire Industrial Community, 1790-1914* (Motherwell, 1986).
See also R.W. Dron, *The Coal-Fields of Scotland* (Glasgow, 1902); R. Page Arnot,
A History of the Scottish Miners from the Earliest Times (London, 1955); and
Alan B. Campbell, *The Lanarkshire Miners: A Social History of Their Trade Un-
ions, 1775-1874* (Edinburgh, 1979).

6. Jean Robinson interviews, 27 April, 27 July 1976. See also Scotland, County of
Lanark, *The Housing Conditions of Miners. Report by the County Medical Officer
1910* (Glasgow, 1910), 140.

7. Jean Robinson interviews, 27 April, 27 July 1976; George MacEachern to
author, undated letter [received 10 June 1992].

8. Arnot, *The Scottish Miners*, 60-2; A.L. Lloyd, *Come All Ye Bold Miners* (London,
1952), 78, 129.

9. Robert Smillie, *My Life for Labour* (London, 1924), 11-12.

10. *Pomphrey's Directory of Wishaw* (Wishaw, 1893), 54-5.

11. Paul MacEwan, "J.B.M.," clipping from *Cape Breton Highlander* [1965?]. See
also MacEwan, *Miners and Steelworkers*, 15-16.

12. McLachlan's statement is in the *Workers' Weekly*, 7 March 1924, and the same information is repeated in the biographical sketch by Woodsworth. However, the
1881 census lists the twelve-year-old McLachlan as a "scholar." A number of explanations are possible: he may have returned to school or attended nights or
part-time, or he may have been receiving private instruction from one of the
middle-class figures who took an interest in him. By the 1937 account of D.N.
Brodie, McLachlan worked as a blacksmith's helper at the age of fourteen, before returning to the pit the following year. See also R.D. Anderson, *Education
and Opportunity in Victorian Scotland* (Oxford, 1983), 127-8, and Smout, *A
Century of the Scottish People*, 95-6, 209-30.

13. Brodie, "McLachlan."

14. Jean Robinson interview, 27 July 1976.

15. Alexander Shields, *A Hind Let Loose: or, an Historical Representation of the Testimonies of the Church of Scotland* (1687); Liam McIlvanney, "Robert Burns and
the Calvinist Radical Tradition," *History Workshop Journal*, 40 (autumn 1995),
137.

16. Jock Purves, *Fair Sunshine: Character Studies of the Scottish Covenanters* (London, 1968); Willie Thompson, "The Kirk and the Cameronians," in M.

Cornforth, ed., *Rebels and Their Causes: Essays in Honour of A.L. Morton* (London, 1978), 93-106. McLachlan's library contained a biography of Cameron, issued in the 1890s in a series of books on "Famous Scots." See also Ian B. Cowan, *The Scottish Covenanters, 1660-1688* (London, 1976). Thomas Carlyle was described as a Cameronian in William Barry, *Heralds of Revolt: Studies in Modern Literature and Dogma* (London, 1909), 74.

17. *Wishaw Baptist Church Centenary, 1871-1971* (n.p., n.d.). I am grateful to the Reverend Noel McCullins, who furnished information concerning family history from the relevant minute books and church registers.

18. Inscription in McLachlan's copy of *The Student's Analytical Greek Testament* (London, n.d.). The inscriptions cited in this and the following paragraph are also from books in McLachlan's library.

19. For a discussion of this text, see chapter 4.

20. Woodsworth, "McLachlan." Woodsworth took a narrow view of the covenanting legacy for organized labour, which contrasts with the more sympathetic comments of Ramsay MacDonald in his introduction to William Stewart, *J. Keir Hardie: A Biography* (London, 1921), especially xvii-xxii.

21. Gawin Kirkham, *The Open-Air Preacher's Handbook* (London, 1890), 20-1, 34, and passim.

22. The account of this conference is from the published report consulted at the NLS: The Lanarkshire Coal Masters' Association, *Report of Conferences with Representatives of the Workmen on 8th and 11th March, 1887, with Appendix of Opinions of the Press* (Glasgow, 1887), especially 13, 36-7, 47-9, 52, 58, 71-3. See also the Hamilton *Advertiser*, 12 March 1887. The identification of McLachlan is circumstantial but conforms to what we know of his early emergence as a labour spokesman; in his 1923 biographical sketch Woodsworth in particular refers to McLachlan's involvement in "an attempt ... to organize the country" in 1889 [sic].

23. Fred Reid, *Keir Hardie: The Making of a Socialist* (London, 1978), 88-101; Arnot, *The Scottish Miners*, 70. I am grateful to R. Page Arnot, Fred Reid, and Alan Campbell for conversations concerning Scottish labour history. In addition to the materials cited, the J.K. Hardie/Emrys Hughes Papers (Dep. 176) and the records of the National Union of Mineworkers, Scottish Area (Dep. 227) were consulted in the NLS.

24. Important studies of this theme are included in Royden Harrison, ed., *The Independent Collier: The Coal Miner as Archetypal Proletarian Reconsidered* (Sussex, 1978): Alan Campbell and Fred Reid, "The Independent Collier in Scotland," 54-74, and Fred Reid, "Alexander MacDonald and the Crisis of the Independent Collier, 1872-1874," 156-79.

25. Reid, *Hardie*, 98.

26. J.B. McLachlan, Jr., interview, 22 April 1976. For discussion of restriction of output as a strike tactic in 1922, with direct reference to his experience in Lanarkshire, see chapter 6.

27. Jean Robinson interview, 27 April 1976; Eva Pemberton to the author, 14 March 1978. For the full citation of the poem, see chapter 8.

28. "Floors That Have Talked to Me," 19.

29. Wally Seccombe, "Patriarchy Stabilized: The Construction of the Male Breadwinner Wage Norm in Nineteenth-Century Britain," *Social History*, vol. 11, no. 1 (January 1986), 53-76. For discussion of the exclusion of women from the coal industry, see Angela V. John, *By the Sweat of Their Brow: Women Workers at Victorian Coal Mines* (London, 1980); and for discussion of the cult of masculinity, see Michael Roper and John Tosh, eds., *Manful Assertions: Masculinities in Britain since 1800* (London, 1991).

30. Seccombe, "Patriarchy Stabilized," 55. See also McLachlan's discussion of the role of women as "the miner's financier" in chapter 4.

31. Jean Robinson, J.B. McLachlan, Jr., interviews, 1976.
32. This account of the strike is based on Arnot, *The Scottish Miners*, 71-88, issues of the Hamilton *Advertiser* and the *Labour Leader* for 1894, and the minutes of the Miners' Federation of Great Britain, 1893, 1894, Department of Manuscripts, NLS.
33. Hamilton *Advertiser*, 15 September 1894.
34. *Labour Leader*, 20 October 1894. Like his *Mines Nationalisation Bill* (Glasgow, 1893), Hardie's discussion of the 1894 strike was also widely circulated as a penny pamphlet: *A word with our collier laddies* (Glasgow, [1895?]).
35. Belle Small, "William Small: Memories, Visions and Work," "William Small The Man," and "Past Work," unpublished manuscripts in the Small Papers (Acc. 3350 (5)), Department of Manuscripts, NLS. There is no direct evidence of McLachlan in these papers, but according to Arnot, *The Scottish Miners*, 91-2, Small in this period was "the teacher, instructor and guide of a generation of the young lions of Lanarkshire."
36. David Lowe, *Souvenirs of Scottish Labour* (Glasgow, 1919), 125.
37. Thomas Carlyle, *Past and Present* (London and Glasgow, n.d. [1843]), 189, 327. See also Thomas Carlyle, *Last Words of Thomas Carlyle on Trades-Unions, Promoterism, the Signs of the Times* (Edinburgh, 1882); and Philip Rosenberg, *The Seventh Hero: Thomas Carlyle and the Theory of Radical Activism* (Cambridge, Mass., 1974).
38. In his biographical sketch, Woodsworth states: "In 1894 there was a seventeen weeks' strike where owing to his activity he was blacklisted and shortly afterward was appointed to an official position." On the other hand, both Jean Robinson and J. B. McLachlan, Jr., stated in interviews in 1976 that their father's emigration was not the direct result of victimization. Some of the changes in location during the 1890s may also have been dictated by the nature of McLachlan's work as a sinker, since his skills in mine development would be in demand in various locations.
39. Jean Robinson interview, 27 July 1976.
40. Stewart, *Hardie*, 151. McLachlan's library included Henry Cloete, *The History of the Great Boer Trek and the Origin of the South African Republics* (London, 1899), and F.W. Reitz, *A Century of Wrong* (n.p., n.d. [1900?]). The clipping noted here referred to the notorious court-martial and execution of Lieutenants Harry Morant and Peter Handcock, an episode recounted in the 1979 film *Breaker Morant*. See also Richard Price, *An Imperial War and the British Working Class* (Toronto, 1972), and Trevor Royle, *The Kitchener Enigma* (London, 1985), chapter 7.
41. My thanks to the late Harry McShane, Glasgow, who recalled the debates on Glasgow Green at the History Workshop meeting at Ruskin College in May 1976. See Harry McShane and Joan Smith, *Harry McShane: No Mean Fighter* (London, 1978). Long was recalled both by McShane and by McLachlan's eldest daughter.
42. H.A. Long, "To the British Sons and Daughters of Toil," in *Mr. Long's Australian Letters* (Glasgow, 1887), 67-70. See also his *Calvinism Popularised: The Five Points Carbonised in a Series of Discussions with Enquirers or Opponents* (London, 1895).
43. *Proceedings at Conference between Representatives of the Coalowners of Scotland and the Scottish Miners' Federation ... 1899*, and subsequent reports for 1900 and 1901, Department of Manuscripts, NLS; Arnot, *The Scottish Miners*, 98-101; Price, *An Imperial War*, 215.
44. Jean Robinson interview, 27 April 1976. See also Jeremy Mouat, *Roaring Days: Rossland's Mines and the History of British Columbia* (Vancouver, 1995).

45. J.B. McLachlan, Jr., interview, 22 April 1976; Jean Robinson interview, 27 April 1976; Reg Whitaker, *Canadian Immigration Policy since Confederation* (Ottawa, 1991), 2.
46. J.B. McLachlan, Jr., interview, 20 April 1976. MacEwan, *Miners and Steelworkers*, 16, states that McLachlan crossed the Atlantic on a tramp steamer and then took a cattleboat from Montreal to Sydney Mines.
47. Jean Robinson interview, 27 July 1976.

Chapter Two

1. Jean Robinson interviews, 27 April, 27 July 1976. For the family history in Sydney Mines, I have also relied on information provided by J.B. McLachlan, Jr., and Thomas McLachlan. McLachlan is listed in the *McAlpine City Directory for Sydney and Cape Breton County* for 1903-4 and 1907-8.
2. Town of Sydney Mines, *Annual Report, 1909*, 37. The history of Sydney Mines is described in John Carey, "Historical Sketch of the Town of Sydney Mines from the Earliest Times to the Present Year (1912)," unpublished manuscript, BI, and in Mrs R.G. Bain, comp., *History of the Town of Sydney Mines* (Sydney Mines, 1951). Additional sources included town-council minutes and annual reports of the town of Sydney Mines. See also D.A. Muise, "The Making of an Industrial Community: Cape Breton Coal Towns, 1867-1900," in Don Macgillivray and Brian Tennyson, eds., *Cape Breton Historical Essays* (Sydney, 1980), 76-94.
3. On the early development of the coal industry see Richard Brown, *The Coal-Fields and Coal Trade of the Island of Cape Breton* (London, 1871); C. Ochiltree Macdonald, *The Coal and Iron Industries of Nova Scotia* (Halifax, 1909); and Stephen J. Hornsby, *Nineteenth Century Cape Breton: A Historical Geography* (Montreal and Kingston, 1992). See also D.A. Muise, "The General Mining Association and Nova Scotia's Coal," *Bulletin of Canadian Studies*, vol. 6, no. 2 / vol. 7, no. 1 (autumn 1983), 71-87; and L.D. McCann, "The Mercantile-Industrial Transition in the Metal Towns of Pictou County, 1857-1931," *Acadiensis*, vol. 10, no. 2 (spring 1981), 29-64.
4. For the impact of the industrial revolution on the region, see T.W. Acheson, "The National Policy and the Industrialization of the Maritimes, 1880-1910," *Acadiensis*, vol. 1, no. 2 (spring 1972), 3-28, and the collaborative history edited by E.R. Forbes and D.A. Muise, *The Atlantic Provinces in Confederation* (Toronto/Fredericton, 1993), chapters 1-5.
5. *Post*, 18 November 1922, Halifax *Herald*, 5 July 1906.
6. On the British Canadian Cooperative Society, see Bain, *Sydney Mines*, 33, and Ian MacPherson, "Patterns in the Maritime Cooperative Movement, 1900-1945," *Acadiensis*, vol. 5, no. 1 (autumn 1975), 67-83. For an interesting case study of British immigration in this period, see A. Ross McCormack, "Networks among British Immigrants and Accommodation to Canadian Society: Winnipeg, 1900-1914," *Histoire sociale/Social History*, vol. 17, no. 34 (November 1984), 357-74.
7. See the contributions by "A Miner," Halifax *Herald*, 14 November, 7 December 1906.
8. See B.T.A. Bell, *The Canadian Mining Manual and Mining Companies' Year Book, 1903* (Ottawa, 1903); F.W. Gray, "The Coal Fields and Coal Industry of Eastern Canada," Canada, Mines Branch, *Bulletin No. 14* (Ottawa, 1917); Alex L. Hay, "Coal-mining Operations in the Sydney Coal-Field," American Institute of Mining and Metallurgical Engineers, *Technical Publication No. 198* (New York, 1929); A.S. McNeil, "Notes on Mining in Submarine Areas at Princess Colliery, Sydney Mines," *Transactions of the Canadian Mining Institute and Mining Society of Nova Scotia*, vol. 24 (1921), 284-91.

9. On child labour, see Robert McIntosh, "The Boys in the Nova Scotia Coal Mines, 1873-1923," *Acadiensis*, vol. 16, no. 2 (spring 1987), 35-50. Data on the ages of the coal miners in 1907 was collected by the Nova Scotia Royal Commission Respecting Old Age Pensions and Miners' Relief Societies and is reported in a later conciliation board report: *Labour Gazette* (August 1909), 211.

10. Ken Pryke, "Labour and Politics: Nova Scotia at Confederation," *Histoire sociale/Social History*, no. 6 (November 1970), 33-55; Ian McKay, "The Crisis of Dependent Development: Class Conflict in the Nova Scotia Coalfields, 1872-1876," in G.S. Kealey, ed., *Class, Gender, and Region: Essays in Canadian Historical Sociology* (St John's, 1988), 9-48. See also David Frank, "The Industrial Folk Song in Cape Breton," *Canadian Folklore Canadien*, vol. 8, no. 1-2 (1986), 27-9.

11. Robert Drummond, *Recollections and Reflections of a Former Trades Union Leader* (n.p., n.d. [1926?]), 72. For the early history of the Provincial Workmen's Association, see Ian McKay, "'By Wisdom, Wile or War': The Provincial Workmen's Association and the Struggle for Working-Class Independence in Nova Scotia, 1879-1897," *Labour/Le Travail*, vol. 18 (fall 1986), 13-62.

12. See John H.M. Laslett, "'A Parting of the Ways': Immigrant Miners and the Rise of Politically Conscious Trade Unionism in Scotland and the American Midwest, 1865-1924," in Laslett, ed., *The United Mine Workers of America: A Model of Industrial Solidarity?* (University Park, Penn., 1996), 417-37.

13. PWA Grand Council Minutes (October 1888), 182-4, Labour Canada Library, Ottawa.

14. Sharon Reilly, "The Provincial Workmen's Association of Nova Scotia, 1879-1898," MA thesis, Dalhousie University, 1979.

15. Robert Drummond, *To the Officers and Members of Keystone Lodge* [printed circular, 1 December 1896], BI.

16. John Moffatt to John Petrie, 11 July 1939, John Petrie Papers, BI.

17. See Ron Crawley, "Class Conflict and the Establishment of the Sydney Steel Industry, 1899-1904," in Donovan, ed., *The Island*, 145-64.

18. Excerpt from court proceeding in Glace Bay, 5 November 1908, box 1, document no. L-35, 6, 11, Edward A. Wieck Papers, Archives of Labor and Urban Affairs, Wayne State University, Detroit, Michigan.

19. Halifax *Herald*, 26 July 1906 [reprinted from the *Mining Record*].

20. Ibid., 18 July 1906.

21. Ibid., 6 August 1906.

22. Ibid., 18 August 1906.

23. PWA Grand Council Minutes (September 1906), 525, 536.

24. PWA Grand Council Minutes (September 1906), 525.

25. Drummond, "The Beginning of Trade Unions in Nova Scotia," *The Evening News* (New Glasgow), 7 July 1924. See also Drummond, *Recollections and Reflections*, 244.

26. "The Merry Xmas Time for Nova Scotia's $1.38 a Day Laborer and His Family," Halifax *Herald*, 24 December 1906, 4. The letter concluded with a quotation from Carlyle's *Past and Present*.

27. J.C. Kenworthy, *From Bondage to Brotherhood: A Message to the Workers* (London, n.d.). Judging from internal evidence, the date of publication was probably between 1893 and 1896, but McLachlan's copy is inscribed with the date 23 June 1905.

28. Halifax *Herald*, 8 April 1907. The references to events in Scotland and characteristic quotations from Burns and Carlyle helped confirm McLachlan as the author of the pseudonymous letters from "A Miner," all of which were dated at Sydney Mines.

29. Halifax *Herald*, 25 August 1906. Also mentioned was a work by J.M. Davidson, *Annals of Toil: Being Labour-History Outlines, Roman and British.* My thanks to Thomas P. Glynn, Auburn University, for identifying the full title of this item, which was published in a four-volume London edition in 1896-98 and a single volume in 1899. I am also grateful to Jaap Kloosterman, International Institute of Social History, who reports that Max Nettlau has described Davidson as a radical Scottish journalist whose writings contained an eclectic "Christian Anarchism."
30. The competition was announced in the Halifax *Herald*, 14 September, with further details on 22 September 1906. The first entries appeared in October and continued into December 1906.
31. Ibid., 6 October 1906. Letter No. 1 was also reprinted on 29 October 1906.
32. Ibid., 11 January 1907, 3 November 1906.
33. Ibid., 23 November 1906.
34. Ibid., 13 March 1907.
35. Ibid., 26 April 1907. On the origins of the act, see Paul Craven, *"An Impartial Umpire": Industrial Relations and the Canadian State, 1900-1911* (Toronto, 1980), especially chapters 8-9.
36. "Where Would Robert Burns Stand Today in Labor Problems," Halifax *Herald*, 24 January 1908, 5.
37. *The United Mine Workers in Nova Scotia. Their Motives and Methods. By a Former Member* (Sydney Mines, 1910), 14. On the secularization of social reform, see Ramsay Cook, *The Regenerators: Social Criticism in Late Victorian English Canada* (Toronto, 1985).
38. There appears to be no evidence to support the claim that McLachlan was an elder of St Andrew's, as stated in MacEwan, *Miners and Steelworkers*, 22. I am grateful to the Reverend Raymond Gillis, who reported that none of the McLachlan family appears in the church records of elders and communicants for the years 1901-10. Mrs Robinson stated that McLachlan did belong to the Baptist Church but had a falling out with the minister: Jean Robinson interview, 27 April 1976. According to the Clyde Avenue Baptist Church records, a [Miss] Jennie M Lochlan [sic] was baptized early in 1909, at a time when the McLachlans' oldest daughter, Jean, was fifteen years old, but there was no record of other family members in the church records. I am grateful to the church clerk, Hugh Smith, for this information.
39. The SPC platform appeared regularly in the *Western Clarion* and *Cotton's Weekly*; see, for instance, *Cotton's Weekly*, 30 April 1914. The "economic programme of the working class" included three main objectives: "(1) the transformation, as rapidly as possible, of capitalist property in the means of wealth production (natural resources, factories, mills, railroads etc.,) into the collective property of the working class; (2) The democratic organization and management of industry by the workers; (3) The establishment, as speedily as possible, of production for use instead of production for profit." On early socialism in the region, see David Frank and Nolan Reilly, "The Emergence of the Socialist Movement in the Maritimes, 1899-1916," *Labour/Le Travail*, vol. 4 (1979), 85-113, and Nicholas Fillmore, *Maritime Radical: The Life and Times of Roscoe Fillmore* (Toronto, 1992). For western developments, see Ross McCormack, *Reformers, Rebels, and Revolutionaries: The Western Canadian Radical Movement, 1899-1919* (Toronto, 1977), and Allen Seager, "Socialists and Workers: The Western Canadian Coal Miners, 1900-1920," *Labour/Le Travail*, vol. 16 (fall 1985), 23-59.
40. *Post*, 29 November 1904, 24 January 1905; Halifax *Herald*, 22 December 1906.
41. Halifax *Herald*, 8 April 1907.

42. The Biblical reference is a common paraphrase of Genesis, 3:19. Carlyle's proposition was cited by McLachlan, along with similar observations by Adam Smith and John Stuart Mill, in a letter in the Halifax *Herald*, 13 September 1906.
43. These observations are based on an examination of McLachlan's personal library. On the influence of North America's oldest socialist publishing house, see Allen Ruff, *"We Called Each Other Comrade": Charles H. Kerr & Company, Radical Publishers* (Urbana, Ill., 1997).
44. "Average Yearly Income of Wage Earners of Canada," Halifax *Herald*, 13 February 1908, 6.
45. PWA Grand Council Minutes (September 1907), 617-19.
46. *Cotton's Weekly*, 1 July 1909.
47. *The United Mine Workers in Nova Scotia. Their Motives and Methods*, 14.
48. *Cotton's Weekly*, 1 July 1909.
49. Hardie's warning was summarized in these words: "In Canada there were all the materials for a great Socialist movement, but, he would say in all kindness, that with the present attitude of the believers in Socialism and the champions of organised Labour pure and simple, it meant a divorce of interests resulting in permanent injury to both": *Labour Leader*, 16 October 1908, 660.
50. On the entry of international unions into Canada, see Robert H. Babcock, *Gompers in Canada: A Study in American Continentalism Before the First World War* (Toronto, 1974). Recent studies of the UMWA include Maier B. Fox, *United We Stand: The United Mine Workers of America, 1890-1990* (Washington, D.C., 1990), and Laslett, ed., *The United Mine Workers of America: A Model of Industrial Solidarity?*
51. Samuel Gompers to John Flett, 18 January 1901, Gompers to John Mitchell, 18 January 1901, Rosa Lee Guard to Flett, 23 January 1901, Samuel Gompers Letterbooks, vol. 41 (1901), 488, 365, Library of Congress, Washington, D.C.
52. *American Federationist* (October 1901), 443; *American Federationist* (January 1902), 43-4.
53. National Executive Board Minutes, UMWA, 8 April 1903, vol. 1, 255, John Mitchell Papers, Catholic University of America, Washington, D.C. The PWA was first discussed as early as 12 February 1901.
54. National Executive Board Minutes, UMWA, 28 August 1904, vol. 2, 78, Mitchell Papers. However, the board did approve support for UMW miners in Alberta and British Columbia during this period.
55. National Executive Board Minutes, UMWA, 2 August 1906, vol. 2, 270, Mitchell Papers; PWA Grand Council Minutes (September 1906), 546. Another issue that surfaced in 1906 was concern over the depletion of the PWA defence fund. McLachlan was subsequently appointed by Drummond Lodge to report on the condition of the fund, and in 1908 he stated: "I was surprised to find that money had been paid out of the Defence Fund, because it had been reported by delegates from Grand Council that no money was to be taken out of the Defence fund for 5 years": Excerpt from court proceeding in Glace Bay, 5 November 1908, box 1, document no. L-35, 7-8, Wieck Papers.
56. PWA Grand Council Minutes (September 1907), 642.
57. PWA Grand Council Minutes (September 1907), 594-5, 600.
58. Nova Scotia, Royal Commission Respecting Old Age Pensions and Miners' Relief Societies, *Report*, in *Journals of the House of Assembly of Nova Scotia* (1908), appendix no. 15, 114-19. Although the report did not adopt McLachlan's proposals, it led to the incorporation of a Nova Scotia Colliery Workers' Provident Society and an Old-Age Pension Board: *Canadian Annual Review, 1908*, 427-8.
59. National Executive Board Minutes, UMWA, 30 October, 21 December 1907, vol. 3, 61-2, 83, Mitchell Papers.
60. National Executive Board Minutes, UMWA, 5 February 1908, vol. 3, 103-4, Mitchell Papers.

61. Meeting of the International Executive Board, UMWA, 30 March 1908, 3-6, Mitchell Papers.
62. Lewis to Morrison, 30 May, Morrison to Flett, 3 June, Morrison to Draper, 3 June, Morrison to Lewis, 3 June 1908, Nat. Union/No. 7 [Miners], National Union Files, AFL-CIO Papers, Washington, D.C.
63. T.L. Lewis to A. McMullan, 4 October 1908, box 1, document no. L-34, Wieck Papers.
64. Canada, House of Commons, *Sessional Papers, 1910*, vol. 19, no. 36, 256-62.
65. PWA Grand Council Minutes (May 1908), 654-67.
66. *Labour Gazette* (July 1908), 12. The total number of votes cast was 5,405, of which 97 were considered spoiled ballots. The most reliable estimate of PWA membership, reported at the Grand Council in September 1907, was 7,000 members. The total workforce in the Nova Scotia coal industry at this time included more than 12,000 men.
67. PWA Grand Council Minutes (September 1908), 674.
68. Halifax *Herald*, 15-19 September 1908.
69. On the key votes the reformers were able to muster twenty-eight votes; even with the support of the ten excluded delegates and the removal of five PWA delegates whose credentials were challenged, their numbers would not have been sufficient to carry the vote. In part, the UMW group was under-represented because much of their support was concentrated in the largest lodges. It also appears that some UMW supporters failed to send delegates to the meeting, assuming that the PWA had been dissolved by the results of the referendum. Article 21 of the PWA constitution, however, provided that the association could not be dissolved "so long as one lodge, with 40 members shall object thereto." See Halifax *Herald*, 18-19 September 1908, and PWA Grand Council Minutes (September 1908), 669-74. There is a discrepancy between the report in the *Herald*, based on information provided by Moffatt, and the Grand Council Minutes, which report a closer standing vote of thirty for and forty-nine against the constitutional amendment.
70. The Grand Council Minutes, held at the Labour Canada Library, are interrupted at this point and the record does not resume until the meeting of 12 September 1911. According to Moffatt, the original minutes were required in subsequent court proceedings. In place of a full report of the September 1908 meetings, the Grand Council Minutes, 668, contain a statement by Moffatt reporting a margin of 418 [sic] votes against the PWA and a statement summarizing the basis for overturning the result: "Objection was taken against the vote in the September meeting and by a large majority carried. It was held that the notice for the May meeting only called for the reforming of the PWA, not its annihilation." A resolution providing for division of the financial assets was ruled out of order at this session, and the PWA also ruled that "no agitation in favour of other labor organizations be permitted in any subordinate lodge": Halifax *Herald*, 18, 19 September 1908.
71. Halifax *Herald*, 18 September 1908.
72. *Labour Leader*, 16 October 1908, 660; Halifax *Herald*, 26 September 1908. Hardie also came to Canada in 1895 and in 1907, but he visited Cape Breton only once.
73. *Labour Leader*, 16 October 1908, 660.
74. *Post*, 29 September 1908. See also MacEwan, *Miners and Steelworkers*, 21-2.
75. *Post*, 29 September 1908.
76. Conversation with Maurice MacDonald, 26 March 1976.

Chapter Three

1. On the early history of District 26, see especially Forsey, *Nova Scotia Coal Industry*, and Wade, "History of District 26, U.M.W.A." Useful accounts of the 1909 strike include Joseph Steele, "The Big Strike, 1909-1910," MA thesis, St Francis Xavier University, 1960, and Dan Moore, "The 1909 Strike in the Nova Scotia Coal Fields," unpublished paper, Carleton University, 1977. Research in this chapter relies on documents from the United Mine Workers of America Papers, which at the time of research were located in the union headquarters in Washington, D.C., and in a warehouse in Alexandria, Virginia. In addition to the published proceedings of UMW conventions, a mixed series of synoptic and stenographic reports recorded the proceedings of the international executive board. Also, an extensive collection of ledger sheets beginning in December 1909 recorded membership levels and dues for all locals, including those in District 26. Correspondence and documents dating from 1911 onwards were included in the President's Correspondence Files for District 26. I am most grateful to Maier B. Fox, research coordinator for the UMWA, for his cooperation in facilitating this work, and to Ian McKay, who collaborated on the research in this collection. This material has since been relocated to an archives at Pennsylvania State University, State College, Penn. The collection is cited as UMWA Papers.
2. *UMWJ*, 6 May 1909, 5.
3. *UMWJ*, 2 December 1909, 7; *International Socialist Review* (June 1910), 1102.
4. *Constitution, District 26, United Mine Workers of America, 1909* [copy at Miners' Memorial Museum, Glace Bay].
5. *UMWJ*, 18 March 1909.
6. A biographical sketch of McDougall appears in *UMWJ*, 14 April 1910; see also *MLH*, 7 June 1924.
7. Jean Robinson interview, 27 April 1976, J.B. McLachlan, Jr., interview, 22 April 1976.
8. *Census of Canada, 1941*, vol. I, table 10; *CMJ*, 11 June 1908. On Glace Bay, see the anniversary booklets published by the town, *Town of Glace Bay: 50 Years* (1951) and *Town of Glace Bay: 75 Years of Progress* (1976). See also David Frank, "Company Town/Labour Town: Local Government in the Cape Breton Coal Towns, 1917-1926," *Histoire sociale/Social History*, vol. 14, no. 27 (May 1981), especially 178-82.
9. "Notes, 1938," A.S. Kendall Papers, PANS. On the early history of Dominion Coal, see Don Macgillivray, "Henry Melville Whitney Comes to Cape Breton: The Saga of a Gilded Age Entrepreneur," *Acadiensis*, vol. 9, no. 1 (autumn 1979), 44-70.
10. Jean Robinson interview, 27 April 1976.
11. Eva Pemberton interview, 27 July 1978. Later they moved to South Street, which was closer to the central part of town.
12. *ELN*, 3 July 1909. The district officers also included an international board member, a position to which James D. McLennan was elected, as well as four subdistrict board members, one board member at large, and two auditors. Unsympathetic observers estimated union membership at no more than 3,000 men: see, for example, *Canadian Annual Review, 1909*, 299. However, according to the ledgers for District 26 in the UMWA Papers, there were a total of 4,500 members on the books in December 1909.
13. *UMWJ*, 2 December 1909. Between 1901 and 1908 AFL membership in Canada increased from about 10,000 to 50,000 members, and it reached 100,000 by 1913: Babcock, *Gompers in Canada*, 222.

14. For the 1908 agreement, see *Labour Gazette* (April 1908), 1222-6. This agreement was renewed in the midst of the strike and extended to the end of 1911: Halifax *Herald*, 6 November 1909.

15. For the reports of these boards, see *Labour Gazette* (May–August 1909).

16. PWA Grand Council Minutes (September 1907), 589. See also Craven, *"An Impartial Umpire."*

17. *UMWJ*, 2 December 1909, 7.

18. *International Socialist Review* (June 1910), 1102.

19. Moore, "The 1909 Strike," 80.

20. J.B. McLachlan to Wilfrid Laurier, 7 July 1909, with enclosure, Wilfrid Laurier Papers, vol. 582, NAC.

21. "Report of the Deputy Minister of Labour on the Industrial Conditions in the Coal Fields of Nova Scotia," House of Commons, *Sessional Papers, 1910*, vol. 19, no. 36A [Acland Report], 17-19.

22. *UMWJ*, 2 December 1909, 7. The strike against Dominion Coal began on 6 July and the strike against the Inverness Railway and Coal Company began on 9 July. In Springhill the strike against the Cumberland Railway and Coal Company began in August.

23. For some details of the military intervention, I am indebted to an MA report by Ian Andrews, "Military Aid to the Civil Power: The Cape Breton Coal Strike of 1909-1910," University of New Brunswick, 1987. For a general discussion of the use of the armed forces in strikes during this period, see Desmond Morton, "Aid to the Civil Power: the Canadian Militia in Support of Social Order, 1867-1914," *Canadian Historical Review*, vol. 51, no. 4 (December 1970), 407-25.

24. Notations in Russell MacPhee Scrapbook, SB 9, BI.

25. Glace Bay Town Council Minutes, 7 July 1909.

26. Toronto *Star*, 3 August 1909.

27. *ELN*, 14 August 1909.

28. Ibid., 12 November 1910.

29. *International Socialist Review* (June 1910), 1102.

30. Acland Report, 20.

31. UMW Executive Board Minutes, 30 March, 26 June, 27-30 September 1909, 23 May 1910 [stenographic], UMWA Papers; *International Socialist Review* (April 1910), 952.

32. Jean Robinson interview, 27 April 1976; McLachlan to Eugene Forsey, 4 March 1926, cited in Forsey, *Nova Scotia Coal Industry*, 26.

33. *UMWJ*, 9 September 1909; Toronto *Star*, 14 July 1909. One example of the union's propaganda effort was addressed to French-speaking coal miners: *A tout ceux qui travaillent pour le moment* [printed circular, 25 August 1909], BI. For a study that stresses the significance of the recruitment of strikebreakers in regional disputes in this period, see Ian McKay, "Strikes in the Maritimes, 1901-1914," *Acadiensis*, vol. 13, no. 1 (autumn 1983), 3-46.

34. Gompers to J. Bergmans, 30 March, 1 April 1910, Gompers to McLachlan, 1 April 1910, Nat. Union/No. 7, National Union Files, AFL-CIO Papers, Washington, D.C.

35. *ELN*, 18 September 1909; *UMWJ*, 21 October 1909; *Labour Gazette* (November 1909), 533.

36. Montreal *Star*, 2 October 1909; *UMWJ*, 16 June 1910; *ELN*, 4 April, 28 May 1910; conversation with Marguerite McDougall, 1976.

37. Halifax *Herald*, 6, 20 October 1909; Rex vs. Cowans and Dick, Record of Proceedings, RG 21, Series A, vol. 32, PANS. On the production of medical evidence, magistrate George Fielding exempted Ross from appearing on the charges; other prominent defendants included Dominion's general manager G.H. Duggan and Scotia's general superintendent T.J. Brown.

38. Halifax *Herald*, 2 November, 23 December 1909; *ELN*, 20 November 1909; *Labour Gazette* (May 1910), 1334. See also clippings in Stephen Dolhanty Collection, BI.

39. *UMWJ*, 7 April 1910, Halifax *Herald*, 16 February 1910; clippings in Dolhanty Collection, BI.

40. Danny Samson, "The Making of a Cape Breton Coal Town: Dependent Development in Inverness, Nova Scotia, 1899-1915," MA thesis, University of New Brunswick, 1988, 144-5. The case was debated at meetings of the TLC in 1911, where delegates called for repeal of the legislation: Craven, "*Impartial Umpire*," 317. For McLachlan's later comment, see *MLH*, 21 October 1921.

41. Moore, "The 1909 Strike," 106-12. Although they had broken with party ranks, both Kendall and Paul were re-elected in the next provincial election.

42. J.W. Longley to W.L.M. King, 31 July, 10 August 1909, William Lyon Mackenzie King Papers, vol. 12, 10989-94, NAC; Acland Report, 11.

43. *International Socialist Review* (June 1910), 1104; UMW Executive Board Minutes [stenographic], 31 March 1910, 37-8, UMWA Papers; Moore, "The 1909 Strike," 115.

44. *ELN*, 9 July 1910.

45. *ELN*, 9 July 1910. A composition by a local UMW officer, Patrick J. Lynch, "Arise Ye Nova Scotia Slaves," dates from the later stages of the strike. The song recorded the mythic significance of the 1909 strike and was collected by folklorist George Korson in 1940. See David Frank, "The Industrial Folk Song in Cape Breton," 33-4.

46. *International Socialist Review* (June 1910), 1104.

47. *Cotton's Weekly*, 15, 29 July 1909; *ELN*, 18 September 1909. The discussion here and in the following paragraphs is based on Frank and Reilly, "Socialist Movement in the Maritimes," especially 101-105.

48. *International Socialist Review* (June 1910), 1104.

49. TLC, *Report of Proceedings, 1909*, 73.

50. *Cotton's Weekly*, 23 December 1909; *Canadian Annual Review, 1909*, 307-8. For an introduction see *Bill Haywood's Book: The Autobiography of William D. Haywood* (New York, 1928).

51. *UMWJ*, 27 October 1910. Also in *ELN*, 12 November 1910.

52. *ELN*, 4 June 1910; *Cotton's Weekly*, 9, 16 June, 1 July 1910.

53. *Western Clarion*, 3 June 1911. The 1911 election is often considered a classic contest over the issue of free trade with the United States, the Liberals supporting reciprocity and the Conservatives defending protectionism.

54. *Western Clarion*, 2 November 1912. On *Cotton's Weekly*, see Frank and Reilly, "Socialist Movement in the Maritimes," 95-6.

55. The visit is reported in MacEwan, *Miners and Steelworkers*, 41-2. MacEwan cites a pamphlet by Cotton, *Sermon to the Working Class*. In 1921 Cotton returned to Glace Bay as editor of the *Martime Labor Herald*: see chapter 5.

56. Edwin Perry to William Watkins, 13 April 1911, John P. White to Watkins, 30 June 1911, White to J.B. McLachlan, 8 September 1911, President's Correspondence File, District 26, 1911, UMWA Papers.

57. "To all Miners and Mine Laborers in and around the Mines of Nova Scotia," 18 April 1911 [printed circular], President's Correspondence, 1911, District 26, UMWA Papers.

58. Nova Scotia, Royal Commission on Coal Mines [Duncan Commission, 1925], "Minutes of Evidence," 1008, PANS; *ELN*, 21 December 1912.

59. *Post*, 25, 26 April 1911, Halifax *Herald*, 26, 27, 28 April 1911.

60. *Post*, 30 June 1911, Halifax *Herald*, 30 June, 1 July 1911. The second charge against Beal was withdrawn.

61. "Minutes of Evidence" [Duncan Commission, 1925], 1011-2. The information about Beal came to light in a libel suit over the question of who had supplied

the liquor for the men who disrupted the union meeting where the shooting took place.

62. McLachlan to Edwin Perry, 9 June 1911, President's Correspondence, 1912 [sic], District 26, UMWA Papers.

63. McLachlan to White, 1 January 1912, President's Correspondence, 1912, District 26, UMWA Papers; *ELN*, 30 December 1911; "Brother Officers and Delegates to the Fourth Annual Convention of District #26, U.M.W.A." [report by William Watkins], President's Correspondence, 1911, District 26, UMWA Papers.

64. McLachlan to White, 1 January 1912, President's Correspondence, 1912, District 26, UMWA Papers.

65. *UMWA 23rd Convention Proceedings, 1912*, vol. 1, 30-1.

66. Watkins to White, 7 March 1912, C.A. Bonnyman to White, 4 May 1912, McLachlan and Bonnyman to White, 10 October 1912, 14 July 1913, President's Correspondence, 1912, 1913, District 26, UMWA Papers.

67. *ELN*, 9 December 1911, 15 June, 28 December 1912, 4 January 1913.

68. *Evening News* (New Glasgow), 7 November, 6 December 1913. I am grateful to Craig Heron, York University, for sharing this evidence.

69. McLachlan to White, 25 August 1914, President's Correspondence, 1914, District 26, UMWA Papers.

70. Edward Gallagher et al. to White, 3 January 1912, White to McLachlan, 6 February 1912, McLachlan to White, 23 February 1912, President's Correspondence, 1912, District 26, UMWA Papers.

71. McLachlan to William Green, 14 November 1914; J.D. McLennan to Kent Foster, 25 October 1914 [copy], President's Correspondence, 1914, District 26, UMWA Papers. The emigration of young men such as Barrett from Newfoundland to the Cape Breton coal mines is discussed in Ron Crawley, "Off to Sydney: Newfoundlanders Emigrate to Industrial Cape Breton, 1890-1914," *Acadiensis*, vol. 17, no. 2 (spring 1988), 27-51.

72. UMW Executive Board Minutes, 2 December 1914, 6 February 1915, UMWA Papers. District 18 (in Alberta and the Crowsnest area of British Columbia) remained in good standing. For western developments, see Allen Seager, "Miners' Struggles in Western Canada, 1890-1930," in Deian R. Hopkin and G.S. Kealey, eds., *Class, Community and the Labour Movement: Wales and Canada, 1850-1930* (St John's, 1989), 160-98.

73. White to McLachlan, 8 February 1915, White to McLennan, 25 February 1915, President's Correspondence, 1915, District 26, UMWA Papers.

74. Acland Report, 21; Forsey, *Nova Scotia Coal Industry*, 27. The others mentioned by Acland were McDougall, the district president, and two organizers from the international union, Patterson and Bousfield.

75. "Minutes of Evidence" [Duncan Commission, 1925], 1165-6. The purchase in 1917 coincided with McLachlan's return to full-time employment as a union official. The distinction between spouses in such a transaction had little financial or legal significance at the time; indeed, the documents in 1919 treated the transactions as if they had been made by the husband. The property included five acres, plus one acre of adjoining land. For these transactions see Book 217, 622-4 (17 August 1917), Book 220, 1-4 (17 August 1917), Book 234, 330-1 (19 August 1919), Registry of Deeds, Cape Breton County, Sydney, N.S.

76. Jean Robinson interview, 27 April 1976, J.B. McLachlan, Jr., interview, 22 April 1976.

77. Birth, marriage, and death registers, H.M. Register House, Edinburgh; Jean Robinson interview, 27 July 1976. On the enforcement of medical restrictions against disabilities under the Immigration Act, see Barbara Roberts, "Doctors and Deports: The Role of the Medical Profession in Canadian Deportation, 1900-1920," *Canadian Ethnic Studies*, vol. 18, no. 3 (1986), 17-36.

78. Interviews with Jean Robinson, 27 April 1976, Elsie Warner, 27 August 1975, Tom McLachlan, 28 April, 21 July 1976. As in the previous chapters, information here and in the following paragraphs is based on a review of McLachlan's book collection.

79. Interviews with Tom McLachlan, 28 April, 21 July 1976.

80. Interviews with Elsie Warner, 27 August 1975, Mary McLachlan Sanger, 25 February 1997.

81. *Working Class Politics* [printed circular, 1916], BI. On this and other electoral efforts, see David Frank, "Working Class Politics: The Election of J.B. McLachlan, 1916-1935," in Donovan, ed., *The Island*, 187-219, 288-92.

82. Untitled document [1924?], J.B. McLachlan File, Records of the Royal Canadian Mounted Police. This file was released to the author by the Canadian Security and Intelligence Service, under the Access to Information Act, Access Request 85-A-58. Documents from this file are cited below by date, and the file is referred to as RCMP File.

83. For the official returns, see Nova Scotia, *Journals of the House of Assembly, 1917*, appendix no. 18, 5-7. The leading candidates in this four-member constituency polled between 6,885 and 7,381 votes.

84. *Post*, 10-23 June 1916.

Chapter 4

1. McLachlan to White, 13 October 1916, President's Correspondence, District 26, 1916, UMWA Papers.

2. "Dom Coal Coy's daily police report, Cape Breton," 27 December 1916, District 26 UMWA Papers, PANS. See also President's Report, United Mine Workers of Nova Scotia, 12 June 1917, District 26 UMWA Papers.

3. "Dom Coal Coy's daily police report, Cape Breton, for April 21st., 1917," District 26 UMWA Papers, PANS. See also President's Report, United Mine Workers of Nova Scotia, 12 June 1917.

4. PWA Grand Council Minutes (12 June 1917), 859-77; John Moffatt, *Grand Secretary Moffatt's Valedictory Report* (n.p., 1917), 1.

5. McLachlan to White, 24 August, 4 September, 8 October 1917, White to McLachlan, 28 August, 13 October 1917, President's Correspondence, District 26, 1917, UMWA Papers.

6. Halifax *Herald*, 30 October 1917.

7. Ibid.

8. *Minutes of the First Annual Convention of the Amalgamated Mine Workers of Nova Scotia* (Sydney, 1917), 6.

9. Halifax *Herald*, 31 December 1917. See also *AMWNS Minutes, 1917*.

10. *CLL*, 29 December 1917. McLachlan had written these words some weeks earlier, in one of the first issues of the new Sydney labour newspaper, but these issues have not survived. The words impressed themselves on the memory of a later correspondent.

11. "Mine Explosion in New Waterford, 1917," *Cape Breton's Magazine*, no. 21 (1978), 1-11, and "New Waterford's Explosion, 1917," *Cape Breton's Magazine*, no. 63 (June 1993), 82.

12. "Mine Explosion in New Waterford, 1917"; *CMJ*, 1 October 1917, 387-8, 15 December 1917, 489, 1 January 1918, 5.

13. *AMWNS Minutes, 1917*, 12; J.B. McLachlan Notebook [1917], in J.L. MacKinnon Papers, "James B. McLachlan" file, box 4, BI; "Mine Explosion in New Waterford, 1917."

14. McLachlan to Robert Borden, 7 November 1917, and enclosed document, "Re New Waterford Explosion," vol. 223, Robert L. Borden Papers, NAC; *CLL*, 9 March 1918. Plans for the construction of the monument in New Waterford

had been approved at the October convention. The decision to include John McKay's figure was regarded as a mark of esteem for a victim against whom there were allegations of blame for the explosion: Halifax *Herald*, 30 October 1917.

15. Halifax *Herald*, 31 December 1917. For the 1918 disaster, see James M. Cameron, *Pictonian Colliers* (Halifax, 1974), 232-8.
16. Minutebook [Amalgamated Mine Workers of Nova Scotia, Springhill local], 11, 18, 25 August, 1 September 1917, 15 June, 17 August, 5 October 1918, St Francis Xavier University Archives, Antigonish.
17. Springhill AMW Minutebook, 25 May, 20 July, 17 August, 16 November 1918.
18. *Labour Gazette* (July 1918), 520-5, *CLL*, 8, 15 June 1918, Halifax *Herald*, 15 June 1918.
19. Halifax *Herald*, 8 January, 21 February 1918.
20. Ibid., 26 February 1918, *CLL*, 30 March, 11 May 1918.
21. *CLL*, 4 May 1918, Halifax *Herald*, 31 December 1917.
22. Halifax *Herald*, 8 July 1918, *Post*, 9 July 1918, *CLL*, 31 August 1918.
23. *Minutes of Second Annual Convention of the AMWNS* (Glace Bay, 1918), Halifax *Herald*, 19-25 November 1918.
24. For the background to this policy, see Donald Avery, *"Dangerous Foreigners": European Immigrant Workers and Labour Radicalism in Canada, 1896-1932* (Toronto, 1979), 69-70.
25. *Minutes of Second Annual Convention of the AMWNS*, passim., 73-8. "Labour and the New Social Order" was adopted by the Labour Party in June 1918; it had been drafted by Sidney Webb and widely circulated for discussion beforehand. The excerpts included in the AMW's Reconstruction Report included sections 7, 8, 9 (in part), 4 (in part), 25 (in part), 23 (in part). See Paul U. Kellogg and Arthur Gleason, *British Labor and the War: Reconstructors for a New World* ([1919] New York, 1972), 395-412. G.D.H. Cole, *A History of the Labour Party from 1914* (New York, 1969), 54-71, notes "its enthusiastic reception in many countries – not least by progressives in the United States."
26. "For Six Years UMW of A International Has Failed to Support N. S. Miners ...," undated clipping [1925?], item #14E0041, Communist Party of Canada Papers, AO.
27. Halifax *Herald*, 31 December 1917.
28. *AMWNS Minutes, 1917*, 7-11, 16.
29. See *CLL*, 15, 29 December 1917. See also David Frank, "The Miner's Financier: Women in the Cape Breton Coal Towns, 1917," *Atlantis*, vol. 8, no. 2 (spring 1983), 137-43.
30. *CLL*, 19 January 1918, *Post*, 21 January 1922.
31. For insights into the gender-specificity of class consciousness among the coal miners, see Steven Penfold, "'Have You No Manhood in You?': Gender and Class in the Cape Breton Coal Towns, 1920-1926," *Acadiensis*, vol. 23, no. 2 (spring 1994), 21-44. See also Seccombe, "Patriarchy Stabilized," and J.A. Mangan and James Walvin, eds., *Manliness and Morality: Middle-class Masculinity in Britain and America, 1800-1940* (New York, 1987). For recent studies of masculinities and working-class history in Canada, see the articles in *Labour/Le Travail*, vol. 42 (fall 1998).
32. *Wages and Hours of Labour in Canada*, no. 3 (Ottawa, 1922), 23-7; David Frank, "Coal Masters and Coal Miners," 90-6, 234. See also Wade, "History of District 26," passim.
33. *Labour Gazette* (February 1920), 129-31. The MacKinnon Award applied only to the miners employed by Dominion Coal, but similar agreements were reached in the following months with the other operators in Nova Scotia: *Labour Gazette* (March 1920), ibid. (April 1920).

34. *Post*, 27 January, 2, 24 February 1920, Halifax *Herald*, 2, 21 February 1920. There were minor modifications to satisfy some of the objections to the original agreement.

35. Halifax *Herald*, 31 December 1917.

36. "Minutes of Evidence" [Duncan Commission, 1925], 1012-13.

37. Frank J. Hayes to McLachlan, 5 November 1917, McLachlan to Hayes, 9 November 1917, Andrew Steele and Neal J. Ferry to Hayes, 19 January 1918, Excerpt from International Executive Board Minutes, 27 January, 13 April 1918, President's Correspondence, District 26, 1918, UMWA Papers.

38. Correspondence printed in *Minutes of the Second Annual Convention of the AMWNS*, 17-21.

39. Mark Workman to Borden, 30 March 1918, Borden Papers.

40. C.A. Magrath to Gideon Robertson, 12 November 1918; see also memo. by Magrath, 2 December 1918, and an unpublished manuscript on fuel control, May 1935, C.A. Magrath Papers, NAC. When Magrath stepped down as fuel controller, McLachlan wrote to thank him "for all the help and assistance you gave us during the dark days of the war": McLachlan to Magrath, 10 February 1919. See also C.A. Magrath, *Final Report of the Fuel Controller, March 1919* (Ottawa, 1919), 52-5.

41. International Executive Board Minutes, 22 March 1919, 166-70, UMWA Papers. As defined in the agreement, this was an eight-hour hoisting day: all men were expected to be in the mine, ready to work, at 7 a.m.; the day's work would end at 3 p.m., at which time men would begin their return travel to the surface; the standard for surface labour would be 7 a.m to 4 p.m., with half an hour for dinner, and machine shop 7 a.m. to 5 p.m. with one hour for dinner.

42. Excerpt from International Executive Board Minutes, 22 March 1919, President's Correspondence, District 26, 1919, UMWA Papers.

43. Ibid.

44. On the rise of Lewis, see Melvyn Dubofsky and Warren Van Tine, *John L. Lewis: A Biography* (New York, 1977), 38-42 and passim.

45. See G.S. Kealey, "1919: The Canadian Labour Revolt," *Labour/Le Travail*, vol. 13 (spring 1984), 11-44, and Nolan Reilly, "The General Strike in Amherst, Nova Scotia, 1919," *Acadiensis*, vol. 9, no. 2 (spring 1980), 56-77.

46. Documents dated 28 October, 31 October 1919, RCMP File. See also G.S. Kealey, "State Repression of Labour and the Left in Canada, 1914-20: The Impact of the First World War," *Canadian Historical Review*, vol. 73, no. 3 (September 1992), 281-314.

47. *Eastern Federationist*, 12 July 1919, *Labor Leader*, 19 July 1919, *Post*, 16 July, 8-12 September 1919; *Minutes of Special Convention of the United Mine Workers of America Held in Sydney, N.S., Aug. 25-29, 1919* (Glace Bay, n.d.), 29.

48. *Post*, 8-12 September 1919, *Debates of the House of Commons*, 9 September 1919, 108, Sydney *Record*, 1 May 1920, Halifax *Herald*, 1 May 1920, RCMP File, 2 May 1920. McLachlan's reading at this time included *The Winnipeg General Sympathetic Strike* (Winnipeg, 1920), which was produced by the defence committee and acknowledged the support of the coal miners. For a recent edition, see Norman Penner, ed., *Winnipeg 1919: The Strikers' Own History of the Winnipeg General Strike* (Toronto, 1973).

49. *Labor Leader*, 16 August 1919, *Post*, 27 August 1919, *Eastern Federationist*, 6 September 1919. See also James Naylor, *The New Democracy: Challenging the Social Order in Industrial Ontario, 1914-1925* (Toronto, 1991), 192-3, and Naylor, "Workers and the State: Experiments in Corporatism after World War One," *Studies in Political Economy*, no. 42 (autumn 1993), 81-111.

50. McLachlan's correspondence on this issue was reviewed and endorsed at the District 26 convention in August: *Minutes of Special Convention, Aug. 25-29, 1919*, 10-17.

51. *Post*, 22 September, 4 October 1919, 9, 14 September 1920; Naylor, *The New Democracy*, 200. See also Tom Traves, "'The Story That Couldn't Be Told': Big Business Buys the TLC," *Ontario Report* (September 1976), 27-9.

52. RCMP File, 11 February, 5 April 1920. On the OBU, see David Bercuson, *Fools and Wise Men: The Rise and Fall of the One Big Union* (Toronto, 1978).

53. RCMP File, 9, 27 March, 10 April 1920 and passim.

54. *Post*, 10, 12 April 1920, RCMP File, 1 May 1920. See also "Re-U.M.W. Convention, Truro and the O.B.U.," RCMP report dated 9 April 1920, vol. 61, Arthur Meighen Papers, NAC.

55. RCMP File, 7 June, 12 August, 24 November, 8 June 1920.

56. RCMP File, 7, 8 June 1920.

57. RCMP File, 8 December 1920, *Post*, 17 December 1920, 20 January 1921. Challenged by one of the radical local leaders in Glace Bay, Baxter himself had made a relatively poor showing and would not be confirmed as president until after a second run-off election in January.

58. Halifax *Herald*, 2 February, 1 May, 23 September 1920. For a discussion, see "The Image: J.B. and the 'Red Years' through the Eyes of the *Halifax Herald*," *New Maritimes*, vol. 6, nos. 4/5 (December 1987-January 1988), 8-9. See also Margaret Conrad, "The Art of Regional Protest: The Political Cartoons of Donald McRitchie, 1904-1937," *Acadiensis*, vol. 21, no. 1 (autumn 1991), 5-29.

59. Clipping from *Atlantic Leader*, September 1919, Stuart McCawley Scrapbook, 65, Miners' Memorial Museum, Glace Bay.

60. *Eastern Federationist*, 16 August 1919. See also *Eastern Federationist*, 13 September 1919.

61. J.B. McLachlan Notebook [1917], BI. On one of the pages there is a marginal notation to "Myre's History"; McLachlan's personal library included a copy of Gustavus Myers, *A History of Canadian Wealth* (Chicago, 1914). Some of these notes may be quotations or paraphrases based on his reading, but it has not been possible to identify published sources for these notes.

62. From more than 100 entries, the judges – who included Robert Baxter and Stuart McCawley of Glace Bay – awarded first place to the one by McLachlan, which was submitted under the pen-name "MINER." As far as can be determined, the *Herald* did not announce the results of the contest nor did it publish the prize-winning essay. See Halifax *Herald*, 17 May 1919, *The Citizen* (Halifax), 2 February 1923, *OBU Bulletin* (Winnipeg), 2 October 1924. The full text is printed in "The Economic Gospel of J.B. McLachlan," *New Maritimes*, vol. 2, no. 4 (December 1983-January 1984), 3.

63. On the social gospel, see Richard Allen, *The Social Passion: Religion and Social Reform in Canada, 1914-1928* (Toronto, 1971). For a contemporary statement by a theological radical from within the church, see Salem Bland, *The New Christianity* ([1920] Toronto, 1973).

Chapter 5

1. "Just Before the Battle, Mother," first published in 1863, was one of Elihu Root's popular songs of the Civil War in the United States. The Wobbly song was entitled "I'm Too Old To Be A Scab" and began to appear in the IWW songbooks in the 1920s. See *Songs of the Workers to Fan the Flames of Discontent* (Chicago, 1973), 21. Also using the same tune was a 1913 song from the Vancouver Island coal miners, "Bowser's Penitents": O'Donnell, *"And Now the Fields Are Green,"* 103-4.

2. See E.J. Hobsbawm, "Trends in the British Labour Movement since 1850," in *Labouring Men: Studies in the History of Labour* (London, 1971), especially the discussion of "spontaneity" and "consciousness" at 334-42; and Antonio Gramsci, *Selections from Political Writings (1910-1920)* (London, 1977), 265-8. See

also David Frank, "Industrial Democracy and Industrial Legality: The United Mine Workers of America in Nova Scotia, 1908-1927," in Laslett, ed., *The United Mine Workers of America: A Model of Industrial Solidarity?*, 438-55. Is it possible that in these years McLachlan's tactics and strategy on numerous issues were informed by familiarity with the writings of an obscure Marxist writing for the radical press in northern Italy? One reporter noted the presence of an Italian magazine in McLachlan's offices, he possessed an Italian dictionary (and also a Kerr edition of Antonio Labriola), there were Italian immigrants in the coal towns who counted themselves among his followers, and McLachlan wore in 1925 a button of the Italian Communist Party! But as Ian McKay has suggested in the case of the Maritime socialist intellectual Colin McKay, whose work contains numerous Gramscian observations, there was parallel thinking among contemporaries who reflected on similar issues: see Ian McKay, ed., *For a Working-Class Culture in Canada: A Selection of Colin McKay's Writings on Sociology and Political Economy, 1897-1939* (St John's/Fredericton, 1996).

3. "Floors That Have Talked to Me," 19-20. For a consideration of the rise of the labour bureaucracy generally, see Mark Leier's study of the Vancouver Trades and Labour Council before the Great War, *Red Flags and Red Tape: The Making of a Labour Bureaucracy* (Toronto, 1995).

4. J.B. McLachlan, Jr., Tom McLachlan, Alice McLachlan, Elsie Warner, interviews, 1975-76.

5. Ibid.; P.M. Nicholson interview, 21 July 1964, T-34, BI; Annie Whitfield interview, 4 May 1975.

6. RCMP File, 8 June 1920.

7. Tom McLachlan interview, 28 April 1976; Annie Whitfield interview, 27 July 1975. The names of family members occur on several occasions in the records of Glace Bay's Knox United Church, PANS; this includes both the father and the mother at the time of their respective deaths in 1937 and 1939. On one occasion McLachlan joked that "Presbyterians is the church we stay away from."

8. *Post*, 14 November 1917, *CLL*, 2, 16 February 1918. On the rise of independent labour politics, see Craig Heron, "Labourism and the Canadian Working Class," *Labour/Le Travail*, vol. 13 (spring 1984), 45-75.

9. Halifax *Herald*, 18 December 1917. For detailed results, see House of Commons, *Sessional Papers, 1920*, no. 13.

10. Frank, "Company Town/Labour Town," 177-96.

11. *CLL*, 6 July 1918, *Labor Leader*, 16 August 1919. See also Frank, "Working-Class Politics." On the beginnings of the Nova Scotia Federation of Labour, see the official report of the proceedings in *Eastern Federationist*, 8, 15, 22 March 1919.

12. For a detailed study of this election across the province, see A.A. MacKenzie, "The Rise and Fall of the Farmer-Labour Party in Nova Scotia," MA thesis, Dalhousie University, 1969.

13. RCMP File, 7 June 1920, *Citizen*, 11 June 1920. See also Suzanne Morton, "Labourism and Economic Action: The Halifax Shipyards Strike of 1920," *Labour/Le Travail*, vol. 22 (fall 1988), 67-98.

14. For the results, see Nova Scotia, *Journals of the House of Assembly, 1921*, appendix no. 32. See also MacKenzie, "Rise and Fall of the Farmer-Labour Party in Nova Scotia," and Frank, "Working-Class Politics," 195-6.

15. *Post*, 11, 12, 14, 21 June 1920, Sydney *Record*, 14 June 1920.

16. G.S. Kealey and Reg Whitaker, eds., *R.C.M.P. Security Bulletins: The Early Years, 1919-1929* (St John's, 1994), 117.

17. *Monetary Times*, 26 March 1920; *New York Times*, 8 April 1945; H.J. Crowe to G.B. Hunter, April 1902, H. Crowe Letterbook, PANS.

18. On the corporation's history, see David Frank, "The Cape Breton Coal Industry and the Rise and Fall of the British Empire Steel Corporation," *Acadiensis*, vol. 7, no. 1 (autumn 1977), 3-34.
19. RCMP File, 12 August 1920.
20. *Labour Gazette* (February 1920), 129-31; McLachlan to Alfred Tonge, 29 March, 23 April, 5 May 1920, and Tonge to McLachlan, 5 April, 1 May, 14 May 1920, President's Office Correspondence, District 26, 1920, UMWA Papers; clipping from Sydney *Record*, 6 October 1920, Alexander Johnston Papers, MG35/1/#426, St Francis Xavier University Archives.
21. Royal Commission to Inquire into Coal Mining Operations in Nova Scotia and New Brunswick, "Proceedings of Conference at Glace Bay, July 20 and 21, 1920" [Quirk Hearings, Glace Bay] and "Minutes of the Royal Commission on Mining, Sitting at Halifax, August 9, 1920, and Following Days" [Quirk Hearings, Halifax], 6, 12, 27-8. For these documents, see File 611.04:6, vols. 141 and 142, RG27 (Department of Labour Records), NAC.
22. Quirk Hearings, Halifax,13
23. Ibid., statement dated 14 August 1920.
24. Ibid., 15, 35-6.
25. RCMP File, 6 September 1920. See *Post*, 4 September 1920, for one local's strike threat.
26. *Labour Gazette* (September 1920), 1168-84.
27. McLachlan to Lewis, 24 September 1920, Lewis to F.A. Ackland [sic], 1 October 1920, President's Office Correspondence, District 26, 1920, UMWA Papers.
28. Lewis to McLachlan, 1, 20 October 1920, President's Office Correspondence, District 26, 1920, UMWA Papers
29. RCMP File, 17 October 1920; *Post*, 29 September, 1 October 1920; McLachlan to Lewis, 15 October 1920, President's Office Correspondence, District 26, 1920, UMWA Papers; RCMP File, 16 October 1920; *Post*, 14, 19 October 1920.
30. RCMP File, 17 October 1920; Lewis to Robertson, 25 October 1920, President's Office Correspondence, District 26, 1920, UMWA Papers.
31. White to Lewis, 6 November 1920, President's Office Correspondence, District 26, 1920, UMWA Papers.
32. "MEMO RE CONFERENCE BETWEEN CERTAIN COLLIERY OPERATORS IN NOVA SCOTIA AND REPRESENTATIVES OF THEIR EMPLOYEES," Montreal, 8 November 1920, President's Office Correspondence, District 26, 1920, UMWA Papers.
33. *Post*, 13, 16, 17 November 1920; RCMP File, 18 November 1920. When Robertson challenged the account, Baxter confirmed McLachlan's report about the threatened use of the police: *Post*, 27 November 1920.
34. *Post*, 19 November 1920.
35. Ibid.
36. Ibid., 20 November 1920, RCMP File, 22 November 1920.
37. *Post*, 1, 2, 3 December 1920.
38. Ibid., 17 December 1920, 15 November 1920. As noted in chapter 4, the other members of the "Big Three" had not fared so well that month. As international board member, Barrett was closely associated with the international union's failure to support a strike; he had gone down to defeat at the hands of the radical Pictou County leader Dan Livingstone. Baxter had also faced a radical opponent and was forced to a second round before his re-election as president was confirmed.
39. RCMP File, 8, 24 December 1920.
40. House of Commons, Special Committee Respecting Future Fuel Supply of Canada, *Official Report of Evidence* (Ottawa, 1921), 776. See also John N. McDougall, *Fuels and the National Policy* (Toronto, 1982), 33-55.
41. *Fuel Supply Hearings*, passim.

42. McLachlan to Borden, 10, 18 July 1921, Borden Papers. See also *Labour Gazette* (March 1919), 308, and E.R. Forbes, *Maritime Rights: The Maritime Rights Movement, 1919-1927: A Study in Canadian Regionalism* (Montreal, 1979), 43.

43. In addition, a representative of the Inverness miners, I.D. MacDougall, was heard on 14 May: *Fuel Supply Hearings*, 643-57.

44. Ibid., 439-40, 504.

45. Ibid., 463-77.

46. Ibid., 477.

47. Ibid., 477-8.

48. Ibid., 478-9.

49. Ibid., 480.

50. Ibid., 480-3.

51. Ibid., 484.

52. Ibid., 485-9.

53. Ibid., 486-90.

54. Ibid., 490-1.

55. Ibid., 491-6.

56. *Globe* (Toronto), 7 May 1921, *Post*, 10 May 1921, *Herald*, 27 April 1921.

57. *Fuel Supply Hearings*, 657-65.

58. Ibid., 748-56.

59. Ibid., 757-62.

60. Ibid., v-x. The Dominion Fuel Board would, however, be established in 1922, and following another round of winter coal shortages, the Commons would pass a resolution in 1923 stating that "no part of Canada should be left dependent on a United States coal supply": see McDougall, *Fuels and the National Policy*, 37, 43-4.

61. Upton Sinclair, *The Brass Check: A Study of American Journalism* (Pasadena, Calif., 1920 [6th edition]), 436.

62. Sinclair, *Brass Check*, 400 [McLachlan's copy].

63. See Ron Verzuh, *Radical Rag: The Pioneer Labour Press in Canada* (Ottawa, 1988).

64. Ibid.; Reid, *Keir Hardie*. On MacDougall, see *Dictionary of Canadian Biography*, vol. 13 (Toronto, 1994).

65. *Minutes of Special Convention, Aug. 25-29, 1919*, 22.

66. Nova Scotia, *Journals of the House of Assembly, 1921*, appendix no. 12, 19; *Articles of Association and By-Laws, Maritime Labor Herald* (Glace Bay, 1921); MLH, 14 October 1921. A list of shareholders at the end of 1924 showed a total of 2,463 shares, the great majority held by the Cape Breton locals of District 26; only 64 shares were held by individuals: *The Maritime Labor Herald Limited, Financial Statement ending December 31st, 1924* (Glace Bay, n.d.)

67. *Post*, 8, 31 August, 23, 29 September 1921. On Cotton, see E.M. Penton, "*Cotton's Weekly* and the Canadian Socialist Revolution, 1909-1914," unpublished manuscript, 1978.

68. *MLH*, 14 October 1921.

69. Ibid., 14 October-3 December 1921.

70. Ibid., 10 December 1921, 29 April 1922, 25 October 1924.

71. *Debates of the House of Commons*, 6 May 1921.

72. RCMP File, 17 August, 9 November 1921. For an earlier account, see Frank, "Working Class Politics," 196-8.

73. *Post*, 6, 15 October 1921.

74. For this election the labour and farmer organizations in Cape Breton North-Victoria also united to endorse a common candidate. In the single-member North riding, the Farmer-Labour candidate was M.A. MacKenzie, a St Ann's native and Sydney alderman sympathetic to the labour cause. The Conservatives decided to make no nomination, and the result was a straight fight

between M.A. MacKenzie and the veteran Liberal D.D. McKenzie. As in the South riding, the Farmer-Labour candidate did better in the industrial district. In the coal and steel town of Sydney Mines, he won 49.5 per cent of the vote; overall he received only 35.4 per cent of the total vote in the constituency.

75. *Post*, 27 October, 1, 9 November 1921.
76. *MLH*, 12 November 1921.
77. Ibid., 12, 19 November 1921.
78. Ibid., 5 November 1921.
79. Ibid., 19 November 1921; *The Casket*, 24 November 1921. For earlier attacks on the labour party, see *The Casket*, 28 July, 11, 25 August 1921.
80. *Post*, 1 November 1921.
81. *MLH*, 3 December 1921.
82. *Post*, 5 December 1921.
83. Ibid., 6 December 1921.
84. Ibid.; *MLH*, 10, 17 December 1921, *Let CARROLL Produce 'THE LETTER!'* [copy of leaflet, 1922], Joseph Nearing Scrapbook. This collection was examined with the kind permission of Mr Nearing.
85. *MLH*, 10 December 1921; E.H. Armstrong to W.F. Carroll, 8 December 1921, vol. 10, F11/3194, E.H. Armstrong Papers, PANS.
86. *MLH*, 10 December 1921.
87. As the labour poet Dawn Fraser wrote a few years later: "McLachlan was fighting and running strong, / And but for a cowardly, cruel wrong, / When somebody told a lot of lies / To fool the workers and blind their eyes ..." See Fraser, *Echoes from Labor's Wars: The Expanded Edition*, 23-4. This general view of the results has been largely accepted by subsequent writers, who have claimed that McLachlan's support among the miners and steelworkers was severely damaged by "the smear campaign of Carroll and his associates" and generally by "lies, deceit, and outright chicanery": MacEwan, *Miners and Steelworkers*, 77, and Mellor, *The Company Store*, 128-38.
88. For the detailed returns, see *Report of the Chief Electoral Officer, Fourteenth General Election, 1921*, House of Commons, *Sessional Papers, 1922*, no. 13.
89. *MLH*, 24 December 1921.
90. *The Casket*, 19 January 1922. See also David Frank, "Joe Wallace, Poet," *New Maritimes*, vol. 4, no. 2 (October 1985), 15.
91. *MLH*, 17, 24 December 1921, Kent Foster to John L. Lewis, 3 May 1920, President's Office Correspondence, District 26, 1920, UMWA Papers.
92. On Woodsworth, see Grace MacInnis, *J.S. Woodsworth: A Man to Remember* (Toronto, 1953), Kenneth McNaught, *A Prophet in Politics: A Biography of J.S. Woodsworth* (Toronto, 1959), Allen Mills, *Fool for Christ: The Political Thought of J.S. Woodsworth* (Toronto, 1991).

Chapter 6

1. Clipping, Stuart McCawley Scrapbook, 33.
2. On McDougall, see *CMJ*, 14 September, 12 October 1923.
3. For an earlier account of the events of 1922 see David Frank, "Class Conflict in the Coal Industry: Cape Breton 1922," in G.S. Kealey and Peter Warrian, eds., *Essays in Canadian Working Class History* (Toronto, 1976), 161-84, 226-31. The wage cut became popularly known as a 37.5 per cent reduction: at the time the Montreal Agreement of 1920 represented a 12.5 per cent improvement in rates; the 1922 rates were to be 25 per cent below this scale. An index of nominal daily wages constructed on the basis 1913=100.0 shows a reduction from 235.9 under the Montreal Agreement to 156.6 on 1 January 1922; an index of real wages, taking into account the movement of prices, shows a reduction from 154.6 in July 1921 to 102.0 in January 1922.

4. *MLH*, 7 January 1922; the legislation is quoted in Ben Selekman, *Postponing Strikes* (New York, 1927), 377-8; Murdock is quoted in Wade, "History of District 26."

5. "Opinion of Mellish, J., UMW et al. vs. Dominion Coal et al.," 10 January 1922, Records of the Supreme Court of Nova Scotia, PANS. There were additional unilateral changes at this time: the company changed contract drivers from tonnage to daily rates and refused to collect union dues from several groups of overground workers, including machine shop workers.

6. *MLH*, 11 February 1922.

7. *Post*, 18 January 1922, MLH, 21 January 1922.

8. *Post*, 23-27 January 1922, *MLH*, 28 January 1922. Subsequently thirteen men were convicted and sentenced to prison terms of two and three years for their part in the raids.

9. F.P. Hanaway to John L. Lewis, 30 January 1922, President's Office Correspondence, District 26, 1922, UMWA Papers.

10. For the text of the report, see *Labour Gazette* (February 1922), 142-81; for McLachlan's data, see 149-61.

11. *Proceedings of the 29th Consecutive and Sixth Biennial Convention of the United Mine Workers of America* (Indianapolis, 1924), vol. I, 447-9, 458; Halifax *Herald*, 27 February 1922.

12. *Labour Gazette* (March 1922), 308-9; *UMWA Proceedings, 1924*, 449-52; *MLH*, 25 March 1922; White to Lewis, 1 March 1922, President's Office Correspondence, District 26, 1922, UMWA Papers. The document, signed only by Baxter, Wolvin and McDougall, is included in President's Correspondence, District 26, 1922, UMWA Papers.

13. Halifax *Chronicle*, 11-16 March 1922.

14. *MLH*, 11 March 1922.

15. William Grant, ed., *The Scottish National Dictionary* (Edinburgh 1931), vol. 2, 6.

16. McLachlan's knowledge of restriction of output was discussed in chapter 1. On the practice in Scotland, see Arnot, *The Scottish Miners*, 17. See also John R. Commons, "Trade Union Regulation and Restriction of Output," *Eleventh Special Report of United States Commissioner of Labour* (Washington, 1904). "It had long been the custom amongst the colliers to meet a reduction of wages or other worsening of conditions by a reduction of output," writes Arnot. "The 'wee darg' was a normal, 'instinctive' reaction to any unfair bargain, especially when trade unions were repressed or not recognized, so that collective bargaining could not take place." For a discussion of organic, tactical, and strategic forms of workers' control in the coal industry in this period, see David Frank, "Contested Terrain: Workers' Control in the Cape Breton Coal Mines in the 1920s," in Craig Heron and Robert Storey, eds., *On the Job: Confronting the Labour Process in Canada* (Kingston and Montreal, 1986), 102-23.

17. *MLH*, 11 February 1922.

18. *The Worker*, 1 May 1922, Halifax *Herald*, 27 February 1922.

19. *MLH*, 18 March 1922.

20. *Post*, 23 March 1922, Halifax *Chronicle*, 20 March 1922. "This is not sabotage, but merely ca'canny," advised the *Maritime Labor Herald*, 1 April 1922.

21. *Post*, 20-31 March 1922, *MLH*, 25 March, 1 April 1922, RCMP File, 1 April 1922.

22. Joseph Nearing interview, September 1975.

23. *MLH*, 25 March 1922.

24. Ibid., 1 April 1922.

25. McLachlan to members of the House of Commons, 20 March 1922, Meighen Papers. See also *MLH*, 25 March, 1 April 1922.

26. *The Canadian Parliamentary Guide, 1922*, 180, 235.

27. The full exchange appears in *MLH*, 25 March 1922, and in *Debates of the House of Commons*, 1922, 512-16.

28. *Debates of the House of Commons*, 1922, 497-545; *Debates of the Senate*, 1922, 50-64.

29. *MLH*, 8, 15 April 1922; E.H. Armstrong to W.S. Fielding, 31 March 1922, vol. 10, F2/2945, Armstrong Papers; R.M. Wolvin to King, 31 March 1922, King to Wolvin, 1 April 1922, King Papers.

30. Interview with Tim Buck, by Mac Reynolds, 21 June 1965, NAC. My thanks to Richard Lochead for locating this item. For an abbreviated account of Buck's 1922 visit, see Tim Buck, *Yours in the Struggle: Reminiscences of Tim Buck* (Toronto, 1977), 114-18.

31. Documents from the founding convention are published in *The Worker*, 15 March 1922. For this period see Ian Angus, *Canadian Bolsheviks: The Early Years of the Communist Party of Canada* (Montreal, 1981), part 1, and Norman Penner, *Canadian Communism: The Stalin Years and Beyond* (Toronto, 1988), 44-69. See also William Rodney, *Soldiers of the International: A History of the Communist Party of Canada, 1919-1929* (Toronto, 1968), and the official history, *Canada's Party of Socialism: History of the Communist Party of Canada, 1921-1976* (Toronto, 1982).

32. *Left-Wing Communism* was serialized in Canada by the *B.C. Federationist* and the *Western Clarion* in 1921: Penner, *Canadian Communism*, 60.

33. *The Worker*, 1 May 1922, Buck, *Yours in the Struggle*, 114. An earlier item from Cape Breton appeared in *The Worker*, 1 April 1922: Marjorie MacInnis, "Grip of Dominion Coal Co." McLachlan's recruitment was the beginning a long relationship, which has been examined in John Manley, "Preaching the Red Stuff: J.B. McLachlan, Communism, and the Cape Breton Miners, 1922-1935," *Labour/Le Travail*, vol. 30 (fall 1992), 65-114.

34. *MLH*, 29 April, 6, 13 May 1922.

35. On Knight, see Bercuson, *Fools and Wise Men*, passim., and Rodney, *Soldiers of the International*, 44-5, 166.

36. *MLH*, 29 April, 17 June 1922, *Post*, 10 June 1922. The date of Knight's arrival is uncertain; according to the *MLH*, 29 April 1922, he was not expected in Glace Bay until the following week, but McLachlan may have met with him in Halifax beforehand. Plans for Knight's visit were mentioned in RCMP files as early as 15 April. The proposal for a government loan to Russia was subsequently endorsed by District 26 but rejected by a 147-56 vote at the annual meeting of the TLC.

37. *MLH*, 22 April 1922, RCMP File, 17 April 1922.

38. RCMP File, 8 June 1922.

39. *MLH*, 21, 28 January, 11 February, 10, 17 June 1922, *Workers' Weekly*, 15, 26 May 1922. In addition there was evidence that Nova Scotia was rapidly recovering its share of the Quebec market and that Wolvin was facing a revolt among shareholders, which was interpreted as a "concerted move on the part of the really big capitalists to get control of Besco" and take it out of the hands of Wolvin and McDougall, "who do not know how to manage the affairs of a big corporation": *MLH*, 24 June 1922.

40. Sydney *Record*, 9 May 1922, *MLH*, 27 May 1922.

41. For the board's report, see *Labour Gazette* (June 1922), 578-90.

42. *Labour Gazette* (February 1922), 178, *MLH*, 3 June 1922.

43. *Post*, 13 June 1922.

44. "Minutes, Third Annual Convention of District 26, UMWA, 20-24 June 1922" [mimeographed copy provided by Joseph Nearing].

45. Ibid., Halifax *Herald*, 24, 26 June 1922, *UMWA Proceedings, 1924*, 452.

46. "Minutes, Third Annual Convention of District 26." See also Halifax *Herald*, 27 June 1922, *MLH*, 1 July 1922, *The Worker*, 1 August 1922.

47. For a specific reference to the Chartist use of the phrase, see the 1839 speech of George Julian Harney in Dorothy Thompson, *The Early Chartists* (London, 1971), 186.
48. Halifax *Herald*, 26 June 1922, *Annual Report on Labour Organization in Canada, 1922*, 156-65.
49. Buck, *Yours in the Struggle*, 118, Buck interview, 1965.
50. John Moffatt to F.A. Acland, 5 August 1922, King Papers.
51. Sydney *Record*, 22 July 1922, Toronto *Star*, 24 July 1922, *Post*, 24 July 1922.
52. Baxter to King, 14 August, King to Baxter, 14 August, Baxter to King, 14 August 1922, King Papers.
53. Montreal *Star*, 15 August 1922; "Minutes of Evidence" [Duncan Commission, 1925], 1047-9.
54. Halifax *Citizen*, 18 August 1922, Halifax *Herald*, 21 August 1922.
55. Montreal *Star*, 16 August 1922.
56. Halifax *Herald*, 21 August 1922. The tellers' report, dated 21 August 1922, is contained in President's Office Correspondence, District 26, 1922, UMWA Papers.
57. Beginning with Wolvin's appeal to King on 14 August 1922, there is extensive correspondence in the King Papers concerning the use of troops. See also Don Macgillivray, "Military Aid to the Civil Power: The Cape Breton Experience in the 1920s," *Acadiensis*, vol. 3, no. 2 (spring 1974), 45-64.
58. Halifax *Herald*, 21 August 1922.
59. Memo of Communications Ottawa-Halifax (GOC, MD#6), August 1922, King Papers; James A. Fraser to Armstrong, 18 August 1922, vol. 8 F11/2661, Armstrong Papers; Halifax *Herald*, 18 August 1922.
60. McLachlan to Murdock, 21 August 1922, King Papers; see also *MLH*, 26 August 1922.
61. McDougall to Lewis, Murdock to Lewis, 15 August 1922, Lewis to McDougall, Lewis to Murdock, Lewis to Baxter (and others), 16, 17 August 1922, President's Office Correspondence, District 26, 1922, UMWA Papers.
62. Barrett to Lewis, 16 August 1922, Baxter to Lewis, 17 August 1922, McDougall to Lewis, 17 August 1922, President's Office Correspondence, District 26, 1922, UMWA Papers.
63. Halifax *Herald*, 28 August-2 September 1922.
64. RCMP File, 7, 8 September 1922.
65. Halifax *Herald*, 2 September 1922.
66. RCMP File, 5 December 1922.
67. Ibid., 16 September 1922.
68. Barrett to Lewis, 26 June 1922, Baxter to Lewis, 8 September 1922, Barrett to Lewis, 26 September 1922, President's Office Correspondence, District 26, 1922, UMWA Papers.
69. Lewis to Livingstone, 20 October 1922, McLachlan to Lewis, 15 December 1922, Lewis to McLachlan, 21 December 1922, President's Office Correspondence, District 26, 1922, UMWA Papers.
70. *MLH*, 14 October 1922, 17 February 1923.
71. McLachlan to J.J. Tompkins, 4 October 1922, Tompkins to W.S. Learned, 20 September, 5 October 1922, J.J. Tompkins Papers, BI; *MLH*, 23, 30 September 1922. On college federation, see John G. Reid, "Mount Allison College: The Reluctant University," *Acadiensis*, vol. 10, no. 1 (autumn 1980), 35-66; and on Jimmy Tompkins, see George Boyle, *Father Tompkins of Nova Scotia* (New York, 1953).
72. *MLH*, 14, 28 October 1922, Halifax *Herald*, 25 October 1922.
73. Tompkins to Ryan, 20 October 1920, Tompkins Papers; *CMJ*, 29 September 1922.
74. *MLH*, 7 October 1922.

75. Ibid.
76. Ibid., 11 November, 2 December 1922; *Citizen*, 8 December 1922; *Annual Report on Labour Organization in Canada, 1922*, 235. Apart from an endorsement by the Alberta Federation of Labour, subsequent editions of the *Maritime Labor Herald* reported little response to this initiative.
77. Manley, "Preaching the Red Stuff," 70. McLachlan's library included an early edition of *Left-Wing Communism*, published by the Marxian Educational Society in Detroit in 1921, which may have been presented to him by Joseph Knight or Tim Buck.
78. Halifax *Herald*, 1 September 1922; H.L. Stewart, "Bolshevism and Jacobinism," *Canadian Magazine*, October 1922, 463-4; inscription by J.W.A. Nicholson in McLachlan's copy of *The New Testament: A New Translation by James Moffatt* (New York 1918).
79. Halifax *Chronicle*, 27 April, 12 April 1922, *MLH*, 18 November 1922, *Mining Record*, 13 September 1922.

Chapter 7

1. *MLH*, 5 May 1923, *Post*, 2 May 1923, Emerson Campbell interview, 27 September 1975.
2. *Post*, 30 January, 27 February 1923, Sydney *Record*, 19 February 1923.
3. "Report of National Convention, February 1923," "Report of Industrial Organizer," files 5, 6, 7, box 11, Communist Party of Canada Papers, NAC. Rodney, *Soldiers of the International*, 61, cites a membership of 4,180 members at the end of 1922.
4. ? [Tim Buck] to Kid Burns, 20 March 1923, file 5, box 8, CPC Papers, NAC. The other Maritime delegates were H.M. Bartholomew and Joe Wallace. *CMJ*, 2 March 1923, confirmed that McLachlan had gone beyond the bounds of free speech in making "anti-social utterances" in Toronto and confirmed his reputation as a "firebrand labour leader."
5. "My Dear Chris" [unidentified letter], 16 March 1923, file 6, box 6, ? [Tim Buck] to Jack Dolan, 29 March 1923, ? [Buck] to Louis Macdonald, 23 April 1923, ? [C. Scott] to Tim [Buck], n.d. [March 1923], file 5, box 8, CPC Papers, NAC.
6. See Alan J. Singer, "'Something of a Man': John L. Lewis, the UMWA, and the CIO, 1919-1943," in Laslett, ed., *The United Mine Workers of America: A Model of Industrial Solidarity?* 110-11: "His attack on Kansas (District 14) and Alexander Howat, its district president, became a model for future campaigns to eliminate opposition and centralize authority."
7. [E[?]. A. Munro to Armstrong, 10 April 1923, Armstrong Papers; *MLH*, 12 May 1923. See also *Debates of the House of Commons*, 1923, 2296, 3155.
8. *Post*, 2 May 1923, *Worker*, 1, 16 May 1923, *MLH*, 5 May 1923. Portions of the quotation from McLachlan were written for *The Worker* in advance of the day and his actual speech was only briefly reported.
9. W.J. McNulty, "The 'Reds' of Eastern Canada," *The Current History Magazine*, vol. 4 (June 1923), 422-4.
10. David Montgomery, *The Fall of the House of Labor: The Workplace, the State, and American Labor Activism, 1865-1925* (New York, 1987), Dubofsky and Van Tine, *John L. Lewis*. The debate with District 26 offered an instructive case study in contrasting views of the significance of industrial legality: see Frank, "Industrial Democracy and Industrial Legality," in Laslett, ed., *The United Mine Workers of America: A Model of Industrial Solidarity?* 438-55.
11. McLachlan to Lewis, 15 December 1922, Lewis to McLachlan, 21 December 1922, President's Office Correspondence, District 26, 1922, UMWA Papers;

Proceedings [stenographic report], international board meeting, 8-12 January 1923 [black bound volume], 9-13, UMWA Papers; *MLH*, 13 January 1923.

12. Proceedings [stenographic report], January 1923 UMWA international board meeting, 8-12 January 1923 [black bound volume], 23-4, UMWA Papers.

13. Ibid., 190-97. See also *American Federationist* (February 1923), 139-41, *UMWJ*, 1 February 1923.

14. McLachlan to Lewis, 2, 3 February 1923, President's Correspondence, District 26, 1923, UMWA Papers.

15. *MLH*, 12 May, 16 June 1923.

16. McLachlan to Lewis, 18 April 1923, President's Correspondence, District 26, 1923, UMWA Papers.

17. *Post*, 7 May 1923.

18. Proceedings [stenographic report], international board meeting, June 1923, 159-75, UMWA Papers; *UMWJ*, 22 June 1923.

19. *MLH*, 9 June 1923.

20. Proceedings [stenographic report], international board meeting, June 1923, 175-85, UMWA Papers.

21. Ibid., 185-7.

22. Ibid., 295-6

23. Ibid., 268-9; Wolvin to Lewis, 20 June 1923, President's Correspondence, District 26, 1923, UMWA Papers.

24. Ibid., 296.

25. Lewis to Wolvin, 22 June 1923, Wolvin to Lewis, 23 June 1923, President's Correspondence, District 26, 1923, UMWA Papers.

26. *MLH*, 3 February 1923. On the steelworkers, see "The 1923 Strike in Steel and the Miners' Sympathy Strike," *Cape Breton's Magazine*, no. 22 (June 1979), 1-9, and Craig Heron, *Working in Steel: The Early Years in Canada, 1883-1935* (Toronto, 1988).

27. This account of the strike is based mainly on newspaper accounts and documents contained in the Strikes and Lockouts Files of the Department of Labour: NAC, RG27, vol. 330, file 8. See in particular Wolvin's correspondence with James Murdock, especially 18 February 1923 informing Murdock of the settlement.

28. *MLH*, 17 February 1923.

29. Forman Waye to C.B. Wade, 16 February 1950, RG21, Series M, no. 25, Reel #13, District 26 UMWA Papers, PANS.

30. *The Worker*, 2 April 1923.

31. Paul McNeil and J.B. McLachlan to King, 29 March 1923, vol. 90, King Papers. See also *Debates of the House of Commons*, 1923, 1704-5.

32. Memorandum by E. McG. Quirk on March 1923 visit to Sydney, RG27, vol. 143, file 611.04:10, NAC.

33. G.H. Murray to Armstrong, 10 April 1923, vol. 11A, file 15, 3828, Armstrong Papers.

34. *Post*, 30 May 1923; *Labor Defender* (March 1934), 4. Charges against Bruce were dismissed in court on 6 June.

35. *Post*, 15, 19 May 1923; W.J. O'Hearn to Armstrong, 20 May 1923, Armstrong Papers.

36. "RCMP Weekly Summary Notes Respecting Revolutionary Organizations and Agitators in Canada, No. 183," vol. 89, J4, King Papers.

37. Ibid.

38. *Post*, 28, 29, 30 June, and 4 July 1923; *MLH*, 7 July 1923. See also McLachlan's account in *The Worker*, 26 March 1932.

39. "RCMP Weekly Summary Notes Respecting Revolutionary Organizations and Agitators in Canada, No. 183."

NOTES 563

40. "The King vs. James B. McLachlan" [transcript of the case in the Supreme Court of Nova Scotia sitting as a Criminal Court of Appeal, 1923], Records of the Department of Justice, NAC, RG13 C2, vol. 1233, 33, 37; *MLH*, 8 September 1923.
41. *MLH*, 7 July 1923.
42. "The King vs. McLachlan," 4-5.
43. Ibid., 45-7.
44. *Post*, 7, 9 July 1923.
45. *Dominion Law Reports*, 4 (1923), 1047-9; *Post*, 12 July 1923. Various documents on the case, including a transcript of the preliminary hearing, are found in the case file at the PANS: RG 39 'C', box 706, file B-164.
46. Jeffery Williams, *Byng of Vimy, General and Governor General* (London, 1983), 280-1, 288-9.
47. On the significance of the *Hector* celebrations in the making of a Scottish myth in Nova Scotia, see Michael Boudreau, "Ship of Dreams," *New Maritimes*, vol. 11, no. 1 (September-October 1992), 6-15.
48. E.M. Macdonald, *Recollections Political and Personal* (Toronto, n.d. [1940?]), esp. 123, 415-17, 487-90.
49. Halifax *Herald*, 18 July 1923.
50. J.W. McLeod to Byng, n.d. [July 1923], vol. 84, King Papers; Viscountess Byng of Vimy, *Up the Stream of Time* (Toronto, 1945), 157-9.
51. *The Worker*, 26 March 1932. See also *Post*, 15 September 1923.
52. Wade, "History of District 26," chapter 4.
53. Williams, *Byng*, 292-3. See also Byng to King, 26 July 1923, King to Byng, 1 August 1923, Byng to King, 5 August 1923, vol. 84, King Papers.
54. King to Macdonald, 17, 18 July 1923, Macdonald to King, 21 July 1923, vol. 90, King Papers.
55. *Post*, 17 September 1923.
56. *The Worker*, 26 March 1932. It is not clear that McLachlan was actually in jail when he received this message, although he makes this assertion in some accounts of the events. According to the records of the county jail, McLachlan was released on 11 July and, although there were a number of court appearances in the interim, he did not return to jail until the end of his trial in October. It is possible that the union leaders had returned to Halifax for a further appearance on their application for bail.
57. Stewart to Lewis, 11, 14 July 1923, President's Office Correspondence, District 26, 1923, UMWA Papers.
58. Lewis to Sherman, 10 July 1923, Livett to Lewis, 10, 13 July 1923, President's Office Correspondence, District 26, 1923, UMWA Papers.
59. Barrett to Lewis, 5, 6 July, 16 July 1923, Lewis to Barrett, 5, 15, 20 July 1923, President's Office Correspondence, District 26, 1923, UMWA Papers. The telegram from Wolvin referred to by Lewis is missing from the file. According to a report in the Montreal press on 19 July, repeated by Tom Bell, Lewis "asked for the co-operation of the British Empire Steel Corporation and that co-operation President Wolvin has readily promised": *Labor Herald*, September 1923, 11.
60. Lewis to Sherman, 17 July 1923, President's Office Correspondence, District 26, 1923; Proceedings of International Executive Board [stenographic report], November 1923, 241-2, UMWA Papers. Lewis's actions were unanimously approved.
61. Lewis to Livingstone, 17 July 1923. See also *Post*, 18 July 1923 and *UMWJ*, 1 August 1923.
62. RCMP File, 8 September 1923.
63. Note by W.H. Measures, 17 July 1923, file #675, vol. 89, J4, King Papers. Lewis later reported that the corporation lodged daily protests, beginning on 5 July:

Proceedings of International Executive Board [stenographic report], November 1923, 240-1, UMWA Papers.

64. *The Worker*, 1 August 1923.
65. *MLH*, 4 August 1923.

Chapter 8

1. *Post*, 18 October 1923; Halifax *Herald*, 4 May 1933.
2. *Post*, 18 October 1923. On Harrington, see *CMJ*, January 1933, 4, and Desmond Morton, *A Peculiar Kind of Politics: Canada's Overseas Ministry in the First World War* (Toronto, 1982), 159, 164-5, 177, 199-200.
3. For opinions of Mellish, see R.A. Kanigsberg, *Trials and Tribulations of a Bluenose Barrister* (Halifax, 1977), 36, and an incomplete letter, probably from a Sydney lawyer, to J.S. Woodsworth, 9 February 1924, J.S. Woodsworth Papers, NAC. See also *The Supreme Court of Nova Scotia and Its Judges, 1754-1978* (Halifax, 1978), 77.
4. Kenneth McNaught, "Political trials and the Canadian Political Tradition," in M.L. Friedland, ed., *Courts and Trials: A Multidisciplinary Approach* (Toronto, 1975), 137-61. The most sophisticated account of the legal implications of the trial is Barry Cahill, "*Howe* (1835), *Dixon* (1920) and *McLachlan* (1923): Comparative Perspectives on the Legal History of Sedition," *UNB Law Journal*, vol. 45 (1996), 281-307. An earlier account is David Frank, "The Trial of J.B. McLachlan," *Historical Papers/ Communications historiques*, 1983, 208-25.
5. Toronto *Star*, 29 August 1923.
6. *TLC Proceedings, 1923*, 92-101. McLachlan did not vote in the roll call but was listed among the absentees.
7. "'Jim' McLachlan, Labor Covenanter," *Post*, 1 October 1923. See also Winnipeg *Tribune*, 20 September 1923.
8. The activities of the Nova Scotia Workers' Defence Committee can be followed in reports and audited statements in the *MLH*. See especially *MLH*, 29 September, 17, 24 November 1923.
9. *Post*, 17 August, 22, 25 September, 3 October 1923. On the Bruce case, see Halifax *Chronicle*, 8 May 1923, *Post*, 30 May 1923, Sydney *Record*, 7 June 1923.
10. "The King vs. James B. McLachlan" [transcript of the case in the Supreme Court of Nova Scotia sitting as a Criminal Court of Appeal, 1923], Records of the Department of Justice, RG13 C2, vol. 1233, NAC, 4; *Statutes of Canada, 1919*, chapter 46, 307-10. James M. Whalen of the National Archives of Canada was most helpful in gaining access to this copy of the trial transcript; no other copies were located. Except where noted otherwise, references to the court proceedings in this chapter are drawn from this document.
11. *Post*, 16 October 1923.
12. On Merkel, see Gwendolyn Davies, "The Song Fishermen: A Regional Poetry Celebration," in L.D. McCann, ed., *People and Place: Studies of Small Town Life in the Maritimes* (Fredericton, 1987), 137-50, and Charles Lynch, *You Can't Print That! Memoirs of a Political Voyeur* (Toronto, 1988), 25-31.
13. J.M. Beck, "'A Fool for a Client': The Trial of Joseph Howe," *Acadiensis*, vol. 3, no. 2 (spring 1974), 34; Skelton to Woodsworth, 28 March 1924, Woodsworth Papers.
14. Fraser, "The Case of Jim McLachlan," *Echoes from Labor's Wars*; *Post*, 19 October 1923; *OBU Bulletin*, 22 November 1923; Tom McLachlan interview, 28 April 1976.
15. Notes from the author's interview with John A. Walker, Halifax, 23 September 1976.
16. Cahill, "*Howe* (1835), *Dixon* (1920) and *McLachlan* (1923)," 295 and passim. Despite vigorous defences, most of the strike leaders charged with seditious

conspiracy were convicted; however, of the two men charged with seditious libel, Dixon was acquitted and the charges against Woodsworth were not pressed.

17. *Post*, 1 November 1923.
18. ? to Woodsworth, 9 February 1924, Woodsworth Papers.
19. *The Worker*, 14 November 1923; *MLH*, 17 November 1923.
20. *OBU Bulletin*, 24 January 1924. See also *Post*, 3 January 1924, *MLH*, 24 January 1924. The message from Mother Jones was actually sent in November, before the appeal was heard: *MLH*, 24 November 1923. For an introduction to "the miners' angel," see *The Autobiography of Mother Jones* (Chicago, 1925).
21. McLachlan wrote out a copy of the endorsement on the back of McCormack's letter, which is preserved in MG1, G76a, BI.
22. McLachlan to Eva, 28, 29 December 1923, letters which I examined with the kind permission of Eva Pemberton.
23. *Nova Scotia Law Reports*, 56 (1924), 413-21; *Canadian Criminal Cases*, vol. 41 (1924), 249-62. The first of these states, incorrectly, that Judge Mellish served as a member of the appeal court on this case.
24. *Dominion Law Reports*, vol. 1 (1924), 1109-12.
25. *Post*, 10 January 1924, *MLH*, 2 February 1924. McLachlan noted that his own diet was better than that of most prisoners: "The loyal miners saw to it that the best food was sent into the jail to him three times a day."
26. "The Maritime Penitentiary," *The University Monthly*, vol. 33 (January 1912), 163-7.
27. "Penitentiary Regulations, 1920," file #1-21-1, pt. 6, vol. 135, RG73, NAC. See also W.S. Hughes to minister of justice, 3 January 1924, ibid.
28. File 25777, RG 13 C2, vol. 1233, NAC.
29. In 1930 there was public controversy about "inadequate medical examination and antiquated hospitalization" at Dorchester when two young inmates died of tuberculosis: *Telegraph Journal* (Saint John), 5 May 1930.
30. G.T. Goad to W.S. Hughes, 2, 4 January, 3 September 1924, file 2-21-9, vol. 92, RG73, NAC.
31. Tom McLachlan interview, 28 April 1976, Jean Robinson interview, 27 July 1976.
32. *The Worker*, 9 April 1927. This is a frequently repeated story, with several variations. The version given here was reported in a story by Becky Buhay, who visited McLachlan in October 1925.
33. *Post*, 18, 19, 22, 24 October 1923.
34. An extensive file of petitions is contained in McLachlan's Remission Register, file no. 25777, RG 13 C2, vol. 1233, NAC. Individual items are cited from this file.
35. *MLH*, 1, 22 December 1923, *Post*, 15 December 1923. In Montreal, CPR workers pledged to pay $100 per month to help support the McLachlan family until he was released: *Post*, 12 January 1924.
36. *MLH*, 12, 19 January 1924. See also McNaught, *A Prophet in Politics*, 176, and *Debates of the House of Commons*, 1924, 61-5.
37. *Post*, 15 January 1924.
38. *The Worker*, 3 December 1923, published the letter, written by another veteran radical, F.J. Peel.
39. Wolvin to King, 10 January 1924, vol. 110, King Papers.
40. File no. 25533, vol. 1233, C2, RG13, NAC.
41. "Minutes of Convention of Penitentiary Officials, Vancouver, 15-20 September 1924," file 1-18-8, vol. 30, RG73, NAC, 24-6, 40, 42.
42. Livingstone to McLachlan, 3 March 1924, MG1 G76b, BI.
43. A typewritten version is contained in the Robinson Papers at the Beaton Institute with the notation "typed by one of his daughters original on back of Livingstone's letter." Was this with all certainty McLachlan's own composition? The authorship has not been traced to any established writer.

44. *Workers' Weekly*, 7 March 1924.
45. RCMP File, 7, 8 March 1924. McLachlan addressed another packed house at the Savoy on Sunday 9 March and then at the Strand in Sydney the following Sunday.
46. McLachlan to Woodsworth, 17 March 1924, Woodsworth Papers.
47. Stenographic report of McLachlan speech, 5 April 1924, vol. 8, F11/2671, Armstrong Papers.
48. McLachlan to Woodsworth, 17 March 1924, Woodsworth Papers.
49. *Workers' Weekly*, 7 March 1924.

Chapter 9

1. *MacLean's Magazine*, 15 January 1925.
2. *MLH*, 8 March 1924, RCMP File, 8, 10, 13, 17, 20 March, 24 May 1924.
3. *ARLOC, 1924*, 147-8.
4. For Buck's report see file 13, box 11, CPC Papers, NAC.
5. *MLH*, 1925, passim. On Bell, see Stewart Smith, *Comrades and Komsomolkas: My Years in the Communist Party of Canada* (Toronto, 1993), 84.
6. *MLH*, 17 May 1924.
7. *MLH*, 20 December 1924.
8. *MLH*, 27 September, 25 October 1924. The circulation of the newspaper at this time was estimated at about 4,000 copies: *MLH*, 8 November 1924.
9. *MLH*, 31 May 1924.
10. On the OBU, see Bercuson, *Fools and Wise Men* and Mary Jordan, *Survival: Labour's Trials and Tribulations in Canada* (Toronto, 1975).
11. David J. Goldberg, *A Tale of Three Cities: Labor Organization and Protest in Paterson, Passaic, and Lawrence, 1916-1921* (New Brunswick, N.J., 1989), 156-64. See also Jordan, *Survival*, chapter 13, and Bercuson, *Fools and Wise Men*, 238-40.
12. *OBU Bulletin*, 24 July, 7 August 1924.
13. *OBU Bulletin*, 21 August 1924, *Post*, 14 August 1924.
14. *MLH*, 14 June, 9, 23 August 1924; A.A. McKay to Ben Legere, 25 August 1924, box 5, folder 6, Ben Legere Papers, Archives of Labor and Urban Affairs, Wayne State University; RCMP File, 8 September 1924. My thanks to David Montgomery for referring me to the Legere Papers.
15. *ARLOC, 1924*, 176-9; McKay to Joseph C. McKinnon, 15 September 1924, McKinnon to McKay, 25 September 1924 [typed copies], box 5, folder 6, Legere Papers.
16. Legere to Leo –, 29 March, 1 April 1925, box 5, folder 7, Legere Papers; "Starving Nova Scotia's Miners," *The Nation*, 1 April 1925, 353-4.
17. William Dalrymple to Lewis, 11 March 1924, Lewis to Louis McCormack, 10 April 1924, President's Office Correspondence, District 26, 1924, UMWA Papers.
18. Lewis to Barrett, 20 February, 1 March 1924, William Green to Lewis, 6 March 1924, President's Office Correspondence, District 26, 1924, UMWA Papers; Executive Board Minutes, April 1924, 150-3, UMWA Papers.
19. Barrett to Lewis, 26 March 1924, Lewis to Barrett, 2 April 1924, Houston to Lewis, 26 March 1924, President's Office Correspondence, District 26, 1924, UMWA Papers.
20. Ind: Org: [Buck] to McLachlan, 30 April [1924 – but incorrectly dated "/25" by an archivist], file 49, box 52, CPC Papers, NAC.
21. *ARLOC, 1924*, 176-9.
22. Circular letter to board members, 5 September 1924, Lewis to Houston, 10 September 1924, President's Office Correspondence, District 26, 1924, UMWA Papers; *MLH*, 27 September 1924.

23. *Post*, 30 September 1924, *MLH*, 11 October 1924. Shortly after taking office, Joseph Nearing ran for the office of international secretary-treasurer on a slate of dissidents opposed to the rule of John L. Lewis.

24. Minutes of Convention of District 26, UMWA, 17-22 November 1924, RG 21A, vol. 42, no. 97 (Sessions of 18-19 November), PANS.

25. Ibid., Morning session, 20 November.

26. Ibid., Sessions of 20-21 November.

27. *MLH*, 3 January 1925. McLurg arranged to reproduce this front page as a paid advertisement in the Halifax papers, with a company response.

28. *MLH*, 17, 31 January, 7, 14 February 1925. For a sustained treatment of this theme, see Frank, "Contested Terrain: Workers' Control in the Cape Breton Coal Mines in the 1920s," 102-23.

29. *Post*, 5 November 1924. For biographical background, see MacEwan, *Miners and Steelworkers*, 127-8, and the corporate magazine *Teamwork* (Sydney), October 1949, 15.

30. *MLH*, 24 January 1925.

31. *Debates of the House of Commons*, 1925, 459ff. The Shelley verse appeared in the *MLH*, 21 February 1925, and the final lines had also appeared on the front page of 26 April 1924.

32. *MLH*, 7 February 1925.

33. *MLH*, 14 February 1925, *Post*, 14, 24 February, 3 March 1925. The *Maritime Labor Herald*, 7 February 1925, greeted the demise of King's "fugitive slave law."

34. *Post*, 3, 4, 6 March 1925.

35. McLachlan to Woodsworth, 6 March 1925, Woodsworth Papers.

36. *Post*, 5, 7, 9 March, 29 April 1925.

37. *Post*, 10 March 1925, *MLH*, 14 March 1925. See also Stuart McCawley, *Standing the Gaff: The Soreness of the Soul of Cape Breton* (Glace Bay, 1925). A slang North Americanism of the early 20th century, "standing the gaff" has entered Canadian English with the meaning "resisting rough treatment."

38. *Debates of the House of Commons*, 1925, 1726-35. See also Terry Crowley, *Agnes Macphail and the Politics of Equality* (Toronto, 1990), 80-2.

39. *Debates of the House of Commons*, 1925, 1731-2.

40. McLeod to Lewis, 25 March 1925, President's Office Correspondence, District 26, 1925, UMWA Papers.

41. Tom Moore to Lewis, 27 March 1925, President's Office Correspondence, District 26, 1925, UMWA Papers.

42. *ARLOC*, 1925, 207-8. See also *MLH*, 4, 11, 18 April 1925, which report the controversy and the local protests in favour of accepting the donation.

43. McLeod to Lewis, 8, 9, 21 April 1925, Lewis to McLeod, 22 April 1925, McLeod to Lewis, 23 April 1925, Lewis to McLeod, 27 April 1925, President's Office Correspondence, District 26, 1925, UMWA Papers; *MLH*, 18 April 1925.

44. RCMP File, 3, 20, 23 April 1925.

45. *OBU Bulletin*, 23 April 1925; McLachlan to Buck, 4 May 1925, box 1, envelope 1, Communist Party of Canada Papers, AO.

46. Jack MacDonald, "Report on Situation in District 26, UMWA," 28 April 1925, box 52, file 49, CPC Papers, NAC.

47. McLachlan to Buck, 4 May 1925.

48. McLachlan to Buck, 26 May 1925, box 1, envelope 1, CPC Papers, AO.

49. *Post*, 3, 4, 5 June 1925; *Labour Gazette* (July 1925), 661-3; McLeod and McKay to Murdock, 30 May 1925, and reply, 1 June 1925, King Papers.

50. *Post*, 6, 7, 16, 22 May, 1, 3 June 1925.

51. *Post*, 11 June 1925.

52. For the events at Waterford Lake, I have relied on Wade, "History of District 26," which had the benefit of interviews with participants and observers; see also *Post*, 10-15 June 1925, and MacEwan, *Miners and Steelworkers*, 137-40. I

have also had the benefit of conversations with residents of New Waterford who recalled the day's events, including one of the sons of William Davis: Robert Davis interview, 24 July 1975. My thanks to Don MacGillivray for sharing research on these events. His biography of William Davis appears in *Dictionary of Canadian Biography*, vol. 15.

53. Robert Davis interview, 24 July 1975; see also "Edith Pelley, William Davis's Daughter," *Cape Breton's Magazine*, no. 60 (June 1992), 45-54.

54. *Post*, 15, 16 June 1925. See also Christina M. Lamey, "Davis Day through the Years: A Cape Breton Coalmining Tradition," *Nova Scotia Historical Review*, vol. 16, no. 2 (1996), 23-33.

55. *Labour Gazette* (August 1925), 771-2; Wade, "History of District 26," chapter 6.

56. *Post*, 20, 28 May 1925; E.N. Rhodes to J.C. Douglas, 3 June 1925, E.N. Rhodes Papers, PANS.

57. *Post*, 3, 6, 10, 13 August 1925; *Labour Gazette* (August 1925), 771-2.

58. Tom McLachlan interview, 28 April 1976; Jean Robinson interview, 27 April 1976.

59. RCMP File, 15, 19 June 1925.

60. Wade, "History of District 26," chapter 6.

61. Copies from the photographic collection, Miners' Memorial Museum, Glace Bay.

62. *Saturday Night*, 5 December 1925.

63. Ibid.

64. *ARLOC, 1925*, 143-4; "Proceedings, Fourth National Convention," file 17, box 11, CPC Papers, NAC, 8, 10.

65. For descriptions of the evolution of the Cape Breton constituencies, see *History of the Federal Electoral Ridings*, 1867-1980, vol. 4 (Ottawa, 1983). See also *Post*, 16 September 1924. Carroll was named to the Supreme Court of Nova Scotia, an appointment that was approved by order-in-council the day before the election (but not announced until after the vote).

66. Election handbill, 1925, RCMP File.

67. On developments in the Conservative Party at this time, see Forbes, *Maritime Rights*. See also David Frank, "The 1920s: Class and Region, Resistance and Accommodation," in Forbes and Muise, eds., *The Atlantic Provinces in Confederation*, 252-61.

68. *Post*, 20 October 1925.

69. Ibid., 28, 29 October 1925

70. Ibid., 21, 28 October 1925.

71. *Report of the Chief Electoral Officer, Fifteenth General Election* (Ottawa, 1926), 317-18.

72. *Post*, 2 August 1926; RCMP File, 2 November 1925.

73. King to Woodsworth, 24 July 1926, L.D. Currie to L.C. Moyer, 19 July, Woodsworth to King, 2 August 1926, King to Woodsworth, 27 August 1926, vol. 165, King Papers.

74. *Report of the Chief Electoral Officer, Sixteenth General Election* (Ottawa, 1927), 318-19.

Chapter 10

1. The proceedings are found in Nova Scotia, Royal Commission on Coal Mines [Duncan Commission, 1925], "Minutes of Evidence," PANS. For McLachlan's appearance, see 950-1194. Among the limited newspaper reports, see especially George Pearson, "Sydney's Great Coal Drama Pure Scotch – With Comedy," *Star Weekly* (Toronto), 5 December 1925, 22. I am grateful to Professor D.A. Muise, Department of History, Carleton University, and his 1994-95 seminar

for listening to an earlier version of this chapter and sharing the results of their own work on the Duncan Commission.

2. Pearson, "Coal Drama," 22.
3. Pearson, "Coal Drama," 22; author's conversation with Joseph Nearing, 1976; *Post*, 16 November 1925.
4. Pearson, "Coal Drama," 22.
5. *Who's Who, 1925* (London, 1925), 841; Halifax *Herald*, 5 October 1925; Pearson, "Coal Drama," 22; *Post*, 23 November 1925; *CMJ*, 13 November 1925, 1061.
6. Rhodes to Borden, 10 July 1925, vol. 281, Borden Papers; G.S. Harrington to L.M.S. Amery [secretary of state for the colonies], 6 August 1925 [copy in MG1 G796, BI]; *Who's Who, 1925*.
7. See F.W.S. Craig, ed., *British Parliamentary Election Results, 1918-1949* (Glasgow, 1969).
8. A.A. Johnston, *Antigonish Diocese Priests and Bishops, 1786-1925* (Antigonish, 1994), 90; Halifax *Herald*, 8 October 1925. My thanks to Kathleen MacKenzie and Dan MacInnes for their assistance.
9. Halifax *Herald*, 8 October 1925; *A Standard Dictionary of Canadian Biography*, vol. 2 (Toronto, 1938), 79-80.
10. Halifax *Herald*, 12, 13, 17 November 1925.
11. "Minutes of Evidence," 952.
12. Ibid., 969-70.
13. Ibid., 997-8, 1006.
14. Ibid., 992.
15. Ibid., 980, 999-1000.
16. Ibid., 1007-8.
17. Ibid., 1022-3.
18. Ibid., 1023-4.
19. Ibid., 1030.
20. Ibid., 1030-1.
21. Ibid., 1048-9.
22. Ibid., 1053-4.
23. Ibid., 1083-4.
24. Ibid., 1072-3.
25. Ibid., 1075.
26. Ibid., 1076.
27. Ibid., 1076-7.
28. Ibid., 1078-9.
29. Ibid., 1084-5.
30. Pearson, "Coal Drama," 22.
31. "Minutes of Evidence," 1087.
32. Ibid., 1089-93.
33. Ibid., 1098.
34. Ibid., 1099-1101.
35. Ibid., 1107.
36. Ibid., 1109-12. For the statement by Pritchard, who was also a pre-war member of the Socialist Party of Canada, see Gloria Montero, *We Stood Together: First-Hand Accounts of Dramatic Events in Canada's Labour Past* (Toronto, 1979), p. 14.
37. "Minutes of Evidence," 1112.
38. Ibid., 1130.
39. Ibid., 1138.
40. Ibid., 1133-4.
41. Ibid., 1135-7.
42. Ibid., 1154-7.
43. Ibid., 1178.

44. Ibid., 1191
45. Ibid., 1182.
46. Ibid., 1190.
47. Ibid., 1181.
48. Ibid., 1193-4.
49. Ibid., 1174-5.
50. Ibid., 1175.
51. Ibid., 1177.
52. *Post*, 19 November 1925, Halifax *Herald*, 19, 20 November 1925.
53. *The Worker*, 5, 19 December 1925.
54. "Minutes of Evidence," 4288-90.
55. Ibid., 1634.
56. Ibid., 2034-6.
57. McLeod to Lewis, 5 December 1925, Lewis to McLeod, 11 December 1925, McLeod to Lewis, 28 December 1925, President's Office Correspondence, District 26, 1925, UMWA Papers.
58. The text of the Duncan Report was published in the Halifax *Herald*, 11 January 1926, 9-12. See also Nova Scotia, *Journals of the House of Assembly*, 1926, vol. 2, appendix no. 37. The report was also published as a supplement to the *Labour Gazette* (January 1926). See especially section 1, "Causes of Recurring Strife and Friction."
59. *MLH*, 30 January 1926.
60. *The Worker*, 30 January 1926.
61. *The Worker*, 30 January 1926, *MLH*, 30 January 1926.
62. *The Worker*, 30 January 1926.
63. Ibid., 30 January 1926.
64. *MLH*, 30 January 1926.
65. *The Worker*, 30 January 1926.
66. Clippings from *Daily Worker* (Chicago), 12 January [sic], 9, 7, 18 February 1926, RCMP File. See also Wade, "History of District 26," chapter 7.
67. *MLH*, 27 March, 24 April 1926.
68. See Frank, "The Cape Breton Coal Industry and the Rise and Fall of the British Empire Steel Corporation," especially 32-3.
69. H.P. MacPherson to A.R. Duncan, 9 December 1939, no. 288, Dr H.P. MacPherson Papers, St Francis Xavier University Archives.
70. See *Who's Who, 1951* (London, 1951), 832. Hugh Dalton is quoted by Stephen Brooke, *Labour's War: The Labour Party during the Second World War* (Oxford, U.K., 1992), 306. See also Angus Calder, *The People's War: Britain, 1939-1945* (London, 1969), 258.
71. *MLH*, 22 May 1926.

Chapter 11

1. Buller to ?, 3 January 1927, box 5, CPC Papers, AO. On Spadina, see Rosemary Donegan, *Spadina Avenue* (Toronto, 1985).
2. For this episode and the free-speech fights generally, see Lita-Rose Betcherman, *The Little Band: The Clashes Between the Communists and the Canadian Establishment, 1928-1932* (Ottawa, 1979). See also Tom Mitchell, "From the Social Gospel to 'the Plain Bread of Leninism': A.E. Smith's Journey to the Left in the Epoch of Reaction After World War I," *Labour/Le Travail*, vol. 33 (spring 1994), 125-51.
3. *The Worker*, 24 November 1928, RCMP File, 28 November 1928, Toronto *Star*, 10, 13 November 1928.
4. Buller to the McLachlan family, 3 December 1928, McLachlan to Buller, 11 December 1928, box 5, CPC Papers, AO. A short biography of Buller is Louise

Watson, *She Never Was Afraid: The Biography of Annie Buller* (Toronto, 1976). See also Joan Sangster, *Dreams of Equality: Women on the Canadian Left, 1920-1950* (Toronto, 1989), where the identification of Buller and Buhay in the picture on 65 is unfortunately reversed.

5. *The Worker*, 16 July 1927.
6. McLachlan to Buller, 17 February 1927, box 5, CPC Papers, AO.
7. *Nova Scotia Miner*, 21 December 1932.
8. Mary McLachlan Sanger interview, 25 February 1997.
9. *The Worker*, 26 March 1927.
10. Harry Campbell to Annie Buller, 15 December 1927, box 5, CPC Papers, AO.
11. MacEwan, *Miners and Steelworkers*, 152-3, *Directory of the Members of the Legislative Assembly of Nova Scotia, 1758-1958* (Halifax, 1958), *Cape Breton Post*, 2 February 1976, *CMJ*, 28 September 1928. Morrison remained in office until 1942.
12. *Post*, 26 September 1928; Nova Scotia, *Journals of the House of Assembly*, 1929, appendix no. 22, 9-13. See also Frank, "Working Class Politics," 203-4.
13. For the international context, see E.H. Carr, *Twilight of Comintern, 1930-1935* (London, 1982).
14. Fourth Plenum, Central Committee, November 1928, file 24, box 11, CPC Papers, NAC. The most detailed discussion of this turn in party history is Angus, *Canadian Bolsheviks*, chapters 9-13.
15. Proceedings, 6th National Convention, box 11, file 26, 132, CPC Papers, NAC.
16. *The Worker*, 9 March 1929.
17. See Tom McEwen, *The Forge Glows Red: From Blacksmith to Revolutionary* (Toronto, 1974). For the authoritative study of the WUL, see John Manley, "Communism and the Canadian Working Class during the Great Depression: The Workers' Unity League, 1930-1936," PhD thesis, Dalhousie University, 1984.
18. "General Correspondence, 1930, District 1," box 1, CPC Papers, AO; Murdoch Clarke interview, 7 November 1973; McEwen, *The Forge Glows Red*, chapter 10.
19. *Nova Scotia Miner*, 14, 28 December 1929, 25 January, 1 March 1930.
20. *Provisional Constitution and By-laws of the Mine Workers' Industrial Union of Nova Scotia* (1930) and *Minutes of the District Convention, Convened by Sub-District No. 1, District 26, U.M.W. of A.* (1930), District 26 UMWA Papers, PANS.
21. *Nova Scotia Miner*, 19 April 1930.
22. Jim Barker to "The Secretariat" [Buck], 11 April 1930, box 1, CPC Papers, AO.
23. *The Worker*, 1, 29 March, 31 May 1930, *Nova Scotia Miner*, 31 May, 7 June 1930, Barker to Ewen [Tom McEwen], 26 May 1930, box 1, CPC Papers, AO.
24. Buck to Barker, 17 April, 13 June 1930, box 1, CPC Papers, AO.
25. Buck to Barker, 13 June 1930, box 1, CPC Papers, AO.
26. Pat Toohey to Ewen, 2 November 1930, Toohey to McLachlan, 10 August 1930, file 27, box 9, CPC Papers, NAC.
27. "Minutes of the IX International Miners' Conference" [2-5 September 1930], 17, box 13, CPC Papers, AO; "Resolution of Profintern Commission on the Mining Situation in Canada and the Perspective of a Canadian Miners' Union" [30 October 1930], box 9, CPC Papers, NAC; "Tasks of the CPC and the WUL in the Organization of the Canadian Miners' Union" [6 October 1930], box 10, CPC Papers, AO. See also Carr, *Twilight of Comintern*, 20-2, which underlines the ambiguities of policy concerning the red unions.
28. Barker to W. Sydney, n.d. [1930], box 5, CPC Papers, AO.
29. Resolutions of Enlarged Central Committee Plenum, February 1931, 16, file 36, box 11, CPC Papers, NAC.
30. Walter Davis et al. to Ewen, 8 June 1931, McLachlan to Buck, 7 June 1931, box 2, CPC Papers, AO.

31. Buller to McLachlan, 24 February 1927, box 5, CPC Papers, AO.
32. Buck to Slutsky, 5 February 1930 [1931], RCMP File.
33. McLachlan to Buck, 9 April 1931, Buck to McLachlan, 26 May 1931, McLachlan to Buck, 7 June 1931, box 2, CPC Papers, AO.
34. *Nova Scotia Miner*, 12 September, 24 October 1931, 7 November 1931; the letter of introduction from Local 4529 was signed by Clarence Gillis: undated clipping [*Nova Scotia Miner*], Joseph Nearing Scrapbook.
35. RCMP File, 23 September, 21, 27 October.
36. *Nova Scotia Miner*, 21 November 1931.
37. *Nova Scotia Miner*, 23 January 1932. The clipping appears among the photographs preceding p. 268 in Mellor, *The Company Store*.
38. *Moscow News*, 7 January 1932, 3. Reprinted in *The Worker*, 30 January 1932. See also Anna Louise Strong, *I Change Worlds* (New York, 1935).
39. *Nova Scotia Miner*, 23, 30 January 1932. Additional reports on his trip appear in *Nova Scotia Miner*, 6, 20 February, 5 March 1932.
40. "Floors That Have Talked to Me," 19-20.
41. Mary McLachlan Sanger interview, 25 February 1997.
42. The passage is a composite reconstructed from the reports of 24 January and 31 January 1932, RCMP File.
43. McNaught, *A Prophet in Politics*, 233; *Star Weekly* (Toronto), 5, 12 December 1931; Toronto *Star*, 9, 11 August 1932.
44. David Caute, *The Fellow-Travellers* (New York, 1973), 11, 62, 66-7, 78-83.
45. RCMP File, 17 January 1932.
46. D.W. Clark to Sydney Rowe, 23 January 1932, Clark to J.H. MacBrien, 23 January 1932, deputy minister to MacBrien, 1 February 1932 and related items, RCMP File. I am grateful to G.S. Kealey for comparing notes here, as the name of the complainant was withheld under my original request for this file.
47. *The Worker*, 6, 13 August 1932, *Workers' Unity* (August-September 1932), and *Labour Defender* (September 1932); Toronto *Star*, 8 August 1932.
48. *The Worker*, 13 August 1932.
49. *Labour Defender* (September 1932).
50. *The Worker*, 6 August 1932.
51. The exchange is reconstructed from evidence in *The Worker*, 6, 13 August 1932, in *Labour Defender* (September 1932), and in an RCMP report dated 31 August 1932 giving McLachlan's account of the event at a public meeting in Sydney on 21 August 1932.
52. Peter Hunter, *Which Side Are You On, Boys: Canadian Life on the Left* (Toronto, 1988), 107. A similar anecdote is reported in Mellor, *The Company Store*, 333.
53. *The Worker*, 13 August 1932.
54. "Report on Conditions in Glace Bay, N.S." [February 1932], 493639-40, box 798, R.B. Bennett Papers, Archives and Special Collections, University of New Brunswick. My thanks to Carol Ferguson for a copy of this document.
55. *Nova Scotia Miner*, 23 January 1932. On the history of the AMW, see Wade, "History of District 26," chapter 9, and Michael Earle, "The Coalminers and their 'Red' Union: The Amalgamated Mine Workers of Nova Scotia, 1932-1936," *Labour/Le Travail*, vol. 22 (fall 1988), 99-137.
56. *ARLOC, 1932*, 30, *Nova Scotia Miner*, 17 September 1932.
57. *ARLOC, 1932*, 30, *Post*, 19-26 September 1932.
58. *Nova Scotia Miner*, 27 August, 1 October 1932.
59. Typed notes of interview with J.B. McLachlan, 26 January 1934, H.L. Stewart Papers, DAL MS2.45.C.2.F.1, Dalhousie University Archives. At Stewart's request, McLachlan reviewed the typed text of his notes and reported: "Your typed statement of our talk is pretty correct. At least that's how it looks to me": McLachlan to Stewart, 5 May 1934, Stewart Papers, DAL MS2.45.C.2.F.2.

60. A.A. McKay to Thomas Kennedy, 5 June 1933, with enclosures [strike circulars from AMW and UMW], William Hayes File, 1933-34, Secretary-Treasurer's Papers, UMWA Papers.
61. *Nova Scotia Miner*, 3 June 1933, Earle, "The Amalgamated Mine Workers of Nova Scotia," 124.
62. *Nova Scotia Miner*, 10 June 1933.
63. *Nova Scotia Miner*, 10, 17, 24 June 1933.
64. McKay to Kennedy, 5, 19 June 1933, Kennedy to McKay, 28 June 1933, William Hayes File, 1933-34, Secretary-Treasurer's Papers, UMWA Papers. Michael Earle, "The Amalgamated Mine Workers of Nova Scotia," 125, has concluded that "in retrospect this appears to have been the decisive crisis in the life of the AMW."
65. *Nova Scotia Miner*, 23 September 1933.
66. "Vote for McLachlan and You Vote for Yourself!" [election leaflet, 1933], MG1, G76a, BI.
67. Glace Bay *Gazette*, 9, 21 August 1933, Sydney *Post-Record*, 10, 22 August 1933.
68. *Nova Scotia Miner*, 26 August 1933.
69. Nova Scotia, *Journals of the House of Assembly*, 1934, appendix no. 30, 12-13; *The Worker*, 2 September 1933. See also Frank, "Working Class Politics," 204-7.
70. *Nova Scotia Miner*, 24 June, 26 August 1933.
71. Ibid., 8 July 1933.

Chapter 12

1. RCMP File, 23 February 1934.
2. *The Worker*, 16 September 1933, *Nova Scotia Miner*, 7 October 1933 [page wrongly dated in original]. The office of national president was created at the 1933 congress. For the amended 1933 constitution, see McEwen, *The Forge Glows Red*, 247-56. On Scarlett, see Don Avery, "British-born 'Radicals' in North America: The Case of Sam Scarlett," *Canadian Ethnic Studies*, vol. 10, no. 2 (1978), 65-85.
3. *Labour Defender* (February 1934), 7. For Buck's account of the trials and imprisonment, see Buck, *Yours in the Struggle*, chapters 16-25.
4. *Nova Scotia Miner*, 28 July, 4 August, 22 September 1934. See also "Minutes of Proceedings of the National Miners' Conference" [30 June, 1 July 1934], reel # 13, District 26 UMWA Papers, PANS.
5. Stewart to McLachlan, 10 September 1934, McLachlan to Stewart, 6 October 1934, Stewart Papers, DAL MS2.45.C.2.F.1, DUA.
6. *Nova Scotia Miner*, 14 July 1934, RCMP File, 19 July 1934.
7. *Nova Scotia Miner*, 28 July 1934, *The Worker*, 29 August 1934.
8. See Manley, "Communism and the Canadian Working Class During the Great Depression."
9. *The Worker*, 5 September 1934.
10. J. Petryshyn, "Class Conflict and Civil Liberties: The Origins and Activities of the Canadian Labour Defence League, 1925-1940," *Labour/Le Travail*, vol. 10 (autumn 1982), 39-63.
11. *The Worker*, 6, 10, 17 October 1934, Penner, *Canadian Communism*, 133-5, Thomas Socknat, *Witness Against War: Pacifism in Canada, 1900-1945* (Toronto, 1987), 163-4.
12. RCMP File, 6 August 1934.
13. RCMP File, 1934, *Nova Scotia Miner*, 4 August, 3 November 1934.
14. *Nova Scotia Miner*, 10, 24 November 1934. Meanwhile in Sydney, M.A. MacKenzie had started publication of *The Steelworker*, another radical weekly aimed at workers in the industrial community.
15. *The Worker*, 13 April 1935.

16. RCMP File, 6 December 1934. See also "Re: Communist Party of Canada, Cape Breton," secret RCMP report, 24 November 1934 [copy provided to the author by Ron Adams, 1977].

17. For discussion of this phase in the history of the AMW, see Wade, "History of District 26," chapter 9, and Earle, "The Amalgamated Mine Workers of Nova Scotia, 1932-1936," especially 122-30.

18. G.S. Harrington to Joseph Nearing, 1 May 1933, Joseph Nearing Scrapbook.

19. William Hayes to Thomas Kennedy, 20 November 1933, and enclosure, clipping from Halifax *Daily Star*, 15 November 1933, William Hayes File, Secretary-Treasurer's Papers, UMWA Papers; *Nova Scotia Miner*, 4, 18 November 1933.

20. *Nova Scotia Miner*, 30 September 1933, 13 January, 31 March 1934.

21. Typed notes of interview with J.B. McLachlan, 26 January 1934, Stewart Papers, DAL MS2.45.C.2.F.1, DUA.

22. *Statutes of Nova Scotia*, 1934, c. 44; see also Sydney *Post-Record*, 17 November 1934.

23. *Nova Scotia Miner*, 5 May 1934, *Statutes of Nova Scotia*, 1927, c. 1, s. 97, and *Statutes of Nova Scotia*, 1934, c. 44. The outline of procedures was brief. The returning officers would apparently be the company officials themselves, possibly the most interested parties in the entire contest, although union representatives were entitled to be present during the count. The definition of the electorate was very general – "employees in or about all mines" – and nothing was said about the exclusion of minor officials not eligible for union membership. No provisions for appeal were provided.

24. *The Worker*, 2 June, 26 September, 14 November 1934, *Nova Scotia Miner*, 29 September 1934.

25. *Nova Scotia Miner*, 10 November 1934.

26. Sydney *Post-Record*, 15, 16, 17, 19 November 1934; *Nova Scotia Miner*, 17, 24 November 1934.

27. Stewart to McLachlan, 29 November 1934, McLachlan to Stewart, 5 November [5 December] 1934, 2.45. C.2 F.2, Stewart Papers, DUA. McLachlan pointed out that the most recently published Mines Report gave the total employment at the mines as 11,884 men. The total vote reported in the card count, however, was 13,105. Meanwhile, there were seven smaller companies where no card counts were taken, including one with 477 employees; another adjustment should be made for the mine officials not eligible for union membership. His revised account of the vote was as follows:

Total Employed at Mines	11884
Voted for AMW in face of Coal Co. intimidation	6312
Balance left for UMW including temporary officials	5572
Majority for AMW	740

28. Earle, "The Amalgamated Mine Workers," 129-30. Earle has concluded that the card counts left the embattled AMW in a condition of extreme frustration: "The AMW was holding most of its membership, but everyone could also see that the UMW was never going to be driven from the district."

29. *Nova Scotia Miner*, 20 April 1935.

30. Ivan Avakumovic, *The Communist Party in Canada: A History* (Toronto, 1975), 115; Penner, *Canadian Communism*, 148-52; Stuart MacIntyre, *Little Moscows: Communism and Working-Class Militancy in Inter-war Britain* (London, 1980).

31. "Elect a Worker to Parliament!" [election leaflet, 1935], RCMP File; *The Communists' Fight for Working Class Unity* [pamphlet, 1934], 39, file 38, box 61, CPC Papers, NAC. See also Frank, "Working-Class Politics," 207-11.

32. *Nova Scotia Miner*, 27 April, 5 May 1935.

33. RCMP File, 1935, passim. See also *The Worker*, 30 April, 12 September, 3 October 1935.
34. *The Worker*, 24 October 1935, *Nova Scotia Miner*, 2 November 1935, RCMP File, 1935, passim.
35. "Why Every Woman Should VOTE FOR MCLACHLAN – The People's Candidate" [election leaflet, 1935, author's collection]; *The Worker*, 24 October 1935; *Toward a Canadian People's Front* [report of November 1935 plenum, Central Committee], 150-1, file 6, box 11, CPC Papers, NAC.
36. Glace Bay *Gazette*, 12, 14 October 1935.
37. Ibid., 15 October 1935; RCMP File, 1935, passim.
38. *Eighteenth General Election, 1935, Report of the Chief Electoral Officer* (Ottawa, 1936), 385-7.
39. *Nova Scotia Miner*, 19 October 1935.
40. Carman Carroll, "The Influence of H.H. Stevens and the Reconstruction Party in Nova Scotia, 1934-1935," MA thesis, University of New Brunswick, 1972, 135-7, 150-1, 196-8, 218. Carroll incorrectly states, at 197, that McLachlan "entered the contest at the last moment," thus ruining Morrison's chances for victory.
41. *The Worker*, 26 October 1935. Morrison himself subsequently became a supporter of the CCF. In 1940 a local united front produced victory in the form of the election of a CCF MP. The coal miner Clarie Gillis, a former AMW officer, was elected with a poll of 11,582 votes in a three-way contest. See Michael Earle and Herb Gamberg, "The United Mine Workers and the Coming of the CCF to Cape Breton," *Acadiensis*, vol. 19, no. 1 (autumn 1989), 3-26. On Gillis, who held the seat until 1957, see Gerry Harrop, *Clarie: Clarence Gillis, M.P., 1940-1957* (Hantsport N.S., 1987).
42. *The Worker*, 24, 26 October 1935. Apart from McLachlan (with 19 per cent of the vote) only Buck in Winnipeg (25 per cent) and Fred Rose in Montreal (16 per cent) showed substantial support. Rose would be elected to the House of Commons in 1943 and again in 1945. Meanwhile, the CCF had received more than ten times as many votes as the Communists and elected seven MPs, all in western Canada.
43. Leftist critics have condemned the turn as a repudiation of the class struggle and a capitulation of the international movement to the domestic and security interests of the Soviet Union: see Fernando Claudin, *The Communist Movement: From Comintern to Cominform* (Harmondsworth, U.K. 1975). More sympathetic historians have emphasized the roots of the popular-front strategy in the labour and anti-fascist movements of the west: see Eric Hobsbawm, *Age of Extremes: The Short Twentieth Century, 1914-1991* (London, 1994), chapter 5.
44. For Canadian studies that underline the significance of this change in policy, see Penner, *Canadian Communism*, and Robert Comeau and Bernard Dionne, *Le droit de se taire: Histoire des communistes au Québec, de la Première Guerre mondiale à la Révolution tranquille* (Montreal, 1989).
45. "Unite the Canadian Trade Union Movement," 28 February 1935, in R.B. Bennett Papers, vol. 420, NAC. See also *The Worker*, 2, 26 March 1935. The Canadian initiative was paralleled internationally by appeals for unity between the Red International and the International Federation of Trade Unions, and McLachlan published several of these documents in the *Nova Scotia Miner*, 18, 25 May 1935. For Canadian developments, see Manley, "Communism and the Canadian Working Class during the Great Depression" especially 259, 314-32, 360-72.
46. *Nova Scotia Miner*, 2 November 1935. In the full report to the Seventh Congress, which McLachlan studied, Dimitrov summarized his view of the united front in the unions: "We are for united class trade unions as one of the major bulwarks of the working class against the offensive of capital and fascism. Our

only condition for uniting the trade unions is: Struggle against capital, against fascism and for internal trade union democracy": Dimitrov, *For a United and Popular Front* (Sofia, n.d.), 164. McLachlan also returned to the pages of Lenin's 1920 pamphlet *Left-Wing Communism*, of which he possessed a 1935 edition.

47. *Toward a Canadian People's Front*, 148-53.
48. *The Worker*, 9 November 1935. See also *Unity* (November 1935).
49. Thomas A. Ewen, *Unity is the Workers' Lifeline* (Toronto, 1935?).
50. *Unity* (December 1935).
51. *The Worker*, 23 November 1935.
52. See Harvey Levenstein, *Communism, Anticommunism and the CIO* (Westport, Conn., 1981), chapters 1-2, and Dubofsky and Van Tine, *John L. Lewis*, chapters 10-11. The Canadian context is discussed in Manley, "Communism and the Canadian Working Class during the Great Depression," and Irving Abella, *Nationalism, Communism and Canadian Labour: The CIO, the Communist Party, and the Canadian Congress of Labour, 1935-1956* (Toronto, 1973).
53. *Unity* (December 1935).
54. Stewart to Local Unions, AMWNS, 4 January 1936, box 51, file 7, Stewart to Sims, 29 January 1936, box 52, file 4, CPC Papers, NAC.
55. Stewart to Sims, 29 January 1936.
56. "Joint Report," file 71, box 51, CPC Papers, NAC.
57. Buller to Sims ["Dear Charlie"], 24 January 1936, box 6, file 9, CPC Papers, NAC.
58. Stewart to Sims, 29 January 1936.
59. Buller to Sims, 24 January 1936, Stewart to Sims, 29 January 1936.
60. Sydney *Post-Record*, 3, 10 February 1936.
61. Ibid., 9, 21 March 1936.
62. Ibid., 30 March 1936.
63. *Nova Scotia Miner*, 21 March 1936.
64. Stewart to Sims, 30 January 1936, box 52, file 74, CPC Papers, NAC. In the latest issue of the WUL magazine *Unity* (January-February 1936), which Stewart had just received, Salsberg was recommending "organic unification with the A.F. of L."; by contrast, Sims offered a more sceptical endorsement of the reform movement. Sims pointed out that in many respects the UMW itself was hardly a model union: "Its industrial structure existed while John L. Lewis and his henchmen were carrying out the rottenest policies of class collaboration, wage reductions, expulsion of militants like J.B. McLachlan, expulsion of whole districts, suspension of district and local charters, etc. No man can deny this. And no miner can forget this either."
65. Stewart to Sims, 30 January 1936.
66. *Nova Scotia Miner*, 21 March 1936. See Manley, "Communism and the Canadian Working Class during the Great Depression," 515-21.
67. *Unity* (January-February 1936), *The Worker*, 6 February 1936, *Daily Clarion*, 18 June 1936.
68. *Nova Scotia Miner*, 8 February, 29 February, 21 March 1936.
69. Alex A. McKay to Thomas Kennedy, 28 March 1936, Secretary-Treasurer's Papers, UMWA Papers.
70. Sydney *Post-Record*, 18 April 1936. In early May 1936 Morrison reported to a local union meeting in Springhill that "the District would be 100% in the near future & they were coming in according to the International constitution"; a proposal to hold an open meeting was rejected and the local agreed that those who had left the UMW must "go through the proper channels, to regain their membership": Minutes, Local Union 4514 (Springhill), 9 May 1936, DUA.
71. Sydney *Post-Record*, 11, 14, 25 May 1936. Stewart himself was subsequently reinstated in the UMW and was elected as a district board member in 1938; he

played a leading part in district politics during the 1940s. Meanwhile, Barrett announced that he was launching libel proceedings in connection with comments in the most recent issue of the *Nova Scotia Miner*: Sydney *Post-Record*, 18 May 1936. This was probably the last issue to have been published. No copies appear to have survived.

72. *George MacEachern: An Autobiography: The Story of a Cape Breton Labour Radical* (Sydney, 1987), 96.

73. McLachlan to Buck, 13 June 1936. The quotations in the following paragraphs are from this document. My thanks to Eva Pemberton for providing a copy of the letter, and to John Manley for sharing his research and insights. For an earlier discussion of this episode, and the full text of the document, see David Frank and John Manley, "The Sad March to the Right: J.B. McLachlan's Resignation from the Communist Party of Canada, 1936," *Labour/Le Travail*, vol. 30 (fall 1992), 115-34, especially 132-4.

74. In withdrawing from the party, Eva Pemberton later stated, her father was not betraying all that he stood for in his life. "My father was not a turncoat," she stated. "I so want that letter to be published so that people will understand why he left": letter to the author from Eva Pemberton, 14 March 1978.

75. Halifax *Herald*, 12, 14 September 1936. It is notable that the Sydney *Post-Record* did not publish an account of Gallacher's visit to Glace Bay, although it did report that Gallacher was prohibited from entering the United States.

76. RCMP File, 11 September 1936.

77. For an account that stresses McLachlan's hostility to the Communist Party, see MacEwan, *Miners and Steelworkers*, 189-90, which was first published in the *Cape Breton Highlander*, 29 May 1968. A similar version is repeated in Mellor, *The Company Store*, 333-7. See also George MacEachern's response to MacEwan in *Cape Breton Highlander*, 26 June 1968, and Michael Earle, "The Legacy: Manipulating the Myth of McLachlan," *New Maritimes*, vol. 6, nos. 4-5 (December 1987-January 1988), 10-13.

Epilogue

1. "Certificate of Death," no. 24345, issued by registrar general, Nova Scotia; D.N. Brodie to J.S. Woodsworth, 27 October 1937, Woodsworth Papers.

2. Glace Bay *Gazette*, 8 November 1937, *Daily Clarion*, 9 November 1937.

3. *Proverbs*, 31:9. The citation was meaningful to McLachlan, for it was cited in W.U. Cotton's *Sermon to the Working Class* (*c.* 1910).

4. *The Steelworker*, 6 November 1937.

5. *The Steelworker*, 6, 13, 20 November 1937.

6. *The Worker*, 4 November 1937, *Clarion*, 5 November 1937.

7. *Clarion*, 5 November 1937.

8. *The Worker*, 4 November 1937, *People's Advocate*, 5 November 1937.

9. MacEwan, *Miners and Steelworkers*, 188-93, and Mellor, *The Company Store*, 333-7. MacEwan also notes the view of McLachlan – "a rip-snortin' Bolshevik all his life" – later expressed by "one worthy" who had known him (probably Eugene Forsey).

10. Brodie to Woodsworth, 27 October 1937.

11. William T. Mercer interview, March 1980. In this interview Mercer stated that he was unaware that McLachlan had left the Communist Party and, contrary to the claim in MacEwan, *Miners and Steelworkers*, 191, that McLachlan did not participate in the 1937 campaign by preparing speeches and other materials for him.

12. For the argument that this tradition is one of the gifts of the Maritimes to Canadian democracy, see Ian McKay, "Of Karl Marx and the Bluenose: Colin

Campbell McKay and the Legacy of Maritime Socialism," *Acadiensis*, vol. 27, no. 2 (spring 1998), 3-25.

13. James Bryson McLachlan [grandson] to Terry McVarish, 16 April 1993, private correspondence. This passage is quoted with the kind permission of Mr McVarish of the J.B. McLachlan Commemorative Society. Mr McLachlan died in 1995.

14. This paragraph borrows, respectfully, from a 1972 commentary by E.P. Thompson, "A Special Case," reprinted in Thompson, *Writing by Candlelight* (London, 1980), 65-76.

Index